THE ENCYCLOPEDIA OF
AMERICAN CRIME

Second Edition
Volume I

THE ENCYCLOPEDIA OF
AMERICAN CRIME

Second Edition
Volume I

Carl Sifakis

Facts On File, Inc.

The Encyclopedia of American Crime, Second Edition

Facts On File, Inc.
11 Penn Plaza
New York, NY 10001

Library of Congress Cataloging-in-Publication Data

Sifakis, Carl.
The Encyclopedia of American Crime / by Carl Sifakis.—2nd ed.
p.   cm.
Includes index.
ISBN 0-8160-4633-6 (Volume 1)
ISBN 0-8160-4634-4 (Volume 2)
ISBN 0-8160-4040-0 (set)
1. Crime—United States—Encyclopedias. I. Title.
HV6789 .S54 2000
364.973'03–dc21   99-058740

Facts On File books are available at special discounts when purchased in bulk quantities for businesses, associations, institutions or sales promotions. Please call our Special Sales Department in New York at (212) 967-8800 or (800) 322-8755.
You can find Facts On File on the World Wide Web at http://www.factsonfile.com

Text design by Cathy Rincon
Cover design by Nora Wertz

Printed in the United States of America

VB FOF 10 9 8 7 6 5 4 3 2 1

This book is printed on acid-free paper.

For Maria Balluff

Contents

VOLUME I

VOLUME II

Acknowledgments

Special thanks concerning this book must be given to Ed Knappman, who thought of the idea and made it work; to Howie Langer, who thought of me; to Joe Reilly; to James Chambers. And of course to my wife, Maria-Luise, whose encouragement, researching, editing and constant checking of facts often passed what should have been the limits of endurance.

Introduction

The history of crime in America is quite simply the history of America. When criminals began arriving in the New World, America, unlike the nations of Europe, had virtually no social structure, customs or institutions of its own. As America grew into a nation, criminals adapted themselves to the emerging institutions, flourished with them, worked within them, corrupted them and, some might even say, were corrupted by them. Criminality started immediately with the arrival of the first white men. If the Viking sagas are given credence, there were eight murders on Day One of the white man's appearance in North America.

New York City became a symbol of urban crime well before the end of the 18th century. Although there are earlier commentaries on crime in the city, an observation by New York printer-journalist John Holt in 1762 is especially illustrative. Holt wrote of "such various attempts to rob, and so many Robberies actually committed, having of late been very frequent within the Circuits of this City, both Day and Night; it is become hazardous for any person to walk in the latter."

Holt's words sound much like a New York newspaper editorial in the 1980s demanding something be done to solve the crime problem. What becomes apparent to any serious student of crime in America is the myth of "the good old days." In Philadelphia in the 18th century, newspapers spoke in awe of the most fearful of all criminals, "those nocturnal Sons of Violence." And even in the good old days, the best of neighborhoods quickly went to hell. This was true of Cherry Street, that wondrous New York thoroughfare lined with splendid mansions, where George Washington resided at the corner of Franklin Square after his inauguration as president of the United States and where, a few doors away, John Hancock lived. Together they strolled amid the street's fragrant cherry trees and spoke of the American Dream. Yet within a few short decades Cherry Street had degenerated into an area jammed with miserable tenements and inhabitants steeped in poverty, vice and criminality. Cherry Street became the domain of the early Irish street gangs, and no honest citizen dared venture where Washington had once casually ambled.

Crime soon developed into an "organized" activity, as gangs found allies and protectors among the aspiring politicians of the day. The politicians realized that properly used, the gangs could win and maintain power for them by intimidating voters at election time. The gangs continued to work with political machines for about 100 years until approximately the start of World War I.

By that time reform movements had taken root in most big cities, and politicians realized that the great street gangs—such as New York's 1,500-member primarily Jewish Eastman gang and the equal numbered Italian Five Points Gang under Paul Kelly—had turned into a liability. No longer could the gangs rob and kill (often to order according to detailed price lists) and expect Tammany or its equivalent in other cities to protect them. With their members subject to frequent arrest and imprisonment, the great gangs started to disintegrate.

What saved the gangs from a complete collapse was a unique development in American history, Prohibition. The Noble Experiment began shortly after the close of World War I, and suddenly, the disintegrating criminal gangs were revived. The attempt to legislate morality was doomed to failure, and in a sad by-product of this ill-advised attempt, the seeds of organized crime were sown. Where once the criminals had been popular just with the politicians, they now became accepted by the public as a whole; the bootleggers were the public's saviors, supplying them with forbidden drink. Al Capone, the bootleg king of Chicago, was cheered at baseball games while Herbert Hoover, the president of the United States, was booed.

More important, the revenues of bootlegging provided the gangsters with wealth they never had accumulated before. No longer could the politicians buy them; now they could and would buy the politicians. In Chicago, Capone would boast about how he owned the police. In New York a young Frank Costello would tell his superior, Lucky Luciano, that the mob owned the police commissioner. Society nurtured the new underworld criminals of the 1920s and then bewailed the relatively insignificant "public enemies" of the 1930s, reflecting a total misunderstanding of the era's crime problem. That misunderstanding continues to the present day.

Not only do we fail to see the genuine menace of crime but we panic over illusions, particularly the specter of a rising crime wave in the 1970s and 1980s. We demand that something be done about crime, that dangerous criminals be put away, ignoring the old lesson that prisons do not reform criminals but make them into worse criminals. Undoubtedly, one reason for this change in attitude is racial bias. Today's prison populations in general have darker skins. Crime is currently personified by a rowdy black youth in sneakers. In our prejudice we see the root problems of crime as an ethnic matter. And in a sense, it is, since crime springs from ghettos and ghettos tend to be inhabited by ethnic minorities. When the Irish were the first people jammed into the ghettos of American cities, they were responsible for the bulk of the crime wave. After the Jews and Italians arrived, they became the nation's leading gangsters. When in history has not most of the crime in America (except for white-collar crime) sprung from the ghettos?

Any crime reporter is familiar with the attitude that has been described as the "Irish cop morality": "Why are these people like animals? Why don't they pull themselves out of the slime the way we did?" Certainly the Irish did, but it took them about a century. Many second- and third-generation Jews do not even know of their heritage of criminality in America, making it one of the nation's best-kept secrets. According to an ethnic self-delusion, spoken not without a measure of pride, among Jews, those among them who became criminals remained in the background, letting others carry out the violence. This myth is clearly contradicted in the persons of such brutal thugs and killers as Monk Eastman, Crazy Butch, Johnny Spanish, Little Kishky, Ike the Blood, Kid Jigger, Kid Dahl, Big Jack Zelig, Gyp the Blood, Lefty Louis, Whitey Lewis, Yoske Nigger, Charley the Cripple, Johnny Levinsky and Dopey Benny; and in a succeeding era by Kid Dropper, Little Augie, Legs Diamond, Dutch Schultz, Waxey Gordon, Meyer Lansky, Bugsy Siegel, Pretty Amberg, Louis Lepke, Gurrah Shapiro, Abe Reles, Pittsburgh Phil Strauss and Buggsy Goldstein. Many drew their first blood as juvenile muggers, preying on citizens alarmed

about the crime wave in their time and insisting things were better in the good old days. (The identities of some Jewish gangsters are lost because they adopted Irish-sounding names. Even the celebrated Monk Eastman, born Edward Osterman, often called himself Edward Delaney, and the notorious turn-of-the-century Italian gang leader Paolo Vaccarelli was likewise better know as Paul Kelly. It was part of the prejudice of the day that even these criminals thought that to be gangsters, they had to have good Irish names.)

Throughout the 1960s, '70s and '80s, the public became aware that crime was increasing enormously. Crime experts thought otherwise, but no matter, the public *knew* crime had gone up compared to the good old days. Actually this was not accurate, but the perception was firmly rooted and its causes were not difficult to find.

One reason is that in the past several decades the public became better informed. The average person today probably watches an hour to an hour and a half of news on television each day, far more than was ever spent reading newspapers in the pre-video period. Crime news is driven home much more forcefully, and in vivid color. This is not to say that the public would be better off uninformed. Television played a similar role during the Vietnam War, subjecting viewers night after night to the horrors of that tragic conflict. As a result, TV was more instrumental in ending the nation's involvement in Vietnam than were the numerous anti-war demonstrations.

Today, television sickens viewers with crime. There is something antiseptic about a three-paragraph news story of a killing. But it is quite different to show a murdered corpse being carried off, with close-ups of bloodstains on a floor or sidewalk. In the good old days, people rarely saw anything like this, so crime now must indeed be worse.

This public misconception naturally carries over to the political arena, with politicians seeking to outdo each other by promising to "get tough with criminals." They talk of taking violent criminals off the streets and locking them up at the same time courts are ordering prison populations reduced because of overcrowding. In the era of a government determined to spend less, various politicians are calling for new prisons. Yet while it costs a minimum of $20,000 a year to house a convict in an existing facility, the per prisoner cost of providing new accommodations is $70,000 to $100,000. The politicians of course realize what they propose will never be done on the scale that would be necessary to take care of the overflow, but the idea represents a "quick fix" for the public's worry.

To focus on the criminal justice system, which has proven incapable of stopping crime in the past, inhibits any serious discussion of the problem. For years, the Federal Drug Enforcement Administration made numerous arrests of major drug dealers in the United States and abroad, and handed out long prison terms. Still, the country is flooded with heroin and cocaine, and their impact on the crime rate is staggering. An addict often requires $200 a day to support his habit. How can he get it except by stealing, and assaulting victims in the process? Researchers at Temple University found recently that 243 heroin users in Baltimore had committed more than half a million crimes over an 11-year period, an annual average of 200 per criminal. Sooner or later, rather than emphasizing the "lock 'em up and throw away the key" attitude, it will become necessary to begin a serious dialogue about other solutions, such as heroin maintenance programs for addicts. Until an effective method of dealing with the drug problem is implemented, addicts will go on committing vast numbers of crimes.

A genuine effort will have to be made to come up with proper standards of probation, parole and sentencing of criminals. New York district attorney Robert M. Morgenthau notes that the law metes out the harshest sentences to second- and third-time offenders, many of whom are by that time in their late twenties—an age when a criminal's illegal activity generally starts to diminish. "From the standpoint of fairness, that's the fairest way to do it," Morgenthau stresses. "But actually he's less of a danger to society than the guy who's 22 or 23 years old, more active and has fewer convictions."

It is not the purpose of this book to attempt to solve the crime problem, but it is important to try to note some of the fallacies of many of the remedies suggested. President Ronald Reagan's labeling of crime as an "American epidemic" requiring a sweeping overhaul of federal criminal laws to "redress the imbalance between the rights of the accused and the rights of the innocent" particularly missed the point, while raising serious constitutional questions. Reagan proposed new drug-trafficking crackdowns and bail-tightening procedures and endorsed legislative proposals that would permit judges to order convicted criminals to make restitution to their victims. This last point requires serious study, not only from the viewpoint of the victim but from that of the accused, since it offers new opportunities for frame-ups by giving a victim a financial motivation for making a positive identification of a suspect, a matter few proponents have yet addressed.

Police claim that their hands are tied because no matter how many arrests they make, the courts continue to put criminals back on the street. But is this not an attempt to draw attention from the fact that the police make an arrest in only one crime out of five?

Furthermore, this 20 percent ratio is bloated with arrests for "easy" crimes, those of murder, aggravated assault and rape, in which the identity of the perpetrator is often readily established.

In the 1990s a sea change concerning crime occurred as the rate of virtually all types of crimes started to decline, and the public has begun to feel better about the situation. Naturally law enforcement officials throughout the country claim that the decline is due to their work, but the more logical assumption is that it in large measure reflects a previous falling birth rate. Experts on such matters say the situation will change in due course and crime will rise as a growing crop of teenagers, important contributors to the crime rate, comes of age.

Still, Americans are satisfied that things are better now, although they remain exercised about the murder rate, which is perceived as more grisly than ever. This more than anything else continues to fuel popularity for capital punishment. Indeed a certain type of murder has come to the fore as one of the major crime problems of the new millennium—that of the serial killer.

When the first edition of this book appeared in the early 1980s, the term *serial killer* had hardly come into vogue, and it was more common to speak of mass murderers. There is no doubt that serial killings have exploded in recent years. Today and for some years now the FBI estimated that of the 5,000 or so killers not apprehended each year, some 3,500 could be the work of serial killers who are not caught. Many crime writers tended to regard such estimates as wildly exaggerated, but as more and more serial killers are apprehended and tied to five, 10, 20 or more slayings, there is much more of a readiness to acknowledge the FBI experts know what they are talking about.

In a way, confirmation of this comes in a study of what is occurring in death houses around the country as condemned men are cleared and released. As of August 1999 there have been 566 executions, while 82 others condemned to die, including some only hours or days from that fate, were discovered to be not guilty. Frequently the condemned had been acting as stand-ins for serial killers or rapists.

This may speak volumes about the efficiency of the justice system to find the guilty rather than imprisoning the innocent, while the real criminal remains free. Much of the saving of lives, a growing number of voices now say, cannot be simply ascribed to the position of capital punishment proponents that "this proves the system works" but rather that *some* of the innocent are freed despite a system that inherently is incapable of being consistently right. In some cases now, in some states, vocal capital punishment proponents have actually joined opponents of the death penalty to propose a moratorium on executions while the matter is studied further. Illinois, where there had been 12 executions and *an equal number of wrongful convictions requiring release of condemned men,* stands out as a glaring example.

What is clear is that these two issues, a more comprehensive study of the problem of serial killers and the use of DNA and other methods to prevent permanent miscarriages of justice, will be hot-button items in coming years.

Along with these will come an increased interest in crime. In such a climate the need for a more systematized study of the history of crime in America should be apparent.

It is not an easy field for historical study. Facts about crime are more obscure than in most other subject fields, and although I have endeavored to weed out misrepresentation and inaccuracies, I probably have not been completely successful. Some crime myths have become so imbedded in our culture that it is probably too late at this date to separate fact from fiction. It may be a hopeless struggle to try to prove that John Dillinger never used a wooden gun to break out of jail. Some of the most respected reference sources to this day inaccurately report that Al Capone was born in Naples, when in fact his birthplace was Brooklyn, New York City.

Criminals not only lie about their deeds but about their lives as well. Efforts to obtain merely birth and death dates of criminals are often frustrating. They give different birthplaces and dates at different times, perhaps in an attempt to assume another identity or to cloud the truth because of deportation concerns. The result is confusion. Deaths are not always reported. Criminals, certainly more so than old soldiers, seem to just fade away.

Police have been known to misrepresent facts, and when convenient, the great historians of crime, news reporters, have also stretched the truth, sometimes entertainingly so. The pressure in the newspaper profession for a daily "fresh angle" undoubtedly has led some reporters to embellish their facts. Paul Schoenstein, one of New York's leading newspaper editors, once said his favorite reporters were those who came back with a news story in which at least addresses didn't turn out to be in the middle of the Hudson River.

Reporters have gained reputations, or at least some journalistic rewards, by knowing how to cater to the public's appetite for sensationalism. The vehicle for their fame has been the "piped" newspaper crime story, the origin of the term deriving from the location of New York police headquarters near Chinatown, where people could journey to dreamland puffing on an opium pipe.

Some of the most fanciful stories have been produced on out-of-town assignments, which provide police reporters with their greatest joy: the chance to escape police headquarters and their city rooms. There is a convenient division of labor on such jobs whereby only one reporter covers the news sources while the rest play cards. At a given moment, all the reporters get the same facts and call their offices at the same time so that no one gets a lead on the rest. Even more important, expense accounts cover lavish living and allow for padding of such imaginary items as hip boots to traipse around with the police in swampy areas.

According to a story that is often told at the Columbia University School of Journalism, in the days when New York City had a dozen-odd newspapers, police reporters were sent to New Jersey to cover a particularly important murder. After several weeks, the investigation began petering out, and the city editors started making rumbles about the reporters returning home. Faced with the loss of their journalistic vacation, the reporters came up with a ruse. One of them obtained an old rusted gun that could not be traced, and they buried it in the backyard of a suspect. Naturally, the police were tipped off and there was a new break in the story, which kept the reporters in New Jersey for another week until it was determined that the gun was not linked to the case.

It is capers like these that cloud the history of crime and make the serious student's task all the harder. Crime is sensational enough, bizarre enough, certainly important enough and sometimes even entertaining enough to require no more than, as Sgt. Joe Friday used to say on TV's long-running *Dragnet* series, "just the facts, ma'am."

A work attempting to cover the full gamut of crime in America is of necessity highly selective. With a mere 2,000 entries how does one cover just murder, with up to 20,000 known cases a year? Only those killings that in some way have become "classics" can be recorded here. Although more words were written about the Hall-Mills murders than any other criminal case up to that time, it remains, in essence, a singularly common crime: the murder of a married man and his paramour while on a tryst. A sensational trial and a not-guilty verdict have given it a special niche in America's criminal history. The Snyder-Gray case also lives in our memories even though it is another rather ordinary murder: a married woman and her lover dispatching the lady's husband, a crime repeated perhaps hundreds of times a year. Still, we remember Snyder-Gray not for what they were—especially Judd Gray, a particularly weak man with little inclination for killing—but for what we the public made of them. In the 1920s the murder they committed was labeled one of the great crimes of the century, a phrase found with monotonous regularity in tabloid headlines.

I've also paid particular attention to recording "firsts" in this work. Along with the Vikings' early depredations is included the case of John Billington, who was convicted of the first murder in the Plymouth colony. Also covered in these volumes are murders of a particularly bizarre nature or those with some important symbolic or historical relevance.

Other murder cases are included because they were trail-blazers in such fields as establishment of insanity pleas or, on a slightly more exotic level, set precedents involving murders by sleepwalkers or victims of hypnotists. The mass murderers of America are also here, including such wholesale practitioners of death as H. H. Holmes, Johann Hoch, Albert Fish, Earle Nelson, Howard Unruh, Charles Starkweather, Carl Panzram, Edmund Kemper, Richard Speck, Charles Whitman, Dean Corll, Joseph Gacy, Albert DeSalvo (the Boston Strangler) and many others.

In the Old West, it is striking to note how little separated the lawmen from the bandit; indeed many readily and frequently passed from one role to the other. I describe men like Wyatt Earp and Wild Bill Hickok, warts and all, often finding little but warts. Such other folk heroes as the James Brothers and Billy the Kid, examined objectively, lose the redeeming qualities often attributed to them.

Any detailed study of the public enemies of the 1930s shows most to be overglamorized, with the possible exception of John Dillinger and one or two others. In the process of deglamorizing them, I inevitably deglamorized those who built the myths around them while they ignored and indeed denied the existence and growth of an organized crime syndicate. Fame in the field of crime is fickle, sticking to some and deserting others. Today, Baron Lamm, a giant among bank robbers, is little remembered, although his influence on Dillinger, who never met him, was enormous.

Even among genuine heroes, fame can be short lived. Few Americans today know the name of Ed Morrell, possibly the most tortured and, later, the most respected convict in the nation's penal history. When he was eventually pardoned, a prison warden wept for joy with him. Excuses are made for Jesse James, and the railroads that he plundered are cast as villains, although James was certainly a cold-blooded murderer. At the same time, the California Outlaws, led by such men as Morrell, Chris Evans and the Sontag brothers, are described in superficial histories as cutthroats while the true villain of the day, the Southern Pacific Railroad, escapes censure.

I've also included important prosecutors and defense attorneys, not all Darrows perhaps but many colorful, brilliant and, in some cases, devious. In examining these practitioners of the law as well as judges and police officers, the inequities in America's judicial history become apparent.

But moral judgments aside, the events and people— the killers, thieves, madams, whores, crooked and honest lawmen and judges, political bosses, syndicate gangsters and even victims—in the annals of crime are worth studying because they are, perhaps much more than we wish to admit, reflections of ourselves and the society we have created.

THE ENCYCLOPEDIA OF
AMERICAN CRIME

Second Edition
Volume I

Abbandando, Frank "the Dasher" (1910–1942)
Murder, Inc. killer

One of Murder, Inc.'s most prolific killers, Frank "the Dasher" Abbandando got his nickname, according to one version, on one of his early hits. He pointed his gun at a huge waterfront character and pulled the trigger, but the weapon didn't fire. Abbandando then made a mad dash to get away, with his intended victim lumbering after him. According to the story, Abbandando ran around a building so fast that he actually came up behind the man. This time he got him with three slugs in the back. Even if this story is legend, it is matter of fact that during the 1930s, Abbandando did a remarkable job of littering the streets of Brooklyn with corpses. No accurate statistics on his kills were ever kept, but he was known to have been involved in probably 50 or so. When he wasn't knocking off mob victims, the Dasher spent his free time raping young girls in the Brownsville and Ocean Hill sections of Brooklyn. In one case he "squared up" with a girl's family by tossing them $25, "or otherwise I buy you all tombstones."

When finally brought to justice as a result of the testimony of informer Abe Reles and several other gang members who turned into stoolies, Abbandando was probably the most unrepentant of the hired killers in court. At one stage in the Dasher's trial, the judge ordered a court officer to stand between himself and Abbandando on the witness stand after the defendant threatened to kill him right in his own court. Still, the Dasher's lawyer tried to cast him in the best possible light, pointing out he had indeed been a star at second base for the Elmira team—the Elmira Reformatory team that was. In his summation he pleaded for the Dasher in the fair name of baseball, arguing: "Ballplayers don't kill people. In all my experience I cannot think of a single baseball player who ever killed anybody—at least so viciously as in this case."

The athletic assassin went to the electric chair on February 19, 1942.

See also: MURDER, INC.; ABE RELES.

Abbott, Burton W. (1928–1957)   murderer

The defendant in one of California's most sensational kidnap-murder trials, 29-year-old Burton W. Abbott was the object of an even more sensational execution, which offered grim proof of the finality of the death sentence.

On April 28, 1955 14-year-old Stephanie Bryan disappeared in Berkeley, Calif. after walking a classmate home. Thirteen days after the hunt for the girl began, the police found one of Stephanie's schoolbooks in a field outside of town. On the evening of July 15, Georgia Abbott was rummaging in the basement of her home when she found a purse and identification card bearing the name of the missing girl. She rushed upstairs and blurted out news of her find to her husband, Burton, and a dinner guest. Police were summoned and a careful search of the premises revealed a number of Stephanie's schoolbooks, her brassiere and her glasses. Neither Burton nor Georgia Abbott could explain the presence of the girl's possessions, but Abbott pointed out that his garage had served as a polling place in May and that anyone of scores of people might have used the opportunity to hide the items on his property.

While the police remained suspicious, they had no other evidence to link Abbott to the girl's disappearance. The Abbotts owned a weekend cabin in the Trinity Mountains, some 300 miles away, and on a hunch, investigators visited the area. Dogs led them to a shallow grave that contained the badly decomposed body of Stephanie Bryan. She had been bludgeoned to death and her panties tied around her neck. Abbott was arrested and charged with kidnapping and murder.

While the case against Abbott was circumstantially strong, the prosecution had difficulty establishing a direct link between the suspect and the victim. However, scientific examination showed that hairs and fibers found in Abbott's car matched those from the girl's head and clothing. Still, there were enough doubts in the case to cause the jury to deliberate for seven days before finding Abbott guilty. He was sentenced to die in the gas chamber. Insisting on his innocence, Abbott filed appeal after appeal, but each was turned down. He was, however, granted several stays—some only hours before his scheduled execution—to launch yet another appeal.

On March 14, 1957 Abbott's last appeal failed and he was taken to the gas chamber at San Quentin. At 11:15 A.M. the tiny gas pellets were exploded beneath Abbott's chair. Just then the telephone "hot line" from Gov. Goodwin Knight's office buzzed Warden Harry Teets. "Hold the execution," a governor's assistant ordered. Warden Teets explained it was too late—the gas had been released. Gov. Knight had ordered a stay for one hour, for a reason never officially explained. It didn't matter. At 11:25 Abbott was dead.

Since then the Abbott case has often been cited by forces opposing capital punishment, not because of the merits of his claim of innocence, but as stark evidence that once the state takes away a person's life, it cannot restore that life.

Abilene, Kansas See SHAME OF ABILENE.

abolitionist riots

Riots against abolitionists were common in the pre–Civil War North, but in New York City such commotions were often engineered by the gangsters of the Bowery and the Five Points in order to provide opportunities for general looting and mischief.

Several minor episodes occurred in 1833, followed by numerous bloody riots the subsequent year. On July 7, 1834 anti-abolitionist mobs attacked a chapel on Chatham Street and the Bowery Theater. Finally routed by the police, the rioters stormed down Rose Street, then a fashionable thoroughfare of mansions, and

attacked the home of Lewis Tappan, a leading antislaver. Tappan escaped but most of the furniture in his house was heaved into the street, doused with oil and set on fire. As the mob ripped pictures from the wall, one rioter suddenly stopped another from throwing a painting on the bonfire. "It's Washington! For God's sake, don't burn Washington!" The mob took up the chant, and the painting was held aloft by a group of thugs who respectfully escorted it to the veranda of a house not under attack, where it was fervently guarded during the rest of the riot.

The worst of the year's violence took place three days later, when the leaders of the anti-abolitionist gangs declared they would destroy any house in the Five Points area that didn't put a candle in the window in denunciation of abolition. By evening, candles flickered from almost every window, but still a dozen buildings were set ablaze and looted. The rioters attacked St. Phillip's Negro Church on Center Street and completely gutted it. A house next door to the church and three across the street were also destroyed. As smoke spread throughout the district, the gangsters turned their frenzy on houses of prostitution, and the occupants of five of them were dragged outside and forced to watch their homes and belongings burned. The women were stripped, passed out to the gang and horribly mistreated. Blacks were pulled from their homes or hiding places and tortured, and an Englishman had both eyes gouged out and his ears cut off.

When troops arrived on the scene a little after one o'clock in the morning, the mob fled. The following night rioters gutted a church on Spring Street whose pastor had supported the antislavery movement, and then barricaded the streets, vowing to battle the soldiers to the death. But when the troops moved on the barricades, the mob turned and ran. For a time thereafter, the riots against abolitionists ceased, resuming in the 1850s.

abortion as a crime stopper controversial theory

As crime continued to drop in the 1990s—and somewhat earlier in some localities—political and law enforcement officials were quick to claim the lion's share of the credit. However, in 1999 a new theory advanced by two highly regarded academics offered a new explanation that would account for as much as half of the drop. It was a firestorm theory that had the distinction of being attacked by all sides of one of the most divisive issues in late 20th-century America—that of abortion.

The thesis advanced by Dr. John J. Donohue 3d of Stanford Law and Dr. Steven D. Levitt of the University of Chicago was that much of the falling crime rates of the 1990s could be attributed to the sharp increase in abortions after the Supreme Court's *Roe v. Wade* decision of 1973. Unsurprisingly, the two researchers were accused of everything from promoting eugenics to outright recommending abortion as a means to reduce crime. When the findings were first reported in the *Chicago Tribune* in August 1999 they resulted in fiery tirades in op-ed columns and radio talk shows. The criticisms came from both sides in the abortion debate.

Joseph Scheidler, executive director of the Pro-Life Action League, denounced the study as "so fraught with stupidity that I hardly know where to start refuting it," adding, "Naturally if you kill off a million and a half people a year, a few criminals will be in that number. So will doctors, philosophers, musicians and artists."

From a different source, the same response was offered. Columnist Carl Rowan wrote, "I've seen a lot of far-fetched and dangerous ideas passed off as 'social research,' but none more shallow and potentially malicious than the claim that the drop in crime in the United States can be attributed to legalized abortions."

Some observers noted that Donohue and Levitt had accomplish the near-impossible of simultaneously infuriating the right and left. Some academics noted that the pair seemed to have discerned an effect but doubted their findings that half the crime reduction came from abortion practices. The debate about the decline was sure to be subjected to academic scrutiny, and the specifics of the pair's findings closely reviewed.

One such finding was that such disparate states as New York, Washington, Alaska and Hawaii were among the first to legalize abortion, and they were the first to experience a decrease in crime. Similarly, the states that legalized abortions in 1969 or 1970 had a cumulative decrease in crime from 1982 to 1997 that was greater than for the rest of the nation. The decline in violent crime was greater by 34.4 percent and in property crime by 35.3 percent. The fall in murders was 16.2 percent greater. In addition, states with the highest abortion rates had larger declines in crime than states with low abortion rates.

Donohue and Levitt concluded that abortion has occurred selectively, decreasing the number of individuals most likely to be at risk of committing future crimes. Fitting that category, the researchers said, were the potential offspring of mothers who were teenagers, unmarried or black, all of whom have higher rates of abortion. Children born to mothers in these groups are statistically at higher risk to turn to crime as adults. The researchers estimated the economic benefit of abortion to society in reducing crime at perhaps "on the order of $30 billion annually."

In response to criticism, Dr. Levitt said: "There's nothing in our paper that either indirectly or directly suggests that we condone denying anyone the right to have children if they want to have children. We've been accused of having a eugenic agenda and it just is not an accurate appraisal of what we're doing at all. If anything, what our paper says is that when you remove a government prohibition against a woman choosing, the woman makes choices that lead to better outcomes for her children."

It was obvious that in future debates neither side on the abortion issue would touch it with, as one observer put it, "a 10-foot pole." However, should the researchers' claims win peer support, it was considered possible that in time they would gain sub-rosa support from elements in the political community.

Abrams, Big Mike (?–1898) murderer

While the Chinese of New York's Chinatown have fought many savage tong wars among themselves, through the years they have tried to avoid violent conflicts with whites. The opposite was not the case, however. White killers were familiar denizens of the Chinatown alleys, always ready to eliminate any man's enemy for a shockingly reasonable price. The most notorious of this ilk was Big Mike Abrams, who roamed the area performing beatings and killings for pay. When work was slow, Abrams would take to street muggings, which, besides earning his keep, further enhanced his reputation.

Big Mike sometimes operated opium-smoking dens on Pell Street and in Coney Island and in his later years settled for a small percentage from such establishments, while contributing nothing to their operation. The fact that a man was a client of one of these dens, however, did not afford him protection in the event Big Mike was offered cash to slug or kill him. Big Mike's most celebrated murders were the knife decapitations of three Chinese before the horrified eyes of onlookers on Pell Street.

Even the dread hatchet men of the tongs feared Big Mike, but finally one of them, Sassy Sam of the Hip Sing Tong, got drunk on rose wine and rice brandy and attacked the awesome killer. Big Mike happened to be unarmed at the time and fled down Pell Street, with Sassy Sam in hot pursuit waving a long ceremonial sword.

Big Mike lost considerable stature after that display of vulnerability. While he did regain a measure of respect by removing the head of Ling Tchen, one of the chiefs of the Hip Sing Tong, the unthinkable—the elimination of Big Mike—began to be considered. Within a month of the death of Ling Tchen, police found Big

Mike dead in bed, his room filled with gas. The windows and door to his room had been sealed from the outside and a line of thin hose from a gas jet in the hall had been stuffed in the keyhole of Big Mike's door.

The Hip Sings were generally credited with killing Big Mike, but the tong never acknowledged the deed, apparently fearful of retribution from other white gangsters.

Abu-Jamal, Mumia   See CAPITAL PUNISHMENT.

Accardo, Anthony Joseph (1906–1992) Chicago mob leader

Today, it may be somewhat hard to believe that someone like "Joe Batters," who, as a young tough, gained his sobriquet for his proficiency with a baseball bat and who served as one of Al Capone's bodyguards, could become the boss of the Chicago mob and be described by his syndicate supporters as having "more brains before breakfast than Al Capone had all day."

Accardo's rise in the Chicago underworld was rapid. When Capone first went to jail for a brief stay in 1929 and named Jake Guzik in charge of administration and Frank Nitti in charge of operations, Accardo was installed as the head of "enforcement." Under him were such brutal characters as Machine Gun Jack McGurn, Tough Tony Capezio, Screwy John Moore, Sam "Golf Bag" Hunt, Red Forsyth and Jimmy Belcastro, the King of the Bombers. Accardo continued to grow in stature in the gang, and when Nitti committed suicide in 1943 rather than go to prison, he became the acknowledged head of the Chicago mob.

At various stages in the 1950s and 1960s, Accardo reportedly had his powers wrested away by Sam "Momo" Giancana, but it is unclear how much Accardo gave up under force and how much he relinquished willingly.

Accardo was always reputed as a leader who believed in iron-clad obedience in the lower ranks but a sharing of power at the top. Under his rule the level of violence in the Chicago underworld dropped to near zero, especially compared to the old Capone days. However, enforcement against alleged informers and those who tried to steal from the syndicate remained strict and awesome. Such was the fate in 1961 of one William "Action" Jackson, a collector for the mob who had developed "sticky" fingers. Action got particularly brutal treatment, ending up stripped naked and hanging by his chained feet from a meat hook in the basement of a Cicero gambling joint. He was beaten on the lower body and genitals with a baseball bat, carved up with a razor and had his eyes burned out with a blow-torch. Following that treatment he was further dissected, and then pictures were taken of his corpse (he had died, according to the coroner's report, not of his wounds but of shock) and distributed in mob centers as a warning of what was in store for a thief.

Accardo's personal fairness, by underworld standards, was of the same sort that inspired so much loyalty in many of Capone's adherents. Noted for his pool playing, Accardo was once victimized in a $1,000 bet by a pool hustler who had wedged up the table and then adjusted his technique accordingly to beat the crime chief. When the hustler was exposed, Accardo blamed only himself. "Let the bum go," he said. "He cheated me fair and square." Accardo's behavior in such matters won him a great amount of affection.

But Accardo also proved most resourceful in dealing with the drug problem, which much of the national syndicate and the Mafia had ruled out of bounds. Some families disobeyed the rule but others enforced it rigorously, killing any who disobeyed or cutting them off from legal and support aid if they were caught. Accardo's solution was to ban all narcotics dealings, but he also ordered that all those involved in dope be given $200 a week out of family funds to help make up their losses.

This "taking care of everybody" approach helped to pacify the Chicago mob; by comparison, gangland murders became much more common in New York, with its five greedy Mafia families. This record of peace may well have been shattered by the 1975 murder of Sam Giancana, but a number of underworld sources insist Accardo was not behind the murder. According to them, the Giancana killing was "a CIA operation all the way," designed to prevent him from speaking about the agency's use of the underworld in a Castro assassination plot.

By the late 1970s Accardo, a multimillionaire, was in semiretirement, living the good life as he traveled from Florida to the West Coast to Chicago looking after his enormous legitimate investments. According to the FBI, the mob's operational authority in Chicago had shifted to Joe Aiuppa, an Accardo gunman buddy from the old days. After that, Joe Batters returned to approve further new leaderships when Aiuppa went to prison. Accardo died in 1992, never having spent a night in jail.

See also: SAM "MOMO" GIANCANA.

accident faking   insurance swindle

Over the years faking accidents to swindle insurance companies has developed into a thriving business. There is no way to gauge accurately the extent of this crime since insurance industry figures are themselves suspect; many observers claim that the companies have a vested interest in minimizing the extent of fraud to deter other attempts and to defend their rate structures. Some calculations of accident frauds place the figure between $20 million and $100 million a year, with most estimates falling in the upper range. It was estimated that one insurance gang in Birmingham, Ala. cleared several million dollars over a seven-year period. Such insurance rings sometimes buy duplicates of legitimate X rays from doctors and then use them to bolster phony claims of industrial, auto and personal injuries.

One of the most incredible operations of this kind worked out of Kirksville, Mo. The swindle involved doctors, lawyers, osteopaths, nurses, insurance agents, a county sheriff, farmers and businessmen. Sixty-six of them were eventually convicted and sentenced. The racket was run by a crooked insurance agent. He favored realism in staging his phony claims; claimants had their wrists broken with crank handles and their fingers smashed with hammers. An osteopath would be called in to compound such injuries by manipulating the bones of the hand and giving injections designed to cause infections. In some cases miscalculations resulted in amputations, but these only increased the size of the award. The men, women and children who willingly pose as the accident victims in such plots are often of limited intelligence, but they are also usually poor and the pool of these volunteer victims increases dramatically during periods of high unemployment.

Faked pedestrian accidents have long been a mainstay of the racket. Sometimes both the victim and the driver are in collusion, but most fakers prefer to utilize an honest driver who can stand up to rigorous investigation because he really is innocent. "Floppers" and "divers" are used when the motorist is not a willing partner in the swindle. A flopper is a person who is adept at feigning being hit by a car going around a corner. Perpetrators insist this is not as hard to do as it would appear. The flopper simply stands in the street and starts crossing as the car makes its turn. Under such circumstances the car is moving relatively slowly, and the flopper bounces off the front fender and flips his body backward to the ground. As the crowd starts to gather, the flopper moan and groans. The premium flopper is one who has an old fracture, preferably a skull fracture since the break will show up in an X ray no matter how old it is. The flopper is naturally schooled in the art of faking serious injury. Just before the accident he will bite his lip open and dab some of the blood into his ear.

"Divers" are considered finer artists than floppers because their act seems more convincing. They work at night so that witnesses can't really see what is happening. As a car approaches, the diver runs into the street and in a crouching position slams the car door with his hand as hard as he can. The resulting loud noise quickly attracts onlookers as the diver lies on the ground, doing the same moaning and groaning act as the flopper.

One of the most bizarre accident swindles involved a father of identical twins. One child was normal but the other quite retarded. Rather than put the unfortunate child into an institution, the father decided to use him as a prop for a swindle scheme. He would take his normal child into stores and when no one was looking, he'd knock something off a shelf and have the child start screaming as though he had been hit on the head. The father would then create a scene and storm out of the store. Later, he would file suit against the store, charging the accident had permanently damaged his child's brain. As proof, he would produce the retarded twin. Settlements were hastily arranged since no company dared take such a case to a jury. The racket worked a number of times until an investigator making a routine check visited the family's home while the parents were out and saw the normal child playing in the backyard.

Adams, Albert J. (1844–1907) numbers king

A famous and colorful New York City gambler, known as the Policy King, Al Adams was the boss of the most extensive numbers game operation in the city.

Dishonesty has been the keynote of policy games from the time they started in England during the 1700s to the present, but Adams gave them a new wrinkle, not only bilking the public but also swindling other numbers operators in order to take over their businesses.

Adams came to New York from his native Rhode Island in the early 1870s and first worked as a railroad brakeman, a job he found much too taxing. He soon became a runner in a policy game operated by Zachariah Simmons. Duly impressed by Adams' penchant for deviousness, the older man took him in as a partner. Adams developed many ways to rig the game to reduce the winners' payoff. After Simmons died, Adams took over his operation and eventually became the boss of the New York policy racket. At the time, there were scores of independent operators. It was common practice for independent policy men to "lay off" numbers that had been bet too heavily for comfort. They would simply shift part of the action to another operator who had light play on the number, thus spreading the risk. When these operators tried to lay off a heavily played number with Adams, he would note the number and claim he already had too much action on it. He would then lay off the same number around the city, even if he actually had little or no action on it. Thus, a number of operators would become vulnerable to that number. Adams' next move was to fix the results so the heavily played number came out, hitting the owners of many policy shops with devastating losses. To make their payoffs, the operators had to seek loans from Adams, who exacted a partnership as the price of a loan, ultimately kicking the operators out entirely. Some policy operators he simply refused to help, forcing them to make their payoffs (many to Adams' undercover bettors) by dipping into the cash reserved for bribes to politicians and the police. Losing their protection, they were immediately shut down, and Adams simply moved in.

In time, it was estimated that Adams ran between 1,000 and 1,100 policy shops in the city. Over the years his payments to the Tweed Ring totaled in the millions. Even after Tweed fell and reformers came in, Adams was able to operate with the connivance of the police. It was not until 1901 that law enforcement authorities were forced to take action against his nefarious operations, raiding his headquarters. Adams was sent to Sing Sing, where he served more than a year.

When he came out, Adams found that he no longer controlled the New York policy game. The battle for control of the business was turning exceedingly violent, and Adams, who had always operated with bribes and trickery, neither needed nor wanted to be involved in wars to the death. He lived out the next few years in luxury in the Ansonia Hotel and amassed a great fortune through land speculation. However, he was estranged from his family, who was ashamed of his past criminality and blamed him for their inability to lead normal, respectable lives. On October 1, 1907 Adams committed suicide in his apartment.

See also: NUMBERS RACKET.

Adler, Polly (1900–1962) New York madam

Often called the last of the great madams, Polly Adler achieved such a measure of esteem that in the 1930s and 1940s she was regarded as one of New York City's most illustrious "official greeters." As she said in her memoirs, "I could boast a clientele culled not only from *Who's Who* and the *Social Register,* but from *Burke's Peerage* and the *Almanach de Gotha.*" Her clients, of course, were not limited to high society; they included politicians, police, writers and gangsters. Among the latter were Dutch Schultz, Frank Costello and Lucky Luciano. The first two were regarded by Polly and her girls as lavish spenders. Luciano was not. If a girl sent by Polly to Luciano's suite in the Waldorf Towers thought she would do much better than the standard

$20 fee, she was disillusioned. Luciano might stuff an extra $5 in her bra at the conclusion of a session, but that was all. As he later recalled: "I didn't want to do nothin' different. What do you think I was gonna do—spoil it for everybody?"

Polly almost always used the real names of her clients when introducing them to her girls; the clients did not object, knowing that their secret was safe with Polly. When Dutch Schultz was on the run from the law in 1933 because of an income tax evasion charge drawn by a young federal prosecutor named Thomas E. Dewey, there were 50,000 wanted posters on him. The gang chief nevertheless continued his regular two or three visits a week to Polly's place and was never betrayed.

Despite some memorable police raids, Polly generally operated with little interference out of lavish apartments in Manhattan's fashionable East 50s and 60s. Long laudatory descriptions of the decor in her opulent "homes" appeared in various publications. One establishment at Madison Avenue and East 55th Street was

The flamboyant Polly Adler managed to appear dowdyish whenever hauled into court on vice charges, a far cry from the way she paraded with her girls through the Broadway nightclubs.

described as having a living room done up in "Louis XVI," a taproom in a military motif colored in red, white and blue, and a dining room that suggested the interior of a seashell. All the baths and "workrooms" were finished in peach and apple green. Free food was always offered and the bar did a thriving business. Many men dropped in just for refreshments and a stimulating chat with the loquacious madam.

Polly became a celebrity in her own right. Interviewed by the press, she commented on various past and present events. Her opinion on Prohibition: "They might as well have been trying to dry up the Atlantic with a post-office blotter." Offer the people what they want, she said, and they will buy it. It was a philosophy that served her as well in her field as it did the bootleggers in their area. Madam Adler routinely made the gossip columns and was a regular at nightclub openings, where she would create a sensation marching in with a bevy of her most beautiful girls. She later recalled: "The clubs were a display window for the girls. I'd make a newspaper column or two, the latest Polly Adler gag would start the rounds and, no matter where we happened to go, some of the club patrons would follow after us and end the evening at the house."

Polly Adler retired from the business in 1944. Encouraged by a number of writer friends, including Robert Benchley, she pursued a writing career after taking a number of college courses, and by the time of her death in 1962, she had become something of a literary light. In her later years Adler, an acknowledged expert on matters sexual, was a dinner companion of Dr. Alfred Kinsey.

Adonis, Joe (1902–1972) syndicate gangster

A member of the governing board of the national crime syndicate from its inception in the early 1930s, Joe Adonis, or simply Joey A., remained a power until he was deported in 1956. While Adonis always insisted that he was born in this country, he was, in fact, born in Montemarano, Italy, on November 22, 1902. Joseph Doto entered the country illegally and adopted the name Adonis to pay tribute to what he regarded to be his handsome looks. After joining a New York street gang, Adonis formed a teenage friendship with the future big names in American crime—Albert Anastasia, Vito Genovese and Lucky Luciano. By the mid-1920s Adonis was the head of the Broadway Mob, which controlled the flow of bootleg liquor in mid-Manhattan, the richest market in the country. While he was the operating head of the mob, he may not have been the real brains, since his partners included Luciano and Frank Costello. However, Adonis continued to rise in

the hierarchy of organized crime because he was loyal and never overambitious. He became a trusted member of the board of the national syndicate, settling disputes between various criminal factions and issuing murder contracts, among other duties. Abe Reles, the informer in the Murder, Inc. case, once told authorities, "Cross Joey Adonis and you cross the national combination." When Luciano went to prison, he left Adonis in nominal charge of the combination's affairs, but he added, "Cooperate with Meyer." Meyer was Meyer Lansky, who became the chief officer in the combination. Adonis proved smart enough to know how to take orders.

Following the end of Prohibition, Adonis extended his domain to include not only the waterfront and gambling rackets in Manhattan but those in Brooklyn and New Jersey as well. He also masterminded a number of jewel thefts, an avocation that amused his big-time confederates. It seemed like a dangerous enterprise but it made Adonis happy. Despite a long career in crime, he did not go to jail until 1951, when, after the Kefauver Committee hearings, he pleaded guilty in New Jersey to violation of the state's gambling laws and received a two-year sentence. In 1956, Adonis, facing federal perjury charges, accepted a deportation order, after his true birthplace had been discovered. Thereafter, he lived out his days lavishly in Milan, Italy, still maintaining ties with the underworld in America and occasionally meeting with Luciano, who resided—also in exile—in Naples.

See also: BROADWAY MOB, MEYER LANSKY, LUCKY LUCIANO.

Adorno, George (1959–   ) youthful murderer

The case history of George Adorno is frequently cited as an example of the breakdown of the criminal justice system in the prosecution of juvenile crime. Adorno first ran afoul of the legal system at the age of four, when he set his sister on fire. After 16 subsequent arrests for theft, Adorno—age 15—was charged with triple murder, which he confessed to before a New York City district attorney in the presence of his sister. The sister had been summoned because Adorno's mother, an immigrant from Puerto Rico, did not speak any English. A juvenile court judge threw out the confession, however, because the mother had not been present. With the murder charge dropped, the judge found Adorno guilty of a lesser offense of robbery, ordered his confinement for three years and, as required by law, had his complete criminal record, including the three murder charges, sealed.

After serving half his sentence, Adorno was released. Nineteen days later, he shot to death Steven Robinson, a black law student who drove a cab to finance his education. When Justice Burton Roberts sentenced him to 15 years to life for the Robinson murder, he commented: "Nothing ever happened to Adorno. He plays the courts like a concert player plays the piano. Is there ever a time when a red light goes on and you say, 'We have to control this person'? So, at age sixteen, he finally gets a three-year sentence and he is out in eighteen months." Under Justice Roberts' sentence, the maximum permitted by the youth's plea of guilty, Adorno became eligible for parole after eight and a half years.

See also: JUVENILE DELINQUENCY.

adultery

One of the most unenforced laws in the country is that concerning the crime of adultery, which, with certain variations in state laws, may be described as sexual intercourse by a married person with someone other than his wife or her husband. In some states adultery is committed only when the married person is the woman.

New York penal law defines the crime as "the sexual intercourse of two persons, either of whom is married to a third person. The offense is deemed a misdemeanor and is punishable by imprisonment in a penitentiary or county jail, for not more than six months or by a fine of not more than two hundred and fifty dollars, or by both." A few states, among them South Dakota, Oklahoma and Vermont, allow for a five-year prison term; in several others, small fines (as low as $10 in Maryland) are the limit of punishment. Such penalties caused Judge Morris Ploscowe to wonder "why legislatures have bothered to include adultery in their penal system if the enjoyment of extramarital intercourse may at most result in a small fine."

The law is, of course, generally incapable of controlling voluntary sexual behavior. According to Dr. Alfred Kinsey, strict enforcement of sex statutes would result in the jailing of 95 percent of the population.

age and crime

Crime, especially violent crime, is for the young in body, not just the young in heart. Perhaps as many as three out of every four street crimes are committed by persons under the age of 25. This phenomenon is hardly a new one; the average western outlaw was shockingly young. Billy the Kid, who was reputed to have killed several men by the time of his 21st birthday, was more the rule than the exception. A criminal act does require a good amount of daring, vigor and rebelliousness, and as Peter W. Lewis and Jack Wright, Jr. point out in *Modern Criminal Justice,* "Society is not often plagued by daring, rebellious old people."

Some of the statistics are shocking indeed. Children under the age of 15 commit more total crimes than do adults over 25. About one-third of all violent crimes are the work of the under-18 group. The under-25 group commits about four out of five robberies, burglaries, larceny thefts and car thefts; three out of every five forcible rapes; and about half of all murders, non-negligent manslaughters and aggravated assaults. Thus, it is fair to speak of what one observer has called a "tidal wave of young criminality." It is impossible to judge whether this represents a break with the past or just reflects age-old patterns, since there are no reliable statistics for the 19th century—much less earlier times—to match with those of the present-day *Uniform Crime Reports.* But it might be pointed out that while organized crime today is largely an over-25 activity, in the 19th century this violent business was largely controlled by the young. The Daybreak Boys, a brutal New York gang, were composed of mostly 20-year-old and younger criminals. Certainly today's school violence must go far to equal that of the Walsh School feud in Chicago from 1881 to 1905.

Much of the "crime wave" that supposedly enveloped the United States from the 1960s onward was little more than a logical development of the age-crime relationship. Irresponsible statements by politicians and law enforcement officials tended to confirm public fear of a new crime wave. The simple fact is that as a result of the postwar baby boom, the under-25 age group grew far faster than the rest of the population and, as always, the increasing number of youngsters committed an increasing number of crimes. Recent crime statistics have shown a decline in crime rates.

Further complicating the use of age-crime statistics are other factors that strongly affect them. For instance, the high crime rate produced by under-15 and under-25 black youths is in part influenced by urbanization. All studies show that the violent crime rate for young blacks who have moved from the South to large urban cities in the North and Midwest is far higher than that for young blacks on a nationwide basis.

Clearly, a study of the relationship between age and crime is necessary as a method for understanding the problem but it hardly provides an answer to it.

See also: DAYBREAK BOYS, JUVENILE DELINQUENCY, WALSH SCHOOL FEUD.

Ah Hoon (?–1909) murder victim

The tong wars of New York's Chinatown were fought with more than guns, hatchets and snickersnee. They were also fought with insult, loss of face and wit. In the 1909–10 war between the Hip Sings and the On Leongs, some of the most telling blows were struck by

MURDER OFFENDERS BY AGE, SEX AND RACE, 1998

Age	Total	Sex		
		Male	Female	Unknown
Total	16,019	10,505	1,241	4,273
Percent distribution[1]	100.0	65.6	7.7	26.7
Under 18[2]	1,169	1,069	100	—
Under 22[2]	3,965	3,675	289	1
18 and over[2]	9,545	8,438	1,105	2
Infant (under 1)	—	—	—	—
1 to 4	1	1	—	—
5 to 8	4	2	2	—
9 to 12	17	14	3	—
13 to 16	594	530	64	—
17 to 19	2,009	1,872	137	—
20 to 24	2,685	2,477	207	1
25 to 29	1,627	1,425	202	—
30 to 34	1,101	946	155	—
35 to 39	890	736	154	—
40 to 44	678	561	117	—
45 to 49	423	351	72	—
50 to 54	260	222	37	1
55 to 59	165	137	28	—
60 to 64	90	79	11	—
65 to 69	58	51	7	—
70 to 74	38	35	3	—
75 and over	74	68	6	—
Unknown	5,305	998	36	4,271

[1] Because of rounding, percentages may not add to total.
[2] Does not include unknown ages.
Source: Federal Bureau of Investigation

the celebrated comic Ah Hoon, who was a member of the On Leongs. Ah Hoon used his performances at the venerable old Chinese Theater on Doyers Street to savage the Hip Sings. Finally, the Hip Sings could take no more insults to their honor and passed the death sentence on the comic. They announced publicly that Ah Hoon would be assassinated on December 30. The On Leongs vowed he would not be. And even the white man got into the act. A police sergeant and two patrolmen appeared on stage with Ah Hoon on December 30. The performance went off without a hitch, and immediately after, Ah Hoon was escorted back to his boarding house on Chatham Square. He was locked in his room and several On Leongs took up guard duty outside the door. Ah Hoon was safe. The only window in his room faced a blank wall across a court.

The On Leongs started celebrating this new loss of face by the Hip Sings, who sulked as the On Leongs paraded through Chinatown. When Ah Hoon's door was unlocked the next morning, his shocked guards found him dead, shot through the head. Subsequent investigation revealed a member of the Hip Sings had been lowered on a chair by a rope from the roof and had shot the comic using a gun equipped with a silencer. Now, the Hip Sings paraded through Chinatown. Ah Hoon's killer was never found.

See also: BLOODY ANGLE, BOW KUM, MOCK DUCK, TONG WARS.

Aiello, Joseph (1891–1930) Chicago mobster

Joseph Aiello and his brothers, Dominick, Antonio and Andrew, were enemies of Al Capone in the struggle for control of organized crime in Chicago. Aiello tried to have Capone killed in somewhat novel ways, e.g., attempting to bribe a restaurant chef $10,000 to put prussic acid in Capone's soup and, on another occasion, offering a reward of $50,000 for Big Al's head.

These efforts called for extraordinary vengeance on Capone's part, and he ordered his enemy killed "real good." On October 23, 1930 Aiello was gunned down on North Kolmar Avenue, struck by 59 bullets, weighing altogether well over a pound.

See also: LOUIS "LITTLE NEW YORK" CAMPAGNA.

Alcatraz of the Rockies   top maximum-security prison

It is the prison confinement convicts fear most—the maximum-security institution called the Alcatraz of the Rockies and, by federal prisoners themselves, "Super Max." That last sobriquet is not complimentary but rather born of something between fear and terror.

Imprisoned Mafia chief John Gotti was confined to Marion Penitentiary, in Illinois, for a life sentence in 1992 because Super Max was not yet completed. At the time, Marion held the top spot as the most feared prison in the country and indeed was cited as being inhumane by Amnesty International. Marion—like Super Max—operates under a quota system calling for the transfer out of lifers to less harsh institutions after they have served 30 months and demonstrate the ability to be subject to discipline. Under that regulation Gotti was eligible for transfer in 1995, but he was kept in Marion. It was well known that his lawyers did not press the issue of his long confinement for fear it would prolong the situation or possibly cause his transfer to what was now the still harsher Super Max.

Located in Florence, Colo., it holds fewer than 400 prisoners and has almost one prison employee per inmate. The plan of the Federal Bureau of Prisons is to modify the behavior of violent prisoners by what can only be described as entombing them in isolation cells for up to 23 hours a day. Unlike other prisons, Super Max is silent. There is an empty fluorescent-lit hallway. There are no shouts and screams across cellblocks, or convicts banging on bars, or even the sound of a radio.

Movements in the prison are restricted by 1,400 electronically controlled gates and viewed by 168 television monitors. It costs about $50,000 a year to incarcerate a prisoner in Super Max—about two and one-half times the $20,000 average cost elsewhere. And Super Max boasts a hefty pricetag at $60 million.

The prisoners in Super Max fall into two basic groups. The smaller one is the so-called bomber wing, in which some of the nation's most notorious offenders, i.e., bomber terrorists, are kept under "multiple locks and keys." Included in this group are Oklahoma City bomber Timothy J. McVeigh, Unabomber Theodore J. Kaczynski, and World Trade bombing mastermind Ramzi Ahmed Yousef. They are held at Super Max not for behavior problems but because authorities say they would very likely face violence in less secure prisons. Another consideration is that Super Max offers far less opportunities for escape.

Primarily, however, Super Max was set up to house the "worst of the worst" among the 100,000 inmates in the federal prison system. Among the Super Max inmates about 35 percent have committed murder in prison, 85 percent have committed assaults in prison and 41 percent have made attempts to escape.

After three years some prisoners who are not transferred out are offered the opportunity of spending more time out of their cells. Among them, there is said to be a strong hatred of Super Max. As one inmate told a *New York Times* reporter: "Prolonged isolation is the worst punishment you can put on a human being. The common denominator among prisoners is rage, pent-up rage, frustration." It was reported that many prisoners stay in their cells and refuse to come out for recreation. They turn jumpy and become enraged when having to deal with people.

There is an occasional prisoner who can be described as adapting to Super Max—or, in prisoner parlance, "beating the system." One would be Charles Harrelson, the father of actor Woody Harrelson, who is serving two consecutive life sentences for murdering a federal judge in the 1970s. His son is trying to obtain a new trial for him. The elder Harrelson finds Super Max somewhat attuned to his interests. He notes that his previous prison did not have a shower in the room but did have a lot of noise. "Peace and quiet here is paramount for people like me who like to write. But for people who can't read and write it must be pure hell. He told the *New York Times*, "They designed this place for sensory deprivation. It's an Orwellian experience."

The Super Max administration claims that the prison has found "no evidence to show that people are deteriorating." Lawyers of inmates see it differently. Lawrence Feitell, who represents Luis Felipe, the leader of the Latin Kings gang in New York, says his client "has retreated into himself, that is where the destruction of his personality is taking place. He has deteriorated to the extent where he prefers to stay in his cell. He takes no recreation."

The real test of how much psychological damage is caused to prisoners probably has to be judged over a longer span of time. It has been noted that by the time Alcatraz was closed in 1963 it was estimated by some that as many as 60 percent of the prisoners were "stir crazy," or insane. And despite its fearful reputation, Alcatraz had eliminated many of its truly restrictive measures, so that today Super Max can be regarded as far more fearful than Alcatraz. While authorities downplay the possibility of personality deterioration under the Super Max regimen, the concept of release to a less restrictive prison (leaving aside the matter of how complete the practice is) is itself a recognition that the prison is not exactly conducive to prisoner well-being.

Prison authorities may be said to be marching to an entirely different drummer, basing the worth of the system on the claim that by concentrating highly violent prisoners in Super Max, there has been a resultant drop in prison violence across the federal prison system.

See also: MARION PENITENTIARY.

Alcatraz prison

In 1868 the U.S. War Department established a prison for hostiles and deserters on a stark little island in San Francisco harbor. The Indians called it "Alka-taz"—the lonely "Island of the Pelicans."

By the 1930s Alcatraz had outlived its usefulness to the War Department, but it filled a new need for the Department of Justice, which wanted a "superprison to hold supercriminals," because there just seemed no way to contain them securely in the rest of the nation's federal penitentiaries. The new federal prison on Alcatraz opened on January 1, 1934 under the wardenship of James A. Johnston. Although the warden had previously earned a reputation as a "penal reformer," he would rule "the Rock" with an iron hand.

Hardened criminals were shipped in large batches from other prisons, the schedules of the trains carrying them kept top secret. The first batch, the so-called Atlanta Boys Convoy, excited the public's imagination, conjuring up wild stories of huge gangster armies plotting to attack the convoy with guns, bombs, flamethrowers and even airplanes in order to free scores of deadly criminals. But the first mass prisoner transfer and those following it went off without a single hitch; by the end of the year, the prison, now called America's Devil's Island housed more than 250 of the most dangerous federal prisoners in the country. The city of San Francisco, which had fought the establishment of a superprison on Alcatraz, now found it had a prime tourist attraction; picture postcards of Alcatraz by the millions—invariably inscribed, "Having wonderful time—wish you were here"—were mailed from the city.

The prisoners, however, wished they were almost anywhere else. Johnston followed the principle of "maximum security and minimum privileges." There were rules, rules, rules, which made Alcatraz into a living but silent hell. A rule of silence, which had to be abandoned after a few years as unworkable, meant the prisoners were not allowed to speak to one another either in the cell house or the mess hall. A single whispered word could bring a guard's gas stick down on a prisoner. But the punishment could be worse; he might

instead be marched off to "the hole" to be kept on a diet of bread and water for however long it pleased the warden and the guards.

A convict was locked up in his Alcatraz cell 14 hours a day, every day without exception. Lockup was at 5:30, lights out was at 9:30 and morning inspection at 6:30. There was no trustee system, and thus no way a convict could win special privileges. While good behavior won no favors, bad behavior was punished with water hosing, gas stick beatings, special handcuffs that tightened with every movement, a strait jacket that left a man numb with cramps for hours, the hole, a brad-and-water diet and, worst of all, the loss of "good time," by which all federal prisoners could have 10 days deducted from their sentence for every 30 days with no infractions. But this harsh treatment proved too much for the prisoners and too difficult for the guards to enforce, even with an incredible ratio of one guard for every three prisoners. Within four years the rule of silence started to be modified, and some other regulations were eased.

Incredibly, despite the prison's security and physical isolation, there were numerous attempts to escape from Alcatraz, but none was successful. In 1937 two convicts, Ralph Roe and Teddy Cole, got out of the workshop area during a heavy fog, climbed a Cyclone fence 10 feet high and then jumped from a bluff 30 feet into the water. They were never seen again, but there is little doubt they were washed to sea. The tide ran very fast that day, and the nearest land was a mile and a quarter away through 40° water. The fact that the two men, habitual criminals, were never arrested again makes it almost certain that they died. Probably the closest anyone came to a successful escape occurred during a 1946 rebellion plotted by a bank robber named Bernie Coy. During the 48 hours of the rebellion, five men died and 15 more were wounded, many seriously, before battle-trained marines stormed ashore and put an end to the affair. Escape attempts proved particularly vicious on Alcatraz because convicts with so little hope of release or quarter were much more likely to kill guards during a break.

Many more prisoners sought to escape the prison by suicide, and several succeeded. Those who failed faced long stays in the hole after being released from the prison hospital. Others escaped the reality of Alcatraz by going insane. According to some estimates, at least 60 percent of the inmates were insane. It remains a moot point whether Al Capone, who arrived there in 1934 from the Atlanta Penitentiary, where he had been serving an 11-year sentence for tax evasion, won parole in 1939 because of the advanced state of his syphilitic condition or because he too had gone stir crazy like so many others.

U.S. Coast Guard aerial photo of Alcatraz furthers its "superprison" image. In truth, it proved to be a crumbling, inefficient institution.

Alcatraz in the 1930s housed not only the truly notorious and dangerous prisoners but also many put there for vindictive reasons, such as Robert Stroud, the Birdman of Alcatraz, who, along with Rufus "Whitey" Franklin, was one of the most ill-treated prisoners in the federal penal system. The inmate roster included the tough gangsters who truly belonged, like Doc Barker, and those who did not, like Machine Gun Kelly, who had never even fired his weapon at anyone. There were also such nontroublesome convicts as former public enemy Alvin "Creepy" Karpis.

Over the years there were many calls for the closing of Alcatraz. Some did so in the name of economy, since it cost twice as much to house a prisoner on Alcatraz than in any other federal prison. Sen. William Langer even charged the government could board inmates "in the Waldorf Astoria cheaper."

By the 1950s Alcatraz had lost its reputation as an escape-proof prison and had become known simply as a place to confine prisoners deemed to be deserving of harsher treatment.

By the time "the Rock" was finally phased out as a federal prison in 1963, it was a crumbling mess and

prisoners could easily dig away at its walls with a dull spoon.

See also: ALCATRAZ PRISON REBELLION, ALCATRAZ PUSH-UPS, ATLANTA BOYS CONVOY, RUFUS "WHITEY" FRANKLIN, JAMES A. JOHNSTON, JAMES LUCAS, RULE OF SILENCE, ROBERT STROUD.

Alcatraz Prison Rebellion

The 1946 Alcatraz Prison Rebellion was a misnomer. It was nothing more or less than a cunning prison escape plot by six men based on the release of the other prisoners in order to confuse and distract the authorities. The attempted breakout, which was foiled after 48 hours, was bloody: five men died and 15 others were wounded, many seriously. To quell the so-called rebellion, trained sharpshooters were flown in from other prisons and battle-trained U.S. marines stormed ashore under the command of Gen. Joseph "Vinegar Joe" Stilwell and Frank Merill, of the famous World War II Marauders.

The mastermind of the plot was one of the least likely of convicts, 46-year-old Bernie Coy, who still had another 16 years to serve for bank robbery. The warden and guards regarded Coy as little more than a Kentucky hillbilly bandit. Coy, however, had spotted a critical weakness in the Alcatraz security system; as a cellhouse orderly, he saw that he could overpower the tier guard, release a few confederates and work his way up to a gun gallery, a floor-to-ceiling cage of bars behind which was housed the one man with weapons in the entire building. The only time this armed guard stepped out of the cage was to inspect D Block, the dreaded isolation section. On May 2, according to a detailed plan, Coy was waiting for the guard when he left the cage and overcame him in a fierce hand-to-hand battle. Inside the gun gallery there was an ample supply of weapons and ammunition.

From here on, Coy's plan was simple. He and his confederates captured all nine guards in the building and placed them in two cells. They then released most of the other convicts but barred the doors so that they could not follow them. Under cover of the resulting confusion, the escapers intended to use hostages to get across the prison yard, seize the prison launch and speed across the bay before an alarm could be sounded. On the mainland, cars would be waiting for them, thanks to the connections of Joseph Paul "Dutch" Cretzer, one of Coy's accomplices. Besides Cretzer, a bank robber, murderer and former Public Enemy No. 4, Coy's accomplices included Sam Shockley, a mental defective and close friend of Cretzer; Marvin Hubbard, a gangling Alabama gunman and close friend of Coy; Miran Edgar "Buddy" Thompson, a robber, murderer and jailbreak artist who previously had escaped from eight prisons; and Clarence Carnes, a 19-year-old Choctaw Indian serving 99 years for kidnapping a farmer across a state line after escaping from a prison where he was doing time for murder.

The plot failed because a prison guard—against orders—had failed to return one corridor key to its place on a keyboard. The escapers then jammed the lock trying to force it open with other keys. Soon, the convicts' timetable ran out and the prison launch left. Coy, accompanied by Hubbard, left Cretzer in charge of the hostages, ordering that none of them be killed, and went off to communicate with Warden James A. Johnston over the prison phone system. Coy had come up with a desperate alternative plan to use the guard hostages to get into the staff living compound, where the guards' families, including 30 young girls, lived. With these hostages, Coy was sure the authorities would have to let him and his confederates off the island.

Back with the hostages, Cretzer knew better. He realized that as soon as the convicts headed in the direction of the family area, the guards on the walls would cut loose, killing the escapers and the guard hostages as well. There was no way the guards would let their families be taken. Besides, Cretzer wanted to kill all the guards. He had not told Coy that he had already killed a guard in a gunfight and that the prison authorities had the body. Cretzer had nothing to lose. Moreover, the deranged Shockley and the cunning Thompson kept goading Cretzer to kill all the guards. Thompson realized that if all nine were dead, there would be nobody alive who could name him as one of the escapers. Only Carnes, obedient to Coy and Hubbard, was opposed. Suddenly, Cretzer exploded in a murderous fury. He fired shot after shot into the two cells holding the guards. All went down. Then he ordered Carnes to go inside to make sure all were dead. Carnes went in at gunpoint and saw most of the guards were alive, but he reported that all were dead. Actually, only one was dead; of the remaining eight, five were gravely wounded and three had escaped injury completely, though they feigned death.

When Coy returned from talking with Warden Johnston, who had stalled for time, he discovered Cretzer's mass shooting. Without the guard hostages, Coy knew there could be no escape. Furious over how their carefully laid plans had been destroyed, Coy and Hubbard stalked Cretzer, who in turn hunted them. Meanwhile, news of the mass break attempt and wild rumors spread throughout San Francisco. Thousands lined the waterfront to watch as 80 marines stormed ashore in full battle dress and guard sharpshooters slipped into the prison. They found the hostages, including one already dead, and brought them out. The seriously wounded five had compresses pressed over their wounds. Some unknown convict had treated them, undoubtedly saving the lives of at least three or four, and then slipped away, never to be identified.

More guard sharpshooters were sent in. Holes were cut in the roof of the building and grenades heaved inside, forcing most prisoners back to their own cell blocks, among them Thompson, Carnes and Shockley. But the remaining trio, Cretzer, Coy and Hubbard, evaded the grenade blasts by moving into the darkened utility corridors, concrete trenches below the cell blocks where plumbing and electric wires were buried. Even gas grenades dropped through the ventilator shafts could not dislodge them or stop them from firing at the guards stalking them.

The trio of convicts did not find one another until almost the end. By then Cretzer had been wounded by bomb shrapnel and Coy by gunfire. According to Clark Howard's *Six Against the Rock* (1977), the most definitive study of the escape, it was Cretzer—not the guards—who killed Coy, jumping out of the shadows and shooting him in the neck, shoulders and face. Cretzer tried to kill Hubbard as well but raced off as guards closed in. Hubbard dragged Coy off into a dark tunnel and remained with him until he died. In the meantime Cretzer was cornered by guards, who finally killed him with grenades and gunfire, 41 hours after the great escape attempt had started. Several hours later, four guards caught up with Hubbard. He died in a barrage of fire, taking one rifle slug in the left eye and another in the left temple.

The investigation that followed the great escape attempt focused on the brutal conditions in the prison. It was found that one prisoner, Whitey Franklin, who had attempted an escape back in 1938 with two others and had received an added life sentence for killing a guard, had spent every day since his conviction, more than seven years, in the hole.

It was almost an anticlimax when the three survivors of the ill-fated plot were brought to trial. Carnes got life to go along with his 99 years, and on December 3, 1948 Thompson and the obviously insane Shockley became the first two men to die in San Quentin's new gas chamber.

See also: BERNARD COY, JOSEPH PAUL "DUTCH" CRETZER, RUFUS "WHITEY" FRANKLIN, JAMES A. JOHNSTON, SAM RICHARD SHOCKLEY, MIRAN EDGAR "BUDDY" THOMPSON.

Alcatraz push-ups   prison "currency"

While Alcatraz had the deserved reputation of being America's toughest federal prison, there were a couple of seemingly odd exceptions to the rugged regimen that produced one of the strangest and most unique practices in American penology. Alcatraz became known as the *best* prison for "eats and smokes." Federal regulations called for a minimum of 2,000 calories per prisoner per day, but on Alcatraz the average was kept between 3,100 and 3,600 daily calories. When Mrs. Homer Cummings, the wife of the attorney general, visited "the Rock" in the mid-1930s, she was served the standard convict dinner—soup, beefaroni, beans, cabbage, onions, chili pods, hot biscuits, ice cream, iced tea and coffee—and exclaimed: "Why, this is more than we eat at home!" It was estimated that the average convict gained 15 to 20 pounds during his stay in the prison, and some put on 40 pounds or more.

Along with this rather lavish menu, Alcatraz had a bountiful smoking program. Each prisoner was issued three packs of cigarettes a week, and when that supply was gone, he could get all the loose tobacco he wanted from free dispensers to roll his own. Thus, in Alcatraz cigarettes lost the currency value and bribing power they enjoyed in other institutions. As a result, the curious practice of paying debts, such as those incurred in gambling games, with so many push-ups developed. This allowed the prisoners to have some action and offered something of an antidote for their overfeeding.

See also: ALCATRAZ PRISON.

alcohol

Drinking, drunkenness and alcoholism are significant factors contributing to crime in the United States. Each year there are about 3 million arrests for drunkenness and drunk driving and for vagrancy, disorderly conduct and other activities that usually involve drunkenness. These so-called direct alcoholism arrests may well account for 30 to 40 percent of all arrests made. Many far more serious crimes are also committed "under the influence," ranging from personal assault to armed robbery and murder. There are no reliable statistics measuring the exact correlation between drinking and homicide, but any veteran police officer knows that a great many domestic quarrels and "in the home murders," the leading category of homicides, are preceded by heavy drinking by one or more of the participants.

A 1974 study divided 3,510 men between the ages of 20 and 30 into drinking and nondrinking categories. The men were asked if they had committed a number of crimes, including car theft, breaking and entering, shoplifting, face-to-face stealing and armed robbery. Among the nondrinkers 16 percent had engaged in shoplifting and 5 percent admitted to breaking and entering. The incidence of all the other types of crime was statistically nonexistent. Among the drinkers in the study, the number of law breakers increased as the survey moved from light or moderate drinkers to heavy users of alcohol.

In the heaviest drinkers category, 18 percent reported engaging in breaking and entering, 56 percent in shoplifting, 9 percent in car theft, 5 percent in stealing and 2 percent in armed robbery.

In a 1974 nationwide study of 191,400 inmates at state correctional facilities, 43 percent said they had been drinking at the time they committed the crime of which they were convicted. About half of these described their drinking as heavy.

Criminologists have long debated whether these and other studies demonstrate whether a person who is under the influence of alcohol will violate laws that he would not violate if he were not intoxicated. No definite conclusions are possible, but there is considerable evidence indicating that a drinker will behave in a "class" manner. Thus, among the middle class and advancing up the socioeconomic ladder, there is generally little economic basis for the commission of crime, especially violent crime, and the tendency is for drunkenness to result in such behavior as singing, telling dirty stories and crying. On the other hand, in the ghettos and among the lower socioeconomic classes, the economic basis for crime increases, and there is a far greater tendency to turn from "happy drunkenness" to the starting of fights and the violation of criminal laws.

Further reading: *Fundamentals of Criminal Investigation* by Charles O'Hara.

Alderisio, Felix "Milwaukee Phil" (1922–1971) hit man

Regarded by many as the top hit man of the Chicago mob, Felix "Milwaukee Phil" Alderisio was popularly given credit for designing the "hitmobile," a car especially geared for committing murder with the least possible interference. Among what may be called its optional features were switches that would turn out the car's front or rear lights to confuse police tails. Another innovation was a secret compartment in a backrest that not only held murder weapons but contained clamps to anchor down handguns, shotguns or rifles for more steady shooting while the vehicle was in motion. Although the Chicago police insisted that Milwaukee Phil was the executioner in well over a dozen gangland hits, no murder charge against him was ever proven. He was, however, finally convicted of extortion and died in prison in 1971.

Aldermen's Wars   Chicago political killings

Even for Chicago, a city noted for its gangland killings and battles, the so-called Aldermen's Wars, between 1916 and 1921, stand out for sheer savagery. In all, 30 men died in the continuous five-year battle fought for control of the 19th, or "Bloody," Ward, which encompassed the city's Little Italy. The political forces that controlled the 19th were entitled to the huge payoffs coming out of Little Italy for various criminal enterprises. With the coming of Prohibition, the production of moonshine alcohol became the area's "cottage industry" and an important source of illicit alcohol for the entire city.

The 19th had been controlled by Johnny "de Pow" Powers, an incorrigible saloonkeeper, protector of criminals and graft-taking alderman from the 1890s on. Despite the transition of much of the area from Irish to Italian, Powers was able to maintain his control and met no serious challenge until 1916, when Anthony D'Andrea mounted a bid against James Bowler, junior alderman from the 19th and a Powers henchman. D'Andrea was less than a pillar of civic virtue himself, although he was a prominent leader in many Italian fra-

ternal societies and a labor union official. The *Chicago Tribune* reported: "Anthony Andrea is the same Antonio D'Andrea, unfrocked priest, linguist, and former power in the old 'red light' district, who in 1903 was released from the penitentiary after serving 13 months on a counterfeit charge. D'Andrea's name has also been connected with a gang of Italian forgers and bank thieves who operated at one time all over the country."

The killings commenced in February 1916. Frank Lombardi, a Powers ward heeler, was shot dead in a saloon. D'Andrea lost his election battle that year, as well as another one in 1919 and a final one in 1921, a direct race against Powers. During all that time, corpses of supporters on both sides filled the streets, and a number of bombings took place, including one set off on the front porch of Powers' home. The Powers forces retaliated with the bombing of a D'Andrea rally, severely injuring five persons. There were subsequent bombings of D'Andrea's headquarters and the home of one of his lieutenants.

One day in March 1921, Paul Labriola, a Powers man who was a court bailiff, walked to work with some apprehension because his name had been listed on the Dead Man's Tree, a poplar on Loomis Street on which both factions had taken to posting the names of slated victims, a grim form of psychological warfare. At Halsted and Congress, Labriola passed four D'Andrea gunmen; as he started across the intersection, he was cut down by a volley of shots. One of the four gunmen walked over to their victim, straddled his body and pumped three more revolver shots into him. Later that day the same four gunmen killed cigar store owner Harry Raimondi, a former D'Andrea man who had switched sides. While the killings and bombings continued, Alderman Bowler declared:

> Conditions in the 19th Ward are terrible. Gunmen are patrolling the streets. I have received threats that I was to be "bumped off" or kidnapped. Alderman Powers' house is guarded day and night. Our men have been met, threatened and slugged. Gunmen and cutthroats have been imported from New York and Buffalo for this campaign of intimidation. Owners of halls have been threatened with death or the destruction of their buildings if they rent their places to us. It is worse than the Middle Ages.

The killings continued after D'Andrea's third election defeat, despite his announcement that he was through with 19th Ward politics. In April 1921 a man named Abraham Wolfson who lived in the apartment across the hall from D'Andrea got a threatening letter that read in part: "You are to move in 15 days. We are going to blow up the building and kill the whole

D'Andrea family. He killed others and we are going to do the same thing. We mean business. You better move and save many lives."

Wolfson showed the note to D'Andrea and then moved out. This gave D'Andrea's enemies what they wanted, an empty apartment from which to watch him. On May 11, just after his bodyguard had driven off, D'Andrea was gunned down as he was about to enter his building.

D'Andrea was the wars' 28th victim. There were to be two more, Andrew Orlando and Joseph Sinacola, D'Andrea's Sicilian "blood brother," both of whom had sworn to avenge their boss' death. Orlando was killed in July and Sinacola in August.

There was only one prosecution for any of the 30 murders committed during the Aldermen's Wars, that of Bloody Angelo Genna for the street corner slaying of Paul Labriola. But nothing much came of it. The numerous witnesses to the murder belatedly realized they hadn't seen a thing.

See also: DEAD MAN'S TREE.

Allen, Bill (?–1882) murderer

A Chicago black man named Bill Allen had the distinction of being hunted by the largest "posse" in American history. On November 30, 1882 Allen killed one black and wounded another, and later that evening he murdered Patrolman Clarence E. Wright, who tried to arrest him. Three days after the incident Allen was located in the basement of a house by Patrolman Patrick Mulvihill, but the fugitive shot Mulvihill through a window and fled. Soon, 200 policemen were scouring the black district of Chicago for Allen. By mid-afternoon, according to a contemporary account, "Upwards of 10,000 people armed with all sorts of weapons from pocket pistols and pitchforks to rifles, were assisting the police in the hunt." At 3:30 that afternoon, Sgt. John Wheeler found Allen in the backyard of a house on West Kinzie Street and killed him in a gunfight. Allen's body was taken in a patrol wagon to the Desplaines police station, and somehow the rumor started that he had been arrested rather than killed. A lynch mob of thousands quickly formed, and when a few officers tried to break up the crowd, they were threatened. "The crowd," one report of the event said, "became frenzied and threatened to tear down the station. Threats and promises were all in vain, and a serious riot seemed inevitable. Chief Doyle mounted the wagon and assured the crowd that the Negro was really dead. They hooted and yelled, shouting that the police were concealing the man and encouraging each other to break in the windows of the station."

The police chief then came up with a way of placating the mob. Allen's body was stripped, laid out on a mattress and put on view through a barred window where it could be seen at the side of the station. A line was formed, and "the crowd passed in eager procession, and were satisfied by a simple glance at the dull, cold face. All afternoon that line moved steadily along, and the officers were busily occupied in keeping it in order. The crowd increased rather than diminished, and until darkness settled down, they were still gazing at the dead murderer. After dark a flaring gas jet at the head of the body brought it out in strong relief, and all night long the line of curious people filed by for a glimpse of the dead." It was 48 hours before Allen's body could be taken off display.

Allen, John (c. 1830–?) "Wickedest Man in New York"

One of the most notorious dives in New York City during the 1850s and 1860s—on a par with such later infamous resorts as the Haymarket, Paresis Hall and McGuirk's Suicide Hall—was John Allen's Dance House at 304 Water Street. Allen himself became widely known as "the Wickedest Man in New York," a sobriquet pinned on him first by Oliver Dyer in *Packard's Monthly*. What brought down the wrath of Dyer and other crusading journalists was not simply the vulgarity and depravity of Allen's establishment but his personal background. Allen came from a pious upper New York State family; three of his brothers were ministers, two Presbyterian preachers and the other a Baptist. He himself had initially pursued a similar ministerial career but soon deserted the Union Theological Seminary for the pleasures and profits of the flesh.

With his new wife, John Allen opened a dance hall–brothel on Water Street, stocking it with 20 prostitutes famed for wearing bells on their ankles and little else. In 10 years of operation, the Allens banked more than $100,000, placing them among the richest vice operators in the city.

Despite his desertion of the cloth, Allen never entirely shed his religious training. While he was a drunk, procurer and thief and was suspected of having committed more than one murder, Allen insisted on providing his lurid establishment with an aura of holiness. All the cubicles in which his ladies entertained customers were furnished with a Bible and other religious tracts. Regular clients were often rewarded with gifts of the New Testament. Before the dance hall opened for business at 1 P.M., Allen would gather his flock of musicians, harlots, bouncers and barkeeps and read passages out of the Scriptures. Hymn singing was a ritual; the favorite of Allen's hookers was

"There Is Rest for the Weary," apparently because it held out a more serene existence for the ladies in the life hereafter.

> There is rest for the weary,
> There is rest for you.
> On the other side of Jordan,
> In the sweet fields of Eden,
> Where the Tree of Life is blooming,
> There is rest for you.

Eventually, when a group of uptown clergymen took over Allen's resort for prayer meetings, it looked as if the religious aspect of the dance hall had gotten out of hand. Allen had apparently embraced religion entirely, and a lot of uptown devout began attending these meetings to bear witness to the reformation of sinners—especially John Allen. Alas, exposés in several newspapers turned up the sad intelligence that Allen, rather than undergoing a religious rebirth, had actually leased out his establishment to the ministers for $350 a month and seemingly provided some newly reformed sinners for 25¢ or 50¢ a head.

In time, the revivalist movement faded and Allen attempted to return his resort to its former infamy, only to find the criminal element no longer had faith in him, figuring anyone so religiously inclined might be untrustworthy. The last public record of Allen was his arrest, along with his wife and some of his prostitutes, for robbing a seaman. Shortly thereafter, the dance hall closed.

Allen's fate is obscured by contradictory legends. One had him finally undergoing a complete reformation and even taking up the cloth, but another placed "the Wickedest Man in New York" practicing his tawdry business in a different city under an assumed name. None of these stories has ever been confirmed.

John Allen rented out his dance hall-bordello for prayer meetings and obligingly provided sinners at 25¢ or 50¢ a head.

Allen, Lizzie (1840–1896) Chicago madam

Next to the fabulous Carrie Watson, Lizzie Allen was Chicago's most successful madam during the 19th century. A native of Milwaukee, she came to Chicago in 1858, at the age of 18, with the clear intention of becoming a madam. She went to work at Mother Herrick's Prairie Queen and, unlike most of the other girls, did not squander her earnings on men. After a stint at another leading brothel, the Senate, Allen opened a house on Wells Street staffed by three prostitutes. Despite the modest nature of the enterprise, she prospered there. Like most other brothel owners, Lizzie was burned out in the Great Chicago Fire of 1871, but she is credited with being the first back in business. She recruited a large staff of unemployed harlots and put them to work in a new house on Congress Street while the carpenters were still working to complete it. With that jump on the competition, Allen accumulated a large fortune and soon became one of the most important madams in the city. In 1878 she formed a relationship with a "solid man," the colorful Christopher Columbus Crabb, and with him as her lover and financial adviser, she flourished still more. In fact, Lizzie Allen was regarded by one local tabloid as "the finest looking woman in Chicago."

In 1888 Allen and Crabb built a 24-room mansion on Lake View Avenue to use as a plush brothel, but police interference doomed the enterprise. They then built an imposing double house at 2131 South Dearborn, which they named the House of Mirrors. Costing $125,000, it was one of the most impressive brothels of its day. (The house was destined to even greater fame under the Everleigh sisters, who took it over in 1900 and made it the most celebrated bawdy house in America.) Lizzie Allen operated the mansion until 1896, when, in poor health, she retired, leasing the property to Effie Hankins. She signed over all her real estate to Crabb and named him the sole beneficiary in her will. The estate was estimated to be worth between $300,000 and $1 million. When Lizzie Allen died on September 2, 1896, she was buried in Rosehill Cemetery. Her tombstone was inscribed, "Perpetual Ease."

See also: CHRISTOPHER COLUMBUS CRABB, EVERLEIGH SISTERS, PRAIRIE QUEEN.

Allen massacre courtroom shoot-out

The bloodiest confrontation ever to take place in an American courtroom occurred on March 14, 1912 at the Carroll Country Courthouse in Hillsville, Va. The Allen clan of the Blue Ridge Mountain area believed in its own code of behavior built around making moonshine, shooting revenuers and—certainly— paying no taxes. One day in 1911 a peace officer arrested a member of the clan for moonshining. Floyd Allen, the uncle of the accused, knocked the officer down and helped his nephew to escape. Uncle Floyd subsequently was charged with assault. It was an unheard-of event—nobody had every dared arrest Floyd Allen before.

The Allen clan immediately began informing citizens throughout the county that Floyd Allen was innocent and had better be found so. It soon became evident that no one in the county was about to find Allen guilty of anything, and the state came up with the legally questionable ploy of importing jurors from elsewhere in Virginia. Floyd Allen was readily found guilty by the imported jurors. At 9 A.M. on March 14, the court convened for sentencing. As Judge Thornton L. Massie started speaking, some 17 Allen men entered the courtroom and stationed themselves at strategic positions. The judge finished his speech and sentenced Floyd Allen to one year. Floyd then addressed the court. "Gentlemen," he said, "I ain't goin'."

With that statement, Floyd Allen pulled out two guns and started shooting: where and at whom varies with each account. Most say that Floyd shot and killed Judge Massie. But some credit his brother Sidna with that killing. In any event, 17 Allens started shooting; some only shot at the ceiling or into the floor and most of the shooting was done by Floyd, Sidna and Floyd's son Claude. In less than 60 seconds at least 75 shots were fired and six people killed—the judge, the sheriff, the commonwealth attorney, a spectator, a juror and a woman witness, ironically for the defense. Eight others were wounded. Among the Allens only Floyd was wounded and he was able to hobble off to a nearby hotel, where he was later taken into custody. This too must have surprised the Allens, who obviously thought their show of force would be enough to allow Floyd to walk from the courtroom. Sidna Allen was so nonchalant about the entire matter that when he ran out of ammunition, he went across the street to buy more in a hardware store. It was closed because the owner was in court.

Virginia authorities moved in rapidly to suppress the Allens once and for all. Floyd and his son Claude were sentenced to death for murder and electrocuted on March 28, 1913. Sidna got 15 years. All the other Allens got lesser sentences; some had insisted they had fired in the air or at the floor, trying deliberately not to kill anyone but merely create panic. A few came up with a novel defense: because the gunsmoke was so thick, it was impossible to aim, and therefore, if anyone was killed, it was purely an accident.

After serving 13 years, Sidna Allen received a pardon in 1926 from Gov. (later Sen.) Harry F. Byrd.

In his memoirs, Sidna insisted the shootings had all been unpremeditated and were originally intended as a bluff to free Floyd Allen. He also claimed the clan had been the object of political persecution in the country for some time. After Sidna's release the Allen clan argued that his pardon indicated the state had admitted they had been framed.

Allison, Clay (1840–1887) gunfighter

One of the most notorious of the western gunfighters, Clay Allison was not an outlaw in the ordinary sense of the word. He called himself a "shootist," apparently in an attempt to indicate he was a professional, like an artist or a dentist. Allison lived on the fringe of the law and according to a personal code governed more by his own belief in honor than by the strictures of the law. Invariably, this meant he killed men "that deserved killin'." In a morbid sense, he may have contributed some of the most entertaining—to observers rather than to victims—shootings in western lore.

One of his more famous duels was with a gunman named Chunk Colbert in 1874. The pair sat eyeball to eyeball in a New Mexico Territory eatery, staring each other down and stirring their coffee with the muzzles of their six-guns. Soon each reholstered his piece and continued to eat. Colbert made the first move to draw but Allison shot him dead just above the right eye. On another occasion Allison led a lynching party against a man named Kennedy who was suspected of killing his own young daughter. Some bones were found on the Kennedy ranch, but there was no definite determination that the bones were human. The matter was still in dispute after the lynching, but that didn't stop Allison from cutting off the dead man's head, impaling it on a pike and riding 29 miles to Cimarron, Kan. to his favorite watering hole, Henry Lambert's saloon.

Allison could best be described as a part-time maniac, since between his vicious killings he was generally a well-mannered rancher. There might have been some excuse for his behavior, however. He had joined the Confederate Army in his native Tennessee but was discharged after sustaining a blow on his skull, which was said to have made him intermittently epileptic and at other times maniacal. After the Civil War, he punched cattle and finally set up the first of his several ranches.

What troubled other men about Allison was his unpredictability. In 1875, although a rancher, he sided with the homesteaders in their battles, clearly out of a sense of fair play, an attitude that enraged other ranchers and stock associations. At the same time Allison was a bitter racist, and in New Mexico he killed a number of Mexican "outlaws." Few, however, even considered challenging him for any of his deeds.

Contemporary drawing depicts Clay Allison's famous shoot-out with another notorious gunman, Chunk Colbert.

Allison continued to devise duels that bordered on lunacy. He once indulged in a fast-draw contest with a gunman named Mace Bowman. After Bowman continually outdrew him, Allison suggested they pull off their boots, strip down to their underwear and take turns shooting at each other's bare feet to see who danced best under fire. Remarkably, the confrontation ended without bloodshed after several hours, each man giving in to exhaustion.

When he got into yet another dispute, Allison arranged to do battle naked in a grave in which each adversary would be armed with a Bowie knife. Both agreed to purchase a tombstone and the winner would see to it that the stone of the loser was suitably engraved. While waiting for the delivery of the tombstone, Allison picked up a wagonload of supplies from Pecos, Tex. to bring back to his ranch. When a sack of grain fell from the moving wagon, he tried to grab it and toppled to the ground. A wagon wheel rolled over his neck, breaking it and killing him.

It was a bizarre ending to a violent life for a man credited, by various counts, with the deaths of 15 to 21 men. A Kansas newspaper had a difficult time trying to evaluate the life of Clay Allison and whether he was "in truth a villain or a gentleman." That was "a question that many never settled to their own satisfaction. Certain it is that many of his stern deeds were for the right as he understood that right to be."

See also: CHUNK COLBERT.

Allison, Dorothy (1925–1999) crime-solving psychic

Among the various psychics who have made the popular press in recent years, one American psychic, a housewife from Nutley, N.J., ranked above all others as having some apparent crime-solving ability. Dorothy Allison's visions of peaceful landscapes containing unfound bodies have turned out to be, as *Newsweek* labeled them, "close approximations of grisly reality." In the past dozen years or so, Mrs. Allison had been consulted by police in well over 100 cases and, by her own count, had helped solve 13 killings and find more than 50 missing persons. Many police departments expressed wholehearted, if befuddled, gratitude. "Seeing is believing," said Anthony Tortora, head of the missing persons division of the Bergen County, N.J. sheriff's office. "Dorothy Allison took us to within 50 yards of where the body was found. She's quite a gal."

Some of Mrs. Allison's "finds" have been accident victims and others have been the victims of foul play. In September 1977 two of her finds turned up in different states just one day apart. She pinpointed a swamp area in New Jersey where 17-year-old Ronald Stica would be found and was able to tell police prior to the discovery of the body that he had been stabbed to death. The day before, the body of 14-year-old Susan Jacobson, missing two years, had turned up inside an oil drum in an abandoned boat yard in Staten Island, N.Y. Mrs. Allison had described the corpse site—although she had never been to Staten Island—as a swampy area, with "twin church steeples and two bridges—but one not for cars" nearby. She said she also saw the letters M A R standing alone. All the elements were there, including the letters M A R painted in red on a nearby large rock.

Perhaps Mrs. Allison's most amazing case was one that began at about 6:30 P.M. on Thursday, July 22, 1976, when Deborah Sue Kline left her job as a hospital aide, got in her car and started for her home in Waynesboro, Pa. She never got there. Months of police investigations proved fruitless. Jane Kline, the girl's mother, finally contacted Mrs. Allison, who agreed to come to Pennsylvania. Quite naturally, the first thing the mother asked was if her daughter was still alive. By the end of the day, Mrs. Allison told her the answer: Debbie was dead. Mrs. Allison put on Debbie's graduation ring "to help me feel her presence." She toured the area with police, reporters and a friend of the Klines.

After a while, she was able to reconstruct the crime. She saw Debbie driving home from the hospital and two cars, a yellow one and a black one, forcing her off the road. According to a local newspaper account: "She was taken from her car in one of the other cars to a place where she was molested. She was taken to another place where she was killed with a knife wound. I saw [at the death site] yellow signs, a dump, burnt houses and a swimming pool. I could see her skeleton. It was not underground. The word 'line' or 'lion' came to me."

On January 26, 1977, three days after Dorothy Allison had returned home, police located the body of Debbie Kline. It was not buried and was in an area where junk was dumped. There were no "burnt houses" but the spot was just off the Fannettsburg–Burnt Cabins Road. In the area were yellow traffic signs warning motorists of steep grades on the road. Near the body was a discarded plastic swimming pool. There was no "lion" but there was a "line"—150 feet away was the line between Huntington and Franklin Counties. And Debbie had been stabbed to death.

Then the police confronted a suspect, in jail at the time on another rape charge. His name was Richard Lee Dodson. Dodson broke down and led them to where the body had been found. He and another man, Ronald Henninger, were charged with the crime. Ken Peiffer, a reporter for the *Record Herald*, said: "She told me, among other clues later proven accurate, the first names of the two men involved, Richard and Ronald. She even told me that one of the men had a middle name of Lee or Leroy."

The police of Washington Township, who were in charge of the case, made Dorothy Allison an honorary member of the police department. The citation given to her reads in part, "Dorothy Allison, through psychic powers, provided clues which contributed to the solving of the crime."

Of course, not all of Dorothy Allison's efforts had been triumphs. She was the first psychic called in by Randolph Hearst after daughter Patty disappeared in Berkeley, Calif. Mrs. Allison turned up little of value while on the West Coast. Still, Hearst did not scoff. "Dorothy couldn't locate Patty," he said, "but she is honest and reputable. I wouldn't laugh at it." Allison died December 1, 1999.

Allman, John (?–1877) the cavalryman killer

The prototypical western cavalryman bad guy, according to a Hollywood historian, "Bad John Allman did as much to make John Ford a great movie director as did John Wayne." The point may have been stretched, but John Allman was just about the worst killer the U.S. Army contributed to the West.

A native of Tennessee, Allman was a violent character throughout his army career. There is some speculation that Allman was not his original name, that he had served elsewhere in uniform under another identity or two until it became wise to change it.

There is no record of exactly how many men Allman killed—"not countin' injuns," as they said in the cavalry. In any case, his last spree substantially reduced the population of the Arizona Territory. In the summer of 1877 Allman got into an argument during a poker game in the cavalry barracks at Prescott, Ariz. When the pistol smoke cleared, Allman and the pot were gone and two army sergeants were dead. A posse soon started out after Bad John and got close to him, close enough for two of its members, Billy Epps and Dave Groat, to be killed by him. Still on the run, Allman was recognized, or at least thought he had been recognized, by two woodcutters, and he promptly shot them dead. Late in August, about two weeks after he had killed the woodcutters, Allman, tired, hungry and broke, rode into Yuma. When he rode out, a bartender named Vince Dundee was dead, and Allman had the contents of the till and as many bottles of whiskey as a man could tote. In Williams, Ariz. Deputy Sheriff Ed Roberts spotted Allman in a saloon, but Bad John's gun was quicker; on his way out, the cavalryman killer stepped right over the dying lawman.

Sheriff Ullman of Coconino County turned over the job of apprehending Allman to a bizarre group of bounty hunters referred to by the press as Outlaw Exterminators, Inc. The Exterminators consisted of five bounty hunters who specialized in going after "dead or alive" quarries and bringing them in dead rather than alive. However, Allman was a hard man to run to ground. Low on bullets, he killed a sheepherder named Tom Dowling for his gun and ammunition. Next he kidnapped a 13-year-old white girl named Ida Phengle and a 12-year-old Hopi girl and raped them both. Allman eventually freed his two young captives but soon found himself pursued by various lawmen, the Exterminators and a Hopi war party. In the end, it was Clay Calhoun, one of the Exterminators, who located Allman among some deserted Indian cliff dwellings on October 11, 1877. According to Calhoun, whose version of what happened was the only one reported, he brought down Allman in a stirring gun fight. This dramatic scenario is hard to credit since Allman had been shot four times, in the mouth, chest, stomach and groin, all in a nice neat line. Any of those shots would have grounded Allman, making the alignment of wounds most unusual for a shoot-out. Some speculated that Allman had more likely been shot while asleep. But speculation aside, the important thing was that Bad John Allman's bloody reign of terror was over, and the particulars of how it happened didn't trouble many people in Arizona.

See also: OUTLAW EXTERMINATORS, INC.

Almodovar, Louisa (1919–1942) murder victim

Terry Almodovar had the misfortune of strangling his estranged wife to death on a certain hill in Central Park in New York City, thereby achieving unlikely fame in botany texts. If he had done it almost anywhere else in the park, in fact on the other side of the same hill, he might not have gone to the electric chair.

When Louisa's body was found on November 2, 1942, the police were certain the murder had been committed either by a park marauder or by the woman's husband. Terry Almodovar insisted that at the time of the murder, fixed at between 9 and 10 o'clock the night before, he was at a dance hall several blocks away. No less than 22 girls backed him up, saying he

was there the whole time. The truth was that he had slipped away long enough to kill his wife, whom he had secretly offered to meet in the park. Her death was desirable because he had been offered marriage by a very wealthy widow.

Almodovar didn't realize the trouble he was in when the police took his suit and gave it to Dr. Alexander O. Gettler of the Medical Examiner's Office. Dr. Gettler made a spectrogram of the dirt from Terry's trousers and another of the dirt from where the body was found. The elements of both were exactly the same. Still, Almodovar insisted he hadn't been in Central Park the night of the murder or at any time within the previous two years. But Dr. Gettler also found some grass spikelets in the suspect's cuffs; these were identified as *Panicum dicoth milleflorium*, and they matched perfectly with similar grass spikelets found at the murder scene. Almodovar insisted they must have been picked up somewhere else—perhaps in Tremont Park in the Bronx, where he'd been recently. At this point Joseph J. Copeland, a professor of botany at City College of New York, took over. This particular kind of grass, *Panicum dicoth*, was extremely rare in the New York area. It grew in three areas in Westchester County, two in Long Island—but only one in New York City: a small section of a hill in Central Park, and not even on the other side of the same hill where the murder had been committed. Confronted with the evidence, Almodovar suddenly remembered he'd gone through Central Park just a couple of months before, in September. Copeland, however, knew that *Panicum dicoth* is a late bloomer. Most of the spikelets found in Almodovar's cuffs couldn't have gotten there before October 10 and probably not before October 15. But they most certainly could have got there on November 1.

The science of botany sent Terry Almodovar to the electric chair on March 9, 1943.

Alta, Utah lawless mining town

For a time, Alta, Utah Territory sported a sign that read, "WELCOME TO THE MEANEST LITTLE TOWN IN THE WEST." The small silver-mining town in the foothills of Utah's Rustler Mountains lived up to its motto. In its heyday during the 1870s, Alta had 26 saloons and a cemetery touted as the largest in any town of that size.

While avalanches claimed the lives of many miners, the largest contingent of corpses buried in the Alta cemetery were the more than 100 victims of gun battles. In 1873 a stranger dressed in black came to town and announced he had the power to resurrect all of the town's dead gunmen. The miners, a superstitious lot, speculated that such a development would only lead to a lot of bullets flying about in vengeance shoot-outs and opted for the status quo. They raised $2,500 in a community collection as a gift for the "resurrection man" contingent on his leaving Alta permanently.

By the early 1900s Alta was a ghost town, its ore mined out, but today it thrives in a new reincarnation as a popular ski resort.

Alterie, Louis "Two Gun" (1892–1935) gangster

The Dion O'Banion gang that dominated Chicago's North Side during the early years of Prohibition was particularly noted for its zaniness (it once "rubbed out" a horse for killing one of its members in a riding mishap), but even for this bunch, Louis "Two Gun" Alterie was wacky. Alterie, whose real name was Leland Verain, owned a ranch in Colorado but came east to join up with O'Banion's gambling and bootlegging operations. He wore two pistols, one on each hip, Wild West–style, and always boasted of his perfect marksmanship with either his left or right hand, often shooting out the lights in saloons to prove his point.

It was Alterie, it was said, who insisted that revenge was required after a leading member of the gang, Nails Morton, had been thrown by a horse in Lincoln Park and kicked to death. He led the gang to the riding stable, and there they kidnapped the horse, took it to the scene of Morton's demise and shot it to death. Alterie was so incensed by the "murder" of his comrade that he first punched the hapless horse in the snout before turning his gun on it.

When Dion O'Banion was assassinated by Capone gunmen, Two Gun Alterie went wild. In a tearful performance at the funeral, Alterie raged to reporters: "I have no idea who killed Deanie, but I would die smiling if only I had a chance to meet the guys who did, any time, any place they mention and I would get at least two or three of them before they got me. If I knew who killed Deanie, I'd shoot it out with the gang of killers before the sun rose in the morning." Asked where the duel should be fought, he suggested Chicago's busiest corner, Madison and State Streets, at noon. Mayor William E. Dever was enraged when he heard of Alterie's words. "Are we still abiding by the code of the Dark Ages?" he demanded.

Earl "Little Hymie" Weiss, successor to O'Banion as head of the mob, ordered Alterie to cool off, stating that because of his rantings political and police pressure was being put on the gang's operations on the North Side. Alterie nodded grandly with a big wink and stayed quiet for about a week. Then he swaggered into a Loop nightclub frequented by reporters and gangsters and, brandishing his two pistols, boasted loudly: "All

12 bullets in these rods have Capone's initials carved on their noses. And if I don't get him, Bugs, Hymie or Schemer will."

For Weiss, who was trying to keep peace with Capone until the right time to strike, Alterie's blustering was just too much. He ordered Bugs Moran to "move" Alterie. Moran went to the cowboy gangster and growled: "You're getting us in bad. You run off at the mouth too much."

Alterie recognized an invitation to leave town when he heard one and returned to his ranch in Colorado, ending his participation in the Chicago gang wars. When he finally came back to Chicago on a visit in 1935, the O'Banion gang had been wiped out except for Moran, and he was no longer a power. Apparently, just for old time's sake, somebody shot Alterie to death.

See also: ANIMAL LYNCHING, GEORGE "BUGS" MORAN, SAMUEL J. "NAILS" MORTON, CHARLES DION "DEANIE" O'BANION.

Altgeld, John P. (1847–1902) Illinois governor

John P. Altgeld, elected governor of Illinois in 1892, was the main player in the final act of the 1886 Haymarket affair, in which a dynamite bomb killed seven policemen and two civilians and wounded 130 others. Altgeld, a wealthy owner of business property, announced he would hear arguments for pardoning three anarchists who had been sentenced to long prison terms for their alleged part in the affair; but no one expected him to free them because it would be an act of political suicide. Four other anarchists had already been hung as a result of Haymarket, and another had committed suicide in his cell.

In June 1893 Altgeld issued a long analysis of the Haymarket trial, attacking the trial judge, Joseph E. Gary, for ruling the prosecution did not have to identify the bomb-thrower or even prove that the actual murderer had been influenced by the anarchist beliefs of the defendants. "In all the centuries during which government has been maintained among men and crime has been punished, no judge in a civilized country has ever laid down such a rule before." Altgeld also referred to the judge's obvious bias in constantly attacking the defendants before the jury. He then issued full pardons for Samuel Fielden, Michael Schwab and Oscar Neebe, declaring them and the five dead men innocent.

While Altgeld was hailed by labor spokesmen, most newspapers condemned him bitterly. The *New York World* caricatured him as an acolyte worshiping the bomb-wielding, black-robed figure of an anarchist. The *Chicago Tribune* denounced Altgeld, who was German, as "not merely an alien by birth, but an alien by temperament and sympathies. He has apparently not a drop of pure American blood in his veins. He does not reason like an American, nor feel like one." The governor was also hanged in effigy.

Altgeld ignored such criticisms, being content he was "merely doing right," but his act turned out to be political suicide. In 1896 he ran for the U.S. Senate but was defeated. Clarence Darrow later tried to set him up in practice as an associate, but Altgeld, no longer rich, was a tired man, and he died in obscurity six years later. His memory was neglected until Vachel Lindsay placed a poem, "The Eagle That Is Forgotten," on his grave; it read in part:

> *Where is that boy, that Heaven-born Bryan,*
> *That Homer Bryan, who sang from the West?*
> *Gone to join the shadows with Altgeld the eagle,*
> *Where the kings and the slaves and the troubadours rest. . . .*

See also: CLARENCE DARROW, HAYMARKET AFFAIR.

Alvord, Burt (1866–1910?) lawman and outlaw

A notorious law officer turned bad, Burt Alvord seems to have enjoyed long simultaneous careers as a lawman and bandit. The son of a roving justice of the peace, Alvord was a youth in Tombstone during the time of the vaunted gunfight at the O.K. Corral. Although only 15, he was astute enough to spot one of the underlying motives for the battle—control of the county sheriff's office, with the special duty of collecting taxes, which might or might not be turned over to the treasury.

When the celebrated lawman John Slaughter was elected sheriff of Cochise County in 1886, Alvord, who was 20 at the time, became his chief deputy and began building a solid reputation as an enforcer of the law, tracking down numerous rustlers and other thieves. There is little doubt, however, that during the same period he was also an outlaw. In time, Slaughter, an honest man, became disenchanted with his deputy. Yet when the sheriff retired from his post in 1890, no crimes had been pinned on Alvord. In the mid-1890s Alvord switched from wearing a badge to rustling cattle in Mexico. But by 1899 he was a constable in Willcox, Arizona Territory despite some murders under his belt. Here Alvord teamed up with Billie Stiles to pull off a number of train robberies and other holdups. The entire Alvord-Stiles gang was captured after a train robbery near Cochise in September 1899, but they escaped from jail and went back in business. Alvord and Stiles were caught again in 1903 but once more broke free. After that, Alvord tried to fake their deaths, even sending coffins allegedly carrying their remains to Tombstone. The trick failed, and the law kept hunting for the two outlaw chiefs. Finally, the Arizona Rangers swept

into Mexico in 1904 and cornered Alvord at Nigger Head Gap. Alvord was wounded and brought back to Arizona. This time he spent two years in prison. Thereafter, Alvord's record becomes murky. He was spotted, according to various stories, all over Latin America and even in Jamaica. When a canal worker in Panama died in 1910, he was said to be Alvord, but the identification was not conclusive.

See also: BILLIE STILES.

Amatuna, Samuzzo "Samoots" (1898–1925)
Chicago gangster and murderer

One of Chicago's most colorful and brutal gangsters during the 1920s, Samuzzo "Samoots" Amatuna for a time held a power base from which he challenged Al Capone's control of crime in the city. In the end, however, Samoots was more remembered for the changes his death brought about in the practices of Chicago-area barber shops.

A professional fiddler and a fop, Samoots was one of the first to conceal a weapon in an instrument case, using this technique with three confederates in the attempted murder of a musicians' union business agent. The proud possessor of 200 monogrammed silk shirts, he once took off in pursuit of the driver of a Chinese laundry delivery wagon after one of his shirts was returned scorched. Samoots pulled his gun to shoot the frightened driver, but at the last moment he was overcome by a spark of humanity and shot the driver's horse instead.

Samoots became the chief bodyguard for the notorious Terrible Gennas, who controlled much of the city's homemade bootleg racket. As they were wiped out or scattered one by one, Samoots moved up in power and in 1925 he seized control of the Unione Siciliana. This group had been a lawful fraternal organization up to the turn of the century, but from then on, it became more and more a front for the criminal operations of Mafia forces. Chicago had the largest number of branches of the Unione, whose 40,000 members represented a potent force as well as an organization to be looted through various rackets, such as manipulation of pension funds. For years the Unione was under the control of Mike Merlo, who knew how to keep peace among the various criminal combines, but after his death in 1924 the Unione presidency became a hot seat. Bloody Angelo Genna took over as president, only to be murdered in May 1925.

Al Capone, who was not a Sicilian and thus not eligible for membership, wanted to place his *consigliere*, Tony Lombardo, in the office but decided to wait for an election. In the meantime Samoots walked into the Unione's offices with two armed confederates, Abe

"Bummy" Goldstein and Eddie Zion, and declared himself elected. Capone was furious at the effrontery, but he soon had more reason to hate Samoots as the latter moved to open a chink in Capone's booze and other operations.

However, Samoots had other enemies such as the O'Banion Irish gang, which was still in power on the North Side even after the death of its leader. On November 13, 1925 Samoots, planning to go to the opera with his fiancée, Rose Pecorara, dropped into a Cicero barbershop for a shave. He was reclining in a barber's chair with a towel over his face when two assassins, believed to be Jim Doherty and Schemer Drucci of the O'Banions, marched in. One of the gunmen fired four shots but, remarkably, missed Samoots with every shot. The frightened target bolted from the barber's chair and tried to dodge four bullets from the second gunman. Each of these shots hit home, and the assassins strode out, leaving their victim near death. Rushed to a hospital, Samoots asked to marry his fiancée from his hospital bed but died before the ceremony started.

Within a few weeks Samoots' aides, Goldstein and Zion, were also killed, and the way was open for Capone's man, Lombardo, to take over the Unione. After Samoots' death, which was the second recent Chicago barbershop assassination, it became common practice for barbers dealing with a gangster clientele never to cover their faces with a towel and to position the chair so that it always faced the entrance. This local custom did not spread to New York, where some two decades later Albert Anastasia was gunned down under similar circumstances.

Amberg, Louis "Pretty" (1898–1935) racketeer and murderer

From the late 1920s until his own violent demise in 1935, Louis "Pretty" Amberg was New York's best-known killer, having dispatched more than 100 victims. Thanks to cunning and dumb luck, however, he was never so much as saddled with a stiff fine for any of his or his brother Joe's murders, although his achievements were common knowledge. His technique of stuffing victims into laundry bags, alive but trussed up in such a way that they strangled themselves, was immortalized by Damon Runyon in several stories in which Pretty Amberg was featured in a thinly fictionalized form.

Pretty, so named because of his ugliness, was brought to America from Russia by his fruit peddler parents. By the age of 10 he was terrorizing his home territory of Brownsville in Brooklyn, New York City, an area that bowed only to genuine toughness and meanness. Young Pretty developed a unique fruit-selling technique: he would kick on a door until the resident opened up and then shove handfuls of fruit and vegetables forward and snarl, "Buy." People bought.

By the time he was 20, Pretty was *the* terror of Brownsville. He was now so ugly that a representative from Ringling Brothers offered him a job with the circus as the missing link. It is the mark of Pretty's intellect or sense of humor that he often bragged about the offer. However, Pretty didn't accept the job because of his involvement in the loansharking business with his brother. Unlike the banks of Brownsville, the Ambergs turned no one down for a loan, but at 20 percent interest a week. Pretty would watch his brother count out the amount of the loan and growl, "I will kill you if you don't pay us back on time."

The Amberg brothers soon became so successful in loansharking that they shifted their operations to around Borough Hall in downtown Brooklyn. The brothers did not desert Brownsville, however. Pretty stalked Pitkin Avenue; for amusement he would walk into a cafeteria and spit in someone's soup. If the diner protested, Pretty would spill the whole bowl in his lap. Even Buggsy Goldstein, shortly to become a prize killer in the fledgling Murder, Inc., once took the soup treatment in silence. Famous Murder, Inc. informer Abe Reles later said, "The word was that Pretty was nutty."

Pretty Amberg's continuing ties with Brownsville were not based solely on sentiment. He took control of all bootlegging in the area, and speakeasies took Pretty's booze or none at all, a business practice Pretty established with a few bombings and frequent use of a lead pipe.

Soon, Pretty was wallowing in money, and he became a lavish-spending, if rather grotesque, figure in New York's night life. Waiters fawned over him because he never tipped less than $100. He was a regular at the Central Park Casino, where in time he became a nodding acquaintance of the city's playboy mayor, James J. Walker. It was Runyon who reported that when the mayor first saw Pretty, he vowed to stay off booze.

Pretty expanded his rackets to include laundry services for Brooklyn businesses. His rates were rather high, but his sales approach was particularly forceful. It was at this time that laundry bags stuffed with corpses started littering Brooklyn streets. One victim was identified as a loanshark debtor of the Ambergs who owed a grand total of $80. Pretty was arrested for that one, but he just laughed: "I tip more than that. Why'd I kill a bum for a lousy 80 bucks?" In fact, it was Pretty's philosophy to kill men who were indebted to him for small amounts so that their loss of life would not cause him to have to write off a major capital investment. It also made an excellent object lesson for more substantial debtors. And while the police knew the particulars, they could not prove them in court and Pretty went free.

By the early 1930s Pretty was considered among the most successful racketeers in the city, one who could withstand any inroads by other kingpins, such as Dutch Schultz and Legs Diamond. Once, Schultz told him, "Pretty, I think I'm going to come in as your partner in Brooklyn."

"Arthur," Pretty was quoted as replying, "why don't you put a gun in your mouth and see how many times you can pull the trigger."

Pretty was famous for such pithy comments. Another big racketeer, Owney Madden, mentioned to Pretty one day that he'd never visited Brownsville in his life and thought he would come out some time and "let you show me the sights." Pretty was carving up a steak at the moment. "Tell you what, Owney," he said matter-of-factly while continuing his meal, "if I ever see you in Brownsville. I'll cut your heart out on the spot." He was even more direct with Legs Diamond, whom he buddied around with. "We'll be pals, Jack," Pretty told Diamond, "but if you ever set foot in Brownsville, I'll kill you and your girlfriend and your missus and your whole damn family."

With the end of Prohibition, however, such threats proved insufficient. Dutch Schultz, without his former bootleg rackets, was down to only a multimillion dollar numbers racket centered in Harlem, and he kept casting greedy glances over at Brooklyn and the Amberg loan-shark operations around Borough Hall. Pretty had by now firmly established himself in the laundry business, but loansharking remained his principal source of funds. He was therefore hardly overjoyed in 1935 when Schultz ensconced his top lieutenants, Frank Dolak and Benny Holinsky, in a new loan office just a block away from the Amberg enterprise. When Pretty stormed into the place, the pair glared back at him defiantly. "We ain't afraid of you," Holinsky said, and Dolak echoed, "That's right, we ain't afraid of you." The statements qualified as famous last words because 24 hours later their bodies, riddled with bullets, were found on a Brooklyn street.

The Ambergs and the Schultz forces faced off for total war. The first to go was Joey Amberg, who was ambushed by Schultz's gunmen. In October 1935 both Amberg and Schultz died. Some historians have insisted that each man was responsible for the other's death. According to this theory Amberg had paid professional killers $25,000 down to kill Schultz and promised them $25,000 more upon completion of the job. In the meantime, however, the fire department, responding to an alarm, found a blazing automobile on a Brooklyn street. In the back seat of the car was the body of a man

roasted beyond all recognition, with wire wrapped around his neck, arms and legs. It took a few days for a positive identification: it was Pretty Amberg. But by the time the identification was made, a couple of killers had gunned down Dutch Schultz in a Newark chop house.

Despite the war, it is not certain that Amberg was killed by Schultz. A more convincing theory attributed Pretty's passing to a gang of armed robbers he had joined and offended by insisting on taking virtually all the loot for himself. Another view held that both Amberg and Schultz were "put to sleep" by the increasingly dominant national crime syndicate bossed by Lucky Luciano and Meyer Lansky.

But whoever was to blame, Pretty Amberg was dead, and as a *Brooklyn Eagle* reporter observed, "There was joy in Brownsville."

Ameer Ben Ali   See "OLD SHAKESPEARE."

American Protective League   vigilantes
With the possible exception of the Sons of Liberty, formed during the American Revolution, the World War I American Protective League (APL) was probably this country's most abusive and lawless patriotic vigilante groups. The league was the brainchild of A. M. Briggs, a Chicago advertising executive, who in March 1917 wrote Bureau of Investigation chief A. Bruce Bielaski to suggest the formation of a volunteer group of patriotic Americans who would aid the bureau in its national defense duties. Not the most perceptive of officials, Bielaski enthusiastically approved the idea, and divisions of the APL were established in every large city in the country, soon achieving a membership of 250,000.

APL members paid their own expenses and sported badges that read, "American Protective League, Secret Service Division." The words *secret service* were removed following the protest of the secretary of the treasury, but Attorney General Thomas W. Gregory defended the league and its patriotic purpose despite the fact that the organization exhibited the worst attributes of a vigilante movement, had a callous disregard of civil rights and even committed lynchings.

In 1917 in Butte, Mont., armed masked men, generally believed to have been league members, invaded the boardinghouse room of Frank Little, a member of the general executive board of the Industrial Workers of the World (IWW), dragged him out into the night and hanged him from a railroad trestle for what was regarded as his unpatriotic beliefs and actions. The Little hanging did not receive particularly bad press. While the *New York Times* called the lynching "deplorable and detestable," it also noted that "IWW agitators are in effect, and perhaps in fact, agents of Germany. The Federal government should make short work of these treasonable conspirators against the United States." A western newspaper declared Butte had "disgraced itself like a gentleman." And on the floor of the House of Representatives, a congressman wondered if those who gave no allegiance to this nation "have any right to 'squeal' when citizens of this country hang one of them occasionally?"

President Woodrow Wilson felt it necessary to warn of "the great danger of citizens taking the law into their own hands," but he did nothing to force Gregory and Bielaski to repudiate the APL. The league continued to make illegal arrests and searches, and its members continually gave the impression they were federal officers. Labor leaders attacked the APL, citing instances of it being used by employers to intimidate strikers. When veteran members of the Bureau of Investigation scoffed at these "voluntary detectives," they were warned that such "slurs" could result in their dismissal.

In August and September of 1918 the league, cooperating with the Bureau of Investigation, the army and local draft boards, launched a great war against "slackers" and deserters, men who failed to answer the call to service after registering for the draft. Small roundup experiments using local police and APL members proved successful in Pittsburgh, Boston and Chicago. Early in September a three-day roundup was staged in New York City. Newspapers ran notices reminding all men between 21 and 31 that they were required to carry their draft cards on their person and that all others should carry proof of their age. No warning, however, was given of an impending roundup. At 7 A.M. on September 3, 1918, a task force of 1,350 soldiers, 1,000 sailors, several hundred policemen and 2,000 APL members struck. During the next three days 50,000 men were hustled out of theaters and restaurants, plucked off street corners and from trolley cars and seized in railway stations and poolhalls. Workers were stopped by bayonet-wielding soldiers as they left work. All were jammed into bull pens for interrogation, left for hours without food and refused the right to make telephone calls to establish their innocence. Frightened wives of out-of-town visitors reported their husbands as kidnapped.

The seizures in general and those by the APL in particular were sharply criticized. The *New York World* condemned "this monstrous invasion of human rights." In the Senate, Sen. Hiram Johnson of California said that "to humiliate 40,000 citizens, to shove them with bayonets, to subject them to prison and summary mili-

tary force, merely because they are 'suspects,' is a spectacle never before presented in the Republic."

The weight of public opinion turned against the APL following the roundups, which resulted in the estimated induction of 1,500 men into the service. President Wilson demanded a report from Attorney General Gregory, who informed the president that he took full and complete responsibility for the raids and that they would continue, although he did deplore the use of extralegal methods. Wilson seemed incapable of moving against Gregory and the APL, but in November 1918 the war ended, eliminating the need for confrontation.

The American Protective League formally dissolved on February 1, 1919.

American Tragedy, An   See CHESTER GILLETTE.

Anastasia, Albert (1903–1957) syndicate gang leader and murderer

The Lord High Executioner of Murder, Inc., Albert Anastasia rose to the top levels of the national crime syndicate and remained there until he himself was murdered in a hit as efficient as any of the countless ones he carried out or planned.

Immediately upon his arrival in the United States in 1920, Anastasia and his brother, Tough Tony Anastasio, became active on the crime-ridden Brooklyn docks and gained a position of power in the longshoremen's union. He demonstrated a penchant for murder at the snap of a finger, an attitude that was not altered even after he spent 18 months in the Sing Sing death house during the early 1920s for killing another longshoreman. He was freed when, at a new trial, the four most important witnesses against him could not be located, a situation that proved permanent.

For Anastasia the solution to any problem was homicide. So it was hardly surprising that he and Louis "Lepke" Buchalter were installed as the executive heads of the enforcement arm of Murder, Inc. The victim toll of Murder, Inc. has been estimated as low as 63 and as high as 400 or 500. Unlike Lepke and many other members of the operation, Anastasia escaped punishment. In a "perfect case" against him, the main prosecution witness—again—vanished. This disappearance of witnesses was a regular occurrence in the Anastasia story, as were killings to advance his career. When in 1951 Anastasia aspired to higher things, he took over the Mangano family, one of New York's five crime families, by murdering Phil Mangano and making Vincent Mangano a permanent missing person.

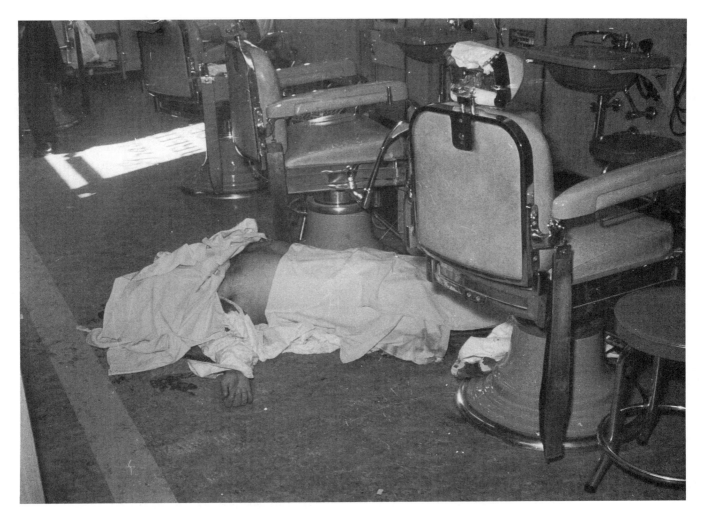

Albert Anastasia, Lord High Executioner of Murder, Inc., was gunned down in a Manhattan hotel barbershop with all the efficiency he himself exhibited in numerous killings.

Anastasia became known as the Mad Hatter because his killings were so promiscuous. He had always been a devoted follower of others, mainly Lucky Luciano and Frank Costello. His devotion to Luciano was legendary. In 1930, when Luciano decided to take over crime in America by destroying the two old-line Mafia factions headed by Giuseppe "Joe the Boss" Masseria and Salvatore Maranzano, he outlined his plan to Anastasia because he knew the Mad Hatter would kill for him. Anastasia promptly grabbed Luciano in a bear hug and kissed him on both cheeks. He said: "Charlie, I been waiting for this day for at least eight years. You're gonna be on top if I have to kill everybody for you. With you there, that's the only way we can have any peace and make the real money." ·

Anastasia's killer instincts could be contained as long as Luciano and Costello were around to control him,

but Luciano was deported in 1946 and a few years later Costello became bogged down by continuous harassment from the authorities. Now in charge of his own crime family, Anastasia really turned kill-crazy. In 1952 he even had a young Brooklyn salesman named Arnold Schuster killed after watching Schuster bragging on television about how he had recognized bank robber Willie Sutton and brought about his capture. "I can't stand squealers!" Anastasia screamed and then ordered his men, "Hit that guy!"

The Schuster killing violated a principal rule of the underworld: we only kill each other. Outsiders—prosecutors, reporters, the general public—were not to be killed unless the very life of the organization was threatened. That clearly was not the case in the Schuster murder. The rest of the underworld, even Anastasia's friends Luciano (now in Italy) and Costello, were horrified, but they dared not move on him because they needed him as a buffer against a new force within the crime structure. Vito Genovese, long number two under Luciano, was making a grab for greater power. Between him and that goal stood Anastasia, a man who had hated him for years. Secretly, Genovese brought to his banner Anastasia's underboss, Carlo Gambino, a frail-looking mobster with unbridled ambition of his own, who in turn recruited Joe Profaci and his Brooklyn crime family.

Before Genovese could move against Anastasia, he needed more support, and he could not move without the tacit agreement of Meyer Lansky, the highest-ranking Jewish member of the national syndicate. Normally, Lansky would not have supported Genovese under any circumstances; their ethnic bitterness was one of the underworld's longest-standing feuds. But Anastasia had recently given Lansky reason to hate him even more. In 1957 Lansky was in full control of gambling in Cuba through his close personal and financial arrangements with that country's dictator, Fulgencio Batista. As was his style of always enhancing his own base within the underworld, Lansky gave a piece of the action to Miami crime boss Santo Trafficante and a number of other Italian-American mobsters. When Anastasia learned of Lansky's largesse, he started to put pressure on him for a huge cut.

Under these circumstances Lansky, who previously had preferred to let Genovese and Anastasia bleed each other to death, okayed the elimination of the latter.

Early on the morning of October 25, 1957 Anastasia entered the barbershop of the Park Sheraton Hotel in New York City and sat down for a quick haircut, shutting his eyes. Anastasia's bodyguard took his car to an underground garage and then conveniently went off for a little stroll. Moments after Anastasia sat down in the barber's chair, two men entered the shop with scarves over their faces. Arthur Grasso, the shop owner, was standing at the entrance by the cash register. He was told, "Keep your mouth shut if you don't want your head blown off." The two men moved to Anastasia's chair and shoved the barber aside. If Anastasia's eye had been open, he would have seen them in the mirror. Suddenly, both guns roared.

Anastasia leaped out of the chair with the first volley and weaved on his feet. Then he saw his attackers and lunged at them—in the mirror. He took several more shots, one in the back of the head, and collapsed dead on the floor.

Officially, the Anastasia killing remains unsolved, although it is known that Joe Profaci gave the contract for the killing to the three homicidal Gallo brothers from Brooklyn.

The double-dealing continued after the Anastasia murder, with Gambino breaking off from Genovese and making his peace with Luciano, Costello and Lansky. A desperate Genovese called an underworld summit meeting at Apalachin, N.Y. to justify the elimination of Anastasia, who, he said, had become so murder-crazed that he had imperiled the entire organization. That meeting ended in disaster following a state police raid, and six months after that, Genovese was arrested on a narcotics rap, one which much of the underworld regarded as a setup. The inside word was that the setup was arranged by Gambino, Luciano, Costello and Lansky. At any rate, Genovese was effectively removed from the scene.

See also: ANTHONY "TOUGH TONY" ANASTASIO; APALACHIN CONFERENCE; FRANK COSTELLO; THOMAS E. DEWEY; CARLO GAMBINO; VITO GENOVESE; CHARLES "LUCKY" LUCIANO; MURDER, INC.; S.S. *NORMANDIE*; FRANK SCALICE; ARNOLD SCHUSTER; FREDERICK J. TENUTO.

Anastasio, Anthony "Tough Tony" (1906–1963)
waterfront racketeer

From the 1930s until his death from natural causes in 1963, Tough Tony Anastasio ruled the New York waterfront with an iron hand as a vice president of the International Longshoremen's Association and head of Local 1814. Much of his real authority derived from the power and reputation of his murderous brother, Albert Anastasia. While Tony kept the original spelling of his last name, he never hesitated to point out he was Albert's brother in order to enhance his own position. Ever loyal to Albert, Tony once cornered a reporter from the *New York World–Telegram and Sun* and asked: "How come you keep writing all those bad things about my brother Albert? He ain't killed nobody in your family . . . yet."

Because would-be rivals knew Tough Tony had the full weight of the mob behind him, they never seriously challenged him. As a result, Tony's word was law. During World War II he could order, with Lucky Luciano's approval, the sabotaging of the French luxury liner SS *Normandie* to panic federal authorities into seeking underworld assistance to help protect the New York waterfront. It was apparently in return for this "good work" that Luciano was transferred from Dannemora to a far less restrictive prison and, after the war, was pardoned by Gov. Thomas E. Dewey. Following Luciano's release Tony had an army of longshoremen on a Brooklyn pier to keep away reporters and others while the top gangland figures gathered to bid Luciano farewell on the day he was being deported to Italy.

See also: CHARLES "LUCKY" LUCIANO, SS *S.*

anatomy and crime

The idea that criminals differ from noncriminals in certain anatomical traits was first expounded by an Italian named Cesare Lombroso, often considered to be the father of criminology. According to Lombroso, such differences turned up in various parts of the body, with criminals typically possessing such features as a long lower jaw, a flattened nose, a scanty beard and an asymmetrical cranium. He did not claim that these stigmata or anomalies themselves caused crime, but rather that they pointed to personalities predisposed to criminal patterns of behavior. Above all, Lombroso insisted that deviations in the shape of the cranium were the most critical.

Over the years Lombroso's views fell into disrepute, but in the 1930s an American anthropologist, E. A. Hooton, attempted to resurrect the Lombrosian theory. He measured thousands of prisoners and a few nonprisoners and found what he considered to be deviations between the two groups. From these studies he concluded, in his *Crime and the Man* (1939), that "the primary cause of crime is biological inferiority." However, other studies failed to find significant differences in physical traits between criminals and noncriminals and the Lombrosian revival gained little support.

Further reading: *"Physical Factors in Criminal Behavior"* by W. Norwood East in the *Journal of Clinical Psychopathy* 8 (1946): 7–36.

Andrews, Shang (c. late 19th century) publisher

During the 1870s and 1880s a sporting character named Shang Andrews launched a series of publications that chronicled the doings of Chicago's prostitutes.

The Walter Winchell–style tidbits were read as avidly by ladies of the evening as the *Chicago Tribune's* social pages were by matrons of prominence. Portraying the ravages of the profession, they are, no doubt, of sociological value today. The following quotations are taken from the *Chicago Street Gazette*, which like *Sporting Life, Chicago Life* and *Chicago Sporting Gazette* among others, made up the Andrews publication list.

Lottie Maynard should not be so fresh with other girls' lovers, or she will hear something to her disadvantage.

Ada Huntley is now happy—she has a new lover—Miss Fresh from Pittsburgh.

Lizzie Allen has put on her fall coat of veneer and varnish, and she is now the finest looking woman in Chicago.

Eva Hawkins is on one of her drunks again.

Miss Kit Thompson of 483 South Clark had better let up on taking other girls' men in her room and buying booze for them.

Lulu Lee, the little streetwalker, has gone into a house to endeavor and reform herself, but we think it will prove a failure.

Lizzie Moss has got sober.

What has become of Bad Millie?

May Willard, why don't you take a rumble to yourself and not be trying to put on so much style around the St. Marks Hotel, for very near all of the boys are on to you; and when you register, please leave the word "New York" out, for we know it's from the Bridewell you are.

We are happy to inform the public that the old-timer, Frankie Warner, has left the city.

Mary McCarthy has gone to the insane asylum.

The true identity of gutter journalist Shang Andrews was never definitely established.

Andrews Committee police corruption inquiry

During the 1890s a spate of investigations around the country revealed that most large cities—Atlanta, Kansas City, Baltimore, Chicago, Los Angeles, San Francisco and Philadelphia—had just as much police corruption as had been found in New York City by the Lexow Committee. Of all the panels set up to hold investigations, the Andrews Committee, which examined the Philadelphia police, had one real distinction: it proved that a city consistently under Republican Party rule could have just as corrupt a police force as any under Democratic Party rule, including that of Tammany Hall.

At the urging of the Citizens' Municipal Association of Philadelphia, a bipartisan reform group, the committee was set up in 1895 by the Pennsylvania Senate with Sen. William H. Andrews of Crawford County as its chairman. In a devastating report issued in May 1897, the committee accused the police of being no more than political agents of various Republican Party factions. Police officers labored hard to see to it that the voters voted right, or not at all. Ballots containing the "wrong" votes were discarded by the hundreds. In some cases policemen got into the booths with voters to make sure they cast their ballots "according to the rules."

In exchange for these and other services rendered to politicians, well-connected officers were exempt from even the threat of departmental discipline and therefore could freely engage in brutality and harassment of citizens as well as offer protection to gambling and prostitution interests. The Andrews Committee's findings were never seriously challenged, but very little came of them. The city's public safety director, while admitting the police force's entanglement with city politics, promised only to deal with the problem in the future. It proved to be an unkept promise. General Smedley D. Butler, appointed public safety director in 1923, found that many, if not most, of Philadelphia's patrolmen were pocketing $150 to $200 a month in payoffs.

See also: LEXOW COMMITTEE.

animal criminals

The history of crime and justice in America is replete with examples of dumb animals being charged and often punished for alleged illegal acts. Perhaps the most famous episode occurred in Erwin, Tenn. in 1916, when a circus elephant named Mary was charged with murder after running amok and killing a man. The dumb beast was hanged from a railroad derrick before a cheering crowd of 5,000 persons. Whether Mary deserved capital punishment might be legally debated on the grounds that she did not know right from wrong, but there are numerous cases of animals being trained to follow a life of crime.

In Chicago in 1953, a resourceful bird fancier trained her pet magpie to enter rooms in a nearby hotel and bring back any bright object it found. The heavy jewelry losses were driving the house detectives crazy, but they were unable to turn up any leads. If it were not for the fact that one day the magpie entered the room of a woman guest who was a particularly light sleeper, the bird fancier and her pet might still be at their winged larceny. The woman, taking a nap after lunch, was awakened by a low noise. She saw a bird flying around the room as though looking for something. It swooped down and picked up a diamond ring lying on a table. When the bird flew out the window, the woman jumped up and got to the window in time to see the bird flying into a neighboring flat. She told her story to the police, and although dubious, they raided the apartment. Their doubts were allayed when they found a fortune in jewelry. The lady bird-lover tearfully admitted all. She had spent arduous years training her bird because magpies, although notorious thieves, can seldom be taught to bring what they steal to a specific spot. Usually they drop their loot in any place that strikes their fancy.

Then there was the case of the chimp cat-burglar. For months in 1952 householders in a New York City neighborhood were being plagued by a series of odd burglaries. In some instances the victims lived in apartments 15 stories up and there seemed to be no means of entry other than a window. One day the son of a city detective happened to see a small figure round a rooftop corner. At first he thought it was a child, but when he looked around the corner, he saw an ape. The boy watched the animal climb through the open skylight of a shop. When it emerged within a matter of seconds, it was carrying a sack; around its neck, packed nearly full. The boy followed the chimp and saw it disappear into a run-down house on another street. He ran home and told his father. Shortly thereafter, the owner of the long-armed, light-fingered animal stood before a judge and told a strange story.

While abroad he had bought a chimpanzee for his children. Chimps are probably the brightest of animals next to humans and his was one of the smartest, he said. He named the chimp Socrates. But then his fortunes took a sudden dive, and it became difficult to provide for his family's needs. One day Socrates went foraging by himself. When he returned, he was munching on a piece of bread and carrying a bagful of pastries. Realizing what had happened, the owner decided to exploit the chimp's latent talents. Socrates was a quick learner, and his master designed a special sack he could use to carry the swag in. Before long, Socrates had the family back in the chips again. The upshot of the case was jail for the chimp owner and a zoo for Socrates.

See also: ANIMAL LYNCHING.

Further reading: *The Criminal Prosecution and Capital Punishment of Animals* by E. R. Evans.

animal lynching

The lynching of animals—cats, dogs, horses, cows, bulls etc.—has a long and brutal history in the United States, but on September 13, 1916 an all-time low in man's inhumanity to beast was reached when Mary, a circus elephant that had killed three men, was hanged from a railroad derrick in Erwin, Tenn. The first attempt to lynch the animal ended after two hours when the derrick's steel cable broke and Mary came crashing down to earth. The second try was successful, and much to the satisfaction of 5,000 spectators, the dumb beast paid the human price demanded for its crimes.

It was not uncommon in the West to kill horses or cattle deemed to have been responsible for the loss of human life. And even the Chicago underworld got into the act. When the celebrated Nails Morton was thrown by a riding horse and killed in Lincoln Park in 1924, his buddies in Dion O'Banion's gang abducted the animal from its stable at gunpoint and took it to the spot where Nails had been killed. There the poor creature was executed, as each of the gangsters solemnly shot it in the head.

During the last century more restraint was shown toward a steer over which an argument regarding its ownership had arisen. Shooting broke out and when the smoke cleared, six men were dead or dying. Because the incident was such a tragedy, it was felt that something other than death was required. The animal was branded with the word MURDER and allowed to live on as grim reminder of the awful occurrence.

See also: LOUIS "TWO GUN" ALTERIE, SAMUEL J. "NAILS" MORTON.

Annenberg, Moses L. (1878–1942) gambling information czar

Moe Annenberg rose from Chicago's South Side slums to become, for a time, the possessor of the largest individual income of any person in the nation. Using methods not everyone considered legal, he was able to capitalize on two American traits, the desire to read newspapers and the eagerness to bet. However, like Al Capone, he ended up in prison for income tax evasion. For the year 1932 the government said Annenberg owed $313,000; he had paid $308. For 1936 Annenberg owed an estimated $1,692,000; he had paid $475,000. Together with interest and penalties his unpaid taxes totaled $9.5 million. And just as was true with Capone, Annenberg's income tax problems were merely a logical consequence of his other activities.

Annenberg, who had cut his teeth in the early Chicago circulation wars, was, in the words of William Randolph Hearst, a "circulation genius." That "genius" meant selling newspapers with an army of sluggers, overturning the competition's delivery trucks, burning their newspapers and roughing up dealers who sold papers under the impression that it was a free country. Moe first worked in the circulation department of the *Chicago Tribune* and later switched his allegiance to Hearst's new papers in town, the *American* and the *Examiner,* serving as circulation manager of the latter from 1904 to 1906. The roster of Moe's sluggers read like a future public enemies list. A typical Annenberg hireling was Frank McErlane. Former Chicago newspaperman George Murray later wrote of the Annenberg-McErlane alliance: "McErlane went on to become the most vicious killer of his time. Moe Annenberg went on to become father of the ambassador to the Court of St. James."

Moving up in the Hearst organization, Annenberg became one of the highest-paid circulation men in the country. His arrangement with Hearst gave him the right to engage in private business dealings on the side, which included his incursion into the racing information field, on both a legal and an illegal basis. In 1922 he bought the *Daily Racing Form,* and by 1926 his various enterprises had become so vast that he quit Hearst and struck out on his own. In a matter of a few years, he had gathered in his domain the *New York Morning Telegraph, Radio Guide, Screen Guide* and the Nation-Wide News Service. He also took over the century-old *Philadelphia Inquirer* and through it became a power in Republican Party politics. According to Annenberg, because these activities occurred during a Democratic era, they got him in trouble with the law. Others said that Nation-Wide News Service gave him his great legal problems, as well as huge profits. The service received its information from telegraph and telephone wires hooked into 29 race tracks and from those tracks into 223 cities in 39 states, where thousands of poolrooms and bookie joints operated in violation of local laws. Annenberg became the fifth largest customer of American Telephone and Telegraph, exceeded only by the three press associations and RCA.

The flow of money simply gushed in, becoming so large that, as the *New York Times* reported, "it apparently did not seem worth while to give the government its share." In 1939 Moe and his only son, Walter, were indicted. Walter pleaded not guilty and Moe attacked the charges against him as politically motivated. But finally, in what some observers called great paternal devotion, Moe declared: "It's the best gamble. I'll take the rap." Moe was in his sixties, and his lawyers were hopeful that his guilty plea would lead to the dropping of charges against his son. The gamble paid off. Moe Annenberg drew a three-year prison term and made a $9.5 million settlement with the government.

Nation-Wide News folded up and Moe Annenberg was succeeded as the country's racing information czar by James M. Ragen, who founded Continental Press Service. Walter Annenberg remained a great publishing power and society figure and went on to become ambassador to England under President Richard Nixon.

See also: JAMES M. RAGEN.

Further reading: *My Last Million Readers* by Emile Gauvreau.

Anselmi and Scalise gangsters

It is impossible to record the criminal activities of Albert Anselmi without also discussing those of John Scalise, the worst pair of killers during the bloody 1920s. Anselmi and Scalise grew up together, played together, worked together, killed together and, fittingly, were slaughtered together. The two resembled that other inseparable pair Mutt and Jeff; Anselmi was short and bulky, Scalise tall and thin. It was this duo who brought to the Chicago underworld the old Sicilian custom of rubbing bullets with garlic; if the shots failed to kill, the resulting gangrene allegedly would. Anselmi and Scalise's medical knowledge was somewhat faulty, although the same could not be said about their homicidal prowess, which was proficient even by Chicago standards.

While in their twenties, Anselmi and Scalise were forced to flee their native Marsala because of a murder charge. The pair turned up in Chicago during the early 1920s and went to work for the Terrible Gennas, a family of killers who had established themselves as the leading bootleggers in the Midwest. Since the Gennas also hailed from Marsala, they welcomed the two to their bosom, having a constant need for reliable torpedoes. Anselmi and Scalise were single-minded of purpose: they planned to make a million dollars each, which they felt would give them enough to fix the case against them in Sicily and allow them to return as rich men. Their killing services came high, but they were extremely efficient. For one killing the Gennas rewarded each of the pair with $10,000 and a $3,000 diamond ring. Scalise, the more romantic of the two, sent his ring to his sweetheart in Sicily. Anselmi reportedly sold his to a jeweler at the point of a gun for $4,000.

Anselmi and Scalise introduced a degree of double-dealing unknown even in the Chicago underworld. True innovators, they introduced the "handshake hit," whereby the short, fat Anselmi would shake hands with the unsuspecting victim and lock his right hand in a tight grip. With the victim's gun hand incapacitated, the taller Scalise would quickly step forward and shoot him in the head. The shorter Anselmi always did the holding because he had a grip of iron and Scalise did the shooting because his height enabled him to get in a head shot regardless of how tall the victim was. Anselmi and Scalise were definitely two of three killers involved in the 1924 assassination of Dion O'Banion, the leading Irish gangster of the era, in which the usually careful gang leader was caught off guard in a handshake just before the funeral of a leading Italian underworld figure.

Some of their other killings were legendary. One victim held his hands in prayer and begged to be spared. They shot off his hands before putting a bullet in his brain. Anselmi and Scalise probably sprayed more pedestrian-mobbed streets than any other pair of kill-happy gunners. They gunned down gangland rivals and police officers with equal ferocity. Once, in the company of several other killers, they noticed that their bullet-filled victim lying on a street managed to raise his head. Chagrined that he was not dead, the two rushed back across the street and, before dozens of witnesses, finished the job.

The only time Anselmi and Scalise wavered in obeying the orders of the Gennas was when they were told to kill Al Capone, for they realized their ultimate reward for such an act would be their own deaths. Instead, they informed Capone of the Gennas' plan and became Capone men while ostensibly still working for the Gennas. When it finally came time for Capone to erase the Gennas, Anselmi and Scalise "set up" one of the brothers and took an active part in killing another.

Capone now welcomed the pair openly into his organization, making them two of his most important bodyguards and gunners. When the mob boss offered to make peace with Hymie Weiss and the rest of the O'Banion gang, his terms proved entirely acceptable. Weiss made only one stipulation: Anselmi and Scalise had to be turned over to the gang for killing Dion O'Banion. Capone rejected the deal, declaring, "I wouldn't do that to a yellow dog."

Several legal attempts were made to get Anselmi and Scalise. They were once charged with the killing of two police detectives, but after three trials, involving a great number of threats against witnesses and jurors, they went free, remarkably, on the ground that they had merely been resisting unwarranted police aggression.

In 1929 they were arrested for taking part in the infamous St. Valentine's Day Massacre, but by the time their trial date arrived, they too had been murdered. How they died is no secret. Capone staged a party in honor of the pair and Joseph "Hop Toad" Giunta, whom he had recently installed as president of Unione Siciliana. At the height of the banquet, Capone stopped the festivities, accused the trio of plotting to murder him and, after having them tied up, beat all three to death with a heavy Indian club. They may well have been conspiring against Capone, but it is just as possible that Capone decided to kill the trio because he feared they were getting too important. Anselmi and Scalise had been appointed as bodyguards for Giunta in his new rule, but Scalise had quickly relegated Giunta to the background and had taken direct charge of the organization's affairs. He was heard to brag, "I am the most powerful man in Chicago." And Anselmi chimed in, "We the big shot now."

It was a fitting collective singular. Anselmi and Scalise, who had so often killed together, died together.

See also: ALPHONSE "SCARFACE AL" CAPONE, GENNA BROTHERS, ANTONIO "THE SCOURGE" LOMBARDO, CHARLES DION "DEANIE" O'BANION, ST. VALENTINE'S DAY MASSACRE.

Anti-Horse Thief Association

A vigilante organization, the Anti-Horse Thief Association was formed at Fort Scott during 1859 to battle the marauders plaguing the border states. After the Civil War these outlaw elements, using sprawling, poorly policed Indian Territory as their base, swept into Kansas and other states to run off herds of horses and cattle. Because of the strength of the outlaws, few lawmen would pursue them further than Marion County in Kansas, and the work fell to the Anti-Horse Thief Associations that proliferated in Kansas and other states. They generally dispensed instant justice on the trail when they caught the rustlers. As the West was tamed and the incidence of horse thievery dropped, the organization stayed on as a social group. Well into the 20th century it was common for a chapter to announce somberly at an annual meeting that no horse thieves had been apprehended during the previous 12 months, a record worthy of a great celebration.

See also: HORSE STEALING.

Apache gangs   mythical Indian outlaw bands

Without doubt one of the most fertile subjects for foreigners' misconceptions of conditions in America has always been crime. This has been true not merely because of purple reporting by several popular writers but also because of the inaccurate opinions of many experts. Typical was the work of Dr. Edmond Locord, one of the great criminologists of France in the early part of this century. Writing in the preface of a book on crime in 1925, Locard discussed crime in various parts of the world; of America he said: "In Texas and California even today one meets roving bands of redskins who live by extortion, pillage, and rapine. They are the Apaches." Thus, foreigners visiting the United States in that period spoke fearsomely of traveling in "Apache Gang" country.

The "Apache dancers," depicting the ways of the brutal French underworld, also derived their name from popular 19th-century misconceptions of the generally peaceful Apache.

Apache Indian job   gangland bombing

Using bombs as a "convincer" has long been a practice of the underworld. Today, organized crime makes great use of firebombs, particularly for what is known in the underworld as an Apache Indian job: when a building is so thoroughly burned that little remains standing other than a chimney and a few smoking timbers, as in the case of Indian burnings of settlers' cabins.

Such firebombings have been common in recent years in New York City to convince, for example, restaurateurs to pay tribute to the little-known but lucrative parsley racket. Restaurants that don't serve parsley with every meal, and indeed with a number of mixed drinks, can look forward to an Apache raid.

Apache Indian jobs have reappeared in the West recently. In 1980 the Montana State Crime Control Commission reported that a New York "parsley king" was involved in restaurant firebombings in that state.

See also: PARSLEY RACKET.

Apache Kid   (1867–?) rapist, robber, murderer

The Apache Kid conducted the worst one-man reign of terror the Arizona Territory and perhaps the entire West ever saw. Until age 20 the Apache Kid adapted well to the white man's world, becoming a sergeant of scouts at the San Carlos Agency under Al Sieber, Arizona's famed Indian fighter. When his father was murdered, tribal law required the young Indian to avenge the crime, and under that law, it would be a legal execution. Although Sieber warned him that such revenge would be illegal under the white man's law, the Apache Kid slipped away with a few followers, located his quarry near a creek and stabbed him to death. The young Indian then surrendered to Sieber, but becoming fearful of his treatment in a hostile white court, he escaped with his followers. After two years on the run, the Apache Kid returned to face a court-martial. He was convicted but won a pardon from President Grover Cleveland. Incensed by this action, the local Indian haters promptly indicted the Kid and several of his band on charges of having killed a whiskey drummer who was trying to sell "fire water" to their people. The Apache Kid was found guilty and given seven years in prison, a remarkably short sentence that indicated the case against him was either weak or that the crime itself was considered by many to be justified. On November 1, 1889 the Apache Kid was being escorted to the prison at Yuma when he overwhelmed his two guards, Sheriff Glen Reynolds and Deputy Bill Holmes, killed them and made his escape. From then on, the Apache Kid became the scourge of the state, leaving a bloody trail of robbery, rape and murder. He struck blindly, victimizing Indians as well as whites. He took many Indian women, and when he tired of them, he cut their throats. Prospectors were robbed and murdered in their mountain cabins; lonely ranches were attacked and their inhabitants killed. It was impossible to get an accurate count of the number of white girls he kidnapped, raped and killed because he was blamed whenever a lone Indian committed a

Originally a sergeant of scouts, the Apache Kid (center) later went on an orgy of robbery, rape, kidnapping and murder, becoming the most-hunted Indian outlaw in the Arizona Territory.

crime, but there was no doubt that most such victims were his. Even a $5,000 bounty on his head failed to stop him, although several whites and Indians alike tried and died in the effort.

The terror ended abruptly in 1894. One night Ed Clark, a prospector and former chief of Wallapai Scouts, awakened at his camp north of Tucson to see two young Indians trying to steal his horse. Clark shot the woman and badly wounded the man, who fled. Clark, whose partner, Billy Diehl, had been killed by the Apache Kid five years earlier, was sure he recognized him. He was equally positive that he had gotten in a killing shot and that the Apache Kid had crawled in some hole to die. Clark's story was plausible, but it was more likely that the Apache Kid realized the tale of his fate gave him the perfect opportunity to fade away. There seems little doubt that he took an Indian woman, went into the Sierra Madre in Mexico and raised a family. He was recognized and spoken to by a number of reliable witnesses well into the 20th century.

Further reading: *Lone War Trail of Apache Kid* by Earle F. Forrest and Edwin B. Hill.

Apalachin Conference   underworld convention

A much-publicized fiasco, the great underworld conference held at Apalachin, N.Y. on November 14, 1957 was in its own way as important for its impact on crime in America as the famous Atlantic City crime meeting in 1929. However, while Atlantic City was famous for what it did, Apalachin's chief significance was what it did not do, namely propel Vito Genovese into the number one spot in the syndicate hierarchy. More accurately, the Apalachin meeting destroyed Genovese, and in hindsight, it is impossible not to regard the events as brilliantly stage-managed.

The bare-bones history of the conference is rather clear cut. It came three weeks after the barbershop assassination of Albert Anastasia, which was arranged by Genovese as part of his plan to become "boss of bosses" both in New York and the nation. Genovese called the conference among other reasons, to justify Anastasia's death and relieve the heat he was getting for the attempt on Frank Costello's life a few months earlier. Most of all, he wanted his position as the syndicate's top man affirmed. But that was against the wishes of other powerful forces.

As it happened, the meeting at the 58-acre estate of mobster Joseph Barbara, Sr. never got off the ground. Before real discussions started, a raid by state police sent the participants scurrying. It was a ludicrous scene: immaculately tailored crime bosses, mostly in their fifties or older and no longer fleet of foot, climbed out windows or bolted through back doors and went racing through woods, burrs and undergrowth in a frantic attempt to escape. How many did is not known, but 58 were caught. The arrest roster bore the names of men whom various law enforcement agencies had tried to corner for years: Genovese, Trafficante, Profaci, Magliocco, Bonanno, Scalish, DeSimone, Riela, Magaddino, Gambino, Miranda, Catena, Ida, Zito, Civello, Colletti, Ormento, Galante. Of the 58, 50 had been arrested some time in their lives; 35 had convictions and 23 had served prison sentences. Eighteen had been involved in murder case investigations; 15 had been arrested for narcotics violations, 30 for gambling, 23 for illegal use of firearms. Newspapers wondered if anyone still thought the Mafia didn't exist.

The public assumption was that the Apalachin meeting was intended as the forum for presenting Genovese with his crown, and much was made of the fact that a total of $300,000 was found on the arrested crime bosses. This, the theory went, was "envelope money" to be given to Genovese. There was considerable reason to dispute that view, however. Few of the participants ever went about with anything less than a fat "roll," and it was known that Carlo Gambino was ready to announce he brought no money for Genovese. Gambino had cooperated with Genovese in the Anastasia assassination in order to take over the latter's crime family, but he had no intention of gaining Genovese as an overboss.

In short, Apalachin seemed likely to produce fireworks and perhaps even open warfare. All of that, however, could be avoided if the meeting were boycotted or sabotaged. The first alternative was partially accomplished, the second completely. Unless one holds to the theory that the crime leaders from Chicago, Detroit and San Francisco had escaped during the raid or were still "on the way," their absence was noteworthy. Lucky Luciano, from his exile in Italy, lobbied strongly against the meeting with some of these people (his voice was still powerful in those very cities), and he coached others on their behavior at the conference, especially Carlo Gambino. Frank Costello also begged off on the grounds that he was constantly being tailed by the authorities. As treasurer for the syndicate, Meyer Lansky was supposed to show but developed, he said, a sore throat that kept him in Florida.

All these absences pointed up the lack of unanimity facing Genovese. And then came the fiasco of the raid—nothing so degrading had ever happened in the underworld's history. Vito Genovese, it was concluded, had led the crime bosses to disaster. The extent of the fury against Genovese was pointed up in a tapped telephone conversation later between Sam Giancana, then head of the Chicago syndicate, and Steve Magaddino, his Buffalo, N.Y. counterpart:

Magaddino: "It never would've happened in your place."

Giancana: "You're fuckin' right it wouldn't. This is the safest territory in the world for a big meet. . . . We got three towns just outside of Chicago with the police chiefs in our pocket. We got this territory locked up tight."

Magaddino's comments were less than gracious considering it was he who had suggested to Genovese that the meeting be held at Apalachin. Host Barbara was a lieutenant in Magaddino's crime family. If Genovese had the feeling he had been set up, there was considerable justification. How much so he did not realize until he and a number of his aides were indicted for narcotics conspiracy six months later. The chief testimony against Genovese was provided by a two-bit heroin pusher named Nelson Cantellops. That an unimportant Puerto Rican street operator could have the goods on a big man like Genovese did not seem logical, but the government gleefully used his testimony to convict the crime boss.

Shortly before he died, Lucky Luciano revealed the secret behind the Cantellops testimony. He said Cantellops had in the past worked for Chicago's Sam Giancana and for Meyer Lansky, both of whom had missed the Apalachin conclave. The pusher had received a $100,000 payoff from Luciano, Gambion, Lansky and Costello. For his $25,000, Costello had insisted that among those convicted had to be Vincente "the Chin" Gigante, the triggerman in the Genovese-inspired attempt on his life.

Apalachin had indeed been the first nail in Genovese's coffin. The coup de grace followed in 1959, when he was sentenced to prison for 15 years. He would die there in 1969.

See also: JOSEPH BARBARA, SR.; VITO GENOVESE.

Arbuckle, Roscoe "Fatty" (1887–1933) accused murderer

Roscoe "Fatty" Arbuckle was at the peak of his career as a comedian, regarded second only to Chaplin, when he was arrested in 1921 for the rape-killing of a delicate young actress named Virginia Rappe, which came to be regarded as Hollywood's worst scandal. The three trials that followed laid bare facts about Arbuckle's private life. What had been amusing on screen for an almost 300-pound buffoon assumed sinister aspects off screen. Somehow the knowledge that Arbuckle had the back seat of his $25,000 Rolls Royce equipped with a built-in toilet came across as more animalistic than humorous when associated with an alleged rapist-murderer.

The facts in the death of 25-year-old Virginia Rappe have never been entirely clear, the picture having been muddled by Hollywood movie studios anxious to protect their investment in a hot comic property. Bribes were paid and witnesses disappeared or changed their stories. But what is clear is that Arbuckle, straight from working on three films without a day off, headed for a session of relaxation in San Francisco with a party of friends, among them Virginia Rappe, who had recently moved up to starring roles on the basis of her delicate beauty rather than any acting ability. Her pretty face at the moment graced the sheet music of "Let Me Call You Sweetheart."

According to some accounts, Virginia thoroughly disliked Arbuckle but kept his company because she felt the fat comedian could aid her career, a common enough belief among aspiring starlets. The young actress was present at a wild party—some later described it as an orgy—that took place in Fatty's St. Francis Hotel suite on September 5, 1921. During the revelry Fatty seized Virginia and hustled her into the bedroom, with the actress showing some or no resistance, according to the conflicting testimony of the witnesses. But what happened next was not disputed.

For 20 minutes no sound was heard from the bedroom and the others in the party simply passed knowing glances. Suddenly, there were hysterical screams and Virginia cried, "I'm dying, he's killing me, I'm dying!"

Arbuckle then walked out of the room wearing Virginia's hat and giggling. "Go in and get her dressed and take her back to her hotel. She makes too much noise."

When the others looked into the bedroom, they saw Virginia's nude, bloody body lying among her ripped clothes. "He hurt me. Roscoe hurt me," she cried. "I'm dying, I'm dying. Roscoe did it."

Arbuckle was unimpressed by Virginia's ravings. "She's acting it up," he said. "She's always been a lousy actress." He warned those present he would throw her out the 12th-story window unless she stopped moaning. Several other women carried Virginia down the hall to another room. Three days later she died.

The three trials of Fatty Arbuckle for felony rape and murder were legal curiosities. At first, courtroom descriptions of what Arbuckle had done were considered so shocking that they were passed back and forth in writing. The official version that Virginia's bladder had been ruptured when the fat man had forced intercourse on her was hardly the complete story. Finally, a witness testified that after the incident Arbuckle had laughingly told others at the party that he had jammed a large jagged piece of ice into her vagina. Later, there was talk about a champagne bottle as well.

The first two trials ended in hung juries, voting 10 to two for acquittal and then 10 to two for conviction. The third trial resulted in a not-guilty verdict, after the jury had deliberated only six minutes. In addition to setting the comedian free, the panel added: "Acquittal is not enough for Roscoe Arbuckle. We feel a great injustice has been done him and there was not the slightest proof to connect him in any way with the commission of any crime." The jurors then stuck around to have their pictures taken with the grateful comic.

While the air was filled with charges that witnesses and jury members had been bribed, the studios set up plans to relaunch Arbuckle's film career. However, it soon became apparent that although a California court had cleared him, the rest of the country did not feel the same way. Theater owners reported that the comedian's unreleased movies would play to empty houses, and his films were junked. Arbuckle spent the next 10 years knocking around in vaudeville and playing second-rate cabarets. He was allowed to direct some minor films under the name of William Goodrich, while he implored the studios to give him another chance. Finally, in 1933 Warner Brothers signed him to do some two-reelers. He finished the first one in New York on June 29. "This is the happiest day of my life," he said. The next morning he was found dead in his hotel room bed of a heart attack.

Argos Lectionary rare manuscript

One of the most-valued Greek manuscripts possessed by an American university is the University of Chicago's Argos Lectionary, a book of parchment leaves containing excerpts from the Bible arranged for church services. The book was purchased by the school in 1930 from the manager of an underworld-controlled nightclub, who had phoned and offered to sell "a Bible with an odd history."

The nightclub manager, however, had something else in mind when he referred to its "odd history." Prohibition-era gunmen had placed their hands on the Bible when they swore their oath of allegiance to Al Capone. The university's experts recognized it as a ninth or 10th-century work—and a masterpiece of singular scholarly import.

Arizona Rangers

Formed much later than the Texas Rangers, the Arizona Rangers were organized in 1901 to assist local officials in maintaining law and order. Headed by Capt. Burton C. Mossman, the 12- to 14-man force achieved a noteworthy record. While aimed at stopping outlaws and rustlers in general, the Arizona Rangers probably would not have been formed had it not been for the depredations of a vicious outlaw and murderer named Augustine Chacon, a 30-notch gunman. The Rangers got their man and many more before being disbanded in 1910, probably in recognition of the fact that the use of such a force was justified only in an era of widespread lawlessness. By doing so, the Arizona Rangers avoided the later criticism of the Texas Rangers as an organization that had outlived its usefulness. Such early groups as the Arizona Rangers and the New Mexico Rangers set the precedent for the present state police organizations.

See also: BURT ALVORD, BURTON C. MOSSMAN.

Arkansas Tom   See ROY DAUGHERTY.

Arkansas toothpick   murder weapon

The popular concept of backwoods feuding and killing is of mountain boys blasting away at each other with their trusty shotguns. True, they all carried shotguns or rifles, but as in the Hatfield-McCoy feud, many of the killings were done with a stiletto-type dagger known as an Arkansas toothpick, the hillbillies' favorite for a "silent job."

Arlington, Josie (1864–1919)   madam

Mary Deubler, better known professionally as Josie Arlington, was perhaps New Orleans' most famous madam. She was certainly regarded as the classiest and her house, the Arlington, gained a reputation as the gaudiest and grandest of bordellos. Her achievement was somewhat remarkable, however, considering her early years in the trade. For nine years, starting at the age of 17, she worked in various brothels on Customhouse Street and Basin Street under the name of Josie Alton. She never stayed long in one place because of her proclivity for brawling with the other girls. In 1886 she engaged in a fierce fight with another prostitute, Beulah Ripley. Josie lost much of her hair, while Beulah staggered from the battle minus

One of Madam Arlington's ads in the *Blue Book*, a turn-of-the-century guide to whoring in New Orleans, heralds the ultimate in brothel furnishings and decor.

her lower lip and half an ear. In 1888 Josie opened her own place at No. 172 Customhouse Street, a house known for having the most quarrelsome residents on the street. The profits enabled Josie to support her lover, Philip Lobrano, who lived in the house, and several members of her family. Lobrano was quite outspoken about relatives living off the income of his women like "a flock of vultures." In 1890, during a fierce brawl in the house involving Josie and all her girls, Lobrano shot and killed Josie's brother, Peter Deubler. New Orleans being New Orleans, Lobrano was acquitted by the courts.

Changing her name to Lobrano d'Arlington, Josie turned over a new leaf. She kicked out her lover, dismissed all her battling prostitutes and announced that henceforth she would fill her establishment with the most gracious of foreign ladies who would entertain only gentlemen of refinement and impeccable taste.

The *Mascot*, a tabloid that reported the doings of the red-light district, trumpeted: "Society is graced by the presence of a bona-fide baroness, direct from the Court at St. Petersburg. The baroness is at present residing incog. at the Chateau Lobrano d'Arlington, and is known as La Belle Stewart." The baroness was soon exposed as being a hoochy-koochy dancer and circus specialist who had graced the Midway at the Chicago World's Fair. Many of Josie Arlington's other imports also proved to be imposters. Despite this, her lavish brothel thrived and when Storyville, a quasi-legal red-light district, was established, Josie opened the Arlington, which was just about the most discriminating in Storyville. Over the next decade Josie Arlington amassed a considerable fortune, which allowed her to buy a mansion in the most fashionable part of New Orleans.

Josie also started to get religion, sending a niece to be educated in a convent. While still in her early forties, she bought a plot in Metarie Cemetery and erected an $8,000 tomb of red marble, with two large flambeaux on top and a crosscut in the back. There was a copper door and carved on it, in bas-relief, was the figure of a kneeling woman, her arms filled with flowers.

Josie leased out the Arlington in 1909 and retired from the business. She died in 1914, at the age of 50, by then Storyville's most-storied madam. Even in death, Josie entertained, in a fashion, the citizenry of New Orleans. The city installed a red traffic light on the street by Metairie Cemetery, and during the night its red glow cast on the two flambeaux gave the illusion of a red light shining over the renowned madam's tomb. Crowds gathered each night to enjoy the spectacle, and nightly sightseeing tours all paused at the cemetery for the show. The city eventually replaced the red light with a white one, making the traffic light one of the most confusing ever installed. In 1924 Josie's niece had the madam's bones transferred to a receiving vault and the gaudy tomb was sold.

See also: STORYVILLE.

Arnold, Keith See GERALD CRAFT.

Arnold, Stephen (c. 1770–?) murderer

Men and women suffering from varying degrees of lunacy have committed murders, and depending on the prevailing mores of their societies, they have received varying punishments. Stephen Arnold, in an event marked by high drama, was one of the first in America to win leniency due to insanity. As a thirtyish schoolteacher in Cooperstown, N.Y., he was a perfectionist who would fly into a mad rage whenever a pupil made

a spelling error. When in 1805 his six-year-old niece, Betsy Van Amburgh, misspelled *gig*, Arnold lost all control of himself, seized a club and beat her to death. Then comprehending what he had done, he fled Cooperstown for Pittsburgh, Pa., where he took up a new identity. Caught later that year, he was returned to Cooperstown to be tried for murder. Since his lawyer could not dispute the obvious facts of the crime, Arnold was convicted in short order and sentenced to be hanged.

Arnold's execution day was a banner event in Cooperstown, with thousands from the surrounding area converging on the town for the big show. According to a contemporary account, marching bands, a company of artillery and a full battalion of infantry led Arnold to the gallows. Flowers and bunting decorated the caissons and even the gallows. While Arnold stood with the noose around his neck, a minister launched into an hour-long sermon on the sins of men letting their tempers race unchecked. Much of the admonishments were quotations from Arnold himself. Now, with the obligatory matters taken care of, the hangman stepped forward—the crowd tensed . . . suddenly the sheriff moved to the condemned man and ceremoniously flung the noose from Arnold's neck. Before the stunned onlookers, the sheriff then read a reprieve for Arnold that he had received from the governor earlier in the morning. The sheriff had let the execution charade continue for three reasons: to show his disagreement with the chief executive's act; to force Arnold to experience the terror of execution for his murderous sin; and not to disappoint entirely the thousands gathered for the event. The crowd's disappointment was great nonetheless, and there was some speculation that the sheriff had acted as he did only so that the local merchants and tavern keepers could still profit from what would prove to be a nonevent. Amidst all the bickering on that point, the concept of temporary insanity and the pros and cons of it were lost on most of the crowd. Arnold was later pardoned for the same reason.

arrest, citizen's

A private citizen has just as much right to arrest a lawbreaker as does a police officer, but these so-called citizen's arrests are actually rife with legal danger to the person making them. A private citizen can arrest another for a crime that is committed or attempted in his or her presence. In addition, a private citizen can arrest a person who has committed a felony even though it was not perpetrated in the arresting citizen's presence. The arresting citizen must inform the person of the arrest and, without undue delay, take him or her before a magistrate or hand him or her over to a police officer. Everything will then have been handled properly—provided the person arrested is later found guilty. If he or she is acquitted or the charges are dropped, the citizen making the arrest can be sued for false arrest, not an uncommon occurrence. As a result, most legal authorities strongly counsel against a citizen's arrest except under the most certain of circumstances.

arrest procedures

Arrest is the taking or detainment of a person by legal authority, preferably by an officer of the law acting with a warrant, a written order signed by a magistrate stating the reason for the arrest. An officer can also make an arrest without a warrant if the crime is a misdemeanor, or lesser offense, committed in his presence or a felony, or major offense, that he may not have witnessed but has reasonable cause to believe the person being arrested has committed.

As soon as the arrested person arrives at the station house, he or she is booked. Booking is the entry of the charge into what is called the "arrest book," more popularly known as the police blotter. At this point, the defendant officially learns the exact charge against him, but in practice, the average person often is so frightened he doesn't grasp the exact words or the desk officer mumbles in such a manner that the accused can't make out the officer's words.

Next comes an "order for admittance and property receipt." The arrested person empties his pockets; everything is itemized and put in an envelope. As a rule, wristwatches may be kept.

Regulations in the average jail permit an arrested person to send local telephone messages to his or her relatives, friends, employer and a lawyer. "Messages" is indeed the right word, since in most places the police make the calls for you. If the arrested person is well behaved, the police wink at the rules and let him or her personally use the phone and even make as many calls as desired. If the arrestee gets nasty, the police will make the call, or at least they say they will. Unfortunately, they sometimes will inform the arrestee the line is busy. The Constitution provides no guarantee that a telephone can't be busy.

If charged with a felony or a misdemeanor, the arrestee is fingerprinted and "mugged." A person can refuse to be fingerprinted, but in most places one can't get bail without going through the procedure. Four sets of fingerprints are made: two for the local police files, one for the state capital and another for the FBI. Four photographs—"mug shots"—are taken, two front view and one left and one right profile. If the arrested person is later found innocent or the charges are dropped, he or she has the right to demand the return of the prints.

Some officers make a point of not doing this, instead offering a phony set of prints. In some states a court order is needed to get back such prints. It's often wise to have a lawyer get a court order even where it is not required; few officers will play games when a court order is involved.

After the arrested person has been booked, printed and mugged, he or she is brought into court for arraignment. Usually, the police are required to bring an arrested person before a judge within 24 hours, but in some areas the rule isn't rigidly enforced. Over a weekend an arrestee can often spend three nights locked up, and there are numerous cases of persons being held two or three weeks before arraignment. At times, court arraignment is used only in felony cases. In any case, the formal charge is made at arraignment, and at the same time, or possibly at a later hearing, the arrested person pleads either guilty or innocent. A magistrate then hears the police case and decides whether it's strong enough to hold the arrested person for the grand jury. If not, the magistrate will dismiss the charge.

The grand jury hearing a case does not necessarily call the defendant before it. It may simply hear the police side and decide that a crime has been committed and that the defendant could have committed it. The grand jury is a body of 12 to 23 citizens, with the average number around 19. For a verdict, 12 jury members must agree. If the grand jury decides there is enough evidence to bring a defendant to trial, it issues a "true bill," or indictment. After that, the defendant is permitted to alter his or her plea, and the judge will set new bail, either larger or smaller, depending on what is deemed appropriate.

For a misdemeanor the arrestee or may not be arraigned in court the next day. In many cities, at the time of booking, the desk officer will order the arrested person to be in court on a given date, possibly two or three weeks later. By agreement with the courts, the police are empowered to collect bail in misdemeanor cases according to fixed rates and allow the defendant's release. Bail is solely for the purpose of guaranteeing that the accused will appear at his or her trial. If the defendant can't raise bail, for either a felony or a misdemeanor charge, it's back to jail, possibly for a long stay until the case comes to court.

See also: BAIL.

arson

If any crime in America can be described as out of control, it is arson. At the end of the 1990s, arson was responsible for killing 700 persons and injuring thousands more each year. The cost to insurance companies was more than $2 billion. From 1970 to 1996 the number of fires due to arson jumped from 120,000 to 500,000. A Senate investigations subcommittee warned, "Long thought by the public to be a sporadic act of greed, arson has evolved into a way of life in many metropolitan areas." The committee said landlords and other building owners who saw property values dropping often overinsured their properties and then arranged to have them burned down by professional firebugs or ghetto gangs in order to obtain quick insurance windfalls.

Pyromania, the act of a compulsive fire-setter, may not have increased as fast as arson for money, but it too is growing. In fact, insurance arsonists are at times the inspiration for pyromaniacs.

Pyromania is a difficult illness to diagnose and one that shows few social patterns.

- The Chicago area had a rash of fires set in 27 different buildings. It turned out to be the work of one of the community's most respected physicians, a dedicated doctor who still made house calls.
- When a large building on the campus of the University of Michigan was set afire, a respected faculty member was apprehended for the crime.
- A Georgia orphanage burned to the ground, and the arsonist turned out to be a society matron who had worked hard to raise money for its construction in the first place. "When I get the urge to set a fire," she declared when caught, "nothing I can do stops me."

Few arsonists start fires with any desire to kill people. They know it will happen sooner or later, but the thought doesn't stop them from committing their crimes.

Recent history's worst proven case of arson was the Ringling Brothers Barnum and Bailey Circus fire in 1944 in Hartford, Conn., in which 168 men, women and children perished. Eventually, a 15-year-old circus roustabout was found to have set the fire. He was caught some six years later after he set another big blaze in East St. Louis. The pyromaniac couldn't really explain why he had started the circus fire; all that could be established was that he had felt picked on by his bosses and that he had had a lifelong preoccupation with fire.

By and large, pyromaniacs can be said to share one or more of four common characteristics: (1) a resentment of authority; (2) the urge for destruction; (3) an inability to show resentment directly; and (4) extremely poor sexual adjustment. One of the leading authorities on the subject, Dr. Nolan D. C. Lewis, has observed: "The pyromaniac can give no rational motive for his incendiary acts. Even though he is aware that he may cause property damage worth hundreds of thousands of dollars, perhaps even be responsible for the deaths of innocent women and children, he feels he *must* set fires. I know of cases where such people have rushed into police stations shouting, 'Stop me before I set another fire!'"

There is considerable evidence to indicate that compulsive arsonists can be cured. In their landmark study, *Pathological Firesetting*, Drs. Nolan Lewis and Helen Yarnell traced 1,071 convicted pyromaniacs. Only 138 of the pyromaniacs had received psychiatric treatment specifically designed to solve their problem. Of these, Lewis and Yarnell concluded, not one was still setting fires.

Ashby, James (c. 1830) riverboat gambler

While the Mississippi was noted for many colorful riverboat gamblers, none was more amazing than old James Ashby, a grizzled sharper skilled at suckering others who superficially seemed much more polished.

Ashby would work with a young confederate, pretending to be father and son returning home after selling off some stock at market. The bumpkin-appearing "son" looked like a perfect victim, easily inveigled into trying his luck at cards, and Ashby pretended to be a fiddle-playing old man teetering on the brink of senility. While the son was gambling, Ashby guzzled white lightning and played snatches of tunes on his fiddle, bemoaning that he no longer remembered how the complete version went. His son proved less dimwitted than he looked, winning hand after hand in defiance of all the odds. "Not for a long time," one historian of the river wrote, "did the gamblers learn that the tunes were signals." Whereupon Ashby retired from Mississippi activities, having grown wealthy by outsharping the sharpers.

Ashley, John (1895–1924) Everglades gangster

Still regarded as a folk hero in the Florida Everglades, John Ashley headed an unlikely band of criminals who, from 1915 to 1924, robbed a total of 40 banks and stole close to a million dollars. Small-town bankers lived in dread of the sight of the Ashley gang bouncing into town in a Model T and out again with the loot, often waving a gin bottle at the citizens as they went. They were also expert hijackers. Rumrunners, not a spineless sort, blanched when Ashley and his crew mounted one of their transports. A state official called Ashley the worst menace to Florida since the war with the Seminoles. The newspapers likened him to Jesse James, and there was indeed a resemblance save that James never flaunted the law quite as openly as John Ashley.

Once the Ashley gang pulled a job, they would separate and head for the Everglades, where no man alive could track John Ashley, a "cracker" who could move through the swamps with the assurance of an urban pedestrian on well-marked city streets. The story was often told of the time a posse of 12 men went after Ashley when he was alone in the swamp. They failed to catch him but ended up racing out of the swamp panic-stricken, two of them wounded. They suddenly had realized that Ashley was tracking them instead of the other way around.

It was exploits of this sort that made Ashley a hero to a great many crackers who inhabited the pine and palmetto backwoods of Florida. He became a symbol of their resentment toward an encroaching civilization, and a popular belief was that Ashley killed only when he was forced to, lived a life of crime only because he was forced into it. And besides, he sure stuck it to all those the crackers detested—the townies, the revenuers, the police, even them big-city rumrunners importing that foreign stuff and taking away white lightnin' markets. In that last endeavor, the Ashley gang did what the U.S. Coast Guard had failed to do. They virtually halted rumrunning between Bimini, a little spit of sand in the Bahamas, and much of Florida's east coast. The smugglers lost so much liquor to the Ashley gang that they transferred their activities elsewhere.

Perhaps what made the gang so engaging was the fact they did their work so haphazardly; in fact, they were just too lazy to do any advance planning. When Ashley robbed a bank, often the extent of his casing the job was to check the bank's hours to make sure it would be open when he got there. Once when the Ashley mob hit a bank in Stuart, Fla. without bothering to bring along a getaway car, they had an excellent reason: no member of the gang at the time knew how to drive! Ashley figured there'd be someone in the bank who had a car parked outside. Which was exactly how things worked out.

Ashley did get caught a couple of times: following one bank robbery, a member of his own gang accidentally shot him in the eye while firing at pursuers. Ashley was captured as he staggered around on the edge of a swamp, clutching his eye and half-crazed with pain. After that, he wore a glass eye.

Instead of being tried for the bank robbery, Ashley was shipped to Miami to stand trial for the murder of a Seminole Indian subchief. There was no hard evidence against Ashley, and he was almost certainly innocent of the murder. The crackers of the swamp knew what was behind it all: the land sellers wanted someone convicted of the killing because they didn't want any Indian trouble scaring away buyers. So why not pin it on John Ashley?

The Ashley gang was incensed and determined to free its leader. Ashley's brother Bob actually made his way into the jailhouse and killed a guard, but he was forced to flee before reaching his brother's cell and was killed shortly thereafter in a fight with police. The frustrated gang then sent an "ultimatum" to the city of Miami that brought the Ashleys nationwide fame. Addressed to the local sheriff, its exact words were

Dear Sir,

We were in your city at the time one of gang Bob Ashley was brutely shot to death by your officers and now your town can expect to feel the results of it any hor, and if John Ashley is not fairly delt with and given a fair trial and turned loose simply for the life of a God-damn Seminole Indian we expect to shoot up the hole God-damn town regardless to what the results might be. we expect to make our appearance at a early date.

The Ashley Gang

It is doubtful the course of Miami justice bent because of this threat, but among the crackers there was a knowing nod of the heads when the murder charge against Ashley was nol-prossed. However, Ashley was convicted of bank robbery and sentenced to 17 years in prison. In a short time, he escaped and returned to take command of his gang.

In 1924 Ashley, tired of bank jobs and the like, pulled one of the most fabulous crimes of the century, though it is little remembered today because the loot turned out to be disappointingly small. During this period of Prohibition most of the rumrunners drew their supplies from the West End Settlement in the Bimini Islands. Ashley decided that instead of going through all the trouble involved in waylaying the rumrunners, it would be a lot less tiring to go to West End and rob whatever money the rumrunners brought there. John and his crew hit the island late one afternoon and within two hours cleaned out all the money the liquor suppliers had on hand. It was the first time in more than 100 years that an American pirate had raided a British crown colony, but Ashley wasn't particularly interested in the distinction. What bothered him was that his master coup had netted a mere $8,000. Just hours before the gang hit the island, an express boat carrying $250,000 in cash had left for Nassau.

Ashley went back to bank robbing, but the end was near. The police now had a stoolpigeon within the gang. His identity has never been established with certainty, but it is widely believed to have been Clarence Middleton, a drug addict member of the gang. The police got a tip in February 1924 that Ashley's father, who'd recently jumped bail on a moonshining charge, was holed up not far from the Ashley home, and that John Ashley was going to visit him.

The hideout was attacked, and Old Man Ashley was killed and a few others wounded. John Ashley, however, escaped. The same source then informed the police that the gang was heading for Jacksonville. A roadblock with a chain and some lanterns was set up at the Sebastian Bridge. It was dark when the Ashley gang's car pulled up. All four men in it—Ashley, Hanford Mobley, Ray Lynn and Clarence Middleton—got out to inspect what they thought was a construction job. A score of gun muzzles were leveled on them. They started to raise their hands.

What happened next is a mystery. The official version is that Ashley made a move for his gun. Twenty law officers fired, and four of the most-wanted men in Florida died. According to another version, told by the crackers, Ashley and the others were handcuffed and then shot to death. This story claims that when their bodies were brought to the funeral parlor, all the dead men's wrists bore the marks of handcuffs.

assassination

Political assassination came late upon the American scene. The first assassination attempt against a U.S. president occurred in 1835 as Andrew Jackson was strolling out of the Capitol. Richard Lawrence, an out-of-work painter, stepped out from behind a pillar and fired two pistols at Jackson, both of which misfired. Lawrence was judged deranged and committed to an insane asylum, although Jackson remained convinced the would-be assassin's act had been part of a Whig conspiracy to kill him.

The next attack on a U.S. president was the assassination of Abraham Lincoln by John Wilkes Booth in 1865. Besides Booth, who was killed by pursuing troops, four others—Lewis Paine, George Atzerodt, David Herold and Mrs. Mary Surratt—were hanged and several others sent to prison. What followed can best be summarized by a phrase from James McKinley's *Assassination in America*, "After Lincoln, the deluge." While Andrew Johnson was president, 13 political officeholders were shot at and 12 of them killed. During Ulysses S. Grant's two terms, from 1869 to 1877, there were 20 attacks, resulting in 11 deaths.

Assassinations became a part of American political life from the late 19th century on. Some important assassinations and attempts included the following:

1881: President James A. Garfield was shot in Washington, D.C. on March 13 by a disappointed office seeker, Charles Julius Gaiteau. Garfield died on September 29 and Gaiteau was hanged in June 1882.

1901: President William McKinley was shot in Buffalo, N.Y. on September 6 by Leon Czolgosz. McKinley died on September 14 and Czolgosz was executed the following month.

1910: New York mayor William J. Gaynor was shot and badly wounded by James J. Gallagher, a disgruntled city employee, but the mayor recovered.

1912: Former President Theodore Roosevelt was shot in Milwaukee by a demented man named John N. Shrank, but Roosevelt was saved when the passage of the bullet was slowed by a folded 50-page speech and the spectacle case in his pocket. The bullet nevertheless, penetrated the former president's chest in too dangerous a position ever to be removed. Shrank was confined in mental institutions until his death in 1943.

1933: President-elect Franklin D. Roosevelt was shot at in Miami, Fla. on February 15 by Joseph Zangara. The shot missed Roosevelt and instead hit and

In what many experts regard as the greatest crime photo ever taken, New York mayor William J. Gaynor is shown seconds after he was shot by a disgruntled city employee in 1910 aboard an ocean liner as he prepared to sail for Europe. Gaynor survived. When Charles Chapin, city editor of the *Evening World*, saw the picture he exclaimed, "Look, what a wonderful thing! Blood all over him—and exclusive too!"

fatally wounded Chicago mayor Anton J. Cermak. Some historians insist Zangara never intended to shoot Roosevelt (despite his own claims to that effect) but had been hired by elements of the Capone mob to get rid of Cermak. The mayor himself clung to that belief on his deathbed. Zangara died in the electric chair in March 1933.

1935: Sen. Huey P. Long of Louisiana was shot and killed by Dr. Carl Austin Weiss, who in turn was cut down by Long's bodyguards.

1950: On November 1 two Puerto Rican nationalists, Oscar Collazo and Griselio Torresola, attempted to storm Blair House to assassinate President Harry S Truman. They never reached Truman but killed a guard, Leslie Coffelt. Torresola was also killed and Collazo wounded. Collazo was sentenced to life imprisonment. In 1979 President Carter granted him clemency and he returned to Puerto Rico.

1963: President John F. Kennedy was shot to death in Dallas, Tex. by Lee Harvey Oswald. Oswald was later assassinated by Jack Ruby while in police custody.

1965: Malcolm X was shotgunned to death in New York City on February 21 by three assassins as he addressed his Organization of Afro-American Unity. Thomas "15X" Johnson and Norman "3X" Butler, both reputed Black Muslim enforcers, and Talmadge Hayer were all convicted of murder and given life imprisonment.

1968: Dr. Martin Luther King, Jr., was gunned down in Memphis, Tenn. on April 4 by James Earl Ray, who was convicted of the shooting and sentenced to 99 years in prison.

1968: Sen. Robert F. Kennedy was fatally shot in Los Angeles on June 5 by Sirhan Sirhan, who was subsequently convicted of the murder and sentenced to life imprisonment.

1972: Gov. George Wallace of Alabama was shot and permanently paralyzed in Laurel, Md. on May 15 by Arthur H. Bremer. Bremer was sentenced to 53 years in prison.

1975: An adherent of Charles Manson, Lynette Alice "Squeaky" Fromme, pointed a gun at President Gerald Ford in Sacramento, Calif. on September 5, but she was immediately seized by a Secret Service agent. Fromme received a sentence of life imprisonment.

1975: In the second attempt on President Ford's life in 17 days, Sara Jane Moore fired a revolver at him in San Francisco, Calif. on September 22, but an onlooker shoved the gun off target. Moore was sentenced to life in prison.

1981: President Ronald Reagan was shot in the left lung on March 30 by 25-year-old John W. Hinckley, Jr., who fired a total of six shots at the president as he left a Washington, D.C. hotel. Reagan's press secretary,

a Secret Service guard and a city policeman were also severely wounded. Reagan recovered.

assault and battery

Assault and battery are two distinct crimes and the distinction is most valuable in the prosecution of criminals. Assault involves the threat or the attempt to use force or violence on another, but its commission does not require the actual use of force. Battery constitutes the actual use of force.

Legally, the distinction is most important, for without it, a holdup man who does not actually manhandle or touch his victim would not be guilty of any crime other than, say, robbery or attempted robbery. Thus, the mere waving of a fist in a person's face constitutes assault, and the employment of that fist raises the crime to assault and battery.

Astor Place Riots

One of the worst riots in New York City's history started on May 10, 1849, ostensibly as an outgrowth of a rather silly theatrical feud between the English tragedian William Charles Macready and the American actor Edwin Forrest. Actually, the riots were fomented by a notorious political rogue, Capt. Isaiah Rynders, who capitalized on the poor's general class hatred and anti-British feeling to regain a measure of public power following the unexpected defeat of his Democratic Party in 1848.

Macready had been chosen instead of Forrest to perform in *Macbeth* at the Astor Place Opera House. When the English actor appeared on stage, he was met by a mob who had gathered in response to a fiery tirade by Capt. Rynders and one of his chief lieutenants, Edward Z. C. Judson, better known as Ned Buntline. Rynders' thugs broke up the performance by hurling rotten eggs, pennies and even chairs onto the stage. Others threw pieces of paper filled with gunpowder in the chandeliers. Macready was driven from the stage but no one was injured. The noted actor was induced by the righteous element, led by Washington Irving and other prominent citizens to try once more on May 10, but Rynders was again prepared.

Offering free drinks, passes and rabble-rousing handbills, Rynders produced a crowd of 10,000 to 15,000. Twenty of Rynders' thugs entered the theater with orders to kidnap the hated foreigner right off the stage. However, the police foiled the plot and locked them all up in the basement, where they unsuccessfully tried to burn down the building. Meanwhile, the mob outside was running wild. They bombarded the barricaded windows of the theater with cobblestones gathered from a nearby sewer excavation and ripped down street lamps to use as clubs, plunging the area into darkness.

The police managed to evacuate the building and got Macready out wearing a disguise, but they couldn't contain the rioting. When Edward Judson was arrested, the mob turned even more violent. Officers were stoned to their knees, and the Seventh Regiment was called into action. Even the cavalrymen were knocked off their horses, and the infantry fell back on the sidewalk on the east side of the opera house. When the crowd tried to seize their muskets, the soldiers were ordered to fire, and several volleys tore into the rioters, who fell by the dozens. Twenty-three persons were killed, and the injury list on both sides totaled more than 120.

The mobs returned the following night determined to wreck and burn the opera house, but they were driven off by reinforced troops and artillery, which had been set up to sweep Broadway and the Bowery. For several days thereafter, crowds gathered in front of the New York Hotel, where Macready had been staying, calling on him to come out and be hanged. However, the actor had rushed to New Rochelle on May 10 and gone on by train to Boston, where he sailed for England, never to return to America.

For his part in fomenting the trouble, Edward Judson was fined $250 and sentenced to a year in the penitentiary. Rynders also was tried for inciting to riot. At the farcical trial, prosecution witnesses retraced the genesis of the plot back to Rynder's Empire Club, where the original plotting had been done, but they could not recall anything involving him directly. The jury acquitted Rynders in two hours and 10 minutes.

See also: EDWARD Z. C. JUDSON.

Atlanta Boys Convoy   mass shipment of convicts

On January 1, 1934 the former military prison on Alcatraz island in San Francisco Bay officially became a federal penitentiary. In the months that followed, this "super cage to hold super criminals" began drawing the worst inmates from other federal prisons, the trouble-makers and those most likely to attempt an escape.

It was decided to ship these dangerous convicts en masse in convoy form from each prison. The first of these, called the Atlanta Boys Convoy, caused an immense amount of excitement throughout the country. On August 14, 1934, 53 tough convicts were taken from their cells in Atlanta Penitentiary, chained hand and foot and loaded into a train composed of special steel coaches with barred windows and wire-meshed doors. This came in a year when the hysteria over gangsters had reached its zenith. Once the plan to move "the

Atlanta boys" became public, there were wild rumors of huge underworld armies mobilizing armored cars, flamethrowers, machine guns and even aircraft to free the convicts.

The government took measures that were appropriate for a military operation in hostile territory. The prisoners were chained to their chairs and refused toilet privileges other than on a carefully planned schedule. While the train's route was unannounced, the mysterious closings of certain stations along the way led to public speculation.

At Alcatraz, Warden James A. Johnston was kept constantly informed of the train's progress. He had stayed up the entire night of the 13th tracking the projected route on a large map. When the train neared Oakland, it was shifted away from the city's busy terminal and switched to a little-used railway yard at Tiburon. The cars were run straight onto a ferry barge and escorted to the Rock by the Coast Guard. The prisoners were in terrible shape, having been chained in close quarters where they could hardly move and certainly couldn't sleep. All were caked in grime and sweat, and most suffered swollen feet from the irons and could hardly walk.

Their bitter journey was over, but their ordeal in the most restrictive federal prison in history was just beginning. When all were finally locked in their cells. Warden Johnston wired Attorney General Homer Cummings, "FIFTY THREE CRATES OF FURNITURE FROM ATLANTA RECEIVED IN GOOD CONDITION—INSTALLED—NO BREAKAGE."

See also: ALCATRAZ PRISON.

Atlanta Centennial Park bombing   case of the wrong suspect

Early in the morning hours of July 27, 1996, television cameras swayed during Olympic Games interviews, and a loud report sounded. It was an explosion. It was a deafening blast that flooded out the rock music in the park. Shrapnel and debris rained down on dancers and onlookers. Bodies were riddled as more than 100 persons were hit. Luckily, only one person, Alice Hawthorne, a 43-year-old African-American business-woman, was fatally wounded. Another 111 persons were treated at local hospitals or at the scene but all recovered. A second death claimed as a result of the explosion was that of Turkish TV cameraman Melih Uzanyol, who suffered a fatal heart attack while attempting to videotape the bombing scene.

The death toll would have been much higher had not a private security firm guard, Richard Jewell, spotted a suspicious looking knapsack and, with other guards, hustled numerous people from the area before the pipebomb in the knapsack exploded. Jewell's alert action was credited with probably saving scores of lives. Television interviewers flocked to the hero guard who said, "I just happened to be at the right place at the right time, and doing the job I was trained to do."

Jewell's day in the sun did not last long. Investigators soon zeroed in on a chief suspect—Richard Jewell. The president of Piedmont College in Demorest, Ga., informed authorities that Jewell had previously been employed there as a campus security guard but had been fired for "infractions," such as once on his own flagging down motorists to give them sobriety tests. Before that Jewell had been a deputy for the Habersham County sheriff's department where following a reprimand for his behavior, he was reduced in rank to jail guard. Since that time he had worked in security guard positions at Piedmont and for other security companies, including the Olympic post he held at the time of the explosion.

It soon became clear that the FBI was determined to nail Jewell for the terrorist bombing (although FBI agents apparently made it appear to Jewell they considered him an ally in the hunt for the culprit). The open speculation fostered by the authorities' actions was that Jewell had himself planted the bomb, then spotted it so that he could then be credited with saving many innocent lives.

Emphasizing the FBI's belief that they had their man, agents made a very public search of the two-bedroom apartment Jewell shared with his mother, taking out box after box of material they found there, including scores of videotapes. Despite this busy-bee activity, the FBI did not charge Jewell with any crime, but he was left twisting in the wind by the agency, which did not dismiss him as a suspect. Eventually Jewell's mother wrote in protest to President Bill Clinton, pointing out her son "is a prisoner in my home."

Attorneys hired by Jewell now went on the offensive, demanding that the government either charge the security guard or that he be given an apology. The most picturesque quote came from one of Jewell's lawyers who raged, "These jerks need to get up off their butts and tell the truth." It took another two months, until October 26, before the Department of Justice officially declared that Jewell was no longer a suspect in the case. It could not be regarded as one of the FBI's most shining hours.

In early 1997 a suburban Atlanta abortion clinic was bombed, and the following month a gay and lesbian bar was similarly hit, so similarly in fact that investigators believed it was the work of the same terrorist. And they had indications that the suspect in the first two cases and probably the Centennial Park bombing was Eric Robert Rudolph. Rudolph was a suspect in other cases as well, but, an adept survivalist, he vanished somewhere in the wilds of the southeastern states. At present the Centennial Park bombing remains in the unsolved files.

Atlanta children murders

Over a period of 24 months, from mid-1979 to mid-1981, a total of 29 young blacks, most of whom were considerably under the age of 20, disappeared in Atlanta, Ga. Twenty-eight of them were found dead. The string of murders terrified the city and galvanized the rest of the country into outpourings of support and sympathy. The main national effort came in the form of green ribbons, "symbolizing life," which appeared on millions of lapels everywhere, worn by blacks and whites. Even shopping bag ladies in New York City were seen wearing the ribbons as well as green-lettered buttons proclaiming "SAVE THE CHILDREN."

Vice President George Bush journeyed to Atlanta to demonstrate an extraordinary degree of national concern. President Ronald Reagan announced the authorization of a $1.5 million grant to aid the investigation, and huge rewards were offered for information leading to the capture of the killer or killers. Celebrities, such as Frank Sinatra and Sammy Davis, Jr., contributed money to pay for investigations and aid to the families of the victims, and thousands of letters containing checks, dollar bills and even coins streamed into Atlanta.

The official manhunt was marked by bickering between local and federal investigators. FBI director William H. Webster riled local feelings when he announced that four of the cases, apparently unrelated to the others, had been solved. The next day a bureau agent in Macon, Ga. said the four children had been killed by their parents. This brought an angry outcry from the public, demanding to know why no arrest had been made. None was made, Atlanta mayor Maynard Jackson said, because there was not enough evidence to justify an arrest. He complained the FBI head had undermined the public's confidence in the investigation.

A large proportion of the deaths were so similar they indicated the likelihood that many of the victims had died by the same hand or hands. Nineteen of the 28 were believed to have died from strangulation or other forms of asphyxiation. Nine were found in rivers, nude or almost nude. More than a dozen had traces of similar fibers, from a blanket or carpet, on their bodies. Evidence of dog hairs was found on a number of the bodies.

Numerous suspects, some found thousands of miles from Atlanta, were quizzed, but without success. Finally, on June 3, 1981 23-year-old Wayne B. Williams was standing in an Atlanta phone booth when FBI agents appeared and "insisted," according to Williams, that he come downtown for questioning. Word of his interrogation spread quickly through Atlanta, and for the first time many felt the hunt for the mass killer might be over. However, after being held for 12 hours, Williams, who had worked as a TV cameraman and part-time talent scout and booking agent, was released. Publicly, officials said there was insufficient evidence to hold him, but privately they implied he was still a definite suspect.

It appears that Williams was picked up because investigators feared he might destroy suspected criminal evidence. During his interrogation Williams submitted to three lie detector tests, which, he later said he was told, indicated "all my answers were deceptive." The findings, Williams explained to the press, might have been caused by his nervousness. Following his release, authorities obtained a warrant to search Williams' home and confiscated a yellow blanket and a purple robe and collected samples of dog hairs and fibers from a bedspread and carpet.

Williams had first come to police attention on May 22. Around 3 A.M. officers staking out a bridge across the Chattahoochee River stopped his car after hearing a loud splash in the water. According to the police, when asked if he had thrown anything into the river, Williams said he had dumped some garbage. However, he subsequently insisted, "I told them I had dropped nothing in the river." Two days later, the body of 27-year-old Nathaniel Cater floated to shore about a mile downstream from the bridge, within 500 yards of where the body of 21-year-old Jimmy Ray Payne had been found the month before.

On June 21 Williams was arrested and charged with murdering Cater. An Atlanta grand jury indicted him on July 17 for both the Payne and Cater slayings. Clearly, the authorities acted as though several of the killings had been solved. In August, Williams pleaded not guilty to the charges.

By September, when the new school year started, there had been no further unaccountable murders of young blacks. Teachers reported that unlike the previous year there was hardly any talk among the pupils about the unsolved murders. A 12-year-old boy, Owen Malone, was quoted as saying: "It seems like it's over. Last year we talked a lot about the case; we got safety tips. The students were afraid of getting snatched." But this year, he observed, "It was all right."

On February 27, 1982 Williams was convicted of the two murders and sentenced to life imprisonment.

Atlantic City Conference   underworld convention

Perhaps the most important criminal conference of the American underworld was held during three days in May 1929 in Atlantic City, N.J. Its deliberations were certainly more important than even the famous conference called in Havana by the deported Lucky Luciano in 1946 or those scheduled for the ill-fated conference in Apalachin, N.Y. in 1957.

The meeting was hosted by the boss of Atlantic City, Nucky Johnson, who was able to guarantee no police interference. For three days the overlords of American crime discussed their future plans in the Hotel President's conference rooms and various hospitality suites, which Johnson kept stocked with whiskey, food and hostesses.

Chicago's Al Capone and his "brain," Greasy Thumb Guzik, attended the conference. Other delegates included King Solomon of Boston, Nig Rosen and Boo-Boo Hoff of Philadelphia, Moe Dalitz and Chuck Polizzi of Cleveland, Abe Bernstein of Detroit's Purple Gang, John Lazia (representing Tom Pendergast) of Kansas City and Longy Zwillman of New Jersey. The biggest contingent represented New York and included Johnny Torrio, Luciano, Frank Costello, Joe Adonis, Louis Lepke, Dutch Schultz, gambler Frank Erickson, Meyer Lansky, Vince Mangano, Frank Scalise and Albert Anastasia. Notably absent and uninvited were the two New York Mafia leaders then engaged in a bloody battle to decide who would be the so-called boss of bosses—Giuseppe "Joe the Boss" Masseria and Salvatore Maranzano. Both were what Luciano and others among the new crop of Italian gangsters referred to contemptuously as "Mustache Petes," men who failed to understand the need to work with non-Italian crime leaders.

At the convention, plans were laid for criminal activity following the end of Prohibition, and it was decided that the gangs would emphasize getting into the legitimate end of the bootlegging business by acquiring distilleries, breweries and import franchises. "After all," Luciano said, "who knew more about the liquor business than us?" It was also determined that gambling would become a major enterprise. The country was sliced up into exclusive franchises for both purposes. Groundwork for deals with Moses Annenberg, who controlled the dissemination of horse racing news, was laid. Labor and protection rackets were also plotted. One thing everyone agreed upon was that all these activities would be apportioned peacefully. The earlier success of the Seven Group on peacefully resolving the bootlegging wars was held up as a model for the future.

It was further agreed that gang violence had to be cooled down. Capone was lectured on the pointless folly of incidents such as the bloody St. Valentine's Day

Massacre, which produced far too much publicity and heat for comfort. Under pressure from the other gang leaders, Capone even agreed to submit to arrest and a short jail term for some minor offense in order to reduce the heat. All the participants concurred that the next logical step would be the establishment of a national crime syndicate; in fact, the meeting ended on this harmonious note. The call for reduced violence was meant seriously, but all understood that the Luciano-Lansky group would have to use considerable force to wrest control from the old Mafia dons. At this task they did not fail.

While the Atlantic City Conference was earthshaking in its effect on the development of American crime syndicates, historians have always been impressed or amused by how casual some of the deliberations were. Many took place on the beach, with the top mobsters in America walking barefoot through the water, their pants legs rolled up, somberly dividing an empire and deciding who was to live and who was to die.

See also: SEVEN GROUP.

Attica prison riot

If not the most violent prison riot in American penal history, the uprising at the Attica State Correctional Facility, 40 miles east of Buffalo, N.Y., in September 1971 was certainly one of the most tragic and most controversial. The riot was finally smashed by a massive assault of 1,500 heavily armed sheriff's deputies, state troopers and prison guards during which 28 prisoners and nine guards being held hostage were killed. State officials claimed that the guards had had their throats cut by the convicts and that one of them had been emasculated.

The riot began on September 9, when about 1,000 prisoners among the inmate population of 2,254 seized a portion of the prison compound, in the process taking more than 30 guards and civilian workers captive. The convicts presented a series of demands, including higher wages and greater political and religious freedom. In addition, they demanded total amnesty and no reprisals for the riot. Negotiations took place between the inmates and Russell G. Oswald, the state commissioner of corrections. Most of the deliberations were handled through the liaison of an "observers committee," consisting of representatives of government, several newspapers, the radical Young Lords and Black Muslims, and other social and professional groups.

Oswald accepted most of the prisoners' demands but refused to fire Attica superintendent Vincent Mancusi and rejected total amnesty. Gov. Nelson Rockefeller also refused the amnesty demand and rejected the requests of the observers committee that he come to Attica and personally join in the negotiations.

Early on the morning of September 13, Oswald read an ultimatum that listed his concessions and demanded the release of the hostages. The prisoners answered by displaying a number of the hostages with knives held to their throats. The bloody but successful assault followed. During the 24 hours after the assault, state officials made much of the convicts' violence and the sadistic murders of the hostages during the attack. Then came the official autopsies, which showed that none of the dead hostages had had their throats cut and none had been mutilated. All had been shot. In further contradiction of the state version, it was found that the prisoners had been in possession of no guns. All the hostages apparently had been killed in the crossfire of the police attackers.

Angered state officials summoned other medical examiners to check the findings of the Monroe County medical examiner, Dr. John F. Edland, who reported state troopers had stood over him while he performed the autopsies, evidently to guard against any cover-up of the supposed throat-slashing evidence. Commissioner Oswald, who previously had told reporters that "atrocities were committed on the hostages," could not believe Dr. Edland's findings. According to one newspaper, "He suggested that some sinister force—conceivably—motivated Dr. Edland to heap blame and shame on the authorities who decided to storm the prison." The other medical examiners called in were also subjected to close observation but concurred in Dr. Edland's findings.

After long public hearings a congressional subcommittee issued a report in June 1973 that criticized the methods used by prison officials and the police and condemned the brutality and inadequate medical treatment given wounded convicts after the attack. Previously, a nine-member citizens fact-finding committee, chaired by Robert B. McKay, dean of New York University Law School, had filed a final report that condemned Rockefeller's failure to go to Attica as well as the chaotic nature of the attack. The committee declared the riot was a spontaneous uprising stemming from legitimate grievances.

The autopsies' findings, as well as the later reports, stunned the small village where the prison stood and most of the guards lived. Hatred toward the prisoners shifted to angry disbelief and in many cases to vitriolic accusations that the authorities had recklessly risked lives by ordering the retaking of the prison.

Several indictments followed, and on December 30, 1976 Gov. Hugh L. Carey pardoned seven former Attica inmates and commuted the sentence of an eighth in a move to "close the book" on the bloody uprising.

Photo shows police and correction officers attempting to reestablish security at Attica, while dead and wounded inmates lie on the catwalks. Some of the wounded did not receive medical treatment for four hours.

He also declared that no disciplinary action would be taken against 20 law officers who had participated in the attack.

The closing of the book was not complete, however. In 1977 the first of a series of lawsuits was filed on behalf of a number of guards who were taken hostage and relatives of hostages who were killed. They contended law enforcement officials used excessive force in retaking the prison and asked $20 million in damages. The trial was delayed a full year after appellate courts ruled the state had to produce the "debriefing" statements the guards and troopers made shortly after the riot. Another delay, possibly for a year or more, was indicated when appeals were filed on behalf of 19 guards and troopers who had been cited for contempt by the trial judge after they took the Fifth Amendment on questions concerning the retaking of the prison.

Eventually these claims were settled, but dragging on were the claims of inmates that they had been horribly abused not only in the retaking of the prison but in the aftermath. The inmates contended that what followed was an orgy of reprisals carried out by prison guards and law enforcement officers, many of the charges later being substantiated. Prisoners were forced to crawl naked over broken glass, and one inmate had a screwdriver shoved repeatedly into his rectum. Possibly the worst abused inmate was Frank B. Smith, who was assaulted, burned and subjected to threats of castration and death. In 2000, Smith, then 66 and working in Queens, N.Y. as a paralegal dedicated to prisoners' rights cases, proclaimed victory in the fight to win a settlement for suffering endured by the prisoners.

While the offered settlement figure of $8 million for the prisoners and $4 million for their lawyers was well below what the ex-prisoners had sought, it seemed certain to win approval by the prisoners who otherwise would see the case dragged out for many more years. By 2000 an estimated 400 of the inmates were already dead, but about 400 others were to share in the awards to be determined on an individual basis by a federal judge. While the awards were expected to vary widely, they would average out to $20,000 per individual. Most of the prisoners were believed to feel that more important than the money award was the fact that the settlement held the government accountable for its actions.

While the settlement proposal was subject to appeals in some cases, it remained obvious that the name Attica and the attending stain would last in the public's conscience for years to come.

Aurora, Nevada   lawless mining town

As far as gold-mining towns went, Aurora, Nev. may not have been much more violent than others, but because accurate records were kept in Aurora, statistics offer considerable evidence on how wild the West really was. Founded in 1860, Aurora's heyday lasted only four years and then the gold seams ran out, but in that time, it managed to bury exactly 65 persons in its graveyard. Half were described as the victims of gunshot, and the rest expired of such afflictions as knife wounds, mining mishaps and "accidents." Aurora lasted another 90 years as a ghost town; the last of its buildings were vandalized in the 1950s.

auto theft

The cost of the stolen car racket in America is now put at more than $4 billion a year, and that figure only includes direct monetary loss, excluding the higher insurance premiums all automobile owners must pay. A motor vehicle is stolen every 25 seconds, and the annual total is now over 1 million, double the total in 1967. Generally, cars are stolen for the salvage value of their parts rather than for direct resale. An automobile that could resell for $10,000 can be taken apart and its component parts sold for almost twice that amount.

While it is true that most auto thefts are perpetrated by teenage joyriders and the large majority of stolen cars are recovered—although often with considerable damage done to them—the recovery rate for professionally stolen cars is close to zero. It is not unusual for a ring of auto thieves to steal and dispose of as many as 2,000 vehicles a year. Some cars are stolen to order; e.g., a ring furnishes autos on specific order from a dealer for immediate delivery to customers. At no time does any of the hot cars have to grace the dealer's lot. Most professional car theft rings have sufficient artistry to alter motor numbers in a manner that will deceive every test but fluoroscope analysis.

Probably the most prolific auto thief was Gabriel "Bla Bla" Vigorito, who masterminded a highly effi-cient organization in the 1930s, '40s and '50s. Bla Bla—so named because of his incessant boasting about his family—did a land office business in hot cars, shipping more than $250,000 worth to Norway alone in the 1930s. He also transported altered stolen vehicles to Russia and Persia and shipped a special order to a warlord general in Sinkiang Province, China.

Standard operating procedure for car thieves is the salvage racket. Auto graveyards and body shops are searched for wrecks of late-model cars already written off by insurance companies. The thieves buy the wrecks for a pittance, but more important, they buy a good and legal title. Then they steal duplicate models of each wreck, install the salvaged serial plate, restamp the motors to coincide with the salvage documents and attach salvaged license plates. The stolen car now has a complete new identity.

While the resale of stolen cars can be profitable, the "chop shop" racket has really come of age, as criminals have learned that on a nationwide black market the sale of parts from completely dismantled stolen cars can be even more lucrative. Once a stolen car has been reduced to its parts, no identification is possible. Just as important is the fact that the gang's operations can undergo a much greater division of labor, so that various members of the outfit do not even know each other. For instance, a spotter merely locates a likely candidate for a theft and then disappears from the scene. The actual heister then shows up to drive the car away to a drop, and another driver sees that the vehicle reaches the chop house. The choppers do their job without ever coming into contact with the sellers, who move the parts back into commerce.

If identification numbers were put on all body components, a responsibility auto manufacturers have resisted, chop shop operators would find life much more difficult. Cynical car thieves claim that automakers have a vested interest in the stolen car racket's continued existence since it puts hundreds of thousands of motorists back in the market well ahead of schedule.

See also: DYER ACT.

Averill, James (?–1889)   lynch victim

Jim Averill, whose lynching along with Cattle Kate Watson helped foment Wyoming's Johnson County War of the 1890s, may or may not have had a shady past when he took advantage of the Homestead Act and settled on the banks of the Sweetwater. There are conflicting reports about his background, but in that respect, he differed little from many of the homesteaders seeking a new start in life. There was even a report that he had attended or been a graduate of Cornell University, or some similar institution of learning. But it was evident that Averill was an articulate man, and he soon became the spokesman of the homesteaders in the Sweetwater Valley. He wrote blistering letters to the *Casper Daily Mail* in which he condemned the power of the cattle barons. When Averill became a leader in a futile fight to stop passage of the Maverick Bill, under which all unbranded cattle were made the property of the Stockmen's Association, it was clear the big cattlemen had to silence him. They did so by lynching Averill and an enterprising prostitute friend of his, Cattle Kate, who had set up a one-girl brothel in a cabin near his. The story the stockmen planted was that Cattle Kate was a big-time bandit queen and Averill her top aide and that the two of them were running a massive rustling operation. The twin lynching proved to be only the opening move in an effort to clear the range of homesteaders, or "rustlers," and led to the Johnson County War.

See also: CATTLE KATE, JOHNSON COUNTY WAR.

Baca, Elfego (1865–1945) *gunfighter and lawman*
In his native New Mexico Territory, Baca, at 19, was the chief participant and main target of one of the truly memorable gun battles of the frontier West. At the time, Frisco, a town in western New Mexico, was constantly being terrorized by cowboys from the Slaughter spread. Among other things the cowhands castrated a Mexican for a prank and then used another man for target practice when he tried to intervene. These stories were told to Baca by his brother-in-law, who was deputy sheriff of Frisco.

Enraged, Baca put on his brother-in-law's badge and on November 30, 1884 headed for Frisco. He found the town living in terror and being constantly shot up by cowboys. When one of them shot Baca's hat off, the self-appointed deputy promptly arrested him. The next day 80 cowboys descended on Frisco to get the "dirty little Mex." Baca placed all the women and children in the church and prepared to meet his attackers in an ancient adobe hut. The gunplay started at 9 A.M. and continued for 36 hours, during which time an estimated 4,000 bullets were poured into the shack. The plucky Baca killed four of his assailants, wounded eight others and came through the battle unscathed. When two regular lawmen appeared, the remaining cowboys retreated and Baca was placed under arrest. Baca was tried twice in connection with the great shoot-out, but even in the Anglo courts, he was found innocent. A hero to his people, Baca was later elected sheriff of Socorro County and enjoyed a political career of 50 years.

badger game *sex swindle*
The badger game is an ancient con, worked in many variations in every land. The standard modus operandi is simple: man picks up woman; woman takes him to a room; woman's "husband" comes in suddenly, confronts lovers and demands satisfaction. He gets it in the form of the frightened lover's money.

Perhaps the greatest organizer of the badger game was a notorious 19th-century New York City gangster named Shang Draper, who was also an accomplished bank robber. In the 1870s Draper operated a saloon on Sixth Avenue at 29th Street. From it he directed the activities of 30 women and girls in a combined badger and panel game operation headquartered at a house in the vicinity of Prince and Wooster Streets.

In the panel game, a thief would sneak into the room while the woman and her male friend were occupied in bed and steal the man's money and valuables from his discarded clothing. The sneak thief would gain entry to the room through a hidden panel in the wall out of sight from the bed.

However, if the man appeared really prosperous, Draper preferred working the badger game, because the stakes were potentially much higher. Draper added a new wrinkle to the game by using young girls, from age nine to about 14. Instead of an angry husband breaking into the room, the young girl's irate "parents" would burst in. The "mother" would immediately seize the child and smash her face, usually her blows would be hard enough to make the child bleed from the nose or mouth. While this convincing act was taking place, the equally angry "father" would shove his fist under the man's nose and say, "I'm going to put you in prison for a hundred years!"

Men victimized by this technique often could be induced to pay thousands in hush money. Draper himself loved to tell about how he stood in a telegraph office with a quivering out-of-towner waiting for his bank to wire him $9,000 so he could pay off a badger game. It was estimated that Draper's badger game conned 100 or more men each month. The police finally broke up Draper's racket in the early 1880s, but the hardy badger game easily survived the demise of his operation.

Another colorful practitioner was a Philadelphian known as "Raymond the Cleric," who found the pose of a betrayed minister-husband to be more lucrative. While he prayed in a corner for divine forgiveness for his errant spouse and her sinful lover, a couple of "members of his congregation" would appear a bit more threatening, and the sinner usually demonstrated his repentance with a hefty contribution.

To this day, the badger game, in its pure form and in dozens of variations, is one of the country's most widely practiced confidence games, although given the compromising position of the victim, one that rarely comes to the attention of the police.

See also: PANEL HOUSES.

Badman from Bodie   western bogeyman

During the last three decades of the 19th century, western mothers would scare their mischievous children into line by invoking the specter of the "Badman from Bodie," who had to have a victim every day. Unlike the more traditional bogeyman, the Badman from Bodie was rooted in reality. Bodie, Calif. was one of the West's most lawless towns reportedly averaging at least one killing a day for 20 years. Even if that estimation was somewhat off, threatening nasty children with the Badman from Bodie was apparently an effective instrument of parental control.

See also: BODIE, CALIFORNIA.

bagman   payoff man

Originally, the word *bagman* was applied to commercial travelers, or salesmen, in England during the 18th century. At first, it was used with the same connotation in America, but the term was gradually applied more to underworld figures who carried large cases or bags in which they toted off stolen goods. These fences often had to pay off the police to operate and carried the bribe money in their bags. Bagman was soon used to describe either the man paying a bribe or the one accepting and subsequently dividing it among all the parties involved.

For years during the heyday of the Capone mob, one of the chores of Jake "Greasy Thumb" Guzik was to sit nightly in Chicago's St. Hubert's Old English Grill and Chop House and hand over money to district police captains or the sergeants who collected the graft for them, as well as the bagmen for various mayors and their aides. Another famous bagman was Joe Cooney, better known as Joe the Coon. He dispensed money within New York City police headquarters for the emerging Lucky Luciano–Frank Costello–Meyer Lansky–Joe Adonis crime empire. It was one thing to distribute payoffs to lower-ranking police officers and politicians but quite another to bring payoffs directly into the office of the police commissioner, as Lucky Luciano was later to reveal. Cooney was chosen for the job because, as a red-haired freckle-faced Irishman, it was easy for him to enter the commissioner's office each week in a maintenance man's uniform to hand over the sum of $10,000 in small bills (later said to have increased to $20,000 a week during the tenures of Joseph A. Warren and Grover A. Whalen). Joe the Coon carried the money in a plain brown bag as though it were his lunch. To make him even more inconspicuous, Luciano instructed Joe to change a lightbulb occasionally.

During the Kefauver Committee crime hearings in 1950–51, Frank Bals, named seventh deputy police commissioner during the reign of Mayor Bill O'Dwyer, admitted (and subsequently retracted) to the committee that while his duties and those of his staff of 12 were to gather intelligence about gambling and corruption in the police department, he and his men played a far different role. Bals stated that they were actually bagmen for the New York Police Department, collecting payoffs from gamblers and doling out the funds throughout police headquarters.

The most famous bag woman in criminal history was Virginia Hill, that bedmate of gangsters, who promptly carried off much of their money to secret bank accounts in Switzerland.

bail

Bail is a method whereby a person awaiting trial on a criminal charge is allowed to go free upon the posting of security sufficient to ensure his or her appearance in court. Most state constitutions specifically provide for the right to bail in all cases except capital crimes. Since the majority of persons arrested cannot come up with sufficient cash to cover a bail bond, they must patronize a surety company or professional bondsmen to obtain bail. The legal cost for such a bond may be 5 or 10 percent of the bail, but many bondsmen demand and get more. These bondsmen justify their exorbitant fees by claiming that because their business involves such a high risk, they would go broke if they had a half-dozen "skips"—persons who fail to make an appearance at the appropriate time—in quick succession.

Exposés of the bail bond racket are common. Criminologists H. E. Barnes and N. K. Teeters state: "Professional bondsmen are usually parties to a questionable, if not downright corrupt, political system and usually have no appreciable assets with which to go to bail for those who must later appear for another hearing. They offer what is called a *straw bond,* that is, they present evidence that collateral exists which is nonexistent or is insufficient for the purpose." In one instance a bondsman in New York City offered as security a piece of property that, according to its street address, would have been in the middle of the Hudson River. Bondsmen have also been found to use the same property as security for 15 to 20 defendants concurrently. In cases where a defendant skipped, a small bribe generally could get the record of the bond removed and the security returned to the bondsman.

In the old days bondsmen were legally permitted to solicit business openly and aggressively; in the process, they put the storied ambulance chaser to shame. Cops in almost every station house tipped off bondsmen whenever there was a bailable arrest, and some even passed out bondsmen's business cards. Sometimes, thanks to a cooperative arresting officer, a bondsman could get to the station before the officer brought in the prisoner for booking. In most jurisdictions today, a bondsman must wait until somebody comes and asks him to put up a bond. Of course, many bondsmen have their methods of circumventing the legal obstacles to soliciting business. They often hire runners to hang around the courthouse and whisper to relatives of prisoners, "I can see that you get a bond fast." If the person bites, the runner guides him to the bondsman. Trying to prove a bondsman hired a runner is, as authorities have found, practically impossible.

When a bondsman posts a bond, he gets all the security he can from the defendant. He will take possession of such things as automobile ownership papers and bankbooks, requiring the accused to sign an agreement that no money may be withdrawn from the account without the bondsman's signature as well. Call girls must often put up their jewelry and furs. Bondsmen have also taken such items as manufacturing dies, bulletproof vests, guns, war souvenirs, pornographic collections, rare comic books, out-of-print books and toupees. One legendary New York bondsman was said to specialize in exceptionally hot items including packets of heroin, police pistols and badges, blackmail material, phony draft cards, stolen license plates and bogus ration books. The tale is often told that he made a fortune renting out counterfeiting plates he was holding against a client's $25,000 bail.

Organized crime has never had any trouble raising bail; a gang will often use one or more bondsmen to handle its bail business. Stitch McCarthy, who for years held the title of Bail Baron of New York, was a close friend of Jack "Legs" Diamond and did most of the bail bonding for Diamond and his men. Once, Mad Dog Coll went gunning for Diamond when Legs was out on bail, and McCarthy became frightened that Diamond might skip out to avoid a fatal battle. Magnanimously, McCarthy insisted Diamond hide out in his home.

Large bonds are meaningless for top crime figures. On one occasion Johnny Torrio's devoted mother paraded into federal district court and calmly peeled off 97 $1,000 bills, four $500 bills and 10 $100 bills to make a cool $100,000 bail for her mobster son. Torrio kissed mom on the cheek and they walked out.

A major criticism of the bail system is that the poor are generally victimized since they usually are unable to provide enough security to satisfy a bondsman. One answer to this—although a judge who resorts to it risks being labeled a low bail jurist—is to limit the bail to the fee that would normally be paid to a bondsman. For the poor the incentive of getting back the equivalent of the bondsman's fee is sufficient to guarantee reappearance. While critics of low bail protest the system simply returns criminals to the streets, they seldom concern themselves about the abuses of high bail. A 43-year-old truck driver in New York who was held on $75,000 bail for two charges of murder remained in jail for 14 months. He was then proved totally innocent. Had he been from a higher-income group, he would not have been falsely imprisoned for more than a year.

The worst abuse of high bail is its use by prosecutors to set a climate for plea bargaining. Legal experts agree that a defendant kept in jail suffers from depression about his fate and becomes less resistant to the prosecution's offer of a lighter sentence, especially when time served is credited against the term involved.

See also: ARREST PROCEDURES.

Bailey, F. Lee (1933–) defense attorney

Not quite as flamboyant as some other present-day criminal defense lawyers, such as Richard "Racehorse" Haynes and Percy Foreman, F. Lee Bailey is nonetheless recognized as one of the best in the business. Virtually a specialist on homicide, he has, at least until recent years, flown from case to case, around the country in his own private jet, causing courtroom foes and some of the more staid members of the bar to nickname him "the Flying Mouth."

Bailey has proven to be a miracle worker in court: he freed Dr. Sam Sheppard after he had been convicted of murdering his wife when represented by other well-regarded attorneys; he won acquittal for army captain Ernest L. Medina on charges of killing South Vietnamese civilians at My Lai; and perhaps most remarkably of all, he prevailed upon the state of Massachusetts to try Albert DeSalvo, the notorious Boston Strangler, on noncapital charges.

Of course, Bailey has had some notable failures—because, his supporters say, he refuses to run away from the really tough cases. Thus, he lost the Patricia Hearst case and one out of two murder cases against Dr. Carl Coppolino. In his courtroom oratory Bailey lacks the bombast typical of some of today's leading defense lawyers. He is not given to cheap moralizing and has been described by *Newsweek* magazine "as unsentimental as a cat, and equally predatory." Bailey is also cunning. In pre-1972 murder cases—before the Supreme Court temporarily halted the death penalty—he went out of his way to get prosecutors to smile amiably during the trial. "To ask for the death penalty successfully," he explained, "a prosecutor must be like an Old Testament figure—deeply serious, righteously angry. No smiling man can properly ask for another man's death."

Bailey is accomplished at what has been long recognized as a defense lawyer's most important function: picking the right jurors. In the first Coppolino trial, one of his notable successes, he asked prospective jurors if they would be prejudiced because the defendant "may have stepped out of line" during his marriage. One man replied, "I step out of line myself occasionally." When the courtroom laughter subsided, the man added, "You look like you might have played around a little yourself."

"Right there and then," Bailey later said, "I knew he was my man, and I grabbed him. For some reason, the prosecution didn't challenge. And when the jury went out, my man dragged his chair to the window and said, 'I vote not guilty. Call me when the rest of you are ready to agree with me.'"

However, Bailey does not rely on such lucky happenstance. At many of his trials he posts beside him a hypnotist aide who advises him on juror selection and who allegedly is able to tell Bailey how a potential female juror will react to a lawyer based on the way she crosses her legs when answering questions.

Some observers say that in recent years the glow has rubbed off Bailey. He reputedly was chosen to defend Patty Hearst only because the family's first choice, Racehorse Haynes, had asked for double the fee Bailey wanted. But Bailey's detractors are no doubt motivated, in large part, by jealousy. His reputation with the public is probably best typified by one prospective juror's comment under questioning: "I think the man's guilty

already. He wouldn't have the most important lawyer in the U.S. otherwise."

See also: ANTHONY H. DESALVO, PATRICIA HEARST.

Baker, Cullen M. (1838–1868) outlaw and murderer

A sallow-faced killer, Cullen Baker did most of his "Civil War fighting" as the head of a Texas gang of outlaws who called themselves Confederate Irregulars in the years immediately after Appomattox. The band was really little more than a group of farm looters, but they pacified their fellow Texans by occasionally killing some Yankee soldiers or upstart "nigger police."

Baker hadn't been much of a patriot during the war. He had been drafted into the Confederate Army in Cass County, where he had lived since the age of four. Actually, being drafted had its advantages: since he had killed a man in Arkansas two years earlier, the army provided a good hiding place for Baker. He soon deserted, however. After killing two Union soldiers in Spanish Bluffs, Tex., Baker figured a good place to hide would be in Lincoln's army, so he joined the Union cause. Not long after, he deserted again and joined a group of Confederate irregulars. After the war Baker saw no reason to stop his activities. He and his gang of vicious gunmen terrorized much of Texas, preying mostly on local farmers. They were still regarded in some circles as local heroes because they were pursued by Northern troops and black police, several of whom they killed in various fights.

Late in 1867, Bill Longley, a young gunfighter on the run from the law, joined the irregulars. He was to become the infamous Wild Bill Longley. Young Longley stayed with Baker about a year, leaving just before Baker's death. During that period Baker had developed a strong liking for a girl named Belle Foster, who did not return his attention but instead focused her affection on a crippled schoolteacher named Thomas Orr. In December 1868 Baker kidnapped Orr at gunpoint and hung him from a tree. Fortunately for Orr, he was found before he strangled to death. This act set local opinion against Baker. Trying to hang Orr hardly qualified as an anti-Yankee act. Orr and a posse of local citizens took off after Baker, and when they cornered him, Orr was given the privilege of shooting him full of holes, permanently dissolving Baker's Confederate Irregulars.

See also: WILLIAM P. LONGLEY.

Baker, Joseph (?–1800) pirate and murderer

Pirates who plied their murderous trade along the American coast around 1800 had one modus operandi that was particularly insidious as well as effective. Used by the freelance pirate Joseph Baker, it called for a sailor to sign aboard a small vessel, subvert a few of the crew, kill the honest sailors in a mutiny and sail for pirate waters, where the craft and cargo could be disposed of at a handsome profit.

Little is known of Baker's early career except that he was a Canadian whose real name apparently was Boulanger. For Baker, piracy was definitely profitable until he tried it on Capt. William Wheland of the schooner *Eliza*. Having joined the small crew, Baker, with the aid of two other sailors named Berrouse and LaCroix, killed the first mate and wounded Capt. Wheland. Wheland was allowed to live after promising that he would sail the ship into pirate waters, since Baker's seamanship did not extend to the art of navigation. A cunning captive, Wheland awaited the proper moment and then managed to lock Baker's confederates below deck. Seizing an ax, the captain drove Baker high into the rigging of the ship and forced him to remain there for 16 days in a deadly game of cat and mouse. By that time Wheland was able to bring his vessel into port. On May 9, 1800 pirates Baker, Berrouse and LaCroix were hanged in Philadelphia.

Baker, Rosetta (1866–1930) murder victim

Few murder trial verdicts were ever based so much on racial stereotypes as that in the Rosetta Baker case, although this was one of the few times the decision went in favor of a member of a minority.

A wealthy San Francisco widow in her sixties, the woman was found dead by her Chinese houseboy, Liu Fook. In the course of their investigation, detectives zeroed in on Liu Fook, who was about the same age as the victim, as the only logical suspect. Witnesses revealed that Liu Fook and his "boss missy" had quarreled often, and on the day of the murder, he had scratches on his face and an injured finger—as though it had been bitten. In addition to that, a broken heel and a shirt button found on the floor beside the body belonged to the houseboy.

In spite of this and still more incriminating evidence, the jury at Liu Fook's trial in 1931 acquitted him. Some of the jurors said they had simply been swayed by the defense lawyer's repeated insistence that Liu Fook could not have been guilty because no Chinese employed in this country had ever murdered his employer. Immediately after the trial, Liu Fook took a fast boat for Hong Kong.

Baker Estate great swindle

One of the most lucrative and enduring swindles in American history began just after the Civil War with the establishment of the first of numerous Baker Estate associations. These associations were joined and supported by victims conned into believing they were the rightful heirs to a $300 million fortune in Philadelphia.

The fortune was entirely imaginary, but one association after another roped in suckers with claims that the estate was just about settled. Exactly how much money victims lost to the criminal operators of the fraud is difficult to calculate; the best estimate is that some 40 different Baker Estate associations took at least a half-million persons for a minimum of $25 million in "legal expenses" during the peak years of the fraud, from 1866 to 1936. During that period the estate swindle had very little interference from the law, but finally in 1936 the federal government launched a vigorous effort to stamp it out through many arrests and a massive publicity campaign. Since then similar con games have appeared from time to time, but none has ever been as successful as the Baker Estate swindle was during its early years.

Baker's Confederate Irregulars See CULLEN M. BAKER.

Bakker, Rev. Jim (1940–) "Praise the Lord for Suckers"

On a par with the bank and Wall Street scoundrels of the 1980s, some in televangelist circles were also grabbing headlines as scamsters. At the top of the list was the Reverend Jim Bakker and his hectic sexual and Ponzi-like shenanigans. Bakker had built up a television network, the PTL (for "Praise the Lord," or "People That Love"), that reached more than 13 million American households.

It was a sexual dalliance that precipitated Bakker's downfall. In December 1980, the youthful-looking Bakker had met a 21-year-old comely brunet named Jessica Hahn, a secretary at a Pentecostal church in Massapequa, N.Y., during a visit to Clearwater, Fla. At the time, Bakker's 19-year marriage to his wife, Tammy Faye, who cohosted his religious television show, was rough going. Bakker and Hahn had sex, and to hear Hahn tell it, she suffered great emotional distress as a result of the encounter. In any event, her pain and suffering were so great that $265,000 was to be paid her as compensation for her silence.

Bakker's secret remained safe for a time; the story was eventually broken in the *Charlotte* (N.C.) *Observer,* a newspaper near the headquarters of the PTL ministry. In addition to the television show featuring Jim and Tammy Faye, the PTL empire included Heritage USA, a Christian resort complex and amusement park in Fort Mill, S.C. In the PTL's peak year, the ministry took in $129 million, and in the recent few years, it had garnered $158 million by offering promises of lifetime vocations—which Bakker could not provide. Instead, huge sums were diverted to the couple, which allowed the Bakkers to live in opulence. In March 1987, Bakker was forced to resign his ministry and later was charged with fraud and conspiracy. At his trial (with Tammy Faye—by now regarded as something of an American original—vowing to stand by her man), a former reservation supervisor at Heritage USA said that in the last year of Bakker's regime at PTL, between 1,300 and 3,700 lifetime contributors had been turned away every month from lodgings that had been promised but did not exist.

Bakker was convicted on all 24 counts against him and sentenced to 45 years in prison and fined $500,000. He would not be eligible for parole for 10 years. In passing sentence, U.S. district judge Robert Porter said, "Those of us who do have religion are sick of being saps for money-grubbing preachers and priests. I just feel like there was massive fraud here, and it's going to have to be punished."

Once again, Tammy Faye promised to stand by her man, but she later filed for divorce and planned to marry a businessman who likewise divorced his wife. In the meantime, Hahn had appeared on the cover of *Playboy* magazine and was paid an estimated $750,000 for a photo display and an interview in which she informed readers that "I'm not a bimbo." She later devoted her talents to hosting a late-night show advising viewers via special 800 numbers how to find "love."

After Jim Bakker was freed, he remarried and devoted himself to activities helping the unfortunate, an undertaking that won him considerable accolades from the media.

Ball, Joe (1892–1938) mass murderer

When it came to ghoulishness, an ex-bootlegger and tavern owner named Joe Ball, of Elmendorf, Tex., was exceptional even for a mass murderer.

In the 1930s Ball ran the Sociable Inn, a watering hole famous for two tourist attractions: the most beautiful waitresses for miles around and the pet alligators Ball kept in a pond in back of the establishment. The high point of the day was feeding time for the alligators, which Ball turned into a regular show, often feeding a live stray dog or cat to the slithering reptiles. It was a performance that could drive even the strongest men to drink, which made the gators as good for business as the pretty waitresses.

Ball's waitresses seemed to be a fickle lot, disappearing without a word to any of the customers. Naturally, they told Ball. Some were getting married, others had sick mothers, still others left for new jobs. Ball was never very enlightening. He merely shrugged and said philosophically, "They come, they go."

Exactly how many really went was never fully established. Later, police were able to find some of the waitresses alive, but 12 or 14 were never found. Most or all of the missing women were murdered by Ball so he would not be hampered in his constant search for a new romance. Some of them had become pregnant and demanded that Ball "do the right thing." His concept of the right thing was to ax them to death. Then, as later evidence would show, he often chopped up the body and fed the incriminating pieces to the alligators.

In 1937 the family of Minnie Mae Gotthardt wrote the local police complaining they had not heard from her for a long time. Some officers dropped in to see Ball. He set up drinks for them and explained that Minnie Mae had left to take another job. A short while later, the police came around again, wondering what happened to another waitress named Julia Turner. She left for the same reason, Ball said. That didn't wash too well because Julia had not packed any of her belongings. However, when Ball explained Julia had had a fight with her roommate and left without packing because he had given her $500 to help out, the law was placated. Then two more waitresses were listed among the missing and the Texas Rangers entered the case. They began compiling a list of Ball's former waitresses and found quite a few who could not be accounted for; their relatives had no idea of where they were.

The investigators were clearly suspicious of Ball but failed to break him down. However, an old black handyman and cook who had worked for Ball for years proved less resistant to the lawmen's questions and confessed helping his boss kill some of the women and dispose of their bodies. He said he did so because he was fearful that Ball would kill him if he refused. When the lawmen showed up at the inn on September 24, 1938 seeking the barrel in which Ball said he kept meat for feeding the alligators, the tavern owner realized the game was up. Before the officers could stop him, Ball rang up a "no sale" on the cash register, pulled out a revolver and shot himself in the head, dying instantly.

The handyman got two years for being an accessory after the fact, and the alligators were carted off to the San Antonio Zoo.

ballooning prison drug-smuggling method

Drugs, especially heroin, are valued commodities in prisons and are brought in usually by a method called "ballooning." The drugs are carried into the prison, usually on visiting days, by "mules," the wives, other relatives or girlfriends of prisoners. The balloon involved is nothing more than the type used at children's parties.

A few grains of heroin or other substances are put in a balloon and a female visitor then hides it, positioned as a tampon would be, in her vagina. Admitted to the prison visiting room, she enters the women's bathroom, removes the balloon and puts it in her mouth. Since visitors are permitted to kiss prisoners at the start of a visit, the inmate takes the balloon into his own mouth and regurgitates it back in his cell or simply waits until the balloon has passed through his system.

The only way to prevent such balloon smuggling would be to bar any physical contact of any sort between an inmate and a visitor.

Banana War battle for control of organized crime

The Banana War of 1964–69 was the most recent significant effort by the head of a leading Mafia family to seize control of the major portion of organized crime. The attack was led by the aging Joseph C. Bonanno, Sr., the head of the small but efficient crime family known by his nickname as the Bananas family.

Joe Bananas' crime interests extended from New York to Canada, Arizona and California; however, as he watched many of the older dons fade away, he decided to strike out for greater glory and illegal revenues. He launched plans to eliminate in one swoop such old-time powers as New York's Tommy Lucchese and Carlo Gambino, Buffalo's Steve Magaddino and even Los Angeles' Frank DeSimone. Bananas involved in the plot an old ally, Giuseppe Magliocco, who agreed despite misgivings and ill health. His loyalty to Bananas was unquestioned. Unfortunately for Bananas, Magliocco passed the hit assignment to an ambitious younger underboss named Joe Colombo, who readily accepted but immediately reported to the other side, seeking a reward. Colombo was rewarded with the leadership of the late Joe Profaci's Brooklyn crime family. But the dons and board members of the Mafia were still faced with the Joe Bananas problem. At a moment's notice he could put 100 gunmen on the streets of Brooklyn and Manhattan. There might be a bloodbath of a magnitude unseen since the days of Capone in the 1920s and the Genovese move for power in the 1950s.

Bananas and Magliocco were summoned to a peace meeting by the underworld commission. Bananas contemptuously didn't show. Magliocco did and begged for mercy. The syndicate leaders decided to let him live, swayed by the fact that he obviously lacked the guts to continue a war and was so ill he would not live long in any case. He was fined $50,000 and stripped of his power, which went to Colombo. A few months later, he died of a heart attack.

Bananas took off for his strongholds out West and in Canada, ignoring a second order to appear before the commission. In October 1964 he returned to Manhattan under a grand jury summons. On the night of October 21, he had dinner with his lawyers. Afterwards as he stepped from a car on Park Avenue, he was seized by two gunmen, shoved into another car and taken away. The newspapers assumed Bananas had been executed.

However, the commission was treating Bananas, an important don, carefully, apparently realizing his death would provoke a full-scale war. If Bananas was frightened, he did not show it. He realized he was in a tight spot and offered a deal. He would retire from the rackets, give up control of his family and move to Arizona. He proposed that his son, Salvatore "Bill" Bonanno, take over, but the proposal was rejected out of hand. The commission members decided Bananas should retire and so should his son. They would pick his successor. Bananas could do little but agree.

When Joe Bananas reappeared in May 1966—19 months after his disappearance—the newspapers treated it as a sort of second coming, but more important, Bananas, instead of retiring, began expanding his family activities into Haiti, working tightly with the Duvalier regime. Meanwhile, the national commission appointed Gaspar DiGregorio to take over Bananas' family, a move that split the group. Many loyalists insisted on sticking with Joe Bananas, and if they could not have him, then his son, Bill.

With a war threatening, DiGregorio called for a peace meeting with Bill Bonanno. It was set for a house on Troutman Street in Brooklyn. When Bill arrived, several riflemen and shotgunners opened up on him and his men. The Bananas gang fired back, but in the dark, everyone's aim was off and there were no casualties.

DiGregorio's failure enraged the national commission and he was removed from power and replaced by a tougher leader, Paul Sciacca. Sciacca couldn't prevent the Bananas forces from striking, and several of his men were wounded in various attacks, with three being machine-gunned to death in a Queens restaurant. Eventually, five others on either side died.

A heart attack in 1968 finally slowed Joe Bananas, and he flew off to his home in Tucson, Ariz. He sent word to his foes that he had decided to retire. But the commission viewed the message as an old and unbelievable story and they continued the war. On several occasions bombs were planted at the Joe Bananas' home as well as the homes of his allies in Arizona. Finally, however, peace was achieved.

The Bananas family kept control of its western interests, but Sciacca, and later Natale Evola, was accepted as the East Coast boss. The war was over. In 1980 Joe Bananas, at the age of 75, was convicted of conspiracy to interfere with a federal grand jury's investigation of his two sons' business operations. By that time Bill Bonanno was in prison for a parole violation. Joe Bananas' dream of power had ended.

It may be that the other Mafia chiefs learned something from the conflict. When another tough mafioso named Carmine Galante started a violent push for power in the late 1970s, he was summarily executed, without ever receiving the opportunity to appear before the board to explain himself.

See also: JOSEPH COLOMBO, SR.

banco swindle

A swindle whose name careless writers often misspelled as *bunco*, which was later applied to all types of confidence games.

Banco was based on the old English gambling pastime of eight-dice cloth. Sharpsters who introduced it in America usually converted it into a card game, which could be manipulated more easily than dice. It was very prevalent in the western gold fields during the 1850s until California vigilantes drove out the gamblers using it to swindle miners. About 1860 banco was introduced in New York City, where the two greatest practitioners of the art—George P. Miller, the King of the Banco Men, and Hungry Joe Lewis—amassed fortunes.

In its card game variation, banco was played on a layout of 43 spaces—42 were numbered and 13 of those contained stars. The remaining space was blank. The 29 unstarred numbers were winning ones, being worth from $2 up to $5,000, depending on the size of the bank. Each player received eight cards numbered from one to six, with the total number in his hand representing the prize. However, if a number with a star came up, he got no prize but could draw again by putting up a certain amount of money. The sucker would generally be allowed to win at first—with no money actually changing hands—until he was ahead a few hundred to a few thousand dollars. Then he would be dealt number 27 which was the so-called conditional prize, meaning he had to stake a sum equal to the amount owed him and draw again or lose all his "winnings." Naturally, he would be dealt a blank or starred card and thereby lose everything.

The pattern of play just described was automatic since the entire banco game was a phony, being played in a "skinning dive" in which all but one of the players were actually confidence operators. The only person not in on the scheme was the sucker who had been steered there.

Miller and Hungry Joe specialized in victimizing bankers, businessmen and other prominent personages. Not only did these victims have plenty of money to lose, they also were likely to be too embarrassed to go to the police. In 1882, Hungry Joe wormed his way into an acquaintanceship with Oscar Wilde, then on a lecture tour of the country. Over several dinners he boasted of the money he had won at banco and then steered the writer to a game. The confidence man later bragged that he had taken Wilde for close to $7,000. Wilde himself, perhaps in a face-saving exercise, later insisted he had lost only $1,500 in cash and had taken care of the rest with a check on which he had stopped payment once he discovered the play was dishonest. Banco died out not because of a dearth of potential victims but rather because con men found they could attract more suckers to fixed horse races or stock market swindles.

Banditti of the Plains, The book

Probably the most explosive book ever to come out of the West, *The Banditti of the Plains* by Asa C. Mercer was a hard-hitting account of the brutal Johnson County War in 1892 between cattlemen and homesteaders.

Mercer, born in 1839, was a longtime editor, author and lawmaker on the frontier. In *Banditti* he placed the blame for the war on some of the richest and most powerful cattlemen of Wyoming, various state officials and even President Benjamin Harrison, whom he accused of being in sympathy with the stockmen. He charged that many important men—naming names and supplying details—were guilty of a long list of crimes from bribery to genocide.

The book itself had a most violent life from the time it appeared in the winter of 1893. It was ruthlessly suppressed and its plates were destroyed. Copies of the book were burned and even the one in the Library of Congress disappeared. At one point, Mercer was jailed for a time for sending "obscene matter" through the mails. Somehow a few copies survived over the years, and in 1954 the University of Oklahoma Press reprinted the book. Thanks to that printing, it can be found today in many libraries. The motion picture *Shane* has been described as being "straight out of *The Banditti of the Plains.*"

As for Mercer, he wrote other books and pamphlets but nothing as potent as *Banditti*. He died in relative obscurity in 1917.

See also: JOHNSON COUNTY WAR.

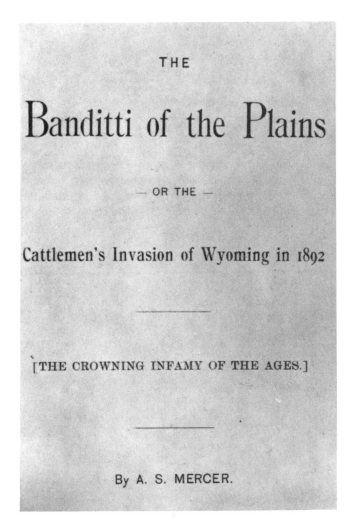

THE

Banditti of the Plains

— OR THE —

Cattlemen's Invasion of Wyoming in 1892

[THE CROWNING INFAMY OF THE AGES.]

By A. S. MERCER.

Title page of *The Banditti of the Plains*, which charged some of Wyoming's greatest cattlemen with mass murder. The book was ruthlessly suppressed and even the copy at the Library of Congress vanished.

bank robberies

The first bank robbery—actually a burglary, since it did not involve the use of threats or violence—in America was pulled by an Englishman named Edward Smith (alias Edward Jones, alias James Smith, alias James Honeyman). Using duplicate keys obtained by a method never fully explained, he entered two doors of the City Bank on Wall Street in New York City on March 19, 1831 and stole $245,000. Because of his free spending and tips from informers, Smith was apprehended quickly and $185,000 of the loot was recovered. On May 11, 1831 he was sentenced to five years at hard labor in Sing Sing, which was a rather light sentence considering the terms handed out later to other bank thieves. It appears Smith was treated somewhat leniently because his crime was unique and the authorities were not prepared to deal with it.

In the ensuing years bank robberies became commonplace. Daylight robberies were the mode of the West, with the first jobs being pulled by the Reno gang, the Jesse James gang, the Youngers and others. In the East the more common practice was nighttime burglaries, including safecrackings, of which the leading practitioners were the notorious George Leonidas Leslie, George Miles Bliss and Mark Shinburn. Bliss and Shinburn led the Bliss Bank Ring, which was especially noted for bribing the police in New York City with a percentage of the loot from each job. In the famous $1.75 million robbery of the Ocean Bank in 1869, the Bliss gang paid a total of $132,300 in bribes to guarantee a nonsolution to the case.

In the 20th century the daylight robberies of the Wild West migrated to the East. The first really great practitioner of the craft, one who stressed meticulous planning, was Herman K. "Baron" Lamm, an ex-Prussian army officer who brought discipline and precision to the field. Lamm never robbed a bank without first drawing up a detailed floor plan of the institution and running his men through a series of full rehearsals, sometimes using a complete mock-up of the bank's interior. His men were drilled in their assignments on a minute-by-minute basis, and they were required to leave a job at a scheduled moment, regardless of the amount of loot scooped up by then. Getaways were staged with equal preciseness. A skilled driver, often a veteran of the car-racing circuit, followed a chart pasted on the dashboard showing the escape route marked block by block, with speedometer readings and alternate turns. Lamm tested each route in various weather conditions. After 13 years of successful bank robberies without a hitch, Lamm was killed in a 1930 robbery that went wrong for freak reasons. In prison, two survivors of his gang were permitted to join a mass escape engineered by what would become the Dillinger mob on the understanding that they would teach Dillinger the details of Baron Lamm's methods.

In the 1930s the bank-robbery business was taken over by the public enemies, led by the likes of Dillinger, Creepy Karpis, the Barker brothers and Baby Face Nelson. The FBI's success in running down these bank-robbing and kidnapping gangs did much to enhance the public image of that previously unimpressive organization.

Since then, probably the only great bank robber has been Slick Willie Sutton, famous for his alleged quote on why he robbed banks: "Because that's where the money is."

Looking at crime statistics, one would conclude that bank robbery is a much more serious problem today than in the 1930s. The dollar take, now totaling between $30 and $40 million annually, far exceeds that of the 1930s and the number of robberies is up many times. However, considering inflation, population expansion, the hugh growth of bank branches in the suburbs—just off main highways—we can see why the crime has apparently increased. The professionals, in fact, have more or less dropped out of the field, leaving it to amateurs, crackpots and persons seized by little more than a sudden impulse to raise money. And where is the money? Still in banks.

Some experts feel that only persons of limited intelligence try to rob banks today because the sophisticated antirobbery devices and other security measures now in use limit the take to a measly average of $1,500 and almost always lead to the capture of the culprit. A random sample of recent robberies supports that conclusion.

- In Queens, New York City an unemployed shoe salesman walked into a bank and handed a teller a note demanding "all your tens, twenties and thirties." When he left, he was followed by a bank officer as he went by foot to a motel a block away from the scene of the crime. He was arrested by police within 15 minutes.
- In Salt Lake City a would-be robber walked up to a teller and asked her to hand over all the money. As she was gathering it up, he fainted.
- In Los Angeles two shotgun-armed robbers made everyone lie down on the floor of the bank. When there was nobody left to gather up the money, the pair hesitated a moment and then fled in panic.

The typical bank robber, according to New York City police and the FBI, is an unemployed man in his early to mid-twenties, often in need of money for debts or drugs. In many cases, especially in Manhattan, the bandit does not show a gun and, indeed, sometimes does not even have one. He simply passes over a note demanding the teller's money or makes a verbal threat.

Most banks instruct tellers to hand over the cash in such instances, rather than risk a shooting situation. However, tellers, being human, react in different ways. One teller became so unnerved that she plopped a wastebasket over her head as a form of protection. The shocked bandit charged out of the bank. In another case a teller by force of habit counted and recounted the money before handling it over to the patient robber.

An FBI official in Los Angeles has called modern bank robbers "young and dumb. By dumb I mean not wise in the ways of the professional holdup man. We've had guys write holdup notes on the back of their own utility bills. Or run out of a bank so excited they can't find their getaway car."

Another FBI man observed: "Twenty years ago the bank robber was looked up to by the other inmates in prison. He was a big shot, and bank robbery was viewed as the class robbery. Not any more."

Because of the changing nature of bank robbers, the FBI in recent years has been reducing its involvement in such cases. Under criticism that such crimes are trivial, easy to solve and do little other than add to the agency's solved total, the agency has been moving more into the field of organized crime and white-collar crime. Embezzlers steal three to five times as much as bank robbers.

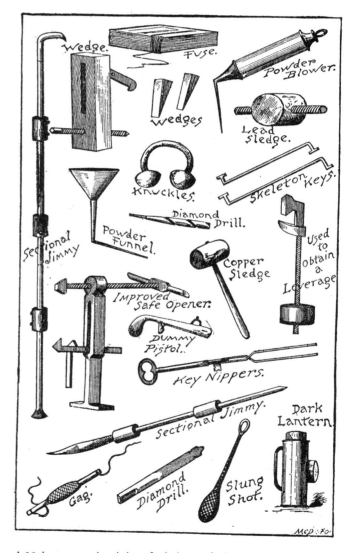

A 19th-century bank burglar's kit included a gag and slung shot to use on watchmen, but the more common procedure was to bribe them.

60

Bank officials have objected to the FBI's withdrawal from the field, however, not so much because the agency is needed that often but because they fear general knowledge of this will simply encourage more attempts. But the fact is that with new antirobbery devices the banks can pretty much take care of themselves. One innovation is a money wrapper that dispenses tear gas. The teller simply activates the device before handing the money over. In an Atlanta, Ga. bank a 19-year-old happily stuffed $5,000 in his waistband and raced out the door. The next moment he collapsed in a coughing, crying fit, ripping at his clothes as he rolled around in the parking lot. By the time he was captured, the young robber had torn off every stitch of clothing.

Consider also the sad plight of two robbers who took money that a teller had secretly doused with a vial of malodorous liquid hidden in the money wrapper. As they drove away, a foul odor infested the car, and in desperation, they abandoned it and ran, still holding the money. But the money will never be spent—it smells too bad.

By the 1990s it became apparent that bank robbery was becoming more and more a juvenile crime, especially considering the huge number of bank robberies masterminded by two young men, Robert S. Brown, 23, and an accomplice, Donzell L. Thompson. The FBI linked the two young men, Los Angeles gang members, to some 175 bank robberies over a four-year period up to 1992. The pair employed teenage boys and trained them to carry out the heists. Brown and Thompson pleaded guilty to a number of counts and were handed federal prison sentences of 30 and 25 years, respectively. Prosecutors said the total number of bank robberies carried out by Brown was the most in the nation's history.

See also: BANK ROBBERIES—BOUNTIES, BLISS BANK RING, JOHN DILLINGER, EDWARD GREEN, JUG MARKERS, HERMAN "BARON" LAMM, GEORGE LEONIDAS LESLIE, LITTLE JOKER, SAFECRACKING, MARK SHINBURN.

bank robberies—bounties

In 1928 a strange invitation to murder was unwittingly issued by a group dedicated to the prevention of crime. At the time, Texas was being plagued by a rash of bank robberies that law enforcement officials were unable to solve. Finally, the state's desperate bankers came up with what was thought to be the perfect deterrent. The Texas Bankers Association had printed and posted in every bank in the state a notice that read:

REWARD
$5,000 for Dead Bank Robbers
Not One Cent For Live Ones

In short order, several bank robbers turned up very dead and rewards were paid out to the local lawmen who brought in the bodies in what was very much a throwback to the bounty system of the Old West. The bankers were happy, and the lawmen were happy. But a Texas Ranger named Frank Hamer, who was to win fame later as the stalker and killer of outlaws Bonnie Parker and Clyde Barrow, was unhappy. Hamer wondered why all the bank robbers had been killed late at night. He also wondered why local lawmen were making all the kills rather than Texas Rangers or U.S. marshals, both of whom had a fairly good record of bringing bank robbers to justice.

Hamer dug into the background of a number of cases and found the "bank robbers" were types such as loners, town bums, drifters passing through or young men who had been drunk earlier in the evening of their demise. The ranger unearthed evidence that these so-called bank robbers had been framed and murdered by crooked lawmen who then collected the rewards. It soon became apparent that there were "murder rings" at work collecting the rewards. When Hamer went to law enforcement officials with his findings, he met with stubborn disbelief. He tried appealing to the Texas Bankers Association for a withdrawal of the reward system. Again, he was rebuffed.

Hamer took his findings to the leading newspapers of the state, including an accusation that the bankers were "bringing about the execution of men by illegal means and for money." The ensuing headlines broke the scandal wide open and led to a grand jury investigation that handed down indictments against two men accused of being the leaders of one of the several murder rings. Hamer arrested them and they subsequently confessed. Only then did the bankers admit their scheme had caused the death of innocent men; the terms of the reward offer were changed to require positive proof that a bank robbery had taken place.

bankruptcy fraud

In recent years bankruptcy scams have become one of the most lucrative activities of organized crime. According to U.S. Justice Department sources, crime syndicates pull off at least 250 such capers every year, each one involving at least $250,000 in goods and materials.

As the racket is generally worked by the New York Mafia crime families, a new company is set up with a "front man" who has no criminal record. "Nut money" of at least $30,000 is deposited in a bank to establish credit, and the company starts ordering supplies that are quickly paid for in full. However, as the orders are increased, the payments slow down a bit until finally a huge order is placed. As soon as these supplies arrive, they are either sold off at extremely low rates or transferred to other business outlets. The nut money is then pulled out of the bank and the operators simply disappear. All the creditors can find is a bankrupt shell of a company.

Perhaps the classic bankruptcy scam was pulled by members of the Vito Genovese crime family, who once took control of a large New York meat wholesale business by advancing the company cash and then insisting on putting in their own president to safeguard the loan. After becoming established, the Mafia operators needed only 10 days to work a $1.3 million swindle. They bought up huge amounts of poultry and meat on credit and sold them off at lowered prices. The mob then pulled out, blithely ordering the cowed management to go into bankruptcy.

Bannack, Montana Territory gold rush town

The site of the Montana Territory's first big gold strike, Bannack was such a violent town in the 1860s that it became "the town nobody wanted." Because territorial borders at the time were imprecise, for a while Bannack was part of Oregon and then Idaho. In 1864 it finally became part of Montana and was even the territorial capital for a period. Murder and thievery were common in Bannack since the time the prospectors panned gold from Grasshopper Creek in 1862. The greatest crook of them all was Henry Plummer, who served both as the local sheriff and the head of a huge gang called the Innocents, which committed almost all the crimes in the area. Plummer planned the gang's jobs and then, as sheriff, proved singularly ineffective at solving any of the crimes. It took the dreaded rope of the Montana Vigilantes to clear up wrongdoing in the area, and they did so by hanging Plummer—from a scaffold he had built himself for executing lawbreakers—and a large number of his Innocents.

After a long spell of noose justice, tranquility prevailed in Bannack. As the gold ran out, the town began to decay. Today, it is a ghost town with just a few well-preserved relics, such as the jail Plummer built.

See also: JOHN X. BEIDLER, HENRY PLUMMER, VIGILANTES OF MONTANA.

Barbara, Joseph, Sr. (1905–1959) Apalachin Conference host

Almost as shadowy as the complete story of the infamous underworld conference at Apalachin, N.Y. in 1957 is the personal history of its host, Joseph Barbara, Sr., at whose rambling estate the meeting took place.

Barbara, who was to rise to the rank of lieutenant in the Magaddino crime family in Buffalo, N.Y., came to the United States from Sicily at the age of 16, and his first job was apparently that of an underworld enforcer. He was arrested in a number of murder cases, once being caught in possession of a submachine gun that had been used in a gang murder in New York. He was also arrested for a number of murders in Pennsylvania. A typical victim was racketeer Sam Wichner, who was lured to Barbara's home in 1933 to confer with Barbara, Santo Volpe and Angelo Valente, Wichner's silent partners in a bootlegging operation. Police said, but couldn't prove, that Barbara strangled Wichner. During his entire career Barbara was only convicted of one crime: the illegal acquisition of 300,000 pounds of sugar in 1946.

After that, Barbara was ostensibly nothing more than a beer and soft drink distributor. He himself insisted he was in poor health and could do nothing more. In fact, virtually all of the 60-odd participants in the 1957 underworld meeting claimed they had gone to Barbara's home to pay a call because he was a cardiac patient. It "just happened," they insisted, that they all picked the same day for their visit.

Investigators were thwarted in their efforts to question Barbara after the Apalachin raid because of his insistence that he was too ill to testify. Finally, the State Investigation Commission sent its own heart specialist to examine Barbara, and in May 1959 a state supreme court justice ordered him to appear before the commission. The following month, however, Barbara died of a heart attack. At the time he was living in a new home in Endicott. His 58-acre estate in Apalachin had been sold for use as a tourist attraction.

See also: APALACHIN CONFERENCE.

Barbe, Warren Gilbert (?–1925) murder victim

To his neighbors in Berkeley, Calif., Charles Henry Schwartz was a remarkable individual. He was a master chemist and during World War I he'd been a spy in Germany for the Allies. After the war he'd taken an important post in a German chemical plant, where he had discovered a process for the manufacture of artificial silk. He smuggled the process into the United States and set up a hush-hush experimental laboratory, in which he often worked into the night. It sounded impressive, but it was all hogwash. Least of all was he a master chemist. But Schwartz found plenty of people willing to give him money in exchange for a piece of the process. When he produced no silk, however, some of his backers started to grumble and talk of fraud.

In 1925 Schwartz began to take an avid interest in a different science—human anatomy. He cultivated a friendship with a traveling evangelist named Warren Gilbert Barbe. Although the facial features of the two men were very dissimilar, they were of the same overall size. Late in July, Barbe disappeared from his usual haunts, but no one gave it a thought. He most likely got the "call" and had "gone into the wilderness" to preach. Meanwhile, Schwartz was very busy in his laboratory. He said he was almost finished with his process and he worried that some international cartel might try to stop his work. He took out a $200,000 insurance policy on his life and allowed no one to enter the laboratory.

In the lab he was very busy altering the dead evangelist into a stand-in corpse for himself. He burned away a section of the corpse's chest because he had a scar in his own chest. He pulled out two teeth from the upper jaw to match his own dental characteristics. He punctured the eyeballs to solve the problem of different color eyes. But all these he regarded as extra precautions, since he planned to blow up his laboratory in order to really make the corpse unidentifiable. In fact, he believed the entire building would be destroyed in the explosion. He soaked the laboratory with several gallons of benzol which, when detonated, would take care of the building and the evidence. Schwartz set up a timing device and left. He couldn't afford to be seen at the site of the explosion. But he stayed close enough to hear the clanging fire trucks approaching as he stepped into a taxi.

Hiding out in Oakland, Schwartz was shocked to discover he was wanted for murder. The body, hardly singed, had been identified. Even three religious pamphlets bearing Barbe's name had survived the blaze. An incompetent chemist, Schwartz didn't realize that benzol fumes rise very slowly. Several more minutes would have been needed to set off the fire properly. A flop as a chemist, an anatomist and a murderer, Schwartz did better in his final endeavor: suicide.

See also: INSURANCE FRAUDS.

Barker, Arizona Clark "Kate" or "Ma"
(1871?–1935) outlaw or mother of outlaws

Kate, or Ma, Barker remains one of the enigmas of the underworld. Was she the brains, indeed the queen mother, of one of the most violent gangs of the 1930s, or was she just a dumpy little old lady whom many of the gangsters of the era considered just plain "Mom"? One version, which belongs to Hollywood and the FBI, presents us with an iron mistress who was feared by her murderous sons as well as numerous other members of the Barker-Karpis gang and who died, tommy gun in hand, in a fabled shoot-out with federal agents. A different viewpoint, held by

other members of the underworld, portrays a doting, worried—although at times ill-tempered—mother whose sole concern was always the safety of her brood. Whatever the truth was, the fact is that Ma Barker was never on any official list of public enemies and indeed was never charged with a crime during her lifetime.

Born to Scotch-Irish parents about 1871 in the Ozark Mountain area near Springfield, Mo.—the area that nurtured Jesse and Frank James—she was saddled with the unlikely name of Arizona, which friends soon shortened to "Arrie" and she herself later switched to Kate. One of her greatest experiences in childhood was seeing Jesse James ride by one day, and she cried with youthful anguish when "that dirty coward" Bob Ford killed Jesse in 1882. The year 1892 was doubly bad for Kate: the Dalton gang was cut down at Coffeyville, Kan., and Kate married an itinerant farm laborer named George Barker. It was not a happy marriage. Kate realized that a penniless sharecropper could never be much of an inspiration for the four boys—Herman, Lloyd, Arthur and Fred—who were born of the union. As the boys grew up in a series of tar paper shacks, Kate made it clear to Barker that she would run the family and she would guide the boys' upbringing. George Barker merely shrugged.

Brought up in this impoverished environment, the boys soon started turning up regularly on police blotters. Ma Barker frequently managed to get her sons released, sometimes weeping hysterically and at other times screaming. As late as 1915, Ma was able to get her eldest, Herman, freed from a highway robbery charge. In the following years the Barkers turned to bank robbery. According to later FBI accounts, Ma planned all the jobs, and the boys and their buddies executed them. Ma supposedly ran things with iron discipline, making the boys memorize a "getaway chart." She herself was said to drive around all the surrounding roads, checking the times needed on them under all weather conditions. During the actual commission of a crime, Ma would once more become the doting mother, weeping for fear that her sons might be hurt. Ma was also said to dominate the gang's personal lives, refusing to allow the presence of any girlfriends. This, to be sure, was nonsense. All of the gang's hideouts were always awash with whores, and Ma did nothing about it. Things hardly could have been otherwise, given the character of her sons and the other top gangsters she sheltered, such as Al Spencer, Ray Terrill, Earl Thayer, Frank Nash, Francis Keating, Tommy Holden and Alvin "Creepy" Karpis. Karpis probably best presented the underworld version of the real Ma Barker. He wrote in his memoirs:

Ma was always somebody in our lives. Love didn't enter into it really. She was somebody we looked after and took with us when we moved from city to city, hideout to hideout.

It's no insult to Ma's memory that she just didn't have the brains or know-how to direct us on a robbery. It wouldn't have occurred to her to get involved in our business, and we always made a point of only discussing our scores when Ma wasn't around. We'd leave her at home when we were arranging a job, or we'd send her to a movie. Ma saw a lot of movies.

In 1927 son Herman was stopped by police near Wichita, Kan. after a robbery. When one officer leaned down to look in Herman's car window, Herman grabbed the policeman around the neck and fired a pistol into his head. A cop on the other side of the car cut loose at Barker, so filling him with bullets that the gangster turned his weapon on himself and finished the job. This development, according to J. Edgar Hoover in a bit of colorful prose, caused Ma to change "from an animal mother of the she-wolf type to a veritable beast of prey." Thereafter, according to the FBI version of events, Ma planed a near-endless string of bank robberies, the kidnappings of millionaires William A. Hamm, Jr. and Edward George Bremer and the murder of her "loving man," Arthur Dunlop. The best evidence indicates that Dunlop was murdered by Ma's sons and other members of the gang, with total disregard for Ma's feelings, because they suspected him of being a "squealer." The FBI claim that Ma was the brain behind the Hamm kidnapping is somewhat tarnished by the fact that the agency first arrested and caused the wrongful prosecution of Roger Touhy and his "Terribles" for the offense before discovering its mistake and correctly pinning the charge on the Barker-Karpis gang.

By 1935 the gang was being intensively pursued by the FBI and other law inforcement agencies. On January 16, Ma and her youngest and favorite son, Freddie, were traced to a cottage hideout at Lake Weir, Fla. A four-hour gun battle ensued, and both Freddie and Ma were shot to death. The official version had Ma manning a submachine gun in the battle, but this is debatable. Freddie was found with 14 bullets in him, indicating he was obviously in the line of fire. There is a discrepancy on how many bullets were in Ma, however. Some accounts said three and others only one—and that one self-inflicted. Cynics have charged that the FBI, having killed a dumpy, insignificant middle-aged woman, quickly promoted her into "Bloody Mama."

See also: BARKER BROTHERS, ALVIN "CREEPY" KARPIS, SHOTGUN GEORGE ZIEGLER.

Ma Barker was either "a veritable beast of prey," as J. Edgar Hoover claimed, or just a dumpy little old mom to a bunch of gangsters, as the latter said.

Barker brothers public enemies

Easily the worst collection of criminal brothers in 20th-century America were the Barkers, or the "Bloody Barkers," as the newspapers not inappropriately called them. Indeed J. Edgar Hoover called the Barker-Karpis gang "the toughest mob we ever cracked." This characterization was close to the truth, whether or not Ma Barker herself, the so-called Bloody Mama, was included. There is considerable controversy over whether Ma Barker was really much of a criminal, but there is no doubt that her brood of four boys—Herman, born 1894; Lloyd, born 1896; Arthur—or "Doc" or "Dock"—born 1899; and Fred, born 1902—were a bloodthirsty lot. Of the four, Doc Barker was probably the leader, the one who commanded the respect of other prominent gangsters of the day.

Doc was both fearless and cold blooded and often killed without provocation or warning. Once when his brother Freddie and a few others of the gang wanted another gang member, William J. Harrison, rubbed out, Doc jumped at the assignment. He took Harrison at gunpoint to an abandoned barn near Ontarioville, Ill., shot him to death and after saturating him and the surrounding area of the barn with gasoline, set fire to the whole thing. He then wrote a note to several of the gang members hiding out in Florida: "I took care of that business for you boys. It was done just as good as if you had did it yourself. I am just like Standard Oil—always at your service. Ha, Ha!"

After several brushes with the law on minor—by Barker family standards—charges, Doc was sentenced to life imprisonment at the Oklahoma State Penitentiary for the murder of a night watchman during a robbery in 1920. In 1927 Herman Barker took his own life after being severely wounded in a shoot-out with police following a robbery. The next severe blow to the Barker family came when Lloyd Barker was arrested for a 1932 mail robbery and sentenced to 25 years in Leavenworth. This left only Freddie free.

Next to Doc, Freddie was the deadliest of the Barkers. He had a rather loose attitude toward killing. Once in Monett, Mo., he and another gangster, Bill Weaver, broke into a garage to steal a car for use in a job. Freddie got behind the wheel, and Weaver slid the garage door open to find himself facing a policeman with gun drawn. Freddie leaned out of the window and promptly shot the officer dead. He later moralized, "That's what comes from stealing these goddamn cars all the time." Freddie did a considerable amount of time for that killing, but he was eventually freed after Ma Barker haunted the parole board, wardens and governors and reputedly spent a significant amount of money.

When Freddie rejoined his mother following his release, he brought with him Alvin "Creepy" Karpis, who proved to be the most important leader of the gang. Each had a mutual respect for the other and they worked well as a team. Ma Barker was equally taken with Karpis and treated him almost as another son, perhaps because she now only had Freddie on the loose. In the meantime, however, Ma also worked on freeing Doc. Remarkably, Doc won a banishment pardon from the governor, which meant he could go free provided he left the state of Oklahoma. J. Edgar Hoover raged over the pardon and even more over the treatment afforded Doc's partner-in-crime, Volney Davis, who was granted an unbelievable "two-year leave of absence."

The Barker-Karpis gang, headed by Creepy, Doc and Freddie, was now ready for full operation. They pulled off an unparalleled number of bank robberies and the like and then moved into the lucrative new field of kidnapping. Their two major jobs were the abductions of William A. Hamm, Jr. and Edward George Bremer, which netted the gang a total of $300,000 in ransoms. Many have claimed Ma Barker was the master planner of both crimes, but none of the facts support this conclusion. Hoover credited the plan to a member of the Barker-Karpis gang named Jack Peifer, while according to Karpis, the Bremer job was the brainchild of Harry Sawyer, a flamboyant character who ran much of the crime in St. Paul, Minn. In all, there were about 25 or 26 members of the Barker-Karpis gang, and Doc and Freddie Barker were only slightly more equal than the rest. None regarded Ma Barker as their leader but did feel she was valuable for renting hideouts and handling payoffs to corrupt officials.

The Hamm and Bremer kidnappings were to prove the downfall of the Barkers and the rest of the gang, triggering one of the most persistent manhunts in history, during which the members were picked off one by one.

On January 8, 1935 Doc Barker was captured by FBI agents led by the legendary Melvin Purvis, the man who got Dillinger. The authorities located Doc by shadowing women he was known to have been in contact with. Eight days later, Freddie Barker was traced to a cottage at Lake Weir in northern Florida, where he was hiding with Ma Barker. Both were killed in a four-hour shoot-out, although there are some reports that Ma Barker actually shot herself when she saw her favorite son riddled with bullets.

In January 1939, Doc Barker, long a troublemaker at Alcatraz, attempted an escape from what was known as America's Devil's Island. He made it into the water before his skull was smashed and his left leg broken by guards' bullets. In the prison hospital he murmured: "I was a fool to try it. I'm all shot to hell." He died the following day, January 14, and was buried in a potter's field on the California mainland.

That left Lloyd Barker the last living brother. He remained in prison until 1947. Two years later, after returning home from his job at a filling station–snack shop, he was shot to death by his wife, with whom he had been feuding.

See also: ARIZONA CLARK "KATE" OR "MA" BARKER, ALVIN "CREEPY" KARPIS, DR. JOSEPH PATRICK MORAN, SHOTGUN GEORGE ZIEGLER.

Barnes, Leroy "Nicky" (1933–) Harlem narcotics king

Born in Harlem of a poor family, Barnes rose rags-to-riches fashion to criminal stardom and what could well be called the position of the first King of the Black Mafia.

He was definitely the King of Harlem. As the *New York Times Magazine* reported: "Checking in at Shalimar, the Gold Lounge, or Small's . . . he will be bowed to, nodded to, but not touched." The juke always got a steady play of "Baaad, Baaad Leroy Brown," which, say Barnes' fans, was written for him. "It's like the Godfather movie," according to a New York police detective who also described Barnes wading through mobs of admirers "being treated like the goddamn Pope."

This idolatry of Barnes was, in a sense, a celebration because he was one of the first blacks to come out on top in the underworld as organized criminal activity shifted—and is still shifting—from Italians to other minority groups. Barnes' rise to power was in large part due to his alliance with Crazy Joey Gallo, a maverick of the Mafia who taught Barnes how to organize a drug empire.

Barnes and Gallo met in New York State's Greenhaven Prison, where the former was doing time for narcotics violations and the latter for extortion. Gallo fed Barnes inside information about the drug world of Harlem, how it was supplied and how one man could take control of it. When Gallo was released, it was agreed that the two would work together. In exchange, Barnes would supply the Brooklyn gangster with black "troops" when he needed them. When Barnes was released, he began importing, with Gallo's help, large amounts of heroin directly from Italian sources. Barnes then set up his own network of "millworkers," who cut the heroin, and deliverers. This gave him control of heroin distribution over large areas in upstate New York, New Jersey, Pennsylvania and even into Canada. Barnes also moved to take over actual street operation in Harlem. Italians were replaced by blacks without bloodshed, also apparently due to Gallo muscle.

In the process Nicky Barnes became not just rich but flamboyantly so, walking around with incredible bankrolls. During one of his arrests, $130,000 cash was found in the trunk of his automobile, of which he had many. Among his possessions were a Mercedes Benz and a Citroen Maserati, and police department files were admittedly incomplete in recording his Cadillacs, Lincoln Continentals and Thunderbirds. Barnes had several apartments in Manhattan, another in the fashionable Riverdale area of the Bronx and at least two in New Jersey. These residences were, of course, in addition to the working apartments Barnes maintained for his drug operation. The *Times* reported that the operations of a typical Barnes heroin plant involved more than a dozen young women and two men. "The . . . women . . . are lined up along the sides of a huge sheet of plate glass that, propped up on pieces of furniture, has become a table. The women are naked, to insure that they will not be tempted to con-

ceal any of the powder they are working over. The lieutenants, trusted, dressed, do not even look at the women. Their eyes, like the eyes of the women, are on the small pyramids of white powder heaped on the plate glass." It would take some 16 hours to cut the heroin. "In those 16 hours, 10 kilos of pure heroin brought from a wholesaler by a trusted representative of one of New York City's major drug dealers for $150,000 has become worth about $630,000. For the dealer, the night's expenses have run about $170,000, including the cash fees to the women and their apartment guardians. Thus the dealer has cleared about $460,000 in profits—all in cash—in an operation that he financed, sanctioned, and arranged, but in which he had no physical part."

While Barnes openly led a lavish life, proving anything against him was not easy. He paid taxes on a quarter of a million dollars in annual "miscellaneous income." Although the IRS insisted he owed much more, substantiating it would not be easy. Barnes had always been good at avoiding conviction; he had a record of 13 arrests but only one had led to a sentence (an abbreviated one) behind bars. This ability to avoid the law's retribution made Barnes something of a cult figure in Harlem and beyond. "Sure, that's the reason the kids loved the guy and wanted to be like him," a newsweekly quoted a federal narcotics agent as saying. "Mr. Untouchable—that's what they called him—was rich, but he was smart too, and sassy about it. The bastard loved to make us cops look like idiots."

Unlike his worshipers, Barnes probably was smart enough to know he'd eventually fall, and in 1978 he did, thanks to a federal narcotics strike force. When brought up for sentencing that year, Barnes rose, squared his shoulders and smiled faintly when he was given life imprisonment plus a $125,000 fine. Barnes appeared to take his fare well, as though, to some observers, he was taking pride in the pivotal role he had played in shifting underworld power from Italians to blacks. The severity of the sentence was fitting. It was as though his importance was being certified by the courts and, according to one reporter, "making him a sort of Muhammed Ali of crime or, even better, the black man's Al Capone."

See also: CRAZY JOE GALLO.

Baron of Arizona   See JAMES ADDISON REAVIS.

barrel murders   early Mafia execution style
The "barrel murders" started turning up in America around 1870. The modus operandi of these killings, which occurred in several large cities, was always the

same. A victim, invariably an Italian, would be killed—either shot, strangled or stabbed—and then stuffed into a barrel, which was then either deposited on a street corner or empty lot or else shipped by rail to a nonexistent address in another city.

It was the barrel murders that first alerted authorities to the existence of the Mafia. The murder technique started by coincidence with the arrival of a fierce pack of brothers, half brothers and brothers-in-law from Corleone, Sicily, the Morellos. Over the next three decades more than 100 barrel murders were traced to the Morellos, who finally abandoned the technique because all such murders merely advertised their criminal activities. Even worse, freelance non-Italian murderers were using the barrel method to divert suspicion from themselves to Italian gangsters.

See also: MORELLO FAMILY.

Barrie, Peter Christian "Paddy" (1888–1935) horse race fixer

Without doubt the most successful horse race fixer in the United States was Paddy Barrie, a skilled "dyer" who applied his handiwork to swindle bettors out of some $6 million from 1926 to 1934.

Barrie's system was perhaps the simplest ever used to fix races. He would buy two horses, one with a very good record and the other a "dog." Then he would "repaint" the fast horse to look like the slow one and enter it in a race under the latter's name. Based on the past performance record of the slow horse, the ringer would generally command odds of 50 to one or even more; because it really outclassed its opponents, the horse would usually win the race easily. Using stencils, bleaches, special dyes and dental instruments, Barrie changed the identity of a champion horse, Aknahton, and ran it under three less-distinguished names at four tracks—Havre de Grace, Agua Caliente, Bowie and Hialeah. The horse made five killings for a gambling syndicate Barrie was working with. It was a feat that led the gamblers to call him "Rembrandt."

The Pinkerton Detective Agency finally unmasked Barrie following an investigation that was started after a leader in the betting syndicate, Nate Raymond, made a drunken spectacle of himself in Broadway clubs and was heard bragging about a "bagged race" worked by an "artist" from England named Paddy. The Pinkertons queried Scotland Yard and learned that a master dyer named Paddy Barrie had disappeared from the British Isles some years previous. An alert went out for Barrie, but he managed to elude capture for another two years by doing the same thing to himself that he did to

horses, adopting disguises and changing his name frequently. One day a Pinkerton operative recognized him at Saratoga race track in New York, and he was bundled off to jail.

Oddly, the laws on horse race gambling and fixing were rather lax and Barrie appeared to have broken no law other than having entered the United States illegally. He was deported back to his native Scotland, where he died less than six month later of a "broken heart," according to a sensational British tabloid, due to constant surveillance aimed at guaranteeing he would never be able to ring another horse.

Because of Barrie's depredations, American tracks adopted such precautions as lip tattoos and other methods of identification to make the ringing in of other horses almost impossible. However, since foreign horses have not been so identified they have been used as ringers in recent years. The disclosure of such fixes has led to close checks on the identification of foreign horses.

Barrow, Clyde   See BONNIE AND CLYDE.

Barrows, Sydney Biddle (1952–) the "Mayflower Madam"

The 1980s infatuation with the sins of the rich and famous extended even to the world of prostitution, a field that was withering not so much due to a rise in morals but because, as one practitioner put it, "the sexual revolution is killing us. There are just too many women willing to just give it away." Thus, the nation's tabloids were thrilled by the appearance of Sydney Biddle Barrows—the "Mayflower Madam."

For the scandal-minded press, the story harkened back to the glorious old days of high-paid sex, "little black books" and erudite madams. Intellectually, the swooning press declared, Barrows could have held her own with Polly Adler, the "Madam Elite" of the 1930s and 1940s. Sydney Barrows, a descendant of two *Mayflower* Pilgrims, also added a new dimension in class: *Social Register* charm and grace.

Thirty-two-year-old Barrows was indicted in December 1984 in New York City for promoting prostitution in the guise of a temporary-employment agency, through which she ran three escort services that actually were expensive call-girl operations. The press was much impressed that the call girls she trained garnered as much as $2,000 a night, in her 20-woman, $1 million-a-year business.

When the tabloids uncovered her connection with the *Mayflower* (which linked her with Elder William Brewster, the minister who had played a leading role in the 1620 Plymouth Rock landing), they quickly dubbed her the "Mayflower Madam."

Barrows pleaded guilty in July 1985 to a lesser charge of fourth-degree promotion of prostitution and paid a $5,000 fine. The press saw this as a plea-bargain deal to suppress those eternal little black books. In fact, under the agreement, the prosecution returned seized documents that bore information about her clients, said to include "scores of prominent businessmen."

Now famous, Barrows appeared on the *Donahue* television show unrepentant and complaining that nobody had gone to jail in the state in the last 100 years for what she had done. She earned the attention of the press by writing about her call-girl business: "As I saw it, this was a sector of the economy that was crying out for the application of good management skills—not to mention a little common sense and decency." She expressed the opinion that all women are prostitutes since they withhold favors from their husband when they are angry. But she assured the eager public that, in her own life, "I am monogamous and rather old-fashioned."

Barrows did qualify as a trailblazer in the world's oldest profession by employing only well-informed, articulate women and letting her ladies choose the nights they wished to work. She even allowed clients to pay for services *after* they were rendered, truly a revolutionary practice in the field.

Barrows was a graduate of New York's Fashion Institute of Technology and had studied business management and merchandising. After a stint as a fashion buyer, she got a job through a friend answering the phone for an escort service. She decided she could do it better with her own service, one with very special wrinkles.

Barrows would not even concede that her *Mayflower* ancestors necessarily would have censured her activities. "Had they lived in a more enlightened era," she opined, "they would have understood that the private behavior of consenting adults is not the business of the state."

When TV host Phil Donahue wondered what Barrows' grandmother—who died after her granddaughter's arrest and conviction—had thought about it all, Barrows answered, "She was not amused."

Her post-business activities proved most rewarding for Barrows. Her book soared to the best-seller lists and was condensed in a top women's magazine, and she remained much sought after for lucrative television appearances.

Sydney Biddle Barrows, the "Mayflower Madam" who ran a plush Manhattan bordello, celebrates after getting off with just a $5,000 fine.

Barter, Rattlesnake Dick (1834–1859) stagecoach robber

Few criminal reputations in the Old West were more enhanced by the Eastern writers whose flowery prose graced the pages of such 19th-century publications as *New York Weekly, Harper's Monthly* and the torrent of dime novels and paperbacks than Rattlesnake Dick's.

The real-life Rattlesnake Dick Barter was more wooly than wild and, alas, hardly an archbadman of the West. Barter was, on the whole, quite incompetent. According to the legend-makers, he was named Rattlesnake Dick because he was so dangerous and devious. No doubt the fact that he was an Englishman operating outside the American law was enough to give him a certain romantic aura. However, Rattlesnake Dick was downright prosaic in comparison with many native American badmen of the period. The real story behind his name was that he had prospected for a short time at Rattlesnake Bar in the Northern Mines area of California. Rattlesnake Dick soon decided, however, that it was easier to steal gold than to dig for it. Here the legend-makers were right, although they failed to note that Rattlesnake Dick had never made a dime at his digs. In 1856, after some small-time stage holdups, Barter hit on what was to prove the most brilliant and, at the same time, most comic criminal scheme of his career. To give him credit due, he masterminded the $80,000 robbery of the Yreka Mine's mule train and managed to organize a gang for that purpose. Rattlesnake Dick did not take part in the actual robbery, which was left to George Skinner and some others, possibly explaining why that part of the scheme worked so well. The Yreka Mine mule train had been regarded as immune from robbers because the mules would always tire out halfway down the mountains and thus make pursuit too easy. Rattlesnake Dick's plan called for him and George Skinner's brother, Cyrus, to meet the robbers on the mountain trail with fresh mules. Clever though the plan was, it left the execution of this phase to Rattlesnake Dick. When George Skinner and his gunmen reached the rendezvous point, there was not a fresh mule in sight. It developed that Rattlesnake Dick and Cy Skinner were already in jail. They had been caught, drunk, trying to steal some mules.

Under the circumstances all George Skinner could think to do was bury most of the stolen gold nuggets and then head off with his crew for some high living over at Folsom. That's where Wells Fargo agents caught up with them. George Skinner was shot dead while in bed with a screaming prostitute and the rest of the gang was similarly liquidated. But with them died the secret of where the stolen gold was buried. Shortly thereafter, Rattlesnake Dick and Cy Skinner broke jail by walking out an open door and went looking for the buried loot. Following an unsuccessful search for it, the pair returned to the stagecoach-robbing business. After some of their hold-ups netted the pair less than $20, Cy Skinner decided he had had enough of the criminal genius of Rattlesnake Dick and went his separate way. Barter continued his bush-league hold-ups until he was shot and killed by a pursuing posse in July 1859. But the legend of Rattlesnake Dick as California's worst bandit between the eras of Murieta and Vasquez lives on, enhanced by the fact that today treasure hunters still scour the California hills for Dick's buried gold.

Bass, Sam (1851–1878) outlaw

Sam Bass was born in Indiana, it was his native home;
At the age of seventeen young Sam began to roam.
Sam first came out to Texas, a cowboy for to be—
A kinder-hearted fellow you seldom ever see.

From "The Ballad of Sam Bass"

Kinder-hearted or not, Sam Bass was an outlaw. While he "came out of Texas, a cowboy for to be," young Bass found life dull and soon opted for crime. He and two other characters, Joel Collins and Jack Davies,

went in for some "easy rustling," taking on 500 cattle on consignment, driving them to market in Kansas in 1876 and then neglecting to settle up with the Texas ranchers who had hired them. With their loot as capital, the trio became pimps and opened a whorehouse in Deadwood, Dakota Territory, a place described as "the most degraded den of infamy that ever cursed the Earth." With that sort or recommendation, the brothel did a thriving business. Nonetheless, Bass, Collins and Davies drank and gambled away their income faster than their prostitutes could make it, so the trio and three of their best bordello customers, Bill Heffridge, Jim Berry and Tom Nixon, formed an outlaw gang and held up a number of stagecoaches. On September 19, 1877 the gang made a big score, robbing a Union Pacific train of $60,000.

With a $10,000 stake, Bass returned to Denton County, Tex. and started a new gang, becoming a folk hero in the process. While he was not exactly a Robin Hood, Bass was loose with the money he stole and if there was one way for a gunman to become popular in Texas, it was for him to be a free spender. For a time, Bass proved to be a real will-o'-the-wisp, impossible for

Photograph shows outlaw Sam Bass (center), although its authenticity has been disputed.

the law to corner and remarkably skillful at extracting hospitality from Texans who looked upon him with affection. As the reward money mounted, however, Bass became a marked man. Finally, one of his own band, Jim Murphy, whose family often gave Bass refuge on their ranch, betrayed him by informing the law that the gang planned a bank robbery in Round Rock. While Murphy ducked for shelter, ambushers killed an outlaw named Seaborn Barnes and shot Sam Bass off his horse. Another outlaw, Frank Jackson, rode back through a fusillade of fire to rescue Bass and carry him out of town.

Bass was found by pursuers the next day; he was lying under a tree, near death. While he clung to life, Texas Rangers questioned him about his accomplices and the location of the loot he was believed to have buried. Bass would not respond, saying only: "Let me go. The world is bobbing around." He died on his 27th birthday. Some treasure hunters still search for the Bass loot, although it is more than likely that the dying Bass told Jackson where to find it. The "Ballad of Sam Bass" is still a Texas favorite, and the outlaw's grave at Round Rock remains an attraction.

See also: FRANK JACKSON, JIM MURPHY.

Bassity, Jerome (1870?–1929) whoremaster

During the long history of prostitution in San Francisco's Barbary Coast, Jerome Bassity stands out as perhaps the owner of more brothels than any other single person in that city. Although he was described by the press as being a "study in depravity" with an intelligence only slightly higher than that of a chimpanzee, Bassity was the veritable lord of the red-light district. In the heyday of the corrupt Ruef machine, especially during the three terms of Mayor Eugene Schmitz from 1901 to 1907, Bassity, whose real name was said to be Jere McGlane, was far and away the most potent figure in the San Francisco underworld.

The newspaper singled him out for special condemnation. The *San Francisco Bulletin* invited its readers to "look at the low, cunning lights in the small, rapacious, vulture-like eyes; look at that low, dull-comprehending brow; the small sensual mouth; the soft puffy fingers with the weak thumb, indicating how he seeks ever his own comfort before others, how his will works only in fits and starts." Despite such publicity, Bassity operated with little or no restraint, from about the turn of the century until 1916, save for two years—1907 to 1909—during a reform administration. In 1909 Mayor P. H. McCarthy took office on a platform designed to "make San Francisco the Paris of America." Bassity aided that cause by operating a 100-cubicle brothel called the Parisian Mansion. While

McCarthy was in office it was openly acknowledged that the city was really ruled by a triumvirate: the mayor, police commissioner and bar owner Harry P. Flannery, and Bassity.

In addition to his brothels, Bassity owned dance halls and other dives, including a notorious Market Street deadfall called the Haymarket that even the streetwalkers refused to enter. Bassity had an interest in the income of at least 200 prostitutes and his own income was estimated to be around $10,000 a month, no trifling sum for the period. A dandy dresser and "diamond ring stud," Bassity reportedly went to bed with a diamond ring on each of his big toes. In his own brothels he claimed and exercised his seigniorial rights whenever a young girl or virgin arrived, but by and large, Bassity patronized his competitors' establishments. His patronage practically amounted to sabotage since he was generally drunk, always armed and frequently concluded a night of debauchery by shooting out the lights or seeing how close he could fire shots to the harlots' toes. Bassity bragged that he squandered most of his income on clothes, jewelry and debauchery, but he predicted the flow of money would never end. In 1916, foreseeing the success of reform efforts to shut down the Barbary Coast, Bassity retired from the sex racket and headed for Mexico, where he unsuccessfully attempted a takeover of the Tijuana race track. He was later charged but not prosecuted for a swindle in California. When he died in 1929, after what was described as "California's most sinful life," he left an estate of less than $10,000.

See also: ABRAHAM RUEF.

Bath, Michigan school bombing

One of the most hideous crimes ever committed in America was the slaying of 37 schoolchildren in 1927 by Andrew Kehoe, the mad bomber of Bath, Mich.

The background to the case was pieced together by the police after the fact, because Kehoe himself did not survive the crime. Kehoe was a farmer, but not a very successful one, barely scraping by even in boom years. When the community of Bath decided to build a new schoolhouse, property owners were assessed a special levy. Kehoe's tax bite came to $300. After he paid up, he no longer could meet his mortgage and faced imminent loss of his house. "It's that school tax," he would tell anyone who would listen. "If it hadn't been for the $300 I had to pay, I'd have the money. That school never should have been built."

Kehoe feuded with school board officials, accusing them of squandering the taxpayers' money. He started telling people he'd have his revenge for that. Night after night Kehoe would be seen near the school. It turned out that he was sneaking in the building and spending hours planting dynamite in safe hiding places.

At 9:43 A.M. on May 18, 1927, the whole building shook. The second floor of the north wing rose in the air and came down, crushing the first floor in an avalanche of battered wreckage. In all, 37 schoolchildren and one teacher died, and some 43 others were very seriously injured.

The explosion brought the townspeople running, while Andy Kehoe sat and watched the whole horrible scene from his parked car. Among the rescuers was the head of the school board, heroically risking his life to bring injured children out of the tottering wreckage. He kept at it until Kehoe beckoned him over to his car. Andy Kehoe still had one more murder card to play. As the school official placed his foot on the running board of the car, Kehoe turned a switch and a violent explosion killed the last two victims of the mad bomber of Bath.

bats prostitutes

"Batting" remains one of the most common forms of streetwalking. A bat is a prostitute who works the streets only at night in sections that are respectable by day. In Chicago during the 1870s, for example, a respectable woman could readily traverse such downtown streets as Randolph, Dearborn and East Monroe during the day and fear no untoward incident. At night, however, she could well be accosted by men in search of a harlot. The hookers operated out of "marble front" business buildings, residing there but remaining undercover until after dark and then venturing forth to entice still available businessmen.

Bats prefer working respectable streets because the fees earned are much better than along more vice-ridden streets. Bats too are generally far nicer looking than their competitors in the business. Typical bat streets in the early 1980s to the present in New York are Lexington Avenue and Madison Avenue from the low 40s to about 48th Street, the so-called prime meat market row.

Battaglia, Sam "Teets" (1908–1973) syndicate gangster

Perhaps the craziest and certainly the deadliest of the four notorious Battaglia brothers who were members of the Chicago mobs, Sam Battaglia was a graduate of the notorious juvenile 42 Gang.

A burglar from the age of 16 and later a muscleman for the mob, he was arrested 25 times, beginning in 1924, on various armed robbery charges and at least seven homicide charges. A huge barrel of a youth, nicknamed Teets because of his muscular chest, Battaglia gained his first major notoriety when he was arrested in

the fall of 1930 on a charge of robbing at gunpoint $15,500 worth of jewelry from the wife of the mayor of Chicago, Mrs. William Hale Thompson. Adding insult to injury, Teets appropriated the gun and badge of her policeman chauffeur. However, a positive identification could not be made, and Teets went free when he insisted he was watching a movie at the time of the robbery and a half-dozen witnesses insisted they were watching him watching the movie.

The robbery occurred on November 17, and, between then and the end of the year, Teets was involved in one fatal killing and one attempted killing. In ensuing years he became one of the mob's most reliable machine gunners and, despite a reputation for being a bit zany, moved steadily up the syndicate ladder. By the 1950s he was the virtual king of the mob's "juice," or loansharking, rackets and supervised a number of gambling joints and prostitution rings.

Sam Battaglia, a tough out of Chicago's Patch district who was always considered stronger on brawn than brains, became a millionaire and the owner of a luxury horse-breeding farm and country estate in Kane County, Ill. In 1967 Battaglia was finally sent away for 15 years on extortion charges, yet he was considered, pending his release, the likely head of the Chicago mob.

See also: FORTY-TWO GANG.

Bayonne-Abriel gang New Orleans waterfront killers

A small band of burglars, wharf rats and professional murderers that terrorized New Orleans in the 1860s, the Bayonne-Abriel gang made up in viciousness what they lacked in numbers. According to one story, the gang once stole a row boat and, after discovering the boat was missing an oar, went out and killed another sailor just for his oars. While they occasionally functioned as shanghaiers, their main operation was a lucrative racket supplying seamen with everything from women and drugs to murder services. It was such a murder-for-hire service that eventually eliminated both leaders, Vincent Bayonne and Pedro Abriel, and led to the gang's dissolution.

Early in June 1869 the mate of a Spanish bark offered Bayonne and Abriel the kingly sum of $6 to kill a sailor who had earned his enmity. With such a prize at stake, Bayonne and Abriel decided to handle the job themselves rather than share it with any of their followers. The pair lured the sailor into a dive for a few drinks and then all three headed down to the levee "for some fun." Fun for the sailor turned out to be getting batted over the head with a club wielded by Bayonne. When Bayonne raised his arm to strike the unconscious man again, Abriel stopped him and said, "Let me finish him."

Bayonne refused, and Abriel struck him in assertion of his rights. The pair struggled fiercely for several minutes until Abriel knocked Bayonne out. By that time the sailor was stirring. Abriel then stabbed him 17 times and heaved the body into the river. Abriel and Bayonne reconciled afterwards but made the mistake of revealing the details of their vicious crime to a man named Isadore Boyd. Boyd's testimony was instrumental in getting the pair convicted and on May 14, 1871, hanged.

Beachy, Hill   See LLOYD MAGRUDER.

Beadle, William (?–1782) murderer

As a murderer, Wethersfield, Conn.'s William Beadle achieved lasting local notoriety not only because of the horrendous nature of his crime but also because of the way he kept coming back to remind local residents of what he'd done. It appeared later that William had planned to wipe out his family—his wife and five children, aged six to 11—for some time. Finally, one night as they slept, he crept upstairs, struck each in the head with an ax and then cut their throats. After this bloodletting, Beadle returned to the kitchen downstairs and sat in a chair at the table. He picked up two pistols, placed one in each ear and pulled both triggers at the same time. The victims were all buried in the town cemetery, but the townspeople had to decide what to do with Beadle. They determined he should be buried secretly and a grave was dug in the frozen December ground down by the river. However, an overflow the following spring disinterred the body. Beadle was again buried secretly, but this time a dog dug up the corpse. Finally, on the third try, the murderer's body stayed buried.

Bean, Roy (c. 1825–1902) saloonkeeper and judge

Billing himself as the "law west of the Pecos," Roy Bean of Texas was without question the most unusual and colorful jurist ever to hold court in America. Bean dispensed justice between poker hands in his saloon-courtroom. He would open a proceeding by declaring: "Hear Ye! Hear Ye! This honorable court's now in session and if any galoot wants a snort before we start, let him step up and name his pizen."

A native of Kentucky, Bean had been a trader, bartender and Confederate guerrilla during the Civil War. (He organized the Free Rovers in the New Mexico Territory, which local residents soon began calling the Forty Thieves, an indication of how much of the booty went to the Confederate cause.) In his late fifties, fat, bewhiskered and whiskey sodden, Bean ambled into the tent town of Vinegaroon in 1882 and got himself appointed justice of the peace, perhaps because he had a copy of the *1879 Revised Statutes of Texas*. When the road gangs moved on from Vinegaroon, Bean went to Langtry, a stopover point on the Southern Pacific. Here Bean, first by appointment and then by elections held in his saloon, was to dispense his bizarre justice for 20 years.

Judge Bean had all sorts of profitable lines. He got $5 a head officiating at inquests, $2 performing marriages and $5 granting divorces. When higher-ups informed him he did not have the authority to divorce people, he was unimpressed. "Well, I married 'em, so I guess I got a right to unmarry 'em if it don't take." When a railroad man with a good record, meaning he was a regular paying customer at Bean's saloon, was hauled in for killing a Chinese laborer, the judge leafed through his dog-eared legal guide and then released the prisoner, ruling, "There ain't a damn line here nowheres that makes it illegal to kill a Chinaman." And when another friend of the judge was charged with shooting a Mexican, Bean's finding was that "it served the deceased right for getting in front of a gun."

Having himself appeared in other courts on occasion, Bean knew that judges from time to time made very flowery speeches, and he endeavored to do the same, adding a flourish or two of his own. Passing sentence on a cattle rustler once, he intoned:

You have been tried by 12 good men and true, not of your peers but as high above you as heaven is of hell, and they have said you are guilty. Time will pass and seasons will come and go. Spring with its wavin' green grass and heaps of sweet-smellin' flowers on every hill and in every dale. Then sultry Summer, with her shimmerin' heat-waves on the baked horizon. And Fall, with her yeller harvest moon and the hills growin' brown and golden under a sinkin' sun. And finally Winter, with its bitin', whinin' wind, and all the land will be mantled with snow. But you won't be here to see any of 'em; not by a damn sight, because it's the order of this court that you be took to the nearest tree and hanged by the neck till you're dead, dead, dead, you olive-colored son of a billy goat.

In 1896 a lamentable oversight occurred in Bean's reelection campaign. He ended up with more votes than there were eligible voters, and as a result, the authorities awarded the office to his hated opponent, Jesus P. Torres. Bean was undaunted by this development and continued to handle cases that originated on his side of town. He died in 1902, a victim of his own rum as much as old age.

See also: BENEDICT'S SENTENCE.

Judge Roy Bean dispensed his special brand of Texas justice seated on a beer keg outside his saloon.

Beauchamp, Jereboam O. (1803–1826) murderer

Few murderers shocked, and yet typified, the genteel antebellum South more than Jereboam O. Beauchamp. A brilliant young lawyer from a leading Kentucky family, Beauchamp created quite a stir in society when he married Ann Cooke, a somewhat withered belle of 38; Beauchamp was but 21. Beside the disparity in age, there were other complications, such as Ann's well-known affair with a leading political figure, Col. Solomon P. Sharp. In 1826 Sharp, a former state attorney general, ran for reelection to the Kentucky House of Representatives. During the campaign Sharp's foes dredged up his old affair with Ann, fully publicizing her charges at the time that he had seduced and impregnated her.

It was stale gossip, but even at this late date, Beauchamp decided Ann's honor had to be avenged. He challenged Sharp, who had maintained a strict silence on the matter, to a duel. Sharp refused, and Beauchamp considered this breach of behavior almost as heinous as his sexual escapade with a woman who was then unmarried.

One day early in 1826, Beauchamp donned a red hood and appeared at the colonel's door. When Sharp appeared, Beauchamp stabbed him to death and fled. However, he had been readily recognized by his garments and was quickly cast into jail in Frankfort. Ann visited

him daily and proclaimed her eternal gratitude for the avenging of her honor. After Beauchamp was sentenced to hang in July, the couple decided to commit suicide together. Ann smuggled in some poison to the cell, but they succeeded only in getting themselves a bit sick.

Jereboam's execution was scheduled for July 7, and the two were permitted to breakfast together. When they were alone, they took turns plunging a knife into each other's stomach. Beauchamp held Ann in his arms as she died, but he did not die. Bleeding profusely, he was dragged from the cell by embarrassed guards, still clinging to his dead wife. It was decided that his execution would go on even though it was not certain if the bleeding prisoner would be able to stand on the scaffold.

Thousands of spectators lined the way to the gallows, fully expecting to see the condemned man sitting on his own coffin in an open cart, as was the custom of the day. Instead, Beauchamp was bundled in a blanket, still clutching his wife's body, and transported in a closed carriage. Once the crowd was appraised of his condition and the circumstances surrounding it, it was appeased. This was truly something different.

Hushed whispers of satisfaction swept through the crowd when Beauchamp managed to climb the steps of the gallows. He weaved precariously, while a band played a favorite selection of the period, "Bonaparte's

Retreat from Moscow," as Beauchamp's last request. His final words were "Farewell, child of sorrow! For you I have lived; for you I die!"

Husband and wife were buried in a common grave. Chiseled in the stone slab was a poem Ann had composed in the death cell:

> He heard her tale of matchless woe,
> And burning for revenge he rose,
> And laid her base seducer low,
> And struck dismay to virtue's foe.
>
> Daughter of virtue! Moist thy tear.
> This tomb of love and honor claim;
> For thy defense the husband here,
> Laid down in youth his life and fame.

Beck, Dave (1894–1993) labor union leader

In the early 1950s David D. Beck was one of the most powerful and respected labor union leaders in the United States. He was president of the country's largest single union, the 1.4 million member International Brotherhood of Teamsters. He was a rich man whose friendship was sought by business executives and statesmen. He boasted that management almost unanimously hailed him as a cooperative labor leader sympathetic to its problems. He was also greedy on a monumental scale.

In his younger years Beck was noted as an aggressive labor leader and an effective bargainer. Founder of the western Conference of Teamsters, he negotiated contracts that became standards for labor settlements throughout the rest of the country. When he became president of the union in 1952, he had seemingly achieved the pinnacle of success, although he had to share his union powers in several areas with tough James R. Hoffa, chairman of the Teamsters Central States Conference. In fact, Hoffa once boasted: "Dave Beck? Hell, I was running it while he was playing big shot. He never knew the score."

Beck knew the score, however, when it came to milking union funds to become a millionaire. He took loans from the union treasury, which he never repaid. With the aid of money from the union, he built for himself an elegant house in the suburbs of Seattle, featuring an artificial waterfall in the backyard and a basement movie theater. He sold it to the Teamsters at twice what it cost to build and then got it back from the union rent-free for his lifetime use. He put the bite on large companies for personal "loans" and gained the reputation of being able to walk off with anything not nailed down.

Beck's downfall came in a confrontation with the Senate Select Committee on Improper Activities in the Labor or Management Field, chaired by Sen. John McClellan of Arkansas with a young Robert F. Kennedy as chief counsel. The McClellan Committee did much to expose the greed of a number of union officials who had often allied themselves with underworld figures and had looted union treasuries for personal gain. Many union officials squirmed under the inquiry, but none more so than the Teamster leadership. Beck, like others, was to infer that the committee and especially the chief counsel were "antilabor," but he came before the investigation declaring: "I have nothing to fear. My record is an open book." He then proceeded to invoke the Fifth Amendment more than 200 times.

In summing up, the committee declared:

> The fall of Dave Beck from a position of eminence in the labor-union movement is not without sadness. When named to head this rich and powerful union, he was given an opportunity to do much good for a great segment of American working men and women. But when temptation faced Dave Beck, he could not turn his back. His thievery in the final analysis became so petty that the committee must wonder at the penuriousness of the man. What would cause a man in such circumstances to succumb to the temptation of using union funds to pay for six pairs of knee drawers for $27.54, or a bow tie for $3.50? In Beck's case, the committee must conclude that he was motivated by an uncontrollable greed.

Exposure of Beck's greed caused him to leave the hearings a broken man. He would soon be imprisoned, although he tried to fend off this fate by refunding huge sums of money to the Teamsters' treasury. By May 1, 1957 he had returned some $370,000, but the next day, with only a few days remaining before the statute of limitations expired, he was indicted on charges of income tax evasion.

Jimmy Hoffa replaced him as president on February 20, 1958, and Beck drew a long prison term. When he came out, he was still worth a considerable amount of money and had intact his $50,000 lifetime pension from the union. Beck still owed the government $1.3 million in back taxes, and the Treasury Department had the right to seize any and all of his assets to satisfy the claim. However, in 1971 John B. Connolly, secretary of the treasury under President Richard Nixon, approved a plan for a moratorium on the payment of the debt. The Teamsters became Nixon's strongest booster in the labor movement.

Beck, Martha (1920–1951) Lonely Hearts Killer

Together with Raymond Martinez Fernandez, 280-pound Martha Beck became infamous in the 1940s as one of the Lonely Hearts Killers. Although the pair was charged with only three murders, they were suspected of committing 17 others.

Both Fernandez and Beck were social misfits who joined several lonely hearts clubs seeking companionship. In addition to companionship, Fernandez sought money from women he became acquainted with. When Fernandez and Beck met through the auspices of a club, they teamed up to make a business of swindling women. While Fernandez wooed the women, Martha played the role of his sister. They mulcted scores of women and simply killed those who proved uncooperative or troublesome. The murders that tripped the pair up were those of Mrs. Janet Fay, a 60-year-old Albany, N.Y. widow, and Mrs. Delphine Downing, an attractive 41-year-old widow from Grand Rapids, Mich., and her 20-month-old child.

Mrs. Fay traveled as fast as she could to Valley Stream, Long Island to meet her husband-to-be (Fernandez) and his sister (Beck) after selling her home in Albany. Once the pair was sure they had all the woman's money, they beat her to death with a hammer and buried her in the cellar of a rented house. The killers then traveled to Grand Rapids and similarly stripped Mrs. Downing of much of her wealth. After feeding her sleeping pills, Fernandez then shot her to death. A few days later Martha Beck drowned the woman's child in the bathtub. The murderous pair then buried both corpses under cement in the cellar.

That chore completed the couple went off to a movie. When they returned, they found the police inside the Downing home. Suspicious neighbors had not seen the woman around for a few days and notified the authorities. Since the cement in the cellar had not yet dried, the bodies were quickly found. The police also discovered traces of the late Mrs. Fay's belongings in the couples' possession and soon obtained a confession to the New York murder as well. Since New York had a death penalty and Michigan did not, the two were tried for the Fay killing. After a 44-day trial, in which the sexual aberrations of Fernandez and Beck provided a field day for the sensational press, they were sentenced to death. On March 8, 1951—their final day of life—Fernandez received a message from Beck that she still loved him, news he exclaimed, that made him "want to burst with joy." Martha Beck was granted her last request. Before she was executed in Sing Sing's electric chair, she had her hair meticulously curled.

The lonely hearts murders led to the tightening of restrictions on the operations of lonely hearts clubs, but most lawmakers conceded little safeguards could be established to protect foolish and romantic people from being swindled and even killed for love's sake.

Becker, Charles (1869–1915) corrupt policeman and murderer

In the 1890s novelist Stephen Crane witnessed a tall, brawny policeman walk up to a prostitute and start beating her to a pulp when she refused to share the proceeds of her last business transaction. Crane would write about this brutish patrolman in his novel titled *Maggie: A Girl of the Streets,* but the real-life officer, Charles Becker, would go on to commit far worse offenses. Becker was known as "the crookedest cop who ever stood behind a shield," no mean accomplishment in the sordid history of New York City police corruption.

He rose to the rank of lieutenant, became personal assistant to dapper police commissioner Rhinelander Waldo, perhaps the most inept holder of that office before or since, and was in charge of the department's special crime squad. In addition to his police function, Becker was also the protégé of Tammany Hall leader Tim Sullivan and aspired to succeed him. Becker used his position to handle all payoffs to the police and politicians from gamblers, prostitutes and other vice operators. His special squad as well as outside gangsters were employed to enforce the payoff rules, providing protection to those who paid and retribution to those who refused.

One gambler who attempted to stand up to Becker was Herman Rosenthal, who ran a betting joint on West 45th Street. Fearful that Rosenthal would set a bad example for other gamblers, Becker kept intensive pressure on him, but the tactic boomeranged. Rosenthal started telling his troubles to reporter Herbert Bayard Swope of the *New York World* and to Charles S. Whitman, Republican district attorney of Manhattan. Soon, Becker realized his position was threatened. He turned to his top underworld henchman, Big Jack Zelig, to take care of Rosenthal before he did any more talking. At the moment, Zelig was in jail, but Becker used his influence to free him. Zelig then arranged for four gunmen—Gyp the Blood, Lefty Louie, Dago Frank and Whitey Lewis—to handle the hit.

The four botched a few attempts, and the frightened Rosenthal sent word to Becker and Zelig that he was finished talking and would leave New York. However, Rosenthal had already talked too much, and on July 16, 1912 the four killers brought him down in a fusillade of bullets outside the Hotel Metropole on West 43rd Street.

An investigation was ordered, and Commissioner Waldo put Becker in charge. With amazing nerve, Becker instructed the police to "lose" the license number of the murderers' car and even attempted to hide an eyewitness to the crime in a police station jail cell. Through a tipster, District Attorney Whitman learned of the witness and, with the help of his own investigators, seized him in a scuffle in the station house.

Eventually, the killers were caught and, in hope of saving their own necks, talked, implicating Zelig. Zelig, in turn, realized his best chance to avoid execution also lay in talking, and he informed on Becker. Allowed free on bail, Zelig was shot and killed by another gangster. However, Whitman, who saw the Rosenthal case as a way of purging police graft and perhaps promoting himself into the governorship, still presented enough evidence to have the four killers convicted and sentenced to death and convicted Becker of being the instigator of the killing.

Becker was granted a new trial amid clear indications that Whitman had promised rewards to various prosecution witnesses in return for their aid in convicting a police officer. Nonetheless, he was found guilty once again and was sentenced to death. As Becker's execution date drew near, his only hope was to obtain clemency from the governor, but unfortunately for him, Whitman had since been elected to that office. He ignored a plea from Becker's wife, who remained faithful to her husband to the end.

Becker's friends insisted that he had been "jobbed" and, whatever his sins, had not masterminded the Rosenthal murder. After Becker was electrocuted on July 7, 1915, in what was probably Sing Sing's clumsiest execution, his wife had attached to the top of his coffin a silver plate with the following inscription:

CHARLES BECKER
MURDERED JULY 7, 1915
BY GOVERNOR WHITMAN

The plate was finally removed when the police convinced Mrs. Becker that she could be prosecuted for criminal libel.

See also: STEPHEN CRANE.

Becker, Jennie (1881–1922) murder victim

Abe Becker was certain he had committed the perfect crime when he bashed in his wife's skull, buried her in a pit and poured corrosive alkali over her body. Instead, it became a criminal-medical text classic. On the night of the murder in April 1922, Becker had taken his wife, Jennie, to a party at a friend's house in New York City and played the role of a loving spouse, stuffing her with canapés, grapes, figs and almonds. On the way home, he lured Jennie out of the car by pretending to have motor trouble. He then struck her over the head with a wrench and carried her dead body

to a prepared grave, where he doused it with alkali. In the ensuing months Becker explained his wife's disappearance by saying she'd run off with another man. He was not even too concerned when the police found Jennie's body, or what they thought was her body, five months later. Proving it would be another matter. The alkali had rendered the body unrecognizable.

In desperation, the police turned the corpse over to the medical examiner's office. Experts found that the alkali had not totally destroyed the stomach. They found the woman had eaten grapes, figs, almonds and some meat-spread sandwiches—the very things Becker had lovingly fed his wife at the party. Becker was undoubtedly frightened now, but he kept insisting the body was not his wife's. Figs are figs, grapes are grapes and almonds are almonds—some other woman had simply eaten the same type of food, he contended. Denials proved worthless, however. Laboratory examination of the meat spread found it matched exactly with the meat spread prepared by the party hostess—according to a private family recipe. Becker died in the electric chair in April 1924.

Beckett sisters   white slave kidnap victims

During the early 1800s, no kidnapping of young girls by the infamous Mississippi River procurers excited the American public as much as that of two teenage sisters, Rose and Mary Beckett of St. Louis, who were abducted by the notorious Sam Purdy gang.

It was the custom of these river procurers to buy up young girls from their impoverished parents and transport them down the Mississippi by flatboat to Natchez, where they were sold at auction to whoremasters from various Southern cities. Only when they could not find enough willing girls available to be "sold down the river"—hence the origin of the phrase—did the procurers go in for actual kidnapping. Such was the fate of the Beckett girls, who wound up at Natchez in early 1805 and were sold off after spirited bidding by various bordello keepers and "floating hog pen" operators. The girls were sold as a set for $400 to the proprietor of a notorious New Orleans establishment called The Swamp.

Here the girls were incarcerated, and here they would have remained had it not been for a reformer named Carlos White, who had tracked the Purdy gang from St. Louis and scoured the New Orleans fleshpots for the Beckett sisters. A man of action, White used force to rescue the two sisters from The Swamp, shooting one of their guards to death and pistol-whipping another while the girls climbed out a window and escaped.

White eventually reunited the pair with their parents and, unlike the fate of most "ruined girls," the Beckett sisters became famous heroines of the day.

See also: SAM PURDY.

Beckwourth, Jim (1800–1866 or 1867) mountaineer and thief

Trader, scout and all-around frontiersman, Jim Beckwourth was easily the most famous of the black adventurers of the West.

Beckwourth was born in Virginia, the son of Sir Jennings Beckwith (who was descended from minor Irish aristocrats) and a mulatto slave woman. In 1822 Beckwourth (the spelling he adopted) appeared in Missouri as a free black man. Two years later, he joined Gen. William Ashley's expedition to the Rocky Mountains. It is difficult to measure Beckwourth's accomplishments because his own accounts make him easily the greatest Indian fighter and lover of Indian women of all time; yet his reputation grew quickly, and migrants coming West in wagon trains bid high for his services as a guide through the Sierras. Beckwourth also did a thriving business supplying these migrants with horses. To that end, he formed the biggest gang of horse thieves in California's history, together with famed mountain men Old Bill Williams and Pegleg Smith. The gang's greatest raid occurred in 1840, when, with a large band of Indians, they slipped undetected over Cajon Pass. On May 14 Juan Perez, the administrator at San Gabriel Mission, reported to the authorities that every ranch in the valley from San Gabriel to San Bernardino had been stripped of its horse stock. Although posses occasionally caught up to the horse thieves, they were beaten off. Finally, a posse of 75 men under Gov. Jose Antonio Carillo cornered the gang at Resting Springs. In the ensuing gun battle, Beckwourth justified the tales of his prowess with a gun, killing or wounding several members of the posse. Scores of horses were killed and others so badly wounded they had to be destroyed, but Beckwourth and company still got away with more than 1,200 head.

Eventually, Beckwourth turned to ranching, managing to build up his stock with stolen horses until 1855, when he barely got out of the state ahead of vigilantes out to hang him. He moved to the Colorado Territory, scouted again for the army and later took up city life in Denver as a storekeeper. This activity bored him, and in 1864 he went back to the wilderness, acting as a guide for John M. Chivington in the infamous Sand Creek Massacre. Perhaps unwisely, Beckwourth then started trading with the Indians again, and in 1866 he was allegedly poisoned by the Crows while visiting

their village. Other reports have him dying in 1867 near Denver.

See also: THOMAS L. "PEGLEG" SMITH, WILLIAM S. "OLD BILL" WILLIAMS.

begging

The practice, or perhaps more correctly the profession, of begging doubtlessly goes back to prehistoric times. It appeared in America almost with the first settlers and continues to the present day. In New York one resourceful entrepreneur, after years of successful panhandling, opened a school in 1979 to teach the art of begging. (Lesson One: On the subway, pick out one target, stand before him and whine loudly, "Please!" If that doesn't work, get on one knee and continue to plead until he does give.)

There have been many legendary beggars in American history. One of the most successful during the 1920s was New York City's "Breadline Charlie," who eschewed use of a harness or other equipment to make him appear crippled or helpless. Instead, he carried in his pocket small chunks of stale bread, and when in a crowd, he would drop a piece on the sidewalk. Then he would "discover" it, let out a scream of ecstasy and gobble it down as though he hadn't eaten in days. This pitiful scene always touched the hearts and purses of passersby.

An earlier faker, George Gray, had earned, by his own confession, at least $10,000 a year for many years around the turn of the century thanks to his incredible ability to feign an epileptic fit or a heart attack, usually in front of the residence of a well-to-do Manhattanite. After one of his many arrests, Gray was taken by police to Presbyterian Hospital, where doctors pronounced him "a curiosity of nature in that he possesses the power of accelerating or retarding his heart action at will." A businessman named Jesse L. Strauss gave police a considerable argument when they tried to roust Gray as he lay writhing on the sidewalk. Strauss had his money in hand and was ready to give it to the unfortunate man so that he could seek medical attention. Gray was wanted as the era's most professional "fit-thrower" by police in a dozen Eastern cities.

Robert I. Ingles was an energetic beggar who toured the country for years on a regular begging beat until his death in a charity ward in New York during the 1950s. On his person was found a pass book showing he had $2,500 in a Manhattan bank. In due course, it was found he had 42 other savings accounts with a total value of well over $100,000.

Rose Dym (born Anna Dym), a nightmarishly homely daughter of a retired Brooklyn pushcart peddler, hit the bright-light district in 1929. She was 17 then, a stage-struck little autograph hunter. Almost immediately, she developed a knack for making a pest of herself, and people gave her whatever she asked for just to get rid of her. Soon, she was asking for money. Her technique worked so well that after a while, she would accept folding money only. Celebrities quailed at Rose's glance. Jack Dempsey once fled his own restaurant when she walked in to put the touch on his customers. In time, Broadway Rose prospered to the extent that she could refuse donations from nobodies with the admonition, "Go get yourself a reputation, jerk, before I'll take your scratch."

Probably the most profitable approach used today is a beggar in a business suit who embarrassedly tells victims he has lost his wallet and needs commuter fare home. Since home is a far way off, a minimum bite is $5. While such a routine can be most remunerative, it probably will never earn the profits attained by a New York beggar who used to pose as a leper. He was a tall, gaunt, olive-skinned man who'd haunt shadowy alleys and emerge only when he saw a prospective sucker coming along. "Mister . . . I'm a leper. . . . Will you drop some money on the sidewalk for me? . . . Will you, please? . . . For a poor leper?" All this time, the "leper" would keep moving toward his quarry, his arms outstretched—and many a poor soul was known to have reacted by dropping his entire wallet and then racing out of harm's way.

Behan, John (c. 1840–?) lawman and Wyatt Earp foe

John Behan was sheriff of Cochise County, Ariz. for only a year from 1881 to 1882, but since that was the period of the Earp-Clanton feud and such events as the gunfight at the O.K. Corral, he is accorded much more attention in western lore than the average crooked sheriff of the day. Behan was a firm enemy of Wyatt Earp, the bone of contention between them being the sheriff's office, which Behan had and Earp wanted. Most sheriffs devoted the bulk of their time to collecting county taxes, leaving the gunfighting to their deputies. Remuneration for the job was largely a percentage of the tax collection, which, combined with a reasonable amount of graft from road-building and other contracts that a sheriff often controlled, could make such a lawman wealthy. At the time, the sheriff's job in Cochise County was worth $30,000 a year and Behan made $40,000.

In his fight to retain control of the office, Behan represented the cowboy and rustler element, or Democratic Party, while Earp represented the saloonkeeper/gambler-townie interests, or generally the Republican forces. It is against this background that events such as the O.K. Corral shoot-out must be seen. To win the support of the out-county elements, Behan allied himself with the Clanton forces and hired some of their gunmen to help in the collection of taxes. Elimination of the Clantons would weaken Behan's hold on his office. Behan tried to stop the shoot-out at the O.K. but was contemptuously ignored by the Earps and Doc Holliday. He could do nothing to prevent the magnificent duel, or callous slaughter, depending on one's viewpoint, that followed.

Despite the killing of one Clanton and two McLowery brothers, the Earps failed to wipe out their enemies, and in the end, they were driven out of Tombstone by a combination of legal charges and public opinion. Behan's triumph was short lived, however. In 1882 he faced charges of financial irregularities and stepped down. After leaving office, he was indicted for continuing to collect taxes after his term.

Behan disappeared before the indictment could be served and nothing was heard about him for a few years. In 1887 he surfaced as a turnkey at the Yuma Penitentiary, where he became something of a hero by helping to quell a prison riot, although in the uproar he locked the warden in with a bunch of knife-brandishing convicts. No effort was made to return him to Cochise County for prosecution. Two years later, Behan came under another cloud when he was suspected of helping some convicts escape. For the second time in his life, Behan found it prudent to fade from the scene.

See also: WYATT EARP, O.K. CORRAL.

Beidler, John X. (1831–1890) Montana vigilante hangman

In the 1860s John Beidler's "long rope" became the terror of Montana's badmen, and Beidler became known as the most zealous vigilante that ever looped a noose. In one six-week period 26 outlaws were hanged, and Beidler's rope did the job in every case.

Beidler, a plump, walrus-faced man, was born in Montjoy, Pa. of German stock. Even to his friends in the West, he was known as a rather joyless person. Some biographers are unsure how much of Beidler's appetite for hanging sprang from a respect for law and order and how much from a morbid pleasure in hanging people. But whatever else was said about Beidler, he was certainly brave enough in taking credit for his acts. He never wore a mask, as did so many other vigilantes. If some of the "boys" ever wanted to get even with him, they knew where to find him.

Beidler's first vigilante act took place in Kansas, where, as the head of a posse, he disabled a gang of lawbreakers by firing a howitzer loaded with printer's type at them. In contradiction to the general description of his somberness, Beidler said, as the victims painfully dug the type slugs out of their bodies, that he saw no need for a necktie party, pointing out they could become good citizens now that "they have the opportunity to learn to read." A few years later, in the Alder Gulch–Bannack area of lawless Montana, Beidler came to the fore as the hanging vigilante. His victims included all the important badmen in the area. Beidler's style was casual in most cases: a handy tree limb or corral gate, the noose tightened and a box kicked out from under the victim's feet. With the coming of more organized law and order, the need for Beidler's long rope ended, and he became a businessman and saloon keeper, later serving as collector of customs for Idaho and Montana. He held that post until his death on January 22, 1890 in Helena.

See also: BANNACK, MONTANA TERRITORY; VIGILANTES OF MONTANA.

Bell, Tom (1825–1856) outlaw doctor

Known as the Outlaw Doc, Tom Bell, whose real name was Thomas J. Hodges, is believed to have been the only physician to ride the western bandit trail. On a criminal job he would carry as many implements as a doctor would carry on a house visit, in one case totaling up to six revolvers and a like number of knives and, presumably because of his superior medical knowledge, a chest protector fashioned from sheet iron.

Born in Rome, Tenn., Bell took part in the Mexican War. During that period he was trained as a doctor and emerged as a fully qualified practitioner. Bell followed the '49ers to California in search of gold but came up empty. He supported himself by gambling at cards, now and then taking time out to treat a gunshot victim. Exactly how or why he turned to crime is not known, but in 1855 he was doing time for theft in Angel Island Prison. There he befriended a vicious criminal named Bill Gristy, and within a matter of weeks the pair engineered an escape. The two then organized their own outlaw gang with five other hard cases and began pulling stage holdups.

On August 12, 1856 Bell and his confederates attempted to hold up the Camptonville-Marysville stage, which had $100,000 in gold bullion aboard. They killed a woman passenger and wounded two men but were beaten back by the stage's shotgun guards who killed two of them. The murder of the woman passenger sparked a huge manhunt for the bandits. There were legal posses under assorted lawmen and illegal posses of vigilantes who vowed to reach the killers first and mete out fast western justice. By the end of September, Gristy had been arrested and, under threat of being handed over to a lynch mob, had turned stoolpigeon in his jail cell, identifying Doc Bell as the main culprit. The official and unofficial posses were quickly back on the trail in a race to locate Bell first. The sheriff of

Stockton came in a close second. He found Doc on October 4, 1856 dangling from a tree on the Nevada City road.

Bender family mass murderers

The Hell Benders, as they came to be called, were the most murderous family America ever produced. They robbed as a family, killed as a family and may well have been slaughtered together as a family. When the Benders moved into Cherryvale in southeastern Kansas during the early 1870s, no one thought ill of them, and in fact, most of the young blades around were much impressed by the beauty of young Kate Bender, whose age was around 18 or 20.

The family consisted of Old Man William John, aged about 60, Ma Bender (no Christian name has ever been ascribed to her), young Kate and her brother, John, who, while older in years, was certainly less mature mentally than his sister. He was actually a moron whose main activity in life appeared to be cackling insanely.

The family maintained a log cabin outside of town consisting of one large room divided by a canvas curtain. They served drink and meals to travelers on one side of the curtain and slept on the other side. At night, they set up some beds on the public side to put up travelers wishing to stay the night. If they served meals to someone they knew, the Benders were most hospitable and sent them cheerfully on their way. However, if the patron was a lone traveler and looked like he had money, he never left the Bender cabin alive. Kate would sit him down on a bench against the canvas curtain and presumably flirt with him until he was smitten—in the most literal sense of the word. Either Old Man Bender or moronic John would be on the other side of the canvas, and when they made out the outline of the man's head, they would bash it in with a sledgehammer.

The dead man would be taken down to the cellar through a trap door and stripped of all money and valuables. Later, the victim would be buried on the grounds around the house, and Ma Bender would plant flowers over the spot.

The Benders' last victim was a Dr. William H. York of Fort Scott, Kan. Passing through Cherryvale in March 1873, he asked for a place where he could eat and perhaps stay the night and was directed to the Benders'. When he disappeared, his brother, a lawyer named Col. A. M. York, followed his trail. He traced Dr. York to Cherryvale and no further. The Benders told Col. York that his brother had never come to their place. Kate Bender invited the colonel to sit a while and she would fix him a cup of tea. She offered him a seat by the canvas, but York said he wanted to ride on past

Cherryvale to see if he could pick up his brother's trail. Then John came in with a jug of cider and suggested the lawyer have a swig before leaving. York refused the offer and said he wanted to cover some ground before night fell. If he failed to pick up his brother's trail, he announced, he would be coming back.

The next day a neighbor rode past the Bender place and noted the door was open and the family wagon nowhere in sight. He went inside and discovered the Benders had gone, belongings and all. When Col. York returned to Cherryvale, the trail gone cold, he was informed of the facts. A group of men went out to the Bender place. They looked in the cellar and found some loose dirt there. They dug and discovered the body of Dr. York.

They started digging around the cabin and found 10 other bodies, all with their skulls crushed. The Benders had something like a two-day start, but if they were in their wagon, they still might be caught. A posse of seven men headed by Col. York started out to scour the surrounding area in the hopes of finding the fugitive family. When they came back some weeks later, they said they had failed to find the Benders. But the posse members were downright uncommunicative about where they had been; they didn't seem to want to talk about it. Col. York lost interest in hunting for the murderous family and took his brother's body with him for reburial.

The news of the Hell Benders spread from coast to coast. Souvenir hunters descended on Cherryvale and soon leveled the Bender place to the ground. Nails and boards said to be from the Benders' house sold for high prices in New York and San Francisco. Months passed, then years, but none of the four Benders turned up. Of course, there was a rash of false identifications. In 1889 Leroy Dick of Cherryvale traveled to Michigan and identified Mrs. Almira Griffith and her daughter, Mrs. Sarah Eliza Davis, as Ma Bender and Kate. They were returned to Kansas, and out of 13 persons, seven agreed with Dick's identification. Proof was then produced that one of the women had been married in Michigan in 1872, and the case against the two women was dropped. There were a number of other false identifications, all of which proved unreliable.

In 1909 George Downer lay dying in a Chicago suburb. He called for his lawyer, and in his last hour, Downer told the lawyer and his wife that he had been a member of the posse that had killed the Benders. After catching up with them, the posse had butchered the family so badly they felt they could not reveal the facts; they therefore buried the Benders in a 20-foot well and covered them over with dirt. In 1910 a man named Harker, dying in a New Mexico cow camp,

confessed he too had helped kill the Benders. He also mentioned the 20-foot well—at that time Downer's confession had not yet become common knowledge. Harker said the posse had taken several thousand dollars from the bodies of the Benders, money they believed to have been stolen from the victims. As late as 1940 the same story surfaced from another source, George Stark, who said his late father had made an identical confession to him but had pledged him to secrecy until after his death.

Were the confessions true? After the 1909 and 1910 confessions a search was made for the well in the area identified by Downer and Harker. But the area had long since been planted with corn. If the Benders were there, they had been plowed under.

Of all the missing members of the Hell Benders, William "Old Man" Bender (c. 1813–1884?) is worth special mention since, if any of the family did survive the manhunt for them and was not killed, it was the elder Bender. If that was what happened, Old Man Bender died in 1884, 11 years after he had fled Kansas. In that year an aged individual who answered to his description and spoke with a German accent, as Bender had, was seized in the Montana Territory for a murder near Salmon, Idaho Territory. The victim's skull had been crushed from behind with a blunt instrument. The method, plus the suspect's physical appearance and the fact that he grew sullen when the name Bender was mentioned, convinced the arresting officers that they had the much-sought Old Man Bender.

The suspect was clamped in ankle irons and tossed in the Salmon jail while the authorities back in Kansas were notified to send someone to make an identification. The next morning the old man was dead. In a desperate effort to escape, he had tried to cut off his foot and had bled to death. Since there was no ice house in town, the sheriff's deputies tried to preserve the body in a calcifying pool. It didn't work, and by the time witnesses arrived from Kansas, identification was no longer possible.

However, since it seemed like a waste to give up such an attraction as a heinous murderer, the dead man's skull, identified as "Bender's skull," was put on display in the Buckthorn Saloon in Salmon, where it remained, an object of many toasts, until the onset of Prohibition in 1920. Then it, like the rest of the Benders, disappeared.

Benedict's Sentence *judge's speech*

Probably the most famous judicial speech ever made in the Old West was the death sentence pronounced by Judge Kirby Benedict and referred to with solemn awe as Benedict's Sentence.

Benedict was an extremely learned man who was appointed to the Supreme Court of New Mexico by President Franklin Pierce in 1853. Previously, he had spent all his adult life in Illinois, where he was a highly regarded member of the bar and a friend of both Abraham Lincoln and Stephen A. Douglas. On the New Mexico bench, Benedict handed down several opinions that are often cited as examples of fine judicial writing, but he is unquestionably best remembered for his sentencing in Taos of Jose Maria Martin. Martin had been convicted of a particularly heinous murder, a verdict with which Benedict fully concurred. Judge Benedict addressed the prisoner as follows:

Jose Maria Martin, stand up. Jose Maria Martin, you have been indicted, tried and convicted, by a jury of your countrymen, of the crime of murder, and the Court is now about to pass upon you the dread sentence of the law. As a usual thing, Jose Maria Martin, it is a painful duty for the Judge of a court of justice to pronounce upon a human being the sentence of death. There is something horrible about it, and the mind of the Court naturally revolts at the performance of such a duty. Happily, however, your case is relieved of all such unpleasant features and the Court takes the positive pleasure in sentencing you to death!

You are a young man, Jose Maria Martin; apparently of good physical condition and robust health. Ordinarily, you might have looked forward to many years of life, and the Court has no doubt you have, and have expected to die at a green old age; but you are about to be cut off in consequence of your own act. Jose Maria Martin, it is now the springtime, in a little while the grass will be springing up green in these beautiful valleys, and, on these broad mesas and mountain sides, flowers will be blooming; birds will be singing their sweet carols, and nature will be pleasant and men will want to stay; but none of this for you, Jose Maria Martin; the flowers will not bloom for you, Jose Maria Martin; the birds will not carol for you, Jose Maria Martin; when these things come to gladden the senses of men, you will be occupying a space about six feet by two beneath the sod, and the green grass and those beautiful flowers will be growing about your lowly head.

The sentence of the Court is that you be taken from this place to the county jail; that you be kept there safely and securely confined, in the custody of the sheriff, until the day appointed for your execution. (Be very careful, Mr. Sheriff, that he have no opportunity to escape and that you have him at the appointed place at the appointed time); that you be so kept, Jose Maria Martin until—(Mr. Clerk, on what day of the month does Friday about two weeks from this time come?

"March 22nd, your honor.") Very well, until Friday, the 22nd day of March, when you will be taken by the sheriff from your place of confinement to some safe and convenient spot within the county (that is in your discretion, Mr. Sheriff, you are only confined to the limits of this county), and that you there be hanged by the neck until you are dead, and the Court was about to add, Jose Maria Martin, 'May God have mercy on your soul,' but the Court will not assume the responsibility of asking an allwise Providence to do that which a jury of your peers has refused to do. The Lord couldn't have mercy on your soul. However, if you affect any religious belief, or are connected with any religious organization, it might be well for you to send for your priest or minister, and get from him—well—such consolation as you can, but the Court advises you to place no reliance upon anything of that kind! Mr. Sheriff, remove the prisoner.

The only footnote to Judge Benedict's sentence was that Jose Maria Martin did escape and never paid the supreme penalty.

See also: ROY BEAN.

Beni, Jules (?–1861) outlaw

An ageless and larcenous Frenchman, Jules Beni operated a trading post near Lodgepole Creek, Colorado Territory around 1850, where anything went with no questions asked. An Eastern reporter called it the "wickedest city on the plains." It wasn't much of a city until a stage station was built next to it and a small settlement sprung up around it. The city became known as Julesburg in honor of old Beni.

The real joke was putting Beni in charge of the stagecoach station; instantly, the line was plagued by holdups. Considering that the bandits always seemed to know which stages carried important money and which didn't, it was only a matter of time until Beni came under suspicion. Beni was dismissed and replaced by Jack Slade, one of the most notorious killers the West ever produced. Needless to say, Slade and Beni did not get along, especially as Beni went about his stagecoach robbing a little more obviously now. The scene was set for a showdown, and Jack Slade came out second best. Beni blasted him with a shotgun and left him for dead, but miraculously, Slade recovered after the doctors had given up on him. That was lucky for Beni because the local citizens had taken him in custody and were getting set to hang him, founder of Julesburg or not. When Slade pulled through Beni was released after promising to vacate the area. He did, only to return about a year later. According to one account—Slade's—Beni tried to kill his adversary again. In any event, whether Beni found Slade or Slade found Beni, the fact was that Slade captured the Frenchman, tied him to a fence post, and used him for target practice. Then Slade killed Beni and cut off his ears as souvenirs. According to most accounts, Slade used one ear as a watch fob and sold the other for drinking money.

Today, Julesburg is a quiet little town of about 25,000 persons with very little of the wickedness that its founders had bequeathed it.

See also: JOSEPH "JACK" SLADE.

Benson family murders   a not-so-ideal son

During the 1980s—the decade of greed—it was inevitable that scandals and homicides among the rich and famous received a great deal of attention. The Benson family murders in Florida were a case in point.

Mrs. Margaret Benson, a 58-year-old widow and heiress to a $10 million tobacco fortune after the death of her wealthy husband in 1980, moved herself and her grown children to a life of self-indulgent ease in Naples, Fla. She supported her children: a married daughter, Carol Lynn Benson Kendall; her older son, Steven; and her young adopted son, Scott. Of the boys, Steven—seemingly the ideal son—was by far the more responsible and dependable and had taken charge of managing the family's affairs. Twenty-one-year-old Scott, by contrast, was always a problem, prone to violence and the use of drugs, snorting cocaine and inhaling nitrous oxide (laughing gas). Given to expensive clothes and flashy sports cars, Scott had difficulty living within a $7,000-a-month allowance. On occasion, he beat his mother and sister, and once the police had to haul him away to a drug-treatment center. Still, the members of the Benson family remained loyal and loving toward him.

In 1985, Steven bought a $215,000 home complete with tennis court and swimming pool, which aroused his mother's suspicions about how he could afford to do so. She began to realize he had been skimming money from a company the family owned. She made plans to have an audit conducted and hinted at disinheriting Steven. One summer day in 1985, the family climbed into their Chrevolet Suburban van for a drive when Steven said he had forgotten something and reentered the Benson mansion. While he was gone, two pipe bombs sent off in the van. Mrs. Benson, now 63, and young Scott died instantly, and Carol was badly injured.

After recovering, Carol told investigators that Steven had made no effort to aid her after the explosion and had shown little emotion at the scene. He was eventually charged with murder. At Steven's trial in 1986, Carol shocked the court by revealing that Scott Benson was actually her son and that her mother—actually Scott's grandmother—had adopted him.

Steven Benson's defense was that the pipe bombs had probably been made by the drug-crazed Scott, who was seeking to destroy the family. The pipe bombs, the defense argued, must have gone off sooner than Scott had anticipated. However, prosecution witnesses contradicted that line of reasoning; one of them testified that Steven had once declared he had learned how to make pipe bombs years before. A purchase order for materials used for such devices was found to bear Steven's finger- and palm prints.

While no one had actually seen Steven plant the bombs, the circumstantial evidence was strong enough for the jury to quickly bring in a guilty verdict. Steven, then 35, was sentenced to two consecutive terms of life imprisonment with no parole for at least 50 years.

Bergdoll, Grover Cleveland (1893–1966)   World War I draft dodger

No draft dodger in American history was as infamous as Grover Cleveland Bergdoll, a handsome Philadelphia millionaire playboy who refused to report to his local draft board in 1917. Bergdoll was not captured until January 1920; eventually, he was sentenced to five years imprisonment. In a bizarre escape, Bergdoll talked his military escort into allowing him to retrieve a gold cache of $105,000 he said was hidden in his home, took them there and then eluded them. Over the next two decades the federal government spent millions of dollars trying to recapture him. Private "vigilantes" tried to kidnap, lynch or murder him. During this time Bergdoll flitted between America and various hideouts in Europe, but remarkably, he spent a large portion of the time hidden in the family mansion in Philadelphia with his wife and children.

An overview of newspaper headlines perhaps best illustrates the comic quality of the desperate hunt. Some read:

SEAS SEARCHED IN BERGDOLL HUNT . . . BERGDOLL DISGUISED AS WOMAN POSSIBLY . . . SEARCH FRUITLESS. . . . BANKER COUNSELS PATIENCE IN BERGDOLL CASE: HAS NO CLUE TO THE FUGITIVE . . . INDIANA MARSHAL SAYS DRAFT DODGER WENT INTO KENTUCKY . . . MAN IN FEMALE GARB TAKEN FOR BERGDOLL . . . BERGDOLL NEARING MEXICO . . . SEEK BERGDOLL IN MOHAWK TOWNS . . . BERGDOLL SUSPECT FREED . . . BERGDOLL CAPTURE HOAX OF SUMMER . . . ONEONTA PRISONER NOT BERGDOLL . . .

BERGDOLL REPORTED NEAR CITY . . . BERGDOLL 'ARRESTED' AGAIN.

Perhaps the most frantic headline of all appeared in the *New York Times:* BERGDOLL'S INITIALS AND ARROW ON TREE.

Finally tiring of the chase, Bergdoll—who had slipped in and out of the country at least a half-dozen times—surrendered on May 27, 1939, sailing into New York aboard the German liner *Bremen.* Reports said he had fled Hitler's Germany to avoid being drafted into the army there; however, as an American citizen, Bergdoll was not subject to German military service. Bergdoll's case was debated in Congress and pressure was put on President Franklin D. Roosevelt to deny amnesty that had been granted to all other draft evaders and deserters. Bergdoll was sentenced to a total of seven years at hard labor. He was released early in 1944. Nineteen years later, suffering mental deterioration, he was confined to a psychiatric hospital in Richmond, Va. He died there on January 27, 1966.

Berger, Meyer (1898–1959) reporter

Although totally lacking the flamboyance of such other great crime reporters as Ike White, Charles MacArthur and Ben Hecht, Meyer "Mike" Berger was probably the greatest of his or any other day. He brought a sense of quiet, self-effacing dignity and a devotion to accuracy for which the field was hardly renowned. All doors were open to Berger, whether they belonged to distinguished citizens or secretive mobsters. Whenever a rampaging horde of crime reporters from the more than 10 New York City newspapers then in existence would descend on the home of a well-known citizen drawn into a criminal investigation, they would shove Berger to the front and announce: "This is Mr. Meyer Berger of the *New York Times.* He would like to ask some questions." This same respect for the *Times* man was shown in a most unusual way by Arthur (Dutch Schultz) Flegenheimer after the reporter had covered one of his many trials. An incensed Schultz sought out Berger, demanded to know if he had written the story in which someone was quoted as saying Dutch was a "pushover for a blonde." Quaking, Berger admitted he was. "Pushover for a blonde!" the gangster raged. "What kind of language is that to use in the *New York Times?*"

Berger was nominated for a Pulitzer Prize in 1932 for his stories on Al Capone's Chicago trial that had captured the character of America's most famous gangster far better than the more so-called definitive efforts. When Abe Reles, the Murder Inc. informer, "went out the window" of a Coney Island hotel in which he was being held under police "safekeeping," Berger climbed out on the ledge where Reles would have stood—if indeed he had gone willingly—and told his readers what Reles saw and heard and what he must have felt. Berger won a Pulitzer Prize for his brilliant coverage of the 1949 shooting of 13 persons in Camden, N.J. by an insane veteran named Howard Unruh. The reporter followed the mad killer's trail, talking to 50 persons who had watched segments of Unruh's movements. The account, written in two and a half hours and running 4,000 words, was printed in the *Times* without any editorial changes.

When Berger died nine years later, very few of his colleagues knew that he had given his prize money to Unruh's aged mother.

Berkman, Alexander (1870–1936) anarchist and would-be assassin

In one of the most tortured assassination attempts ever, anarchist Alexander Berkman tried but failed to kill a leading industrialist of the late 19th century.

Few men were more hated by labor and radical forces in this country than Henry Clay Frick, chairman and strongman of the Carnegie Steel Co., who was blamed as much or more for the company's abysmal working conditions as his partner, Andrew Carnegie.

During the terrible Homestead Steel Strike of 1892, Carnegie left for a vacation in Scotland to avoid being around when the great labor crisis erupted over the workers' refusal to accept a reduction in wages. Carnegie wanted the strike crushed by any means, and no one was more capable and indeed eager to do so than Frick. He recruited a private army of 300 Pinkertons and fortified the company's mills at Homestead, Pa. Then, under cover of night, he sent the Pinkertons by barge up the Monongahela River. They opened fire on the strikers without warning, killing several, including a small boy, and wounding scores of others. The strikers countered with burning oil, dynamite and homemade cannon. With his army stymied, Frick turned to the governor for aid and 8,000 militiamen were dispatched to the scene.

During the stalemate Frick continued his opposition to unionization despite a rising anger in the country. On July 23, 1892 Frick was in his private office with his chief aide, John Leishman, planning company strategy when a young man posing as an agent for a New York "employment firm" received permission to enter.

Actually, the man was 21-year-old Alexander Berkman, a fiery anarchist and lover of another famous anarchist, Emma Goldman. Berkman was outraged at Frick's behavior during the strike and resolved to assassinate him as an act of liberation on behalf of his working comrades. He first tried to do so by making a bomb but failed to produce a workable model. Emma then went into the streets as a prostitute to raise money in order to buy a gun. She was picked up by a kindly older man who guessed her amateur status and sent her home with $10. With that, Berkman bought the assassination weapon.

The actual attempt was best described by a contemporary account in *Harper's Weekly:*

> Mr. Frick had been sitting with his face half turned from the door, his right leg thrown over the arm of his chair . . . and almost before he had realized the presence of a third party in the room, the man fired at him. The aim had been for the brain, but the sudden turning of the chairman spoiled it, and the bullet ploughed its way into the left side of his neck. The shock staggered Mr. Frick. Mr. Leishman jumped up and faced the assailant. As he did so another shot was fired and a second bullet entered Mr. Frick's neck, but on the left side. Again the aim had been bad. Mr. Leishman, who is a small man, sprang around the desk, and just as the assailant was firing the third time, he seized his hand and threw it upward and back. The bullet embedded itself in the ceiling back of where the man was standing . . . Mr. Frick recovered almost instantly from the two shots and ran to the assistance of Leishman, who was grappling with the would-be assassin . . . The exertion made the blood spurt from his wounds and it dyed the clothing of the assailant.
>
> The struggle lasted fully two minutes. Not a word was spoken by any one, and no cry had been uttered. The fast-increasing crowd in the street looked up at it open-mouthed and apparently paralyzed (Frick's upper-floor office could be readily seen into from across the street). There were no calls for the police and no apparent sign of excitement, only spellbound interest. The three men swayed to and fro in struggle, getting all the time nearer to the windows. Once the assailant managed to shake himself loose, but before he could bring his revolver again into play, Mr. Leishman knocked his knees from under him, and the combined weight of himself and Mr. Frick bore the man to the floor. In the fall, he succeeded in loosening one hand and with it he drew an old-fashioned dirk-knife from his pocket and began slashing with it. He held it in his left hand. Mr. Frick was trying to hold him on that side. Again and again, the knife plunged into Mr. Frick until seven distinct wounds had been made, and then Mr. Frick succeeded in catching and holding the arm.
>
> At the first sign of the knife the crowd in the street seemed to recover itself and there were loud calls of "Police!" "Fire!" The clerks in the main office recov-

Anarchist Alexander Berkman is shown after his assassination attempt on steel magnate Henry Clay Frick during the Homestead Steel Strike of 1892.

ered from their stupefaction, and rushed pell-mell into the office of their chief. Deputy Sheriff May, who happened to be in the office, was in the lead. He drew a revolver, and was about to use it, when Mr. Frick cried: "Don't shoot! Don't kill him! The law will punish him." The deputy's hand was seized and held by one of the clerks, while half a dozen others fell on the prostrate assailant. The police were in the office in a few minutes and took the man away. Fully two thousand people had gathered in the street, and there were cries of "Shoot him! Lynch him!"

Despite a total of nine wounds, Frick was back at his desk within a week, but Berkman spent 14 years in prison before being pardoned in 1906. Like most acts of terrorism, his attack on Frick had not helped the intended beneficiaries. In fact, the strikers generally denounced the act, though many with seemingly little conviction. From 1906 until 1919, when they were deported in the Red Scare roundups, Berkman and Goldman became the primary spokespersons for American anarchism. They were sent back to their native Russia, where they were welcomed by the new Soviet government, but the incompatibility of anarchism and communism soon forced them both to leave. Berkman settled first in Sweden, then Germany and finally in France. He continued his anarchist writing and organized and edited many of Goldman's work. He did some translating and ghostwriting for European and American publishers but needed contributions from friends and comrades to survive. Both despondent and ill, he committed suicide in 1936. H. L. Mencken wrote of Berkman that he was a "transparently honest man . . . a shrewder and a braver spirit than has been seen in public among us since the Civil War."

Berkowitz, David R.   See "SON OF SAM."

Berman, Otto "Abbadabba" (1889–1935) policy game fixer

Few rackets have ever produced as much money for underworld coffers as the numbers game, and although the profit slice is 40 percent or more, crime bosses have always searched for ways to give the suckers even less of a break.

Otto "Abbadabba" Berman was for a time a magician at this, as his nickname indicates. During the 1930s Berman devised a system for rigging the results of the game so that only a lesser-played number would win. He worked for Dutch Schultz, the crime czar who controlled the bulk of the numbers game in New York, including most of the action in black Harlem. At the time, the winning number was derived from the betting statistics at various race tracks. The underworld could not control the figures at the New York tracks, but during the periods when those courses were closed, the number was based on the results from tracks that the underworld had successfully infiltrated, such as New Orleans' Fair Grounds, Chicago's Hawthorne and Cincinnati's Coney Island. Berman was able to figure out how much money to put into the mutual machines to have a low-played number come out. It was estimated that Abbadabba's magic added 10 percent to every million dollars a day the underworld took in.

In 1935 Dutch Schultz was assassinated by vote of the Luciano-Lansky national crime syndicate, allegedly because Schultz had announced he intended to kill Thomas E. Dewey, whose racket-busting activities were hampering underworld operations. Luciano especially was concerned about the ramifications of killing a man of Dewey's stature. His concern, however, was no doubt heightened by the opportunity he saw to take over the Schultz numbers racket. Schultz and three of his favorite underlings were cut down at the Palace Chophouse in Newark while having dinner. Unfortunately for the mob, one of those shot with Schultz was Berman. His loss was to cost the mob literally millions of dollars a year, for while others tried to imitate the technique of what Luciano's aide, Vito Genovese, called "the Yid adding machine," few approached even a fraction of his results.

See also: NUMBERS RACKET, DUTCH SCHULTZ.

Berrett-Molway taxi cab case   murder trial

The murder trial of two men, Clement Molway and Louis Berrett, both Boston taxi drivers, in February 1934 is memorable for the sobering second thoughts it caused the jury. Eight undisputed eyewitnesses identified the pair as the men who murdered an employee of the Paramount Theatre in Lynn, Mass. Just before the case was to go to the jury, a man convicted with two others in another robbery-murder confessed to the crime. Berrett and Molway were freed and won compensation. Newspapers widely reported the deep impression made on the jurors, who admitted they would have convicted the innocent men. Typical was the following comment of the jury foreman, Hosea E. Bradstreet:

Those witnesses were so positive of their identification that it was only natural that we should be misled. While I sat at the trial I somehow hated the thought of sending those two men to the electric chair; but we were sworn to perform our duty and we would have done it—to the best of our ability. . . . This trial has taught me one thing. Before I was a firm believer in capital punishment, I'm not now.

Bertillon system   criminal identification method

From the mid-1880s through 1904 or 1905 the standard method of criminal identification in the United States was the system invented in 1883 by Alphonse Bertillon, a Frenchman. Bertillon concluded there were 12 measurements on an adult that do not change, such as the length and width of the head, the length of the left foot, left forearm and left little finger, and so on. Criminals were photographed and measured according to this method, and records were compiled on the assumption that no two people would ever look alike and have exactly the same measurements. There were several flaws in the Bertillon system, not the least being that more than one arresting officer often made entry of a subject's "pedigree" and the material would be contradictory. The real death knell for the system came when two prisoners lodged in the same penitentiary were found to have the same Bertillon measurements, looked alike and even had virtually the same names. The Will West–William West case was the prime factor in convincing law authorities to switch to fingerprinting as an identification method.

See also: FINGERPRINTING, "WEST BROTHERS."

Bethea, Rainey (1914–1936) last publicly executed man

The last public execution in America was held in 1936. The victim was a 22-year-old black man named Rainey Bethea, and his execution at Owensboro, Ky. remains one of the most shameful episodes in U.S. history.

Because Rainey had killed a 70-year-old white woman, public opinion was at a fever pitch, and the county sheriff, a woman named Florence Thompson, decided to stage the execution in an open field so that thousands of witnesses could be accommodated. By the night before the execution, Owensboro was swamped with visitors from all over the country; by dawn more than 20,000 persons had gathered at the execution site. Only six blacks were present—virtually all the local blacks had fled the town during the previous night's drunken revelry, which was punctuated by calls for a mass lynching. Each time the hangman tested the scaffold, it snapped open to the appreciative cheers of the crowd. Bethea reached the scaffold at 5:12 A.M. and the execution moved briskly, authorities now fearing the crowd might get out of hand. When the bolt snapped, a joyous roar swept over the field and the crowd surged closer. Souvenir hunters almost immediately attacked the dangling, still-warm body, stripping off pieces of the condemned man's clothing and in some instances trying to carve out chunks of flesh. Meanwhile, doctors fought their way through the melee to certify Bethea's death and then cried out that his heart was still beating. The spectators groaned and pulled back, waiting. Bethea was finally pronounced dead at 5:45, and once more the souvenir hunters charged forward, a great scuffle taking place for possession of the death hood.

See also: EXECUTIONS, PUBLIC.

Bickford, Maria (1823–1845) murder victim

The murder of Maria Bickford by Albert Tirrell in Boston on October 27, 1845 was noteworthy because the young man was of the Weymouth Tirrells, one of New England's wealthiest and most socially prominent families. However, the case was to become even more noteworthy since it represented the first effective use of sleepwalking as a defense.

The 25-year-old Tirrell was the bane of his family. Although married, he was notorious for picking up a whore and going off with her for a week or longer at a time. In one of the family's constant efforts to get Albert to reform, they sent him on the road as a representative for one of the Tirrell businesses, Tirrell's Triumphant Footwear. Exactly how providing Albert with such an ideal opportunity for whoring would lead to his reformation was, at least in retrospect, a mystery. In New Bedford, Mass., he met 23-year-old Maria Bickford and was soon pursuing his usual desires. But in the case of this woman, it was a matter of true love; Tirrell brought Bickford back to Boston, ensconcing her in a waterfront flat where he could visit her regularly, while continuing to pretend to his family that he had indeed become a solid citizen.

However, the Tirrell-Bickford love affair was not a quiet one. They screamed, fought, got drunk frequently and eventually were evicted for boisterous behavior. Tirrell's conduct became the talk of Boston. The family could no longer ignore this, and finally, Tirrell's wife and brother-in-law brought criminal charges of adultery against him. In the year 1845 in Boston, adultery was a word spoken only in whispers. Indeed, the act was punishable by a fine and six months imprisonment. Even worse, a convicted man would almost certainly be treated as a pariah, shunned by society. Painfully aware of this, Tirrell was most contrite when visited in his cell by the family. "He implored his young wife for forgiveness," says an account of the day. The fact that he was in the process of "drying out" added to the heart-rending scene. Finally, on October 20 the family, including Tirrell's wife and brother-in-law, capitulated. They withdrew the charges and the prodigal son was turned loose upon signing a bond promising to "keep the peace and observe propriety in his behavior."

Back home for an hour, Tirrell kissed his wife and said he had to go out "on business." Like a homing pigeon, he headed for the house of Joel Lawrence on Cedar Lane in the Beacon Hill district, where Maria Bickford had taken up residence. Tirrell brought with him a demijohn of rum. During the reunion of the lovers that followed, landlord Lawrence later said that he thought the house was falling down. Eventually, the lovers quieted a bit until the following evening. Then the revelry started again but soon turned into a nasty quarrel when Tirrell found some letters written to Maria by a new admirer. Over the next several evenings the pair's frolicking was increasingly interrupted by harsh arguments, a matter compounded when a Miss Priscilla Moody from down the hall, unaware that Tirrell was around one afternoon, dropped by to ask Maria to help her out since she had two gentlemen calling on her shortly. When Tirrell erupted in anger, Maria just laughed and said if she did anything like that, it would just be "funning."

The Tirrell-Bickford funning came to an end at 4:30 the morning of October 27. Smoke was seen pouring out of Maria's window, and the landlord, who had been awakened about an hour earlier by another of the incessant screaming matches between the lovers, broke in. Someone had deliberately set fire to the room. It was not Maria. She was lying on the floor, totally nude, her throat slit almost from ear to ear. When Lawrence viewed the scene, he shouted out, "Where's Albert?"

Albert had headed for the Boston docks, he joined a ship's crew and sailed away as a common seaman. It was not until February 27, 1846 that he was apprehended aboard the schooner *Cathay* in New York and returned to Boston to face murder charges. There was little reason to doubt that Tirrell would be convicted. There were witnesses who saw him leave the Lawrence house moments before the fire. Those who had seen him testified that he wore no shirt under his coat—his bloody shirt had been found in the murder room. An acquaintance of Tirrell's, Sam Head, told of how young Albert had turned up at his home and asked, "Sam—how came I here?" He stank of rum.

With such a strong case against him, Tirrell was considered as good as convicted. Nevertheless, the Tirrell family decided to strive mightily to save the errant son, recoiling in horror from the stigma that would attach to all if Albert were hanged for murder. The Honorable Rufus B. Choate was retained to defend Albert. Choate, then at the height of his oratorical powers, was rightly considered a courtroom wizard, but everyone was convinced that in this case he was espousing a hopeless cause. It would take a miracle to save Tirrell. Which was exactly what Choate came up with.

Choate stunned the court when he conceded that his client had indeed killed "this unfortunate woman." However, the lawyer said, "I will prove that he cannot be held responsible under the law because he was asleep at the time." While the courtroom buzzed with an argument never heard before in an American court of law, Choate continued:

I do not mean, of course, that he was asleep in the usual physical sense. He was mentally asleep. Although he was capable of physical movement and action, he had no knowledge or judgment of what he was doing. His mental and moral faculties were in deepest slumber. He was a man in somnambulism, acting in a dream. Gentlemen, I will show that the defendant Tirrell has been a sleepwalker since early youth, and that while in a condition of somnambulism that often lasted for many hours, he performed feats of almost incredible complexity and dexterity.

Witness after witness took the stand to tell of Tirrell's past sleepwalking escapades and accomplishments. His mother said her son had first shown sleepwalking tendencies at the age of three. He had been found in the kitchen sound asleep smearing jam on the walls. He started sleepwalking regularly. Mrs. Tirrell took to tying his son to his bed, but the boy showed a slumbrous ability to untie knots he could not undo when awake. After the lad had been discovered to have climbed out of his bedroom window and perched precariously on the porch roof, Mrs. Tirrell, according to the testimony of a workman, ordered an iron grill over the window "to keep the tyke from killing himself."

The family physician reported that at the age of 10, the sleepwalking boy, barefoot and in only his nightgown, had been found in the late hours of a winter night just as he completed building a snowman. "The boy came near dying of pneumonia as a result of that," the doctor testified.

According to the evidence presented, Tirrell's sleepwalking escapades became less frequent in adulthood but tended to be more dangerous and violent. His wife Cynthia awoke one night to find him trying to strangle her. Her desperate screams awakened him, and he expressed surprise and contrition, begged her forgiveness and then lapsed into a peaceful sleep. A sailor from the *Cathay* told of watching the sleeping and stark-naked Tirrell cross the ice-covered deck of the vessel, climb high in the mast and then come down safely, all the while acting "like a man in his sleep."

Lawyer Choate then recalled the words of Samuel Head, who had seen Tirrell shortly after Maria Bickford's murder. "He seemed like a man coming out of a stupor. He said, 'Sam, how came I here?'"

Despite the prosecution's attempts to knock down Choate's unique defense of his client, the jury was duly impressed. It took less than two hours to bring in a verdict that established a legal milestone. Albert Tirrell was found not guilty and freed. As time passed, the Tirrell verdict did not sit well with the public, which clearly felt the family money had gotten him off. A man who could slit a pretty girl's throat and—allegedly—not remember it was, general opinion held, more likely rum soaked than in a somnambulistic trance. Finally, bowing to public opinion, the family had Albert confined where he would no longer be a danger, sleeping or awake.

See also: SLEEPWALKING AND CRIME.

bicycle police

Late in the 19th century most big-city police departments found they could not adequately patrol their communities with just police on foot or on horseback. What they needed was a "motorized" force on bicycle. Typical was the New York Bicycle Squad formed in 1895 after police commissioner Theodore Roosevelt angrily declared the traffic of "steam carriages," the forerunner of the automobile; huge horse-drawn trucks; and bicycles had made Eighth Avenue and the waterfront area unsafe for pedestrians. To regulate traffic in these areas, he assigned bicycles to four officers. The speed limit for all vehicles was set at eight miles an hour, and speeders were flagged down by a traffic cop on a bike who would demand to see the driver's license.

By 1902 the Bicycle Squad was enlarged to 100 men, and Commissioner Thomas Andrew could proudly announce a total of 1,366 arrests that year of "civilian wheelmen who persisted in risking the lives and limbs of others by 'scorching' along the Central Park drives." He added that a great many of these "bicyclist-scorchers were also of that despicable breed known as 'mashers.'"

By 1910 the horseless carriages had ceased being the mere playthings of the very wealthy and eccentric and were starting to choke the city streets. The Bicycle Squad did heroic work trying to contain these automobile "speed demons." It did not occur to anyone until 1912 to provide the police with automobiles so that they could give chase to other such vehicles. In that year the Traffic Division was established. Still, the Bicycle Squad hung on, providing sundry services until finally being abandoned in 1934. Rather than sell hun-

A New York City bicycle cop runs down one of the new automobile "speed demons" around the turn of the century.

dreds of bicycles to commercial dealers, the police auctioned them off to city kids, with some of the police bikes going for a mere 25¢. Of course many police departments today have on hand a few bicycles for special duty, such as during traffic gridlock.

Biddle brothers   murderers and death-row escapees

Ed and Jack Biddle escaped from the Allegheny County Jail on January 30, 1902, 16 days before they were to be executed for the killing of a store owner and a police detective. When details of the escape became known, it scandalized Pittsburgh and much of the rest of the country since the escape was engineered by 26-year-old Katherine Scoffel, the warden's wife. She had come to their death cells a month earlier, as was her custom, to try to bring religion to doomed men and had fallen in love with Ed Biddle, eight years her junior. Mrs. Scoffel supplied the brothers with guns and hacksaws and led them to freedom through the warden's home, which had a private entrance to the institution. She had drugged her husband so he would be asleep and made sure their four children were not home at the time.

Two guards were shot superficially and another was overpowered during the breakout; when they were found, the alarm was sounded. The warden, apprised of the facts, notified the police of the Biddle brothers' escape and told them to arrest his wife as an accomplice. Then he wrote a letter of resignation, gathered up his children and left the prison for the last time.

Meanwhile, the three fugitives made it as far as Butler, Pa., switching from the carriage Mrs. Scoffel had secured for them to a stolen sleigh. They were stopped by a seven-man roadblock, and in a furious gun battle 26-year-old Jack Biddle was shot dead. Ed Biddle was hit three times in the lung. As he was dying, Katherine Scoffel begged him to shoot her. He did so, but while Biddle died a few hours after being taken into custody, Mrs. Scoffel survived. When she recovered, she was tried and sentenced to serve two years in the penitentiary of which she had once been the first lady. Asked during her trial how a woman of her standing could love a vicious criminal like Ed Biddle, she said: "I can forgive anything he's done. Except one. I can forgive his killings, his robberies, anything. But I cannot forgive him for failing to kill me so that I could be with him forever in death."

Katherine Scoffel was released from prison in 18 months and lived until 1926, ostracized and in disgrace. Often through the years, she would see an advertisement in a newspaper for a performance of a melodrama about the case. It was called *The Biddle Boys* and played to capacity houses for many years.

Big Store major confidence game operation

Prior to 1900, swindles were pretty much "short cons" in which the victim was cheated for a few dollars, perhaps a few hundred and occasionally a few thousand. It was difficult to keep the sucker in tow long enough to make a really big killing. Buck Boatright, an ingenious gambler and the originator of a little con game called the smack, solved this problem by devising the most elaborate and successful confidence racket ever invented.

Boatright's plan was to set up a permanent base of operations, either an office or a store with seemingly respectable or authentic trimmings as well as many employees and "customers." Here the sucker could be skinned with near-scientific precision. Boatright set up his operation with the backing of a number of con men who became his partners. The first requirement was to establish a protected territory in which police and politicians would cooperate for either a flat payoff or a percentage of the take. Boatright's selection was Webb City, Mo., where in 1900 he opened what was to become known as the Big Store.

Boatright's operation was a fake gambling club, featuring among other things fixed sporting events (generally foot races or fights). So convincing was the atmosphere in Boatright's establishment, which soon spawned a branch in Council Bluffs, Iowa, that a sucker almost never suspected he was losing his money in a completely play-act arena where everyone except the victim was a member of the gang.

After the sucker was roped in by being allowed to win a few small bets, he then was informed of a big fix and induced to bet thousands, only to watch as something unforeseen went wrong. In a footrace or fight the participant the victim was betting on might suddenly "drop dead," triggering a false panic since such sporting events were illegal. In other cases the victim would be kissed off when the two operators who suckered him in, and who allegedly lost their money with his, got into an argument that would end with one pulling a gun and "killing" the other. In this play-acted "sting" the shot con man would slump to the floor with blood gushing from his mouth. This would really be chicken blood secreted in a pouch in the man's mouth and bitten open at the right moment. It was an act well calculated to put the sucker "on the run" since, while he had intended only to break the law against illegal betting, he now believed he was an accessory to murder.

Although the big store would seem to be an operation that could fleece only the most gullible, it was carried off with such convincing performances that many men of business and wealth were easily taken, never for a moment suspecting a swindle. Perhaps the greatest of all big store operators was Lou Blonger, a master fixer, who for four decades made Denver, Colo. the "con man's capital of America."

See also: DOLLAR STORE, SMACK GAME.

bigamy

Few crimes are as welcome to newspaper editors as bigamy, the act of ceremonially marrying another person when already legally married. Although the typical state statute exacts up to five years imprisonment for the offense, few bigamists are ever punished, usually getting off with a stern lecture provided they make amends by speedily annulling the illegitimate marriage. Meanwhile, the newspapers have their human interest story, especially when, as often happens, the bigamist's spouses violently denounce or attack one another.

One such case involved two women who went at each other in a Chicago courthouse corridor, pulling hair, gouging and biting. "I'm still in love with him," wife number one announced to reporters, after the two battling women were separated. "I'll help him all I can." Which is how things turned out. Since he was her husband first, she got him while the second wife got only an annulment. Triumphantly, in fact, wife number one paid the $500 fine her errant husband faced for his misdeeds.

It is not unusual to find a bigamist with six or eight spouses who still does not end up with a prison sentence, unless he or she is also guilty of stealing his or her spouses' money or defrauding them of their fortunes. Few prosecuting attorneys will expend much energy on bigamy complaints because as many as a dozen investigators would have to be put on a single bigamy case full time to clear the tangled web. Another discouraging factor is that bigamists often have wives and families in different states. As a result, for every bigamist finally hauled into court, possibly as many as a hundred or more go free and undetected.

Many bigamists have bizarre or zany reasons for committing the crime. Often, they have concocted and sold their spouses wildly improbable tales to sustain their deception. This was the case of a Washington woman who married two Canadian navy seamen, assuring each that she had a twin sister who had married the other. When it was discovered that both "twins" had identical cuts on a finger, her double life was exposed.

Courting exposure, indeed, seems very common among bigamists. A gray-haired 52-year-old night watchman was clapped in the county jail in New Haven, Conn. for having two wives—living a mere block from each other. He was exposed when a long distance call for one wife mistakenly went to the other.

One Michigan bigamist got caught when his wife went by a photographer's shop and spotted a picture of her husband and a stunning young bride. A Massachussetts man's bigamy was revealed when two of his wives met in court while both were bringing action against him for nonsupport.

Harried bigamists often find themselves mired deep in serious crime before long. The "flying lothario" of Memphis made the headlines from coast to coast after it was found he kept one wife in Tennessee and another in California, commuting back and forth each week by plane in order to spend weekdays in Memphis and weekends in Los Angeles. Travel costs murdered him, and he finally confessed to stealing $19,000 from the Memphis firm where he worked as a cashier.

Few bigamists are exceptionally attractive. In fact, some of the country's most successful bigamists are bald and fortyish, both in age and waistline. Master swindler and bigamist Sigmund Engel was only coming into his prime when he was arrested at the age of 73. At the other end of the scale was a 17-year-old schoolboy who had already walked up the aisle three times, evidently incapable of saying no to older women.

Probably the only way to end bigamy would be to enact a proposal made in recent years by several district attorneys that a central national office be established to receive notice of and record every marriage made anywhere in the country. In addition, every person being married would have to be fingerprinted. Obviously, while this would effectively stop the bigamists, the proposal's disregard for American concepts of civil liberties outweighs its usefulness as a measure to eliminate bigamy.

Biler Avenue Chicago vice district

From the 1870s until the turn of the century, Pacific Avenue, nicknamed Biler Avenue, was "one of the most disreputable streets in the city, built up with hastily constructed tenements which were occupied by the most depraved of men and women, black, white and mixed." Yet it was still held in particular fondness by the reigning political powers. Biler Avenue and its side streets were filled with bordellos of the lowest class and lowest price in the city. A typical establishment was Dan Webster's big groggery and bagnio at Nos. 130–132, which the *Chicago Times* called an "infernal hell hole. There it is that the rottenest, vilest, filthiest strumpets, black and white, reeking with corruption, are bundled together, catering indiscriminately to the lust of all." What made the activities of the establishment most noteworthy was, as the *Times* discovered, that the building was owned by Michael C. Hickey, the superintendent of police. Because of the stir caused by the *Times* exposé, Hickey was hauled before the Police Board for trial, but he was acquitted of any wrongdoing since there was no way a superintendent of police could possibly have known about the character of his tenants. An even more startling revelation was that an entire block on Harrison Street was the property of Mayor Carter Harrison.

"Our Carter" the *Times* said, "owns the entire block between Clark Street and Pacific Avenue. On the corner of Clark, and running west to the middle of the block, stands a hotel. The other half of the block is occupied by four or five ordinary frame houses. One is used for a lager-beer saloon, another for a restaurant, still another for a tobacco store, a fourth as a hotel on a small scale, and right among these, as snug as a bug, Our Carter has allowed a number of gay damsels to nestle down, and they are rather homely ones at that."

Even that last withering comment was not enough to keep Carter Harrison from becoming a five-term mayor. Biler Avenue thus typified Chicago's tolerance of political venality, an attitude that was to last for many decades.

See also: CARTER HARRISON.

Billee, John (?–1890) western murderer

The idea of bringing in a badman dead or alive was an Old West concept that did not usually apply to deputy federal marshals. For each prisoner brought back, the marshal was paid the sum of $2 plus a mileage allowance of 6¢ per mile going and 10¢ coming back provided he had his man. Out of this sum, the marshal had to pay all his own expenses and feed his prisoner. However, if he lost his prisoner or was forced to kill him, the lawman lost his fee and mileage allowance! The system encouraged marshals to try their best to keep their quarry alive.

A noted case that underscored the point involved John Billee, who killed a man named W. P. Williams in April 1888 and buried the corpse in a ravine in the Kiamichi Mountains. Federal deputies caught up with Billee in a wide sweep during which they also netted four other wanted men. On their way back to Fort Smith, deputies Perry DuVall, Will Ayers and James Wilkerson stopped with their prisoners to spend the night at a deserted two-room cabin outside Muskogee, Okla. in Indian Territory.

Deputy Ayers, with three prisoners chained to him, bedded down in the front room along with Deputy DuVal, who had Billee in tow. Deputy Wilkerson and the fifth prisoner slept in the small rear room of the cabin. About 3 A.M. Billee worked out of one of his handcuffs and managed to reach DuVal's revolver. He fired but in the darkness only succeeded in wounding DuVall in the head. He then turned the gun on Ayers before the deputy had a chance to react out of his sleep, shooting him in the right nipple. Meanwhile Wilkerson had rolled over into a sitting position in the doorway of the next room and Billee put a shot into his back. Ayers then lunged at the outlaw and battled Billee to keep him from getting off another shot. While this was going on, Wilkerson leveled his own gun and aimed carefully at the outlaw, trying to get off an incapacitating, rather than a fatal, shot, which he did. By keeping Billee alive long enough for him to meet his doom on the gallows at Fort Smith on January 16, 1890, the three wounded deputies were able to collect their fee for the outlaw.

Billington, John (?–1630) America's first murderer

Even before the Pilgrims landed at Plymouth Rock in 1620, Capt. Miles Standish had already had his fill of one John Billington aboard the *Mayflower*. Standish reprimanded Billington, a foul-mouthed brawler from the London slums, and eventually was forced to make an example of the man by having his feet and neck tied together. There is no evidence that this punishment had any lasting effect on Billington, who became the scourge of the Plymouth colony, starting feuds with a number of settlers.

One Pilgrim who refused to knuckle under to Billington's bullying was John Newcomen, a neighbor, and the pair became mortal enemies. Finally, one day in 1630 Billington ambushed Newcomen while he was out in the woods hunting, shooting him dead with a blunderbuss from behind a rock. Billington was quickly seized, tried by the Pilgrims and summarily hanged. Ironically, many Americans today proudly trace their ancestry back to the *Mayflower* and Billington, the American colonies' first murderer.

Billy the Kid (1859–1881) outlaw

There has probably been more written about Billy the Kid than any other outlaw, which perhaps explains why so little of his true story can be accurately reconstructed.

Hyperbole has been added to lies until we are left with a portrait of a young outlaw said to have killed 21 men during his 21 years. The number is an exaggeration. He did not kill a man at the age of 12 for insulting his mother as is often stated. Probably the first man the New York–born youngster—whose real name is believed to have been either William Bonney or Henry McCarty—killed was a bully named Frank "Windy" Cahill, who had called him a "pimp and a son of a bitch." Billy gunned him down on the spot. He was

arrested but almost immediately escaped from jail. In fact, he frequently escaped from jails, which probably helped to give him a romantic air. There was certainly nothing romantic about his looks. He was small, with prominent front teeth and a short, fuzzy upper lip, almost a harelip, which gave him a perpetual smile. He smiled when he killed and his smile made him look pathological, which he probably was. One moment he was good natured and the next he displayed an explosive temper.

Famous "flopped," i.e., reversed, portrait of Billy the Kid started the legend that he was left-handed.

An enthusiastic *Police Gazette* artist was so awed by the Kid's exploits that he awarded him two right hands.

Beginning in his early teens, Billy supported himself by gambling and, when the cards ran wrong, by stealing anything from clothes to cattle. After his mother died in 1874, Billy was completely on his own. Following the Cahill killing and a few others, according to some historians, Billy hired out as a cowboy to an English gentleman rancher, John Tunstall. It was a smart move by Tunstall since Billy had been stealing his stock. Billy looked upon the Englishman as a father figure, even though Tunstall was only five or six years older. Tunstall, on the other hand, said he saw good in Billy and was determined to make a man out of him. When the Lincoln County War for much of the New Mexico Territory backcountry and the Pecos Valley broke out soon afterwards, Tunstall became a leading figure on one side. Allied with Alexander McSween and cattle king John Chisum against the business interests of the

county dominated by Lawrence G. Murphy, James J. Dolan and James H. Riley, Tunstall turned out to be the first major casualty, shot down in February 1878 by gunmen supposedly deputized to arrest him on a trumped up charge.

Billy saw the killing from a distance but could do nothing about it. He was deeply affected by Tunstall's murder. "He was the only man that ever treated me like I was free-born and white," he said. Over Tunstall's grave he swore, "I'll get every son-of-a-bitch who helped kill John if it's the last thing I do."

With that pledge Billy the Kid became the chief killer of the Lincoln County War, lining up with McSween. When the opposing forces besieged the town of Lincoln for several days, Billy killed numerous enemies. McSween was murdered during the siege and his death ended the war, as Chisum saw he lacked the power to

92

win by himself. Billy the Kid went back to rustling and organized a gang of gunfighters and cutthroats. He robbed Chisum's cattle as well as others'. Eventually, Gov. Lew Wallace offered an amnesty to all participants in the Lincoln County War, and for a time, Billy considered accepting it. But he was leery of the "formality" of the trial he would have to face and stayed on the loose. He permanently lost his chance to go straight after killing a lawman.

Billy and his gang killed several more men over the next year or so but suffered their losses as well. Sheriff Pat Garrett stalked Billy and in one ambush killed Billy's close friend Tom O'Folliard, whom he mistook for the Kid. In December 1880 Charlie Bowdre died in an ambush at Stinking Springs, New Mexico Territory. Trapped by Garrett and his posse, Billy and several of his confederates were forced to surrender. Billy was convicted of the murder of Sheriff William Brady and sentenced to hang. Confined in a top-floor room of the Lincoln County Courthouse, he made a sensational escape, killing deputies James Bell, whom he liked, and sadistic Bob Olinger, whom he hated. He shot Olinger down like a dog in the street outside the courthouse and fled.

Billy was a hero to those who shared his sympathies in the Lincoln County War and to Mexicans, among whom he often hid out.

Finally, Garrett located Billy the Kid hiding at old Fort Sumner. When Billy walked into a darkened room, Garrett shot him down without giving him a chance to surrender. He was buried in a common grave with his two buddies, O'Folliard and Bowdre. The gravestone bore the inscription "Pals."

After Billy the Kid died, the legend-makers went to work. The first book about him appeared three weeks after his death. Most of his biographers probably had never been west of New York. Sheriff Garrett contributed a volume, which greatly built up Billy and in the process, of course, the man who had gotten him. Serious students of Billy the Kid have been mystified by his place in the folklore of the country. His crimes were largely unimaginative and cold blooded. He lacked the verve and style that marked Jesse James, for instance, and seldom inspired the loyalty that James did.

See also: CHARLIE BOWDRE, PATRICK FLOYD GARRETT, JOE GRANT, LINCOLN COUNTY WAR, TOM O'FOLLIARD, ROBERT OLINGER, DAVE RUDABAUGH, JOHN TUNSTALL.

Binaggio, Charles (1909–1950) political leader and murder victim

The murder of Charley Binaggio and his number one muscleman, Charley Gargotta, on April 6, 1950 shocked Kansas City, Mo., where Binaggio was the acknowledged political and crime boss. He was found stretched out in a swivel chair at the First District Democratic Club, his face blood soaked and four bullets in his head. Garotta lay on the floor nearby, the same number of slugs in his head. Overlooking the grisly scene were large portraits of President Harry Truman and Gov. Forest Smith. The bullet wounds in the heads of both men were arranged in two straight rows, or "two deuces." In dice parlance, this is called Little Joe. It is also the insignia the underworld stamps on welshers when it wants the world to know that the murder was done by the mob. Clearly, Binaggio had welshed on a promise to the national crime syndicate.

Only 41 at the time of his murder, Binaggio was recognized as a political "comer." He had been born in Beaumont, Tex. As a youngster he became a drifter and was arrested twice in Denver for carrying a concealed weapon and for vagrancy. At age 23 Binaggio landed in Kansas City and joined the operations of North Side leader Johnny Lazia, who delivered votes for Democratic boss Tom Pendergast. Lazia's reward was control of gambling, vice, liquor and racing wires in the North Side. Binaggio continued to climb the criminal ladder even after Lazia's assassination in 1934. By 1944 he controlled all the North Side wards.

In 1946 Binaggio made a splash on the national scene when President Truman ordered a purge of Congressman Roger C. Slaughter for voting against administration bills. Truman called in Jim Pendergast, the late Tom's nephew successor, and ordered the nomination of Enos Axtell. Slaughter lost in the primary, but the *Kansas City Star* soon charged wholesale ballot fraud. During several probes launched on both the national and state level, a woman election watcher was shot to death on the porch of her home. Just before state hearings were scheduled to start, the safe at City Hall in Kansas City was dynamited and fraudulent ballot evidence was destroyed.

Both the ballot frauds and the City Hall bombing were believed to have been masterminded by Binaggio. However, he was never indicted and only one minor hanger-on, "Snags" Klein, went to prison, for a short term. Thereafter, a power struggle broke out between Jim Pendergast and Binaggio. The former proved to be lacking the astuteness of his late uncle, and by 1948 it was obvious that Kansas City was becoming Binaggio's town. However, Binaggio still needed a lot of funds to beat Pendergast's entrenched machine, and he spread the word throughout the underworld that once his man was elected governor, he would give gambling and other "wide-open" interests free rein in the state. More than $200,000 flowed in from gangland sources to help Binaggio's plans. Forrest Smith was elected governor and Binaggio claimed credit. But Binaggio found he could not deliver on his promise to the underworld, a fact that was now common knowledge. A St. Louis newspaper broke the story that the understanding he had with the underworld called for opening up both Kansas City and St. Louis, but that the St. Louis police commissioner had blocked every one of his moves. Binaggio was forced to stall for time on his underworld agreement. The time expired, and it was obvious that Binaggio was in deep trouble. The mobs had realized that their $200,000 was a write-off. All that remained was the payoff. It was Little Joe for Binaggio and Gargotta.

Bioff, Willie Morris (1900–1955) labor racketeer and stool pigeon

A noted union racketeer and ex-pimp, Willie Bioff masterminded, with George Browne, the Chicago syndicate's extortion of an estimated $6.5 million from the Hollywood movie studios in the 1930s. Bioff was eventually convicted because of the crusading activities of right-wing columnist Westbrook Pegler, who discovered Bioff as a "guest of honor" at a lavish Hollywood party and remembered him as a two-bit panderer during his own apprenticeship as a Chicago reporter.

Bioff became a pimp no later than the age of 10, when he began collecting money from other schoolboys for enjoying the favors of his "girls" on a table at the local poolhall. By his mid-teens Bioff had an entire string of prostitutes working for him and was a familiar sight in Chicago's vice-ridden Levee area, wearing gaudy silk shirts and offering a girl for every purpose. While Bioff knew the virtue of paying for police protection, some of his activities proved just too much, and he served jail time for brutalizing his prostitutes. Yet somehow, as just seemed to happen in Chicago, Bioff escaped serving one six-month term he was sentenced to.

In the meantime, while maintaining his vice activities, Bioff moved up in the Capone mob as a union slugger, a job he performed so well that he was promoted steadily up the ladder, eventually being installed by the mob as president of the International Alliance of Theatrical Stage Employes and Motion Picture Operators. In this position, Bioff teamed up with George Browne to terrorize studio executives by threatening to shut down all moviemaking. The result was enormous payoffs by the movie moguls to Bioff, Browne and numerous other members of the Capone syndicate.

It was at this stage that Pegler started digging into Bioff's record and publicizing his unsavory past. Despite charges of Pegler's antiunionism, Bioff was forced to serve his old six-month vice sentence, although while doing his time in the Chicago House of Correction, he was provided with a private office and a tub of iced beer renewed each day.

Thanks to Pegler's efforts Bioff and Browne were convicted in 1941 of violating antiracketeering laws. Each of the pair drew a 10-year sentence. It was not a fate either appreciated, and both testified for the government in the prosecution of many top members of the syndicate, men like Frank Nitti, Phil D'Andrea, Paul Ricca, Charlie Gioe, Lou Kaufman and John Roselli.

The defense attacked Bioff's character and demanded to know why he had lied to previous grand juries. "I am just a low, uncouth person," he replied sadly. "I'm a low-type sort of man."

Because of his testimony the top members of the Chicago syndicate went to prison. The exception was Nitti who committed suicide instead. As these crime figures went in, Bioff and Browne went out. Browne ran and hid. Bioff also traveled, finally settling in Phoenix, Ariz. under the name of William Nelson.

Bioff's nature was to court the centers of power, and in 1952 he and his wife contributed $5,000 to the senatorial campaign of a department store heir named Barry Goldwater. After the election a warm friendship developed between Arizona's new senator and Bioff-Nelson. Just two weeks before Bioff's untimely demise, Goldwater, an accomplished air force pilot, flew Bioff and his wife to Las Vegas and back. On November 4, 1955, Bioff went out the kitchen door of his home and climbed into his small pickup truck. His wife waved to him. Bioff waved back, then tramped on the starter. There was a blast and a flash. The truck was demolished, as was Willie Bioff. It was a little late in coming, but syndicate vengeance had been exacted.

See also: PROCURING.

Bird Cage Theatre   Tombstone night spot and "shooting gallery"

One of the more wicked establishments in Tombstone, Ariz. during the 1880s was the Bird Cage Theatre. A performance of *H.M.S. Pinafore* might grace its stage while harlots plied their trade in 12 tiny balcony boxes. An act more in keeping with the place was the appearance of Fatima, who belly-danced to raucous western acclaim in 1882.

The owners of the theater, Bill and Lottie Hutchinson, made it a rule that the audience had to check their shooting irons upon entering, but unfortunately, the regulation was not always obeyed, often with tragic consequences. In one wild shoot-out 12 men were reportedly left dead. Care was required in the selection of the repertoire, since if too evil a villain appeared on the stage, he might soon be forced to dodge lead from outraged members of the audience. There is no accurate record of the numbers of fatalities that occurred in the Bird Cage, but while it never equaled the fabulous Oriental Saloon as a shooting gallery, it certainly provided the setting for a good many death scenes on both sides of the footlights.

See also: TOMBSTONE, ARIZONA TERRITORY.

Birdman of Alcatraz   See ROBERT FRANKLIN STROUD.

Bisbee (Arizona) kidnapping

Without doubt, the largest mass kidnapping in American history occurred in 1917 in Bisbee, Ariz., once the greatest copper boom town in the country. In that year the Industrial Workers of the World, or Wobblies, staged a general strike, which, given the economy of the town, meant primarily a strike against Phelps-Dodge Copper. What happened next is not in dispute by labor historians. The company bankrolled an operation by Sheriff Harry Wheeler that gathered the largest posse in the West's history to run the strikers out of town. In a midnight raid more than 2,000 strikers were rounded up; some 1,200 of them were jammed into cattle cars and shipped off across the desert into New Mexico. This mass abduction broke the strike and started the Wobblies on a steady decline within the union movement. As for the criminal aspects—the action was clearly an act of kidnapping—Phelps-Dodge was credited with using its gigantic financial power in Arizona to ensure that not a single man went to prison for the outrageous act.

Bisbee Massacre   robbery carnage

Probably few robberies exercised the West more than what became known as the infamous Bisbee Massacre, which some historians have claimed marked the swing of the Arizona Territory from anarchy to law and order.

On the evening of December 8, 1883, five masked men rode into the mining town of Bisbee and dismounted at the store of A. A. Castanda. They wore long overcoats to cover the rifles they carried. Two of the men entered the store, which was about to close. There were six customers still inside and one of them, J. C. Tappenier, reached for his gun when he saw the intruders produce their rifles. He went down in a blast of rifle fire that alerted the whole town. As curious townsfolk poured into the street to see what was going on, three lookouts outside the store started shooting to clear them away. Two men and a woman were killed in the raking fire, bringing the total death count to four, with several others wounded, before the five thieves

In the view of many in the Old West, confession did not cleanse the soul. John Heath was dragged from Tombstone's jail and lynched for his part in the Bisbee Massacre despite the fact that his confession led to the capture of five other perpetrators.

rode out of town with $3,000 in cash and various pieces of jewelry.

A sheriff's posse from Tombstone took off in pursuit of the bandits, numbering among its ranks a tracker named John Heath. Some thought Heath did an excellent job of getting the posse to run in circles. Suspicion also focused on him for a number of other reasons, one being a report that he had been suspected of heading an outlaw gang some time earlier in Brewery Gulch.

These suspicions were not unfounded. Once jailed and subjected to some persuasion. Heath admitted knowing about the robbery plans. It was not clear whether he was merely in on the planning or had indeed done most of it, but in any event, Heath was now "cooperative" and spilled out the names of those involved: Daniel Kelley, Daniel Dowd, James "Tex" Howard, William Delaney and Comer Sample. After some months all five were rounded up, given a speedy trial and sentenced to hang.

Heath, without whose admissions the others would not have been apprehended, was extended leniency and given a life sentence. Arizonians found it difficult to accept this concept of law and order. western beliefs did not hold that a man's soul was made any less black through confession. On February 22, 1884 an irate mob of several hundred broke into the Tombstone jail, and when they were finished, John Heath dangled lifeless from a telegraph pole. In the cemetery at Tombstone, Heath's marker can still be read. "John Heath, taken from County Jail and lynched by Bisbee mob in Tombstone, Feb. 22nd, 1884."

See also: DANIEL KELLEY.

Bismarck Hall   New York dive

Of all the vicious establishments that abounded in New York's Bowery in the post–Civil War period, one that had a uniquely Old World flavor was Bismarck Hall. Low physically as well as morally, the Hall had an annex in a string of cavelike rooms buried under the sidewalk where ladies employed in the dive could entertain gentlemen. Following an Old World custom, the operator of the dive supposedly often "bought" his inmates by paying them a small sum of money binding them to him for several years. While such an agreement, of course, would have had little standing in court, its terms were quite well enforced; the girls were not allowed off the premises unless they left a "deposit" that guaranteed their return. Bismarck Hall achieved a measure of renown when Grand Duke Alexis of Russia, visiting it in the 1870s while slumming, or, as the practice was then known, "elephant hunting," recognized a Russian countess who had fallen on hard times and was working there as a "waiter girl." According to the story, he bought the freedom of this unnamed noblewoman and took her back to Russia and her former position of grace.

Black Bart   (1830–1917?)   stagecoach robber

One of the most colorful, daring and unconventional bandits of the Old West was Charles E. Bolton, better known as Black Bart, the poet laureate of outlawry. By the best count, he pulled 27 stagecoach holdups in California from 1874 to 1883. But he prided himself on never robbing a stagecoach passenger. After each robbery Black Bart would send the coach on its way and then stroll off on foot, since he greatly disliked horses. Wearing a duster and a flour-sack mask and carrying an empty shotgun, he would step out into the road and shout to the stage driver, "Throw down your box or

die." Sometimes he would issue orders to his men in the bushes to open fire if the driver refused. The driver would see a half-dozen rifles in the shadows and would do as he was told. Actually, the rifles were never more than broomstick handles. After each holdup Black Bart would leave behind bits of doggerel that won him a reputation as a poet. One typical poem read:

> *Here I lay me down to sleep*
> *To await the coming morrow*
> *Perhaps success, perhaps defeat*
> *and everlasting sorrow*

> *I've labored long and hard for bred [sic]*
> *For honor and for riches*
> *But on my corns too long you've tred*
> *You fine-haired Sons of Bitches*

> *Let come what will, I'll try it on*
> *My condition can't be worse*
> *And if there's money in that box*
> *'Tis munny in my purse.*
> *Black Bart, the Po-8.*

Black Bart was captured on November 3, 1883, after a robbery that had netted him $4,800. A rider came by during the robbery and fired at the outlaw, forcing him to flee so rapidly he dropped his handkerchief. Detectives traced the laundry mark, F.O.X. 7, until it led them to a man named Charles E. Bolton in San Francisco. The *San Francisco Bulletin* described him as "a distinguished-looking gentleman who walked erect as a soldier and carried a gold-knobbed cane." At first, Bolton denied being Black Bart but finally confessed. He was sentenced to 10 years in San Quentin but was released on January 21, 1888, with time off for good behavior. When a reporter asked him if he intended to go on writing poetry, Black Bart snapped, "Young man, didn't you just hear me say I will commit no more crimes?" According to the report, which had a romantic air, Wells Fargo settled an annuity on Black Bart for his agreement to rob no more stagecoaches. There is no additional information about him. One account had him living out his days in Nevada, and another said he died in 1917 in New York City.

Black Dahlia   (1925–1947)   murder victim

The 1947 case of Elizabeth Short, better known as the Black Dahlia, is unsolved but still actively pursued, principally because it has had more "confessions" than any other case in California history.

In a sense, Elizabeth Short was typical of the young girls who flooded Los Angeles: she was from a broken home, with an unhappy lovelife, consumed with a desire for a Hollywood career. She had, as they said in

Hollywood, a gimmick. She always dressed completely in black. It was one way to grab attention, but she certainly had others. She understood the meaning of the casting couch and would go to bed with any man who had even the most tenuous connection with the studios. They started calling her the Black Dahlia, and in the zany world of moviemaking, she might eventually have gained enough of a reputation to make it despite a lack of acting ability.

On January 15, 1947 her nude corpse was found in a garbage-strewn vacant lot in a Los Angeles suburb. She had been badly mutilated and her body had been crudely cut in half. Deep into the thigh of the 22-year-old victim, the killer had carved the initials "BD," presumably for Black Dahlia. It took the police some time to identify the severed corpse as Elizabeth Short, or the Black Dahlia, but no time at all to make several arrests. The murder seemed to excite the public and produced a rash of confessions. In fact, the police were overwhelmed by men and women coming forward to claim credit for the brutal act. Most of the confessions were soon discounted because the self-proclaimed murderers demonstrated a lack of knowledge about various aspects of the case. Yet, still more confessors came forward. One woman walked into a station house and said "The Black Dahlia stole my man, so I killed her and cut her up." A husband whose wife had deserted him said he was the killer in the hope that if he made himself notorious and got his picture in the papers, his wife would return to him. Another sent the police a letter made out of pasted-up letters from magazines, offering to meet them and give them information. He signed the message "Black Dahlia Avenger." But he never kept the rendezvous. Another writer sent a message reading: "Here are Dahlia's belongings. Letter to follow." Enclosed were Elizabeth Short's Social Security card and birth certificate and her address book—with one page missing. Unfortunately, no letter followed. The most promising confession appeared to be that made by a 29-year-old army corporal, who talked loudly and convincingly of knowing her. He appeared quite knowledgeable about the facts of the case and insisted, "When I get drunk, I get rough with women." After an intensive investigation, the police wrote him off as an unbalanced personality. As the confessions continued to pour in, all efforts to keep an accurate count were dropped, and to this day the Black Dahlia case remains unsolved.

Black Hand extortion racket

"The Society of the Black Hand" was one of the sillier journalistic hoaxes of its time. Contrary to what newspapers of the era published, there was no such Society of the Black Hand, but that was undoubtedly of little comfort to Black Hand victims.

Recalcitrant victims of this extortion racket were shot, poisoned, dynamited or maimed; more pliant targets willingly turned over their funds after receiving a demand for money usually outlined at the bottom with a hand that had been dipped in black ink, a menacing sight sure to produce an icy feeling around a victim's heart. Actually, there once had been a Society of the Black Hand—not in New York, not in Italy, not even in Sicily, but in Spain. It originated in the days of the Inquisition, when like such genuine Italian secret societies as the Camorra and Mafia, it was organized as a force for good, trying to fight the oppression of its day. In later centuries the Mafia and the Camorra turned into criminal bodies, while the Society of the Black Hand in Spain simply withered away. But for New York City newspapermen, *La Mano Nera,* or the Black Hand, had a nice ring to it; it was easy to remember and lurid. Thus was reborn the Black Hand. Reporters and some detectives wasted their time trying to trace suspects' family trees to tie them to some Black Hand Society. In reality, the Black Hand was simply an extortion racket practiced in the Little Italy sections of numerous American cities. The senders would threaten the recipient or his family and would warn that they would kill or maim a family member as a starter. Usually, the letter was signed with some sort of ominous symbol, such as a skull and crossbones or knives, hatchets or sabers dripping blood. Once the newspapers publicized the symbol of a black hand, that symbol became standard.

Certainly, Black Handers, many of whom were Mafia and Camorra gangsters, often killed if they did not receive their payoff, although more often they might at first catch a victim's child and cut off a finger as a convincer. A typical victim of a Black Hand operation was a wealthy Brooklyn butcher named Gaetano Costa, who in 1905 got a Black Hand letter that read: "You have more money than we have. We know of your wealth and that you are alone in this country. We want $1,000, which you are to put in a loaf of bread and hand to a man who comes in to buy meat and pulls out a red handkerchief." Costa, unlike his neighbors, refused to pay and was shot dead one morning as he worked behind his counter. His killers were never caught, although it was suspected that gangsters working for Lupo the Wolf, a Black Hand chieftain in Italian Harlem, were behind it.

Lupo was regarded as the biggest Black Hander in New York City, and years later, an infamous Murder Stable, which he owned on East 107th Street in Manhattan, was discovered to be the burial place for at least 60 victims, many of them individuals who had refused to pay Black Hand extortion demands. Lupo's power sprang from his shrewd use of terror. Strutting around Italian Harlem, the man exuded cruelty, and it was the custom for residents, at the very mention of his name, to cross themselves and extend their fingers in an effort to ward off his spell.

Within Italian-American society almost anyone could be a Black Hand victim. While on a triumphal engagement at the Metropolitan Opera shortly before World War I, tenor Enrico Caruso got a Black Hand demand for $2,000, which he paid, regarding an appeal to the police as useless if not foolhardy. However, his payment of the money led to a new demand for $15,000 more. This time the tenor notified the authorities because he realized paying the money would only lead to further, even greater demands. Under police direction, Caruso left the money beneath the steps of a factory as the extortionists had ordered. When two prominent Italian businessmen tried to retrieve the loot, they were arrested. Both went to prison in one of the few successful prosecutions of Black Hand criminals. Caruso was kept under guard for a number of years thereafter on the theory that he faced Black Hand retribution, but it never came, because his extortioners were no more than independent operators who had no connection with a crime family or the nonexistent Society of the Black Hand.

A New Orleans Black Hander, Paul Di Cristina, considered himself so immune from interference by the law that he delivered his Black Hand notes in person. His victims always quaked and paid—all except Pietro Pepitone, a grocer. He informed Di Cristina's strong-arm men that he would not pay. So the boss came around personally to collect. When Di Cristina alighted from his wagon in front of the grocer's store, Pepitone picked up a shotgun, stepped out on the sidewalk and blasted the Black Hander to death.

It has been estimated that at least 80 different Black Hand gangs operated in Chicago, totally unrelated to one another except that their messages to their victims were always the same, "Pay or Die."

Virtually all the Black Hand gangs were wiped out or disappeared around 1920. The leaders of the Cardinelli Black Handers were executed in Chicago; the DiGiovanni mob leaders were convicted in Kansas City, Lupo the Wolf got 30 years in New York, albeit for counterfeiting rather than Black Hand crimes. Some observers of the crime scene have attributed the decline of the Black Hand racket to the rise of the big-money rackets under the scourge of Prohibition; there was so much more money available in bootlegging, rumrunning and hijacking that the extortionists couldn't be bothered anymore with what was by comparison a penny-ante racket. However, that was hardly the whole answer. The fact was that Prohibition brought the Italian immigrants into close contact with the feared police for the first time. Most Little Italy sections around the country turned alcohol making into a "cottage industry," with its attendant odors, smoke and fumes. That meant the neighborhood policeman had to be paid off. And when you paid off a man, you had the right to ask him for a favor, such as taking care of this Black Hander who was bothering you.

See also: ENRICO CARUSO, DEATH CORNER, LUPO THE WOLF, SHOTGUN MAN, WHITE HAND SOCIETY.

Black Maria   police van
The Black Maria (pronounced Ma-rye-ah) police van originated in Boston, Mass. In 1847 a newspaper informed its readers that a "new Black Maria" had been put into service. There is no record of Black Marias necessarily being painted black; the origin of the term most likely referred to a huge black woman, Maria Lee, who ran a lodging house for sailors during the period. Since the woman was generally called Black Maria and her establishment was among the most unruly in the city, it was assumed that a police van loaded with boisterous offenders was coming from Black Maria's.

Black Sox Scandal   baseball betting coup
Before 1919 the fixing of baseball games for betting purposes was by no means unheard of. But in that year it went too far; the "unthinkable" happened: a World Series was fixed by eight star players for the Chicago White Sox who managed to lose the series to the underdog Cincinnati Redlegs five games to three (the series that year was being played in an experimental nine-game set).

All the details of what was to be called the Black Sox Scandal were never fully exposed, primarily because there was an attempted cover-up by the baseball establishment, in general, and White Sox owner Charles A. Comiskey, in particular. The offending players were not even suspended until there were only three games left to play in the following season, when confessions by three players to the grand jury forced Comiskey to act.

The throwing of the series appears to have been thought of initially by Chicago first baseman Charles Arnold "Chick" Gandil, who passed the word to Boston gamblers that he could line up several teammates for a lucrative killing. The other players involved were Eddie Cicotte and Claude Williams, star pitchers who between them had won 52 games during the season; left fielder Shoeless Joe Jackson; center fielder Oscar Felsch; third baseman George "Buck" Weaver;

shortstop Charles "Swede" Risbergand; and utility infielder Fred McMullin. The gamblers first approached were Joseph "Sport" Sullivan of Boston and William "Sleepy Bill" Burns of New York. Because they felt they needed more capital to finance a gigantic killing, they approached the country's leading gambler, Arnold "the Brain" Rothstein. It is debatable whether or not Rothstein entered the plot or turned them down and then simply went ahead and bet at least $60,000 on Cincinnati (and collected $270,000) because he knew the fix was in and saw no need to pay out any bribe money himself. In any event, the main operator behind the fix became Abe Attell, the ex-featherweight boxing champion. A caller to Attell's hotel suite in Cincinnati later told of seeing money stacked on every horizontal surface in the room, on tables, dresser tops and chair seats, after the Reds won the first game.

In the first two games Cicotte's invincible "shine ball" failed him, and he was knocked out in the fourth inning; Williams was uncharacteristically wild and lost 4–2. By the end of the second game, rumors of the fix were rampant, and the Reds were big favorites to take the series. It was impossible to find a professional bookmaker who would bet on Chicago, that action being played strictly by amateur bettors. It took a year-long grand jury investigation to crack the case, with confessions coming from Jackson, Cicotte and Williams. Comiskey was forced to fire all the players except Gandil, who had already "retired."

Testimony showed that most of the players had gotten $5,000 for their parts in the fix, while Gandil had kept $35,000 for himself. How many hundreds of thousands the gamblers made was never really determined. When several of the players left the grand jury room, a group of small boys awaited them. One said to Shoeless Joe Jackson: "It ain't true, is it, Joe?"

"Yes, boys," the outfielder replied, "I'm afraid it is."

The conversation has come down in folklore as the boy wailing plaintively, "Say it ain't so, Joe."

Another bit of folklore is that the baseball establishment excised this cancer as quickly as possible. In fact, the baseball magnates provided legal aid to the players, and indeed, the jury acquitted them and carried some of the defendants out of the courtroom on their shoulders. However, Judge Kenesaw Mountain Landis, appointed commissioner to oversee the integrity of "the Game," was not satisfied. He never let any of the players don a Comiskey uniform again.

See also: ARNOLD ROTHSTEIN.

Blackbeard (?–1718) pirate

No pirate in American history enjoys quite as ferocious a reputation as Edward Teach (or Thack or Thatch) of the 14 wives and the pigtailed beard. A contemporary pirate historian, Capt. Charles Johnson, offered the following description:

> This beard was black, which he suffered to grow of an extravagant length, as to breadth, it came up to his eyes. He was accustomed to twist it with ribbons, in small tails . . . and turn them about his ears. In time of action he wore a sling over his shoulders, with three brace of pistols hanging in holsters like bandoliers, and stuck slow-burning lighted matches under his hat, which, appearing on each side of his face, his eyes naturally looking fierce and wild, made him altogether such a figure that imagination cannot form an idea of a fury from hell to look more frightful.

Not much is known about Blackbeard's early life. He was generally believed to have been born in Bristol, England, although some claimed he was from Jamaica or the Carolinas and "of very creditable parents." Blackbeard himself boasted his parents were even bigger rascals than he, keeping a grogshop and specializing in giving sailors knockout drops and then shanghaiing them. In any event, Blackbeard went to sea at a young age and served on English privateers during Queen Anne's War (1702–13), eventually gathering a group of cutthroats on a ship of his own. When peace came, Blackbeard turned pirate and came to command five ships and crews totaling 400 to 500. By 1716 Blackbeard enjoyed the protection of Gov. Charles Eden of Carolina, who thereafter shared in a portion of the booty taken. Blackbeard preyed on shipping all along the American coast line from New England down to the West Indies. In one of his more daring raids, he once blockaded the port of Charleston, S.C., finally accepting a ransom in drugs and medications.

Under a pardon granted by Gov. Eden, Blackbeard became a familiar figure in what is now North Carolina. At the time he had 13 wives, scattered around various ports. In Bath, N.C. he took bride number 14, a blond-haired girl just turned 15. The marriage barely outlasted the honeymoon when Blackbeard brought a number of his ruffians along for a visit at his new in-laws' plantation. His young wife finally fled and hid with friends. Despite the pirates' lavish spending, the people of Bath soon were disenchanted with Blackbeard, finding that he and his crew made free with their houses and women and demanded all kinds of requisitions from them. Despairing because of the pirate's close ties to the royal governor, several Carolinians appealed to Gov. Alexander Spotswood of Virginia for help. Spotswood could not interfere in another colony but resolved to do something

An old print depicts the bloody end of Blackbeard the Pirate.

about Blackbeard at sea, since the pirate was notorious for attacking Virginian shipping. Spotswood commissioned a young lieutenant named Robert Maynard to conduct a hunt. Maynard finally located the pirate at anchor near Ocracoke Island, off North Carolina. On November 21, 1718 Blackbeard was killed in a fierce battle in which he took five bullets and 25 cutlass wounds before a seaman struck him from behind and sliced his head off. When Maynard sailed back to Virginia, Blackbeard's bloody head was hung by the hair from the bowsprit of his ship for all to see.

Stories of Blackbeard's buried treasure have tantalized fortune hunters for 250 years. Legend places some of his many hoards in such locations as Ocracoke Island; the Isles of Shoals off New Hampshire; Plum Point, N.C.; under the Blackbeard Tree on the island of New Providence in the Bahamas; Ossabaw Island, Ga.; under a walnut in Burlington, N.J.; and the island of Trinidad. None has ever been found.

See also: MAJOR STEDE BONNET, PIRACY.

blackmail

Blackmail, the extortion of money from a victim by threats of public disclosure, censure or exposure to ridicule, is not a frequent crime, if judged by the numbers reported to the police. In one year the New York district attorney reported only four cases had reached his office. However, during that same period three of the larger detective agencies in the city handled more than 50 cases, none of which had been reported to the authorities—and at the time, there were also 300 private detectives in the city. Since even a small agency will get eight or 10 blackmail cases a year, it is evident that police statistics on the crime are meaningless, with perhaps only one in 20 or 50 cases reported. Furthermore, there is no way of measuring how many other victims are too frightened even to enlist the service of a private agency and instead pay off.

Most blackmail cases are based on modern versions of the badger game and involve the sexual misadventures of the victim, complete with pictures. The second largest category is probably homosexual cases, and many of the remainder relate to business shenanigans. A classic example of the latter involved a Brooklyn businessman who faked company expenses to beat the Internal Revenue Service on his income. Unfortunately for him, the businessman let his secretary help with the doctoring, and shortly afterward, the secretary decided she would work only from 11:30 A.M. until 3:00 P.M., with two hours or so for lunch. She doubled her own salary, the balance being off the books. Ironically, the secretary ran afoul of the tax men, and the blackmail case came to light.

Many blackmailers are freelancers such as a brother and sister team who blackmailed a university professor in Massachusetts for $21,000 by claiming that he had fathered the woman's son or a prostitute who milked the son of a former governor for $40,000. However, there have been a number of organized blackmail rings. The most successful of these was the Forcier-Gaffney gang, which extracted at least $2 million from wealthy homosexuals over a period of 15 years. The ring was smashed when one victim finally had the courage to go to the police. Organized crime often uses blackmail in its bankruptcy scams, first getting something on a businessman and using it as a wedge to become his "partner." At the petty end of professional blackmailers was a Midwestern ring that concentrated on housewives who shopped in supermarkets. They spied on the women until they spotted one slipping small items into her purse or coat pocket. Outside the store they would confront her under the guise of being police detectives. They would settle for all the money the woman had on her plus, of course, the groceries.

Blackmail is a crime with a long history. According to the Greek historian Xenophon, blackmailing was so pervasive some 2,300 years ago that many prominent and wealthy citizens of Athens went into exile to escape the exactions of its perpetrators. He also tells us of another victim who subsequently lost all his money in a commercial venture and thus, happily, no longer was compelled to live in fear of the blackmailers. Even today that is probably the most foolproof protection.

Bliss Bank Ring   criminal-police alliance

Crime's golden age in America started with the end of the Civil War, as thousands of wastrels and rogues schooled in the rough-and-tumble of wartime criminality came home determined never to work for a living again. While great gangs had existed in the cities long before the war, the crime specialist emerged during the postwar period. Mobs formed to practice one particular brand of crime, and among the most highly rewarded were the bank burglar gangs. Since the great street gangs had often allied themselves with political protectors and carried out many chores for them, such as winning elections through voter intimidation, it was only logical that the new crime mobs would work with the authorities.

The Bliss Bank Ring, bossed by two leading thieves, George Miles Bliss and Mark Shinburn, was probably the biggest bank mob to appreciate the virtue of working with the law. It was common practice for the Bliss gang to pay off the police with about 10 percent of the loot, somewhat less if the score was exceptionally large. "If we spoil them with too much money," Shinburn said, "they won't be hungry for more."

They hardly needed to worry. The appetite of the police seemed insatiable, and they often squabbled about their individual shares. Capt. John Young, chief of the Detective Bureau of the New York Police Department, finally quit in disgust rather than share the $17,500 cut given him by the Bliss forces for one robbery. The extent of the gang's involvement in police bribery was perhaps best exhibited after Young's departure. Bliss lobbied openly for Detective Jim Irving to be put in charge of the bureau, personally stating his case to Boss Tweed of Tammany Hall. The friction over bribes within the bureau was such, he warned, that some disgruntled member might go to reform-minded Samuel Tilden with the facts. "Put Detective Jim Irving at the head of the Detective Bureau," Bliss told Tweed, "and you'll switch the whole business to safety. If not, I can't say what will happen."

Tweed saw the merits in Bliss' argument, and Irving was given the post, whereupon the bank ring entered its most prosperous period. With the cooperation of the police, the ring pulled off the famous $2.75 million raid on the Ocean Bank located at Fulton and Greenwich Streets, in 1869. The breakdown of bribes paid to police was revealed later by confessions:

James Irving, head of Detective Bureau	$17,000
John McCord, detective	$17,000
George Radford, detective	$17,000
James Kelso, detective	$17,000
Philip Farley, detective	$17,000
John Jordan, captain of the Sixth Precinct and later superintendent of police	$17,000
George Elder, detective	$17,000
Inspector Johnson	$1,800
One other detective	$1,000
Frank Houghtaling, clerk of Jefferson Market Police Court	$10,000
John Browne	$500
Total	$132,000

For this sum of money the police not only did not harrass the Bliss gang but also performed yeoman service in trying to pin the job on the George Leonidas Leslie gang, an outfit notorious for being niggardly in the payment of bribes.

The Bliss Ring survived even the fall of Boss Tweed in 1873, but when Thomas F. Byrnes became head of the Detective Bureau in 1880 and outlawed the alliance between the police and the bank burglars, the gang fell apart. Many members were arrested, and Bliss himself was captured and sentenced to prison for the robbery of a Vermont bank. Penniless when released, he spent his final years writing exposés of crime. Only Shinburn survived the ring's demise, fleeing to Europe, where for years he lived the life of a count, having bought the title with the proceeds of some of his crimes.

See also: MARK SHINBURN.

Bloody Angle   New York murder site

During the great tong wars fought in the early 20th century in New York's Chinatown, the area became an armed camp. Mott Street became the stronghold of the On Leong Tong, while Pell Street belonged to the Hip Sing Tong. Doyers Street was a sort of no-man's-land with a certain sharp turn that journalists labeled the Bloody Angle. The police later estimated that more men were murdered there than at any other spot in New York City and most likely the entire United States. Only the foolhardy ventured past it after dark. The Bloody Angle was ideal for an ambush, with too abrupt a turn for a pedestrian to see ahead. Armed with a snicker-snee, or hatchet, sharpened to a razor's edge, a *boo how doy,* or hatchet man, could strike before the victim had time to cry out, lay the weapon across his throat and flee through an arcade to safety.

See also: AH HOON, BOW KUM, MOCK DUCK, SNICKER-SNEE, TONG WARS.

Bloody Tubs   criminal gang

One of the most vicious gangs in Baltimore, Md. during the mid-1800s, the Bloody Tubs sold their election-influencing services to the highest political bidder. They earned their name from their habit of dunking political opponents in the slaughterhouse tubs. Like another vicious gang of criminals, the Bloody Inks, whose turf extended from Baltimore to Philadelphia, they so terrified voters with their brutal methods that many persons were afraid to come to the polls.

The heyday of both the Bloody Tubs and the Bloody Inks ran from 1857 to 1870. By the end of this period, their crimes were so outrageous that even the most callous politicians could no longer offer them protection or make use of their services. Stripped of their political protection, the Bloody Tubs fell to the mercy of police "head smashers" and retired from the field.

Bloomingdale-Morgan affair   perversion in high places

This sex scandal caused considerable dismay in the Reagan White House and concluded later in a savaqe murder that was judged to be unconnected to it. The scandal erupted when a beautiful playgirl-model filed a $10 million palimony suit in 1982. Thirty-year-old Vicki Morgan filed the claim against multimillionaire Alfred Bloomingdale and later against his estate, charging she had long been "kept" by him for sexual perversions and sadomasochistic orgies. Bloomingdale was the scion of the Bloomingdale's department store family and a longtime friend of Ronald Reagan. His wife, Betsy, was a particularly close friend of the president's wife, Nancy.

The affair had started in 1970 when Morgan was 17 and Bloomingdale was 53. Bloomingdale had spotted Morgan on Sunset Boulevard and followed her into a restaurant and struck up a conversation with her. He insisted on having her phone number before he would leave. Morgan later said, "He was so persistent, I had lunch with him."

Lunch was not what the encounter was all about, and within a week of "wooing," Morgan was mired into Bloomingdale's bizarre world of leather and chains, with Bloomingdale as a demanding dungeon master. Vicki stripped naked along with as many as three other women so that Bloomingdale could whip them and have them engage in an endless number of sexual "games."

The end result: Vicki "found herself falling in love" with Bloomingdale. If love was not enough, there was the matter of compensation. Bloomingdale paid Morgan's rent, provided her with spending money to the tune of a trifling—for him—$18,000 a month and got her launched on a movie career that never amounted to much. This went on for 12 years.

For all his weird activities Bloomingdale still had time to do his thing on the social circuit. He extended his fame and fortune by developing the Diners Club credit card. For a time he was also a Hollywood agent and producer and was a big booster of actor Ronald Reagan's career in state and, later, national politics. After Reagan became president, Bloomingdale, as a member of Reagan's "kitchen cabinet" of political advisers, harbored hopes of becoming ambassador to France. However, he got no such appointment, and it was said later by some observers, this was because the public image–conscious president was obviously aware of his pal's swinging lifestyle. A year later, Bloomingdale became a member of Reagan's Foreign Intelligence Advisory Board, composed of "trustworthy and distinguished citizens outside the government" who reviewed the operations of U.S. intelligence and counterintelligence agencies.

Early in 1982, the 66-year-old Bloomingdale was diagnosed with throat cancer and hospitalized. It was during this period that his wife discovered he had been providing Morgan an $18,000 monthly allowance. Furious, Mrs. Betsy Bloomingdale had the payments stopped. Morgan countered by filing a $5 million palimony suit, claiming she was Bloomingdale's confidante, business partner and traveling companion. Shortly after, she raised the ante another $5 million for Betsy having cut off her $18,000 stipend.

Before the case came to court, Bloomingdale died, on August 20, 1982. The following month, a court threw out most of the $10 million claim, declaring the relationship had been no more than a "wealthy, older

Vicki Morgan's long-running love affair with multimillionaire Alfred Bloomingdale bared perversions in high political and social circles.

paramour and a young, well-paid mistress." The judge permitted to stand Morgan's claim that she had a written contract guaranteeing her a $10,000 payment each month as a partner in Bloomingdale's business interests.

While litigation against the Bloomingdale estate continued, the depressed and angry Morgan moved into a North Hollywood condominium, which she eventually shared with an old friend, Marvin Pancoast, a homosexual with major psychological problems of his own. The condominium became the site of frequent drug and drinking bouts. Arguments between the two over money, mainly that Pancoast could not come up with his share of the expenses, became tense.

On July 7, 1983 Pancoast used a baseball bat to beat Morgan to death. He notified the police and confessed to the crime, but later recanted.

Meanwhile, the embarrassing political fallout continued when an attorney practicing criminal law announced he had been asked to represent Pancoast at this trial and said he had videotapes showing Bloomingdale and Morgan in group and sadomasochistic sex with a number of top government officials. The lawyer said one person so involved "would definitely embarrass the president, just like Mr. Bloomingdale did."

Shortly thereafter, he insisted the tapes had been stolen, and the following day porno publisher Larry Flynt said he had a deal with the lawyer to pay $1 million for the tapes, but that the lawyer never showed up to complete the deal. The lawyer later denied having talked to Flynt. The tape story was considered to be a hoax and the lawyer was charged with having filed a false report.

Pancoast pleaded innocent to the murder of Vicki Morgan by reason of insanity. Records indicated that over the previous 13 years, he had been diagnosed as masochistic, manic-depressive and psychotic-depressive. It turned out he had once even confessed to the Sharon Tate and related murders, which actually were committed by the Charles Manson family. Besides trying to discredit Pancoast's previous confession, the defense also stressed that others had had reasons to murder Morgan because of her claims of depraved sex with government officials. The jury rejected such theories and convicted Pancoast. He was sentenced to 26 years to life in prison.

In December 1984, a jury finally ordered the Bloomingdale estate to pay $200,000 to Morgan's estate, on the grounds that Bloomingdale had promised in a letter in February 1982 to pay $240,000 for Morgan to spend time with him in the hospital during his terminal illness. Morgan had received $40,000 before these funds also had been cut off. Under the law, the money went to her 15-year-old son, who had been fathered during an affair Morgan conducted during a brief breakup with Bloomingdale early on in their relationship.

blue-sky laws

In 1911 the state of Kansas passed the first law to protect the public from the marketing of deceitful stock or shares in worthless, often imaginary enterprises. The "blue-sky" nickname was given to them by a state legislator who demanded that the rules placed on investment concerns "should be as far reaching as the blue sky." The Kansas law and those enacted by other states were vigorously challenged by investment and banking interests until the Supreme Court upheld them in a 1917 ruling. The High Court bolstered the nickname by denouncing fraudulent investment schemes "which have no more basis than so many feet of 'blue sky.'"

Bodie, California   lawless gold-mining camp

Gold placers were first discovered in Bodie in 1859, but since the town was isolated on the eastern slope of the Sierra Nevada, it didn't boom until 1870, when rich veins started showing up. The population quickly mushroomed to some 15,000, drawn by what would eventually prove to be some $100 million worth of ore over the next two decades. With fortunes to be made and stolen overnight, Bodie became perhaps the most lawless, corrupt and vice-ridden town in the West. Three breweries working 24 hours a day, were needed to service some 35 saloons. There were also some 60 bordellos in action on a 24-hour basis, home, according of one historian's account, to no less than 1,800 prostitutes. With a total population of only 15,500, it was clear what the remaining 13,200 were doing when they weren't drinking, digging or killing each other. Violent deaths in such an atmosphere were understandably frequent, and in fact, it was said that Bodie always had "a man for breakfast." Men were killed for their gold in arguments over who paid for the last beer, for being line-jumpers at brothels and, now and then, in disputes about the facts of some previous killing. When one entire Sunday passed without a fatality, folks in Bodie spoke with pride of the "Christian spirit" that had overtaken the town.

Bodie did not live long enough to be tamed. After 1880 the gold finds became less lucrative and by the turn of the century much of the town was empty and forlorn. Some slight mining activity continued up to World War II, but most of the town's well-preserved but unused wooden structures were burned in a fire in 1932. Today Bodie is nothing more than a ghost town with a bloody past.

See also: BADMAN FROM BODIE.

Boesky, Ivan (1937–)   "Ivan the Terrible" of stock deals

Until the mid-1980s Ivan Boesky was regarded as the most controversial high-rolling stock speculator on Wall Street. Few such operators were more feared than "Ivan the Terrible," as he was called. Boesky gambled tens of millions on risky securities deals. Later, when the secrets of his methods were uncovered, he was regarded as one of the biggest crooks in the financial world.

The son of a Russian immigrant in Detroit, Boesky was graduated from law school in 1962 and moved to New York four years later. He did stints in an investment firm and then a brokerage house, and then was attracted to the wild world of risk arbitrage—risking huge sums buying and selling stocks of companies that appeared to be likely to merge or be taken over by other firms.

Boesky launched his own arbitrage firm with $700,000 in capital, and 11 years later had a financial empire worth some $2 billion. He lived with his wife and four children in a 10-bedroom mansion on a 200-acre estate in suburban Westchester County and maintained a lavish river-view apartment in Manhattan. Corporations competed to get him on their boards, and he gave huge sums to charities while making increasing profits on his stock dealings.

Unfortunately, Boesky didn't do this on the up-and-up. He sought out insider tips and paid generously for such illegal information. In May 1986, Dennis Levine, one of Boesky's key illegal sources and a wheeler-dealer in his own right, was trapped by government investigators and started to "sing." The man he gave to the government was Boesky, and Boesky in November of that year made an agreement to pay $100 million in penalties for violating securities laws. To cut his potential prison time, Boesky started to outwarble Levine and turned in his fellow lawbreakers. He even agreed to let investigators tape his phone conversations as he carried out his stock deals. Numerous heads rolled as a result, and Drexel Burnham Lambert, one of the giant financial institutions on Wall Street, plunged to near collapse, turning into a shell of its former self.

In a plea bargain Boesky got off with a three-year sentence, saying he was "deeply ashamed" of his past actions. Many observers thought he had paid a very tiny price for the ruined financial fortunes of so many shareholders. Even his $100 million penalty—the largest of its type in history—left him a most wealthy man. When he left prison, Boesky did, however, face a host of legal actions undertaken by ex-partners and victimized shareholders.

See also: DENNIS LEVINE.

Bolber-Petrillo murder ring

The Bolber-Petrillo murder ring, which reaped a fortune from insurance killings in the Italian community of Philadelphia during the 1930s, is an excellent example of why murder statistics are not to be trusted. The ring disposed of an estimated 30 to 50 victims before police suspicions over just one or two brought about the killers' downfall. From a statistical viewpoint, the case is often cited as an indication that the generally accepted figure of 20,000 murder victims a year may be greatly understated and that a truer figure would be 20,000 known homicides a year and 20,000 undiscovered ones.

Neither Dr. Morris Bolber nor his two cousins, Paul and Herman Petrillo, were much interested in such a statistical overview, being content to rake in a goodly income from the occupation of murder during the Depression, a period when most forms of business were hardly rewarding.

The original murder scheme was hatched by Dr. Bolber and Paul Petrillo in 1932, when they decided to have Petrillo seduce Mrs. Anthony Giscobbe, the wife of one of the doctor's patients. The woman had often complained to Dr. Bolber of her husband's infidelities. When she fell in love with Petrillo, she also rather enthusiastically agreed to a plan to kill her husband for the $10,000 insurance on his life. Since the errant Mr. Giscobbe often staggered home dead drunk, it was a relatively simple matter to undress him and leave him all night by an open window in the dead of winter. Eventually, the husband succumbed to pneumonia, and the grieving widow and Dr. Bolber each netted $5,000. Perhaps the only sad development for the widow was that immediately upon completion of this financial transaction, Paul Petrillo lost all amorous interest in her. The slick-haired Petrillo had moved on to conquer new lonely wives, all of whom had husbands not long for this world.

Since the plotters found that few Italian husbands carried much, if any, insurance, they decided to add a new wrinkle to the operation by recruiting Petrillo's cousin, Herman Petrillo, an actor of some accomplishment with church groups, to impersonate the husbands and apply for insurance. Naturally, the wives were required to screen their husbands' mail and weed out all insurance correspondence. After a few premium payments were made, the husbands were efficiently dispatched. A roofer named Lorenzo was heaved off an eight-story building by the Petrillos in an on-the-job accident that doubled the payment on his life. To make the death more convincing, the Petrillos gave the roofer some French postcards before shoving him off the roof, making it rather obvious that the victim had been distracted by them when he misstepped.

After a dozen or so murders, the plotters recruited a valuable new accomplice, Carino Favato, a faith healer known as the Witch in her own bailiwick. The Witch had murdered three of her own husbands and apparently been consulted by female clients who wished to be rid of their spouses. The Witch poisoned them for a price. However, when Dr. Bolber pointed out that she had erred grievously by not adding the insurance wrinkle to the operation, the Witch was duly impressed, readily agreed to a liaison and was able to supply the names of quite a few potential victims.

The ring went busily about committing murder, most often by poison or by Dr. Bolber's favorite method, "natural means," a canvas bag filled with sand that, when artfully applied, caused a fatal cerebral hemorrhage without any telltale marks. By 1937 the ring's death toll may easily have approached 50, at least 30 of which were rather well documented later on.

A recently released convict in need of money called on Herman Petrillo with a scheme by which they could both make money. Herman was not impressed, mainly because he already had a very good thing going. "Dig up somebody we can murder for some insurance and you can make some dough with us," he told the ex-convict earnestly. The ex-con was frightened of murder and informed the police. The ring's members were rounded up, and with unseemly eagerness, each agreed to inform on all the others in the hope of gaining leniency. Although some wives went to prison, others were permitted to turn state's evidence. Dr. Bolber and the Witch were sentenced to life imprisonment and the Petrillos were executed.

Bolles, Don (1929–1976) murder victim

Don Bolles, award-winning investigative reporter for the *Arizona Republic*, was fatally wounded when a bomb exploded in his car on June 2, 1976. He died 11 days later after having lost both legs and his right arm in the explosion. At the time of the explosion, Bolles told eyewitnesses and paramedics that he "was working on a Mafia story." He also said "John Adamson did it" and mentioned "Emprise," a Buffalo, N.Y. sports conglomerate that had been linked to organized crime and operated dog racing tracks in Arizona. Adamson was a 32-year-old professional racing dog owner.

In December, Adamson confessed a murder-for-hire plot, implicating Max Dunlap, a wealthy Phoenix contractor, and James Robison, a Phoenix plumber. Adamson signed a statement alleging that Dunlap had hired him for $10,000 to kill Bolles because his writings had irritated Kemper Marley, Sr., a 74-year-old rancher and wholesale liquor distributor and one of the richest men in the state. Adamson also claimed Dunlap wanted the reporter killed before Bolles made a scheduled trip to San Diego the following month. The significance of the trip was never established. According to Adamson, he invited Bolles to a Phoenix hotel and then placed a bomb under his car. His statement further declared that Robison detonated the explosive charge from several hundred feet away by use of a radio transmitter.

After Bolles' death, a group of journalists called Investigative Reporters and Editors, Inc. came to the state and wrote about corruption and other criminal matters. Meanwhile, Adamson was allowed to plead guilty to second-degree murder and was sentenced to 20 years and two months. Dunlap and Robison were convicted in 1977 of first-degree murder, mainly on Adamson's testimony, and were sentenced to death. In February 1980 the convictions of the two men, still professing their innocence, were overturned by the Arizona Supreme Court because the trial judge had not permitted the defense to question Adamson about his criminal activities unrelated to the murder.

The state announced plans to retry the pair but in June 1980 asked for dismissal of the charges "without" prejudice because Adamson had refused to testify against them. Adamson indicated he wished a better deal for himself. He was retried alone and found guilty. The state announced plans to push for the death sentence and then allow Adamson to serve a life term if he would once more agree to testify. Many observers felt, however, the Bolles murder case would never be brought to a satisfactory conclusion.

Don Bolles remains the only American reporter believed to have been killed by what is considered "organized crime." *Chicago Tribune* reporter Jake Lingle suffered the same fate in 1930, but his death was not due to his endeavors as a journalist but rather to his own criminal involvement in the rackets.

Bolton, Charles E. SEE BLACK BART.

bombings (aerial) See BOOTLEGGING.

Bonanno, Joseph C. See BANANA WAR.

Bonnet, Jeanne (1841–1876) gangster
Also known as the Little Frog Catcher, Jeanne Bonnet was a bizarre character who founded one of California's strangest criminal gangs, composed only of women. Jeanne got her nickname from the way she made an honest living—catching frogs in the marshes of San Mateo County. She had other unusual habits, including wearing men's clothing and regularly visiting the leading bagnios of the Barbary Coast. Whether her interests were truly or solely sexual became a cloudy issue in view of later events. She formed a gang of women recruited from the brothels, from which they all fled on a single night. A dozen of them joined her, holing up in a shack on the San Francisco waterfront south of Market Street. They lived by robbing, stickups, shoplifting and other forms of thievery, swearing off prostitution completely and having nothing to do with men, except, of course, as victims. The gang crumbled in less than a year, however, when Jeanne Bonnet was found shot to death with a bullet through her heart. The police concluded she had been murdered by one or more of the pimps whose ladies she had taken, thus ending an early, if criminal, experiment in women's liberation.

Bonnet, Major Stede (c. 1670–1718) the Gentleman Pirate
Aside from Blackbeard, Major Stede Bonnet, the so-called Gentleman Pirate, was probably the worst scourge in American coastal waters during the early 1700s, the halcyon years of piracy. Blackbeard's reputation for violence was largely exaggerated, while Bonnet was, in fact, more of a bloodthirsty killer than a gentleman. In pirate legend, it is Blackbeard who made victims walk the plank and then laughed hideously as the poor souls struggled in the water and finally submerged. Actually, it was never proven that Blackbeard made anyone walk the plank. Bonnet, on the other hand, did, having read hundreds of pirate stories and decided that was one of the things a bloody pirate should do.

The information on Bonnet's life is sketchy and not necessarily trustworthy. He was supposedly a man of good family and education who had fought in Queen Anne's War until it ended in 1713, when he retired in middle age to an estate he had bought on the island of Barbados. For no apparent reason, he decided to turn pirate. One historian of the period assures us he "was driven to it by a nagging wife." In any event, Bonnet went about becoming a buccaneer in a most unpiratical fashion: he bought and outfitted a vessel with his own money.

Shortly thereafter, he formed an alliance with Blackbeard, a valuable ally since he was under the protection of Carolina governor Charles Eden. Blackbeard's interest in Bonnet seemed limited to the latter's possession of a vessel that was worth adding to his fleet. Blackbeard insisted on bringing Bonnet aboard his own vessel,

Queen Anne's Revenge, as number two in charge of all pirate activities. It apparently took Bonnet some time to figure out that Blackbeard had simply appropriated his ship and put one of his own men in charge.

Eventually, Bonnet got another vessel and started a one-man crime wave of the sea, looting ships from New England to the Spanish Main. Like Blackbeard, Bonnet maintained control of his crew through threats and violence. Bonnet's crew required merciless discipline, perhaps because the men had little respect for their captain's seamanship. Once when Blackbeard cheated Bonnet out of his share of booty and set sail, Bonnet started out for what is now North Carolina in pursuit but instead wound up in Bermuda.

When Blackbeard was killed on November 21, 1718, Bonnet became a most-hunted buccaneer along the Atlantic Coast. He lasted only until the following December 18, when he was hanged in Charleston. Bonnet had been easily captured after running his ship aground.

See also: BLACKBEARD, PIRACY.

Bonney, William H. See BILLY THE KID.

Bonnie and Clyde   public enemies

As professional thieves, Bonnie and Clyde—Bonnie Parker and Clyde Barrow—never qualified as public enemies. Most of their thefts were of the minor-league variety: grocery stores, filling stations, luncheonettes and a few small-town banks. Their greatest haul was no more than $3,500. But they were brutal, killing at least 13 persons and escaping police ambushes with incredible pluck.

In a sense, Clyde Barrow was cut from a heroic mold, unlike many other gangsters of the 1930s, such as Baby Face Nelson, Pretty Boy Floyd and even John Dillinger. When trapped, he never abandoned his woman, often fighting his way back to her and leading her to safety. It was an odd relationship: a homosexual and a near nymphomaniac.

Born in extreme poverty in Texas in 1909, Clyde followed his older brother into crime, first stealing turkeys and then graduating to cars. The pair committed several robberies in the Dallas area. Finally, after holding up a gas station in Denton, Tex., they were forced to make a 90-mile-an-hour run from the police with Clyde behind the wheel. Buck was shot during the chase, and when Clyde wrecked the car in a ditch, he left Buck for the law, fearing his brother would bleed to death otherwise. Buck got five years.

In January 1930 Clyde met 90-pound, golden-haired 19-year-old Bonnie Parker, who was "sort of married"

to a convict, Roy Thornton, serving 99 years for murder. Bonnie described herself in that period as "bored crapless." They started living together, and Clyde tried to support them by playing the saxophone. It was a futile effort and he quickly reverted to robbery. It wasn't long before Dallas lawmen arrested Clyde for a burglary in Waco: he had left his fingerprints behind. The judge sentenced him to two years.

Buck Barrow escaped from prison, and he and his wife, Blanche, joined up with Bonnie. On a visit soon afterwards, Bonnie passed a narrow-handle .38 Colt through the jail bars to Clyde. After he made his break, Bonnie stayed put for a while to keep the law occupied. The law caught up with Clyde in Ohio.

This time Barrow was sent to the prison farm at Eastham, Tex., one of the most brutal institutions in the state. Clyde endured many tortures there and became a far more hardened criminal and a confirmed homosexual. He served 20 months, gaining a pardon after his mother tearfully pleaded his cause with Gov. Ross Sterling. Clyde Barrow said he would never see the inside of a prison again. "I'll die first," he said, and he was right.

Following Clyde's release, Bonnie teamed up with him on various robberies, but after a confrontation with the police, they became separated and Bonnie was caught. She served three months for the robbery of a car the couple had seized trying to escape. Clyde went on committing robberies and killed his first two lawmen in Atoka, Okla.

When Bonnie rejoined him, they fell in with a gunman named Ray Hamilton, an incorrigible young thief and killer who in many ways was a more spectacular criminal than Clyde. His relationship with Bonnie and Clyde, however, was more meaningful than just the addition of greater firepower on their holdups. Hamilton regularly slept with Bonnie and at times with Clyde as well. It was, by all accounts, a well-adjusted triangle, at least for brief periods. Eventually, the sexual pressures probably became too much for the three, and Hamilton broke away. Both Bonnie and Clyde apparently needed a more submissive love partner; Hamilton was just too tough to give them their way. After leaving them the last time, he pulled off a long string of crimes and several jailbreaks before finally dying in the electric chair in 1935.

While Bonnie and Clyde's robberies continued to be on the minor side, their escapades were often extremely violent. They stuck up a butcher, and when the man came at Clyde with a cleaver, Clyde avoided the blow and emptied his gun into him. In November 1932 the pair held up a filling station and kidnapped the attendant, William Daniel Jones. After learning who his captors were, Jones joined up with them and replaced Ray Hamilton in their affections. He later described his experience as "18 months of hell."

Meanwhile, Buck Barrow had been in and out of jail again, this time pardoned by the new governor, Mrs. Miriam "Ma" Ferguson, who had granted pardons to some 2,000 felons during an earlier term. With Buck and Blanche in tow, the gang now numbered five and was ready for the big time. Brandishing newly obtained machine guns, they held up a loan company office in Kansas City. They had been identified, and their exploits made front-page news from coast to coast, which pleased Bonnie no end. She deluged newspapers with samples of her "poetry." Editors eagerly printed her poem "The Story of Suicide Sal." They also printed pictures of her smoking a cigar and brandishing a machine gun. Bonnie said these were "horsing around" pictures and resented the light in which the newspapers had put them. During their getaways the gang often kidnapped lawmen, one of whom was chief of police Percy Boyd. When they let him go, Bonnie told Boyd: "Tell the public I don't smoke cigars. It's the bunk."

Bonnie and Clyde are snapped in a playful mood. Gag photos such as these did much to capture the public's attention.

They fought their way out of a trap in Joplin, Mo., killing two officers, but it was apparent that the gang could not continue to escape capture or death. In July 1933 the gang was hiding out in the deserted fair grounds in Dexter, Iowa when a posse closed in. Buck Barrow was fatally wounded and Blanche captured. Bonnie and Jones were also wounded, but Clyde got both of them away.

In the next few months, Bonnie and Clyde killed four more lawmen. During this period Jones took the first opportunity to desert them. When picked up in late 1933, he told of his incredible career of crime and suffering with the pair and begged to be sent to prison, where he would be safe from Bonnie and Clyde. The law obliged.

Bonnie knew the end was near. She mailed newspapers "The Ballad of Bonnie and Clyde," which concluded:

The road gets dimmer and dimmer,
Sometimes you can hardly see,
Still it's fight man to man,
And do all you can,
For they know they can never be free.

If they try to act like citizens,
And rent them a nice little flat,
About the third night they are invited to fight,
By a submachine-gun rat-tat-tat.

They don't think they are too tough or desperate,
They know the law always wins,
They have been shot at before
But they do not ignore
That death is the wages of sin.

From heartbreaks some people have suffered,
From weariness some people have died,
But take it all and all,
Our troubles are small,
Till we get like Bonnie and Clyde.

Some day they will go down together,
And they will bury them side by side.
To a few it means grief,
To the law it's relief
But it's death to Bonnie and Clyde.

The pair stayed on the run until May 23, 1934, when they attempted to hook up with Henry Methvin, a convict they had freed once while busting out Ray Hamilton in a daring prison raid. With the law closing in on all sides, they felt Methvin was the only one left outside of family whom they could trust. But Methvin sold them out, informing the law about a roadside rendezvous he was to have with them. In exchange, he was not prosecuted for charges pending against him in Louisiana and Texas.

A trap was set up at Gibland, La., near the Texas border, under the command of Capt. Frank Hamer of the Texas Highway Patrol, an ex–Texas Ranger who for the past three and a half months had been assigned exclusively to tracking down Bonnie and Clyde. Hamer and five other lawmen waited at an embankment armed with a Browning automatic rifle, three automatic shotguns and two rifles.

Bonnie and Clyde drove up to the rendezvous site. Clyde was driving in his socks; Bonnie was munching on a sandwich. They had in their car a shotgun, a revolver, 11 pistols, three Browning automatic rifles and 2,000 rounds of ammunition.

There is some argument about whether they were given a chance to surrender or even knew they had run into a trap. The lawmen opened fire and the pair died instantly. They dug 25 bullets out of Clyde and 23 out of Bonnie.

See also: FRANK HAMER, RAY HAMILTON.

Boodle Gang   early New York hijackers

It may well be that the American crime of hijacking was originated by an 1850s New York street gang known as the Boodle Gang. These toughs raided food provision wagons that passed through their area on the lower West Side. When the wagons started detouring around the Boodle Gang's territory, they descended on the Centre (later changed to Center) Market and became the most efficient of the butcher cart mobs. About a dozen thugs would ride up to a large butcher shop and charge inside. Seizing a whole carcass of beef, they would fling it on their cart and then whip their horses at breakneck speed down the street. The gang's activities did not meet with disfavor in their neighborhood since immediately after a raid a number of stores would offer meats at bargain prices.

In the 1860s the Boodlers perfected their methods and invaded the financial district to rob messengers of their money and securities, a haul more rewarding than meat carcasses. In January 1866 two gang members knocked down a messenger, grabbed his satchel and escaped on a speeding butcher's cart with $14,000 in cash. As they fled, the gang stopped all pursuit by clogging up Beekman Street with three other carts.

The technique was a perfect model for the hijackers of the following century. The police were not particularly successful at rounding up the Boodlers, but the gang eventually disappeared because it could not withstand the depredations of other area gangs, especially the Potashes, who sought to reserve the best criminal activities and territories for themselves.

book whippings

During colonial days books that were deemed offensive were also considered "criminal" in themselves and therefore subject to criminal punishment in addition to being burned. In a typical Massachusetts case, a book was sentenced "to be publicly whipt with 40 stripes, save one, and then burnt." In 1754 the hangman was assigned to perform that same task on a pamphlet that criticized the court. The public punishment was carried out in the middle of Boston's King Street.

Boorn brothers   wrong men convicted of murder

The case of the Boorn brothers has been cited countless times by those warning against the perils of both capital punishment and false confessions.

In 1819 the village of Manchester in Vermont was rocked by a murder trial, described at the time as being "attended by such multitudes" that it had to be held in the Congregational church since the court house was "by a very great deal too small." Seven years earlier, during the War of 1812, a man named Russell Colvin had disappeared from his home after 18 years of a presumably happy marriage that produced a string of numerous and presumably happy children. Folks thought it odd at the time but did nothing about it until old Amos Boorn had a dream in 1819 that was to become most famous. Old Amos was the uncle of Colvin's wife. Three times on a single night in May, Colvin appeared in the old man's dream and informed him that he had been murdered and was willing to name names and places. His murderers, the spirit announced, were Stephen and Jesse Boorn, his brothers-in-law and Amos' own nephews. The murder place was the Boorn farm and "I'm buried there under the stump of a tree."

By October the brothers had been tried, convicted and sentenced to death. Naturally, the state of Vermont had more evidence than just Uncle Amos' dream. Buried in the earth inside the Boorn barn had been found a large knife, a penknife and a button. The knives were identified by Mrs. Colvin as the property of her husband. Then there were the bones found by a dog digging at the base of a stump on the farm. The first announcement was that they "might have been human." Two doctors later said they belonged to an animal, but they had to admit that two toenails found among the bones had "the appearance of belonging to a human foot." Then Jesse, in shackles for three months, made a confession and his brother Stephen followed some weeks later. According to Stephen's written admission, they had murdered Colvin after a fierce argument, buried him, dug up his bones some years later and "throwed them in the river."

At their trial both brothers repudiated their confessions, insisting they had made them simply as a bid for clemency when they saw how inflamed public opinion against them was. Their mother, Mrs. Barney Boorn, was excommunicated from the Baptist church. The state legislature was then petitioned for a commutation of the sentences to life imprisonment. The petition was granted Jesse but denied his brother, who was slated to hang January 28, 1820.

One of the Boorns' attorneys attempted a final gamble; he decided to advertise for Russell Colvin. An advertisement thus appeared in the *Rutland Herald* under the headline "MURDER":

Printers of newspapers throughout the United States are desired to publish that Stephen Boorn, of Manchester, in Vermont, is sentenced to be executed for the murder of Russell Colvin, who has been absent about seven years. Any person who can give information of said Colvin, may save the life of an innocent by making immediate communication.

There followed a short description of the supposed victim. Among the newspapers that picked up the item was the *New York Post,* and it was read aloud one night in a New York hotel to James Whelpley, a former Manchester resident, who began telling stories about the village idiot Colvin. Within earshot of Whelpley was Taber Chadwick. Chadwick realized that his brother-in-law, William Polhemus, who owned a farm in Dover, N.J., had working for him a weak-minded man who called himself Russell Colvin. In late December 1819 Colvin was returned to Manchester. There he confronted Stephen Boorn, whose legs were still fettered in irons.

Colvin looked at the fetters and asked, "What's them for?"

"Because they say I killed you," Stephen said.

"You never did," Russell said in all seriousness. "Jesse threw a shoe at me once, but it didn't hurt me any."

The case was reopened and the Boorns were cleared. In 1820 the brothers petitioned the legislature for compensation for their false conviction and close call with the hangman. Their request was turned down. It was pointed out that both brothers had made false confessions, no matter how desperate their situation, which had helped to convict them.

boot camps A solution whose time came and went

In 1995 it was looked upon as the most promising idea in the battle against serious juvenile crime. Dubbed the Leadership Challenge, it began in Mary-land and called for boot camp programs for teenage criminals. Boot camps had existed before, but this was an ambitious extension of the idea under the aegis of Lt. Gov. Kathleen Kennedy Townsend of Maryland, who previously had been a former assistant attorney general in the Clinton administration where she had studied the boot camp idea and determined it represented "a cost-effective intermediate punishment."

It was thought that military-style discipline would improve juvenile rehabilitation programs. Several other states quickly followed the Maryland program. The results were pathetic, as determined by a national study of such state boot camps that revealed a shockingly high recidivism rate, ranging from 64 to 75 percent.

If asked, the men who ran *genuine* boot camps could have predicted that the juvenile programs would not work. "The key reason we are successful," noted Sgt. Maj. Ford Kinsley, who supervised drill instructors at the Marine Corps' recruitment base at Parris Island, S.C., "is that we have a clientele down here that chose to be here on their own. They are not here because a judge said you should go here. Our population comes with a lot more positive attitudes." He explained that when "a kid graduates from Parris Island, he is just beginning a four- or five-year enlistment in the Marine Corps. It is not like they spend 11 months here and we just throw them out onto the streets."

Besides the high recidivist rates, the juvenile boot camps were plagued by scandals of routine and brutal beatings of inmates by guards. In Maryland, Gov. Parris N. Glendening and Lt. Gov. Townsend suspended the state's camps and fired the top five juvenile justice officials. Soured by similar results, officials in Colorado, North Dakota and Arizona dropped their programs, and others scaled back their efforts amid predictions that they too would fold eventually. In Georgia a Justice Department investigation concluded the state's "paramilitary boot camp model is not only ineffective, but harmful."

A number of experts regarded the boot camp experiments as nothing more than cynical political maneuvers. Dr. David M. Altschuler of the Institute for Policy Studies at Johns Hopkins University described them as "just another knee-jerk reaction, a way to get tough with juveniles that resonated with the public and became a political answer." And Gerald Wells, a senior associate at the Koch Institute, stated, "People thought boot camps shaped up a lot of servicemen during three wars. But just because you place someone in a highly structured environment with discipline, does not mean once they get home, and out of that, they will be model citizens."

Perhaps the major problem with boot camps was the budget issue. Get-tough ideas resonate with the public, but when it came to the extra expense involved in follow-up, the money was not there. Besides with a drop in the juvenile crime rate since 1994, along with the country's overall drop in the juvenile population, it became even harder to interest voters to pay for individualized rehabilitation.

As a result the 27,000 young people who were sent to boot camps each year were largely sent to prison instead. Gerald Wells warned that as bad as boot camps proved to be, "once you start incarcerating kids, you have lost. But unfortunately, that is where we seem headed."

Boot Hill

Almost all Americans believe that every gunslinging western community had its Boot Hill, where all the victims of lead poisoning were buried. The fact is that the "Boot Hill industry" is a 20th-century development. There really was only one Boot Hill and that was at Dodge City. The name referred to a slight rise used as a temporary burial spot and alluded to the custom of burying a corpse there with his boots curled up and placed under his head as a sort of permanent pillow. In due course, Dodge's Prairie Grove Cemetery was completed, and in 1879 the 25 or so inhabitants of Boot Hill were transferred to the new burial grounds.

Most communities didn't know they were supposed to have a Boot Hill until they read modern western novels and saw movies about the Wild West and became aware of the demands of the tourist industry. Along with newly christened Boot Hills came such graveyard graffiti as "Died of lead poisoning" and, for a cattle rustler, "Too many irons in the fire." One of the superattractions of the West is the 20th-century Boot Hill in Tombstone, Ariz., where visitors are welcomed to the burial sites of Tom and Frank McLowery and Billie Clanton, who all died in the famous gunfight at the O.K. Corral. With a certain pride it is claimed that among the graveyard's residents are Dan Dowd, Red Sample, Tex Howard, Bill DeLaney and Dan Kelly, all of whom were "hanged legally," an accomplishment of sorts. In one of the more exploitative events at Tombstone, one promoter tried to sell square-inch plots of Boot Hill cemetery but was squelched by the city council.

See also: LESTER MOORE.

Booth, John Wilkes   See ABRAHAM LINCOLN—ASSASSINATION.

bootlegging

Bootlegging was and is a major pastime in America. Because it remains an illegal enterprise, however, no reliable figures on its scope have ever been established.

The term *bootlegging* derives from the custom of the early Indian traders who carried a bottle of liquor in their boot since such traffic with the red man was either illegal or frowned upon. Hence, a bootlegger came to mean a person engaged in illegal liquor deliveries. Naturally, bootleggers thrived most during Prohibition, from January 16, 1920 until repeal of the 18th Amendment on December 3, 1933. The best guess was that during the Prohibition period Americans annually consumed at least 100 million gallons of bootleg liquor.

Great profits were derived from bootlegging during Prohibition. In the larger cities powerful bootlegging gangs arose to meet demand and to fight bloody wars for control of the huge income. Much of the liquor was smuggled across the border from Canada or Mexico or brought in by boat. Many of the gangs found it necessary to produce their own alcohol to assure themselves of a steady supply and established illegal distilleries and breweries, activities that would be impossible without political and police cooperation.

Prohibition made possible the rise of the "Chicago gangster" and the domination of that city and the entire Midwest by the Capone gang, but only after the gang had eliminated many tough competitors, such as the Dion O'Banion mob and the Bloody Gennas. It has been estimated that more than 1,000 men died as a result of the bootleg wars in Chicago alone.

In Williamson County, Ill. another bloody war was fought, perhaps even more constant and murderously inventive than those in Chicago, Detroit, Philadelphia or New York. It was also the scene of an incredible American first. On November 12, 1926 the farmhouse belonging to a prominent family of bootleggers was subjected to an aerial bombing by a rival bootlegging family. Three projectiles were dropped, but since all failed to explode, no damage occurred and there were no complaints and no arrests. Still, it was the first and only time real bombs were dropped from a plane in the United States in a genuine effort to destroy human life.

Many of the great American fortunes derived from bootlegging activities, as leading businesses, like the criminals themselves, could not resist the lure of huge revenues. In 1930 a federal grand jury uncovered the largest liquor ring of the era. Thirty-one corporations and 158 individuals were cited in Chicago, New York, Cleveland, Detroit, St. Louis, Philadelphia, St. Paul, Minneapolis, Los Angeles and North Bergen, N.J. and charged with the diversion of more than 7 million gal-

The U.S. Coast Guard stopped thousands of boats attempting to bring in bootleg liquor. Despite many shoot-outs and arrests most rumrunners easily reached the shore.

lons of alcohol in seven years. Their total business in bootlegging was put in excess of $50 million.

With the repeal of Prohibition, bootlegging did not simply fade away. Bootleggers have always operated and probably always will. By not paying alcohol taxes the bootlegger is able to put out a more reasonably priced product of "mountain dew," or "white lightning." In 1958 the government seized 15,000 stills, although by the 1970s the figure stood at about only 10 percent of that figure. It is difficult, however, to dismiss bootlegging and moonshining as playful larks; hundreds of tipplers of bootlegged alcohol die each year from poisoning.

One of the more frightful instances occurred in Atlanta, Ga. in October 1951, when a bootlegger used

54 gallons of methyl alcohol to mix up a large batch of moonshine. The liquor was sold all over Atlanta, some to an Auburn Avenue nightclub. One Sunday night a man named Eliza Foster walked into the club and downed a shot. A half hour later he dropped dead. He was the first to go. A little while after that, two more went. A man died in his car, a bottle of this same batch on the seat beside him. Another casualty, a little old lady, died in her rocking chair, a bottle of the bad liquor lying spilled at her feet. In all, 13 people died that day, and hundreds of others, feeling miserable and some already blind or writhing on stretchers, jammed into Grady Memorial Hospital. Tortured, frightened people fell to their knees in prayer, expecting to die, and by Monday night 14 more had passed away, raising the

total to 27. By the end of the week, there were 35 dead—three were children. The figure finally reached 42. There was no reliable estimate of the number of people who went blind. Altogether, however, at least 500 persons were seriously affected. After the mass poisonings the sale of legal whiskey went up 51.2 percent in Atlanta. But the tragedy in that city was not an unusual event. Just two weeks later eight persons in Revere, Mass. died from another batch of poisoned liquor.

There are no accurate national figures on how many deaths are caused each year by poisoned moonshine, but the number of deaths plus those permanently blinded or paralyzed is certainly in the hundreds. Moonshining operations and stills are turned up not only in the backwoods but in the big cities as well. In virtually all these cases a frightening disrespect for human life is exhibited. Producers seeking to cut costs often dilute their moonshine with rubbing alcohol. Some shortcut artists even add lye to the whiskey to give it a sting, and even more callous individuals mix in ether and fuel oil.

Some experts calculate that as much as 20 percent of all alcohol consumed in this country is illicit moonshine, basing their estimates on the government's open admission that it finds no more than one-third to one-half of all illegal stills, a figure that others believe high.

See also: HAMS, PROHIBITION, RUM ROW.

Borden, Lizzie (1860–1927) accused murderess

A well-respected, religious spinster of 32, Lizzie Borden of Fall River, Mass. became without doubt America's most celebrated accused female murderer, charged with the 1892 killing of her father, Andrew, and her stepmother, Abby.

On August 3 of that year, Mr. and Mrs. Borden were both taken ill with severe stomach pains. Lizzie had bought some prussic acid just a short time before, but no connection was ever developed.

Between 9 and 9:30 on August 4, a hot, sweltering morning, someone entered a second-story bedroom of the Borden house and axed Abby Borden to death, bashing her skull 19 times. At the time, Lizzie's sister Emma was away from home, and the only ones known to be in the house besides the victim were Lizzie and Bridget Sullivan, the Irish maid. If either of them was the murderer, they certainly concealed it from the other for the next hour to 90 minutes, each going about their business without indicating any knowledge of the body in the bedroom. At about 10:30 Andrew Borden returned home from his business activities. He lay down on a sofa in the downstairs sitting room to take a nap, and the murderer crept up on him and hit him 10 times with an ax, killing him.

The police charged Lizzie Borden with committing the crimes, strictly on circumstantial evidence, not all of it very strong. For one thing, although the walls of both murder rooms were splashed with blood, no blood was found on Lizzie or her clothes. There was a theory that Lizzie had stripped naked to do the deeds and then had put her clothes back on, but that certainly would have involved a great risk of her being seen by the maid. The authorities claimed but never really proved that Lizzie had burned a dress in the kitchen stove a few days after the murders.

After being held in jail for nearly a year, Lizzie was subjected to a 13-day trial, with the entire nation hanging on every word. Rather than play down the gruesome nature of the murders, her defense attorney stressed this aspect. He then pointed to the prim, very feminine, charity-minded Lizzie and said: "To find her guilty, you must believe she is a fiend. Gentlemen, does she look it?"

The verdict in the case of Lizzie Borden, perhaps this country's most enduring cause célèbre, was not guilty. The jury had needed only an hour to arrive at it.

Lizzie made one statement to the press expressing her elation but then refused to say any more, even though reporters parked in front of the Borden home for weeks and weeks, searching for more morsels to feed their hungry readers. Lizzie enjoyed a considerable public sympathy during her ordeal and through her acquittal, but over the years public opinion seemed to turn, with more and more people regarding her as guilty. After a time she was considered guilty, as the popular rhyme went, of the charge that she "gave her mother forty whacks."

Lizzie and Emma inherited their parents' $500,000 estate, but they soon sold the house and moved into a lavish mansion in Fall River. Lizzie returned to her charitable works. Although she demanded anonymity, it is believed she financed several college educations.

In 1905 Emma moved out of the mansion after an argument. She too had lived under a cloud, and there was even speculation that she was the killer. At the time of the murder, Emma had been staying overnight with friends, but some authorities on the Borden case insisted she could have returned home, committed the crimes and returned to her friends' unseen.

The sisters never spoke again. When Lizzie died in 1927, she left nothing to Emma. Aside from some bequests to servants, she willed the bulk of her estate, $30,000 in cash and large holdings in stocks, to the Animal Rescue Leagues of Fall River and Washington, D.C. She was buried in the family plot beside her mother, father and stepmother.

Bordenmania   impact of Lizzie Borden case

No murder case in American history caused more public repercussions than that involving Lizzie Borden, the 32-year-old spinster who was tried and acquitted of killing her father and stepmother with an ax in their home in Fall River, Mass. in 1892. The case was the subject of an endless number of books, magazine articles and newspaper accounts. Edmund Pearson explained the public's fascination with the case may have resulted from its very "purity." The murders, and Lizzie's guilt or innocence, were uncomplicated by such sins as ambition, robbery, greed, lust or other usual homicidal motives. Innocent or guilty, Lizzie became an American hero.

The verse and doggerel on the case varied from the anonymous children's jump rope rhyme:

> *Lizzie Borden took an ax*
> *And gave her mother forty whacks;*
> *When she saw what she had done,*
> *She gave her father forty-one.*

to A. L. Bixby's almost endearing:

> *There's no evidence of guilt,*
> *Lizzie Borden,*
> *That should make your spirit wilt,*
> *Lizzie Borden;*
> *Many do not think that you,*
> *Chopped your father's head in two,*
> *It's so hard a thing to do,*
> *Lizzie Borden.*

The *New York Times* informed its readers that controversy over Lizzie Borden's innocence or guilt was directly responsible for 1,900 divorces. Such was the grip of "Bordenmania" on the entire nation.

Borne, Henry   See DUTCH HENRY.

Boston, Patience (1713–1735)   first woman hanged in Maine

In Puritan New England, Patience Boston was often cited from the pulpit as proof of how one sin begets another. She was first caught lying, then swearing, then being drunk, then stealing and finally committing murder. In 1735 Boston killed eight-year-old Benjamin Trot of Falmouth by picking him up and throwing him down a well to drown after he had accidentally tramped on her toe. There was only a minimum of debate about sparing her life because she was a woman, a fact certainly outweighed by her heinous past record as a liar, curser, drunk and petty thief. She was hanged in York on July 24, 1735, the first woman to suffer that fate in what is now Maine.

Boston police strike

On September 9, 1919 a union of policemen in Boston went on strike; 1,117 out of 1,544 patrolmen walked off their jobs after the police commissioner refused to recognize their right to join the American Federation of Labor (AFL). Under an unusual law, the police commissioner was appointed by the governor of the state rather than the mayor of the city and thus had much more freedom. Although Mayor Andrew J. Peters and a citizens committee made compromise proposals on pay and working conditions to head off the strike, the police commissioner rejected them. The resulting strike left Boston virtually unprotected and riots, robberies and lootings followed.

Before the strike began, Mayor Peters and James J. Storrow, the head of the citizens committee, had urged Gov. Calvin Coolidge to act, but he had refused. When rioting broke out, the mayor called out Boston contingents of the militia, established order and broke the strike. Then Gov. Coolidge ordered the commissioner to take charge of the police once more and called out the entire Massachusetts militia. With the police union defeated, AFL head Samuel Gompers tried to win back the jobs of the strikers, who had all been fired. Coolidge responded with a statement that made him famous, won him the vice-presidential nomination in 1920 and paved the way for his subsequent succession to the presidency. "There is no right to strike against the public safety by anybody, anywhere, any time," Coolidge said.

Boston Strangler   See ALBERT H. DESALVO.

Botkin, Cordelia (1854–1910)   poisoner

A poisoner convicted in one of the most sensational trials of the 1890s, Cordelia Botkin may well have been, as the Sunday supplement writers later referred to her, the original Red Hot Mama. Certainly her triangle love affair earned her a reputation as a truly wanton woman as well as a murderess.

A stocky, fleshy woman living in San Francisco, she nonetheless seemed to have all the charms necessary to lure a successful journalist named John Presley Dunning away from his wife and child for a life of gambling and whoring. In 1896 Dunning's wife had had enough and returned to her parents in Dover, Del. While that should have pleased Botkin, she still feared Dunning's wife might someday lure him back, and she deluged Mrs. Dunning with anonymous threatening letters, advising her against trying to rejoin her husband.

In 1898 Dunning got an assignment covering the Spanish-American War, and Botkin grew more certain he would not return to her. Her depression gave way to murderous thoughts. She went out and bought a box of chocolates, a lace handkerchief and two ounces of arsenic. She spent several hours inserting arsenic into each piece of candy. She enclosed the handkerchief and a note that read "With love to yourself and baby—Mrs. C." and tied up the whole package with pink ribbons. The next day she mailed the "gift" to Mrs. Mary Dunning in Delaware.

When the box arrived, Mrs. Dunning puzzled over the identity of the "Mrs. C." who had sent the candy. She thought of several people it might have been. But having a sweet tooth, she didn't hesitate long before polishing off the box. Her sister, Mrs. Joshua Deane, joined in. Twenty-four hours later both women were dead. The deaths did not help Botkin's lovelife, however, because the box of candy was eventually traced back to her in San Francisco.

After a lurid trial that satisfied even the most avid readers of the sensational press, she was found guilty of murder on December 31, 1898 and sentenced to life imprisonment. She died in San Quentin in 1910.

bounties See BANK ROBBERIES—BOUNTIES; JOHN BILLEE; OUTLAW EXTERMINATORS, INC.

bounty jumping Civil War racket
During the Civil War enterprising individuals and organized gangs reaped a fortune collecting bounties for enlisting in the Union Army and then immediately deserting. The cycle would then be repeated, generally in another congressional district or state, for amounts that varied from $100 to as much as $1,000.

One specialist in this racket was caught after 32 enlistments and desertions, a record that drew him a four-year prison term. A notorious Chicago underworld character named Mike McDonald operated a bounty racket on an organized basis, recruiting hoodlums to sign up for service. McDonald collected a commission each time and shuttled the men around to different areas for repeat tries, keeping track of his "campaigns" on a large war map with tacks indicating where each hoodlum was assigned. Profits from this racket provided McDonald with the capital to set up several gambling houses after the war.

There are some estimates that perhaps nearly half of all desertions from the Union Army, which totaled 268,000, were really cases of bounty jumping. While such figures are most likely too high, considering the large number of draftee desertions, they are at least indicative of how widespread the crime was.

See also: MICHAEL CASSIUS "MIKE" MCDONALD.

Bow Kum (1889–1909) murder victim
Bow Kum, meaning "Little Sweet Flower," was a beautiful slave girl of 15 when she was illegally brought into the United States by a wealthy San Francisco Chinese, Low Hee, who had paid a Canton slave merchant the unheard of sum of $3,000 for her. The American authorities found out about Bow Kum some three years later and despite Low Hee's valid bill of sale, placed her in a home. Bow Kum was finally released when she married another man, Tchin Len, who took her to New York. A dispute broke out between Low Hee and Tchin Len on the matter of compensation and soon involved three groups: the On Leong Tong, an alliance of the Hip Sing Tong and a fraternal organization called the Four Brothers. These groups were already at odds on such matters as the control of gambling in various parts of New York's Chinatown. As the dispute appeared beyond settlement, the On Leongs murdered Bow Kum on April 15, 1909, and the first of Chinatown's great tong wars broke out.

One typical killing spree took place in the venerable Chinese Theater on Doyers Street on New Year's night during a supposed truce in the fighting that had been arranged for the biggest Chinese celebration of the year. The performance went along smoothly until a celebrant in the audience suddenly tossed a bunch of lighted firecrackers into the air. This caused a brief commotion before things quieted down. As the audience filed out at the end of the performance, five men remained in their seats. They all had bullets in their heads. The banging of the firecrackers had drowned out the cracks of the revolvers of five Hip Sings behind five On Leongs.

Police estimates of casualties during the war were put at about 350 before the tongs came to a peace settlement in late 1910 and the war over Little Sweet Flower ended.

See also: AH HOON, BLOODY ANGLE, MOCK DUCK, TONG WARS.

Bowdre, Charlie (c. 1853–1880) accomplice of Billy the Kid
Charlie Bowdre's grave is among the most visited in the country, but only because he shares it in common with Billy the Kid. They, together with another of the Kid's sidekicks, Tom O'Folliard, lie in Old Fort Sumner, N.M. under a stone marker bearing the inscription "Pals."

Bowdre, somewhat older than the Kid, seems to have always been fascinated by him. A cowboy drifter, he settled in New Mexico Territory in the late 1870s and married a pretty Mexican girl named Manuela. He apparently wanted to retire from the wild life, but with the outbreak of the Lincoln County War, he took up his guns on behalf of the Tunstall-McSween group and joined forces with Billy the Kid. By the time the war ended, Bowdre was convinced that Billy was the smartest and toughest man ever to ride a horse. When the Kid said they were going into the cattle-rustling trade, Bowdre went along without question. But his blind faith in Billy came to an abrupt halt on December 21, 1880, when a posse headed by Pat Garrett cornered the Kid's gang in a deserted farmhouse at Stinking Springs. In the gunfight that ensued Billy shoved Bowdre, who had been hit five times, through the door of the house, saying: "They have murdered you, Charlie, but you can get revenge. Kill some of the sons of bitches before you go." Bowdre lived only long enough to pick up another couple of bullets; lunge forward mumbling, "I wish . . . I wish"; and die. A short while later, Billy the Kid surrendered to Garrett. The gunfight at Stinking Springs perhaps gives the inscription "Pals" an ironic twist.

See also: BILLY THE KID, PATRICK FLOYD GARRETT, LINCOLN COUNTY WAR.

Bowers, J. Milton (1843–1904) accused murderer

The Bowers case, involving a handsome young San Francisco doctor who lost three wives to early deaths, was one of the 19th century's most sensational, controversial and protracted. The doctor, J. Milton Bowers, was convicted of murder and later cleared, although not to the satisfaction of the police or a substantial portion of the public.

Bowers' third wife, 29-year-old Cecelia, had been ill for two months before dying from what appeared to be an abscess of the liver. Dr. Bowers appeared appropriately grief stricken over the death of his wife of three years. But an anonymous letter triggered an investigation, and an autopsy was ordered. When the body was found to contain phosphorus, Bowers was charged with murder. He was pilloried in the press, and the public seemed obsessed with the fact that Cecelia was the third of Bowers' wives to die after a short-lived marriage. In addition, all three had been duly insured. There were also charges that Bowers was a criminal abortionist. At Bowers' trial much damning evidence was presented by his brother-in-law, Henry Benhayon, who testified that the doctor had prevented his wife from receiving outside care during much of her illness. Bowers was convicted of first-degree murder and incarcerated pending a decision on his appeal for a new trial.

In October 1887 Henry Benhayon was found dead in a rooming house. Police discovered a bottle of potassium cyanide and three suicide notes. One of the notes, addressed to the coroner, confessed that Benhayon had poisoned Mrs. Bowers. While this sensational development appeared to clear Dr. Bowers, the police were not convinced that the suicide note was genuine or that Benhayon's death was a suicide. Tracing purchases of potassium cyanide, the police located a druggist who identified one John Dimmig as a purchaser. They then discovered that Dimmig had visited Bowers in his jail cell.

Although he denied having bought the poison or being involved in Benhayon's death, Dimmig was charged with murder. The first trial ended in a hung jury. In the meantime, Dr. Bowers' motions for a new trial were rejected. Dimmig was tried again in late 1888 and acquitted. In August 1889 Dr. Bowers was released from jail, where he had been confined for four years. He eventually married a fourth time, and when he died in 1904 at the age of 61, the murder of Cecelia Bowers was still being carried in police files as "unsolved."

Bowery Boys early New York gang

One of the toughest gangs in New York during the early 1800s was the famed Bowery Boys, who, as native Americans, did battle with the dreaded Irish gangs, especially the Dead Rabbits and their satellites. On occasion, they also fought the police.

Unlike the other great gangs, the Bowery Boys were not loafers and bums—except on Sundays and holidays. Nor were they criminals, except once in a while, until the Civil War. The average Bowery Boy was a burly ruffian who worked as a butcher or apprentice mechanic or perhaps a bouncer in a Bowery saloon or dance cellar. Almost always, he was a volunteer fireman, an avocation that gave the Bowery Boys important political pull since the firemen were strong allies of Tammany Hall and thus had important influence on the running of city government. The Bowery Boys were especially valuable allies on election day when their rough activities often determined voting results.

The Bowery Boys' hatred of Irish gangs and of foreigners in general was implacable, and they campaigned strongly for those candidates who ran against naturalization laws and favored their repeal so that Irish voters could be stripped of their citizenship. The Bowery Boys worked on behalf of such candidates with blackjacks in hand and voted early and often themselves in every election.

The Bowery Boys' greatest fight was a two-day battle on July 4 and 5, 1857, when allied with forces of the anti-Irish Native American Party, they withstood an invasion of the Bowery by the Dead Rabbits and the Plug Uglies and other gangs from the Five Points area. With more than 1,000 combatants taking part, the police lacked sufficient manpower or backbone to stop the fighting throughout the first day and much of the second. Officially, eight gang members died and another 100 were injured, but it was known that both sides dragged off a considerable number of corpses for secret burials in their own bailiwicks.

During the Draft Riots the Bowery Boys took part in much of the criminality loosed on the city. After that, the gang splintered into various smaller groups, almost all involved in illegal pursuits.

See also: DEAD RABBITS, DRAFT RIOTS.

bowie knife

Fashioned either by the famed Jim Bowie or his brother Rezin P. Bowie, the bowie knife was the West's most popular close-combat weapon before being supplanted by the six-shooter. The Mississippi pirates disemboweled their victims with it; the early river gamblers settled disputes with it; the Texas Rangers carried it as a sidearm; and the men of the mountains and the West hunted with it, slaughtered animals with it, cut wood with it and ate with it.

The knife was baptized in blood by Jim Bowie in the famous Sandbar Duel fought on the Mississippi near Natchez in 1827. Jim Bowie, appearing only as a second for one of the participants, joined in a murderous melee that broke out and killed a second for the rival party with a 15-inch-blade knife. He butchered his opponent so efficiently that word of his wicked weapon spread rapidly. The homemade knife had originally been fashioned from a large blacksmith's rasp, but given its new notoriety, the Bowie brothers sent it to a Philadelphia cutlery manufacturer who shaped and polished it to their instructions and christened it a bowie knife.

An authentic bowie knife was anywhere from 15 to 20 inches in overall length with a blade of 9 to 15 inches, sharpened only on one side to the curve of the tip and then on both sides to the tip. A handguard of brass allowed the knife wielder to thrust or parry and slide his hand down over the blade as the situation required. Weighing 2 pounds or more, it could be used for brute force or deft lethality.

Once the weapon became popular, more than a dozen cutlers started producing it, each claiming to have been the originator. There was, however, no dispute over the knife's intended use. A Sheffield, England manufacturer catered to the market perfectly by inscribing on the blade the legend "America Can and Must be Ruled by Americans."

See also: SANDBAR DUEL.

Boyd, Jabez (?–1845) murderer

Eventually to be known as the American Jekyll and Hyde, Jabez Boyd was always judged to be a highly religious man in his community, but it appears that he used his church-going activities to learn when potential victims would be abroad with sums of money on their person or in their homes. He would then strike accordingly.

One night in 1845, Boyd waylaid Wesley Patton in Westchester, Pa. When Patton resisted and possibly recognized Boyd, the latter clubbed him to death. Unknown to Boyd, another man witnessed the crime and identified him. When Boyd was apprehended the next day, he was sitting in a church pew "with a hymn book in his hand, and from which he was singing with apparent composure." He was hanged forthwith.

When four decades later Robert Louis Stevenson created *The Strange Case of Dr. Jekyll and Mr. Hyde*, an enterprising American journalist tried to resurrect Boyd as the source of Stevenson's inspiration. This thesis had and has nothing to recommend it other than increased circulation, since Stevenson was known to have based his tale of "man's double being" on Deacon William Brodie, an 18th-century Scotsman who, while a respected member of the Edinburgh town council, led a gang of criminals.

Boyle, W. A. "Tony" (1902–1985) labor leader and murderer

In labor's worst murder scandal during recent years, rivaling the disappearance of ex-Teamsters boss Jimmy Hoffa, United Mine Workers (UMW) president Tony Boyle was convicted of the 1969 murder of union rival Joseph Yablonski and Yablonski's wife and daughter. On December 31, 1969, seven months after the 59-year-old Yablonski, a union rebel, announced he would oppose Boyle for the UMW leadership, he, his wife, Margaret, 57, and their daughter Charlotte, 25, were shot to death while they slept in their Clarksville, Pa. home.

Boyle, angered by the grass roots opposition to his reign, ordered Yablonski's assassination after a heated board meeting in Washington the previous June. The plot began to unravel when William Turnblazer, a lawyer and former UMW District 19 president, admitted his role in the conspiracy. He testified that the order was given as Boyle, Turnblazer and Albert Pass stood outside an elevator. At his first trial in 1974 in Media, Pa. Boyle insisted no such meeting had taken place, but he was found guilty. Three others pleaded guilty, including Pass, who was sentenced to three consecutive life prison terms. Boyle got the same sentence.

Boyle's conviction was overturned by the Pennsylvania Supreme Court because the presentation of certain evidence had not been permitted. A retrial in 1978 ended with the same verdict, and the same sentence was again imposed on Boyle, then 77 and suffering from heart disease. He died in 1985.

Brady gang   public enemies

Although they are little remembered now, the Brady gang were the most sought criminals in the United States, following the fall of such 1930s gangsters as Dillinger, Baby Face Nelson, Pretty Boy Floyd, Bonnie and Clyde, and the Barker-Karpis mob. By eradicating the Brady gang, the FBI disarmed the critics of its methods. Before that, J. Edgar Hoover had been attacked on the floor of the U.S. Senate as being a personal coward, the FBI had been criticized for killing John Dillinger without giving him a "chance"; and when Hoover made his famed foray to New Orleans to arrest Alvin Karpis personally, the newspapers gleefully reported that none of the host of FBI agents making the arrest had thought of bringing along a pair of handcuffs.

The Brady gang began in Indiana during the early 1930s, when three former lonewolves—Al Brady, Clarence Shaffer and James Dalhover—teamed up to terrorize the Midwest. While the other public enemies fell one by one, Brady and his two friends left a trail of holdups of banks and other establishments during which they killed two clerks and three police officers. They had been captured once but had escaped jail and by the end of 1937 were the most hunted men in the country. Feeling the "heat," the trio moved into virgin territory in Maine. In October 1937 they entered a sporting goods store in Bangor and asked for two revolvers of a certain make. The clerk waiting on them recognized the three as the Brady gang and said the weapons would be in stock the following week. On October 12, 1937 the trio returned and were recognized by an employee, who immediately pulled a hidden cord that caused a suspended show card to drop in the store window. At that instant four FBI men, guns drawn, jumped from hiding places under the counter and surprised the gangsters, who turned and charged out the door. They were immediately hit with a hail of bullets fired by 16 other FBI agents hidden across the street. Brady and Shaffer died instantly; Dalhover lived long enough to be executed. More important, the FBI received no criticism for the ambush of the gang. In part, that was because none of the gangsters ever exhibited the verve and flair of John Dillinger. But it was also true that the public took the Brady gang for what they were, brutal murderers. The days of romanticizing public enemies was over.

branding   punishment for crime

Branding as a punishment for crimes was never as widely used in the New World as in Europe, but it was a standard form of punishment in colonial America. In the Massachusetts colony the wearing of signs or initials on a person's outermost garment was in effect a method of symbolic branding. Thus, in Boston in 1639 Richard Wilson had to wear a T for theft of "money and diverse small things" from his master, and about the same time in Plymouth, Katheren Aines, a married woman, was required to wear a B for bawd "for her unclean and laciviouse behavior with . . . William Paule."

A number of crimes were considered so heinous that branding was mandatory even for a first offense. Burglary of a dwelling house called for the letter B to be branded on a culprit's forehead. A second such offense required a second branding and whipping. A third offense called for the death penalty. Counterfeiting was considered such a danger that the offender was branded on his right cheek with an F for forger. It was presumed that such a branding would be proper warning to any potential victims to beware of their money or supposed legal records.

With proper application, branding of course produced a permanent scar, but the punishment was considered so awesome that several constables took to using a light touch or an iron not heated sufficiently to destroy the tissue.

Officially, the branding iron was last used on Jonathan Walker, who in 1844 had the letters S.S. (for slave stealer) burned into the palm of his right hand; however, the practice of branding continued as an acceptable form of punishment in the informal miners courts in the West and in the military, especially during the Civil War. On October 10, 1863 a Union artillery brigade held a mass branding of those being drummed out of the service for deserting their batteries. The brigade was assembled in the form of a hollow square facing inward, with a battery forge in the center. A battery blacksmith heated irons, and the letter D was burned into the convicted men's left hips. Significantly, the army had by this time restricted branding to relatively unseen parts of the body. Miners courts, acting in a lawless environment, were not as lenient. Generally, these courts believed in only two penalties, hanging and expulsion from the community. When this later punishment was decreed, the convicted man was often branded on the forehead, face or hands to give due warning to other communities of his unsavory character. This extralegal form of punishment disappeared by the 1880s and 1890s.

See also: JONATHAN WALKER.

Further reading: *Crime and Punishment in Early Massachusetts* by Edwin Powers.

Bras Coupe (?–1837) slave outlaw

In the 1820s one of the most famous slaves in New Orleans was Squier, an exceptionally talented Bamboula dancer. His master was Gen. William de Buys, well known as an indulgent slave owner. The general was all the more indulgent of a famous slave like Squier. He taught Squier to shoot and let him go hunting alone in the forests and swamps. A big and powerful man, Squier became adept at firing a rifle with either hand, something that would stand him in good stead later on. He also became accustomed to the feeling of freedom. So much so, that he ran away. When he was caught, he escaped again. In 1834 Squier was shot by a patrol of planters hunting slaves in the swamps, and his right arm was amputated. As soon as his wound had healed, Squier ran away again, determined never to be retaken. He organized a gang of escaped blacks and—what truly terrified New Orleans—some renegade whites. Now known as Bras Coupe, the escaped slave led his gang on frequent robbery and murdering raids around the outskirts of New Orleans. For nearly three years Bras Coupe was the scourge of New Orleans, a hobgoblin used by mothers and nurses to frighten their children. The New Orleans *Picayune* described him as "a semi-devil and fiend in human shape" and called his life "one of crime and depravity." What frightened the slave owners most, of course, was the fact that Bras Coupe became a hero to the other blacks. They endowed Bras Coupe with superhuman powers. In the instant folklore that sprung up around him, the veritable superman was fireproof and, having now lost his one weak arm, invulnerable to wounds. Hunters who tried to take him in the swamp stood in awe as their bullets flattened against his chest while he laughed. Sometimes the bullets whizzed off Bras Coupe's chest and came flying back at the hunters. When a detachment of soldiers invaded his lair, they were swallowed up in a cloud of mist and never seen again. Bras Coupe was said to paralyze with a mere glance and to nourish himself on human flesh.

Bras Coupe's mythic qualities were tarnished on April 6, 1837, when he was shot by two hunters. But he escaped and it was assumed, would surely survive since he knew all the miraculous herbs that could be found in the swamps. On July 19 of the same year, the legend came to a tawdry end. A Spanish fisherman, Francisco Garcia, long considered to be in league with the slave-outlaw, brought Bras Coupe's body into New Orleans on a mule-drawn cart. He said Bras Coupe had fired on him from the shore of the Bayou St. John. Infuriated, Garcia said he had come ashore and beat the slave renegade's brains out with a club. The weight of evidence, however pointed to the conclusion that Bras Coupe had been murdered as he slept in Garcia's hut. Garcia demanded the $2,000 reward that had been posted for the outlaw; but however much the whites had feared the man they called the Brigand of the Swamp, they had little stomach for the Spaniard's act. He was given only $250 and told to leave. The body of Bras Coupe was displayed for two days in the Place d'Armes so that several thousand slaves could be brought to view it as an object lesson.

Breakenridge, William (1846–1931) western lawman

An opponent of the Earps, Deputy Sheriff Billy Breakenridge of Tombstone was a "survivor" of the Tombstone feuds and certainly one of the few lawmen ever to hire known outlaws to act as his bodyguards.

A native of Wisconsin, Breakenridge served in the U.S. Cavalry and later made an unsuccessful attempt at prospecting. In 1880 he was a deputy to Sheriff John Behan, a law officer often at odds with Wyatt Earp and accused of being in league with the notorious Clantons and Curly Bill Brocius, the leaders of the "cowboy element," which was more or less a synonym for rustlers. Breakenridge's main duty was the collection of taxes, an occupation not noted for longevity in the area around Tombstone. To solve this problem, Breakenridge approached Curly Bill and asked him to act as his bodyguard while he made his rounds in outlaw territory. On the surface, Curly Bill's agreement appeared to be a lark, but it was far more likely that the outlaw was interested in cementing his relations with Behan.

In all the violence of the Tombstone feuds, including the famous gunfight at the O.K. Corral, Breakenridge, although not loved by the Earp faction, at least managed to avoid antagonizing the Earps to the point of provoking a showdown. As a result, and in spite of the "Behan stain," Breakenridge continued to hold down various law enforcement jobs, working as a U.S. marshal and as a special agent for the Southern Pacific Railroad. He died in 1931, six years after a much publicized "reconciliation" with Wyatt Earp.

See also: JOHN BEHAN.

Bredell, Baldwin See COUNTERFEITING.

Bremer, Arthur Herman (1950–) would-be assassin

On the afternoon of May 15, 1972, George Wallace was campaigning at a Laurel, Md. shopping center in his quest for the Democratic presidential nomination. He left the bulletproof podium and was shaking hands with people when a young blond man called several times, "Hey, George, over here!" Wallace moved toward that area, and the youth pulled a gun and fired several shots at Wallace, hitting him four times. In the ensuing struggle with Wallace's guards, the assassin emptied his weapon, wounding three others, all of whom recovered. Wallace himself remained paralyzed afterwards because of a bullet that lodged near the spinal column.

The would-be assassin was identified—how soon was to be a matter of some concern later—as Arthur H. Bremer, a young man in his twenties who had been a janitor's assistant and a busboy in Milwaukee, Wis. In November 1971 Bremer had been charged by Milwaukee police with carrying a concealed weapon, but this was reduced to a disorderly conduct charge and the gun confiscated. Shortly thereafter, he went out and bought two other guns.

On March 1, 1972 Bremer started following the Wallace campaign trail. During that period he spent about $5,000, although his total earnings for 1971–72 came to only $1,611. At times, he left the Wallace trail. On April 7 and 8 he stayed at the Waldorf-Astoria Hotel in New York, where Hubert Humphrey was staying. Bremer then traveled to Ottawa, Canada, where he stayed at the expensive Lord Elgin. He also checked into a number of motor inns along the Wallace campaign route. Where he got the money for the bills has remained a mystery, especially since it was established that he had not received any money from his parents.

As is customary in such cases, Bremer was initially reported to be a "loner," but that does not appear to have been very accurate. He had quite a few friends in Milwaukee, including Dennis Cassini, an individual officials never got to question. He was found dead of a heroin overdose, his body locked in the trunk of his own automobile. Although this was reported to the FBI, there is no indication that its director, L. Patrick Gray, ordered any inquiry into the matter. Other odd facts or circumstances developed. Bremer had been seen in Ludington, Mich. in the company of a man described as having a "New Joisey brogue." Roger Gordon, who was a former member of the Secret Army Organization (SAO), a right-wing intelligence organization, said the man was Anthony Ulasewicz, a White House operative later to win fame in the Watergate scandal. Gordon later left the country.

There were prominent reports that White House aide Charles W. Colson ordered E. Howard Hunt (two more Watergate personalities) to break into Bremer's apartment and plant Black Panther Party and Angela Davis literature. More explosive than that charge was the allegation that the order was given within one hour of the attempt to kill Wallace.

Commenting on these details in an interview with Barbara Walters, Wallace said: "So I just wondered, if that were the case, how did anyone know where he lived within an hour after I was shot?"

A practical political result of the attempted assassination of Wallace was to force him out of the 1972 race, in which he was expected to run as a third-party candidate. A week before the election, voters were polled on how they would have voted had Wallace run. The results were Nixon, 44 percent; McGovern, 41 percent; Wallace, 15 percent. Such a result, because of how the vote broke down, would likely have thrown the election into the House of Representatives, where Wallace would have had considerable influence. With Wallace out of the race, virtually all his supporters went to President Nixon.

Arthur Bremer has steadfastly refused to state why he shot Wallace. He was sentenced to 63 years, over objections by his attorneys that he was unbalanced. He has been described as a loner in the Maryland State Penitentiary, working in the print shop.

"Bremer does not give interviews," Warden George Collins said in 1979. "In fact, he won't even see his mother. She came in all the way from Milwaukee at Christmas, and he talked to her for about five minutes and went on back down inside. He just doesn't want to be bothered. He just doesn't want any hassle." The warden did add Bremer was "a very good inmate, so far as obeying institution rules is concerned."

Brennan, Molly (?1853–1875) murder victim

A dance hall girl at the Lady Gay gambling saloon in Sweetwater, Tex., Molly Brennan participated in a love triangle that provided western folklore and Hollywood with one of the most oft-used clichés ever.

A character named Melvin King, who was a sergeant with the 4th Cavalry when he wasn't beating up or shooting up folks, was romantically inclined toward Molly. Once while on leave, King rode up to Kansas to visit friends, which put him far out of sight and out of mind for Molly, who then took an interest in a civilian scout for the army named Bat Masterson. Returning from his leave, King was already in a foul mood, having come out second best in a dispute with Wyatt Earp, and he was spoiling for a fight. When he heard about Molly's fickleness, he rode hell-for-leather toward

Sweetwater. King stormed into the Lady Gay to find Molly and Bat on the dance floor. Masterson barely had time to unclinch from Molly as King drew his gun. At the same time King fired, Molly threw her body in front of Masterson and took the bullet in her stomach. King's second shot shattered Masterson's pelvis, but as Bat was falling, he drew his .45 and shot King dead. Molly Brennan died shortly afterward as a result of her wound.

An unkind chronicler said that out of respect for Molly, Bat Masterson avoided all romantic entanglements for a month. Considering the condition of Masterson's pelvis, this was almost certainly both untrue and ungracious. It became the custom at the Lady Gay for the men to toast the memory of Molly Brennan, and her sacrifice went on to be reenacted in scores of Hollywood shoot-'em-ups.

briefcase agents early FBI men

During the early years of the FBI, agents were not permitted, under ordinary circumstances, to carry a gun or make an arrest, other than those an average citizen could make. If they needed to arrest someone, they were required to seek local assistance. Such restrictions on federal agents made sense in terms of preventing the rise of a national police force, but in actual practice they led the underworld to regard the FBI as an impotent force. FBI men became known as "briefcase agents," because that was about the only equipment they could carry. The requirement that the FBI seek local assistance in making arrests proved to be a serious drawback because of the widespread corruption among many local police departments. By the time agents arrived to arrest a suspect, he often had already fled the scene thanks to the local police "pipeline." The FBI was forced to select carefully among the various jurisdictions before attempting an arrest.

While the rise of the public enemies brought about some demands for unshackling the briefcase agents, two crimes in particular led to federal passage of a package of crime laws by 1934 that widened the scope of the FBI and gave its agents the right to carry firearms and make arrests. These were the Lindbergh baby kidnapping and the Kansas City Massacre.

Briggen, Joseph (c. 1850–1903) mass murderer

One of this country's most awesome mass murderers, Joseph Briggen committed his crimes for many years on a small ranch in a remote California valley.

Briggen barely made a living on his Sierra Morena Ranch. Certainly he was never prosperous enough to keep more than one hired hand at a time. In fact, were it not for his prime Berkshire swine, for which he almost invariably won the coveted blue ribbon at the state fair in Sacramento, Briggen's ranching would probably have been considered a total loss.

At state fair time, however, he was in his glory, his prize swine attracting top dollar. When he was asked about how he raised them, Briggen would say the secret was all in their care and feeding. But his recipe for the latter was something he would share with no one, other than to say they got prime feed only.

There was good reason for Briggen to guard his secret. The truth was a grisly story. He hired homeless men as his helpers, recruiting them on a customary trip to the Embarcadero section of San Francisco. A down-and-outer would jump at the chance for a good job with room and board, and Briggen could keep him several weeks if not months before the man would demand his back pay. Then Briggen would kill him, chop up the body and feed it to his prize swine. In his twisted mind, Briggen had become convinced it was this diet of human flesh that made his swine prize winners. He was finally exposed in early 1902, when his newest hired hand, a youth named Steve Korad, who had arrived very enthusiastic about finding work, looked around his room and found two severed human fingers from a previous victim that Briggen had carelessly dropped behind the bed. Korad raced off in the night and notified the law. When authorities dug up Briggen's ranch, their search turned up the bones of at least a dozen victims, but they were sure they had not found them all. The pigpen itself yielded up several bones, including one dead man's skull.

Briggen was convicted in August 1902 and sentenced to life. He died in San Quentin shortly thereafter.

Briggs, Hattie (c. 1880–1890s) madam

In vice-ridden Chicago during the 1880s and 1890s, the most famous madams were Carrie Watson and Lizzie Allen, but a black madam ("as ugly as anyone could imagine," according to one contemporary account) named Hattie Briggs enjoyed almost equal notoriety, being the subject of a never-ending string of newspaper articles.

Six feet tall and weighing about 225 pounds, Hattie cut an arresting figure in the long scarlet coat she always wore. She ran two brothels, one on Clark Street and another on Custom House Place, where her girls were available for 25¢. However, rare indeed was the customer who got out of either of these dens without being robbed. Scorning such slow-moving, indirect robbery methods as the sliding panels used in some other establishments, Hattie's technique was quick and most direct. She would simply seize a customer and slam him up against a wall a few times, strip him of his money and toss him out into the street. Although Hattie was raided several times a week, she got off with minor fines; few victimized customers cared to appear in court to testify against her.

While the newspapers constantly wrote exposés of her activities, it took the police some 10 years to drive her from the city; some cynical newsmen saw this as proof of police corruption. Indeed, Hattie's downfall resulted more from her insulting the police than from her breaking the law. In the early 1890s Hattie took a young black thief and gambler, William Smith, as a lover. She set him up in the saloon business and dressed him gaudily in patent-leather shoes with white spats, lavender pants, white vest, yellow shirt, bright blue coat and, of course, a silk hat. She adorned him with diamond pins and rings. Smith soon became very "big for his britches" and bragged that Hattie intended to make him the "biggest black boy in Chicago." Indeed, Hattie announced that she was making so much money she intended to buy up all the brothels and saloons in the city's vice centers for Smith, elect him mayor and abolish the police force.

This may have been the insult the police could not abide because a force of 20 patrolmen raided Smith's main saloon and, following a desperate battle, arrested the great man and 22 of his henchmen. After Smith's liquor license was revoked, the still-smarting police turned their rage on Hattie Briggs, arresting her 10 to 20 times a day with blanket warrants. After lasting about half a month, Hattie finally hired a moving van and shipped off her girls and their bedding to a new place in suburban Lemont. According to later reports, Hattie moved south to a place where the law was said to be more considerate of hard-working madams.

See also: PANEL HOUSE.

Brink's robbery

The Great Brink's Robbery of 1950 was two years in the making. For 24 months, 11 middle-aged Bostonians, seven of them heretofore no more than petty thieves, worked on the robbery of the Brink's North Terminal Garage. They entered the garage at night and walked about in their stocking feet, measuring distances, locating doors, determining which way they opened, all beneath unsuspecting guards. On one occasion they removed the locks from the doors, fitted keys to them and then replaced the locks. They even went so far as to break into a burglar alarm company in order to make a closer study of the alarm system used

by Brink's. In December 1949 they ran through a complete dress rehearsal. Finally, they decided they were ready.

On the appointed day, January 17, 1950, the bandits entered the garage dressed in simulated Brink's uniforms, rubber Halloween masks, and crepe-soled shoes or rubber overshoes. They made their way to the counting room and relieved five very surprised employees of $2.7 million in cash, checks and securities. The cash alone came to $1,218,211. In less than 15 minutes they were gone.

The plan had been to keep a low profile for six years until the statute of limitations ran out, but one of the bandits, Joseph "Specs" O'Keefe, felt he had been gypped out of his fair share. He demanded another $63,000. The others refused but then started worrying he would turn informer. A professional hit man, Elmer "Trigger" Burke, was assigned to shut O'Keefe up permanently. Burke chased O'Keefe through the streets of Boston in a wild nighttime shoot-out, firing at him with a machine gun. O'Keefe was wounded in the arm and chest but escaped, although Burke was sure he had finished him off. The hit man was seized by police before he could correct his error.

O'Keefe took offense at the effort to kill him and eventually started talking to the law; by then the FBI had spent $25 million investigating the caper. As a result of O'Keefe's talking to the police, eight of the plotters were convicted and given life sentences.

In 1980 an $18 million movie titled *The Brink's Job* was released. It was played partly for laughs. On hand for the showing in Boston were two of the three surviving members of the original bandit group. Both had served 14 years for the crime before being released.

"I'm glad they made something light out of it," said 72-year-old Thomas "Sandy" Richardson. "Yeah, people need a few laughs these days."

Seventy-year-old Adolph "Jazz" Maffie wasn't completely sold. "I thought it was all right. But only thing is that it wasn't that much fun. That was hard work, that kind of job."

"Yeah," Sandy said.

See also: ELMER "TRIGGER" BURKE.

Bristol Bill (c. 1840) bank robber and counterfeiter

Perhaps one of the most mysterious criminals in American history was the notorious Bristol Bill, who operated during the 1840s in New York and Boston. His true identity was never known to police in this country, although the London police know exactly who he was. They refused to reveal it, however, because Bill's influential father, a member of the British Parliament, did

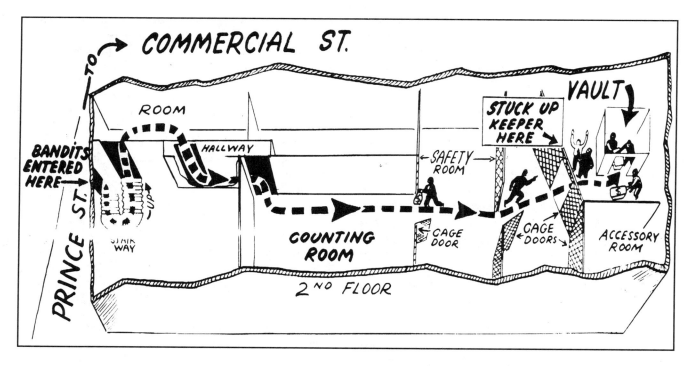

A diagram shows the route taken by the bandits in the Great Brink's Robbery in 1950, which netted them $2.7 million in cash, checks and securities.

not want the family name dishonored. It was established that Bristol Bill had escaped from the British penal colony in Sydney, Australia; his true identity had not been known there either.

In New York, Bristol Bill teamed up with another ex-Sidney prisoner, James Stuart, better known as English Jim, who had served 12 years down under. It was later estimated that the pair robbed more banks in the area from New York to Boston than any other criminals of their era.

By the late 1840s, after several close brushes with pursuing detectives, they decided to pursue their calling in the relative safety of Vermont. Within a matter of several weeks during the fall of 1849, they robbed six banks, floated a huge quantity of counterfeit money and swindled a number of businessmen. However, the small-town police of Vermont proved sharper than their big-city brethren and captured Bristol Bill. English Jim escaped, fleeing to California, where he became one of that state's top criminals before being captured and hanged by vigilantes. Bristol Bill was sent to prison for 14 years. His later life proved as enigmatic as his earlier history, and his true identity was never learned on this side of the Atlantic.

Broadway Mob   rumrunners

One of the most important components that eventually were merged into the national crime syndicate was the Broadway Mob of the 1920s. Officially run by Joe Adonis (his real name was Joseph Doto but he went under the name "Adonis" because he was proud of his looks), the Broadway gang boasted a board of directors that included such future big shots as Frank Costello and Lucky Luciano. It totally controlled the flow of bootleg liquor in the great center of Manhattan.

Luciano brought in the Bug and Meyer Mob, run by Meyer Lansky and Bugsy Siegel, to provide protection for the gang's convoys. Adonis and Costello soon decided that it made more sense and was cheaper to bring Lansky and Siegel in as partners. This new interethnic Broadway Mob soon dominated bootlegging in New York, supplying good whiskey to all the top speakeasies, including Jack White's, Jack and Charlie's "21" Club, the Silver Slipper, Sherman Billingsley's Stork Club and others. While not all the whiskey was "right off the boat" as claimed, even the liquor produced in Waxey Gordon's Philadelphia distilleries was far better than the local rotgut. The

Broadway Mob invested in some of the best speak-easies and thus had a special interest in keeping the liquor supplies of good quality. It was through the workings of the Broadway Mob that the syndicate's top mobsters came to own some of Manhattan's most valuable real estate, a situation unchanged even to the present day.

See also: JOE ADONIS.

Brocius, William B. "Curly Bill" (1857–1882)
western outlaw

A brutal outlaw whose real name was William B. Graham, Curly Bill Brocius, or Brocious, was the most important gunfighter in the Clanton gang and, as such was frequently at odds in Tombstone with the Earps. Curly Bill was probably the one Clanton man Earp feared most, and it was said the Earps provoked the famous or infamous gunfight at the O.K. Corral because Brocius was not around.

When Old Man Clanton died, Curly Bill became the de facto leader of the gang, having far more ability, brains and guts than Ike Clanton. He would have been a more imposing outlaw except for a lack of ambition. Curly Bill preferred commiting crimes that required little effort on his part. He was quite content to capture a Mexican muleteer in the hills, take all his money and torture him to death.

Brocius killed Marshal Fred White on the streets of Tombstone in a confrontation with that lawman and his deputy, Virgil Earp. It was a matter of dispute whether Curly Bill killed the marshal with a cunning maneuver of his six-gun as he was handing it over to White or whether White caused his own death by seizing the gun by the barrel. Virgil Earp said it was murder; a jury decided on accidental death.

In July 1881 two Clanton gunmen, Bill Leonard and Harry Head, were killed trying to hold up the store of William and Isaac Haslett in Hauchita, New Mexico Territory. The brothers were hailed as heroes, but they didn't have much time to enjoy their fame before Curly Bill and Johnny Ringo rode into town and shot them both dead. Later that same month Brocius led his men on a particularly vicious murder spree, ambushing a Mexican trail herd in the San Luis Pass and killing 14 *vaqueros*. Actually, six of the victims fell in the first volley and the rest surrendered, only to be tortured to death before their cattle were driven off.

After the O.K. Corral gunfight, Curly Bill took part in an assassination attempt on Virgil Earp and the successful ambush of Morgan Earp, both for handsome pay provided by Ike Clanton. After those killings and a couple of stagecoach robberies, Brocius,

in one of the frequent ironies of law enforcement in Tombstone, was sent off to the hills armed with a warrant for the arrest of Wyatt Earp that had been issued by Earp's foe Sheriff John Behan. Earp was in the hills at the same time looking for Brocius. Their respective bands met at Iron Springs, a waterhole in the Whetstone Mountains. Earp told Brocius he was taking him in, and Curly Bill said he had a warrant for Earp. The latter ended this legal impasse by blowing Brocius to pieces with a double blast from his shotgun.

See also: JOSEPH ISAAC "IKE" CLANTON, NEWMAN H. "OLD MAN" CLANTON, WYATT EARP.

broken homes and crime

For years the broken home, one altered by divorce, desertion or death, has been considered a major cause of delinquency and subsequent criminal behavior by children. Overall, various studies have indicated that 40 percent of juvenile delinquents, give or take 10 percent or so, come from broken homes, which is at least double the percentage of children from broken homes in the general population. Among male delinquents in cases closed by the Los Angeles Probation Department, 58 percent of those institutionalized came from broken homes.

However, it has become apparent on the basis of several studies that the judicial process tends to select children from broken homes for institutionalization, adding an important distortion to the figures. More recent studies have concluded that the impact of a broken home may not be very significant on white males, although some researchers insist there is an important impact on white females and on blacks compared to whites in general. But even in these cases, the differences may be more apparent than real, as is suggested in a 1972 Florida study by Roland J. Chilton and Gerald E. Markle. It found that the so-called differences in delinquency rates between white boys and girls are primarily in the areas of ungovernability, truancy and running away from home and that statistical differences between the sexes virtually disappear for behavior that would be considered a crime if committed by an adult.

Among black children distinctions between the seriousness of the offense tend to disappear, suggesting that for black youths the home situation may be less significant as a cause of major misconduct, which is considerably higher among blacks than among whites. The Florida study found that in low-income families, white or black, the seriousness of the offense was not determined by the family situation, suggesting that the family's overall economic condition rather than its composition is more relevant to the development of delinquency.

Brooks, William L. "Buffalo Bill" (?1832–1874)
lawman and horse thief

There are those who say that William Brooks could have been the greatest and most efficient lawman the West had ever seen before he himself went bad.

The life of Brooks, called Buffalo Bill because his prowess as a buffalo hunter nearly equaled that of William F. Cody, is steeped in controversy. Little is known about his early life, although he was apparently born in Ohio. Brooks' story really begins in the late 1860s, when he was reputed to have killed several men in gunfights. After a stint as a stage driver, he became marshal of Newton, Kan. in 1872, reportedly at the age of 40. The town wanted a "mature man" for the job and Brooks seemed to fit the bill. Yet some biographers insist he was in his twenties at the time. Brooks' six-guns made quite an impression in Newton, and he was soon offered the chance to clean up Dodge City. In his first month on the job there, Brooks was involved in some 15 gunfights, killing or wounding numerous "hard cases." One of the men he killed had four brothers, who then came gunning for Brooks; with just four shots—according to the legend—Brooks dispatched them all.

In any event, Brooks had gone far in taming Dodge and had he continued, Wyatt Earp would never have gotten the opportunity to achieve his later fame there. However, power seemed to have corrupted Brooks. He killed a few men he ought not have, one for merely being his rival for the affections of a dance hall girl. Brooks then backed down in a shoot-out with a tough character named Kirk Jordan and left Dodge. Some say it was this loss of face that turned Brooks bad and led him to engage in many illegal enterprises. According to one popular story, Brooks made a try for the marshal's job in Butte, Mont., but his reputation and an opponent named Morgan Earp defeated him. The legend says Brooks' defeat rankled him to the point that he went gunning for Morgan Earp and was killed in a classic gunfight at high noon, with the two men firing at once and one dropping in the dust. That would have been a far more glorious ending for Buffalo Bill Brooks than what actually happened.

The facts are that no such duel ever took place—Brooks' time ran out long before the alleged fight. In early 1874 he returned to his old employer, the Southwestern Stage Co., as a driver. A few months later, the company lost its mail contract to a competitor, and Brooks was out of a job. Late in June 1874 a number of mules and horses belonging to the competing company were stolen. About a month after that, Brooks and two others were arrested for the thefts. Before they could be brought to trial, they were lynched the night of July 29, 1874. Brooks' motive, it became apparent, was to cripple the rival company and win back the mail contract for his former employer. All in all, it was an ignoble end for the man who just two years before had been known as the toughest gun in Dodge City.

Brown, Hendry (?1850–1884) lawman and outlaw

Several men in the history of the West have made a transition from outlaw to lawman or vice versa, but Hendry Brown seemed to flit back and forth so much it was difficult to say which one he was at any particular time.

Brown was first heard of when he was operating in Texas as an illegal whiskey peddler. He said then that he had been a lawman in the panhandle, which may or may not have been true. What is true is that later on he did some posse duty with the McSween forces during the Lincoln County War in New Mexico, which might have qualified him as a lawman except that he spent a good deal of this time riding with Billy the Kid.

After the Lincoln County War cooled, Brown split from Billy the Kid, deciding that the outlaw life offered little promise of longevity. He drifted over to Tascosa, Tex., where he magically ended up as town constable. But that activity soon bored Brown, and he hit the outlaw trail, working his way up to Kansas. After a while, Brown figured that the lawman game was, all in all, a better bet, and using his credentials as a constable in Texas, he became a deputy marshal at Caldwell. He killed a couple of men in the line of duty and soon picked up the marshal's star. He was holding that job when in 1884 fickleness overtook him again. With three confederates he plotted out a bank robbery at Medicine Lodge in April of that year. It was a bloody affair, with Brown gunning down the bank president and another member of the gang killing a teller. The four bandits fled but they never made it back to cover in Caldwell. A hard-riding and fast-shooting posse cornered them and took them back to the local jail. They never survived the night—a large mob overwhelmed the guards and hanged all four from the same tree.

Brown, Sam (?–1861) Virginia City killer

Vicious even by the standards of the frontier, Sam Brown was said to have killed some 13 men in the streets and barrooms of Virginia City, Nev. The stocky red-bearded killer always carried a huge bowie knife slung from his gun belt. Proficient with the use of both knife and revolver, Brown killed without provocation. There is no record of him ever challenging a man as well armed as himself, and he never invited anyone to do fair battle. He killed only when he knew he was in no danger himself. One of his more revolting crimes took place in a C Street saloon in 1861. A pleasant young miner named McKenzie accidentally bumped his elbow at the bar. Brown turned to see who had offended him and spotted McKenzie, a man Brown knew had not been around long enough to make any close friends who would stand up for him. Seizing the youth by the throat, Brown, according to a contemporary account, "ran a knife into his victim, and then turned it around, completely cutting the heart out, then wiped his bloody knife and lay down on a billiard table and went to sleep."

Finally, Brown picked the wrong would-be victim, a farmer named Vansickle. On July 6, 1861, Brown's birthday, the killer boasted between whiskeys that he would "have a man for supper." He decided on Vansickle, who quickly made off for his farm, with Brown in bloodthirsty pursuit. By the time Brown reached the farmhouse, Vansickle had just enough time to dash inside and grab a shotgun. When the farmer came back to his doorway with the weapon, Brown, not relishing such resistance, climbed back on his horse and rode off to town. However, Vansickle was not prepared to let the matter rest. He decided he'd have to kill Brown to prevent him from trying again. As Brown dismounted in front of a saloon, Vansickle rode up. A contemporary account states, "Upon seeing his pursuer, mortal terror seized upon the ruffian; abject, unutterable fear sealed his lips; a spasmodic, agonizing yell of despair forced itself from his mouth. . . ." Vansickle leveled his shotgun and blasted his tormentor with both barrels. An inquest the next day found that Vansickle "had shown good sense, and, instead of deserving punishment, he should be rewarded for having thus rid the community of this brutal and cowardly villain."

Brown, William   See ALEXANDER WILLIAM HOLMES.

Brown's Chicken mass murders   classic botched investigation

One of 1990s most horrific cases of mass murder, it remained unsolved and has been cited by some crime experts as one of the worst fumbled investigations ever conducted by police. On January 8, 1993 workers of the day shift of Brown's Chicken & Pasta Restaurant in

what was called the sleepy Chicago suburb of Palatine arrived and were mystified to find the entire overnight crew had mysteriously disappeared.

Only when they opened the restaurant coolers did they discover the terrible truth. Seven bodies were stacked in the coolers: the entire workforce of five employees and the two owners of the franchise operation. All had been methodically slaughtered. Clearly it was one of the most gruesome robberies ever committed, and also one of the most baffling, since the perpetrators obviously were intent on leaving no witnesses.

In the O. J. Simpson case a few years later much was made—successfully—by the defense in the criminal case that much of the evidence had been contaminated by inept investigators. However, the Simpson case could be held up as towering efficiency compared to the Brown investigation. Local authorities were determined to produce quick charges, and an innocent former employee was held and grilled for a considerable waste of time while some insisted the trail was allowed to grow cold.

In *Homicide: 100 Years of Murder in America*, Gini Graham Scott, Ph.D., reflected the opinion of a number of experts in declaring: "There must have been telltale evidence left behind, but whatever it might have been was smudged over or trampled by the eager but inexperienced police. . . . By the time a task force of experienced officers from other communities took charge, it was too late to solve the murders."

Brown's Hole   western outlaw refuge

Brown's Hole was one of the great western outlaw hideouts, lying some 250 miles southwest of Hole in the Wall. Accessible only by little-known roads that wound through deserts and over mountains, it lay at the junction of what is now eastern Utah, western Colorado and southern Wyoming. Brown's Hole, rather than Hole in the Wall, was Butch Cassidy's favorite hideout. It was here that the scattered elements of Cassidy's Wild Bunch knew they could always renew contact. What Butch liked best about it was that "the tax collector doesn't come around too often."

Brownsville affair   mass punishment

One of America's most callous miscarriages of justice occurred in 1906 after an unidentified group of men shot up stores and homes around Fort Brown in Brownsville, Tex., where three companies of black soldiers were stationed. The shootings happened around midnight on August 13 and resulted in the death of a local resident and the severe wounding of a policeman.

Despite the fact that the incident had taken place in the dark, a number of witnesses said the shooting had been done by soldiers, and the following morning some cartridges of U.S. Army specifications were found outside the fort. The company commanders instituted an immediate inspection of all the soldiers' rifles but concluded none had been fired, and an inventory check indicated that none of the fort's cartridges were missing.

Several grand jury and military inquiries failed to pin the blame on any specific individuals. On October 4 President Theodore Roosevelt ordered an ultimatum be read to the troops, who had since been transferred to Fort Reno, warning that all would be ordered discharged "without honor" unless they handed over the guilty parties. When all continued to maintain their innocence, the entire group of 167 enlisted men were accused of a "conspiracy of silence" and discharged "without honor." None were afforded any opportunity to confront their accusers and none were ever proved guilty of being involved in the crime. The Senate Committee on Military Affairs later held hearings that were critical of the president's actions, and a military court of inquiry in 1909 announced that 14 of the soldiers would be allowed to reenlist, but the reasoning behind this decision was not revealed. The record of the discharges stood for 66 years until September 22, 1972, when secretary of the army Robert F. Froehlke issued a directive changing them from "without honor" to "honorable."

Buccieri, Fiore "Fifi" (1904–1973) syndicate killer

A top enforcer for the Chicago syndicate, Fiore "Fifi" Buccieri was considered to be mob leader Sam Giancana's personal hit man. No complete record of Fifi's kills have been recorded, although federal agents who had bugged a house in Florida being used to plan a murder heard Buccieri reminisce about a number of killings. Among other principles he espoused was that ammunition for shotguns used in an assassination should be "fresh." Fifi was particularly lighthearted about the gruesome demise of William "Action" Jackson, a 300-pound collector for the mob's loansharking operation who was suspected of holding out some of the money and of being an informant for federal authorities. Jackson was hung from a meat hook, stripped and shot in the knee. Then, Buccieri recalled, the boys decided "to have a little bit of fun." Jackson was worked over with ice picks, baseball bats and a blow torch. Fifi got hold of an electric cattle prod and jammed it up Jackson's rectum. The fat victim lived for two days, but even at that, Fifi was "sorry the big slob died so soon." Buccieri took photographs of the

mutilated corpse and passed them around as reminders to other mobsters not to stray from mob rule.

Fifi was a graduate of Chicago's worst juvenile gang, the 42ers. He was a hulking, gravel-voiced punk who attracted younger kids by his dapper dress and his affection of wearing wide-brimmed hats similar to those worn by movie gangsters. He attached himself to another up-and-coming 42er, Sam Giancana, who eventually rose to the top position in the Chicago outfit. Fifi became Giancana's personal executioner and his loyal ally during the power struggles for mob leadership.

The law never made Buccieri crack. During one federal probe investigators tried to elicit mob information by questioning Fifi about his brother Frank, also involved in mob affairs. They even questioned Fifi about the fact that his brother had a girlfriend who had been a Playboy bunny and a centerfold nude in *Playboy* magazine and that he had given her a horse as a present. Fifi's answer, which became a classic in underworld circles was, "I take the Fifth on the horse and the broad."

Fifi died of cancer in 1973, and Giancana was assassinated two years later. There was speculation at the time that the mob—if the Giancana killing was a mob caper and not a CIA operation, as the underworld has insisted—would never have dared move against Giancana while Fifi Buccieri was alive.

Buchalter, Louis "Lepke" (1897–1944) syndicate leader and murderer

The only national crime czar and kingpin of the rackets ever to go to the electric chair, Louis "Lepke" Buchalter graduated from sneak thievery during his youth on New York's Lower East Side to become one of the founders of the national crime syndicate. Through control of the tailors and cutters unions, Lepke milked millions from the New York garment industry. Part of Lepke's power sprung from his control of Murder, Inc., the Brooklyn "troop" of specialist killers who serviced the syndicate. Thus, Thomas E. Dewey referred to Lepke as "the worst industrial racketeer in America," and J. Edgar Hoover called him "the most dangerous criminal in the United States."

In the early 1920s, while most gangsters were attracted by the huge fortunes to be made in booze, Lepke chose a different route to underworld fame and wealth. He and another thug, Jacob "Gurrah" Shapiro, linked up with the era's top labor racketeer, "Little Augie" Orgen, to offer strike-breaking services to garment industry employers. Little Augie was shot dead in 1927, but Lepke and Shapiro prospered, especially after refining their operations so that they could serve both sides, assuming the added duties of union organizers and eventually taking control of union locals.

The union racketeers extended their operations to control the bakery drivers' union and levied a penny "tax" per loaf on bakers to guarantee their products got to market fresh. To greater or lesser degrees, Lepke moved into other industries, especially in league with Tommy Lucchese, a mobster with close ties to Lucky Luciano. Their extortion rackets expanded to tough on such businesses as handbags, shoes, millinery, poultry, cleaning and dyeing, leather, restaurants and others until it was estimated legitimate businesses were paying Lepke up to $10 million a year just so they could operate without trouble.

The Lucchese connection gave Lepke an "in" with the budding crime syndicate being formed by Luciano, Meyer Lansky, Frank Costello, Joe Adonis, Dutch Schultz and others. The new organization recognized the need for an enforcement branch within its framework. Lepke was put in charge of it, with Albert Anastasia as second in command. The choice of Anastasia was obvious; he was a madman whose philosophy could be summed up in three words—kill, kill, kill. And the election of Lepke over him was equally logical. Lepke was the greatest exponent of violence in the rackets; an associate once noted, "Lep loves to hurt people." Under Lepke and Anastasia the enforcement branch, later dubbed Murder, Inc. by the newspapers, carried out hundreds of hits for the syndicate.

Lepke courted trouble with the law, living lavishly and relishing the spotlight. Thomas Dewey, then an ambitious special prosecutor, zeroed in on him once he had convicted Luciano. And while Dewey went after him for bakery extortion, the federal government stalked him for restraint-of-trade violations. Then the federal Narcotics Bureau began gathering proof that Lepke was the head of a narcotics-smuggling operation that was involved in massive bribing of U.S. customs agents. Free on bail, Lepke decided to go into hiding. While a nationwide manhunt was organized to catch him, he continued to control his union rackets from various Brooklyn hideouts, where he was being hidden by Anastasia.

The continued manhunt, however, put extraordinary pressure on the entire syndicate and hamstrung their operations. Mayor Fiorello LaGuardia turned the screw even tighter by ordering his police commissioner, Lewis Valentine, to go to war on "hoodlums." The problem got so bad that it was brought to the attention of Luciano, then confined at Dannemora Prison but still the top voice in the organization. Luciano agreed that Lepke had to give himself up, but there was a problem: Lepke realized Dewey could convict him of enough charges to keep him in prison for life. Therefore, Luciano decided that Lepke would

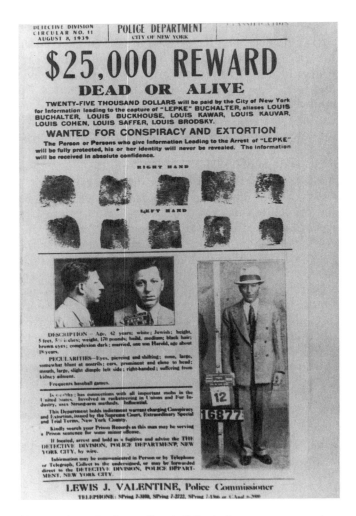

The manhunt for Louis "Lepke" Buchalter was among the most intensive ever, one that ended only when other leaders of organized crime betrayed him.

have to be fooled into surrendering. He arranged for an emissary Lepke trusted, Moe "Dimples" Wolensky, to carry a message that a deal had been worked out with J. Edgar Hoover whereby if he surrendered directly to the FBI chief, he would be tried on the federal narcotics charge only and not handed over to Dewey.

Lepke bought the story and surrendered on a Manhattan street to gossip columnist Walter Winchell and Hoover. As soon as he entered their car and Hoover spoke to him, Lepke realized he had been double-crossed. Lepke was convicted on federal charges of narcotics conspiracy and sentenced to 14 years at Leavenworth but was then turned over to Dewey who succeeded in getting another conviction that resulted in a 39-year-to-life sentence.

Unfortunately for Lepke, while he was behind bars, the story of Murder, Inc. broke, mainly because of information supplied by squealer, Abe Reles, one of the group's leading killers. Lepke was tied in as the leader of the killer troop and was specifically linked to the 1936 murder of a Brooklyn candy store owner named Joe Rosen, a former trucker in the garment district who had been forced out of business by Lepke. Instead of bearing his loss in silence, Rosen began making noise about going to the district attorney's office. Lepke handed out a contract on Rosen to two of his chief aides, Mendy Weiss and Louis Capone, and to Pittsburgh Phil Strauss. Rosen ended up with 17 bullets in his corpse.

Even though Reles was killed in a mysterious fall from a window in a hotel where he was being kept under police guard, authorities had more than enough evidence to convict Lepke, Weiss and Capone (Strauss had already been sentenced to death for another murder). Through various appeals, Lepke staved off execution until March 1944. Shortly before his death the newspapers were filled with speculation that Lepke was talking about corrupt political and labor officials he had had dealings with and that if he really "opened up" he could blow the roof off the country, among other things delivering what one newspaper called "a prominent labor leader, powerful in national politics, as a man who had inspired several crimes." In thinly disguised sidebar stories, that labor leader was readily identifiable as Sidney Hillman, then an intimate advi-ser to President Franklin D. Roosevelt. Lepke himself was quoted as saying: "If I would talk, a lot of big people would get hurt. When I say big, I mean big. The names would surprise you." The *New York Mirror* reported, "It is said Lepke offered material to Governor Dewey that would make him an unbeatable presidential candidate."

On the afternoon of the execution, Lepke released his version of the facts. He had his wife read a statement that he had dictated: "I am anxious to have it clearly understood that I did not offer to talk and give information in exchange for any promise of commutation of my death sentence. I did not ask for that! . . . The one and only thing I have asked for is to have a commission appointed to examine the facts. If that examination does not show that I am not guilty, I am willing to go to the chair, regardless of what information I have given or can give."

Clearly Lepke had given some information, but it had not been enough, and now he was eager to inform the syndicate he was not going to talk about crime matters. If he did, he realized, no member of his family would be spared.

On March 4, 1944 Lepke silently followed Capone and Weiss to the chair.

See also: THOMAS E. DEWEY; JEWISH MAFIA; MURDER, INC.; JACOB "LITTLE AUGIE" ORGEN; JACOB "GURRAH" SHAPIRO; WALTER WINCHELL.

Buchanan, Dr. Robert (?1855–1895) murderer

Dr. Robert Buchanan, one of New York's most famous 19th-century killers, was a vain murderer who modeled his crime on a similar one committed by a young medical student, Carlyle Harris, for which the latter went to the chair. Dr. Buchanan, possessing higher scientific knowledge than that of a mere medical student, improved on Harris' method but also went to the chair.

Buchanan's background is a bit murky. He had lied about his age and education so that he could practice medicine in Canada without a license. When he got caught, he went to Chicago for a couple of years and then returned to Halifax, Nova Scotia, where he married the daughter of a wealthy manufacturer. Buchanan talked his in-laws into sending him to Edinburgh, Scotland to complete his medical education. When he returned, he and his wife moved to New York, where he set up a modest practice in Greenwich Village.

By 1890 when he divorced his wife and sent her back to Nova Scotia, Buchanan had developed a taste for the seamier side of life and had formed an attachment with big, fat, ugly Annie Sutherland, who lived in the Village but ran a call house in Newark. Annie had one very redeeming quality: she had $50,000 in the bank. When he proposed marriage, Annie Sutherland jumped at the chance. For her, marrying a doctor meant respectability. For Dr. Buchanan, the marriage meant $50,000.

About that time the Carlyle Harris case was coming to trial. Harris, a medical student had secretly married a young girl named Helen Potts. After tiring of her, he disposed of Helen by poisoning her with morphine. He had been caught because a doctor noticed her pupils were pin points, the universal sign of morphine poisoning.

One evening Buchanan was drinking in Macomber's, a Village watering hole. He slammed a fist on the bar and said: "And I tell you Carlyle Harris was a fool! If Harris had known anything about medicine, he could have gotten away with it easily."

"How, Doc?" a drinking companion asked.

"Never mind," said Buchanan. "We of the profession cannot have laymen mindful of such information."

Buchanan would say no more, but he was in fact to put his opinion to the test. In 1892 he announced he was going to Edinburgh by himself, but four days before he was scheduled to leave, he canceled the trip because his wife had taken sick. Buchanan promptly called in not one but two other physicians to treat her. Both of them were with her when she died. Clearly, the doctors had no reason to view the woman's death as anything other than apoplexy, the result of a cerebral hemorrhage; their patient did not appear to have been poisoned since her pupils were not contracted. Apoplexy and morphine poisoning produced similar symptoms except for that one basic difference: in apoplexy there is no change in the pupils of the eyes, but in morphine poisoning the pupils greatly contract.

Some of Mrs. Buchanan's friends, from her brothel in Newark, were sure the doctor had not only married her for her money but had also killed her for it. Although the police wouldn't listen to such shady characters maligning an apparently respectable medical man, Ike White, a star reporter for the *New York World* who had a reputation for breaking cases, did listen. He had worked on the Carlyle Harris case and was intrigued by the story of a doctor who had married a madam.

White asked the physicians who had attended Mrs. Buchanan about her symptoms and raised the possibility of morphine poisoning; he was told that the woman's pupils had definitely not contracted. An average investigator or reporter might have given up right there, but White kept checking. He discovered that a mere three months after Mrs. Buchanan's death, the doctor had announced he was going to Edinburgh. Instead, he went back to Nova Scotia and remarried his first wife. The major difference in the doctor's present marital condition was that he was $50,000 better off. There was a story here, and White knew it.

He also knew that in the 1890s, before the psychiatric couch came into vogue, the average man imparted his deepest secrets to either his priest or his bartender. He also knew that Dr. Buchanan was not a churchgoer. This theory is what finally led the reporter to Macomber's. He talked with Old Man Macomber about a number of things, including sports, current events, murders—especially the Carlyle Harris case—and people in the neighborhood who had died, such as Mrs. Buchanan. Finally, the matter of Dr. Buchanan's statement about Harris' stupidity was raised.

"Now how could Harris not have been found out?" White said derisively.

The bartender leaned forward. "The doc told me," he said. "One night he said he wouldn't tell anybody how it could be done, but by closing time he was so plastered he whispered to me that if I'd set up one for him, he'd tell just me. I did and he said, 'If you've ever

been to the eye doctor, and he's put drops in your eyes, chances are the eye drops were atropine, which makes the pupils dilate or enlarge. If Harris had used some atropine when he gave his wife the morphine, his wife's eyes would have ended up looking normal, and no one would have suspected.'"

White ran his story, and Dr. Buchanan was indicted. An autopsy showed that his wife had in fact been killed by morphine poisoning. At his trial the prosecution went so far as to kill a cat in the courtroom with morphine and then administer atropine to show how the pin pointing could be prevented.

On July 1, 1895 Dr. Buchanan went to the electric chair as a result of drunken remarks he never remembered making.

See also: ISAAC DEFOREST "IKE" WHITE.

Buck gang   Indian murderers

The Rufus Buck gang, five semiliterate, half-black, half-Creek Indians, lasted only two weeks in the old Indian territory of Arkansas-Oklahoma. While their crimes were shocking, they are best remembered by the enemies they made.

Rufus Buck and his four confederates—Lewis Davis, Sam Sampson, Maoma July and Luckey Davis—were all under the age of 20 when they started their depredations on July 28, 1895. A deputy marshal made the mistake of looking at them suspiciously and died in a hail of rifle fire. Over the next 13 days they carried out a series of holdups of stores and ranches around Fort Smith and committed several rapes, in one case threatening to drown a woman's babies unless she submitted. They held up a drummer, or salesman, named Callahan and gave him a "sporting chance" to escape if he could outrun their fire. He did, and in frustration, the gang turned their guns on Callahan's young black helper, killing him without the same sporting offer.

Not only whites but Creek Indians as well were incensed by the gang's actions. On August 10 the five were trapped in a grove outside of Muskogee where they were dividing some loot. The posse that tracked them down was composed of lawmen and a company of Creek Light Horse (Indian police).

They were brought to trial before Hanging Judge Parker, although the Creeks sorely wanted to try the gang and mete out Indian justice. None of the gang or their five appointed lawyers had much to say. One attorney's total summation was, "May it please the court and the gentlemen of the jury, you have heard the evidence. I have nothing to say." The jury rendered its verdict without even sitting down in the jury room, and the five were duly hanged on July 1, 1896.

After the execution a picture of Rufus Buck's mother was found in his cell. On the back of it he had written this poem:

MY dreAM—

i,dremP'T, i, wAs, in, HeAven,
Among, THe Angels, FAir:
i,d, neAr, seen, none, so HAndsome,
THAT TWine, in goLden, HAir:
THeY, Looked, so, neAT,
And; sAng, so, sweeT
And, PLAY,d, THe, THe, goLden, HArp,
i, wAs, ABouT, To, Pick, An, Angel ouT,
And, TAke, Her, To, mY HeaRT:
BuT, THe, momenT, i, BegAn, To, PLea,
i,THougHT, oF, You, mY, Love,
THere, Was, none, i,d seen, so, BeAuTiFuLL,

On, eArTH, or, HeAven, ABove.
gooDl By, My, Dear, Wife . . anD MoTHer

All. so. My sisTers.
RUFUS, BUCK
Youse. Truley

We are told by one of Hanging Judge Parker's more maudlin biographers that the poem "brought tears to Parker's dimming eyes."

See also: ISAAC C. "HANGING JUDGE" PARKER.

Buckminster, Fred (1863–1943) con man

One of the most fabled of American con men, Fred Buckminster started on the "bunco trail" while still a teenager. He was to be a swindler the rest of his life, completing his last prison term at the age of 75. In an era of hard money, he stole a minimum of $3 million.

He worked for 20 years with another fabulous fraud, Artist Yellow Kid Weil, together developing and pulling off some of the most famous con games of all time. They worked variations of the "fixed" prize fight and horse race swindles, utilizing a "big store," or phony betting shop, to trim the suckers. Everyone in the establishment other than the victim was a fake, betting and collecting on phony races. On some occasions Buckminster and Weil would turn things around and swindle a genuine betting parlor; one of them would get the results of a race at the western Union office while the other placed a bet before the hotel bookie joint received the results. They swindled "Palmer House" Ryan, operator of the Stockade, a horse-betting establishment in the woods outside Chicago, by having a railroad engineer toot out the winner in code as his train passed the Stockade.

Buckminster discovered early in his career that the easiest person to cheat was another thief, amateur or professional. He victimized dishonest bankers, seeking out those who had been accused of cheating customers. He would pose as a depositor with some stocks that he would leave for safekeeping and then would permit himself to be "swindled" out of them after the banker was fed false information that the stock had suddenly ballooned in value.

As Buckminster once put it, "When I see a crook, I see nothing but dollar signs."

Buckminster's greatest swindle of other swindlers was a racket he worked with Kid Dimes, a leading gimmick man who fixed roulette wheels for crooked gambling houses. Buckminster was probably the first man to "fix" a fixed roulette wheel. In 1918 the Kid was busy rigging a wheel for the King George Club, a crooked gambling joint in Chicago's Loop area populated by con men who steered suckers there nightly.

The wheel Kid Dimes constructed allowed the croupier to let the ball stop in any of three numbers he desired, giving him complete control in picking red or black, odd or even or the winning set of numbers. On Buckminster's instructions, Kid Dimes added another button at the customer's end of the table that would cancel out the croupier's choice and magnetize the ball into the number 8 slot.

Outfitting himself in a 10-gallon hat, Buckminster posed as a Texan looking for some gambling action and soon was steered into the King George. With a con man at each elbow, he began playing the wheel. Despite their egging and his swagger about being a Texas oilman, he made only small bets. The house let him win a few while the con men kept working on him to set up a killing. Finally, Fred rose to the bait. He plunked down a roll of $10,000 on a bet covering numbers 7 through 12. The odds against Fred winning were 5-to-1. But of course there was no danger of that. Then just before the croupier rolled his roll, Fred tossed a fat $1,000 bill on number 8 "for good luck."

As the wheel spun, the croupier hit the secret button that guaranteed the ball would stop in a safe number in the 30s. At the same time, Fred pushed his button, canceling out the croupier's action. The little ball came to rest on number 8.

A loud cry went up in the place. Nobody had seen a hit like that. Five-to-1 on the combination bet and 35-to-1 on the number bet paid a total profit of $85,000. The croupier was stunned. A hurried conference was held, but Buckminster was relaxed. With so many suckers in the place, the house could do nothing but pay off. Others pounded on his back, congratulating him. Fred announced he hadn't had enough and continued to play further until he lost back $5,000. In the process, he also removed the secret button from under the table. Then he walked out, promising the con men to return the next evening. Naturally, he did not come back.

The gambling house owners were furious and sent for Kid Dimes to explain what went wrong. Kid Dimes was a picture of innocence as he inspected the table. He emerged from under the table holding a dead battery. Shaking his head in disdain, he said: "Why don't you people change batteries at least once a week to be safe? At a dime a throw you ought to even be able to afford to change batteries every night."

Over the next decade, whenever things cooled down, Buckminster and Kid Dimes worked that racket on several gambling houses. Buckminster once estimated it netted close to $750,000.

Despite his successes, Buckminster spent a great many of his adult years in prison. He was acutely aware of how greatly the odds favored the police over the crook. "A copper can make a thousand mistakes but a crook only one to get put away," he said sadly when he got out of prison the last time. At the age of 76, Buckminster retired from the rackets. In 1941 he did a series of memoirs for a detective magazine. He raised one of the checks given him for the use of his byline from $100 to $1,000 and cashed it. The publishing house took it philosophically and did not prosecute. Sending a dying old man back to prison made little sense, and it did seem a little late for Buckminster to alter his ways.

See also: JOSEPH "YELLOW KID" WEIL.

Buffalino, Russell A. (1903–) mob leader

Although labeled by the McClellan Committee as "one of the most ruthless and powerful leaders of the Mafia in the United States," Russell A. Buffalino has remained a prime example of the shadowy crime kingpin about whom much is suspected but little proved. Centering his activities around Pittstown Pa., Buffalino was long considered the Mafia "family boss" of organized crime in much of that state. His activities reportedly also extended into upstate New York and New Jersey, where he was described as an active participant in labor racketeering and a behind-the-scenes power in Teamsters' affairs. It is known that the government has long regarded Buffalino as the prime suspect in ordering the "disappearance" of ex-Teamster head Jimmy Hoffa. He also reputedly was involved in peddling drugs and fencing stolen jewelry. Although he had a record of arrests dating back to 1927 on such charges as receiving stolen goods, petty larceny and conspiracy to obstruct justice, he was not convicted of a serious offense until 1977, when he was sentenced to four years for extortion after threatening a man who owed $25,000 to a jeweler. The evidence against Buffalino was uncovered as part of the federal government's efforts to link him to the possible

murder of Hoffa. Later he drew a long sentence for murder and was regarded as the oldest top mafioso behind bars.

Buffalo Blacks murders   racist homicides

In the 1980s a rash of murders of blacks by one man led to the commencement of explosive racial panic and retribution, which may have been curbed only by the solution of the crimes. Known as the "Buffalo Blacks murders," the deadly spree spread far beyond that upstate New York city, sometimes as far as to Georgia, and produced an atmosphere of bigotry and animosity in areas considered relatively free of such feelings. Eventually one man acknowledged responsibility for 13 deaths, with others unsolved but still perhaps connected with his rampage—or inspired by it.

The killings started when a 14-year-old African-American youth was shot outside a Buffalo supermarket by a white man. The next day a 32-year-old man was also shot to death in a fast-food restaurant in a Buffalo suburb. There was another killing that night, and then a fourth victim fell in nearby Niagara Falls. All had been shot with a .22-caliber weapon, and the crimes were headlined as the work of the ".22-caliber killer."

Panic seized the black community, which complained about nonexistent police protection in their areas. White motorists were pelted by blacks, a cross was burned in Buffalo and fears grew that some paramilitary racist groups were behind the violence.

The killings resumed on October 8 when the body of a 71-year-old black cabbie was found in the trunk of his car, his heart ripped out. The next day another black taxi driver was found by the Niagara River. His heart was also ripped out.

On October 10 there was another frightening occurrence. A white stranger appeared at the bedside of a black patient recuperating from an illness in a Buffalo hospital. He snarled, "I hate niggers." The stranger started to strangle the patient but was frightened off by the appearance of a nurse. The patient's description of his assailant seemed to match those given by eyewitnesses in the .22-caliber killings.

There were no more attacks in the Buffalo area. Then, on December 22, a series of knife slashings by a white man of five blacks and one Hispanic occurred in a brief period in New York City. Two survived the onslaughts, but four of the victims died. The press dubbed the attacker the "Midtown Slasher." While the police hunt was on in New York City, a 31-year-old black man was stabbed to death in Buffalo on December 29. The next day the same fate befell a black victim in Rochester. Over the next two days there were three more attacks on blacks, but they survived.

By January 6 authorities declared that the stabbings were "probably linked" to the .22-caliber killings. The police now had a theory but no suspect. That changed on January 20 when white private Joseph Christopher was charged with the slashing of a black GI at Fort Benning, Georgia. Christopher was from Buffalo and a search of his former residence turned up .22-caliber ammunition, a gun barrel and two sawed-off rifle stocks. Investigators established that he had joined the army in November, after the Buffalo shootings, and was on leave from December 19 to January 4 and that he arrived in New York by bus on December 20 just before the slashings started.

In May Christopher, who was hospitalized with self-inflicted wounds, bragged to a nurse that he had been involved in the September shootings. He was charged with four of the shooting deaths, and in New York he was indicted in one of the slashing murders and a non-fatal attack.

Christopher waived a jury trial in Buffalo and went to trial before a judge. In December 1981 he was found to be mentally incompetent to stand trial, but that decision was later reversed and he was convicted of three counts of first-degree murder and sentenced to 60 years in prison. That finding was also reversed on grounds the judge had improperly barred testimony indicating mental incompetence. However, three months later a Manhattan jury rejected Christopher's claim of insanity, and the terrors of the .22-caliber killings and the Midtown slashings reached their legal conclusion.

buffaloing   method of police brutality in the old West

Described several times in western lore as "the gentle art of bending a revolver barrel around a lawbreaker's skull," buffaloing was a common treatment given cowboys by vicious "townie" lawmen. Two confirmed practitioners of the method were Wild Bill Hickok and Wyatt Earp. This technique was rarely anything other than pure brutality, since the victim was generally in custody and disarmed when the "head creasing" took place. The term evidently derived from the contemptuous attitude many lawmen had toward cowboys, regarding them as so dimwitted that they were as easy targets for a slugging as a buffalo was for a hunter's gun. Earp carried the practice to such excess that one Texas cattleman put a $1,000 bounty on his head because of his treatment of the rancher's cowboys.

See also: GEORGE HOYT.

Bug and Meyer Mob   early Lansky gang

Started in 1921 by Meyer Lansky, who was the brains, and Bugsy Siegel, who provided the muscle, the Bug and Meyer Mob was the forerunner of Murder, Inc.

Lansky and Siegel had been inseparable buddies since childhood in New York City. Together they formed a stolen car combine, in time supplying cars to various gangs. As their gang of tough Jewish hoods grew, Lansky began renting out drivers for the cars and then hit men who might be needed. They also took on the job of protecting bootleg gangs' booze convoys, occasionally hijacking shipments for another gang. The Bug and Meyer Mob's rates were high, and in time some bootleggers figured out it would be cheaper simply to bring them into the operation and give them a slice of the take.

Lucky Luciano, thanks to a friendship with Lansky that was to last his lifetime, made good use of the mob. The Bug and Meyer forces protected Luciano from assassination until he was ready to move against the "Mustache Petes" of the old Mafia forces. As the head of a group of Jewish gunmen posing as police detectives, Siegel assassinated Salvatore Maranzano, thereby making Luciano the number one Italian gangster in the country. After that, the need for the Bug and Meyer Mob ended, and all its members moved on to lucrative positions with the newly established Luciano-Lansky crime syndicate.

Years later when Lansky attempted to gain refuge from U.S. law in Israel, he tried to paint the Bug and Meyer Mob as just a collection of poor Jewish boys he had organized to protect other Jews from the vicious Irish gangs of the period. This revisionist version of history has little evidence to support it. The Bug and Meyer Mob was a group of killers, the first of organized crime's Murder, Inc. troops, and many of its "graduates" played godfatherly roles when the Brooklyn version of that organization was established in the 1930s under Lepke and Anastasia.

See also: MEYER LANSKY, BENJAMIN "BUGSY" SIEGEL.

bugging   See WIRETAPPING AND BUGGING.

Bulette, Julia (1832–1867)   madam and murder victim

Julia Bulette was the reigning madam of Virginia City, Nev. during the town's wide-open mining days, and her murder in 1867 became a cause célèbre of the time. In a larger sense, it marked the beginning of the taming of the West.

It is hard to separate fact from legend when talking about Julia. In later years it was believed that she was buried in a solid silver coffin, that a parlor car on the

Virginia and Truckee Railroad was named in her honor, that she was enormously rich and that she charged as much as $1,000 a night for her company. Probably only the last two items were really true.

This beauty of Creole origin turned up in Virginia City in 1859, when it was no more than a town of clapboard houses and tents inhabited by 6,000 miners and a handful of women. Julia immediately set up business as a prostitute, starting to entertain men as soon as a floor was laid for her cabin, while other grateful miners went about putting up the walls and roof. Julia's enterprise flourished and within a year she employed six other girls to handle business. She opened a parlor house that became the town's center of elegance, one that offered French cuisine and wines and had fresh flowers brought in daily from the West Coast by Wells Fargo. Julia was made an honorary member of the Virginia City Fire Co., the only woman so honored, and on the Fourth of July, she led the parade through town, riding a fire truck adorned with roses.

Much beloved by miners, mine owners and railroad tycoons, Julia was frequently pictured as the prostitute with the Golden Heart. Her praises were often sung by a young reporter for the *Territorial Enterprise* who had just adopted the pen name of Mark Twain. During the Civil War she was one of the biggest contributors to fund-raisers for the Sanitation Fund, the Red Cross of its day. When a fever epidemic hit the area, Julia turned her pleasure palace into a hospital and pawned much of her jewelry and furs to raise money to care for and feed the sick. After the sickness passed, the establishment returned to its fabled bagnio status.

During her early years in town, Julia always sat in the orchestra of the local theater surrounded by a swarm of admirers, but with the arrival of more virtuous ladies and gentlemen in Virginia City, she was forced to sit in a box on the side, curtained off from their cold stares. Civilization was coming to the West, and Julia's days as queen of Virginia City society were clearly coming to an end.

On January 20, 1867 Julia was found strangled in her bed, most of her valuables gone. She had been murdered by either a thief or a client.

The miners of Virginia City were outraged. Quickly, suspect after suspect, 12 in all, were arrested, questioned and finally released after proving their innocence. Had one been judged guilty in those angry days just following murder, a lynching would have resulted, despite the attitudes of the more righteous elements.

Unable to bring the culprit to justice, the men of Virginia City gave Julia Bulette the biggest funeral the town had ever seen. All mines, mills and stores were shut down and draped in black bunting. Led by the fire company and the Metropolitan Brass Band, the cortege paraded through town with hundreds of weeping men in the line of march. We are told that the respectable women of the town shuttered their windows for fear of seeing their own husbands in the procession. After Julia's body was laid in the ground, the band marched back to town, playing the rollicking "The Girl I Left Behind Me."

Several months after the murder, the culprit, John Millain, described in the local press as a "trail louse," was captured following an attempt to rob and kill another madam. Many of Julia's jewels and other prize possessions were found on him. Despite his claims that others were responsible for the murder, Millain was convicted after a quick trial.

The community attitude toward Millain was probably best reflected in the district attorney's summation to the jury:

Although this community has, in times past, seen blood run like water, yet in most cases there was some cause brought forward in justification of the deed, some pretext. But on the morning of the 20th of January last, this community, so hardened by previous deeds of blood, was struck dumb with horror by a deed which carried dread to the heart of everyone—a deed more fiendish, more horrible than ever before perpetrated on this side of the snowy Sierra. Julia Bulette was found lying dead in her bed, foully murdered, and stiff and cold in her clotted gore. True, she was a woman of easy virtue. Yet hundreds in this city have had cause to bless her name for her many acts of kindness and charity. So much worse the crime. That woman probably had more real, warm friends in this community than any other; yet there was found at last a human being so fiendish and base as to crawl to her bedside in the dead hour of the night, and with violent hands, beat and strangle her to death—not for revenge, but in order to plunder her of these very articles of clothing and jewelry we see before us. What inhuman, unparalled barbarity!

That philosophy reflected the thinking of virtually the entire male population of Virginia City, but not that of some of the women. During his confinement in jail, many of the good ladies of the area virtually lionized Millain, bringing him delicacies to fortify his spirits. A woman's committee went so far as to circulate a petition for commutation of his sentence. The *Territorial Enterprise* was incensed by the effort, commenting: "We believe that the man will be hung. If he is not, we do not know where a fit subject for hanging is to be found."

After Millain was sentenced to be hanged on April 24, 1868, so many people wished to attend the event that it had to be shifted to a great natural ampitheater one mile to the north of the city. On that day all the mines on the Comstock shut down once again; it was the second major holiday Julia Bulette had provided.

Bummers western gang

The Bummers were an organized band of outlaws who robbed, raped and terrorized Auraria, Colorado Territory from about 1855 to 1860, much as the Plummer gang did a few years later in Bannack, Montana Territory.

In 1860 the Bummers were wiped out by a vigilante committee of just 10 townsmen in alliance with the local sheriff, who made no pretense about observing legal niceties. The sheriff whose name went unrecorded by the chroniclers of the day, would approach two or three Bummers and arrest them on some minor charge, and since the outlaws knew they would be released shortly, they offered no resistance, right up to the moment when a noose was suddenly slipped around their necks. After a few such multiple hangings, the Bummers who hadn't been hung fled and law and order came to Auraria.

Bunch, Eugene "Captain Gerald" (?1850–1889) train robber

A former schoolteacher who decided there was more money in robbing trains, Eugene Bunch became the notorious Captain Gerald, scourge of the railroads of Texas, Louisiana and Mississippi during the 1880s.

He staged his first robbery in 1888, when he climbed aboard a Southern Express train outside New Orleans and quietly informed the express car guard that he would blow his brains out if he didn't open the safe. Departing with $10,000 in currency and bonds, he told the guard to inform the railroad line that Captain Gerald would be back. Wanted posters described this Captain Gerald as "soft-spoken." After he gained notoriety and a certain popularity with a few more robberies, Bunch was described by the newspapers as being "handsome and daring."

Bunch moved on to Texas, where he became a society darling and extremely popular with the ladies. He passed himself off as a Captain Bunch, a former newspaper editor from Virginia, and he spent an honest six months running a local newspaper. Bunch also had a torrid affair with the daughter of a former governor of Texas. When the train-robbing urge hit him again, Bunch ended up in Mississippi and the girl followed

him, dutifully awaiting his return from each holdup. By now, however, Pinkerton detectives were closing in on Captain Gerald and had even connected him with Captain Bunch.

In 1889 Bunch ceased his lone wolf operations and recruited five gunfighters to form a gang. One was captured and betrayed the gang's hiding place on a small island in a Mississippi swamp. Bunch and two of his gang were ambushed while they were eating. His two confederates were shot before they could even rise from the table. Attempting to make a run for it, Bunch was shot dead in a spirited gun battle. The revelations about Captain Bunch, needless to say, sent shock waves through Texas society.

Bundy, Ted (1947–1989) the charming human monster

The standard description of the average serial killer is that he has, especially in the eyes of neighbors, the behavior patterns of a "creep." In some atypical instances, however, the serial killer comes across differently. Ted Bundy certainly belongs to this "different" class. As one journalist noted: "The moment he stepped into the courtroom in Utah . . . those who saw him for the first time agreed with those who had known him for all of his twenty-eight years. There must have been some terrible mistake."

It was no mistake, as Robert Keppel, an expert who worked on serial killer investigations, noted: "Bundy [later] said he had a Ph.D. in serial killing. He taught us that a serial killer can appear to be absolutely normal, the guy next door. It's very simple. He liked to kill."

Ted Bundy was to leave a scar on the American psyche from 1974 to 1989, when he was finally executed in Florida. His first batch of kills, eight of them, started in 1974, as young women disappeared from Seattle streets. They had been lured into a beige Volkswagen by a presentable young man named Ted. A police computer search turned up nearly 3,000 owners of light-colored Volkswagens in Seattle, and Bundy's name cropped up among them. But while many were questioned and checked on, Bundy was not. Why should he have been? He was of impeccable character, with numerous good points:

- He had worked as a counselor at a crisis clinic.
- He had become an assistant director of the Seattle Crime Prevention Advisory Commission.
- He had written a rape prevention pamphlet for women.
- He had gotten a letter of commendation from the governor of Washington for once capturing a purse snatcher in a shopping mall.

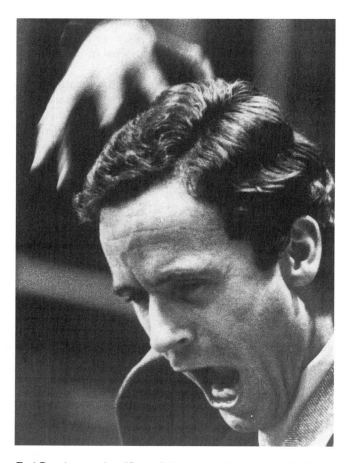

Ted Bundy struck a "Dracula" pose as the judge left the courtroom following a jury recommendation that Bundy be sentenced to die in the electric chair.

Bundy was very active in the Republican Party and won the title of Mr. Up-and-Coming Republican. A former state party chairman who knew Bundy well and recruited him as his assistant said: "If you can't trust someone like Ted Bundy, you can't trust anyone—your parents, your wife, anyone."

Presumably, Seattle lost a fine resource when Bundy left the area and moved on to Salt Lake City and became a Mormon. The killings followed him.

Bundy's first arrest came in October 1975 when a 19-year-old woman identified him in a police lineup as the man who had tried to handcuff her and pull her into his car one night in Murray, Utah. Bundy had been picked up for a traffic violation, and when handcuffs were found in the car, police thought back to the attempted kidnapping of the young woman. Bundy was convicted in the case and given a one- to 15-year prison sentence. While the case was pending, police in Colorado became convinced Bundy had murdered Caryn Campbell, a nurse who had been vacationing in

Aspen almost a year earlier. Campbell had been missing for five weeks before her body turned up in a snowbank. She had been raped, bludgeoned to death, and then ravaged almost beyond recognition by wild animals.

Bundy was extradited to Colorado but was never to stand trial for the Campbell murder. Instead he escaped twice. The first break occurred when Bundy was alone in a room in the county courthouse in Aspen. He jumped from a second-story window and disappeared, not to be recaptured until a week later. Although Bundy was charged with a vile crime, his exploit made him a folk hero in some quarters, a perverse public reaction expressed on future occasions. Six months later, still awaiting trial, Bundy outwitted his jailers again, this time wiggling through a lighting panel in the ceiling of his cell. The opening was only 18 inches wide, and in order to make good his escape, Bundy had managed to lose 35 pounds.

While authorities pressed their search for the fugitive, Bundy made his way across the country to Tallahassee, Fla. Using a phony name and stolen cars and credit cards, he moved into a rooming house on the outskirts of Florida State University. The lodging was just four blocks from the Chi Omega sorority house.

Less than two weeks after arriving in Florida, Bundy invaded the sorority house. He was dressed in black and carried a heavy wooden club. Two co-eds were to die in the house. They were found to have been gnawed badly, but unlike Campbell, they bore bite marks not from wild animals but from their wild *human* attacker. Particularly gnawed up was Lisa Levy, who bore teeth marks on one of her breasts and on her buttocks. She had been beaten, bitten, and strangled in her bed. Another sorority member, Margaret Bowman, met the same grisly fate. The bite marks, investigators realized, were appalling evidence of the killer's psychotic fervor at the moment of the kills.

Levy and Bowman were not the only victims in the Chi Omega house that night. Another co-ed was also attacked and beaten unconscious, but she recovered. Meanwhile, Bundy moved on like a wraith in the night, and six blocks farther on, a young actress was beaten and raped in her bed. She also survived but could offer no description of her attacker.

During the ensuing investigation, several residents in Bundy's rooming house were suspected of the killings, although Bundy was not. Evidently, he was considered a cut above the rest. At the time, the fact that Bundy had very crooked teeth went unnoticed.

Three weeks after the sorority house invasion, Bundy stole a white van and drove to Jacksonville, where he attempted to abduct a 14-year-old girl. He was forced to drive off when the girl's brother appeared. The brother and sister were quick enough to make a note of the van's license plate.

Three days later, 12-year-old Kimberly Leach disappeared from her Lake City junior high school in the middle of the day. Her corpse was not found for two months. When it was discovered, Kimberly was described as having been the victim of "homicidal violence to the neck region."

By now, police in Washington State, Utah, Colorado and Florida were coming to grasp that a *single* killer was responsible for at least 18 murders in their jurisdictions. Bundy had been the prime suspect in the Campbell murder in Colorado, and he was now being sought for many others as well. He moved on to Pensacola, driving yet another stolen VW and unaware that the FBI had just listed him on its Ten Most Wanted list. The car Bundy was driving was recognized by police as a stolen vehicle, and he was seized when he tried to flee on foot. At first, the police did not know whom they had caught, as Bundy gave a false name. But they did know that he was involved somehow in other cases: They found the plates from the van in which the 14-year-old Jacksonville girl had nearly been abducted.

Thirty-six hours after Bundy's arrest, he was identified. The authorities had hit the jackpot.

Florida law officials charged Bundy with the murders of Lisa Levy and Margaret Bowman. An impression made of Bundy's teeth showed that his crooked bite marks matched perfectly those found on Lisa Levy's buttocks.

Bundy pleaded not guilty to the Chi Omega murders and once again was perversely celebrated by those with a twisted and maudlin viewpoint when, as an ex–law student, he conducted part of his own defense. It took the jury just seven hours to find Bundy guilty on a variety of counts. The teeth bite evidence was the most damning, but in addition, a hair in the panty hose mask worn during the attack on the actress the same night as the sorority house killings was found to be indistinguishable from Bundy's.

When asked if he had anything to say before sentencing, Bundy, with tears in his eyes, declared: "I find it somewhat absurd to ask for mercy for something I did not do. The sentence is not a sentence of me. It's a sentence of someone who is not standing here today." Bundy's mother was quoted as saying, "There will be appeal after appeal after appeal."

Even the judge exhibited a certain sympathy for Bundy when passing the death sentence, saying: "Take care of yourself, young man. I say that to you sincerely. It's a tragedy to this court to see such a total waste of humanity. You'd have made a good lawyer. I bear you no animosity, believe me. But you went the wrong way,

partner. Take care of yourself." On a radio talk show one commentator wondered if the judge would have been pleased to have Bundy give his daughter driving lessons.

A year later, Bundy was convicted of the murder of Kimberly Leach, whose body had been found half-buried near a state park. The van he was driving at the time contained leaves and soil matching samples near the burial site. Also, bloodstains in the van matched the blood type of the murdered girl.

There were a number of appeals put forward by Bundy. In the process, he accumulated a large body of supporters, including a number of lawyers and journalists who had followed the trials.

The string ran out at last for Bundy in 1989. In a final interview, Bundy confessed to 28 additional murders. On the night of his electrocution, there were 100 newspeople circulating the crowd outside the prison. It was one of a few cases where those favoring execution far outnumbered those opposed. Signs raised in celebration bore messages such as "Buckle up, Bundy, it's the law" and "roast in peace."

Buntline, Ned   See EDWARD Z. C. JUDSON.

Burdell, Dr. Harvey (1811–1857)   murder victim

The murder of Dr. Harvey Burdell was New York's most sensational case during the 1850s, marked by too many suspects and too many motives, and ending with the public paying P. T. Barnum a fortune to view a baby whose claim to fame was not having been fathered by the late dentist Burdell.

In 1857 Dr. Burdell, at the age of 46, was no pillar of righteousness in the community. When the police relayed news of Burdell's murder to his own brother, Theo, the man declared, "I am not surprised, for he was a dirty"—here even the more sensational of the city's press concealed the words— "... .. . .!"

As the police pressed their investigation, they found that no one seemed to have a good word to say about the departed wealthy dentist. He was described as a sly scoundrel, an accomplished thief, a slick cheat, a welsher, a cheap swindler, a liar "whose word was not worth a cough," a man who quarreled with everyone including his patients. One redoubtable Irishman even insisted Burdell had been a secret agent in the pay of the British government. And why not? Anything was possible when speaking of a man who could woo a girl, go to the church to marry her, pull her father aside and say the wedding was off unless he was paid $20,000, and indeed call the wedding off if no agreement in principle was reached.

Dr. Burdell was paid back in full by his murderer; he died in painful and lingering fashion. He had been stabbed 12 times, and sometime during that ritual, in between or afterward, the murderer or murderess paused to strangle him for good measure. He was found in the master bedroom of his Bond Street home by a young boy who came each morning to make a fire in the fireplace. The boy had trouble pushing open the door to the bedroom, and the obstruction turned out to be Burdell's body. The place was spattered with blood.

There were three other people living in the Burdell mansion. One was a comely widow, Mrs. Emma Cunningham, who, on a sublet deal with the dentist, rented out rooms to boarders. She was about the most distressed person the police found. When informed of the crime, she shrugged and said, "Well those things happen."

A bachelor businessman, John J. Eckel, who rented a room in the house, was not quite as heartbroken. In fact, a contemporary historian insisted he danced a jig when he learned of Burdell's passing. The other tenant was George Snodgrass, who was the son of a Presbyterian minister, a shy and effeminate-looking youth, broke into a big smile when told about the murder and supposedly went out to celebrate, got drunk and tried to attack a hulking longshoreman. Snodgrass was to become a prime suspect after the police found various female undergarments, which he evidently liked to wear, secreted in his rooms. This struck the lawmen as somehow highly significant in a murder investigation.

But there were other major suspects. Dr. Burdell was known to owe a bundle to Honest John Burke, the crookedest gambler in town. Honest John took the loss of his money quite well when informed of his patsy's death. As a matter of fact, he ordered drinks set up for everyone in his favorite tavern, including the officers who brought him the tidings. A rich old Connecticut Yankee, Spawl, now living in New York, had much the same reaction as Honest John, although he didn't spend any money to exhibit his joy. Dr. Burdell had also pursued his daughter, Miss Lucy Spawl, until Spawl sent him away. Burdell had become so incensed that he beat up the old man.

Unfortunately for the police, Honest John, Spawl and several other suspects all had alibis for the time of the murder. This left authorities with the three persons living in the Burdell mansion, Cunningham, Eckel and Snodgrass. And in fact, since the house was shut tight from the inside and the fireplace boy had his own key to get in, the murder certainly appeared to be an inside job. If it hadn't been, then how had the killer entered and left?

Mrs. Cunningham became a prime suspect when she suddenly laid claim to a widow's portion of Burdell's estate, stating she had married him secretly a short time before his murder. She even produced a rather senile minister to attest to the marriage. Yes, the minister said, he had married the woman to a Harvey Burdell. But he wasn't at all sure if this Burdell fellow resembled the deceased. In fact, the minister allowed that the groom looked a little like roomer Eckel.

The coroner decided there wasn't all that strong a case against any of the three alone, so he ruled all three were involved in the murder and should be charged. The prosecutor in the case was A. Oakley Hall, a district attorney who was later to become the most rapacious and, according to some, the most dishonest district attorney in the history of New York City, known as O. K. Haul. But at this stage of the game, Hall was merely out to make a name for himself so he could pave the way for his future misdeeds.

Mrs. Cunningham was to be tried first, under Hall's plan, and her supposed confederates later. One reason for this was that doctors had found Burdell had been stabbed by a left-handed person—and Mrs. Cunningham, or Mrs. Burdell, was left-handed. But aside from that detail and motive and opportunity, there was little direct evidence linking the woman with the crime.

All the while the district attorney was presenting his case, the defendant sat in a chair demurely knitting little blue and pink things. Finally, Hall had had enough and he protested this bizarre behavior. Emma's lawyer, Henry L. Clinton, a descendant of a former vice-president of the United States, defended his client's action. Mrs. Burdell—as he insisted on calling her—was pregnant and would soon be giving birth to the deceased's child.

In the end, that as much as anything caused the jury to bring in a not-guilty verdict. With the woman free, the prosecution gave up efforts to convict the two men. The men quickly disappeared, but Mrs. Cunningham-Burdell stayed much in evidence, pressing her claim to the Burdell fortune. Now that she was with child, she stood to inherit virtually the entire estate. Her pregnancy, however, had an odd quality to it. She seemed to grow bigger, but she would not permit her doctor to examine her. She was, she said, of the old, old school, and no male hands would ever touch her body.

Finally, the doctor decided he was being used and went to the district attorney to say he suspected the woman was stuffing her dress with cushions. The authorities put a watch on her and soon found she was dickering to buy a new-born baby. She offered a young unmarried girl about to give birth $1,000 if she would slip her baby right over to the Burdell home. The girl took the money, and as soon as her baby was born, it was sent over to the alleged Mrs. Burdell, who planned to inform her doctor that a little event had happened during the night. But the police were watching and stormed into the bedroom of the bogus mother-to-be and arrested her.

Many people thought that since Mrs. Cunningham wasn't pregnant, it somehow meant she had indeed murdered Burdell. But the fact was she had been acquitted of that charge. Fraud charges were brought against her but they were later dropped. The Burdell case was to remain unsolved, although for many years the press continued to present various theories. The *Police Gazette* came out with an exclusive that the murderer was a man named Lewis, who had just been executed in New Jersey for another murder. Lewis had told the Gazette that he had done the job by mistake, meaning to kill another Burdell.

Whoever did kill Dr. Burdell, now firmly established as New York's favorite murder victim, never paid for his sins, but at least the guilty party did not gain financially from his or her crime. The only one to make out well moneywise was the bogus Burdell baby. Her mother, already $1,000 ahead on the deal, rented her out for $25 a week to P. T. Barnum, who displayed the tot at his museum for all the eager New Yorkers wishing to see what a baby impostor looked like.

Burke, Elmer "Trigger" (1917–1958) hit man

In the 1950s the most reliable hit man used by the underworld was Elmer "Trigger" Burke, who often said there were only two things in this world that he loved—money and machine guns. In trouble as a youth, he was advised by his older hoodlum brother, Charlie, to join the army in order to avoid being sent to prison for the robbery of a New York City grocery. Fighting in Europe during World War II, he distinguished himself, earning his nickname of Trigger by storming a German machine-gun nest and killing eight enemy soldiers. When his lieutenant reached the scene, he found Burke still blazing away and told him to stop because "those bastards are dead."

"You're goddamn right they are," Burke replied, slinging his weapon.

When Burke returned to his native Hell's Kitchen in New York City, he again moved in mob circles and through his brother's good offices became a freelance killer for a number of gangs. These killings he handled with precision, but he proved less adept at committing his own robberies. He was sentenced to two years at Sing Sing for a liquor store holdup. While Burke was in prison, his brother was murdered. The police nabbed a man named George Goll for the job but released him for insufficient evidence. Via the grapevine, Burke

informed Goll that he did not believe the accusation against him. When he got out of prison, he found Goll on a Manhattan street and put two bullets into the back of his head.

Burke also committed a number of other murders mostly on paid assignments but occasionally gratis. He apparently killed Edward "Poochy" Walsh on July 23, 1952 out of nothing more than personal pique. He entered a bar where Poochy was holding forth, stuck a revolver in his face and blew his victim away with three slugs. "Don't call me Trigger no more," he said. "Call me Killer."

For the rest of Trigger Burke's days before his arrest, he was a wanted man, but he remained readily available to the underworld for hit duty. In June 1954 Burke was assigned to eradicate Joseph "Specs" O'Keefe, reputedly a wayward member of the gang that had pulled the $2.7 million Brinks robbery and believed to be about ready to provide the police with details and names of those involved. It was one of the few jobs Burke messed up. In a wild machine-gun spree through the streets of Boston, Burke loosed blast after blast at the fleeing O'Keefe but managed only to wound him. O'Keefe survived and identified his attacker. Trigger Burke became the most hunted outlaw of the era for all of 24 hours.

Contrary to expectations, Burke did not leave Boston; he apparently had more assignments. The next day another hoodlum, George O'Brien, was found fatally wounded just three miles from the scene of the Burke-O'Keefe shooting spree. And that evening a Boston detective arrested Burke "on suspicion." Burke looked at him and said, "You've made a better pinch than you think, copper."

Burke was clapped in the 104-year-old Suffolk County Prison on Charles Street and remained there until he was able to escape three months later with the help of two gunmen who broke into the prison through a carriage shed and two unused emergency doors.

Burke's escape electrified the nation, but his freedom was short lived. A year later, he was captured by the FBI in Charleston, S.C. while waiting for a bus. He was unarmed and offered no resistance. Burke's attorneys resisted efforts to extradite him to New York for the Walsh killing, insisting he go instead to Massachusetts to face charges of carrying a machine gun and breaking out of jail. New York won out. On January 9, 1958 Burke went to the electric chair, after a last meal of a giant steak followed by a half-dozen cigars. He spent his remaining hours going over 144 newspaper clippings of his exploits. Burke advised the warden to preserve them all "for history's sake."

See also: BRINK'S ROBBERY.

Burke, William (1870–?) "Philadelphia's Jean Valjean"

William Burke was one of the most tragic figures in American criminality, whose fate earned him the title of Philadelphia's Jean Valjean. Burke did not, however, enjoy the final happiness of his fictional counterpart. In his early years in Boston Burke had a different nickname, the Prince of Flatworkers, which he had earned by robbing an estimated 300 to 400 houses and apartments in that city. Finally caught, he served seven years in the Charlestown state prison under another name.

Upon completion of his sentence Burke settled in Philadelphia, where he lived an honest life and saved up enough to open a cigar store. He married and in 1911 was elected to the city council on a reform slate. Burke might have continued his upright life with his past shrouded in secrecy had not a former fellow convict from Charlestown recognized him. The man blackmailed Burke to the point that he finally resigned from office and confessed his criminal record, retiring then to a bitter obscurity.

Burns, Robert Elliott (1890–1965) chain gang fugitive

Author of *I Am a Fugitive from a Georgia Chain Gang*, Robert Elliott Burns, through his book and a subsequent movie about his life, was responsible for the exposure and eventually the end of the inhumane Georgia chain gang system.

Out of a job as a World War I veteran, Burns, together with two strangers, burglarized $5.80 from a grocery store. For this crime he was sentenced to six-to-10 years on the chain gang. In June 1922 Burns made a dramatic escape and was not located until 1930, by which time he had risen to a high post on a magazine in Chicago. Burns voluntarily returned to Georgia after being promised by state officials that he would get a pardon. Instead, he was returned to the chain gang. Burns then did what no other prisoner had done—he escaped the chain gang a second time, assuming a double life in New Jersey. During this period Burns began writing magazine articles describing his personal story and exposing chain gang conditions. These articles were expanded into a book, and in 1932 a movie about his prison life starring Paul Muni evoked much public sympathy.

Georgia officials, however, were outraged. Finally locating Burns later that year, they demanded his extradition. Gov. A. Harry Moore of New Jersey held a special hearing in the Senate Chamber of the State House at Trenton. Heading Burns' defense was Clarence Darrow, and the hearing soon turned into a trial of Georgia's penal system. Described in chilling detail was the "sweat box," a barrel with iron staves on top, in which "insolent" prisoners were kept, often with near-fatal

results. It was revealed that prison cages built for 18 men actually housed 34 convicts. Bolstered with endorsements by several other governors, Gov. Moore rejected the extradition request. Burns was a free man inside New Jersey. Still Georgia did not cease its efforts to recapture its most publicized fugitive. In 1941, Gov. Eugene Talmadge tried again to win custody of Burns, citing improvements made in the penal system. These claims were countered by penal reformers who said the changes were in name only, not in fact.

In 1945, Gov. Ellis Arnall finally ended the chain gang system and invited Burns to return to Georgia. He did, and Arnall immediately commuted his sentence to time served. A free man at last, Burns returned to his New Jersey home and thereafter continued to lend support to penal reform movements until his death 10 years later.

See also: CHAIN GANGS.

Burns, William J. (1858–1932) detective

Few detectives in history have led as checkered a career as William J. Burns, founder of the detective agency that bears his name. He was also the "star of the United States Secret Service" and later the discredited head of the Bureau of Investigation, forerunner of the present FBI. Both in government and private work, Burns may have been the most politicized detective the country has ever seen. Samuel Gompers, the head of the American Federation of Labor, regarded him as an enemy of labor, a frame-up man and faker of evidence. Yet during their head-on clash over the 1910 bombing of the *Los Angeles Times* building, it was Gompers who lost face when the McNamara brothers, two labor officials, were convicted of the murderous plot. Burns emerged to great accolades, with the *New York Times* referring to him as "the greatest detective certainly, and perhaps the only really great detective, the only detective of genius whom the country has produced."

Similarly the great attorney, Clarence Darrow, who also tangled with Burns in the McNamara case, came within an eyelash of being sent to prison on a charge of jury tampering. But during his career Burns himself narrowly missed being imprisoned on such charges as kidnapping and jury tampering, once being lucky to escape with a mere fine against his agency for keeping under surveillance the jurors in the trial of oil man Harry Sinclair. Throughout his career, Burns served the establishment, or at least those elements within the establishment he deemed proper. Generally, this meant those with a strong antilabor bias and pro–Eastern Republican leanings.

Few could quarrel with Burns' early detective career as a member of the U.S. Secret Service, when he cracked many important counterfeiting cases, especially the Bredell-Taylor ring. In 1905 Burns was put in charge of investigating the great western land fraud, in which tens of thousands of acres of public lands were illegally fenced or bought under false representations. Through Burns' efforts Oregon senator John H. Mitchell and Oregon representative John N. Williamson, both Republicans, were convicted and right-wing Republicans never forgave Burns. Years later, considerable evidence indicated that some of the investigations and prosecutions were so corrupt and politically tainted that many regarded them as worse than the charges brought against those eventually convicted.

In 1906 Burns left government service to conduct an investigation of corruption in San Francisco, one that would ultimately wreck the machine and send Boss Abe Ruef to prison. Later, he cracked the *Los Angeles Times* bombing, which many regarded as the greatest bit of detective work in American history, by tracing bomb fragments to the McNamara brothers. However, Burns' stunning accomplishment in the case became somewhat tarnished when, some say at the instigation of *Times* owner Harrison Gray Otis, he attempted to prove the McNamara's lawyer, Clarence Darrow, had attempted to bribe two jurors. The charge was a bit far fetched considering Darrow was at the time preparing to have the McNamara brothers plead guilty in order to save them from execution.

The move failed when Darrow, taking over his own case in summation, made a speech lasting a day and a half that has been cited as matching the eloquence of William Jennings Bryan's "Cross of Gold" oration. "Burns!" Darrow sneered throughout. "Burns with his pack of hounds. The steel trust with its gold. All arrayed against me. I stood alone for the poor and weak. Will it be the gray dim walls of San Quentin? My life has been all too human, but I have been a friend to the helpless. I have cried their cause."

Near the conclusion, Darrow cried: "Oh, you wild insane members of the steel trust. . . . Oh, you bloodhounds of detectives who do your masters' evil bidding. Oh, you district attorneys. You know not what you do."

Right then, it was said, Burns knew he was beaten. The jury came in with a not-guilty verdict after only one ballot. Another trial for the alleged bribing of the second juror ended in a hung jury, and the local authorities, Otis and Burns gave up their attempt to jail Darrow.

Despite this defeat, Burns' detective agency was flourishing. He had succeeded in wresting the plum of the profession, the contract with the American Bankers Association for the protection of its 11,000 member banks, from the much larger and more powerful Pinkertons. Burns' disdain for the Pinkertons was limitless. He regarded his competitors as cowardly, taking on only "safe" cases and never going against local public opinion. To Burns' credit, he was willing to buck public opinion in the case of a young Jewish businessman in Georgia, Leo Frank, who was convicted of raping and murdering a 14-year-old white girl, Mary Phagan, and sentenced to death. During their investigation Burns and one of his assistants were almost lynched by a mob. Because of evidence uncovered by the detectives, Frank's death sentence was commuted, but he was later kidnapped from his prison cell and hanged.

From 1912 through the war years, Burns compiled an impressive record of uprooting political corruption in a number of states, leading to indictments of many lawmakers and political figures. In 1913 he exposed bribe taking in Canada in the Quebec Legislature.

In 1921 Burns was appointed to a position that should have been the capstone of his career, head of the Bureau of Investigation, then an organization that was inept at best and corruption-ridden at worst. It cannot be said that Burns improved matters; in fact, the bureau became overrun with agents urged on Burns by the very figures who were to become involved in the Teapot Dome Scandal. About the only laudable accomplishment of the bureau under Burns was an effective prosecution of the Ku Klux Klan, which Burns had come to hate in the aftermath of the Leo Frank case. However, his famed ability to detect fraud and graft failed him completely as the "Ohio Gang" took over during the Harding administration. Burns apparently saw nothing while corrupt friends of Harding looted the Veteran's Bureau and the Alien Property Claims Bureau. The former bloodhound failed to uncover Secretary of the Interior Albert Fall's blatant selling off of the Teapot Dome and Elk Hills government oil reserves to the highest bribers.

In 1924 Burns resigned in disgrace and was succeeded by a young assistant, J. Edgar Hoover. Burns remained on the front pages as head of his private agency; he was accused in 1927 of jury tampering in the acquittal of oilman Harry Sinclair, charged as one of the bribers of Secretary of the Interior Fall. Burns had accepted an assignment from Sinclair to keep the jurors under surveillance. An angry federal judge ruled that the jury shadowing was itself a form of jury tampering.

Burns' angry response, which perhaps all too well summarized his own career, was, "My men didn't do anything for Harry Sinclair that I haven't done for the federal government hundreds of times!"

Burns died in April 1932.

See also: LEO FRANK, LAND FRAUDS, *LOS ANGELES TIMES* BOMBING, GASTON BULLOCK MEANS, EARL ROGERS.

Burr-Hamilton duel

The most famous duel in this country's history was between Alexander Hamilton and Vice President Aaron Burr on the banks of the Hudson River at Weehawken, N.J. on July 11, 1804.

There had been a festering hatred between the two men since 1801, when Hamilton refused to join in the conspiracy to keep Thomas Jefferson from the presidency and persuaded a number of key Federalist congressmen to choose Jefferson in the runoff against Burr, whom Hamilton called "a cold-blooded Cataline." At the signal, Burr fired, and Hamilton rumbled forward mortally wounded. Hamilton's gun had discharged into the air, and many of his supporters claimed he had deliberately fired high. A coroner's jury called for Burr's arrest, but he fled to the South. After the duel, Hamilton's reputation was enhanced, while Burr became an outcast. A typical poem attacking him read:

> *Oh Burr, oh Burr, what hast thou done,*
> *Thou hast shooted dead great Hamilton!*
> *You hid among a bunch of thistle*
> *And shooted him dead with a great hoss pistol!*

Burrow, Rube (1856–1890) train robber and murderer

Reuben Houston Burrow, the leader of the notorious Burrow gang of the 1880s, developed the same sort of mystique that Jesse James enjoyed. The balladeers and legend-makers, for instance, celebrated the time Rube and brother Jim drove off the miserly banker out to foreclose on a widow's mortgage; of course, they also robbed him for their own gain.

A daring criminal, Rube several times pulled off one of the most difficult of criminal endeavors: robbing a train single-handed. Generally, however, he worked with a gang that included his brother, James, another pair of brothers, Will and Leonard Brock, and various other "hard cases."

The Burrow brothers were born in Alabama and eventually moved to Texas, where they led rather tranquil existences as small farmers for about 14 years before suddenly turning to crime, perhaps because of tales they had heard about a so-called glamorous and lately lamented outlaw named Sam Bass. In any event, they went about robbing trains until they became the subject of ballads, especially after the brothers made a habit of robbing the same train at the same spot on a number of occasions. In

February 1888 the Burrows were captured, but Rube broke jail and escaped. With an accomplice named Lewis Waldrip, who may have been Leonard Brock, Rube spent most of the next several months trying to break Jim Burrow out of his Little Rock, Ark. prison, but his brother died there from consumption in December. Forced eastward by his pursuers, Rube Barrow continued his train-robbing activities in Florida and Alabama. In 1890 he pulled one of his lone wolf jobs. As he confidently strode to his horse to ride off once more into the darkness, a Southern Express detective took his head off with a shotgun blast.

Burton, Mary (?–?) false informer

An 18th-century prostitute and thief named Mary Burton had a more chilling record as an informer than even the girls involved in the Salem witchcraft hysteria. Finding herself in prison in 1741, Burton, also known as Margaret Kelly, sought and won her freedom by concocting a story about an imaginary "Negro criminal plot" in New York City. Because blacks, slave and free, comprised a large segment of the population, any talk of concerted action by them provoked fears on the part of the whites. Given that climate, the general rule was that any testimony by a white woman, regardless of her character or motive, was sufficient to convict a black. Mary Burton also found that every new accusation she made added to her prestige. As a result, 71 blacks were transported away, 20 were hanged and 14 others were burned at the stake. As was the case in the Salem executions, the general dignity with which many of the condemned died finally sparked doubt in the public's mind, and Mary Burton's charges were later simply ignored.

Burts, Matthew (1878–1925) train robber

A minor member of the notorious Burt Alvord–Billy Stiles outlaw band, Burts deserves an entry of his own since, thanks to a cunning strategem by law officers, he was responsible for the gang's complete breakup.

Burts was suspected of being one of the robbers who held up the Southern Pacific train near Cochise, Arizona Territory on September 9, 1899 but it couldn't be proved. Constable Grover of Pearce devised what might be called a reverse undercover operation: he hired Burts as a deputy. Totally unsuspecting any ulterior motive, the dim-witted Burts, got rip-roarin' drunk with Grover and his cronies and slowly spilled out details of the robbery until he had made what amounted to a complete confession and had named all the other robbers. With Alvord and Stiles identified, the days of their criminal enterprises were numbered. For being an unwitting informer, Burts was rewarded with a prison term instead of the rope. He served his time and then moved on to California, where he engaged in the cattle business. Despite years of honest living, Burts still died violently; he was shot dead in 1925 in a grazing rights dispute with a neighboring rancher.

See also: BURT ALVORD, BILLIE STILES.

bushwhacker

Originally bushwhacker had no more meaning than backwoodsman, but the backwoods became the scene of so much criminal violence, starting with the 18th-century depredations of Joseph Hare, Sam Mason and the Harpe brothers along the Natchez Trace, that every bushwhacker had to be regarded as a potential attacker. By the time of the maraudings of Quantrill and his Raiders during the Civil War, bushwhacker had already come to mean a backwoods outlaw.

Buster from Chicago (?–1931) hit man

Perhaps the most brutal and efficient hit man the Mafia ever had was known simply as "Buster from Chicago." Because of his prowess at murder, he was imported into New York by the Maranzano forces to do battle with the dominant power of Giuseppe "Joe the Boss" Masseria during the Castellammarese War of 1930–31. In true Hollywood fashion, no one ever knew Buster's real identity, and his appearance belied that of a professional killer. He looked and dressed like a college boy and carried with him, in the proper Chicago tradition, a submachine gun in a violin case. How many men he killed during that war or earlier in Chicago was never determined, but Buster had a reputation of always succeeding in a hit and doing it with a flair that other gangsters admired. On an assignment to "take out" Peter "the Clutching Hand" Morello, Buster found him and a visitor in Morello's office. He shot Morello, but his victim was tough. He got up and danced around the office trying to avoid further shots. Getting into the spirit of things, Buster backed off and for a while tried to wing Morello shooting gallery style before finally finishing him for good. Then, without a word, Buster turned to the visitor, one Giuseppe Pariano, who had stood frozen during the macabre scene, and killed him also.

Joe Valachi, the celebrated informer, marveled at Buster's shooting ability, which was equally masterful with machine guns, pistols or shotguns. Buster was the main shotgunner in the shooting of two top Masseria aides: Alfred Mineo and Steve Ferrigno,

cut down in the Bronx on November 5, 1930. After the hit he and the two other gunmen with him scattered, but a police officer cut him off just a block from the murder scene. Excitedly, Buster told him there had been a shooting down the street. The officer raced that way and Buster the other. Another of Buster's victims was James Catania, alias Joe Baker, who was killed on February 3, 1931 as he stood on a street corner talking to his wife. Buster had been loathe to do the shooting in front of the victim's wife but couldn't resist such an open target. He was proud of the fact that every shot hit the victim and none the woman.

Buster lived through the Castellammarese War and the victory of Maranzano, but when Maranzano died in a 1931 plot that brought Lucky Luciano to real power, Buster's days were numbered, probably because he was not respectful toward the Mafia captains. He was amused by, rather than in awe of, the structure and rituals of the Mafia. In September 1931 the nonbeliever was killed in a poolhall on the Lower East Side and his body toted away for dumping. Just as Buster's early history is a mystery, so too is his final resting place.

See also: JOSEPH VALACHI.

Butcher, Jake (1937–) the $700-million bank man

Of all the high finance scam operators whose depredations came to the fore in what came to be known in financial circles as the "Greedy 1980s," Jake Butcher had the distinction of being the most punished by the law, ending up with much more prison time than such offenders as Ivan Boesky, Michael Milken, and Charles Keating, Jr., among others.

Jacob "Jake" Franklin Butcher was a former Democratic candidate for governor of Tennessee and organizer of the 1982 World's Fair in Knoxville. Considered a respected figure in Tennessee banking circles, Butcher defrauded his own banks (he controlled 26 in Tennessee and Kentucky) of millions of dollars so that many of them failed and went bankrupt. Butcher's depredations, which financed his flamboyant lifestyle—such as the purchase of such "toys" as a 60-foot yacht for a mere $400,000—ended up costing the Federal Deposit Insurance Corporation (FDIC) well over $700 million, with Butcher and his wife having personal debts of more than $200 million.

It was said at the time that by his actions alone, Butcher had destroyed the deep-held faith that people had put in their banks since the reforms of the 1930s. The public grasped clearly the threats to their banks and savings and that they would have to pay for FDIC losses through their taxes. As a result, there was universal praise for the sentence imposed on Butcher—two 20-year concurrent terms, the maximum allowed.

Butterworth, Mary (1686–1775) counterfeiter

One of the first successful counterfeiting rings in America was masterminded by a woman, probably the first of her sex to practice the art in the New World. In 1716 30-year-old Mary Butterworth started her monumental fraud right in her own kitchen in the Plymouth colony, copying the Rhode Island pound "bills of credit." Using a hot iron and some starched muslin, she simply reproduced the image onto a blank paper. With several confederates of artistic bent, she filled in the images with quill pens and then passed them on through a pipeline, which included a local justice who was above suspicion.

It is impossible to establish any firm money figure on the scope of the profits realized, but the bills reportedly caused considerable financial havoc in Rhode Island, and the operation must have been extensive. The so-called kitchen counterfeiters stayed in existence for seven years before Mary Butterworth was arrested along with a half-dozen others. However, while a number of bogus bills were found and the counterfeiter's tools located in the woman's kitchen, no hard evidence could be produced proving the bills had been there. Eventually, Butterworth and the others were released for lack of evidence. She was closely watched for many years thereafter to prevent any resumption of the counterfeiting. Thus, tranquility was restored to the New England financial scene.

Byrnes, Thomas F. (1842–1910) New York police inspector

Although he served briefly as chief of police in New York City, Thomas F. Byrnes really made his mark while serving as chief of detectives and chief inspector of the force in the 1880s and 1890s, during which time he was easily the most renowned American policeman of the era. What he lacked in honesty he more than made up for in flamboyance. It has been said that Byrnes embodied all that was good and all that was bad in the 19th-century policeman.

Born in Ireland in 1842, he was brought to New York as a child. During the Civil War he fought for two years in the Union Army before joining the police force in 1863. By 1870 he had moved up to captain, a rank generally achieved only by playing according to the accepted rules, which meant collecting bribes and passing along the proper share to police higher-ups and to the right politicians at Boss Tweed's Tammany Hall. In 1880 Byrnes became head of the Detective Bureau after

solving the record $3-million robbery of the Manhattan Bank. He had rounded up most of the loot and several of the burglars and been applauded by Tammany for his work, especially since the Leslie mob, which pulled the job, had neglected to fork over the standard police-politician cut for such a caper, generally 10 percent of the take.

As head of the Detective Bureau, Byrnes outlawed such cooperation between crooks and police and set as his first goal the elimination of bank robberies in the Wall Street area. He had received more than acclaim after solving the Manhattan Bank job. Several grateful bankers had gotten together and "invested" a large sum of money for him from which he collected the profits. This was not to be considered a reward because rewards had to be approved by and shared with police superiors, not to mention that a certain percentage of rewards had to be given to the police pension fund. Byrnes appreciated the sentiments of the bankers and decided to show his gratitude by ordering all professional criminals to stay out of the Wall Street area. To enforce this edict, he ordered his men to arrest or at least blackjack any professional thief found south of Fulton Street, the demarcation known to criminals as Byrnes' Dead Line.

Byrnes further aided the prominent bankers and stockbrokers by always proving cooperative in hushing up any personal scandals. If he reduced the incidence of major crimes in the Wall Street area, Byrnes was also responsible for a novel treatment of crime elsewhere in the city. He more or less legalized crime, or more precisely, he kept it within acceptable limits by using some criminals to oversee or suppress other criminals, giving each a protected area in which to operate. In return, for this right, the criminals paid Byrnes far less than the previous levels of graft but were required to perform certain other duties on request. For instance, if a prominent person had his pocket picked or was robbed by foodpads, all Byrnes had to do was ask for the return of the loot and it was on his desk within 24 hours.

A gullible public regarded such feats as examples of keen detective work, and overall, Byrnes' stature was enhanced. Byrnes appreciated the value of public relations and became a romantic figure in print. He collaborated on a number of books, and one of his own, *Professional Criminals of America* became a best-seller. In his day, Byrnes got as much mileage out of denouncing foreign-born anarchists as did J. Edgar Hoover upon his discovery of the communist menace.

Byrnes realized that if he catered to a privileged few, he had carte blanche to do whatever he wished with all others. In the 1880s he was considered second only to Inspector Alexander "Clubber" Williams in his devotion to the practice of the third degree. Byrnes was, to journalist Lincoln Steffens, "Simple, no complication at all—a man who would buy you or beat you, as you might choose, but get you he would."

Byrnes' downfall came about in the mid-1890s because of the opposition of reformer Theodore Roosevelt, at the time a member of the four-man board of police commissioners, and because of the findings of the Lexow Committee. Writing to Henry Cabot Lodge, Roosevelt announced: "I think I shall move against Byrnes at once. I thoroughly distrust him, and cannot do any thorough work while he remains. It will be a hard fight, and I have no idea how it will come out."

As it was, Byrnes retired about a month later, in June of 1895. He had had a particularly trying time before the Lexow Committee, which heard testimony indicating that Byrnes permitted widespread corruption within the Detective Bureau. His men were notorious for refusing to undertake robbery investigations unless the victim first posted a reward. Byrnes was personally pressed to explain how he had accumulated $350,000 in real estate, $292,000 in his wife's name. His top salary had been $5,000 a year and no more than a quarter of his huge estate could be attributed to the "gratuities" of the Wall Street crowd.

Despite these embarrassments, Byrnes made a pitch at staying on as chief of police, assuring Roosevelt and the other reformers that he could run a department free of all corruption. His own failings, he said, were due to being trapped in a foul system. His offer was rejected.

See also: BLISS BANK RING, DEAD LINE, OLD SHAKE-SPEARE.

cackle-bladder con man's trick

Probably the most efficient method ever devised by confidence men to "blow the mark off," i.e., to get rid of a victim after fleecing him is the use of a "cackle-bladder." The victim is lured into a supposedly sure thing such as betting on what he is assured to be a fixed horse race. He is steered to a phony betting parlor where everyone is an actor playing a role, from the supposed tellers to the bettors winning and losing fortunes. Naturally, the horse he bets on loses, but before the mark can remonstrate another supposed loser, who is actually in on the scheme, turns on the con man playing the role of the chief conspirator. He screams he has been ruined, pulls a gun and shoots the con man dead. There seems no doubt the man is dead as blood literally gushes from his mouth. Everyone starts to scatter, and so does the bilked victim. Not only has he lost his money, but even worse, he's now involved in a homicide. Sometimes the supposed murderer will flee with the mark, even conning the sucker into leaving the city with him. Eventually, of course, the mark decides he is better off to part company with a man who has committed murder and who could now drag him into prison as an accessory.

This type of scam is made convincing through the use of a cackle-bladder, a tiny bag of chicken blood concealed in the mouth and bitten open at the appropriate moment. The gimmick was also used in the last century at fixed running races and boxing matches as well, where the "sure thing" runner or boxer whom the sucker had bet on seemed to drop dead. Since gambling on such races or fights was illegal and all the bettors were therefore liable to imprisonment, everyone, including the gullible victim, fled when the faking runner or boxer dropped.

While the cackle-bladder is only used on rare occasions in contemporary confidence games, it remains a favorite with insurance accident fakers, who use the dramatic spurt of blood to convince witnesses that they have really been injured.

Calamity Jane (1852–1903) woman "outlaw"

Few works touching on female criminality in America and especially in the West fail to include Martha Jane Cannary, best known as Calamity Jane. However, her inclusion in such studies is a miscarriage of justice, since it has been clearly demonstrated that the extent of her lawless behavior was limited to disorderly conduct, drunkenness and stints of prostitution, such as her 1875 tour of duty at E. Coffey's "hog farm" near Fort Laramie.

Calamity's "autobiography" is full of shoot-'em-up exploits and, of course, a torrid love affair with Wild Bill Hickok. Actually, it is doubtful that Hickok ever considered this muscular, big-boned girl who dressed like a man anything other than an occasional member of his entourage. After Hickok's death in 1876, Calamity Jane became a living legend: "the White Devil of the Yellowstone," as one dime novel called her. The last 25 years of her life were spent peddling her autobiography and other books about her for a few pennies, whoring and appearing in various Wild West shows, from which she was invariably fired for drunkenness. In 1900 a newspaper editor found her sick in a brothel and nursed her back to health. Calamity was dying in a

Public drunk and prostitute Calamity Jane picked up occasional change in her last years posing for tourists at the gravesite of her "lover," Wild Bill Hickok.

hotel room in Terry, not far from Deadwood, S. Dak. in the summer of 1903. On August 2 her eyes fluttered open and she asked the date. Upon being told, she nodded and said: "It's the 27th anniversary of Bill's [Hickok's] death. Bury me next to Bill." They did and recorded her death on August 2, although she had not died until August 3. But then the facts never have been permitted to cloud the Calamity Jane legend.

See also: WILD BILL HICKOK.

Calico Jim (?–1897?) shanghai operator

Shanghaiing of men was an old San Francisco custom and one of its most proficient practitioners, along with the infamous Shanghai Kelly, was Calico Jim. A Chilean whose real name was said to be Reuben, Jim ran a saloon and crimping joint at Battery Point, from

which a great many men were sent on long sea voyages. During the 1890s the San Francisco police received so many complaints against Jim that they began paying him close attention. Evidently not close enough, however, because a policeman sent to arrest him didn't come back. Another tried and also never returned. A total of six police officers went to the saloon and disappeared; all had taken a sea cruise, compliments of Calico Jim. Feeling now that his days in the business were limited, Jim sold out and returned to his native Chile.

It was many months before the policemen made their way back to home port. It has been said that they pooled their money, drew lots and sent one of their number off to Chile to hunt down Calico Jim. After many months of hunting, according to the story, the policeman found Jim on a street corner in Callao, Chile and shot him six times, one for each officer he had shanghaied. There is some doubt about the truth of this account, although it gained a great deal of currency. For years the police department insisted there was no record of six officers being shanghaied. But jaded citizens of San Francisco contended they knew a cover-up when they heard one.

See also: SHANGHAI KELLY.

California Outlaws   anti-railroad band

Perhaps the nearest thing this country ever saw to the Robin Hood legend was the California Outlaws, a misnomer for the small ranchers and mountain people of the San Joaquin Valley who did battle in the latter part of the 19th century with the Southern Pacific Railroad, or the "Octopus," as it was commonly known and described in the Frank Norris novel of that title. The railroad was laying its tracks through several western states, and from its standpoint, all intervening land had to be acquired for this purpose, no matter by what means. If the railroad passed through farmland or the home of some settler, the property was condemned, and the helpless owner had to accept the pittance offered him or get nothing. The railroad imported gunmen from the East to do battle for it, and any act committed by the company was considered legal, including such atrocities as the "slaughter of Mussel Slough," in which seven settlers were shot and killed in 1880. The result was a virtual civil war, as the landowners of the San Joaquin Valley banded together to fight the "enveloping tentacles of the Octopus engulfing their lands," as one historian put it. Undercover agents of the railroad moved in among the settlers to spy on and single out troublemakers to be dealt with.

Under their leaders, Chris Evans and the Sontag brothers, George and John, the California Outlaws began robbing Southern Pacific trains. They would stop the trains on lonely stretches and, ignoring the passengers and the U.S. mails, rob only the railroad's safe in the express car. The raids went on for years. Railroad detectives under the notorious Big Bill Smith and lawmen under U.S. marshal George C. Gard engaged in an unseemly bounty competition for bringing in, or more often killing, individual members of the Outlaws. In time, the Outlaws dwindled down to a band of 24 men, plus a 25th named Ed Morrell who worked as a spy for them among the railroad detectives. Morrell, later immortalized by Jack London in *The Star Rover,* was able to save the Outlaws from several traps, but after he was exposed, the band was destroyed. John Sontag was killed in a shoot-out with a posse of railroad gunmen. Chris Evans went to prison under a life sentence; George Sontag died attempting to escape from Folsom Prison. Ed Morrell, later to become famous as the most

tortured prisoner in the history of American penology, drew a life term but was pardoned in 1907.

See also: CHRISTOPHER EVANS, ED MORRELL, SONTAG BROTHERS.

Campagna, Louis "Little New York"   (1900–1955)
gangster

Considered by Al Capone to be his most reliable bodyguard, Louis "Little New York" Campagna was a stubby little mobster who, thanks more to his steel nerves than his brainpower, rose to the top echelon of syndicate crime.

During the Chicago mob's movie studio extortion days, Campagna walked into a jail and stiffened a wilting gang member, Willie Bioff, who had announced he wanted to quit the rackets. In a menacing voice few could equal, Campagna said, "Whoever quits us, quits feet first." Later, after Bioff cracked, sending several top syndicate men, including Campagna, to prison, Little New York always bemoaned the fact that his associates had vetoed a "feet first" proposal regarding Bioff.

Al Capone had imported Campagna in 1927 from New York, where he had cut his criminal teeth as a teenager in the Five Points Gang and been convicted of bank robbery at 19. Capone dubbed him Little New York merely to demonstrate his ability to import all the gunners he needed. Campagna soon demonstrated his nerve following an unsuccessful plot by the Aiello brothers to assassinate Capone. Shortly thereafter, Joseph Aiello and one of his gunmen were taken to the Chicago Detective Bureau lockup. Campagna promptly surrounded the bureau with a dozen gunmen, and he and two others approached the building, shifting weapons from holsters to side pockets. A policeman recognized Campagna and, realizing he was laying siege to the building, sounded the alarm. A score of detectives rushed out to seize the trio and hustled them into the building before their accomplices could come to their aid.

Campagna was lodged in a cell next to Aiello while a detective who understood the Sicilian dialect posed as a prisoner in another cell. He heard Campagna say: "You're dead, dear friend, you're dead. You won't get up to the end of the street still walking."

Aiello was quaking with fear. "Can't we settle this?" he pleaded. "Give me fourteen days and I'll sell my stores, my house and everything and quit Chicago for good. Can't we settle it? Think of my wife and baby."

Campagna was unmoved. "You dirty rat! You've broken faith with us twice now. You started this. We'll finish it."

It was no idle threat. When Aiello was later found shot down on the street, 59 slugs, more than a pound of bullets, were dug out of his body.

At the height of the assassination scare against Capone, the gang boss made Campagna his main bodyguard. At night, the devoted little killer slept on a cot just outside Capone's bedroom door. Anyone going in would have to climb over Campagna's body.

In the 1930s and early 1940s, Campagna became a key figure in the mob's union rackets and extortion plots against Hollywood movie studios. Along with six others, Campagna was convicted of conspiracy to extort $1 million from studio executives and sentenced to 10 years. He served one-third of his sentence and was paroled to a firestorm of protest by Chicago newspapers. In later years Campagna played the role of a gentleman farmer on an 800-acre spread near Fowler, Ind. He died of a heart attack aboard a pleasure cruiser off Miami in 1955.

Campbell, Bertram (1886–1946) wrong man

The case of Bertram Campbell demonstrates as well as any the near impossibility of achieving adequate compensation for wrongfully convicted individuals.

Before his conviction, Campbell had been a securities salesman and customer's man for several New York brokerage houses. In February 1938, New York City police detectives visited Campbell in his apartment in Freeport, Long Island and brought him to the city for questioning. There five bank tellers identified him as a forger who had recently cashed two checks for $4,160 under the name of George Workmaster. He was convicted of the charge and served three years and four months of a five-to-10-year sentence in Sing Sing, all the time maintaining his innocence. Released on parole late in 1941, Campbell, a sick and broken man, eked out a rather miserable existence as a bookkeeper. In early 1945 he happened to read a newspaper story that the FBI had arrested a forger in Kentucky. The man's method of operation brought Campbell up sharply. It fitted perfectly with the one used in the crimes of which he had been convicted. Campbell contacted a lawyer, who learned that the forger had been brought to New York for arraignment. The lawyer rounded up the five bank employees and took them to see the forger, Alexander D. L. Thiel. Three of them immediately

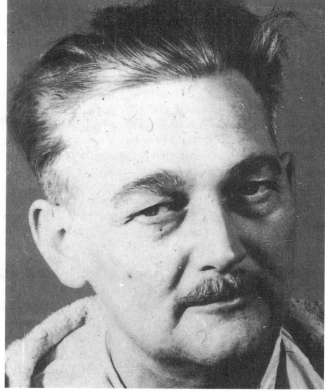

Often cited as an example of the dangers of faulty eyewitness testimony, Bertram Campbell (left) was identified as a forger by five bank tellers and sent to prison. Later, Alexander Thiel (right), a professional check passer, was determined to be the guilty party.

admitted they had been in error, that Thiel was the man.

Thiel, now a drug addict, readily confessed. To the FBI he had been "Mr. X," who in 40 years had duped banks the country over for upwards of $600,000. After months of delay Campbell was pardoned and awarded $40,000 for earnings lost and $75,000 for disgrace and humiliation suffered. All in all, it seemed about as satisfactory a conclusion to a sad case as was possible. However, Campbell's tribulations were not over. Nassau County officials slapped Campbell with a $4,000 bill for welfare payments made to his wife while he had been wrongfully imprisoned. Then, just 82 days after he had won the $115,000, Campbell died of a stroke, which doctors speculated was the result of the strain of his years in prison.

See also: ALEXANDER THIEL.

Canada Bill   See WILLIAM "CANADA BILL" JONES.

Canal Street   Buffalo vice center

"For sheer wickedness, vice and crime there is no need to go any further west than here," a 19th-century historian said of Canal Street in Buffalo, N.Y. It was quite a claim to make about a thoroughfare but two blocks long.

Born with the Erie Canal, Canal Street was set off on a jutting piece of land, segregated from the rest of Buffalo by 40 feet of murky water. On quiet summer nights Buffalonians could stroll casually along the canal and gaze across at the street that never lost its light from dusk to dawn. They could hear boisterous noises of ribaldry and wonder if at that moment, somewhere on Canal Street, someone was in the process of being killed, a likely occurrence on a street that boasted 93 saloons, three combination grocery-saloons and 15 dives known as concert halls. More than half these establishments had portions of their premises given over to prostitution, with an estimated 400 practitioners of that art on hand around the clock.

Canal Street grew up with the Erie Canal, which cut across New York State and linked up the Hudson with the Great Lakes. The street sucked gold from the rugged sailors of the Lakes and the lusty canalers and in return provided a bawdiness unrivaled even in the tenderloin sections of far bigger cities. An early clergyman thundered from his pulpit that it should be called Market Street because the fruits of any vice could be purchased along its cobble-stoned length. The ladies of Canal Street knew how to get a man's money, and they were not averse to slitting his throat if need be. In the end, the residents of the street usually got every penny a

man had, leaving him without even enough with which to buy a mug of beer. Canal Street was said to be the birthplace of the word *mugging*. When a man had been so sheared that he didn't even have the price of a mug of beer, he would walk outside and waylay a passerby or "mug" him.

The worst dives on Canal Street were those places on the East Side whose rear areas extended on wooden pilings over the canal. Unsuspecting canalers and lakers were hustled there by painted women who charged exorbitant prices for their services. However, if a man had money, but was uncooperative about parting with it, he was fed an overdose of knockout drops. He then was hauled into a backroom, stripped of all his clothes and dumped naked down a slicked wooden chute into the canal with hardly an incriminating splash. Eventually he would turn up floating face down in the murky water. The police would know no more than that he had been killed in one of about 100 places and listed the victim as a "floater." In one week in 1863 no less than 14 floaters were fished out of the canal, five on one morning alone.

Canal Street lived on protection. One time there was a report, undoubtedly true, that several leading politicians had had a little two-day party in one of the street's leading bordellos, which helped explain why no concerted effort was made to drive out the scarlet women. For many years about all the politicians would grant the citizens of Buffalo was a segregation ruling that denied such ladies the right to go any further uptown than the liberty pole, which marked the entrance to Buffalo proper in those days. So long as the prostitutes remained in the Canal Street area, they were safe.

In 1870 a young reformer named Grover Cleveland was elected sheriff of Erie County after making campaign promises to clean up Canal Street. Cleveland tried to keep his word but was singularly ineffective. The saloon keepers and brothel owners of the street paid out so much money to the right political forces in Buffalo that Cleveland's campaign was fruitless. If he made arrests, politically controlled judges immediately released the prisoners for "lack of evidence." Cleveland went on to become president of the United States. He was once asked what was the greatest disappointment of his life; he stated that it was not failing to be reelected president in 1888 but rather being unable to wipe out the scourge of Canal Street.

Both before and after Cleveland, Canal Street went its own murderous way, regarding all type of crime as hardly worthy of special notice. When Fat Charley Ott, the proprietor of The Only Theater, a sort of combination concert hall, saloon, dance hall and assignation hotel, came to a bad end, the street handled it in typical fashion. Fat Charley had a propensity for padding the bill of a client who appeared in possession of less than all his faculties. One sweltering night in the 1890s, he made the mistake of trying it on a certain bearded laker. After letting out an angry howl that filled the Only, the laker reached across the bar, seized Fat Charley by the hair and with brute force hauled Charley to him. Like many a lakeman, he carried a Spanish knife, a nasty, two-edged slicer that was worn up the sleeve, attached by a leather thong. He whipped it out. Fat Charley struggled to get loose, but his unhappy patron wasn't letting go. At the time, there were some two dozen other patrons in the Only. They gaped in motionless horror as the bearded lakeman decapitated Charley Ott with one swipe.

The murderer strode out of the Only as the other customers froze. Someone allowed that perhaps the police should be informed. Others agreed but suggested that perhaps they should have a drink in memory of the dear departed. They had one, another and then another. When in due course the police arrived, the Only was empty save for the two parts of Fat Charley, a looted till and scores of empty liquor bottles. And some wag had even left a sign on the door that read CLOSED ON ACCOUNT OF ILLNESS.

It was said, not without good reason, that the females of Canal Street were far more deadly than the males. There was, for instance, Gallow May Moore, a blond hellion who could throw her garter stiletto with unerring accuracy; any man who tried to leave her without paying the premiums could count on awesome retribution. Her favorite trick was to pin an unchivalrous gentleman to a wall with a stiletto, empty his pockets, kiss him goodbye and leaving him dangling as she went out to live it up on his roll, with enough set aside for a new knife.

Then there was Frosty Face Emma, described as a handsome woman much sought after by men. She had, however, one disconcerting habit. For a time she could drink liquor as though she had a hollow leg, and a gentleman would wait impatiently for her to enter a more compliant phase, which unfortunately never happened. At a certain level of consumption, she turned into a vicious man-hater. A man's only hope was that he had not as yet adjourned with her to a more secluded atmosphere before she exploded. Otherwise, there was little chance he would be seen alive again. One historian states Emma assassinated at least seven lovers and cut up many others. The law never did get anything on Emma, however. Her victims couldn't or wouldn't talk, and Canal Street had its own rules: nobody ever told anything to the law about anybody.

Fittingly, Emma got her just deserts in a knife battle with a redhead called Deadly Dora. If there was one thing Dora wouldn't tolerate, it was another woman stealing a man from her. She had latched on to a blue-eyed Swedish sailor for whom she developed a genuine affection. Emma tried to cut in and knives flashed. They fished Emma's body out of the canal a few days later.

A time came when Buffalonians could thank the girls of Canal Street for preventing the city from being overrun by prostitutes. It happened during Pan-American Year, when all Buffalo was in a Mardi Gras spirit in celebration of the turn of the century. Up till then the several hundred prostitutes in and around Canal Street had the territory to themselves, but with the celebration hundreds of sinful ladies from New York City headed for the bonanza town of the North. One day, bag and baggage, they poured from a train at the Terrace railroad station, directly across from the canal, and attempted to move in.

The women were all colorfully dressed, and canalers paused in their labors to give them a cheering welcome. They circulated among the men with friendly words that happy days had indeed come to Buffalo. The gay arrival, however, also had been seen by the women of Canal Street, and like an army, they swarmed out of the dives and bordellos to descend on the train station. Many carried stillettos, clubs, planks or chairs.

It was a battle the likes of which Buffalo had never seen before. Before it was over, close to 100 ladies were in various degrees of undress. A dedicated reporter counted eight females stripped totally raw. Two dozen girls had to be hospitalized, many with awful knife slashes across their faces. The paddy wagon made a total of 32 trips to the Franklin Street Station, hauling off battling participants. By nightfall the battle was over, and the New York ladies, no match for the denizens of Canal Street, jammed back into the station and took the next train out.

Pan-American Year was the last really big one for Canal Street. Buffalo was changing. Erie Canal traffic was dipping, and as the railroads took over more, fewer and fewer Great Lakes freighters docked. Consequently, fewer sailors and canalers hit Canal Street. The joints began to shutter. In 1908 a citizens' movement increased the pressure on the police to clean up Canal Street once and for all. Raids increased, and foreign immigrants began to flood into Canal Street, soon outnumbering the criminal element. In 1915 the name of the street was changed to Dante Place. In peculiarly American style, the area became an ordinary slum, breeding its own type of vice and crime. But the whores and whoremasters were gone, and Canal Street, with its incredible century of murder, mayhem, vice and corruption, was just a memory.

See also: FLOATERS, MUGGING, YORKY OF THE GREAT LAKES.

Candelaria, Nevada   lawless mining town

Of all the mining camps that sprang up in Nevada in the 1860s and '70s, Candelaria deserves special mention because for a quarter of a century it officially had only seven murders. That was remarkable for a town that boasted 10 whorehouses running around the clock and that sold whiskey by the gallon. In fact, fatal shootings were extremely common, and recorders of the town's history put the death toll in the several hundreds. More so than any other mining camp where the law was seldom found, the public relations–minded authorities of Candelaria were inclined to write off almost any shooting as a matter of self-defense. Of the seven killings officially listed as murders, none was ever solved.

Canton, Frank M.   (1849–1927)   outlaw, lawman and vigilante leader

One of the villains or heroes of the Johnson County War in Wyoming Territory, depending on one's outlook, Frank M. Canton was proof that an evil man who was good to the right people could do all right for himself in the Old West.

While his early life was at the time a mystery, Canton turned up in Wyoming in 1880 and became a small rancher; two years later, he was elected sheriff. As a lawman, he ran up an impressive record tracking down rustlers, although some objected that many of the so-called rustlers were in no shape to answer formal charges after facing Canton's six-guns. After two terms Canton found himself voted out of office. He was so bitter that when approached by Wyoming's wealthy stockmen to head up their vigilante war against rustlers in Johnson County, Canton accepted even though he knew the real objective of the war was to intimidate the small ranchers responsible for electing him to office. These ranchers, actually homesteaders with a few head of cattle, had incurred the wrath of the absentee cattle barons of Cheyenne, who were determined to rewrite the traditional law of the range that a maverick, or unbranded, steer belonged to the man with the longest rope. With Maj. Frank Wolcott, Canton led the big cattlemen's paid vigilantes in numerous attacks and lynchings in Johnson County. They were finally beaten, however, by a ragtag but straight-shooting army of homesteaders, who won the sympathy of most of the nation.

During the period of the Johnson County War, Canton, slender, cold eyed and sinister looking in a long capelike coat, was described by a companion as a man who "only thought of guns and killings . . . they seemed to be on his mind all the time . . . he couldn't sleep. He was always jumping up and saying . . . 'Do you hear them? . . . Get on your guns.' But it wasn't anything—just the wind or the horses."

The fact that Canton was able to switch sides with so few second thoughts can be partially explained by the gunfighter ethics of the day. However, it was later proved that he had switched sides more than once. Canton's real name was Joseph Horner, the son of a Virginia doctor who came to Texas after the Civil War. By his mid-twenties Horner had run up a criminal record of bank robbery, rustling and assault with intent to kill. In 1874 he fled Texas after killing a soldier in a saloon brawl. Between that time and his appearance in Wyoming, Horner had engaged in a number of illegal enterprises. After his Wyoming days—there was no way he could remain there, being generally regarded as a hired killer—Horner, using the name Canton, became an undersheriff in Pawnee County, Okla. and then a deputy U.S. marshal in Alaska. He later returned to the States and was employed by the Texas Cattle Raisers' Association. It has been suggested that through this organization's good offices a long-missing fugitive named Joe Horner received a pardon from the governor of Texas. Perhaps in deference to the feelings of ill-will back in Wyoming, it was not revealed that Horner was Canton until he died in 1927.

See also: CATTLE KATE, NATHAN D. CHAMPION, JOHNSON COUNTY WAR, RED SASH GANG.

capital punishment

When on January 17, 1977 Gary Gilmore was led before a firing squad and shot to death, the execution marked the return of capital punishment in the United States after a 10-year hiatus.

It is often assumed that executions stopped because of a ruling by the U.S. Supreme Court, but in fact, executions ceased basically because of a combination of public disapproval and the growing reluctance of juries to convict in cases involving mandatory death sentences. Thus, while there were 152 executions in 1947, the number dropped to seven by 1965 and to just one in 1967. It was only at this stage that the Supreme Court agreed to hear arguments in two cases challenging the basic precepts of capital punishment. Certainly, the strongest evidence that the High Court follows election results or public opinion can be seen in its rulings concerning capital punishment, both pro and con. In 1967 public opinion was overwhelmingly opposed to the death penalty, and the High Court was eventually to rule that way. When by 1976 public opinion had shifted in the opposite direction, the Court veered toward that view, even while admitting that the primary argument always made for the death penalty, that it is a deterrent to murder and other capital crimes, was faulty.

Capital punishment in the American colonies was patterned after the English system, but the early settlers, with some lamentable exceptions, soon broke away from the full implementation of the death penalty for such crimes as witchcraft, blasphemy, fornication, various "crimes against nature" and "man stealing." Murder and thievery, major or petty, remained firm cause for execution.

In 1834 Pennsylvania banned public executions, and in 1847 Michigan became the first state to abolish the death penalty. Other states joined the abolition movement, although the death penalty made a strong comeback during periods of great wars, the Civil War and the two world wars. By 1971 39 of the 54 U.S. jurisdictions (the 50 states, the District of Columbia, Puerto Rico, the Virgin Islands and the federal jurisdiction) carried the death penalty on the books for as many as eight capital crimes: espionage, treason, murder, rape, kidnapping, arson, train wrecking and robbery. In most states the number of offenses for which the penalty was imposed ranged from one to four.

The principal argument presented by advocates of capital punishment is that it satisfies society's need for retribution and retaliation and serves as a deterrent to the commission of murder. Moreover, it is the only certain process for the elimination of deviants. The arguments of the abolitionists are many. It is a weapon used primarily against the blacks and other racial minorities and the poor ("Rich men never burn" is a death house saying). As a deterrent, they insist, capital punishment doesn't work. In some states the murder rate actually decreased when the death penalty was abolished. Overall, it appears that the murder rate in states with or without the death penalty is, over a period of time, about the same. In states where murders do increase (both in states with and without capital punishment), the causes for the increase are apparently due to societal or cultural variations or changes. If a state moves to a greater heterogeneous mix, the murder rate will go up, death penalty or no. Abolitionists also argue against the deterrent theory on the ground that the crimes it punishes result from irrational impulses, not cool calculation. As Gary Gilmore commented about his murder of two young strangers: "Murder is just a thing of itself, a rage, and rage is not reason, so why does it matter who? It vents a rage." Most of the men who have been on death row insisted they murdered without any thought of the consequences. Furthermore, it has been shown that mass murderers move blithely from states without the death penalty to states with it.

There have even been a number of murders committed because the death penalty exists. According to the Washington Research Project, an Oklahoma farmer who had shot to death a total stranger simply explained to police, "I was tired of living." In 1961 a convicted Oklahoma murderer, James French, who had been tried three times for one homicide, strangled his cellmate in order to speed his own execution along. In 1938 Robert West, who had helped build Missouri's gas chamber, killed a young girl and, after turning himself in, said his only motive for murdering the victim was to be able to die in the gas chamber. When John Spenkelink died in the electric chair in May 1979, he became the first person executed in Florida in 15 years. A later study of the six-month period before and after his execution, when the public controversy about the issue was at its peak, showed that homicides in the state increased 14 percent.

Opponents of the death penalty also argue for rehabilitation over execution. Probably no prison warden would deny that murderers are often the most easily rehabilitated and best-behaved convicts. Additionally, cases of murder committed by paroled murderers are most rare, especially when compared with repeaters of other types of crimes.

It was against this background that in 1972 the Supreme Court ruled the death penalty as practiced was unconstitutional, in violation of the Eighth Amendment ban on cruel and unusual punishment, particularly in the way judges and juries arbitrarily and infrequently imposed it. The immediate impact of the Court's decision was that the death sentence for 648 men and women then on death row was commuted to life imprisonment. Almost immediately, supporters of capital punishment launched a counterattack. By 1976 public opinion, upset by sensational murders little different from those of earlier years, had turned once more in favor of the death penalty.

A not-unmindful Supreme Court took the hint and announced in a new ruling the same year that execution methods in the United States were not inherently "cruel and unusual" punishment as prohibited by the Constitution. The Court even cited various public opinion polls indicating that Americans favored capital punishment by a two-to-one margin. However, at the same time, the Supreme Court agreed there was little proof the death penalty deters the commission of capital crimes. Fundamentally, the Court decreed that retribution and punishment alone were sufficient reasons to impose the death penalty. In other words, the concept of the state "getting even" for killing by killing had become a worthwhile value. Left unanswered by the Court was how, if society has the right to take a life as retribution, this could fail to reinforce a murderer in his firm belief that he has a right to "get even" with his victim. Surveys indicate that 84 percent of all homicides are motivated by the murderer's desire to exact retribution for some real or imagined offense committed by the victim.

The reimposition of the death penalty in the United States puts this country in the opposite camp from such western nations, 41 in all, as England, Germany, Italy, Switzerland, the Netherlands, Israel, the Dominican Republic, Honduras, Costa Rica and Ecuador. Among the United States' bedfellows are Russia, China, Libya, Iraq, Iran, Castro's Cuba, Chile and Saudi Arabia.

Perhaps remarkably, the Supreme Court has never regarded execution in itself as "cruel and unusual punishment" when the possibility of error is considered. Proponents of the death penalty give assurances that the likelihood of a mistake can be ruled out because the judicial process in capital cases is allegedly so much more exact, thus eliminating the type of error that turns up in so many "wrong man" cases involving lesser crimes. Of course, innocent men have been executed. Years afterward, official decrees of one sort or another have cleared some of the Mollie Maguires, the Haymarket martyrs, and Sacco and Vanzetti, but these are causes célèbres. As many legal authorities have commented, the interest in clearing the average innocent man after he is executed dwindles to nil. What we are left with is some of the more bizarre ways innocent persons have been saved from execution. In 1894 Will Purvis was saved from hanging in Mississippi simply because the knot around his neck slipped and he dropped unharmed. The execution was postponed because the onlookers became unruly, some taking it as a sign from the Divine that Purvis was innocent. In the period before his execution was rescheduled, Purvis escaped from custody and surrendered only when a new governor agreed to commute his sentence to life imprisonment. Twenty-two years later, in 1920, Purvis was proven innocent by a deathbed confession of the real murderer, whose story was found to check in every detail. For his tribulations, Purvis was awarded $5,000 by the state legislature.

In Florida in 1902 J. B. Brown mounted the scaffold still protesting his innocence for having murdered one Harry Wesson. Chagrined officials called off the execution when the sheriff, as required by law, started reading the death warrant and discovered that through a clerical error it listed as the man to be executed not Brown but the foreman of the jury that had convicted him. While officials argued about whether or not to proceed with the execution, Brown's ordeal on the scaffold created a nationwide stir, and the governor bowed to demands that the condemned man's sentence be commuted to life. In 1913 a man named J. J. Johnson confessed on his deathbed that it was he who had killed Wesson, even revealing where he'd hidden some of the victim's personal effects. Brown was pardoned and awarded compensation of $2,492, to be paid in monthly $25 installments.

By the turn of the century it was obvious various jurisdictions were going to have to loosen the purse strings for damages significantly as scores of condemned men have been cleared after years of appeals while they were on death row. The state of Illinois in recent years has been obliged to release six such condemned men out of 12 because it was later determined they were not guilty. Advances in DNA techniques have led to the freeing of scores of condemned persons.

Yet at the same time the majority voices within the criminal justice system continue to campaign for a cutoff of appeals from the death sentence so that justice can be done for the sake of the victims and their families. Generally these parties propose a five-year limit on delays of executions. Fairly or not these limitations have sometimes recently been referred to as "the Bush brothers program" calling for faster executions. Critics tend to cite any number of cases in which the final acquittal process took and takes longer than that to finally win out. Texas governor George W. Bush and Florida governor Jeb Bush represented "high execution" states, Texas being first and Florida third.

Of course, such high execution states have records for wrong man death row inmates. The fact remains, as Congressman Don Edwards of California has noted, "Most of the releases from death row over the past twenty years came only after many years and many failed appeals. The average length of time between conviction and release was almost seven years." Some releases come in unusual ways, even in what has been described as random ways. Filmmaker Errol Morris went to Texas to do a documentary on Dr. James Grigson, the controversial and some said notorious "Dr. Death." Grigson claimed 100 percent certainty for his courtroom predictions that a particular defendant would kill again. One man he made such a prediction about was Randall Dale Adams. During his work on Dr. Grigson, Morris became interested in the case of Randall Adams and in his investigation uncovered layers of prosecutorial misconduct in the cases. Morris eventually obtained a virtual confession to the murder Adams had been accused of by another person. Morris's 1988 movie, *The Thin Blue Line*, did much to free Adams the following year.

Another Texas "death row alumnus" who exceeded the five-year rule was Clarence Brandley who was convicted in 1981 for the rape-murder of 16-year-old high school girl. The police zeroed in on Brandley who was the only black custodian at the school, the rest being white. Hair left at the crime scene clearly implicated a white man, but the prosecution relied heavily instead on the testimony of two chief witnesses. Later one of the two key witnesses recanted his statements at the original trial, saying at a later appeal hearing that the prosecution and the police had pressured him into implicating Brandley. The other witness confessed the crime, and Brandley was released in 1990. Had a five-year rule been in effect, Brandley would have been dead four years before his release.

Another capital case that received much attention in recent years involved Anthony Porter who was convicted in 1983 of a double murder in Chicago witnessed by several persons. Porter's lawyer lost several appeals but two days before his execution date in 1998 Porter got a stay because of his limited mental capacity. Porter was freed in 1999 after journalism professor David Protess assigned students to investigate the prosecution of the case. A number of the witnesses recanted their testimony, and another man confessed. Porter had exceeded the five-year rule by 11 years. Professor Protess' students also exonerated two other death row inmates. The question was whether this was something the public should regard as laudable or whether, as the *New York Times* noted, "No system that requires college students to provide justice can be called functional."

Numerous experts have claimed one should not believe that somehow murder prosecutions are always more carefully considered because of the implications of the possible death penalty. Gregory Wilhoit was not released until six years after his conviction in 1987 in Oklahoma. He was convicted of murdering his estranged wife in her sleep. An expert for the prosecution declared that Wilhoit's teeth matched bite marks on the victim's body. On appeal it was ruled that Wilhoit's lawyer did not challenge that testimony and, as an appeals court later ruled, the lawyer was "suffering from alcohol dependence and abuse and brain damage during his representation of appellant." At a new trial a year after the so-called five-year rule would have run out, 11 experts testified that the bite marks did not match, and Wilhoit was released.

Despite this, observers agree there was no way a politician can be too supportive of the death penalty as well over 70 percent of the public approved of it. And the rule is the quicker the better. Thus in Texas, aside from distasteful headlines, there was little outcry from the public in December 1999 when officials chose to remove a hospitalized inmate from intensive care, where he had been taken after a suicide attempt, and fly him directly to the death chamber rather than stay the execution. The joke went around that the condemned man was not to collect $200 for passing Go.

On the other hand Texas officials seemed eager to help a prisoner with a special request, such as one inmate whose lawyers failed to have him declared incompetent for execution when he asked to be put to death on the night of the full moon. Officials deemed it a request worth granting.

Perhaps the most controversial execution under George W. Bush involved that of Karla Faye Tucker, who was condemned for her role in two killings. It appeared Tucker had undergone a death row conversion to Christianity. She married the prison chaplain and was acknowledged to have become a model inmate. Many Evangelical Christians regarded her conversion as clear proof of the transforming power of God, and religious leaders like Pat Robertson and Pope John Paul II called on Gov. Bush to grant clemency. He did not, despite his own well-known religious awakening in helping him swear off alcohol and right the course of his own life.

Later after Tucker was executed, Bush was portrayed in a *Talk* magazine interview as mocking the woman's appearance on television with Larry King in which she asked the governor to spare her. The magazine reported that Bush had imitated her in a whimpering voice. After the article, Bush campaign aides insisted the magazine reporter had misread his comments, but the magazine stood by the article.

The fact remains what riles the public the most is indications that condemned men are delaying their executions by an endless string of appeals. For pro-executions forces the number one case of this type at the turn of the century was the case of Mumia Abu-Jamal, a convicted cop killer sentenced to death. Abu-Jamal's supporters insist he is not guilty and that he was convicted because of his political beliefs and the determination of the police and prosecution to be rid of him. A black journalist in Philadelphia, Abu-Jamal, became a political symbol after the murder of a Philadelphia policeman, Daniel Faulkner, on December 9, 1981.

At age 15, Abu-Jamal was a member of the Black Panther Party and minister of information for the Philadelphia chapter. When the party fell apart, Abu-Jamal turned to broadcasting and by age 25 was one of the top figures in local radio and interviewed many top luminaries such as Jesse Jackson. He won a Peabody award for his coverage of the pope's visit, was president of the Philadelphia Association of Black Journalists and was called "one to watch" by *Philadelphia* magazine.

However, Abu-Jamal never compromised on his beliefs—which led the *Philadelphia Inquirer* to call him "an eloquent activist not afraid to raise his voice." This led to his undoing, as his positions caused him to lose jobs at black stations, and he was forced to drive a cab to support his family. His supporters charged Abu-Jamal was consistently subjected to police harassment, including, they said, a cocked finger and a "bang, bang" from a smirking cop.

Thus the scene was set for the deadly events of 1981. Officer Faulkner stopped a Volkswagen driven by Abu-Jamal's brother and an altercation ensued. The brother hit the officer, and Faulkner began beating him with a 17-inch flashlight. Abu-Jamal was nearby in his cab and ran over, armed with a .38. Shots were fired. Abu-Jamal was hit and Faulkner died. The question was had Abu-Jamal shot the officer. Several witnesses saw another shooter flee the scene. Jamal's weapon, found nearby was empty save for five shell casings. However, at the time the bullets could not be tied to Abu-Jamal's gun, and incredibly the police failed to smell the gun barrel to see if it had been fired.

But the police did have an eyewitness, one Robert Chobert, a cabbie, who said he saw Abu-Jamal "standing over him [Faulkner] and firing shots into him." The problem was that Chobert said the shooter had raced from the scene before being captured, but the police said the wounded Abu-Jamal had not run at all. Two other police witnesses also had contradictions in their testimony. Abu-Jamal's supporters pointed out Chobert had reasons to be a good police witness. He was at the time on probation and was driving that night with a suspended license.

None of this did the defendant any good since he was brought to trial before Albert F. Sabo, a judge labeled by the *Philadelphia Inquirer* as a "defendant's nightmare," having sentenced more men to death (31 to date, only two of them white) than any other sitting jurist in the nation. A fellow judge once called Sabo's courtroom a "vacation for prosecutors" because of a bias for convictions. Terry Bisson, writing in *New York Newsday,* called the murder trial "a policeman's dream." Denied the right to represent himself, Abu-Jamal was defended by an attorney since labelled incompetent but who had actually handled about 20 homicide cases and felt restrained by Abu-Jamal's demands for a defense on a political rather than legal basis.

Abu-Jamal's supporters have since his conviction asked for a new trial before an unbiased judge. Attorney Leonard Weinglass filed a motion to have Judge Sabo removed from the case because, he said, Sabo could not provide even the "appearance of fairness." In Sabo's courtroom, said journalist Bisson, "Mumia's Black Panther history was waved like a bloody flag: Had he said, 'All power to the people?' Yes, he admitted he had said that. . . . Thus with Judge Sabo's help, an award-winning radical journalist with no criminal record was portrayed as a police assassin lying in wait since age 15. After Mumia's conviction, Sabo instructed the jury: 'You are not being asked to kill anybody' by imposing the death penalty, since the defendant will get 'appeal after appeal after appeal.' Such instruction,

grounds for reversal since *Caldwell v. Mississippi,* was allowed in Mumia's case."

By the time he had been on death row for 13 years, Abu-Jamal was a cult hero to many and disparaged by others as the only classic radical-chic cause to survive into the 1990s. Among those who have rallied to Abu-Jamal's cause have been Norman Mailer, Cornell West, Ed Asner, Whoopi Goldberg, Susan Sarandon, and Oliver Stone. Others, less likely to be regarded as liberal "bleeding hearts," such as Stewart Taylor, Jr., of the *National Journal,* supported Abu-Jamal's call for a new trial, labeling his trial "grotesquely unfair."

Meanwhile the pros and cons of the case persisted. The *Yale Law Review* published one of Abu-Jamal's articles. National Public Radio's *All Things Considered* scheduled a series on the condemned man's commentaries (but then canceled it following objections from the Fraternal Order of Police). When Abu-Jamal's book, *Live From Death Row,* appeared, it was greeted with a boycott, and a skywriter circled the Boston offices of the publisher with a trailer proclaiming "Addison-Wesley Supports Cop Killers." In the anti–Abu-Jamal campaign, journalist Bisson reported, "Officer Faulkner's widow has gone on TV claiming that Mumia smiled at her when her husband's bloody shirt was shown—even though the record shows that Mumia wasn't in the courtroom that day." (In fact, during his trial Mumia was kept in a holding cell, reading about his own trial in the newspapers.)

Still, the controversy roared on. In 1999 Evergreen State College in Washington State featured Abu-Jamal's voice at its commencement. Abu-Jamal was heard via audiotape from death row in Pennsylvania. Naturally, pro-execution forces were outraged. The battle for a new trial for Abu-Jamal had become by the turn of the century a testament to the fact that the battle over capital punishment would not cease any time soon.

See also: DNA EVIDENCE, EXECUTION, METHODS OF.

Further reading: *The Death Penalty In America,* edited by Hugo A. Bedau; *Capital Punishment,* edited by Thorsten Sellen.

capital punishment of children   a concept in flux

The school shootings of children by children during the late 1990s into the new millennium have produced outrage on the part of many elements of the public, and there is growing demand for harsher punishment of children—such as life sentences and even the death penalty. This attitude seems to be eroding the long-held view that youngsters, of various ages, should be treated less harshly or that there be minimum age restrictions to severe punishments.

Several states provide no minimum age for execution but do require that age be a factor in sentencing. Among these states are Arizona, Arkansas, Colorado, Florida, Maryland, Mississippi, New Mexico, Pennsylvania, South Carolina, Washington and Wyoming. Three other states have no minimum age for executions, and age is not a factor in sentencing. They are Delaware, Oklahoma and South Dakota.

States that include a specific age for executions of children are as follows:

18 years: California, Connecticut, Illinois, Nebraska, Ohio, Tennessee

17 years: Georgia, New Hampshire, Texas

16 years: Montana, Nevada

15 years: Louisiana, Virginia

14 years: Alabama, Idaho, Kentucky, Missouri, New Jersey, North Carolina, Utah

10 years: Indiana

However, as more states have or are coming on line for the death penalty, it is possible that some alterations will have to be made in the above listings. Depending on the states, the procedures are still subject to judicial appeal and may or may not include any minimum age standards.

Standards for executions of juveniles in this country derived from English law. The United Kingdom long sanctioned the death penalty for teens and preteens for such varied crimes as murder, rape, theft and picking pockets, but reports of many such death sentences pronounced was hardly an indication of those carried out. Richard Streib noted in 1995, "Research at Old Bailey revealed that although more than one hundred youths had been sentenced to death from 1801 to 1836, none had been executed. While some cases do exist, it appears settled that execution of youths was never at any time common in England."

In America the first documented execution of a juvenile took place in Roxbury, Mass., in 1642. Thomas Graunger went to the scaffold for having sodomized a cow and a horse. The all-male jury sentenced him under the Old Testament law described in Leviticus 20:15.

From the 1890s through the 1920s executions of juveniles numbered from 20 to 27 per decade, 1.6 percent to 2.3 percent of all executions. In the 1930s the number of juvenile executions rose to 41, in line with the general pickup in executions during that period. Naturally as public support for capital punishment waned, and indeed was outlawed for a number of years, juvenile executions dropped off. As the recent public support for both capital punishment for adults and an equally fervent demand for executions of juveniles grows, it appears likely that more of the young will face that grim fate. What cannot be disputed is a report of Amnesty International that noted, "The USA carries out more executions of juvenile offenders (people sentenced to death for a crime they committed when they were under the age of 18) than almost any other country in the world."

Capone, Alphonse "Scarface Al" (1899–1947) gang leader

Al Capone was a mindless, brutal and obscure Brooklyn hood in his teens, but by the age of 26 he had become the most powerful crime boss of his day and could boast that he "owned" Chicago, that city of gangsters, during the Prohibition years.

At its zenith the Capone mob had probably upward of 1,000 members, most of them experienced gunmen, but this represented only a portion of Capone's overall empire. Capone often proclaimed, "I own the police," and it was true. Few estimates would place less than half the police on the mob's payroll in one way or another. Capone's hold on the politicians was probably greater. He had "in his pocket" aldermen, state's attorneys, mayors, legislators, governors and even congressmen. The Capone organization's domination of Chicago and such suburban areas as Cicero, Ill. was absolute. When Capone wanted a big vote in elections, he got out the vote; when he wanted to control the election returns, his gangsters intimidated and terrorized thousands of voters. The politicians he put in power were expected to act the way the Big Fellow desired. The mayor of Cicero once took an independent action. Capone caught him on the steps of City Hall and beat him to a pulp; a police officer standing nearby had to look elsewhere to avoid seeing the violence.

Capone was born in Brooklyn in 1899 and attended school through the sixth grade, when he beat up his teacher, got beaten by the principal and quit. After that, he learned his lessons in the streets, especially with the tough teenage James Street gang, run by an older criminal, Johnny Torrio, as a subsidiary of the notorious Five Points Gang, to which Capone eventually graduated. Among his closest friends, both in school and in the gang, was a kid who grew up to become a major crime boss, Lucky Luciano, and the two remained lifelong friends.

When he was in his late teens, Capone was hired by Torrio as a bouncer in a saloon-brothel he ran in Brooklyn. Capone picked up a huge scar on his left cheek in an altercation with a tough hood named Frank Galluccio, who slashed him with a knife in a dispute about a girl. Later, Capone would claim he got the

This mug shot of Al Capone was taken in 1929 in Philadelphia, where he allowed the police to arrest him in order to "take off some heat" brought on by the St. Valentine's Day Massacre.

wound serving with the "Lost Battalion" in France during World War I, but he was never in the army.

In 1920 Torrio, who had relocated in Chicago to help his uncle, Big Jim Colosimo, the city's leading whoremaster, ply his trade, summoned Capone to come and help him. What Torrio wanted to do was take advantage of Prohibition and gain control of the booze racket, an endeavor that promised profits in the millions. But he was being thwarted by Colosimo, who was so rich and content he saw no need to expand. Torrio soon decided Colosimo would have to be eliminated so that he could use Big Jim's organization for his criminal plans. He and Capone plotted Colosimo's murder and imported New York talent to do the job.

The Torrio-Capone combine was then on the move, taking over some mobs that bowed to their threats and going to war with those that failed to cooperate. Their biggest coup was the assassination in 1924 of Dion O'Banion, the head of the largely Irish North Side Gang, utilizing the talents of Frankie Yale of Brooklyn, the same man who had rubbed out Colosimo. However, the O'Banion killing resulted in all-out war with the rest of the North Siders. Torrio was badly shot in an ambush and hovered near death in a hospital for days. When he got out in February 1925, he told Capone, "Al, it's all yours," and retired back to Brooklyn with an estimated $30 million.

It was a sobering experience for the 26-year-old Capone, who found he now needed to use brains instead of muscle to run things. He had to become a

top executive, bossing a firm employing more than 1,000 persons with a weekly payroll of over $300,000. He demonstrated he could do this as well as work with other ethnic groups, such as the Jews, the Irish, the Poles and the blacks. Capone appreciated any man provided he was a hustler, crook or killer, and he never discriminated against any of them because of their religion, race or national origin, being perhaps the underworld's first equal opportunity employer.

Capone's secret of success was to limit his mob's activities mainly to rackets that enjoyed strong demand from the public: liquor, gambling and prostitution. Give the people what they want and you have to gain a measure of popularity. Al Capone was cheered when he went to the ball park. Herbert Hoover was not.

Capone surrounded himself with men in whom he could place his trust, a quality he in turn inspired in many of his underlings. He was even smart enough to hire Galluccio, the thug who had scarred him, as a bodyguard, an act that demonstrated to the underworld the Big Fellow's magnanimity. Still, he faced many assassination attempts, including an effort to poison his soup. In September 1926 the O'Banions sent an entire convoy of cars loaded with machine-gunners past Capone's Cicero hotel headquarters. They poured in 1,000 rounds, but Capone escaped injury.

One by one, Capone had his North Side enemies eliminated, and he did the same to others who resisted bending to his will. His most famous killing involved treachery within his own organization. Hop Toad Giunta and Capone's two most competent killers, John Scalise and Albert Anselmi, were showing signs of planning to go independent. Capone invited them to a banquet in their honor and, at the climax of the evening, produced an Indian club with which he bashed their brains in.

By this time, Capone started to look invincible, but he erred terribly when he ordered the St. Valentine's Day Massacre in an effort to kill Bugs Moran, the last major force among the old O'Banions. Seven men were machine-gunned to death by Capone hit men masquerading as police officers. Suddenly, the public had had enough of the savage bootleg wars. Washington began applying intense pressure, and while he could not be convicted of murder, Capone was nailed for income tax evasion and sentenced to the federal prison at Atlanta for 11 years.

He was transferred to Alcatraz in 1934 and within a few years his health began to deteriorate. When released in 1939, he was a helpless paretic, a condition generally attributed to the ravages of syphillis contracted in his early whorehouse days. Chances are he had also gone "stir crazy," a comm on fate among Alcatraz inmates.

Capone retired to his mansion in Miami Beach, no longer capable of running the Chicago mob. For several years he wavered between lucidity and mental inertia. He died on January 25, 1947.

Al Capone had left an imprint on America and the rest of the world. Even in the minds of foreigners, he was the "Chicago gangster" personified. His impact on Chicago was significant and long lasting. During his reign Capone ordered the extermination of more than 500 men, and an estimated 1,000 died in his bootleg wars. The pattern of violence he set and the organization he built did not disappear with either his imprisonment or death. It is still not dead.

See also: ANTHONY JOSEPH ACCARDO; JOSEPH AIELLO; ALCATRAZ PRISON; LOUIS "TWO GUN" ALTERIE; ANSELMI AND SCALISE; BOOTLEGGING; LOUIS "LITTLE NEW YORK" CAMPAGNA; FRANK CAPONE; JAMES CAPONE; RALPH "BOTTLES" CAPONE; CICERO, ILL.; VINCENT "SCHEMER" DRUCCI; FIVE POINTS GANG; GENNA BROTHERS; GREAT DEPRESSION; JAKE "GREASY THUMB" GUZIK; HAWTHORNE INN; MIKE "DE PIKE" HEITLER; HERBERT HOOVER; ALFRED "JAKE" LINGLE; ANTONIO "THE SCOURGE" LOMBARDO; JAMES LUCAS; "COUNT" VICTOR LUSTIG; MACHINE GUN JACK MCGURN; GEORGE "BUGS" MORAN; ELIOT NESS; FRANK NITTI; CHARLES DION "DEANIE" O'BANION; PINEAPPLE PRIMARY; PAUL "THE WAITER" RICCA; JOHN TORRIO; ROGER "TERRIBLE" TOUHY; HYMIE WEISS; WHITE HAND GANG; FRANK J. WILSON; FRANKIE YALE.

Capone, Frank (1895–1924) brother of Al Capone

Had Frank (Salvatore) Capone, Al Capone's elder brother, survived until the latter's climb to the pinnacle of power, it might well be that he would have been just as famous—Frank Capone's killer instincts and savagery exceeded those of his brother. Despite Al's acknowledged ruthlessness, he was a man who would try to deal before he tried to kill. Frank Capone never exhibited such patience. "You never get no back talk from no corpse," he used to say, a sentiment made all the more ominous by his quiet, almost bankerlike demeanor.

Frank's labors on behalf of his mentor Johnny Torrio and his brother Al were generally employed in situations where persuasion had failed and force was called for. Such was the case in the 1924 city election in Cicero, Ill., where the Democratic Party had actually dared to mount a serious effort against the Torrio/Capone-backed regime of Joseph Z. Klenha. What ensued on April 1 was one of the most terror-filled elections in American history. Frank Capone showed his great ability as a political campaigner by leading an assault on election eve against the Democratic candidate for town clerk, William K. Pflaum,

beseiging him in his office, roughing him up and finally destroying his office. At polling places during the balloting, a thug would sidle up to a voter waiting in line to cast his or her ballot and inquire as to the person's preferences. If the voter gave the wrong answer, the thug ripped the ballot from the person's hand and marked it properly. The thug then waited, fingering a revolver, until the voter dropped the ballot into the box. Voters who still protested were simply slugged and carried from the polling place to vote another day. When honest election officials and poll watchers objected, they too were slugged, kidnapped and held until the voting ended. Three men were shot dead, and another had his throat cut. A policeman was blackjacked. Michael Gavin, a Democratic campaign worker, was shot in both legs and carted off to be held prisoner in the basement of a mob-owned hotel in Chicago. Eight other balky Democrats kept him company and ministered to his wounds.

By late afternoon a group of honest citizens appealed to the courts for assistance and County Judge Edmund K. Jarecki swore in 70 Chicago policemen as deputy sheriffs. Over the next several hours officers and Capone's followers fought a series of battles. A police squad commanded by Detective Sgt. William Cusick pulled up in front of a polling place near the Hawthorne works of the Western Electric Co. where Al and Frank Capone, Charles Fischetti, a cousin, and Dave Hedlin were "campaigning" with drawn revolvers. In that era unmarked police cars were long limousines no different in appearance from the type gangsters used, and Al Capone, Fischetti and Hedlin hesitated at the sight of the vehicle, unsure whether its occupants were police officers or merely gangsters who supported the anti-Klenha ticket. Frank Capone exhibited no such inhibitions and immediately opened fire on an officer at virtually point-blank range. Frank missed and the officer and another policeman responded with double blasts from their shotguns, killing the elder Capone instantly. Al Capone fled the scene.

Frank Capone was given the biggest underworld funeral Chicago had ever seen up till then, even eclipsing that of Big Jim Colosimo a few years earlier. His coffin was silver-plated, satin-lined and surrounded by $20,000 worth of flowers. The *Chicago Tribune* called the affair fitting enough for a "distinguished statesman." In deference to the sad occasion, every saloon, gambling joint and whorehouse in Cicero closed down for two solid hours. But perhaps the crowning tribute to Frank Capone was the election returns. The entire Klenha slate was swept back into office by overwhelming margins.

Capone, James (1887–1952) brother of Al Capone and lawman

Referred to by the newspapers as the "white sheep" of the family, James Capone was not precisely a model citizen—except in comparison. He disappeared from the Capone family fold in 1905, when he was 18, and considering what later became of the other Capone brothers, it was probably a good thing. Jim Capone did not surface again until 1940, when—broke, missing an eye and unable to support a wife and several children—he wrote to Ralph Capone, still a mighty power in the Chicago mob. He later visited with Ralph, who thereafter sent him monthly support checks, and with Al, who was in sickly retirement in Florida. Only then did Jim's wife learn for the first time that her husband was the brother of the notorious Al Capone. The newspapers also soon learned the facts, at least as Jim Capone told them. According to Jim's own account, he had spent most of his years as an enforcer of the law and was known in Nebraska as Richard James "Two-Gun" Hart because of his prowess with a gun. The loss of an eye he falsely attributed to a gunfight with gangsters.

While the newspapers played up this white sheep story, the real facts were hardly as flattering to Two-Gun Hart. Capone-Hart had joined a circus and later bummed all over the United States and Central America. In 1919 he dropped off a freight in Homer, Neb. and settled there. He married Kathleen Winch, the daughter of a grocer, and eventually had four sons. During this period he told such vivid tales of his war exploits, although he had never served in the armed forces, that the awed local American Legion post made him their commander.

Hart's popularity was such that he was named the town's marshal and after two years became a state sheriff. In 1922 he joined the Indian Service as a special officer supervising the Omaha and Winnebago tribes to prevent the sale of liquor to them. Hart earned a reputation for cruelty to the Indians and was eventually transferred to Sioux City, Iowa, where he killed an Indian in a saloon brawl but was not prosecuted. It was in a later melee with other Indians that Hart lost an eye. Transferred to Idaho, he was charged with yet another murder, but the case was finally dropped.

Returning to his marshal's job in Homer, Hart eventually lost his badge when store owners began noticing steady shrinkage of their stocks. As marshal, Hart was furnished keys to all business places. He also lost his position as commander of the American Legion post when other members finally thought of asking for proof of his war record. When he couldn't even prove he was a veteran, he was expelled. Without income and evicted from one house for nonpayment of rent, the Hart family went on relief. It was then that Hart got in

touch with the other Capones. With the help he received from them and the money he got for telling his fanciful stories to the newspapers, Hart-Capone was able to live out the rest of his years in reasonable comfort, although by the time of his death in 1952 he was totally blind.

Capone, Ralph "Bottles" (1893–1974) brother of Al Capone

The most durable of the Capone brothers, Ralph "Bottles" Capone was a loyal aide to his younger brother Al, and like the mob chieftain, he did a stretch for income tax evasion. Afterward, he got out, Ralph rejoined the Capone mob. In 1950 the United Press stated that "in his own right [Ralph Capone] is now one of the overlords of the national syndicate which controls gambling, vice and other rackets." That statement was somewhat of an exaggeration. Ralph was always given a position of honor within the group as well as excellent sources of income, partly to provide for Big Al's sickly retirement in Florida after his release from prison. But Ralph was never on the same level as the leaders of the national syndicate, such as Lucky Luciano or Meyer Lansky, or the heads of the Chicago mob, such as Tony Accardo, Paul Ricca, Jake Guzik and Sam Giancana.

Part of Ralph's income through the years came from his longtime legitimate business: distributing bottled water in Chicago, an activity that won him the nickname Bottles. Ralph's investment in bottling plants stemmed from a plan Al had devised to gain monopoly control of the soda water and ginger ale used in mixed drinks.

In the early 1950s Ralph was questioned by the Kefauver Committee at great length. A short while later, his son, Ralph, Jr., committed suicide. Young Ralph had been haunted by the Capone name through school and a long string of jobs, and he had always tried to keep his identity secret but without success. The Capone name was not easily shaken by either the son or the father. Even in his eighties, Ralph Capone was still being described as an important member of the mob.

Car Barn Gang

The Car Barn Gang, the last gang in America to declare open war on the police, was clearly an organization born in the wrong era. The Car Barners harkened back to the post–Civil War days when criminal bands operated in most big cities on the basis of pure terror and often engaged in pitched battles or vindictive strikes against the police. Organized in late 1911 in New York

160

City, the Car Barners recruited mostly the young toughs who infested the East River docks, fighting, stealing and rolling drunks. As a gang, they became vicious gunmen and highwaymen, staging daring daylight robberies and holding up trolley cars with the same Wild West techniques used in earlier days on stagecoaches.

The first the police knew of the existence of an organized gang was the appearance of placards near the old car barns around Second Avenue and East 97th Street. The signs read:

Notice
COPS KEEP OUT!
NO POLICEMAN WILL HEREAFTER
BE ALLOWED IN THIS BLOCK
By Order of
THE CAR BARN GANG.

The police soon learned the Car Barners were most serious about their edict after a half-dozen officers who had ventured into the forbidden zone were either stabbed or had their skulls fractured. Following that, the police never patrolled the area in groups of less than four or five, leading to the vaudevillian comic's famous joke that the police were insisting on police protection.

The primary captain of the Car Barners was one Big Bill Lingley, widely renowned as a burglar and desperado. He seldom ventured forth with less than two revolvers, a blackjack and a slungshot, which he used to attack a likely citizen or a police officer. Big Bill's principal confederate was Freddie Muehfeldt, a youth who, although from a good family and a background of considerable Sunday School work, at age 17 had taken up a wastrel life on the docks. Big Bill determined to make over Muehfeldt, who became known as the Kid, in his own image. They became the twin terrors of the Car Barners' domain from East 90th Street to 100th and from Third Avenue to the East River. Almost by themselves, they were said to make the area as unsafe for honest folk as the notorious Hell's Kitchen section.

The Car Barn Gang ranged far afield in their depredations and would often make an incredible sweep robbing saloons from Manhattan's 14th Street all the way up to the Bronx. The Kid would simply walk behind the bar and tap the till while Big Bill and a dozen or so stalwarts isolated the bouncers. If a barkeep objected to the Kid's action, he would receive a liquor bottle across his skull from the teenaged gangster. Often the saloon keepers who got advanced warning of the approach of the Car Barners, realizing that resistance was foolhardy, would reduce the amount of cash in the till and hope the gangsters would be mollified with their take.

Meanwhile, the war between the Car Barners and the police raged on. Finally, the police strong-arm squad was sent into the area to clean out the gang.

They clubbed the gangsters unmercifully, but neither side could get the better of the other as long as Big Bill and the Kid were in the forefront of the battles. Eventually, however, the pair killed a Bronx liquor dispenser making a valiant effort to protect his receipts and were arrested for murder.

Big Bill and the Kid, not yet 21, were executed for the crime, and by the onset of World War I, the dispirited Car Barners collapsed under persistent police attacks.

Cardiff Giant   scientific hoax

The Cardiff Giant, allegedly the fossilized remains of an authentic giant who in ancient times walked the earth in the area of what has become New York State, was one of the most lucrative hoaxes in history.

George Hull, a former cigar maker from Binghampton, N.Y., conceived the plot to create the the giant. In 1868 he obtained a five-ton block of gypsum in Iowa and had it fashioned into the shape of a huge man by a stonecutter in Chicago. He then shipped the statue to the farm of a cousin, William Newell, near Cardiff, N.Y., where after a year the latter duly "discovered" it. It is not clear whether the pair had first concocted their plot as a swindle or if, as he would later state, Hull had had the giant built to ridicule clergymen who were always quoting from Genesis about a supersized race— "There were giants in the earth in those days."

A Syracuse newspaper headlined the find as "A Wonderful Discovery," and the pair pitched a tent and began exhibiting the giant, charging 5¢ for a view. News of the find flashed across the country and indeed around the world. Thousands swarmed to see it and admission was raised to 50¢ and then to $1. Meanwhile, most experts were convinced the Cardiff Giant was genuine. Two Yale professors, a paleontologist and a chemist, agreed it was a true fossil. The director of the New York State Museum thought the giant was really a statue but indeed most ancient and the "the most remarkable object yet brought to light in this country." Others, including Oliver Wendell Holmes and Ralph Waldo Emerson, concurred. Still, a few were doubtful; the president of Cornell University felt the giant was made of gypsum and thought there were hints of a sculptor's chisel. But the crowds, now arriving by special trains, continued to grow, and P. T. Barnum, the great showman, offered $60,000 to lease the object from Newell for three months. The farmer refused. Undeterred, Barnum hired a sculptor, Professor Carl C. F. Otto, to make an exact copy of the giant.

When Hull and Newell brought their giant to New York in 1871 for exhibit, they discovered Barnum was already displaying his version in Brooklyn. While they hauled Barnum into court, newspapermen were tracing Hull's activities and uncovered his purchase of gypsum in Iowa. They located the stonecutter in Chicago, one Edward Salle, who admitted to carving the giant, aging it with sand, ink and sulfuric acid, and punching pores into it with darning needles. Faced with the growing evidence of fraud, Hull confessed. Barnum now was able to avoid prosecution by claiming all he had done was show the hoax of a hoax.

Thanks to their fraud, Hull and Newell netted about $33,000 after building expenses of $2,200. Barnum, who continued showing his version for years, made much more. Today, the Cardiff Giant, Hull's authentic fake, is on display at the Farmers' Museum in Cooperstown, N.Y.

Cardinella, Salvatore "Sam" (1880–1921) murderer

One of the most terrifying and obese criminals in Chicago history and chief of a gang that even the beer barons of Prohibition were fearful of crossing, Sam Cardinella was the mastermind of an incredible plot of self-resuscitation. Known as Il Diavolo, or "the Devil," Cardinella was one of the city's most powerful Black Handers until police cracked down on that racket, whereupon he and his gang turned to banditry and violent crime. Il Diavolo's top triggerman was Nicholas Viana, better known as the Choir Boy, an accomplished murderer at the age of 18. The gang committed 20 murders and well over 100 holdups before Cardinella, Viana and Frank Campione were captured and sentenced to be hanged. But the Cardinella story did not end there.

In his death cell at the Cook County Jail, Cardinella went on a hunger strike and lost 40 pounds. Only 11 minutes before Cardinella was slated to die, Lt. John Norton, who had apprehended him, received a telephone tip that Cardinella's friends "are going to revive him after the execution." Norton quickly gathered a squad of detectives and hurried to the prison, posting men at the rear entrances where the bodies were taken out. A hearse turned into the alley and stopped. The officers surrounded the vehicle and opened the back door. Inside were a doctor and a nurse, dressed in white.

"What does a dead man need with medical attention?" Norton wanted to know, but he got no answer. The hearse contained a rubber mattress filled with hot water and heated by pads attached to batteries. At the head of the bed was an oxygen tank. There was also a basket jammed with hot-water bottles and a shelf loaded with syringes and stimulants.

Rushing into the jail, Norton found Cardinella laid out on a slab and his relatives eagerly signing papers for possession of the body. Norton bluntly announced that the body would be held for 24 hours, and though Cardinella's relatives screamed in anger, they were powerless.

Later, medical men agreed Cardinella's neck had not been broken when the trap was sprung: his body had been too light. Death had resulted from choking. The doctors said that had sufficient heat been applied to the body quickly, he might have been revived.

card trick suicide   inventive way of avoiding execution

William Kogut, San Quentin death row convict #1651, is seldom remembered today except in the folklore of the notorious prison he inhabited, but his final exploit would alter the practices followed in numerous death rows around the country.

When Kogut entered San Quentin Penitentiary in 1930 sentenced to death by hanging for the lethal stabbing a woman, he openly boasted he would never be executed, that he would instead die by his own hand. The sentencing judge did not dismiss the threat but instead warned authorities to deprive him of all weapons or tools that would facilitate a suicide attempt. In San Quentin the guards kept an unusually close watch on Kogut, whose only diversion was playing solitaire with one of the two decks of cards he was permitted to keep in his cell.

One Sunday morning not long before his scheduled execution, the prison was ripped by a terrific explosion. Guards rushed to death row and discovered Kogut lying in a pool of blood, his face little more than a blob. It took the coroner and a group of chemists several days to figure out how Kogut had managed to kill himself. He had in days previous been playing solitaire—or so it seemed. Unobserved by guards, he was busily scraping off all the red spots on the cards—the hearts and diamonds—with his thumbnail. Then he soaked that residue in water in his tin cup, producing a wet pulp. This he poured into a hollow knob from his cot and then he plugged the knob with a second knob. Now Kogut had what he wanted—a potential deadly bomb. The bits of playing cards were made of cellulose and nitrate, and when mixed with a solvent formed pyroxylin, an explosive that could be set off by heat. What he had was a primitive homemade pipe bomb.

On the night of October 9, 1930 Kogut put his bomb in his tin cup and placed it on the small heater in his cell. Then he laid his head on the cup and waited for the inevitable explosion that cheated the hangman.

Kogut's card suicide trick can never be duplicated in San Quentin or, in fact, any other death row. Condemned prisoners are still allowed playing cards, but the decks are routinely collected and checked.

Carlton, Handsome Harry (?–1888) murderer

Handsome, blue-eyed Harry Carlton was a dapper murderer who had a date with the hangman late in 1888. However, after his sentence had been pronounced, the New York legislature decided that no convicted murderer would be hanged after June 4, 1888 and that from January 1 of the following year on, the state would use the electric chair for capital punishment. The lawmakers' intention was that anyone with a death sentence who was still alive on June 4 would be executed the next year in the electric chair. But that was not the way they had written the statute. Instead, the law was phrased to say that nobody could be hanged after June 4, 1888 and that "electrocution shall apply to all convictions punishable by death on or after January 1st." Carlton's lawyer was quick to spot the loophole. He demanded that Handsome Harry be freed. Death happened to be the only punishment on the books for murder—unless the jury recommended mercy, which in Handsome Harry's case it had not. If a person committed murder, as Harry had, and got no sympathy from the jury, he or she had to die. However unintentionally, the language of the new law stated that persons who committed murder before June 4, 1888 not only could not be hanged but moreover could not be punished at all.

Handsome Harry became an instant worldwide cause célèbre and his case shook the very foundation of law in New York State. If he were let go, it would mean that for a seven-month period murder was legal in the state! The dispute was rushed to the Supreme Court. In a marked departure from the High Court's traditional respect for legalisms, it ruled that while the interpretation of the law by Carlton's attorney might be technically correct, no slipup by the legislature could be allowed to endanger human lives. Hanging, the Supreme Court held, remained in force until replaced by the electric chair. On a gray morning two days before Christmas, Carlton swung from the gibbet in the Tombs courtyard in New York City. After the execution a newspaper commented, "We are not at all sure that this hanging was entirely legal but it certainly was justice."

See also: HOWE AND HUMMEL.

carnival gyps

Probably half the people in this country visit a carnival or fair of some kind during the course of a year; yet the so-called games of skill or chance they play are obviously among the most lucrative gyps practiced today. None of the games played are susceptible to being beaten, either by skill or chance. All of them are or can be rigged. The television program *60 Minutes* once devoted an entire segment to the exposure of just one gyp game, "razzle," an involved form of gambling in which the customer can never win.

The "gaff," or fix, is applied to every game or built right into it, as is the case with various coin-pitch games in which a player wins a prize if his coin lands inside a square or circle without touching a line. In this game valuable prizes can theoretically be won, but the house percentage has been mathematically worked out as 80 percent—compared to a little over 1 percent for casino dice, 2.5 to 5 percent for roulette and 15 percent or so for one-armed bandits.

Milk bottle toss is a notorious gaff game, although the proprietor or a shill, or phony player, will always be seen winning. The object of the game is to knock six imitation milk bottles off a podium with three baseballs. Knocking them down is not sufficient—they must be knocked completely off the table. The key to the gyp is that three of the six bottles arranged in pyramid form are lead-weighted at the bottom. When these three are placed at the bottom row, or base, they will do no more than fall over even when hit directly, and the player loses. Yet it's relatively simple for the operator of the game to demonstrate how easy it is to win. He throws the three baseballs and the six bottles topple to the floor, but his assistant has simply stacked the six bottles so that three non-lead-weighted bottles are on the bottom row and the weighted ones are on top. A mere brushing will topple the weighted bottles to the floor.

Even games with a guaranteed prize are gaffed. The most common variation of this is the "string game," in which all prizes are attached to strings that feed into a crossbar, or collar. The player pulls a tab for one of the strings on the opposite side of the collar and wins whatever prize pops up. The operator demonstrates the honesty of the game by grabbing all the strings on the other side of the collar and pulling them so that every prize, including very valuable ones, jump up to tempt the public. The trick: the strings attached to the valuable ones are "dead-enders," reaching the collar but not extending to any of the tabs on the other side.

One of the most exotic gaffed games, and a very popular one at big carnivals because it seemingly can't be fixed, is the "mouse game." The public bets on which of 60 numbered holes a mouse will enter, and the prize is quite a good one. A mouse is placed on a wheel, covered with a tin can and spun around vigorously so that when liberated, it is weaving almost drunkenly. Then completely unrehearsed, the mouse heads for the numbered holes. Meanwhile, the operator of the game has made a quick survey of the board and judged whether more money is bet on odd or even numbers. With a foot pedal, he simply closes either the odd or even holes, thereby greatly increasing the house's winnings, especially if the mouse enters an unplayed number. If the mouse, staggering around the holes, butts his head against a closed-off hole, it simply backs off and heads for another opening. This does not look suspicious to the public because the mouse has been moving erratically all along. Finally, the creature enters a hole. Whether or not there is money bet on it, the house almost always wins much more than it loses.

Carpenter, Richard (1929–1956) murderer

The object of one of the greatest manhunts in American criminal history, Richard Carpenter was the real-life villain of Hollywood's *The Desperate Hours,* holding a Chicago family hostage and forcing them to hide him in a drama reported in headlines around the world after he was finally caught.

The Sunday supplements still carry stories of Carpenter as a prime example of a "mama's boy" turned killer. His probation report showed he was passionately fond of his mother and would always come to her as a child, sit on her lap and moan, "Mother, I'm terribly lonely."

In 1951 Carpenter had begun to make excursions into crime. He was finally arrested for pulling a gun on a taxi driver and robbing him of $8; he got a year in jail. On her visits to the prison, Carpenter's mother brought him cakes and other sweets, which he shared with nobody. He made no friends among his fellow prisoners. His cellmates tagged him Mama's Boy and savagely never let him forget it. When Carpenter was released, he vowed never to fool around with crime or guns again. He became a cabbie, earning about $80 a week. His streak of puritanism showed through when he refused any fare to a gambling joint or brothel. He remained his lone wolf self but occasionally would take his sisters and a girl cousin to a skating rink or the movies. While he couldn't skate, he didn't approve of the girls going out alone at night. Carpenter always bought clothes for the girls, although he neglected himself to the point of going around in tatters. In addition, he always kept his grandfather supplied with three cigars a day. Suddenly, his thin veneer of sanity cracked.

On December 4, 1953 Carpenter stole a car, which he later wrecked, and held up a grocery for $100. From that day on, he never returned to his home or saw his family. He ran up a string of more than 70 heists and became a cop killer in August 1955, gunning down a police detective who attempted to arrest him on a Chicago subway. Once, he was recognized and almost caught in a downtown movie theater by an off-duty policeman named Clarence Kerr, who happened to be there with his wife. When Kerr ordered Carpenter into the lobby and demanded identification, Carpenter

faked a stumble and came up shooting, hitting Kerr in the chest and wounding him badly. Kerr was able to fire one shot off at the fleeing Carpenter, injuring him in the leg. Before passing out, Kerr gasped to his wife: "It was Carpenter—Carpenter—I know it was Carpenter."

The manhunt for Carpenter, pressed by Chicago police for more than a year, intensified, with the fugitive's picture splashed across television screens. While police cars wailed through the streets, Carpenter took refuge in the house of a truck driver and his family and threatened to kill them all unless they kept him hidden. But Carpenter was really not that much of a menace to his captives. He yearned for a family environment and ended up trusting the truck driver and his wife too much. They managed to elude his watch long enough to get out of the house and call the police. Within minutes 30 police cars surrounded the house. Carpenter was able to flee through a barrage of bullets and made it across the roof to another building, where he took refuge in a room. When police burst in on him, Carpenter tried unsuccessfully to pretend he was the real occupant of the room.

After his arrest, he said: "I'm sorry about one thing—I didn't do a single thing to make my mother and my sisters proud. It was a lousy life I led—but it is too late now. . . . I'll go to the chair, but I hope I can see my mother before I die."

Carpenter got his wish before dying in the electric chair on March 16, 1956.

Carroll's orgy Prohibition offense

What may have been the silliest arrest in the entire era of Prohibition, but one with tragic personal consequences, was that of Broadway producer Earl Carroll for an "orgy" held on February 22, 1926 at the Earl Carroll Theatre after a performance of his *Vanities.*

With typical Broadway irreverence, Carroll was honoring the Countess Vera Cathcart, who had just beaten an Immigration Service effort to prevent her from remaining in this country on the grounds of "moral turpitude" because of her sensational divorce from the earl of Cathcart. Climaxing the party onstage, a bathtub was filled with champagne and a nude model climbed in while men eagerly waited to fill their glasses or at least ogle at the naked beauty. When reports of the big bash got out, producer Carroll was hauled before a federal grand jury to explain his unique violation of the Volstead Act. Carroll tried to avoid prosecution by declaring there was no champagne in the bathtub, merely ginger ale. For this heinous distortion, he was convicted of perjury, fined $2,000 and sentenced to the federal prison at Atlanta for a year and a day. Carroll suffered a nervous breakdown on the way to the penitentiary. Because of his mental state, his fellow prisoners were ordered never to mention bathtubs in his presence. He was released after serving four months.

Carson, Ann (1790–1838) counterfeiter

A strange set of circumstances turned Ann Carson into one of early America's most notorious female criminals. The daughter of a naval officer, she was the lovely and vivacious wife of Capt. John Carson of the U.S. Army, who disappeared in 1810 on a mission in the West against the Indians. Carson was listed as presumed dead. In 1812 Ann Carson met Lt. Richard Smith, who was stationed near her home in Philadelphia. After a short courtship they were married and lived happily until January 20, 1816, when her first husband arrived at his home and banged loudly on the door. He told Smith who he was. Smith, who later insisted he had been confused, drew a revolver and shot Carson dead. Within days Smith was brought to trial, and it was soon evident that everyone assumed he had killed Carson rather than give up his wife.

While the trial was going on, Ann Carson made a desperate attempt to kidnap the governor of Pennsylvania, Simon Snyder, and hold him as a hostage to gain her second husband's release. She failed, and Smith was convicted and, on February 4, 1816, hanged. Ann Carson lost all respect for law and order and became the head of a band of hardened criminals. Drawing on her military background, she organized the gang under strict regulations that made them most effective. While they engaged in some violent crimes, Ann Carson's gang were most competent at counterfeiting, passing notes for six years with brilliant efficiency. After they were finally rounded up, all were given long prison terms in 1823. Ann Carson died in Philadelphia Prison in 1838 while working on her memoirs.

Caruso, Enrico (1873–1921) Black Hand extortion victim

Few Italians coming to America around the turn of the 20th century expected to escape the terrors and tribulations they had experienced at the hands of criminals in their native country. Rich or poor they could expect threats on their lives—so-called Black Hand threats that promised death unless they paid money. These were not the work of any "Black Hand Society" but extortions performed by the Mafia or other criminals, and not even the most famous were immune. During a triumphal engagement at the Metropolitan Opera shortly before World War I, the great Italian tenor Enrico Caruso received a Black Hand letter, with the imprint of a black hand and a dagger, demanding

$2,000. The singer quietly paid, considering an appeal to the police both useless and foolhardy.

However, when this payment was followed by a new demand for $15,000, Caruso knew he had no choice but to go to the police. If he did not, he realized the criminals would continue to increase their demands and drain him dry. Caruso had been instructed to leave the money under the steps of a factory, and after the police set a trap, he did so. Two prominent Italian businessmen were seized when they tried to retrieve the loot. The two were convicted of extortion and sent to prison—one of the few successful prosecutions of Black Hand criminals. Even so, Caruso was considered to be in such great danger in case the criminals sought their usual vengeance on an informer that he was kept under police and private detective protection, both in this country and in Europe, for several years.

See also: BLACK HAND.

Casey, James P. (?–1856) murderer

One of the most famous and infamous victims of the San Francisco Committee of Vigilance, James Casey was the editor of the *Sunday Times* and a member of the city's Board of Supervisors during what many regard as the most politically corrupt decade in San Francisco's history. Ruffians, outlaws, thieves and murderers controlled the city in the 1850s and were protected by equally crooked politicians, one of whom was Casey.

An arch rival of Casey was James King, editor of the *Evening Bulletin,* who publicized Casey's involvement with corrupt elements and his previous history, which included serving 18 months in Sing Sing prison for larceny. In 1855 King's voice was the most virulent in calling for the reestablishment of the 1851 vigilance committee to clean up the city. On May 14, 1856 King launched a vigorous attack against Casey and said he deserved "having his neck stretched." As King left his newspaper's offices later that day, Casey accosted him, shoved a revolver against his chest and ordered him to "draw and defend yourself." Casey then shot and mortally wounded his foe without even giving him a chance to draw a weapon, which in any case he did not have. After the shooting Casey was taken into custody. However, fearing the political powers would permit him to escape justice, the vigilance committee swung into action. A thousand men enrolled in a special armed force, and militiamen guarding Casey in jail wired their resignation to the governor, stacked their arms and joined the vigilantes. King clung to life for six days before dying on May 20. He was buried two days later, with an estimated 15,000 to 20,000 men and women following his body to the grave. By the time the last of

Drawing shows James Casey being conveyed through heckling San Franciscans to be hanged by the vigilance committee.

the throng returned to the city, Casey and another murderer, Charles Cora, were hanged from the windows of the vigilante headquarters on makeshift gallows.

Casey's political friends buried him and had inscribed on his tombstone, "May God Forgive My Persecutors." It should also be noted that in the two months following Casey's execution, not a single murder occurred in San Francisco, a period of tranquility never again experienced in that city.

cash machine rackets

The explosive growth in bank and store cash machines in recent years has inevitably fostered various criminal means of exploiting them. While there have been occasional murders resulting from crooks forcing victims to hand over their personal codes so as to allow them to extract money from the machines, this is not a frequent occurrence since banks generally limit the amount of money that can be withdrawn in any one day from any one account. As a result nonviolent but ingenious scam artists represent the more common cash machine predators.

Not long ago in New York City, a bankcard customer approached a cash machine during evening hours and found a handwritten sign reading: "Sorry for the inconvenience. Minimum withdrawal $300." This happened to be the maximum withdrawal permitted from the machine.

The customer wanted much less cash but given the alternative opted to withdraw $300. He inserted the card, punched out his code and saw the bills drop into a withdrawal slot. However, the man soon discovered he could not raise the slot cover to retrieve his money. Puzzled for a time, he finally noticed two tiny screws inserted on either side of the slot cover that effectively sealed it. The man left the outer bank lobby in search of a policeman. After going only one block in an unsuccessful search, he returned to find the screws removed and his $300 gone.

Bankcard machines are designed to thwart theft, but with every new safety technique, thieves refine their methods. In this case the bank announced it would alter the slot cover design, but experts regarded this as an unsatisfactory solution. The slot covers on some machines had replaced certain types of money dispensers that dropped the cash through an open slot. These were plugged by thieves using various wax sprays and the like. Money could be cleared out by the thieves at their leisure after a customer attempting to make a withdrawal left. Most cash machines have a special telephone connection to the bank machine's main office, enabling a customer to call on the spot when such a caper is suspected. To counter this, crooks simply put the communication system out of service.

Security experts and police advise bankcard customers to be wary when using cash machines, and to walk away from any machine that seems to have any sort of unusual problem. It is recommended that a card user frequent only a machine that has been observed to be in good working order from use by a previous customer.

Cassidy, Butch (1866–1937?) outlaw leader

Robert LeRoy Parker, alias Butch Cassidy, is without doubt the most romantic character to come out of the outlaw West. He combined the daring of Jesse James with the free spirit of Bill Doolin and, indeed, his Wild Bunch had much in common with the latter's Oklahombres. What is most amazing about Parker's appeal is that he never killed anyone, and American hero worship has usually been reserved for more efficient bloodletters. But Cassidy had other ingratiating qualities. He could prevent Kid Curry from shooting a resisting railroad express car guard by saying: "Let him alone, Kid. A man with his nerve deserves not to be shot." In 1894, when Cassidy was convicted of horse stealing and sentenced to two years, he requested permission to leave his jail cell unescorted for the night before he was to be transferred to the state prison. "I give you my word I'll be back." Incredibly, permission was granted and sure enough the next morning Cassidy returned. He never revealed where he went or whom he visited; he simply turned in his guns and went off to prison.

Born in 1866 in Utah Territory, young Bob Parker was raised on his Mormon father's remote ranch. As a teenager he came under the influence of an old-time rustler named Mike Cassidy and rode with him in the early 1880s in Colorado. Later, he went to work for a mining outfit in Telluride, Colo., and fell in with bad company, taking up rustling and pulling small bank jobs. Strictly speaking, Cassidy's Wild Bunch was not formed until his release from prison in 1896, although his earlier gang, which included the likes of Tom McCarty and Matt Warner, was cut from the same fun-loving mold.

In 1896 Cassidy (Parker had by then adopted the name of his old mentor) turned up in a desperado haven called Brown's Hole. There and in Hole in the Wall, he met many other young criminals who became part of the loosely-knit Wild Bunch. They included Kid Curry (Harvey Logan), the Sundance Kid (Harry Longbaugh), Harry Tracy, Matt Warner, Elzy Lay, Deaf Charley Hanks and Ben Kilpatrick. From the very first, Cassidy was regarded as the leader of the gang, commanding respect as much by being able to exercise restraint as by his more than competent shooting. He was a superb planner of crimes and had the gift for being able to use the best ideas of others, especially Elzy Lay, who was probably the smartest of the group and Cassidy's best and most trusted friend.

The Wild Bunch's first important train robbery, after a number of bank jobs and stock thefts, was that of a Union Pacific train near Wilcox, Wyo. on June 2, 1899. The gang detached the express car and blasted it open with a dynamite charge, enough to get in but not to kill a plucky guard inside who was determined to resist. Throughout his career Cassidy could boast he had never killed a man, although the same could not be said for the rest of his gang despite his best efforts to restrain them. The Wilcox robbery netted $30,000. The Wild Bunch quickly pulled three more train robberies, and Cassidy's fame spread. While Pinkerton detectives tracked him, the Union Pacific considered another way of containing Cassidy—offering to buy him off by obtaining a pardon for him and

giving him a job as an express guard at a very high salary, presumably as a no-show job. Cassidy himself probably queered that deal by robbing yet another train just as negotiations through intermediaries were beginning.

The railroad then sent its own band of gunfighters after Cassidy and his gang. Equipped with high-powered rifles, these manhunters took up the chase utilizing a high-speed train. A number of the gang were either killed or arrested, and Cassidy realized it was only a matter of time until he too would be run into the ground. In late 1901 Cassidy, accompanied by the Sundance Kid and his lady, the celebrated Etta Place, fled to New York and the following year headed for South America. Much has been speculated about the relationship between Etta, Butch and Sundance, but there is little doubt that Etta was basically Sundance's woman. Butch once told an acquaintance, "She was the best housekeeper in the Pampas, but she was a whore at heart."

Etta was also the hard-riding partner who joined with the two men on their many holdups in Argentina. In between jobs Butch and Sundance flirted with going straight and became close friends with a young mining man, Percy Seibert, who in time came to learn their identities, a secret he kept. Cassidy often spoke earnestly to Seibert about changing his life, and the mining man encouraged him. In 1907 Etta Place returned to the States for reasons of health. Sundance took her back but rejoined Cassidy in 1908. Forced to move on because they had been identified, the pair went to Bolivia, where, according to more or less the official Pinkerton version, they were killed in 1911 by Bolivian troops after being cornered following a robbery. In a variation of this story the Sundance Kid was killed but Cassidy escaped and eventually returned to the United States.

Seibert identified two American bank robbers killed in Bolivia as Cassidy and Sundance. But his identification was rebutted in a 1975 book—*Butch Cassidy, My Brother*—by Butch Cassidy's sister, Lula Parker Betenson, who insisted her brother came home and lived out a good life until his death in the 1930s. According to his sister, Cassidy visited his family on a number of occasions and rendezvoused many times with his old buddies Warner and Lay, who had mended their ways. She said Butch felt that Seibert had willfully misidentified the two bandits just to give him and Sundance another chance. Overall, the evidence appears that Cassidy did not die in Bolivia, but that he returned around 1910, married and spent some time in the Mexican Revolution as a mercenary, all under the name of William Thadeus Phillips. If Cassidy was Phillips, he died in Spangle, Wash. in 1937.

Castellammarese War Mafia power struggle

During much of the 1920s the Mafia in New York was dominated by one man, Giuseppe "Joe the Boss" Masseria, who could quite logically be considered the "boss of bosses." However, Masseria was a crude, obscene leader who was increasingly hated by the young, second-generation mafiosi around town. They resented what they considered his stupidity and insistence on putting personal power and the old Sicilian virtues of "respect" and "dignity" ahead of the quest for money. Like other old "Mustache Petes," Masseria was violently opposed to working with the powerful, non-Italian gangs, even though the high profits of such cooperation were obvious.

What these young rebels objected to even more was the needless and constant struggle for power within the Mafia. Under these old-time gang leaders, Mafia gunmen not only fought other ethnic groups but also warred among themselves, with Sicilians battling Neapolitans and, even worse, Sicilians battling Sicilians who had immigrated from other parts of the island or from other villages.

By 1928 Masseria had become concerned about the growing power of mafiosi from the west coast Sicilian town of Castellammare del Golfo. Several of these Castellammarese rose to power in other American cities, especially Cleveland and Buffalo, but their main source of strength lay in Brooklyn, where many of the rackets were controlled by Salvatore Maranzano, a tough mafioso in his own right who aspired to the title of boss of bosses himself. Soon, the war for control of New York rackets broke out between the two groups.

In the Masseria organization were such rising talents as Lucky Luciano, Vito Genovese, Frank Costello, Albert Anastasia, Joe Adonis, Carlo Gambino and Willie Moretti. Under the Maranzano banner were such future crime leaders as Joe Profaci, Joe Bonanno, Tommy Lucchese, Gaetano Gagliano and Joe Magliocco. However, few of these men owed much allegiance to their respective bosses, wanting only for the Castellammarese War, as the struggle was called, to be brought to a conclusion.

Thus, while Masseria men killed Maranzano supporters and vice versa, a secret underground developed in the two camps, attracting men who realized that both leaders would have to be eliminated to achieve the peace needed to organize crime the way they knew it should be. The leader in this rebellion was Lucky Luciano, who developed a strong rapport with his young counterparts in the Maranzano organization, especially with Tommy Lucchese, who kept him informed of all secret developments.

Finally, Luciano planned and carried out the assassination of Joe the Boss in a Coney Island restaurant. Luciano, then number two in command to Masseria, simply stepped into the men's room just before four of his supporters, Vito Genovese, Joe Adonis, Albert Anastasia and Bugsy Siegel, loaned to Luciano for the operation by his closest Jewish confederate, Meyer Lansky, walked in and gunned down Joe the Boss.

When the police arrived, Joe the Boss was dead, and Luciano, having emerged from the men's room, was unhelpful. The standard report quoted in newspapers around the country was that Luciano said he had heard the shooting and "as soon as I finished drying my hands, I walked out to see what it was all about." A bit of journalistic censorship was involved. Luciano's actual comment was: "I was in the can taking a leak. I always take a long leak."

With Masseria eliminated, Luciano and his cohorts contacted Maranzano with a peace offering, one that was accepted with the clear understanding that Maranzano was now the boss of bosses. However, Maranzano was smart enough to realize that what had happened to Masseria would also happen to him unless he struck first. He therefore planned a series of assassinations that would eliminate not only Luciano and his second-in-command, Vito Genovese, but also many others, including Al Capone in Chicago, Willie Moretti, Joe Adonis, Frank Costello and Dutch Schultz, one of Luciano's non-Italian associates. According to his battle plan, Maranzano would emerge from such a bloodbath as the undisputed crime boss in America.

However, Luciano and Lansky anticipated Maranzano's moves, and on September 10, 1931, just hours before a psychopathic killer named Vincent "Mad Dog" Coll was to begin the Maranzano purge, four Jewish gangsters supplied by Lansky walked into Maranzano's office in the guise of detectives and shot and stabbed Maranzano to death.

The Castellammarese War thus ended with the two contending forces vanquished. The young rebels under Lucky Luciano took over. While Luciano made use of such terms as "Cosa Nostra," or "our thing," as a sort of Mafia carryover, the day of the Mafia was really finished. The new crime boss formed lasting alliances with non-Italian gangsters, and the national crime syndicate, or "organized crime," was born, taking control and continuing to this day.

Castellano, Paul (1915–1985) murdered "boss of bosses"

Whatever may be said of Paul Castellano, the head of the Gambino crime family, he must be acknowledged to have enjoyed "great press." This was never more obvious than at his death. When Castellano and his driver, Tommy Bilotti, were hit Mafia style in front of a steakhouse on New York's East Side on December 16, 1985, the news made headlines around the country. "Big Paul" Castellano was hailed as the Mafia's "boss of bosses," and "the most feared don in America." In fact, he was not the most feared don in America, although perhaps the most hated by other mafiosi, and he was never the so-called boss of bosses. That the 6-foot-2 Castellano actually believed he deserved the dubious distinction may explain why he was taken out more easily than any other crime boss.

Despite all the buildup given Castellano, he never had total control of the Gambino family, but rather only of what was accorded him by his enemies. Castellano had come to power only through his connection to the previous and much heralded and respected boss Carlo Gambino. Gambino was a true power within the Mafia and rightfully could have been heralded as the boss of bosses. But like Lucky Luciano decades earlier, Gambino opted for de facto power rather than an ephemeral moniker.

A sick man in his last years, Gambino settled on Castellano to succeed him, although he knew Paul was not the man for the job on the basis either of right or ability. What Castellano had going for him was blood; he was Carlo's cousin, and in addition the husband of Gambino's sister. Everyone in all the crime families expected that the mantle would be passed to Gambino's underboss Aniello Dellacroce, a tough, heartless killer who could prevent incursions into the family's operations.

Gambino, a master manipulator, knew that if Dellacroce fought for the top spot, Castellano would be destroyed. It is unclear whether Gambino knew that Dellacroce was already suffering from cancer (certainly Dellacroce's allies probably did not know). What Gambino did know was that killing Dellacroce would solve nothing. The Young Turks under John Gotti, followers of Dellacroce, had the power to destroy Castellano, and Dellacroce was the only man who could keep them in line. What Gambino had to do was make Dellacroce Castellano's life insurance policy. Gambino pulled that off by offering Dellacroce and his faction total control of the family's Manhattan activities as a sort of crime family within a crime family. It was an offer Dellacroce could not refuse.

Gambino sought further support for Castellano through his friendship with Funzi Tieri, who then headed the Genovese crime family. That group had been the number one family in the Mafia since the days of Luciano, Frank Costello and Vito Genovese, but Gambino had maneuvered his family to the pinnacle of power without alienating Tieri. Tieri promised Gambino he would not do anything to shake Castellano from power. He kept his word, but Tieri was a master criminal, and inevitably the Genovese family reasserted its top position among the mobs. In a sense Castellano presided over a decline of the Gambinos.

However, Tieri died in 1981 and lesser, and perhaps divided, leadership weakened the Genovese family and allowed the Gambino mobsters to regain rackets and territories that the Genovese could not maintain. Over the next few years Castellano actually did start thinking he was the boss of bosses.

But on December 2, Dellacroce died of the cancer wracking his body. Apparently Castellano did not realize how vulnerable he now was without the life insurance Gambino had provided him. One of the big knocks made against Castellano by other mobsters in the family was that he was weak, hesitant, didn't go for the kill when it was required. A smart Mafia boss would have moved instantly and started killing the competition. It was as though Castellano thought he was in some sort of corporate proxy fight. He thought he could name the none-too-bright Bilotti his underboss and then start breaking up and isolating the Gotti crew.

John Gotti had a different idea. Even before Dellacroce was buried, he or his representatives were meeting with other Mafia families in New York and elsewhere, getting approval for what had to be done. The Gottis were smart enough to offer other mobsters a "piece of Paul." It probably wasn't necessary, considering the contempt in which Castellano was held. All the mobs had been stunned when they learned that Castellano had allowed his 17-room mansion on Staten Island to be bugged by the FBI. And when the tapes were revealed it was learned that Castellano had talked disparagingly about all of them.

That was bad enough, but Castellano had blabbed about Mafia business with almost anyone who entered his home. He told Bilotti things that violated the mob's need-to-know code. He even told his maid (and mistress) things she wasn't to know. More important than that, it was clear that Castellano was even more of a menace, since he was under indictment on a number of racketeering counts. The boys had to worry if the 70-year-old Castellano could take prison and the knowledge he'd never enjoy his twilight years as a free man. Under such circumstances a weak boss like Big Paul could start talking.

Gotti moved with astonishing speed. Two weeks after Dellacroce died, Castellano came to Sparks Steak

House on East 46th Street to meet three men and discuss family affairs and no doubt outline his future plans. At least one of the three men who was already there knew what was going to happen. As Castellano and Bilotti stepped out of their Lincoln limousine, neither of them armed, and not even accompanied by a backup car of armed gunmen for protection, three men wearing trenchcoats and fur hats approached, pulled out semiautomatic handguns and shot both men repeatedly in the face. One of the assassins stopped long enough to pump a coup de grâce into Castellano's head. The gunmen walked rapidly away, one talking into a walkie-talkie. They got into a waiting dark car that quickly disappeared.

John Gotti then was driven past the scene to make sure everything had gone as planned. It most certainly had, thanks to Castellano's absolute lack of any semblance of precaution. Apparently he thought as the boss of bosses he could walk on water. As it was, only his car blocked his body from ending up in the gutter.

The media promised their audience that the murder of the so-called boss of bosses was certain to trigger a family war as the Castellano forces wreaked their vengeance. There turned out to be no Castellano supporters. The transfer of power went smoothly, proving that in the Mafia at least, there was nothing like violence to promote peace.

castration as punishment

Castration is a much discussed and little-used method of punishment for criminality. There are no overall statistics available, and the best that can be determined is that during the 20th century it has been used several hundred times in California and less frequently in some other states. Because of new interpretations of existing law and malpractice, it is highly unlikely to be used much in the future, although one occasionally reads a newspaper item of a prisoner being offered or indeed suggesting the use of castration as an alternate to a long prison term. In California in 1975 two convicted child molesters, Paul de la Haye and Joseph Kenner, requested they be castrated instead of being given what was likely to be a life sentence. The sentencing judge readily agreed, but the operations were canceled when the urologist retained to perform them was advised by a group of colleagues at University Hospital in San Diego that he most likely would be open to a lawsuit for assault and battery and probably would not be covered by malpractice insurance. The county urological society gave the doctor the same advice.

Aside from these legal restrictions there is a growing philosophical opposition to the practice, despite an occasional flamboyant outburst by an isolated jurist.

The sentiment is probably best summarized by Aryeh Neier, executive director of the American Civil Liberties Union, in a book entitled *Crime and Punishment:* "But an overriding purpose of the criminal law should be to prevent citizens from committing physical violence against each other. It cannot be useful to that end for the state to set an example of violence against its own citizens. If prison is more barbarous to the victim, at least citizens cannot readily mimic the state by holding other citizens behind bars."

Of course when castration is tried, the results are not always what is hoped for. Fifteen years after convicted rapist Joseph Frank Smith agreed to "chemical castration" as a condition for probation, he pleaded guilty to new crimes in late 1998. Prior to that Smith had been celebrated as a "poster man" for the success of chemical castration.

He had been convicted in San Antonio in 1983 for twice raping the same woman. Smith accepted an offer to be subjected to impotence-causing injections in exchange for probation. Smith moved to the Richmond area in 1984 and appeared on television's *60 Minutes* and stood as a logical example of how to treat rapists. According to officials at Johns Hopkins University Hospital in Baltimore, where he commuted for treatment at the time, it was reported that chemical castration suppressed the sexual appetite of offenders and made them more susceptible to treatment.

At the time of his latest two convictions, Smith, a 45-year-old truck driver, was said by authorities to have possibly been responsible for as many as 75 additional sex-related crimes since 1987.

cat burglar

A general public misconception is that a so-called catman, or cat burglar, is an acrobatic daredevil who burglarizes private homes. Very few of these talented criminals would waste their skills on so pedestrian a target, even if it was the mansion of a millionaire. The cat burglar's habitat is the urban skyscraper, which he climbs by means of ropes and scaling ladders. His targets are jewelry salesrooms, fur shops and cash-heavy businesses deemed safe from window-entry burglary because of their location on high floors.

A catman of extraordinary ability was a character named Slippery Augie Smith, who plagued businesses and baffled New York City police in the 1950s and 1960s. The police suspected they had catman trouble after an epidemic of baffling burglaries. There were no signs of forcible entry, and insurance companies were balking at paying claims for so many burglary losses. At first, the heists looked like inside jobs. In three instances bookkeepers who had the combinations of rifled safes were fired. It struck the police as odd, however, that three trusted employees should all go bad at about the same time.

Then one Saturday night, protective agency patrolmen answering an automatic alarm on West 28th Street came across an intruder on the 14th floor and raced after him down a corridor. Without hesitation the man crawled through an open window at the front of the building, hung from the sill for a moment and, to the officers' horror, let go. The guards called for an ambulance and went to the street to help remove the gory remains. The only trouble was there were no remains—just a moccasin. When the police arrived a few minutes later, the only explanation seemed to be that the burglar had fallen 14 stories and walked away. The agency patrolmen swore they'd seen the man disappear from the ledge.

The mystery was finally solved when the other moccasin was found on the 13th floor under a heavy pivot window that swung out from the middle of the frame. The thief had dropped to this open slanted window directly below and slid down it like a chute into the 13th floor hallway. While the guards were rushing to the street, the catman had blithely made his getaway over the roof.

The next weekend the catman went into action again. Fifteen Persian lamb coats were stolen from the same building where he had put on his high-diving act. Unable to make off with all the loot in one trip, he stashed 10 of the coats under a water tower on the roof. The police found the coats and immediately staked lookouts all around, hoping to nab the thief when he returned for the rest of the haul. But the catman apparently surveyed the scene from another roof and spotted the police trap. After several futile nights the police gave up and returned the coats to the owner. The very next night, the catman struck and made off with the same 10 coats.

Months marked by more improbable burglaries went by before the police got a break. Finally, they received a tip from the desk clerk at a hotel on 27th Street that a salesman guest was renting a top-floor room by the week but occupied it only from Friday night to Monday morning. The routine made no sense since salesmen don't do any business in the garment area on weekends; moreover, if someone wanted a room for a fling on the town, he'd be more likely to rent space nearer the Times Square area. After obtaining a search warrant, police entered the hotel room. A fast check indicated they had found their catman. The room contained a cache of ropes, ladders and stolen loot, including those elusive Persian lamb coats.

When Slippery Augie, a 23-year-old ex-sailor, strolled into the room a few hours later, he found himself under arrest, with no chance to make a fast break to the window. Realizing he faced a long prison stretch, Augie talked, not without an air of pride. He said he got his thrills suspended high above the street. He also explained how he had been able to make his safecracking robberies look like inside jobs. "Most of these businessmen were so sure nobody could get into their places except through the door, which was protected by burglar alarms, they would leave the safe combination around someplace handy," he said. "Some pasted them in the upper left-hand drawer of their desks. Others filed the figures under S."

Catania curse   fate of Mafia victim's family

A Sunday supplement phrase invented to describe the sorry plight of the Catanias, father and son, who met the same fate at the hands of Mafia executioners 29 years apart, it nevertheless reflects the primitive law of survival pervading that criminal organization.

Joe Catania was a Mafia capo who ran the southern Brooklyn docks area in 1902. This position made him extremely valuable to New York's first Mafia family, the Morellos, in their counterfeit money distribution setup. The bogus money was printed in Sicily and then concealed in olive oil shipments that were sent to Catania's piers. From there the bills went to Pittsburgh, Buffalo, Chicago and New Orleans, where they were passed by Mafia organizations. The only threat to the arrangement was Catania himself, whose increasing addiction to the bottle weakened his sense of discretion. When his saloon remarks became too open, Catania was subject to a special Mafia trial—one that the defendant knew nothing about—and his execution was ordered. His body was found near the Gowanus docks inside a barrel, his throat slit from ear to ear. He had also been so savagely beaten that all major bones in his body were broken, a clear Mafia signal for all to maintain silence.

At the time of his father's assassination, Joseph "Joe the Baker" Catania was only a babe in arms. He grew up in the rackets, as was his right since he was related by blood to the Morello family. On February 3, 1931, just after he kissed his wife good-bye, Joe the Baker was gunned down in the Bronx by Joe Valachi and the mysterious "Buster from Chicago." Much was made about Joe the Baker being a victim of the Masseria-Maranzano war for control of New York, but the fact was that Catania had been marked for death when his father died. It was a Mafia custom that members of a family were supposed to avenge killings of their kin. Joe the Baker, therefore, was supposed to kill his father's assassins. On the other hand, when someone in the Mafia had cause to eliminate Joe the Baker for reasons unrelated to his father's killing, in this case his hijacking of certain bootleg whiskey trucks, they found ready allies among the kin of old Joe Catania's murderers.

Cattle Kate (1862–1889) prostitute and alleged rustler

Ella Watson, known as Cattle Kate, was an enterprising young prostitute from Kansas who settled in the Wyoming cow country. With a partner of sorts, Jim Averill, she did a thriving business in cattle, which was the coin of the realm for cowboys paying her for services rendered.

It would of course have been highly unusual if the cowboys limited their payments to cows they held clear title to. For a time, Cattle Kate was tolerated by all, including the big stockmen, who understood that men on the range needed certain diversions and cattle losses of this sort were merely the price of doing business, that era's equivalent of cheating on expense accounts. However, the blizzards of 1888 thinned out

Rendering of the lynching of Cattle Kate and Jim Averill appeared in a publication sympathetic with the interests of the big cattlemen.

the herds, and the big stockmen felt they could no longer stand such losses. One July day in 1889 a wealthy and arrogant cattleman named Albert Bothwell and 10 others decided to do something about the matter. They kidnapped Cattle Kate from her cabin, picked up Averill, who had become something of a spokesman for the small homesteaders fencing off the wide-open range, and threatened to hang them. It appears there was no real plan for a lynching but rather just a desire to frighten the duo. Unfortunately for them, neither Cattle Kate nor Averill took the threats seriously, even when nooses were put around their necks. They were then shoved into space, apparently just to carry the scare tactics a step further. But as the pair slowly strangled, no one made a move to cut them down. The lynchings stirred up an outcry from citizens that Bothwell and his friends had not anticipated, but Bothwell's fellow stockmen hastily came up with a new justification for the act. Stories were planted in the friendly Cheyenne press that Cattle Kate was a mean, gun-toting bandit queen and Averill her business manager. They were accused of systematically looting the range, with her red-light activities a mere cover for their crimes. Cattle Kate became a criminal adventuress worthy of front-page coverage in even the *Police Gazette*. The *Cheyenne Weekly Mail* observed that the lynchings indicated the time had come "when men would take the law into their own hands." The whitewash, the cattle barons soon saw, was effective enough cover for them to launch a major attack on the homesteaders in Johnson County, Wyo. Others were accused of running rustling operations similar to Cattle Kate's and, it was said, would have to be dealt with. Thus, the lynching of a 26-year-old prostitute provided the rationale for what was to become the Johnson County War.

See also: JAMES AVERILL, JOHNSON COUNTY WAR.

cattle rustling

The principal business of the American West was cattle raising, and, quite naturally, the number one crime was cattle rustling. Actually, the Indians did much of the early stealing, mainly because they realized that if the white man could not keep his cattle, he could not occupy the Indian hunting grounds. Many Indians also felt that stealing cattle made up in some small way for the newcomers' slaughter of the buffalo. In due course, it became the main illegal activity of many outlaws. Mexican bandits frequently raided the Texan and later the American side of the Rio Grande and, according to official claims made to the Mexican government, rustled 145,298 cattle from the King and Kennedy ranches. Turnabout seemed fair play. Numerous Texas stockmen built their vast herds by stealing animals from Mexican-owned ranches on either side of the border. Often going to Mexico on a "buying trip" meant stealing great herds and swimming them across the Rio Grande at night. Such herds, in fact, came to be called "wet stock."

Having so accumulated much of their herds, these same stockmen were nonetheless enraged by the relatively insignificant losses caused by other American rustlers. Yet, cattle rustling never provoked the venom that horse stealing did. The stealing of one neighbor's stock by another, however, was universally condemned, unless the other was a hated absentee owner, in which case the prohibition did not apply. A small rancher often would start his herd using a "rope with a wide loop," an accepted practice when restricted to unbranded animals. As Bill Nye wrote in his *Laramie Boomerang* in 1883: "A guileless tenderfoot came to Wyoming, leading a single steer and carrying a branding iron. Now he is the opulent possessor of 600 head of fine cattle—the ostensible progeny of that one steer."

The great cattle wars were essentially fought by the hired guns of big ranchers out to eliminate thefts by smaller ranchers and cowboys "to get a start in the business." This type of conflict was epitomized by Wyoming's bloody Johnson County War, which took place in an area where local jurors simply would not convict local citizens for cutting a few animals out of a big ranchman's stock. Many alleged rustlers died of "hemp fever" for no other reason than that they had arrived on the scene at the wrong time. Just a few years earlier the very men now doing the "stringing up" had been committing the same crimes; in fact; that's how they had gotten started in the business. In the end, cattle rustling was stamped out by these extreme measures. "Range detectives," who were often no more than hired guns, barbed wire fences, and the forceful closing of the range put an end to this traditional method of breaking into the ranching business.

See also: JOHNSON COUNTY WAR, WET STOCK.

cave-in-rock pirates

The great commercial route that opened the frontier in the early 19th century was down the Ohio and Mississippi Rivers to the port of New Orleans. The two rivers teemed with pirates who falsely marked the channels so that rafts and keelboats would run aground or crash into the rocks. When this wasn't practical, the boats were attacked from skiffs and canoes. The most treacherous stretch was on the Kentucky shore of the Ohio from Red Bank to Smithland, where the king of the local pirates was Bully Wilson.

A Virginian, Wilson set up his headquarters in a cave near the head of Hurricane Bars. Beckoning thirsty travelers to shore was the following sign:

WILSON'S LIQUOR VAULT
and
HOUSE FOR ENTERTAINMENT

The unwary who paused there rarely resumed their voyage. Wilson's place was known as Cave-in-Rock, and the only visitors who could stop there in safety were pirates, robbers, slave stealers and murderers. And if they were alone and were known to have a hoard of loot with them, they were not particularly safe either. But the main purpose of Cave-in-Rock was to prey on river traffic, and Bully Wilson always had 80 to 100 men ready to swoop down on helpless vessels. Whenever a craft was taken, all aboard were killed, and the boat, manned by a pirate crew, would sail on to New Orleans to sell its goods. The river pirates dominated the waterways until the mid-1820s, when the boatmen organized to fight back.

In July 1824 the crews of about a dozen flatboats, about 80 men in all, hid in the cargo box of a single boat and floated down the river. The boat was soon attacked by a force of about 30 pirates, coming out in canoes and skiffs. As the pirates swept aboard the flatboat, the hidden men stormed out of the cargo box. Ten pirates were killed and another 12 captured. They were blindfolded and forced to walk the plank in 20 feet of water. As the helpless men surfaced, crewmen armed with rifles stood on the cargo box and shot them. The end result of such punitive expeditions finally broke the power of Bully Wilson and other pirates, so that the waterways were relatively free of piracy and safe for commerce after 1825.

See also: COLONEL PLUG, PIRACY.

Center Street   New York vice district

For many decades the site of New York Police Headquarters, Center Street had an unwholesome history. Its creation traces back to the financial crisis of the winter of 1807–8, when business virtually ground to a halt because of the weather. The out-of-work elements were near starvation, and because of mob riots for jobs and food, the city began its first public works program to create employment. Large work gangs were set to draining and filling a pond and marshland known as the Collect. When the work was finally completed and the earth settled, the area was opened for settlement. The first street created was called Collect Street; later, it was renamed Rynders Street for Capt. Isaiah Rynders, the corrupt political boss of the

Sixth Ward and protector of the gangsters that inhabited the Five Points section. For well over half a decade, the street was known as one of the wickedest in the city and contained virtually nothing but saloons and brothels. Even with a determined effort to rid the area of vice, unsavory elements remained when most of the worst dives were closed and the name changed to Centre Street (later altered to Center). But the real cleanup was not made until police headquarters was situated there and the criminals decided to move a few blocks away.

Cermak, Anton J. (1873–1933) Chicago mayor and murder victim

Mayor Anton J. Cermak of Chicago was with Franklin D. Roosevelt in Miami on February 15, 1933 when Joseph Zangara attempted to assassinate the president-elect and fatally shot Cermak instead. Cermak became a martyr.

At the time he was shot, Cermak cried, "The President, get him away!" He told Roosevelt, "I'm glad it was me instead of you." Roosevelt, who cradled the wounded mayor, said: "I held him all the way to the hospital and his pulse constantly improved. . . . I remember I said, 'Tony, keep quiet—don't move—it won't hurt you if you keep quiet and remain perfectly still.'"

Cermak lingered for three weeks. From his deathbed the mayor expounded a theory, long held by some historians after his death, that he, not Roosevelt, was the intended victim all the time. Judge John H. Lyle, probably as knowledgeable as any non-Mafia man on the subject of Chicago crime, stated categorically, "Zangara was a Mafia killer, sent from Sicily to do a job and sworn to silence." It was not an outlandish theory, the concept of the sacrificial hit man having a long history in the annals of the Mafia.

In theory, Cermak was a great reformer, but that must be measured in light of what constituted reform in Chicago. Born in Prague and brought to America when he was one year old, Cermak went into politics at an early age and soon won the nickname Ten Percent Tony, since that figure was said to be his standard skim in kickbacks and other deals. By the time Cermak had served three terms in the state legislature, he was worth $1 million. Before he took office as mayor, his net worth was $7 million. In the words of a contemporary writer, Cermak was guilty of using "surreptitious means such as wire taps, mail drops, surveillance and stool pigeons to ferret out information concerning the weaknesses and foibles of administrative and political friends, taking great pains to learn the identities of his enemies."

Cermak did not attempt to purge Chicago of gansterism but only of the Capone element, which he sought to replace with others who had supported his campaign, headed by Gentleman Teddy Newberry. Some writers have claimed that Cermak moved to take over all crime in Chicago after the imprisonment of Al Capone. Later court testimony indicated that the mayor had dispatched some "tough cops" to eradicate Frank Nitti, Capone's regent during his absence. Nitti was searched, found to be unarmed and was about to be handcuffed when an officer leveled his gun at the gangster and shot him three times in the neck and back. The officer then shot himself in the finger. Nitti was taken to the hospital to die, and the police announced he had been wounded while resisting arrest, as the officer's injured finger proved. Unfortunately for the mayor, Nitti recovered and a full-scale war ensued, one of the early victims being Cermak's favorite gangster, Newberry. At the time, Cermak was taking the sun in Florida on a rather extended vacation, said to have been so arranged to keep him away from the Capone gangsters. Cermak had left Chicago for Florida on December 21, 1932, and he was still there February 15, 1933. Some cynics suggested that the mayor was seeking the protective wing of the president-elect to stay alive. Others contended that Cermak was merely cementing relations with the incoming administration and just possibly talking to Roosevelt's campaign manager, James J. Farley, about an indictment said to be pending against him for income tax evasion.

Zangara, who had been overwhelmed by guards and the crowd after firing the shots, died in the electric chair on March 21, 1933. He insisted Roosevelt was the man he had meant to kill.

See also: JOSEPH ZANGARA.

Cero-Gallo case wrong man case

In one of the most-twisted "wrong man" cases in history, Gangi Cero, a young Italian seaman was found guilty of murder in Massachusetts and sentenced to die in September 1928. Cero's sympathetic employer, Samuel Gallo, provided his own lawyer, who unsuccessfully tried to save the defendant. On the night scheduled for the execution, a witness was found who identified the murderer as Gallo. Cero was granted a reprieve. Gallo was then indicted, and both he and Cero were brought to trial together. Cero was quickly found not guilty, but Gallo was convicted. Gallo, however, won a new trial, and after the main witness against him left the country, he too was acquitted.

Chadwick, Cassie (1857–1907) swindler

One of the most audacious swindles ever worked in this country was accomplished in the 1890s by a Canadian woman and incorrigible thief, Mrs. Cassie Chadwick, who married into Cleveland society. She was, she hinted, the illegitimate daughter of Andrew Carnegie, the steel magnate. In fact, she did more than hint—she flashed all sorts of promissory notes supposedly signed by Carnegie and then deposited some $7 million worth of allegedly valid securities in a Cleveland bank. She told the banker to keep her secret, which meant, of course, that the news spread like wildfire throughout the banking community and soon among the city's social set. Clearly, Mrs. Chadwick was somebody, and she was invited to the best functions. Bankers too volunteered their services without asking. Yes, Mrs. Chadwick acknowledged, she might be able to use a little loan or two against future payments from her tycoon father. She took a few small loans, all under $100,000, and repaid them promptly by taking out other loans from different banks and private lenders. She then went whole hog, borrowing millions. Mrs. Chadwick paid high interest, but with all that Carnegie money behind her, she seemed good for it.

The hoax was simplicity itself, being so outrageous that it was never questioned. Certainly, no one was going to approach Carnegie for confirmation. The Chadwicks now traveled frequently to Europe and, when they were in Cleveland, entertained lavishly. Mrs. Chadwick was also a leading public benefactor. In less than a decade, it was later estimated, she took banks and private lenders for upwards of $20 million.

The bubble burst in 1904, when the *Cleveland Press* heard of a Boston creditor who had become dubious about getting his money back. The newspaper checked on Mrs. Chadwick's background and found out her real name was Elizabeth Bigley, a convicted forger who had been pardoned in 1893 by Gov. William McKinley of Ohio. When the news came out, Charles T. Beckwith, president of the Citizens National Bank of Oberlin, to whose institution Mrs. Chadwick owed $1.25 million, promptly keeled over from heart failure. There was a run on the bank and on scores of others that were found to have made loans to the woman.

Mrs. Chadwick, who was in New York on a spending spree when the unpleasantness surfaced, was arrested and extradited back to Cleveland, where she was tried and sentenced to 10 years in prison. She died there in 1907. It was believed at the time of her death that many of her victims had still not come forth, some individuals hoping to avoid ridicule and the banks to avoid runs. Remarkably, there were still those who firmly believed that Mrs. Chadwick was indeed Carnegie's daughter and that he would in due course make good on her debts. All of which made Cassie Chadwick's swindle among the most enduring ever concocted.

chain gangs

The use of chain gangs for convict labor was not, as the public now generally believes, an invention of the Southern states; the custom was practiced in both the North and in England during the 18th century. The Southern states, having used the method to some extent in antebellum years, embraced the custom wholeheartedly in the post–Civil War era as an important source of revenue during their financial distress. Convicts were turned over to leasees, who not only chained a prisoner's two legs together but chained him as well to several other prisoners, lessening the chances of escape. Public protests against the inhumane treatment of chain gang convicts led to a sharp reduction of the practice. However, the advent of the automobile and the need for many new roads led to a great resurgence of chain gang labor; by the early part of the 20th century, a major part of the prisoner force in several states labored in road gangs. Exposés of conditions became common, the most potent being that written by an escaped convict, Robert Elliott Burns, who authored *I Am a Fugitive from a Georgia Chain Gang*, a bestselling book that was made into an important movie in the 1930s. Reform pressures no doubt forced some states to reduce greatly or discontinue chain gangs, but in truth, their virtual elimination was due to a form of "automation." New road-making machinery simply rendered chain gang labor obsolete.

In the late 1940s Georgia became the last state to eliminate the practice, although in later years it was still reported to exist for small details of brief duration.

See also: ROBERT ELLIOTT BURNS, CONVICT LABOR SYSTEM.

Champion, Nathan D. (1857–1892) victim of Johnson County War

Even today in some quarters of Wyoming, the name of Nate Champion is a hallowed one, that of a man killed solely because he defied the great cattle barons. Others regard him as a cunning rustler, the head of the notorious Red Sash Gang that allegedly stole thousands of head of cattle. Whatever the truth may be, it is certain that he was on a "death list" composed by the executive committee of the Wyoming Stock Growers' Association on the basis of "nominations" received from members.

Champion, a powerfully built man, had been a trail-herder for several years until the early 1880s when he collected his pay after a drive and settled in Johnson County. Similar to many others, Champion became a homesteader and built up a little herd of cattle, thus earning the enmity of the cattle barons, who wanted an open range for their huge herds. These absentee cattle-men sent Pinkerton agents onto the range and were assured by them that there was organized rustling of their stock in Johnson County, mainly the work of the Red Sash Gang bossed by Nate Champion. Other observers believed that the charge was a self-serving lie and the only connection Champion had with any myth-ical Red Sashers was the fact that he, like a great many other homesteaders who came up from Texas, wore a *vaquero*-type red sash.

In the early morning hours of April 11, 1892, a small army of about 50 gunmen, most hired for the occasion, attacked Champion's cabin, which he shared with a cowboy named Nick Ray. Ray went outside in the snow to chop some wood and was cut down by a hail of bullets. Champion rushed out and hauled the severely wounded Ray to safety. He then kept up a bar-rage of fire that held off his attackers. By afternoon Ray had died, but so had two of the invaders and several others were wounded.

During lulls in the battle Champion kept a diary of his ordeal. One entry read: "Boys, there is bullets com-ing like hail. They are shooting from the table and river and back of the house." Another went: "Boys, I feel pretty lonesome just now. I wish there was someone here with me so we could watch all sides at once." The final entry was made that evening, about 12 hours after the first attack. "Well, they have just got through shelling the house like hail. I heard them splitting wood. I guess they are going to fire the house to-night. I think I will make a break when night comes, if alive. Shooting again. It's not night yet. The house is all fired. Goodbye, boys, if I never see you again."

Champion signed his pathetic diary and then charged out the back door, firing two guns. How many bullets cut him down could not be determined because his dead body was strung up and used for target prac-tice. Later, 28 bullets were removed from the body. Champion's slayers also pinned a card on the body—"Rustlers beware."

The killings of Champion and Ray were the opening shots in the Johnson County War, one in which the cat-tle barons' mercenary army would go down to ignoble defeat. Because a reporter accompanying the stockmen's hired army found their victim's diary, Nate Champion was to emerge as the folk hero of the struggle.

See also: JOHNSON COUNTY WAR, RED SASH GANG.

Chapin, Charles E. See ROSE MAN OF SING SING.

Chapman, Gerald (1892 or 1893–1926) robber and murderer

The term "Public Enemy No. 1" was first coined by a newspaperman to describe Gerald Chapman, the most popular criminal in the country for a time in the 1920s. When his picture was flashed in movie newsreels, the audience responded with thunderous applause, a phe-nomenon not repeated until Franklin D. Roosevelt was perceived by moviegoers in the 1930s as the savior of the nation.

Even the *New York Times*, on April 7, 1923, editori-alized under the heading "Something Almost Heroical":

> *It is getting to be rather difficult to keep in mind that fact that Gerald Chapman is a thoroughly bad man, whose right place is in jail. The difficulty arises from the fact that in his battle with the law he shows qualities—courage, persistence, ingenuity and skill—which it is impossible not to admire. The result is that unless one is careful one finds one's self hoping that he isn't caught, and, so great are the odds against him, that the struggle seems somehow unfair. . . . The temptation is strong to lament that such a man should make of his abilities and peculiarities such miserable employment as devot-ing them to theft. There must be some explanation of that, however, and the probability is that he is defective. But it does seem hard that his punishment for his crimes should be increased because of his attempts to evade it. That he hates imprisonment is only human, and that he takes desperate risks in his efforts to get out is rather to his credit than his discredit—from every standpoint except the safety of society.*

Thus did the *Times* come down on the side of law and order, but it was a close decision.

Gerald Chapman had that way about him. An accomplished criminal a dozen or so years older than Chapman, Dutch Anderson, similarly impressed with young Chapman when both were doing time in New York's Auburn Prison, taught him all he knew about committing crimes and was eventually to become his willing underling. When the pair got out within two months of each other, they teamed up as con men and made about $100,000 trimming suckers in Chicago with varied swindles. They returned to New York City to live the high life, with their hotel suite a parade ground for showgirls, whores and impressionable young things.

In 1921 they got together with an old Auburn crony, Charley Loeber, and robbed a mail truck in New York City in a daring escapade with Chapman jumping from a moving car onto the running board of the truck and, gun in hand, forcing the driver to stop. The trio made off with five sacks of registered mail containing $1,424,129 in cash and securities, the greatest mail theft up to that time.

Chapman and Anderson fenced the securities slowly while living the good life, but Loeber proved incapable of handling the fruits of such a big-time heist and was caught disposing of his loot. When he was nabbed, he implicated Chapman and Anderson, and unaware of any danger, they were easily captured. The pair had been on a jaunt upstate, robbing five banks just to stay in shape.

Taken to the main post office building for questioning, Chapman made his first electrifying attempt at an escape. In the midst of the interrogation of Anderson and himself, Chapman, in the middle of a yawn, leaped from his chair, said "Sorry, gentlemen", and dashed to a window, stepped over the sill and disappeared.

"He's jumped," someone yelled, and everyone rushed to the window. However, they did not see what they had expected on the ground 75 feet below. There was no spread-eagled body.

Gerald Chapman might have escaped had not a detective noticed a cleaning woman in a building across the street frantically pointing to one side. Chapman had stepped onto a ledge and wormed his way down to another open window. He was captured four offices away.

Both men were convicted and sentenced to 25 years in the Atlanta Penitentiary. Chapman refused to testify, but one of his lawyers, Grace F. Crampton, reported later:

Chapman's philosophy of life excused his crimes. He told me that he did not believe it as sinful to hold up a mail truck or rob a store as it was to speculate on Wall Street and probably steal money from widows and orphans and poorly paid teachers. "At least we do not take money from poor people," he said to me. "What we steal hurts nobody. Everything that is sent by mail or express is fully insured and in the end the sender loses nothing. The man who comes out the winner on Wall Street is respected, and he is envied for his yachts and cars and homes, while we are hunted and despised. I think I am the more honorable of the two.

After seven months in Atlanta, Chapman escaped. He feigned illness by drinking a disinfectant, overpowered a guard and went out the window using bedsheets for a ladder. He was free only two days before being cornered by a posse and shot in the arm, hip and back. One bullet had penetrated his kidney. He was taken back to the prison hospital for a real reason this time. Yet, though it was feared he might die, Chapman escaped the same way six days later. The authorities were sure they would find his body shortly, but Chapman made a clean break.

Two months later, Dutch Anderson tunneled out of Atlanta, and the team was back in business as two of the most wanted men in the country. The *Times* was not the only publication having difficulty managing restraint in its admiration of Chapman. Meanwhile, Chapman, separated for security reasons from Anderson, made the mistake of teaming up with one Walter J. Shean, the black-sheep son of a wealthy hotel owner and a fledgling criminal. They attempted to hold up a department store in New Britain, Conn., on October 12, 1924, and in the process one of the bandits shot and killed a police officer. Shean was captured and, with some pride, proclaimed, "My pal was Gerald Chapman."

Finally, Chapman was caught in December in Muncie, Ind. and returned to federal prison under incredibly tight security. For a time the government refused to turn over Chapman to Connecticut for trial, fearing he would escape, but finally it relented. The trial was an event that had the country going haywire. Chapman fan clubs sprang up, and at least four or five bouquets arrived each day at the front door of the prison where he was kept during the trial.

It didn't help Chapman, nor did his claim that he had never been in New Britain and never even met Shean. He was found guilty and sentenced to death.

Meanwhile, Dutch Anderson was going off his rocker. Convinced that Chapman had been betrayed by a man named Ben Hance, who had once shielded the pair in Muncie, Anderson killed Hance and his wife. He then tried to assassinate Shean, but he was too well guarded and Anderson could not get near him. Anderson was finally recognized by a policeman in Muskegon, Mich. Both went for their guns at the same time, and each killed the other.

Chapman's execution was postponed a couple of times. In his death cell he whiled away the time writing epigrams ("The more we learn, the less we discover we know") and poetry (his favorite poet was Shelley). A poem of his, "Reward," was released by one of his lawyers, who said, "I do this because I don't want people to think Chapman was merely a bandit with nothing in his head." It read in part:

Comes peace at last! The drums have beat disray,
No armistice of hours, but ever and ever
The slow dispersing legions of decay,
Under the muffled skies, tell all is over.
Returns the husbandman, returns the lover,
To reap the quiet harvest of alway,

The bright-plumed stars those wide fields
may not cover
Though wings beat on forever and a day. . . .

Chapman was hanged on April 6, 1926.

Chapman, Mrs. James (1874–1922) murder victim

When on December 27, 1922 Mr. and Mrs. James A. Chapman opened a package they thought was a Christmas present arriving late in the mail, the parcel exploded in Mrs. Chapman's face, fatally injuring her and crippling her husband. Thus began a case that the Winconsin Supreme Court, in rejecting the convicted murderer's appeal, was to call unrivaled for being "so replete with scientific presentation of actualities." And indeed, the bomb murderer, John Magnuson, never did have a chance, as one clue after another, developed in brilliant scientific fashion, blared his guilt.

The wrapping paper that the dynamite package came in had been burst apart in the explosion and much of it was stained with blood and powder, but the handwritten name and address had only been torn apart. These scraps were turned over to John F. Tyrrell, then considered the country's number one examiner of questioned documents. Tyrrell reassembled the writing, which read, "J. A. Chapman, R. I, Marsfilld, [sic] Wis." From this tiny scrap of evidence Tyrrell reached a startling number of conclusions. The writing was stilted, as though the writer had deliberately attempted to disguise it. Tyrrell studied the spacing, slope, alignment, pressure and rhythm of the script and determined this was not the case. It had been written the best its author, who was not used to writing very much, could manage. The misspelling of the town name indicated the writer had simply spelled it phonetically. Tyrrell concluded the writer was a foreigner, most likely a Swede. There was only one Swede in the community, John Magnuson, and he had a long-running dispute with Chapman concerning a creek drain.

Tyrrell had only begun to make conclusions. He also determined the writing had been done with a medium smooth-pointed fountain pen. The ink was an odd mixture, mostly Carter's black ink with a slight trace of Sanford's blue-black fluid ink. When postal inspectors armed with a search warrant inspected the Magnuson home, they found that the man's daughter had a fountain pen with the very point Tyrrell had described. She always used Sanford's ink but had loaned her bottle of ink to a schoolmate who, when it ran dry, had refilled it with Carter's black ink, producing the exact mixture Tyrrell had discovered on the death package.

Then the iron-bomb remnants were turned over to two professors at the University of Wisconsin, who polished them and matched their tell-tale properties with metal found in Magnuson's barn workshop. Fragments of the wood portions of the bomb were sent to Arthur Koehler, a wood expert who was to give vital testimony in the Lindbergh kidnapping. He identified the wood as elm. On the floor of his workshop, Magnuson had elm lumber and wood shavings with the same cellular structure as the scraps from the bomb.

The jury convicted Magnuson on the very first ballot, and given the mound of scientific evidence, it was hardly surprising that the high court of Wisconsin saw no reason to set aside his life sentence.

Chapman, John T. (1832–?) train robber

A respected resident of Reno and superintendent of a Sunday school, John Chapman, together with Jack Davis, masterminded the robbery of the Central Pacific's Train No. 1 on November 4, 1870, the first train holdup in the Far West.

Chapman's arrest for the robbery, which occurred near Verdi, Nev. came as a shock to the good folks of Reno, who never suspected him of being anything other than a pillar of the community. True, it was known that he was often in the company of a deadbeat and gambler named Jack Davis, but it was assumed he was out to save the soul of that sharper. The facts were the other way around; Davis had introduced Chapman to a number of hard cases ready to make some money in any logical six-gun manner. When Chapman unveiled a plan to hold up a train, something the Reno gang had pioneered just four years earlier in Indiana, they all agreed enthusiastically. Since such robberies were not common at the time, the gang had little trouble. They boarded the train just as it was about to pull out of Verdi, overpowered the conductor and engineer and forced their way into the express car after uncoupling that car and the engine from the rest of the train. The messenger in the express car gave up without a struggle, and the gang broke into treasure boxes containing $41,600 in coins and escaped with their loot.

Chapman and Davis hadn't counted on their accomplices acting like cowpokes at trail's end, spending money so fast that they had to attract the attention of the Wells Fargo detectives. Under intensive questioning, two of the gang confessed and led detectives to some of the buried loot. Davis and Chapman were arrested, stunning Reno. Chapman put on a defiant front, denying all, but Davis saw that was useless and confessed. Davis got 10 years, but Chapman was given 20.

On September 28, 1871, nine months after he had gone to prison, Chapman led three of his men in a prison break; however, he and two of the others were recaptured after a brief period and given an extra year for their escape. The former Sunday school superintendent served his entire sentence. Upon his release he advised the current crop of train robbers to cease their wicked ways and find God. With that, he dropped from sight, although he was named as a likely suspect in several train holdups, including two in widely separated places within eight hours of each other.

See also: JACK DAVIS.

Chapman, Mark David (1955–) murderer of John Lennon

The murder of 40-year-old rock star John Lennon, a former member of the Beatles, on December 8, 1980 by Mark David Chapman was a long time in the making. Chapman had waited all that wintry day and evening in front of the Dakota, a celebrated New York apartment building, where the singer and his wife, Yoko Ono, lived. He had come prepared for the weather, wearing two pairs of long underwear, a jacket, an overcoat and a hat. He also carried a .38-caliber Charter Arms revolver.

Chapman had been living in Honolulu since 1977, arriving there from Decatur, Ga., his home state, and had apparently been afflicted with John Lennon fantasies for a considerable period. Lennon's wife was Japanese, and although Chapman's wife was not Japanese, she was of Japanese descent. In the fall of 1980 Chapman decided to "retire," at the age of 25. After all, Lennon was retired. Later, a psychiatrist would testify that the more Chapman imitated Lennon, "the more he came to believe he was John Lennon." He eventually began to look upon Lennon as a "phony."

In September 1980 Chapman sold a Norman Rockwell lithograph for $7,500, paid off a number of debts and kept $5,000 for a "a job" he had to do. He contacted the Federal Aviation Administration to inquire about the best way to transport a revolver by plane. He was advised that he should put the gun in his baggage but was warned that the change in air pressure could damage any bullets. When Chapman left his job as a security guard at a Honolulu condominium development for the last time, he scrawled the name John Lennon on the sign-out sheet. On October 29 he flew to New York, taking a gun but no bullets.

Frustrated in New York by an inability to obtain bullets for his weapon or to gain access to Lennon, Chapman left on November 12 or 13 to return to Honolulu. After his arrival there he made an appointment at the Makiki Mental Health Clinic for November 26 but didn't keep it. On December 6 he flew back to New York.

Two days later, Chapman waited outside the Dakota for Lennon to appear. About 4:30 P.M. the singer and his wife left the building. When he saw the couple, Chapman held up his copy of Lennon's recently released Double Fantasy album, and Lennon stopped to autograph it. After the Lennons departed, the doorman asked Chapman why he lingered, and he said he wanted to wait to get Yoko Ono's autograph as well.

At 11 P.M. Lennon and his wife returned. Chapman stepped out of the darkness and said, "Mr. Lennon." As Lennon turned, Chapman fired his revolver five times. Four bullets struck Lennon, killing him. When the police arrived, Chapman was reading his copy of Catcher in the Rye by J. D. Salinger.

A few weeks later, John W. Hinckley, Jr. recited into a tape recorder: "I just want to say goodbye to the old year, which was nothing, total misery, total death. John Lennon is dead, the world is over, forget it." In March 1981 Hinckley attempted to assassinate President Ronald Reagan.

Chapman pleaded guilty to the Lennon killing. On August 24, 1981, appearing in court with what looked to be a bullet-proof vest underneath his T-shirt, evidently to protect him from possible retribution by distraught Lennon fans, he was sentenced to 20 years to life. Under New York State law he would have to stay in prison for 20 years before becoming eligible for parole.

Chappleau, Joseph Ernst (1850–1911) murderer

Joseph Chappleau was the first man sentenced to die in the electric chair, but he escaped that fate in 1889 when the new-fangled instrument of death was not completed in time for his execution, and his sentence was commuted to life imprisonment. In his memoirs, the famous warden of Sing Sing, Lewis E. Lawes, later credited Chappleau with doing more to shape his philosophy of modern penology than any other man. While Lawes was a rookie guard at Clinton Prison in New York in 1905, Chappleau was credited with saving his life in a prison yard melee.

A New York farmer, Chappleau had been found guilty of the murder of a neighbor named Tabor over some poisoned cows. The real motive for the murder, according to local gossip, was not the poisoning of the cows but an affair between Tabor and Chappleau's wife. Once his sentence had been commuted, Chappleau became a prisoner uniquely popular with other convicts and the guards. None regarded him as a true criminal but rather a man trapped by fate. Lawes came to regard Chappleau as the perfect example of a murderer not likely ever to commit another crime and perhaps the best possible argument against capital punishment, a penalty Chappleau had escaped for purely technical reasons. When Chappleau died in the prison hospital at Clinton in 1911, guards and prisoners alike declared their happiness that he had been released from the burdens of his life.

See also: WILLIAM KEMMLER, LEWIS E. LAWES.

Charlton Street Gang Hudson River pirates

In early New York virtually all pirate activity was restricted to the East River, where the prime loot was the stores of relatively small craft. On the West Side, only a daring bunch of ruffians called the Charlton Street Gang worked the Hudson River, but they did it with a vengeance, actually flying the Jolly Roger and making forays as far upriver as Poughkeepsie, attacking riverside mansions and even kidnapping men, women and children for ransom. In the 1860s the Charlton Streeters found the pickings on their side of Manhattan slim because the Hudson piers were reserved for ocean vessels and shippers kept an army of watchmen on duty to protect their property. With looting in the immediate city area not very rewarding, gang leaders were forced to cast their eyes upstream. It is doubtful if their ambitions would ever have become as grandiose as they did without the inspiration of an attractive but deadly haridan named Sadie the Goat. She convinced them in 1869 that to be successful river pirates, they had to have a first-class sloop of their own, one that could outrun pursuers. The gang promptly went out and stole one.

The gang flew the Jolly Roger from the masthead, finding that its appearance frightened residents along the Hudson from the Harlem River to Poughkeepsie and tended to encourage flight rather than resistance. The Charlton Streeters soon had a lucrative enterprise going, looting farmhouses and mansions. Learning that Julius Caesar had once been held for ransom by pirates, Sadie involved the gang in kidnapping. She cut a sinister figure pacing the deck, issuing orders. According to the sensationalist press of the day, Sadie on several occasions made men walk the plank in proper piratical style.

After a number of murders had been committed, the desperate riverside residents finally organized vigilante posses to battle the pirates. Their ranks thinned by a number of musket battles, the Charlton Streeters returned to their home base and restricted their activities to more ordinary urban crimes. Sadie the Goat left the group in disgust with its timidity.

See also: GALLUS MAG, PIRACY.

check passing

Not long ago a professional check passer, a forger who writes worthless checks, in New York, was asked why he only passed his rubbery works of art in bars and taverns. Paraphrasing Willie Sutton, who supposedly said one robs banks "because that's where the money is," the check passer declared, "Because that's where the crooks are." The check passer's technique was simple enough, relying as it did on human greed. He would enter a saloon, appearing well bombed, and hoist a few. Then he would produce what appeared to be his paycheck drawn on the account of a well-known local firm and in an apparent stupor, ask the bartender to cash it. Normally, the barkeep would be reluctant to cash a check for an unknown party, but since in this case the customer could barely stand erect, he would find it too appetizing to pass up. The bartender would cash the check and invariably shortchange the purported drunk $10 or $20, figuring he was too far gone to notice. The check passer would hoist one more and stagger out of the place, heading for another bar to repeat his routine.

The check passer stated he generally could cash eight to 10 bad checks an evening and get turned down in no more than two or three places. He had found a new wrinkle to make one of this country's most common and easiest crimes even easier.

Check forgery is so common, in fact, that no one really knows how extensive it is. Spokesmen for surety companies have put the losses at $400 million to $1 billion, and those estimates are probably too low, since a great many businesses have one to a dozen had checks tucked away unreported. With the value of checks written annually now totaling a few trillion dollars, the bogus-check business is currently the most lucrative field available to a smooth-mannered con man, or even to people with a lot less finesse.

In Washington, D.C. a few years ago, a 14-year-old boy walked into a small store and made a few inexpensive purchases with a government check that eventually bounced. It had been stolen, but the shopkeeper had no one to blame but himself. The rightful recipient was an 83-year-old woman, and the check had been clearly marked "Old Age and Survivor's Insurance."

Once, in Cleveland, Ohio, the story goes, a bad-check artist handed a bank clerk a check to cash after signing it "Santa Claus." He got his money.

Another comic check passer liked to sign his phony masterpieces, "N. O. Good." No one ever caught on—in time. And a Bedford, Ind. grocer, who was not too quick, accepted a check signed "U. R. Hooked." Fun-loving check passers have used bum checks drawn on such institutions as the East Bank of the Mississippi.

The interesting fact about all these cases is the ridiculous chances the bad-check writer will take, so sure is he that the sucker will bite at his bait. Not all forgers are so cocky and contemptuous of their victims, but these incidents do point out what check passers have learned: with the proper approach and in many cases, without, a person can have far less trouble cashing a bad check than a good one.

The professional operator runs into absolutely no trouble 95 percent of the time as long as he has a gimmick to distract suspicion. A California forger cashed 200 bad checks by pretending to be a physician. He found that by passing checks that carried such corner notations as "In Payment for Tonsils" or "Balance over Blue Cross," he was seldom questioned. In big cities he often entered a store dressed in a doctor's white coat in order to give the impression that he had just stepped out of his office in a nearby building to get a check cashed.

One of the most prolific bogus-check passers was Courtney Townsend Taylor, who was most active in the 1940s and 1950s. In Chicago he once went down a certain street and cashed a check in every other store the whole length of the street. On the return trip he hit all the stores he had missed. Caught once in Mobile, Ala., he pulled a fountain pen from his pocket while he was being frisked for a weapon and said: "This is the only gun I need. I can get all the money I want with it."

Nobody knows how many rubber-check artists are operating, but one estimate placed the figure at around 2,500 full timers. Roughly two-thirds of all phony checks sent to the FBI are quickly identified as the work of known forgers by examining a file of about 60,000 current fraudulent check signatures. The rest are the product of amateurs.

Check passing is the type of crime that gets into a practitioner's blood. Rapists and muggers may slow down over the years and quit by the time they start graying at the temples. Check passers simply mellow. Their dignified look turns into a plus. Although in his seventies, Joseph W. Martin had no trouble separating thousands of dollars from gullible check cashers until his arrest in 1952 by the FBI. An actor, Martin had actually played in more than 500 motion pictures during more honest times, including a 1932 film in which he portrayed President Warren Harding. As a check passer, he simply carried on acting. His favorite technique was turning up at bar association meetings and cashing checks with his "colleagues." He was arrested in New York while posing as a lawyer from Nebraska attending a meeting of the American Bar Association in the Waldorf-Astoria.

Experts consider the late Alexander Thiel the most accomplished forger of modern times. Also high on the list is Frederick Emerson Peters. However, the great-granddaddy of all check chiselers clearly was Jim the

Penman, who was born Alonzo James Whitman in 1854. He dissipated an inherited fortune, amassed an illegal million, became a state senator in Minnesota, received an honorary degree from Hamilton College and was almost elected to its board of trustees. He also passed thousands of bad checks. During his career, Jim the Penman was arrested 43 times, indicted 27, convicted 11. Once while doing a stretch in Auburn Prison, he was assigned to teach in the prison school—until it was discovered he was teaching forgery.

See also: FREDERICK EMERSON PETERS, ALEXANDER THIEL.

Cherokee Bill (1876–1896) holdup man and murderer

It was often said that the man Hanging Judge Isaac Parker most enjoyed sending to the gallows was Crawford Goldsby, a part-Cherokee, part-white, part-Mexican and part-black murderer better known as Cherokee Bill, who killed 13 men before his 20th birthday.

Goldsby came to live with a foster mother at Fort Gibson, Okla. when he was seven years old. The woman imbued the boy with the credo: "Stand up for your rights. Don't let anybody impose on you." When he was 18, he followed her advice. He shot a man who beat him up at a dance. The man lived, but Goldsby fled to Indian Territory and soon joined the outlaw band of Bill and Jim Cook. In June 1894 the Cooks and Goldsby shot their way out of a posse trap after Goldsby killed a member of the law party, Sequoyah Houston.

After that, the killings came fast, and Goldsby became known and hunted as Cherokee Bill. The young killer had a dozen notches on his gun before he was betrayed by a couple of supposed friends while he was paying a courting call on a young girl. The duo, Ike Rogers and Clint Scales, clubbed him unconscious and collected $1,300 in reward money. Cherokee Bill was speedily tried before Judge Parker for just one of his crimes and sentenced to be hanged. However, his lawyer succeeded in delaying the execution through several appeals. While the murderer was still being held in his prison cell, he somehow got hold of a gun and attempted to make an escape. The attempt failed, although Cherokee Bill did kill a prison guard, Lawrence Keating, the father of four children.

The escape effort roused Judge Parker to a fit of anger. He blamed the guard's death on the U.S. Supreme Court and told reporters that the High Court's obsession with the "flimsiest technicalities" was allowing the 60 "murderers" then in his Fort Smith jail to fight off their executions—Cherokee Bill among them. Parker brought the outlaw to trial for the guard's murder without waiting for the outcome of his appeal on the previous conviction. The judge found Cherokee Bill guilty of this second charge and sentenced him to death, but again the execution was forestalled by appeals. Finally, though, the first appeal went against the defendant, and on March 17, 1896, with Judge Parker watching the execution from his office window, Cherokee Bill mounted the gallows. Asked if he had any last words, the young murderer replied, "I came here to die, not to make a speech." Cherokee Bill paid for his 13 murders, but it appeared later that he was responsible for one more. Ike Rogers, one of the men who betrayed him, was murdered. The crime was believed to have been the work of Cherokee Bill's young brother, Clarence Goldsby, in an act of vengeance. If Clarence was the killer, he was never brought to justice.

See also: ISAAC C. "HANGING JUDGE" PARKER.

Cherry Hill Gang Gay Nineties criminals

A vicious bunch of thieves and killers, the Cherry Hill Gang were the "dandies" of the New York underworld in the 1890s. Members of the gang were seldom seen in other than dress suits and often carried walking sticks, metal-weighted of course. Disguised in the height of fashion, they found it easy to get within striking range of a well-heeled gentleman and attack before their victim had a chance to be alarmed.

The Cherry Hillers were also responsible for provoking others to crime out of envy. Other gangs often tried to match their sartorial splendor and would go to any lengths to do so. When the Batavia Street Gang announced plans to hold a ball at New Irving Hall, the Cherry Hillers announced they were obtaining new wardrobes for the occasion. As hosts, the Batavians felt required to match or surpass the Cherry Hillers in dress. To raise funds the night before the gala social affair, the gangsters smashed a window of Segal's jewelry store on New Chambers Street and carried off 44 gold rings. They sold them the following morning, but more than a dozen of the gangsters were caught by police as they were being fitted for new suits at a Division Street tailor shop. On the night of the big event, the leading lights of the Batavia Street Gang languished in the Tombs while the elegant dandies of Cherry Hill were once again the hit of the ball.

Chessman, Caryl (1921–1960) executed sex offender

During the 1950s the case of Caryl Chessman produced one of the most intense anti–capital punishment campaigns in history. Certainly no case since that of Sacco and Vanzetti produced such furor. Protests came from all levels of society. Millions of persons in Brazil, 2.5 million in São Paulo alone, and thousands more in Switzerland signed petitions pleading for his life. The queen of Belgium made a special plea for Chessman, as did Aldous Huxley, Pablo Casals, Eleanor Roosevelt, Dr. Karl Menninger, Arthur Koestler, André Maurois and François Mauriac. Added to those names were Max Ascoli, Harry Elmer Barnes, Ray Bradbury, Norman Corwin, William Inge, Norman Mailer, Dwight MacDonald, Clifford Odets, Christopher Isherwood, Carey McWilliams, Billy Graham, Harry Golden and Robert Frost.

In January 1948 Chessman, then 27, had been on parole for just six weeks from California's Folsom Prison when he was arrested in Los Angeles as the suspected Red-Light Bandit. This marauder approached victims parked in lonely spots, flashing a red light resembling that of a police car. He would rob the driver and sometimes drive off with the woman and force her to perform sexual acts with him. Chessman made a confession, which he later said had been extracted from him by police torture.

He was found guilty under California's "Little Lindbergh" law, which provided for the death penalty in cases of kidnapping "with bodily harm." Chessman had killed nobody and had held nobody for ransom. Since the jury brought in a verdict of guilty without a recommendation of mercy, he was automatically sentenced to death in the gas chamber. There were many who thought Chessman's punishment was excessive for a felon who had not murdered anyone.

Chessman was sent to death row at San Quentin, and his first execution date was set for March 28, 1952. Then began the famous drama of Cell 2455, Death Row. That prison address became the title of a best-selling book by Chessman, which sold a half-million copies and was translated into a dozen languages. It was one of four he would write, often smuggling out manuscripts after he had been forbidden to publish any further. With the success of his first book, Chessman retained a group of lawyers to help him with his appeals, which previously he had handled on his own, having "read or skimmed 10,000 law books."

The fight went on for 12 years. It finally ended in defeat when Gov. Edmund G. Brown, a stated opponent of capital punishment, insisted his hands were tied and he would not save Chessman. By then Chessman had survived eight scheduled dates of execution, some by only a matter of hours. On May 2, 1960 he entered the gas chamber at San Quentin. At that moment federal judge Louis E. Goodman granted Chessman's attorneys a delay of at least 30 minutes to argue their case. He asked his secretary to telephone the warden at San Quentin. As the prison number passed through several persons, a digit was inadver-

Convict-author Caryl Chessman (left) appears in court in 1957 in a futile attempt to win a new trial.

tently omitted. After being verified, the number had to be redialed. By the time the call was put through, Associate Warden Louis Nelson said the cyanide pellets had just been dropped.

Inside the gas chamber, Caryl Chessman had turned to a female supporter who was there as a witness, and his lips formed a final message: "Take it easy . . . It's all right . . . Tell Rosalie [one of his attorneys] good-bye. . . ."

After the pellets dropped, Chessman managed to strain at the binds in order to see if his message had been understood. The woman, a reporter, nodded. Chessman half-smiled and winked.

Chessman had one more signal to give. Just before he lost consciousness, he turned to reporter Will Stevens of the *San Francisco Examiner*. He had agreed to give the newsman a signal if a gas chamber death was a form of agony. Chessman moved his head up and down, staring at Stevens. It was the signal that death in the gas chamber was agony.

One news account of the execution started, "Sex-terrorist Carol Chessman ended his 12-year fight for life today with a wink and a smile."

Chicago amnesia discouragement of witnesses
During the gang wars in Chicago during the 1920s, successful prosecution of murderers and other law-breakers often proved almost impossible. The gangsters themselves never would impart information to the police, even when dying. Despite the fact that a number of eyewitnesses might step forward initially to do their civic duty, by the time of the trial these witnesses almost invariably had been "reached" by bribes, threats or outright attempts on their lives. As a result, some witnesses even had trouble remembering their own names on the stand. Gang leader Dion O'Banion, an accomplished practitioner of the art of witness discouragement, observed puckishly: "We have a new disease in town. It's called Chicago amnesia."

Chicago fire looting
Without question the greatest rampage of criminality sparked by an American disaster occurred during the 24 hours of the Great Chicago Fire on October 8–9, 1871.

The *Chicago Post* perhaps best set the scene:

The people were mad. Despite the police—indeed, the police were powerless—they crowded upon frail coigns of vantage, as fences and high sidewalks propped on wooded piles, which fell beneath their weight, and hurled them, bruised and bleeding, in the dust. They stumbled over broken furniture and fell, and were trampled under foot. Seized with wild and causeless panics, they surged together, backwards and forwards, in the narrow streets, cursing, threatening, imploring, fighting to get free. Liquor flowed like water; for the saloons were broken open and despoiled, and men on all sides were to be seen frenzied with drink. . . . Everywhere dust, smoke, flame, heat, thunder of falling shouts, braying of trumpets, wind, tumult, and uproar.

And into this human cauldron the criminals swarmed. Hoodlums, prostitutes, thieves hunting alone or in packs snatched all they wanted from drays and carriages. They broke into stores and homes and stuffed their pockets with money and jewelry. Men ran about wearing as many as a dozen women's rings and bracelets. They broke into saloons and guzzled down liquor to fortify their criminal daring. "They smashed windows with their naked hands," the *Post* reported, "regardless of the wounds inflicted, and with bloody fingers rifled till and shelf and cellar, fighting viciously for the spoils of their forage. Women, hollow-eyed and brazen-faced, with filthy drapery tied over them, their clothes in tatters and their feet in troddenover slippers, moved here and there—scolding, stealing, fighting; laughing at the beautiful and splendid crash of walls and falling roofs."

When the courthouse caught fire, guards released 350 prisoners from the basement jail and then watched helplessly as they descended in a single horde on a jewelry store and looted every stone, every watch in the place. William Walker, a Chicago reporter, added his eyewitness account:

As the night wore on, and the terrors aggregated into an intensity of misery, the thieves, amateur and professional, dropped all pretense at concealment and plied their knavish calling undaunted by any fear of immediate retribution. They would storm into stores, smash away at the safes, and if, as happily was almost always the case, they failed to effect an opening, they would turn their attention to securing all of value from the stock that could conveniently be made away with, and then slouch off in search of further booty. The promise of a share in the spoils gave them the assistance of rascally express-drivers, who stood with their wagons before doors of stores, and waited as composedly for a load of stolen property to be piled in as if they were receiving the honestly-acquired goods of the best man in town. . . . The scenes of robbery were not confined to the sacking of stores. Burglars would raid into the private dwellings that lay in the track of the coming destruction, and snatch . . . anything which their practical senses told them would be of value. Interference was useless. The scoundrels . . . were inflamed with drink, and were alarmingly demonstrative in the flourishing of deadly weapons. Sometimes women and children, and not infrequently men, would be stopped as they were bearing from their homes objects of especial worth, and the articles would be torn from their grasp by gangs of these wretches.

Besides the looting, which the authorities were unable to thwart, trouble developed from a new source. By the time the conflagration was burning itself out on the night of October 9, firebugs took to the streets trying to start new blazes, some for the thrill of it and others because they had seen how fire created opportunities for looting. Seven men were shot after being caught setting fires and another was stoned to death by an angry mob, his body left on the street as a warning to others. For the next 13 days Chicago was patrolled by 2,400 regular and special policemen, six companies of state militia and four companies of U.S. Army troops, all under Gen. Phil Sheridan, who placed the city under martial law. Perhaps the most significant comment on the aftermath of the Chicago Fire was a historian's observation that "no part of Chicago was rebuilt more quickly than the saloons, brothels, gambling-houses, and other resorts and habitations of the underworld."

Chicago May (1876–1935) Queen of the Badger Game

May Churchill Sharpe did not invent the badger game, whereby a gentleman is invited to a lady's room to be "done for" and ends up being "done out" of his money through blackmail or simple robbery, but she was its most accomplished practitioner in the 1890s.

Born in Dublin, Ireland in 1876, May Sharpe spent six years in a convent school before running off to America, with 60 pounds from her father's strongbox as traveling money. Within a year after arriving in New York in the spring of 1889, she was living the fast life as the mistress of Dal Churchill. Churchill eventually married her and took her west. He was "a robber, highwayman, safecracker, cattle rustler and general all-round crook," according to May, and also a member of the Dalton gang. May was sublimely happy for an exciting year. Then Dal fouled up a train robbery and ended up hanging from vigilantes' rope near Phoenix, Ariz.

Widowed at 15, May went to Chicago, where with her looks she became the Queen of the Badger Game. At first, she operated as a loner, choosing her victims from hotels, night spots and other places where good-time Charlies congregated. Because of the publicity involved and the resultant effect on their families, most of the men who took her to a hotel wouldn't dream of going to the police after she had robbed them. May would also steal a sucker's valuable papers and write him, asking if he remembered the gay time they almost had together and wondering if he wanted his papers back. She would threaten, if ignored, to take the matter up with the wives. The tactic got results, and the errant husbands would give the money to an underworld pickup man sent by May. She would then deliver the papers. She never double-crossed a sucker a second time. She took him in the badger game and then once with a spot of blackmail, but then she let him off the hook.

Later, May took to using male accomplices and an older woman posing as her mother. The "mother" would catch May and her gentleman and shriek for help, which would come in the form of a hulking relative or neighbor. There would be no escape for the unfortunate victim until he paid. By her 16th birthday Chicago May had made $100,000, and by 17 she had run that up to $300,000.

Deciding the really big money was in New York, May transferred her operations there in the early 1890s. She frequented a famous criminal hangout, Considine's, which was also a slumming spot for sportsmen and literary and theatrical personalities. One evening she spotted a bushy-haired man with a drooping mustache. Thinking of him as a likely victim, she inquired about his identity and learned he was the celebrated author Mark Twain. May immediately started boning up on her Tom Sawyer and Huck Finn, and one night, done up in finery, she strolled over to Twain and introduced herself as Lady May Avery of England. She said she so admired Twain's work and had to meet him. The next evening Lady Avery dined with Twain and amused him greatly. It was well known that Twain was highly appreciative of the spicier things in life, and May expected him to jump at the bait when she invited him to visit her in Connecticut. Twain's eyes twinkled, but he shook his head.

"I'm sorry, dear lady," he said, "but I'm off to Washington in the morning and then am going West for an extended period."

Chicago May was crushed. However, the real crusher came when Twain got up to leave. He kissed her hand and whispered to her: "May I thank you, my dear lady, for a most amusing time. Of course, I don't believe a word of your story that you are an English noblewoman."

Such defeats were rare for May, especially after she formed a business relationship with Sgt. Charles Becker, New York's notorious cop-crook who was to die in the electric chair for murder. Becker fed May victims and took a 25 percent cut of the revenues.

A few years after the turn of the century, Becker advised Chicago May to pull out of New York because of an impending reform wave, and she moved to London, where she met the accomplished bank robber Eddie Guerin. She helped him rob some $250,000 from the Paris branch of the American Express Co. However, the couple had a falling out and were eventually caught by French police. Eddie Guerin was sent to Devil's Island, from which he later made a sensational escape. May did a short stint in an English jail for transporting the American Express loot to London and then was kicked out of the country. She returned to the United States, but she was pushing 40. Hard-living had left her with wrinkles, puffs and rheumy eyes. There was no way she could be the Chicago May of the badger game.

The road the rest of the way was down. There were a number of arrests and convictions for various thefts, even petty larceny. For a time, May's fortunes picked up. She ran what she called a "nice house" in Philadelphia, where she used to entertain the prostitutes with tales of her exploits as Chicago May. However, a reform movement put her out of business.

Rather belatedly, May came to the conclusion that crime did not pay and wrote her autobiography in 1928. In an amused air, she noted: "My old friends, in the police write me letters of encouragement. Christians feel called upon to send me platitudes. Reformers insist upon drawing their pet theories to my attention. Professional crooks berate and praise me. Beggars importune me. Sycophants lather me with adulation. The rich . . . and others . . . patronize me."

But May was actually trying to live in her past. Her real life was nothing like that. The last newspaper clipping about her tells the whole story. She was arrested in Detroit during the early 1930s for soliciting male pedestrians, asking the bargain price of $2. She died a few years later.

Chicago piano   tommy gun

The Chicago piano, or tommy gun, first gained underworld acceptance in the Chicago gang wars of the 1920s. Some historians insist its first use came in the shooting of Jim Doherty and Tom Duffy, gunmen of the O'Donnell gang, and William H. McSwiggin, an assistant state's attorney, on April 27, 1926 in front of the Pony Inn in Cicero. Supposedly, Al Capone handled the weapon personally. However, the likelihood is that the Chicago piano was introduced by the Polish Saltis-McErlane gang that controlled the Southwest Side of Chicago. After Joe Saltis and Frank McErlane demonstrated the Chicago piano's awesome potential, every Chicago gangster wanted one. And it was easy to see why. The weapon was light, weighing only $8\frac{1}{2}$ pounds, easy to operate and could fire up to a thousand .45-caliber cartridges a minute. Furthermore, it cost a mere $175 by mail order. When the federal government slapped controls on the sale of the guns, gangsters still managed to get all they wanted through a thriving black market, although the price soared to thousands of dollars.

Chicago Street Gazette   See SHANG ANDREWS.

Chicago Times   sensationalist newspaper

If any one 19th-century newspaper can be singled out as the most devoted to the coverage of crime news, it would have to be the *Chicago Times*, which was founded in 1854 to promote the political career of Sen. Stephen A. Douglas, a role it continued to fulfill until it was sold to Cyrus H. McCormick, the reaper manufacturer, in 1860. A year later, McCormick sold the newspaper to Wilbur F. Storey of Vermont, who made it into an antiwar publication upon the issuance of the Emancipation Proclamation, which Storey regarded as a deceitful act because it switched the war's aims. To silence Storey's blasts at President Lincoln, Gen. Ambrose Burnside seized the *Times*, provoking one of the great civil liberties controversies of the Civil War. Mobs formed at the *Times* to support the army action, while Copperhead forces swarmed around the *Chicago*

Tribune office and threatened to burn down that newspaper's building unless the *Times* was allowed to publish. Tempers were dampened when Lincoln revoked Gen. Burnside's order of suppression, and the *Times* appeared again.

However, it was after the war that the *Times* emerged, under Storey, as one of the great muckracking and crusading newspapers, carrying on a steady fight against crime and political corruption, exposing the growing accommodation between the underworld and politicians and identifying reputable citizens who allowed their property to be used for immoral purposes. Storey's staff reporters originated or popularized many phrases that were to become criminal vernacular. The word *racket* appears to have been born in the *Times* on October 24, 1876, when the newspaper carried a story that noted, "big thieves are boldly traversing our streets by day, planning their racket." The *Times* headline style on criminal matters was certainly colorful as well as prejudicial. When on September 10, 1872 a notorious hoodlum named Christopher Rafferty was found guilty of the murder of Patrolman Patrick O'Meara, Storey's paper turned nearly poetic with the following headline:

SHUT OFF HIS WIND

A Satisfactory Job for Jack Ketch at Last.
The Hangman's Rope Awarded to
Christopher Rafferty.
Now, Do Not Reprieve Nor Pardon Him.
Nor Give Him a New Trial.
And, in the Name of All That's Decent,
Don't Commute His Sentence.
The Jury Concludes, in Just Twenty Minutes,
To String the Ruffian Up.

Perhaps an even more colorful headline, one still quoted in journalistic circles, appeared on November 27, 1875; it read:

JERKED TO JESUS

Four Senegambian Butchers Were
Wafted to Heaven on Yes-
terday from Scaffolds.
Two of Them, in Louisiana, Died with
the Sweet Confidence of
Pious People.
While Yet Two Others, in Mississippi, Expired
Exhorting the Public to Beware of
Sisters-In-Law.

Sometimes Storey's outspoken attitudes on crime and morality got him in deep trouble. When the noted burlesque actress Lydia Thompson appeared at Crosby's Opera House with her troupe of "English Blondes," the *Times* denounced the young maids for "capering lasciviously and uttering gross indecencies." The *Times* added that Miss Thompson was not much better than a common strumpet and that Chicagoans would do well to run her out of their city. When Storey refused to retract the statements, Miss Thompson caught him in front of his home on Wabash Avenue and beat him severely with a horsewhip.

Chicken Ranch   the best little whorehouse in Texas

A Texas institution that was around almost as long as the Alamo, the Chicken Ranch was never a ranch during all its 129 years of existence, although chickens sometimes pecked around its front yard. Its last and most famous proprietor, gun-toting Miss Edna Milton, called the establishment in La Grange a boarding house. The boarders were all very attractive young women in cocktail dresses, and their guests included any man who happened to have $10. The Chicken Ranch was closed down in 1973 after a television newsman from Houston publicized what many people in Texas knew it to be, and the "exposé" eventually forced the governor to order it shuttered.

The Chicken Ranch went on to live again in a highly successful Broadway musical called *The Best Little Whorehouse in Texas,* with Miss Edna acting as an adviser for the show and doing a short walk-on part. The newsman whose story doomed the ranch, Marvin Zindler, was portrayed on Broadway as Melvin P. Thorpe, a crusading reporter with an American flag necktie. In 1978 the Small Business Administration ordered an auction of the ranch's fixtures. A bag of brass tokens bearing the legend "Good for All Night" sold for $30.

Chinese riots

When the Chinese first arrived in this country in about 1850, they were greeted warmly, especially in San Francisco, where they worked for very low wages as household servants and menials. Within a year or two, as their numbers increased, the Chinese became one of the most hated ethnic groups because they allegedly took jobs away from "Americans," mostly other ethnics who had also come to America from foreign shores. The wanton killing of Chinese probably was even less hindered by legal sanctions than the slaughter of Indians or Mexican "greasers." The saying "not having a Chinaman's chance" had a very awesome meaning for a "chink," "heathen," "celestial," "coolie," "moon face" or "slant-eyes" meeting a white man with a gun. Riots became common, with particularly bloody ones occurring in Los Angeles, San Francisco, Denver, Seattle, Rock Springs, Wyo. and Pierce City, Idaho. Cities

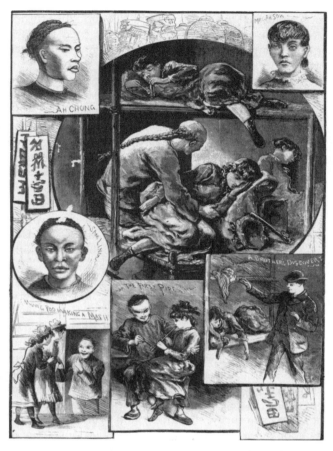

Scandal sheets of the 19th century constantly fanned public opinion against the Chinese by depicting their alleged corrupting influence on young white females.

like Tacoma, Wash. expelled their entire Chinese populations. The main opposition to the Chinese was economic, since such employers as the Union Pacific preferred to hire Chinese because, besides being docile, they worked for low pay and were satisfied with a bowl of rice. However, their large numbers and their insistence on maintaining their own customs—an attitude not really different than those of all other ethnic groups—became an added irritant. Not surprisingly, the Chinese were unmoved by efforts to Christianize them, one missionary observing, "They were unable to distinguish between our mobs and our Christian workers and could not be expected to favor or tolerate our religion. They had no way of knowing that Christianity was a religion of love, not one of bowie knife, insult, and the worst oppression the world has yet seen." Henry Ward Beecher's comment was more sarcastic: "We have clubbed them, stoned them, burned their houses and murdered some of them; yet they refuse to be converted. I do not know any way, except to blow them up with nitroglycerin, if we are ever to get them to Heaven."

It would probably be impossible to try to estimate the hundreds or thousands of Chinese who were murdered by whites in this country during the 19th century since most newspapers did not regard the killing of a Chinese as newsworthy. Diaries of 49ers in California constantly refer in passing to the killing of a "chink" here or there. Practically no white man was ever convicted of killing a Chinese; the crude Texas judge Roy Bean once dismissed a case because he said he found no statutory restriction against the activity. Lawmen in general showed no inclination to ascertain the facts in the violent death of any Chinese. Perhaps the 19th-century attitude in the West is best summed up in a ballad still popular around the turn of the century:

> Old John Martin Duffy was judge of the court
> In a small mining town in the West;
> Although he knew nothing about rules of the law,
> At judging he was one of the best.
>
> One night in the winter a murder occurred,
> And the blacksmith was accused of the crime;
> We caught him red-handed and give him three trials,
> But the verdict was "guilty" each time.
>
> Now he was the only good blacksmith we had
> And we wanted to spare him his life,
> So Duffy stood up in the court like a lord
> And with these words he settled the strife:
>
> "I move we dismiss him, he's needed in town";
> Then he spoke out these words which have gained him renown:
> "We've got two Chinese laundrymen, everyone knows;
> Why not save the poor blacksmith and hang one of those?"

Eventually, anti-Chinese violence petered out, although not for any commendable reason. First, President Chester A. Arthur signed a bill suspending Chinese immigration. Second, the focus of bigotry shifted to newer immigrant groups, such as the Japanese.

See also: ROY BEAN.

LOS ANGELES
One of California's bloodiest and most barbaric mob actions occurred on October 4, 1871, when a huge group of whites—men, women and children—rampaged through Calle de los Negros, or "Nigger Alley," which had become the city's Chinatown. Ostensibly, the reason for the riot was to avenge the death of a white who had been killed in the cross fire of fighting between two rival Chinese gangs, or tongs. But it was clear that this was little more than a rationale for an explosion of racially motivated violence. On the day of

the riot, hundreds of people charged through Nigger Alley smashing windows and battering down doors. Any Chinese seized was beaten or stabbed. When one Chinese man broke free of his tormentors and tried to run away, he was shot down in the street. Having thus tasted blood, the crowd grabbed another Chinese and hauled him through the streets to a corral, where they hanged him. Other victims were pulled over the cobblestoned streets with a rope around their necks until they died.

Perhaps the most shocking killing, one that drew international attention, was that of an elderly Chinese doctor named Gene Tong. When caught by the mob, he pleaded to be spared and offered several thousand dollars he was carrying in exchange for his life. The rioters just laughed and hanged him anyway. As the old man was choking to death, several women in the crowd stepped forward and ripped off his trousers to get at his money. Someone also severed his ring finger with a bowie knife when a diamond ring would not slip off readily.

The death toll in the 1871 massacre was placed at 20 to 25, with many more injured, and it was estimated that the rioters had robbed and looted every room, every strongbox, every trunk in all Chinatown. A grand jury investigation condemned the mob for "disgracing our city" and charged that the authorities had failed to perform their duty properly, but not one person was ever brought to trial. Not surprisingly therefore, a few years later, after the first initial shock and revulsion had passed, Anti-Coolie Clubs began to spring up in the city. Finally stung by charges of intolerance, the officials of Los Angeles did something: they changed the name of Nigger Alley to Los Angeles Street.

PIERCE CITY, IDAHO TERRITORY

Compared to some anti-Chinese massacres, the slaughter at Pierce City, Idaho Territory was, as one participant put it, "small potatoes." However, it is most illustrative of the brutal and inhuman attitude of whites toward Asians.

On September 10, 1885 the body of a white merchant, D. M. Frazier, was found "chopped to pieces in his own store." A vigilante mob was formed quickly and on no apparent evidence, deduced the crime had been committed by two Chinese merchants who were in competition with the victim. The Chinese partners were seized and tortured until each accused the other of committing the crime. The verdict was that both should be hanged, and as long as they were hanging them, the vigilantes thought it would be a good idea to get rid of three other undesirable Chinese—a gambler, a barber, described as "hard featured," and a "parasite," meaning a local camp prostitute. Cooler heads among the

mob convinced the others that the five should be turned over to the law so that they could be tried formally before being hanged. That night when a half-dozen lawmen set out with the prisoners for the county seat, they were stopped by a large mob of masked men who abducted the five. It seems some discussion among the vigilantes had led to the conclusion that the three additional prisoners would most likely not be hanged for the murder and that perhaps the confessions extracted from the two merchants by torture might also be disallowed in a courtroom. Direct action would solve that problem, and all five were hanged, if somewhat inefficiently and slowly, from a pole placed between the forks of two pine trees. The incident triggered wholesale expulsions of Chinese from a number of Idaho towns with the tacit approval of high government officials.

When news of the lynchings spread, the Department of State received a protest from the Chinese government, but it was six months before the territorial governor E. A. Stevenson, arrived in Pierce City to launch an investigation. The "investigation" consisted solely of talking to anti-Chinese elements and announcing he had failed to discover the identities of any perpetrators of the lynchings. He did express regret at the hangings but added, "The Chinese hanged were the identical parties, who so cruelly, shockingly and brutally murdered without the least provocation (except jealousy) one of the best citizens of Idaho." The governor also insisted that deportation was the only solution to the Chinese problem, since "their low, filthy habits, their highbinder piratical societies, together with their low dens of infamy, prostitution and opium smoking, have disgusted our people."

After the Pierce City affair a prodeportation movement seemed to be gaining ground in Washington, but by this time a new wave of immigrants, this one from Japan, had started to arrive and hostility was shifted away from the Chinese to meet this new menace. Deportation of the Chinese was forgotten, and they went on to become one of the most law-abiding ethnic groups in America.

ROCK SPRINGS, WYOMING TERRITORY

As terrible as the slaughter was in the Los Angeles Chinese massacre of 1871, it did not compare with the mob riot in Rock Springs, Wyoming Territory in 1885.

When the main line of the Union Pacific was completed in 1869, many of the Chinese laborers settled in the railroad town of Rock Springs. In 1885 there were 500 Chinese in Rock Springs, the great majority working in the Union Pacific coal mines. In fact, the Chinese were the majority in the mines, and this led to friction as unemployment grew in the white community. When on September 2 a white miner and two Chinese got into an altercation underground, the fighting soon spread in the shaft among other miners, leaving one Chinese killed and three others severely injured. Word of the battle was passed above ground, and a heavily armed mob of white miners formed for the destruction of Chinatown. The Chinese had no reason to expect an attack and were easily routed from their dugouts and shacks. One white miner's diary recalled, "Bullets followed the fleeing Chinese and sixteen of them were killed brutally, while the other casualties met an even more horrible fate the same evening when some of the citizens satisfied their murderous instincts and inhumanly slew the few remaining Chinese for the money which their victims had hidden on their persons, after setting fire to the buildings to hide their crimes." The entire Chinatown section was burned to the ground and "the smell that arose from the smoking ruins was horribly suggestive of burning flesh." Overall, the death toll was put at 50, or 10 percent of the Chinese community.

The *Rock Springs Independent* put out an extra edition the following day and sided with the anti-Chinese forces. It especially complimented saloon operators for shutting down during the riot: "It cannot be said that a 'drunken mob' drove out the Chinamen. Everyone was sober, and we did not see a case of drunkness. All of the stores in town were closed, and men, women and children were out watching the hurried exit of John Chinaman and everyone seemed glad to see them on the wing."

Because of demands by the Union Pacific, federal troops were called in and took over the task of feeding the destitute Chinese wandering about the countryside. Many of the men involved in the massacre were identified; instead of being prosecuted, they were paid off by the railroad, given train tickets and "strongly advised" by the commander of the troops to leave the state. The federal troops remained on duty in Rock Springs for the next 13 years, finally departing at the start of the Spanish-American War in 1898.

Chivington, John M. (1821–1894) leader of massacre

The minister-soldier who commanded the infamous Sand Creek Indian Massacre in 1864, John Chivington was court-martialed but acquitted. To escape further military justice, he resigned from the army. Most authorities on Chivington say that he was hated the rest of his life, unable to escape the stigma of his deeds, unable to find employment. The truth, however, was that the man once tried for the wanton slaughter of 450 Indian men, women and children later became a lawman. For many years until his death, he held the job of

undersheriff in Denver, Colo., where he did his duty, so it is said, with honor and fairness and was respected by all those who worked with him.

Choctaw legacy, the con game

Fleecing Indians became a major sport for con men during the 1930s. Most of these swindles were based on telling the victims that under old treaties Indians were entitled to $1,000 each for their deceased relatives and that the only thing needed was to get an enabling act through Congress. The Indians could finance the lobbying necessary to pass the act for a mere $5 apiece.

A notorious sharper, Odie Moore, worked the scheme to perfection in Neshoba County, Miss., promising the Indians great rewards due them because of the breaking of the Dancing Rabbit Treaty of 1839. Since there had been wide intermarriage between whites and Choctaws over the decades, thousands of white suckers added their $5 contributions. Moore's fanciful association managed to come up with a slogan, promising "$1,000 for every dollar." A number of young whites even sought out girls with traces of Choctaw blood in them to get on the promised gravy train.

Moore's victims gave and gave from the time he started his swindle in 1930 until his death in 1945, and even after that, many remained sure their promised windfall would soon be forthcoming.

Chowchilla school bus kidnapping

The greatest kidnap for ransom plot in terms of numbers of victims in the United States took place on July 15, 1976 near the town of Chowchilla, Calif. By blocking the road with a van, three stocking-masked armed men stopped a school bus containing 19 girls and seven boys returning from a summer school session. While one of the three masked men drove the bus off and hid it in a dried-out creek bed, the 26 children and the bus driver were herded into the van used for the blockade and a second van driven up from a hiding place. The driver and the children, who ranged in age from six to 14 years, were driven around for more than 11 hours and finally brought to a rock quarry near Livermore, less than 100 miles from the kidnap site.

There they were all transferred to a large moving van that had been buried in an isolated section of the quarry. Tarpaulins were stretched from the two small vans to the roof of the buried van so that the prisoners could not see where they were. A hole had been cut in the roof of the buried van, and the children were forced to climb down a ladder into their underground prison. Before each child was transferred, his or her name and age were recorded and a personal item or bit of clothing was taken, obviously for proof later that the kidnappers indeed held them prisoner.

The bus driver was given a flashlight and ordered into the moving van, which was then sealed off with large sheets of metal, plywood, dirt and other debris. The van, 25 feet long and 8 feet wide, had been well furnished for accommodation of the prisoners, containing a portable toilet and supplies of water, bread, potato chips and breakfast cereal. There were a number of matresses, and ventilation was provided by 4-inch rubber tubing, with air pumped in and out by two battery-driven fans.

Later that day a police air search located the abandoned school bus, but there was no trace of the children, and terror gripped the Chowchilla area. Twenty-four hours went by without a ransom demand from the kidnappers, who were apparently determined to fuel the parents' anxiety further so that the state would be forced to make payment immediately. However, the kidnappers' plans went awry when, 16 hours after their imprisonment in the large van, the driver and some of the older children managed to dig their way out. When all the children were pulled free, the group walked toward lights in the distance. They found a quarry employee, who immediately called the police. The Chowchilla children's ordeal was over.

It took the authorities 12 days to round up the three kidnappers involved. The day before the kidnapping a woman had jotted down the license number—1C91414—of a small van near what was to prove to be the site of the abduction. She had become suspicious of the van's occupants. The school bus driver underwent voluntary hypnosis and was able to recall the license number of one of the vans—1C91414—and all but one digit of the other. The numbers were eventually traced to an Oakland car dealer, and the large buried van to a Palo Alto firm, which had sold it to one Mark Hall. Employees at the Palo Alto and Oakland firms identified the purchaser from photographs as Frederick Newhall Woods, IV, the son of the owner of the rock quarry. Some of the children recalled hearing their abductors use the names Fred and James, and since Woods was known to be close friends with two brothers named James and Richard Allen Schoenfeld, sons of a prominent Atherton podiatrist, warrants were issued for them as well. Richard Allen Schoenfeld surrendered to authorities on July 23, and his older brother was captured on July 29. On the same day, Woods was arrested by Royal Canadian Mounted Police in Vancouver.

The defendants chose a court trial rather than a jury trial, feeling that jurors would be hostile because the victims had been children. Evidence indicated that the trio had worked on the details of the kidnapping for an entire year before setting it in motion. All three were convicted of 24 counts of kidnapping and three of kidnapping with bodily harm. Richard Allen Schoenfeld got life imprisonment, and brother James and Woods drew life with a stipulation barring parole.

Christie, Ned (1867?–1892) Indian outlaw

Along with the Apache Kid, Ned Christie, a full-blooded Cherokee, became one of the most wanted Indian outlaws in the West.

A bright youth, Christie served in the Cherokee tribal legislature, but in 1885 he became an outlaw in a big way. For some unknown reason, he killed Deputy U.S. Marshal Dan Maples and vanished into the Cookson Hills of the Oklahoma Indian Territory. In that area he functioned as a horse thief, rumrunner, bandit and murderer, although there is no doubt that, as was the case with the Apache Kid, just about any crime committed in the territory by a young Indian was pinned on him.

It took Hanging Judge Parker's deputies seven years to catch up with Ned, who was cornered by U.S. marshals Heck Thomas and Paden Tolbert in a log fort near Tahlequah on November 1, 1892. Finding Ned and flushing him out were two different matters, however, as the fort

Photograph of the lifeless body of Indian outlaw Ned Christie nailed up to an old door became the most popular pinup in the Oklahoma Territory during the 1890s.

was close to impregnable. The marshals sent all the way to Kansas for an army cannon and then set about the task of blasting out the Indian outlaw with the aid of about 20 reinforcements. They pumped an estimated 2,000 bullets into the fortress that did no damage at all; the cannon proved even less helpful. The logs held firm and the cannon balls had the disconcerting habit of bouncing back at the besiegers. Twenty-four hours of battle had not added up to a day of glory for the law. Finally, the attackers used dynamite to breach the walls. Although shellshocked, the Indian came out fighting, riding hard and pumping away with his Winchester. With some 20 guns trained on him, Ned Christie was blasted off his mount, full of holes and dead.

The killing of Oklahoma's most wanted Indian desperado deserved special artistic commemoration. His body was allowed to harden somewhat into a pre–rigor mortis pose, propped up against an old door with his rifle cradled in his hands, and then his picture was taken. Ned Christie became the most popular pinup in Oklahoma during the 1890s.

See also: HECK THOMAS.

Cicero, Ill. mob-controlled Chicago suburb

In the heyday of the Capone mob, Cicero was known as the syndicate's town. Al Capone's private guard in Cicero totaled about 800 gunmen, while the town's police force numbered about 50. Any officer who considered standing up to the Capone gang thought twice because every official from the major down to the dogcatcher was believed to follow Capone's orders without question. Once when the mayor dared to displease Capone, the mob chieftain knocked His Honor down on the steps of the town hall and kicked him unmercifully in the groin. A Cicero policeman watched the entire procedure, reportedly looking quite embarrassed.

In 1924 the Democrats dared to put up candidates opposing the Klenha slate, which with bipartisan backing had ruled the town for three terms. The Capone forces sent in hundreds of gangsters to guarantee the proper election results. On the eve of the election, William F. Pflaum, the Democratic candidate for town clerk, was roughed up in his office and the place was totally wrecked. On election day gangsters in seven-passenger black limousines patrolled the streets, terrorizing the citizenry. Persons known to favor the Democrats were beaten. Capone men walked up and down lines of voters asking people how they intended to vote. If they gave a wrong answer, their ballots would be snatched from their hands and marked properly by the mobsters. Then a Capone hood, fingering a revolver in his coat pocket, would stand beside the voter until he or she dropped the ballot into the box.

Honest poll watchers and election officials were simply kidnapped and held until the polls closed. A Democratic campaign worker, Michael Gavin, was shot through both legs; policemen were blackjacked.

Terrified Cicero citizens appealed to the courts for aid. Cook County judge Edmund K. Jarecki deputized 70 Chicago patrolmen, nine squads of motorized police and five squads of detectives and sent them to the beleaguered town. That afternoon and evening pitched battles were fought between gangsters and police. Frank Capone, Al's brother, took aim at officers piling out of an unmarked black limousine and squeezed the trigger of his automatic, but it clicked on an empty chamber. Before he could pull the trigger again, two lawmen blasted him with their shotguns.

When Al buried Frank a few days later, he could at least console himself with the knowledge that his brother had not died in vain. The Klenha slate carried the election by a huge margin.

See also: AL CAPONE, FRANK CAPONE, HAWTHORNE INN.

Cimarron County Seat War

While the Cimarron County Seat War in Kansas in 1889 may not have been the most murderous of the struggles of this kind, it has often been cited as the prototype of the county seat wars that bloodied Kansas and several other states during the land boom era, especially in the 1880s.

In October 1887 Cimmaron had been voted the seat of Gray County, a decision that did not please Asa T. Soule, a leading citizen of Ingalls, the town that had competed with Cimarron for the designation. Soule had invested heavily in Ingalls real estate and knew that if Ingalls became the county seat, his holdings would soar in value. At the time, custom dictated that the possession of the county court records established the legal location of the county seat. Promising a $1,000 reward, Soule got Sheriff Bill Tilghman to deputize a gang of hired guns and go after the records. Tilghman and more than a dozen gunfighters, including Neal Brown and Jim and Tom Masterson, arrived in Cimarron in the early hours of January 13, 1889. While several stood guard outside, the two Mastersons and Brown broke into the courthouse and began hauling out the records. They had almost completed the job when a Cimarron resident spotted them and sounded the alarm. The awakened Cimarron citizenry pushed guns out of scores of windows and opened fire. Four Ingalls invaders went down in the fusillade. Their bodies were tossed into a wagon loaded with the court records and the invaders fled. The Mastersons and Brown were left trapped inside the courthouse. A gunfight consumed the entire next day, with more than 200 armed men keeping the trio pinned down. Talk of lynching filled the air after a resident died and three others were badly hurt, but in the end, nothing happened. By that time two of the trapped men had been identified as the Mastersons, and the news of their plight went out over the telegraph lines, reaching their noted brother, Bat Masterson, in Denver. He immediately wired Cimarron warning the townspeople to release the trio or he would lead an army of gunfighters to level the town. It was no idle threat. Bat commanded the loyalty of scores of noted gunmen, such as the Earps, Doc Holliday, Luke Short and others, men whom ordinary citizens could never stand up to. Thus, the following morning the trapped trio was allowed to leave town under a flag of truce.

By its forceful action, Ingalls did indeed become the county seat and held on to this honor until 1893, when it was passed back to Cimarron following another election. On this occasion there was no warring, however. Hard economic times had punctured the land bubble. Within a few years the populations of both Cimarron and Ingalls dropped to a few hundred souls each, and the bitter struggle had proved meaningless.

See also: COUNTY SEAT WARS.

Cincinnati riots

A common public perception in 19th-century big-city America was that enforcment agencies and the courts were corrupt and that criminals could often buy their freedom or mild sentences. This view, hardly unjustified, led to the organization of many vigilance committees and to frequent and bloody riots.

One of the worst of these took place in Cincinnati, Ohio in 1884. The public had been outraged by the action of the criminal courts, which in the previous year had sentenced to death only four persons out of 50 convicted of capital crimes. On March 28, 1884 a huge mob stormed the jail where two youths who had been let off with manslaughter convictions were being held. They lynched the pair and were finally dispersed by a militia company. The following night mobs formed again to perform additional acts of "instant justice." Stores were looted of guns, the jail attacked and the courthouse set afire and almost totally destroyed. The rioters were eventually driven off after a pitched battle with troops. Violence continued the third day, a Sunday, and that night the mobs, which now contained large numbers of criminals protesting for law and order and looting stores at the same time, again battled the militia. Soldiers were rushed in from all parts of the state and streets were barricaded to isolate the mobs. Vicious fighting continued for three more days before

the barricades could be removed and street-car service restored. The death toll in the rioting was at least 45 persons with 138 more badly injured. Despite the riots, Cincinnati retained its reputation as a wide-open city during the immediate ensuing years.

circus grifting

Compared to circuses in other countries, the American version has relied much more on criminal enterprises and fake exhibits and less on talented performers. A prime source of revenue in 19th-century circuses was gambling, particularly such crooked pastimes as the shell game, three-card monte and eight-dice cloth. Some seemingly ran independently of the circus management, but all paid a certain percentage of their take for the right to operate on the circus grounds. For these circus cons to thrive required four basic ingredients: grifters, victims, a dishonest circus management and public officials open to bribes. None were ever hard to come by.

The arrival of a circus in a community meant that within the next day or two many residents would find themselves swindled out of much of their ready cash, just as several church sermons the previous Sunday had warned. What the gambling grifters didn't take, circus shortchangers and pickpockets would. As late as 1900, many of the small circuses that traveled about the country still made each ticket seller pay up to $35 a week for the job because shortchanging the excited "rubes" on ticket sales was so easy and profitable. The pickpocketing franchise was sold to professional thieves, and to assist them in their chores, the master of ceremonies would make it a point to warn patrons about pickpockets. As a result, most men would quickly feel their wallets and thus reveal to the watchful crooks in which pocket they carried their cash. When a circus pulled up stakes, the grifters would ride out in the "privilege car," one lined with steel to protect them from angered rubes taken by the gambling grifts.

Criminologists have attributed the dishonest inclinations of the American circus to its more mobile existence compared to its European counterparts, especially the English circus, which stayed rooted in one place for much longer periods of time. The footloose lifestyle of American circuses encouraged a criminal business thrust. Many circuses in early years were ideal fences for stolen horses. Knowing they would be gone from an area the next day, circus employees became notorious for stealing from farms, barns and clotheslines.

Any one-shot method for improving profits would do. Balloon sellers typically hired an assistant to blow tacks at balloons in order to create an instant demand by howling children for a second or third sale. Many of the exhibits were outright frauds, particularly in small circuses, which used grifters because they could be paid far less than, for example, talented acrobats. Thus, the "Siamese twins" were simply two individuals held together by a flesh-colored belt while on display. As soon as that exhibit closed, the twins could hurry off, one to be perhaps a clown and the other to work, say, at the refreshment stand.

Circus grifting was an accepted practice in virtually all circuses until the 1880s and in all except Ringling's up to 1900. By as late as 1930, only the large circuses were free of grifting. The change did not come about as a result of a sudden reformation of the circuses or because public officials were less willing to take bribes or due to any growing sophistication among the customers. In earlier years a circus changed its name frequently so that it could return the following year to a community that it had angered on a previous trip. But as circuses grew, their very name became more of an asset than the revenues brought in by grifting. Faced with the necessity of making a choice, the bigger outfits, reluctantly, gave up grifting.

See also: CARNIVAL GYPS, SHELL GAME, THREE-CARD MONTE.

Ciucci, Vincent (1925–1962) murderer

The Ciucci case is often cited by critics of the court system as an example of justice delayed. Vincent Ciucci of Chicago was found guilty of having murdered his wife and three young children because he had fallen in love with an 18-year-old girl and wanted his freedom. He chloroformed his wife and three children on the night of December 4, 1953 and then shot each in the head. After the killings he set his apartment ablaze, apparently in the futile hope that the flames would eradicate all evidence of the shootings.

Although the case seemed open-and-shut and the jury quickly found Ciucci guilty, the wheels of justice moved slowly. Ingenious appeals and constant applications for commutation kept Ciucci alive for almost nine years until his execution in 1962. While these delays did not equal the 12 years on death row served by California's Caryl Chessman, the Ciucci case was criticized from all sides, by those who felt constant appeals were making a mockery of the death penalty and by opponents of capital punishment who condemned a system of justice that could make any defendant go through such a long ordeal. The Ciucci case contributed to the public's disenchantment with capital punishment in the 1960s, an attitude not reversed until the mid-1970s, when the death penalty once more became regarded as the cure-all for crime.

Civil War gold hoax

Perhaps the most audacious illegal money scheme of the Civil War period was perpetrated by a professional newspaperman, Joseph Howard, city editor of the *Brooklyn Eagle,* who concocted a false proclamation by President Abraham Lincoln. The hoax, in the words of one witness, "angered Lincoln more than almost any other occurrence of the war period."

Working with a reporter named Francis A. Mallison, Howard forged an Associated Press dispatch of the supposed proclamation that began, "In all seasons of exigency it becomes a nation carefully to scrutinize its line of conduct, humbly to approach the Throne of Grace, and meekly to improve forgiveness, wisdom, and guidance." The document, recounting the military stalemate in Virginia and disastrous news from Louisiana, called for a national day of "fasting, humiliation and prayer" eight days hence, on May 26, 1864. The real crushing news in the proclamation was the drafting of an additional 400,000 men.

Howard realized such a doleful pronouncement would shake the financial community to its roots, upset the stock market and undoubtedly cause a rise in price of gold. Days before he and Mallison unleashed their hoax, Howard bought a considerable amount of gold on margins, much of it apparently under other names, so that the best estimate of his profits could only be put at "many, many thousands of dollars."

The schemers used young boys to deliver the bogus AP dispatch to various New York newspapers. The news was so startling that several of the publications decided to confirm the facts before printing the story. However, two papers, the *World* and the *Journal of Commerce,* were pressed by deadlines and tore down their makeup at the last moment to get the story out. Quite as Howard had expected, the stock exchange "was thrown into a violent fever." The price of gold instantly shot up 10 percent. Fortunes were made and lost before the hoax was exposed.

Incensed by the false story, President Lincoln, Secretary of State William H. Seward and Secretary of War Edwin M. Stanton ordered the two newspapers seized. Only two days later, on May 20, the trail led to Howard and Mallison when it became apparent that the newspapers had been the victims rather than the perpetrators of an act that in Stanton's words "distinguished [them] by the violence of their opposition to the Administration."

The clearing of the newspapers led to a firestorm of protest against President Lincoln's initial seizure of them. Lincoln, locked in a battle for renomination and reelection, found the charges of suppression of the free press particularly embarrassing. Almost forgotten in the controversy were the culprits, Howard and

Mallison, who were confined in Fort Lafayette. Finally, Howard's father, an elder of Henry Ward Beecher's church, prevailed upon the famous minister to petition Lincoln for mercy. Beecher told Lincoln that the 35-year-old Howard was "the only spotted child of a large family" and his only guilt was "the hope of making some *money*." Finally, after the culprits had been confined for less than three months, Lincoln ordered their release.

The freeing of the gold hoaxers many not have been as magnanimous as it appeared on the surface. Ironically, when the report of the phony proclamation was published, an as yet unreleased proclamation lay on Lincoln's desk. It called for the draft of 300,000 more men. When Lincoln saw the adverse effect of the bogus report on the people and on the financial markets, he postponed all call-up plans for an additional two months.

Claiborne, Billy (1860–1882) gunfighter and rustler

Billy Claiborne is most noted as a survivor of the gunfight at the O.K. Corral.

Claiborne was a young gunslinger who insisted on being called Billy the Kid after the death of the more famous bearer of that name in July 1881. It is recorded that each of the three men who laughed in Claiborne's face over that pretension paid with his life. The last doubter to die was Jim Hickey, and Claiborne was arrested for his murder. Incarcerated in San Pedro, Arizona Territory, Claiborne, a member of the Clanton gang of rustlers, was busted out of jail by Ike Clanton and the McLowery brothers on October 22, 1881. At the time, a showdown was fast approaching with the Earp forces, and Ike Clanton undoubtedly wanted all the guns he could get.

Claiborne's two guns proved of questionable value. The gunfight at the O.K. Corral took place four days later, and as nearly as can be determined, Claiborne got off one or two wild shots in the general direction of Virgil Earp and then fled for the sanctuary of C. S. Fly's photography studio. Ike Clanton himself had little ground for complaint since he also sought shelter there while his brother Billy and the McLowery brothers were being gunned down.

It was a while before Claiborne again insisted on being referred to as Billy the Kid. While drunk in Tombstone's Oriental Saloon on November 14, 1882, he made the same demand of Buckskin Frank Leslie, a pitiless gunfighter who may well have killed more of the Clanton gang than the Earps ever did. Leslie, then serving as a sort of combination barman and bouncer, stepped outside on the street with Billy the Kid, II and shot him dead. Claiborne had

managed to live to be one year older than his self-proclaimed namesake.

See also: BUCKSKIN FRANK LESLIE, O.K. CORRAL, ORIENTAL SALOON.

claim jumping

Few crimes in the mining communities of the West were considered more reprehensible than that of claim jumping, stealing another man's goldfield property before he had a chance to record it officially.

Filing a claim was not really the legalistic ritual it might seem. The district recorder was often a merchant or saloon keeper, and once a man had filed his claim, he still had to protect it. A typical sign read, "CLAME NOTISE—Jim Brown of Missoury takes this ground; jumpers will be shot." If by chance Brown or a counterpart did shoot a jumper, a miners court would readily clear him and most likely set up a bottle for him at the local saloon. Claim jumpers were not treated leniently. A frequent punishment called for a jumper to have his ears cut off so that, said one miner's diary, he would "not hear about no more strikes." When a stranger showed up in gold-strike country, he would not be welcomed if he had a reputation as a claim jumper. "Preventative hangings" were not unheard of in such circumstances. Overall, however, it must be said that the miners and their courts generally settled claim-jumping problems in a fair and equitable manner. When the law became fully established years later, few miners court findings were ever upset.

See also: SOAPY SMITH.

Clanton, Joseph Isaac "Ike" (?–1887) outlaw

Son of the notorious Old Man Clanton, Ike became nominal head of the Clanton gang following the death of his father in July 1881, but he was not that strong a personality and ranked no better than second in command to Curly Bill Brocius. While Ike Clanton hated the Earps and others of the "townie/gambler" element and plotted against them, he never really sought a confrontation with them. In the noted gunfight at the O.K. Corral on October 26, 1881, Ike aligned with Billy Claiborne, the McLowery brothers and his younger brother Billy against the Earps and Doc Holliday. Ike begged that the shooting be stopped and then fled, leaving Billy Clanton and the McLowerys to be killed. A few months later, Ike was involved in the plan to kill Virgil Earp, and although it failed, the shooting left Virgil maimed for life. While Ike was not present when Morgan Earp was murdered in March 1882, there is little doubt he was in on the planning.

After the Earps left Tombstone later that same year under considerable pressure from the citizens, Ike Clanton and brother Finn became scarce in the area as well, and rumor had it that Wyatt Earp must have killed Ike. Within a year, however, Ike was back at work rustling cattle, continuing to operate without trouble from the law until the new sheriff of Apache County, Commodore Perry Owens, led a posse that trapped the Clanton rustlers at their camp on the Blue River. Finn Clanton was captured and received a long prison term, but Ike fought to the end and was killed.

See also: WYATT EARP, O.K. CORRAL, COMMODORE PERRY OWENS.

Clanton, Newman H. "Old Man" (?–1881) outlaw clan leader

A Texan of a hazy but definitely bloody past, Newman "Old Man" Clanton settled his family in the 1870s on a ranch at Lewis Springs, Arizona Territory, which was stocked with a constantly changing supply of stolen cattle. Old Man Clanton directed the lawless activities of the family and numerous hangers-on. The Clanton gang swept into Mexico and Texas to undertake robberies of stagecoaches and bullion pack trains. Besides his three sons, Ike, Finn and young Billy, important members of the gang included such cutthroats as Johnny Ringo, Curly Bill Brocius and the McLowery brothers, Tom and Frank. Clanton also maintained a spy network on both sides of the border that advised him on potential victims. One of the Old Man's worst depredations was the Guadalupe Canyon Massacre in July 1881, in which he and his men slaughtered 19 Mexicans escorting a mule train loaded with $75,000 in silver bullion. That vicious act made Old Man Clanton just about the most hated of all *gringos*. But about two weeks later, a large posse of Mexicans ambushed the old man and five of his gang as they were driving a herd of stolen cattle through the same Guadalupe Canyon. Only one of the gang, a man named Earnshaw, got away.

See also: GUADALUPE CANYON MASSACRE.

Clanton, William (c. 1865–1881) outlaw

The only Clanton to die at the O.K. Corral, young Billy Clanton was considered by many the bravest of the family. While the Earp supporters always sought to claim that Billy was 17 or 19 at the time of the O.K. Corral fight, the anti-Earps have tended to set his age between 13 and 15 at most and thus claim that Wyatt Earp killed a "baby." Billy Clanton was deserted by his brother, Ike, and Billy Claiborne, and the McLowerys staggered off as they were hit. His right hand shattered

by a shot, Billy shifted his gun to his left hand and kept fighting alone. He shot Virgil Earp through the leg. Then Wyatt Earp put the sixth bullet in Billy Clanton, and he went down. Billy worked his way up to his knees and tried to level his .45, allegedly pleading, "Just one more shot, God, just one more shot." Finally, he fell back to the dirt, and the Earps and Holliday all held their fire.

Billy Clanton's reputed last words were: "Pull off my boots. I promised my mother I'd never die with my boots on."

See also: O.K. CORRAL.

Clark, Douglas (1959–) the "Sunset Slayer"

Perhaps the most infamous serial killer of recent years, Ted Bundy left his mark in the chronicles of serial killings in many ways, particularly as an inspiration to "copy-cat" criminals. It is apparent that a sometime factory worker named Douglas Daniel Clark—the "Sunset Slayer"—had been much impressed by Bundy's murder spree and sought to imitate it. His murders, often in company of his lover, Carol Mary Bundy (no relation of Ted Bundy), began in 1980 and were far more ghoulish than those of his role model.

Calling himself the "king of the one-night stands," he dated either women older than himself or young girls between ages 10 and 15. However, sexual liaisons, even kinky ones, hardly sated his desires, which ran to dark reflections on rape, mutilation, murder and necrophilia. In 1980, Clark met Carol Bundy, a vocational nurse in Burbank, who at age 37 was a half-dozen years older than he, and she became his willing accomplice in his gruesome activities. When their game turned deadly, Carol cruised the Sunset Strip looking for prostitutes—with a strong preference for blonds—for Clark to murder and then engage in depraved sexual acts. Clark and Carol committed about 10 known murders in this fashion; at times, the heads of their decapitated victims were stored in a refrigerator for later gory fun and games. In one case, Carol later confessed to making up one face with cosmetics, saying, "We had a lot of fun with her. I washed her up like a Barbie with makeup."

Typical of Clark's killings were those of two half sisters, 16-year-old Cynthia Chandler and 15-year-old Gina Narano, who vanished from a beach. They were later found on the side of the Ventura Freeway in Los Angeles, each shot in the head. Gleefully, Clark described to Carol how he had had forced sex with the girls before killing them.

Carol clearly had become a murder slave for Clark, a fairly common occurrence among female consorts of serial killers, but she was also responsible for his eventual capture. In the past, she had had a romantic attachment with an apartment house superintendent and part-time singer in country and western bars, John Robert Murray. On a date with Murray after her murderous involvement with Clark, a liquored-up Carol let too much slip out about Clark and their doings. Murray said he might well go to the police about it all, a prospect that threw Carol into a panic. On August 5, 1980 she set up a midnight rendezvous with Murray in his van near the bar where he was doing a gig. She shot him in the head. Murray's body turned up four days later with nine stab wounds and deep slashes across his buttocks. The head was missing, removed by Carol and Clark to prevent any ballistics identification.

Two days after the discovery of the corpse, Carol sank into a state of depression, crying out on her job to another nurse, "I can't take it anymore. I'm supposed to save lives, not take them." Her coworker reported her comments to the police, who arrested Carol and in a search of her home found shocking pictures involving Clark and young girls. Clark was arrested at his job, where police found a pistol that ballistics tests linked to five of the known victims of the Sunset Slayer.

According to Carol, Clark claimed he had killed at least 50 young girls both before and after meeting her and that he hoped to hit 100 before he inevitably was caught. At his trial, Clark tried to shift the Sunset Slayings to Carol and victim Murray, claiming it was they who were ardent fans of Ted Bundy. The jury believed otherwise. Clark was sentenced to death and joined the growing list of condemned prisoners waiting for years for execution with the restored California death penalty. Carol first claimed insanity but then admitted her part in some of the slayings, including that of John Murray, and she was sentenced to a total of 52 years in prison.

Clark, James G. (1924–) sheriff and smuggler

Using electric cattle prods on demonstrators during the Selma, Ala. desegregation protests of the 1960s, Sheriff James G. Clark of Dallas County became a symbol of resistance to black voting rights.

Following passage of the Voting Rights Act of 1965, Clark was defeated for sheriff. After that, he himself got into trouble with the law. In 1978 he was charged with marijuana smuggling after officials confiscated about three tons of the drug aboard a DC-3 that had landed in Montgomery, Ala. in May of that year. The marijuana, valued at $4.3 million, had been flown in from Colombia. Pleading guilty to the charge, Clark was sentenced to two years in federal prison. At the time of his sentencing in December 1978, four charges of fraud and one of racketeering were also pending against him, in an unrelated case in New York City.

Clark's Battalion   New Orleans posse

In 1800 Spain, which had held New Orleans and the rest of the Louisiana province for 30 years, ceded the area back to France. However, the French were slow taking possession, the reason becoming clear with the purchase of Louisiana by the United States in 1803. During that three-year period, and especially in the final year, law and order crumbled. The Spaniards remained in nominal control but had lost all interest in maintaining the peace. On November 3, 1803 Spanish troops sailed for Havana, leaving the city with no organized protection and facing the likelihood of full-scale rioting and looting by the lower and criminal elements.

To fill this vacuum, the American consul, Daniel Clark, organized a battalion of 300 men, Americans living in the city and Creoles. The battalion had no clear legal code and in effect meted out posse justice to offenders, utilizing pillories located on Chartres Street. Major offenders were warned they faced the American hangman as soon as full authority was established. With a few French officials, Clark supervised the imposition of several regulations that were in keeping with American law and provided residents with a foretaste of U.S. rule. Among the ordinances adopted were ones outlawing profanity and the driving of carts on Sunday. Other regulations established curfews for slaves and sailors, which banned them from the streets after 8 P.M. without a written pass from their owners or commanding officers. With the official takeover by the United States on December 17, 1803, these new laws-by-posse became permanent.

Cleary, Katherine (1954–1973) "Looking for Mr. Goodbar murder"

This was, in a sense, the murder of an era, when the sexual revolution was increasingly embraced by young people. Twenty-eight-year-old Katherine Cleary was haunting Manhattan's Upper West Side looking to find a man for some casual sex. In Tweed's bar, she met Joe Willie Sampson, who had a sexual hang-up: trying to go "straight" despite a homosexual orientation. Cleary invited Sampson back to her apartment. When Sampson proved unable to perform sexually, Cleary derided him. In a rage Sampson beat her to the floor and, seizing a carving knife, stabbed her several times until the knife broke. He jammed a candle into her vagina and left. Taken into custody, the following May Simpson hanged himself in his cell.

The protagonist in Judith Rossner's novel *Looking for Mr. Goodbar* was patterned on Simpson.

Clifton, Dan (?1865–1896?) outlaw

Better known as Dynamite Dick, Dan Clifton was a small-time Oklahoma Indian Territory safe blower, holdup man and rustler who hooked up with the Doolin gang in 1892. He was involved in all the gang's jobs from then on and had three fingers shot off during the Doolins' famous battle with the law at Ingalls, Okla. in 1893. A reward of $3,500 was put on Dynamite Dick's head, and he became the most "killed" outlaw in America, as reward-hungry posses kept trying to pin his identification on any shot-up corpse. Some overlooked the matter of the three missing fingers, while the more knowledgeable would simply cut three off, alas often the wrong three.

In all likelihood, Dynamite Dick was tracked down in 1896 near Blackwell, Okla. and shot dead. While there were three fingers missing on the corpse, considerable speculation arose that the dead man was still not Dynamite Dick but another outlaw named Buck McGregg.

Cline, Alfred L. (1888–1948) bluebeard

One of the most successful criminals at marrying and murdering widows for their money was Alfred L. Cline, until the law cut off his career in California in 1945.

His modus operandi remained constant, and he is known to have killed eight unfortunate wives after he had convinced them to will their estates to him. Cline would take his brides on a lavish vacation and in some smart hotel get them to drink a glass of buttermilk that he had laced with a heavy amount of a sleep-producing drug. He would follow this up a few hours later with a fatal dose of the drug, but in the meantime he would call the house physician and inform him that "Mrs. Cline has had another heart attack." When he resummoned the doctor shortly thereafter, his wife would be dead, and the doctor, prepared for that event, would not be suspicious and would issue a death certificate, citing heart failure as the cause.

Eventually, many of the facts about Cline's crimes surfaced, but the law invariably foundered on one key element. Cline always had his wives' bodies cremated, a process that destroyed all evidence of the poison he had used. However, the authorities were able to prove that he had used forgery to get his hands on his wives' money, and for this he was sentenced to 126 years in prison. Cline died in California's Folsom Prison in 1948.

Clum, John P. (1851–1932) Indian agent and publisher

One of the most colorful men of the Old West, John Clum was born near Claverack, N.Y. At the age of 23 he was an Indian agent on the San Carlos Reservation, where he is generally credited with developing the concept of the Indian police. The principle of giving Indians armed authority was not one that came easily to many whites, and Clum and other Indian agents who tried it found themselves involved in many imbroglios with the power structure. Of all the agents, Clum, not surprisingly, had the most effective Indian police force. He resigned from the Indian Service in 1878 because of the government's hardening line toward the Indians.

In 1880 in Tombstone, Arizona Territory, he founded one of the West's most colorful and outspoken newspapers, the *Tombstone Epitaph,* which became known as the town's pro-Earp publication. Publisher Clum was often a more worthy citizen than the elements he supported at times—Earp and Doc Holliday, for instance, were little more than corrupt lawmen and murderers—and there is little doubt that his newspaper did much to bring law and order to the area. Selling out his interests in the *Epitaph* in 1882, Clum left the area

John Clum poses with some of his highly regarded Indian police.

after the death of his wife and daughter to become assistant editor of the *San Francisco Examiner*. He died in 1932, two years after making a sentimental return to Tombstone.

See also: WYATT EARP, INDIAN POLICE, TOMBSTONE EPITAPH.

Clutter family murders *In Cold Blood* case

The Clutter family murders in 1959 were a brutal, senseless affair that became the subject of Truman Capote's best-selling book *In Cold Blood*.

The Clutters were sought out, robbed and killed by two ex-jailbirds and vagrants named Richard E. Hickock and Perry E. Smith. Hickock had learned of the Clutters while sharing a prison cell with a convict named Floyd Wells, who had once worked for Clutter, a well-to-do wheat farmer in Holcomb, Kan. Hickock pumped Wells about Clutter's wealth and whether he kept a safe in his home and how much money he was likely to have on hand. When Hickock was paroled from the Kansas State Penitentiary, he hooked up with Smith, and the two headed for the Clutter home. They invaded it on November 15, 1959. After terrorizing the family, the pair killed Clutter and his wife, Bonnie, both 45, daughter Nancy, 16, and son Kenyon, 15. Clutter's body was found in the basement of his home with his throat cut and shot in the head. His wife and two children had been killed with shotgun blasts at close range. All the victims were bound by the wrists.

When news of the murders reached the penitentiary, Wells went to the warden and told him of Hickock's interest in the Clutters. This put the police on Hickock's trail, and he and Smith were captured in Las Vegas. Both men made confessions, each trying to shift more of the blame on the other. While they had expected to find $10,000, they had netted less than $50 for the four murders. Smith said of Clutter: "He was a nice gentleman. . . . I thought so right up to the moment I cut his throat."

At the trial the jury was urged by the prosecuting attorney not to be "chicken-hearted" and to find them guilty of first-degree murder. The jury did so, and after a number of appeals, Hickock, 33, and Smoth, 36, were hanged in April 1965.

cockfighting

A generally illegal but much practiced sport, cockfighting was imported into the United States from the Spanish islands and Mexico. During the 19th century it became a common weekend entertainment in many parts of the South and West. Some cocks were armed with steel spurs to make their battles more bloody and furious.

Cockfighting has never been stamped out, and secret matches are still held in large cities for big-money prizes. Not long ago, police in Los Angeles broke up a cockfighting gambling ring and freed some two dozen cocks that had fought in matches for stakes of up to $10,000. Similar arrests have been made in Chicago and New York, where vacant buildings in deserted slum areas have been turned into exhibition halls. Cockfighting has outlasted dogfighting because it is easier to maintain secretly and because much of the action takes place in barrios, where police investigation is generally unpopular.

While local laws generally ban cockfighting, proposals in Congress have called for action on a federal level, which has brought protests from congressmen representing Mexican-American areas. A Texas congressman denounced a successful House vote to ban interstate transportation of birds and the use of the mails for the promotion of cockfighting, citing "the ethnic and cultural background of some of us."

Coe, George Washington (1856–1941) gunfighter

A sidekick of Billy the Kid, George Coe took part in most of Billy's battles during New Mexico's Lincoln County War in the late 1870s, barely escaping death when severely wounded in the gunfight at Blazer's Mill. He accepted amnesty when it was offered by the new governor of the territory, Lew Wallace, and thereafter lived a long and peaceful life, becoming the last survivor of that great commercial conflict for the wealth and riches of New Mexico.

In 1934 Coe had his reminiscences ghost-written in a book called *Frontier Fighter*, which offered a rather cleaned-up portrait of Billy the Kid. One observation said Billy was as fine as any "college-bred youth and with his humorous and pleasing personality got to be a community favorite. In fact, Billy was so popular there wasn't enough of him to go around."

Coe, Phil (?–1871) gambler and Wild Bill Hickok victim

A Texas dandy, Coe was the Hollywood prototype of the western gambler, handsome and elegant with neatly trimmed beard, gold-headed cane and derby hat. His killing by Wild Bill Hickok tarnished the latter's reputation as a fair gunfighter more than any of Hickok's other shootings.

Little is known of Coe's origins because "he told as many stories about his past as there were cards in a deck," but he was a fixture on the gambling circuit of the 1860s and early 1870s and prospered. In 1871 Coe turned up in Abilene, Kan. with a vicious gunfighter named Ben Thompson, and they opened the Bull's Head

Tavern and Gambling Saloon. The establishment thrived, and this put the partners in conflict with Wild Bill Hickok, who, as town marshal, was also the protector of the Alamo, the leading gambling emporium in the town. Coe charged that his fellow Texans up on cattle drives were being cheated at the Alamo's tables while Hickok looked the other way; the marshal charged in turn that Coe ran a crooked game.

The tension was further heightened by what became known as the *Shame of Abilene*. Coe and Thompson had the front of their establishment painted with a huge bull, with even larger genitalia. If some considered the representation offensive, Coe and Thompson found it boosted business greatly. Within weeks, reports of the *Shame of Abilene* were even being carried in the Eastern press. Finally, Hickok, prodded by the more genteel elements as well as the other gambling interests, ordered Coe to remove the painting or at least reduce the size of the more offending parts to scale. When Coe refused, Hickok, armed with paint can and brush, did the job himself, revealing perhaps some overlooked talents.

There has been much speculation that the argument over the bull painting was the cause of the Hickok-Coe gun duel, but it appears more likely that the showdown stemmed from Hickok's desire to win control of the lion's share of Abilene's gambling business. The trouble came to a head on October 5, 1871, at a time when Ben Thompson, whose skills with a gun more closely approached Hickok's than did Coe's, was out of town. Coe was bidding a liquid farewell to a bunch of Texas cowboys. They wound up in front of the Alamo, where Coe fired a shot from his gun. Hickok hurried out of the saloon, there being an ordinance against carrying firearms inside the town limits. Putting away his weapon, Coe explained that he had just shot at a stray dog, and Hickok reprimanded him. Some anti-Hickok observers have suggested that Coe's explanation only infuriated Hickok more, since as marshal he collected 25¢ for each stray he killed and Coe was thus threatening to cut the marshal's paycheck. What happened next is a matter of dispute. The Texans all insisted that when Coe turned away, Hickok whipped out a pair of derringers and shot him. The other version was that Hickok did not shoot until Coe pulled his gun and fired point blank at him. In any event, Hickok's image as a gunfighter was soon tarnished by a charge that he was "trigger-happy." As Coe fell mortally wounded, Hickok heard loud bootsteps behind him and, thinking he was being attacked from behind, whirled and fired again. He shot his own deputy, Mike Williams, who was rushing to his aid. Williams died a few minutes later stretched out on a poker table in the Alamo, while Hickok continued to curse the dying Coe. One rather maudlin pro-Hickok recorded of the events added:

"Tears are the safety valves of a woman's soul. Without them she could not survive. Sometimes they and strong men also. 'Jesus wept.' declares the Gospel. So did Wild Bill." In reality, there was little doubt Hickok was determined to kill Coe; he simply got more than he bargained for in the process.

See also: WILD BILL HICKOK, *SHAME OF ABILENE*, BEN THOMPSON.

coffin, double-decker   Mafia body disposal method

From the time of its first appearance in America during the 19th century, the Mafia has been most inventive in the ways it disposes of the bodies of murder victims; a great many are finally listed in official records as missing, instead of dead. Some victims have been fitted with "concrete overcoats" or ground up in garbage shredders. Top New York mafioso Tony Bender is believed now to be either part of a large Manhattan skyscraper or of the recently crumbling West Side Highway (an in-joke in certain Mafia circles is that "dagos make lousy roads").

Perhaps the quaintest of all body disposal devices is the "double-decker coffin." A murder victim is taken to one of the mob's cooperative undertakers who constructs a special panel in a coffin he has ready for an about-to-be-buried corpse. The unwanted murder victim is placed in the bottom of the coffin and a panel is put over the body. Then the right corpse is placed on top. After a properly mournful funeral, the two corpses are buried together. No undertaker has ever been convicted as a result of this method because he can always claim the mob must have dug open the grave after burial and put in the extra corpse. The undertaker cooperating with the mob on such a matter is assured of the proper financial reward because the crime family will see to it that he gets a good deal of their regular business thrown his way.

Cohen, Mickey (1913–1976)   gangster

One of the most shot-at gangsters of the 1940s and 1950s, Mickey Cohen was the gambling czar of the West Coast, succeeding to that position after the underworld execution of Bugsy Siegel, Cohen's mentor, in 1947 by "persons unknown." Those unknown persons were members of the national syndicate. Cohen later did battle with them, especially the syndicate's Los Angeles representative, Jack Dragna, refusing to turn over a cut of the proceeds from his bookmaking operations despite a series of attempts on his life.

Cohen lived in a mansion surrounded with an electrified fence and spotlights. On two occasions his home was dynamited. While he survived both times, he bemoaned the loss of much of his 200-suit wardrobe in one of the blasts.

Noted for his colorful and fiery comments, Cohen told television interviewer Mike Wallace, "I have killed no man that in the first place didn't deserve killing by the standards of our way of life." When asked to name the California politicians who had once protected his gambling interests, he refused, stating, "that is not my way of life."

Cohen wasn't any more communicative when he appeared before the Kefauver Committee's hearings on organized crime in 1950. When asked by Sen. Charles Tobey, "Is is not a fact that you live extravagantly . . . surrounded by violence?" Cohen responded "Whadda ya mean, 'surrounded by violence'? People are shooting at *me*."

When pressed on how he had obtained a $35,000 loan without putting up collateral from a Hollywood banker, Mickey quipped, "I guess he just likes me."

In 1958 Cohen, ever the publicity hound, gave the newspapers love letters written by actress Lana Turner to Johnny Stompanato, her gangster lover and a former Cohen bodyguard who was stabbed to death by Turner's teenage daughter. What upset Mickey was the fact that he had been struck with the bill for Stompanato's funeral.

The Internal Revenue Service nailed Cohen twice for income tax violations. He served four years the first time and did 10 years of a 15-year term the second time. Released in 1972, he announced his intention to go straight. Cohen didn't have too much choice in the matter since he was partly paralyzed as the result of a head injury inflicted by a fellow convict in the federal penitentiary at Atlanta in 1963. In 1974 Cohen attracted attention by campaigning for prison reform and, later, by stating he had been in touch with people who knew the whereabouts of kidnap victim Patricia Hearst.

Cohen died of natural causes in 1976.

Colbert, Chunk (?–1874) gunfighter and outlaw

Chunk Colbert was a gunfighter credited with killing seven men, but he is best remembered for taking part in one of the most famed gun duels in the history of the West.

The man Colbert challenged in an obvious effort to become known as one of the truly great gunfighters was an accomplished duelist and outlaw named Clay Allison, whose own killings eventually totaled somewhere between 15 to 21. Colbert rode from the Colorado to the New Mexico Territory just to face down Allison. Once there he invited Allison to dine with him at the Colfax County Inn. As the duel was immortalized by Hollywood and John Wayne, the pair, eyeball to eyeball, stirred their coffee and whiskey with the muzzles of their six-guns. Each reholstered their piece, still eyeing the other carefully, and started to eat. In a telltale sign, Colbert reached for his coffee cup with his left hand. Below the table he was moving up his gun with his right hand. Allison detected the move and went for his own gun. Desperate, Colbert fired before his gun had cleared the table top and the slug plowed into the wood. Allison shot him directly over the right eye, and then, the story goes, calmly proceeded to finish his meal as his foe's body was being removed.

Later, Allison was asked why he had sat down to eat with a man he knew was determined to kill him. "Because," he said, "I didn't want to send a man to hell on an empty stomach."

See also: CLAY ALLISON.

Coleman, Edward (?–1839) murderer

A fierce New York gangster, Edward Coleman became one of the city's most hated murderers for killing one of New York's favorite street characters.

The Hot Corn Girls of the early 19th century were the predecessors of the hot dog and peanut vendors of today, but they also had a certain aura of romance about them. Appearing mostly in the Five Points section of early New York, the Hot Corn Girls sold hot ears of corn from wooden buckets that hung from their shoulders. All successful Hot Corn Girls were of striking beauty; they had to be because of the intense competition. They strode through the streets barefoot in calico dresses and plaid shawls singing:

Hot Corn! Hot Corn!
Here's your lily white corn.
All you that's got money—
Poor me that's got none—
Come buy my lily hot corn
And let me go home.

The young bloods of the city would vie for the favors of a Hot Corn Girl. Many duels were fought over them. The more artistic suitors celebrated their beauty in story and verse. If a man had an aversion for work and a handsome wife, he could live a life of leisure by sending her forth with a cedar bucket full of corn. Such a husband, however, might find he would have to trail behind her to fend off the blades who tried to flirt with his Hot Corn Girl.

Edward Coleman wooed and won a truly beautiful member of this elite group, one so fetching that she was called the Pretty Hot Corn Girl. He married her after winning battles with about a dozen other suitors. The marriage was a short one, though. Coleman became enraged when he found her earnings were less than he had expected. He beat her so badly that she died. He was arrested, convicted and, on January 12, 1839, became the first man to be executed in the newly completed Tombs prison, a punishment much applauded by a public who still knew the victim only by the name of the Pretty Hot Corn Girl.

Coll, Vincent "Mad Dog" (1909–1932) gangster and murderer

Alternately known as Mad Dog and the Mad Mick, Vincent Coll stands as the best remembered of the so-called baby-faced killers of the 1930s. On another level, he was typical of the latter-day Irish gangsters who resisted the growth of organized crime, fighting a bloody war for an independent existence.

Some have described Coll as at least half-demented, with no regard for human life. Others have said he had no regard for even his own life, exhibiting a death wish as he invaded the far stronger gangland empires of Dutch Schultz, Legs Diamond and Owney Madden. With mindless nerve, he even accepted a commission to assassinate Lucky Luciano, Vito Genovese, Frank Costello and Joe Adonis. He was hired by Salvatore Maranzano, then the Mafia's "boss of bosses," who wished to rid himself of the young Turks he knew were plotting against him. Maranzano wanted the killings done by a non-Italian so that he could insist he was above the bloodshed. Coll drew a $25,000 advance and was on his way to Maranzano's office, where a trap was being laid for Luciano and Genovese. Luciano learned of the plot and had Maranzano killed first. When Coll got there, he found he had lost his murder contract, but being ahead $25,000, he walked off content.

Vince Coll emerged from the Irish ghetto of New York's Hell's Kitchen, where criminal activity was an accepted mode of behavior. In his early twenties, he and his brother Peter hired out as rumrunners to Dutch Schultz at $150 a week each. As he told his brother, the job was merely a way of learning the ropes before they either started up a bootleg empire of their own or simply took over the Dutchman's. Within a short time, Coll was demanding a cut of the action from Schultz, a proposal that was angrily rejected. The Coll brothers then started laying the groundwork for their own organization. As the fate of Vincent Barelli, a Schultz hood, and Mary Smith, Barelli's girlfriend, proved, Vince Coll was prepared to use gratuitous violence to accomplish his goal. The Coll brothers and Mary's brother, Carmine, had attended the same Hell's Kitchen grade school, and on the basis of this connection, Mary got Barelli to attend a meeting with the plotting broth-

ers. When Barelli refused to desert Schultz, Coll shot him and Mary.

Schultz was unaware of the scheming and still regarded the Coll brothers as being in his stable. After Vince was arrested for violating the Sullivan Law against carrying weapons, Schultz put up $10,000 bail. He became duly incensed when Coll promptly jumped bail; as a moral lesson, the beer baron had Peter Coll murdered. This launched the bitter Coll-Schultz war, in which at least 20 gunmen were killed. An exact count was impossible since the Castellammarese War for control of the New York Mafia was raging at the same time and the police had difficulty figuring out which corpse resulted from which feud.

Even though he had less firepower, Coll held his own against the Schultz forces. Constantly pressed for cash, he raised it in desperate fashion by kidnapping mobster kingpins attached to the Legs Diamond and Owney Madden gangs and collecting huge ransoms for their freedom. Thus, Coll was soon being hunted by a large portion of the New York underworld. In July 1932 Coll won his sobriquet of Mad Dog when he tried to gun down several Schultz gangsters on East 107th Street. Riding by them in a car, Coll cut loose a machine-gun blast that missed the gangsters but hit five small children, aged five to seven, leaving them writhing on the ground, some shot as many as five times. Five-year-old Michael Vengalli died, most of his stomach blown away.

The public was indignant, and orders went out to the police to bring in Mad Dog Coll dead or alive. Realizing he would be caught sooner or later, Coll kidnapped yet another Owney Madden aide and collected $30,000 in ransom. He used this money to hire the top lawyer of the day, Samuel Leibowitz, to defend him. Remarkably, Coll was acquitted of the murder charge after the masterful Leibowitz somehow seemed to make the eyewitnesses, rather than his client, the defendants. The Mad Dog was back on the streets.

Later, the underworld put a $50,000 reward out for the trigger-happy youth. Schultz gunners almost cornered Coll on four occasions but he fought his way to safety each time. Then one day late in 1932, Coll was in a drug store telephone booth talking to Owney Madden, threatening to kill him unless he was given money. Madden kept talking to him while the call was traced. Coll was still in the phone booth when a black automobile pulled up outside the drug store. One man stood outside on the street and another just inside the door. A third with something bulging under his overcoat strode toward the phone booth. Coll saw him as the man leveled a tommy gun at him. In his cramped position Coll was unable to react as the man squeezed the trigger.

At the autopsy 15 steel-jacketed bullets were removed from Coll's face, chest and stomach.

See also: SAMUEL S. LEIBOWITZ, OWNEY "THE KILLER" MADDEN, SALVATORE MARANZANO.

College Kidnappers Chicago gang

During the early-1930s heyday of the kidnapping gangs, one combine that operated in unique fashion was the so-called College Kidnappers of Chicago. They specialized in snatching only underworld characters, who not only could afford to pay but also were not likely to complain to the police.

The gang got its name because most of its members were college graduates; the leader, Theodore "Handsome Jack" Klutas, was an alumnus of the University of Illinois. The modus operandi of the gang was to pick up gossip in underworld circles about who had made a big "score." They would then kidnap the individual and release him only when they received a slice of the loot. Quite often, members of the Chicago mob were their victims, a pattern that earned the College Kidnappers the enmity of the Capone operation. But Klutas and his men had little fear of organized crime and continued their onslaughts, reportedly pulling in more than $500,000 dollars in ransom money between 1930 and 1933.

In 1933 a hot rumor, later proven to have some basis in fact, spread that the College Kidnappers had merged the Dillinger gang into their operations. Faced with this disturbing news, the Capone forces decided to try to buy off the kidnappers and persuaded one of the kidnappers, Julius "Babe" Jones, to approach Klutas to arrange a deal. Klutas told Jones he would consider it but, as soon as Jones left, ordered his assassination. The attempt was made by first stealing Jones' car and then faking a telephone call, allegedly from the Joliet police, to tell him that his car had been found and could be picked up at a local garage. Jones, an old hand at College Kidnapper tricks, was suspicious and drove by the garage dressed as a woman. As he expected, he spotted two gang members parked in a car opposite the garage, ready to gun him down when he appeared.

Now trapped between the College Kidnappers and the Capones, Jones could only turn to the police, informing them about a number of the gang's hideouts. One was a brick bungalow in Bellwood. When two squads of detectives stormed the bungalow, they captured two wanted criminals. One was Walter Dietrich, one of 10 convicts Dillinger had helped to break out of the Michigan City Prison. Dietrich refused to say where Klutas was or whether he alone or the rest of the Dillinger gang had joined the College Kidnappers. Meanwhile, acting on Jones' information, the police rounded up several other gang members, but not Klutas.

Later that same day a stakeout at the Bellwood bungalow paid off. A car pulled up, and Klutas boldly strode up the walkway. As Klutas pushed open the door, four police officers trained guns on him, including Sgt. Joe Healy's machine gun. Healy said: "Hands up. Police officers."

Klutas, who had always vowed never to be taken alive, reached under his overcoat for a gun. Healy loosed a burst of machine-gun bullets into the gangster's chest. Klutas was thrown clear off the bungalow porch to the sidewalk. He was dead, and the College Kidnappers were finished.

Collins, Dapper Don (1880–1950) confidence man

The archetypal smooth operator who uses his charms to seduce women and defraud them of their wealth, Dapper Don Collins was a notorious rogue who, by his own admission, "could never pass up a score," large or small. He swindled women by reversing the old badger game, so that they were extorted when he was "arrested" by confederates posing as law officers. The police impersonators would say he was a Mann Act violator or suspected procurer for white slavers. To protect the honor of the woman, usually upper class and perhaps married, he would give the bogus officers all his cash, only to be visibly shaken when they announced it was not enough. The panicky woman, facing sure ruin if the case was publicized, could be counted on to contribute her money, jewelry and furs.

Born in Atlanta, Ga. as Robert Arthur Tourbillon, he affected a number of aliases for his various cons but became best known as Dapper Don Collins, because according to his confederates, he was a dandy who could "sweet talk a lady" or anyone else for that matter. He often used a phony police badge and pretended to be a police officer, one who, of course, was always open to a bribe. Dapper Don first arrived in New York around the turn of the century after an unrewarding circus career riding a bicycle around in a cage full of lions. He gravitated to the notorious Broadway poolroom of Curly Bennett, where he befriended most of the metropolitan underworld.

Dapper Don soon became a gang leader, forming the first of his blackmail rings for extorting money from women. Besides his various confidence games, he masterminded train robberies and drug-smuggling and alien-smuggling operations and later, with the onset of Prohibition, was a top bootlegger and rumrunner. Collins often used a luxury yacht for rumrunning and bringing in aliens. In one of his more audacious exploits, he once entrapped a society woman aboard the yatch by having phony law enforcement raiders seize him on Mann Act violation for transporting the woman from Connecticut for "illicit purposes." They shook the woman down for $7,000 in cash and diamonds. Before the raiders left the yacht, they seized three aliens Collins had brought into the country from a ship offshore. Dapper Don had already collected $1,000 from each of them, but now the "law officers" confiscated the rest of their personal fortunes as a pay-off for not taking them into custody. Because Collins was fearful of overlooking some of their money, he even had his men take all the victims' luggage with them to search at their leisure.

While he bossed many of these grandiose schemes, Collins could not pass up even the smallest take. For a time, he headed a "punch mob" on Manhattan's West Side that specialized in looting nickels from pay telephones. One of his extraordinary cons occurred in 1920 during the hunt for a Railway Express agent who had skipped out of his job with $6,000. While police hunted the agent, Dapper Don came across him first. He immediately turned copper and swindled the thief out of his haul in return for letting him go free, appropriating as well the man's watch, ring and tiepin.

While Collins occasionally did time for various capers, he usually beat the rap for his blackmail exploits because his victims refused to testify against him. He retained the Great Mouthpiece, Bill Fallon, to defend him on a number of charges and usually went free. The pair were constant companions on Broadway.

According to Gene Fowler in *The Great Mouthpiece*, when Fallon was asked why he chummed with such a notorious individual, he replied: "Because he is a philosopher as well as the Chesterfield of crime. He performs in a gentlemanly manner. This first bit of philosophy he ever dropped in my company made me laugh and made me like him. We were discussing whether any man is normal; precisely sane; and what sanity consists of. Collins said: 'Between the ages of sixteen and sixty, no man is entirely sane. The only time any man between those ages is sane is during the first ten minutes after he has concluded the supreme love gesture. Fifteen minutes after, and the old insanity creeps back again'!"

Part of his success with the ladies stemmed from his reputation as the biggest spender and fashion plate on Broadway. It cost him plenty. What Collins netted from one gullible but adoring lady one day he might blow the next on another lady. Once Collins set up a Maryland matron and took off to Atlantic City with her. He was then to guide her to Washington for the kill. Instead, he stayed in Atlantic City for a week with her. At the end of that week of bliss, he kissed her good-bye and went to Washington alone. He had four

confederates in this operation and had to pay them $350 apiece for a caper that was intended to net a $10,000 profit.

In 1924, with the police hunting him for a number of capers, Dapper Don transferred his operations to Europe and seduced several women in Berlin and Paris. In the French capital, he took up with Mrs. Helen Petterson, former wife of Otto Young Heyworth, and extracted money from her under a number of ruses. Moreover, during a New Year's party at the Hotel Majestic, he flipped her out of a third-floor window. She broke her leg in the fall, and Collins was hustled off to prison for that offense and failure to pay his hotel bill. Undaunted, Mrs. Petterson limped from her hospital room at Neuilly to visit Collins, announcing, "We are going to be married." However, some New York police officers were in France to pick up a suspect in another case and spotted Collins in the prison. They promptly arranged for his extradition to the States on a robbery charge. Dapper Don was brought home in grand style aboard the steamship *Paris*, sharing a fine stateroom with a New York detective. Passengers knew that one of the two was a crook, but most believed the detective was the guilty party.

Back home, Collins beat the rap but later did short stretches on a couple of other charges. Dapper Don then got involved in a liquor-smuggling operation with another top confidence operator, Count Victor Lustig, supplying the notorious Legs Diamond with booze. They worked a label-switching dodge that enabled them to cheat the gangster out of thousands of dollars. Eventually, Diamond found out about the swindle, and the pair had to go into hiding. For a time, Collins left the country again, but in 1929 he came back and was caught swindling a New Jersey farmer out of $30,000. He was sent to prison for three years. When he came out, a lot of the old Dapper Don was gone, as indeed was the pre-Depression era that nurtured him. He was over 50, paunchy around the waist and looking tired, perhaps having lost some of his self-confidence. He told the press he was reforming.

That was impossible; he was plain tired. In 1939 Dapper Don, then a drug addict, was far gone, and his swindles were petty. Long ago, Collins had learned the danger of going after small potatoes. Unlike big people, little victims scream. He swindled an immigrant woman out of a few hundred dollars by pretending to be an immigration official and threatening to deport her husband. For this unimportant caper Collins drew the longest sentence of his career, 15 to 30 years.

The newspapers reported that Dapper Don started off on his train ride up the river as light hearted and debonair as ever. But that was newspaper hyperbole. Collins was old and beat. "The only way I'll ever come out again," he told the officer escorting him, "is feet first."

He was right. He died in Attica Prison in June 1950 and was buried in a pauper's grave. No one attended the funeral.

Collins, John Norman (1947–) Michigan co-ed murderer

For a time it appeared that the murders of seven co-eds in the Ypsilanti area between August 1967 and July 1969 would never be solved. The victims had been shot, strangled or beaten to death and then sexually mutilated. There were no clues, and even the importing of Peter Hurkos, the Dutch "psychic detective," failed to provide any fruitful leads. With the seventh murder, that of 18-year-old Karen Sue Beckemann, the police had what appeared to be a logical suspect in 22-year-old John Norman Collins, an Eastern Michigan University student and motorcycle enthusiast. Karen Sue had been seen with him shortly before her disappearance, and other students told of hearing things Collins had said that hinted he might be the Michigan co-ed killer.

Collins was arrested but soon released because there was no solid evidence against him. Like so many other suspects, he seemed to be just another odd character caught up in the investigation. The eventual case against Collins resulted from a discovery made by a relative, his aunt, Mrs. Dana Loucks. Mr. and Mrs. Loucks had gone away on vacation and let Collins use their home. When they returned, Mrs. Loucks found some dark stains in the basement. She pointed them out to her husband, who was a member of the Ypsilanti police force. The stains proved to be blood, of the same type as that of Karen Sue, who had been killed while the Loucks were away. The police then searched the basement and discovered some male hair clippings, which matched hair clippings found on Karen Sue's underwear. It developed that Mrs. Loucks cut the hair of her two boys in the basement. Based on the hair clippings, the blood stains and Collins' admission that he had used the Loucks' basement during the time they were on vacation, Collins was brought to trial in Ann Arbor in 1970. He was convicted and given a life sentence.

Collins, Walter (1919–1928) kidnap and murder victim

Nine-year-old Walter Collins suffered the sad fate of being kidnapped and murdered by a maniac on March 10, 1928, although his body was not found until the following year. However, it was his widowed mother's fate rather than that of the unfortunate child's, that made Walter's case so bizarre.

When Walter disappeared, a nationwide search for him was launched, and some five months later, a boy who looked exactly like him was picked up in Lee, Mass. The boy was a runaway and readily identified himself as the missing Walter Collins. In the period before he was turned over to Mrs. Collins, someone, whose identity was never learned, coached him so that he could pass himself off as Walter. This meant knowing little details that allowed the boy to discuss Walter's past with relatives and friends. It took Mrs. Collins three weeks to become suspicious that the boy was not Walter. She then measured his height and found he was an inch and a half shorter than her son had been before he disappeared. Convinced she had an impostor on her hands, Mrs. Collins went to the police, demanding that this strange boy be taken away. The police promptly committed the woman to a psychopathic institution for observation. Mrs. Collins was kept there almost a week before doctors became convinced she was sane and released her. Finally, the boy confessed his impersonation. Mrs. Collins sued the authorities who had had her wrongly committed and was awarded $10,800.

Colombo, Joseph, Sr. (1914–1978) murdered mafioso

There were those in the underworld who said that Joe Colombo, the head of one of the Mafia's biggest crime families, had to come to a bad end. He was a lightweight in a killers' world. Colombo's rise to power had been achieved through neither muscle nor brain power but by the simple expedient of being what was regarded as a "fink." When Joe Bananas made a powerful push in the 1960s to take over the whole New York Mafia, he planned the murder of the entire top echelon of the crime syndicate's ruling board. Bananas gave the assignment to his ally Giuseppe Magliocco, who had fallen heir to Joe Profaci's Brooklyn crime family, and Magliocco in turn ordered his ambitious underboss, Colombo, to carry out the hit contracts.

Colombo was probably too frightened to make the hits and also judged Magliocco a sure loser, so instead, he betrayed the plot to the leading would-be New York victims, Carlo Gambino and Tommy Lucchese. Eventually, the old guard won the ensuing Banana War, and Colombo was rewarded by being put in charge of the Profaci family. Colombo soon found he had his hands full trying to deal with an insurrection led by the upstart Joey Gallo and his brothers.

At the same time, Colombo went off on an illconceived program to improve the image of Italian Americans by forming the Italian-American Civil Rights League. Colombo's idea was that this organization would make Italian Americans proud of their heritage and that in unity they would be able to fight the

Mafia boss Joseph Colombo, Sr., holding umbrella, pickets FBI headquarters in 1971 as part of his Italian-American Civil Rights League activities.

authorities' alleged victimization of them. The league was also intended to fight the Italian gangster stereotype. Other Mafia leaders looked upon Colombo's efforts with distaste. They had long ago learned that denying the existence of the Mafia was another way of calling attention to it. Ignoring their displeasure, Colombo went ahead with a giant rally on June 29, 1970 at Columbus Circle. It was a smashing success, with 50,000 persons in attendance. And it was too powerful a demonstration to be ignored by the politicians. Even Gov. Nelson Rockefeller accepted honorary membership in the league, despite its Colombo imprint.

Joe Colombo came out of it appearing, to himself at least, a hero. He laid new plans for extending the league's power. Meanwhile, some of Colombo's lieutenants fretted over the declining revenues of the family while the chief spent ever more time pushing the league instead of minding criminal business. These men approached the other families who were upset by Colombo's activities, and they agreed that he had become more than a mere tribulation. The leading voice among them was Carlo Gambino, whose life had been saved by Colombo's finking. Gratitude was one thing and business another.

It was decided to let the Gallo forces have a shot at Colombo. Joey Gallo jumped at the chance. The second Unity Day rally of the league was set for June 28, 1971. Gallo knew he and his men could not get close enough to kill Colombo, but he had other sources of strength. Of all the Italian racketeers, Joe Gallo was the only one who had genuine power in the black gangster movement in Harlem.

On the morning of the 28th, Joe Colombo showed up early at the rally, as the crowd was just starting to form. A black man, Jerome A. Johnson, wearing a newspaper photographer's badge neared. When he was within a step of Colombo, he pulled out a pistol and fired three quick shots into the gang leader's head. Instantly, Colombo's bodyguards gunned down the assassin.

Johnson died on the spot. Colombo did not, but he suffered such brain damage that he turned into a vegetable. He died seven years later in an upstate hospital.

See also: BANANA WAR, CRAZY JOE GALLO.

Colonel Plug (?–1820?) river pirate

With Bully Wilson, Col. Plug was one of the two most important pirates who preyed on boat traffic along the Ohio and Mississippi Rivers. A bewhiskered giant whose real name was Fluger, Col. Plug boasted he had been a colonel in the American Revolution. Plug's modus operandi was to hide aboard a flatboat that was tied up for the night. When it got going in the morning, he would dig out the caulking between the planks and bore holes in the bottom. Col. Plug would time his work so that the boat would be scuttled opposite his hideout. His gang would row out to the flatboat in skiffs, supposedly coming to the rescue. The only person to be rescued would be Col. Plug, of course, along with the cargo; the crew and passengers would be left to drown, or, if they resisted, to be shot. Col. Plug was active for many years until, according to the legend, he bored too many holes one day and the boat he was sabotaging went to the bottom before Plug could climb out of the hold. At least, so the story was told in pirate circles, presumably accurate since suddenly Col. Plug ceased to be a scourge of the rivers.

See also: CAVE-IN-ROCK PIRATES, PIRACY.

colonial punishment

Punishment for crime tended to be less severe in colonial America than in the countries from which most colonists had come. The New England colonies and the Quaker settlements in West Jersey and Pennsylvania had punishments that in general were less harsh than those used in New York and the South. In New England the main thrust of punishment came in the form of humiliation; thus when Mary Mandame of Plymouth became the supposed first female sex offender in 1639, she was required to wear a badge of shame on her left sleeve. Had she failed to do so, she would have been branded in the face with a hot iron, but the mere threat of this punishment brought compliance in almost all cases. Vagrancy brought punishment in the stocks, while the ducking stool was held ready for the scold. More serious crimes brought stricter penalties. Murder and witchcraft called for hanging, and burglars were branded.

The same crime called for far different punishments in various jurisdictions. Theft in New York was punishable by multiple restitution and whipping, but in numerous Southern colonies the death penalty was often exacted when the sum taken was more than 12 pence. In several New England settlements a gentleman could commit the following offenses and be fined a sum equivalent to $10: lie eight times; swear four times; beat his wife twice; or criticize a court once.

In the Massachusetts Bay Colony in the early 18th century punishment did not end with a mere flogging or confinement in the stocks. After initial punishment offenders were then required to wear on their arm or bosom for a year or many years a large letter cut from scarlet cloth. The letter identified the crime for which the offender had been punished, such as A for adultery, B for blasphemy, D for drunkenness, I for incest, P for poisoning, R for rape, T for thievery. However, it was soon decided that this punishment was too inhumane and it was abandoned.

Whippings were often carried to excess, with the result that the convicted person often was left crippled for life. In New England an attempt was made to prevent this abuse by limiting the number of lashes to 39, as called for under Mosaic law. Contrary to common belief, no one, not even a witch, was burned at the stake in New England. However, burning and quartering were practiced in New York and the South. In the great Negro Plot of 1741 in New York, many blacks were put to the stake. Quartering was generally applied for treason and to blacks. In Maryland a black who murdered an overseer was punished by having a hand cut off, then hanging and finally quartering.

Perhaps the sternest punishments were carried out in Virginia. A slave who ran away might have an ear nailed to the pillory and then cut off. Criticism of the authorities in that colony meant an offender could be pilloried with a placard, lose both ears, do a year's service for the colony or have his ears nailed to the pillory. The most common punishment for the offense was being laid "neck and hells" in irons and then heavily fined. Virginia probably decreed more castrations of blacks than did any other colony.

See also: BOOK WHIPPINGS, BRANDING, FLOGGING, MARY MANDAME, MUTILATION, PILLORY, SALEM WITCHCRAFT TRIALS.

Colt, John C. (1819–1842?) murderer

John C. Colt was the central figure in a classic murder case in 1841 that started with a solution but concluded in a mystery.

Colt was a member of one of New York's millionaire merchant families and the brother of Samuel Colt, inventor of the Colt revolver and the Colt repeating rifle. At 22 John was tall, slim and handsome, with curly blond hair and steel gray eyes. The darling of society, he fancied himself a writer of sorts and numbered among his close friends Edgar Allan Poe, Washington Irving, James Fenimore Cooper, John Howard Payne, George Palmer Putnam and Lewis Clark.

Despite his literary bent, Colt had a quick, uncertain temper, and in a nasty argument he killed Samuel Adams, a printer he had hired to produce a book of his. Colt was tried speedily and sentenced to be hanged. There were those who said Colt would never hang, that his family was too powerful. Press exposés of Colt's treatment in the city's new prison, the Tombs, informed the public that Colt lived an exceedingly happy life for a condemned man. He had flowers on his table and a pet canary. A young Charles Dana reported: "In a patent extension chair he lolls smoking an aromatic Havana. . . . He has on an elegant dress-gown, faced with cherry-colored silk, and his feet are encased in delicately worked slippers." His food was "not cooked in the Tombs, but brought in from a hotel. It consists of a variety of dishes—quail on toast, game pates, reed birds, ortolans, fowl, vegetables, coffee, cognac."

The greatest concession to Colt's grand station was the permission granted by prison authorities that he be allowed to marry his fiancée Caroline Henshaw on the morning of November 18, the day of his execution. Newspaper announcements of the bizarre nuptials-gallows ceremony brought out thousands of thrill seekers who jammed Centre (later Center) Street at dawn. Miss Henshaw was forced to come by carriage to a side street entrance to the Tombs at about 11:30. During the actual wedding ceremony, carpenters assembling the gallows in the courtyard politely suspended their hammering, a fact a guard relayed to the crowd outside. The crowd moaned at that. It moaned again when word was passed, "They're married." Other news was passed as it happened. "The guests have gone. . . . There are silk curtains across the cell door. . . . They've ordered champagne. . . . They're testing the gallows!"

Shortly after 1 P.M. the new Mrs. Colt was advised that she had to leave, and she did so "smiling bravely." Later, there would be much conjecture over whether Caroline slipped her groom a large dagger with which he could stab himself in the heart and thus escape the noose. At 3:30 P.M. the Rev. Henry Anton, who had officiated at the wedding, was ordered to offer his final services to the condemned man. At that moment the tinder-dry wooden cupola atop the adjacent Hall of Justice mysteriously caught fire. Within three minutes smoke was pouring into the interior of the prison. Panic broke out and several guards raced out of the building. Convicts banged on their bars and begged to be let out, and some apparently were by the few remaining keepers. In the smoke-filled confusion, Rev. Anton rushed up to Sheriff Monmouth Hart and cried: "Mr. Colt is dead! He has a dagger in his heart!"

Instead of proceeding to the cell, the sheriff rushed around in search of the doctor who was there to pronounce Colt dead after his now unnecessary execution. At 7 P.M. a hurriedly convened coroner's jury officially declared Colt had committed suicide. It was a remarkable hearing, with no official identification of Colt being made. Not even Rev. Anton was called to testify. The body was released and buried that same night in the yard of St. Mark's Church. Afterward, the recently widowed Mrs. Colt disappeared.

At first, the newspapers focused on the source of the death dagger, including in the speculation every member of the wedding party. Only when it later was conceded by officials that a number of prisoners had escaped during the fire, did it suddenly occur to anyone that Colt could have escaped in the confusion—if there was a body to substitute for him.

The *New York Herald* commented, "We have no doubt that Governor Seward will order an investigation at once into this most unheard of, most unparalleled tragedy." No investigation was ever held, however, although even George Walling, who was appointed chief of police shortly therafter, gave considerable credence to the idea of a substitute corpse. So too did Colt's friends. In 1849 Edgar Allan Poe received an unsigned manuscript from Texas written in the unmistakable hand of John Colt. He took the manuscript to Lewis Clark, editor of *The Knickerbocker* magazine, and found Clark too had gotten a copy. They concluded it was Colt's way of letting them know he was alive and still trying for a literary career. Then in 1852 Samuel Everett, a close friend of Colt, returned from a visit to California and told others in the Colt circle of friends that he had met John Colt while horseback riding in the Santa Clara Valley. According to Everett, Colt lived in a magnificent hacienda with his wife, the former Caroline Henshaw.

Many students of crime dismiss the substitute corpse theory and regard Everett's story as apocryphal, insisting it was just an exotic fillip to an incredible tale. Others find the chain of events too mired in coincidence. That Colt should commit suicide just at the moment of a mysterious fire during which several prisoners escaped, they say, staggers the imagination. And why did the widowed Mrs. Colt disappear from New York City after her husband's death?

See also: TOMBS PRISON.

Colt .45   early police weapon

Well into the 19th century, lawmen relied almost solely on nightsticks and muskets for weapons. In 1830 James D. Colt, while on a voyage at sea, whittled a wooden model of a new-style six-shot handgun. When he returned home, he started production but soon found that few law enforcement officers had much interest in the weapon. The one consistent buyer was the Texas Rangers. During the war with Mexico in 1846, the Texas Rangers refused to fight without their beloved Colts. This brought added fame to the Colt six-shooter, and after the war most lawmen in the West used the weapon. They continued to do so until the first decade of the 20th century, when they switched to the smaller but potent .38-caliber Smith and Wesson, which most policemen in the rest of the country had already adopted as the basic firearm.

Commission, The   organized crime overseers

There is the mistaken impression that Organized Crime, in capital letters, is ruled by something called The Commission, also in capital letters, which is the ruling body of the Mafia. In point of fact, the Mafia is not organized crime (or the national crime syndicate) and above all, the commission does not rule over the forces of crime with the powers of life and death. Organized crime is not a monolith but rather a confederation of forces, and the commission is the body charged with seeing it remains no more than a confederation. It restrains itself from interfering with the internal operations of any member gang or crime family.

While the Mafia supplies many or most of the members of the commission, it does not totally control it, just as it does not fully control organized crime. The commission is composed of nine members drawn mostly from the 24 crime families that blanket the United States. While many of the commission members are rotated from this pool of 24 families, some non-Mafia members, e.g., the late Meyer Lansky, remained a regular and powerful participant in all syndicate discussions. For a time in the late 1940s and early 1950s the commission was dominated by the so-called Big Six, including Tony Accardo and Greasy Jake Guzik of the Chicago mob, the heirs of Al Capone. (While dominated by Mafia types, the Chicago mob, with its heavy Jewish and Irish membership, never really qualified as a Mafia crime family.) Frank Costello, the so-called Prime Minister of the Underworld, who recognized the need for a broader base of support for the Mafia, was also one of the Big Six. Joe Adonis was another member, one whose power spread from Brooklyn to New Jersey and was closely tied to Costello's interests. The remaining two members were,

like Guzik, Jews: Meyer Lansky and Abner "Longy" Zwillman. Zwillman had been a Prohibition bootleg king who later infiltrated a number of legal enterprises and frequently played an important role in naming governors, attorneys general and mayors in New Jersey, political clout that made him vital to the commission. Lansky, of course, was for decades vital to the syndicate in handling gambling enterprises for criminal elements in Miami, New Orleans, Las Vegas, the Bahamas, Saratoga, N.Y. and, in pre-Castro days, Cuba.

While Hollywood has never failed to portray the commission as ruthless and efficient, the group has by the very nature of its composition and assigned duties been somewhat less than all powerful. The commission's more notable failures include its inability to stifle the Profaci-Gallo war in Brooklyn and the more explosive Banana war, in which Joseph "Joe Bananas" Bonanno came close to becoming a new "boss of bosses." On the whole, however, the commission has undoubtedly done much to keep crime organized and operating in relative harmony.

See also: MAFIA.

"Company, girls!"   brothel phrase

For over a century the traditional call of harlots to work in American houses of prostitution has been a madam's shout of "Company, girls!" Many historians of the subject have mistakenly credited the origin of the custom to a San Francisco madam named Tessie Wall; however, the call preceded Miss Tessie by at least three decades and appears to have been sounded first in San Francisco in a Sacramento Street brothel run by Madame Bertha Kahn. A large woman with a vibrant contralto voice, she would stride to the foot of the stairs and shout, "Company, girls!"

It had a certain genteel quality compared to such earlier calls as "All whores!" And in fact, Madame Bertha's establishment became one of the most popular of the 1870s. Her girls were dressed in red sandals, matching red velvet caps and long lacey white nightgowns. Unlike other bagnios, Madame Bertha's sold no liquor, and no obscene talk or rough conduct was permitted. Each bedroom bore a sign reading, "No Vulgarity Allowed in This Establishment." It is said that Madame Bertha also introduced to San Francisco charge accounts for regular customers. But she is best remembered for forbidding the prodding and feeling of the merchandise, which was the practice in other houses, and insisting her girls be refined in greeting company and in turn be treated as ladies by the company.

computer crime

Computer crime is the least understood of all illegal activities because it is so new and steeped in a technology not as yet fully developed. The difficulty of detecting computer fraud has attracted many criminal minds. Some known swindles are monumental, such as the 64,000 fake insurance policies created between 1964 and 1973 on the Equity Funding Corp.'s computer. That operation involved $2 billion.

The main weakness in a computer system is that a criminal can perpetrate a fraud once he or she has learned the code or password that will activate the system. In one case a bank employee simply programmed the firm's computer to divert over $120,000 from various customers' accounts to those of two friends. A clever scheme was pulled off by a programmer who ordered a computer to deduct sums from many accounts and credit them to dummy accounts, which he then emptied. In another case a bank employee embezzled more than $1 million to finance his betting on horse racing and basketball games. Ironically, his computer-based system for handicapping the horses proved nowhere near as efficient as his money diversion scheme.

With the discovery of each new method, computer practices are changed to prevent such fraud. Some sophisticated systems use fingerprints or voiceprints as a method of insuring their integrity, and the FBI has computer fraud experts who conduct training seminars for police officers and businessmen to combat this new type of crime. But it is obvious that computer fraud is itself a growth industry.

See also: INTERNET CRIME.

Comstock, Anthony (1844–1915) censor

The "great American bluenose," Anthony Comstock conducted a lifetime crusade against vice—as he saw it. He was responsible for the arrest of at least 3,000 persons for obscenity, destroyed 160 tons of "obscene literature" and got the Department of the Interior to fire Walt Whitman for publishing *Leaves of Grass* and the city of New York to ban Margaret Sanger's books on birth control. He proudly boasted that he had caused 16 persons to be hounded to death, either through fear or suicide, under his relentless attacks. He caused George Bernard Shaw to coin the word *Comstockery*, which is defined in the *American College Dictionary* as "over-zealous censorship of the fine arts and literature, often mistaking outspokenly honest works for salacious productions."

At the age of 18, Comstock started his crusade against sin by breaking into a liquor store in New Canaan, Conn. and opening the spigots on all the kegs.

Throughout the ensuing years, in concert with the Young Men's Christian Association, he launched a campaign against pornography. In 1873 he established the New York Society for the Suppression of Vice and labored as its secretary until his death 42 years later. In that same year Congress passed the Comstock Act, which banned obscene materials, including rubber prophylactics, from the mails. The post office appointed Comstock a special agent charged with enforcing the new law. As a result of his activities, publishers stripped their books of any explicit language, e.g., *pregnant* became *enceinte*.

What constituted pornography or sin was determined by Comstock's fanatical puritanism. Female crusader Victoria Claflin Woodhull was hauled into court for what Comstock considered a "crime," her exposure of a love affair between clergyman Henry Ward Beecher and a parishioner's wife. In 1905 Comstock instituted actions against George Bernard Shaw's play *Mrs. Warren's Profession.* Shaw, who had already invented the word *Comstockery*, warmed to this opportunity to do battle with the censor, declaring: "Comstockery is the world's standing joke at the expense of the U.S. It confirms the deepseated conviction of the Old World that America is a provincial place, a second-rate country town." The resultant publicity made the play a box office sensation. Such was also the case when Comstock leveled his sights at the innocuous nude painting *September Morn*, by Paul Chabas. The publicity generated by Comstock's blasts made the painting a monumental success, after it had been rejected as being too tame for a barber shop calendar.

In 1915 President Woodrow Wilson named Comstock the U.S. representative to the International Purity Congress in San Francisco. Although in failing health, Comstock was a fiery figure at the congress. But he lost a humiliating battle in that city's courts during the congress when he arrested some department-store window dressers for putting clothes on five bare models in full view of passersby. A San Francisco judge listened to the charges the next morning and promptly dismissed the case. "Mr. Comstock," said the judge, "I think you're nuts."

Comstock came back home and died shortly after, on September 21, 1915. He was buried in Brooklyn, New York City, his epitaph reading, "In memory of a fearless witness."

See also: MADAME RESTELL, SEPTEMBER MORN.

confessions

In the "old days," as veteran policemen will admit, the standard way for the police to extract confessions was through the time-honored "third degree." In the 1920s one of New York's legendary cops, Johnny Broderick, imparted the keen deductive processes he used to solve a certain case. "Ah, it was nothing," he said. "All I did was bat around some guys until they told me what I wanted to know." Four decades before that, Chief Inspector Alexander S. Williams, better known as "Clubber" Williams, explained to his men the art of cracking cases with just three words, "Beat, beat, beat."

Some years ago a California police authority once listed the only three possible results of third-degree treatment: the suspect would finally confess to anything, guilty or not; he would go insane; or he would die. Since by the 1930s too much of this had occurred, a presidential fact-finding group known as the Wickersham Commission was assigned to investigate the extent of third-degree practices around the country. Its report of brutal treatment in 29 large cities from coast to coast led to such a public outcry that many police departments finally mended their ways, or at least, forced confessions dropped in a number of cities.

The pattern of reform however, was mixed, particularly because in some cities the practice was more entrenched than in others. Even in recent times the saying in Philadelphia was, "If you get arrested in this town, your only defense may be the telephone company." It was meant literally. According to official findings, one of the methods used by Philadelphia police to question a suspect was to put a telephone book on his head and then hammer on it. Somehow, guilty or not, the record shows quite a few suspects confessed under this treatment.

The record also indicates that telephone book interrogation was not the only one employed by the Philadelphia police. A case in point occurred in October 1975. At that time the family of Radames Santiago was on the alert because of several recent firebombings in their neighborhood and had stationed a 14-year-old youth to keep guard on their tiny porch during the night. At 3:20 one morning a Molotov cocktail, a bottle filled with gasoline and stuffed with a flaming rag, crashed through the window of the house. As the screams of Mrs. Santiago and her four children filled the night, a passerby, 26-year-old Robert "Reds" Wilkinson, returning home from celebrating his first wedding anniversary, rang a fire alarm. By the time the fire engines arrived, the screams had stopped—Mrs. Santiago and her children were dead.

It didn't take the police long to latch on to a suspect. According to an old axiom, an arsonist often turns in the alarm to his own handiwork. That, as far as the police were concerned, pointed the finger of guilt at Wilkinson. The only thing needed was that he be interrogated and make a confession. Wilkinson did not get the telephone book treatment. Instead, before each question someone slapped him hard across the face. Wilkinson, with no police record at all, insisted he did not do the firebombing. Another slap, another question. Then with each slap Wilkinson was warned that unless he confessed, "You'll never see your wife and baby again."

While this was going on, Mrs. Wilkinson was being abused in another room. A police officer constantly screamed at her: "We already know your husband did it. Tell us the truth, or you'll never see your baby again."

Hour after hour the slapping went on. And at the same time, seven other "witnesses" were also being verbally abused and beaten until they gave "evidence" against Wilkinson. They all fell in line, and after nine solid hours of punishment, Wilkinson did the only thing he was by then capable of doing: he confessed.

The case seemed air-tight. The culprit had confessed, and there was a host of witnesses against him. The 14-year-old boy who was standing guard positively identified Wilkinson as the firebomber. Wilkinson was sent to prison for murder and arson, but fortunately for him a later federal investigation cleared him of any involvement in the case. All the witnesses admitted they had been pressured by the police into giving false testimony. The 14-year-old guard had fallen asleep and was too ashamed to admit it; when the police informed him Wilkinson was guilty, he was all too willing to agree with them.

While third-degree confessions obviously still occur, they are definitely on the decline, as much because of the sloppiness of the method as due to public revulsion. J. Edgar Hoover once stated: "My indignation against the third degree arises from practical as well as humanitarian reasons. No matter how viciously they beat and abuse their suspects, the average third-degree officer manages to convict only about one out of every five prisoners whom he takes into court. That is a record of 20 percent efficiency."

In comparison, the FBI's record on confessions has always been phenomenal. An agency that gets about 97 convictions out of every 100 arrests, the FBI has actually gone into court with confessions in up to 94 percent of its cases during some periods. Yet, as American Civil Liberties Union counsel Morris L. Ernst, a veteran of countless battles involving violations of an individual's civil rights has stated, the charge of third degree "is almost never raised against the FBI."

What the FBI employs instead is a psychological approach, often using what is known as the "one-two" or "Mutt-and-Jeff" technique. A typical case was one in which the agency was called when a batch of rifles was stolen from an army post. The military officers had a suspect, the only person who logically could have taken and disposed of the rifles with ease. But they had no proof. The agents knew that to get a confession, they had to find the emotional key to the suspect's mind. Usually, it's love or pride or even a happy memory of a childhood incident.

The agents tried one trick after another but couldn't get the suspect talking. Then the man was asked how long he had been in the army.

"Nine years," the soldier answered with pride.

The FBI men knew they had their angle. Isn't it a joke, one of them said, how the army couldn't even clear up a little matter like some missing rifles without having to call in the FBI. "Does this brass think all we have to do is stuff like this?" The conversation continued to set the pattern of thought that it was almost disloyal for anyone to put the army in such a spot, making it a laughing stock. After about an hour or so, the FBI men left the room and told the company commander to go inside. The soldier saluted him and said: "Sir, I stole those rifles. I wouldn't tell those bastards, but I want to tell you."

Most police forces now use variations of the one-two or Mutt and Jeff to get confessions. The first detective to question the suspect will generally come on strong, talking tough and trying to antagonize or frighten him. His teammate then moves in gently, befriending the suspect. The second man stands out as a friend in a sea of foes and becomes, so to speak, the prisoner's father confessor. Sometimes the friendly detective pretends to be on the outs with the suspect's chief tormentor. He may, if the prisoner's condition has made him so gullible as to believe almost anything, suggest that the tough officer is out for his scalp, trying to boot him off the squad or even off the force. Both he and the suspect are thus kindred souls, oppressed by the same villain. The whole thrust of the approach is to find a way to "stick it to" the enemy detective. The friendly one tells the suspect, "If you are going to confess, say you'll only do it if *he* leaves the room." In the Mutt-and-Jeff technique, this brings on a strong emotional response that can produce a fast confession before the feeling wears off.

Men who have succumbed to the Mutt and Jeff often wonder afterwards what made them "be sucker enough to confess." However, members of the psychiatric fraternity, realizing the effect of the technique, have invented the term *menticide* for this shrewd wearing down of a suspect's mind. Anyone, experts say, can be made to confess to anything if the pressure is great enough.

Even the new tightened rules that require officers to inform a suspect of his right to have counsel present during interrogation can be gotten around by the sort of emotional response evoked by this new-wave type of police questioning, a method that in large part has rendered the third degree obsolete.

See also: CONFESSIONS, FALSE.

confessions, false

In Chicago during the 1950s a pregnant woman was viciously slain and her body dumped in a snowbank. Almost immediately a factory worker came forth and confessed. He stood a good chance of becoming a modern-day lynching victim since a spirit of vengeance dominated the woman's neighborhood. That sentiment dissipated, however, when a 19-year-old sailor at the Great Lakes Naval Station also confessed to the slaying. This second confession turned out to be the real one.

In 1961 a young widow in New York tearfully told police she had killed her husband several years earlier. His death had been attributed to natural causes. The body was exhumed and an autopsy performed. The man had died of natural causes, and psychiatrists found the woman was merely suffering from delusions that stemmed from a guilt complex that she had failed to be a good wife to her late husband.

Both of these persons could easily have been convicted of the crimes to which they so eagerly confessed. Throughout hundreds of years of legal history, the confession has been viewed by the courts and society as the "queen of proofs" of criminal guilt. Yet, each year probably thousands of persons in this country confess to crimes that they did not, and could not, have committed. Why do they do it? Some are neurotics who will confess to any crime just for the excitement of being the center of attention; for example, more than 200 persons confessed to the Lindbergh baby kidnapping. Others are motivated by bizarre guilt feelings for some other incident, often trivial; they seek punishment, consciously or subconsciously, for a crime they did not commit.

Whenever legal experts discuss false confessions, the subject of the mutiny of the *Hermione* is raised. The *Hermione* was a British frigate captained by a harsh disciplinarian named Pigot. In September 1797 the seething anger of the crew erupted against Pigot and his officers. The men of the *Hermione* not only murdered the captain and the officers, they butchered them. The crew then sailed to an enemy port, but one young midshipman escaped and got back to England. He identified many of the offenders, and some of them were run down and hanged.

Many innocent sailors confessed to taking part in the *Hermione* mutiny. One admiralty officer later wrote:

In my own experience, I have known, on separate occasions, more than six sailors who voluntarily confessed to having struck the first blow at Captain Pigot. These men detailed all the horrid circumstances of the mutiny with extreme minuteness and perfect accuracy. Nevertheless, not one of them had even been in the ship, nor had so much as seen Captain Pigot in their lives. They had obtained from their messmates the particulars of the story. When long on a foreign station, hungering and thirsting for home, their minds became enfeebled. At length, they actually believed themselves guilty of the crime over which they had so long brooded, and submitted with a gloomy pleasure to being sent to England in irons for judgment. At the Admiralty, we were always able to detect and establish their innocence.

The last sentiment was, of course, self-serving and perhaps not shared by all. Sir Samuel Romilly related the fate of another seaman who confessed to taking part in the same incident. He was executed. Later, Sir Samuel learned that when the mutiny had taken place on the *Hermione,* the sailor was at Portsmouth aboard the *Marlborough.*

American criminal history is replete with persons confessing to crimes and indeed to noncrimes. The classic case of the latter occurred in Vermont during the 19th century, when two brothers, Stephen and Jesse Boorn, confessed in colorful detail the slaying of Russell Colvin, their brother-in-law. They were both sentenced to death, but Jesse, in recognition of the fact that he had confessed first, had his sentence commuted to life. Stephen's hanging was only postponed when Colvin fortuitously returned home after an absence of seven years, during which time he had had no idea that he had been "murdered."

Probably the great-granddaddy of all cases involving false confessions was the Los Angeles murder of Elizabeth Short in 1947. The case was to become famous as the Black Dahlia murder. The police took full written confessions from at least 38 suspects, and after more than 200 others had telephoned their admissions of guilt and offers to surrender, the police stopped keeping count of confessions.

In the Black Dahlia case the number of confessions was attributable to the sadistic nature of the crime. Such vile crimes invariably produce great numbers of confessions, as though the neurotic confessors literally beg for the spotlight of revulsion and contempt. Many, experts say, are made by persons propelled by a death wish and eager to find the most spectacular method of committing suicide, e.g., in the Black Dahlia case, going to the gas chamber. Others have different motivations. When a girl named Selma Graff was bludgeoned to death by a burglar in Brooklyn during the

1950s, the police got the usual rash of phony confessions. One of them came from a young ex-con out on probation for auto theft. He carried within him a vicious hatred for his mother, who was always so embarrassed by his criminal traits and who at the moment was threatening to notify his parole officer that he had been visiting bars. So he walked into police headquarters and gave himself up for the Graff killing. His story proved to be a hoax when he was unable to supply the murder weapon and could not describe the Graff home accurately. Finally admitting his falsehood, he said he gladly would have gotten himself convicted of the murder, even gone to the chair, in order to torment his mother.

Privately, even some former prosecutors say all confessions should be suspect, that it is illogical to expect that a police officer who has worked hard to extract a confession from a suspect will be just as diligent in his efforts to test whether the confession is true or not. More often, the police and prosecutors have clung to discredited confessions in an effort to convict someone who later proved to be an innocent man. A case in point was George Whitmore, Jr., the man who was wrongly accused of the notorious "career girl" sex slayings of Janice Wylie and Emily Hoffert in their Manhattan apartment in 1963. Whitmore-type incidents, especially repudiated confessions, were cited by the Supreme Court in the landmark Miranda decision, which led to curbs on police powers to interrogate suspects. Some attorneys, such as O. John Rogge, a former assistant attorney general of the United States and author of the book *Why Men Confess,* hold to the theory that no repudiated confession should ever be used in court. They believe that the Supreme Court is gradually moving, perhaps with some steps backward from time to time, in that direction. Quite naturally, prosecuting attorneys claim that such action will make convictions next to impossible to obtain.

See also: BLACK DAHLIA, BOORN BROTHERS, HAROLD ISRAEL, JANICE WYLIE.

Connors, Babe (1856–1918) St. Louis madam

Outside of the bagnios of New Orleans, no brothel contributed more to the arts than the famous St. Louis parlor of a plump mulatto madam named Babe Connors. More than most practitioners of her trade, Babe thought of her places, especially her famous Palace, which she opened in 1898, not only as houses of sexual pleasure but also as centers of entertainment, mostly erotic of course, but musical as well. The Palace itself was a work of art, featuring magnificent crystal chandeliers, extremely expensive rugs, tapestries and objets d'art. Babe staged renowned shows in which her most lovely octoroons danced on a mirrored floor wearing elegant evening gowns and no underclothes. But the highlight of the show was always music and song. For years Babe presented the incredible old black singer Mama Lou. Mama, who wore the traditional calico dress, gingham apron and bright bandana, gave forth with famous downhome field songs and blues. Music-loving whites flocked to Babe Connors' establishment to listen to Mama Lou. Even the great Ignace Paderewski journeyed to hear Mama Lou and accompany her on the parlor piano in the early 1890s. Virtually all of Mama Lou's songs were obscene, but many provided the original melodies for such later hits as "Bully Song" and "Hot Time in the Old Town Tonight."

While Babe Connors' resorts, such as the Palace on Chestnut Street and the earlier Castle on Sixth Street, were among the most lavish in the country, racial law and custom restricted their profit level to about a third or less than what other great houses of the period netted. But even as $5 houses, Babe Connors' famed resorts produced revenues that made her among the most illustrious women of her kind and allowed her to live in fun-loving elegance. Her open carriage was one of the sights at Forest Park, where Babe, bedecked with feathered boa and parasol, rode by in regal splendor, nodding her head only at those gentlemen who acknowledged her first. In her later years Babe converted to Catholicism and, unlike most of her scarlet sisters, was permitted burial in consecrated ground.

conscience fund   anonymous donation money

Every day the U.S. Treasury receives money, often anonymously, from persons who, having stolen or otherwise withheld money from the government, have become conscious-stricken and have decided to pay up. *Conscience money* is the popular term for these sums, although it enters the records as "Miscellaneous receipts: Moneys received from persons unknown." Sums received have varied from as little as 1¢ to $80,000.

One immigrant wrote that he had achieved success in his adopted country and was therefore upset because he had avoided a tax payment of $30 some 30 years previous. He enclosed $50 to cover the payment on the principal plus interest. Most contributors do indeed add the interest. Some go to unusual lengths to make sure their money goes where it truly belongs this time. One man, taking care that the money was not stolen in the mail or up on receipt, cut a total of $250 in half and sent the halves to two separate government bureaus with an explanation of his actions. Another sent in only

a half of each bill and demanded a receipt for these before sending the other half.

Many of the donors to the conscience fund are former government employees weighed down by the knowledge that they illegally appropriated government supplies or money. Other persons confess failing to pay certain taxes and customs duties or even under-stamping mail. Remarkably, very few say their conscience money is to cover income tax underpayments.

The biggest contribution ever made came from an anonymous donor of a total of $80,000. Sending in $30,000 as his final installment, the person wrote:

This amount makes a sum aggregating $80,000 which I have sent the United States, or four times the amount which I stole years ago. I have hesitated about sending all this money because I think it does not really belong to the government, but conscience has given me no rest until I have consummated the four-fold return like Zacchaeus, the Publican of old. That every thief may understand the awfulness of the sin of stealing is the sincere wish of a penitent. Let no one claim any of this amount on any pretext.

When details of this donation were printed, a woman wrote in to claim part of it. She said her husband, a habitual drunkard, was the anonymous donor and had sent in $15,000 too much. She demanded its return. Treasury investigators checked out the woman's claim and found it spurious.

No effort is made by the government to otherwise determine the identity of a donor. The official government position is that it will not prosecute persons making restitution. If requested, it will even mail a formal receipt—with no questions asked. This attitude of non-prosecution is not necessarily all that high minded. It is recognized that if prosecutions were undertaken, the flow of conscience money would cease.

consigliere   Mafia "hearing officer"

The press and various books revealing the "inside" story on organized crime have spread a fundamental misconception about the post of *consigliere* in the Mafia. He is often pictured as the operating brains of a crime family, the adviser to the don, the master planner. The role is far less important. Originally, it was little more than a public relations invention of Lucky Luciano, probably the most brilliant leader the Mafia ever produced.

By 1932 Luciano had risen to the zenith of power, having engineered the murders of Giuseppe "Joe the Boss" Masseria and Salvatore Maranzano on the Night of the Sicilian Vespers. With these killings Luciano became in fact if not in name the new "boss of bosses," a position previously held by Masseria and then Maranzano.

It was now in Luciano's interests to bring the killings to a halt; he therefore announced the establishment of the position of *consigliere,* with one to be named in each crime family. The function of the *consigliere* was that of a hearing officer who would have to clear any plan to knock off a member of the Mafia before a hit could be made. Thus, it would be possible for everyone to get back to plucking the fruits of crime and to reduce intrafamily warfare. If he disapproved because the reasons for the killing were unjust, there would be no hit. It was a marvelous cosmetic device that gave Mafia members a sense of "law and order." In actuality, no hearing officer would ever dare interfere with the orders of the top bosses, and the record shows that none ever has. But the position hangs on to this day, having long ago served Luciano's purposes and fostered an image of himself as Lucky the Just.

contract   mob killing assignment

The word *contract* has graduated from argot into common English. However, underworld murders by hire are arranged through an elaborate technique little understood by the general public. The importance of the use of a contract is the protection it affords the party ordering the execution. He is completely isolated from the trigger man, never talking to him about the job. Instead, he lets the contract to a second party. This person then selects the hit man, or killer. Even this person will sometimes have the order passed by another party. All negotiations are handled one to one so that even if someone in the line of command eventually talks, the authorities still do not have the vital corrobative witness required to make a case against whomever he informs on.

This shrewd procedure protected Albert Anastasia, the Lord High Executioner of Murder, Inc., again and again. The same caution protected the planners of the October 1957 rub-out of Anastasia himself, even though the name of the man who ordered it was no secret to the police. Anastasia was eliminated as part of Vito Genovese's strategy to take control of the major portion of New York crime. In a cunning stroke, Genovese gave the contract to Carlo Gambino, the number two man in Anastasia's crime family. Gambino was ambitious and saw he would ascend to Anastasia's throne if the crime boss was eliminated. Gambino accepted the contract but in turn protected himself by passing it on to Joe Profaci, another top Mafia leader. Profaci then picked as hit men the three brothers,

Crazy Joey, Larry and Albert "Kid Blast" Gallo. It has never been fully established whether Crazy Joey and Larry personally carried out the famed execution of Anastasia in a Manhattan hotel barber shop or whether they merely acted as spotters, pointing out the victim to the person whom they may have passed the hit contract to.

This near-scientific method of parceling out contracts explains why virtually all gang murders end up unsolved. In Chicago from 1919 until February 1, 1967, there were approximately 1,000 gangland executions, but only in 13 of these cases was there a conviction.

convict labor system

Throughout the years and in different jurisdictions, various forms of convict labor systems developed. In the earliest form, manufacturers supplied prisons with raw materials, supervised the work of the convicts and marketed the goods they made. The pay for the convicts' labor went to the state. Then some states switched to piece work, whereby the prison authorities supervised the work and got paid on delivery of the finished products.

Early in the 19th century leasing convicts for work outside prison walls became common, especially in mines and sawmills and for railroad construction. The employers paid a lump sum for the leased workers and were responsible for board and discipline. Excesses and abuses marked this system, as prisoners were generally overworked, underfed and often brutalized. The system continued to grow well into the latter half of the century, when union opposition became fierce and frequently turned violent, more against the outside employers than against the convicts, a notable instance occurring in Tennessee in 1891–92. Consequently, the convict lease system virtually died in the first decade of the 20th century.

Ironically, the working conditions of the convicts did not improve as the prisons switched to turning out goods themselves and, when this foundered because of business opposition, to manufacturing items solely for governmental use. The states proved to be harsh exploiters of convict labor. In the South especially, states found a new outlet for leasing, providing convicts to the counties for road construction. This produced the great excesses of the Southern chain gangs. Since World War II, when most chain gang abuses ended, convicts have labored producing goods for the use of the state and other political subdivisions. The prisoners are paid only enough to buy cigarettes or candy, an irritant said to be the cause of much convict discontent. Reformers insist this dissatisfaction will continue until prisoners' pay is raised enough to let them provide some assistance to their families.

See also: CHAIN GANGS, CONVICT LEASE BATTLES.

convict lease battles

Probably few methods of strikebreaking during the 19th century aroused the ire of unionists more than that of the convict lease system, whereby employers could rent convict labor from the state whenever faced with a work stoppage.

The procedure was in very wide use in Tennessee, where it always set off violent conflicts with civilian workers. One of the state's greatest confrontations was an escalating battle during 1891–92. In Briceville mine owners leased 40 convicts to take over a mine idled by a strike and had them rip down the miners' houses and erect a stockade for themselves. Ten days later, on July 15, 1891, 300 heavily armed miners overwhelmed the stockade, marched the convicts, their guards and some management officials to the railroad station and put them on a train to Knoxville. The following day the convicts were brought back, escorted by 125 militiamen led personally by the governor. Outrage spread through the surrounding area, and on July 20 a force of 2,000 miners confronted the militia and again succeeded in marching them and the convicts to the depot and sending them all back to Knoxville. The governor responded by sending in 600 militiamen, but a truce was agreed upon to allow the legislature to hold a special session for the purpose of repealing the convict lease law. Under lobbying by business interests, however, the legislators failed to act, and the miners returned to the use of force. In early October they evicted several hundred convicts and burned three stockades to the ground. In December the governor brought the convicts back and had Fort Anderson built. This was a permanent military barracks, guarded by 175 troopers and a Gatling gun and surrounded by trenches. Matters festered for the next several months, while the nation's attention focused on the great Homestead steel strike in Pennsylvania. In August 1892 similar trouble developed at the Oliver Springs mine in Anderson County. When miners marched on the convicts' stockade, the guards fired and several miners were wounded. Miners poured into the area, marched on the stockade again and forced the guards to lay down their arms. The strikers followed their usual practice of burning the facility to the ground and returning the convicts and their guards to Knoxville. The miners then marched on Fort Anderson and placed it under siege. The arrival of 500 soldiers routed the miners, and they were taken into custody and locked up in churches, schoolhouses and railroad cars. The

revolt had been crushed but local juries soon released all the miners. It was clear that resistance was too great to the convict lease system and that it could not be made to work; soon thereafter, it was abolished.

Cook, David J. (1842–1907) lawman

A remarkable western crime fighter, Dave Cook never achieved the press of an Earp, Hickok or Masterson, but it was not for lack of trying. His memoirs, published in 1882 under the title of *Hands Up! or Twenty Years of Detective Work in the Mountains and on the Plains,* is an almost incredible account of robbery, shoot-outs and bloodletting that stakes his claim to being one of the most violent characters of the West, even allowing for a certain amount of exaggeration. Cook did make a total of 3,000 arrests, many, of course, for minor offenses, and that meant contending with a lot of quick tempers and quick triggers.

Cook was born in Indiana in 1842, and after working as a farmhand in the corn belt, he moved on to Colorado in 1859. Joining the Colorado Cavalry in the Civil War, he was assigned to detective duty tracking spies, gold smugglers and the like and earned himself enough of a reputation to become city marshal of Denver in 1866. Subsequently, he served as a federal marshal and later as a range private eye. Cook was credited with almost single-handedly wiping out the Musgrove-Franklin gang that terrorized Colorado in the 1860s, running down Musgrove in 1868 and holding him in jail to lure Franklin into a rescue attempt. Franklin arrived in Denver with that idea in mind, but Cook learned he was hiding out in the Overland Hotel and burst into his room to find the outlaw lying on the bed with nothing on except a pair of long johns and a gun belt. When Franklin went for his piece, Cook, to use his own words, sent "a ball crashing through his very heart."

If Cook had a failing, it appears to have been a singular propensity to lose his prisoners to lynchers. But that may have been one of his maxims for staying alive. Another was, "Never hit a man over the head with a pistol, because afterward you may want to use your weapon and find it disabled." Thanks to such rules, one of the most gunfight-prone lawmen the West ever saw was able to die with his boots off. He passed away on April 2, 1907.

See also: LEE H. MUSGROVE.

Cook, Dr. Frederick A. (1865–1940) explorer and land fraud conspirator

Dr. Frederick A. Cook is most famous for his dispute with Commodore Robert E. Peary over who was the first to reach the North Pole. For a brief time, Dr. Cook was hailed throughout the world after announcing he had reached the North Pole. However, shortly thereafter, Peary made the same claim and labeled all of Cook's claims false. In the controversy that followed, Peary clearly gained the upper hand, and Cook was to keep only a few believers. He returned home disheartened and in disgrace, and things were to get worse for him. In the 1920s Cook's name was used to promote a Texas oil-land sale that was branded fraudulent. While there was much reason to believe that Cook was not an active member of the fraud, he had a famous name and thus made an excellent target. He was convicted of using the mails to defraud and sentenced to 14 years. After working as a prison doctor in Leavenworth, he was released in 1931. Considering that the lands in question were now selling at prices well above the so-called fraud figure, it would indeed have been unseemly to hold him longer. President Franklin D. Roosevelt granted Dr. Cook a presidential pardon shortly before the latter's death in 1940.

Cook, William (1929–1952) mass murderer

Few mass murderers have ever gone on a worse bloodletting spree than the one 21-year-old Billy Cook launched on December 30, 1950. On that day, Cook, posing as a hitchhiker, forced a motorist at gunpoint to get into the trunk of his own car and then drove off. Over the next two weeks Cook went on a senseless killing rampage. He kidnapped nearly a dozen people, including a deputy sheriff; murdered six in cold blood, including three children; attempted other killings; and generally terrorized the Southwest border area.

A hell raiser as a child, Cook was in and out of reform schools. He sported a tattooed letter between the knuckle and first joint of each finger of each hand, and when he held his hands together, the letters spelled H-A-R-D-L-U-C-K, an obvious form of self-pity that in retrospect psychologists said fostered a feeling of persecution. He clearly turned this feeling outward, even shrieking to his lawyer in the San Quentin death house, "I hate them; I hate their guts—everybody!"

Cook exhibited that feeling from the moment he kidnapped his first victim, a motorist, near Lubbock, Tex. Luckily for the motorist, he was able to force open the trunk and escaped on a small road. Far less lucky was the family of Carl Mosser. Mosser, his wife, Thelma, and their three small children were on a motor trip from Illinois to New Mexico when they picked up the killer. Cook soon produced a gun and forced Mosser to drive on. Following the gunman's mercurial directions, they went to Carlsbad, N.M., to El Paso, to Houston. After a time, Cook shot and killed all five of them and, for good measure, the family dog. He dumped their bodies in an abandoned mine shaft just outside Joplin, Mo.

Eventually, the Mossers' car was found abandoned near Tulsa, Okla. The car was a complete shambles, the upholstery bloodsoaked and ripped open by bullets. Then their bodies were discovered. But Cook left something in the car besides bullets, a receipt for a gun he had bought. The killer's identity was learned and a massive manhunt was launched. Cook headed for California and there kidnapped a deputy sheriff who had almost captured him. He forced the deputy to drive him around while he bragged about killing the Mosser family.

After a 40-mile ride in the deputy's car, Cook ordered the lawman to stop. "Out," he ordered his prisoner. Then he forced the deputy to lie down in a gully and tied his hands behind him. "I won't bother to tie your feet because I'm going to put a bullet through your head anyway," Cook said.

The mass murderer was just having his joke. He drove off as the officer waited for the shot that would kill him. A short time later, Cook stopped another motorist, Robert Dewey, whom he did kill. With the alarm for him covering the western half of the country, Cook headed into Mexico, kidnapping two other men. In the little town of Santa Rosalía, 400 miles below the border, Cook, with his hostages in tow, was recognized

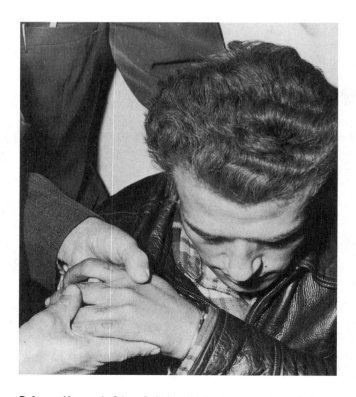

Police officers hold up left hand of mass murderer Billy Cook to show "Hard Luck" tattoo across his fingers.

by the police chief. The officer simply walked up to Cook, snatched a gun from the killer's belt and placed him under arrest. Cook was rushed back to the border and turned over to FBI agents. On December 12, 1952 he died in the gas chamber at San Quentin for the Dewey murder.

Cookson Hills, Oklahoma   outlaw hideout

Ranking with such outlaw refuges as Hole in the Wall and Robber's Roost, the Cookson Hills of Oklahoma have harbored badmen of all kinds over the last two centuries.

With its endless peaks and twisted gullies, the Cooksons have served as the hideout for the Bandit Queen, Belle Starr, and, in this century, for public enemy Pretty Boy Floyd. In 1979 the hills again made the news when a 57-year-old army air corps deserter from World War II came out after hiding there for 36 years. Pvt. D. B. Benson had hidden in one abandoned shack or temporary shelter after another ever since going AWOL from the service in June 1943. From time to time he roamed the woods and mountains into Arkansas but was rarely seen. While newsmen were amazed at his feat, lawmen were not. "A lawbreaker can get lost in those hills for all his life and live off the land without ever being caught," one said.

Cooley, Scott   (1845–?)   Texas Ranger and murderer

The man who ignited the Mason County War of 1875, Scott Cooley is often cited as the type of gunslinger who never should have been a Texas Ranger. To be fair to the Rangers, it should be pointed out that Cooley's major offenses occurred after he left that organization, where his record was nondescript. Cooley had been attracted to big money, which in Texas during the 1870s meant cattle money, and he became close with a number of cattlemen, including Timothy Williamson of Mason County.

In September 1875 Williamson was shot to death by a mob as he was being taken to jail for rustling by Deputy Sheriff John Worley. This was the official start of the Mason County War, although it might have ended there. Most similar wars in the Old West generally sprang from obvious monetary motives, such as cattleman vs. cattleman, or vs. sheep man, or vs. homesteader. If the Mason County warfare began that way, it soon became a matter of friends choosing sides. Williamson was Cooley's friend, and the latter blamed Worley for being involved in the killing. Riding to the lawman's home, he shot him dead and then cut off his ears, which he showed around as an example of what awaited all the anti-Williamsons in the county. Cooley

was good to his word, and several more murders were attributed to him and his friends, just as others were linked to Williamson's enemies. About a year later, the Texas Rangers were sent in and the fighting ended. But Cooley never was brought to justice for his crimes. What happened to him is not known, although there was talk that he was killed in 1876. However, the record shows the Rangers continued to hunt for him long after that, without success.

See also: FRANK JONES, MASON COUNTY WAR, TEXAS RANGERS.

Coons, William   (1838–1881)   murderer and western lynch victim

The "stringing up" of William Coons, a relatively minor outlaw in the Old West, was, besides having a touch of rather macabre humor, illustrative of the region's theory and practice of lynching, which was that the man with the fewest friends got hanged more readily.

Coons, a homesteader, spent two years working his land in Lincoln County, N.M. without incident; the only bad mark against him during this time was a suspicion that he was doing a spot of rustling and hog stealing on the side. Then in 1881 Coons got into a dispute with John Flemming, a neighbor, over water rights. One day in April he rode over to Flemming's place and shot him dead. Since Flemming was hit in the chest, Coons claimed that Flemming had gone for his gun first. In point of fact, according to witnesses, Coons drew on Flemming and started shooting while his neighbor's back was turned. After Coons missed several shots, Flemming turned around and was hit full in the chest. However, when Sheriff Pat Garrett investigated, the witnesses couldn't be found, having fled out of fear of Coons. Flemming's friends started some lynch talk, but Coons had his supporters, and the matter became a Mexican standoff. The following month Coons celebrated his 43rd birthday with about a dozen supporters. Quite a few other apparent well-wishers showed up at Coons' home, and it appeared the Flemming people had decided to let the past be forgotten. When the Coons people were "plastered good," the Flemming forces all drew guns, herded the drunken celebrants into a bedroom and locked them up. Bill Coons suddenly found himself facing an impromptu court, with the evidence of the eyewitnesses now presented against him. He was found guilty and sentenced to be hanged forthwith from a tree outside his house. Since it was Coons' birthday, however, the members of the court and jury felt obliged to help the condemned man finish off the party's supply of whiskey. Then, in further deference to the occasion, an improvised band formed to play at the hanging. Since there were more Flemming supporters than Coons' men in Lincoln County, no arrests were ever made for the lynching.

See also: LYNCHING.

"Cooper, D. B." (?–?) legendary airline hijacker

A hijacker who commandeered an airliner, collected a $200,000 ransom and then apparently parachuted to earth, "D. B. Cooper" achieved folk hero status in the Pacific Northwest. His daring 1971 exploit made him the perpetrator of the nation's only unsolved skyjacking. D. B. Cooper T-shirts were sold, and books about his crime were written. The community of Ariel, Wash., near the spot where Cooper was believed to have landed, has held annual daylong celebrations on the anniversary of the crime.

On Thanksgiving eve 1971, a man calling himself D. B. Cooper bought a ticket for a Northwest Orient Airlines flight from Portland, Ore. to Seattle, Wash. Once airborne, Cooper, wearing dark glasses, told a flight attendant he had a bomb in his briefcase and demanded $200,000 in $20 bills and four parachutes. After the plane, a 727 Trijet, landed in Seattle, the hijacker released the 36 passengers and all but three of the crew upon receipt of the ransom money. He then ordered the 727 be flown to Reno, Nev. When the plane landed in Reno, there was no trace of Cooper, but the rear exit door under the tail was open. The FBI theorized that Cooper, dressed only in a business suit and street shoes, jumped from the plane over southwest Washington into a howling wind and a freezing rain.

Did D. B. Cooper survive? Although the FBI never said so officially, it was known to have felt that the hijacker-extortionist had most likely perished in the plunge. However, no body has ever been found. The $200,000 in ransom had been paid in marked bills, none of which turned up until 1980, when a few thousand dollars was discovered partially buried along the north bank of the Columbia River near Vancouver, Wash. The bills had been dug up by children playing in the sand during a family picnic. It was unclear whether the money had been buried there or washed downstream years ago from a Columbia River tributary. While the find reinvigorated the investigation of the case, the true believers in D. B. Cooper refused to accept the theory that the money had been blown away when Cooper died on impact. They felt it could have been lost or, because it was a small portion of the loot, deliberately discarded by Cooper in an effort to make it appear he had not survived. Obviously, as far as the legend goes, until a body is found and identified, D. B. Cooper lives!

cooping police sleeping on duty

Few rule infractions are more common on major city police forces than that of sleeping on duty.

In 1969 a major exposé in New York City revealed that the custom was so ritualized that some officers showed up for the duty lineup armed with pillows and alarm clocks. Newspapers ran pictures of police officers sleeping in patrol cars in Brooklyn's Fort Greene Park. The practice is known as "cooping" in New York and has different names in other localities. In Boston on-duty carnapping is known as "holing," and in Atlanta policemen have been described as seeking out "pits," usually in lovers' lanes or in a tunnel under the city. An investigation of "huddling" in Washington, D.C. revealed that a harassed headquarters could only awaken drowsy officers by activating the shrill buzzers on their walkie-talkies.

Cooping has been a problem ever since there have been police forces in this country. The earliest form of protection in most cities in this country was a guardian of the peace, often a private citizen drafted for the chore, who was little more than a night watchman assigned to patrol a given area. He was provided with a small wooden shanty in which to take short respites from the weather, and of course, many slept on the job. It became a favorite sport of the young bloods of the 17th and 18th centuries to sneak up on such a cooper, bind the shed with rope and uproot it and then drag it away a goodly distance, much to the guard's embarrassment and disgrace among his neighbors.

The highest-ranking police officer ever charged with the offense of cooping in New York was a Brooklyn police captain, who was allegedly caught napping while on duty in 1980. Facing charges of "conduct unbecoming an officer," he submitted his resignation. Earlier that year a lieutenant was suspended for sleeping on duty, becoming for a time the highest-ranking officer caught cooping. Two months later, 11 officers in a station house were charged with snoozing on the job. In 1978 six other New York City officers had been found guilty of the charge and given fines ranging from $1,052 to $2,880.

While most officers deny it vehemently, some experts view the two-man police car as the worst invitation possible to cooping, since one officer can remain by the car radio while the other goes off to snooze.

Copeland, James (c. 1815–1857) land pirate and hired killer

The most feared outlaw in Mississippi during the 1840s, James Copeland bossed a vicious gang of "land pirate" highwaymen and hired killers, yet was welcomed within a certain strata of high society in the state. This resulted from his performing several "chores" for one of the state's most arrogant, powerful and corrupt families, the Wages, great landowners around Augusta.

Being under the protection of the Wages gave Copeland virtual immunity from the law, but he finally committed an act so brazen that he had to be arrested. When Gale H. Wages and another man were killed by one James Harvey, the elder Wages paid Copeland $1,000 to avenge his son's death. Taking on the chore eagerly, Copeland shot Harvey in the head on July 15, 1848. However, he was identified as the killer, quickly tried, convicted and sentenced to be hanged. That Old Man Wages had paid Copeland to do the job was common knowledge, but Copeland refused to say anything and for his silence won the full support of the Wages clan. He thus stayed alive for nine years, such being the power of the family. Even when he was finally executed on October 30, 1857, the famed land pirate said nothing to implicate any of the Wages in his crime.

copper slang for policeman

The origin of the word *copper*, referring to a police officer, most probably goes back to Jacob Hays, the first high constable of New York City in the early 19th century, who introduced the badge system for policemen.

According to Detective Alfred Young, official historian of the New York Police Department: "The badge then was a five-pointed star. Different metals were used for different ranks. Brass was for patrolmen, silver for lieutenants and captains, gold for the commissioner. But everybody with a beef always went to the sergeant. He was the guy with the copper star. So whenever a problem came up, they just said, 'Take it to the copper,' and the name just sort of stuck."

Coppola, Michael "Trigger Mike" (1904–1966)
syndicate gangster

Trigger Mike Coppola was successful in the Luciano-Genovese crime family because he was a raging sadist and thus an excellent enforcer.

When Vito Genovese fled a possible murder rap and Luciano was sent to prison in the 1930s, Coppola ran much of the crime family's rackets, including the lush artichoke racket, levying an underworld tribute on the vegetable no Italian family wanted to do without, and a goodly portion of the Harlem numbers racket. He was said to net something around $1 million a year. An oft-told underworld tale concerns the time Coppola woke up in the middle of the night remembering he had left a package in the freezer of one of his favorite night spots.

A hurried phone call brought the package to his door and he spent the rest of the night thawing out $219,000 of mob money, which he had to dispense in the morning.

There is considerable evidence that Coppola would do anything and kill anybody to advance his fortunes or protect himself. His first wife, according to the subsequent testimony of his second wife, Ann, happened to overhear her husband discussing with another gangster the impending murder of a Republican political worker, Joseph Scottoriggio. She was called to testify against her husband in the case, but her appearance was postponed because of her impending pregnancy. She gave birth to a baby daughter and conveniently died afterward in her hospital bed. Coppola's second wife later charged that Trigger Mike had her killed to prevent her from talking.

Ann Coppola's marriage to Trigger Mike was a nightmare highlighted by mental and physical abuse. At their honeymoon party Coppola took a shot at her for the entertainment of the guests. In 1960 Ann discovered her husband was giving drugs to her teenage daughter by a prior marriage. She filed for divorce and testified in an income tax case against Coppola, who sent strongarm men to kidnap and beat her up. She was found badly mauled on an isolated beach, recovered and continued to testify against him. Finally, Trigger Mike gave in and pleaded guilty; he was sent to Atlanta Penitentiary.

Ann Coppola, who had squirreled away something like $250,000 of Trigger Mike's underworld money, fled to Europe to escape the mob's hit men. In Rome in 1962 Ann Coppola stopped running. She wrote a last letter to Internal Revenue, addressing certain portions of it to Attorney General Robert F. Kennedy. She penned a farewell to Trigger Mike as well, saying: "Mike Coppola, someday, somehow, a person or God or the law shall catch up with you, you yellow-bellied bastard. You are the lowest and biggest coward I have had the misfortune to meet." Then she wrote in lipstick on the wall above her hotel bed: "I have always suffered, I am going to kill myself. Forget me." She took a dozen sleeping pills and lapsed quietly into death.

Trigger Mike was released from prison the following year and died in 1966 of natural causes.

Coppolino, Dr. Carl (1933–) murderer

Two of the most sensational murder trials in the 1960s involved Dr. Carl Coppolino, an anesthesiologist charged with murdering his wife and, in a separate case, a male patient with whose wife he had had an affair.

The doctor was the first alleged to have used succinylcholine chloride to commit a murder. The drug commonly was used during operations to keep patients' muscles from trembling; an excessive dose could paralyze the muscles of the lungs, causing death. However, saying that and proving it in court were two different matters because when injected into the body, succinylcholine chloride broke down into its component parts and, for all practical purposes, disappeared.

Coppolino had given up his practice in anesthesiology at the age of 30, retiring because of heart trouble. Although the insurance company in time would become suspicious that he was faking his ailment, it paid him benefits of $22,000 a year. Coppolino and his wife moved from New Jersey to Sarasota, Fla., where they lived rather comfortably. Carmela Coppolino was a doctor herself, and between her practice and Carl's insurance payments, they had no trouble making ends meet, including covering the cost of a new $65,000 insurance policy taken out on Carmela's life. In 1965 Carmela died. A local doctor who knew Coppolino was some kind of expert on heart problems accepted his word that Carmela had had such an ailment and put down heart attack as the cause of her death.

Perhaps the matter would have ended there had Coppolino not married a 38-year-old divorcée named Mary Gibson. Hearing of the marriage, an older woman named Marjorie Farber, a widow then living in Sarasota who had been a neighbor of the Coppolinos in New Jersey, came forward and accused the doctor of killing his first wife. He had also, she said, killed her husband in 1963. According to Marge Farber, she and Coppolino had carried on a torrid love affair, and because he was jealous of her husband, the doctor had murdered him. She said she had watched the whole thing. Coppolino gave Farber, a retired army colonel, an injection of some drug that was supposed to kill him. When it failed to take effect quickly enough, the doctor took a bed pillow and smothered the unconscious man. The death was passed off as coronary thrombosis.

After an extensive investigation, Dr. Coppolino was indicted for murder both in Florida and New Jersey. He was tried first in the Farber case but won an acquittal. No trace of any poison had been found in the dead man's body, and the only testimony against the doctor came from a scorned woman.

Florida authorities decided to press their case, which, on the surface at least, looked weaker. There was no eyewitness to the alleged crime, and there appeared to be no proof as to the cause of death. The Florida trial was dominated by scientific evidence. Dr. Milton Helpern, the New York City medical examiner, did an autopsy on Carmela's body and found that she had been in good health and had not suffered a heart attack. He also found that she had been given an injection in her left buttock just prior to death. Next, Dr. Joseph Umberger, the toxicologist in the Medical Examiner's Office took over, attempting to identify any poison in Carmela Coppolino's body. Dr. Umberger set about finding a method to identify the drug succinylcholine chloride—or its component parts—in the corpse in quantities or qualities that could only be explained by an injection. For six months he worked with tissue from the victim's liver, kidneys, brain and other organs and finally, using spectrography, found succinic acid, one of the components of the drug, in her brain.

Dr. Umberger was on the witness stand for two and a half days, mostly under withering cross-examination by the defense, which contended that succinic acid is present in every brain. Dr. Umberger agreed but pointed out that such acid is "bound," that is, tied to the proteins and perhaps other substances in human tissue. But the type of succinic acid Dr. Umberger had discovered in the woman's body was "unbound," or what he preferred to call "store-bought," and this could only have gotten there by injection.

Coppolino was found guilty of second-degree murder and given a life sentence.

Corbett, Boston (1822–?) killer of John Wilkes Booth

An army sergeant named Boston Corbett, whose name has always figured prominently in logical or illogical Lincoln conspiracy plots, was one of the pursuers of John Wilkes Booth, the man who assassinated the president. When Booth was trapped in a tobacco-curing barn near Port Royal, Va., Corbett shot and killed him after the structure was set afire. Did Corbett shoot Booth because, as he claimed, God had told him to or because he was part of a conspiratorial cover-up, as some later investigators claimed? There is little doubt that Corbett suffered from serious disorders that led to further unstable behavior and criminality. He later castrated himself so that he might better "resist sin." After he fired two pistols into a crowded session of the Kansas legislature, Corbett was committed to a mental institution. He escaped and vanished from sight forever.

Corey, Giles (1612–1692) Salem witchcraft trial victim

Of all the victims of the Salem witchcraft hysteria, none died a worse death than 80-year-old Giles Corey. Corey made a strange martyr. Like most people of his day, he believed in evil spirits and had originally accused his wife of witchcraft. However, when he himself was

A soldier with mental problems, Boston Corbett was credited with shooting John Wilkes Booth after the assassination of President Abraham Lincoln, and since that time he has figured in a number of Lincoln conspiracy theories.

accused in the madness, he protested by contemptuous silence. Under English law a defendant had three chances to plead, and if he did not, he or she could not be tried but was subject to a judicial sentence of death. Giles entered the court and stood mute, causing the judges to order a judicial finding. He was stretched out on the ground and weights were placed on his chest. Nevertheless, he refused to utter a word for the two days he suffered before dying. Only near the end did he gasp, "More weight!" so that he might die sooner. After Corey's death the townspeople's uneasiness about the trials turned to revulsion, and his demise hastened the end of the witchcraft trials.

Corey's fate has been portrayed in Arthur Miller's play *The Crucible* and in a ballad written in 1692. The latter goes in part:

> *"Giles Corey," said ye Magistrates,*
> *"What hast thou hearde to pleade,*
> *To those who now accuse thy soule*
> *Of Crymes and horrid Deed?"*

> *Giles Corey he sayde not a Word,*
> *No single Word spake he;*
> *"Giles Corey," sayeth ye Magistrates,*
> *"We'll press it out of thee!"*

> *They got them then a heavy Beam*
> *They layde it on his Breast,*
> *They loaded it with heavy Stones,*
> *And hard upon him presst.*

> *"More weight!" now sayde this wretched Man,*
> *"More weight" again he cryde,*
> *And he did not Confession make*
> *But wickedly, he dyed.*

See also: SALEM WITCHCRAFT TRIALS.

Further reading: *Capital Punishment, U.S.A.* by Elinor Lander Horwitz.

Corll, Dean (1940–1973) mass murderer

Many people who knew Dean Corll of Houston, Tex. thought of him as a friendly sort of guy, but there was another Dean Corll, a homosexual murderer of at least 27 young boys in that city's "crime of the century" during the early 1970s. Corll used two teenage boys, Elmer Wayne Henley and David Brooks, to steer young victims to him. They would get the victim drunk and then Corll would take over.

The victim would revive to find himself stripped naked, gagged and spread-eagled on a plywood plank. His legs and arms would be secured by handcuffs and nylon ropes. A radio would be going full blast and there would be plastic sheeting on the floor to take care of the blood. Sometimes Corll would kill his victim in as little as 10 minutes, but other times he'd stretch it out for as long as 24 hours or even more. On occasions, perversely, he would suddenly cut the boy loose and explain, laughing, that he was just kidding, seeing if he could scare the youth. But for the murder victims, there was a wooden "body box" on hand in which the slain boys were transported to a city boat shed, a Gulf Coast beach or a wooded area in East Texas for disposal.

On August 7, 1973, 17-year-old Henley shot and killed Corll in self-defense because of fear the sadistic murderer intended to turn on him and Brooks. The police investigation soon implicated Henley and Brooks in the murderous reign of terror, and the pair admitted they had been paid from $5 to $10 for each adolescent boy they had recruited for Corll. For their parts in the crimes, Brooks, convicted on one count, got life imprisonment and Henley, convicted on nine counts, got a total of 594 years. By then the Houston police had recovered somewhat from the criticism heaped on them when the murders were discovered. In most cases, when the victims were reported missing to the police, worried relatives had been informed they had probably run off and "joined those hippies in California."

Henley, who was not charged in the Corll killing, won a new trial in 1979 but was convicted for a second time.

Cornett, Brack (1859–1888) western outlaw

A little-remembered south Texas bank and train robber, Brack Cornett, a fast-shooting cowboy from

Louisiana, deserves recognition as a criminal far ahead of his time. He was the most advanced of the western outlaws at "casing" a job and plotting an escape route, especially compared to the prevailing criminal technique of shoot-'em-up-and-ride. Cornett would have his gang travel the escape route several times, noting each possible cut-off, a method not seen again in bank robbing until the 20th-century days of Baron Lamm, John Dillinger and the Barkers. Because he was a pioneer, Cornett's modus operandi stood out like a sore thumb and led to his downfall. His gang was seen riding hell-for-leather near Pearsall, Tex. by a rancher who suspected they had just pulled something. He reported them but no crime had been committed, and they were written off as some cowpokes in a hurry. When a train was robbed a few days later and the gang rode off hell-for-leather in the direction of Pearsall, the report was recalled. It took sheriff's deputies a while to track down some fast riders, but on February 12, 1888 they located Cornett hiding out on a ranch near Pearsall and, when he refused to surrender, killed him in a spirited gunfight.

Corona, Juan (1934) mass murderer

A Mexican labor contractor who had started out as a migrant fruit picker, Juan Corona was convicted of the murder of 25 migrant workers in 1970-71, becoming labeled as the greatest captured mass killer in California history. (There is speculation that the uncaptured "Zodiac Killer" may have killed almost twice as many people.)

All Corona's victims were transient laborers between the ages of 40 and 68. They had been mutilated, usually with a machete, and buried in peach orchards and along a river bank in Yuba County. Unfortunately for Corona, some of his bank deposit slips and receipts had apparently been found buried with some of the victims, leading the authorities directly to him.

Bloodstained weapons and clothing were found in his home, including two butcher's knives, a machete, a pistol, a jacket and some shorts. The most sensational evidence, however, was what the prosecution called Corona's "death list," a ledger containing the names of many of the victims with a date after them.

In January 1973 Corona was found guilty and sentenced to 25 consecutive life terms, a somewhat meaningless exercise in overkill since he technically would become eligible for parole in 1980. Later that year he was attacked in his prison cell and stabbed 32 times, causing him to lose the sight of one eye. In 1978 a new trial was ordered for Corona on the grounds that his lawyer had failed to provide him with an adequate defense by not presenting what the appeals court called

an "obvious" insanity plea. The court emphasized it did not doubt the correctness of the guilty verdict, but it insisted Corona was entitled to an insanity defense. Corona was sent to a mental facility for observation to see if he could eventually be put on trial again. In the early 1980s he was still there and was found guilty again.

corpus delicti

Technically, a corpus delicti refers to "the body of the crime," which in homicide cases means first that death has occurred and second that the death was caused by a criminal agency. Typical of the laws in other states, the New York penal law demands the following in all homicide cases: "No person can be convicted of murder or manslaughter unless the death of the person alleged to have been killed and the fact of the killing by the defendant, as alleged, are each established as independent facts; the former by direct proof, and the latter beyond a reasonable doubt."

Naturally, a number of murderers have escaped prosecution because they succeeded in getting rid of the body *without anyone seeing it*. The law is not required to produce the actual body, however, if it can produce witnesses who saw the body and can thus testify that a crime had been committed. In one case neighbors heard shooting in a Bronx luncheonette and saw several men carry a body from the establishment to a car. Although the body was never found, the testimony of the witnesses was sufficient to prove that a murder had occurred. A corpus delicti can also be proved if bone or body fragments necessary to human life can be identified.

Cortez, Gregorio (1875–1916) fugitive

Mexicans in Texas still sing the "Ballad of Gregorio Cortez." In the song, the hero, pistol in hand, defiantly declares, "Ah, so many mounted Rangers just to take one Mexican!"

Cortez came to Texas with his family when he was 12. He worked as a ranch hand until he and his brother took over a farm. In 1901 the Karnes County sheriff came to arrest the brothers on charges of horse stealing. Gregorio Cortez denied the charges and refused to surrender. The sheriff opened fire and wounded his brother. Gregorio then shot and killed the sheriff. Fearing Texas justice, which was undoubtedly prejudiced in its treatment of Mexicans, Cortez fled. He was to fight off posse after posse, some with up to 300 men, that tried to take him. The chase covered more than 400 miles. During it he became a hero to his compatriots, fighting for his and their rights. A posse caught Cortez close to the Mexican border and in the ensuing battle he killed another sheriff.

The legal battle on Cortez's behalf lasted four years, with hundreds of Mexicans contributing to his defense fund. They looked upon Cortez's act as a protest against American injustice. He was cleared in the killing of the first sheriff but sentenced to life imprisonment for killing the second. Protests continued until in 1913, at the age of 38, he was freed. He died three years later but the "Ballad of Gregorio Cortez" preserves his memory.

Cortina, Juan (1824–1892) bandit and Mexican patriot

Juan Cortina, a Mexican born on the Texas side of the Rio Grande, was, in the view of Anglo Texans, one of the worst bandits that state had ever seen. In the Mexican view, he was a daring patriot unafraid to stand up to the *gringos* who stole everything the Mexicans had.

Cortina was heir to a huge spread that spanned both sides of the Rio Grande; as such, he became a leader of the Mexican community. Mexicans and Mexican property were fair game in Texas, and land grabbers began whittling away at the Cortina spread. By the time Cortina had reached manhood, he had killed a number of these land grabbers, and there was a warrant out for his arrest.

Cortina was living on the family ranch near Brownsville, but although it was no mystery where he was, no one seemed too interested in invading that stronghold to take him. On September 13, 1859 he came upon the marshal of Brownsville brutally beating a former employee of the Cortina ranch. He wounded the officer and helped the beaten Mexican to escape. Brownsville boiled over this "greaser insult," and there was talk of going out and capturing Cortina. Instead, on September 28 Cortina, at the head of an army of 1,000 cutthroats, captured Brownsville. According to the Texan version, Cortina then summarily executed several men. The Mexican version was that the only killings occurred while Brownsville was being seized. What is not in dispute is that Cortina held the town for ransom, demanding $100,000 under threat of burning it to the ground. Eventually, influenced by less volatile members of his family, he relented, withdrawing to the town limits and keeping it under siege. A Brownsville citizen slipped through the cordon and summoned aid in the form of U.S. troops, Texas Rangers and civilian volunteers. Cortina and his men routed this force in a battle at Palo Alto, but by December 1859 he was compelled to keep constantly on the move, harassed by superior forces. Still, Cortina was able to capture Edinburg, and then Rio Grande City, from which he extracted a ransom of $100,000 in gold. By Christmas Day a large contingent of Texas Rangers was able to force Cortina across the border into Mexico, but neither the Rangers nor the U.S. Army was able to keep him from periodically raiding far into Texas over the next several years.

Cortina and his men were regarded by Texans as that state's worst cattle rustlers, making off with an estimated 900,000 animals in their raids. From the Mexican viewpoint, Cortina was merely making up in a small degree for the cattle previously stolen from Mexicans. During his later years in Mexico, Cortina's fortunes ran to extremes. He was a general in the army of President Benito Juárez and then served as military governor of the state of Tamaulipas. In 1875, with the emergence of the Díaz regime, Cortina was imprisoned and remained there until 1890. He lived out the last two years of his life in retirement on the border with Texas.

See also: LEANDER H. MCNELLY.

Cosa Nostra

The Mafia, pure and simple, by another name: Cosa Nostra—literally, "Our Thing." For many years FBI chief J. Edgar Hoover insisted there was no such thing as organized crime or the Mafia. Says crime historian Richard Hammer, "In order to get Hoover off the hook, a new name had to be created, hence Cosa Nostra."

See also: MAFIA.

Costello, Frank (1891–1973) Prime Minister of the Underworld

No syndicate criminal in this country ever enjoyed as much political pull as did Frank Costello, who was the advocate within the national crime syndicate of the "big fix." He believed in buying favors and even paying for them in advance. Scores of political leaders and judges were beholden to him. An entire array of New York's Tammany Hall bosses "owed" him. They ranged from Christy Sullivan to Mike Kennedy, from Frank Rosetti to Bert Stand and from Hugo Rogers to Carmine DeSapio. Costello had done them favors, had raised money for them, had delivered votes that really counted. And when it came time to make appointments, Costello practically exercised the equivalent of the Senate's prerogatives to advise and consent. Tammany kingpin Rogers put it best when he said, "If Costello wanted me, he would send for me."

It was the same with judges. In 1943 Manhattan district attorney Frank Hogan obtained a wiretap on Costello's telephone. Investigators were treated to this enlightening conversation on August 23 between

At the pinnacle of his power during the Kefauver Committee hearings in the early 1950s, Frank Costello, as Prime Minister of the Underworld, was the mob's representative in dealings with politicians, judges and the police.

Costello and Thomas Aurelio just minutes after the latter had learned he was getting the Democratic nomination to become a state supreme court justice:

"How are you, and thanks for everything," Aurelio said.

"Congratulations," Costello answered. "It went over perfect. When I tell you something is in the bag, you can rest assured."

"It was perfect," Aurelio said. "It was fine."

"Well, we will all have to get together and have dinner some night real soon."

"That would be fine," the judge-to-be said. "But right now I want to assure you of my loyalty for all you have done. It is unwavering."

Despite the disclosure of the wiretap, the grateful Aurelio went on to be elected to the judgeship after beating back disbarment proceedings. Clearly, when Costello said something was in the bag, it was in the bag.

Born Franceso Castiglia in Calabria, Italy in 1891, he came to New York with his family at age four. At 21 he had a police record of two arrests for assault and robbery. At 24 he was sentenced to a year in prison for carrying a gun. He did not return to prison for another 37 years. Beginning in the early days of Prohibition, his best friends were Lucky Luciano, a Sicilian, and Meyer Lansky, a Polish Jew. These three were to become the most important figures in the formation of the national crime syndicate during the 1930s. While Luciano and Lansky did most of the organizing among criminals, Costello's mission was to develop contacts and influence among the police and politicians. By the mid-1920s the trio's varied criminal enterprises, mostly bootlegging and gambling, were making them rich. To protect these interests, they were paying, through Costello, $10,000 a week in "grease" directly into the police commissioner's office. Within a few years, during the regimes of commissioners Joseph A. Warren and Grover A. Whalen, the amount rose to $20,000 a week. In 1929, just after the stock market crash, Costello told Luciano he had to advance Whalen $30,000 to cover his margin calls in the market. "What could I do?" Costello told Luciano. "I hadda give it to him. We own him."

No one ever questioned whether Costello always dispensed mob money the way it was intended. Costello was a man of honor on such matters. Besides, the results were there for the mob to see, with cases never brought to court, complaints dropped and so on.

Costello became the most vital cog in the national crime syndicate after the forceful purging of the old mafiosi or "Mustache Petes." The gangs cooperated, and Costello supplied the protection. As part of his reward, Costello got the rights to gambling in the lucrative New Orleans area.

He was respected by all the crime family heads and was considered the Prime Minister of the Underworld, the man who dealt with the "foreign dignitaries"—the police, judges and politicos. Much has been made of the fact that Costello was not a murderer, but he sat in on all syndicate decisions concerning major hits, and while he may have often been a moderating force, he was a party to murder plans. His general reluctance to use violence was not due to squeamishness; it was just that he felt hitting a man over the head with a wad of greenbacks could be more persuasive than using a blackjack.

One of the prime accomplishments of the Kefauver investigation during the 1950s was the exposure of Costello's vast influence in government. While he insisted that only his hands be shown on television, that minor subterfuge could hardly cover up his activities. When he left the stand, Costello knew his term as prime minister was at an end. He was too hot for everyone, those who appreciated the mob's favors and the mob itself.

Through the 1950s, with Luciano deported to Italy, Joe Adonis being harassed and facing the same fate, and Costello facing tax raps that would finally send him to prison, Vito Genovese moved to take over the syndicate. In 1957 Genovese engineered an attempt to assassinate Costello; he survived by perhaps an inch or two, his assailant's bullets just grazing his scalp. Later that same year Genovese arranged the rub-out of Albert Anastasia, the Lord High Executioner of Murder, Inc. and a devoted follower of Costello and Luciano.

It looked like Genovese was in. Meanwhile, Costello really wanted out, to retire in peace and concentrate on his battles with the government about his citizenship and tax problems. But Genovese's blueprint for power was soon destroyed. Costello, Lansky, Carlo Gambino and Luciano masterminded a drug

operation that involved Genovese. As soon as he was mired deeply in it, evidence was turned over to prosecutors, and in 1959 Genovese went to prison for a term of 15 years. He would die there in 1969. During this period Costello did a short stint in Atlanta Penitentiary, the same one Genovese was in; it was said the two had a sentimental reconciliation there. Genovese may have been sincere, but Costello certainly was not. When he left prison, he felt no pangs of sorrow for Genovese.

Costello went into quiet retirement after that, living the life of a Long Island squire until his death in 1973.

See also: APALACHIN CONFERENCE, CARLO GAMBINO, VITO GENOVESE, VINCENT "THE CHIN" GIGANTE, KEFAUVER INVESTIGATION, MEYER LANSKY, CHARLES "LUCKY" LUCIANO, WILLIE MORETTI, SLOT MACHINES, WIRETAPPING AND BUGGING.

Coster, F. Donald   See PHILIP MUSICA.

Cotroni gang   Mafia's "body importers"
Based in Montreal, Canada, the Cotroni gang has a tremendous impact on crime in the United States, its main function being to import for the Mafia new blood, mainly Sicilians who have proved tougher and more reliable than second- and third-generation American recruits. The mass importation of native Sicilians was started in the 1960s by the late "boss of bosses" Carlo Gambino, who felt there was a need for tough young recruits still schooled in the old Mafia codes and, above all, "hungry" and not as anxious to move to the suburbs.

According to Canadian police, the Cotroni gang provides aliens with a pipeline into the United States for a fee that runs between $2,000 and $3,000. It is easy for aliens to get into Canada since the only thing needed for a three-month stay without a visa is $300 in cash and a Canadian address where they can be reached. The Cotronis supply the addresses and have little trouble moving their immigrants across the border.

Many of the mobsters recently arrested by police have been new Mafia faces, all recent arrivals, which has led to fears that American police will lose track of mob operations as these unknown newcomers take on more and more of the Mafia's street duties.

counterfeiting
Throughout American history there have always been people who have thought the best way to make money is, simply, to make money.

Mary Butterworth, the kitchen counterfeiter, may have been the first. This housewife with seven children operated a highly successful counterfeiting ring in Plymouth colony during the early 1700s.

The comparatively crude paper money used in colonial times, "Continental currency," was so frequently and successfully faked that it gave rise to the saying, "Not worth a Continental." During the Civil War, it was estimated that a good third of the currency in circulation was "funny money." The counterfeiter's chore was made much easier because some 11,600 state banks across the nation designed and printed their own currency. Finally, in 1863 the nation adopted a uniform currency.

Counterfeiting today is hardly a lost art, but few stay successful at it for very long. In 1976 the Secret Service made a record haul in the Bronx, New York City, arresting six suspects who had run off $20 million in what was characterized as "highly passable" bills. This followed on the heels of raids in Los Angeles that netted four men with more than $8 million worth of bogus bills. The main worry of the government today is that sophisticated new photographic and printing equipment will permit counterfeiters, as never before, to approximate the intricate whorls, loops and crosshatching that makes American paper money just about the most difficult in the world to imitate. In recent years, the government has introduced new bills said to be even more counterfeit-proof, but that must be tested over time, while understanding that all moneys have always been duplicated.

In a typical counterfeiting operation, distribution is handled by an army of wholesalers, distributors and passers. The standard breakdown calls for the counterfeiters to sell their output to wholesalers for 12 percent of face value. The wholesaler then has the job of reselling the bills to distributors for 25 percent. The distributors turn it over to street-level passers for 35 percent.

Although counterfeiting is punishable by up to 15 years in prison and a $10,000 fine and Treasury officials estimate that almost 90 percent of all bad-money makers are jailed in less than a year, counterfeiters, big and small, still keep trying their luck. There are those who will print fake $1 bills despite the rather high overhead involved. It took the Secret Service 10 years to catch up with a lone operator who passed fake $1 bills in New York. He was an elderly former janitor who circulated only eight or 10 ones every few days, making it a point never to pass them twice at the same place. He explained later that he "didn't want to stick anybody for more than a dollar."

Some even try their hand at counterfeiting coins, even though breaking even is nearly impossible in these inflationary times. In the past, however, coin counterfeiting was big business. In 1883 a deaf-mute named

Joshua Tatum made a small fortune by slightly altering the original liberty head nickel and passing it for 100 times its real value. On the face of the nickel was a woman's head wearing a liberty headpiece. On the other side was the motto E. *Pluribus Unum* and a large V. The V, the Roman numeral five, was the only indication of the coin's value to be found on the nickel. Tatum noted that the liberty head nickel closely resembled in design and size the half eagle, or $5 gold piece, which was then in general circulation. The face of the latter also displayed a woman's head with a liberty headpiece. On the reverse side was the sign of value, Five D., indicating $5. About the only difference was the color: the nickel had a silvery appearance, and the half eagle, gold. Tatum began gold-plating nickels by the thousand and then buying 5¢ items all over the East Coast. Invariably, he got $4.95 in change. On occasion, a merchant would flip the coin over, note the V for five and assume it was a newly issued $5 gold piece. He couldn't prove it by Tatum, who was a deaf-mute. When Tatum was finally caught, the courts freed him because he was a deaf-mute. The authorities could never prove Tatum had ever asked for change, and there were no laws on the book prohibiting a person from gold-plating a nickel. The law was changed accordingly and an emergency session of Congress was called to alter the design of the nickel.

Students of the fine art of counterfeiting contend that the true craftsmen are all in their graves. There were, for example, artists like Baldwin Bredell and Arthur Taylor, who in the late 1890s turned out such perfect $100 bills that the government had to withdraw from circulation the entire issue of $26 million in Monroe-head bills. Sent to Moyamensing Prison, Bredell and Taylor astounded the experts by pulling off a moneymaking caper so amazing that Treasury Department experts at first refused to concede it possible. Within several months of their arrival in the prison, Bredell and Taylor began turning out counterfeit $20 bills at night in their cell. To do this, they needed to have supplies smuggled in. One of Taylor's relatives brought books and magazines on his weekly visits. These hid engraving tools, steel plates, files and vials of acids. Another smuggled in a kerosene lamp piece by piece and some magnifying glasses hidden in a basket of cookies. The printing press they needed was made to specifications the counterfeiters drew up and had smuggled out. Getting the press in was easy because it was the size of a cigar box. Since Bredell's wife was pregnant, she became just a bit more expecting. Inks were a different problem. With their former workshop under government padlock, there was no way to get the special bleaches and inks that were needed. One couldn't buy the proper ink legitimately without the government knowing about it, so the pair stole the bleaches they needed from the prison laundry and then their relatives started bringing fruits and flowers. From the dried fruits and berries and the green leaves of the flowers, they made their own ink.

Soon the Bredell-Taylor $20s—virtually as good as Uncle Sam's—started turning up. What the pair hadn't counted on was that John E. Wilkie, the chief of the U.S. Secret Service, would spot the work as being too good to be anybody's but theirs. Naturally, Wilkie assumed the plates had been prepared by the pair before their arrest and they were just being used now, so he put a watch on relatives of Taylor and Bredell, and after one was caught passing some of the fake $20s, Wilkie uncovered the whole story. The experts called in by the Secret Service scoffed at the possibility that Bredell and Taylor could have produced such work in prison. They insisted it could not have been done without a camera, a huge workroom and an 8-ton press. Only when the prisoners reenacted their feat were the experts convinced.

In recognition of their extraordinary talents, Chief Wilkie decided to help the pair get a new start in life when they were released. He got financial backing for a mechanical engraving machine Taylor had perfected, starting the ex-counterfeiter on the way to becoming a prosperous manufacturer. Bredell went on to establish a leading engraving and lithography plant and also became rich. The two master counterfeiters were lured away from their illicit activities the only way the government could think of—by making them rich, legally.

Today, there are no counterfeiting geniuses such as Taylor and Bredell or Jim the Penman, perhaps the only counterfeiter in history to make top-grade notes simply by drawing them. Using a fine camel's hair brush, he made phony bills by tracing them from genuine notes that he placed before a strong light. Criminal craftsmen of such caliber, to the U.S. government's relief, are a dying breed.

See also: MARY BUTTERWORTH, "COUNT" VICTOR LUSTIG.

Further reading: *Money of Their Own* by Murray Teign Bloom.

county seat wars Midwest boomtown violence

Encouraged by unscrupulous speculators during the land boom in several western states following the Civil War, fierce struggles broke out between various communities over the location of county seats. Obviously, the prestige of being the county seat would add to the value of a town's property and deadly wars were fought to win this distinction. Kansas alone had 28 of these disputes, and others cropped up in Nebraska and North and South Dakota. The ultimate decision on the location of a county seat was left to local elections, but both sides would use bribes, trickery and fraud to fix the results as well as hire professional gunmen to intimidate voters. Even civic-minded citizens resorted to importing gunslingers to protect the polls. Unfortunately, whatever the result, the losing side seldom accepted it. A common practice was to invade the winning town and simply attempt to steal the courthouse records, a typical case being the invasion of Cimarron by Ingalls forces in Gray County, Kan. In one case an attempt was made to jack up a wooden courthouse on rollers and physically cart away the entire building.

One of the bloodiest confrontations involved Hugoton and Woodsdale in Stevens County, Kan. The sheriff and three Woodsdale citizens were murdered by Hugoton men on July 25, 1888, and Woodsdale prosecutor Col. Sam N. Wood was assassinated in Hugoton in 1891. As was often the case in county seat wars, all murder charges eventually were dropped. In the end, Hugoton became the county seat. At Coronado in Wichita County, Kan., three Leoti residents died in a street battle in 1887, but not in vain; their community eventually won the war. Finally, bad economic times and the ensuing collapse of the short-grass land boom brought an end to the county seat wars.

See also: CIMARRON COUNTY SEAT WAR.

Courtright, Longhair Jim (1845?–1887) western lawman and murderer

A prime example of a lawman gone bad, Jim Courtright, variously reported as being born in Iowa or Illinois between 1845 and 1848, was a popular two-gun sheriff in Fort Worth, Tex., but after two years on the job, he was fired in 1878 for drinking. Courtright bounced around to a few other jobs as a lawman, but his brooding nature was such that these rarely lasted for long. Eventually, he drifted into a job as a guard for the American Mining Co., in whose employ he killed two would-be robbers in 1883. News of this exploit reached the attention of a New Mexico rancher named Logan, who had been Courtright's old Civil War commander. Logan offered him a job as a ranch foreman, but Courtright's real assignment would be to rid Logan's range of squatters. He got off to a fast start by promptly shooting two unarmed nesters. Because there had been witnesses, Courtright was forced to flee. He was arrested in Fort Worth and held for extradition. Courtright knew the jail routine well, and after being smuggled a pair of pistols, he escaped, fleeing to South America. After three years he returned to face trial, but by that time the witnesses against him had scattered, and he was easily acquitted. Returning to Fort Worth, he set up the T.I.C. Commercial Detective Agency. Finding little demand for his services, Courtright used the agency as a guise to demand protection money from the town's various gambling halls and saloons. For this ploy to be successful, a 100 percent record of collection was necessary; it was Courtright's misfortune that an emporium called the White Elephant Saloon was run by a pint-sized gambler named Luke Short, one of the West's grand masters of the six-gun. On February 8, 1887 Courtright sent a messenger into the White Elephant demanding that Short step outside. Short did, and moments later, Courtright called out, "Don't try to pull a gun on me." Courtright clearly was laying the legal basis for a claim that he was acting in self-defense. The matter was academic, however. Courtright started to draw one gun, but Short shot his thumb off as he tried to trip back the hammer. This was not a trick shot; Short's aim was slightly off on his first blast. As Courtright went to pull his other gun, Short was on target with three more shots, two in the chest and one in the forehead.

See also: LUKE SHORT.

Coy, Bernard Paul (1900–1946) bank robber and Alcatraz Prison Rebellion leader

Bernie Coy was 46, with 16 years more to go on a 25-year sentence for bank robbery, when he masterminded the famous breakout-rebellion attempt from Alcatraz in May 1946.

Regarded as little more than an ignorant Kentucky hillbilly, Coy initially was not considered smart enough to be the mastermind behind the escape attempt. During the 48-hour break attempt, prison officials were sure the leader of the plot was Dutch Cretzer, a former Public Enemy No. 4 doing a life sentence. Unlike Coy, Cretzer was a brutal killer and hard to control, but Coy needed him in the escape because of Cretzer's outside connections, who could arrange a getaway once they reached the mainland.

In fact, as a subsequent investigation proved, the entire escape plot was Coy's. He secretly designed and had built a bar spreader made from plumbing fixtures and valve parts and concealed it until the time of the break, both incredible accomplishments in security-conscious Alcatraz. With the bar spread, Coy was able to break into the gun gallery, where the only weapons in the cell block were kept, overpower the guard and arm his accomplices. There is no doubt the escapers, having turned loose a great number of other convicts to make things look like a prison riot rather than break, could have made it across the prison yard to the wharf and then aboard the prison launch. Coy's plan adhered to a strict timetable that took advantage of the very guard procedure designed to prevent escapes. His plan foundered, ironically, because one guard disobeyed the rules and failed to put the key to the last door back on its rack. He had it in his pocket and, when taken hostage, managed to hide it in a cell. The escapers took nine guards hostage, but because of one locked door, Coy's plan failed and the prison launch left the island before they had a chance to reach it. Although the break and riot lasted 48 hours, Coy lost control of his men, and Dutch Cretzer, who all along chafed at taking orders from Coy, "a hick hillbilly," shot up the hostages while Coy was trying to negotiate over the phone with the warden. Throughout the remainder of the rebellion, Cretzer spent his time trying to find and kill Coy and Marv Hubbard, a con who supported Coy, while Coy tried to hunt down Cretzer. As marines and the guards bombarded the prison with grenades and raked the cell blocks with rifle and shotgun fire, the grim duel continued. Although popular accounts to this day often insist that the three ringleaders joined together and fought the attacking guards to the death deep within the underground tunnels of the prison, the fact was that Cretzer killed Coy and then died in a final confrontation with a host of attackers, who also killed the wounded Hubbard.

See also: ALCATRAZ PRISON REBELLION, JOSEPH PAUL "DUTCH" CRETZER.

Crabb, Christopher Columbus (1852–1935) "solid man"

It is generally acknowledged that the most eminent and successful "solid man" in the history of American vice was Christopher Columbus Crabb, whom Chicago mayor Carter Harrison, Jr. described as "an imposing looking rooster." Remarkably, Crabb was able to function as lover and financial manager for more than one madam at the same time.

Crabb was a $14-a-week clerk in Marshall Field's department store when he met Lizzie Allen in 1878. Lizzie was one of the city's top madams, operating brothels just a cut in quality below those of the famous Carrie Watson. Crabb had been a lover to several of Lizzie's prostitutes, and while he was not a pimp, the ladies lavished gifts upon him. At the age of 38, Lizzie had at last found her true love and promptly smothered Crabb with kindness.

Crabb was known as a square-shooter in Chicago vice circles, a man who could be trusted to handle madams' or harlots' money. He was constantly urging various madams to give their workers a better break, and while he would be most helpful in initiating a new girl "into the business," he would just as willingly aid others who wanted to get out. While his affair with Lizzie Allen was blossoming, Crabb apparently played the same role with another madam, Mollie Fitch. When the latter died a few years later, she left Crabb $150,000. In 1890 Crabb and Lizzie spent $125,000 to build a large double house at 2131 South Dearborn Street, which was later taken over by the Everleigh sisters and became the nation's most famous bordello. Under Lizzie, the resort was called the House of Mirrors. When she retired in 1896, Lizzie signed over all her property to Crabb and died later that same year. Crabb buried her in Rosehill Cemetery and had her tombstone inscribed, "Perpetual Ease."

The press estimated that Crabb inherited well over $300,000 from Lizzie. He spent the later years of his life as a sort of elder statesman in vice circles, and when he died on January 5, 1935, he left an estate of $416,589.81, three quarters of which he bequeathed to the Illinois Masonic Orphans' Home.

See also: LIZZIE ALLEN, EVERLEIGH SISTERS.

Craft, Gerald (1965–1973) kidnap victim

Although not very well known in white circles, the kidnap-murders of eight-year-old Gerald Craft and six-year-old Keith Arnold in Detroit on December 1, 1973 stand as the "black Lindbergh case."

Gerald Craft was actually a familiar face to most of the country's whites, being famous, if anonymously, for a television commercial in which he gobbled down big helpings of fried chicken with a devilish grin on his face. On that December 1, a Saturday afternoon, Gerald was playing football with a friend, Keith, in front of his grandmother's house when both suddenly disappeared. The next day a hoarsely whispered telephone call demanded a ransom of $53,000 for the return of the children. This was an amount the families could not pay. With the help of the Detroit police, a bogus package of ransom money was dropped at a designated spot, which the police staked out. Two men came to retrieve it, but officers moved too slowly to capture them before they drove off. Two days later, the bodies of the two boys, both shot twice, were found in a field near Detroit's Metropolitan Airport.

The *Detroit News* offered a $5,000 reward for information leading to the capture of the kidnappers and set up a "secret witness" phone number for informers. Within a week the information received through this source led to the arrest of three 21-year-old men and a teenage girl and the solution of the case. The girl provided evidence that convicted the men, Byron Smith, Geary Gilmore and Jerome Holloway. All three were given mandatory life sentences.

As big a news splash as the kidnapping made in the black press around the country, few whites ever heard much about it.

Crane, Stephen (1870–1900) writer and police victim

Few writers have suffered as much harassment from the police as did Stephen Crane during the last four years of his life. Crane's troubles began in September 1896, when the author, already famous for his book *The Red Badge of Courage,* visited the vice-ridden tenderloin section of Manhattan to collect material for a series of sketches on the district. A tall, broad-shouldered policeman named Charles Becker walked up to a free-lance prostitute, Dora Clark, and started beating her to a pulp. Becker over the years was to become famous as "the crookedest cop who ever stood behind a shield," and in 1915 he died in the electric chair for the murder of gambler Herman Rosenthal. His prime concern during his days in the tenderloin was not to drive out the prostitutes but to make sure he got his share of their income.

Dora Clark was definitely not soliciting when Becker started roughing her up and arrested her. Crane, having witnessed the entire incident, so testified at her hearing. The Clark woman complained she had been subjected to Becker's constant harassment and demands for money. The judge chose to believe Crane over Becker and released the woman.

Becker was brought up on police departmental charges before Commissioner Frederick Grant, who at the time was considered one of the department's looser administrators and an opponent of reforms advocated by another commissioner, Theodore Roosevelt. Becker's defense tried to shift the case to one against Crane, accusing him of regularly consorting with prostitutes and of being an opium smoker. Despite attacks by the newspapers, Commissioner Grant allowed a long line of questioning on such points, causing the *Brooklyn Daily Eagle* to lament that "the reputation of private citizens is permitted to be assailed without comment or protest, while so much is done to shield one of a body of men that collectively was lately shown to be one of the most corrupt, brutal, incompetent organizations in the world." Other newspapers joined in observing that the rank treatment of Crane showed the police had hardly reformed since the revelations of their crookedness by the Lexow Committee two years previously.

Becker escaped without suffering any major penalties for his conduct, and the police thereafter kept up a steady campaign of intimidation and harassment against Crane. His rooms were raided, and police insisted they had found opium there. (The conventional wisdom was that they had brought the opium with them.) The police vendetta against Crane reached such intensity that the author was forced to flee the city for a time. As soon as he returned, the police resumed their persecution of him. When a policeman saw Crane at the theater with a woman, he loudly accused her of being a "goddam French whore" and only beat a retreat after realizing the other member of the Crane party was a priest.

By 1898 the malicious attacks on Crane again forced him to leave the city. When next he returned, there was no need for the police to reactivate their campaign a third time. Crane was dying of tuberculosis.

See also: CHARLES BECKER.

Crater, Joseph Force (1889–1937?) missing judge

On August 6, 1930 a portly 41-year-old man wearing a high-collared shirt, brown pin-striped double-breasted suit and extremely polished and pointed shoes stepped into a taxi in front of a Manhattan restaurant, waved good-bye to a friend and rode off into history, to become known as America's greatest vanishing act. The man was Justice Joseph Force Crater of the New York Supreme Court. From that day forth, Crater was never seen again—alive or dead. His disappearance provided grist for the mills of jokers, playwrights, graffiti writers, cartoonists and amateur detectives over the next half century.

Crater was born in Easton, Pa., graduated from Lafayette College and earned a law degree at Columbia University. He established a successful New York practice and formed important political connections, later rising to the presidency of the Cayuga Democratic Club, an important part of the Tammany organization. In April 1930 Gov. Franklin D. Roosevelt appointed him to the New York Supreme Court.

Crater cut short a vacation in Maine to return to the city in order to take care of some business. He was seen in his court chambers on August 5 and 6 and had his aide cash two checks for him totaling $5,150. Later that day he met some friends at a restaurant and then stepped into the taxi and oblivion.

The investigation into his disappearance eventually mushroomed into a months-long grand jury probe that quizzed hundreds of witnesses but produced no leads to explain what happened to him. One theory was developed about why he had vanished. The grand jury uncovered considerable evidence of corruption in the Cayuga Democratic Club, which brought on the much publicized Seabury probe.

Meanwhile, the tantalizing mysteries of the case continued. Under New York City law, cabbies were required to keep records of all their trips, starting

Twenty-five years after Judge Joseph Force Crater's disappearance, his wife, since remarried, calls for a renewal of the hunt for him.

points and destinations. But despite many appeals from the police, a $5,000 reward offered by the city and a $2,500 reward offered by the New York World, the cabbie who picked up Judge Crater never came forward nor offered any information concerning the case. If he had, Crater's movements could have been traced at least one more step.

On countless occasions in the 1930s, the case seemed to be a fraction of an inch from being solved, but each lead fizzled. There was no limit to the type of leads the police ran down over the years. The missing Crater was identified wrongly as a gold prospector in the California desert country; a human torch who died of self-inflicted burns in Leavenworth, Kan.; a skeleton at Walden, Vt.; an unidentified murder victim in Westchester County, N.Y.; a man who hanged himself from a tree less than 15 miles from the Crater summer home at Belgrade Lakes, Maine; an amnesia victim in the Missouri State Insane Asylum; a sufferer of "daytime somnambulism."

Then again he was a Hollywood race tout; a free-spending American tourist in Italy; an ill-shaven door-to-door beggar in Illinois ("I didn't pull his whiskers but I'm pretty sure they were false," one Chicago housewife bubbled to police). Perhaps the best of all was the GI who returned from overseas in 1946 with the emphatic intelligence that Crater was operating a bingo game in North Africa for a strictly Arab clientele.

Jokers, of course, got into the act. Assistant Chief John J. Sullivan was sitting at his desk one day when a call from Montreal was switched to him. A very calm voice said: "I can't tell you my name, because I don't care to get mixed up in it, but Judge Crater is now in room 761 at my hotel. I am in the hotel now, but I don't dare give you my name." In a matter of minutes Sullivan had the Montreal police breaking into the room of a honeymooning couple.

Throughout the country a number of dying bums felt compelled to make deathbed confessions, each admitting that he was the judge. One in the Midwest, who lived long enough for the police to question him, admitted finally that he was just trying to "get myself a decent burial instead of being laid in that pauper's plot all the other boys end up in."

In 1937 Judge Crater was ruled legally dead, and his widow remarried. At the time, it was estimated the hunt for Crater had expended 300,000 Depression dollars. Even by the 1950s the Judge Crater legend had not faded. Former police commissioner Edward P. Mulrooney, under whose supervision the case was first investigated, revealed he still carried a picture of Crater in his pocket at all times. "You never know but that someday you might run into him," he said. "I'd give my right arm to find him." During the following decade the police were still up to the search, digging up a Yonkers, N.Y. backyard in the hope of finding the judge's bones. Nothing came of it.

Crazy Butch gang

During the 1890s and first few years of the 20th century, the most efficient gang of young criminals in New York City was the Crazy Butch gang. Crazy Butch, the leader of the gang, had been tossed into the world at the tender age of eight. Renouncing his alcoholic parents, he never acknowledged his family name. After surviving for two years as a shoeshine boy, Crazy Butch became a pickpocket. When he was about 13, Butch stole a dog, which he named Rabbi, and trained it to steal handbags from careless women's hands. Rabbi would snatch a purse, race through the streets until it lost any pursuers and then meet Crazy Butch at Willett and Stanton Streets, tail wagging and the purse clenched in its teeth.

In his late teens Crazy Butch switched his operation from a dog to a gang of 20 to 30 youths, whom he trained to prowl the streets snatching handbags and muffs. Butch would lead his minions down a street on a bicycle, bump into a pedestrian, preferably a little old lady, and alight to help her up while at the same time berating her as a careless walker. As people pressed in to see what was happening, Crazy Butch's boys would thread through the mob rifling pockets and purses. When the crowd was completely milked or a policeman appeared, Butch would apologize to his victim and pedal away. At the gang's headquarters, his protégés would turn in their spoils, and Crazy Butch would reward each with a few pennies.

By the turn of the century, Crazy Butch and many of his followers had advanced to such adult occupations as musclemen, sluggers and, on occasion, paid murderers, often pursuing their criminal endeavors in bicycle teams. A subchief under the celebrated Monk Eastman, Crazy Butch held his followers, some 60 strong, always at the ready should they be needed to do battle with the Five Points Gang of Paul Kelly, whose ranks already included a young hoodlum named Johnny Torrio and would soon be graced by such names as Luciano, Yale and Capone. Crazy Butch demanded his men be ready for action at all times. Once, hearing the Five Pointers were preparing an onslaught, Crazy Butch decided to test his boys' preparedness. So, one night Crazy Butch and three of his men charged up the stairs and into the hall of the gang's Forsyth Street headquarters, blazing away with two revolvers each. The gang members, who were boozing or playing cards, either went out the windows or down the backstairs. Little Kishky, who had been sitting on a window sill, was so startled he fell backwards out the window and was killed. Crazy Butch was furious; he wanted his men better prepared for action than that.

Crazy Butch survived a number of gun battles with the Five Pointers and other gangsters under Humpty Jackson, but his own gang and the great Eastman gang started falling apart at the same time. In 1904 both he and Eastman disappeared from the scene. Eastman was sentenced to 10 years in prison for robbery, and Crazy Butch was killed by Harry the Soldier in a fight over a girl, an expert shoplifter called the Darby Kid.

Crazy Butch is seldom remembered today in criminal histories, but he trained many of the early 20th-century gangsters and especially the sluggers of the union wars. Big Jack Zelig had started out under Crazy Butch. In fact, that notorious bruiser had always quaked under Butch's rage.

See also: MONK EASTMAN.

Crazy Eddie's insane fraud   *their prices and their stock offerings were truly insane*

In the 1980s few television pitches bombarded Easterners more than of Crazy Eddie's, an appliance and hi-fi chain that declared ad nauseum "our prices are insane." And they were—and so was their accounting system, their tax payments and their Wall Street deals.

Crazy Eddie's went public at a time when Wall Street was mad about rapidly growing companies. In effect, proprietor Eddie Antar and his cousin Sam were telling the best brains in the financial community: "You want super growth, we got super growth."

The Antars realized that super growth thanks to Sam Antar's creative accounting. As the law was later to determine, the Antars had been skimming money from the business for years. In fact, they were making money not only from actual profits but just as lucratively from avoiding sales taxes. It was as near to a Marx Brothers operation as possible. But then an even more insane inspiration hit the Antars:

"Why don't we go public?" Why not indeed.

Of course, to be a super growth company they had to show explosive profits. Nothing was easier for the boys. All that had to be done was to cut back on the family skimming. With the abrupt reduction in the skim, profits seemingly ballooned from $1.7 million to $4.6 million. That figure for 1984 truly astounded Wall Street brokers, and a public stock offering was a resounding success. The Antars had barely warmed up.

In the quest for more imaginary profits, the family bought up imaginary merchandise so that gross profits by 1986 had soared to the level of 40 percent. For a second time Wall Street put out a stock issue that was even more successful than the first.

Alas for the Antars and their investors, there was no way Sam Antar could produce more bogus profits. Hungry Wall Streeters now were expecting an additional $20–$30 million for 1987.

"My pencil is only so long," Sam informed Eddie. The boys tried to move inventories from store to store so that auditors would count the same goods time after time. Unfortunately, that was the end of the road. Auditors were not that insane.

Jail sentences followed, but this did not end the Antar saga. In later years Sam Antar made speeches to such groups as the National Association of Fraud Examiners, outlining the crookedness of Crazy Eddie's. His theme to the experts and to credulous investors was that fraud is so easy—insanely so.

Credit Mobilier Scandal   first great robber baron plot

A financial unit set up to finance the construction costs of the Union Pacific, Credit Mobilier was the cause of one of the greatest congressional scandals of the 19th century.

In order to get favorable legislation on land grants and rights-of-way, Credit Mobilier "sold" company stock at half price to key congressmen—"where it

would do the most good." The chief bagman in the operation was Rep. Oakes Ames of Massachusetts, a principal officer of Credit Mobilier. When the *New York Sun* broke the scandal in 1872, it was determined that among those whose goodwill Ames had managed to buy was Vice President Schuyler Colfax (who had been speaker of the House at the time of his alleged involvement), Sen. Henry Wilson and Rep. James A. Garfield. A congressional committee investigating the case concluded that the Credit Mobilier stockholders, including the congressmen involved, had reaped $23 million in ill-gotten profits. Garfield survived the scandal and went on to be elected president in 1880. Ames, however, fell victim to a censure motion in the House and returned home to Massachusetts, broken hearted but still maintaining his innocence.

Some later economic historians concluded that Credit Mobilier's profits totaled "only $13 million to $16 million" and were not "excessive" by the standards of the day. Ames is described by some of these historians as being guilty of no more than a "grievous error of judgment." Nonetheless, the label of "robber baron" has remained attached to him.

creep joint   crooked brothel

Much of the prostitution activity in San Francisco during the 19th century was conducted in what were called cribs or cowyard cubicles. When business was brisk, a customer was not permitted time to undress, even to remove his footwear. Instead, a piece of oilcloth was spread along the bottom of the bed to keep the man's boots from soiling the bedding. Of course, all customers were required to remove their hats, since no self-respecting prostitute would consider entertaining a man with his hat on.

One type of crib that never forbade the removal of clothing by customers was the so-called creep joint. Here men were encouraged to hang everything in a closet that was attached to the back wall of the crib. The back walls, however, were really doors, and while the customer was otherwise occupied, an accomplice of the woman would open the door and steal all the man's money and valuables.

Creep joints may or may not have originated first in San Francisco, but at least in that city the rip-off was carried out with a certain amount of style and a touch of sympathy; a dime was always left in the man's clothing for his carfare home. Few men ever taken in creep joints attempted to put up a fight. It was common knowledge that such cribs had a push-button alarm attached to a nearby barroom which, if activated, would bring the saloon bouncer and several other toughs over to manhandle the protesting victim.

See also: BADGER GAME, PANEL HOUSE.

Cretzer, Joseph Paul "Dutch" (1911–1946) bank bandit and murderer

One of the key figures in the Alcatraz Prison Rebellion of 1946, the Rock's greatest break-out attempt, Dutch Cretzer was the country's top bank bandit of the late 1930s and Public Enemy No. 4.

The Cretzer gang laid waste to banks all along the West Coast up to the time their leader was captured in 1939. Sent to the federal prison on McNeil Island in the state of Washington, Cretzer attempted an escape by crashing a truck through a gate but was caught. Brought to trial in Tacoma for the attempt, he was quickly found guilty and given five additional years. As he was being led from the court, Cretzer clubbed a federal marshal with his handcuffed hands, killing him. He then picked up the dead lawman's gun and leveled it at the judge, intending to use him as a hostage. But before he could reach the judge, a court bailiff returning to the room jammed his gun into Cretzer's neck and disarmed him. Cretzer was convicted of murdering the federal marshal but escaped the death sentence because his victim had actually died of a heart attack during the assault on him.

Given a life term, Cretzer was taken in chains to Alcatraz, where within nine months he attempted another escape. He and another convict, Crazy Sam Shockley, overpowered a guard and tried to drill through a barred window in a prison workshop. In a speedboat nearby, two men were fishing, or at least they appeared to be fishing. They were really Cretzer gang members, and under some canvas aboard the boat were four submachine guns. The drilling of the bars was unsuccessful, however, and the convicts were found by other guards.

Cretzer was put in solitary for the next five years, an unusually harsh punishment in any federal penitentiary other than Alcatraz. But even that didn't stop Cretzer from once more joining an escape attempt after he was returned to the main cell house in March 1946. He once told a Seattle detective who came to see him about a bank job he had pulled: "I can't stand living at Alcatraz. I was reared in San Francisco, and being able to see the city lights go on each evening from my cell . . . I can't stand that. I'll make a break from here one day. And if I don't get killed in the trying, I'll kill myself."

Within days of returning to the cell house, Cretzer threw in with a Kentucky bank robber named Bernie Coy who had plotted out the most intricate escape plan ever devised in the prison. Coy had designed and built a bar spreader made from plumbing fixtures and valve parts and had figured out a way to break into the cell house gun gallery, where the only weapons in the building were kept. This acquisition of weapons was the one thing no previous Alcatraz breakout attempt had ever achieved. Coy had planned out a minute-by-minute, step-by-step escape route that would get himself, Cretzer and four others through Alcatraz's tight security net, across the prison yard and to the wharf, where they would seize a prison launch when it was just about to sail. They could make the mainland quickly, and then Cretzer's gang would pick them up in fast getaway cars before the authorities would have time to react.

Cretzer went into the deal even though he had a problem accepting Coy, whom he regarded as a "hick hillbilly," giving the orders. The great Alcatraz Prison Rebellion started on May 2, 1946 when the six plotters took over the cell block and freed the prisoners to confuse matters for prison officials. Once armed, they quickly took nine guards hostage. Cretzer, without Coy's knowledge and despite orders against any killing, shot and killed another guard. The plotters almost made it to freedom, Coy's plan failing only at the last corridor door because a guard had, against prison rules, kept the key to the door in his pocket instead of returning it to its proper peg. Coy's delicate timetable collapsed, and the prison launch left the island before the escapers could locate the key.

Cretzer went wild at the plan's failure and during Coy's absence turned his guns on the nine hostages, killing only one but severely wounding several others. Thinking he had killed them all, Cretzer retreated into an isolated part of the prison. Three of the plotters then slipped back to their cells as Cretzer, Coy and another prisoner, Marv Hubbard, tried to devise alternate escape plans. In a bizarre development Cretzer stalked Coy and his friend Hubbard, determined to kill them, while they in turn hunted him. Meanwhile, the released prisoners started a full-scale riot, and alarmed officials called in sharpshooter guards from other prisons as well as a detachment of battle-outfitted marines. The "battle of Alcatraz" raged for almost 48 hours, as hundreds of grenades and gas bombs were dropped through holes in the roof to try to subdue the rampaging convicts. During this time Cretzer moved deeper into the bowels of the prison, attempting to find a way out along the sewer lines. Coy and Hubbard made their way to the same area, and it was here that all three men would die. According to some accounts, guards cornered them and a fierce gun battle ensued. Fanciful stories of this hit-and-run confrontation have Cretzer cackling insanely as he fired at the pursuers and screaming, "Hey, this is fun!" with Coy responding, "Yeah, and there's more coming."

Nothing like this happened. In a darkened tunnel Coy walked right into Cretzer, who shot him dead. The maddened Cretzer also tried to kill Hubbard but was driven off by the guards. A short time later, Cretzer was trapped and shot to death. So was Hubbard. The great crashout attempt was over.

See also: ALCATRAZ PRISON REBELLION, BERNARD PAUL COY, SAM SHOCKLEY, MIRAN "BUDDY" THOMPSON.

crime clocks FBI statistical device

Probably no FBI method of publicizing crime statistics is more controversial than its so-called crime clocks, whereby an anxious public is given such intelligence as "there is a rape in this country every (14, 13, 12) minutes" or "someone is robbed every (5½, 5, 4½) minutes," etc.

What is most severely criticized about these crime clocks is that each year the time between the occurrence of such offenses almost inevitably shrinks, indicating an apparently constant increase in crime. The fallacy in the presentation is that no allowance is made for a steadily growing population, which may well mean more crimes statistically but not necessarily proportionally. Perhaps an even more germane criticism is based on the fact that an enormous number of all violent crimes are committed by teenagers, and in periods of rapid growth of this age group, the crime clock figures present a far greater distortion.

Much better than crime clocks, insist some critics, would be comparative figures to indicate the risk of violent attack from strangers, which is one of the less likely hazards facing the average American. For instance, the risk of death from reported cases of willful homicide until recently was about one in 20,000 and now less, and a scant 25 percent of such murders are committed by strangers, all the rest being the work of the victim's family or friends. An average American is about 15 times more likely to be killed in a car crash. Rather than reduce crime statistics to mere minutes or seconds, critics prefer to note that the average chance of one being the victim of a crime of violence is roughly once in 400 years.

Crimmins, Alice (1939–) convicted child killer

One of New York's most lurid criminal cases started on July 14, 1965, when a 26-year-old mother and divorcée, Alice Crimmins, reported her two young children, four-year-old Alice Marie and five-year-old Edmund, were missing from her Queens apartment, apparently abducted. Both children were later found dead. The girl had clearly been murdered by strangulation, but the boy's body was too decomposed to ascertain the cause of his death.

However, the kidnapping theory was soon abandoned, and investigators focused on the possibility that Alice Crimmins had killed her daughter in a fit of anger

and then, with the aid of gangsters, murdered her son because he had witnessed the strangulation of his sister.

Originally tried in 1968 on a charge of killing her daughter, Alice Crimmins was found guilty of first-degree manslaughter in a trial spiced with lurid testimony about the defendant's extramarital affairs and "swinging" lifestyle. Many courtroom observers were surprised at the verdict and expressed the opinion that the manslaughter case had been rather weak and the woman had been convicted mainly because of her style of living, which much of the public found offensive.

Crimmins was sentenced to five to 20 years, but the guilty verdict was set aside after it was learned that several jurors had visited the scene of the alleged slayings on their own. When Crimmins was retried in 1971, she was charged with murdering both her daughter and her son. After a five-week trial she was convicted of manslaughter in the case of her daughter, for which she was given five to 20 years, and first-degree murder of her son, for which she drew life. An assistant district attorney was overheard to say he was "stunned" by the severity of the murder verdict. Eventually, higher courts threw out the murder conviction because of insufficient evidence but found there was "overwhelming proof" that Mrs. Crimmins had killed her daughter. As a result, her life sentence was lifted and she was left with the term of five to 20 years on the manslaughter count.

Early in 1975 newspapers reported that Crimmins was in a work-release program working as a secretary for an undisclosed Queens company while living in a Manhattan medium-security residential facility. She had also been allowed to marry Anthony Grace, a wealthy contractor who admitted he had been having an affair with her at the time of her daughter's death and on whose yacht she had been spending her summer weekends while on the work-release program. Later that same year Crimmins was granted a parole after serving the minimum five years of her sentence.

Crittenden, Thomas T. (1832–1909) Missouri governor

The governor of Missouri during the last years of the Jesse James gang's reign, Thomas Crittenden clearly conspired with the Ford brothers to kill the noted criminal leader, an act that was to have a profound effect on his political career.

By 1882 the James gang was in disarray, most of its stalwart members either killed or jailed, and Jesse and Frank James were forced to rely on such less trustworthy accomplices as Dick Little and Bob and Charles Ford. By late 1881 Dick Little was secretly negotiating to surrender. Either through him or others, the Ford brothers had begun dickering with Gov. Crittenden about the $10,000 reward offered for Jesse James, dead or alive. They eventually met with Crittenden, and it later became a common belief that he actually gave the Ford brothers a written guarantee that they would be pardoned and given the reward money if they killed James. No such document ever surfaced, but when on April 3, 1882 Bob Ford shot the outlaw leader, Crittenden kept his part of the bargain, granting the Fords pardons and the reward money.

Crittenden clearly expected to be applauded for ridding the state of Jesse James and so was not prepared for maudlin support given to the murderous outlaw. "Good-Bye, Jesse!" wailed the *Kansas City Journal;* "Jesse By Jehovah," cried the *St. Joseph Gazette.* But the governor did not help his cause by telling the *St. Louis Republican* after the killing: "I have no excuse to make, no apologies to render to any living man for the part I have played in this bloody drama . . . I am not regretful of his death, and have no censure for the boys who removed him. They deserve credit, is my candid, solemn opinion. Why should these Ford boys be so abused?"

Such are not the statements of political heroes. When in 1882 Frank James stalked into the governor's office, unstrapped his guns and announced it was the first time he had done that since his days riding with Quantrill, the governor's stock plummeted further. Mobs cheered Frank James as he stood on train platforms on his way back to stand trial in Clay County. Crittenden was booed.

Crittenden had hoped to win another term as governor and then to pick up the mantle of the illustrious George Vest in the U.S. Senate, but the "James vote" was now against him, and his party refused even to renominate him for governor, leaving his political career in ruins. By contrast, when Frank James announced his support for Rough Rider Teddy Roosevelt after the turn of the century, the Missouri newspapers considered the endorsement important news and a boost for TR.

See also: CHARLES FORD, ROBERT NEWTON FORD, JAMES BROTHERS, DICK LITTLE.

Crowley, Francis "Two Gun" (1911–1931) murderer

Francis "Two Gun" Crowley was perhaps the nearest thing America produced to a 20th-century counterpart of Billy the Kid. The only differences were that Crowley lived two years less and the Kid was never involved in as fierce a gun battle as Crowley was. In a short but violent criminal career, Crowley engineered a bank robbery, shot down a storekeeper in one of several holdups, was involved in the murder of Virginia Banner, a dance hall hostess who had turned down his partner-in-crime, and killed Frederick Hirsch, a policeman who had asked him for identification in a deserted spot near North Merrick, Long Island.

By then the newspapers had labeled the sallow-faced 19-year-old Two Gun Crowley, a reputation he would enhance in the most savage gun battle in the history of New York City. On May 7, 1931, in what was termed the "siege on West 90th Street," Crowley traded bullets with 300 police attackers from his hideout room, while his 16-year-old girlfriend, Helen Walsh, and his partner, Rudolph Duringer, cowered under a bed. The police poured more than 700 bullets into the room, blasting away brick and mortar from the building's facade. In response, Crowley raced from window to window firing back and throwing tear gas cannisters lobbed into his room back to the street, where they overcame a number of his besiegers. Fifteen thousand persons jammed against police barricades, often seeming about to press through the barriers into the "no-man's-land" where the battle raged. More leaned out of neighboring windows, using pillows as armrests. It was violent Dodge City transferred to a Depression-weary Manhattan, an event to be savored. Finally, Crowley, shot four times and weakened by tear gas, was overwhelmed by a police assault squad that smashed through his door.

At his trial Crowley lived up to his press notices with an air of bravado, bantering with reporters, officers and the judge. He smirked when sentenced to the electric chair. In Sing Sing, Crowley maintained that attitude for a while. He fashioned a club out of a tightly wrapped magazine bound with wire from his cot and tried to slug a guard and escape from the death house. He set fire to his cell. He took off his clothes, stuffed the toilet with them and flooded the cell. Warden Lewis E. Lawes ordered Crowley be kept naked. Still, the youth looked for violence. He placed grains of sugar on the floor, and whenever a fly settled there, he would kill it and laugh.

Then slowly, Crowley changed. A starling flew into the cell, and Crowley didn't kill it. He fed it, and each day the bird returned. "The prisoner had tamed the bird," Lawes noted. "But more surprising was the fact that the tiny bird tamed the bandit." The warden allowed Crowley all his former privileges, and they talked for hours. Lawes saw Crowley for what he was, a pathetic youth with a mental age of 10, born illegitimately and deserted by his mother. The only mother he had ever known was a woman who took him from a foundling home. He had had to work since the age of 12.

Shortly before he was to be executed, a press syndicate offered him $5,000 for his signature on a series of articles already written that purported to tell his life story. Crowley rejected the deal, telling Lawes, "If mother [meaning his foster mother] had that five grand when I was a kid, maybe things would have been different."

A few hours before he died, Crowley pointed to a large water bug running around his cell floor. "See that?" he said to Lawes. "I was about to kill it. Several times I wanted to crush it. It's a dirty looking thing. But then I decided to give it a chance and let it live." Lawes doubted if Crowley even grasped the significance of his remark.

He went to his death without the braggadocio of the newspaper-bred Two Gun Crowley. "Give my love to mother," he called out to Lawes as the hood went over his head.

Cunanan, Andrew (1969–1977) murderer of Gianni Versace

Andrew Cunanan was, if there is such a thing, just an average multiple killer—until he gained notoriety from shooting and killing famed fashion designer Gianni Versace outside his Florida mansion. Clues left at the scene soon identified Cunanan as the killer, just as telltale evidence of his identity clumsily littered the scenes of crimes he'd committed previously.

To the sensation-hungry media, such behavior was reflective of his stature as one of the most daring and brilliant criminals of the century: he disdained covering things up because he knew he could always elude his hunters, utilizing among other attributes his mastery of the art of disguise. One had to assume he was like that "damned elusive" Scarlet Pimpernel—here, there and everywhere—and the police, like the French, knew not where.

In *Three Month Fever: The Andrew Cunanan Story* Gary Indiana noted that Cunanan's killing of Versace instantly made him a world-famous "diabolic icon." According to Indiana, the tabloid press magnified the stories of his many disguises, among other matters, to fashion "a homosexual golem to absorb every scary fantasy about the gay community."

Cunanan did indeed spin his disguises and deceptions through a lifetime of lies going back to childhood to aggrandize his relatively humdrum existence. Thus at times he could pose as the son of a Filipino plantation owner who had fled from the oppression of the Ferdinand Marcos regime, or as having a multimillionaire Israeli father who doted on him and gave him anything he wanted, or then again that he was himself a major international drug dealer. In point of fact Cunanan's father had fled the States after embezzling $106,000 from his company, after which his mother was reduced to living in public housing in Eureka, Ill.

As for his being a major drug dealer, for a time he was actually a drugstore clerk who sold prescription drugs such as Prozac and Xanax on the street. Flashiness and lies were part of his nature, and none of his acquaintances took him seriously for long, forcing him to constantly reinvent himself.

While still in his teens he learned the art of living off very rich men. It would be wrong to say that Cunanan was a simple hustler. He was rather a compensated companion. He was very good looking and lent a touch of class to the men he escorted, being well-versed in current events, fine wines and etiquette. His companions tended to be very friendly and generous to him. With younger men Cunanan was apparently into sado-masochism.

Thus Cunanan reinvented himself to accommodate two different lifestyles. His most successful and fruitful relationship with an older man was with an arts patron in San Diego who moved among the La Jolla elite. There were lavish gifts for Cunanan as well as a grand tour of Europe with his patron. Then Cunanan mixed his two lifestyles. He complained to his millionaire friend that he was worth more. He got a hefty allowance, a lavish apartment and more, but he was not satisfied. Now his patron started viewing him as more of a cheap hustler than a cherished companion. The millionaire kicked him out, giving him severance variously stated to have been $15,000 or $50,000. Cunanan was crushed. He realized it would be harder to reestablish himself in social circles. He was getting older and going to paunch. He tried to maintain his ties to younger friends and companions.

One was David Madsen, a young blond architect from Minnesota. Madsen wanted to end his relationship with Cunanan, suspecting him of being involved in some "shady dealings." Madsen headed back to Minnesota in April 1997. Now low on funds and overdrawn on his credit cards, Cunanan managed to scrape up the money for a one-way ticket to Minneapolis. Madsen took his visitor to dinner but seemed to maintain a certain aloofness. Cunanan found Madsen now had become closer to another friend, Jeffrey Trail, whom he did not like and had that feeling returned from Trail. Trail often objected to Cunanan's use of drugs. Fresh from rejection by his wealthy patron, Cunanan suspected there was no way he could be a part of the Madsen-Trail relationship.

Now the situation became unclear. Cunanan invited Trail to come to Madsen's loft apartment. It is unclear if Madsen was present. What was a fact was that Cunanan beat Trail to death with a claw hammer and rolled the corpse in a carpet and stayed with it for two days. On the second day, Madsen reappeared. The pair were seen walking a dog and later, without the dog, the pair drove to a lake outside Minneapolis. Cunanan shot Madsen with Trail's pistol and dumped the body where it was later found by fishermen.

Authorities readily determined that Cunanan was staying with Madsen but had disappeared. Plenty of evidence was found to link him to the two murders.

But where was Andrew Cunanan?

It turned out Cunanan had moved on to Chicago. Somehow he got to know Lee Miglin, one of Chicago's most successful real estate developers. Apparently Cunanan used a fake gun to force the millionaire into his garage, where he was bound and eventually murdered, his throat cut with a bow saw. Miglin was wrapped in masking tape in bondage mask style. There were also wounds from a garden tool on Miglin's body, indicating Cunanan had tortured him to reveal where his money and some gold coins were. Then Cunanan drove off in Miglin's green Lexus.

Again there were plenty of clues left that linked Cunanan, the murderer of Madsen and Trail, to the Miglin murder as well. Madsen's red jeep was left behind. Again Cunanan was gone.

How he wound up in a Civil War cemetery in Pennsville, N.J., not far from Philadelphia, was never determined except that he may have decided he needed new wheels. He shot caretaker William Reese to death in the cemetery office, deserted the Lexus as too hot and made off with a pickup truck.

Because most, but not all, his victims were gay, homosexuals around the country grew rather tense about meeting young, dark-haired men.

It was known that Cunanan spent a few days in Manhattan and then passed through Florence, S.C. But where was he bound?

In *Homicide: 100 Years of Murder in America*, Gini Graham Scott, Ph.D., surmised: "Knowing what we do now, there seems only one reason Cunanan went all the way to Miami: He was going to kill Versace because—there seems no other explanation—he admired him yet had no way to enter his circle of friends."

It has never been established that Cunanan knew Versace. Cunanan had been present at a lavish party in San Francisco to greet the fashion designer in celebration of the work he'd done on a production of the Richard Strauss opera *Cappricio*. According to Cunanan, Versace had thought he recognized him and introduced himself but that he, Cunanan, brushed him off, saying, "If you're Versace, I'm Coco Chanel." That would have been a typical claim for Cunanan to make, true or not.

In Miami Beach Gianni Versace went about his life. He never suspected his lavish mansion and grounds in South Beach were being watched. On Tuesday morning, Versace left to buy some publications at a newsstand, then turned around and walked back home. He was in the process of inserting a key in the lock to the gate when, innocuous in black shorts, gray T-shirt, black cap and white tennis shoes, Cunanan stepped up behind him. He fired two shots, leaving the designer dying.

Again there were tons of clues identifying the culprit, fingerprints and more. And now knowing what part of the country he was in the law could marshal its forces in vast numbers. Authorities located a garage where Cunanan had stored the cemetery pickup. He had a considerable library of clippings there covering the manhunt for him.

The question was whether Cunanan was still in the Miami area. Was he not, the media noted, a master of disguise? He could be anywhere. The tabloids were very grateful when some authorities speculated that Cunanan might be disguised as a woman.

While the authorities pressed their search, Cunanan had broken into a houseboat moored across from the luxury hotels and condos on Collins Avenue. It had been lavishly furnished by the owner, a Las Vegas club operator. Cunanan was comfortably ensconced in surroundings of wealth. It was where he always wanted to be. But where could he go next? The media had no problem; he was a serial killer who would continue with his killing spree.

But the shadows were closing in on Cunanan. He had all the fame he could ever hope to achieve. He was at a dead end. He knew sooner or later such vessels are checked for intruders. There was no way he dared leave and there was no way he dared stay.

Finally a caretaker did show up and spotted signs of an intrusion. He called police. A SWAT team responded and moved slowly through the boat. They found Cunanan's body propped up on two pillows in the bedroom of the master cabin on the second level. He was dead, his gun in his lap.

The search for the master killer who had dared so often for the authorities to catch him—or was so clumsy he left a parcel of clues wherever he went—was over.

Fittingly, the houseboat Cunanan occupied was demolished in January 1998. But the legend of a mythic killer still remains.

Cunninghams' revenge

In 1855 a band of 13 Mexican bandits, Juan Navarro's band, raided the Arizona ranch of Dave Cunningham and made off with his daughter, 15-year-old Mary. Cunningham and his two sons, John and Adrian, took up the pursuit and soon discovered the sad fate of the girl. She had been raped, and then she and her pinto pony had been forced over a precipice. The trail of the bandits showed they were headed for Mexico. The older Cunningham turned back. He had a wife and ranch to take care of. The two boys went on in what a president of the United States would later call "the most audacious feat ever brought to my attention."

They tracked Navarro's band to the town of Naco and then on to Agua Prieta, where the gang had taken over a cantina. One bandit came outside to relieve himself, and the brothers stabbed him to death with their razor-sharp skinning knives. Soon, another bandit came out to call to the first one. He met the same fate. Two other bandits emerged, accompanied by a woman. John jumped on one, neatly slitting his throat. Adrian, however, missed his man, who drew a long knife and gashed Adrian's arm before John came to the rescue and stabbed the bandit. The woman began screaming and the brothers fled. The remaining nine-man Navarro band did not give chase but rode off, after shooting up the town in anger. They obviously were not sure who or how many men had done the killings.

Eventually, after a run-in with the Mexican police, who were suspicious of their reasons for being in Mexico, the brothers again caught up with Navarro's band heading toward their home base at Chihuahua. They crept close to the bandits' sleeping camp and opened fire. The brothers did not know how many they had killed until dawn, when they found five corpses and the tracks of four horses. Navarro was among the missing. Now, however, Navarro knew he was being hunted and set a trap for the two brothers. One bandit rode ahead with the four horses while Navarro and the other two bandits waited in ambush. In the ensuing shoot-out two bandits were killed, but Adrian was badly wounded in the leg. The brothers continued their pursuit with Adrian suffering in agony. Only Navarro and one other bandit were left. The Cunninghams had no choice but to make their way to Chihuahua openly, even though they knew Navarro would be waiting for them. Gangrene had infected Adrian's leg, and when they reached the town, a doctor said there was no alternative but amputation. Meanwhile, John Cunningham went out searching for the two bandits. He found them in a cantina. On the lookout for any American, they were instantly suspicious of him and may or may not have recognized him. When John walked out of the cantina, Navarro and the other bandit followed him. Outside, John Cunningham whirled, drew two sixguns and opened fire. Both Mexicans dropped, and John stepped over them and fired several more shots into their bodies.

John Cunningham was arrested, but no charges could be pressed against Adrian. While they languished in Chihuahua, a detachment of U.S. cavalry under Maj. Ben Hunt, returning from a mission to Mexico City, passed through and heard of the affair. Maj. Hunt went to see the Cunninghams. The niceties of Mexican law did not impress Hunt; with a veiled threat of force, he secured the release of John Cunningham and returned the brothers to the United States. The Mexican government filed a protest, saying that what the brothers had done amounted to an armed incursion into Mexican sovereignty. A complete report of the affair was made to President Franklin Pierce, who decided that the Cunninghams would not be extradited to Mexico. He called their bloody ride "the most audacious feat ever brought to my attention." Eventually, Mexico let the matter drop.

Curry, Big Nose George (1841–1882) outlaw and murderer

Often confused with Kid Curry (Harvey Logan), Big Nose George Curry (alias Flat Nose George Parrott, alias George Manuse) stands in his own right as not only a prolific stagecoach and train robber but also as the biggest cattle rustler of the 1870s in the Powder River region, Wyoming Territory. Harvey Logan, one of the most prominent of the Wild Bunch, was so taken with Big Nose's criminal career that he appropriated Curry as a nickname for himself.

Big Nose Curry was finally apprehended for the 1880 holdup of a Union Pacific train and the killing of two deputy sheriffs; he was sentenced to hang on April 3, 1882 in Rawlins, Wyo. A week before his slated execution, Big Nose broke out of jail but was immediately captured by a mob that, taking unkindly to condemned men escaping, resolved to hang him on the spot. Big Nose was ordered to climb a ladder set against a lamp post, put a rope around his own neck and jump. Big Nose did, but the rope broke. While some of the mob said another rope should be secured, others felt it wasn't worth the effort and shot Big Nose to death as he lay on the ground.

Even in death, Big Nose had a role to play. The local druggist, Dr. J. E. Osborne, who was also the coroner, performed an autopsy on the badman and in the process helped himself to some of his parts. He peeled off the hide from Big Nose's chest, tanned it and made a pair of slippers, which were still on display in a Rawlins bank during the 1970s. Osborne, who incidentally went on to become governor of Wyoming, fashioned other tanned hide from the outlaw into a tobacco pouch. When he had finished skinning Big Nose, Osborne dropped the rest of the corpse into a barrel of alcohol, put it out behind his premises and forgot about it. The barrel was rediscovered in 1950 and caused quite a stir until the dry bones therein were identified as the old badman Big Nose Curry.

Custom House Place Chicago vice district

Of all the "brothel streets" in Chicago during the 19th century, the one that gave the police the most trouble was Custom House Place. Besides the standard bordellos, the street contained an abundance of panel houses, where, by use of sliding panels, a male customer's possessions would be stolen while he was involved with a prostitute. A study in 1890 revealed there were almost 200 panel houses on Custom House Place, Plymouth Place, and Clark and State Streets, with the greatest number on Custom House Place.

Probably the most notorious business on Custom House Place was at No. 202, a resort that functioned as a standard brothel, as a panel house and as a meeting place for some of the worst female ruffians of the 1880s and 1890s. The house was run by Lizzie Davenport, probably the biggest operator of panel houses in the city and certainly the wealthiest. Among the women who headquartered at No. 202 were Emma Ford, her sister Pearl Smith, Flossie Moore and Mary White, better known as the Strangler. All these women functioned as panel house workers, street muggers and holdup artists. The Strangler was estimated by police to have stolen more than $50,000 in less than three years. Inside No. 202 it was quite common for 10 to 15 robberies to take place in a night. Because the house was subject to frequent police raids, Lizzie Davenport protected her ladies by installing a closet made of 3-inch oak planks with a massive door, where they could hide. Detective Clifton Wooldridge became the darling of the press when he rousted the women by boring holes in the door and blowing pepper inside. Through such sterling police work, one of Chicago's most notorious houses was finally shuttered.

See also: EMMA FORD, FLOSSIE MOORE, PANEL HOUSES, CLIFTON WOOLDRIDGE.

Cutler lie detector decision

Although lie detector findings are generally not accepted as evidence in courtroom proceedings, based on a landmark decision in *Frye v. United States,* there has been an occasional ruling the other way. A breakthrough of sorts occurred in California in 1972. Raymond Christopher Cutler was stopped by a deputy U.S. marshal in the Los Angeles International Airport when the officer became suspicious of a suitcase Cutler was carrying. The marshal requested permission to open the suitcase for inspection and Cutler's response was to be a point of contention later. The marshal said Cutler had agreed, and Cutler said he had not. In any event, the suitcase was opened and found to contain marijuana.

Cutler's defense was based on the claim that his luggage had been searched illegally since he had refused permission. With the consent of Superior Court judge Allan Miller, both men, the defendant and the marshal, were subjected to lie detector tests. The examiner reported that Cutler's claim of having denied permission for his luggage to be searched was truthful, and on this basis the defendant was freed. Judge Miller ruled that since scientific tests had demonstrated the accuracy of lie detector equipment and techniques, rules preventing the use of lie detector findings as evidence should be changed. It was a surprising decision, one that sparked the district attorney's immediate notice of an intention to appeal. However, no appeal was made. It soon appeared, observers noted, that the decision in the Cutler case would have no impact on other cases, which provided more sweeping precedents.

Ironically, shortly after the Cutler decision California governor Edmund Brown, Jr., signed into law a bill that ran contrary to the spirit of the Cutler case. The law, referred to as the police officers' bill of rights, gave law enforcement officers the right to refuse to take a lie detector test without fear that such refusal could be held against them.

See also: *FRYE V. UNITED STATES,* LIE DETECTOR.

Cyclone Louie (1882–1908) Coney Island strongman and murderer

Using the name Cyclone Louie, Vach Lewis was a noted professional strongman who was always available for a hit assignment, thereby earning the title of the Coney Island Killer in the early 1900s. When two men were found strangled on the beach one morning with their necks virtually wrung like chickens, all Coney Island knew Cyclone Louie had done the deed. So too did the police, but two dancing girls and six other members of their family insisted the strongman had spent the entire night under their tender ministrations after he had allegedly wrenched his back while wrapping an iron bar around his neck. There Cyclone Louie lay moaning, too weak to unwrap the cursed metal. The police were forced to drop the charge against Louie, who shortly thereafter regained his strength and unbent the iron bar.

While Cyclone Louie's murder services involved a substantial fee, he rendered similar duty without charge for Kid Twist, the last great leader of the Eastman gang before it fractionalized upon his killing. The big, hulking Cyclone Louie followed Kid Twist around like a loyal dog, marveling at his mental superiority. There were those who said that Cyclone Louie would never meet his mental equal. But although he wasn't bright, Cyclone Louie was nonetheless useful to Kid Twist. One service he performed was the elimination of "the Bottler," the partner of Kid Twist and Kid Dahl in the operation of a profitable crooked card game in a Suf-

Firing a shot into President William McKinley's stomach, assassin Leon Czolgosz cries, "I done my duty."

folk Street house on Manhattan's Lower East Side. Twist and Dahl had simply declared themselves in on the Bottler's operation and later decided to declare the Bottler out. Thus, at the time of the Bottler's murder Kid Twist was in the Delancey Street police station arguing with the desk sergeant for the release of a fellow gangster who had purposely got himself arrested, and Kid Dahl was in a Houston Street restaurant involved in a loud argument with the proprietor. With those alibis firmly in place, Cyclone Louie walked in on the card game and shot the Bottler dead in front of 20 players, each of whom later claimed either to have been elsewhere or, if they admitted being there, to have been looking in the other direction.

Cyclone Louie died in the service of Kid Twist on May 14, 1908 while making the rounds of Coney Island dives. The pair ran into a mortal enemy of Twist's, Louie the Lump, in one dive and ordered him to jump out the window, a rather unfriendly suggestion since they were on the second floor of the building. Louie the Lump was forced to leap but survived and, being a member of the Five Points Gang, quickly put in a call to Manhattan for reinforcements. Twenty gunmen answered the summons and stationed themselves outside the dive, where Twist and Cyclone Louie were drinking themselves senseless. When the pair emerged from the joint, Louie the Lump shot Kid Twist in the brain. Cyclone Louie tried to run for it but was cut down by a Five Point volley and tumbled dead atop his beloved mentor. Later, every Five Pointer involved insisted his bullet struck Cyclone Louie. The police do not seem to have made an accurate count of the bullets that brought about Cyclone Louie's demise. The only one ever arrested for the crime was Louie the Lump. The killer's lawyer made a fervent, if somewhat tortured, plea of self-defense, which evidently had some effect since Louie the Lump was sent to prison for a mere 11 months.

See also: KID TWIST.

Czolgosz, Leon (1873–1901) McKinley assassin

The crowd at the Pan-American Exposition in Buffalo, N.Y. at noon on September 6, 1901 was jubilant over the opportunity to meet William McKinley, the president of the United States, face to face. They queued up excitedly after the president had agreed to shake hands with all comers. At the end of the line was a dark little man of 28, his right hand swathed in a white bandage. When he was about sixth in line, the man lowered his head to keep from being spotted. He had lived in nearby West Seneca for some time and was known to police as a dangerous anarchist.

The president was smiling as he stepped toward Czolgosz. Czolgosz waited until he was just a few feet from the president and then flipped a pistol out from under the phony bandage and fired. The first shot hit a button and bounced away, but the second penetrated the president's abdomen. McKinley stiffened a moment but did not lose consciousness as guards and soldiers pounced on his attacker. "I done my duty," Czolgosz cried. A guard took careful aim and smashed his fist into Czolgosz's face. "Be easy with him boys," the president said weakly.

Eight days later, McKinley died of gangrene of the pancreas. Latter-day opinion contended that bungled medical care was as much the cause of death as Czolgosz's bullet. Nine days after the president's death, Czolgosz was put on trial, a matter in which the defendant took no interest. He said nothing to his court-appointed lawyers, refused to take the stand and showed no reaction when a verdict of guilty was announced. All he would do was affirm his anarchist beliefs, even though long before the assassination an anarchist publication, *Free Society*, had urged others to avoid him, denouncing Czolgosz as a dangerous crank and possibly a spy or police agent.

When Czolgosz went to the electric chair at Auburn Prison, he said: "I killed the President because he was the enemy of the good people—the good working people. I am not sorry for my crime." When he was placed in his coffin, sulfuric acid was poured on his body, and experts predicted his corpse would decompose in 12 hours.

After McKinley's death, the third presidential assassination in 36 years, the new president, Theodore Roosevelt, ordered the U.S. Secret Service to take over full responsibility for guarding the chief executive.

Dahmer, Jeffrey (1960–1994)   the underinvestigated killer
In February 1992, 31-year-old Jeffrey L. Dahmer was convicted of the murder of 15 young men and boys (plus another one in a later prosecution), most of them killed right in his apartment. Far from being on the alert for a serial killer, the Milwaukee police did nothing to catch Dahmer early on—and actually were subjected to national outrage as being virtually guilty themselves of ignorant complicity *before* the fact!

In one case, a Dahmer victim escaped naked and bloodied from the killer's apartment and raced screaming down the street. Three police officers who "investigated" simply decided the matter was no more than a quarrel between gay lovers and turned the victim back over to Dahmer without so much as checking out his apartment. Dahmer took his victim in tow and after terrorizing him for a few hours, he got around to butchering him. It would be charged that if the victim had been white, rather than a member of a minority— in this case, a Laotian—the police would have been more competent in the investigation.

Meanwhile Dahmer went on luring victims to his home, drugging them, killing them to perform primitive lobotomies by drilling holes in their heads in an effort to make them into zombie-like sex slaves. Dahmer also engaged in frightful practices of cannibalism and necrophilia, descriptions of which are best left to medical texts.

On July 22, 1991 two police officers stopped a black man running with a set of handcuffs around one wrist. The man, near hysteria, told them a white man with a big knife was saying he was going to cut out his heart. The officers went to Dahmer's home and asked to enter. Dahmer, having consumed a large amount of beer, did not object, and the officers found a knife under a bed in the two-room apartment. In a dresser

Jeffrey Dahmer, killer of 16 young men and boys, was actually caught once by Milwaukee police but was inexplicably let go. (Reuters/Corbis-Bettmann)

drawer there were scores of photographs of homosexual acts and other pictures of apparently dead male bodies and body parts. Opening the refrigerator, the police found a human head. (It became a bit of talk radio black humor that this find made the police somewhat suspicious.)

Dahmer was taken into custody, and detectives and technicians took over a frightening search of the premises. Body parts turned up in drawers, coolers, closets, boxes and a large plastic drum. Checking missing persons reports, authorities were able to determine the identities of the victims, ranging in age from late teens to 30 years old. The victims were mostly black but some were white, Hispanic, Laotian and American Indian.

Since Wisconsin had no death penalty, Dahmer was given 15 life sentences, plus one more for a fatal beating of an 18-year-old in Ohio. Only technically was Dahmer spared execution. He and another prisoner, Jesse Anderson, a wife killer, were attacked by prisoners while they were cleaning a washroom and shower area in Columbia Correctional Center in Portage. Both were killed with a metal club wielded by Christopher Searver, who was doing life for robbery-murder.

Even in death, Dahmer did not escape a bizarre circumstance: Shackles were kept on him during his autopsy as though there was some fear that he might rise from the dead to kill again. His brain was preserved for forensic study.

Dalton, J. Frank   See JESSE JAMES—IMPOSTORS.

Dalton brothers   outlaws

The outlaw Dalton brothers might have become great bandits in the tradition of their cousins, the Younger brothers, who rode with Jesse James, had they not come into the Wild West just as it was taming down. Law and order were taking over, but the Daltons refused to believe it. They were driven to make a name for themselves.

Oddly enough, four of the brothers—Frank, Gratton, Robert and Emmett—first pinned on U.S. marshal badges for Hanging Judge Parker's court in Fort Smith, Ark., and Frank was killed in the line of duty. Evidently, the surviving brothers plus younger William were unimpressed by Judge Parker's hang-'em-high policies and decided to hit the outlaw trail. They headed for California, where they pulled a few small capers and then tried a train robbery in 1891. Bill was caught and sent to prison for 25 years. Grat was given the same sentence but escaped and rejoined Bob and Emmett, and they hightailed it back east.

Contemporary rendering depicts the bloody demise of the Dalton gang in Death Alley, Coffeyville, Kan

In Oklahoma the trio started up a gang that took in such worthies as Charlie Bryant, Charley Pierce, George Newcomb and Bill Doolin, who was to become a more distinguished outlaw than any of the Daltons. They pulled a few minor jobs, during which Doolin was starting to think the Daltons were nothing like their kinfolk, the Youngers.

The brothers, for their part, were determined to do something big to make the West stand up and take notice of them, and they came up with the idea of the great Coffeyville Raid. They decided to hit the Kansas town and pull a double bank job, robbing two institutions at the same time. It made sense to them, one entrance into town, one escape from town and double profits. Six men started out on the raid, but Doolin pulled out when his horse went lame, perhaps thinking, What am I doing with clowns like these?

On October 5, 1892 the three Daltons plus Dick Broadwell and Bill Powers rode into the Coffeyville town plaza and set about holding up the Condon and First National banks. They had done no recent scouting

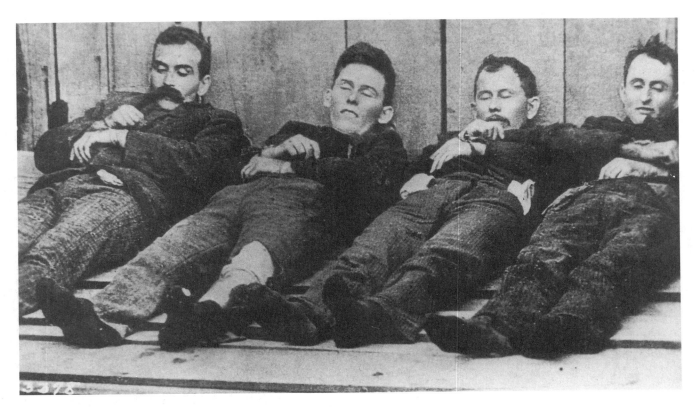

The end of the Daltons. Photo shows corpses of (left to right) Bill Powers, Bob Dalton, Grat Dalton and Dick Broadwell.

and found the hitching posts in front of both banks had been removed because workmen were busy on the street. The bandits had to leave their horses in an alley—Death Alley, it would be called later—about a block away. They came out of Death Alley carrying Winchesters and broke off in two groups to head for the banks. The scene was noted by a local citizen, Alec McKenna, who thought he even recognized one or two of the men as Daltons. Watching from a distance, McKenna spotted weapons being pointed in one of the banks and sounded the alarm. The robbers still might have gotten away in time had they not had to wait around for a time lock to open one of the safes.

By the time the gang emerged from the two banks, half the town was armed and laying for them. In the next two hectic minutes, four citizens of Coffeyville died from the outlaws' gunfire, but the Dalton gang would ride no more. None of them survived the race through Death Alley, although they did make it to their horses. Charlie Connelly, the town marshal, traded bullets with Grat Dalton, and both fell dead. Broadwell was shot out of his saddle, and both Powers and Bob Dalton were gunned down by John Kloehr, a livery stable owner.

Only Emmett made it to the end of the alley and could have gotten away, but in a show of brotherly devotion, he turned back to try to save Bob, whom he idolized. Dying, Bob moaned: "Don't mind me, boy. I'm done for. Don't surrender! Die game!"

Emmett was still trying to pull Bob up in the saddle when he was felled by 18 buckshot in the back. Of the five, only Emmett survived. He was sentenced to life in the Kansas State Penitentiary. Ironically, his act of pointless heroism at Coffeyville gave the Daltons their greatest claim to fame.

In 1895 Bill Dalton, released from prison, was killed by a posse in Oklahoma Territory. Emmett Dalton was pardoned in 1907 and moved to California, where he prospered as a building contractor. He also did some writing for the movies and appeared in small roles in some of his own epics. His main literary work was entitled *When the Daltons Rode*, which appeared in 1931, six years before the last of the Daltons died. It purported to be a true account of the Daltons' activities but has never been regarded as overly accurate or incisive. The fact is the Daltons never understood they had been born a quarter of a century too late. Emmett showed that in 1910 when a New York reporter asked his expert opinion on how to keep the city cleansed of crime. The reformed outlaw earnestly advised, "Guard the entrances to the town."

Daly, John (1839–1864) Western outlaw

The head of perhaps the most vicious gang to terrorize the Nevada gold fields in the 1860s, John Daly, a young gunfighter from California who followed the gold trail, firmly believed in what might be called "criminal vigilantism." He felt that resistance by law-abiding elements called for their lynching. Because of these fear tactics, the Daly gang operated with a great deal of impunity and left a trail of robbery and murder from Aurora to Carson City. In 1863 one of Daly's confederates, Jim Sears, tried some horse stealing and was shot dead by an employee of William R. Johnson. Daly promptly held Johnson responsible for this act of resistance and prepared to exercise his form of vigilante justice. On February 1, 1864 Daly and three of his men cornered Johnson and made an example of him by cutting his throat and setting his body aflame. Daly later boasted of the work of "us vigilantes," but it developed that what he had accomplished was not the quashing of all resistance but the planting of a powerful suggestion. The Citizens' Protective Association was set up, and exactly one week after the Johnson assassination, Daly and three members of his gang, Johnny McDowell, William Buckley and Jim Masterson, were seized separately before they suspected what was afoot and were summarily hanged outside Aurora's Armory Hall.

Dance of Death   famed multiple hangings

Probably no simultaneous public hangings in the 19th century produced more protests than the celebrated Dance of Death at Fort Smith, Ark. on September 3, 1875.

Six condemned men had been found guilty in Hanging Judge Parker's so-called Court of the Damned and were sentenced to die on a special 12-man gallows constructed by George Maledon, who became known as Parker's Lord High Executioner. This first multiuse of the gallows brought out a crowd of 5,000 eager citizens. Jamming into the fort compound, families came by the wagonload from as far as 50 to 60 miles away to witness the first dispensation of Parker-style justice. Youngsters mounted the walls of the fort for a better view; however, the more comfortable vantage points were reserved for gentlemen of the press from St. Louis, Kansas City, Philadelphia, New York and Boston, among others.

At exactly 9:30 A.M. the six men were brought to the gallows. One, a Cherokee named Smoker Mankiller, had been found guilty of killing his white neighbor but protested to the end that he had not done so, his unfor-

tunate name notwithstanding. Sam Fooy, a half-breed who had murdered a schoolteacher during a robbery, had made peace with himself and was ready, even eager, to die. John Whittingham, who had clubbed and knifed a drinking companion to death, left behind a written condemnation of "demon rum." Edmund Campbell, convicted of a double-passion slaying, had nothing to say. James H. Moore, a horse thief and murderer, spotted a friend in the crowd, waved and called, "Good-bye, Sandy." And Dan Evans, who had killed an 18-year-old for his boots, surveyed the throng from the high platform and opined, "There are worse men here than me."

After prayers led by four local clergymen, Maledon slipped black masks over the men's heads and adjusted the nooses of specially ordered Kentucky hemp rope around their necks. He clambered down the 12 steps and pressed the trigger-release. Six bodies hurtled into an 8-foot drop. Not a single body twitched. All had died instantly of broken necks rather than suffering slow strangulation. Hangman Maledon was proud of his handiwork and certainly the local citizenry was satisfied both with the show and the demonstration of quick, unyielding justice.

The hangings received coast-to-coast newspaper coverage, and the reaction was generally far from laudatory. Newspaper readers were horrified over the simultaneous public hangings, although most probably, they would readily have accepted such executions if performed separately. Judge Parker bore the brunt of the public revulsion, being regarded as a monster who enjoyed wholesale executions and gaining for the first time the sobriquet of Hanging Parker, a name that would stick to him during the 21 years of his judicial reign. Despite the criticism, Parker and Maledon continued their brand of legal retribution, although never again would six doomed men do the Dance of Death at one time. Thereafter, the top number was five.

See also: GEORGE MALEDON, ISAAC "HANGING JUDGE" PARKER.

Daniels, James (?–1865) murderer and vigilante victim

Called the "vigilante's experiment," murderer James Daniels was the first prisoner of the famous Montana Vigilance Committee of the 1860s to be turned over to the law instead of being promptly lynched. The experiment was not a glowing success and the vigilantes did not make the same mistake twice—at least not with the same man.

A bad-tempered Californian, Daniels stabbed to death a man named Gartley in a dispute over cards. When she heard of her husband's death, Mrs. Gartley suffered a fatal heart attack. Normally, Daniels would have faced quick vigilante action, but times were changing in the territory, and many citizens—even vigilance committee members—were convinced the politic thing to do was to hand over Daniels for trial in the regular courts of justice. And they prevailed.

In view of the extenuating circumstance—both men had gone after each other at the same time—Daniels was found guilty only of murder in the second degree and was sent to prison for three years. If that conclusion galled a number of citizens, it was nothing compared to the feelings aroused when Daniels was granted a pardon after only a few months. It appeared that the pardon may have resulted from a clerical error, but the matter was soon academic. Daniels returned to the scene of his crime and made it clear he intended to wage war on the vigilantes who had brought him to justice. In Daniels' case such loose talk was a capital matter, and he was seized by vigilantes on his first night in Helena and hanged forthwith. It was a considerable length of time before the vigilantes decided their experiment with established justice was worth trying again.

See also: PROFESSOR THOMAS J. DIMSDALE.

Daniels, Murl (1924–1949) mass murderer

With another parolee, Murl Daniels committed a series of senseless murders in Ohio in 1948, making him the quarry in what came to be labeled the "greatest manhunt in Ohio history."

Both Daniels, a psychopath, and his partner, John Coulter West, had done time at the Mansfield Reformatory, where, said Daniels, they had formed a compact that they would return someday to "take care" of one or more of the guards who had mistreated them. At the time, Daniels was serving a one-to-25-year term for a stickup and West, a feeble-minded man, was doing a one-to-seven-year stretch for stealing tires off a truck. Some critics of the American justice and penal systems have said that Daniels never should have been paroled, while others have insisted that the state was negligent in permitting an inmate such as West to mingle with a dangerous psychopath like Daniels.

When the two were paroled, they teamed up to commit stickups throughout the Midwest, finally killing a tavern owner during a robbery. They continued to rove the Midwest, committing several more holdups before they remembered their compact about killing some of their former guards. They headed for Mansfield, especially determined to kill a guard named Harris. But they were unable to locate him. They then decided to get Harris' address from his superior, John Elmer Niebel, who was in charge of the reformatory farm. They awakened Niebel about midnight and decided they would have to hold him and his wife and daughter until after they had killed Har-

ris. They took the three of them to a cornfield outside of town and ordered them to take off their clothes, in order to make it more difficult for them to give an alarm if they worked themselves loose from their bindings, but then the pair realized that they had neglected to bring any rope with them. So instead, they shot and killed all three and fled to Cleveland. When they were identified as the killers an intensive manhunt was mounted. Daniels and West raced around the state, killing a farmer to get his car and later a truck driver for his truck.

They almost made it out of the state with the truck, a haulaway carrying new Studebaker cars. They were waved through a number of police roadblocks until one sheriff realized that the truck was headed back toward the auto plant instead away from it. The two were ordered to stop, and West started shooting, hitting a guard before he himself was killed. Daniels surrendered meekly and went to the electric chair on January 3, 1949.

Danites alleged Mormon murder squads

There was a time when almost every anti-Mormon in the West was certain that the Mormon Church had a special terrorist killer squad charged with the violent eradication of all those who opposed the Mormons. According to the belief, Brigham Young had organized these Destroying Angels, or Danites, who operated as a separate cell of the church and took on all assignments involving death or violence. In an interview with Horace Greeley, Young emphatically denied their existence. Real or not, the story of the Danites was widely believed, and every Mormon charged with a crime would be labeled a Danite. The belief, of course, kept anti-Mormonism at fever pitch for many years.

Dannan, Emmanuel (1843–1851) murder victim, folk hero

Known as the "boy who wouldn't lie," eight-year-old Emmanuel Dannan became an instant Wisconsin folk hero when he was killed by his adopted parents, Samuel Norton and his wife, in 1851. Both of Emmanuel's English-immigrant parents died before he was five years old, and he was saved from the poorhouse by an uncle, who unfortunately died a year later. The Samuel Nortons then adopted the child.

Emmanuel was eight when he happened to see his stepparents murder a peddler. The Nortons ordered the boy to lie to the police, but he said he would not. He was hanged by his wrists from the rafters of the family's log cabin deep in the woods and beaten with willow switches for two hours. During his ordeal the only thing the boy would say was, "Pa, I will not lie!" After two hours the boy's spirit was still unbroken, but his body was and he died. The facts came out in an investigation, and the Nortons were both sent to prison for seven years, while Emmanuel's tale spread throughout the area.

There was talk of erecting a monument to his memory, and a total of $1,099.94 was collected, only to be siphoned off by a fund-raiser. Over the years the story of Emmanuel Dannan's bravery became part of the state's folklore, and finally, on May 2, 1954 a monument was erected in his memory at Montello, Wis. The inscription read, "Blessed are they which are persecuted for righteousness sake, for theirs is the kingdom of Heaven." Since then, Truth Day in Montello has been celebrated every May 2.

Darrow, Clarence Seward (1857–1938) defense lawyer

America's greatest lawyer, Clarence Darrow, had been practicing before the bar for 16 years when in 1894 he took on the case of a convicted murderer who was appealing to a higher court. Darrow lost and the man, Robert Prendergast, was hanged. He was the first—and last—Darrow client to be executed, although the famous lawyer represented more than 50 accused murderers, many of whom were definitely guilty.

Born in the Ohio farmlands in 1857, Darrow's formal education ended after he finished the equivalent of one year of high school. He continued to study law books at night, however, and saved up enough money to go to law school. In 1878 Darrow was admitted to the bar and soon became a political reformer, backing the ill-fated John Peter Altgeld's efforts in Illinois. Later, he was a well-paid corporation lawyer, but his natural sympathies lay with the working man, and in 1894 he rejected the business world to defend labor leader Eugene V. Debs in connection with the Pullman strike. He earned the permanent enmity of business when in 1906 he successfully defended radical labor leader Big Bill Haywood on a murder charge. However, he was forced to plead labor men James McNamara and John J. McNamara guilty in the 1910 bombing of the *Los Angeles Times*, a decision that had a shattering effect on the Western labor movement. The unions refused to pay him his $50,000 fee in the case, and the prosecution, prodded by *Times* publisher and rabid anti-union-

The Great Defender, Clarence Darrow, is shown in shirt sleeves, at the Monkey Trial. Standing behind him in light jacket is schoolteacher John Scopes.

ist Harrison Gray Otis, tried to convict him of jury tampering. Darrow beat the charges, but he never again took a labor-related case.

He continued to achieve considerable success, however, in leading criminal cases. Darrow's secret, he admitted, was his ability to pick a jury, which he considered the most important part of any case. "Get the right men in the box," he said, "and the rest is window dressing." Darrow would seldom accept a German or a Swede for a jury. A German, he felt, was too bullheaded and too "law and order" oriented and a Swede also too stubborn. His favorite jurors were Irishmen and Jews. Both, he felt, were highly emotional and easily moved to sympathy. He often said the perfect jury was six Irishmen and six Jews. "Give me that combination in the box," he remarked often, "and I could get Judas Iscariot off with a five dollar fine."

Darrow also preferred older men to younger ones. An older man, he said, was more sympathetic to the jams other men got into. In important cases Darrow assigned investigators to look into the lives of prospective jurors and would come into court with a dossier on all the veniremen, aware of their foibles, their likes and dislikes, and their prejudices. Through the years Darrow was never troubled by the testimony of experts against his clients. His handling of a medical witness called to testify that an accident victim would soon be up and around was typical; it ran:

> "You came here from out of town to testify for the company, Doctor?"
> "Yes."
> "And you had a nice trip?"
> "Yes, Mr. Darrow."
> "How much are you getting for testifying, Doctor—over and above the expenses of your trip?"
> "Three hundred dollars."

Darrow then turned to the jury, raised his eyebrows and, still looking at the jurors rather than the witness, growled, "That will be all, Doctor."

Once Darrow implied that an expert was a money grubber, he never deigned to concern himself with what the witness had to say—and usually neither did the jury.

There is no record of how much money Darrow made in a year. There were years when he made over $100,000, but others when, bogged down in cases with penniless clients, he netted very little. Even in what was perhaps his most famous case—that of thrill-slayers Nathan Leopold and Richard Loeb in 1924, two wealthy Chicago youths whom he saved from execution—his clients, the boys' parents, reneged on paying him the major part of his fee.

The Leopold and Loeb case showed Darrow's courtroom genius at its best, passing up a jury trial in favor of making his case to a judge. From experience, Darrow knew that while a juror might convict and thus doom a defendant if his vote was only $1/12$ of the decision, that same juror would draw back if his vote alone was the deciding factor. He shrewdly viewed the judge, a humane jurist, John Caverly, as no different than the average juror.

Although both sides presented expert psychiatric testimony, Darrow knew in the end that he would have to sway the judge with his summation, in part because he himself probably recognized his two clients were homicidal. Throughout the trial Darrow had had trouble keeping them from smirking in court and hamming it up for photographers outside the court. Public opinion had been against the two rich boys from the beginning and became even more so because of their mannerisms during the trial.

For two days Darrow summarized his case, maintaining his clients were not murderers but two boys who had taken a human life because they were mentally and morally sick, victims of complicated, often misunderstood forces, buried deep in their past. He ended by declaring: "Your Honor, if these two boys hang, *you* must order them to hang. It will be entirely up to *you*, Your Honor. There must be no division of responsibility here, Your Honor. The sentencing of these boys to die must be an act on *your* part alone. Such a sentencing must be your own cold, deliberate, premeditated act, without the slightest chance to shift any part of the responsibility. Your Honor alone stands between these boys and the trap door of the scaffold."

Darrow's gamble of bypassing a jury trial worked. The judge sentenced the pair to life imprisonment.

The following year Darrow won worldwide acclaim in Tennessee's famous Monkey Trial, in which he dueled with William Jennings Bryan over the theory of evolution. Darrow's client, a young schoolteacher named John Scopes, was convicted of teaching evolution, a decision that was almost inevitable considering the time and the place, and fined $100, but the famous lawyer clearly won the case against Bryan in the world of public opinion.

Darrow published his autobiography in 1932, six years before he died at the age of 81.

See also: JOHN P. ALTGELD, WILLIAM J. BURNS, WILLIAM D. "BIG BILL" HAYWOOD, *LOS ANGELES TIMES* BOMBING, LEOPOLD AND LOEB, MASSIE CASE, MISTAKEN IDENTITY, HARRY ORCHARD, EARL ROGERS, JOHN T. SCOPES.

Daugherty, Roy (1871–1924) outlaw

One of the few Western bank robbers to make the transition from riding a horse to driving an automobile in his line of work, Roy Daugherty, better known as

Arkansas Tom, was born in to a very religious Missouri family; two of his older brothers became preachers. Leaving home in his early teens, he turned up in Oklahoma Territory and by 1892 was riding with the notorious Doolin gang.

He was with Bill Doolin and his men in the epic Battle of Ingalls on September 1, 1893 and was the only member of the gang captured there. While the other gang members were in Murray's Saloon, Arkansas Tom was sleeping in his room at the Pierce Hotel when a possee of 13 lawmen headed by Jim Masterson, Bat's brother, came thundering into town. When the shooting started, Arkansas Tom climbed up on the hotel roof for a better overview and from there killed Deputy Tom Houston and probably killed Deputy Ike Steel. His sharpshooting permitted the rest of the Doolin gang to fight their way out of town with only one man wounded, but Arkansas Tom was trapped on the hotel roof. An hour-long shoot-out ended when Tom Masterson got hold of several sticks of dynamite and threatened to blow up the entire building and Arkansas with it. Arkansas Tom laid down his arms and surrendered.

For his part in the Battle of Ingalls, Daugherty was sentenced to 50 years in prison, but he was paroled in 1910, in large part due to the efforts of his preacher brothers. Arkansas Tom vowed to go straight after that. Nonetheless, he took part in a bank job in Neosho, Mo. in 1916. Sent back to prison, he was not released until November 11, 1921. Arkansas Tom was soon identified as having been involved in another bank stickup, this time in Asbury, Mo., but he managed to stay out of the way of the law until August 6, 1924, when a young policeman recognized him in Joplin, Mo. Arkansas had managed the switch from horses to cars in bank robberies easily enough, but the switch in clothing fashions was more difficult for the old-fashioned gunfighter. Back in his younger days, Arkansas Tom was quite a fast draw, but in 1924 it wasn't common practice to walk around with hip holsters. While fast-draw Tom was trying to claw his shooting iron out of his back pocket, the policeman easily cut him down.

See also: DOOLIN GANG; INGALLS, OKLAHOMA TERRITORY, BATTLE OF.

d'Autremont brothers See EDWARD OSCAR HEINRICH.

Davis, Angela (1944–) political activist and accused murderess
Few political figures in recent years have been so enmeshed in a criminal case as black activist Angela Davis, a former acting assistant professor of philosophy at the University of California at Los Angeles. In 1972 Davis was charged with kidnapping, murder and conspiracy in connection with the highly publicized shoot-out at the Marin County Courthouse in San Raphael, Calif. in August 1970. Before she was brought to trial, Davis fled and was placed on the FBI's list of the 10 most wanted fugitives.

Born in Birmingham, Ala., Davis took part, with her mother, in civil rights demonstrations during the mid-1950s. After graduation from Brandeis University and two years of postgraduate study in West Germany, she enrolled in the University of California at San Diego in 1967 to study under marxist philosopher Herbert Marcuse. Growing more radical in her political beliefs, Davis became involved with a number of militant black organizations, including the Black Panthers. In 1968 she joined the Communist Party. The following year Davis was hired to teach four courses in philosophy at UCLA. Within a few short months she was dismissed from her position after her membership in the Communist Party was revealed by an ex-FBI informer. She won reinstatement under court order and in 1969–70 her courses were described as among the most popular on campus. The school administration monitored her classes and found them "excellent," but the Board of Regents, which included Gov. Ronald Reagan, refused to reappoint her.

What most upset the regents was her speeches in support of the Soledad Brothers, the name given to a group of black prisoners at Soledad Prison who had organized a marxist revolutionary collective among the convicts. Three of the Brothers, George Jackson, Fleeta Drumgo and John Cluchette, were accused of murdering a white prison guard a short time after three other blacks involved in a fistfight had been shot dead by a tower guard, an action the local district attorney had labeled justifiable homicide.

Davis became a principal figure in the Soledad Brothers' Defense Committee, organized in support of the three prisoners. She established a clandestine correspondence with George Jackson even before meeting him. Eventually, the charges against Jackson, Drumgo and Cluchette were dismissed.

Meanwhile, after receiving threats against her life, Davis legally bought several guns for the defense of Soledad House, her base during the trial of the trio. On August 7, 1970 Jonathan Jackson, George's teenage brother, and Davis' constant companion during this period, took the guns Davis had purchased and entered the Marin County Courthouse, where a San Quentin prisoner, James McClain, was on trial for a prison stabbing. Jackson's plan was to free McClain and two other inmates there to testify in McClain's defense and to take white hostages who would be held as ransom for the release of the Soledad Brothers. Passing guns to the three convicts, Jackson supervised the taking of five hostages from the courthouse, including Judge Harold Haley and District Attorney Gary Thomas. A gunfight erupted in the parking lot and Judge Haley, Jackson and two of the inmates were killed, while Thomas was badly wounded and left permanently paralyzed.

Because the guns were owned by her, Davis was indicted on charges of murder, kidnapping and conspiracy. She went into hiding and became the object of a nationwide search. Two months later, she was captured by the FBI in a New York City motel and extradited back to California. While she was held without bail in California, a worldwide Free Angela movement sprang up. Finally, Davis was released on $102,000 bail.

During her trial, which finally began on February 28, 1972 after a series of procedural delays, the prosecution's case proved to be astonishingly fragile, based on the premise that Davis' "passion for George Jackson"—who had been killed in August of the previous year while allegedly attempting to escape from prison—had led her to plot the courthouse kidnappings. The defense countered that there was absolutely no evidence linking Davis to the kidnapping or to the planning of it. On June 4, 1972 a jury of 11 whites and one Mexican-American acquitted her on all counts following 13 hours of deliberation.

Davis, Jack (?1845–1879?) train robber

On November 4, 1870 Jack Davis, a leader of the Davis-Chapman gang, pulled the first train robbery in the Far West, holding up the Central Pacific's Train No. 1 near Verdi, Nev. The job netted more than $40,000.

As successful as he was at train robbing, Davis was a failure at most other criminal endeavors. He appeared as a not too successful gambler around Virginia City in the late 1860s. Davis was suspected of having taken part in some small-time stagecoach holdups but the charges never stuck. Early in 1870 he linked up with John Chapman, the superintendent of a Sunday school in Reno, and together they plotted to imitate the train-robbing exploits of the Reno gang of Indiana. Their first robbery was a success, but careless free spending by some of the gang eventually led to their capture. Davis was sentenced to 10 years and Chapman to 20.

Davis got out after serving less than six years and went back on the outlaw trail, joining up with a couple of young hard cases named Joel Collins and Sam Bass from Texas; the latter would go on to become a legend on his own. With a few other men, the trio went into the stagecoach-robbing business, a line that had never proved too remunerative for Davis. And it certainly

would prove no different now. Western historians have delighted in telling of the gang's misadventures. The first stage they attempted to hold up just never stopped despite their murderous gunplay. The next two stages did stop, but the first was devoid of passengers, gold or cash. The second yielded only $30 from four flat-broke passengers; the road agents gave each $1 for breakfast money. Another stage robbery brought in a gold watch and $3. The one after that produced $6. The gang was clearly operating at a loss, and Davis suggested they try a train. Bass was dubious but did concede that Davis had a record of a big score in the train-robbing field.

Surprisingly, the gang executed a train holdup at Big Springs, Neb., on September 18, 1877 that was a crowning success, the loot totaling $60,000. The gang then scattered. Collins and two others were shot down in gunfights with the law, and only Davis, Bass and one other member avoided pursuers. Davis drifted on to New Orleans, where he presumably dropped his $10,000 share of the loot at the gaming tables. In any event, by 1879 he was back in Nevada robbing stagecoaches with his accustomed lack of success. In fact, his bad luck in this field may have resulted in his death. A bandit tried to hold up a stage at Willow station and wounded one of the guards. The other guard was Eugene Blair, a legendary Wells Fargo shotgun rider with an amazing record of dispatching road agents. He did so in this case with two hefty charges from a scattergun in the bandit's face, which made recognition of the outlaw impossible. Blair insisted he had a look at the man first and it was Jack Davis. However, there were reports as late as 1920 that Davis was alive in Nicaragua.

See also: SAM BASS, JOHN T. CHAPMAN.

Day, Gertie (1895–1915) murder victim

The 1915 murder of Gertie Day is memorable mainly because her killer was trapped thanks to his ignorance of the unusual properties of dynamite. Her killing followed the pattern of *An American Tragedy*: a young girl gets pregnant, tells her lover and is murdered by him. In Gertie's case her lover was more than two decades older, George Morton Field, the richest man in Mustoch, Kan., a small community 30 miles west of Atchison.

Field was also the religious leader of the community, having contributed generously to local church building funds. When a visiting preacher was not on hand, Field often gave the sermon from the pulpit. They were frequently of the fire-and-brimstone variety, promising damnation to all sinners. Field, however, was not one to heed his own dire warnings and seduced young, rosy-cheeked Gertie, whose full alto voice was the pride of the church choir.

Unfortunately, Gertie became pregnant and informed Field he had better find a solution to her problem. Gertie agreed to accept $2,000 and leave the area, but Field soon realized he would be open to blackmail from the girl and decided to kill her, thus protecting his good name for sure. He journeyed to Kansas City to purchase all the necessary ingredients for a bomb and then arranged a meeting with Gertie at the church late one night.

While Gertie awaited her $2,000, Field crept under the wooden church and planted his paper-wrapped homemade bomb. He returned home just as the bomb exploded, killing Gertie and totally demolishing the church.

Field felt free of suspicion, not realizing that he had unwittingly wrapped the dynamite bomb in paper on which he had started to compose a new church sermon. As is often the case in dynamite explosions, the material closest to the dynamite was not totally destroyed. Sheriff James R. Carter, a famous Kansas peace officer of the time, found enough of the sermon text to realize that Field was implicated, a fact confirmed when store clerks in Kansas City identified him as the man who had bought the makings of a bomb. Field was sentenced to life imprisonment and died in 1926.

Daybreak Boys   New York criminal gang

Although no member was much over the age of 20, the Daybreak Boys were among the most desperate New York gangs in the 1850s. It was said that no one could join the gang until he had killed at least one man, but this was an exaggeration since some members were as young as 12 or even 10 and hadn't yet advanced to homicide. However, once in the gang, such delinquents were quickly initiated in the practice. Police estimated conservatively that from 1850 to 1852 alone the gang committed at least 20 murders—and more likely over 40—and stole loot worth $200,000. What made the gang so fearsome was its habit of scuttling ships just to demonstrate its power and willingness to kill even when there was no hope for gain. The roster of leaders of the gang was a who's who of the most dangerous criminals in New York during the 1850s: Nicholas Saul, Bill Howlett, Patsy the Barber, Slobbery Jim, Cowlegged Sam McCarthy and Sow Madden.

In time, the depredations of the Daybreak Boys became so troublesome the police declared a virtual war on them and killed with an abandon that matched the tactics of the Daybreakers themselves. Three offi-

cers named Blair, Spratt and Gilbert killed 12 of the gang in various gun battles in 1858. By the end of 1859 the gang, having lost so many of its leaders, broke up, although individual members still remained dangerous criminals on their own for years afterward.

De Feo, Ronald, Jr. (1951–) mass murderer

In November 1974 Ronald De Feo, Jr., stunned Amityville, Long Island by shooting to death his mother, father, two brothers and two sisters as they slept. It marked the start of what can only be described as a "murder groupie" rage.

The type of killings De Feo perpetrated is hardly unusual on police blotters, yet his crime supposedly made the house haunted. The alleged ghostly experiences of its next owners were described in a book, *The Amityville Horror*, which became a best-seller.

As for De Feo himself, no more than a necessary prop in the ghostly tales that followed, he tried unsuccessfully to plead insanity and was sentenced in 1975 to a total of 150 years imprisonment.

de Kaplany, Dr. Geza (1926–) murderer

Dubbed the Acid Doctor, Dr. Geza de Kaplany committed what one expert called "the most horrendous single murder in American history" and caused a further scandal when he was paroled. Dr. de Kaplany was an anesthetist at a San Jose, Calif. hospital. He wooed and eventually married his 25-year-old fiancée, Hajna, a part-time model and leading beauty of California's Hungarian community, largely on the basis of his professional status. The marriage proved a failure. Exactly why is not absolutely clear: according to the prosecution in the subsequent murder trial, de Kaplany was unable to consummate the marriage, but the defense contended his love had been rejected. For whatever reason, de Kaplany decided in his own words, "to ruin her beauty."

He assembled an elaborate torture kit in their honeymoon apartment and, on the evening of August 27, 1962, even stopped off to get a manicure so as not to puncture the rubber gloves he would wear. Exactly what de Kaplany did early the following morning, during what he called "my one-hour crackup" is best left to the medical texts. In any event, neighbors in the building got annoyed by loud music from the de Kaplany apartment, and despite the music, they could hear some terrible wailing. The police were summoned, and they took Hajna away, her once lovely face and body now covered with third-degree, corrosive burns. Careless ambulance attendants burned their own hands moving her body.

The bedroom resembled a torture chamber, the bedclothes virtually disintegrated in acid. There were bottles of nitric, sulfuric and hydrochloric acids in a leather case. Also found were rubber gloves, a roll of adhesive tape and a note that read, "If you want to live—do not shout; do what I tell you; or else you will die."

Hajna did die but only after suffering excruciating pain for three weeks in a hospital, with her mother praying for her death and nurses unable to look at de Kaplany's handiwork.

During his trial, at which he pleaded both "not guilty" and "not guilty by reason of insanity," de Kaplany denied wanting to kill his wife, only to mar her looks. He was convicted and escaped with just one life sentence because the jury was assured by a spokesman for the state prison system that he would be classified a "special interest prisoner," that is, someone almost certain never to be paroled. To add to that precaution, the judge ordered that photographs of de Kaplany's wife's body be kept in his file. Later on, it was discovered the pictures had not remained there very long.

Many Californians were both amazed and shocked when they heard an announcement in 1976 that de Kaplany had been paroled and quietly put aboard a plane to Taiwan. Pressed for an explanation, the Adult Authority, the state parole board, said that de Kaplany had been released six months ahead of any possible scheduled parole because a missionary hospital in Taiwan urgently needed the skills of a cardiac specialist. Since de Kaplany was not a heart specialist but an anesthesiologist whose skills had wasted for 13 years and whose medical license had been revoked, the explanation seemed implausible. The uproar over the parole of a murderer many people thought would never be released from prison was tempered only by the fact that he prudently had been sent out of the country.

De Palma, William (1938–) wrong man

A former federal convict, William De Palma holds the record for receiving the highest compensation ever awarded to a man wrongfully convicted of a crime. The Whittier, Calif. native agreed on August 12, 1975 to a $750,000 settlement for 16 months wrongful imprisonment at McNeil Island Prison in Washington. De Palma had been found guilty of armed robbery and given a 15-year sentence in 1968 on the basis of forged fingerprint evidence.

dead line   Fulton Street, New York City

Attempting to contain a growing wave of bank robberies in the financial district, Inspector Thomas F. Byrnes of the New York City police announced on March 12, 1880 the establishment of a "dead line" at Fulton Street. He said known criminals would be "dead," i.e., arrested, if they were found south of the line. The plan, like so many others by Byrnes, who was always more flamboyant than effective, proved to be a dud. But the officer is credited by some scholars with popularizing the word *deadline* in America.

dead man's eyes   superstition

An old story has it that the last thing a murder victim sees is his killer and that this image remains imprinted on the retina. Some superstitious murderers have gone to considerable trouble to shoot out a victim's eyes in order to destroy such imaginary evidence. Monk Eastman, a famed gangster and murderer at the turn of the century, supposedly heard the theory discussed once and suddenly remembered it after his next murder. He thereupon reclimbed three flights of stairs and shot out the dead man's eyes.

The origin of the superstition is unknown, but it came into renewed vogue around 1900, when criminals had become impressed with such scientific advances as fingerprinting, which was making police detection more effective. Even now, there are a few reports of murder victims found with their eyes shot out each year.

dead man's hand   aces and eights

A poker hand of a pair of aces and a pair of eights has been known in American culture as a "dead man's hand" ever since Jack McCall shot Wild Bill Hickok in the back of the head on August 2, 1876 as Hickok held those cards in a poker game in Carl Mann's saloon in Deadwood, S.D.

See also: WILD BILL HICKOK, JACK MCCALL.

Dead Man's Tree   Chicago "murder announcement" site

During the infamous Aldermen's Wars that wracked Chicago's 19th Ward, the so-called Bloody Ward, from 1916 to 1921, a poplar tree on Loomis Street in Little Italy became famous as the Dead Man's Tree. Both sides, those supporting John "Johnny de Pow" Powers and those backing Tony D'Andrea, took to announcing the impending death of a victim by posting his name on the tree, a notice that, if it did not completely shatter his nerve, at least offered the marked man an opportunity to set his affairs in order. In a majority of the 30 deaths that occurred during the wars, the victim's name had been written on the tree; none of these deaths were ever solved.

See also: ALDERMEN'S WARS.

Dead Rabbits   early New York gang

From the 1820s until their final decline in the 1870s, the Dead Rabbits were a huge gang of criminals who controlled much of the Lower East Side, excluding the Bowery, and achieved great renown as thieves and thugs. When they went on looting forays or to do battle with other gangs, their leaders carried a dead rabbit impaled on a pike. The Dead Rabbits were also noted political sluggers, supporting pro-Irish candidates. They were given credit for controlling the voting booths in 1856 when Tammany Hall's Fernando Wood was reelected mayor during an election in which at least 10,000 fraudulent votes were cast. Wood won by a little more than 9,000 votes.

The main foes of the Dead Rabbits were the Bowery Boys, who were aligned with the anti-Irish Native American Party, and the two organizations, each with satellite supporters, fought many pitched battles. The greatest of these occurred on July 4 and 5, 1857, when the Dead Rabbits and the Plug Uglies and several other Five Points gangs marched into the Bowery to loot stores and do battle with the Bowery Boys. Armed with knives, pistols, clubs, iron bars and huge paving blocks, they attacked a Bowery Boys headquarters, putting a small contingent of the enemy to rout. When the news of the outrage spread, the Bowery Boys, in alliance with the Atlantic Guards and other gangsters determined to protect the sanctity of the Bowery, poured out of their holes onto Bayard Street to engage in the most desperate and largest free-for-all in the city's history.

The police made an early and feeble effort to control the fighting but merely took a few prisoners before wisely retreating. By this time the fighting forces had grown to an estimated strength of about 400 to 500 on each side. The *New York Times* reported:

Brick-bats, stones and clubs were flying thickly around and from the windows in all directions, and men ran wildly about brandishing firearms. Wounded men lay on the sidewalks and were trampled upon. Now the Rabbits would make a combined rush and force their antagonists up Bayard Street to the Bowery. Then the fugitives, being reinforced, would turn on their pursuers and compel a retreat to Mulberry, Elizabeth and Baxter streets.

While the rioting was going on, other gangsters used the opportunity to attack households and stores along the Bowery and several other streets, and residents and storeowners had to barricade their buildings and fight off attacks with shotguns and pistols. In the afternoon a much larger force of police moved into the area and cleared the streets, forcing the rioters into the houses and up to the roofs. One gangster who refused to surrender fell from the roof of a house onto Baxter Street. As he lay there, his head in a pool of blood, his foes stomped him to death. As soon as the police retreated with more prisoners, the fighting resumed. It continued until three regiments of troops were brought into action the next day. At that point, eight rioters were dead and more than 100 wounded, half of whom required long hospitalization. More of their dead were carried off by both sides and it was common knowledge that several new graves decorated the underground passages and cellars of the Five Points and Paradise Square.

Small bands of the rioters continued battling for another week, while the general citizenry demanded something be done to curb the criminal elements. The Dead Rabbits resented descriptions of themselves as criminals and so informed the press. The *Times* reported:

We are requested by the Dead Rabbits to state that the Dead Rabbit club members are not thieves, that they did not participate in the riot with the Bowery Boys, and that the fight in Mulberry street was between the Roach Guards of Mulberry street and the Atlantic Guards of the Bowery. The Dead Rabbits are sensitive on points of honor, we are assured, and wouldn't allow a thief to live on their beat, much less be a member of their club.

Nonetheless, several noted sluggers of the Dead Rabbits, and the Bowery Boys as well, were never seen alive again.

See also: BOWERY BOYS, ROACH GUARDS.

Death Corner   Chicago murder locale

During the heyday of the Black Hand, this loose society of extortionists terrorized Italian communities in America, demanding money from designated victims and promising them death if they refused. The most dangerous locale in Chicago's Little Italy at this time was the intersection of Milton and Oak Streets, nicknamed Death Corner because so many Black Hand victims were slain there. In one 15-month period, from January 1, 1910 until March 26, 1911, 38 Black Hand murders occurred there.

There never was one official Black Hand organization; rather the extortions and killings were carried out on a freelance basis by various criminals. It is likely that some so-called Black Hand murders were really private affairs and disguised as Black Hand matters to confuse the police. Whatever the case, none of the 38 murders were ever solved, and there were many residents of Little Italy who would always go blocks out of their way to avoid passing Death Corner.

See also: BLACK HAND, SHOTGUN MAN, WHITE HAND SOCIETY.

debtors, imprisonment of

The practice of imprisoning debtors was an English custom readily imported into the American colonies, and it also became common that such persons could be sold into service for periods of time in order to pay off their debts. However, this method of discharging debts was eliminated during the early years of the 19th century thanks to a backlash against the imprisonment of debtors that had started about 1775 (more than a century after similar outcries in England). By 1800 strong reform movements were active and some state legislatures passed poor debtor and insolvency laws that were liberal. "Prison limits" for debtors posting bonds sometimes extended throughout an entire county. Yet despite these improvements, the most common crime in America was debt, and more than 75,000 debtors a year were sent to prison for the offense. The amount owed had little to do with the sentence. A survey in one Pennsylvania penitentiary in 1829 revealed that there were almost 100 prisoners serving sentences for owing amounts of less than $1.

It became clear to reformers that the only true cure was the absolute and total ban on jailing debtors, and laws were passed totally banning imprisonment of debtors or at least greatly restricting the rules under which imprisonment was called for. In 1821 Kentucky became the first state to act, followed by New York a decade later. North Carolina, South Carolina and Florida were the last to act, constitutionally forbidding imprisonment for simple debt in 1868.

Deep Nightstick   secret informant

As famous as Deep Throat in the Watergate scandal was Deep Nightstick in a newspaper investigation of police brutality in Philadelphia during the mid-1970s. The investigation was given much of the credit for ending the mayoral career of controversial tough ex-cop Frank L. Rizzo.

In 1976 a new court reporter for the *Philadelphia Inquirer*, Jonathan Neumann, observed that although murder suspects routinely testified to brutal beatings by the police, officials never bothered to investigate. Later, Neumann, a former New Yorker, asked an editor about this strange situation and was told, "Welcome to Philadelphia."

Neumann and another young reporter, William Marimow, began digging into the subject of police brutality and produced a series of articles that would win them a Pulitzer Prize in 1978. Much of their information was to come from Deep Nightstick, a secret source with close ties to the police department who provided them leads that kept their investigations on course. Checking the records of 433 homicide cases between 1974 and 1977, they found confessions and statements in 80 cases were thrown out because of illegal interrogations, but no action had been taken against the policemen involved. By the time the pair won their journalistic prize, nine officers had been convicted, three had been acquitted, three were under indictment, seven were under arrest and two others had pleaded guilty to departmental misconduct charges.

In 1979 Mayor Rizzo tried to effect a change in the city charter that would allow him to run for a third four-year term in November 1979. However, the police brutality charges became a dominant issue in the campaign for the charter revision, and Rizzo lost by a two-to-one margin.

See also: FRANK L. RIZZO.

Deep Throat   Watergate informant

Without doubt the most famous informer in U.S. history, Deep Throat, named after the title of what has been described as a landmark pornographic film of the early 1960s, remains unidentified. He was the chief source of *Washington Post* reporters Robert Woodward and Carl Bernstein during their investigation of the break-in at the Democratic Party's headquarters in the Watergate office complex, which toppled the administration of President Richard Nixon and sent a number of his top aides, including a former attorney general—the first ever—to prison.

Defenbach, Marie (?–1900)   murder victim

A young Chicago model named Marie Defenbach may have been the most gullible murder victim in American history. Marie got involved in a plot to bilk 10 insurance companies out of $70,000 by faking her own death. She named her three accomplices as beneficiaries and then moved into a boarding house under another name. According to the plan, the brains of the conspiracy, Dr. August M. Unger, would give her a special medicine that would induce a deathlike sleep and later he would revive her. Meanwhile, another body would be substituted for cremation. For her troubles, Marie was to get half of the $70,000, whereupon she would depart on a tour of Europe. Remarkably, Marie accepted the plan, not considering that her three accomplices would get twice as much money if they really killed her. On August 25, 1900 Marie took the medicine and died in severe agony 15 minutes later. Dr. Unger signed the death certificate. The three conspirators then proceded to collect all the insurance money. But an uncle of the girl investigated her disappearance and uncovered the bizarre plot with the aid of private detectives. One of the three killers turned state's evidence, and Dr. Unger and the third accomplice, Frank Brown, were sentenced to five years in prison for fraud. The murder itself could not be proved against them, however.

Dekker, Albert (1905–1968) accidental or deliberate death?

The death of veteran actor Albert Dekker in early May 1968 had the element that the tabloids love best in Hollywood scandals—kinkiness. Dekker, long famed for his career in the theater and later in top Hollywood films, was in a sense best known to a generation of young moviegoers for playing the title role in *Dr. Cyclops,* about a mad scientist who shrinks people to doll size. Perhaps that Cyclops association somehow fit the gruesome death he suffered.

Dekker was found in a scene that was called a "grotesque nightmare." Police had to break into the bathroom of his Hollywood apartment, where they found him dead and naked except for some female underwear. His wrists were handcuffed and he was bound with leather ropes around his neck, chest, waist and ankles. There were punctures on his arms and buttocks caused by a hypodermic needle that lay beside the body. Scrawled on his body with bright red lipstick were a number of words, among which the tamer were *whip* and *slave.* There was a drawing of a vagina on his lower stomach. He had been choked to death by the leather rope.

If Dekker was into kink, it was something neither his friends nor his longtime fiancée, fashion model Geraldine Saunders, seemed to know. It was Saunders, unable to reach him by phone the previous two days, who had sounded the alarm.

In the entertainment world Dekker was known to be cultured and intellectual. He had served two years in the 1940s in the California legislature as a liberal Democrat. His liberal stance and his attacks on Sen. Joseph McCarthy led to his being blacklisted as an actor for several years. During the last year of his life, although his career was very much on track, Dekker was despondent over the death of his 16-year-old son Jan, who fatally shot himself accidentally.

The official verdict on Albert Dekker's death was first said to be suicide but was later changed to accidental death. This seemed to be rather logical since the bathroom door had been chainlocked from the inside. But many observers found the idea unconvincing, declaring that Harry Houdini, and lesser sorts, would

Albert Dekker won great fame in "mad" and kinky roles. In that sense his death was his kinkiest role ever.

know it is as easy to lock a chainlock from the outside as from the inside. And Houdini certainly could have escaped the restraints on Dekker but might have had a bit more difficulty getting in them without help of some sort. The way Dekker was bound and choked indicated 1) that he had not been alone and 2) that he was unconscious at the time of his death.

Then there was the drug that had certainly been injected in him. Officials could not identify it.

On a more prosaic crime level, it was known that Dekker had $70,000 in cash in his apartment. The money was missing, as was an expensive camera.

But to officials an autoerotic asphyxiation thesis was more fitting to write *fini* to the life of an actor who had played so many spooky roles.

DeLorean, John (1925–) accused multimillionaire drug smuggler

He was one of the most flamboyant automotive entrepreneurs to come out of Detroit. He was also perhaps the only American multimillionaire ever busted for alleged drug trafficking. Federal authorities were reportedly ecstatic over netting such a big fish in a huge sting operation. However, the results did not turn out the way the government wanted.

John DeLorean was reputed to be both a wunderkind and incorrigible playboy. From the very beginning of his career in the automotive industry at Chrysler he showed the signs of developing into a swashbuckler—"hustler" not seeming to suitably reflect his style. From Chrysler DeLorean shifted to Packard and was by then generally known as a real "comer." In 1956 DeLorean hopped to General Motors and at age 44 was general manager of the Chevrolet division. In 1972 he was a vice president with much more expanded duties. Observers of the automotive scene cast him as a logical candidate to eventually become president of GM if he could keep his personal ardor under control. But DeLorean took his own measure of his status; he regarded most of GM's leadership as dinosaurs. He felt he could do wonders for company policies without their interference, and he ignored objections to his "fast lane" lifestyle, which included marrying a 20-year-old fashion model. In 1973 after a divorce he married 22-year-old fashion model Cristina Ferrare.

About this time GM and DeLorean came to a parting of the ways. DeLorean resigned from his post, which paid him $650,000 a year in salary and bonuses. The way DeLorean told it, he "fired" GM.

DeLorean was by then totally involved in developing his "dream car"—a state-of-the-art sports car. He made an offer to the British government that it could not refuse. Britain was to invest $110 million for his dream car, and he would build a "showcase" auto factory in Belfast where thousands of jobs would go to that strife-torn and unemployment-ridden area. The British government coughed up loads of grants and low-interest loans, and, attracted by DeLorean's reputation for genius, a number of rich American investors put up additional backing.

The first of DeLorean's gleaming products came off the assembly line in 1981, most of the cars targeted for the American market at a then eye-popping $25,000. Unfortunately for DeLorean and his govern-

Flamboyant automotive hot shot John DeLorean produced his "dream car," which turned out to be a bust. Then he was accused of being the only American multimillionaire ever busted for alleged drug trafficking.

mental and private backers, the roll-out coincided with a worldwide recession. Sales were, to say the least, disappointing.

The following year the British government could no longer keep a stiff upper lip and was obliged to put DeLorean's company in receivership. Later the Belfast factory was to be shut down permanently.

However, when the shoe dropped it was not then DeLorean's major worry. The very day of the announcement of the shutdown, DeLorean was arrested in Los Angeles by federal authorities, who charged him as being involved in a $50-million cocaine deal. It was a shocking story for the American and British public.

Federal prosecutors were sure they had an iron-clad case. They had videotapes involving DeLorean and federal agents posing as drug dealers going over details of the negotiations. When authorities broke in on the scene and arrested DeLorean, he was defiant, declaring, "I am absolutely an innocent man" and that the case was "a pure frame-up and FBI cheap shot."

Usually sting operations of this type easily go the prosecution's way, since, to use a law enforcement phrase, a "dog was caught with the meat in his mouth." But after a 22-week trial in which DeLorean was charged with conspiracy to sell $24 million worth of cocaine, as well as other charges involving possession and distribution of drugs, proved no easy sell to the jury. The defense made much of what it called improper entrapment and that federal agents had set up DeLorean because he was known to be desperate for funds to bail out his ailing dream car enterprise. At the time a congressional inquiry had subjected such stings to severe criticism. The jury felt the same way about the DeLorean case and voted not guilty on all charges.

Clearly enraged by the verdict, prosecutors brought new charges accusing their elusive quarry with wire and mail fraud, interstate transportation of stolen money and income-tax evasion. DeLorean was accused of funneling millions into a Dutch bank. However, once again a federal jury was not buying the charges and cleared DeLorean on all counts.

All told, DeLorean's company owed more than $100 million to creditors, and finally a federal bankruptcy court okayed an agreement under which a shade more than $9 million settled the company's debt.

In later years John DeLorean lived in reclusion in his New Jersey mansion.

Demara, Ferdinand Waldo, Jr. (1921–1982) impostor

Known as the greatest impostor in 20th-century America, Ferdinand Waldo Demara, Jr. had a compulsion to impersonate people. A high school dropout, he was nonetheless able in the 1940s to masquerade success-

fully as a doctor of philosophy named Robert L. French and to teach college psychology classes. He also passed himself off as Cecil Boyce Haman, a zoology Ph.D.; a Trappist monk in a Kentucky monastery; a biologist doing cancer research in a Seattle, Wash. institution; a law student; a hospital orderly; an American soldier; an American sailor; a recreational officer at a maximum security prison in Texas; a two-time "convert" to Catholicism (although he was born a Roman Catholic); and a deputy sheriff.

Demara's greatest impersonation occurred during the Korean War, when he assumed the role of a lieutenant-surgeon with the Canadian navy and successfully performed a number of major operations under severe battle conditions. Demara would bone up on medical books aboard ship and then remove tonsils, pull teeth and amputate limbs. In his most accomplished operation, he successfully removed a bullet from within a fraction of an inch of the heart of a wounded South Korean soldier. When he finished the skillful operation, a small cheer went up from fascinated spectators.

However, news stories about the amazing medical lieutenant wired back to Canada finally resulted in Demara's exposure, and he was ordered back to Victoria. Incredibly, the Canadian navy decided that Demara had enlisted under a false name; it didn't occur to them that he was not actually a doctor. As a result, he was merely discharged with all pay due him and asked to leave the country.

In 1956 Demara was caught posing as an accredited teacher at a school in Maine. He served a few months in jail for "cheating by false premises." His longest prison term for any offense was 18 months. Demara was the subject of a book and then a Hollywood movie starring Tony Curtis. When asked why he engaged in a lifetime of impersonations, Demara said, "Rascality, pure rascality."

Dennison, Stephen (1909–) candy thief

One of the most bizarre miscarriages of justice in American history occurred in 1925, when 16-year-old Stephen Dennison was sent to a reformatory for stealing a $5 box of candy in New York. Treated brutally in the institution, Dennison became known as a rebellious troublemaker. He was transferred to the state prison, and because of continuous minor infractions, he had years and years added on to his original sentence. Incredibly, Dennison ended up doing a total of 34 years for having committed no crime greater than stealing a box of candy. After he was finally found "buried alive" in a prison cell, he was released in 1959. It took Dennison seven years in the courts to win compensation: the New York Court of Claims granted him $115,000. The court said, "No amount of money could compensate Dennison for the injuries he suffered and the scars he bears." So it allotted him a little over $3,000 for each year he spent behind bars.

Denver's "Spiderman" Murderer   See PHILIP PETERS.

Depression, the Great   (1929–1940)

On the surface, it would seem that the underworld should have been a victim not a beneficiary of the Great Depression of the 1930s. Generally, this was not the case because the goods and services it provided—liquor, sex, drugs and gambling—all boomed when everything else went bust, avidly craved by Americans caught in the hopelessness of an economic system gone to pot.

While businessmen, small and large were ruined by "cash flow" problems and the banks were shutting down, the underworld was flush with greenbacks. Where could strapped businessmen readily get the money needed to tide them over? Only the underworld extended credit so generously, making loansharking one of organized crime's most lucrative fields. Moreover, during the 1930s the underworld's grip on corrupt unions strengthened, as workers, desperate to keep their jobs, willingly kicked in more dues and paid more assessments even if they knew the money went straight into gangster's pockets.

Al Capone played a role as a "socially responsible" gangster, taking care of many of Chicago's unemployed. A Capone storefront on State Street offered food and warmth for the destitute. It was, Capone informed reporters, his civic duty to do his share to help the jobless. Capone's Loop soup kitchen dispensed 120,000 meals at a cost of $12,000. On Thanksgiving Day, Capone proudly announced he was donating 5,000 turkeys.

Capone turned his famous soup kitchen into a great publicity campaign. As it turned out, the charity really hadn't cost him very much. Coffee roasters and blenders in Chicago had been leaned on to supply that commodity. Various bakeries were required to provide day-old doughnuts and pastries. The hearty meat dishes were gratis from the packinghouses, and the South Water Market Commission merchants pitched in the potatoes and vegetables. They were all assigned regular quotas, and those who objected that the amount was too much were informed the Big Fellow was very concerned that their trucks were not wrecked or their tires slashed.

Capone also knew how to squeeze a bit of profit out of all this unemployment. In December 1930 the price of beer to the speakeasies, which cost an estimated $4 a barrel to produce, was raised from $55 to $60, allegedly to help finance aid for the poor. The Loop's speakeasy operators were informed by Capone's salesmen, "The Big Fellow says we've all got to tighten our belts a little to help those poor guys who haven't got any jobs."

derrick, the Folsom   prison torture

The "derrick" was used in various forms at many prisons but nowhere more freely than at California's Folsom Prison. Around 1900 it was estimated that an average of 10 men were on the derrick day in and day out the year round. Sentences on the derrick might be for as long as 50 hours, but the maximum length a man could stand it was about five hours a day, so long sentences had to be stretched out over 10 days.

Located in the prison dungeon, the derrick was a block and tackle suspended from a balcony over the convict's head. The prisoner's arms would be yanked backward and a pair of handcuffs snapped on his wrists. Then a guard would pull a rope attached to the handcuffs, drawing the prisoner upward. When the victim's heels were just off the floor, the attendant would give the rope a sharp jerk and then tie it fast to a cleat on the side of the wall. The weight of the prisoner's body would make the handcuffs bite deeply into his wrists as he swung limply from the block and tackle. Then the guard would release an inch or so of slack so that the prisoner could get a steadying position, the tips of his shoes barely resting on the flagstones of the dungeon. Prisoners who had suffered on the derrick said later that after the initial pain, they were overcome by a sense of reeling drunkenness, followed by the return of pain which steadily increased to an excruciating level.

A prisoner's ordeal on the derrick might continue for two and a half hours in the morning and then resume for two and a half hours in the afternoon. Once sentenced to punishment on the derrick, only severe medical reasons justified its interruption or suspension. A common ailment caused by the punishment was bleeding from a prisoner's kidneys. The prison doctor would be summoned when a prisoner's shoes were soggy with blood. This might gain the prisoner a three-day respite in the prison hospital, but he would then be returned to the dungeon to complete his punishment. The derrick remained in use at Folsom until 1911, when an outraged legislature outlawed all forms of corporal punishment at places of detention. However, it was believed that some limited forms of derrick punishment continued thereafter for a number of years.

derringer

The derringer might be called the Saturday Night Special of the 19th century. The original $3 version was produced around 1850 by a Philadelphia gunsmith named Henry Deringer, Jr., who turned out some versions that were only 3¾ inches long and thus easily concealed by a professional gambler in his vest pocket or up his sleeve, an outlaw in his boot or a prostitute in her garter. Most were one-shot affairs and accurate only at a range of less than 6 feet, which was generally more than sufficient for its purposes.

Since Deringer had failed to patent his model, dozens of other gunsmiths began putting out imitations shortly after the appearance of what is now called the Deringer-derringer. The only thing these manufacturers did to conceal their theft was to add an *r* to the name of the weapon. One of the more popular competing models was E. Remington and Sons' over-and-under double-barreled version, which was in continuous production from 1865 to 1935.

Despite the fact that the derringer was tiny to hold, it had an unusually large caliber, .50 the largest and .41 the most common, and was thus a real killer at close range. The derringer inspired such other quaint weapons as the muff pistol and the pepperbox revolver in the constant hunt for sneakier ways to kill.

See also: MUFF PISTOL, PEPPERBOX REVOLVER, SATURDAY NIGHT SPECIAL.

DeSalvo, Albert H. (1933–1973) Boston Strangler

Between June 1962 and January 1964, a mass murderer who became known as the Boston Strangler killed 13 women in Boston, Mass. He used various devices to talk his way into the homes of women living alone and then sexually assaulted and strangled them. The first murder, that of 55-year-old divorcée Anna Slesers in June 1962, was typical. She was found sprawled on the floor of her apartment, strangled with the cord from her own housecoat. In some of the other cases, there was a hint of a robbery attempt, but police concluded this was merely a blind to cover up the clear sexual motivations of the murderer.

As the murders continued, a hysteria developed among Boston women, and many would never open a door to a stranger's knock. While the police pressed their hunt and brought in numerous suspects, the crimes continued up to January 1964, when they suddenly stopped without explanation. Then in October the Strangler struck again, molesting a young woman in her home after gaining entrance by pretending to be a detective. But although he threatened her with a knife, he left without killing her. The victim was able to identify her attacker as Albert DeSalvo, who had been released from prison in April 1962 after serving time for indecent assault. When his photograph appeared in the papers, scores of women reported to police that he was the man who had assaulted them.

The Boston Strangler, Albert DeSalvo, dances with senior citizen in a 1972 prison affair sponsored by a volunteer community agency "trying to show how both these neglected groups of people (senior citizens and prisoners) can help each other." DeSalvo was stabbed to death the following year by one or more of his fellow inmates.

There still was no direct proof that DeSalvo was the Boston Strangler until he made a confession, relating scores of details no one but the murderer could have known.

After his incarceration for life, a weird interest in the quotations of the Boston Strangler continued. Some, in letters by DeSalvo, were auctioned off, while others were recorded by reporters who had managed to have themselves confined in cells near him. Two sample quotes:

"Ha, they even know me in the Soviet Union."

"Boston people are sexpots, they all love sex. . . . Most broads are just waiting to get so-called raped."

Copies of a paperback about him, which DeSalvo attempted to slip to female visitors at the institution where he was confined for a time, were inscribed with the dedication, "Can't wait to get my hands around your throat."

Apparently, some of his fellow inmates at the Walpole State Prison, where he was confined in 1973, had somewhat similar feelings about him. He was found dead in his cell, stabbed 16 times by an unidentified convict or convicts.

See also: F. LEE BAILEY.

Devil's River Valley   Texas outlaw hideout

While Hole in the Wall and Robbers' Roost were the most fabled outlaw hideouts in the West, neither was any meaner than Devil's River Valley in the alkali section of southwestern Texas. The *St. Louis Star* once reported of the refuge: "For many years it has been known to convicts from the Texas Penitentiary that if they could reach the Devil's River country after escaping there would be small danger of being recaptured. It is probable that no other portion of the West harbors so many notorious characters as this particular section. In fact, some of them boast that should they be arrested it would be impossible for the arresting officer to take them out on account of the intervention of friends." It was an unnecessary boast since no such attempt was ever made.

Devine, John   See SHANGHAI CHICKEN.

Devol, George (1829–1902) riverboat gambler

With Canada Bill Jones, George Devol was probably the most talented of the riverboat gamblers, an expert not only at three-card monte but also at poker, seven-up and other card games, especially faro, in which he was the bank and could control the flimflamming. By his own estimate in his 1887 autobiography, *Forty Years a Gambler on the Mississippi*, he made more than $2 million but, like most others in his profession, could not hold on to it, losing most of it in casino faro games. He described himself as "a cabin boy in 1839; could steal cards and cheat the boys at eleven; stack a deck at fourteen . . . fought more rough-and-tumble fights than any man in America, and was the most daring gambler in the world." And the amount of exaggeration was not too great.

Devol's most constant partner was Canada Bill Jones, and the pair made a perfect team. Devol dressed like a fashion plate while Canada Bill acted and dressed like a lout with an intelligence level somewhere below that of moron. Together with Canada Bill and two others, Devol formed a riverboat combine that netted each of the participants $200,000 a year by the time the group broke up. While he was not, and most likely no one was, as great a manipulator at three-card monte as Canada Bill, Devol was nonetheless a master at card skullduggery. On one occasion, in a friendly poker game with four other gamblers he rang in four cold

decks on the same hand and dealt each of the other players a set of four aces. He then sat back and watched the fireworks. Each of the gamblers felt he had been hit with a hand that comes once in a lifetime, and soon, everything the gamblers owned was in the pot. When the hilarious showdown came, it took them hours to sort out who owned what.

Like all cardsharps, Devol appreciated a sucker who lost magnanimously, but not surprisingly, he often met the opposite kind. A sore loser once pulled a gun on Devol, who extricated himself from the dilemma by "using my head." He butted his foe unconscious. Devol was probably correct when he said he engaged in more rough-and-tumble fights than any other man in America. He usually did so as a "butter." Devol was the proud possessor of a massive, dome-shaped cranium that made an awesome weapon. Besides using it against sore-losing gamblers, he won many a bet in butting contests against various strongmen and circus performers, including the famed Billy Carroll of Robinson's Circus, billed as "the man with the thick skull, or the great butter." When Carroll recovered consciousness, he placed his hand on the gambler's head and said, "Gentlemen, I have found my papa at last."

After more than 40 years of gambling on the great rivers and in the Wild West, Devol married late in life. Between his wife and a militant mother-in-law, he was pressured to give up gambling and settle down in Cincinnati. In 1887 he published his memoirs. More or less retired from gambling, he sneaked away for an occasional poker game and allegedly slipped into Kentucky now and then to trim the racetrack suckers at monte. He celebrated his 60th birthday by winning a bet that he could batter an oak whiskey cast to splinters with his hard head. When Devol cashed in his chips in 1902, the *Cincinnati Enquirer* reported that he had won and lost more money than any other gambler in American history. Whether that was true or not, George Devol typified his lusty era.

See also: WILLIAM "CANADA BILL" JONES, THREE-CARD MONTE.

Dewey, Thomas E. (1902–1971) prosecutor and near assassination victim

Thomas E. Dewey was only one of several prosecutors, especially in New York State, to use his crime-fighting prowess to advance himself politically, moving on to the governorship and twice running for president, in 1944 and 1948. Dewey had started off as a Wall Street lawyer, and observers would note that as a prosecutor of industrialists, businessmen and financiers, he showed limited brilliance and effectiveness. In prosecuting gangsters, however, the Dewey zeal was limitless and telling. In various roles—U.S. attorney, special prosecutor and district attorney—he clapped in prison the likes of Waxey Gordon, Louis Lepke, Gurrah Shapiro and Lucky Luciano.

Before he got Luciano, Dewey set his sights on Dutch Schultz, the king of Harlem policy rackets and numerous other criminal enterprises. Although the Dutchman was a brilliant criminal leader, he was also a bit of a flake, fond of solving pressing problems with a gun. When Dewey's investigators closed in on his operations, Schultz went before the national board of the crime syndicate to demand that the prosecutor be assassinated as a solution to both Schultz's present problems and the future ones of others. When the crime syndicate was formed, a firm rule was agreed upon, as Luciano stated it, that "we wouldn't hit newspaper guys or cops or DAs. We don't want the kind of trouble everybody'd get."

Led by the forces of Luciano and Lansky, the crime board voted down Schultz. "I still say he ought to be hit," the mad dog underworld leader is reported to have snarled in defiance. "And if nobody else is gonna do it, I'm gonna hit him myself."

At first, the syndicate decided that Schultz was simply blowing off steam, but then it was discovered in October 1935 that Schultz was setting an assassination plot in place. He had Dewey's Fifth Avenue apartment staked out by a man who posed each morning as the father of a child pedaling a velocipede. What could be less suspicious than a devoted parent strolling with his offspring? Dewey and the two body guards always at his side passed them without suspicion on their way to a nearby drug store, where Dewey made his first phone call of the morning to his office from one of several booths. He did not use his home phone for fear it might be tapped.

Once the "caser" with the child learned this, a murder plot was worked out; a killer carrying a gun with a silencer would be inside the drug store first and shoot Dewey when he entered one of the booths. Dewey's bodyguards waiting outside would not be aware of a thing as the killer walked out past them.

Schultz's mistake was involving Albert Anastasia in the plot. Anastasia was close to Luciano, and although he also favored killing Dewey, he would never betray Luciano. He passed the word about the plot to Luciano and others in the syndicate. Luciano was horrified. So were most of the others. An immediate trial was held and the death sentence passed on the absent Schultz. According to Martin A. Gosch and Richard Hammer in *The Last Testament of Lucky Luciano*, Meyer Lansky, while not casting a dissenting vote, told Luciano: "Charlie, as your Jewish *consigliere*, I want to remind you of something. Right now, Schultz is your cover. If Dutch is eliminated, you're gonna stand out like a

naked guy who just lost his clothes. The way La Guardia and the rest of them guys've been screamin' about you, it's ten to one they'll be after you next."

Luciano allowed that Lansky could be right, but the syndicate had no other choice than to eliminate Schultz. The vote taken was unanimous On October 23, 1935 Schultz was shot to death in a chop house in Newark, N.J.

Dewey did not learn of his "almost assassination" until 1940, when it was revealed to him by Murder, Inc. prosecutor Burton Turkus. Dewey listened impassively to the step-by-step details, but his eyes widened perceptibly when mention was made of the proud papa with the tot on the velocipede. After five years he apparently still remembered them.

By that time, as a result of Dewey's efforts, Lucky Luciano had been sent to prison for 30 to 50 years on a charge of compulsory prostitution, the longest sentence ever handed out for such an offense. After the end of World War II, Dewey backed a parole board's recommendation that Luciano be released, an action for which Dewey was roundly criticized by political opponents. The move was made because of Luciano's aid to the war effort, Dewey said, but it may also have been based to some degree on what had to remain an unspoken gratitude for Luciano's having saved his life. Perhaps somewhat ingraciously, Luciano to his dying day insisted there was yet another reason; the mob had contributed $90,000 in small bills to Dewey's campaign fund.

See also: LOUIS "LEPKE" BUCHALTER, CHARLES "LUCKY" LUCIANO, DUTCH SCHULTZ, JACOB "GURRAH" SHAPIRO.

Diamond, Jack "Legs" (1896–1931) racketeer and murderer

Two things often said about Jack "Legs" Diamond, one of the most notorious gangsters of the 1920s, was that "the only woman who ever loved him was his mother and she died when he was a kid" and "the bullet hasn't been made that can kill Legs Diamond." Both were inaccurate. Although he was a brutal killer, quite a few women loved Legs, especially his wife, Alice, and his showgirl mistress, Kiki Roberts. While he was indeed called the Clay Pigeon of the Underworld, he was the ultimate proof that no one can live forever with bullets constantly being fired at him.

Legs' main problem in life was that almost everyone in the underworld hated him. He was a double-crosser, a chiseler, a man totally incapable of keeping his word. At various times, he fought with most of the leading criminals in New York, thinking nothing of continually increasing his roster of enemies.

Legs started out as a sneak thief in his early teens, heisting packages off the backs of delivery trucks and outracing pursuers, thus gaining his nickname. In the early 1920s Legs had moved up to work for Little Augie Orgen, the top labor racketeer in the city, after he arranged the death of Nathan Kaplan, better known as Kid Dropper. Little Augie turned over to Diamond his smaller bootlegging enterprises. It appears that Augie was the last important gangster Diamond was loyal to. He acted as his bodyguard and even took some bullets in his arm and leg when Little Augie was shot down on a Lower East Side street in 1927. That loyalty did not extend to seeking vengeance for the death of his boss, however, even though Diamond had recognized the killers—Louis Lepke and Gurrah Shapiro. When he got out of the hospital, he made peace with them. They got what they wanted—the labor rackets—and Diamond took over the rest of Little Augie's bootleg business and his narcotics trade.

Suddenly, Legs Diamond was a big-timer, a sport on Broadway. He even opened his own joint, the Hotsy Totsy Club, a second-floor bistro on Broadway in the 50s.

Legs Diamond, in pin stripes, was considered "unkillable" by the underworld and "unconvictable" by the law. The theory proved to be half true.

The club provided Diamond with a cover, and he often invited underworld rivals to peace meetings there. Many of the overly trusting gangsters were murdered in a back room. In 1929 Diamond committed a murder that really demonstrated his recklessness and total lack of conscience. He and his lieutenant, Charles Entratta, murdered a hoodlum named Red Cassidy right at the bar in front of a number of employees and patrons. Diamond and Entratta were forced to flee. Then from hiding, they decided to eliminate the law's case against them. Four witnesses who had seen the killing were in turn murdered, three customers and the club bartender. Four other persons, including the hat-check girl, simply disappeared and were never heard from again. Apparently, Diamond and Entratta had no fear that the missing witnesses might suddenly turn up again because the two resurfaced, confident the police no longer had a case against them.

However, Legs' forced retirement caused complications. The notorious Dutch Schultz had moved in on Diamond's rackets while he was gone, and what the Dutchman took, he seldom gave back. It led to a full-scale war between the two. Schultz was never a popular figure with the rest of the underworld, but no one complained about his efforts to kill Diamond.

There were many who were convinced that Diamond couldn't be killed. It had always been that way. In October 1924 some unknown gunmen had peppered his head with birdshot and put a bullet in his heel. Diamond then drove himself to Mt. Sinai Hospital and had his wounds taken care of. The second near miss was the attack on Little Augie. Diamond had lost so much blood from wounds in his arm and leg that he was not expected to survive. The war with Schultz added to his battle injuries. Shortly after he killed a couple of Schultz's men in October 1930, Legs was curled up in a cozy suite with showgirl Kiki Roberts when gunmen broke in and pumped five bullets into him. Kiki was unhurt.

Legs was rushed to a hospital and, to the amazement of doctors, survived. In April 1931 Diamond was ambushed as he left a roadside inn. He got a bullet in the lung, another in the back, a third in the liver and a fourth in the arm. Once again, surgeons gave up on him, but again he recovered.

By this time, Diamond himself was convinced he couldn't be killed. He let it be known that once he was all better, he intended to take a bigger slice of the action in Manhattan. Legs indicated he was not satisfied with what he had gotten when criminal mastermind Arnold Rothstein was murdered and his empire divided. He served notice on Joey Fay that he wanted more of the nightclub rackets and on Waxey Gordon that he deserved more of the bootlegging and moonshining business.

All of this made it rather difficult to determine whose troops paid him a fatal visit on December 18,

1931. Diamond was hiding away in a room in Albany, N.Y. that only a few confederates knew about. He was sound asleep when two gunmen slipped into the room. One held him by the ears and the other shot him three times in the head. This time Diamond was absolutely dead.

See also: HOTSY TOTSY CLUB, JACOB "LITTLE AUGIE" ORGEN, DUTCH SCHULTZ.

diamond switch   confidence theft game

Considered to be superstars of shoplifters, diamond switch experts, often women, victimize top jewelry stores by feigning interest in the purchase of a diamond. The thief will examine the stone and, when the salesperson's attention is distracted, substitute a worthless or inferior stone for the genuine article. The thief then makes a hasty exit before the switch is discovered.

The prowess of these operators was pointed out not long ago by a woman who had cheated two leading jewelry stores on New York's Fifth Avenue. Handsomely dressed in a fur coat, the woman considered the purchase of an $18,000 ring but after some thought decided it was too expensive. She handed the clerk back a cheaper diamond, one worth only about $7,500. Since the two stones were cut alike and determination of the full quality of the costlier diamond required more than examination by the naked eye, no suspicions were aroused until some time after the supposed customer had departed. Meanwhile, the same thief had entered a second store to inspect a $35,000 diamond, for which she neatly substituted the $18,000 stone. By the time both stores discovered their losses, the woman was long gone from Fifth Avenue.

Dillinger, John Herbert (1903–1934)   public enemy

John Dillinger was the consummate public enemy, certainly the "superstar" gangster of the 1930s. But what is really amazing is that he achieved this status in a criminal career that spanned a mere 11 months, from September 1933 to July 1934. Dillinger and his mob—he actually was not the leader but merely a member among equals of the first so-called Dillinger mob—robbed between 10 and 20 banks. They also plundered three police arsenals, engaged in three spectacular jail breaks and fought their way out of police traps, murdering 10 men and wounding seven others in the process. This last fact was never considered very important by the public, just as Missourians did not hold such indiscretions against Jesse James a half-century earlier.

Dillinger captured the public's imagination with his style and verve; he displayed dash and derring-do in a spectacular but apocryphal "wooden gun" jail escape,

had a casual impudence toward authority and often displayed a form of chivalry during robberies, especially flirting with older women bystanders, that turned him into a Depression-day Robin Hood. After all, he just robbed banks, not people, and on occasion told depositors to hang on to their money, that all the gang wanted was the bank's money. Undoubtedly, Dillinger was smart enough to understand such behavior stood him well with the public and could conceivably help him out of a tight spot someday.

Dillinger was a master bank robber. His gang's jobs were all well planned and timed to precision. During his nine-year stretch in prison for attempting to rob a grocer, he had learned the meticulous "Baron Lamm method" of bank robbery, named after a former Prussian army officer turned American criminal, which called for careful casing of a bank beforehand, pretested and timed getaway routes, and the like. Dillinger followed the technique to the utmost detail but added his own daring touches. The day before one robbery, two of his men cased a bank posing as journalists and were taken on a grand tour of the institution by its chief officer. During another caper the townsfolk thought they were witnessing a rehearsal for the filming of a movie; a "movie director"—reputedly Homer Van Meter, the daring clown of the gang—had visited the scene the day before to publicize the event.

The product of an unhappy home life—John's mother died when he was three and his father subsequently remarried—young Dillinger became a juvenile delinquent. As a member of a youth gang called the Dirty Dozen, he was charged with stealing coal from the Pennsylvania Railroad's gondolas to sell to residents of his Indianapolis neighborhood; he was in the sixth grade at the time.

So far as the record shows, Dillinger did not get involved in serious crime until 1924, following a stint in the navy from which he just "walked away." That year he and an older, more seasoned criminal, Ed Singleton, attempted to rob a grocer whom they knew carried the day's receipts on him. The two men accosted their victim, B. F. Morgan, on a darkened street, and Dillinger, armed with a .32, struck him on the head with a bolt wrapped in a handkerchief. The grocer stayed erect and struggled, and Dillinger's gun went off. The hapless robbers then fled. Apprehended quickly, Dillinger drew a sentence of 10 to 20 years, although he had been assured by the local prosecutor that as a first offender, he would be treated lightly if he pleaded guilty. Dillinger's accomplice, 10 years older, was brought before a different judge and drew a far shorter sentence; he was released after doing two years. Dillinger ended up serving nine and the experience embittered him.

In 1934 Indiana governor Paul V. McNutt's secretary, Wayne Coy, would observe: "There does not seem to me to be any escape from the fact that the State of Indiana made John Dillinger the Public Enemy that he is today. The Indiana constitution provides that our penal code shall be reformative and not vindictive. . . . Instead of reforming the prisoner, the penal institutions provided him with an education in crime."

Doing time first in the Indiana State Reformatory at Pendleton and then in the state prison at Michigan City, Dillinger came in contact with criminals who became his mentors and later his accomplices, among them accomplished bank robbers like Harry Pierpont, John Hamilton, Homer Van Meter, Far Charley Makley, Russell Clark and Walter Dietrich. Despite his youth and relative inexperience, Dillinger was accepted as a member of this clique of hardened criminals because of his personal trustworthiness and willingness to help other prisoners. These were qualities much respected by men behind bars, even causing Pierpont, the group's nominal leader, to overlook a failing in Dillinger that he tolerated in no other associate—having an "old lady" prison lover.

Several members of the Pierpont clique had unsuccessfully attempted to break out of the prison, leading most of them to conclude their only chance for escape was a scheme based on having aid from outside and making the proper payoffs inside. Dillinger, soon to be paroled, was designated the "outside man." As such, he would have to raise a lot of money and fast, and the group, which included a number of "jugmarkers" (men who had knowledge of good banks to be robbed), told him how to go about it. Pierpont and others also supplied him with names of trustworthy accomplices to use on various capers. Dillinger's duties were to get enough money to make the proper payoffs, buy guns, obtain getaway cars and clothes, and find a hideout for the escapees. With only limited experience but a vast amount of criminal knowledge, Dillinger emerged from prison to become the greatest public enemy in the history of American crime.

He was released in May 1933, after a petition bearing the signatures of almost 200 residents of his adopted hometown of Mooresville, Ind., including that of his grocer victim, was presented to the governor. Dillinger immediately set about committing robberies to raise the funds needed for the mass escape. Many of his capers were pulled with criminals little more experienced than he was and were badly bungled, often clearing less than $100. But Dillinger kept trying for bigger scores and finally pulled off a bank robbery that netted $10,600, no small sum for a bank in a Depression-racked area, and then a payroll heist that yielded more than $24,000. He now had enough funds to spring the Pierpont group, being totally unmindful at the time that Capt. Matt Leach of the Indiana State Police had identified him as the busy holdup artist. Leach had an alarm out for Dillinger and had just missed catching him on a number of occasions.

Meanwhile, Dillinger gave a large part of the escape money to Mary Kinder, a 22-year-old woman whose brother was one of the convicts slated to be in on the escape and who would become Pierpont's mistress. The complete story about the Michigan City breakout of 10 convicts was never fully revealed. Payoffs were made, that much is certain. In addition, Dillinger traveled to Chicago, where through an intermediary he bribed the foreman of a thread-making firm to conceal several guns in a barrel of thread destined for the prison's shirt shop. The barrel was marked with a red X so that the escapees would recognize it.

On September 26, 1933 Pierpont and nine others took several hostages and made their way out of the prison, a feat that resulted in all sorts of political recriminations in Indiana. The new McNutt administration contended that holdover Republican guards or some who had been dismissed must have been involved, but the former Republican governor, Harry Leslie, blamed the breakout on the 69 new guards appointed by the Democrats. It mattered little to the Pierpont bunch. They were free. It mattered less to Dillinger. He had in the meantime been captured in Dayton, Ohio while visiting one of several new girlfriends.

The Pierpont bunch were stunned when they learned from Mary Kinder that Dillinger had been arrested. There was no question of what they were going to do about it. Dillinger had kept his word and freed them, and now they were going to free him. They planned a raid on the jail in Lima, Ohio where Dillinger was being held. Dillinger had been informed of the escape plot in advance and asked that another of his girlfriends, Evelyn "Billie" Frechette, a half Indian in her mid-twenties, be waiting for him when he got out.

The grateful Pierpont would deny Dillinger nothing. Billie, the wife of a bank robber then in Leavenworth, was brought to an apartment in Cincinnati to await Dillinger's release. On October 12, Columbus Day, Pierpont, Makley and Clark broke into the Lima Jail, mortally wounded Sheriff Jess Sarber and freed Dillinger. On the way out of the jail, Dillinger paused to look at the dying sheriff, who had treated him kindly and whom Dillinger had developed an affection for, and said sharply to Pierpont, "Did you have to do that?"

Pierpont shrugged. He might not have taken such a rebuke from another man, but he genuinely liked and respected Dillinger.

The "Dillinger mob" was now ready for action, although at the time, it should have been called the

John Dillinger (second from left) is photographed at arraignment in Arizona, the last time he would be taken alive.

"Pierpont mob." Dubbing it the Dillinger mob was the idea of lawman Matt Leach, who thought he might produce friction between the pair by making Dillinger into a greater criminal than he was. However, Leach's ploy failed. Nothing would come between Dillinger and Pierpont, and in fact, the latter wanted Dillinger to assume a more active leadership. He quickly grasped that Dillinger inspired confidence, trust and loyalty, vital qualities in a criminal organization, and could bring peace between feuding gangsters.

The mob pulled off a string of somewhere between 10 to 20 bank robberies; the number could not be determined because the gangsters never confessed which ones they had perpetrated and which were falsely attributed to them. This first so-called Dillinger mob functioned until January 1934, by which time the gang, after going to Florida for a rest, had moved to Tucson, Ariz. Several members were captured there by police work that was partly brilliant, partly pure luck and partly a result of tips from persons who recognized some of the gang from detective magazine pictures.

Dillinger was caught with Billie Frechette. Pierpont, Makley and Clark were taken with Mary Kinder and another woman. The three men were shipped to Ohio to be charged with the murder of Sheriff Sarber. Dillinger was flown to Chicago, where that city's entire "Dillinger Squad," 40 officers permanently assigned to the job of capturing him, and 85 other policemen met the plane. A 13-car convoy then took America's most famous prisoner to an "escape-proof" jail in Crown Point, Ind.

It was here that Dillinger was to electrify the nation with his famous "wooden gun" escape. According to the first version of the story, he used a knife to whittle a wooden gun out of the top of a washboard, colored it with shoe polish and used it to escape. But how did America's number one criminal get hold of a knife in jail? All right, change that to a razor blade. Both versions were sheer nonsense. Dillinger's wooden gun was a real one. The true story behind his escape from the Crown Point Jail was that his lawyer, an incredible rogue named Louis Piquett, had met with a prominent

Indiana judge on the grounds of the Century of Progress in Chicago and handed over an envelope containing several thousand of dollars. In return, the judge agreed to smuggle a gun into the jail. Dillinger used the gun to capture and lock up several guards and then made his way to the warden's office, where he grabbed two machine guns.

He gave one of the machine guns to a black prisoner, 35-year-old Herbert Youngblood, and together they locked up several more officers; snatched the car of a lady sheriff, Mrs. Lillian Holley, from the jail parking lot; and made good their escape, taking two hostages with them. Dillinger later released the two hostages, giving one, an auto mechanic, $4 for his troubles.

Naturally, the supposed wooden gun escape made headlines. Sometime later, however, a secret investigation conducted by the Hargrave Secret Service of Chicago on orders of Gov. McNutt turned up the true story about the gun. McNutt and Attorney General Philip Lutz, Jr. decided not to reveal the information because they quite properly didn't want Dillinger to know that certain informants whom he might trust again in the future had talked to private detectives. By the time Dillinger was killed, the judge too had died, and the findings about the gun never were made public.

Meanwhile, Dillinger basked in the glory of the wooden gun story and sought to perpetuate it. In a letter to his sister, he told her not to worry about him and that he was "having a lot of fun." Concerning the gun, he added:

> . . . [the reports] I had a real forty five Thats just a lot of hooey to cover up because they don't like to admit that I locked eight Deputys and a dozen trustys up with my wooden gun before I got my hands on the two machine guns. I showed everyone the wooden gun after I got a hold of the machine guns and you should have seen thire faces. Ha! Ha! Ha! Pulling that off was worth ten years of my life. Ha! Ha!

Dillinger's intention obviously was to cover up the fact that a real gun had been smuggled to him and to satisfy his ego. It was not the only time he had done that. Dillinger had often tormented his chief pursuer, Matt Leach, with phone calls and letters. And on one occasion he supposedly sent a book entitled *How to Be a Detective* to the excitable Leach. When he was captured in Arizona, Dillinger had been asked if he had in fact sent the book. He replied, "I was there when it was sent." That too was sheer nonsense. The book had been sent to Leach as a practical joke by Jack Cejnar, the bureau chief of the International News Service in Indianapolis.

After their escape Dillinger and Youngblood immediately separated. Thirteen days later, on March 16,

1934, Youngblood was mortally wounded in a gun battle with lawmen in Port Huron, Mich. As evidence of the loyalty Dillinger inspired in men, the dying Youngblood falsely told police that Dillinger had been with him the day before.

Immediately, Dillinger put together the real Dillinger mob, including among others Van Meter, jugmarker Eddie Green, Hamilton, Tommy Carroll and a newcomer, a short, violent-tempered punk named Lester Gillis, better known as Baby Face Nelson. It took considerable skill on Dillinger's part to keep Nelson and Van Meter, and occasionally some of the others, from shooting at one another. Dillinger undoubtedly disliked Nelson but he needed him. Nelson was the sort who would never desert his post in a robbery, and Dillinger had to commit several robberies fast. He had to get money to provide a legal defense for Pierpont, Makley and Clark, who were to be tried for murdering Sheriff Sarber.

Dillinger sent the money, but it did little good. All three were convicted: Clark got life and the other two were sentenced to the electric chair.

Time was running out for Dillinger as well. The same month as his breakout from the Crown Point Jail, he barely escaped in a barrage of machine-gun fire during a confrontation with FBI agents in St. Paul. Dillinger was wounded in the leg, but Billie Frechette drove him to safety. The next month, April 1934, Dillinger and the rest of the mob were hiding out at Little Bohemia Lodge, a closed summer resort about 50 miles north of Rhinelander, Wis., when the FBI closed in. Warned by barking dogs, Dillinger and his men escaped. Baby Face Nelson killed Special Agent W. Carter Baum and wounded another agent and a local police officer. The FBI wound up capturing only three of the mob's women, who were found hiding in the basement. They also managed to shoot two innocent bystanders, a salesman and a Civilian Conservation Corps (CCC) cook, and kill another young CCC worker, all of whom they thought were escaping gangsters.

It was a debacle for the FBI and, in a sense, another laurel for Dillinger. Will Rogers got into the act, writing, "Well, they had Dillinger surrounded and was all ready to shoot him when he come out, but another bunch of folks come out ahead, so they just shot them instead. Dillinger is going to accidentally get with some innocent bystanders some time, then he will get shot."

Dillinger and Van Meter both submitted to plastic surgery to alter their faces and fingerprints. Neither job was overly effective. Ironically, Dillinger "died" on the operating cot. Given a general anesthetic, he swallowed his tongue and stopped breathing. One of the panicky outlaw doctors managed to pull out his tongue with a forceps and applied artificial respirations, and Dillinger started breathing again.

By this time Hamilton had died of wounds received in a shoot-out with pursuing officers, and while Dillinger was recovering from the plastic surgery, Tommy Carroll was killed near Waterloo, Iowa. The mob was falling apart, and Dillinger could only think of making a few big scores and then fleeing to Mexico.

Still, Dillinger's facial surgery gave him enough confidence to venture openly in the streets. Using the identity of Jimmy Lawrence, he took up with a 26-year-old Chicago waitress named Polly Hamilton. Polly shared rooms with a friend, Anna Sage, whose real name was Ana Cumpanis. Sage had come to America from Romania just after the war and had operated whorehouses in Gary, Ind., and East Chicago, Ill. She had twice been convicted of operating a disorderly house but had won pardons from Indiana governor Leslie. Recently, however, Sage had been convicted a third time and Gov. McNutt had refused her request for a pardon. The Immigration Bureau was seeking to deport her as an undesirable alien.

Dillinger felt safe with Polly Hamilton and Anna Sage; he had never had trouble with women betraying him. It is doubtful that Hamilton knew his true identity, but Anna Sage soon discovered it. Dillinger felt comfortable talking to her. She was 42, an older woman and perhaps even a mother figure for him. Sage listened to his stories and ramblings and perhaps would not have informed on him merely because there was a $10,000 reward for his capture. But through a police contact in East Chicago, she made a deal with the FBI to betray Dillinger in exchange for a promise that the deportation proceedings against her would be dropped and the reward money would be given to her. Melvin Purvis, agent in charge of the Chicago office of the FBI, agreed to help with those matters as far as possible.

On July 22, 1934 Dillinger took the two women to a Chicago movie. Earlier in the day Sage had called the FBI to tell them about Dillinger's plans, but at that time she did not know which of two movies they would attend. The FBI staked out both and waited. As planned, Sage dressed in red so that the FBI men would recognize her. The agents at the Biograph Theater saw Dillinger and the two women enter. FBI inspector Sam Cowley, in charge of the nationwide hunt for Dillinger, telephoned J. Edgar Hoover and the decision was not to try to take Dillinger inside the movie house but to wait until he came out. When Dillinger and the women walked out of the theater, Purvis lit a cigar, the signal that identified Dillinger. Then he called on Dillinger to halt. The gangster looked about suddenly, and he saw that his female companions had vanished. In that brief instant he must have realized he had been betrayed by a woman. He pulled a Colt automatic from his right pants pocket and sprinted for the alley at the side of the movie house. Three FBI agents fired. They wounded two women passing, but they also shot Dillinger. One bullet went through his left side, another tore through his stooped back and came out his right eye. Dillinger fell dead.

Within a few months the second Dillinger mob was completely wiped out. Eddie Green was shot by the FBI. A month after Dillinger died, Homer Van Meter was also killed in an alley, this one in St. Paul, after being betrayed by friends. In November, Baby Face Nelson killed two FBI agents but died himself of wounds received in the gun battle. Meanwhile, Pierpont and Makley attempted to escape from the death house at the Ohio State Prison in Columbus by imitating Dillinger's mythical wooden gun ruse. With guns carved out of soap, they succeeded in overpowering one guard and were trying to batter their way out through the door leading from the death house when a riot squad opened fire. Makley was killed and Pierpont wounded. A month later, Pierpont died in the electric chair.

See also: JOHN HERBERT DILLINGER—DOUBLE, DIRTY DOZEN GANG, JUG MARKERS, HERMAN "BARON" LAMM, GEORGE "BABY FACE" NELSON, PUBLIC ENEMIES, MELVIN PURVIS, ED SINGLETON, WOODEN GUN ESCAPES, HERBERT YOUNGBLOOD.

Dillinger, John Herbert—double

The death of John Dillinger in July 1934 marked the end of crime's greatest folk hero of the 20th century, and it was therefore hardly surprising that his death was not accepted by many. This has been a common behavioral reaction. For decades there were people who believed Jesse James had not been shot by Bob Ford, that a substitute corpse had been used. And for decades one "real Jesse James" after another turned up. In the cases of the Apache Kid and Butch Cassidy, the weight of opinion seems to favor the theory that they survived their alleged demises, but the identification of their corpses was far more controversial.

The disbelief about John Dillinger started instantly after his death and continued for years. In a book entitled *Dillinger: Dead or Alive?* (1970), Jay Robert Nash and Ron Offen made perhaps the most complete case that the great public enemy had not been killed by FBI agents. Their basic premise was that the FBI had been duped into thinking the dead man was Dillinger, and when the agency discovered otherwise, it could do nothing but develop a massive cover-up.

What makes this case less than totally acceptable is the number of people such a plot would have required. Certainly Anna Sage, "the woman in red," and her East Chicago police contact or contacts. And someone would have had to have planted a phony Dillinger fingerprint card days before the killing. According to this theory, "Jimmy Lawrence" was not a Dillinger alias but the name of a real minor hoodlum whose career was rather hazy.

Proponents of the fake Dillinger theory make much of glaring discrepancies found in Dillinger's autopsy report, which was allegedly lost for more than 30 years. For instance, in the report the dead man's eyes were listed as brown, Dillinger's were blue. But this was an autopsy performed in Cook County during the 1930s, a time when coroners' findings nationwide were notorious for being replete with errors. The autopsy was performed in a "looney bin" atmosphere. A reporter for the *Chicago Tribune* appeared in news photos propping up Dillinger's head and was identified as the "coroner." Even after the autopsy was performed, Dillinger's brain was actually "mislaid" for a time. If all errors made in autopsies of that period were taken seriously, probably just half the victims of violent deaths could really have been considered dead.

Another question that must be raised is how John Dillinger lived happily ever after and on what. By all accounts, he had less than $10,000 available to him for a final, permanent escape. Could he stay away from crime forever? And if he could not, would he not have been identified sooner or later? And what of Anna Sage? Despite promises made to her by the FBI, she was deported back to her native Romania. She could undoubtedly have bought a reprieve from that fate had she come forward with the true facts about a Dillinger hoax.

In sum, the "Dillinger lives" theory appears to be a case of wishful thinking, one fostered by the fact that John Dillinger was too good—or too bad—to be allowed to die.

Dimsdale, Professor Thomas J. (1831–1866)
vigilante chronicler

Just as John X. Beidler is remembered as the hangman of the famous Vigilantes of Montana, Professor Thomas J. Dimsdale stands as their authorized biographer.

A consumptive English professor and Oxford graduate, Dimsdale settled in Virginia City, Mont. in search of a healthful mountain climate. After running a private school for a time, he was named Montana's first superintendent of public instruction in 1864 by the territorial governor. In August of that year he also became editor of the *Montana Post,* the first important newspaper in the territory, and he regularly chronicled the doings of the Montana vigilantes, offering what folks considered "book learning" justification for rope justice.

When in 1865 a bully named James Daniels killed another man in a dispute over cards and the victim's wife died of a heart attack on hearing the news, Dimsdale approved the vigilantes' decision to turn the defendant over to the law for the exacting of justice. However, he was as incensed as the rest of the community when Daniels got only a three-year sentence and was pardoned after serving just a few months. The pardoned killer returned to Helena and went about threatening to take vengeance on the vigilantes who had caught him. As a result of this misbehavior, the vigilantes seized him a second time and hanged him without recourse to the courts. While Dimsdale agreed that the "politic and the proper course would have been to arrest him and hold him for the action of the authorities," he could not condemn the lynching. He wrote in the *Post:*

> When escaped murderers utter threats of murder against peaceable citizens, mountain law is apt to be administered without much regard to technicalities, and when a man says he is going to kill any one, in a mining country, it is understood that he means what he says, and must abide the consequences. Two human beings had fallen victims to his thirst of blood—the husband and the wife. Three more were threatened; but the action of the Vigilantes prevented the commission of the contemplated atrocities. To have waited for the consummation of his avowed purpose, after what he had done before, would have been shutting the stable door after the steed was stolen.

And, Dimsdale added, Daniels was hanged "not because he was pardoned, but because he was unfit to live in the community."

Dimsdale's articles in the *Post* provided an instant history of the vigilante movement and certainly the most authoritative accounts on the subject. In 1866 a large number of them were collected and published in book form under the title of *Vigilantes of Montana,* the first book published in the territory. Dimsdale died on September 22, 1866, at the age of 35, just after the book's appearance. Although copies of the original edition are extremely rare, the book was republished in 1953 by the University of Oklahoma Press.

See also: JAMES DANIELS, VIGILANTES OF MONTANA.

Dio, Johnny (1915–1979) labor racketeer

Johnny Dio, whose real name was John DioGuardi, rose from the ranks of the old Murder, Inc. to become organized crime's most notorious labor racketeer. He was always believed to have been responsible for the acid blinding of labor communist Victor Reisel in 1956. According to the police theory, Dio had ordered the acid blinding of Reisel because Teamster official Jimmy Hoffa had said in a moment of rage that something should be done about the labor writer's probing columns. Dio reputedly carried out Hoffa's wishes in order to curry favor with him. In any event, Dio was arrested; but the case never came to trial.

Years earlier Thomas E. Dewey, then New York's racket-busting special prosecutor, called Dio "a young gorilla who began his career at the age of 15." As a protégé of the leaders of the old Brooklyn Murder, Inc. syndicate, Dio became an important mobster by the age of 20 and a gang chieftain at 24. In the mid-1950s Senate investigators named Teamster head Hoffa and Dio as the co-organizers of the paper locals of the union that eventually seized control of the lucrative airport trucking business in New York City. Finally, Dio was convicted and sentenced to 15 years in prison for stock fraud. He died in a Pennsylvania hospital after being moved there from the federal penitentiary at Lewisburg, Pa. Although he had been front-page copy for years, Dio's death escaped public attention for several days, even though a paid death notice appeared in the *New York Daily News*.

Dirty Dozen Gang   Indianapolis kids' gang

In 1913 a spokesman for the Pennsylvania Railroad declared that a neighborhood kid gang in the Oak Hill section of Indianapolis was "the worst on our entire right-of-way," but at the time, he could hardly have known why. What started out as little more than a typical neighborhood gang of 10-year-olds had soon turned into a band of minor criminals. One of their biggest illegal activities was stealing tons of coal from railroad gondolas on the belt line that ran through the area and selling it at bargain rates to local homeowners and residents.

The Dirty Dozen were finally caught by railroad detectives. When hauled into juvenile court, all except one of them was frightened. The leader of the gang, chewing gum, faced the judge with arms folded and a slouch cap over one eye. Angrily, the judge ordered him to take the gum from his mouth and the cap from his head. With a crooked smirk, the youth did both and then stuck the gum on the cap's peak.

"Your mind is crippled," the judge said to 10-year-old John Dillinger.

See also: JOHN DILLINGER.

Dix, Dorothea Lynde (1802–1887) prison reformer

In 1841 Dorothea Dix, a consumptive 39-year-old teacher went to the East Cambridge, Mass. House of Correction to teach Sunday school to the convicts and emerged to become the "angel of mercy" of prison reform. From that point on, she spent almost five decades of her life improving conditions for prisoners, the insane and the mentally ill. She found that prison inmates lived in the most inhumane conditions, chained naked and whipped with rods. She started a crusade, traveling the breadth of the country inspecting prisons, jails and almshouses and presenting her findings to legislative bodies. She told about how convicts and those having committed no crime other than being insane were imprisoned in cages, cellars, stalls and closets. More than any one person, she effected enormous improvements almost everywhere she went.

There was only a brief hiatus in her reform work when she was appointed superintendent of women nurses for the North during the Civil War. Immediately after the war she resumed her prison reform crusade. She even journeyed to England and elsewhere in Europe, where her initiative and perserverance brought reforms in every country she visited. She died in Trenton, N.J. on July 17, 1887, active to the end stopping prison horrors wherever she found them.

DNA evidence   convicting the guilty, freeing the innocent

The crime was probably as worthy of the death penalty as any. Robert Lee Miller, Jr., was convicted by an Oklahoma jury in 1988 for the rape and asphyxiation of two women, 92-year-old Zelma Cutler and 83-year-old Anne Laura Fowler. Miller was sentenced to death in 1988 and remained under that sentence for 10 years until a judge dismissed the case because of insufficient evidence. "Insufficient" was not quite the word for it. DNA in a semen sample turned out not to match Miller's DNA but did match that of an already convicted rapist.

DNA has revolutionized the field of crime. It has frequently convicted the guilty and in many cases kept innocent people from being prosecuted; in fact, it has often freed the innocent. However DNA testing involves utilizing human beings in the process and therein can lie the rub. There remains a crying need for competence and thoroughness during an investigation. Robert Hayes was convicted in 1991 in Florida for the rape and murder of a coworker. The conviction was based largely on DNA evidence taken from hair found in the victim's hands. Hayes was released in 1997 by the Florida Supreme Court when it was learned the hair was from a white man. Hayes was black.

DNA could be said to have had its birth in 1953 when English physicist M. H. F. Wilkins, together with Francis Crick and an American. John Watson, worked on the acids comprising the cell nucleus. They discovered DNA.

The great breakthrough in crime detection occurred in 1984 when Dr. Alec Jeffreys in England came up with chemical typing of "genetic fingerprints." Through Dr. Jeffreys' research it was established that the only persons in the world with identical "bar codes" were identical twins.

Dr. Jeffreys first applied the technique in paternity cases and in 1987 he made the great breakthrough in a murder case. Colin Pitchfork raped and strangled two teenagers three years apart. In a sweep that would never get compliance in the United States but did in Britain, authorities gained the cooperation of 4,600 men for blood samples. Pitchfork realized something was up although he did not understand what was involved and got a stand-in to give blood for him. Unfortunately, the police discovered the trickery and Jeffreys got his man.

Within a short time DNA testing started being used extensively in the United States. The FBI started doing DNA testing in rape and rape-homicide cases in 1989. The agency only gets the cases when there has been an arrest or an indictment and then does DNA testing to confirm or exclude the suspect. In one out of four cases where they get a result, the primary suspect is excluded.

The noted DNA expert Barry Scheck, has asked, "How many of those people would have been convicted had there been no DNA testing?"

Scheck is codirector, with Peter Neufeld, of the Innocence Project at the Benjamin N. Cardozo School of Law in Manhattan. As of 1999 well over 60 persons, more than half of them with the aid of project, had their convictions overturned because of DNA testing. In eight of those cases, the convicts were on death row. More important, thousands of others, said Scheck, "have been exonerated after an arrest, in the middle of a trial, things like that." Still, in 70 percent of the Innocence Project cases, the evidence the investigators wished to test could not be located.

On August 23, 1999 the *New York Times* stated that since capital punishment was reinstated by the United States Supreme Court there had been 566 executions, and at the same time 82 awaiting executions were exonerated—one in seven. There was no estimate of how many of those executed had been afforded the opportunity to use DNA evidence. This was not to be unexpected. Back in 1957, in *Not Guilty*, a trailblazing book examining the extent of wrongful convictions, Judge Jerome Frank, noted, "No one knows how many innocent men, erroneously convicted of murder, have been put to death by American governments. For . . . once a convicted man is dead, all interest in vindicating him usually evaporates." A "scorecard" of sorts could be offered by the death penalty experiences in Illinois to show 12 persons executed and in that same period 12 other inmates exonerated.

It is not always easy to free a defendant even after it has been proved that he is not guilty. There have been cases of prosecutors simply refusing to drop the charges even after the defendant has been released. In other cases it is a matter of gamesmanship to even introduce DNA evidence. This is especially the case when there is what some critics call "quickie deadlines" on new evidence. In Virginia the statute of limitations is 21 days, which left Earl Washington, Jr., in hard luck. In 1994 his DNA testing arrived too late. An optimist might say he still had some good luck. Subsequently his sentence was commuted to life imprisonment. David Botkins, a spokesman for Mark Earley, Virginia's attorney general, announced, "The inmates who have been granted clemency and had their death sentences commuted show the system works."

Some reformers do not see this as making the system work, and they have called for federal legislation to guarantee inmates an opportunity to require DNA testing. At the time only New York and Illinois offered such requirements.

Above all, this would require that DNA testing be done correctly. In the celebrated murder trial of ex-football star O. J. Simpson, Barry Scheck persuaded the jury in the criminal proceeding to disregard DNA evidence offered by the prosecution by demonstrating how such evidence could be misused.

Also required would be the fair use of the DNA evidence. In 1992 Randall Padgett was convicted of the stabbing death of his estranged wife. Virtually the entire case against Padgett was based on blood samples left at the scene, which were tested for DNA. It turned out the FBI crime laboratory had concluded the blood was not Padgett's. The Alabama prosecutors simply suppressed that fact. Padgett was acquitted at a retrial and was released after spending five years on death row.

There were indications by late 1999 that a bit of a sea change was taking place concerning the death penalty, especially in light of the DNA record. In some cases reforms were even supported by vocal death-penalty supporters. In Illinois, the house passed a resolution calling for a moratorium on executions and for the formation of an independent group to study how the death penalty was being applied in the state. In Nebraska, death penalty foes and proponents joined forces to pass a law that would stop executions for two years.

But in other jurisdictions the push remained strong for speedier executions. In fact, in August 1999 a conference organized by the United States Court of Appeals for the 11th Circuit, known to attorneys as hard-line, was held to find ways to expedite capital punishment. Some states have cut financing, in some cases to zero, for lawyers representing death row inmates for their appeals.

Calling for the rights to every death row inmate to have access to DNA testing, a decent attorney and the opportunity to introduce evidence of innocence no matter when it is uncovered, the *New York Times* editorialized: "It is the rare death-row inmate who does not claim to be innocent. But many states are finding, to their horror, that it is not a rarity that this claim is true . . . A wrongful conviction, of course, means that the real killer has gone free."

And of course the *Times* reiterated the long-standing view of reformers: "There is no way to know how many innocent people have been executed because the dead do not search for champions to prove their case."

Against this, many death penalty supporters tend to demand a date certain on all executions. A fairly standard call is for a definite cut-off after five years of conviction. Proponents argue that the absence of a date-certain provision makes a mockery of capital punishment. One who might have fallen victim to such a schedule for death would be Gregory Wilhoit, who was convicted in 1987 for killing his estranged wife in her sleep in Oklahoma. The prosecution relied on an expert who testified that Wilhoit's teeth matched bite marks on the victim's body. Later the state appeals court ruled that Wilhoit's counsel had failed to challenge the expert's claim. The court said at the time he—the defense attorney was "suffering from alcohol dependence and abuse and brain damage during his representation of appellant." At a new trial, 11 experts were brought in to testify that the bite marks did not match, and Wilhoit was freed.

However, this was six years later—beyond the so-called five-year limit.

Doane gang   Revolutionary War outlaws

The American Revolution was the first golden age for criminality in this country. The turmoil produced by the shifting fortunes of war created the ideal setting for bands of cattle rustlers, horse thieves and highway robbers. If a criminal stole from the British, he could count on the sympathies and sometimes even the active support of revolutionaries; if he preyed on known enemies of England, he was to the British a supporter of the Crown. Into this law enforcement vacuum stepped the notorious Doanes (sometimes called Doans), who left a trail of plunder through eastern Pennsylvania and parts of New Jersey.

Commanded by raw-boned Moses Doane, a fierce-looking man with long hair and a fur hat, the gang, composed of five of his brothers and as many as 10 to 15 others, became the terror of Bucks County, Pa. especially. Moses Doane declared himself a Tory so that upon the anticipated triumph of the British, he and his confederates would be labeled Loyalists and free from the threat of punishment. On that basis, the Doanes

stole only from the patriot side, but at no time was any of their loot delivered to His Majesty's forces. Their most daring robbery took place on a cold, windy night in October 1781, when 16 members of the gang boldly rode into Newtown, Pa. and headed directly for the home of John Hart, Esq., the treasurer of Bucks County, who was in the habit of hiding government funds in his home for fear of seizure by the British. Terrifying Hart and threatening his children, Moses Doane forced him to reveal the various hiding places of a total of about $4,500 in today's currency, then little short of a king's ransom. The robbery showed how proficient the Doane spy service was. Whenever and wherever in Bucks County a hoard of patriot money was to be found, the Doanes soon knew it. Tax collectors who changed their appointed rounds found that such intelligence was not long kept from the Doanes. Ironically, the Newtown robbery coincided with the collapse of Moses Doane's strategy of aligning himself with the British cause. Just three days previously, Cornwallis had surrendered at Yorktown, dooming the hopes of the Crown. The Doanes were now labeled outlaws by the recognized forces of law and order and were on the run. Their forays continued for several years, but they had few safe refuges other than caves, there being as many storied Doane cave hideouts in Pennsylvania as there were Jesse James caves in Missouri.

From 1783 on, wanted posters for various gang members dotted the Pennsylvania and New Jersey countryside. Before that, the Doanes had intimidated the local inhabitants by exacting vengeance on the nearest inhabitant to any wanted poster. If an individual didn't remove the poster, he faced a visit from the Doanes, one he would not forget—if he survived it. But by 1783 fear of the Doanes was fading, and additionally, some gang members, such as the fabled James "Sandy Flash" Fitzpatrick, had split off with gangs of their own. Fitzpatrick was hanged in 1787. On September 24, 1788 Abraham and Levy Doane, by then more critical to the gang than Moses, were executed on the Philadelphia Commons. A short time thereafter, Moses Doane was also caught and hanged.

See also: JAMES FITZPATRICK.

Doan's Store

While much can be said about lawlessness in the Old West, the fact remains that overall the frontier was composed of honest folk, as exemplified by the existence of Doan's Store, located at the Red River crossing just north of Vernon, Tex. Founded in 1874 by two brothers, Jonathan and Corwin Doan, the store sold supplies and clothing on credit and loaned out money to hundreds and hundreds of trail drivers and cowboys, all without collateral and to many men who were complete strangers.

Author J. Frank Dobie insisted that in almost two decades of business, the Doan brothers never lost a cent to any of their customers and that cowboys would ride hundreds of miles to pay up their accounts. And of course, it was the very clear code of the West that Doane's Store could and would never be robbed and that anyone who did so would have no place to hide.

Dobbs, Johnny (?–1892) bank robber and murderer

Johnny Dobbs was one of the most successful crooks in America during the 19th century. A colorful fence, bank robber and murderer, he was credited by authorities with netting himself at least $1 million over a 20-year criminal career.

During his youth Dobbs, whose real name was Michael Kerrigan, served in the Patsy Conroy gang of river pirates and then became a bank burglar of renown, working with the likes of Worcester Sam Perris Shang Draper, Red Leary, Jimmy Hope, Jimmy Brady, Banjo Pete Emerson, Abe Coakley and the King of the Bank Robbers, George Leonidas Leslie, in whose murder Dobbs later participated. Dobbs played a key role in the celebrated $2.7 million robbery of New York's Manhattan Savings Institution in 1878. He reportedly took part in bank jobs all over the East that netted perhaps $8 million in loot.

With a portion of his revenues, Dobbs opened a saloon at 100 Mott Street, just a short distance from police headquarters, and blatantly operated there as one of the biggest fences in New York. He supposedly fenced over $2 million in hot money and securities, keeping about $650,000 as his own share. When asked once why crooks congregated right by police headquarters, he replied, "The nearer the church the closer to God."

Dobbs and his accomplices murdered Leslie because they believed the King of the Bank Robbers was informing on them in exchange for the opportunity to start a new life elsewhere. Although he was not convicted of the murder, Dobbs was sent to prison for a number of robberies and spent most of the 1880s in various institutions. A week after he was discharged from the Massachusetts State Prison, he was found lying in a gutter in New York City and taken to Bellevue Hospital's alcoholic ward. He died there broke on May 15, 1892. To pay for his burial, one of Dobbs' former mistresses pawned an expensive brooch he had presented to her in happier days.

See also: GEORGE LEONIDAS LESLIE.

Doctors' Mob   great New York riot

On a Sunday evening in April 1788, a strange and bloody riot developed after a young medical student, annoyed by several children peering in the window of the New York Hospital in lower Manhattan, picked up the arm of a corpse he had just dissected and pointed it at them. "This is your mother's hand," he yelled. "I just dug it up. Watch out or I'll smack you with it." Ironically, one child among those who scattered upon hearing that terrifying threat had just lost his mother. He rushed home and told his father of the event. The man rushed to the cemetery where his wife had recently been buried, and by the greatest of coincidences, the grave was open and the woman's body gone. In a rage, the man headed for the hospital, telling his friends on the way what had transpired. Within minutes he was joined by an angry mob of hundreds.

Armed with torches, bricks and ropes, the members of the mob screamed for the doctors to come out. Dressed in street clothes most of the physicians slipped out by mingling with the crowd. Frustrated, the mob stormed the hospital and wrecked tables holding valuable specimens. One doctor and three students who remained behind to try to stop them barely escaped with their lives and were put in jail by the sheriff to protect them.

The mob's fury was not spent, and the rioters spilled back into the street looking for doctors. They attacked many doctors' homes. One of the homes was that of Sir John Temple, who was not a physician, but "Sir John" sounded like "surgeon." The medical student whose jest started the riot, John Hicks, Jr., was almost cornered in a physician's house but escaped over the rooftops.

On the following morning, April 14, authorities fully expected the riot to be over, but the mob's violence increased and scores of doctors were forced to leave the city. Later in the day a huge, ugly mob moved toward Columbia College in search of more grisly specimens and the "savage experimenters" who had gathered them. Several prominent citizens tried to intervene to end the madness. Alexander Hamilton was shoved aside. John Jay was knocked unconscious with a rock.

Meanwhile, Gov. George Clinton had called out the militia and prepared to use force to put down the violence. Baron Friedrich von Steuben, a hero of the Revolution and one of the most popular men in the city, begged the governor to hold off. Standing in front of the troops, he said he would try to dissuade the rioters. For his efforts the baron got hit on the head with a brick. In a quick turnabout, Steuben got to his knees and shouted, "Fire, Clinton, fire!"

The militia cut loose and 20 rioters fell in the first volley alone. In all, eight rioters were killed and dozens more injured.

Still, the riot continued until the morning of the 15th, when the mob was at last sated and returning physicians could tend the wounded rioters. Laws were passed giving medical researchers access to the bodies of executed persons, but this hardly fulfilled the need, and grave robbing remained a serious problem for many years, although no more bloody riots such as the Doctors' Mob incident occurred.

Dodge City, Kansas

In 1872 the railroad gangs of the Atchison, Topeka and Santa Fe Railroad turned a small hole-in-the-ground oasis where whiskey peddlers camped into what became probably the biggest, bawdiest, brawliest train town America ever saw. Located on the Arkansas River a few miles from the military reservation at Fort Dodge, the new town sprouted makeshift saloons and gambling dens in dugouts or tents on both sides of the tracks. Soon, rickety buildings were going up. The place was christened Dodge City and labeled the "queen of cow towns," the "wickedest little city in America," the "Gomorrah of the Plains" and, perhaps most picturesque of all, the "beautiful, bibulous Babylon of the frontier." It was all these and more. The mecca of buffalo hunters and trail herders, Dodge City became a wanton paradise of gamblers, gunmen and harlots. As one journalist reported: "No restriction is placed on licentiousness. The town is full of prostitutes and brothels." Another quotable remark made by an observer was "All they raise around Dodge City is cattle and hell." The terms *boot hill* and *red-light district* were born there. Wyatt Earp, Bat Masterson and company, the lawmen of Dodge, were called the Fighting Pimps, which should explain some of what was allowed in Dodge. Through a man named Ned Buntline, Earp achieved his first nationwide fame in Dodge, although he killed but one man there. Buntline, a journalistic rogue, came to Dodge in 1876 and with his writings did for Earp what he also did for Wild Bill Hickok and Buffalo Bill. Earp, according to Buntline, was all good and Dodge was all bad. Buntline was wrong on the first item but at least half right on the second.

Good or bad, Dodge had to be because it was a vital cattle center. With the years, it tamed down as the West itself did. Today, it is still a cattle center of some 14,000 people.

See also: DODGE CITY PEACE COMMISSION, WYATT EARP, LUKE MCGLUE, RED-LIGHT DISTRICT.

Dodge City Peace Commission   gunmen

The Dodge City Peace Commission was anything but what its name implied. It was a conglomeration of some of the toughest and meanest gunfighters of the West—Wyatt Earp, Luke Short, Doc Holliday, Bat Masterson, Shotgun Collins and others—who threatened to drown Dodge City in a sea of blood in defense of the institutions they held dear, namely gambling and prostitution.

During its early years Dodge City was dominated by a political group of saloon keepers, brothel owners and gamblers that became known as "the Gang." The Gang, especially under Mayor "Dog" Kelly, maintained their idea of a wide-open town by utilizing the guns of Earp, Masterson and Short. By the early 1880s times were changing in Kansas. For one thing, the forces of prohibition were gaining in the state, although not in Dodge. Still, there were reformers trying to change Dodge, primarily by warring on prostitution, the lifeblood of an open cattle town.

In 1883 the "reformers" under Lawrence E. Deger pushed through ordinances against prostitution and vagrancy, the latter instituted as a way of harassing gunfighters and gamblers. The first crackdown was made against the Long Branch Saloon, owned by Luke Short and W. H. Harris, two of the out-of-power Dodge City Gang. The reform party itself contained other saloon elements, especially those of A. B. Webster, who was the chief business rival of Short and Harris, and the new laws seemed to be enforced unevenly. Of course, the reformers could argue a start had to be

Members of the Dodge City Peace Commission were dedicated to preserving gambling and prostitution in Dodge City. Seated, left to right: Charles E. Bassett, Wyatt Earp, M. C. Clark and Neal Brown. Standing, left to right: W. H. Harris. Luke Short and Bat Masterson.

made somewhere. Somewhere came with the arrest of three singers from the Long Branch, known as "horizontal singers," on prostitution charges.

Those arrests marked the start of the so-called Dodge City War. Luke Short was fighting mad at the arrest of his ladies and tried to shoot L. C. Hartman, the lawman who had taken them into custody. Hartman survived the fusillade only because he accidentally slipped to the ground. Short was later arrested for attempted murder and released on bond. When Mayor Deger learned that Short and a half dozen of his supporters were composing a "death list" and that some reformers were talking of setting up a vigilante group, he ordered Short and his men run out of town.

Short took his side of the argument to the governor and the newspapers. Both sides deluged the state capital with petitions supporting their views. Short threatened open warfare, and when the governor made it clear he would not send troops in to protect Dodge, Short acted. First Wyatt Earp and Bat Masterson, two of Short's oldest friends, showed up to lend a hand in Topeka and plan strategy. Suddenly, the citizens of Dodge found Doc Holliday was in town. And there were others to back up Holliday—Charlie Bassett, Neal Brown, Shotgun Collins, Rowdy Joe Lowe and others.

While a nervous governor sent in the adjutant general on a fact-finding mission, Earp and Masterson escorted Short into town. Hysteria started building. A local newspaper gave its readers some of the foreboding facts:

A brief history of these gentlemen who will meet here tomorrow will explain the gravity of the situation. At the head is Bat Masterson. He is credited with having killed one man for every year of his life. This may be exaggerated, but he is certainly entitled to a record of a dozen or more. He is a cool, brave man, pleasant in his manners, but terrible in a fight. Doc Holliday is another famous killer. Among the desperate men of the West, he is looked upon with the respect born of awe, for he has killed in single combat no less than eight desperadoes. He was the chief character in the Earp war at Tombstone, where the celebrated brothers, aided by Holliday, broke up the terrible rustlers.

Wyatt Earp is equally famous in the cheerful business of depopulating the country. He has killed within our personal knowledge six men, and he is popularly accredited with relegating to the dust no less than ten of his fellow men. Shotgun Collins was a Wells, Fargo & Co. messenger, and obtained his name from the peculiar weapon he used, a sawed-off shotgun. He has killed two men in Montana and two in Arizona, but beyond this his exploits are not known. Luke Short,

for whom these men have rallied, is a noted man himself. He has killed several men and is utterly devoid of fear.

While there was considerable exaggeration in the biographies of many of the gunfighters, it was obvious the Short-Earp forces had the firepower to make the O.K. Corral fight a Sunday school outing by comparison. With each hour their legions grew. The citizenry learned of the arrival of gunmen now known only as Cold Chuck Johnny, Dynamite Sam, Black Jack Bill, Three-Fingered Dave, Six-Toed Pete and, most ominously, Dark Alley Jim. They began thinking that the militia would be unable to handle such skilled gunfighters even if it did intervene. Faced with this bleak outlook, the reformers in Dodge capitulated. Short and Harris were invited back to run the Long Branch as they had in the good old days. Prostitution was saved and Dodge City remained a wide-open town.

Later, seven of the Short supporters posed for a victory photograph and labeled themselves the Dodge City Peace Commissioners. Through the years, and especially thanks to Hollywood, the impression took hold that the peace commissioners had something to do with peace and law and order.

See also: LUKE SHORT.

dogfighting

Dogfighting is an illegal sport that is now almost completely eradicated in this country, unlike cockfighting, which continues. Nonetheless, it has a long and terrible tradition in America. Although illegal in almost every state, dogfighting contests were common in every part of the country during the 19th century, and thousands of dogs suffered horrible deaths. Dog stealing became a major criminal activity, as gangsters used every means possible to provide enough animals to keep up with demand. Most top fighting dogs were imported from England or bred from that country's stock. Championship battles often generated as much betting action as did prize fights. Some of the most infamous dogfighting arenas in the country were Hanly's Dog Pit and Bill Swan's Saloon and Rat Pit in New Orleans and Kit Burns' Sportsmen's Hall in New York.

Fights were not only staged between dogs but also with wharf rats, which were brought in to battle dogs after being starved for a considerable length of time. Generally, fighting terriers could handle the rats but occasionally one would start to flee after taking several nips from the rodents. The rooting of the crowd would then shift in favor of the rats, as the spectators hoped to see an execution by them. In a contest at Bill Swan's establishment in 1879, a dog named Modoc killed 36 rats in two minutes and 58 seconds, but good as that was, it hardly equaled the record of a dog named Jacko, who in 1862 had killed 60 rats in two minutes, 43 seconds. The same year, Jacko set his all-time endurance record by disposing of 200 rats in 14 minutes, 37 seconds.

Probably America's greatest dogfight was that staged at the Garr farm near Louisville, Ky. on October 19, 1881. The battle was fought under *The Police Gazette's* revised rules for dogfighting with the purse of $2,000 being held by Richard K. Fox, the owner of that publication. While the match was illegal and in danger of being halted, the contest enjoyed such advance publicity that bets were made on it from coast to coast. The Ohio and Mississippi Railroad ran special excursion trains that brought dogfight fanatics from places as distant as New York and New Orleans. It became apparent that if authorities stopped the battle, they would face rioting in Louisville by disgruntled fans.

The contestants were New York's Cockney Charlie Loyod's brindled, white dog Pilot and Louisville's "Colonel" Louis Kreiger's white battler Crib. Because the fight was for the title of "American champion," the winner was required to kill his foe. Therefore, the brutal and inhumane fight lasted one hour and 25 minutes before Pilot emerged victorious. Pilot became as well known as the famous bare-knuckled boxing champion of the era John L. Sullivan.

By the turn of the century, interest in dogfighting had given way to boxing, which had become somewhat more civilized with the introduction of boxing gloves and three-minute rounds.

Dolan, Dandy Johnny (c. 1850–1876) gangster and murderer

One of the most imaginative and brutal gangsters of the 19th century, Dandy Johnny Dolan probably qualified as the Thomas Edison of the underworld. A renowned member of the Whyos, a gang that dominated crime in New York during the decades following the Civil War, Dolan came up with a host of innovative methods to maim and kill, his prize invention being a great advance in the technique of gouging out eyes. Dolan produced an apparatus, made of copper and worn on the thumb, that could do the gruesome job with dispatch. It served the Whyos well both in criminal endeavors and in battles with other gangs. Dolan also designed special fighting boots for himself with sections of a sharp ax blade imbedded in the soles. A simple stomping of a downed enemy produced an ending both gory and mortal.

Dolan's downfall came when James H. Noe, a brush manufacturer, caught him in the process of robbing his factory. The gangster managed to get away by using his terrible eye gouger on Noe and then beating his victim to death with an iron bar. Later, Dolan proudly displayed eyes to admiring members of the Whyos. The police did not catch Dolan with the eyes, but they did find him in possession of Noe's cane, which had a metal handle carved in the likeness of a monkey, as well as his watch and chain. This evidence was enough to doom Dolan, and he was hanged on April 21, 1876.

See also: WHYOS.

Dollar Store first "big store" swindle

In 1867 a stocky, red-whiskered, friendly man named Ben Marks opened the Dollar Store in Cheyenne, Wyo., where everything in stock sold for that price. Marks, however, was not interested in merchandising but in confidence games, and what he started would develop into the "big store," the grift that was to become the technique used in most great confidence rackets for the next 100 years.

In the windows of his store, Marks featured all sorts of useful price-worthy items, but sales proved few and far between since the pitch was used merely to draw gullible travelers and immigrants into the store. A pioneer exponent of three-card monte and other swindles, Marks had confederates operating several games complete with shills who appeared to be winning. Many a wagon train settler stepped into the store to buy a sturdy shovel and left minus most of his stake for a new life in the West. Ben Marks' cheating Dollar Store in time graduated into the big store concept, the phony gambling club, horse parlor or fake brokerage and other "stings" in which the gullible were separated from thousands of dollars. Ironically, among the scores of dollar stores that sprang up to imitate Ben Marks' pioneer venture was one in Chicago that grew into a great modern department store. Its founder had originally leased the building for a monte operation but discovered he could actually sell cheap and flashy goods at a dollar and make more profits than he could at monte.

See also: BIG STORE, THREE-CARD MONTE.

Donahue, Cornelius "Lame Johnny" (1850–1878) outlaw, lawman and lynch victim

Long an enigma in the Dakotas, Cornelius Donahue had the distinction of having Lame Johnny Creek in the Black Hills named after him, no doubt because of his

275

other claim to fame, that of being the victim of one of the strangest lynchings in American history.

Donahue was a college-trained Philadelphian who went to Texas to satisfy his romantic dreams of being a cowboy. Because he suffered from a deformity that earned him the nickname Lame Johnny, he found that he commanded very poor pay and soon turned to stealing horses. When he puled out of Texas in the mid-1870s, he was a much wanted thief. Lame Johnny moved north to Deadwood in Dakota Territory and showed enough talent with a gun to become a deputy sheriff. Later, he worked for a mining company until he was recognized in early 1878 by a rider from Texas. Oddly, he was not sent back to Texas, probably because he had been so popular, but he lost his job and finally reverted to horse stealing, perhaps doing some stage robbing as well. In 1878 a livestock detective named Frank Smith caught Lame Johnny stealing horses from the Pine Ridge Indian Reservation. Smith and his prisoner boarded a stage bound for Deadwood, where he was to be lodged in jail, but on the trip the coach was halted by a masked man who rescued Lame Johnny. At least that's what was thought until Johnny was found hanging from a tree the next day. It appeared he had been spirited away and lynched by a mob of one. No one could figure it out. Perhaps, according to one theory, Lame Johnny had done something really terrible in Texas that merited his fatal treatment at the hands of a mysterious kidnapper. But the puzzle remained unsolved; the miners named a creek after Lame Johnny and let it go at that.

Donner Party   murder and cannibalism

The tragic fate of the Donner Party, a group of California-bound settlers who split off from a wagon train at Fort Bridger, Wyo. remains the ultimate horror story of America's westward migration.

Following the lead of George Donner, the 89-member caravan took the so-called Hastings Cut-off, a supposed shortcut that was instead to bring them to tragedy. Progress was slow through the rugged Wasatch Mountains, and many of the settlers' horses and oxen died on the tortuous trek. Bickering broke out and a number of killings resulted. One of the organizers of the group, James Reed, killed a young man named James Snyder in an argument. At first, the other members of the wagon train favored hanging Reed but later decided merely to banish him, and he was forced to leave behind his wife and children and continue on his own.

By the end of October 1846, the Donner Party was compelled to camp at what was then called Truckee Lake, now known as Donner Lake, because 20- to 60-foot snows had stopped the wagon train from making it through their last obstacle, the Sierra Nevada. Desperately, the pioneers built shelters and tried to last through the winter by killing their remaining animals to augment the dwindling food supply. However, it soon became apparent that they would starve, and a party of 17 men and five women started out on foot to try to break out of the mountains and get help. One of them died along the way and the others ate his flesh to survive. Only two Indian guides refused to partake of the human flesh. They decided to leave the rest of the party, suspecting they would be killed next to provide more food, but were quickly located and murdered. Meanwhile, members of the party at Donner Lake started dying and the survivors there also resorted to cannibalism to keep themselves alive. Then the murdering started. No one ever found out who died naturally and who was killed.

Finally, the escape party made it through the mountains to an Indian camp and then to an outpost. Rescuers from the outpost set out back across the mountains. One of them was James Reed, who heroically led the largest rescue team and found his wife and two of his children (another child had died and was eaten). It was not until April 17, 1847 that the last of the travelers were saved; by that time, of the 89 emigrants only 45 still survived.

It soon became evident that a number of the dead had been murdered to provide food, while whole legs of oxen lay untouched in the snow not far away. The weakened pioneers had lacked the strength to dig up the meat. The villain of the party was made out to be Lewis Keseberg, who was found lying beside a simmering pot containing the liver and lungs of a small boy. Other parts of human flesh were scattered around the floor of his cabin, and a contemporary account described his "lair" as "containing buckets of blood, about a gallon, and parts of human flesh strewn all around."

After the rescue Keseberg was charged with committing six murders, robbing the dead George Donner of his gold and cannibalizing several bodies. Denying all the charges except that of cannibalism, he described what had happened: "Five of my companions had died in my cabin, and their stark and ghastly bodies lay there day and night, seemingly gazing at me with their glazed and staring eyes. I was too weak to move them had I tried."

He insisted he had resorted to flesh eating as a last desperate act.

I cannot describe the unutterable repugnance with which I tasted the first mouthful of flesh. There is an instinct in our nature that revolts at the thought of touching, much less eating, a corpse. It makes my blood curdle to think of it. It has been told that I boasted of my shame—said that I enjoyed this horrid food, and that I remarked that human flesh was more palatable than California beef. This is a falsehood. It is a horrible, revolting falsehood. This food was never otherwise than loathsome, insipid, and disgusting."

A court freed Keseberg, but he suffered the rest of his life from public disrepute. Whenever children saw him, they shouted: "Stone him! Stone him!" In a sense, Keseberg was the last victim of the ill-fated Donner Party.

Doolin, Bill (1863–1896) outlaw leader

Probably the most popular of the Western outlaws with the public was not Butch Cassidy, Jesse James or Sam Bass but Bill Doolin, the leader of the Oklahombres of the 1890s.

An Arkansas-born cowboy, Doolin punched cattle in Wyoming and later in Oklahoma for the HX (Halsell) Ranch, the breeding ground for a lot of future badmen. Doolin hit the outlaw trail in 1891 with the Daltons. He enjoyed the easy money but clearly was never too sure how smart the brothers were. Doolin started out with the gang for the famed raid on Coffeyville, Kan., where the brothers sought to recapture the lost glory of the James boys and the Youngers by holding up two banks at the same time—a stupid play as far as Doolin was concerned. Fortunately, or conveniently, for him, his horse turned lame and he was forced to turn back. The Daltons were annihilated in Coffeyville, and Doolin alone went back to Oklahoma to form a new band of robbers.

The new Doolin gang reflected much of their leader's personality. They were friendly and fun-loving except when cornered—then they shot to kill. The gang even operated under a code of honor that barred shooting a tracking lawman in the back. Indeed, when the redoubtable lawman Bill Tilghman once appeared unexpectedly in the gang's camp, Doolin saved his life by telling his men to put down their weapons. Doolin knew the Oklahoma badlands section called Hell's Fringe like the back of his hand and always led pursuers on a merry chase there. He was aided too by his popularity with residents, counting on warnings from them whenever posses were in the area. Warned in time, Doolin and his men beat off and escaped a huge posse in the famed Battle of Ingalls in September 1893.

Early in 1894 Doolin married a minister's daughter and under her influence started to settle down to honest pursuits. The Oklahombres began splintering, individuals or pairs going their separate ways. But Doolin had too long a record, having committed too many robberies, for the law to forget him. Bill Tilghman cap-tured him in a Eureka Springs, Ark. bathhouse after a fierce half-hour fight in which neither man used a gun. When Tilghman brought Doolin to Guthrie, Okla., 5,000 people crowded the town to greet Doolin. They all but ignored the brave marshal as they pressed in to touch the famed outlaw and ask him for autographs. Doolin was bigger than life, and he proved that by promptly escaping from the Guthrie jail, freeing 37 prisoners in the process.

Doolin fled to New Mexico, where, it was learned 40 years later, he was sheltered at the ranch of the famous novelist Eugene Manlove Rhodes. There he saved his host from being killed by a wild horse. By 1896 Doolin and his wife had settled in a small house near Lawton, Okla.; at this point the outlaw was in very poor health due to consumption.

For years there have been two versions of Doolin's death. The original story was that Heck Thomas caught up with Doolin on a dark night as the outlaw walked down a road, cradling a Winchester in one arm while leading a wagon driven by his wife. Doolin fired first and Marshal Thomas blasted him to death with a shotgun.

Years later a second version surfaced. There had been no confrontation on a dusty road. Thomas had pushed through the door of the Doolin home to find the outlaw's wife in tears. Doolin was dead, she said. Thomas walked into the bedroom to find Doolin's still-warm body. He was dead and that meant no reward money. Quickly, Thomas leveled his shotgun and fired. Then, after concocting the story about a shooting on a road, he claimed a reward. It was not, however, an act of greed on Thomas' part. Like many other law officers, he respected Bill Doolin and did not wish to see his widow and young boy live in poverty. He gave the $5,000 reward money to the widow.

See also: DOOLIN GANG; INGALLS, OKLAHOMA TERRITORY, BATTLE OF; HENRY ANDREW "HECK" THOMAS; BILL TILGHMAN.

Doolin gang

While Western criminals were often the object of a great deal of hero-worship, one outlaw band that was genuinely respected during the 1890s, not only by the public but by law officers as well, was the Doolins of the Oklahoma Territory. Neither Bill Doolin nor any of the members ever claimed they "were forced into crime," admitting they were in it for the sheer devilry.

The gang was formed by Bill Doolin, who had ridden on a number of bank jobs with the Daltons, but unlike the Daltons, members of the Doolin bunch were good at their trade. They took their work seriously and practiced hard before a bank robbery, gunning a target tree as they rode past and dropping to one side of their mounts as they dodged imaginary bullets. They seldom had to hide in their home areas, such as Rock Fort and Ingalls, where friendly residents provided a network of spies that informed them whenever the law was coming. The gang clearly won the great Battle of Ingalls, beating a posse of about twice its size. Although some of the leading lawmen of the era, respected names like Tilghman, Madsen, Thomas, Ledbetter, Jim Masterson, captured a few gang members, the group, including Bill Doolin, dissolved of its own accord to follow more peaceful pursuits.

See also: ROY DAUGHERTY; BILL DOOLIN; INGALLS, OKLAHOMA TERRITORY, BATTLE OF; GEORGE "BITTER CREEK" NEWCOMB; ROSE OF CIMARRON.

door-knocker thieves   colonial lawbreakers

One of the most prevalent types of theft in colonial days was stealing brass knockers from the doors of fashionable homes. Professional criminals netted considerable profits from such crimes, disposing of their loot to receivers of stolen goods who transported the knockers to another colony for resale. Door-knocker thefts became such a rage that even well-to-do youths took up the crime as a form of sport, making it perhaps the first form of middle-class crime in America. A Philadelphia newspaper in 1773 reported that "wonton Frolicks of sundry intoxicated Bucks and Blades of the City" resulted in the theft of scores of brass knockers from various homes. That same year, in a story datelined Philadelphia, the *Newport Mercury* told of how "three of our Philadelphia Bucks, in the Night, lately attacked one of our Watchmen with swords" while he was attempting to prevent their nefarious deeds. However, "before he got relief they wounded him, of which Wounds he died. One of them made his escape, two were taken; one of those a reputable Merchant's Son in the City; the other a Merchant's Clerk, unknown to me. Various Opinions concerning them, what will be their fate. They are, I hear, loaded with Irons in the Dungeon."

The record appears incomplete regarding the ultimate fate of the perpetrators of this vicious crime, but knocker thievery finally was eliminated through the efforts of one Daniel King, who invented a knocker "the Construction of which is peculiarly singular, and which will stand Proof against the United Attacks of those nocturnal Sons of Violence."

Doty, Sile (1800–1876)   king of the hotel thieves

One of the great "lock men" of crime, Sile Doty was the first thief to develop the complete burglar kit. He bought locks by the dozen, took them apart, studied them and then designed skeleton keys to fit the various types. He also perfected a set of pliers that could be inserted in a door to turn a key on the other side. With these impressive improvements in the art of burglary, Doty was able to boast that he could break into any hotel room in any establishment in the country. In 1835, for example, Doty hit the United States Hotel in Detroit, which was then the state capital, and burglarized the rooms of about a dozen state legislators.

Because of his great success as the King of the Hotel Thieves, Doty in later years set up a criminal network that included crooked hotel managers and clerks, who steered him on to likely victims, and corrupt sheriffs and judges, who protected him in case of a hitch. With this apparatus in place, Doty branched into circulating counterfeit money, but his first love remained anything to do with locks. He designed handcuffs and sold them to sheriffs and then sold criminals special keys that could open the cuffs even while they were being worn.

Doty liked to claim he "made crime pay," but despite all his brilliance and his payoffs, he spent 20 years of his life—on and off—behind bars before retiring at 72 and writing his memoirs.

Draft Riots

Beginning early on the morning of July 13, 1863 and continuing for three more bloody days, great riots broke out in New York City, leaving, according to the best estimates, 2,000 dead and another 8,000 wounded. The cause of the rioting was indignation over President Lincoln's draft, fanned by racial hatred, Irish resentment at occupying the lowest level of the social and economic order, and the greed of the great criminal gangs of the Bowery and the Five Points, which saw a chance to loot the city much as had been done during the earlier anti-abolitionist and anti-English Astor Place riots of the 1830s and 1840s.

There were minor disturbances of the peace in opposition to the draft in Boston, Mass., Portsmouth, N.H., Rutland, Vt. and Wooster, Ohio, but none approached the size or ferocity of the New York riots. There the city's poor, largely Irish, allied with the Democrats in opposition to the war, rioted to protest the draft, which they saw as trading rich men's money for poor men's blood through a provision in the law that allowed a potential draftee to buy out of the service for $300. Since this was a monumental sum to the Irish, it meant they had to do the fighting and dying in the conflict between the North and the South.

What had started out as violent protest against the draft turned by the second day into savage lynching of blacks—the cause of the war in the Irish poor's eyes—and wholesale looting, as rioters and criminals sought

Burning of the Second Avenue Armory caused many deaths.

Great throngs—estimated to be between 50,000 and 70,000 persons in all—stormed across Manhattan from the Hudson to the East Rivers, looting stores, burning buildings and beating every black they saw. At least three black men were hanged before sundown of the first day, and thereafter, the sight of bodies hanging from lampposts and trees were common throughout the city. The blacks' bodies were all viciously mutilated, slashed with knives and beaten with clubs. Often, they were mere charred skeletons, the handiwork of the most ferocious element in all early American riots—women. Trailing behind the men, they poured oil into the knife wounds of victims and set the corpses ablaze, dancing beneath the awesome human torches, singing obscene songs and telling antiblack jokes.

The black settlements were the scene of much of the violence, the target of those of the rioters more concerned with bloodletting than looting. A house of prostitution on Water Street was burned and its occupants tortured because they refused to reveal the hiding place of a black servant. In New Bowery three black men were cornered on a rooftop and the building set afire. For a time the men clung by their fingers to the gutters while the mob below chanted for them to fall. When they did, they were stomped to death.

Meanwhile, as other groups of rioters attacked armories in search of weapons and police stations in anger at the police resistance to them, a mob sought to destroy the offices of Horace Greeley's prodraft *New York Tribune*. They started several blazes that forced the

to seize armory supplies, overpowering and then torturing, mutilating and murdering defending soldiers. Some saw in the great riots a Roman Catholic insurrection, which they were not, although along with the "No Draft" signs were some that sang the praises of the pope and proclaimed, "Down with the Protestants." Considerable church properties of various Protestant faiths were among the 100 buildings burned to the ground by the rioters, but none belonging to the Catholic faith were touched. Lone Catholic priests turned back rioters bent on looting and killing, but Catholic archbishop Hughes refused to counsel the rioters to disband until the fourth day, when the violence had run its course. On that day he addressed a pastoral letter entitled "Archbishop Hughes to the Men of New York, who are called in many of the papers rioters." Later, the archbishop was to acknowledge that he had "spak too late."

The rioters were bent on mayhem, and some of their crimes were heinous indeed. Policemen and soldiers were murdered, and the children of the rioters picked the bodies clean of every stitch of clothing, proudly wearing the bloodstained garments as badges of honor.

Drawing shows the corpse of a policeman killed in the riot being abused by children and women following in the wake of the mob.

By the second day most of the rioters' fury was taken out on blacks, many of whom were lynched.

staff to flee by the back stairway. Greeley was compelled to take refuge under a table in a Park Row restaurant. A police garrison of 100 men retook the newspaper's premises and extinguished the fires, and the following day 100 marines and sailors took up guard in and around the building, which bristled with Gatling guns and a howitzer posted at the main entrance.

By late evening the mobs moved further uptown, leaving the scene behind them filled with numerous fires. At 11 o'clock a great thunder and lightning storm extinguished the blazes. Had it not, many historians believe the city would have been subjected to a conflagration far worse than the Great Chicago Fire a few years hence. Complicating the firefighting was the fact that several fire units had joined the rioters and others were driven away from many of the blazes by the rampaging mobs.

Probably the greatest hero of the first day of the riots was Patrolman George Rallings, who learned of a mob's plan to attack the Negro Orphanage at 43rd Street and Fifth Avenue where 260 children of freed slaves were sheltered. He spirited the children away before the building was torched. Only one tiny black girl was killed by the ax-wielding rioters. Overlooked in the exodus, she was found hiding under a bed and axed to death.

The fighting over the ensuing three days reflected the tides of military battle, as first the rioters and then the police and various militia units took control of an area. A pitched battle that left an estimated 50 dead was fought at barricades on Ninth Avenue until the police finally gained control of the thoroughfare. Rioters captured Col. H. J. O'Brien of the Eleventh New York Volunteers, tied a rope around his ankles and dragged him back and forth over the cobblestones. A Catholic priest intervened long enough to administer the last rites and then departed. For three hours the rioters tortured O'Brien, slashing him with knives and dropping stones on his body. He was then allowed to lie suffering in the afternoon sun until sundown, when another mob descended on him and inflicted new tortures. Finally, he was dragged to his own backyard, where a group of vicious Five Points Gang women squatted around him and mutilated him with knives until at last he was dead.

On July 15 militia regiments sent toward Gettysburg were ordered back to the city, and by the end of the 16th, the rioters had been quelled. The losses by various military units were never disclosed, but the toll of dead and wounded was believed to have been at least 350. The overall casualties in the riots, 2,000 dead and 8,000 wounded, were greater than those suffered at such famous Civil War battles as Bull Run and Shiloh; virtually every member of the police force had suffered some sort of injury. The number of blacks lynched, including bodies found and others missing, was believed to total 88. Property losses probably exceeded $5 million. Among the 100 buildings totally burned were a Protestant mission, the Negro Orphanage, an armory, three police stations, three provost marshals' offices as well as factories, stores and dwellings. Another 200 buildings were looted and partially damaged.

Even while the riots were going on and in the days following them, Democratic politicians seeking to embarrass a Republican president and a Republican mayor, demanded the police and troops be withdrawn from their districts because they were "killing the people." As a result of political influence almost all of the hundreds of prisoners taken in the last two days of the riots were released. This was especially true of the gang leaders of the Five Points and the waterfront who were caught leading looting expeditions during the fighting. In the end, only 20 men out of the thousands of rioters were brought to trial. Nineteen of them were convicted and sentenced to an average of five years in prison. No one was convicted of murder.

On August 19, the city now filled with troops, the draft drawings resumed, and those who could not pay $300 were sent off to war.

Driscoll, Danny (?1860–1888) gang leader and murderer

The last great New York ruffian gang of the 19th century was the Whyos, captained jointly in their heyday by Danny Lyons and Danny Driscoll. In the 1880s Lyons and Driscoll reportedly mandated that a potential member of the gang had to kill at least one man. It is perhaps fitting that this brutal pair were themselves hanged within eight months each other.

Driscoll went first. In 1887 he and tough Five Points gangster Johnny McCarthy became involved in a shooting dispute over whom a young prostitute, Breezy Garrity, was working for. Breezy made the mistake of standing around to see who the winner would be, presumably to hand over to him her recent receipts. In the fusillade one of Driscoll's stray shots struck and killed her. It was clearly a case of unintentional homicide, and by most measures of justice Driscoll should have escaped with something less than the ultimate penalty. However, the authorities had been after Driscoll for years on suspicion of several murders and were not going to allow a golden opportunity such as this to slip away because of legal niceties. The prosecution hardly had to remind the jurors of the many atrocities committed by the Whyos, since everyone living in New York ventured out in constant fear of these gangsters. Driscoll, screaming outrage and frame-up, was sentenced to death, and on January 23, 1888 he was hanged in the Tombs.

See also: DANNY LYONS, WHYOS.

drop swindle

A notorious con game employing a variety of techniques is the drop swindle. A "dropper" drops a wallet at the heels of a likely victim and then pretends to find it. The wallet is stuffed with counterfeit money. Pleading that he is in a hurry, the dropper offers to sell the wallet to the victim, saying something like: "There's a couple of hundred bucks in there. The guy who lost it will probably give half the dough as a reward just to get the rest of it and his IDs back. Tell you what, give me fifty and you can take care of returning the wallet to him and get the rest of the reward." Naturally, like most cons, this racket appeals to a victim's larcenous streak since he has the option of simply keeping the wallet. One of the most famous practitioners of this swindle was Nathan Kaplan, better known as Kid Dropper, who, after earning his nickname practicing the swindle in his youth, went on to become the most famous gangster in New York City during the early 1920s.

While the drop swindle is well worn, it remains viable. Almost any big city police force will handle a few dozen complaints of the scam annually, and of course, the unreported cases are undoubtedly far more numerous.

See also: KID DROPPER.

Drucci, Vincent "Schemer" (1895–1927) bootlegger and murderer

One of the chief lieutenants in Dion O'Banion's North Side Gang during the 1920s, Drucci took charge of the Chicago outfit after O'Banion and his successor, Hymie Weiss, were assassinated by the Capone forces.

In one sense, Drucci was Capone's toughest rival in that opposing gang, because he was, as Capone put it, "a bedbug." The Schemer had earned his nickname because of his imaginative but totally off-the-wall ideas for robbing banks and kidnapping millionaires. He was also a tough kill. In a street duel with ambushing Capone gunners, he traded shot for shot with them while giggling and dancing a jig to avoid the bullets that sprayed the pavement around him. When a police car appeared on the scene, the Capone gunmen sped off in their car, but the Schemer had not had enough. Despite a slight leg wound, he hopped on the running board of a passing car, poked his gun at the motorist's head and yelled, "Follow that goddamn car." Police had to drag him off the car. When questioned, Drucci claimed it was not an underworld battle but a stickup. "They wanted my roll," he said, flashing a wad of $13,500.

With Drucci at the head of the O'Banion gang, Capone had to beef up protection for himself, since the Schemer was capable of any wild plot to get at him. According to one unconfirmed story, Drucci actually cornered Capone alone in a Turkish bath and almost strangled him to death before the gang leader's bodyguards showed up. The Schemer escaped stark naked, hopped in his car and drove off.

Frustrated in his efforts to get Big Al, Drucci decided to hurt him as best he could. A few weeks later, he had Theodore "the Greek" Anton, the owner of a popular restaurant over a Capone headquarters, the Hawthorne Smoke Shop, kidnapped. Anton was an honest man who idolized Capone for what he considered the gangster's tenderheartedness, such as his practice of buying all a newsboy's papers for $20 and sending him home. Capone was eating in the restaurant when Anton was snatched by lurking O'Banionites. He understood what it meant and sat in a booth the rest of the evening crying inconsolably.

Anton's body was found in quicklime. He had been tortured and then shot.

Capone vowed to kill Drucci, but the next several murder attempts were made by the Schemer. As a matter of fact, the Capone gang never did get Drucci. He was arrested on April 5, 1927 for perpetrating some election day violence against reformers seeking to supplant the William Hale Thompson machine. Put in a squad car, Drucci got enraged because a detective, Dan Healy, had dared lay a hand on him. He screamed, "I'll get you for this!" and tried to wrestle the detective's gun away. The officer pulled his hand free and pumped four quick shots into Drucci's body.

The O'Banionites wanted Healy charged with murder. "Murder?" asked Chief of Detectives William Schoemaker. "We're having a medal struck for Healy."

The North Siders gave Drucci a marvelous funeral. He lay in state a day and a night in a $10,000 casket of aluminum and silver at the undertaking establishment of Assistant State's Attorney John A. Sbarbaro. The walls of the room were hidden by masses of flowers; the dominant floral design was a throne of white and purple blooms with the inscription "Our Pal." After Drucci was buried, his blond wife declared proudly, "A cop bumped him off like a dog, but we gave him a king's funeral."

See also: SAMUEL J. "NAILS" MORTON; CHARLES DION "DEANIE" O'BANION; STANDARD OIL BUILDING, BATTLES OF THE; HYMIE WEISS.

drug racket

The drug racket is among the most lucrative of all criminal activities. It has long attracted much of the Mafia's attention and is the prime activity of both the new black and Latin American criminal combines. The potential profits involved are truly staggering. It is said to be one of the most tempting sources of potential police corruption. In the early years of his reign over the FBI, J. Edgar Hoover fought desperately and successfully to keep narcotics control out of the hands of his agency. He was known to have felt that corruption and bribery were virtually inevitable in the policing of this field.

It would be pure guesswork to attempt to put a total dollar value on the drug racket. According to the Drug Enforcement Administration, the average heroin junkie needs some 50 milligrams of the drug each day to satisfy his habit. A rule of thumb sets the average cost of such a habit at $65 a day or $24,000 a year. Since there are between 100,000 to 150,000 hard-core heroin users in the country, this aspect alone makes narcotics at least a $2.5 billion dollar business.

Of course, heroin is just a small part of the drug trade. The Senate Internal Securities Subcommittee has placed the number of regular pot users at more than 10 million. Another 25 million have smoked marijuana at some time or other, indicating that public hostility toward marijuana today is probably not much more severe than that toward whiskey during Prohibition. This public acceptance has done wonders for the marijuana seller. He can charge excessive prices because he is dealing in an illegal product, yet the high public acceptance of the drug lessens the amount he must pay for protection and the risk he has to take.

The drug racket's profit margins up the distribution ladder work much like European value-added taxes but in vastly greater percentages. The importer goes out of the country and obtains 5 kilograms of "pure heroin," which really means about 80 percent pure, for a total price of $250,000. Adding quinine and milk sugar, he

cuts the purity to 40 percent, doubling his supply. This he will sell at $65,000 a kilo, earning a profit of $400,000, or a gain of 160 percent on his investment. The heroin is passed on to the big supplier, who further dilutes the product, so that each kilo he has bought becomes 1.6 kilos. The drug is sold in quarter-kilo bags for $15,000 each, netting the big supplier a total of $300,000. From the supplier the heroin goes to the pushers, who then dilute the product to about 5 percent pure and retail the stuff in $5 and $10 units. The profit for the pushers is about $300,000. Thus, besides recouping the original investment, the 5 kilograms of heroin has produced a million dollars in illegal profits throughout the distribution pipeline.

drugs in prisons

Perhaps the most constant cat-and-mouse game played in jails and prisons today involves the smuggling of drugs. New prisoners must be searched thoroughly to prevent illegal drugs from being slipped into penal institutions in the hair, ears or mouth. All body cavities and the groin area must be searched. Even if such searches were 100 percent effective, however, the flow of drugs into the jails still would be of flood-like proportions. Jail authorities have found prisoners trying to conceal narcotics by saturating handkerchiefs, pants pockets and shirts with them and then reironing. Relatives bringing a tie for a prisoner to wear to court may well have soaked it in a concentration of narcotics.

When female visitors are allowed to kiss prisoners, they sometimes pass packets of drugs by mouth. Prisoners have been known to swallow balloons filled with narcotics that can be retrieved after a bowel movement. Visitors have discarded cigarette butts filled with narcotics. There have been cases of narcotics being thrown over jail walls inside rubber balls or even dropped from low-flying helicopters.

Of course, prisoners have their own explanation for why some police guards are so determined to stop the flow of drugs into an institution. They say it is because these guards want to be the convicts' only—and high-priced—suppliers.

Dry Tortugas Prison

Although its correct name was Fort Jefferson, the most-dreaded federal prison of its day was generally called by the name of the Florida coral islet on which it was situated, Dry Tortugas. Built in 1846 originally as a fort, it turned out to be a fiasco—at a reported cost of $1 per brick—when it was determined that the water around it was too shallow for enemy ships ever to get within cannon range. The government then simply converted it into a prison, and Dry Tortugas became a hellhole for everyone in it—prisoners, guards, soldiers and officials. Mosquitoes swarmed over the place and were considered a terrible nuisance, but the yellow fever that abounded was never attributed to these insects. The prison was hit with periodic epidemics during which men often died faster than they could be buried.

The guards and soldiers stationed there treated the prisoners brutally, a behavior fueled in part by the terrible living conditions they themselves had to endure. It was an open secret that the government sent to Dry Tortugas those prisoners who deserved "special treatment." That certainly was the case with Dr. Samuel Mudd, the physician who set John Wilkes Booth's leg after he had assassinated Abraham Lincoln. Prison officials specifically instructed the guards to be exceptionally harsh with "that Lincoln murderer." Mudd, however, was to nurse the garrison and prisoners through a yellow fever epidemic and thereby win the gratitude of the officials. He was pardoned in 1869 after his humanitarian acts became known, and the resulting publicity about conditions in the hellhole led to its abandonment in the early 1870s. The prison became a national monument in 1934.

See also: DR. SAMUEL MUDD.

drygulch

The best location for killing a man in the West was at a place he would have to come to sooner or later, and in dry, arid country that meant a waterhole. The attacker could hide in the waterhole's protective cover and shoot the victim before he could quench his thirst. Even if he missed or only wounded the victim, the killer could hold the key ground until the man died or surrendered to get a drink, hence the origin of the term *drygulch*.

Duggan, Sandford S. C. (1845–1868) woman beater

Sandford Duggan was one of a hated breed in the West, a lawman turned outlaw and murderer. Yet his life ended swinging from a rope not because of the murders or holdups he had committed but rather for woman beating.

A Pennsylvanian who developed an itchy trigger finger after migrating west, Duggan was still in his teens when he murdered his first man in a Black Hawk, Colo. saloon. He got away before a miners court could convene and wound up in Denver, where he was soon living off the earnings of a young prostitute named Kittie Wells, who willingly supported him. Duggan banged her around regularly and one night he pistol-whipped her almost to death. Such actions toward women, respectable or otherwise, were not tolerated in the West, where families were in such short supply. Duggan

was arrested before a lynching could be arranged, but the next morning a judge freed him on a technicality. A miners lynch mob formed immediately, but Duggan again avoided capture and made it out of town.

He fled east to Laramie City, a Union Pacific end-of-track town. Apparently in such urgent need of a lawman that they had no time to check into Duggan's background, the town's authorities named him marshal. However, in due course a traveler from Denver revealed the details of the Kittie Wells affair, and Duggan was stripped of his badge.

The facts of the case have been lost, but not long afterwards, Duggan was given 24 hours to get out of town. Once again, the alleged offense was woman beating. Duggan then rode the holdup trail until he was captured at Golden by Marshal Dave Cook, who took him back to Denver. This was a double stroke of bad luck for Duggan: he was hated in Denver and Dave Cook had the misfortune, or perhaps the knack, of often losing prisoners to lynch mobs.

That's exactly what happened to Duggan. He was dragged out of jail and quickly strung up from a cottonwood tree. Someone tacked a sign on his corpse that read, "woman beater."

Duke's Restaurant mob headquarters

If any building or place during the 1940s and 1950s could have been called the underworld's Capitol, it would have been Duke's Restaurant, 73 Palisades Avenue, Cliffside Park, N.J. It became a prime topic of inquiry during the historic Kefauver Committee's probe of organized crime in the early 1950s. Duke's was the meeting place, and safe sanctuary, for the leaders of the national crime syndicate. Presiding over all affairs at Duke's was one of the top leaders of crime in New York and New Jersey, Joe Adonis.

Casual visitors to Duke's, which was across the street from the popular Palisades Amusement Park, found it to be a typical Italian restaurant. It had a long bar and booths and served tasty meals. Most did not suspect that to the rear of the public dining area there was a sliding panel with an "ice box door," typical of the nearly indestructible and soundproof barriers used by illegal gambling establishments. Behind the panel there was what could be called the control room from which the Mafia and much of organized crime planned and directed their operations.

Much of the surveillance of Duke's was done by various federal agencies, mainly the Internal Revenue Service and the Bureau of Narcotics, and by Manhattan district attorney Frank Hogan's staff. It was not an easy undertaking. These investigators found that once they had crossed the George Washington Bridge into

New Jersey, they were shadowed, hounded, badgered and even picked up by various local police departments. A car of investigators parked outside of Duke's to keep an eye on the alleged diners entering and leaving were often harassed by police telling them to move on, even after they displayed their credentials. Duke's obviously was set it unfriendly territory for New York and federal investigators.

Meanwhile, inside the restaurant's chamber the likes of Adonis and Albert Anastasia presided over criminal activities, collecting the revenues from various enterprises, arranging "hits," handling "affairs at the table," which were trials of syndicate soldiers for various alleged offenses. On Tuesday, known as the "big day," the top leaders of crime in America came in for their "cabinet" meetings. During the late 1940s and early 1950s, when the syndicate's national commission was dominated by the so-called Big Six, the top men converged on Duke's. Flying in from the Midwest were Tony Accardo and Greasy Jake Guzik, the representatives of Chicago's Capone mob. The remaining four came from the East. They were Adonis; Frank Costello; Meyer Lansky, who could be coming from anywhere since he handled the mob's gambling interests in Saratoga, N.Y., Miami and Las Vegas; and Longy Zwillman, the boss of New Jersey, who had a powerful voice in naming the state's governors and, more important, its attorneys general.

Duke's even survived the prying of the Kefauver Committee. Gangster Willie Moretti insisted he went there for the food and ambience, which was, he said with a straight face, "like Lindy's on Broadway." Tony Bender took the Fifth Amendment rather than reveal if he had ever been in Duke's, insisting even a visit to a restaurant could be incriminating.

Duke's lost its significance when Adonis was deported in 1957. It was, in the words of one newspaperman, "something like the British burning the White House."

Duncan's Saloon   Chicago pickpocket haven

From 1890 through most of the first decade of the 20th century, Duncan's Saloon on Chicago's State Street was the best-known hangout for pickpockets and professional tramps in the United States. The proprietor, Bob Duncan, had long been heralded by the Chicago press as the King of the Pickpockets, but he had retired from active duty to serve as a sort of unofficial greeter for traveling pickpocketing mobs. No less than 20 professional mobs headquartered at Duncan's place, not only for sociability but also because Duncan had developed considerable clout as a fixer with the police. Duncan supposedly could arrange matters so that an individual mob enjoyed free hunting in specified locales. Furthermore he could even fix it so that a police officer would be on hand to confuse victims.

Professional hoboes also used Duncan's place as a rendezvous and mail drop and always saved whatever money they had for a spree in the establishment. One of the most illustrious knights of the road to headquarter at the saloon was Wyoming Slivers. Slivers retired from the road life in 1896, when he married a rich widow in Minnesota. Mrs. Slivers died a couple of years later, leaving him a nest egg of $10,000. Slivers immediately repaired to Duncan's Saloon and, with about 20 of his cronies, staged a six-month spree with the money. Ten of the hoboes died of delirium tremens, and Slivers came through the orgy minus an ear and three fingers lost in fistfights.

Duncan's Saloon closed following one of Chicago's periodic graft investigations, and it was believed that Duncan then returned to his light-fingered trade.

Durrant, William Henry Theodore (1872–1898)
murderer

William "Theo" Durrant, who became famous in this country and Europe as the Demon in the Belfry for the murder of two young women in San Francisco in 1895, was as close to a real-life Jekyll and Hyde as America ever produced.

At 23 Theo was an excellent student in his senior class of Cooper Medical College and a dedicated member of the Emanuel Baptist Church, functioning as assistant Sunday school superintendent, Sunday usher, church librarian and secretary of the young people's Christian Endeavor Society. Whenever there were repairs to be made on the church, Theo could be counted on to offer his services. Several times a week, in his less sane moments, Theo patronized the notorious brothels on Commercial Street, regarded as far more degenerate than those elsewhere in the city. Theo's custom was to bring with him a sack or small crate containing a chicken or pigeon; during the high point of the evening's debauch, he would slit the bird's throat and let the blood trickle over himself. The only hint of Theo's other life was some gossip that he had attempted to kiss girls at church socials.

On April 3, 1895 Theo was seen entering the church with 18-year-old Blanche Lamont, a high school student who often spoke of becoming a teacher. Inside the church Theo excused himself, saying he had a chore to perform. He returned a moment later, stripped naked. When the girl resisted him, Durrant killed her in a frenzy, strangling her and mutilating her body. He then dragged the body up to the belfry and hid it. Two hours later, he calmly appeared at a Christian Endeavor meeting.

Theo was questioned when Blanche was reported missing, but he earnestly informed the police that it was his theory that white slavers might have kidnapped her and installed her in a brothel somewhere in San Francisco or perhaps shipped her to some faraway locality. Nothing much would have developed from the investigation had not Theo struck again that same month, killing 20-year-old Minnie Williams in the church after some naked trysts. Minnie, unlike Blanche, had responded to Theo's bizarre wooing, but he murdered her just as well. He slashed the body with a knife and left it hidden behind a door in the blood-spattered church library, where it was found the next day. The theory was that Theo might have told her about Blanche's murder, and Minnie responded by saying she was going to the police.

Again, Theo had been seen with a young woman who later disappeared or was murdered, but he denied any knowledge of the crime. However, police found Minnie's purse hidden in a suit pocket in his closet, and they finally trekked up to the belfry and found Blanche Lamont's body as well.

Theo's trial was a spectacle, perhaps the first to receive sensational "sob-sister" coverage. William Randolph Hearst's *Examiner* printed a front-page sketch of Theo's hands so that its readers could recognize the "hands of murder." A "sweet pea girl" appeared at each session of the court and offered Theo a bouquet of flowers. This was either a defense tactic or a newspaper trick to generate reader interest. In all, 125 witnesses testified, including Theo himself, who thought he had convinced the jury with his denials of guilt. He was nonetheless found guilty on the first ballot. Appeals delayed the execution for almost three years until January 7, 1898, when Durrant was hanged.

On the scaffold, Theo told the hangman, "Don't put that rope on, my boy, until I talk." The sheriff merely waved to the hangman to continue his work, and Theo was hanged without further ado. The newspapers were somewhat peeved at being deprived of some final words from the fiendish killer, but they were able to report one final macabre incident.

Theo's mother and father had apparently reveled in their notoriety during the trial. After the hanging they called for their son's body. While waiting in a prison anteroom, the couple was offered some food by the warden. When the body arrived, with Theo's face contorted in a hideous grimace, they sat eating not 5 feet from the open coffin. Hearst's newspaper reported that at one point Mother Durrant said, "Papa, I'd like some more of that roast."

Dutch Henry (?–c. 1930) western horse thief

In the Old West, where stealing a man's horse was considered the equivalent of cutting off a man's legs, it was

The Demon in the Belfry is depicted carrying a beautiful victim to his hiding place in the bell tower.

remarkable that a man like Dutch Henry could live to a ripe old age as the King of Horse Thieves, with an estimated 300 men working for him in his prime.

Dutch Henry, whose real name was Henry Borne, was of German extraction. He first turns up as a member of the 7th Cavalry, which he quit in the late 1860s. Apparently, he had greater expectations in another line of work because he was soon arrested at Fort Smith, Ark. for stealing 20 government mules. Sentenced to a long term at hard labor in 1868, Dutch Henry broke prison three months later and went into the horse-stealing business in earnest. He soon was hiring men to steal whole herds at a time for him. No deal being too small for Dutch Henry, a thief with but a single pilfered animal would find him a ready, if tight-fisted, customer. Legends about Dutch Henry abound; one of the best-known tales concerns Henry selling a sheriff one of his own stolen horses.

Dutch Henry had his run-ins with the law but seemed to lead a charmed life. In 1874 he was wounded in a gunfight after being found in possession of a large number of stolen horses—but he was not prosecuted. Bat Masterson arrested Dutch Henry in 1878 and brought him to Dodge City for trial only to see the horse thief beat the charge. The way Dutch Henry always told it, he was a victim just as much as the original owner of the property. Nobody really believed that, and a "Dutch Henry" became another name for a stolen horse. Eventually, the champion horse stealer's luck ran out, and authorities in Arkansas tied Dutch Henry to the long-escaped Henry Borne. Henry was sent back to prison, and other jurisdictions later seized him to serve terms in their area. As a result, Dutch Henry was out of circulation for well over 20 years. By that time the horse-stealing trade was in its decline, better law enforcement and something called the horseless carriage sealing its fate. Dutch Henry just faded away, although a number of old-timers insisted they saw him alive in Arkansas and elsewhere as late as 1930 and heard that he died shortly after that. Be that as it may, Dutch Henry's name lived on as a part of American culture, preserved in Hollywood movies as the favorite name used by uninventive screen writers for a villain and, almost always, for a horse thief.

See also: HORSE STEALING.

Dutch Mob 19th-century pickpocket gang

One of the largest gangs of pickpockets and muggers ever to operate in an American city, the Dutch Mob, under the cunning leadership of Little Freddie, Sheeney Mike and Johnny Irving, controlled the area just east of New York's Bowery from Houston Street to Fifth Street for about a decade beginning in 1867.

At its peak the gang consisted of 300 members, all professional pickpockets, who used varied methods to rob victims. A common practice would be to stage a street fight that attracted viewers who were then stripped of their wallets as they watched the action. In other instances a few of the gang would pick a fight with a victim and threaten to beat him up, but before they could, the cowed victim would be "rescued" by other members of the mob who would deftly pick his pockets while rushing him to safety. In time, the newspapers referred to the entire area from Houston to Fifth as "pickpocket paradise." Under a newly appointed precinct captain, Anthony J. Allaire, the police finally acted to clean up the district in 1877. Allaire's technique was simple enough; he sent in flying squads of police with orders to club anyone in the area resembling a pickpocket or mugger. The strategy worked and the Dutch Mob soon dwindled to a few. Irving moved into a new line of work, becoming a bank robber.

See also: PICKPOCKETING.

Dyer, Mary (?–1660) executed Quaker martyr

A Quaker who became a religious martyr, Mary Dyer may have been the only person ever executed in America simply to test a law. Dyer came to America about 1635 with her husband, William Dyer, and settled in Boston. In 1650 she went back to England on a visit and there was converted to Quakerism. When she returned to New England to spread the Quaker word, she was imprisoned in Boston and later banished. In 1657 Dyer was banished from the New Haven settlement. At this time the Massachusetts Bay Colony passed a law that made a visit following banishment punishable by death. Nevertheless, Mary Dyer returned to visit and minister to other jailed Quakers. She was arrested and condemned to death but was saved through the efforts of her son. In May 1660 Mary Dyer returned to Massachusetts once again, determined to see if the death penalty would ever be enforced and confident that it would not be. She was again seized and, on June 1, 1660, hanged on the Boston Common.

Dyer Act auto theft law

Following World War I Congress became upset about the shocking growth of a new crime, automobile theft. The previous year 29,399 cars had been stolen in 21 cities, and 5,541 of them were never recovered. The theft problem already had proved too great for local authorities to handle, since they legally could not pursue a stolen vehicle across a state line. So, in an effort to curb car thefts, legislation was introduced making it a federal offense to transport a stolen automobile across a state line.

Although it produced a long debate over states rights, the National Motor Vehicle Theft Act, or Dyer Act, was passed in 1919. It hardly solved the problem, however, as the number of thefts mushroomed with the growth of automobile use. Between 1935 and 1955 an estimated 4 million vehicles were stolen; by 1994 the rate was up to 1.5 million per year. And auto theft has continued to present a major problem for law enforcement officials.

The real impact of the Dyer Act was in its effect on the criminal justice system in general, bringing the FBI into areas of law enforcement never originally intended as part of its bailiwick. The public enemies of the early 1930s often needed to steal a car to pull off a bank robbery or some other crime and then escape across state borders. This provided the legal authority for the FBI to enter the chase.

See also: AUTO THEFT.

Earle, Willie (1922–1947) lynch victim

One of the most shocking cases of a Southern jury refusing to convict whites for the lynching of a black man occurred following the 1947 killing of 25-year-old Willie Earle in South Carolina.

Earle was picked up for questioning following the fatal stabbing of a cab driver near Liberty, S.C. He was taken to the Pickens County Jail, where he was interrogated and protested his innocence. Earle was not charged with the slaying, but word spread of his arrest, and outraged cabbies gathered in Greenville to discuss the murder of a fellow driver. Soon, a large mob, armed with shotguns and knives, formed a convoy and headed for the jail. They broke into the jail and forced the jailer to open Earle's cell. Earle was dragged screaming to an automobile and taken in convoy to Saluda Dam, where he was "questioned" and "confessed." The prisoner was then driven to Bramlett Road in Greenville County and viciously put to death there. Earle was stabbed several times and one lyncher shattered the butt of his shotgun on the victim's skull. Others in the mob knife-gouged huge chunks of flesh from Earle's body. Only then was the pathetic prisoner finished off with several shotgun blasts. Satisfied, the lynchers drove home.

The killing shocked the nation and indeed most people in South Carolina. The FBI was called and cleared the jailer of violating Earle's civil rights, finding that he had not willingly released the prisoner. However, the agency cooperated with local authorities in identifying 28 persons among the lynch mob. Twenty-six of these confessed their part in the lynching. Gov. Strom Thurmond named a special prosecutor and pledged that justice would be done, a feeling, observers agreed, that was shared by most residents of the state.

Nevertheless, the result of the trial reflected the longstanding behavior of juries in cases where whites were accused of lynching blacks. The defense offered no testimony whatsoever, and despite the confessions, all the defendants were found "not guilty."

Earp, James C. (1841–1926) brother of Wyatt

The eldest of the Earp brothers, James Earp came home from the Civil War in 1863 so severely wounded that he could not become a lawman like his other brothers. However, he was always linked to his brothers' shadier activities, generally looking after their gambling and saloon interests, while his wife ran an Earp-protected brothel. James died in San Francisco in 1926.

Earp, Morgan (1851–1882) lawman

The brother of Wyatt Earp and participant in the famous, or infamous, gunfight at the O.K. Corral, Morgan Earp was an erstwhile lawman in his own right.

Born in Iowa, he started his career as a deputy town marshal in Dodge City, Kan. in 1876. He later worked in Dodge as a deputy sheriff and developed a reputation as an efficient gunman. Morgan Earp then moved on to Butte, Mont., where he became even more famous as a "town tamer." He apparently dispatched more than a few gunfighters, although the so-called classic gun duel he reputedly had with Billy Brooks in 1880 was no doubt fictional since Brooks had been hanged some six years earlier. If Earp killed a man named Billy Brooks, it was some nonentity. Later that year Morgan joined his brothers Virgil and Wyatt in Tombstone and became a shotgun rider on Wells Fargo coaches. In October 1881 the Earp and Clanton forces had their famous shoot-out at the O.K. Corral, and Morgan was wounded in the battle. He was still recuperating on the night of March 17, 1882 when he went to Bob Hatch's billiard saloon on Allen Street. Morgan was lining up a shot when a hail of .45 slugs smashed through the glass-windowed door and into his back, shattering his spine. He died about 30 minutes later on the sofa in Bob Hatch's office.

Within a short time of Morgan Earp's murder, Wyatt Earp gained vengeance by killing at least three men apparently involved in the crime, Deputy Sheriff Frank Stilwell, Wild Bill Brocius (although others besides Wyatt Earp are suspected of the Brocius killing) and Florentino Cruz, who had been paid $25 for holding the horses.

See also: WILLIAM L. BROOKS, VIRGIL EARP, WYATT EARP, O.K. CORRAL.

Earp, Virgil W. (1843–1906) lawman

After serving with the Union during the Civil War, Virgil Earp divided his time between being a prospector and lawman. In 1877, after serving as deputy town marshal of Dodge City, Kan., Virgil moved to Prescott, Arizona Territory to try the mining business. Because of his enthusiasm about the chances of becoming rich there, his brothers James and lawmen Wyatt and Morgan followed him. The brothers all settled in Tombstone, and in 1881 Virgil became temporary marshal when the former holder of the position died of "lead poisoning." During this period the growing conflict between the gambler forces in Tombstone, represented by the Earps, and the cowboy forces, represented by the Clanton family, climaxed in the gunfight at the O.K. Corral; the war continued long afterward.

Like his brother Morgan, Virgil was wounded at the O.K. Corral, and a few months later, he was the object of an ambush shooting. Hit by five shotgun blasts, Virgil was temporarily paralyzed and lost the use of his left arm permanently. When brother Morgan was murdered in February 1882, Wyatt put Virgil and his family on a train out of the state, and Wyatt and young brother Warren concentrated on avenging the two crimes. Wyatt Earp succeeded but was also forced to flee Arizona. The Earps didn't return to the territory until around the turn of the century, and shortly after Warren Earp came back, he was murdered. It is said Virgil Earp exacted vengeance for that killing in due course. Virgil had by that time returned to Prescott,

Ariz., where he was even asked to run for sheriff. He declined, and there was some speculation that he couldn't win with the Earp name. Virgil Earp died of pneumonia early in 1906.

See also: MORGAN EARP, WYATT EARP, O.K. CORRAL.

Earp, Warren B. (1855–1900) lawman

The baby brother of the Earp family, Warren never achieved the fame or notoriety of Wyatt, Virgil or Morgan, arriving in Tombstone, Ariz. just after the gunfight at the O.K. Corral in 1881. He did serve, however, as deputy federal marshal for a while and aided Wyatt in the hunt for Morgan Earp's assassins. After the Earps left, or were run out of, Arizona in 1882, Warren went with them to California. In 1900 he returned to Arizona to become a cattle detective. It was not a wise move. A few months later, he was killed in Wilcox in a saloon gunfight with a man named Johnny Boyett. The shooting seemed linked with the troubles at Tombstone's O.K. Corral and the revenge slayings that followed the Morgan Earp murder.

Virgil Earp let it be known that he intended to kill the man responsible, and he didn't mean Boyett. Chroniclers of the Earp family agree Virgil did just that in 1905, although the victim's identity was never officially revealed. The Earps had become a little more circumspect in taking their vengeance.

Earp, Wyatt Berry Stapp (1848–1929) gunfighter, pimp, lawman

Few Western characters are credited with more heroic deeds than Wyatt Earp. His legendary stature, however, is almost entirely a product of the 20th century. Those who knew him best treated him differently. They drove him out of California for horse stealing; they fired him from his job as a policeman in Wichita for pocketing fines; they chased him out of Arizona after the gunfight, or slaughter, at the O.K. Corral and the ensuing murders. About the only place he wasn't kicked out of was Dodge City; he left voluntarily for not exactly heroic reasons.

Earp belonged to a clan of brothers: James, Virgil, Morgan and Warren. Natives of Illinois, the Earps moved to California in 1864 by wagon train. Wyatt's jobs there included stagecoach driver, bartender and gambler. In 1871 he was indicted for horse stealing, paid $500 bail and took off for greener pastures doing stints as a buffalo hunter. In Wichita, Kan. he became a lawman and, according to some biographers, performed many a valiant deed. But he apparently made no important arrests and eventually came under a cloud of suspicion when fines he collected never seemed to end up in the town treasury. He was dismissed from his post in 1874 and drifted into Dodge City, Kan., where he served as a deputy marshal from 1876 to 1879. Again, the legend tells how he cleaned up Dodge and gunned down many a varmint in the process. In reality, however, he had only one kill during all his years in Dodge, and that was of a drunken cowboy named George Hoy or Hoyt, who may or may not have been trying to gun down Earp for a bounty put on him by a Texas cattleman. The Dodge City cleanup by Earp and his friend Bat Masterson was strictly a part-time thing. Both supplemented their income working as cardsharps and procurers and became known as the Fighting Pimps. Earp had a piece of the action in most of the whorehouses south of the "deadline," the railroad tracks that bisected Dodge. He probably was at least half owner of the brothel-saloon that belonged to his brother James. James' wife ran the brothel, while James took care of the gambling and saloon end of the business. The couple always trailed after Earp and set up shop wherever he was a lawman.

In 1879 Dodge City kind of settled down—meaning that the Earps' brothel profits weren't what they used to be—and Wyatt decided to try something more lucrative. He headed for the rich silver-strike area of the Arizona Territory. On the way, Earp stopped off in Mobeetie, Tex., where, with the aid of Mysterious Dave Mather, he perpetrated a gold brick swindle on gullible cowboys and was run out of town by Deputy Sheriff James McIntire. Moving on to Tombstone, Wyatt set himself up as a saloon keeper. Brother James became a bartender, and several of the Earp women opened brothels. When Virgil was named temporary town marshal upon the death of the marshal, Wyatt became his deputy. When he later lost out on appointment to the sheriff's office of the newly created Cochise County, Wyatt consoled himself by becoming a part owner in the fabulously successful Oriental Saloon, amazingly without any monetary investment, a clear indication of his shakedown ability and the value attached to the protection he could offer such an establishment.

By early 1881 the Earps—four of the brothers now on hand in various capacities—became involved in a feud with the out-county cowboy element led by the Clanton family. The Earps drew to their banner a character as unsavory as any of the Clanton family killers, the murderous Doc Holliday. There are experts who insist the trouble between the two groups resulted from the Earps' rigid enforcement of the law, mainly to protect their casino and vice interests, and infringement on the Clanton ring's rustling and stage-robbing activities.

Really serious trouble broke out in March 1881, when the Kinnear and Co. stage was attacked and two men killed. Wyatt Earp went after the killers and named a trio of gunmen as suspects. In June, however, Doc Holliday was arrested as one of the suspects in the robbery and murders. The charges were dropped as unproven, but the incident sapped the Earps' popularity. More and more citizens believed the Earps were involved in various criminal activities, including stage robberies.

It was this climate of antagonism that actually led to the great gunfight at the O.K. Corral on October 26, 1881, in which three of the Clanton gang—the two McLowery brothers and Billy Clanton—were killed. The battle later brought fame to Wyatt Earp, then a deputy U.S. marshal, but the local Earp-supporting *Tombstone Epitaph* gave it only page-three coverage at the time, possibly because the Earps could have been brought up on murder charges for the killings. There were and still are considerable doubts about whether two of their opponents were even armed, but there is no doubt the Earps provoked the shoot-out.

The gunfight did not end the Earp-Clanton feud but merely intensified it. In its aftermath, Clanton supporters separately ambushed Virgil and Morgan Earp, fatally wounding Morgan. In revenge, Wyatt Earp shot and killed Frank Stilwell, who was known to have been involved in Morgan's death. He then led a posse that shot to death Florentino Cruz, another man involved in the ambush. It is unclear whether Wyatt also killed Curly Bill Brocius, the reigning head of the Clanton gang. With a warrant for murder hanging over his head, Wyatt was forced to flee Arizona, and the rest of the Earps followed.

In 1883 Earp turned up in Dodge City as part of the celebrated but short-lived Dodge City Peace Commission, really a terrorist action to force the return of gambling and prostitution interests to the town. It is interesting to note that the local newspaper did not remember Earp as the man who had "cleaned up" Dodge but as a man "famous in the cheerful business of depopulating the country."

In 1884 Wyatt was living in Idaho Territory, where he and his brother James operated a couple of saloons, and became involved in a combine that specialized in claim jumping. Shortly thereafter, Wyatt saw the merits of moving on to California, where he spent the rest of his days except for four years when he was a saloon keeper in Alaska during the gold rush. In the 1920s Earp hung around the movie lots of Hollywood, befriending Tom Mix and William S. Hart in an effort to get them to do his life story. Studio producers and directors exploited him for information about the Wild West days without ever paying him. In 1927 Earp finally began setting down the facts for an enthusiastic young writer, Stuart Lake, who produced a highly fanciful biography that established the ill-deserved legend of Wyatt Earp. Earp died on January 13, 1929, before the book appeared.

See also: JOHN BEHAN; JOSEPH ISAAC "IKE" CLANTON; WILLIAM CLANTON; DODGE CITY, KANSAS; DODGE CITY PEACE COMMISSION; MORGAN EARP; VIRGIL W. EARP; GOLD BRICK SWINDLE; JOHN HENRY "DOC" HOLLIDAY; WILLIAM B. "BAT" MASTERSON; MIKE MEAGER; ORIENTAL SALOON AND GAMBLING HOUSE; JOHNNY RINGO.

East Texas Regulator War (1841–1844) vigilante conflict

The establishment of a Regulator vigilante movement in 1840 in Shelby County eventually resulted in turning much of eastern Texas into a battlefield. The need for vigilantes was as acute in Shelby County as anywhere in the West. The area was overrun with thieves, counterfeiters, murderers and corrupt county officials, who made law and order virtually impossible to maintain. Unfortunately, the leadership of the Regulators fell to Charles Jackson, a steamboat operator suspected of rather shady dealings, and it appears he created the Regulators as much for gaining personal control of the country as for ridding it of outlaws. When Jackson was cut down by an assassin, the leadership passed to Watt Moorman, a man with even less scruples than Jackson. Soon, the Regulators descended to the level of the outlaws they had been founded to drive out. In 1841 a countermovement of moderators appeared on the scene to curb the excesses of the Regulators, but both sides attracted criminal elements to their banners. While Regulators and Moderators theoretically battled outlaws and other villains, they began to spend more time warring with each other. In a short while, the entire county became involved; every man had to align with one side or the other and often found himself fighting with his neighbor or even his own relatives. To their credit, the Moderators cleaned their ranks of outlaw forces over the next three years, and by 1844 they were poised for a wholesale shooting war with the Regulators. President Sam Houston of the Republic of Texas prevented a certain bloodbath by sending in the militia, and the outbreak of the Mexican War further defused matters. In all, 18 deaths were officially attributed to the vigilante war; the number of severely wounded or permanently crippled was put in the hundreds. Thereafter, many blood feuds among Regulator and Moderator partisans continued for several decades and the hatreds kept alive lasted into this century.

See also: REGULATORS AND MODERATORS.

Eastman, Monk (1873–1920) great gang leader

There are those authorities on crime who consider Monk Eastman the greatest gangster this country ever produced. Historian Herbert Asbury called him "the prince of gangsters" and "as brave a thug as ever shot an enemy in the back."

Eastman was the boss of the last great primarily Jewish street gang in New York City, able to field 1,200 to 1,500 vicious gangsters on short notice. The Eastmans wiped out the remnants of the brutal Whyos, a truly murderous collection of thugs, near the end of the last century and were always ready to do battle with Paul Kelly's notorious gangsters, the great Italian Five Points Gang. After the turn of the century, the Five Pointers boasted on their roster such future devotees of mayhem and violence as Johnny Torrio, Al Capone, Lucky Luciano and Frankie Yale. Yet, in comparison to Eastman's crew they were choir boys.

In appearance, Eastman looked precisely the way a gangster should—squat, massive, bullet-headed, with a busted nose and a pair of cauliflower ears. And his behavior was worse than his appearance. He deserted his home area in the Williamsburg section of Brooklyn, where his respectable Jewish restaurateur father had set up a pet store for him, and headed for the crime-ridden fleshpots of lower Manhattan. He was to become a legend.

In the early 1890s Eastman became a bouncer at a rough dance hall, New Irving Hall, where a girl might well get raped by a number of the boys if not by her date. Eastman patrolled his domain with a huge bludgeon, a blackjack in his hip pocket and brass knuckles on each hand. He was always proud of the fact that during the six months of his reign no less than 50 men required the attention of surgeons and that jocular ambulance drivers referred to the accident ward of Bellevue Hospital as the Eastman Pavilion. Eastman kept close count of the victims he clubbed and notched each assault on his club. One night an inoffensive little man was sitting at the bar drinking beer when Eastman walked up to him and cracked his scalp open with a mighty swipe. When asked why he'd done so, he replied, "Well, I had 49 nicks in me stick, an' I wanted to make it an even 50."

If that seemed a bit antisocial, at least Monk could pride himself on his near-Victorian treatment of women. He never once struck a woman with his club, no matter how trying she became. At most, he simply blackened her eyes with his hammy fist. "I only gave her a little poke," he would exclaim. "Just enough to put a shanty on her glimmer. But I always takes off me knucks first."

With behavior such as that, Monk Eastman became a legend on the East Side, and other young bloods took to imitating him in speech and manner. Of course, from such personal magnetism great leaders are born, and Eastman soon gathered around him a band of hoodlums eager to do his bidding. It didn't take long before he told them to go forth, beat up some citizens and bring back some money.

From then on, Eastman's gang grew rapidly. He and his men took over much of the crime on the Lower East Side, engaging in robberies, burglaries, assault, muggings and murder for pay. Eastman seized control of many of the gambling dens and houses of prostitution, and even individual streetwalkers and hoodlums had to pay him for the privilege of operating in his turf. Although a crude savage, Eastman was smart enough to ingratiate himself with Tammany Hall and, in exchange for protection and a regular stipend, handled any chore required. On election day he furnished the largest contingent of voters, his own men, who voted early and often, and then blackjacked any honest citizen who was considering voting against Eastman's patrons. Whenever Eastman or his men got in trouble, Tammany Hall lawyers appeared in court for them. Bail was posted and promptly forfeited until the case was expunged from the records.

As rich and powerful as he became, Eastman could never resist doing violence himself, sometimes even personally carrying out a blackjacking commission. "I like to beat up a guy once in a while," he used to say. "It keeps me hand in."

In one confrontation with the hated Five Pointers, Eastman was shot twice in the stomach and left for dead, but he climbed to his feet and staggered to Gouverneur Hospital, plugging a gaping wound with his fingers. Eastman hovered near death but, in keeping with underworld tradition, would not name his assailant. When he got out, Eastman personally shot the Five Pointer and dumped his body in the gutter.

In time, the Eastmans appeared to be winning the war with the Five Pointers and also routing the forces of another major gang leader, Humpty Jackson, but in 1904 Eastman caused his own downfall by holding up a expensively dressed young man who had overimbibed. It was a robbery Eastman did not have to commit but could not resist. Unfortunately for the gangster, the victim was a scion of wealth whose family had hired a Pinkerton to follow him for his protection. Seeing Eastman accost the young man, the detective opened fire on him, and the gangster fled right into the arms of a policeman, who knocked him out before recognizing him.

If Eastman expected aid from Tammany, he was sadly disappointed. In view of the rising spirit of reform, the political bosses were happy for the chance to be rid of him. The great gangster was shipped off in ignominy to do 10 years in Sing Sing. When he was released, he found his power was gone. The Eastmans had factionalized a dozen ways, as the times would no longer support great street gangs. Eastman could not

One of the most famous turn-of-the-century gang leaders, Monk Eastman once clubbed a hapless bar patron because "I had 49 nicks in me stick, an' I wanted to make it an even 50."

understand what had happened. But World War I proved to be a godsend for him, and he went off to fight. When he returned, he was awarded a pardon by Gov. Al Smith, who signed an executive order restoring him to full citizenship.

In December 1920 Eastman was shot dead by a corrupt Prohibition agent with whom he was running a penny-ante bootlegging and dope-selling operation.

See also: CRAZY BUTCH GANG.

Edwards Heirs Association swindle

As much as any of the incredible "heirs swindle," the one involving the so-called Edwards estate was among the most durable. Its operation was handed down from father to son and lasted for decades.

The swindle was the brainchild of Dr. Herbert H. Edwards of Cleveland, Ohio, who in the 1880s maintained with much fervor that he was a descendant of Robert Edwards, a colonial merchant who had willed to his heirs 65 acres of Manhattan Island, right in the middle of which eventually had been erected the Woolworth Building. It was obvious that this bit of real estate had become one of the most valuable in the world. The Edwards estate was apparently worth not millions, but billions.

Dr. Edwards formed the Edwards Heirs Association, which was passed down from father to son, taking in $26 annually from each of thousands of people named Edwards as dues to fight for their legal rights. Naturally, every member of the association believed he would receive at least a thousand times what he had put in when a settlement was reached, an event that was always just about to be achieved. The association was also noted for having a great fete each year, which members attended by the hundreds, to celebrate the profits soon to come. The suckers even had their own anthem, which they sang with leather-lunged joy:

We have rallied here in blissful state
Our jubilee to celebrate.
When fortune kindly on us smiled,
The Edwards Heirs now reconciled.
Our president deserves our praise,
For strenuous work through dreary days,
In consummating our affairs
and rounding up the Edwards heirs.

We're Robert Edward's legal heirs,
And cheerfully we take our shares.
Then let us shout with joy and glee
And celebrate the jubilee.

Finally, after several decades of successful operation, the great swindle was smashed by the post office. The members of the association never saw any of the promised rewards, but they could at least recall their annual hangovers, perhaps still with some measure of fondness.

Egan's Rats   St. Louis gang

First organized in St. Louis about 1900 by Jellyroll Egan, the Rats became the most feared gang in the city. Egan specialized in renting out his men as "legbreakers" to anti-union businessmen. When such activities became less profitable about 1920, Dinty Colbeck, who had taken over the reins from the late founder, turned Egan's Rats in new criminal directions. Operating out of a poolhall called Buckley's, Colbeck controlled bootlegging operations in the St. Louis–Kansas City area and masterminded a number of spectacular safecracking and jewelry thefts, many with the aid of the best safecracker of the 1920s, Red Rudensky.

Dinty Colbeck cut a flamboyant figure in St. Louis and paid enormous bribes to crooked politicians and policemen to allow his enterprises to operate without harassment. Approaching an officer on the street, he was known to pull out a big wad of bills and say, "Want a bribe, officer?"

Like many of the other independent gangs that had been given a new life by Prohibition, Egan's Rats could not cope with the changing crime scene of the post-bootlegging 1930s. Colbeck was killed by rival gangsters and the surviving Rats had to find new homes in other criminal combinations.

Einstein, Isadore   See IZZY AND MOE.

electric shock as crime punishment   controversial proposal

In the constant search for new, or the reworking of older, methods for punishing crime, there has been a renewed effort to restore corporal punishment in place of jail time and the like. Some scholars insist that corporal punishment is more humane and less expensive than incarceration.

One of the more controversial suggestions has been made by a leading authority on punishment, Graeme Newman, who offers electric shock as a general punishment. Electric shock, says Newman, inflicts punishment only where it belongs—on the offender rather than on his family, who also suffers when he is sent to prison. Among the benefits, according to Newman, is that the public is spared the expense of incarceration and of families becoming dependent on welfare. Under the electric shock proposal, all offenders would receive the same penalty for the same crime and no added penalty would be applied because of previous crimes. According to Newman, this would make the punishment fit the crime, not the criminal. And such corporal punishment would work on the offender's body, not on his mind. Newman's ideas, expounded in a 1983 book, have not gone very far.

Further reading: *Just and Painful: A Case for the Corporal Punishment of Criminals* by Graeme Newman.

Electrolytic Marine Salts Company   See GOLD ACCUMULATOR SWINDLE.

Elwell, Joseph Bowne   (1875–1920)   murder victim

Joseph Bowne Elwell was *the* bridge expert of the day and a notorious ladies' man. He was the author of *Elwell on Bridge* and *Elwell's Advanced Bridge,* or so it seemed. In fact, the books were written by his wife, later ex-wife, Helen Darby, whose high social position gave Elwell entrée into the world of society. This was vital for Elwell because the bridge books did not really bring in the kind of money needed to afford him the really good life. Elwell was basically a card hustler who milked the rich. With his ill-won wealth he established himself as one of them, becoming the owner of a racing stable, a yacht, an art collection and several cars.

Elwell was also the owner of what the tabloids referred to after his death as a "love index," a roster of 53 women, married and single, who boasted both high social affiliations and considerable allure. He maintained another list for male acquaintances and more run-of-the-mill females. Clearly, Elwell was a womanizer, a fact that proved to be something of a minor mystery in itself since after death he was revealed to have been toothless and bald, owning a collection of no less than 40 toupees.

Early one morning in 1920, just as dawn crept over Manhattan's West 70th Street, someone put a .45-caliber bullet into Elwell's head as he was reading a letter in his study. His housekeeper found him near death when she came to work; he was not wearing his toupee or his false teeth. The housekeeper, Marie Larsen, was a devoted servant who, while doctors labored over Elwell, hid a pink kimono she found in the house. Later, it was discovered, but the young lady who owned it had an alibi for the time of the shooting. Almost all of the ladies on the love index and those in Elwell's larger file had been sound asleep at the time of the murder.

The newspapers had a field day with this first sex-and-murder scandal of the decade. All sorts of filmy underclothes were found secreted in Elwell's bedroom. It undoubtedly took a keen mind to remember which belonged to whom and perhaps a slip of this kind is what did Elwell in. All sorts of theories developed, featuring jealous women, their husbands or other lovers, gambling rings, gambling victims, mysterious spies (according to this postulation, Elwell, who had been a secret government agent in the war, was killed by spies he had uncovered) and even rival horse owners. One could have a pick of suspects and motives, but the public clearly preferred the idea that some fashionable matron (or her daughter) committed the murder for reasons of passion. Yet a .45 was hardly a woman's weapon and Elwell, a notoriously vain man, would never have admitted a female to his presence without putting in his teeth and donning his toupee. The answer to that argument was, of course, that a woman murderer might use a .45 and then remove his plates and wig precisely to make it look like the work of a man. Russel Crouse, the playwright and a former crime reporter, who had a keen eye for such things, once observed, "'Cherchez la femme!' will echo every time the murder of Joseph Bowne Elwell is mentioned. And the fact that she will never be found will not still the whispers."

See also: CHARLES NORRIS.

embezzlement

The most enduring crime magazine article is probably the embezzlement story. There is something so eternal about the crime, probably because its root causes are deeply related to basic human failings. At times a writer will explain the motive for embezzlement in terms of the "three W's" or the "three R's"—it's all the same whether one speaks of wine, women and wagering or rum, redheads and race horses. The fact is that sex and greed can drive many people to steal large amounts of money, and they frequently do. Recent estimates place embezzlement losses at more than $4 billion a year.

Typical embezzlers work at a bank or other business institution for years or even decades before they are finally exposed—if ever. As a cashier, John F. Wagner, was able to skim somewhat more than $1.1 million from the First National Bank of Cecil, Pa., by juggling the bank's books for at least a score of years until he committed suicide in 1950. The vice president of a bank in Baton Rouge, La. kept up his looting for a dozen years. When he was finally caught, he said: "I'm glad it's finally over. These past twelve years of living under the constant strain of wondering when I'd eventually get caught have cost me more than any amount of money could be worth."

Some embezzlers don't like the strain of wondering if and when the Federal Deposit Insurance Corporation auditors will come calling. Richard H. Crowe, an assistant branch manager of a New York bank, was that type. So he simply went to the vault one Friday in the late 1940s, stuffed $883,000 into a bag and went home to dinner. The following Monday he was nowhere to be found. However, such runaways are generally not difficult to find, and often all the FBI has to do is determine where a man with a lot of extra spending money is most likely to turn up. Agents found Crowe in a plush bar in Daytona Beach, Fla.

Perhaps the classic bank embezzlement, with certainly the brashest motive of all, was that committed by bank president Ludwig R. Schlekat. Out of the $719,000 in cash supposedly on hand at the Parnassus National Bank of New Kensington, Pa., Schlekat managed to appropriate no less than $600,000, accumulating the sum over a 23-year period. When the shortage was found by bank examiners in 1947, it was determined that Schlekat had used $100,000 for his own better living. What had happened to the rest? Well, when Schlekat started working for the bank as an apprentice clerk at the age of 17 he had had only one ambition: to rise to bank president. After the bank's owner became eager to retire, Schlekat used the bulk of the $600,000 to purchase the bank through two nonexistent individuals who supposedly lived in Cleveland. Schlekat had simply used the bank's own money to buy the institution for himself. Then he had the bogus owners make him president. He was caught, tried and given a prison term of 10 years.

Generally, bankers and other business officials insist that people continue to embezzle because of the light sentences that are often imposed. It would be a somewhat more telling argument if all banks paid employees decent wages. In a classic case of that sort some years ago, federal judge Frank L. Kloeb refused to sentence a cashier of an Ohio bank who had been convicted of embezzling $7,500 over a 10-year period ending in 1941. The judge hit the ceiling when he learned that the man had started as a cashier in 1920 at an annual salary of $1,080 and 22 years later he had been earning no more than $1,900 a year. The cashier had stopped his embezzlements as his salary started to rise faster, and he was not found out until many years later.

The judge simply deferred sentencing indefinitely and refused even to put the cashier on probation, because that would have made him a criminal. "If I had the authority," the judge said, "I would sentence the bank officers and the Board of Directors to read the story of Scrooge at Christmas and think of the defendant."

Experts say women are just as likely to become embezzlers as men are. Bankers claim it is very common for middle-aged spinsters to resort to juggling the books. Having gone through life with perhaps little or no romance, such women may be desperate for companionship at this stage. In their eagerness to cement new friendships, they bestow gifts with reckless abandon. That old cliché of a shocked banker asking a trusted employee-turned-embezzler—"Was it a woman?"—definitely has its reverse—"Was it a man?"

As a rule, women are more generous with their loot than men. One trusted bookkeeper who stole $30,000 with the aid of some skillful record doctoring gave most of it to fellow employees in the form of salary increases.

The boom in computers in recent years has opened up new vistas for embezzlers. One bank employee developed a computerized money-diversion scheme to steal more than $1 million, which he used to finance his gambling. It seemed he also had a computer system for handicapping the horses, but unfortunately for him, it was less efficient than his embezzlement operation.

Computer embezzlement has even become a problem within the Internal Revenue Service. One IRS computer programmer set up a system that funneled unclaimed tax credits into a relative's account, and another IRS programmer computer-transferred to his own account checks being held for taxpayers whose mailing addresses could not be determined.

In the precomputer era it was estimated that there were at least 200 ways to embezzle money from a bank without danger of immediate exposure. Now, in an era of advancing technology, the ways cannot be counted. According to John Rankine, IBM's director of data security, "The data security job will never be done—after all, there will never be a bank that absolutely can't be robbed."

See also: COMPUTER CRIME, JOHN F. WAGNER.

Emma Mine fraud

In the West's great scramble for the riches of silver ore from the 1870s to the end of the 19th century, there was scant exploitation by legitimate mining interests of Utah's silver deposits. The origin of this strange diffidence toward a profitable opportunity was the notorious Emma Silver Mining Co. bubble, which had caused investors to lose millions, some in this country and even more in England.

With the first sign of a silver strike in Little Cottonwood Canyon in 1868, a mining speculator, James E. Lyon of New York, moved in to take effective control. He in turn had to yield a good deal of it to San Francisco mining interests, and they then brought in Trevor W. Park of Vermont and Gen. H. Henry Baxter of New York. To protect his interests, Lyon introduced Sen. William M. Stewart of Nevada into the combine, which by then had decided to sell stock in the mine in England. Important names were added to the operation. Professor Benjamin Silliman, Jr. of Yale, for a fee of $25,000, issued a favorable report on the mine's ore deposits. The board of directors of the British company included three members of Parliament, the U.S. minister to the Court of St. James and a former president of the New York Central Railroad, among others. Marketing of the company's stock was handled by Baron Albert Grant, a London financier of dubious ethical standards but a brilliant salesman, who was paid a fee of £170,000 for his troubles. It was a small price since the income from floating the stock was something like £600,000. All the American operators did extremely well, with the possible exception of the original investor, James Lyon. His supposed protector, Sen. Stewart, was able to buy him out for £50,000, half of what Lyon had been promised.

For a time, even the English investors did well, as the stock in the Emma Silver Mining Company, Ltd., quickly moved from £20 to £50. Then a rival firm, the Illinois Tunnel Co., announced the Emma claim had not been recorded correctly and that the English company was mining the ore from the claim to pay the dividends on its stock. Even more shocking was the revelation that the owner of Illinois Tunnel was Trevor W. Park, who was also a member of the board of Emma Mining and who had made one of the biggest profits in the entire deal. All sorts of suits were then filed, especially after 1872, when Emma Mining announced its ore deposits had run out. In the end, everyone who had been in the original combine made and kept money and all the shareholders in Emma Mining lost their money except for a total of $150,000, which Park offered in 1877 for all outstanding shares. Park continued to mine Emma for a number of years and is believed to have made that money back easily. In any event, the Emma

Mine scandal was to frighten off virtually all investment in Utah mines by outsiders for some three decades, and the fraud was often cited as an example of "Yankee ingenuity."

Espinosa brothers   murderers

In 1861 three Mexican brothers and some other kin invaded Colorado with the announced purpose of killing 600 Americans. This vendetta, they said, was to make up—at the rate of 100 to one—for the loss of life suffered by the Espinosa family during the Mexican War. By mid-1863 the three brothers, Felipe, Julián and Victorio, had managed to dispatch 26 Americans. Their typical victims were freighters, prospectors, sawmill workers or soldiers whom they had caught alone. While vengeance was supposedly the first order of the day, the Espinosas saw to it that their victims were also worth robbing; their soldier-victims, for instance, had generally been waylaid right after payday.

With 574 victims to go, Felipe Espinosa, the leader and most audacious member of the family, sent a message to the territorial governor, offering to quit the murderous campaign if the Espinosas were given a land grant of 5,000 acres and made captains in the Colorado Volunteers. Such an offer was hardly likely to be accepted, as Felipe most certainly knew, and probably represented a bold attempt to put the best possible face on the criminal acts. The governor responded by placing a reward of $2,500 on Felipe's head.

The killings went on and terror gripped the territory. Groups of vigilante miners rode hell-for-leather around the countryside trying to corner the Espinosas and hanged more than one suspect, even some who quite clearly were not Mexicans. Finally, however, they did catch Victorio Espinosa in the Fairplay–California Gulch area and strung him up. Later they staged a drunken celebration because they mistakenly believed their victim was Felipe, without whom the Espinosas were thought to be incapable of continuing their murderous activities.

When the terror did not end, it was obvious Felipe was still alive. He continued to elude posses of miners and army patrols. Finally, the army commissioned a storied scout named Tom Tobin to bring in the Espinosas with the aid of a 15-soldier detail. Late in 1863, Tobin successfully tracked down the remaining two Espinosa brothers, but at the last moment he slipped away from the troopers because he did not want to share the reward money with them. Tobin cornered Felipe and Julián Espinosa at Indian Creek and shot them dead before they could return his fire. He cut off their heads as proof he had gotten the right men and returned to Fort Garland to claim his reward.

However, because of a shortage of cash in the territorial coffers, Tobin was given only $1,500 and some buckskins.

For several years pickled "Espinosa heads" were exhibited around the West. Long after, in 1955, Kit Carson III labeled these exhibits, some still around, as fakes. Carson said Tom Tobin, his maternal grandfather, had always insisted the heads had been buried behind Fort Garland and never removed.

Estes, Billie Sol (1925–)   con man

In the 1960s Billie Sol Estes, a flamboyant Texas "salesman" and political supporter of President Lyndon Johnson, became famous as a prototypical big-time swindler after being convicted of inducing farmers to invest in fertilizer tanks that never existed. He was sentenced to 15 years and paroled in 1971 after serving six years. Under the terms of his parole, Estes was not allowed to engage in promotional schemes, but almost immediately he was implicated in some financial dealings that involved allegations of fraud. In August 1979 Estes was sentenced to two five-year federal prison terms to be served consecutively following his conviction for bilking investors by borrowing money and using as collateral oil field cleaning equipment that was nonexistent. One of his victims, J. H. Burkett, an Abilene used-car dealer who lent Estes his life savings of $50,000 shortly after meeting him in 1975, said: "I met him in church, in Bible study in Abilene, and he struck me as a very nice guy. He seemed very humble, very earnest, remorseful. I was very impressed by him, and I still am, but in a different way. The man is the world's best salesman. Just go and meet him, and you'll find out. He'll sell you something."

Following his 1979 conviction Estes told the judge: "I love this country. I'd rather be in prison here than free anywhere else in the world." He said that whether or not he went to jail, he would pay the money he owed, including $10 million in back taxes, to the government. Estes claimed he had more than a million friends and could raise $10 from each of them. There were those who said he probably could.

Estes was always a spellbinder. In a 1961 interview he once outlined his personal philosophy, which apparently won him devoted followers. "You win by losing, hold on by letting go, increase by diminishing, and multiply by dividing. These are the principles that have brought me success."

Evans, Charles (?–1875)   murderer

In another era or in another jurisdiction, Charles, or Daniel (as he was sometimes called), Evans might not

295

have ended up on the end of a rope, thereby helping to make Isaac C. Parker's reputation as "the hanging judge."

Long known as a thief and horse stealer, Evans was arrested in April 1875 for the murder of an 18-year-old boy named Seabolt. The body was found in Indian Territory, Oklahoma, bootless and with an empty wallet nearby. Evans was arrested when he was found in possession of Seabolt's horse. At his trial he insisted he had bought the horse. Since all the evidence against him was circumstantial, he was found not guilty. However, the presiding judge who was resigning and leaving the area, failed to sign certain legal papers, so that Evans had to be held over for a new trial. In June he was brought before a new judge, Isaac C. Parker, who was later to become known as the Hanging Judge. Parker could have ruled that Evans was being exposed to double jeopardy, but such legalisms seldom influenced him and he ordered a trial.

Evans was sure of acquittal and came into court all dolled up to celebrate his forthcoming freedom. The dead man's father was in the courtroom, and when he looked down at the boots the defendant was wearing, he realized they were his son's. Judge Parker sentenced Evans to hang and no doubt noted to himself how a legal technicality had almost freed a guilty man.

See also: ISAAC C. "HANGING JUDGE" PARKER.

Evans, Christopher (1847–1917) anti-railroad outlaw

Called affectionately the Old Chief by many residents of the San Joaquin Valley, Chris Evans, together with the Sontag brothers, led the California Outlaws, a group of train robbers who carried on a fierce war with the Southern Pacific Railroad, looting its express cars but never victimizing any of its passengers.

A veteran of many gun battles with railroad and federal posses, Evans survived a number of wounds, including one that blinded his right eye, but kept up his relentless campaign against the railroad. After George Sontag was captured, Evans and John Sontag were forced up into the hills where they were finally cornered by a huge posse in the famous Battle of Simpsons Flat. The gunfight raged for eight hours, with Evans and Sontag dashing from tree to tree and holding off the army of pursuers. Two Tulare County deputies were killed and a number wounded, but in the end, John Sontag lay dying and Evans was "too filled with lead to run any more." Although expected to die, Evans survived and was lodged in jail in Fresno.

In his autobiography, written many years later, Ed Morrell, a member of the outlaws who worked as a spy inside the ranks of railroad detectives, said that their boss, Big Bill Smith, decided it would be best if Evans died trying to escape, despite the fact that he could barely walk or ride. He ordered Morrell to go to Evans and arrange for a jail break, during which Evans would be shot. Morrell said he frustrated the plan by helping Evans to escape 24 hours ahead of schedule.

While Morrell carried, or half-dragged, Evans for weeks, Smith flooded the valley and surrounding hills with hundreds of agents. Eventually, the fugitives were forced to take refuge in a farmhouse. Although many residents of the area were sympathizers and hid them willingly, there was now a huge reward offered for their capture, and they were betrayed. Chris Evans was quickly sentenced to life imprisonment. So was Morrell, who later was subjected to brutal torture in prison. When word of Morrell's ordeal got out, he was pardoned in 1907 and became a national hero and a champion of prison reform. Evans was paroled in 1911 and quietly lived the last six years of his life with his family in Portland, Ore.

See also: CALIFORNIA OUTLAWS, ED MORRELL, SONTAG BROTHERS.

Everleigh sisters madams

Some experts on the subject insist there has not been a genuine bordello in America since 1910, when Chicago's Everleigh Club, run by sisters Ada and Minna Everleigh, shut its doors. And when it did, the sisters, still in their early thirties, retired with, among other things, $1 million in cash; perhaps $250,000 in jewelry, much of which had come from grateful clients; paintings, statues, rare books, rugs and other valuables for which they had paid $150,000; about 50 brass beds inlaid with marble and fitted with specially designed matresses and springs; and 25 gold-plated spittoons worth $650 apiece. For the Everleighs the wages of sin had been enormous.

Coming from a small Kentucky town, the Everleighs inherited about $35,000 between them. Everleigh was not their real name—it may have been Lester—but one they adopted in honor of their grandmother, who signed her letters, "Everly Yours." For a time the sisters joined a theatrical troupe while they looked for a nice town in which to invest their money. Early in 1898 they decided on Omaha, Neb., then readying for the Trans-Mississippi Exposition, which was expected to bring big crowds. At the time, Ada was 23 and Minna not quite 21, but they were hard-headed businesswomen and coolly analyzed what type of business would please a fun-seeking exposition crowd. So they went out and bought a whorehouse, a field in which they had no experience. They brought in all new girls and charged the highest prices in Omaha. It worked during the exposition, but when the crowds left, the sisters found out there was no way the sports of Omaha were going to pay $10 for a girl and $12 for a bottle of wine. So they packed up and moved to Chicago. The sisters bought the lease to and girls at the brothel of Madam Effie Hankins at 2131-3 South Dearborn Street for $55,000. On February 1, 1900 they opened the incredible Everleigh Club. Describing it, the *Chicago Tribune* said, "No house of courtesans in the world was so richly furnished, so well advertised, and so continuously patronized by men of wealth and slight morals."

On opening night the club took in $1,000. Never again were revenues so small, as word got around about the fabulous services offered. Separate soundproof parlors were called the Gold, Silver, Copper, Moorish, Red, Green, Rose, Blue, Oriental, Chinese, Egyptian and Japanese rooms and were appropriately furnished. The *Tribune* described the Japanese Room as "a harlot's dream of what a Japanese palace might look like." Every room had a fountain that squirted a jet of perfume into the air.

Quite naturally, the charges were hardly cheap for the era, ranging from $10 to $25 to $50, depending on how long a client wished to avail himself of a prostitute's company. The $10 price was really little more than the cost of admission; if a man failed to spend at least $50, he was told not to return. The costs of running such a magnificent house—which included a library, an art gallery, a dining room, rooms where three orchestras played and a Turkish ballroom with a huge indoor fountain—were enormous. Overhead ran to $75,000 a year, including $30,000 for servants, music and entertainment and probably protection, since the sisters were never bothered and the name of the club did not appear on the police lists of bawdy houses. Also on the payroll were 15 to 25 cooks. This was an excellent investment because, while a good sport might spend $50 or $100, and gentleman throwing a dinner party for a small group of friends (with wine at $12 a bottle) could easily run up a tab of $1,500 for an evening's fun.

Madame Minna met each visitor in the grand hallway, clad in a silk gown and bedecked with jewels, including a diamond dog collar. The sisters permitted no lineup of their girls but had them drift from parlor to parlor, talking to a man only after a formal introduction. Everleigh Club prostitutes were much sought after by other bordellos and a girl who made it in the club had her future assured in the business—if she did not go directly from the business to marriage of a wealthy patron.

"I talk with each applicant myself," Ada once explained. "She must have worked somewhere else before coming here. We do not like amateurs. . . . To get in a girl must have a good face and figure, must be in perfect health, must understand what it is to act like a lady. If she is addicted to drugs, or to drink, we do not want her." For the girls the work was lighter and the pay higher than elsewhere, so the sisters always had a waiting list of applicants. Those accepted got regular classes in dress, manners and makeup and had to read books from the establishment's library.

A man who partied at the Everleigh Club even once could boast of it for years. The real secret of the sister's success was their understanding of male chauvinism and fantasies. One much appreciated gimmick used at times was to have butterflies to flit about the house. As a rival madam, Cleo Maitland, observed, "No man is going to forget he got his behind fanned by a butterfly at the Everleigh Club."

The list of celebrities who patronized the club was almost endless. Prince Henry of Prussia enjoyed a mighty orgy there in 1902, and repeat callers included John Barrymore, Ring Lardner, heavyweight boxing champion James J. "Gentleman Jim" Corbett, George Ade, Percy Hammond and Bet-A-Million Gates. One of the rave reviews of the establishment was offered by newsman Jack Lait, who said, "Minna and Ada Everleigh are to pleasure what Christ was to Christianity."

Other madams and whoremasters were jealous of the sisters' success and tried to fabricate charges of clients being robbed or drugged there, but the Everleighs paid the highest graft in the city and the authorities would not listen to such nonsense. One resourceful bordello operator, Ed Weiss, opened up next door to the Everleigh Club and put taxi drivers on his payrolls so that when a particularly drunken sport asked to be taken there, he would be deposited at the Weiss place instead without knowing the difference.

The great reform drive against vice in Chicago in 1910 forced the Everleigh Club to close. The sisters had no intention of doing battle with the authorities, who were under attack from do-gooders. Most Everleigh clients could not believe such a palace of pleasure would ever go out of business. The trauma was much worse for them than for the sisters, who took a year's grand tour of Europe and on their return settled in New York City in a fashionable home off Central Park. They lived out their lives in genteel fashion, Minna dying in 1948 and Ada in 1960.

See also: FRIENDLY FRIENDS, NATHANIEL FORD MOORE, WEISS CLUB.

execution, methods of

Aside from a few early and isolated instances of executions by crushing with weights, drawing and quartering or burning at the stake (these last two almost exclusively punishments reserved for blacks), the death penalty in America has been accomplished by four basic methods: hanging, the electric chair, the gas chamber and the firing squad.

These methods can be discussed in their general order of chronological usage and popularity.

HANGING

Allowing for possible changes and the reimposition of the death penalty following the Supreme Court's 1976 approval of executions, hanging is in vogue in a half-dozen states, although at one time its use was almost universal. The main argument against hanging is that it is far more cruel and painful than other methods; on the other hand, proponents of hanging argue that its very repulsiveness makes it more of a deterrent. Of course, were this latter viewpoint true, hanging should have eliminated murder and other capital crimes centuries ago.

Years of practice and refinement have gone into the technique in an effort to achieve what is known as a "clean" hanging. Here is how things go if a clean hanging occurs—which, according to experts, happens in a minority of the cases. First of all, there is no longer the embarrassment of the rope slipping from the crossbeam since it is now attached to a chain suspended from the gallows crossbeam. The noose is adjusted so that the knot is positioned extremely tightly behind the victim's left ear, and a black hood is placed over his head so that witnesses will be spared the condemned man's final grimaces. In some states the hangman does not spring the trapdoor himself. His job is limited to fixing the knot, binding the legs together to prevent disconcerting kicking and centering the doomed man correctly over the trapdoor. Then he gives a signal and three men in a little booth on the platform each cut a string, only one of which springs the trapdoor. When the door occurs, the knot ideally will strike behind the left ear, instantly knocking the doomed man unconscious. If things work to perfection, just the right number of small bones of the cervical vertebrae in the neck are broken so that the head is not ripped off. The bones should then collapse on the spinal cord, cutting off oxygen to the brain and paralyzing the rest of the body. Rapid brain death follows. This is what can be considered a "clean" clean hanging. It doesn't happen all that often. There are other hangings that are still clean enough.

In the average clean job, the victim's thrashing at the end of the rope lasts for but a few minutes. His wheezing can be heard but never reaches the fever pitch of a botched job. The stench, however, may be rather troublesome, since the victim often urinates, defecates and ejaculates at the same time. The resultant odors, mixed with an overwhelming one of perspiration, is somewhat sickening, especially as human waste runs down the victim's legs and drops to the floor. Finally, after a rela-

Many printed accounts and renderings of 19th century hangings afforded that form of execution a romantic flavor devoid of reality.

tively short few minutes, the dying man's violent shudders subside and the rope stops dancing. There is one final jerk, just a bit of twitching and quiet.

So much for the good work. Former San Quentin warden Clinton Duffy, who witnessed 60 hangings, describes most hanging as being of the less than clean variety. In a "dirty" hanging the condemned man will strangle to death slowly, a vile process that can take as long as a quarter of an hour. His wheezing is extremely loud, and indescribable, save to someone who has heard the hysterical squealing of a dying pig. The victim may even bob up and down on the rope like a yo-yo as he fights for air. Sometimes his legs, even when bound together, whip far out in search of a perch. It may become necessary for a guard to seize the man's legs and hold them steady so that his violent churnings do not break the rope, a development that might upset the witnesses. When death finally comes, it may be difficult to determine for whom the agony was worse—the condemned or the witnesses.

Of course, sometimes things get even messier. A poorly placed knot occasionally gouges out a chunk of the face and head and witnesses see this gory mess drop to the floor. When the noted outlaw Black Jack Ketchum was hanged in New Mexico in 1901, he shouted out as the hood went over his face, "Let her rip!" The rope did so, decapitating Ketchum as he hurtled into space.

The same thing happened during the 1930s in West Virginia when a wife murderer named Frank Myer was hanged. Myer was a bad hanging victim, being heavyset with short neck and what were described as "soft bones." When the trapdoor opened, Myer's body crashed to the concrete floor, followed by a second thud as his head landed nearby. Several of the witnesses got sick as the head rolled a few feet in their direction, and after the execution some of them allowed they would never again attend a hanging.

The sheer messiness of hangings finally led to the abandonment of the method by most states, which opted for either the electric chair or the gas chamber. One state, Utah, just couldn't sever its sentimental attachment to hanging, but it at least has offered the condemned a choice, the noose or the firing squad. The rope has lost out in that popularity contest as well.

SHOOTING

Most condemned men in Utah opt for the firing squad over hanging, two of the most illustrious examples being labor hero Joe Hill, almost certainly executed for a crime he did not commit, and Gary Gilmore, the first man executed after the Supreme Court's reimposition of the death penalty. In some respects, death by firing squad is the most "humane" method of all. The condemned man is strapped down in a chair against an oval-shaped canvas-covered wall. A doctor locates the heart precisely and pins a cloth target directly over it. Unless the victim objects, he is hooded.

Just 20 feet away in a canvas enclosure, five sharpshooters are given .30-caliber rifles, each loaded with a single cartridge. One, however, receives a blank so that each marksmen can later rationalize he did not do the killing. They place their weapons through slits in the canvas, and when the order is given, they fire in unison. Four bullets thump into the heart, making death virtually instantaneous and probably painless. With such a fine method for killing, it may be surprising that more jurisdictions haven't switched to death by shooting, but there are good reasons. One is the fact that the execution is bloody, and society generally does not like a mess around to remind it that a human being has just been slaughtered. But even more important is that sometimes the marksmen turn "chicken" or "cheat." If a marksman wants to make sure he does not fire the fatal bullet, he will aim "off-heart" and thus be able to figure that the victim died long before his shot could have taken any effect. In 1951 the height of official embarrassment was achieved when all four marksmen hit the victim, Elisio J. Mares, on the right side of the chest. He bled to death slowly. Because of such inefficiencies, death by firing squad never will gain much popularity.

ELECTRIC CHAIR

When in May 1979 30-year-old John Spenkelink became the first man in more than a dozen years to die in Florida's electric chair, there was some worry that

"Old Sparky" as some called the venerable electric chair at the state prison at Raiford, might not be up to the task, having been in disuse for 15 years. The worry was groundless. Old Sparky worked beautifully. The Spenkelink execution was not without fault, however. A venetian blind was dropped over the window through which witnesses were supposed to watch Spenkelink being brought to the chair and strapped in. Evidently, he staged a battle royal with his guards. When the blind was opened, he was strapped down with a gag in his mouth. It was something that shouldn't happen. Death house guards are supposed to know how to handle a condemned man and be able to con him into dying easy, but Spenkelink had carried on in such macabre fashion that it was thought wise to spare the witnesses this sight. However, the guards too had had a 15-year layoff.

More than 1,000 men and women have gone to the hot seat since its introduction in 1890, and the history of electrocution is dotted with ghoulish and bizarre incidents. In Florida in 1926 a condemned man named Jim Williams was in the chair waiting for death when an argument broke out between Warden John S. Blitch and Sheriff R. J. Hancock, each of whom insisted it was the other's duty to throw the switch. The argument went on for 20 minutes until poor Williams collapsed. He was carried back to his cell while the dispute went to the courts. Eventually, a ruling was made that the

Early version of the electric chair.

sheriff had to do the job, but by then the Board of Pardons decided Williams had done enough penance and commuted his death sentence to life imprisonment.

During World War II two convicted murderers, Clifford Haas and Paul Sewell, beat the death sentence when one state switched to electrocution from hanging. The War Production Board said the materials required for the chair could be better used fighting the Japanese and the Nazis and refused to grant a priority. No chair, no killing.

The usual electric chair has two legs in back and a heavier single leg in front, all bolted to the floor. The extrawide arms are fitted with straps to hold the arms of the victim rigid. Other straps go around his chest and abdomen. The wiring around the chair is covered with rubber matting. Actually, the electric chair is a rather simple contraption, as indicated by the fact that some Southern states have used portable or mobile chairs.

In Mississippi the chair was carried around in a van with its own generators and controls so that it could be brought into the courtroom where the defendant was convicted. A power line lead from the truck's generators into the packed courtroom. When a newsman once told Sen. Theodore G. Bilbo that the practice was little different than lynching, he responded, "Ah, this is pretty tame compared to a lynching."

Ideally, an electrocution is a three-minute drill, with the prisoner strapped into the chair quickly. Inexperienced guards practice with the straps in advance to avoid fumbling delays. The so-called humane character of electrocution is probably best measured by what the witnesses are spared rather than what happens to the condemned person. A tight mask is placed over the prisoner's face to hide the facial contortions when the "juice" is turned on. The mask is especially tight around the eyes to keep them from popping out of their sockets.

Two popular myths about the execution chamber almost never happen. There are no long good-byes or last statements, although a famous gangster of the 1930s, Two-Gun Crowley, did manage, "Give my love to mother." And the lights never dim in the rest of the prison, because the chair is always powered by a separate source. Hollywood prefers the light-dimming routine because it gives a scriptwriter an opportunity to stage a prisoner protest or achieve special dramatic effect.

Once he is sure everyone is clear of the chair, the executioner throws a switch and the raging current pitches the victim against the bindings with terrible force. His hair stands up and his flesh turns the color of beets. If the executioner fails to flip the switch when the prisoner's lungs are empty, there is a "gurgling" noise as air is forced from the lungs by the shock of the current. The first jolt, executioners have learned by trial and error, should be 2,000 volts or slightly more, after

which it is cut back to 1,000 volts to prevent what witnesses might take as unseemly burning of the body. At this stage the victim may pass waste. The tradition of a last hearty meal for the condemned is truly a tribulation for the executioner. Almost certainly, mouth foam will seep out from under the hood. Often, the electrical jolt may be repeated to make sure the victim is dead. It is a worthwhile precaution. When Arthur Lee Grimes was executed in Alabama in 1954, the doctor found his heart still beating. He stepped back and waited for it to stop, but instead of expiring, Grimes started to shudder violently and thrash against the straps. He started to come back to consciousness, gasping and sucking in air. It took seven full minutes of juice, six massive jolts in all, to end his life.

Proponents of electrocution find such lapses as the Grimes execution lamentable, just as they did the world's first electrocution, that of William Kemmler in New York in 1890. In the 1880s a state legislative commission was established to decide if hanging should be abolished. After viewing a number of hangings, including that of a woman who slowly strangled to death, the members decided the noose had to go. But it is doubtful they would have conceived of the electric chair had it not been for a monumental battle over business profits. Thomas A. Edison and George Westinghouse were competing for domination of the then-budding electric power industry. Edison had developed the first electric power system in 1882 by the use of low-tension, direct current (DC). Two years later, Westinghouse came out with his alternating current (AC) system, which utilized light, easily installed wires compared to the expensive heavy-wire installation required for DC. Faced with an opposing product that was clearly superior, Edison decided his best hope lay in disparaging AC in the public's eye and dispatched a young engineer, Harold P. Brown, to stage shows around the country demonstrating the system's death-dealing potential. Brown shocked people by electrocuting stray dogs and cats and even horses. When he took his show to Albany, the special commission asked if he could kill an orangutan. He could and he did. The poor orangutan even caught fire, but that didn't deter the commission from coming up with the concept of an electric chair. A human being wasn't covered with hair and so was not likely to catch fire. The electric chair was born.

Kemmler's execution was not a happy one. A first jolt of 17 seconds failed to kill him and shocked doctors watched Kemmler's breast heave and his heart resume beating. Panic ensued in the execution chamber and finally the current was turned on again for another 70 seconds at 1,300 volts. Some of the witnesses fainted, and another retched and bolted from the room. Finally, William Kemmler was good and dead. Unfortunately, the flesh on Kemmler's back was badly burned and his muscles carbonized. When his body was autopsied, a witness described his flesh as well-cooked beef.

Despite worldwide protests of the tortures involved in the new method of extermination, the electric chair was here to stay. In time, executioners learned to watch the condemned person's hands. When they turn pink, other parts of the body, nearer to the source of the electrical charge, are far darker and closer to being burned. Unfortunately, in later years "overburning" still occurred.

To the public there was something fascinating about botched-up jobs; thus when the first electrocutions of four murderers took place at Sing Sing in 1891, the roads from Ossining to the prison were jammed with tourists and sightseers hoping that something would go wrong. But the chair worked four times without a hitch. In 1903 disaster struck at Clinton Prison when one of three brothers executed, Fred Van Wormer, started to move in the autopsy room. A rush call brought the executioner, Robert P. Elliott, back to the prison. By the time he got there, Van Wormer had expired, but everyone agreed it made sense not to take any chances. The dead man was hauled back to the chair and given another 1,700 volts.

Survival after death in the electric chair has always been an intriguing idea. When Ruth Snyder was executed along with her lover Judd Gray for the murder of her husband, her lawyer sought a court order to prevent the performance of an autopsy on her body, a legal requirement to determine the cause of death. The lawyer planned to revive her with adrenalin. The idea was never tried out because the courts rejected the move. A number of condemned persons have swallowed all types of metal objects under the belief that somehow this would cause the electric chair to "short." In the 1950s a prisoner named Donald Snyder entered his Sing Sing death cell weighing 150 pounds and soon started eating and eating and eating. He had come up with the novel idea of getting too fat to fit into the chair. Weightwise he did remarkably, eventually tipping the scales at over 300 pounds. His request for the traditional last meal was, "Pork chops, eggs and plenty of 'em!" He spent his last few hours speculating with a guard how the newspapers would go wild when it turned out he couldn't be executed.

It remained for a New York tabloid to write finis to Snyder's bizarre plan: "The hot seat fitted him as though it had been made to order."

Contrary to all the evidence of botched executions, burnings, gasping for air and continuing heartbeats, there are many experts who insist that electrocution is immediate and painless. They can perhaps take comfort in the case of Harry Roberts, a New York slayer who

informed the prison doctor as he was strapped into the chair: "Doc, my last act is going to be for science. We'll see how fast this juice really works. The moment I feel it, I'll wiggle this finger." It never wiggled.

A more or less authoritative source, depending on one's viewpoint, would be Dr. Harold W. Kipp, who, as chief medical officer of Sing Sing, attended more than 200 executions. Dr. Kipp said: "The effect of electricity is instantaneous brain death. What observers see are muscle contractions, not agony."

Not all medical authorities agreed with this enthusiasm for electrocution and the hunt was on for yet a new more humane method of killing. They found it in the gas chamber, and during the 1920s and 1930s it was hyped as truly superior to electrocution and hanging.

By the late 1990s only four states still required execution death by electrocution—Florida, Alabama, Georgia and Nebraska. Two others, Kentucky and Tennessee, switched to offering condemned men an execution of choice, electrocution and lethal injection.

In recent cases years protest against the electric chair centered mainly on Florida where the chair had led to botched executions from time to time. In a 1967 incident, flames and smoke arose from Pedro Medina's head when the electric current was turned on. The cause was said to be the sponges in the chair's headpiece. A one-year moratorium was imposed on executions after that, and an autopsy report insisted Medina had died instantly and suffered no pain from the fire. The Florida Supreme Court ruled by a 4-3 vote that electric chair executions, even in Medina's case did not violate the ban on cruel and unusual punishment. (Around the country courts have been singularly unable to find much in the way of cruel and unusual punishments, even when hanging victims ended up having their heads ripped off when the body was dropped, or slow strangulation followed.)

Then in 1990 and 1997 flames shot out of masks of the inmates and the smell of burned flesh filled the witness room. Similar malfunctions had occurred in other states. The next botch-up involved Allen Lee Davis who had blood seep through his shirt and the buckle holes of the chest strap. Bloody photographs of Davis were posted on the Internet and were to be considered in a U.S. Supreme Court review to determine if electrocution was a violation of the Constitution.

These gruesome examples of a malfunctioning chair led to further claims that Florida was incapable of carrying out executions competently, and the Supreme Court was set to review the state's electric chair practices to decide if Florida was engaging in cruel and unusual punishment. The Jeb Bush administration at first sought to give condemned men the right to choose between the electric chair and lethal injection. By that time the state legislature had quite enough of the controversy and voted unanimously in the senate and by 102 to 5 in the house to get rid of the chair.

GAS CHAMBER

First employed in Nevada, the gas chamber was eventually adopted by eight other states—Arizona, Colorado, Maryland, Mississippi, Missouri, North Carolina, Wyoming and California. The most famous gas chamber is the one at San Quentin. Built in 1938, it has been the site of some of the nation's most dramatic executions, including those of Barbara Graham, Caryl Chessman and Button W. Abbott, whose gassing in 1957 was almost stayed by an order of Gov. Goodwin Knight. When the phone call came from the governor's office, the gas pellets had already been dropped behind his chair, so the execution proceeded.

The gas chamber is designed with two chairs so that two executions can take place at the same time. (Double executions almost certainly guarantee newspapers good quotes. When kidnapper and murderess Bonnie Heady died in the Missouri gas chamber along with her partner, Carl Austin Hall, she asked guards not to strap in her man too tightly. "You got plenty of room, honey?" Heady asked. Hall replied, "Yes, Mama." Thus satisfied, the woman smiled and sat back to breathe the deadly fumes.) Under the chairs are shallow pans into which tubes from a small vestibule are fed a mixture of water and sulfuric acid. A lever is pulled, and bags with 16 1-ounce cyanide pellets are dropped into the mixture. Fumes rise swiftly, and the victim dies quickly—once in a while. Some reporters who have covered various types of executions regard the gas chamber as the most vile and inhumane of all.

Essentially, the victim strangles to death without the courtesy of a rope. He is forced to do it to himself as he battles for oxygen that is no longer there, except in a "frozen" state that is useless to the body. The condemned person is often told that as soon as he smells an odor resembling rotten eggs, he should count to 10 and then take several deep breaths. This, he is told, will cause him to pass out quickly and die without pain. It doesn't happen that way. Human instinct, the body's instinct, is to live. The victim will gasp and wheeze, struggling for air. His mouth opens and shuts like a beached fish. Often, he screams or sobs. Choking, he thrashes about. He pulls on his bonds. Occasionally, it is said, a victim will break an arm free, usually in the process severing the skin, so that his blood may spurt over the windows through which the witnesses are watching.

The asphyxiation process is slow. The thrashing victim's face turns purple, his eyes bulge. He starts to drool. A swollen tongue hangs out. But death still hasn't occurred. The death process takes eight or nine minutes. The record, although statistics are not definitive on the matter, appears to be 11 minutes in a North Carolina execution.

Caryl Chessman's ordeal of dying in 1960 may not have been the most unusual but it received greater media coverage than most other executions. He tried to make his dying easy, inhaling as quickly and deeply as he could. By prearrangement with a newsman witness, Chessman was to signal if the pain became agony. Shortly after his ordeal began, Chessman looked towards the reporter and nodded his head vigorously, the signal the dying process was indeed agonizing. Finally, his head slumped to his chest and his tongue popped out.

A woman reporter on the scene described what happened next:

> I thought he must be dead but no, there was another agonizing period during which he choked on the gas. And again. And then again. There was a long period, another deep gasp. At the fourth such straining, Chessman's head lolled in a half circle, coming forward so that he faced downward with his chin almost touching his chest. This must be the end. But the dying went on.
>
> A deep gasp, then his head came up for an instant, dropped forward again. After two or three deep breaths, which seemed something like sobs, a trembling set up throughout his body. Along the line of his broad shoulders, down the arms to his fingers, I could see the tremor run. Then I saw his pale face grow suddenly paler, though I had not thought that it could be after his 12 years in prison. A little saliva came from his lips, spotted the white shirt that a condemned man wears for his last appearance. Even more color drained from his face and the furrows in his head smoothed out a little. And I knew he was dead. . . .

There seemed to be some sentiment among the witnesses to the Chessman execution that death in the gas chamber was not really the painless process it was billed as. None of the methods of executions used in this country really are. And the search for the perfect method continues.

INJECTION

The newest method of capital punishment in the United States is death by injection, or what the inhabitants of the death rows in the various states opting for it refer to sardonically as "the ultimate high." Under an Oklahoma law passed in 1977, death is to occur by the continuous intravenous injection of "an ultrashort-acting barbituarate in combination with a chemical paralytic agent." Death would be almost instantaneous, with the condemned man simply falling asleep and expiring.

Officially, death would be attributable to coronary arrest.

In 1977 Texas joined Oklahoma in passing death-by-drug legislation, and Idaho and New Mexico followed later. Other states have considered similar action. Because of appeals on death sentences, no such executions had been carried out by mid-1981, although 200 men were under such sentence, and it was believed injection executions might not begin until well into the decade.

The routine, however, had been well planned. In the Oklahoma State Penitentiary at McAlester, there would be no more "last-mile" walk through the basement to the electric chair. Instead, the doomed man would be strapped onto a stretcher and transported, head propped up, to the third floor of the administration building to be executed there in view of about 30 persons. Among them would be six newsmen and five persons chosen by the condemned.

The executioner would be one of three unidentified medical technicians. They would stand behind a panel through which a tube would be passed and connected to the condemned person's arm or leg. The three technicians would inject a dark fluid into the tube, but none would know which of them was injecting the lethal substance.

In essence, this would be similar in approach to the firing squad technique of supplying one marksman with a blank. The argument has been made that execution by injection is more humane than any other method of legal killing, but it must be noted that as society becomes more "humane," the anonymity of the procedure increases to a point where the actual killing is done by only one man in three.

The American Medical Association passed a resolution in 1980 labeling participation in such executions by doctors unethical. However, in 1982 the first execution by injection was carried out in Texas. It was a botched affair. Prison employees had considerable difficulty in trying to pierce with a large needle the badly scarred veins of the condemned man, and blood splattered all over the sheets. Among those witnessing the fouled-up attempt was the prison doctor. For a first-time try it was not, however, as bungled as the first electrocution, that of Willie Kemmler.

Since that time injection has become the execution method of choice for both officials and condemned men, at latest count in 21 states. Some states offer doomed men a choice of execution: Missouri and North Carolina by gas chamber; Montana and Washington by hanging; Idaho and Montana by firing squad.

In 1980 when some of the more rabid advocates of capital punishment, including some in Congress, proposed that the exacting of the death penalty be shown on television, opponents of capital punishment were appalled. Why, it is hard to understand. It was not the

student demonstrations or the draft card burners who stopped the Vietnam War. Rather, it was television. Through the constant showing on the evening news of the blood and violence occurring in a senseless conflict, the American public sickened of that conflict. The same thing would happen after a dozen or so execution spectaculars were viewed on the home screen. The public turned against the death penalty from 1945 to the mid-1960s without being exposed to the full graphic horrors of executions. The impact of television showings are readily predictable—and not even the death penalty could survive the public's reaction to such exposure.

See also: JOHN X. BEIDLER, CAPITAL PUNISHMENT, CARYL CHESSMAN, GARY MARK GILMORE, GEE JON, WILLIAM KEMMLER, GEORGE MALEDON, MONSIEUR NEW YORK.

execution of children   See CAPITAL PUNISHMENT OF CHILDREN.

executions, public
From the time of the first execution in this country's history in 1630, that of John Billington, one of the original pilgrims on the Mayflower, Americans followed the European custom of public executions on the dubious theory that such legal killings would serve as a warning to others.

Throughout the years such public executions were no more than circuses, drawing proportionally a far greater audience than Sunday football games. In the Old West many hangings were reserved for the weekend so that as many people as possible would be free for the festivities. When in 1824 a hatchet murderer named John Johnson was hanged in New York City at 13th Street and Second Avenue, journals of the day reported that some 50,000 spectators attended the execution. Perhaps the most spectacular hanging in New York took place on Bedloe's Island, now the home of the Statue of Liberty, where the murderer Albert E. Hicks was executed on July 13, 1860 not merely for the edification of those squeezed on the island for the event but for thousands more who jammed aboard a mass of ships, from small craft to large excursion vessels, that filled the water around the island. Hawkers paddled in rowboats between the craft selling their wares.

In due course, many communities and many sheriffs banned public executions, finding that they could run a ghoulish sort of black market selling invitations to private executions at hefty prices. However, the custom of public executions stretched into the present century, even extending to electrocutions. In some states, primarily Southern ones, a portable electric chair was brought into the courtroom and the condemned man was executed there before as many spectators as could get inside. The current was fed into the courtroom from a van-type truck equipped with the necessary generators. A journalist once asked Sen. Theodore G. Bilbo of Mississippi if he did not think such executions were little different than lynchings. "Ah," Bilbo replied, "this is pretty tame compared to a lynching."

The last public execution in the United States took place in Owensboro, Ky. in 1936, when a 22-year-old black named Rainey Bethea was hanged for the murder of a 70-year-old white woman. Some 20,000 persons crowded into the town for the big event, and when Bethea was pronounced dead, souvenir hunters fought over the hood that covered his head, ripped off pieces of his clothing and even tried to cut chunks of flesh from his hanging body.

See also: CAPITAL PUNISHMENT, RAINEY BETHEA, JOHN BILLINGTON, ALBERT E. HICKS.

extortion   See BLACK HAND.

eye gouging

Eye gouging was a common crime in pre-20th-century America, especially in the big cities, where Irish gangsters used the technique—often against Englishmen—and on the frontier, where it was a part of the so-called rough-and-tumble style of fighting and much used against the Indians. In his diary Maj. Eluries Beatty tells of witnessing one eye gouging in Louisville, Ky. In 1791: "One of these . . . gougers, a perfect bully; all the country round stood in awe of him, for he was so dextrous in these matters that he had, in his time, taken out five eyes, bit off two or three noses and ears and spit them in their faces."

So despised did this cruel practice become that vigorous laws were passed in many jurisdictions specifically to combat it. In the Northwest Territory a law was promulgated stating:

Whosoever . . . shall voluntarily, maliciously, and on purpose, pull out or put out an eye while fighting or otherwise . . . shall be sentenced to undergo confinement in jail . . . and shall also pay a fine of not less than fifty dollars and not exceeding one thousand dollars, one fourth of which shall be for the use of the Territory, and three fourths . . . to the use of the party grieved, and for want of means of payment, the offender shall be sold into service by the court . . . for any time not exceeding five years, the purchaser finding him food and raiment during the term.

Such punishment was perhaps the only reason a white man on the frontier could be sold into servitude.

Gouging was not easy to eradicate. As late as the 1870s a New York gangster named Dandy Johnny Dolan became celebrated for the invention of an improved eye gouger made of copper and worn on the thumb for instant use. Dolan was hanged in 1876, and for the next quarter century, magistrates meted out heavy penalties against eye gougers. The public became particularly exercised about the practice, and political leaders, who relied on and supported the great gangs of the city, passed the word that eye gouging was out. A criminal caught in possession of a pistol, two or three knives and a pair of brass knuckles had no great fear of the law provided he had the proper political protection, but if he was found with eye gougers, he would be abandoned by his patrons and given severe punishment. Over the years the practice of eye gouging faded away, proof perhaps that rigid enforcement of the laws could in fact eliminate a considerable amount of crime.

Fahy, William J. (1886–1943) postal inspector and criminal mastermind

The robbery of the eight-car mail train of the Chicago, Milwaukee and St. Paul Railroad on June 12, 1924 at Roundout, Ill., proved memorable in the annals of the U.S. Postal Service for a reason greater than the mere fact that $2,059,612 in loot had been taken. It was a case that shook the service to its core.

What particularly upset the postal service was that the robbers, six masked men, had known precisely when the most loot would be aboard. Had they struck earlier or later, the amount would have been far less. The robbers clearly had good information.

Put in charge of the case was Bill Fahy, a slim, well-dressed postal inspector of 40 with a confident and alert attitude. He had cracked a number of tough cases as a member of both the Philadelphia and the Chicago offices and was considered the fair-haired boy of the service. If anyone could solve the Roundout mess, he could.

However, Fahy proved a total disappointment. His investigation was a disaster, following clues down one blind alley after another. Soon, the other agents on the case began striking out on their own investigations. They caught some professional thieves with a portion of the loot. They named the others involved and admitted the gang had inside information. The robbers had a contact in the postal service, but the six never knew his identity.

Suspicion centered on the 18 mail clerks aboard the train. Fahy and his men checked on all of them. But one of the captured gang members said their informer had made it clear he was running the show and was getting the biggest cut. It hardly seemed likely that a mere postal clerk could have that much muscle with a gang of professional criminals. Finally, the other investigators discovered that Fahy had been secretly trying to break down the witnesses' positive identifications of the criminals. That only made sense if Fahy was the inside man.

A trap was baited. Fahy was told a high postal service official was coming to town with a lead on where one of the fugitives of the gang was hiding. The fugitive was Jimmy Murray, the contact man in the gang who had dealt with the postal service insider. When Fahy heard the news, he went home and telephoned a certain C. Anderson at the Ambassador Hotel in Chicago. In a wire-tapped conversation he told Anderson to lie low, that someone was in town who apparently had a lead on his whereabouts. With that, Murray was nabbed, and so was Bill Fahy. Fahy was convicted along with the other robbers and sentenced to 25 years in prison.

He was released in 1937, still proclaiming his innocence and saying he had been "framed by my criminal and professional enemies." He had earlier rejected a commutation offered in exchange for an admission of guilt. Fahy said he was going to prove his innocence but he never did. He died in 1943.

faked deaths See INSURANCE FRAUD—FAKED DEATHS.

Fall, Albert Bacon (1861–1944) political grafter

The central figure in the Teapot Dome scandal, Secretary of the Interior Albert B. Fall was the most tragic figure in the Harding administration. Unlike many of the other grafters, his motive was not so much avarice as a genuine need for money. There is evidence that he resisted temptation until he saw clear cases of corruption by Attorney General Harry M. Daugherty and the rest of the Ohio Gang.

Born in Frankfort, Ky. in 1861, Fall was forced by ill health to move to a Western climate. He taught school for a short time in Indian Territory in the Oklahoma area and then became a cattle drive rider, later trying his hand at mining and oil prospecting. In New Mexico he became a close friend of Edward L. Doheny, was admitted to the bar and started to develop a huge ranch at Three Rivers, N.M.

Fall also turned to politics, holding several positions in the territorial government, and in 1912, after New Mexico had achieved statehood, he became one of the state's first two senators. In 1921 his friend Warren Harding named him to the cabinet as secretary of the interior. It was a welcomed opportunity for Fall, whose

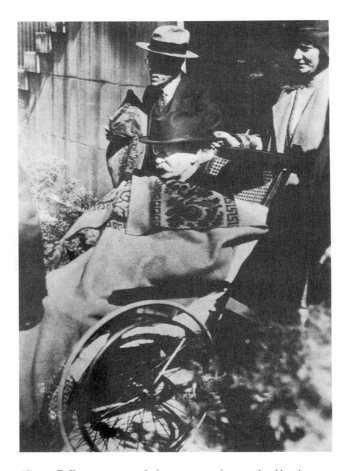

Albert Fall, secretary of the interior during the Harding administration, was broken physically by the time of his conviction and imprisonment and remained an invalid the rest of his years.

personal fortunes had sagged badly. His ranch needed many repairs and improvements, and all his properties were heavily mortgaged. In 1922 Fall secretly leased the Elk Hills, Calif. and the Teapot Dome, Wyo. oil lands, which were held by the government as a reserve in case of war, to Doheny's Pan-American Co. and Harry F. Sinclair's Mammoth Oil Co. It is doubtful if Fall would have done this had it not been for his long friendship with Doheny. Furthermore, Congress had authorized the leasing of the oil lands, although not the secret way Fall had gone about it or, of course, as a quid pro quo for bribes. Doheny gave Fall $100,000, and Sinclair arranged to have Fall receive a "loan" of $260,000 in Liberty Bonds.

The affair became public when a Wyoming oil man wrote his congressman demanding to know how Sinclair had leased Teapot Dome without competitive bidding. In the resulting senatorial inquiry the story of the payoffs to Fall was unraveled. Fall at first insisted that he had gotten the $100,000 as a loan from the eccentric millionaire Edward B. McLean. When McLean then surprised him by denying such a loan, Fall admitted getting the money "in a black bag" from Doheny.

Over the next several years Fall went on trial eight times, sometimes with Doheny or Sinclair and sometimes alone. On the witness stand, Doheny told a tale of how the two young friends started out together, with one eventually striking it rich in oil while the other had nothing but bad luck. "Why shouldn't I lend him $100,000 and tear his name off the note?" he asked. "He was an old friend." Then Doheny called the $100,000 "a mere bagatelle," and the newspapers and public were outraged. It was said that remark did more to doom Fall than any evidence against him. While the two oil men were finally acquitted of the charges against them (Sinclair did get nine months for contempt for having a Burns detective follow the jurors during one trial), Fall was convicted, drawing a year in prison and a fine of $100,000. The money penalty was dropped when Fall signed a pauper's oath, and because he was suffering from tuberculosis, he was allowed to serve his sentence in the New Mexico State Penitentiary, into which Fall, his face ashen, was carried on a stretcher. He came out of the prison an invalid, needing the constant attention of his family until he died poverty-stricken in El Paso in 1944.

See also: OHIO GANG, TEAPOT DOME.

Fallon, William J. (1886–1927) defense attorney

William Joseph Fallon was New York's greatest criminal lawyer during the Roaring Twenties. Fallon was the Great Mouthpiece, as his biography by Gene Fowler was entitled, for pimps, madams, prostitutes, thieves, stock swindlers, second-story men, gangsters and murderers. Few Fallon clients ever spent a day in jail pending trial. Even if a Fallon client were not acquitted, he almost certainly benefitted from long delays due to hung juries. The novelist Donald Henderson Clarke called Fallon "the Jail Robber."

A large number of Fallon's cases never made it to a courtroom. Fallon paid off cops and bought people working in district attorneys' offices who could see to it that the evidence against his clients disappeared. On one occasion, during a court recess, the prosecutor was called to the telephone; he took along his briefcase, which contained the prosecution's case against the defendant. On the telephone, he was startled to hear an anonymous female voice inform him his wife was guilty of infidelity. The prosecutor walked out of the telephone booth in a daze and down the corridor. When he remembered his briefcase and went back for it, it had "disappeared." In court, Fallon demanded the trial continue; without the state's key evidence, his client was cleared.

Unlike those defense lawyers who never take on murder cases when the evidence is overwhelming, in order to protect their claim of never losing a client to the electric chair, Fallon took on any number of individuals who seemed doomed. Still, not one of his clients ever went to the chair. In 12 years before the New York bar, he defended about 100 murderers. About 60 percent of them were acquitted, and the rest got off with comparatively light sentences. Fallon's technique was to badger prosecutors and judges, confuse prosecution witnesses, and fool jurors. Above all, his specialty was producing a hung jury. He would address his entire summation to a single juror, picking out the one he judged to be most susceptible to such flattery. After some years a Hearst newspaper would point to Fallon's almost endless record of cases with juries hung by 1-to-11 votes. When he judged his skills were not winning the battle, Fallon was not above bribing a juror. He often paid them off in the courthouse elevator, giving them half in advance and half afterwards. He reputedly never made a second payment.

His courtroom performances were replete with trickery. In one case he defended a Russian who stood accused of arson and against whom the case looked strong indeed. The man twice previously had been convicted of setting fire to stores he had owned in attempts to bilk insurance companies. Fallon realized his only hope was to discredit the prosecution's witnesses. A fireman testified to entering the burning structure and smelling kerosene on a number of wet rags. Fallon insisted the rags were soaked with water and demanded the fireman submit to a test to see if he could tell the difference. The lawyer produced five bot-

tles number 1, 2, 3, 4 and 5 and asked the fireman to sniff the contents of each and say if it was kerosene or water. The fireman sniffed bottle number 1 and announced it was kerosene. So too were bottles 2, 3, 4 and 5, he declared.

Fallon then took a sip of bottle number 5 and told the jury: "The contents of this bottle does not taste like kerosene to me. This bottle—this bottle that the gentleman on the witness stand would have you believe contains kerosene—doesn't contain kerosene at all. It contains water. When you get into the jury room, I wish you would all help yourself to a taste of its contents. If what you taste in the slightest resembles kerosene, I think it is your duty to convict my client. If what you taste is water, then it is your duty to acquit my client."

Fallon's client was of course acquitted because the liquid was pure water. What he had done was to have the fireman inhale deeply of the first four bottles all of which contained kerosene. Then when he sniffed the water, the fumes from the first four bottles were still in his nostrils.

In 1924 Fallon himself was brought to trial for allegedly bribing a juror in one of his 1-to-11 specialties. Reporters for Hearst's *New York American* had followed a number of jurors who had voted the Fallon way until they found one who was spending an unseemly amount of money after being the lone holdout in a jury hearing the case against two stock swindlers. It appeared Fallon had extracted $25,000 from his clients for the bribing of the juror, offered the man $5,000, given him $2,500 and kept the balance.

The juror confessed, and Fallon was brought up on charges. The famous lawyer ran his own defense, even putting himself on the stand, and proceeded to make William Randolph Hearst, rather than William Joseph Fallon, the defendant. The lawyer insisted Hearst had trumped up the charges because he, Fallon, had gone to Mexico and uncovered the birth certificates of twins fathered by Hearst with a well-known Hollywood actress. While the jurors sat agog at the testimony, the prosecution tried to knock out all references to Hearst. But the point had been scored. It took the jury only five hours, with time out for dinner, to bring in a not-guilty verdict.

Fallon bounded out of his chair and thanked each juror, and then as the crowds of well-wishers thinned out, he approached the press table, where Nat Ferber, the *American* reporter who had dug up the case against him, was sitting. "Nat," he whispered, "I promise you I'll never bribe another juror!"

Actually, Fallon went on operating the way he always had for another couple of years, but by then drink was taking its toll. He died in 1927 of heart disease complicated by alcoholism. He was only 41.

Fanny Hill case   American obscenity prosecution

The American edition of John Cleland's English classic of soft pornography, *Fanny Hill, or the Memoirs of a Woman of Pleasure*, became the subject of the first obscenity trial of a book in the United States.

In 1821, 71 years after *Fanny Hill* first appeared in Britain, printer Peter Holmes, the American publisher of the book, was found guilty of smut peddling. Three years later, the state got around to writing a law that defined and outlawed obscenity. In 1963 G. P. Putnam's Sons republished the work and was promptly taken to court. After winning in the first court and then losing in the second, *Fanny Hill* won her final emancipation by a vote of four to three in New York's Court of Appeals.

Farrington brothers   outlaws

It has been estimated that at least 25 young Missourians turned to a life of crime when they saw the public adulation that was lavished on the James brothers. Two of these were the Farrington brothers, Levi and Hilary. Like the James boys, they were ex-Confederate guerrillas who had taken part in Quantrill's bloody raid on Lawrence, Kan. Later, they rode under George Todd. These two bearded, hardly literate giants witnessed what "ole Jesse and Frank were adoin" and saw no reason they couldn't do the same. They, however, lacked the flair of the James brothers, being nothing more than brutish killers, and never basked in the hero worship accorded to Jesse and Frank. Nonetheless, they were skillful riders and gunmen and their crimes cut a wide swath from Missouri and Tennessee down into Mississippi.

In 1870 they teamed up with another bloody pair, William Barton and William Taylor; flagged down the Mobile and Ohio flyer at Union City; and robbed the express car of $20,000. As they continued their depredations and recruited new members to their gang, Pinkertons and express company detectives picked up their trail and finally cornered the gang in a hideout deep in the canebreaks at Lester's Landing in Mississippi. The raiders, headed by William Pinkerton, the son of the founder of the agency, and Pat O'Connell, considered the best express company detective of the time, captured five gang members after a gunfight but then discovered the Farringtons had pulled out two hours earlier. Weeks later, Pinkerton and O'Connell cornered Hilary Farrington in a farmhouse in Verona, Mo. and captured him after a daylong gun battle. Extraditing him to Union City, Tenn., his captors placed Hilary aboard the sternwheeler *Illinois*. When he attempted a nighttime escape, he fell overboard in a battle with William Pinkerton and was crushed to death by the vessel's stern paddle.

In 1871 Levi Farrington was taken by the Pinkertons during a hand-to-hand battle in the town square in Farmingdale, Ill. Crowds gathered, but unlike the admiration people showed for the James boys, they wanted to string Levi up. The Pinkertons held off the mob at gunpoint and got their prisoner back to Union City. They could have saved themselves the trip, however. A large band of nightriders seized Levi Farrington from the sheriff and hanged him from a tree near the main gate of the Union City cemetery.

Faurot, Joseph A.   (1872–1942)   father of fingerprinting

Joseph Faurot is regarded as the father of fingerprinting in the United States, although he was a lowly member of the New York Police Department when the system was introduced in St. Louis. However, it was Faurot's insistence on the system that shook up the brass of the nation's biggest, and often most complacent, police department and literally forced it into accepting the new scientific method.

Fingerprinting had been an attraction at the 1904 Louisiana Purchase Exposition in St. Louis, where it was demonstrated by experts sent from London's Scotland Yard. St. Louis police officials were so impressed they sent a man to London to study the method and subsequently installed the first American system. Meanwhile, a 32-year-old detective sergeant in the New York Police Department, Joseph Faurot, was bombarding his superiors with proposals that they adopt the system. Faurot finally prevailed upon Commissioner William McAdoo to grant him permission to go to London and study fingerprinting. When Faurot returned, he discovered McAdoo was no longer commissioner and that the current brass had little interest in new methods.

Faurot had realized the enormous value of fingerprinting in Europe and refused to stop lobbying for its use in New York. He got his first break when the suite of a socially prominent person in the Waldorf-Astoria was burglarized. Important pressure was put on the police to solve the theft, and Faurot was given permission to fingerprint several suspects. The prints were sent on to Scotland Yard, and in due course, one of the suspects was identified as Henry Johnson, an international hotel jewelry thief. Johnson was intensively questioned and finally confessed, leading officers to the hidden loot.

In 1908 Faurot used fingerprinting to crack a murder case. A nurse named Nellie Quinn had been choked to death in her room. By the time Faurot arrived, the policeman on the beat and several others had entered the premises, and since they understood nothing about fingerprints, they touched many things in the room. Fortunately, they had not touched a whiskey bottle on the table. Faurot confirmed this by matching the officers' prints against those on the bottle. Some of the prints were the nurse's but there was another set of fingerprints that could not be identified. After fingerprinting friends and neighbors of the slain woman, he discovered the owner of the prints—a man—on the bottle. Since the nurse had bought the bottle the evening of the murder, that placed the murderer in the murder room on the evening of the crime. Confronted with the evidence, the man confessed.

The shadow on Faurot's accomplishments in both cases was that convictions were obtained because of the culprit's confessions and not because of the fingerprint evidence. Until convictions could be obtained on the basis of fingerprint evidence, the technique had an uncertain future. The precedent-setting case turned out to be a prosaic burglary in 1911. A suspect taken into custody had an alibi, but Faurot's fingerprinting method identified him as the guilty party. The trial judge seemed dubious about the worth of fingerprint evidence. Faurot, however, offered a demonstration. While he left the courtroom, some 15 men in the room (various court attendants and lawyers) pressed their fingers on an ink pad and then put their prints on paper. One of the 15 then put his prints on a glass. When Faurot returned to the room, he quickly matched the prints on the glass with the correct set on paper. Both the judge and jury were impressed, and the defendant was found guilty.

Fingerprint evidence had been tested by a court and accepted, and a new method of identification had been firmly established. Armed with this success, Faurot went on to establish the police department's fingerprint bureau and through the years provided the evidence that convicted thousands of criminals. By the time he retired in 1930, he had risen to the rank of deputy commissioner and had been acknowledged as the father of fingerprinting in the United States.

See also: FINGERPRINTING.

fence   receiver of stolen property

Without fences to buy stolen goods, criminals would find many types of thefts unprofitable. Yet despite their key position in the world of crime, the receivers of stolen property seldom face much risk. During one year in New York State some 6,400 persons were arrested for criminal possession of stolen property, but only 30 of those arrested actually served time. This tolerance of fences is all the more incredible in light of the fact that many criminals work in collaboration with them and "steal to order" what the fence can resell at the time. Obviously, rather than just a passive link in the commission of a crime, the fence is often closer to being its

mastermind. Unquestionably, fences enjoy most of the fruits of crime, generally paying the professional thief no more than 25 percent of the loot's value, and much less if the crime has generated "heat."

The operation of one California fence ring, which became the largest collector of stolen property throughout the entire state, was so lucrative that the head of the ring used mink stoles for rugs in his office and lined the dashboard of his car with other expensive stolen furs.

Fagin-type receivers of stolen goods appeared in America during earliest colonial days; an individual named Silas is recorded as one of the pioneering practitioners in Massachusetts, being subjected to floggings, brandings and the stocks in the 1660s and 1670s. Possibly the most important stamping ground for fences in the 19th century was the so-called Thieves' Exchange in New York City during the 1860s, a dive located near Houston Street and Broadway. Each night criminals and fences would gather there to lift glasses in crooked camaraderie while dickering over price. The exchange operated with the connivance of the politicians and police, who were paid by the fences for the right to operate. Journalists of the period alleged that some important politicians and police officials even garnered commissions on a fence's gross business. Criminals with an illegal plan could even shop around for a fence to furnish the capital needed for the enterprise. Despite frequent exposés, the Thieves' Exchange prospered until the turn of the century, when police shut it down because of public outrage.

The most prosperous fence in American history was Fredericka "Marm" Mandelbaum, who from 1854 to 1884 so dominated the fencing racket that she has been described as the first in the country to put crime on a syndicated basis. She bossed the operations of several gangs of bank robbers, blackmailers and confidence men and even operated special schools for advanced courses in burglary and safe blowing. She also ran special classes for young boys and girls to learn the art of pickpocketing and sneak thievery. She enjoyed great esteem in the underworld as one who never betrayed a confidence. A leading thief, Banjo Pete Emerson, once said, "She was scheming and dishonest as the day is long, but she could be like an angel to the worst devil as long as he played square with her."

Marm's chief competitor was a stooped little man named Travelling Mike Grady, who went about the streets of New York with a peddler's box on his shoulder. It was always stuffed with such items as bonds, pearls and diamonds, all stolen and purchased from crooks by Travelling Mike, who never ventured forth with less than $10,000 in cash to buy purloined loot. It should be noted that neither Marm Mandelbaum nor

Travelling Mike ended up in prison but rather lived out their time in lavish retirement, although Marm was inconvenienced to the point where she was forced to flee to the safety of Canada.

Today, police have found that maintaining their own fence operation and using undercover officers to pose as big-time buyers are excellent ways to round up professional thieves and recover stolen property. Such antifencing ruses are funded by federal grants from the Law Enforcement Assistance Administration. During the life of one such front in Washington, D.C. in the 1960s, the police took in a huge amount of stolen items at extremely low prices. Some of the loot included televisions, radios, stereos, cameras, sound recorders, antiques, kitchen appliances, typewriters, calculators, guns, cars, credit cards, savings bonds and government checks. After many months of operation, the supposed fancers held a party to celebrate the success of their ring, and the thieves showed up in droves to take part. They arrived in luxury cars, many in black tie. As they passed from one room to the next, uniformed police placed them under arrest and hauled them off to jail. It was most disconcerting to the thieves, who thought all along they were working with Mafia figures.

See also: GRADY GANG, FREDERICKA "MARM" MANDELBAUM, STING, THIEVES' EXCHANGE.

fence stealing

Although widely practiced, the stripping of fences is hardly considered much of a crime and is often the work of children seeking supplies for building a clubhouse. But in past years it was a serious problem, being among other things a way to obtain firewood and a method to encourage a farmer's stock to "stray."

In this sense, fence stealing was considered a serious offense that called for very severe penalties. A 1659 ordinance in New Amsterdam reveals how stern the colonial punishment for the crime was. It read, "No person shall strip the fences of posts or rails under penalty of being whipped and branded, and for the second, of punishment with the cord until death ensues."

Ferguson Rangers   Texas Ranger cronyism

Probably the most scandalized law enforcement agency in American history was the Texas Rangers from 1933 to 1935, when every officer in service was fired and replaced by cronies of newly elected Gov. Miriam "Ma" Ferguson. The force thus became known as Ferguson Rangers. The Texas Rangers had made the mistake of becoming politicized to the extent of openly backing Gov. Ross Sterling in his race for reelection against former Gov. Miriam Ferguson. Ma Ferguson won and, as one of her first acts, dismissed all 44 rangers in service and put in her close political friends.

During the previous 15 years the Texas Rangers had received considerable criticism for the way they allegedly did and did not enforce law and order, but the record of the Ferguson Rangers made any previous abuses pale. Within a year a Ranger captain had been charged with theft and embezzlement, another had been convicted of murder and several others were found to have seized illegal gambling equipment and set up their own illicit betting enterprises. Undismayed by these scandals, Gov. Ferguson handed out special commissions, and in time, there were 3,000 active "Special Rangers," with the right to carry weapons and exercise other police privileges.

In 1935, following the succession of James Allred to the governorship the Texas Rangers lost their independent status and were made part of the Department of Public Safety. In a thorough housecleaning, their numbers were reduced to about 40.

See also: TEXAS RANGERS.

Fernandez, Manuel (?–1873) murderer

A young troublemaker named Manuel Fernandez stabbed a Yuma, Ariz. storekeeper to death in December 1872. Yet, he avoided the obligatory and rapid lynching that normally would have followed, especially for Mexicans. Instead, he became the first man to be hanged legally in the Arizona Territory. By all accounts, the long waiting period was difficult to bear for a number of "rope-minded" citizens, but after Fernandez was duly and properly executed on May 3, 1873, the general opinion was that the delay hadn't "hurt too bad."

Fernandez, Raymond Martinez   See MARTHA BECK.

Ferris, Danny   See JAILHOUSE SHOPPING NETWORK.

Fields, Vina (?1865–?) madam

The concept of the madam with the "heart of gold" is, of course, more fancy than fact; yet if one woman of that calling had to be singled out for the characteristic, it would be Vina Fields, a black madam who flourished during the last two decades of the 19th century in Chicago. About her, even the antivice muckraker William T. Stead conceded, "She is probably as good as any woman can be who conducts so bad a business."

Vina Fields maintained the largest brothel of the day in Chicago, one that generally had no fewer than 40 prostitutes and as many as 70 or 80 during the World's Fair of 1893. Madame Fields employed black harlots only but allowed patronage by whites only. From 1885 until just about the end of the century, she operated a fancy house on Custom House Place, and during that time, no man ever complained to the police about being robbed there. Vina insisted she never paid a penny in protection money, which may have been the only time she told a lie. Hers was the one house in Chicago where black prostitutes could count on getting a fair shake, drawing a far larger percentage of the take than elsewhere. Because of her generosity, she could also maintain strict discipline. In a famous book on corruption and vice, *If Christ Came to Chicago*, Stead wrote, "The rules and regulations of the Fields house, which are printed and posted in every room, enforce decorum and decency with pains and penalties which could be hardly more strict if they were drawn up for the regulation of a Sunday School." Fields permitted no drunkenness, no soliciting from the windows and no overexposure in the parlors or hallways. She held a court every three days, and girls who had broken rules were fined, ordered to perform menial duties, banned from the parlor or, for major infractions, evicted from the house.

Stead further commented:

Strange though it may appear, [she] has acquired the respect of nearly all who know her. An old experienced police matron emphatically declared that 'Vina is a good woman,' and I think it will be admitted by all who know her, that she is probably as good as any woman can be who conducts so bad a business. . . . She is bringing up her daughter who knows nothing of the life of her mother in the virginal seclusion of a convent school, and she contributes of her bounty to maintain her unfortunate sisters whose husbands down south are among the hosts of unemployed. Nor is her bounty confined to her own family. Every day this whole winter [1893–94] she had fed a hungry, ragged regiment of the out-of-work. The day before I called, 201 men had had free dinners of her providing."

There are many tales, though all unsubstantiated, about what became of Vina Fields in her later years.

See also: WILLIAM T. STEAD.

Finch, Mrs. Barbara (1923–1959) murder victim

The murder of Mrs. Barbara Finch by her California doctor husband and his mistress was one of the most sensational in recent decades. The case required three jury trials before a verdict was given.

Dr. Raymond Bernard Finch and his wife were prominent in social circles in Los Angeles and popular members of the Los Angeles Tennis Club. By 1957 the couple had drifted apart and Dr. Finch, using another name, rented an apartment where he regularly met with a 20-year-old married ex-model, Carole Tregoff. In 1958 Tregoff got a divorce, but Finch's wife refused to give him one.

Finally, she decided to seek a divorce. Under California divorce laws, when the grounds for divorce are desertion, cruelty or adultery, the courts can award all the property to the innocent party instead of dividing it equally. Suing on grounds of desertion, Mrs. Finch claimed all the property, including her husband's interest in a medical center, and demanded heavy alimony. If she won, Dr. Finch would have been left in virtual poverty.

Thereafter, according to later court testimony, Dr. Finch and Tregoff sought to obtain compromising evidence against the doctor's wife and, for that purpose, involved a petty crook named John Patrick Cody to make love to her. Later, according to Cody, he was offered money to kill Mrs. Finch. Cody said Carole Tregoff offered him $1,400 to shoot her. He claimed she stated, "If you don't kill her, Dr. Finch will . . . and if he won't, I'll do it."

On July 18, 1959 Dr. Finch and Carole Tregoff drove to the Finch home for a conference with Mrs. Finch. There was a shot, and Mrs. Finch lay dead on the driveway with a .38 bullet in her back. Dr. Finch's version was that during an argument his wife had pointed a gun at him and he had seized it and tossed it over his shoulder. The gun went off, he said, and fatally wounded his wife.

The prosecution's version was somewhat different. It claimed the pair had come to the Finch home with a so-called murder kit for the purpose of killing Mrs. Finch. The first plan, according to the prosecution, called for injecting an air bubble in her bloodstream; and if that failed, injecting a lethal dose of sodium seconal. An alternate plan, the prosecution contended, involved driving the unconscious woman over a cliff in back of the house. The prosecution contended the shooting was deliberate and presented scientific testimony that "the woman was in flight" when shot.

Dr. Finch took the stand and, with tears coursing down his face, gave a heartrending version of his wife's last words to him after the "accident." They were: "I'm sorry . . . I should have listened to you . . . I love you . . . take care of the kids. . . ." It was a rather novel defense, almost as though the victim was apologizing for being killed.

Nevertheless, the doctor's testimony was effective, resulting in a hung jury after eight days of deliberations. Finch and Tregoff, who had not spoken a word

311

to each other throughout the trial, were retried a second time and again the jury failed to agree. On the third try, Dr. Finch was convicted of first-degree murder and Carole Tregoff of second-degree. Both were sentenced to life imprisonment. As they left the courtroom, Finch tried to kiss Tregoff but she turned away. Carole Tregoff was paroled in 1969; she never answered any of the many letters Finch wrote to her. Dr. Finch was freed in 1971.

fingerprint forgeries   See WILLIAM DE PALMA.

fingerprinting

The art of fingerprinting as a means of identification is a very old one. The ancient Chinese used a thumbprint in clay as an identifying seal, and a clay tablet in a British museum tells the tale of a Babylonian officer ordered to make arrests and obtain the defendants' fingerprints. In 1882 a geologist in New Mexico put his fingerprint on his claims and then signed his name across the print to protect against forgery. It was probably this incident that got Mark Twain to solve a crime through the use of fingerprints in a remarkable story called *Pudd'nhead Wilson*.

In the story, lawyer Pudd'nhead Wilson tells the jury:

Every human being carries with him from his cradle to his grave certain physical marks which do not change their character, and by which he can always be identified—and that without shade of doubt or question. These marks are his signature, his physiological autograph, so to speak, and this autograph cannot be counterfeited, nor can he disguise it or hide it away, nor can it become illegible by the wear and mutations of time . . . . This autograph consists of the delicate lines or corrugations with which Nature marks the insides of the hands and the soles of the feet. If you will look at the balls of your fingers . . . you will observe that these dainty curving lines lie close together, like those that indicate the borders of oceans in maps, and that they form various clearly-defined patterns, such as arches, circules, long curves, whorles, etc., and that these patterns differ on the different fingers. . . . One twin's patterns are never the same as his fellow-twin's patterns. . . . You have often heard of twins who were so exactly alike that when dressed alike their own parents could not tell them apart. Yet there was never a twin born into this world that did not carry from birth to death a sure identifier in this mysterious and marvelous natal autograph.

Twain accepted the worth of fingerprints long before any police department in this country or elsewhere did. Beginning in the 1880s, the primary identification method used by all police agencies was a system developed by the French criminologist Alphonse Bertillon. The Bertillon system compiled information on several physical features of a subject based on the assumption that a combination of measurements, photos and other

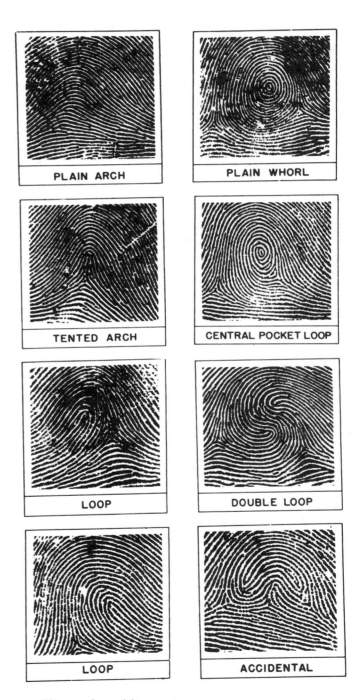

An FBI sampling of fingerprint patterns.

data would always be distinct for different individuals. It was a theory considered valid for only two decades, however. In 1903 two American criminals imprisoned in Leavenworth, one named William West and the other Willie West, were found to have the same Bertillon measurements. That discovery greatly undercut the validity of the Bertillon system. The fingerprints of the two Wests were taken and found to be totally dissimilar.

Scotland Yard pioneered development of a fingerprinting system in the late 1890s, and in 1904 a New York detective sergeant, Joseph A. Faurot, began to press for its adoption in this country, eventually becoming known as the father of American fingerprinting. Today, it is estimated that well over 1,000 fugitives a month are identified through fingerprint files. Unquestionably, numerous criminals would give the bulk of their loot to change their prints. That, however, is an almost impossible task, unless one is willing to destroy not only the prints but most of the fingers as well. Gangster John Dillinger paid a renegade doctor $5,000 to sear his prints with acid. Yet within a few agonizing weeks, after the doctor had wisely moved on, identical ridges grew back in place. After Dillinger was killed by FBI agents, identification of his body was a simple matter for fingerprint technicians.

The only American criminal known to have successfully obliterated his prints was a minor bandit named Robert James "Roscoe" Pitts, who accomplished the task in the 1940s. Once he became famous as the "man without fingerprints," however, he was a marked man. Whenever a robbery occurred in which no prints were found, Pitts automatically became a top suspect. He eventually was apprehended for a robbery and sent to prison for 20 years. While Pitts had eliminated his fingerprints, he had failed to prevent his identification. The doctor he used had erased his fingerprints down to the first joint, but when Pitts had been officially fingerprinted, the prints had inadvertently extended below the crease into the second joint. That area is not normally considered in the classification process, but it is actually just as unique as the primary, first-joint print. Pitts never would have been able to deny his identity.

The facts and fallacies about fingerprints are legion. Only in the movies do detectives pick up guns with handkerchiefs or by sliding a pencil under the trigger guard so as not to smudge fingerprints. Nor do killers wipe a "rod" clean after using it. In not one case in 1,000 will a usable set of prints be found on a gun.

Normally, the finding of a single fingerprint is useless since fingerprints must be classified by full sets and a partial would create an incredible search problem unless it belonged to a person who was already a sus-

pect. Yet a single print found on a gas can put the FBI on the trail of Doc Barker and his gang, who had abducted a banker and released him. The banker remembered the men had refueled their car on the road with gas cans. The FBI found the discarded cans and got one clear impression, that of Doc Barker.

Once, a small portion of a print proved sufficient to doom a criminal in Alabama. A woman was criminally assaulted one night, fighting her attacker until beaten unconscious. When a doctor later treated her wounds, he found a small piece of skin lodged between her lower teeth. Under a microscope, its whorls suggested it might be a piece of a man's fingertip. A number of suspects were brought in and one had a bit of flesh torn from his left middle finger. The man, Major Preston, insisted he had injured his finger at work. His fingerprints were on file, however, and when the whorls on the bit of flesh were compared with the print of his left middle finger on the card, they matched exactly. Preston was convicted and executed.

Actually, duplicate fingerprints could possibly turn up. An expert once estimated the chances were "one in two quadrillion; a sum representing one million times the earth's population." Probably half the population of the United States have their fingerprints on file somewhere and thus could have their identities traced. An "inquiring reporter" once queried a half-dozen persons on the street about whether they had any objection to universal fingerprinting. Only two of the six didn't object, and one was a policeman. One of the others said, "Who knows, I might yet become another Dillinger . . . I wouldn't want my prints on file." Despite intensive campaigns, especially by the FBI, in favor of universal fingerprinting based on the value it has had in identifications following disasters, the American people have been notoriously unimpressed.

A not unfounded fear is the possibility of the planting of fingerprints. Experts have demonstrated how it could be done, and while some fingerprint men claim they can spot such plants, tests made to verify such claims have turned up a rating of less than 50 percent, statistically below even the law of averages.

See also: JOSEPH A. FAUROT, "WEST BROTHERS."

Fink, Isidor (c. 1899–1932) suspected murder victim

The killing of Isidor Fink on March 9, 1929 in a tiny little laundry he operated on East 132nd Street in New York City has remained one of the most perplexing in the history of American crime. Alfred Hitchcock wrote about it and undoubtedly toyed with the idea of filming it but failed to come up with a logical solution. Ben Hecht wrote *The Mystery of the Fabulous Laundryman*, but that short story hardly pleased the locked-room addicts seeking a plausible explanation.

Fink kept the doors and windows of his one-room laundry locked at all times because of fear of robberies. A woman napping next door heard three shots in rapid succession and then something heavy, like a body, thud to the floor. She called police. When Patrolman Albert Kattenborn arrived, he found the door bolted and was unable to enter. He lifted a small boy up to the transom, but the boy found it locked. He smashed the glass, climbed inside and opened the door. Fink was dead on the floor. Patrolman Kattenborn let no one else enter and made the boy wait until detectives showed up. Fink had two bullet wounds in the chest and one in the left wrist. The immediate conclusion of the detectives was that he must have committed suicide since it was evident that no one could have gotten out of the room.

The problem with that solution was the suicide gun. It was nowhere to be found, and Fink had died almost instantly. The small boy was searched to make sure he had not secreted the weapon on his person. Then the police set about searching the room. Perhaps Fink had tied the gun to some sort of elastic device that pulled it out of sight. They literally ripped the room apart. No gun. No loose boards. No hidden panels. No trap doors. A squad of specially picked sleuths was sent up from headquarters to solve the mystery. At first, they worked with vigor, then with some irritation and finally in total bewilderment. Reluctantly, the police accepted the fact that they had a case of murder, one that through the years became a favorite of the Sunday supplements. About the most profound conclusion ever to be drawn from the Fink case was the published comment of a detective after a year's work on the puzzle: "That damn two-for-a-cent mystery gives me the creeps!"

fire bombing   See APACHE INDIAN JOB.

Fish, Albert (1870–1936) mass murderer and cannibal
A harmless-looking house painter in New York City, Albert Fish was a degenerate who admitted molesting more than 400 children over a span of 20 years. Fish, labeled by the press as the "inhuman monster," was described by one shocked psychiatrist as a man of "unparalleled perversity. There was no known perversion that he did not practice and practice frequently."

Fish had a personal and married life that was odd, to say the least. He enjoyed sticking needles into himself, spanking himself with a nail-studded paddle or having children beat him until he bled. He appreciated children because of their innocence and because, as he once put

it, "They don't tell." Certainly, the 15 to 17 children he murdered never told.

He got married when he was 28. It lasted for about 20 years before his wife ran off with a half-wit. She returned about a year later and asked to move back in with her lover. Fish said she could stay but her lover could not. Later, he discovered his wife had hidden her lover in the attic. He kicked him out and again told his wife she could stay, but she went off with her lover and Fish never saw her again. Fish had six children. They were aware their father was a bit peculiar, but he was kind to them and never beat them. The children had seen him use his nailed paddle on himself, but they assumed he must be sane, if somewhat eccentric, since they knew he had been under psychiatric observation a number of times and had always been discharged by the doctors.

His occupation as a house painter allowed him to move from town to town and gave him access to cellars and deserted buildings. By his own count, he committed offenses in at least 23 states. He had some close calls. In St. Louis Fish had almost been caught with a small boy he had been torturing for days but escaped just in time. There were narrow squeaks in Virginia and in Delaware and several in New York. Children disappeared with a kindly old man never to be seen again; others were found brutally mutilated. He was questioned several times but was never a serious suspect.

At a very minimum, he killed and ate at least 15 children. His last such victim apparently was a 12-year-old New York City girl, Grace Budd, whom he lured from her parents in 1928 by telling them he was bringing her to a party a friend was giving for a daughter. He cut up her body and cooked the parts in a stew with onions and carrots. It took him nine days to eat most of her. He buried what was left. It was six years before he was caught for that crime. The police were baffled by the case, but Fish could not resist writing Mrs. Budd to tell her what he'd done. He didn't sign the letter, but the police readily traced him. Fish acted as though he had been waiting for them for a long time. He immediately confessed and led them to a spot in White Plains where they found the girl's bones. He also confessed to a number of additional cannibal murders.

Fish's trial consisted of a long parade of psychiatric specialists. Only Dr. Frederic Wertham and two other defense experts insisted he was insane. Fish was judged guilty and sane enough to die in the electric chair. The prospect excited Fish. "What a thrill that will be if I have to die in the electric chair," he said with a broad smile. "It will be the supreme thrill. The only one I haven't tried." When he did go to the chair on January 16, 1936, he was described by the press as being positively joyful. He even helped adjust the electrodes when he was being strapped down.

The newspapers had one more ghoulish report for their readers. The first massive jolt of electricity failed to kill Fish. The theory was that the 400 plus needles he had inserted into his body over the years had apparently caused a short circuit. A second potent jolt was needed to complete the job.

Fisher, John King (1854–1884) gunman and lawman

John King Fisher was one of the 19th century's controversial gunmen for whom Texas was famous or infamous, becoming a popular hero to some and a callous murderer to others. Fisher once shot a man in the head because he wanted to see if a bullet would bounce off his bald pate. Perhaps his mean streak was best illustrated by the sign he erected at a crossroads when he established his own spread in southern Texas: "This is King Fisher's Road—Take the other one." The sign became something of a landmark and was considered no idle threat. In 1878 Fisher said he was responsible for killing seven men in gunfights, not counting Mexicans.

Fisher's first scrape with the law occurred in 1870, when at the age of 16 he drew a two-year term for robbery but served only four months. Gaining a pardon, he worked as a cowboy for a few years and then started his own spread, which became headquarters for an unsavory crew of rustlers, killers and deadbeats. He formed an alliance with Mexican rustlers, but after a dispute on a division of the spoils, he pistol-whipped one, shot a second as he went for his gun and then gunned down two others who were just sitting on a fence. During Fisher's "ranching" days he reputedly formed a partnership with an *insurrecto* named Porfirio Díaz, who later became president-dictator of Mexico, whereby Díaz delivered stolen Mexican cattle to Fisher and received Fisher's rustled American beef. On both sides of the border there were stock buyers who were not particularly mindful of brands if they were from the other country.

Fisher frequently was arrested on murder charges and was subject to considerable Texas Ranger harassment, but he was inevitably found not guilty or the charges were dismissed for lack of evidence. Then King Fisher made a sudden transformation: he got religion and in 1881 became a lawman, appointed deputy sheriff of Uvalde County. There were those who insisted he backslid a bit now and then, but in 1883 he made plans to run for sheriff the following year. In March 1884 Fisher went to Austin, the state capital, on official business and ran into an old gunman buddy, the crazed Ben Thompson. The pair rode together to San Antonio, where they entered the Vaudeville Variety Theater, a gambling hall whose proprietor, Jack Harris, Thompson had murdered some two years previously.

Thompson and Fisher had a drink at the bar and then repaired to a box upstairs to watch the variety show. They were joined in the box by bouncer Jacob Coy and two of Harris' former partners, Billy Simms and Joe Foster. Thompson made several nasty remarks about the Harris killing and then playfully jammed his six-gun into Foster's mouth, whereupon bouncer Coy moved in and seized the cylinder. There was a moment of tense silence, and Fisher made a remark about leaving before things got out of hand. Suddenly, there was a blaze of fire and Thompson was dead, with nine slugs in him. King Fisher went down in a hail of 13 bullets.

Some suggested that but for his chance meeting with Thompson, the reformed King Fisher would have lived out a full life as a respected rancher and lawman. Not everyone was sorry about Fisher's demise. A woman whose son Fisher had killed came to the Uvalde cemetery on every anniversary of her son's death, set a brush fire atop Fisher's grave and danced "with devilish glee" around it.

See also: BEN THOMPSON.

Fitzpatrick, James "The Sandy Flash" (c. 1760–1787) early highwayman

The first of America's "romantic" criminals, James Fitzpatrick was a handsome young Irishman who was for a time a member of the Doane gang, the first important band of criminals in this country, before splitting off to form his own gang in the early 1780s. Preying on wealthy landowners mainly in Chester and Delaware Counties, Pa., he cut a dashing figure, so much so that he would become the "Sandy Flash" of Bayard Taylor's *Story of Kennett*, a 19th-century best-seller. By 1785 a reward of 200 pounds, a king's ransom in those days, was placed on the Sandy Flash, but fear of betrayal and arrest did not faze him. One day, with the kind of daring that Jesse James would exhibit a century later, Fitzpatrick calmly rode his big black stallion into the center of Chester, Pa. and took his meal at the Unicorn Tavern. Present at the bar were several members of the posses searching for him. Fitzpatrick bought drinks for his hunters, who regaled the tavern crown with what they would do to the Sandy Flash when they captured him. Fitzpatrick could get away with such feats of courage because, like Jesse James, he was a man without a face, with no unusual features by which to be recognized. However, his luck eventually ran out and he was cornered by a posse and taken prisoner. The fair maidens of two counties wept, we are told, when the Sandy Flash was hanged in the Old Chester Jail in January 1787.

See also: DOANE GANG.

Fitzpatrick, Richie (1880–1905) gangster and murderer

One of the few non-Jews to achieve high stature in the Eastman gang, the last great Jewish outfit to dominate crime in New York City, Richie Fitzpatrick, a lethal young Irishman, won the appreciation of leader Monk Eastman because of his great cunning at killing. Once assigned by Eastman to eradicate the owner of a Chrystie Street dive, Fitzpatrick pulled a cunning ruse long before the brothers Corleone thought of it in *The Godfather*—he had a gun planted in the toilet of the dive. Immediately suspect when he walked in, Fitzpatrick permitted himself to be searched and then informed the dive operator that Eastman had ordered him assassinated. He said he was defecting from the Eastman ranks and was thus willing to aid the dive owner. Fitzpatrick's story was accepted, and he joined in a round of drinks, swearing allegiance to his new allies. His next move was to heed the call of nature. When Fitzpatrick emerged from the toilet, he shot the dive operator dead and fled before his henchman could react.

When Eastman was taken by the law for a 1904 attempted robbery, the leadership of the gang fell to an uneasy combination of Fitzpatrick and Kid Twist, so named because of his criminal cunning. It was soon obvious that the pair would have to settle the leadership problem violently, and the gang began to divide into warring factions. The Kid suggested a peace conference in a Chrystie Street dive. Fitzpatrick accepted with alacrity, and the underworld awaited to see what deceit he would conceive to eliminate his foe. Unfortunately for Fitzpatrick the Kid too was noted for his trickery. As the talks began, the lights suddenly went out and a revolver blazed. When the police reached the scene, Fitzpatrick was alone in the back room with his arms folded across his chest and a bullet in his heart.

The underworld applauded the treachery; Kid Twist, the saying went, "had twisted first."

See also: KID TWIST.

Five Points New York City crime district

Every account of crime in old New York is replete with references to the Five Points and the gangs and crimes it spawned. It was the incubator of crime in the city for an entire century. Its early history was tame enough, being a relatively homey place at the junction of Cross, Anthony, Little Water, Orange and Mulberry Streets. In the center of the Five Points was Paradise Square where the poor people of the city came for their fresh air and recreation. By the 1820s the area had turned first seedy and then vile, and the Five Points became a hellhole of impoverished humanity that produced crime in awesome, if predictable, numbers. By the time of the Civil War, the Points and Paradise Square area housed no less than 270 saloons, and many times that number of dance halls, houses of prostitution and green-groceries that dispensed more liquor than vegetables or other provisions. It was already described as a slum section far more wicked than even the Whitechapel district of London.

Perhaps Charles Dickens offered the most graphic picture of the district in his *American Notes*:

Let us go on again, and plunge into the Five Points. This is the place; these narrow ways diverging to the right and left, and reeking everywhere with dirt and filth. Such lives as are led here, bear the same fruit here as elsewhere. The coarse and bloated faces at the doors have counterparts at home and all the whole world over. Debauchery has made the very houses prematurely old. See how the rotten beams are tumbling down, and how the patched and broken windows seem to scowl dimly, like eyes that have been hurt in drunken frays. Many of these pigs live here. Do they ever wonder why their masters walk upright instead of going on all-fours, and why they talk instead of grunting?

So far, nearly every house is a low tavern, and on the barroom walls are colored prints of Washington and Queen Victoria, and the American Eagle. Among the pigeon-holes that hold the bottles are pieces of plate glass and colored paper, for there is in some sort a taste for decoration even here. And as seamen frequent these haunts, there are maritime pictures by the dozen; of partings between sailors and their lady-loves; portraits of William of the ballad and his black-eyed Susan; of Will Watch, the bold smuggler; of Paul Jones, the pirate, and the like; on which the painted eyes of Queen Victoria, and of Washington to boot, rest in a strange companionship. . . .

From every corner, as you glance about you in these dark streets, some figure crawls half-awakened, as if the judgment hour were near at hand, and every obscure grave were giving up its dead. Where dogs would howl to lie men and women and boys slink off to sleep, forcing the dislodged rats to move away in quest of better lodgings. Here, too, are lanes and alleys paved with mud knee-deep; underground chambers where they dance and game; the walls bedecked with rough designs of ships, of forts, and flags, and American Eagles out of number; ruined houses, open to the street, whence through wide gaps in the walls other ruins loom upon the eye, as though the world of vice and misery had nothing else to show; hideous tenements which take their names from robbery and murder; all that is loathsome, drooping and decayed is here.

The teeming Five Points in 1829.

This was the Five Points that gave New York such gangs as the Dead Rabbits, Chichesters, Plug Uglies and Roach Guards and, much later, the dreaded Whyos and the Five Points Gang. From the ranks of the Five Pointers came such fledgling gangsters as Johnny Torrio, Frankie Yale, Lucky Luciano and Al Capone, an impressive result of 100 years of crime breeding.

Today, the old Five Points section takes in parts of Chinatown and Little Italy and a large portion is taken up by Columbus Park. Much of the area consists of decaying housing that the former residents of the Five Points would have considered luxury apartments.

See also: LITTLE WATER STREET, OLD BREWERY.

Five Points Gang   pre-Prohibition New York gang

The last great pre-Prohibition gang in New York City was a 1,500-man collection of eye-gouging terrorists called the Five Points Gang. They carried on in the tradition of those 19th-century cutthroats the Whyos and their predecessors, such as the Dead Rabbits. Bossed by an ex-bantamweight prizefighter, Paul Kelly (né Paolo Antonini Vaccarelli), the gang's gunners and musclemen hired out to businessmen as strikebreakers or to other

mobs as murderers for hire. Probably more modern-day gang leaders emerged from the Five Pointers than any other similar organization.

Kelly's headquarters was in his own New Brighton Dance Hall on Great Jones Street, one of Manhattan's more lavish fleshpots and a mecca for slumming socialites eager to meet a famous gangster. Kelly was an urbane man who spoke fluent Italian, French and Spanish, dressed like a fashion plate and had manners that fit easily into polite society. One of Kelly's top aides was a short youngster, Johnny Torrio, who was to become "the Brain" of the underworld. Under Kelly's direction Torrio developed a subgang called the James Street Gang. His recruits included such ambitious youths as Al Capone, Lucky Luciano and Frankie Yale. All of them were eventually moved up into the Five Pointers, which by 1915 was fast deteriorating because of a lack of rackets to sustain them. Kelly moved off to waterfront labor racketeering and Torrio and Capone to Chicago, while Luciano and Yale remained in New York. All achieved new power and authority through the fruits of Prohibition, a bizarre experiment that provided fresh impetus to gangsterism in America.

See also: JOHN TORRIO.

flaking   police slang for frame-up

This is the term used by policemen and private detectives to describe the framing of an individual. When it is done, the police officers usually justify it as being a service to society; since the victim has committed so many other crimes, it hardly matters if the facts of a crime he is actually charged with are a fabrication.

Naturally, not all law enforcement officials engage in the practice. Deputy Chief Fire Marshal John Barracato of New York relates in a book called *Arson!* about how he was urged to participate in a flaking by another fire marshal and refused. He says, "To me flaking was the most heinous violation of a cop's honor."

Flaking was heavily practiced in the heyday of union organizing in this country, when private detectives framed unionists, often based on the belief that unionism did a worker more harm than good, and that even if a unionist was not actually guilty of a certain act of labor violence, he was undoubtedly responsible for others.

Flamingo Hotel

Known as the casino that made Las Vegas, the Flamingo was the brainchild of mobster Bugsy Siegel. Siegel had come to the West Coast in the late 1930s to handle the mob's betting empire. During the war years he began envisaging a new gambling empire, one that could turn the Nevada sands into gold dust. Gambling was legal in Nevada, where the main attraction was Reno, offering diversion to passing tourists and individuals waiting for their divorce decrees. Siegel saw Las Vegas, then no more than a highway rest stop with some diners, gas stations and a sprinkling of slot machines, as a lavish new gambling oasis.

Bugsy had little trouble convincing Meyer Lansky, treasurer of the national crime syndicate, that his vision was a great idea, and several big city mobs laid out money to build a new casino-hotel, which was to be called the Flamingo, the nickname of Virginia Hill, Siegel's girlfriend and the former bedmate of a number of top mobsters.

During the construction of the Flamingo, Siegel assured building contractor Del E. Webb, who had become nervous about the mob's involvement, that he had nothing to fear because "we only kill each other." At the time Bugsy didn't realize how accurate his statement would prove to be. In the short run, the Flamingo was a disaster, mainly because in the immediate postwar years it was an idea ahead of its time. It would take considerable patience to make it a success, but Siegel had no time. Not only had he failed to produce the profits the mob expected on its $6 million investment, but it appeared he had been skimming off the construction funds. When Siegel refused to make good, indeed could not make good, he was rubbed out.

After Siegel's execution the mob continued to support the Flamingo and eventually saw it grow and prosper. The syndicate poured millions more into Las Vegas, building one successful casino after another.

See also: LAS VEGAS, BENJAMIN "BUGSY" SIEGEL.

floaters   murder victims

Almost every waterfront city in America during the 18th and 19th centuries came to know the term *floater*, used to describe a corpse found floating in the water after meeting with foul play. It was a term imported from England to refer to such crimes, which were common along the Thames in London.

The "floater" capital of the United States was probably Buffalo, N.Y., the terminus of the Erie Canal beginning in 1825. The canal at Buffalo was probably the most crime-infested waterway in the country, and murder victims were dumped there with monotonous regularity. The primary source of this pollution was the dives of Canal Street, whose rear areas extended over the canal, supported by wooden dock pilings. Unsuspecting canalers and lakers were hustled to these places by shills to be trimmed with exorbitant prices. However, if a man had a bundle and was uncooperative about parting with it, he was fed enough knockout drops to put a team of horses to sleep.

He would be hauled into a back room, stripped of all his clothes and dumped naked down a slick wooden chute into the canal with hardly an incriminating splash. Not even the cold water would be enough to revive him, and he eventually would be discovered floating face down in the murky water. The police would know no more than that he had been killed in one of about 100 places on Canal Street and would close the file on the case by listing the victim as a "floater." In one week in 1863 no fewer than 14 floaters were fished out of the canal, five on one morning alone.

floating hog ranches   riverboat bordellos

While from time to time it may have existed in other countries, the floating brothel was fully developed on the Mississippi and later migrated to the waterways of the Far West.

The riverboat brothels made their first appearance along the riverfronts of New Orleans and Natchez-under-the-Hill, where the flatboat crews couldn't even wait to get ashore to enjoy feminine companionship. It was customary for flatboats to be sold once their cargoes were unloaded, and many were turned into bagnios, with prostitutes entertaining customers in narrow cubicles built into the cargo boxes. On occasion there was not even time for that, and the harlots made ready for business on deck with only a tarpaulin cover.

When prostitutes started west, following the frontier, they shunned travel on horseback or by coach, which represented a waste of valuable time. Instead, a typical madam would travel overland with her girls until reaching the next waterway and then purchase any kind of available craft to do business while floating westward. Since the brothels of the West were called hog ranches, such boats were known as floating hog ranches; and it has been said that among the most welcome calls on parts of the frontier was one announcing, "Hog ranch a'coming!"

flogging

Almost from the beginning, the whipping post was a common fixture in colonial America. Since prisons did not come into being until much later, flogging or whipping became the most common form of punishment. Initially, "knout," which was made of knotted rawhide, was used, but it was later replaced by several bound leather strips, referred to as the cat-o'-nine-tails. The development of prisons did not result in a great

Although the whipping post was condemned by reformers after the Revolution as an "English" device, its use continued in the 19th century and, to some extent, in more recent times.

decrease in floggings; since mere confinement was not regarded as a complete enough punishment, offenders got both flogged and imprisoned. Floggings were brutal affairs that often left the victim crippled or, at the very least, permanently scarred. The Quakers were the first to ban the practice, and after the Revolutionary War, reformers made some headway against the whipping post by calling it an "English" device.

The custom died slowly, however, always gaining new life along the frontier, where there was a need for a quick form of justice. In the mining camps of the West, justice had to be fast so that a man could get back to hunting for his fortune, and a malefactor faced either hanging or whipping (or, to a lesser extent, amputation). There simply were no other choices, and in that sense, the whip undoubtedly saved many men from the noose. Floggings virtually disappeared in the 20th century, although Maryland, which had abandoned flogging around the turn of the century, reinstituted it in 1933, at a judge's discretion, for wife beaters, and Delaware continued its use prior to a prison sentence for a number of offenses. But while the custom died outside of prison, it remained a form of punishment for recalcitrant convicts. With the introduction of modern ideas of penology, floggings in prisons tended to be abolished, although a few institutions in the South have admitted its use and others are believed to practice it secretly.

Flores, Juan (1835–1857) outlaw and murderer

Unlike Joaquin Murieta, there was nothing fictional about Juan Flores, one of California's most spectacular and bloodthirsty villains. He was no more than a minor rustler and horse thief when he was put away in San Quentin in 1856. If he had served out his term, he probably would have remained a smalltimer, but Flores and a number of other prisoners escaped. Their method of escape made Flores a well-known figure, held in awe by both the public and other outlaws.

Flores viewed the walls of San Quentin and decided escape that way was difficult and dangerous, if not impossible. But he soon found a weak spot in the prison's security. When the opportunity came, Flores and a group of followers stormed aboard a provision ship tied up at the prison wharf, took control of the vessel and managed to sail off, erratically, but successfully in the end.

The fugitives were unsophisticated, to put it kindly, since they seriously debated sailing their stolen vessel to Australia to "take over the country." Instead, the winds and tides settled the matter, and they landed farther down the California coast. Because of his new fame, Flores, now an outlaw leader, had little trouble recruiting a gang of 50 guns within a few days, including a fairly noted badman named Andrés Fontes. From their hideout in the hills around San Juan Capistrano, the gang terrorized the area south of Los Angeles. They held up stagecoaches and mining supply wagons and invaded small towns to loot stores. Flores also led the gang in kidnapping or waylaying travelers and holding them for ransom. When a German settler wouldn't or couldn't meet his ransom demands, Flores paraded him into the plaza at San Juan Capistrano and summarily shot him to death as a warning to future victims to be more cooperative.

A posse headed by Sheriff James R. Barton went out after Flores in January 1857 and only three members of the posse came back alive. Sheriff Barton was not among them, having been gunned down by Fontes. Since the outlaw attacked Americans and Mexicans alike, he was soon hunted by posses of both nationalities. Led by Don Andrés Pico, a 50-man Mexican-American posse armed with lances routed the gang in one encounter, killing and capturing several of its members, but both Flores and Fontes escaped. On February 1 Flores was finally run to ground by a 40-man posse headed by a Doc Gentry. Held prisoner in a ranch house, Flores broke free but, unarmed, was easily recaptured two days later. He was brought back to Los Angeles, and on February 14, by what was described as a "popular vote," the 22-year-old outlaw was sentenced to hang, the penalty being exacted forthwith. Fontes made it back to Mexico but soon died there in a gunfight.

Flour Riots   New York mob action

The Great New York Fire of December 1835 was largely responsible for bringing on the Panic of 1837, as banks failed and insurance companies went bankrupt, and set the stage for the bloody Flour Riots of 1837. Because many employers in New York could not rebuild, thousands were thrown out of work and economic activities ground slowly down. There was also a falloff in the supplies of food, and by the autumn of 1836 the price of a barrel of flour had risen first to $7 a barrel and then to the unheard-of sum of $12. Actual starvation developed in the slum areas of the Five Points and the Bowery as bread, a staple of the poor's diet, disappeared. By February 1837 the flour depot at Troy, N.Y. had on hand only 4,000 barrels of flour as opposed to the usual 30,000, and it was predicted the price would rise to $20 a barrel or more. New York newspapers denounced as gougers certain merchants who allegedly were hoarding great amounts of grain and flour, waiting for bigger profits.

On February 10 an enormous mob attending a meeting in City Hall Park moved en masse on the big wheat and flour store of Eli Hart & Co. on Washington Street.

Despite defenses by the watchmen, the huge mob battered down the doors and began throwing barrels of flour, sacks of wheat and watchmen out the windows. Several watchmen were seriously injured, and the flour and wheat were spilled out of their containers and scattered by the rioters. They destroyed an estimated 1,000 bushels of wheat and 500 barrels of flour before they were driven off by a large contingent of police supported by two companies of national guardsmen. The rioters scattered, carrying off their dead and wounded. However, the mob simply poured across the city and launched a new attack on the store of S. H. Herrick & Co. Once again, a large amount of flour and wheat was destroyed before the rioters were dispersed. Ironically, very few of the mob made an attempt or even thought to carry off any of the precious flour. And the following day the price of flour increased another dollar.

The Flour Riots did little to alleviate the condition of the poor, who, like their counterparts a century later, simply learned to make do on less until the country emerged from its economic woes.

Floyd, Charles Arthur "Pretty Boy" (1901–1934)
public enemy

Raised in the Cherokee Indian Territory of Oklahoma, Public Enemy No. 1 Charles "Pretty Boy" Floyd was probably the last of the great "social bandits" in America. Just as Billy the Kid was idolized by the poor Mexican herdsmen and villagers of New Mexico, and the James brothers could do no wrong as far as Southern sympathizers in Missouri were concerned, so too was Floyd, the Robin Hood of the Cookson Hills, the hero of the sharecroppers of eastern Oklahoma. As Pa Joad in John Steinbeck's *The Grapes of Wrath* said: "When Floyd was loose and goin' wild, law said we got to give him up—an' nobody give him up. Sometimes a fella got to sift the law."

Unlike other gangsters of the 1920s and the Depression era, Floyd was known as a hard worker who might never have gone wrong if he had been able to find legitimate work. In 1924 things were already tough for sharecroppers in eastern Oklahoma when Floyd married a 16-year-old girl. The following year, his wife pregnant, Floyd turned to crime, got caught pulling a $5,000 payroll robbery and drew a three-year sentence. Released after serving slightly half that time, he committed bank and payroll robberies on his own until hooking up with a few professionals. Working his way east, Floyd and another criminal were arrested in 1930 for the robbery of a Sylvania, Ohio bank, and Floyd was given 10 to 25 years. However, on his way to the Ohio State Penitentiary, Floyd leaped through an open train window, rolled down an embankment just 10 miles from the prison gates and escaped. His fame back in Oklahoma was now established, he would never spend another day behind bars during the rest of his short life.

Floyd made his way to Toledo, Ohio, where he joined forces with Bill "the Killer" Miller, who had been recommended as trustworthy. Floyd's idea was for the pair to go about robbing banks. Bill the Killer—the slayer of at least five men—was four years younger than Floyd but still regarded him as a young punk who needed "seasoning." Miller probably did more than anyone else to turn Floyd from a quick-triggered gunman into a future public enemy. Bill the Killer took Floyd to Michigan, where they limited themselves to $100 to $300 jobs, holding up filling stations and lone farmers. Only then did they move on to some small bank robberies.

By the time they reached Kansas City, the pair had enough of a poke to retire for a time to the splendor and safety of Mother Ash's place, a brothel of considerable standing. Some say it was from the ladies at Mother Ash's that Floyd first picked up his nickname Pretty Boy; others claimed the hill folk had so named him because in his teens he always went around with a pocket comb to neaten up his "slick as axle grease" pompadour. However it started, Floyd always hated the nickname. He did, however, love the girls at Mother Ash's, especially the madam's daughter-in-law, Rose. Bill the Killer was much impressed with Rose's sister, Beulah Bird. This proved to be a deadly double triangle because the sisters were married to Wallace and William Ash, the madam's sons, gangsters in their own right who doubled as bouncers at the establishment. Floyd and his partner solved the problem by murdering both brothers and setting off with the girls in tow on a string of bank robberies.

In Bowling Green, Ohio the quartet attracted police attention. Floyd shot and killed Chief of Police Carl Galliher and wounded another officer, but he was the only one to leave the scene of the shoot-out. Bill the Killer was fatally shot and the two girls were wounded.

Immediately after that incident Floyd returned to Oklahoma and hooked up with 40-year-old George Birdwell, an ex–church deacon turned outlaw. By this time Pretty Boy was regarded as a hero by many in the Cookson Hills and the surrounding area, who saw him as a modern Robin Hood. Rejoicing in this role, Floyd would sprinkle money out the car window as he and Birdwell and whatever aides they recruited rode off after robbing a small-town bank. And inside the bank, he always tried to locate and rip up any first mortgages he could find, hoping they had not as yet been recorded.

The Pretty Boy Floyd legend flowered best in his hometown of Sallisaw. Once he wrote the sheriff there:

"I'm coming to see my mother. If you're smart you won't try to stop me." The sheriff was smart. On another occasion, apparently on a dare, Floyd returned home just to prove he could rob the bank there.

He casually stepped from a car with a machine gun tucked under his arm, and, recognizing some friends lounging outside the barbershop, waved to them.

"How de," one called. "What you doin' in town?"

"How you, Newt," Floyd replied. "Going to rob the bank."

"Give 'em hell," another admirer yelled. Floyd did.

Most Floyd-Birdwell forays were far from picturesque and harmless. They killed often during their robberies, but none of this tarnished Floyd's reputation. He remained a hero while public opinion blamed all the cold-blooded murders on Birdwell.

Late in 1932 Birdwell was killed pulling a bank robbery in which Floyd had not participated. After that, Floyd gravitated back to big-city crime in Kansas City. He became a prime suspect in the notorious Kansas City Massacre of June 18, 1933, in which four lawmen and their prisoner, Frank "Jelly" Nash, were machine-gunned to death. Floyd was incensed by the charge and wrote to the police and newspapers denying any complicity in the massacre. Subsequent disclosures combined with his uncharacteristically vehement denial indicated Floyd probably was innocent.

Innocent or guilty, Floyd had only a little over a year to live. Labeled Public Enemy No. 1, he reportedly was forced to disguise himself as a woman to avoid detection (he had attended Birdwell's funeral in such garb). For a short time, Pretty Boy apparently hooked up with the Dillinger gang, but he generally operated with his own gang, with Adam Richetti as his main partner.

Floyd avoided several police traps set after tips from informers, further building his legend. Meanwhile, his wife was cashing in on the legend: early in 1934 Mrs. Ruby Floyd and her nine-year-old son toured the country promoting a film called Crime Doesn't Pay.

In October 1934 Floyd and Richetti were spotted in a wooded area near Wellsville, Ohio. The local police captured Richetti, but once again Floyd escaped. With Richetti identified, FBI agents under Melvin Purvis descended on the area, determined to tighten the ring on Floyd. On October 22 Floyd was cornered in a cornfield near East Liverpool. He ran in a zigzag pattern across the field, hoping to throw off the lawmen's aim, but went down with eight bullets in him.

Purvis hovered over the dying gangster and said, "You're Pretty Boy Floyd." Even as his life ebbed away, the gangster took offense at the nickname. "I'm Charles Arthur Floyd," he snapped. Another agent asked if he took part in the Kansas City Massacre. Floyd raised himself up and uttered several obscenities, adding, "I won't tell you nothing." He died almost immediately thereafter.

See also: KANSAS CITY MASSACRE, BILL "THE KILLER" MILLER.

Ford, Charles (1858–1884) plotter in the assassination of Jesse James

While it was Charley Ford's brother, Bob, who killed Jesse James, there have always been those who felt that Charley deserves more infamy than he has received.

"I saw the governor," Charley testified at the inquest after James' murder, "and he said $10,000 had been offered for Jesse's death, I went back and told Bob and he said that if I was willing to go, all right. Then we saddled up and rode over to the Samuel place. . . ."

Thus did Charley outline the script for the killing of Jesse James. There is much to indicate that contacting Gov. Thomas T. Crittenden of Missouri was more Charley's idea than Bob's, and many Missourians felt that older brother Charley knew how to manipulate his younger brother. Certainly, things did work out somewhat better for Charley, at least on the surface. He allowed Bob to get the credit, or discredit, for the assassination, but shared equally in the reward and enjoyed an equal share of the profits in their stage appearances as *The Outlaws of Missouri*. Yet, virtually all the boos, catcalls and ripe fruit were directed at brother Bob.

Charley was found dead in his Richmond, Mo. hotel room on May 6, 1884, a suicide, according to the coroner. Quite naturally, his death was thought to be an act of remorse by a man who had been denounced as having one of "the blackest hearts in Creation."

See also: THOMAS T. CRITTENDEN, ROBERT NEWTON FORD, JAMES BROTHERS.

Ford, Emma (c. 1870–?) female crook

Detective Clifton Wooldridge, a turn-of-the-century historian of criminality in Chicago, described a black woman named Emma Ford as the most dangerous strong-arm woman in the city. In point of fact, it would be a close call between Emma and another black woman, Flossie Moore, with whom she maintained a sometimes-friendly, sometimes-unfriendly rivalry.

Emma was a highly successful pickpocket and panel-house worker, but her first love was always violent street muggings. Operating alone or teaming up with her sister, Pearl Smith, Emma would prowl Chicago's South Side and attack men with razors, brass knuckles, knives, guns and sawed-off baseball bats. One of her favorite tactics when a victim did not prove instantly submissive was to slash his knuckles with a razor. Emma Ford had an imposing air about her, being over 6 feet tall and weighing more than 200 pounds. She had both strength and pantherlike agility. According to detective Wooldridge: "She would never submit to arrest except at the point of a revolver. No two men on the police force were strong enough to handle her, and she was dreaded by all of them." While incarcerated in Denver before coming to Chicago, she once seized a prison guard by the hair, lifted him off the floor and plucked out his whiskers one by one. In the Cook County Jail she once held a guard submerged in a water trough until he almost drowned. On another occasion she badly scarred six other female convicts with a hot iron. Every time she was released from jail, the word would spread rapidly, and unhappily, throughout the Levee that "Emma Ford's loose again."

Emma terrorized the South Side area until 1903, when she vanished. Speculation had it that she had been set on by a half-dozen male toughs and sent to her reward, or had returned to Denver, or had gone to New York, or had found a "loving man" and gone off to raise a family. In any event, Chicago did not see her again.

See also: CUSTOM HOUSE PLACE, FLOSSIE MOORE, PANEL HOUSES, CLIFTON WOOLDRIDGE.

Ford, Robert Newton (1860–1892) assassin of Jesse James

Bob Ford was the "dirty rotten coward who shot Mr. Howard" of American ballad folklore, Mr. Howard being the alias used in 1882 by the outlaw Jesse James.

At 22, Bob Ford was a minor member of the James gang as well as a cousin of the Jameses. At the time, the James gang had broken into factions and Jesse was in the process of reorganizing it to rob a bank in Platte City. Jesse didn't trust Bob Ford or his brother Charley, but he was scraping the bottom of the barrel for gunmen. It was a fatal mistake. The Ford brothers were in negotiations, either through Charley or through an intermediary, with Missouri governor Thomas Crittenden, who was offering them pardons and $10,000 in reward money for bringing in Jesse James dead.

When Jesse, or "Mr. Howard," welcomed the brothers into his home on the outskirts of St. Joseph, Mo., he did so wearing his gun harness, which he kept on till he finished breakfast. Then Jesse walked into the parlor to talk to the Fords, by this time a little more relaxed. He took off his holster and tossed it aside and then got up on a chair to straighten out a picture. It was a chance Bob Ford knew he would not likely get again. He drew his single-action Colt .44 and thumbed back the hammer. The slight sound was enough to make Jesse start to turn around. Ford's gun blasted and the famed outlaw tumbled to the floor, instantly dead. His wife, Zerelda, rushed from the kitchen to cradle the bloody head of her dead husband.

Ford said in a stunned voice, still unable to comprehend that he had killed the great outlaw, "It went off accidentally," to which Zerelda James replied, "Yes, I guess it did."

Charley Ford was already out the door to telegraph Gov. Crittenden. Ford quickly surrendered and was tried and convicted of murder. However, the governor, true to his word, pardoned both Fords and saw that Bob got his reward money. Crittenden was sure his actions in the matter would be applauded, but instead, public opinion turned on him, and his political career was wrecked.

Bob Ford and his brother hit the entertainment trail to tell the story of how Jesse James had been killed. Audiences flocked to see the act, mainly to hiss and boo Bob. In September 1882 the pair appeared at Bunnell's Museum in New York. The *Police Gazette* reported: "They will give exhibitions of how they did up Jesse James and sold his cold meat for the reward of $10,000. As the 'Jesse James Avengers' are said to be upon their track, the museum will be put in a state of defense. Manager Starr will wear an armor-lined shirt and will be seated on a Gatling gun while taking tickets. Any suspicious person attempting to pass him will be put on the deadhead list."

A few years later, especially after Charley Ford committed suicide in 1884, Bob took heavily to drink—due to a guilty conscience, some said—and then married. He moved west and opened a saloon and gambling joint in Walsenburg, Colo. In 1892 the Fords were operating a new saloon-whorehouse in Creede, Colo., where they separated the miners from their silver. Mrs. Ford ran the sex side of the business while Ford handled the bar and the gambling. He also handled the rough stuff, especially from other gambling interests trying to drive him out. Chief among these was Jefferson "Soapy" Smith, a con man and killer who was to become famous later for his depredations in the Klondike.

On the afternoon of June 8, 1892, a man carrying a double-barreled shotgun stepped into Ford's tent saloon and, without a word, raised it up and blew the killer of Jesse James away. The man was Edward O'Kelly, who was related by marriage to the Younger brothers and thus sort of kin to Jesse James. There was some question about whether that was the reason he had killed Ford or whether there was some private grudge between them or whether Soapy Smith had paid him to eliminate the competition. In any event, O'Kelly was sent to prison for 20 years. Since his act was rather popular, it was hardly surprising that he was granted a full pardon after serving just two years.

When Bob Ford, the slayer of Jesse James, began making personal appearances after the shooting, crowds turned out to hiss and boo.

Nobody seemed to mourn the "dirty rotten coward who shot Mr. Howard," and Jesse James admirers, whose numbers were then legion, observed with some satisfaction that Bob Ford had not lived to be as old as his celebrated victim.

See also: THOMAS T. CRITTENDEN, CHARLES FORD, JAMES BROTHERS, EDWARD O'KELLY.

Foreman, Percy (1904–1988) defense attorney

Perhaps the greatest accolade that can be heaped on a defense attorney comes not from judges, prosecutors, students of the law or even grateful clients but from other defense lawyers. One who stands in the front ranks of the profession, Texas attorney Richard "Racehorse" Haynes says he has tried to pattern himself after his idol, Percy Foreman. In recent years any list of leading criminal lawyers would count Haynes, Edward Bennett Williams, F. Lee Bailey and, of course, Foreman on the fingers of the first hand.

Foreman, operating out of Houston, clearly deserved this distinction. In a legal career that spanned five decades, he represented more than 1,500 capital case defendants and lost probably less than five percent to prison and only one to the executioner.

In the courtroom Foreman often came across at first as a somewhat ridiculous-looking figure, a hulking 6-feet 4-inch 250 pounder with baggy pants. However, he certainly did well by the vast majority of his clients, with his grandstanding methods getting many a defendant off when earlier courtroom wisdom had declared that a conviction was inescapable. In one case, Foreman's client was a woman who had killed her husband, a cattleman, because he had used a whip on her. Addressing the jury, the lawyer picked up the long black whip from the counsel table and cracked it continuously. When he finished, the jury was ready and willing to vote the lady a medal of honor.

It had long been Foreman's tack to save his client by focusing on the murder victim as a person most deserving of being killed. He worked wonders in the 1966 scandal-ridden trial of Candy Mossler by portraying murder victim Jacques Mossler as a "depraved" deviate who could have been killed by many different persons. Mossler was acquitted and then engaged in a long and stormy quarrel with Foreman for the return of jewels she had given him as security. His final fee worked out to something like $200,000 and assorted baubles.

Over the years Foreman accepted all sorts of security for later payment of fees, including a few dozen pianos, five elephants and a pool table (fittingly, since the lady in the case said she shot her husband because he was always playing pool). While Foreman always had a reputation for showing no mercy when billing the well-heeled, he often represented penniless defendants without charge.

At times, Foreman, like most great defense lawyers, seemed cynical about the law. He was fond of quoting Aaron Burr, who defined the law as "whatever is boldly asserted and plausibly maintained." However, Foreman, like his brethren of the craft, knew that it is the state which does most of the asserting, leaving the average defendant at a disadvantage.

What made Foreman a great legal light was his ability to understand human reasoning and communicate with jurors. That and, of course, the knack of picking the right jurors. He once said: "If you have a drunken-driver client, you ask a prospective juror if he's ever been a member of a temperance organization. If he simply says no, pay no attention. But if he says no and gives a little grin at the same time, grab him!"

Formby gang   Chicago youth gang

Contrary to popular opinion, the term *Chicago gangster* did not first come into vogue with the appearance of the Capone mob in the 1920s but some two decades earlier, when young punks had virtually taken over the community. Typical gangs included the Car Barn Bandits, the Market Streeters, the Briscoes, the Feinberg gang, the Trilby gang, the Brady gang, and the Formby gang, perhaps the most brutal of all.

Not a single member of the Formby gang was 20 years old, yet they committed a number of the city's most vicious crimes, including murder. Headed by a trio of young toughs—David Kelly, 16, Bill Dulfer, 17, and Jimmy Formby, 18—the gang committed hundreds of burglaries and robberies. Formby and Dulfer were the top "gunners" of the gang; the former murdered a street car conductor in 1904 and the latter slayed two men while the gang held up a saloon. Dulfer boasted of gunning down both victims at the same time. "I didn't even have to aim to hit 'em," he said. "Just held a gun in each hand and let go. They both went down. I saw 'em fall, that was all I wanted." When he was captured by the police, he asked that he be charged with murder rather than robbery. "I'm a killer, not a robber," he insisted.

While Dulfer and Formby got long prison terms, the city's problem with their gang or others like it was far from over. In 1906 the *Chicago Tribune* reported the young gangster menace was worse than ever: "It is not unusual for a boy six years old to be arrested for a serious offense. Boys who should be at home learning their ABC's are often found with cheap revolvers and knives." In one police precinct, the newspaper found, arrests of boys under the age of 16 for serious crimes totaled about 60 per month.

The newspaper concluded, "Chicago is terrorized by . . . criminals who have helped to make the name 'Chicago' a by-word for crime-breeding throughout the country." It was from these fields that the O'Donnells, the O'Banions, the Lakes, the Druggans and finally the Torrios and the Capones plucked so many of their members and perpetuated the concept of the Chicago gangster.

Fort Smith Elevator   frontier newspaper

It has become common today to speak with disapproval of Judge Isaac Parker, better known as Hanging Parker, but it should be remembered that he was dealing in one of the most lawless areas of the country, the territory west of Fort Smith, Ark. The man reflected the times, and the support and adulation he enjoyed was considerable among those who wanted the territory "civilized." While Parker may have been attacked by the Eastern press, he had enthusiastic grass-roots support. For example, it is hard to find a critical comment on the judge and the justice he dispensed at Fort Smith in the columns of the city's leading newspaper, the *Elevator*. Its comments proved that Parker was not an aberration but rather a reflection of the inhabitants' mood; his justice was their justice. When Lincoln Sprole was sentenced for the brutal double murder of a farmer and his young son, the *Elevator* commented, "It is only to be regretted that he has not two necks to break instead of one." It was the sort of statement Hanging Parker would make from the bench. The *Elevator* expressed wry satisfaction with Parker justice following the conviction of Crawford Goldsby, better known as Cherokee Bill, noting that the defendant had been found guilty of only one murder but was wanted in four other states for murder and adding, "He will hardly be wanted by any other state after they get through with him here."

When Cherokee Bill escaped the hangman because of appeals to the Supreme Court and eventually murdered a jailer, the *Elevator* ranted (some say the words were secretly written by Parker himself):

For the benefit of those who may not understand why Cherokee Bill was not hanged (why he was allowed to remain alive long enough to commit another brutal murder), we will say that his case was appealed to the Supreme Court of the United States upon what is known in law as technicalities—little instruments sometimes used by lawyers to protect the rights of litigants but oftener used to defeat the ends of justice. It will remain there until the bald-headed and big-bellied respectables who compose that body get ready to look into its merits. . . .

See also: ISAAC C. "HANGING JUDGE" PARKER.

Fortune Society

Recognizing that one way to reduce crime is to maximize the opportunities for those who have been in trouble in the past, the Fortune Society, formed in 1967, is probably the most well-known ex-convict rehabilitation organization in America.

At the heart of the society's program is a one-to-one counseling program, ex-offender to ex-offender, that aims through tutoring programs to raise educational levels and encourage development of careers. Over 1,500 new persons each year come to the Fortune Society's offices in New York for help; of these about 100 are teenagers, most with arrest and conviction records.

The organization evolved from a 1967 off-Broadway play, *Fortune and Men's Eyes,* written by an ex-convict, John Herbert. The play's producer, David Rothenberg, developed a weekly forum to permit audiences to learn about prison life and problems. Ex-cons joined these theatrical forums, and they learned how little the

"square world" knew about the prison experience. Members of the audience began inviting ex-convict panels to address their church or school groups. The Fortune Society at first operated out of a desk in founder and executive director David Rothenberg's office but by 1980 had offices on Park Avenue South with a full-time staff of 18 ex-cons and nine others plus hundreds of volunteers. The society has been successful in finding jobs for about 300 ex-offenders a year. It does not claim to have a magic formula for crime prevention and reduction but rather shares those experiences that have worked in practice. In many instances other programs and localities have utilized elements of the Fortune Society's program.

fortune-teller swindles   See HANDKERCHIEF SWITCH.

Forty Little Thieves   19th-century juvenile gang

Of all the New York juvenile gangs of the mid-19th century, few equaled the viciousness of the Forty Little Thieves, who took the name of the first adult criminal gang in the city with a disciplined membership. The Forty Little Thieves were often used by grown criminals as lookouts or decoys or to enter places to be burglarized through openings that would not admit an adult, but the gang members, aged eight to about 13, committed a number of major crimes on their own, especially looting the wharves. Their leader was a tough little vixen named Wild Maggie Carson, a street orphan who supposedly took her first bath at the age of nine. Under her leadership the gang, according to the police, committed a number of murders, but none was ever proved.

In her 13th year, Wild Maggie went through a remarkable reformation when the Rev. L. M. Pease opened a mission in the Five Points section in 1850 for the very purpose of saving juveniles. Under Pease, Wild Maggie learned the joy of sewing buttons on shirts and became as efficient a seamstress as she had been a mugger. When she was 15, Maggie was adopted by a good family, and she eventually married well. Wild Maggie was the exception rather than the rule, as most of the Forty Little Thieves grew up to join the great gangs of the Civil War era.

Forty Thieves   19th century New York gang

The first criminal gang in New York City with a disciplined membership and an acknowledged leadership was the Forty Thieves, a group of Lower East Side Irish immigrants who served as political sluggers as well as muggers and holdup men.

The gang, which was formed in the early 1820s, met regularly in a grocery speakeasy run by a colorful wench named Rosanna Peers on what is now Center Street. In that speakeasy their chieftain, Edward Coleman, would parcel out assignments and criminal beats to the stickup artists. Each man was expected to bring in a certain amount of loot and knew that if he consistently missed his quota, there was a number of younger criminals in the area eager for the opportunity to join the Thieves.

It was perhaps unrealistic to think that a gang of that size could maintain such discipline in an area as lush as early New York, and indeed, by 1850 the Forty Thieves had just about dissolved as a result of individual members striking out on their own or joining other bigger, more loosely organized gangs. Oddly, the name Forty Thieves then passed on to the Tammany Hall politicians, who by 1850 had begun their systematic looting of the city treasury. The Common Council of 1850 was given the sobriquet Forty Thieves, an affront to the remnants of the old gang of strong-arm robbers, who regarded themselves as much more honorable than politicians.

Forty-Two Gang   Chicago juvenile gang

Perhaps the worst juvenile gang ever produced by this country, the 42 Gang out of the "Patch," or Littly Italy, section of Chicago became a source of recruits for the Chicago mobs in the post–Al Capone era.

Even among the wild juvenile gangs of the 1920s, the 42ers were known as crazy, willing to do anything for a quick buck. They stripped cars, knocked over cigar stores, held up nightclubs, slipped into peddlers' stables and stole from their carts or killed their horses, hacking off the hind legs to sell as horse meat. Many neighborhood Italian girls idolized the 42ers, not only becoming their sexual playthings but also going along with them on their nightly crime capers to act as lookouts or "gun girls," secreting the gangsters' weapons under their skirts until needed so that the boys would be "clean" if stopped by police.

The gang derived its name from the story of Ali Baba and the Forty Thieves, which had always fascinated the members. In 1925 they decided to go Ali Baba two better and called themselves the 42 Gang, an exaggerated figure since at their "founding" meeting there were only 24 members. But in ensuing years their numbers did grow to about 42. The violence-prone gang committed any number of murders, including stoolies and policemen among their victims, but paid a high price. In 1931 University of Chicago sociologists conducted a study of the gang and came up with some staggering statistics. More than 30 of those considered to be the original 42ers had either been killed or maimed or were doing time for such crimes as murder, rape, armed robbery or other felonies.

In 1928, when a number of 42ers were confined to the boys reformatory at St. Charles, the institution's head, Maj. William J. Butler, received a long-distance phone call from Chicago. "This is the 42 Gang," he was informed. "Unless you let our pals go, we'll come down there and kill everybody we see. We've got plenty of men and some machine guns." Butler was inclined to laugh off the threat until Chicago police told him the 42ers probably meant it. The state militia was called out to guard the school, and Butler armed himself with a gun. A few days later, a 42er advance guard of three punks headed by Crazy Patsy Steffanelli was picked up outside the reformatory walls. Crazy Patsy readily admitted harboring plans to machine-gun his buddies to freedom. The incident brought forth a spate of stories about the 42ers, pointing out they should not be sent to St. Charles (an institution meant primarily for wayward boys rather than hardened criminals), even those of a tender age. The *Chicago Tribune* editorialized that the 42ers were a separate criminal class and should be sent either to such higher institutions as Joliet or to the electric chair.

The great ambition of the 42ers was to receive recognition from the big bootleggers and the Caponeites, and after a successful caper they would turn up in mob hangouts, dressed to the hilt and spending money like water. While the big bootleggers occasionally used them as beer runners or drivers, they still regarded the 42ers as "those crazy boys."

But even the Capone men could eventually be convinced by enough accomplishments. It was one of the "mooniest" of the gang, Sam Giancana, who finally made it into the syndicate, winning the support of its two top men, Paul Ricca and Tony Accardo, who took Giancana on as his driver. When Giancana finally proved he could curb his temper and wild behavior and be a disciplined, cunning gangster, he quickly moved up the organizational ladder, eventually becoming head of the entire outfit. And with Giancana's climb, the remnants of the 42 Gang were integrated into the mob.

See also: SAM "TEETS" BATTAGLIA, FIORE "FIFI" BUCCIERI, SAM "MOMO" GIANCANA.

Fountain, Albert Jennings (1838–1896)   murder victim

The Wild West's most celebrated unsolved murder was that of Col. Albert Jennings Fountain and his eight-year-old son, who were killed on January 31, 1896 in New Mexico Territory.

A world traveler, former journalist and leading lawyer, Fountain had been appointed a territorial judge and during his judicial career had sent a number of well-connected men to the penitentiary. At the time of his murder, the judge was deeply involved in a Lincoln County grand jury investigation of cattle rustling that was expected to implicate certain prominent individuals. Returning to their home at Las Cruces, Fountain and his child disappeared along the Tularosa–Las Cruces road. Their bodies were not found for several days. Eventually, three men—Oliver Lee, William McNew and James Gililland—were charged with the murders but acquitted. In Lincoln County, there was a widely held suspicion, which persists to this day, that a political enemy of Fountain, a youthful Albert B. Fall, later to be involved in the Teapot Dome scandal, was implicated in the killings.

Had the Fountain murders occurred less than two decades before, at the time of the Lincoln County War, the incident would no doubt have erupted into another bloody frontier war, in which suspicions were investigated with six-gun and rifle. Historian W. Eugene Hollon theorized on this change in climate: "Maybe it was because the Southwest had finally reached the point in civilization where its people no longer would tolerate wholesale violence. And maybe too, in this corner of the vanishing frontier, the law had finally begun to arise over the ruin wrought by generations of lawlessness."

See also: ALBERT B. FALL.

Further reading: *The Life and Death of Colonel Albert Jennings Fountain* by A. M. Gibson.

Four Deuces   Capone mob gambling den

One of the most notorious "pleasure" joints run by the Capone mob was a four-story structure on Chicago's South Wabash Avenue. The first floor was given over to a bar, and gambling activities occupied the next two. The fourth floor sported a lavish bordello. It was also the scene of numerous murders.

The Four Deuces was not without competition, especially from the nearby Frolics Club, which dispensed both liquor and women at lower prices. This unfair competition was dealt with in an imaginative fashion. One night when a murder occurred in the Four Deuces, the boys lugged the body over to the Frolics and stuffed it into the furnace. One of the Capone men then called the police with an irate complaint that the Frolics was running an illegal crematorium. The police rushed over and found evidence of a corpse in the furnace. The Frolics was promptly padlocked, and the authorities ripped it apart in search of more corpses. None were found, but the Frolics never reopened.

"Four Hundred" assassination list   Secret Service suspects

In the social world, the Four Hundred is a reference to status, but the "400" listing put together by the Secret Service's Protective Research Section refers to the most active potential political assassins in this country. Obviously, the 400 is not a complete or definitive grouping, but it does represent an effort to glean the most likely candidates for political violence out of a computer listing of 30,000 suspects maintained by the Secret Service.

Most of the persons on the larger list have made verbal or written threats against the president or are suspect for some other reason. They are routinely checked on whenever the president visits their locality. Members of the 400 are subjected to closer scrutiny. Since they are often mentally disturbed or have a history of violence, every effort is made to keep them far away from a presidential appearance. If legal or family restraints prove ineffective, the 400 suspect is put under close surveillance, an operation which may require the work of as many as 15 agents on a 24-hour basis.

Watching the 400 to make sure they don't harm the president can be dangerous for the agents. Many of them are well known to the agents, and this familiarity is a danger in itself. A case in point occurred in 1979. That year the Secret Service had Joseph Hugh Ryan committed to a mental hospital outside Washington, D.C. after he tried to break through a gate at the White House. Following his release, Ryan turned up in the Denver, Colo. office of the Secret Service to complain that he was being harassed by agents. Stewart Watkins tried to calm him down, but when the agent moved close to him, Ryan draw a .45-caliber pistol from under his coat and shot Watkins twice, killing him. Another agent then shot Ryan dead as the killer tried to turn his weapon on him.

Of course, neither the 400 grouping nor the larger computer listing is foolproof. Sara Jane Moore did not qualify for either of them despite the fact that she had threatened to kill President Gerald Ford and had one of her guns confiscated by San Francisco police the day before she took a potshot at the president in 1975. Moore was interviewed by two Secret Service agents but found to be "not of sufficient protective interest to warrant surveillance." Although she had a long history of erratic behavior, her name was not put on the computer listing because of the fact that she was simultaneously an informer for the FBI, the San Francisco police and the Treasury Department's Bureau of Alcohol, Tobacco and Firearms. It is possible that the Secret Service considered Moore's "kookie behavior" merely a cover for her other activities.

See also: SECRET SERVICE.

Francis, Willy (1930–1947) double execution case

If everything had gone normally in the execution of Willy Francis in Louisiana, the only unusual note in the matter would have been that he had paid the supreme penalty at a rather young age. However, the Willy Francis case was to result in a landmark decision on what constitutes cruel and unusual punishment.

A 17-year-old boy, Francis was sentenced to the electric chair for a murder he had committed when he was 15. As it turned out, he went to the chair twice. The first effort was botched when a malfunction in the chair caused him to receive an insufficient electric shock. Willy was returned to his death cell. When the state of Louisiana prepared to electrocute him a second time, his lawyers appealed to the Supreme Court that subjecting the youth to a second ordeal in the chair was cruel and unusual punishment. The Supreme Court ruled by a vote of five to four that since the first unsuccessful electrocution was only cruel because of an accident, it "did not make the subsequent execution any more cruel in the constitutional sense than any other execution." In May 1947, about a year after the first try, the chair worked fine.

Further reading: *Death and the Supreme Court* by Barrett Prettyman, Jr.

Frank, Leo (1884–1915) lynch victim

Probably the most infamous anti-Semitic lynching in America was that of Leo Frank, a 29-year-old Atlanta businessman. Frank, Brooklyn-born, a graduate of Cornell and president of the Atlanta chapter of B'nai B'rith, managed the National Pencil Co. factory for his wife's uncle. On Saturday, April 26, 1913, Confederate Memorial Day, the factory was shut, but Frank was there catching up on paperwork. At noon, as he later told police, 14-year-old Mary Phagan, all dressed up to go to the holiday parade, entered the plant to pick up her wages. Frank said she left immediately, but her body was found in the basement sometime after. She had been strangled and beaten. Penciled notes found by the body were supposedly written by the girl. One, addressed to "Mum," described her murderer as "a long, tall, sleam, black negro . . . that long tall black negro did buy his slef."

The next day Leo Frank was charged with the rape-slaying. James Conley, a semiliterate Negro employed at the factory made some startling accusations against Frank, among them that he had been summoned by the white man, shown Mary's dead body and told to carry it to the basement. In addition, he charged that Frank had ordered him to write the notes. At Frank's trial Conley also said that he had often seen Frank performing acts of sexual perversion with a number of young girls who worked at the factory.

Lynch law pervaded the atmosphere during the 30-day trial. Mobs cheered the prosecutor and harangued the defense attorneys—"If the Jew doesn't hang, we'll hang you." A newspaper editorial declared: "Our little girl—*ours* by the eternal God!—has been pursued to a hideous death by this filthy perverted Jew from New York."

While the jury deliberated, crowds outside the courthouse kept chanting the "Jew monster" had to hang. Frank was found guilty and sentenced to death.

Leo Frank defense committees were formed in various parts of the nation. In Chicago 415,000 persons signed petitions asking Georgia's governor John M. Slaton to commute the death sentence, but the chief executive was also under considerable pressure, and threats of death, not to do so. The Frank defense brought in William J. Burns, perhaps the nation's leading detective, to investigate, and he turned up considerable proof of a police frame-up. The police would not open any of their records to Burns other than those he obtained with a court order; on one occasion Burns and his assistant barely escaped from a lynch mob determined to make the case against Frank stand. Ironically, this was perhaps the first murder case in the South in which the word of a black was taken over that of a white man.

Burns discovered a witness, a black woman, who had been Conley's lover from time to time, and she signed a statement that Conley had told her he had killed the white girl. She also had 100 sexual explicit love notes from Conley in which he had described himself performing the very acts he later accused Frank of. In response to the Burns findings, Gov. Slaton commuted Frank's death sentence; it proved to be an act of political suicide. "The Annie Maude Carter notes, which were not before the jury, were powerful evidence in behalf of the defendant," he wrote. "These letters are the most obscene and lecherous I have ever read."

A Northern newspaper editorial announced, "The reign of terror in Georgia is over." But it was not. On August 17, 1915, two months after the commutation, 25 members of a secret vigilante group—the Knights of Mary Phagan—entered the Milledgeville Prison Farm and, without any resistance from armed prison guards, took Frank away with them on a ghastly 175-mile ride to Marietta, the murdered girl's hometown. Leo Frank was lynched there before a howling, gloating mob. The lynchers then proudly posed for pictures around the hanging corpse.

Two months after the hanging, the Knights of Mary Phagan congregated on the top of Stone Mountain near Atlanta to burn a cross and sing a folk song that had materialized out of the tragedy.

Little Mary Phagan
Went to town one day,
Went to the pencil factory
To get her little pay.
Leo Frank, he met her
With an evil heart and grin. . . .

There are many versions of the verses that followed, and it is still sung today in rural pockets of Georgia.

See also: WILLIAM J. BURNS.

Franklin, Rufus "Whitey" (1912–?) bank robber and murderer

Whitey Franklin was probably America's most mistreated federal prisoner, even more so than Robert Stroud, the Birdman of Alcatraz.

A lean, slow-talking Alabaman, he first ran afoul of the law in 1927, when at age 15 he was arrested for stealing a car and sentenced to a chain gang. He later served another year for carrying a gun and, before he was 18, drew a life sentence for murder. Having oversentenced him as a youth, the state of Alabama made up for it, in a manner of speaking, by paroling him from his life sentence after he had served about six years. A fully committed criminal by then, he was arrested for bank robbery within two months of his release and ended up at Alcatraz doing 30 years.

On May 23, 1938 Franklin led two other convicts, Jimmy Lucas and Tom "Sandy" Limerick, on a desperate and foolish prison escape attempt. In the process, Franklin apparently bludgeoned a guard to death with a hammer. The escape, however, failed. Limerick was killed, Lucas surrendered and Franklin ended up trapped on barb wire atop the prison's furniture factory roof with bullets in both his shoulders.

Franklin and Lucas were both tried for the guard's murder and, much to the disgust of Alcatraz guards, got life sentences instead of the death penalty. Although the prosecution had considerable circumstantial evidence that Franklin was the killer, the jury had some doubts and recommended a life sentence for both defendants.

Lucas suffered much harsh treatment through the years, but it was nothing compared to what Franklin received. He was put into an isolation cell, which convicts called the hole, totally cut off from all contact with the rest of the prison. It was always assumed by the rest of the prisoners that Franklin was beaten regularly by the guards and physically and mentally abused in many other ways. In 1946, following the great revolt at Alcatraz, an investigation of prison conditions found that Whitey Franklin was still in his solitary cell—after seven years and 21 days straight. His skin was dry and had a pasty look from his long years of confinement.

When reporters asked Warden James A. Johnston how long the prisoner would remain in solitary, Johnston (frequently described in magazines and newspapers as "stern but fair") replied, "As long as necessary for discipline." Sometime after the public revelation of Franklin's fate, he was transferred to an electrically locked isolation cell, where he would remain. He was fed the same prison fare as other convicts, a treatment he had not received earlier, and on rare occasions was taken for a walk in the exercise yard, but he never saw another prisoner and his guards did not say a word to him. In time, few of the Alcatraz prisoners even remembered him.

It must be assumed that Franklin is now dead, since it is doubtful he ever would have been granted a parole. In 1977 author Clark Howard, who was writing a book on the 1946 revolt, attempted to find out from the U.S. Bureau of Prisons if either Franklin or Lucas was still alive and, if so, still confined in prison or free. He was informed that neither man was within the federal prison system. Subsequent requests to determine whether they had died in prison brought no response.

See also: JAMES LUCAS.

Franks, Bobby See LEOPOLD AND LOEB.

Frazer-Miller feud Texas lawmen's duels

One of the most storied feuds in Texas involved two lawmen of the early 1890s, G. A. "Bud" Frazer and Killin' Jim Miller.

Frazer was elected sheriff of Reeves County in 1890 and shortly thereafter appointed Miller, a Pecos hotel owner, as his deputy. At the time, Miller already had the nickname of Killin' Jim, apparently having gunned down a number of men, but in Pecos he seemed to lead a respectable life. When Miller killed a Mexican prisoner in 1892, Frazer fired him. Miller claimed the Mexican had resisted arrest, but the real reason for the killing was that the prisoner knew Miller was engaged in mule stealing.

Frazer also had Miller charged with livestock theft, but since it was Miller's word against that of a "dead Mex," he was soon freed. Later that year Miller ran against Frazer for the sheriff's post but lost. A short while after, Miller was named city marshal of Pecos, and the feud between the two men festered. Finally, in a violent confrontation Frazer shot Miller in the arm in a duel on a Pecos street. Miller, his gun incapacitated, fired back but managed only to wing a spectator. Frazer then emptied his pistol into his foe's chest and walked away, certain he had killed him. He was rather surprised later to hear that Miller had recovered.

A few months afterward, Frazer lost his race for a third term and moved on to the New Mexico Territory. He returned in December 1894 and encountered Miller. The inevitable shoot-out occurred and Frazer again got the best of it, hitting Miller in the arm and leg. He then pumped two more shots into the wounded man's chest, but incredibly, Miller would not go down. Frazer fled the scene. It became a part of Texas folklore that Miller's life had been saved in the two duels because he had worn a hidden steel breastplate.

Frazer would have needed more than a breastplate to save him in the pair's third and final confrontation on September 14, 1896, when he was visiting his family in Toyah, Tex. Miller spotted Frazer playing cards in a saloon and blasted him with a shotgun from outside the door, blowing away most of his head and face. When Frazer's sister came at Miller with a gun, the gunfighter warned her, "I'll give you what your brother got—I'll shoot you right in the face!"

Miller was tried for Frazer's murder, but the first trial ended in a hung jury because of the argument that the victim had started the shooting feud more than two years earlier. In a second trial, however, Miller was convicted, but that verdict was set aside on appeal. No more legal action was taken against Miller, who went on to become one of the West's most feared professional killers—he once boasted his victims totaled 51—until he was lynched in 1909 in Ada, Okla. after his murder-for-pay of another ex-lawman.

Frenchy   See OLD SHAKESPEARE.

Frick, Henry Clay   See ALEXANDER BERKMAN.

Friendly Friends   Chicago madams' association

In the early 1900s a group of "better class" madams in Chicago formed a trade society "to protect our interests," which meant, among other things, controlling prices and competition and, most important, seeing they got their money's worth for the protection they bought.

The Friendly Friends specifically did not invite the most successful madams of the era, the Everleigh sisters, to join. In fact, most of their proceedings were given over to investigating ways of eliminating the fabulous Everleigh Club, the city's most renowned brothel, which took away so much of the "cream" of the business from their own fashionable establishments. The Friendly Friends were reportedly behind a number of plots to frame the Everleighs in various ways. When a young male member of a leading Chicago family accidentally shot himself in his home in 1905, a story spread that the man had really been the victim of a shooting in the Everleigh Club. The rumor was later put to rest after it was revealed that a black vice operator, Pony Moore, had offered one of the Everleigh Club's courtesans $20,000 to sign an affidavit confirming the alleged shooting. It was generally agreed that most of the money for the bribe plus whatever went to Moore had come from the Friendly Friends.

The leaders of the society were madams Zoe Millard, Georgie Spencer and Vic Shaw. Madam Millard was the most disturbed of all by the Everleigh competition and once administered a frightful battering to one of her prize bawds for speaking nicely of the Everleighs. Madam Spencer was the hell raiser of the group, ready with a complaint to the police whenever anything occurred that displeased her. Her wrath intensified greatly when police pressure increased as a result of public indignation over the vice in Chicago's Levee area. "Redolent of riches and ablaze with diamonds," according to one account, she stormed into the office of police captain Max Nootbaar, hammered on his desk with her jeweled fist and declared: "Listen to me, policeman! I'm rich. I own a hotel that's worth forty-five thousand dollars. I own a flat worth forty thousand, and these stones I'm wearing are worth another fifteen thousand. I'd like to see you interfere with my business."

Capt. Nootbaar was that rare bird, an honest Chicago police officer, and he eventually drove Madam Spencer into wealthy retirement in California.

Of all the Friendly Friends, Vic Shaw held on the longest, trying to keep the society in business even after the shuttering of the Levee district. She continued later with a lavish call house on South Michigan Avenue. As late as 1938 when she was about 70 years old, she turned up operating a similar resort on the North Side.

See also: EVERLEIGH SISTERS, NATHANIEL FORD MOORE.

Frisco Sue   (1853–?) stagecoach robber

Despite the Hollywood concept of the cowgirl hellion, the number of Western badwomen can be counted on one's fingers. The facts about even those who really existed have been steeped in the stuff of which legends are made. One of the real female villains was a lady known simply as Frisco Sue, a former San Francisco dance hall shill and prostitute, supposedly of breathtaking beauty.

In 1876, at the age of 23, Frisco Sue left for the Nevada gold fields, not to trim the miners, as other prostitutes did, but rather to reform herself. Sue decided she could escape her dreary profession by turning to a career of violent crime. Realizing she could not work alone, she shopped around for a suitable partner and finally settled on a minor road agent named Sims Talbot. If Talbot had any misgivings about working with a woman, Frisco Sue had, we are assured by various biographers of the day, all the necessary charms to make him forget them.

Sue's plans were to become very rich and transport herself to a new life in Europe, posing as an orphaned heiress. But that dream was to founder in the reality of her life of crime. The couple's first effort at stagecoach robbing netted them only $500—Sue had rolled society drunks for more than that in her California days. She was furious, and Talbot had a hard time calming her down. But he quickly hit upon a daring scheme that appealed to her. Now that the stage had been robbed, Talbot explained, the line would be confident it would not be robbed again right away and would therefore put on board a valuable shipment. So the couple held up the same stagecoach on its return run. Talbot's strategic thinking was less than perfect: this time the stage carried two shotgunners. Talbot had barely time to announce, "Hands up!" when he was blasted out of his saddle, shot dead. Frisco Sue was captured and sent to prison for three years. The Western press would not let her legend die, however, and there was always a story about some blade's plans to bust the lady free. It didn't happen. Frisco Sue served her time and then disappeared. According to one oft-told tale, she was seen a number of years later in San Francisco, married to a millionaire, but then the West always liked stories that ended with a happy and ironic twist.

Frye v. United States   lie detector ruling

Almost without exception, courts have refused to accept lie detector findings as evidence in courtroom proceedings, generally falling back of the landmark decision in *Frye v. United States*, ironically one that would have saved an innocent man from prison had it gone the other way.

In 1920 Dr. Robert Brown, a leading physician in Washington, D.C. was shot to death in his office. An arrest was finally made about a year later. Police said a robbery suspect, a young black named James Alphonse Frye, had confessed to the murder. Before the trial Frye repudiated his confession, saying he had made it only because he had been offered half the reward if he was convicted. Frye's young lawyers asked Dr. William M. Marston, a pioneer polygraphist, to conduct a test with his newly perfected lie detector. Acting without fee, Marston did so and was surprised to find that his examination agreed with Frye's claims of innocence.

At Frye's trial the defense team tried to introduce Marston's evidence but was overruled by the judge. Even the offer to submit the defendant to a new test in the courtroom was rejected. Frye was found guilty, but only of second-degree murder; the jury had apparently been impressed by the mention of the lie detector test in open court. He was sentenced to life imprisonment. Appeals of the case resulted in a federal court ruling that lie detector findings were in a "twilight zone" and lacked reliability and validity.

Finally, after Frye had been in prison for three years, another man confessed to the murder of Dr. Brown, and after an intensive investigation, Frye was released. However, his freedom did not erase the federal appellate court decision that remains a legal precedent to this day.

See also: LIE DETECTOR.

Fugmann, Michael (1884–1937)   murderer

Veterans of the bloody coal mine union organizing days of the 1930s in Wilkes-Barre, Pa. still remember with horror the frightful Easter season of 1936, when wholesale death came through the mails.

The first of six Easter gifts, each apparently a box of cigars, came to the home of Tom Maloney on the morning of Good Friday. Maloney had left his position as a leader of a union of anthracite coal miners to join John L. Lewis' United Mine Workers of America. When Maloney opened the box, it blew up, killing him and his four-year-old son. Meanwhile, a second homemade bomb in a cigar box was being delivered via parcel post to 70-year-old Mike Gallagher, who died instantly when he opened it.

A third package was received by Luther Kniffen, former sheriff of Luzerne County, who made a mistake that saved his life. Inadvertently, he slit the box open from the rear, and, turning back the lid, found himself staring at two sticks of dynamite, a detonator cap and a trigger mechanism attached to the front of the lid. Authorities immediately sent out a citywide alert, and three other persons who had gotten cigar box-sized parcels in the mail notified postal officials. The boxes were opened under full precautions and discovered also to contain booby-trap bombs.

At first, there seemed to be little chance of finding the bomber. The cigar boxes were of a common type, and while dynamite and detonator caps might be traced in a big city, they were too readily available to be traced in a coal-mining area.

There was one clue, however, in the form of the small pieces of wood used in making the bombs. Just a few days before the bombings, Bruno Richard Hauptmann had been executed for the kidnap-murder of 20-month-old Charles Lindbergh, Jr. Probably the most damning evidence against him had been the testimony of Arthur Koehler, an expert on woods, who had traced one rung of the ladder used in the crime to the Hauptmann home. Koehler was summoned to Wilkes-Barre by postal authorities and asked to study the wood scraps. He soon traced the wood to the home of one of the many suspects in the case. Slats from which the bits of wood had been cut were found in the home of a miner named Michael Fugmann, an independent unionist opposed to the United Mine Workers. Found guilty of the crime, Fugmann went to the electric chair in June 1937, suffering the same fate as Hauptmann on much the same evidence.

See also: ARTHUR KOEHLER.

funerals of gangsters

When Dion O'Banion, Chicago's notorious Irish gangster, went to his grave in 1924, a newspaper commented, "Presidents are buried with less to-do." His bronze and silver casket, made to order in Philadelphia and rushed to Chicago by express car, cost $10,000. Forty thousand persons passed through an undertaker's chapel to view the body as it "lay in state," as the *Chicago Tribune* put it.

To the "Dead March" from *Saul*, the pallbearers—triggermen Two Gun Alterie, Hymie Weiss, Bugs Moran, Schemer Drucci and Frank Gusenberg, and labor racketeer Maxie Eisen, president of the Kosher Meat Peddlers' Association—bore the casket to the hearse. Close behind them came Johnny Torrio, Al Capone and their henchmen. Despite the solemnity of the occasion, police plainsclothesmen were still fearful of a shoot-out and circulated among the gangsters confiscating firearms.

The funeral procession was about a mile long, with 26 cars and trucks carrying flowers, including particularly garish ones sent by Torrio, Capone and the Genna brothers, all of whom probably had been involved in planning O'Banion's murder. Some 10,000 persons followed the hearse, jamming every trolley car to the Mount Carmel area, where the cemetery was situated. At the cemetery 5,000 to 10,000 more spectators waited.

"It was one of the most nauseating things I've ever seen happen in Chicago," commented Judge John H. Lyle, an honest Chicago jurist—somewhat of a rarity in that area.

The O'Banion funeral typified the gaudy gangster funerals of the 1920s. Similar, though not quite as lavish, treatment was given to any number of the O'Banion gang, as one after another went to his reward.

Before the O'Banion funeral, with its 26-vehicle flower procession, a previously deceased member of the gang, Nails Morton, had been honored with 20 cars. When Hymie Weiss departed, the flower train dropped to 18 vehicles; a patient Bugs Moran had to explain to the grieving widow that since the passing of Morton and O'Banion, 30 others in the gang had expired, obviously reducing the number of donors and, consequently, the amount of flowers. After Schemer Drucci was shot dead by a police officer, his funeral was a touch less impressive than Weiss', although he still was buried under a blanket of 3,500 flowers. His widow commented, "A cop bumped him off like a dog, but we gave him a king's funeral."

Attendance at gangster funerals by public officeholders was more or less obligatory during this period. After all, the underworld had bought them and therefore, had a right to call on them. Thus, when Big Jim Colosimo, the great whoremaster and mentor of Johnny Torrio—who with Al Capone plotted his demise—was assassinated in 1920, the honorary and active pallbearers included two congressmen, three judges, a future federal judge, a state representative, 10 aldermen and a host of other politicians and community leaders. Mayor Big Bill Thompson sent personal representatives to express his heartfelt loss. It made sense, considering the fact that Colosimo's organization had piled up huge votes for Thompson and his Republican allies. In his eulogy of Big Jim, Alderman Bathhouse John Coughlin of the First Ward said: "Jim wasn't a bad fellow. You know what he did? He fixed up an old farmhouse for broken-down prostitutes. They rested up and got back in shape and he never charged them a cent."

Into the 1930s the big gangster funeral was considered a must. "That's what buddies are for," one mobster explained to a reporter. However, by the time Al Capone died in 1947, low key was the vogue, and it has been basically that way ever since. The only untoward events at such affairs are scuffles between mobsters and reporters and photographers.

When Frank Costello died in 1973, his widow saw to it that his unsavory friends stayed away from the funeral. The burial ceremony was over in a few minutes. The only person to approach her was a cousin of Frank. Hat in hand, he whispered what she expected to be words of condolence. "What are you going to do with Frank's clothes?" he asked. Mrs. Costello walked on without bothering to answer.

Fury, Bridget (1837–1872?) ruffian and murderer

With the exception of Mary Jane "Bricktop" Jackson, the toughest woman in New Orleans during the years just before and after the Civil War was a vicious free-lance prostitute, mugger and pickpocket known as Bridget Fury. Her real name was Delia Swift and she was born in Cincinnati. There, by the age of 13, she had become an accomplished criminal, working in a dance house where her father was a fiddler. When her father killed a girl in a fit of passion, Bridget moved on to New Orleans, where she plied her trade with a fighting fury that earned her her nickname and established her as a leading criminal of the French Quarter. For a time she teamed up with Bricktop Jackson and a few other vicious women in a gang that could best any group of sailor bullies.

In 1858 she murdered a man and was sent to prison for life but was freed in a general amnesty in 1862. Bridget immediately went back to her belligerent ways. After a few years she decided the violent life did not pay enough, so with money raised from cracking skulls, she opened a brothel on Dryades Street in the late 1860s. In 1869 she was arrested on charges of robbing some $700 from two Texans visiting her house and was sent to prison for several months. Upon her release she found her brothel being run by others. A few years earlier Bridget Fury would have torn the place apart getting her due, but by then she was older and perhaps weary. Within another year she had turned into a gutter hag who was pulled in for drunkenness every two or three days. She was last seen around 1872 in such a state of deterioration that it was said she couldn't live more than a few weeks. The estimate was no doubt correct and after a brief time she was seen no more.

See also: MARY JANE "BRICKTOP" JACKSON.

Gacy, John Wayne (1942–1994) mass murderer

Charged with 33 killings, more than any other mass murderer in American history, John Gacy was a building contractor who lived in a neat three-bedroom brick-fronted house in Knollwood Park Township, Ill., a Chicago suburb. During the period from 1972 to 1978, Gacy, who was in his thirties, murdered 33 boys and young men whom he had lured to his home with the promise of a job. After having sexual relations with them, he killed them and disposed of their bodies in a variety of ways.

Gacy was arrested in December 1978, when authorities traced a missing youth, 15-year-old Robert Piest, to his home. Twice-married, twice-divorced, he had come under suspicion after police learned that he had once served 18 months in an Iowa prison for sodomy with a teenage boy. By the time the killer was apprehended, however, young Piest was dead. Under questioning, following the discovery of three skeletons on his property, Gacy made a rambling statement. He had strangled the Piest boy and tossed his body in the Des Plaines River. Police began searching for victims and found three bodies in his garage, fished four out of the river and discovered 28 buried beneath the crawl space under his house. Of these, he was charged with a total of 33 deaths. It was clear that Gacy himself didn't know the exact count.

At his trial in March 1980, the chief issue was whether Gacy was a cold-blooded murderer who planned the killings or a mentally unbalanced man who lacked the capacity for understanding his actions. He was convicted and, on March 13, 1980, sentenced to the electric chair. At the time, the last execution in Illinois had occurred in 1962. He was finally executed in 1994.

Galante, Carmine (1910–1979) murdered mafioso

After the death of Vito Genovese in 1969, Carmine Galante was considered to be the most ruthless and brutal of Mafia leaders. It could only be guessed how many murders he had committed during a life of crime that dated back to 1921. He was known to have carried out many killings for Genovese, including the 1943 murder of radical journalist Carlo Tresca in New York. (Genovese was in Italy at the time and seeking to curry favor with Benito Mussolini, who was enraged by Tresca's antifascist activities.) Galante eventually became an underboss in the Joe Bananas family, specializing in narcotics trade.

He was finally sent to prison for 20 years on a narcotics charge. While serving time, he plotted to seize power from the other Mafia families in New York upon his release and was considered fearsome and capable enough to have done so. Even from prison, he ran the Bananas family, in which he had ascended to power in 1974, issuing orders to an estimated 200 members, among them many of the top gunners in the country.

The Bananas family had been nothing but grief for the other crime families in New York and elsewhere in the country. In 1964 its retired head, Joe Bananas, had plotted to eliminate virtually the entire governing board of the Mafia and take over. After waging a bloody five-year war, he gave up. Now, it appeared certain Galante would make the same try. Galante talked less than

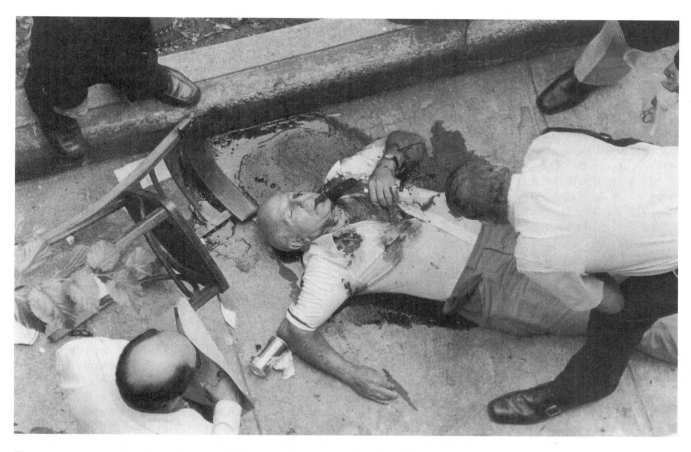

The assassination of mafioso Carmine Galante in the garden of a Brooklyn restaurant in 1979 was said to have solved the underworld's "Cigar" problem.

Bananas, believing the best policy was kill, kill, kill. Freed in 1979, he was gathering strength and making demands backed up with threats.

According to the underworld grapevine, a number of crime leaders held a meeting in Boca Raton, Fla. to decide the "Cigar" problem (Galante was noted for always having a large cigar in his mouth). Mob leaders not present were consulted about whether or not to issue a contract on him. Those said to have been involved included such big shots as Jerry Catena, Santo Trafficante, Phil Rastelli and Frank Tieri. Even the retired Joe Bananas was consulted and okayed the contract on Galante.

On July 12, 1979 Galante had just finished the main course of a meal in the outdoor rear area of an Italian restaurant in Brooklyn. His cigar was in his mouth and he held a glass of wine in his right hand. Three masked men suddenly came through the indoor restaurant into the courtyard.

"Get him, Sal!" one of the masked men said and a hood with a double-barreled shotgun stepped forward and fired two blasts into the gangster. Galante died with his cigar still in his mouth.

A joke that made the rounds in the underworld asked, What's the first thing Galante would do if he could come back to earth alive? Answer: Have dessert.

See also: VITO GENOVESE, CARLO TRESCA.

Gallatin Street   New Orleans crime area

From 1840 until 1880 Gallatin Street in New Orleans was described as having more crime per square foot than any street in America. Indeed, it had the distinction of not containing a single legitimate enterprise anywhere on its two-block length. Running from Ursuline Avenue to Barracks, it offered enough debaucheries from dusk to dawn to sate the country boys, city slickers, sailors and steamboat men seeking varied pleasures. Such visitors, one historian noted, were in turn sought out by "a horde of harlots, sneak thieves, garroters who openly carried their deadly strangling cords, and footpads with slung shots looped about their wrists." There were barrelhouses where for 5¢ a man bought no mere glass of liquor but all the booze he could drink, dance houses that were also bordellos and sailors' boarding houses from which seamen were at times shanghaied. It was often said that a miracle man in New Orleans was one who could enter Gallatin at Ursuline with money in his pocket and emerge at Barracks with his cash and skull untapped. At times, the police entered the street by day in large armed groups but were nowhere to be seen after sunset.

Much of the mayhem on Gallatin Street was the work of the Live Oak Boys, a gang formed in 1858 by one Red Bill Wilson, a vicious thug who always concealed a knife in his bushy red beard. The Live Oak Boys were not a disciplined bunch. While they collected protection from virtually every house on the street, that was no guarantee they would not smash such a place to pieces when they had a mind to, which proved a rather common occurrence. Then too, they considered any payment they received from an establishment null and void if the proprietor of a rival business offered them a bounty to shut down the competition.

Despite such depredations, any resort on Gallatin was invariably a gold mine. Typical was Archie Murphy's, which in a decade of operation left the proprietor in a state a newspaper described as one of "extreme wealth." Murphy achieved that happy status by encouraging his girls "not to allow any sucker to get away." One of his more skillful harpies was Lizzie Collins. A foolhardy farmer once bragged to Lizzie that he had $110 in gold tied in a handkerchief around his leg. He shrewdly refused all drinks but jumped at Lizzie's invitation to go upstairs. As the couple entered Lizzie's room, three other harlots jumped on the man and held him while Lizzie poured whiskey down his throat. When the farmer was helpless, Lizzie retrieved the handkerchief with the gold and then called on the Murphy bouncers to toss the farmer into the alley. The farmer pressed charges and Lizzie was arrested, but the case was dismissed when the farmer could produce no evidence other than his word.

Lizzie Collins went on to suffer a bizarre fate. Years of drink addled her brain and she developed a mania for stealing items that Archie Murphy found little use for. Instead of taking a man's money, she would drug or knock him out and then cut all the buttons off his pants. Archie Murphy tried to get Lizzie to mend her ways, but he finally kicked her out. For some years thereafter, Lizzie stalked Gallatin Street practicing her strange pastime, becoming one additional peril for visitors to the street.

See also: BRIDGET FURY, MARY JANE "BRICKTOP" JACKSON, LIVE OAK BOYS.

Gallo, Crazy Joe (1929–1972) Brooklyn Mafia leader

Joseph Gallo was nicknamed Crazy Joe by rival Mafia figures who considered him "flaky" and hard to deal with. Crazy was all that and mean besides, but at the same time he was among the most perceptive of the new breed of underworld leaders. In the 1960s Crazy Joe recognized the changing tides in the underworld, the steady shift in power from Italian to black and sought to reach an accommodation with the emerging power structure, much in the fashion that Meyer Lansky had recognized the decline of Jewish gangsterism in the 1920s and allied with the Italian Mafia, under which he continued to prosper. In prison, Crazy Joe befriended black criminals. He attempted to break down convict color lines by having a black barber cut his hair; he became friends with Leroy "Nicky" Barnes and tutored him on taking over control of the drug racket in New York's Harlem and then far beyond; he sent released black prisoners to work. In all this, Crazy Joe realized nothing was permanent in crime. Years before, he had questioned the stranglehold the older underworld element had on various activities. "Who gave Louisiana to Frank Costello?" he once demanded in a conversation taped by law enforcement officials.

Crazy Joe started his criminal career at the age of 17, accumulating such charges as assault, burglary and kidnapping. He moved up rapidly in the Carlo Gambino family and was believed to be the chief gunman in the murder of Albert Anastasia in 1957. Gallo went to war against the Profaci family, a war that took more than a dozen lives, because he felt the Gallos were entitled to a bigger slice of the rackets in Brooklyn. After Profaci died and Joe Colombo, Sr. became head of the Profaci family, the war continued. When Colombo was shot and "vegetabled," to use Gallo's term, the murderer turned out to be a black man, Jerome A. Johnson. Gallo was immediately brought in for questioning because of his ability to recruit black troops whenever he needed them. But nothing could be proved against him and he was released.

On April 7, 1972 Crazy Joe left the safe confines of his Brooklyn territory and went to Umberto's Clam House in New York's Little Italy to celebrate his 43rd birthday. It seemed safe. There was always a tacit agreement within the Mafia that no rubouts would take place in Little Italy. In Crazy Joe's case, however, an exception was made. The Gallo party was seated at two tables when a man walked in with a .38-caliber pistol in his hand. Women screamed and customers hit the floor as the killer opened up on Gallo. Gallo's two bodyguards fired back. In all, some 20 shots were fired before the assassin fled. Mortally wounded, Gallo staggered out the front door and collapsed and died in the middle of the street—one block from police headquarters.

See also: LEROY "NICKY" BARNES, JOSEPH COLOMBO, SR.

Gallows Hill execution spot

A hill on the outskirts of Salem, Mass. was the site where a score of persons were hanged in 1692 during the witchcraft delusions. From that time on, it was known as Gallows Hill, even though during the period of public remorse attempts were made to give it another name. While there have been many other American towns with similarly named hills, Salem's has the distinction of being the oldest by far.

See also: SALEM WITCHCRAFT TRIALS.

Gallus Mag (c. 1860s) female thug

Described by New York police as the most savage female ruffian of the period from just before to just after the Civil War, Gallus Mag was a towering six-footer known as the Queen of the Waterfront. Her antecedents were English, but little else was known about her. At times, she would refuse to give any information and, on other occasions, would provide varying and contradictory stories. Once when a saloon habitué asked Gallus Mag her age, she punished him for his nosiness by smashing his skull with a mallet, chewing off his ear and throwing him into the street.

Gallus Mag, who earned her nickname by wearing galluses, or suspenders, to hold her skirt up, held sway in the legendary Hole-In-The-Wall Saloon on New York City's Water Street, where she was a partner with One-Armed Charley Monell and acted as bouncer. The saloon was a "bucket of blood" where more men were said to have been robbed or killed than in any other watering hole of that era. Despite her duty to keep the peace, Gallus Mag was a prime cause of the violence. She would stalk the dive looking for trouble and was well prepared for it, with a pistol always tucked into her skirt and a bludgeon strapped to her wrist. Whenever she found a man violating the rules of the place, such as robbing a stranger without a permit from the management, she would immediately crack him over the head. Her custom was to then seize the offender's ear between her teeth and drag him out the door. If her victim dared to struggle, she would bite his ear off. Gallus Mag became infamous for this act and kept all such severed ears in a huge jar of alcohol behind the bar, a trophy collection that was one of the more gory sights on the crime-ridden waterfront.

Gallus Mag's only real female competition was the notorious Sadie the Goat, so named because when she spotted a likely victim for a mugging she would lower her head and butt him in the stomach. A blow to the head would end the victim's resistance, and Sadie would rifle his pockets at leisure. One day Sadie attempted to butt her way to a victory over Gallus Mag, but a mallet proved more than a match for Sadie the Goat's skull. Gallus Mag chewed off her rival's ear, and Sadie fled the East Side waterfront in disgrace. The vanquished warrior later achieved great fame as the leader of the Charlton Street pirates on the West Side, who terrorized the Hudson River for many miles north of the city. When the Charlton Streeters were finally broken up, Sadie the Goat returned to the East Side and made her peace with Gallus Mag, accepting Mag's primacy as the queen of the area. This total surrender so impressed Gallus Mag that she magnanimously fished around in her alcohol jar of ears and returned Sadie's severed member to her.

Gallus Mag's reign on the East Side waterfront ran from the late 1850s to 1871, when the Hole-In-The-Wall was closed because of the numerous murders and other crimes committed there. Many tales circulated about Gallus Mag's subsequent fate: one that she found true love with a poor young man and another that she found true love with a rich old man. Whatever her fate, the waterfront was never the same after her reign.

See also: HOLE-IN-THE-WALL SALOON.

Gambi, Vincent (?–1819) pirate

A contemporary—at times a follower and at times a foe—of Jean Lafitte, Vincent Gambi, a surly, hot-blooded Italian, was easily the worst cutthroat to sail the Gulf of Mexico during the first two decades of the 19th century. While Lafitte and many of the other pirates headquartering in the "pirates' home" of Barataria Bay and the islands off Louisiana were more or less privateers under commission to Cartagena, which was then revolting against Spain, Gambi often boasted he was a genuine bloody pirate, and he was. By 1810 he was known to have murdered a score of men with his favorite weapon, a broadax.

When Lafitte became the acknowledged leader of the Baratarian pirates about that time, Gambi was the only captain who occasionally challenged his authority. Unlike Lafitte, Gambi wished to attack all shipping, including that of the United States, ignoring the consideration that American merchants were the prime purchasers of the Baratarian freebooters' loot.

Once, Gambi attempted to overthrow Lafitte and had his lieutenant announce loudly, "The men of Gambi take orders only from Gambi!" Lafitte answered that display of dissension by drawing a pistol and shooting the man dead. Gambi immediately lost interest in any thought of revolt. Even after the Americans finally drove the pirates from their Baratarian bases in 1814, Gambi followed Lafitte in pledging to support Gen. Andrew Jackson at the Battle of New Orleans. Lafitte's motive was undoubtedly financial and political; Gambi's was simply to satisfy his urge for violence. He was credited with more killings than any other pirate taking part in the battle.

Following the successful conclusion of the war against the British, Gambi, like the other Baratarians, was granted a full pardon with all the rights of an American citizen, but by early 1816 he, Lafitte and many of the others had tired of New Orleans city life. Lafitte went off with perhaps 1,000 followers to found a community on an island that later became Galveston, Tex., but Gambi set off on his own to earn a new fortune and greater infamy as a pirate. He succeeded, plundering and sinking a score of ships over the next three years. In 1819 Gambi was slaughtered by his own men with his own ax as he slept on a pile of stolen gold, which, as was his wont, he had divided by a method that defied the standard rules of mathematics.

See also: JEAN LAFITTE, PIRACY, PIRATES' HOME.

Gambino, Carlo (1902–1976) Mafia chieftain

Whether Gambino ever was the so-called boss of bosses, assuming the existence of any such character, is debatable, but he was without doubt the head of New York's most powerful crime family as well as the model for Mario Puzo's *Godfather*. Gambino, a youthful companion of Lucky Luciano and Meyer Lansky, rose through the underworld ranks to become the underboss to Albert Anastasia in the 1940s and 1950s.

It is generally believed that Vito Genovese ordered the execution of Anastasia after winning the approval of Gambino. From the time of Anastasia's murder in 1957 and the forced retirement of Frank Costello after a botched assassination attempt on his life, Genovese became the most powerful Mafia figure in New York, allegedly controlling all five major New York crime families. However, Genovese's reign was a short one. He was convicted in a narcotics case, which was reputedly "set up" by Costello, Lansky and Luciano, and sentenced to 15 years in prison. Although he continued to control syndicate operations from behind bars, several others, including Gambino, were able to increase their power. By the time Genovese died in prison of natural causes in 1969, Gambino had emerged as the strongest family leader in New York. By judicious alliances and killings, he eventually became the dominant chieftain of the five families, although it is doubtful he ever attained the fictional Godfather status.

The short, bulb-nosed Gambino, however, did display many of the personal traits of the Godfather. There was the same ruthless cunning, the Long Island

retreat, the tomatoes planted in the garden and the excursions to fruit stands in Italian neighborhoods. Even in death, Gambino resembled the Godfather. After he died of a heart attack in October 1976, the hundreds of mourners at his funeral were cordoned off from reporters and strangers by hard-faced men who easily convinced onlookers that it would be impolite to intrude on the grief of the family, friends and associates of Carlo Gambino.

See also: ALBERT ANASTASIA; APALACHIN CONFERENCE; JOSEPH COLOMBO, SR.; VITO GENOVESE.

gambler's belt

Employed by crooked gamblers in the 19th century, the so-called gambler's belt was a lethal body device of considerable firepower used to discourage any attempt by a victim to recover his losses forcibly.

The belt appeared in gambling dens in Philadelphia, Cincinnati and Chicago and proved popular on the Mississippi and in the West. In a typical version, a body belt was fitted with three small-caliber revolvers that could be fired simultaneously by operating a trigger mechanism hidden on the wearer's right side. Naturally, when fired, the device destroyed the wearer's trousers but did far worse damage to his foe, who would be struck by three shots in the abdomen. According to one account, an unnamed gambler in Nevada used such a belt to kill a miner objecting to his method of dealing, and the other miners gathered around, expressing wonder at the device's design. On reflection, they decided it gave the gambler an unfair advantage in the gunfight, so they marched him out to the street and hanged him.

gangs and gangsters

The terms *gangs* and *gangsters* are used in this book— and in almost every other book on the subject of American crime—in the loose modern definitions and not in their specific original meanings. Thus, Jesse James had a "gang," and John Dillinger had a "gang" and was a "gangster." Originally, and strictly, the words applied to 19th-century organizations that were virtual armies. The Gophers, for instance, could field 500 fighting men, every one a fierce thug and eager killer. Yet, by the standards of the time, the size of the Gophers was unremarkable. Another New York gang, the Dead Rabbits, mobilized far greater numbers. So did other gangs in all parts of the country: the Sydney Ducks, Whyos, Bloody Tubs, Bowery Boys, Roach Guards, Potato Peelers, Plug Uglies and so on. In 1850 the New York police estimated the city gangs totaled about 30,000 men and women. These gangs consisted of bruisers, brawlers and thugs who could and did paralyze American cities when they rampaged. On a more routine basis, a gang might commit a dozen or more robberies of business places and homes each night, and some gangs were good for 30 to 50 street muggings every evening. They often killed, but simply in the course of business with little homicidal intent. If a victim had a weak skull, it was his misfortune. Eventually, many gangs found and met a demand in the marketplace for their murderous abilities. The Whyos, among others, rented themselves out as primitive forerunners of Murder, Inc., committing mayhem according to a set fee schedule.

In the same era there were specialized groups of more sophisticated criminals who perpetuated spectacular and amazing crimes. They were called "mobs" and ranged in number from as few as three or four individuals up to about 15 or so. By this usage, the 1930s saw the Dillinger "mob" in action.

True gangs are still with us, although but for a quirk of history they might well have vanished as they did in many other advanced countries. The true era of the great gangs ran 90 years, roughly from 1825 to 1915. They flourished almost unopposed until the Civil War, when they finally met some police effort to contain them. This was no easy task since many of the gangs had strong political connections as a result of their ability to provide votes for the political forces protecting them and, more important, to dissuade voters from opposing their patrons. Where the gangs were contained, it was basically through the raw force of police beatings and improved educational, economic and social conditions. By the second decade of the 20th century, the reform-minded citizenry in most big cities had brought about wholesale destruction of the gangs. In New York during 1914–15 some 300 gangsters, including the best-known underworld figures of the day were shipped off to prison. The great gangs crumbled. The Whyos were no more, and the last great New York gang, the Five Pointers, were losing the revenues required to keep a large criminal combine alive. After the World War I it seem doubtful if the big gangs could ever recover. But Prohibition provided the gangsters with a public-approved criminal activity, bootlegging, around which to regroup and which made the likes of Al Capone a hero worthy of being cheered at baseball games. The Mafia crime families were able to flourish and the national crime syndicate was born. They were so well organized that after the repeal of Prohibition they could move en masse into the new criminal activities of the 20th century. Thus, the traditions of the old gangs are preserved today in the various Mafia crime families, the new Purple Gang and the massive but less well-known black narcotics gangs.

Of course, almost every ethnic group has its own gangs, some of whom can be said to dominate crime and drug activities in many cities. There are the imported criminals of South America and the so-called Russian Mafia, to cite just two. Then there are America's homegrown gangs, whose members from their early teens dominate the crime rates in many large cities (and who have spread their activities into smaller cities and rural communities).

Actually these gangs are little different from earlier gangs, and they thrive on their ability to amass huge sums of money. Just as earlier gangs engaged in bootlegging during Prohibition, recent street gangs have profited from dealing in drugs. City youth gangs develop and are nurtured in blighted communities, where unemployment, family disorganization, neighborhood traditions of gang delinquency are common. Gangs provide acceptance and protection to inner-city youth. In 1985 there were an estimated 400 gangs in Los Angeles compared to 800—with 90,000 members—in 1990. There are three major Latino gangs, the Latin Kings, which started out as a fraternal organization in the 1940s, the Los Netas and the Los Solidos. All engage in many criminal activities and constantly war on each other for turf and profits.

The two major African-American gangs in Los Angeles are the Crips and Bloods. Ironically the Crips grew out of the fights at dances organized to keep young people off the streets. The Bloods were organized in opposition to the Crips, and one of their rules calls for every member to sign the gang charter in his own blood.

In Los Angeles County, there are an estimated 157,000 Crips and Bloods in 1,100 chapters and related gangs who kill each other at a clip of two a day and are arrested at the rate of 50,000 a year. By 1996 in Los Angeles the battle between the Crips and Bloods took at least 3,000 lives and wounded and maimed thousands of others. As Ben Sonder reported in *Gangs*, "Wheelchairs are a common sight in South Central Los Angeles." By that time there were as many as 100,000 affiliated with these two groups, and their competition spread up and down the West Coast from San Francisco to Seattle. There are chapters of both groups in Phoenix, Denver, Houston, Albuquerque, Omaha, Amarillo and Colorado Springs. In Salt Lake City the crime rate tripled from 1992 and 1993, in great measure because of these gang chapters. In York, Pa. Crips were hauling in $40,000 in crack sales per week.

The surest way to leave the gang life is, of course, death, either by murder or overdosing on drugs. At first the Bloods had a rule against using drugs themselves, but then members defiantly decided that how they lived their lives was their own business.

There is little chance for gang members to "resign." The saying is "Blood in, blood out." The few members who do get out have to do it slowly, maintaining their loyalty to the gang even as they gradually become somewhat legitimate, with a job and family. Similarly, those who go on to become rappers of varying degrees of success, often do not escape, or even want to escape their past. A prime example was rap star Tupak Shakur, who remained mired in gang warfare and died violently.

Efforts are constantly made to reform gang members, but as in all criminal organization activities, the glue that keeps them active and violent is the millions they make that none of the individuals can earn any other way. Gangs have always lived by the law of the money jungle.

See also: TUPAK SHAKUR.

Garcia, Manuel Philip (?–1821) murderer

As a murder, Manuel Garcia's crime was rather ordinary, but it led to the introduction of a new method of detection in this country that has been widely used ever since. Garcia killed Peter Lagoardette, a rival highwayman and burglar in the Norfolk, Va. area, in a feud over a woman. He had induced another bandit, Jose Castillano, to help him lure the victim to an abandoned house, where Garcia hacked Lagoardette to death and the pair cut up the body and burned it in the fireplace. The job was so messy both killers had to leave their blood-drenched shirts behind.

When the neighbors were attracted by smoke coming from the chimney of an abandoned house, they investigated and found Lagoardette's partially burned torso and limbs. They also found the shirts, which were turned over to the sheriff. That lawman had been reading a recent newspaper account from England describing how a murderer's clothing had been traced through laundry marks. The same was done in the Lagoardette case, and the trail led straight to Garcia and Castillano. Apparently, it was the first time a laundry mark had been used to apprehend a murderer in the United States, and Virginia newspapers were at first ecstatic about the method and then somewhat somber as they speculated that many murderers henceforth would undoubtedly do their foul business in an undressed state. The two murderers were hanged in Norfolk on July 1, 1821.

Gardner, Roy (1888–1940) escape artist

As a criminal, Roy Gardner was less than a master, getting himself caught frequently. The problem for the law was not catching him but holding him. One of the leading columnists of the early 1920s, S. Jay Kaufman, wrote in the *New York World:* "There is no end of fascinating questions in the career of this extraordinary man. How often do we find a criminal who has taught Emerson and Thoreau, fought for liberty across the border, knocked down the great Jim Jeffries, written a book of scholarship that is a classic in its field? Roy Gardner is Renaissance man born too late in a world he never made. He is a man of whom they make legends, and we are in need of legends to brighten this dreary world."

Roy Gardner was America's greatest escape artist during the Roaring Twenties, and as he slipped in and out of the hands of the law, he produced one fantastic newspaper headline after another. Born in 1888, the son of a well-to-do Detroit businessman, Gardner appeared to have a brilliant future when he graduated from college with honors. He showed a strong literary bent and at a very early age became a faculty member of a Midwestern college. His record in the English department was outstanding, and a work he published on 17th-century literature was very well received.

By all rights, Roy Gardner should have become a fixture in the academic world and lived out a useful educational career, but youthful enthusiasm and a craving for adventure caused him to drop out. He went to Mexico to live with the revolutionaries. In 1908 Gardner was caught bringing ammunition to the Carranza army and was sentenced to death after a summary government trial. He escaped from the military prison at Hermosillo before the execution could be carried out. Three other Americans escaped with him. Later, two were wounded and recaptured, but Gardner and the other American made it away clean.

Having no desire to return to the university life, Roy headed to the West Coast and took a fling at prizefighting becoming a sparring partner for James J. Jeffries. It was through his acquaintances in the boxing world that Gardner turned to crime. With two others, he pulled a $19,000 van robbery. Afterward, one of his accomplices was caught and he implicated Gardner, who spent two years in San Quentin as a result.

When he got out, he went straight and got married. Gardner opened his own welding shop in Oakland, Calif. and prospered until the shop burned to the ground. He had no insurance. Thereafter, Gardner went to Los Angeles and took a job as a welder. He also started to do some serious writing, but after a while, honest work ceased to interest him. He robbed a mail truck in San Diego, netting only a small sum of money, and was soon caught.

Gardner played the role of the flippant criminal, answering the judge with Shakespearean quotes and constantly showing off his literary knowledge. The judge was unimpressed and sentenced him to 25 years at the federal penitentiary on McNeil Island, Wash. Gardner was stunned at the sentence. Then he regained his composure. "You'll never get me there," he shouted as he was being led away. No one paid him any mind.

But Roy Gardner was right. He overpowered his train guards, seized their weapons and hopped off the train as it neared Portland, Ore. While a vast manhunt for him was launched in the Pacific Northwest, he went east through Canada, holed up in Minneapolis and eventually moved to Davenport, Iowa, where he took a job as a welding instructor. Soon, the old restlessness surfaced, and he returned to Napa, Calif., where his wife lived under constant surveillance. He slipped past the stakeout to see her and sneaked away again. A neighbor spotted him and called the police, but despite an intensive hunt, with his picture splashed across the newspapers, Gardner escaped.

In May 1921 he robbed a Southern Pacific mail car of $200,000 in cash and securities. By not fleeing the area, however, he again proved to be a poor thief. Six days later, he was caught in a Roseville gambling room, betting big and bragging about how smart he was. When apprehended, Gardner had only a small amount of his loot and refused to say where the rest was.

Another 25 years was added to his sentence, and the law put him on a train for McNeil Island once more and once more failed to get him there. Already the newspapers had dubbed him the Escaping Professor and printed his boast that he would not be taken as far as Tacoma, Wash.

On the train Gardner asked his two guards for permission to go to the toilet. The officers, being cautious, accompanied him and kept another prisoner handcuffed to him. The four trooped to the men's room, one of the large types of the 1920s. Nothing untoward happened until they moved to the sink. Suddenly, using his free hand, Gardner pulled a gun from under the sink. He and the other prisoner, Norris Pryor, handcuffed the officers and taped their mouths shut with the tape that had been used to secure the gun in its hiding place. How it got there Gardner never revealed. As the train slowed in the Vancouver yards, Gardner and Pryor jumped off, disappearing in the misty rain.

Gardner's escape made headlines across the country, and he became one of the nation's most glorified criminals. Unfortunately for him, he became so recognizable that he was readily recaptured. The newspapers speculated about how far the law would succeed in transporting Gardner this time, but the authorities took no chances. He was shackled to two unarmed officers and guarded at a distance by two others. When he entered the prison, one journalist mourned "the end of a legend."

It wasn't. On Labor Day 1921 Gardner was watching a baseball game from the bleachers of the prison ball field. As all eyes were focused on the field, he and two other convicts dropped through the bleacher seats to the ground. They cut through the barbed wire fence with wire cutters Gardner had stolen from the machine shop and raced for undergrowth 50 yards from the fence. If they made that, they would have a chance. The tower guards didn't see them until they were halfway there. In the fusillade of bullets that followed, Gardner's two companions went down. Gardner was wounded in the left leg but made the bushes. He hid out there until dark while guards searched for him and police craft circled the island. What they didn't know was that Gardner had retraced his escape route and was hiding out in the prison barn. He treated his wound, which was not too serious, and milked a cow whenever he got hungry.

Gardner stayed hidden for 48 hours, by which time it was decided he had reached the mainland. Only then did he move to the water's edge, drift $2\frac{1}{2}$ miles to Fox Island and from there swim to the mainland. He vanished for a few weeks and then was back in the headlines. Audaciously, he had addressed a letter to President Warren Harding offering a deal. He wanted his sentences suspended so that he could return to his wife and young children "to start life anew." In return, he promised to pay back to the government some $250,000 in loot, which he said he had salted away.

It made good newspaper copy but had no results. The president naturally ignored the offer.

Gardner was now 33 years old. Somewhere between his escape from the prison in September and November 15, all the fight went out of him. He tried to hold up a mail clerk on a train in Arizona but was easily overpowered. This time he was sent to Leavenworth, his sentence now having reached 75 years. He never escaped custody again. Gardner's reputation earned him a transfer to the new maximum security federal prison at Alcatraz in 1934, but he was sent back to Leavenworth two years later because of his good behavior. Two years after that, he was freed. The newspapers speculated investigators wanted him to lead them to his stolen money hoard, but the real reason for his release was his poor health. Thereafter, Gardner lived alone in a rundown hotel in San Francisco, his wife having died years before. In January 1940, at the age of 52, the Escaping Professor made his final break to freedom. He turned on the gas.

Garfield, James A.   See CHARLES JULIUS GUITEAU.

341

Garfield portrait swindle

Shortly after the assassination of President James A. Garfield in 1881, some 200 newspapers carried an advertisement that was to become a minor classic swindle. The ad offered the grieving public what seemed to be a rare portrait of the dead president, stating:

I have secured the authorized steel engravings of the late President Garfield, executed by the United States Government, approved by the President of the United States, by Congress and by every member of the President's family as the most faithful of all portraits of the President. It was executed by the Government's most expert steel engravers, and I will send a copy from the original plate, in full colors approved by the Government, postpaid, for one dollar each.

To every eager person sending a dollar, the swindler fulfilled his promises to the letter by mailing back an engraving of President Garfield on a 5¢ postage stamp.

Following the Garfield portrait swindle, con men went on to pull the same racket countless times in endless variations involving other notable persons and subjects that have appeared on commemorative stamps, sometimes also promising "suitable mounting," which meant putting the stamp on an index card.

garment area crime   See HIJACKING, SNEAK THIEVERY.

Garrett, Patrick Floyd (1850–1908) lawman and killer of Billy the Kid

To sum up Pat Garrett's career as a lawman, he was at his best on a manhunt only when he killed from ambush, a trait he exhibited constantly while tracking his greatest prize, Billy the Kid. While stalking the Kid, Garrett, then sheriff of Lincoln County, plotted an ambush from the old hospital at Fort Sumner, New Mexico Territory, where the wife of one of the Kid's gang members, Charlie Bowdre, was confined. When the gang appeared and Garrett thought he spotted the Kid, he ordered his men to open fire, but the wrong man, Tom O'Folliard, was mortally wounded. Four days later, Garrett set another ambush outside an abandoned rock house near Stinking Springs, N.M. He passed the word that the ambushers were to shoot Billy the Kid when he walked outside at dawn. As dawn broke, Charlie Bowdre came out, and since he was of the same general appearance and size as the Kid, Garrett signaled for the shooting to commence. Bowdre too was fatally wounded. It was a needless killing and a needless ambush. The Kid and his gang

were trapped and eventually did the only thing they could do, surrender.

Garrett always thought ambush. When he caught up with Billy on July 14, 1881, following the young gunman's escape from custody, Garrett shot him to death as the unsuspecting outlaw walked into a darkened room in his stocking feet with his gun tucked in his belt. He then ran triumphantly out of the building shouting gleefully: "I killed the Kid! I killed the Kid!"

Garrett gained nationwide fame for the killing, especially far from New Mexico, where he was not all that popular. In fact, he was denied renomination as sheriff by the Democratic political powers, who undoubtedly were not happy about the way he had killed the Kid from ambush. In addition, Gov. Lew Wallace appeared to have put obstacles in the way of Garrett's collecting the reward for Billy, and Garrett finally had to lobby in Santa Fe to get a special act through the state legislature awarding him $500.

There is reason to think Garrett lived in fear that some fan of the Kid would take revenge on him. When he became cattle boss on a large ranch, he ordered that no cowhand be allowed to carry a six-shooter. Several cowboys who resented the order said it was clearly given because Garrett was afraid to turn his back on them. In 1889 he ran for sheriff in Chavez County but lost, the stigma of Billy the Kid still clinging to him. Embittered, he pulled up stakes and moved to Uvalde County, Tex., where he befriended John Nance Garner, a future vice president of the United States then in his thirties and already a political power. With Cactus Jack's help, he was elected a county commissioner and held that post until 1897, when old friends in Dona Ana County got him to return to New Mexico. Garrett became sheriff of Las Cruces County and held the office for one term. When he was not renominated, he returned to ranching until Teddy Roosevelt, who admired law-and-order types, named him a customs collector in El Paso. For some unknown reason, he fell from presidential favor and was not reappointed in 1905. Following his return to farming, Garrett got involved in a feud and was shot to death in 1908. That killing, like many of Garrett's, was controversial. A neighbor, Wayne Brazel, admitted he had killed Garrett but said it was in self-defense, a version backed up by a witness, Carl Adamson. However, it was evident that Garrett had been shot in the back of the head while heeding a call of nature. There was considerable reason to believe that the real murderer was Killin' Jim Miller, a professional hired gun, and that he had been assigned the task by Adamson, who wanted Garrett's land. Officially, Brazel was charged in the killing and cleared.

Today, Garrett is remembered only for the killing of Billy the Kid and is generally better thought of than he

Pat Garrett's fanciful biography of Billy the Kid served to enhance his own reputation as well as that of the young outlaw.

was at the time. Part of the reason for this is Garrett's contribution to Western history, *An Authentic Life of Billy the Kid,* a book written in Garrett's name by an itinerant journalist, Ash Upson. In the preface Garrett assured his readers, "I am incited to this labor by an impulse to correct the thousand false statements which have appeared in the public newspapers and in yellow-covered cheap novels."

He nonetheless proceeded to deliver a version full of falsehoods. One piece of misinformation was that Billy the Kid had killed his first man at the age of 12 to avenge an insult to his mother. He was also mistaken when he said the Kid rescued a wagon train by routing marauding Indians with an ax, and Billy never rode 81

miles in six hours to get a buddy out of a Texas jail, as Garrett claimed. In praise of himself, Garrett loftily claimed credit for delivering to New Mexico "a season of peace and prosperity to which she has ever, heretofore, been a stranger."

See also: BILLY THE KID.

Gas House Gang 19th-century New York gang

A vicious group of street thugs, the Gas House Gang originally controlled the Gas House district around New York's East 35th Street, but in an unusual criminal migration just before the start of the 20th century, the gang moved southward to take control of Third Avenue from 11th Street to 18th Streets.

During their heyday over the next dozen or so years, the Gas Housers, numbering about 200, controlled the area with an iron fist, extracting tribute from saloon keepers and businessmen, running gambling games and so on. Whenever they failed to find enough entertainment and riches in their immediate neighborhoods, they would invade other gang precincts and take what they wanted. Usually, they met little resistance because other gangs, even larger ones, knew any war with the Gas Housers would be debilitating.

Essentially, however, the Gas Housers remained true street thugs, revelling most in muggings; in their prime they averaged some 30 street holdups a night. The term *Gas House Gang* entered the English vernacular as a description for a bunch of brawling rowdies; thus when some years later the St. Louis Cardinals baseball team developed into the rowdies of the diamond, they quite naturally became known as the Gas House Gang.

Gebhardt, Dr. Fritz (1895–1935) murder victim

The first murder verdict in America with an anti-Nazi tone was given in the case of Dr. Fritz Gebhardt, who in 1934 had met and wooed an American woman, Laura Parr, on a sea cruise. Within a year both were living in the Beekman Tower in New York City, Laura on the 19th floor and Gebhardt on the 21st.

On November 25, 1935 Gebhardt telephoned Laura and asked her to come to his apartment because he was feeling ill. When she arrived in her nightclothes, Gebhardt made a miraculous recovery. It was then that he suggested Laura engage in what she regarded as an immoral act. When she refused, according to her later testimony, he threatened her with a gun. Laura seized the gun and shot Gebhardt dead.

The press initially judged Laura guilty, labeling her the Icy Blonde. The *New York Daily Mirror* ran Laura's picture on the editorial page with the caption "With Such a Lady—Be Careful." The *New York World–*

Telegram asked, "Can True Love Yield to Murderous Hatred?" Even the *New York Times* found interest in the case so intense that it devoted four columns to it just prior to the trial.

At the onset of the trial, public opinion was against Laura Parr, but this changed as her defense lawyer, the legendary Samuel Leibowitz, developed his case. The lawyer succeeded in putting on trial not only the victim, a German businessman, but the entire Nazi regime as well. In fact, while prospective jurors were being questioned, it appeared as though the accused was German philosopher Friedrich Wilhelm Nietzsche, then dead some 36 years. During the trial itself, for a time the real defendant seemed to be Field Marshal Hermann Goering. (During World War I Dr. Gebhardt had served with distinction in the Richtofen Squadron, where he became friendly with a young pilot named Hermann Goering.) Somehow even the personal peccadillos of brutal Brownshirt chief Ernest Roehm became part of the case, although there was no record of Roehm ever residing in the Beekman Tower.

By the end of the trial, the choice was clear; the jury could vote for the supermen of the German master race or for American womanhood. When Laura Parr was found not guilty, women spectators squealed in delight. "The defendant is discharged," the judge announced stiffly and left the bench. It was one of the few times in a New York court when a jury was not thanked by the presiding judge for its labors.

See also: SAMUEL S. LEIBOWITZ.

Geidel, Paul (1894–?) longest-term convict

It is believed that no one ever served more time in an American prison than Paul Geidel, who was found guilty of the 1911 murder of a wealthy guest in a New York City hotel where he worked as a porter. Geidel, who was 17 years old at the time, was sentenced to 20 years to life in Clinton Prison. In May 1980, 68 years and seven months later, he was released from the Fishkill Correctional Facility, to which he had been transferred, and was sent to live out his remaining days in a nursing home.

Gein, Edward (1906–1984) murderer

Few murderers in the 20th century have evoked such horror as Ed Gein, a Wisconsin farmer, in the 1950s. Indeed his career inspired the movie *Psycho*. Gein worked the family farm at Plainfield, Wis. with his brother Henry and his elderly mother, who always insisted that her two boys never marry. His mother died in 1945, and brother Henry followed her within a year, leaving Ed alone on his farm with his strange fantasies.

Gein developed a strong interest in female anatomy and, greatly affected by Christine Jorgensen's successful transsexual operation, apparently wanted to change his sex. He developed a morbid need to acquire women's bodies in order to study the anatomical structure of female organs, and to satisfy that desire, he took to digging up female corpses from their graves.

To aid in this secret task, Gein recruited a lame-witted old farmer, assuring him that their ghoulish activities would advance the cause of science. The old man helped Gein bring the corpses to a shed next to his farmhouse. Here, Gein skinned the bodies and sometimes even donned the skin and walked around his house so clad for hours. He also kept parts of the bodies as trophies, mounting the heads, hearts, livers and sex organs. When the doting farmer was committed to an old-age home, Gein was faced with the task of gathering the corpses on his own—or finding some easier way to collect bodies than exhuming them from all those graves. Some time in the early 1950s, he apparently decided it would be simpler to kill fresh victims rather than go through all the trouble of digging graves

Later, Gein would helpfully try to name his victims, but he suffered from a lack of memory on the subject and could recall only two for certain. In 1954 Gein walked into a bar run by 51-year-old Mary Hogan in Pine Grove and, seeing her alone, pulled out a pistol and shot her in the head. He piled her body on a sled and took her home. Subsequently, he accumulated some other bodies, although after his arrest he couldn't remember if he had killed them or dug them up. In November 1957 he killed Mrs. Bernice Worden, the operator of a hardware store in Plainfield. Ironically, the night before the murder Gein had mentioned to Mrs. Worden's son, who happened to be a deputy sheriff, that he would have to buy some antifreeze. The following evening the deputy went to his mother's store and found her missing. There was some blood on the floor and a half-written receipt for a purchase of antifreeze, and the cash register was gone.

Mrs. Worden's son remembered his conversation with Gein, and the latter's farm was searched. There the authorities found all sorts of grim relics, including bracelets made of human skin, a sewn-up skull fashioned into a soup bowl and dozens of other gruesome remains from at least 15 bodies. Gein admitted the grave robbings and the murders but was most upset when accused of robbing the cash register from his last victim's store. "I'm no robber," he said indignantly. "I took the money and the register only because I wanted to see how the machine worked."

Gein was committed for life to an institution for the criminally insane. For some years the Gein farmhouse was regarded a place of horror until finally the local people burned it to the ground.

Geller, Max   See GREEN PARROT MURDER.

Gem Saloon, gunfight at the

While the O.K. Corral is the most famous shoot-out site in America, far more deadly gun duels and killings took place at the infamous Gem Saloon in El Paso, Tex. It was here in January 1877 that Pink Higgins outdrew Merritt Horrell, chalking up another death in the Horrell-Higgins feud. But just as there was *the* gunfight at the O.K. Corral, so too was there *the* gunfight at the Gem, one that probably had more stock elements than any of a score of famous duels: right against wrong, a man bucking incredible odds, mistaken identity, black Western humor and a prime example of the art of gunfighting.

The duel or more correctly, duels were fought on April 14, 1884. On that day a gambler and dandy named Bill Raynor, who had gained his reputation as a gunfighter by planting eight foes in the ground, turned "mean" and walked through town looking for a fight. Given his reputation, he found no takers. After challenging every man in a barbershop, he moved on to the Gem. He sauntered into the saloon's gambling room and finally provoked one faro player, Bob Rennick, into demanding Raynor stop leaning on him. Raynor told him he was stepping out to the bar to have a drink and was then coming back in to kill him. The other players advised Rennick to move away from the table so they could continue their game in peace. Rennick checked his six-gun, moved to the wall and began watching the doorway. A minute or so later, Raynor burst into the room, his guns blazing. Four shots splintered the chair Rennick had vacated; Rennick stepped out from the wall and answered with two shots that caught Raynor in the stomach and chest. Raynor staggered out to the street and collapsed in the arms of a noted visitor in town, Wyatt Earp, asking Earp to inform his mother that he had "died game."

Raynor was taken to the doctor's office, where his friend Buck Linn rushed to him, inquiring about who had shot him. Raynor gave a garbled answer that indicated the man who had gunned him down was Bob Cahill. Linn vowed to take vengeance on his friend's alleged assailant. When this news got back to the Gem, Cahill, an inoffensive gambler who had never shot a gun, became petrified. A friend named Dan Tipton handed Cahill a loaded .45, and Wyatt Earp gave him a fast lesson in gunfighting, to wit: stay calm, take plenty of time aiming and shoot for the belly button. This was standard advice, but observers could not tell how much of it the frightened Cahill had absorbed. Five minutes later, Buck Linn entered the saloon. After spotting the little gambler, he pulled his gun and fired four fast shots from a distance of 12 to 15 feet. All missed. Cahill aimed his .45 and sighted in on Linn's belt buckle when he was about 8 feet away. His aim was high, and he shot Linn right through the heart.

Thus ended the Gem's most famous shoot-out, although Raynor did not expire for 48 hours. On the chance that he might recover, both Rennick and Cahill, who had pushed their luck to the limit, rode hard for Mexico. The two victors had popular support, one drunk at the bar proclaiming: "I'm damned glad Bill got it. He should have been killed years ago." From the silence that greeted his comment, the drunk realized there was still the chance that Raynor might recover. He added quickly, "If Bill gets well, what I said don't go." But Raynor, fortunately for the drunk, didn't make it.

The *El Paso Herald* stated: "The victims had no one to blame but themselves. Their train of life collided with loaded revolvers and they have gone down forever in the smash-up. Thus endeth the first chapter of our spring fights."

gemstone   Watergate code word

The code word for the break-in at the Democratic National Committee's headquarters in the Watergate complex in Washington, D.C. was gemstone. Five men were caught in the ill-conceived, still not fully explained operation that resulted in the toppling of the Nixon administration, with Richard Nixon forced to resign the presidency and several of his top associates sent to prison.

Genna brothers   Prohibition-era Chicago family gang

The Genna brothers, known as the Terrible Gennas, were the first Chicago gang to jump into moonshining in a big way with the advent of Prohibition. Most of the brothers had been Black Hand extortionists preying on the residents of the city's Little Italy section, but in 1919 they realized there was more money putting people to work producing illegal alcohol, and they turned Little Italy into one large cottage moonshining industry.

The brothers Genna—Bloody Angelo, Tony the Gentleman, Mike the Devil, Pete, Sam and Jim—had come to Chicago from Sicily in 1910. Five of them were typical Sicilian killers—haughty, vicious, treacherous, murderous and devoutly religious. They carried their crucifixes in the same pocket with their pistols. The "different" Genna was Tony the Gentleman, or, as he was sometimes called, Tony the Aristocrat. He studied architecture, constructed model tenements for poor Italian immigrants, was a leading patron of the opera and lived elegantly in a downtown hotel. Tony had strong personal convictions against killing and never did a job himself, although he attended all family councils at which rub-outs were planned. When Johnny Torrio and Al Capone were setting up their operation, the two feared the Gennas more than any other gang because they commanded the most savage set of killers. Among them were Sam "Smoots" Amatuna, the gangland dandy who loved music almost as much as he loved committing murder; Giuseppe "the Cavalier" Nerone, a university graduate and mathematics teacher turned gunman; and the celebrated murder duo John Scalise and Albert Anselmi, who introduced the practice of rubbing bullets with garlic in the hope of inducing gangrene should the victim survive the initial gunshot wound.

Combined with the Gennas' constant application of deadly force was their ability to corrupt the police. In 1925 a confession by their office manager indicated the brothers had on their payroll five police captains and some 400 uniformed officers, mostly from the Maxwell Street station, as well as many plainclothesmen from headquarters and the state attorney's office. The Gennas' booze-making operation grossed $350,000 a month, and the six brothers netted a clear monthly profit of $150,000. When Johnny Torrio brought most of the gangs together under one umbrella, the Gennas were the hardest to control. Ever devious, they constantly flooded other gangs' areas with their cheap booze, underselling them with terrible rotgut. A three-way competition soon developed among the Gennas, the North Side O'Banions and the Torrio-Capone mob.

Eventually the Gennas started getting picked off one by one, especially after Anselmi and Scalise deserted their banner to join the Capone forces.

Bloody Angelo Genna fell victim on May 25, 1925 to North Side gangsters who had followed his roadster through Chicago streets. When Angelo first became aware of them, he picked up speed. But in his desperate haste to get away, he smashed into a lamppost and was pinned behind the wheel, unable to do anything but watch as the pursuing black sedan glided to a stop by him and three shotguns blasted him apart.

Mike Genna vowed vengeance on the O'Banions who had done the job. The following month he and Anselmi and Scalise were out hunting for North Siders. What Mike Genna didn't known was that he was being taken for a ride by the pair, who had secretly defected to Capone. The three got caught in a gunfight with police. Anselmi and Scalise killed two officers, wounded a third and fled, leaving a wounded Genna to be captured by

police. As Mike Genna was being placed on a stretcher, he cut loose a powerful kick with his good leg and knocked out one of the attendants. "Take that, you dirty son of a bitch," he snarled. He died two hours later.

Tony the Gentleman, the real brains of the Terrible Gennas, realizing that Anselmi and Scalise had deserted, knew he was next. Just as he was about to leave the city, he arranged for a final meeting with his supporter Nerone on a darkened street corner. He did not know that Nerone also had defected. When Tony Genna emerged from his car, Nerone grasped his hand in a steel-like handshake. Just then one or two gunmen stepped out of the darkness and filled Tony with bullets. Tony the Gentleman lingered for days before dying.

The power of the Gennas was now broken. The three surviving brothers fled, Sam and Pete to hideouts outside Chicago and Jim all the way back to Sicily. In Palermo, Jim Genna got two years for stealing the jewels that adorned the statue of the Madonna di Trapani.

Eventually, the three brothers came back to Chicago but avoided the rackets. They ran an olive oil and cheese importing firm, finishing out their days in relative obscurity.

See also: ANSELMI AND SCALISE, ALPHONSE "SCARFACE AL" CAPONE, MAXWELL STREET POLICE STATION.

Genovese, Kitty (1935–1964) murder victim

The events surrounding the murder of Kitty Genovese, a 28-year-old woman from Queens, New York City, were more bizarre than the brutal crime itself, in which a killer stalked and killed his victim in three separate attacks over a 35-minute period. The attacks occurred after 3 A.M. on March 13, 1964. The killer, 29-year-old Winston Moseley, walked away after first stabbing the woman on Austin Street in the middle-class section of Kew Gardens. As Kitty Genovese staggered around the short block toward the entrance to her home, her assailant returned in his car, looked for her in doorways, found her and stabbed her again. He drove off but in a few minutes came back to find the woman in a hallway at the foot of a staircase. He stabbed her a third time, fatally, and drove off.

The crime itself was not all that unusual. What made the Genovese case different is that at least 37 persons witnessed all or part of the attacks but not one of them called the police.

After the first attack, the victim shrieked: "Oh, my God, he stabbed me! Please help me! Please help me!" Lights went on in several apartments in a 10-story apartment house across the street. A man yelled out: "Let that girl alone!"

It was enough to make Moseley walk away. When he returned the first time and stabbed her again, Kitty Genovese screamed: "I'm dying! I'm dying!" Again lights went on and again windows went up. Many persons saw Moseley, but still no one called the police. After Moseley finished off his victim on the third try, the first call to the police was made.

Eventually, Moseley was caught and sentenced to the electric chair, which because of the law on capital punishment at the time, meant in effect a life sentence. What remained puzzling to police, newspaper reporters and psychologists was why nobody had called the police earlier. The man who finally placed the first call had done so with trepidation. Before he made the call, he telephoned a friend in Nassau County to seek his advice on what to do. After some deliberation it was decided he should telephone the police. The comments gotten from some witnesses were perhaps instructive of the noninvolvement instincts present in contemporary American society. Among the statements were: "I didn't want to get involved"; "Frankly, we were afraid"; "I didn't want my husband to get involved"; "I don't know"; "I was tired. I went back to bed"; "Get away or I'll throw you down the steps."

Another was possibly the most instructive: "The last time I complained to the police, I was sent to a concentration camp." Kew Gardens contained a high concentration of former victims of the Nazis in Europe, and a common characteristic of many was that the last thing one did was have anything to do with the symbols of authority.

Genovese, Vito (1897–1969) Mafia chieftain

Vito "Don Vito" Genovese was probably the most awesome of the Mafia dons. He is credited with being the moving force that put the Mafia in the narcotics business, a shift some others, such as Frank Costello and, despite the contentions of federal narcotics investigators, Lucky Luciano, strongly opposed. Genovese, who started out in the shadow of Luciano in the early 1920s, rose to the top of the syndicate crime empire by killing off his many rivals. He is known to have ordered the deaths of Willie Moretti in 1951, Steve Franse in 1953 and Albert Anastasia in 1957. He was the obvious mastermind behind the attempt on the life of Frank Costello, which eventually led to the latter's retirement.

Genovese was always a cunning criminal. Faced with a murder charge in 1937, he fled to Italy, where he ingratiated himself with Benito Mussolini despite the fascist leader's ruthless campaign to wipe out the Italian Mafia. Genovese became the chief drug supplier for Mussolini's foreign minister and son-in-law, Count Ciano. During the war, to further gain Mussolini's favor, Genovese ordered the execution of Il Duce's longtime nemesis, radical editor Carlo Tresca, in New York City, a hit carried out by a Genovese underling, Carmine Galante.

In 1944, with the Mussolini regime crumbling, Genovese turned up as an interpreter for the army's intelligence service. Due to his energetic and diligent efforts, a number of black market operatives were caught in southern Italy. However, the military's pleasure with Genovese's performance vanished when it was discovered that as he unearthed the black marketeers and put them out of business, he simply took over their rackets.

Genovese returned to the United States after the war, when the witnesses to the murder charge against him had been dealt with. He took control of the Luciano family and, with his mentor now in exile, set about making himself the dominant figure in the American underworld. To do that, he had to gain dominance over the five New York crime families, eliminate Frank Costello and lessen the influence of Meyer Lansky, all the while paying lip service to Luciano.

It took Genovese almost a decade to solidify his position to the point that he could attempt this takeover, in the process gaining needed revenues from the narcotics trade. By 1957 he was ready to move. He first ordered the execution of Costello, whose importance in the underworld had diminished as a result of the Kefauver hearings. The plot failed and Costello was only slightly wounded. A few months later, however, another of his assassination orders was spectacularly successful. Albert Anastasia was shot to death as he sat in a barber's chair in a New York hotel. At the time, Anastasia was Costello's most important ally, and without him the fabled Prime Minister of the Underworld appeared helpless.

Later that year Genovese sought to solidify his new power by calling the famed Apalachin Conference in upstate New York. That meeting ended in a fiasco when the state police raided it and took dozens of leading Mafia dons into custody. Genovese was not perceptive enough to realize the meeting had been sabotaged by enemies far smarter and craftier than he, including Costello, Lansky, Luciano and Carlo Gambino, the heir to the Anastasia crime family. Gambino and Lansky had cooperated with Genovese in the elimination of Anastasia for their own reasons—Gambino to gain new power for himself and Lansky to eliminate the pressure the kill-crazy Anastasia was putting on him for a share of his vast Cuban gambling profits.

In these four, Genovese was facing the top double-dealers of the underworld. They understood better than Genovese that war between the two camps would be senseless, leading only to trouble for all. Instead, they plotted to eliminate Genovese by cunning and treachery. They decided to set him up for a federal drug bust, but the narcotics agents who were tipped off muffed the opportunity and Genovese slipped away. The underworld conspirators then arranged a trap that even allowed for the government's ineptitude. The four pitched in a $100,000 kitty and paid a minor Puerto Rican dope pusher named Nelson Cantellops to implicate Genovese in a deal. Although it was not logical that an unimportant street pusher like Cantellops would have the type of inside information to put away a power like Genovese, the government gladly accepted his testimony and convicted Genovese. In 1959 he was sentenced to the Atlanta Penitentiary for 15 years. According to underworld informer Joe Valachi, Genovese continued to direct the activities of his crime family from behind bars, but there is no doubt his influence lessened. Unquestionably, his effort to become the top boss of the underworld had been a disaster.

It was said that Genovese and Costello, sent to the Atlanta Penitentiary on tax charges, later held a tearful reconciliation in prison. If so, Genovese didn't understand the role Costello had played in his downfall; the facts of the plot were not revealed until Luciano broke his silence on the matter shortly before he died in 1962. When Genovese died in 1969, still a federal prisoner on a trumped-up charge, he was proof that mere brawn would never be enough to take over organized crime in America.

See also: ALBERT ANASTASIA, APALACHIN CONFERENCE, FRANK COSTELLO, CARMINE GALANTE, CARLO GAMBINO, PETER LATEMPA, CHARLES "LUCKY" LUCIANO, WILLIE MORETTI, CARLO TRESCA, JOSEPH M. VALACHI.

Gentle Annie   See ANNIE STAFFORD.

Gentlemen's Riot

Easily the "classiest" riot in American history was staged in 1835 in Boston by the "broadcloth mob," a crowd of 3,000 wealthy and socially prominent men, most of whom were dressed in broadcloth. On October 21 they gathered to protest a lecture being given by the famous English abolitionist George Thompson on behalf of the Boston Female Anti-Slavery Society. The mob planned to tar and feather the speaker, but Thompson had been forewarned and fled the city. The mob, angered at losing the victim, vented its frustration on William Lloyd Garrison, who published the anti-slavery newspaper *Liberator*. Garrison was bound with ropes and hauled away some distance, and by this time it was probably uncertain if the intent was a tar and feathering or a hanging. Garrison, however, was rescued by a number of friends and the police who carried

him through the crowd to the city jail and kept him there overnight for protection. The disturbance became known as the Gentlemen's Riot. No convictions ever resulted.

George, Christian   (?–1724) cult leader and accused murderer

Christian George was one of the first to preach free love in the New World and died at the end of a rope because of it.

A religious fanatic from Switzerland, he preached his free love faith to the citizens of Charleston, S.C. He soon gathered a small sect of faithful believers and lead them to the Orange Quarter of South Carolina late in 1723 to set up a love commune. Among George's converts were a young couple, Peter and Judith Dutartre. The free love zealot apparently impressed the woman considerably with his gospel, so much so that she was soon pregnant with George's child. News of this "Devil's child" shocked the good burghers of Charleston, who, led by Justice Symmons, formed a posse to destroy George's love camp. Rather than submit to arrest, George ordered his followers to barricade their camp and resist. The Charleston forces stormed the commune's fortification but were beaten back. Then Peter Dutartre seized a musket and shot Justice Symmons dead. The next attack succeeded and the free love congregation was captured.

While the killing of Justice Symmons was a lone act by Peter Dutartre, the real quarry for Charleston justice was Christian George, who, it was feared, might lead other gullible persons from the path of morality. Dutartre, Christian George and a third cult member, Peter Rombert, were put on trial together, and after a two-day hearing all three were sentenced to hang. The verdict was carried out the following day. The citizens of Charleston then burned the love commune to the ground and returned to their own churches, content that morality had carried the day against the teachings of the Devil.

Giancana, Sam "Momo"   (1908–1975) syndicate leader

Considered by many to have been the most ruthless Mafia killer in the country, Sam "Momo" Giancana was for years the crime boss of Chicago and was suspected of involvement in various CIA plots to assassinate Cuban premier Fidel Castro.

Giancana's arrest record dated back to 1925, when he was a gun runner for Al Capone. Unlike other crime bosses, whose arrest records were usually short, Giancana was a "doer," with more than 70 arrests for everything from assault and bookmaking to bombing and suspicion of murder. He served prison sentences for auto theft, operation of an illegal still and burglary. During World War II he was asked by the draft board how he made his living; Giancana replied: "Me? I steal." He was rejected for service as "a constitutional psychopath."

According to well-publicized charges, Giancana was recruited in 1960 by the U.S. Central Intelligence Agency to "hit" Fidel Castro. Some say Giancana deliberately botched the assignment because he still had hopes of rebuilding the Mafia's gambling business in Cuba. In 1975 the Giancana-CIA connection talk was so widespread that the crime boss was about to be summoned before a Senate investigating committee. Before Giancana could appear, gunmen entered his fortresslike home in Chicago's Oak Park suburb and put seven bullets in him. CIA director William Colby announced forthwith, "We had nothing to do with it." Newsmen contacting unofficial spokesmen for the syndicate got the same response from that source.

See also: ANTHONY JOSEPH ACCARDO, APALACHIN CONFERENCE, FIORE "FIFI" BUCCIERI, FORTY-TWO GANG, PAUL "THE WAITER" RICCA.

Gibbs, Charles (c. 1800–1831) pirate

Officially credited with the murder of 400 victims, a Rhode Islander named Charles Gibbs stands high on any list of American pirates, even if, as is probable, the total number of killings attributed to him was greatly exaggerated.

His modus operandi rarely varied. He would sign on a ship and pilfer what supplies he could whenever the vessel hit port. If he found the cargo aboard worthwhile, he would recruit a few other seamen aboard to join him, and they would murder the captain, first mate and whomever else in the crew they thought would harbor any feelings of loyalty. Since crews of the average vessel generally numbered less than 10, three or four murders usually were sufficient for Gibbs' purpose. When he was captured, Gibbs bragged that he often was able to keep all the booty for himself by frightening off the seamen who had helped him.

Gibbs' biggest haul was his last one, some $50,000 worth of cargo seized from the *Vineyard*, which he had signed on in New Orleans on November 1, 1830 for a run to Philadelphia. Together with the ship's cook, Thomas Wansley, and three others, Gibbs murdered Capt. William Thornby and First Mate William Roberts off Cape Hatteras, N.C. After the mutineers landed, the three sailors who had joined Gibbs and Wansley went to the authorities, explaining they had agreed to join in the piracy only because they realized they would be killed if they had refused. Gibbs and

Wansley were captured and convicted. Much to the delight of the press, Gibbs added one gory confession after another to his murderous exploits. Some were definitely true; others were somewhat doubtful. In any event, Gibbs achieved celebrity by the time he and Wansley were hanged on Ellis Island on April 22, 1831. Thousands watched the spectacle from pleasure boats and fireboats off-shore.

Gigante, Vincent "the Chin" (1926–) mobster

Vincent "the Chin" Gigante was a hulking 300-pound gangster generally credited as the hit man in the famous attempt to assassinate crime boss Frank Costello in 1957. According to popular theory, the hit was masterminded by Vito Genovese to seize the leadership of organized crime in New York. Gigante reportedly took target practice daily in a Greenwich Village basement in preparation for his big opportunity.

On May 2, 1957 Costello returned to his apartment building on Central Park West at the corner of 72nd Street. As he did, a large black Cadillac pulled to the curb, and a huge man got out and hurried ahead of Costello into the building. When Costello entered the lobby, the big man stepped from behind a pillar and produced a .38-caliber revolver. Just before firing, he called out, "This is for you, Frank."

At the sound of the man's voice, Costello turned, and by that movement saved his own life. The bullet tore through the right side of his scalp just above the ear. The fat man raced off for the waiting Cadillac, satisfied he had killed his target. Costello, although needing hospitalization, was not seriously hurt. Maintaining the underworld code, he refused to name his assailant. However, the apartment house doorman had gotten a good look at the blubbery gunman, and based on his evidence, an alert went out for the Chin. He was not readily found. According to the later statement of underworld informer Joe Valachi, "The Chin was just taken somewhere up in the country to lose some weight."

When that body beautifying was completed, Gigante surrendered, saying he understood the law was looking for him. It was thus a trim and slim Chin who went on trial for attempted murder, but Costello refused to identify him and the doorman either wouldn't or couldn't. The Chin left the court a free man.

It was supposedly the Chin's farewell to the big time, his last moment in the spotlight, but he was involved in a struggle far greater than himself. Powerful Mafia forces lined up on two sides—Genovese and his men on one side and the aging Costello, the deported Lucky Luciano and the crafty Meyer Lansky on the other. On the surface, peace was arranged. Genovese, who wanted Costello eliminated to ease his path to total power, agreed that Costello would no longer be threatened and would be allowed to retire on his racket revenues. Costello and his allies consented to the arrangement, and apparently to show good faith, the Chin was even invited to a number of Costello parties.

However, the Costello-Luciano-Lansky axis joined by the cunning Carlo Gambino were determined to get rid of Genovese and concocted a plot whereby he would be handed over to federal narcotics detectives in a tidy drug-smuggling plot. Part of the strategy called for the payment of $100,000 to a minor dope pusher, Nelson Cantellops, to implicate Genovese. Costello contributed $25,000 to the kitty with only one proviso: the Chin had to be involved as well. Everything went according to the script: in 1959 Genovese got 15 years, and 24 of his aides, including the Chin, received long prison terms as well.

In the 1970s various printed accounts claimed Gigante was still alive, although, according to underworld sources, suffering from a mental ailment and frequently regressing back to childhood. Actually he had risen to the rank of *consigliere* under Genovese family crime boss Frank "Funzi" Tieri. In fact, in 1987 with the conviction of the next family boss, Fat Tony Salerno, Gigante was named acting boss, this despite the fact that he sometimes walked on the street in Little Italy in his bathrobe, mumbling incoherently. Both the family soldiers and the police saw this behavior as a dodge to avoid possible later future prosecution. Under Gigante the Genovese family became once more the most powerful of all, eclipsing the Gambino family under John Gotti, with whom he had a running battle for power. Eventually Gigante's "dummy act" collapsed under attack by federal prosecutors, and in December 1997 he was sent to prison for 12 years, making it unlikely at his age that he would resume control of his family, presuming he survived his term.

See also: APALACHIN CONFERENCE, FRANK COSTELLO, VITO GENOVESE.

Gillette, Chester (1884–1908) murderer

Chester Gillette was the real-life Clyde Griffiths of Theodore Dreiser's classic novel *An American Tragedy*.

An ambitious factory worker who wanted to make it into high society, Gillette worked at his uncle's skirt factory in Cortland, N.Y. As the relative of a well-to-do businessman in town—Gillette had been deserted at the age of 14 by his own parents, who had gone off around the country to spread the Salvation Army gospel—he was accepted into local society and could look ahead to the time when he would marry a wealthy girl. Those future plans, however, did not prevent Gillette from partaking in the pleasures of the present, especially an affair with Billie Brown, an 18-year-old secretary at the factory.

Things went along well for the 22-year-old youth up to the time he received a letter from Billie saying she was pregnant. She did not ask Gillette to marry her but kept sending him heart-rending letters, which were intended sooner or later to persuade him to "do the right thing." Gillette ignored Billie's plight until she wrote warning him that she would tell his uncle. Seeing his world threatened, Gillette informed Billie he not only would do right by her but also intended to take her on a glorious holiday.

On July 8 the couple spent the night in Utica, registering in a hotel as man and wife, and from there moved on to the North Woods section of the southern Adirondacks. After some time at Tupper Lake, they moved on to Big Moose Lake, where Gillette asked for "any old hotel where they have boats to rent." They were sent to the Glenmore Hotel, where Billie registered under her right name while Gillette used a phony. They got separate rooms.

On the morning of July 11, the couple took along a picnic lunch and a tennis racket and rowed out on the large lake. Chester Gillette was not seen again until almost 8 o'clock that evening; Billie Brown was never seen alive again. Her body washed ashore at Big Moose Lake on July 14. The medical report revealed that she had died from blows to her face, which had been badly battered, not from drowning. The same day, Gillette was arrested for murder at the Arrowhead Hotel on Eagle Bay, where he had since registered. Under some newturned moss on the shore, the police found a buried tennis racket and asserted it was what Gillette had used to kill Billie. He denied it and told many conflicting stories. One was that Billie had committed suicide by jumping overboard; another was that the boat had capsized accidentally and that she had drowned after hitting her face on the side of the boat.

During Gillette's trial, which lasted 22 days, 109 witnesses appeared. So many of them came from the Cortland skirt factory that it had to shut down. Numerous women said they could not believe this charming, calm and handsome young man was capable of murder. From his cell Gillette sold photos of himself for $5 apiece and thus could afford to have his meals sent in from the local inn. Despite what his female supporters thought, the jury found differently, convicting him of premeditated murder. After more than a year of appeals, Chester Gillette went to the electric chair at Auburn Prison on March 30, 1908, refusing to admit his guilt.

Gilmore, Gary Mark (1940–1977) murderer

In 1977 Gary Gilmore, age 36, became the first man to be executed in the United States in about a decade. His death followed the reinstatement of the death penalty, which had been outlawed in 1972, under constitutional limits set by the Supreme Court.

Gilmore had been convicted of murdering a Utah gas station attendant and a motel clerk in July 1976. His case attracted worldwide attention not only because his execution would mark the return of capital punishment but also because he disparaged groups and individuals opposed to capital punishment who tried to block his execution. One stay was granted by the Supreme Court on the request of Gilmore's mother. The High Court ruled that the state of Utah was required to prove the prisoner, who had twice attempted suicide in his cell, had been of sound mind when he waived his right to appeal his death sentence. In its final decision, however, the Supreme Court ruled five to four that Utah's capital punishment law was constitutionally sound.

While a last-minute effort was made to get the High Court to prevent his execution, Gilmore went to his death on January 17, 1977 before a firing squad in the Utah State Prison at Point of the Mountain. The condemned man spent his last hours with his family and attorneys and showed little tension until he learned that a federal judge had granted a restraining order delaying the execution. However, a few hours later, a federal appeals court reversed that order.

Meanwhile, as lawyers again petitioned the Supreme Court to halt the proceedings, Gilmore was removed from his cell to a warehouse on the prison grounds. He was strapped in a chair on a raised platform, and a black paper target with a white circle was pinned to his T-shirt directly over his heart. Asked by the warden if he had anything more to say, Gilmore responded, "Let's do it." At 8:07 A.M. five men armed with .30-caliber rifles fired from a cubicle 10 yards in front of Gilmore. One of the rifles contained a blank cartridge and each of the other four had a real bullet. All four bullets pierced Gilmore's heart, but he lived a full two minutes after the shooting.

The final Supreme Court ruling against Gilmore had been handed down at 8:04, just three minutes prior to the shooting. Prison officials later admitted the execution had taken place before they had received word of the verdict on the appeal to the Supreme Court.

Gilmore's life and execution were scrutinized in detail in a best-selling book, *Executioner's Song*, by novelist Norman Mailer.

See also: CAPITAL PUNISHMENT.

Ging, Katherine "Kitty" (1867–1894) victim of hypnotic murder

Criminologists have often cited the killing of 27-year-old Kitty Ging in Minneapolis, Minn. in 1894 as an authentic case of hypnosis being used to cause a murder. The facts are hazy at best and certainly subject to various interpretations.

Early that year Harry T. Hayward, a smooth-talking local wastrel, had completed a course in hypnotism and tried out his techniques both on Kitty Ging and on Claus Blixt, a dim-witted building engineer and handyman. Eventually, Haywood induced Kitty to give him several thousand dollars, all her ready cash, so that he could "invest" it for her. How much of this was due to "hypnotic powers" and how much to the sheer weight of his personality cannot be measured. In any event, he also was able in time to get Kitty to make him the beneficiary of two $5,000 life insurance policies.

Meanwhile, Hayward was spending long sessions with Blixt too. "He always made me look into his eyes," the simple-minded Blixt later said. "He said that unless I looked into his eyes, I couldn't understand what he was saying." What Hayward was usually saying was that crime paid and was easy. Blixt insisted Hayward "induced" him to set fire to a vacant factory building on which Kitty Ging held a mortgage. She collected $1,500 in insurance and the money eventually found its way into Hayward's pockets. Since Hayward gave some of the money to Blixt, it was unclear how much of Blixt's acts had been due to his own greed and how much to Hayward's hypnotic powers.

Hayward now began to plot Kitty Ging's murder so that he could collect her life insurance. Apparently, he had less than total confidence in his power to induce Blixt to carry out the crime because he first approached his own brother, Adry Hayward, to commit the murder while he established an iron-clad alibi. The astounded Adry rejected the proposition. He later said: "I don't know why I listened when Harry talked to me of this dreadful thing. He kept looking at me as he talked, and sometimes I felt as if I was being hypnotized. When I refused, he talked about getting Blixt to help him. He said Blixt was so simple-minded that he could easily be influenced."

Adry related his conversation with his brother to a lawyer friend of the family, who simply ignored the story as too preposterous until Kitty Ging's body, her head crushed in and a bullet wound behind her ear, was found on the evening of December 3, 1894. The lawyer then took his information to the Hennepin County district attorney's office, and Blixt and Adry and Harry Hayward were brought in for questioning. Hayward proved to be a tough man to crack, possessing a perfect alibi for the time of the murder: attendance at the Grand Opera House.

For a while, Adry attempted to shield his brother, and Blixt insisted he was not involved in any way. Finally, Blixt broke and admitted murdering Kitty Ging, arranging to do so at a time when Harry Howard had an alibi. He said that before his act he had spent several long sessions with Hayward during which he was told over and over again that murder was an easy crime to commit and get away with. After Blixt's admission, Adry talked, and finally, Harry Hayward confessed to masterminding Kitty's murder, saying his mistake "was in not killing Blixt, as I had originally intended."

Claus Blixt was sentenced to life imprisonment and Harry Hayward, "the hypnotic plotter," was condemned to die on December 11, 1895. His execution proved as bizarre as his crime. He promised to cause no trouble if the scaffold was painted bright red and the rope dipped in red dye. The authorities agreed to these requests but refused to allow him to wear red clothing or to use a red hood in place of the traditional black. On the scaffold Hayward recited a prayer and asked God's forgiveness for his sins. Then he shouted: "Don't pay any attention to that! I just said it to oblige one of my lawyers. I didn't mean a word of it! I stand pat. . . ."

At that moment the outraged executioner, without waiting for his signal, sprang the trap.

Glanton, John J. (c. 1815–1850) scalp hunter and murderer

Of all the men who operated in the bloody business of scalp hunting, probably the most successful was a Tennessee-born thug who had escaped prison in Nashville in 1845 while doing time for murder and taken refuge in the Army during the Mexican War. When mustered out in 1848, he organized a band of those who were described in Texas as "border scum" and went into the scalp-hunting business in a big way. It was estimated that Glanton and his men took in about $100,000 for scalps, which meant slaughtering well over 1,000 Indians since the going rate for Apache scalps paid by the Mexican governor of Chihuahua was $100 for a male, $50 for a female and $25 for a child.

What spoiled their lucrative business was the discovery by both Mexican and U.S. authorities that they were taking a lot of "suspect" scalps, apparently lifted from the heads of Mexicans and Americans of a dark complexion. Rewards of more than $75,000 were posted on Glanton and various confederates, forcing the gang to flee west to the California border on the Colorado River. There, Glanton engaged in a running war with the Yuma Indians for control of ferrying opera-

tions across the river. Learning that the Indians charged covered-wagon immigrants a small sum to cross the river, Glanton realized he could exact exorbitant sums if he eliminated the Indian competition. Initially, the killing margin favored Glanton, but on April 23, 1850 a large force of Yumas overwhelmed Glanton and his men and killed all but three of them. The massacre of whites by the Indians brought an army detachment to the scene to quell the "uprising," but when the victims were found to be Glanton and his men, peace was restored. When Fort Yuma was built later in the year, it was named in honor of the Indians who had wiped out one of the West's bloodiest gangs. The Yuma received no reward money, however. Paying a reward to Indians for killing whites, even those with a price on their heads, would have been regarded as an outrage.

See also: SCALP HUNTING.

Glatman, Harvey Murray (1928–1959) rapist and murderer

By masquerading as a detective magazine photographer, Harvey Glatman, a particularly sadistic California murderer in the 1950s, got three young women to pose for the usual "bound-and-gagged" stuff and, after sexually abusing them and taking many pictures, strangled them to death. Glatman was the classic example of a mama's boy turned killer. He had previously done time in New York State for a string of "phantom bandit" attacks on lone women and been imprisoned in Colorado for aggravated assaults on women. After each run-in with the law, Glatman fell back on his aged mother, who paid for his psychiatric treatment for five years. In 1957 his mother gave him the money to attend a television repairman's school in Los Angeles and supplied him with funds to open a TV repair shop.

Glatman's murder victims were two young photographic models and an attractive lonely hearts club divorcée. On separate occasions he had succeeded in convincing 19-year-old model Judy Dull and 24-year-old model Ruth Rita Mercado that he was a photographer on assignment for a detective magazine. With his third victim, divorcée Shirley Bridgeport, he simply made a date. In each case, after gaining their confidence, he then lured the women to his home, pulled out a gun and tied them up. After sexually assaulting his victims, he took lewd pictures of them. Later, he drove each of the three women into the desert, where he inflicted additional perversities on them for many more hours before finally killing them.

"I used the same five-foot length of sash cord for all three," he later said, almost gloatingly. "I kept it in my car with the gun. . . . I made them lie on their stomachs. Then I tied their ankles together, looped the end of the cord about their necks and pulled until they were dead."

Two other women almost suffered the same fate. One escaped when she grew suspicious of Glatman's actions. The other, 28-year-old Lorraine Vigil, offered desperate resistance when he pointed a gun at her and tried to tie her up on the shoulder of the Santa Ana Freeway. Although shot in the leg, she managed to pull the gun from Glatman's hand and had it pointed at him when a highway patrolman arrived on the scene.

Glatman eagerly described his murderous acts and seemed to bear no remorse for them. His main concern was keeping his 69-year-old mother from attending his trial. "It would have been too hard on her," he said after his conviction. He refused to cooperate with lawyers trying to appeal his case, announcing in San Quentin's death row that he wanted to die. "It's better this way," he said. "I knew this is the way it would be." Glatman was executed in the gas chamber on August 18, 1959, undoubtedly pleased that a number of publications had engaged in spirited, if unseemly, bidding to publish the photographs he had taken of his victims.

G-men slang for FBI agents

The use of the term *G-man* to describe an FBI man was bestowed, according to agency historians, by public enemy George "Machine Gun" Kelly when he was captured in 1933 in a Memphis boarding house. Trapped without his weapon, Kelly was described as screaming, "It's the government men—don't shoot, G-men, don't shoot!"

Actually, a Memphis police sergeant, W. J. Raney, was the man who broke in on Kelly and jammed a shotgun in his stomach. Kelly said, "I've been waiting for you." Additionally, some accounts indicate that during the 19th century members of the underworld referred to other government agents, notably the Secret Service, as G-men.

See also: GEORGE R. "MACHINE GUN" KELLY.

Goad, John (?–1907) gun-toting preacher

An itinerant Baptist preacher, John Goad roamed the Nevada gold camps in the 1870s lecturing against sin and crime and backing up his words with what was to become famous throughout the West as the "John Goad Bible."

In his preaching he would denounce the lawless element in the area by name, and such denunciation often brought attempts at retaliation. As protection, Goad carried a loaded derringer in a hollowed-out Bible and would not hesitate to use it when the situation required. In a typical instance a local ruffian named

Mike Fink was hired by the drink-and-prostitution crowd in Carson City, Nev. to break up Goad's meeting and promptly got a ball in the chest for his troubles. That sort of gunsmoke preaching earned Goad proper respect in time, and when John Goad came to town, the lawless element made no effort to silence him.

Gohl, Billy (1860?–1928) mass murderer

Billy Gohl undoubtedly belongs somewhere near the top of any list of the most deadly American mass murderers, having killed a minimum of 40 men and almost certainly many more.

Gohl was always mysterious about himself. He turned up in the spring of 1903 in Aberdeen, Wash. as a delegate of the Sailors' Union of the Pacific. Nobody among Aberdeen's 12,000 inhabitants knew him, and he seems to have told differing tales of his labor and maritime past, although that was not unusual in a wide-open town like Aberdeen. He was a squat, bull-necked man with a shaven head and an almost angelic-looking face. But everyone realized that Billy Gohl was a man who could take care of himself and that earned him respect in the Sailors' Union.

As a union official, Gohl performed all sorts of chores for seamen. The union office was generally the first stop for sailors from schooners and four-riggers arriving in port. The seamen would check with Gohl for mail and would leave their valuables with him when they went carousing. Since this would often be their first shore leave in months, their pay generally came to rather large sums. Union delegates always kept the money in the safe until the sailors called for it. Billy Gohl just kept it.

Gohl's technique was to murder a seaman as soon as he showed up, before he had time to make friends. He would look out the window to see if anyone had seen the man enter the union office; if not, and if the sailor had turned in enough cash or other valuables to make the effort worthwhile, Gohl would simply take a gun from his desk drawer and shoot the man through the head. From there on, Gohl had everything down to a science.

He cleaned the gun, searched the corpse for additional money and stripped the body of all identification. Gohl's office was on the second floor of a building whose rear extended out over the Wishkah River, which fed into Gray's Harbor. Supported by stilts, the house had a trapdoor with a chute leading to the water. Down the chute went the corpse to be carried away by the rapid river current. If and when the body bobbed to the surface, it would be miles out in the harbor.

After 1903 Aberdeen began to be known by sailors as a "port of missing men," but no one thought to attribute that sad turn of events to Billy Gohl. Between

1909 and 1912 a total of 41 "floaters" were fished out of the water. Most were believed to be merchant seamen, and the most upset man in town was invariably Billy Gohl, demanding the law do something. He was finally trapped when one of his victims was traced to his office and no further. Gohl had shot the man as soon as he entered his office. When he searched the body, he found a gold watch with the name August Schleuter of Hamburg, Germany engraved on it. Gohl decided it would be too incriminating to keep and returned it to the body. When the corpse drifted ashore, Gohl identified Schleuter as one of his men. It took the law weeks to find out the truth, which as good as convicted Gohl. It turned out the victim really was a Danish seaman named Fred Nielssen. He had bought a watch in Hamburg, and the name of the watchmaker was August Schleuter.

In 1913 Gohl was convicted of two murders but only laughed when asked to make a complete roster of his victims. He avoided execution because the year before, the state of Washington had eliminated capital punishment. Gohl's mass murder spree was used as an argument for its restoration, even though he had committed his murders while the death penalty had been in effect. In 1914 the death penalty was restored. Gohl died in prison in 1928.

gold accumulator swindle

A monumental fraud perpetrated on hard-headed New Englanders in 1897 involved a so-called gold accumulator, which allegedly mined gold from the ocean. The scheme was the work of a veteran English con man named Charles E. Fisher and a Connecticut Baptist minister named Prescott Ford Jernegan. Jernegan may well have been a dupe at the beginning of the operation, but by the time it reached fruition, he proved just as adept as Fisher at holding on to his ill-gotten gains.

Fisher, it seemed, had a secret invention to extract the gold eddying about in Passamaquoddy Bay near the town of Lubec, Maine. Fisher's gold accumulator was painted with mercury and another "secret compound" and lowered into the water. When the device was raised the following day, it was crusted with thin flakes of gold. Fisher and Jernegan demonstrated the device on several occasions to some extremely dubious Yankee businessmen, who insisted on guarding the scene of the demonstration all night to prevent any tampering. However, they were unaware that Fisher, who had been a deep-sea diver back in England, would swim to the accumulator during the night and plant the grains of gold.

Eventually, shares in the Electrolytic Marine Salts Co. were sold to a gullible public. The value of the initial issue of 350,000 shares at $1 a share soon climbed to $50 a share as New Englanders rushed to get in on a good thing. In addition, a grateful board of directors voted to give Fisher and Jernegan $200,000 each for their services. All this took place on the basis of $25,000 having been "mined," but it was apparent that the process could just go on forever. It went on only until Fisher quietly disposed of his shares of stock, added that money to his $200,000 and left for Boston "to get more supplies." He didn't return and suddenly the gold accumulator didn't accumulate any more gold.

Rev. Jernegan announced he was off in search of Fisher and disappeared with his $200,000-plus as well. His search apparently took him to France, where he was later found living in luxury with his family. The irate board of directors of the marine salts company demanded the French government take him into custody. It did, but the minister was soon released. It was obvious that the $200,000 had been legally voted him and there was no way to force him to return it. All that appeared to have gone wrong was that an apparent gold-mining procedure had run dry.

Jernegan finally came back to America and actually returned $175,000 to the swindled stockholders. This represented what he said was left of the $200,000. He continued to live well thereafter in the Philippines and Hawaii, undoubtedly on the revenues from the sale of his bloated stockholdings. When Jernegan died in 1942, there was a report circulated that Charlie Fisher had been living in the South Seas as a rich American. According to the story, Fisher had been caught fooling around with the wife of a tribal chieftain and that he and she had been killed according to tribal custom. Apparently, the still-living investors in the Electrolytic Marine Salts Co. were determined to have their revenge, real or fancied.

gold brick swindle   confidence game

The gold brick swindle is a hardy perennial that just will not die. The victim buys what he thinks are gold brick ingots and ends up with worthless lead or brass. Most big-city bunco squads handle several such cases each year.

The origin of the gold brick swindle is unknown but probably started in the California gold fields during the 1850s. Wyatt Earp and Mysterious Dave Mather got involved in the game in Mobeetie, Tex. in 1878, after Earp learned how well the racket worked in Kansas. A fabulous young swindler, Reed Waddell, brought the racket to New York in 1880 and trimmed some rather bright and supposedly sharp businessmen with it. Waddell's bricks certainly looked real, being triple gold-plated and marked in the manner of a regulation brick from the United States Assayer's Office, with the letters "U.S." at one end and, below that, the name of the assayer and the weight and fineness of the bullion. Waddell's operation included a phony assayer's office where the brick was supposedly tested. If the sucker hesitated, Waddell would get angry, pull a slug from the brick and insist the victim take it to any jeweler of his choice. As part of the ruse, Waddell had sunk a slug of pure gold into the center of the lead brick, but the trick always worked and his victim would become eager to buy. In all, he took in some $350,000 over the next dozen years. Another ring, headed by Tom O'Brien, netted $100,000 in just five months working the World's Fair in Chicago in 1893. Waddell and O'Brien then joined forces and took the scam to Europe, where O'Brien killed Waddell in an argument over the division of the proceeds from one of their swindles.

Perhaps the greatest swindle of this nature occurred in Texas, where from 1932 to 1935 two crooks, one posing as a minister, victimized a wealthy widow. They told her that gold had been buried in various spots on her vast ranch about 100 years earlier and that ancient maps to the locations could be bought from an old man in Mexico. The widow gave them enough money to buy one map, and sure enough, they came back with some gold bricks. Over the next three years the widow gave them $300,000 and they dug up what was allegedly $4 million in gold. Since at this time the hoarding of gold was illegal, the woman didn't dare attempt to cash in the bricks and therefore never learned they were fake. The con men's downfall came about because of their wild spending, which caused a government agent to investigate the source of their money. The swindle was thus uncovered, and the two crooks were sent to prison.

See also: REED WADDELL.

Goldsby, Crawford   See CHEROKEE BILL.

"Gone to Texas"   western saying

"Gone to Texas" was a euphemism that expressed one important motivation for the Western migration and a fact most people on the frontier knew: that a great many of those who went to Texas or elsewhere in the West were running from something. In fact, an early settler, W. B. Dewees, related in his memoirs that it was common to ask a man why he had fled his home. "Few persons feel insulted at such a question. They generally answer for some crime or other which they have committed. If they deny having committed any crime or say they did not run away, they are looked upon suspiciously."

An Easterner visiting Texas, Frederick Law Olmsted, wrote:

In the rapid settlement of the country, many an adventurer crossed the border, spurred by love of liberty, forfeited at home, rather than drawn by a love of adventure or of rich soil. Probably a more reckless and vicious crew was seldom gathered than that which peopled some parts of Eastern Texas at the time of its first resistance to the Mexican government. 'G.T.T.' (gone to Texas) was the slang appendage . . . to every man's name who had disappeared before the discovery of some rascality. Did a man emigrate thither, everyone was on the watch for the discreditable reason to turn up.

G.T.T. was the way of the rascal and the felon but it was also part of the way America was built.

Gonzales, Thomas A. (1878–1956)   medical examiner

Dr. Thomas A. Gonzales, chief medical examiner of New York City from 1937 to 1954, was recognized as one of the country's foremost forensic pathologists. His evidence convicted hundreds of murderers and saved a number of other innocent men, some of whom were accused of crimes that never happened. Often Dr. Gonzales needed only a moment's view of the corpse to tell immediately, for instance, that a husband who strangled his wife had tried to make it appear a case of suicide by gas inhalation.

Clearing an innocent suspect gave Dr. Gonzales the most satisfaction. Such was the case when an elderly tenant was found dead 15 minutes after he had had a heated argument with a muscular real estate agent over the rent and repairs. The old man's body was discovered just inside the door of his apartment, his face bruised and marked and his scalp deeply gashed. Several pieces of furniture in the foyer were overturned or moved out of position. Police learned of the angry dispute from neighbors and arrested the agent. He denied striking the old tenant, but the case against him was strong indeed. There was the confrontation, the obvious signs of a fight, a witness in the hallway who said no one entered the apartment after the agent left and the fact that the victim was dead just a quarter of an hour later.

Dr. Gonzales inspected the scene, diagrammed the position of the furniture and then performed an autopsy. As a result, charges against the real estate man were dropped. The old man had not been beaten to death. He had suffered a heart attack and stumbled around the foyer, displacing the furniture in his death throes. The diagrams of the furniture placement demonstrated how the old man had suffered each of the injuries he received.

Dr. Gonzales, a tall, spare man, was one of the top assistants to Dr. Charles Norris, who founded the Medical Examiner's Office in 1918. He took over following Dr. Norris' death in 1935, first as acting head and later as the chief medical examiner, after outscoring all other competitors in the tests given for the position. During his career he testified in many famous cases in New York and elsewhere in the country and coauthored *Legal Medicine and Toxicology*, still regarded as a classic in the field. He often said only medicine could solve many cases.

One common puzzle in many violent deaths was whether the cause had been homicide or suicide. He once proved that a man who had allegedly stabbed himself through his shirt had actually been murdered. (Suicides, he found, almost invariably preferred to strip away their clothing before stabbing themselves.) In another case Gonzales solved a stabbing that had police baffled. A man was found stabbed through the heart in a third-floor bathroom that was locked from the inside. The only window had been painted shut. It was clearly a case of suicide except there was no knife. The case was a stumper for the detectives but not for the medical examiner. "Never mind what happened here," he told the police. "See if you can find out about a knife fight anywhere in the area." The police checked and found that the victim had been stabbed in an altercation. As Dr. Gonzales later explained, it was quite possible for a man stabbed in the heart to walk a block, climb a couple of flights of stairs, lock himself in a bathroom and then finally collapse. Such victims often head for the bathroom to clean themselves up, not realizing they have been fatally wounded.

Dr. Gonzales retired in 1954 and died two years later.

See also: CHARLES NORRIS.

Gooch, Arthur (1909–1936) outlaw and kidnapper

The first man ever to die under the so-called Lindbergh Law of the 1930s, which made kidnapping for ransom a capital offense even if no harm came to the victim, Arthur Gooch was considered by many persons to have gotten a "raw deal." On November 26, 1934 Gooch and a partner in crime were stopped by two police officers for routine interrogation at a Paradise, Tex. gas station. In an ensuing gunfight Gooch and his partner seriously wounded one officer and then forced the two lawmen to drive them across the state line into Oklahoma. There they ran into a force of federal agents involved in another case and a second gun battle broke out. Gooch's confederate was killed and Gooch himself captured. The officers were freed unharmed.

Federal authorities pressed for the death penalty in the Gooch case to determine the constitutionality of the law and to enhance its deterrent effects. However, the case was clearly not the right one to serve their purposes. Much to the chagrin of the authorities, a large part of the press ignored the trial. No one had been killed and no ransom passed. Nevertheless, Gooch was eventually convicted and sentenced to death.

Gooch's attorneys appealed the verdict to the Supreme Court on the ground that he had not committed a kidnapping for ransom and therefore should not have been sentenced to die. In February 1936 the Supreme Court held that the kidnapping of a police officer was adequately covered by the phrase "for ransom, reward, or otherwise." The precedent-setting aspect of the Gooch decision was compromised by the fact that although Gooch was executed on June 19—an event that drew relatively minor attention—it became quite common for juries in federal cases to recommend mercy when bringing in guilty verdicts for capital offenses.

See also: LINDBERGH LAW.

good-time laws

Good-time laws, by which a convict can appreciably reduce his sentence based on good conduct in prison, have generally not fulfilled their promise. The average good-time law prescribes the deduction of one month for the first year of satisfactory behavior, two months for the second and so on until, from the sixth year on, a convict can earn six months off his sentence for every year of good behavior. Unfortunately, such a formula is of more value to a long-term offender than to a short-termer, who is often a first offender and thus a more likely candidate for rehabilitation. In the eyes of convicts, good-time laws seem to be intended less to benefit the prisoner or his reformation than to assist the prison administration in extracting labor from convicts and maintaining discipline.

New York State appears to have started the first good-time law in 1817, under which a first-term convict doing up to five years could reduce his sentence by one-fourth. But there is no record of the system ever actually being used. Similarly, relatively unused statutes appeared over the next few decades in Connecticut, Tennessee and Ohio. The good-time principle gained a more effective foothold in Australia and France. But after the Civil War good-time laws spread rapidly, following the example of the "Irish system," by which a prisoner could win his freedom by earning a certain number of "marks," or credits. By 1868 24 states had passed such laws, and today they are the norm.

In addition to this reduction of sentence by statute, in most states convicts can earn "industrial good time" for taking part in prison industries and "merit good time" for especially good behavior such as taking part in medical experiments and the like. These reductions generally affect only the amount of the time served before an inmate is entitled to his first parole hearing rather than the sentence itself. Thus, when a prisoner is subsequently passed over for parole, he may feel he has been "conned" by the system. Reformers often criticize industrial good time on the grounds that many convicts apply for the benefits and accept shop work instead of training programs which develop the skills, the trades and, more important, the attitudes required to reintegrate them into society upon release.

Another problem with good-time laws is that convicts view the benefits as a right, especially in prisons where a new inmate is immediately credited with his maximum time off and then this figure is reduced whenever he violates prison rules. The practice can encourage prisoners to believe that society constantly discriminates against them by taking away good time, an attitude that is at least partially the cause of many prison riots.

Gophers New York gang

One of the last of the all-Irish gangs of New York, the Gophers were the kings of Hell's Kitchen until they disintegrated in the changing society of the pre–World War era. The Gophers controlled the territory between Seventh and Eleventh Avenues from 42nd Street to 14th Street. Brawlers, muggers and thieves, they gained their name because they liked to hide out in basements and cellars. With an ability to summon 500 gangsters to their banner, they were not a force to be dismissed lightly by the police or other gangsters.

They were such hell raisers and so fickle in their allegiance that no one could emerge as the single leader of the gang. Thus, the Gophers never produced a gangster with the stature of Monk Eastman, the greatest villain of the period. Among the most prominent Gophers, however, there were numerous subleaders, such a Newburg Gallagher, Stumpy Malarkey, Happy Jack Mulraney and Marty Brennan.

Another celebrated Gopher was One-Lung Curran, who in due course expired due to this deficiency. Once when his girlfriend wailed that she was without a coat for the chilly fall weather, Curran strode up to the first policeman he saw and blackjacked him to the ground. He stripped off the officer's uniform coat and presented it to his mistress, who, being an adept seamstress, converted it into a military-style lady's jacket. This event caused such a fashion sensation in Gopher society that

thugs by the dozen soon were out on the streets clubbing and stripping policemen.

In brute power and violence, the police could seldom match the Gophers. To do so would have accomplished little anyway, since the gang enjoyed a measure of protection from the ward's politicians, who found the Gophers of immense assistance during elections. They however, were too anarchistic to exploit this advantage to the fullest, feeling that with raw power they could achieve anything they wanted.

The Gophers had no reason to fear the police when they looted the New York Central Railroad freight cars along Eleventh Avenue. But while they might enjoy a measure of tolerance from public officials, they failed to grasp the extent of corporate power and the railroad's ability to field a virtual army against them. The New York Central's special force was staffed with many former policemen who had suffered insults and injuries from the gangsters and who were anxious for the opportunity to retaliate. Railroad property became a no-man's land, and the company detectives began to venture further afield to devastate Hell's Kitchen itself. The Gophers were smashed, their prestige savaged and their unity crushed. Gallagher and Brennan went to Sing Sing, and many others were killed or maimed. Factions of the Gophers joined other criminal combines, but these were organizations that specialized in purely criminal ventures and wasted neither time nor strength on unprofitable street bashings. An era of American criminality was ending.

See also: LADY GOPHERS.

Gordon, Captain Nathaniel (?–1862) pirate

A big, bluff adventurer, Capt. Nathaniel Gordon plied the trade of piracy long after it had declined as a popular criminal endeavor. In the mid-1800s former pirates concentrated on smuggling slaves into the country, bringing in as many as 15,000 per year and reaping enormous profits. In the forefront of this activity were Gordon and his daredevil crew aboard the 500-ton *Erie*. How bloody a business they were engaged in is best revealed by the statistics concerning the cargo. The *Erie* regularly transported approximately 1,000 black captives, but because of the appalling conditions no more than 700 or so would survive the journey. Finally captured on a slave run by the American ship *Mohican*, Gordon was quickly convicted and sentenced to be hanged.

Since the last death penalty for piracy had been carried out some 40 years earlier, protestors insisted it was unfair to execute Gordon for a crime considered virtually extinct. His supporters petitioned President Abraham Lincoln for a pardon, but they failed to consider the political realities. With the nation at war over the matter of slavery, it would have been impossible for Lincoln even to consider pardoning Gordon while Northern soldiers were dying fighting the slave states. Gordon was duly executed in the Tombs in New York City on March 8, 1862. As one last token of fear of a disappearing breed of criminals, authorities packed the prison with armed guards to foil a buccaneer-style rescue attempt, which the newspapers insisted was sure to be made. Unfortunately for Gordon, there were no pirates left. Nathaniel Gordon was the last man hanged for piracy in the United States.

See also: PIRACY.

Gordon, Vivian (1899–1931) murder victim

The murder of Vivian Gordon was one of New York City's gaudiest cases, so shocking that it wrecked the lives of several others and even led to the abrupt end of the corrupt administration of Mayor Jimmy Walker. At the same time, it brought to prominence Samuel Seabury, a lawyer and ex-jurist whose name was to become synonymous with governmental honesty and integrity as a result of the Seabury Investigations. Much of the evidence in the Seabury probe came from a number of "little black books" belonging to Vivian. In them she had kept a day-by-day account of her sexual and criminal doings, which included blackmailing several gentlemen. When revealed, they destroyed the personal and private lives of many men. They also destroyed Vivian's 16-year-old daughter.

Vivian Gordon was born Benita Franklin in Detroit, the daughter of John Franklin, former warden of the Illinois State Penitentiary in Joliet, and was brought up under strict supervision, which included being sent to a convent school in Canada. Eventually, she rebelled and ran away, determined to pursue an acting and modeling career, and later, she married briefly and had a daughter. In 1923 Benita was arrested for prostitution by Patrolman Andrew G. McLaughlin. McLaughlin was a crooked cop who was subsequently found to have banked—on a yearly salary of $3,000—an average of $1,500 monthly. Benita was hauled before a magistrate, H. Stanley Renaud, and became, allegedly, just one of 24 girls without legal representation whom Renaud wrongfully sentenced. Both McLaughlin and Renaud later became targets of the Seabury probe. Benita always insisted she was innocent of the McLaughlin charge, even in later years when, as Vivian Gordon, she was no longer innocent of very much.

Whatever validity her claim of innocence to that charge had, Vivian Gordon became a hooker, and while she branched out into numerous other illegal enterprises, such as being part backer in a stock swindle and financing bank robbery schemes, her steadiest scam was blackmailing men after taking them to hotel rooms. She kept a diary loaded with names, dates and details and put the bite on many an anxious gentleman. During much of her career Vivian worked with a particularly nasty individual named Harry Stein. Later, Stein would be charged with her murder but acquitted; convicted of another woman's murder and serve time for it; and finally executed in the electric chair for a robbery-murder.

While Vivian was living a purple present, she was determined to prove to her teenage daughter that she was a good woman. This and the fact that she felt she had been double-crossed by some politicians in a vice blackmailing scheme prompted her to take the story of her criminal life to the Seabury investigators. In a meeting with one of Seabury's young aides, Irving Ben Cooper, she laid out charges against the police vice squad, including a number of officers who were on her bribe payroll. She claimed her diaries contained explosive evidence against several important men, many of whom were public officials. Cooper listened to her shocking story and told her to gather up all her evidence and bring it to the probers the following week. Vivian said she would. On February 27, 1931 she was found dead in Van Cortlandt Park, strangled with a length of clothesline looped around her neck three times.

Her death became a sensation and loosed the Seabury Investigations with the full support of Gov. Franklin D. Roosevelt. Her diaries were found and led to explosive hearings. They revealed the names of officers on her payroll and, more important, the names of many public officials with indications of the prices for which they could be "bought." The ever-widening probe finally included Mayor Walker who was accused of being "on the take" from a number of business interests.

Under pressure, the police came up with a solution to the Gordon murder, charging Harry Stein and one Samuel Greenberg. They had witnesses who said Stein had tried to pawn Vivian's mink coat and diamond ring just a few hours after the murder. And they had the testimony of Harry Schlitten, who allegedly drove the death car, a Cadillac limousine rented by Stein for the occasion. According to Schlitten, Stein had told him that a party, who turned out to be Vivian Gordon, had to be killed to oblige another party and that Greenberg, posing as a diamond merchant to lure the victim along, would be picked up as they drove toward the Bronx. When Greenberg got in the car, Vivian supposedly said to him, "Where have you been all my life?"

The trio, sitting in back of the limousine, killed off a bottle of bourbon and then the men, said Schlitten, killed off the lady. He said Vivian struggled quite a bit and then he heard Stein say, "She's finished now." He looked back and saw Stein with his hand on the rope.

They dumped the body in the park, the informer said, and drove back to Manhattan.

Not too surprisingly for the era, Stein and Greenberg were found not guilty. Their lawyer, the famous Samuel Leibowitz, went into one of his favorite routines, postulating a "police frame-up," which worked very well amidst the Seabury probe's constant revelations of police venality. Some detectives complained bitterly about Stein beating their "perfect case" and pointed out later that if he had been convicted, he wouldn't have been around to commit several other murders, one of which was to send him to the electric chair in 1955.

That was only one of the misfortunes to result from Vivian Gordon's murder. There was also the tragedy of Vivian's teenage daughter, Benita. Although teachers and classmates at her high school tried to shield her from the details, she read every line about the case in the newspapers. The girl became more and more withdrawn, but she too kept a diary. There were a series of pitiful entries, including one on March 1 that said, "I guess I will have to change my name."

Two days later, she made a final entry: "March 3, 2:15 P.M. . . . I'm tired . . . I've decided to give it all up . . . I am turning on the gas."

See also: SEABURY INVESTIGATION.

Gordon, Waxey (Irving Wexler) (1888–1952)
Prohibition beer baron

One of the top three or four Prohibition bootleggers, Irving Wexler, better known as Waxey Gordon, was a multimillionaire by the end of the 1920s and then fell to depths almost unparalleled in underworld history.

He got his nickname as a kid pickpocket because he could slip a mark's wallet out of his pocket as if it were coated with wax. Although still a small-timer, Gordon moved up in the underworld as a strikebreaker, whoremaster and, at times, a dope dealer.

As it did for so many other criminals of the era, Prohibition made Waxey Gordon a big-timer. First in junior partnership with Mr. Big, Arnold Rothstein, and finally in charge after buying Rothstein out, Gordon was one of the leading illegal liquor importers on the East Coast. His personal income ran somewhere between $1 million and $2 million a year, and he owned blocks of real estate in New York and Philadelphia. He also owned nightclubs, speakeasies, gambling casinos and a fleet of ocean-going rumrunners and lived in a castle, complete with moat, in southern New Jersey. His distilleries in Philadelphia cut, reblended and rebottled booze for dozens of leading bootleggers around the country. He was able to charge an arm and a leg for his supplies, often cutting himself in for a piece of his customer's action. Since one could not really hide major operations like distilleries and breweries, Gordon became probably the biggest graft-paying criminal in the East. When New Jersey reformers grew upset about the noise made by trucks rumbling out of his illicit breweries, Waxey paid off politicians so that his beer could be pumped through pressure hoses in the sewer systems of Elizabeth, Paterson and Union City.

Gordon was so powerful that he even forced his way into a "shotgun-partnership" with the Luciano-Costello-Lansky-Siegel forces in New York, although tension between himself and Lansky grew so intense that they would not even sit at the same table with each other. In the 1930s Gordon feuded with Dutch Schultz, and when it looked like the end of Prohibition was nearing, the two turned to open warfare for control of legitimate beer distribution rights in New York.

By this time, Gordon had won the title of New York's Public Enemy No. 1, an accolade belied by his short, dumpy appearance and the meager wisps of hair on his dome. Outside of Schultz, one of the most violence-prone gangsters of the era, few wanted to take on Gordon in gangland combat, especially since Waxey enjoyed extreme loyalty from his men, who refused to be bought out or to engage in takeover attempts.

There is little doubt that the Luciano-Lansky forces brought about Gordon's downfall by getting the law to do their dirty work for them. Gordon was tossed to the income tax wolves. Meyer Lansky's brother Jake and others, according to the underworld gossip, fed the tax men information about Gordon's operations. The government's case, presented by a young federal prosecutor named Thomas E. Dewey, showed that the Prohibition bootleg baron took in $2 million a year, all the while reporting a net income of just $8,125 annually. Convicted in December 1930, Waxey got 10 years, which finished him as a major underworld operator. Just as they were to do with others, the Luciano-Lansky forces moved to take over Gordon's rackets.

When Gordon was released from Leavenworth in 1940, he announced to reporters: "Waxey Gordon is dead. From now on, it's Irving Wexler, salesman." Actually, it proved to be Waxey Gordon, salesman, hawking one of his old lines, narcotics. In 1951 Gordon, now a small-timer, was nailed as he delivered a $6,300 package of heroin to a federal narcotics stool pigeon.

Among the arresting officers the aged gangster recognized Sgt. Johnny Cottone. He broke down sobbing. "My God, Johnny," he pleaded. "Shoot me. Don't take me in for junk. Let me run, and then shoot me!" One of the old man's younger confederates started weeping too. He pulled $2,500 from his pockets and ripped two diamond rings off his fingers. "Take this," he cried. "Take me. Take the whole business. Just let Pop go."

To the end, Waxey Gordon enjoyed the loyalty of his men. In December the 63-year-old Gordon was sentenced to two terms of 25 years to life. He was sent to Alcatraz, a fate the aged criminal hardly deserved. Six months later, on June 24, 1952, he died there of a heart attack.

Gordon-Gordon, Lord (?–1873) swindler

One of America's most audacious confidence operators was a Scotsman who, masquerading as Lord Gordon-Gordon, swindled some of America's greatest robber barons, including Jay Gould, out of $1 million in negotiable securities. Gordon-Gordon never revealed his real identity. Instead, he spread the word through intermediaries that he was the heir of the great Earl of Gordon, cousin of the Campbells, collateral relative of Lord Byron and proud descendant of the Lochinvar and the ancient kings of the Highlanders.

Gordon-Gordon's first known peccadillo occurred in 1868 in Edinburgh, where, under the equally fanciful name of Lord Glencairn, he swindled a jeweler out of £25,000. Then in 1871, as Lord Gordon-Gordon, he appeared in Minneapolis and opened a bank account with $40,000 from his jewelry swindle. He set up representatives of the Northern Pacific Railroad for a swindle by declaring he was in search of immense areas of good lands on which to settle his overpopulated Scottish tenantry. He suggested he could use upwards of a half-million acres, the very answer to the railroad's dreams. Since the company in its push westward was sorely pressed for capital, it did all it could to woo several millions from Gordon-Gordon. He was wined, dined and taken on lavish hunting expeditions. How much hard cash Gordon-Gordon managed to pocket was never known, but the "trinkets" given him in one instance were worth $40,000. After some three months Gordon-Gordon had picked out all the land he wished to buy, and he told the railroad executives he was returning to New York to arrange for the transfer of funds from Scotland to make the purchase. He left Minneapolis not only with fond farewells but also with special letters of introduction from Col. John S. Loomis, the line's land commissioner, to Jay Gould, then fighting for control of the Erie Railroad, and Horace Greeley, a stockholder in the Erie and a business associate of Gould.

Lord Gordon-Gordon portrayed himself as a potential savior to Gould, just as he had to the Northern Pacific. He let Greeley believe he was a substantial holder of Erie stock and also the holder of proxies from a number of European friends, enough to provide Gould with the margin of victory. But Gordon-Gordon had a price for his aid. He wanted the management of the railroad reformed and an active voice for himself, but, he generously added, he was prepared to leave Gould in charge. Gould was ecstatic—and grateful. He handed over to Gordon-Gordon $1 million in negotiable securities and cash in "a pooling of interests" that could only be considered a bribe.

Soon after this transaction, large chuncks of stock began appearing for sale. Gordon-Gordon was quickly cashing in on his profits from the gullible Gould. Convinced he had been swindled, Gould sued Gordon-Gordon, who immediately threw in with Gould's business rivals. But time was running out for Gordon-Gordon. On the witness stand he cheerfully reeled off the names of important European personages he knew and represented in the Erie deal. Before his references could be checked, he decamped to Canada with a large portion of Gould's money.

When located in Canada, Gordon-Gordon had little trouble convincing the authorities there that he was a man of high breeding and that charges by various Americans, Gould in New York and railroaders in Minnesota, were ill founded and malicious. He told people in Fort Garry, Manitoba that he intended to invest huge sums in the area and that the Americans were being vindictive because he would not utilize the funds in their country.

Convinced they would never get the scoundrel back to face charges by any legal means, a group of Minnesotan railroaders, perhaps financed by Gould, attempted to kidnap Gordon-Gordon. They actually snatched him in July 1873 and were only apprehended at the border by a group of the swindler's friends and a contingent of Northwest Mounted Police. The kidnappers, including two future governors of Minnesota and three future congressmen, were clapped into prison and allowed no bail.

The Gordon-Gordon affair blew up into an international incident. Gov. Austin of Minnesota ordered the state militia to be ready to march and demanded the return of the kidnap party. Thousands of Minnesotans volunteered for an invading expeditionary force. Finally, negotiations between President Ulysses S. Grant and his secretary of state, Hamilton Fish, and Canadian prime minister Sir John MacDonald produced an agreement in the interests of international amity that allowed the raiding party to go free on bail. Gordon-Gordon was safe in Canada, since the treaties between the United States and that country did not provide for extradition for such minor offenses as larceny and embezzlement.

All might have gone well for Gordon-Gordon had not news of the incident reached Edinburgh. The owners of Marshall and Son, Jewelers became convinced that the description of Lord Gordon-Gordon matched that of the long-gone Lord Glencairn. They dispatched a clerk who had dealt with His Lordship to check up on Gordon-Gordon in person. He made a firm identification and the master swindler was ordered returned to England to clear up the matter. Gordon-Gordon undertook a legal battle, but when it was obvious he had lost, he shot himself to death.

Gotti, John (1940–) imprisoned godfather and former "Teflon Don"

Certainly the most storied and important "godfather" in American organized crime in the 1980s and 1990s, John Gotti could well have become the "boss of bosses," even though that is nothing more than a mythical title bestowed by the media and some prosecutors. Gotti was cut from the old mold, a type not seen in New York Mafia circles since the demise of the vicious Albert Anastasia, the "Lord High Executioner" of Murder Inc., and the mobster Gotti most admired.

On one occasion Gotti was overheard chastising an underling for failing to return his phone calls. "Follow orders," he snarled, "or I'll blow up your house." The mobster, thoroughly terrified, swore it would not happen again. "You bet it won't," Gotti responded, "I got to make an example of somebody. Don't let it be you." Veteran officers agreed that if they shut their eyes and heard the words, they would have been sure it was the ghost of Albert Anastasia talking.

By 1985 Gotti was considered the top capo, or lieutenant, in the Gambino crime family, the most powerful Mafia outfit in the country. He bossed a number of lucrative rackets, including those at John F. Kennedy airport as well as other Gambino operations in much of the New York metropolitan area. Additionally he was the favorite of underboss Aniello Dellacroce, an aging but brutal mafioso. As much as Dellacroce admired Gotti, boss Paul Castellano hated—and feared—him.

Gotti moved up the mob ladder in 1972 when the nephew of Carlo Gambino was kidnapped by Irish gangsters who demanded a $350,000 ransom. When part of the ransom was paid, the kidnappers killed the Gambino kin. The FBI grabbed two suspects but not the third one, James McBratney, on whom Gambino put out a contract. Gotti was part of a mob execution squad that caught up with McBratney in a Staten Island bar. Gotti was convicted of his part in the job and drew a seven-year prison sentence. When he got out Gotti was embraced by Gambino, who moved him steadily up the crime family ladder. In about 1978 or 1979 Gotti became a capo and top associate of Dellacroce. Like many others in the family Gotti felt Dellacroce

Mob boss John Gotti in a victory pose after beating a case during his "Teflon Don" period.

should succeed the dying Gambino, but the latter wanted his kin, Castellano, to succeed him.

Dellacroce kept Gotti in line in this period, since he, Dellacroce, knew he was dying of cancer. He urged Gotti to be patient, a characteristic which was not Gotti's strong suit. And neither was gentility. He was once quoted complaining to another mafioso: "Can you beat this—they're telling me I'm too tough for the job. Can you imagine what our thing [Cosa Nostra] is coming to?"

When Dellacroce died in early December 1985, there was no stopping Gotti. Two weeks later Paul Castellano was murdered outside a Manhattan steakhouse on Gotti's orders, Gotti audaciously riding past the murder scene to make sure everything had gone off without a hitch. Normally, the killing of a boss has severe ramifications, but not in this case. Castellano was under indictment and faced a likely long prison sentence as he approached age 70. Many in the crime family were not sure that "Big Paul" could take it. It was thought likely that Castellano might crack and flip for the government. That was one of the lines Gotti used on members of the family as well as other crime families. No one had any problems with Castellano being erased.

Gotti was in, now the godfather of the most powerful crime family in the country, or what had been so until Castellano's misrule had weakened it to the extent that the Genovese crime family was at least its equal or even its superior.

Gotti became known as the "Dapper Don." As one police veteran stated, "He [operated] in style, brutal perhaps, but suave. Gotti looks like a movie star. He wears hand-tailored clothes, drives a big black Lincoln and likes good restaurants."

In 1986 Gotti became the target of federal prosecutors on charges that could take him out of action. But Gotti probably marked a new trend in the Mafia—back to younger bosses, as was common in the 1920s and '30s. In recent years the mobs were concerned about the older dons taking heat. If even one talked, the damage would be enormous. A 20-year prison term wasn't too bad if young leaders got out in seven with good behavior. Everyone knew Gotti was tough enough to take it. Not that Gotti couldn't exhibit coolness. When entering a federal courtroom he insisted on a female radio reporter entering before him. "I was brought up to hold doors open for ladies," he said.

He had a different disposition in family "business," ordering murder after murder without a qualm.

The government clearly had Gotti dead to rights on some major criminal charges, yet three times in a row, Gotti beat the rap, perhaps not always without certain dishonest means. But in any event, the media now had a new nickname for him. He was the "Teflon Don," against whom charges bounced harmlessly off.

Finally the FBI built a solid case against Gotti, involving some 100 hours of incriminating tapes in which Gotti spoke openly about many murders and sundry criminal activities. The game now involved the RICO statutes, which meant if convicted Gotti was gone for good. Even better for the FBI they were able to "flip" Sammy "the Bull" Gravano, Gotti's underboss, a criminal as vicious as Gotti himself. In fact, Gravano had to get on the witness stand and admit to having committed 19 murders. In the deal Gravano made with the government, Gravano "walked" while Gotti was convicted in 1992 and sentenced to life without parole.

For a time Gotti sought to continue to run the family through his son John Gotti, Jr., but that went awry when the younger Gotti was indicted on other charges. Still Gotti appeared to have an influence on his crime family, even though he was probably now hated as much as Castellano had been. From the mobsters viewpoint, the main charge against Gotti could be summed up in one word—stupidity.

Even the boys in the mob could count. In the brief time before Gotti was tucked away in jail, the membership of the family seemed to have dropped from 250 wise guys to about 150 (not counting the associates and wise guy wanna-bes who numbered at least 10 times as many). With Gotti in charge, the family had gained a reputation for dapperness (by Gotti's decree), but the boss's imposing presence on the TV nightly news exposed many capos and soldiers to scrutiny by law enforcement officials. Gotti insisted his top guys constantly show up at the mob's Ravenite headquarters on Mulberry Street, even though the FBI had the area blanketed with FBI cameras. The appearance of these mobsters proved an incredible boon to law enforcement, allowing them to be identified. Many of the wise guys knew that quiet discretion was the correct call, but who was going to contradict Gotti? Failure to show up brought the certain guarantee of a Gotti hit sentence on them.

Clearly all the Gambinos hated Sammy the Bull for ratting, but they privately acknowledged Gravano's charge that the boss's arrogance had done much to bring down not only himself but major portions of the organization.

Law enforcement officials generally believed that Gotti's attitude would eventually make him and his son less imposing figures in the Gambino family, which some federal officials had pronounced doomed. By the very late 1990s, however, it was conceded by much of the media and a number of prosecutors that the Gambino family was still a power. Indeed, crime would probably march on with or without the Gotti influence.

See also: PAUL CASTELLANO, "SAMMY THE BULL" GRAVANO, MAFIA, MAFIA AT THE TURN OF THE CENTURY.

grabbers 19th-century New York procurer gangs

Grabbers was the popular name given in the 1860s and 1870s to the procurer gangs operating in New York. The two most important gangs were those headed by Red Light Lizzie, perhaps the most noted procurer of the time, and her principal rival, the brazen Hester Jane Haskins, also known as Jane the Grabber. Both gangs operated out of business offices and each month sent a circular out to clients advertising their newest wares.

Procuring was generally tolerated by the police so long as the grabbers followed the usual procedure of sending out "talent scouts" to outlying villages upstate and surrounding states to lure young girls to the metropolis with promises of high-paying jobs. The girls were then "broken into the life."

A "grabber scandal" of sorts erupted in 1875 when the Haskins woman began specializing in recruiting girls from good families, the better-paying brothel clients being much enticed by having the company of females of refinement. Too many girls disappeared, however, which created quite a stir. Jane the Grabber was arrested with a number of her minions and sent to prison. Upon their release they were "rousted" out of New York by the police apparently because of intolerance for procurers who could not understand certain class distinctions.

See also: PROCURING.

Grady gang 19th-century sneak thief gang

During the 1860s the art of sneak thievery achieved new heights thanks to a New York gang of thieves masterminded by John D. Grady, better known as Travelling Mike.

Travelling Mike, perhaps the number two fence of the era, after the infamous Marm Mandelbaum, was a stooped, dour-faced little man who padded the streets winter and summer wearing a heavy overcoat and carrying a peddler's box on his shoulder. Mike's box did not contain the standard peddler's stock of needles and other small articles, but rather pearls, diamonds and bonds, all stolen property. He never ventured out with less than $10,000 with which to make his daily purchases from various criminals. Mike was frequently to be seen at the notorious Thieves' Exchange, near Broadway and Houston Street, where fences and criminals met each night and dickered openly in the buying and selling of stolen goods.

To drum up more business, Travelling Mike organized his own gang and planned their jobs. His most famous underling was "Billy the Kid" Burke, a brilliant sneak thief who was arrested 100 times before his 26th birthday but was still able to retire, according to legend, a wealthy man. Mike engineered a raid on the money hoard of Rufus L. Lord, a grasping and penurious financier of the day. Worth $4 million, Lord spent his time clipping coupons and counting his hoard of money in a dingy office at 38 Exchange Place. He was so miserly that he wore tattered and patched clothing and would not light his office with more than one candle at a time. Yet in business he was extremely cunning and was supposedly able to milk the last penny out of any adversary.

In March 1866 Travelling Mike approached Lord about securing a loan for an alleged business venture, and long discussions were held about terms. Finally, on March 7 the fence returned to Lord's office accompanied by his minions, Greedy Jake Rand, Eddie Pettengill, Hod Ennis and Boston Pet Anderson. When Travelling Mike offered to put up high-class security for the loan and suggested an interest rate of 20 percent, Lord bounded from his chair and seized him by the lapels, imploring him to close the deal immediately. While the anxious Lord was thus distracted, Boston Pet and Pettengill slipped in the darkness to the huge safe the financier often absentmindedly left open and made off with two tin boxes. Travelling Mike then agreed to close the deal and said he would return in an hour to sign the necessary papers.

When the gang opened the tin boxes, they counted loot totaling $1.9 million in cash and negotiable securi-

ties. Rand, Pettengill, Ennis and Boston Pet instantly joined Billy the Kid Burke in wealthy retirement, while only Travelling Mike continued in the rackets.

Mike did not consider the Lord caper his crowning achievement. He learned that his archrival, Marm Mandelbaum, had trailblazed a new business method in crime by forming a gang whose members were paid strictly on salary, with all the loot going to her. Travelling Mike, with devious acumen, approached her criminals and purchased much of their loot at extremely low prices. Since the gangsters would have netted nothing extra otherwise, both they and Travelling Mike profited. Only Marm was victimized. When she learned of the plot against her, she dissolved her gang and railed about the lack of honor among thieves, with Travelling Mike specifically in mind.

Graham, Barbara (1923–1955) murderess

Barbara Graham was a call girl and murderess who worked with a California gang of notoriously savage robbers and killers who often tortured their victims to extract loot from them. She was subsequently immortalized in *I Want to Live!*, perhaps the phoniest movie ever made about a female criminal.

Admittedly, Barbara was the product of an unhappy childhood. When she was two years old, her mother was sent to a reformatory for wayward girls, and Barbara was raised in a rather indifferent manner by neighbors. Later, mother and daughter were reunited, but Barbara ran away at the age of nine. Ironically, she ended up doing time in the same institution where her mother had been confined.

Barbara was drawn into organized crime circles in the 1940s. In 1947 she was a star call girl in San Francisco for Sally Stanford, the city's most infamous madam. Following her fourth marriage, to a man named Henry Graham, she gave birth to her third child and took up drugs. She also joined a murderous robbery ring headed by Jack Santos. Santos' gang included Emmett Perkins, second-in-command, a brute as vicious as Santos himself; John L. True, a deep-sea diver who later turned state's evidence; and Baxter Shorter, who eventually tried to turn state's evidence, was kidnapped and was never seen again.

Among the crimes the gang committed were the December 1951 torture and robbery of a gold buyer, Andrew Colner, and his wife; the December 1951 murder of Edmund Hansen, a gold miner; the October 1952 murder of a grocer, Guard Young, his two little daughters and a neighbor's child; and the March 1953 brutal beating murder of Mrs. Mabel Monahan, a 63-year-old crippled Burbank widow believed to have had a large amount of jewels.

Of these crimes the only one that Barbara Graham was definitely tied to, primarily by True's confession, was the Monahan killing. She was to get the gang into the house by asking to use the telephone. According to True, the original plan called for the four men to crowd in as soon as the door was opened, tie up, gag and blindfold Mrs. Monahan and then ransack the house, grab the treasure and leave. The plan went awry when Barbara ran amok.

She struck the widow to the ground, seized her by the hair and began beating her over the head with the butt of the gun she was carrying. The old woman, bewildered and in agony, started moaning, "Oh, no, no, no!" One of the men egged Barbara on, "Give her more!" She did, cracking her skull and killing her. Later, a veteran prosecutor was to tell a jury the victim looked "as if she had been hit with a heavy truck traveling at high speed. The savage brutality of the attack is like nothing I have seen in 20 years of experience. I can scarcely believe that human beings could do that to an elderly woman against whom they had nothing, merely because they wanted money."

The gang, however, got no money. There was no large sum in the house and no valuable jewelry. They had simply been misinformed.

At her trial Barbara tried to prove her innocence by producing two alibis, both of which were probably false. Meanwhile, a police officer posing as an underworld agent offered to furnish her another alibi if she paid $25,000. Barbara agreed, and the plot was then exposed in court complete with taped recordings. Barbara lost her composure and cried out chokingly: "Oh, have you ever been desperate? Do you know what it means not to know what to do?"

On June 3, 1955 Barbara Graham, Santos and Perkins died in the San Quentin gas chamber. Barbara asked for a blindfold. "I don't want to have to look at people," she said bitterly.

In 1958 actress Susan Hayward won an Academy Award for her film portrayal of Barbara Graham.

Graham, John Gilbert (1932–1957) mass murderer

John Graham was a typical, if awesome, example of the plane saboteurs most active in the 1950s and 1960s who placed bombs on airliners to collect the insurance on a single passenger. He thought nothing of the fact that he had to kill 43 other persons because he wanted to murder his mother, Mrs. Daisy King of Denver, Colo.

On November 1, 1955 Graham placed a time bomb made with 25 sticks of dynamite in his mother's luggage before she boarded a DC-6B at Stapleton Airport. The plane was aloft only 10 minutes before it crashed in flames. When traces of a bomb device were found, suspicion soon focused on young Graham because he had attracted so much attention to himself in the terminal before flight time buying insurance policies on his mother's life from a vending machine. He had nervously spoiled a number of them and kept buying more, finally salvaging $37,500 worth.

When the FBI found material used to make bombs in his home, Graham confessed the plane sabotage. Public speculation as to how anyone would kill in such a manner and take the lives of so many innocents brought a simple explanation from a psychologist: "People actually have very few restraints concerning a person they have no intimate knowledge of. A mine disaster that claims 120 lives doesn't really impress many people. But should a neighbor fall from a ladder and die, the effect on these same people is tremendous."

Certainly, Graham showed no remorse about all his victims, being more concerned about his mother. Mrs. King had been going to visit her daughter in Alaska and, planning to go hunting, she had carried a box of

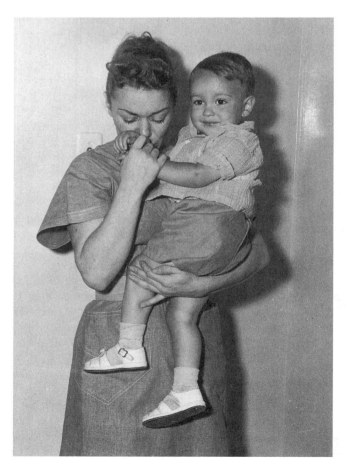

Barbara Graham, on trial for murder, posed for photographers with her 19-month-old son.

shotgun shells on board the plane. Graham laughed, "Can't you just see Mother when all those shells began to go off in the plane?"

At his trial Graham, found sane but resentful of his mother's neglect when he was a child, recanted his confession but was convicted by the overwhelming evidence. He refused to take any steps to appeal his death sentence and went silently to the gas chamber on January 11, 1957.

Graham-Tewksbury feud   sheepmen-cattlemen war

Some historians have insisted that the Graham-Tewksbury feud, sometimes known as the Pleasant Valley War, of 1886–92 was nothing more than a family feud; but the fact remains that it escalated into a great sheepman-cattleman confrontation that was to leave Arizona's Tonto Basin a "dark and bloody ground."

The Grahams and Tewksburys were both small-time ranchers who had built their stock with a "long rope," that is stealing their cattle rather than raising it. There is reason to believe the two neighboring families engaged in this operation as a joint enterprise, with all the stolen stock being hidden on Graham land. When it came time to divide their loot, however, the Tewksburys discovered the Grahams had registered all of them in their own brand. The Tewksburys were left a ranch without cattle, while the Grahams suddenly were able to move in big cattlemen circles.

Not surprisingly, some shooting resulted, but the leaders of each family, John D. Tewksbury and Tom Graham, argued for restraint. Still, the Tewksburys thirsted for revenge and finally came up with a reprisal that not only enraged the Grahams but all the other cattlemen in the basin. They made a deal with some big sheepmen to bring their flocks into Pleasant Valley in a deliberate effort to ruin the Grahams' grazing land. The conflict suddenly was bigger than a family feud, and all the cattlemen took up arms to drive out the sheepmen. Gunfighters lent their services to the side that reflected their economic interest. Not illogically, confirmed cattle rustlers joined in the fight against the sheep invasion since their livelihood, as well as that of honest cattlemen, was imperiled.

Initially, the war was limited to the killing of sheep, which were stampeded over cliffs, burned in the brush or shot to death by night-riding gunmen. Inevitably, human life was lost, and the war escalated. Five cowboys called on the Tewksbury ranch in what was later claimed to be a peaceful visit. As they were leaving, two of them were shot dead by Jim Tewksbury, the deadliest of his family. Tewksbury claimed the two were in the process of turning and drawing on him. While Tom

Graham still tried to stem the violence, another cattleman gunfighter attempted to kill Jim Tewksbury and paid with his life. When Billy Graham, 18, the youngest of the family, was gunned down by a deputy sheriff who sympathized with the Tewksburys, Tom Graham gave up and personally joined the fight, leading a raid on the Tewksbury ranch and offering a reward of $500 for every sheepherder and $1,000 for every Tewksbury killed. In the raid John Tewksbury, Sr. and Jr. and Bill Jacobs were murdered, but Jim, brother Ed and a number of supporters escaped. The cattlemen then allowed hogs to feed on two of the corpses.

Although from then on, the Tewksburys were outnumbered, they generally had the best of it, and more cattlemen than sheepmen died thereafter. In 1888 Jim Tewksbury died of consumption. Nonetheless, Ed Tewksbury had enough supporters to fight on until by 1889 only he and Tom Graham were left of their respective families. The sheep were driven out, but so was Graham, who remorsefully moved away from the valley. He returned in 1892 to settle some affairs and was ambushed and killed, some witnesses said, by Ed Tewksbury and John Rhodes. The case against Rhodes was not very strong and he was released, but Ed Tewksbury, the last survivor of the feud, was charged with murder. He was convicted but the verdict was thrown out on a technicality. The second trial ended in a hung jury, and finally, in 1896 the charges were dropped.

Until he died in 1904, Ed Tewksbury was a constable in Globe, Arizona Territory and deputy sheriff of Gila County.

The story of the feud has been told many times in many ways, including Zane Grey's rendition in his novel *To the Last Man*. But while the personal conflict of the Grahams and Tewksburys had provoked the war, the battle between cattlemen and sheepmen was repeated in many other areas of the country. This age-old conflict only ended when the cattlemen discovered they could indeed allow sheep to graze on the same lands with cattle if scientific agricultural techniques were applied. Then, ironically, the cattlemen began raising the previously hated "woolies" themselves.

See also: COMMODORE PERRY OWENS.

Grand Central fruit stand swindle

One of the most bald-faced swindles in history occurred in 1929 when two well-to-do Italian fruit dealers bought the rights to convert the information booth at New York's Grand Central Station into a fruit stand. It all began when a well-dressed stranger dropped into their bustling fruit store in midtown and presented them with his card:

T. Remington Grenfell
Vice President
GRAND CENTRAL
HOLDING CORPORATION

Mr. Grenfell told the fruit dealers, Tony and Nick Fortunato, that they had been selected, after an intensive investigation, to be offered the rights to the information booth. He explained that the railroad was upset because too many travelers were jamming the big circular booth in the center of the station to ask unnecessary questions. So, it had decided to let the ticket sellers answer all questions and this opened up the information booth for commercial use, ideally as a fruit stand. The rental would be $2,000 a week with the first year's rent paid in advance. The $100,000 payment did not faze the Fortunato brothers—in 25 years in the country they had amassed a goodly fortune through hard work, without ever really catching on to the sharp American ways—but they did ask for time to think it over.

Mr. Grenfell was somewhat curt. He said that wouldn't be possible. He mentioned the name of a nearby competitor of the Fortunato brothers and said he was to get second option if they refused. Quickly, the brothers agreed. It seemed like a good opportunity. While $2,000 a week was certainly high rental, the traffic at Grand Central was enormous. Besides the ordinary fruit sales, travelers would undoubtedly be buying expensive baskets to give as gifts.

The brothers followed Mr. Grenfell into a building connected with Grand Central to the door of a suite of offices that bore the legend:

Wilson A. Blodgett
President
GRAND CENTRAL
HOLDING CORPORATION

They were ushered past a blond secretary into Mr. Blodgett's office. Blodgett was a very busy man and could not spend much time on such a trifling matter. When the brothers again hesitated, Mr. Blodgett seemed to take it that they would have trouble raising the $100,000. Imperiously, he started to dismiss them, but thanks to Mr. Grenfell's intercession and the brothers' hasty assurances, he relented. It was agreed that the brothers would close the deal the following morning by presenting a certified check for the full amount.

The next morning the transaction went like clockwork. The check changed hands and the papers were signed. The brothers were to take possession at 9 A.M. on April 1, coincidentally April Fool's Day.

Shortly before the appointed hour, Tony and Nick Fortunato arrived at the station accompanied by a small gang of carpenters. Some remodeling was, of course, necessary to transform the information booth into a plush fruit stand. Eager to get started, the brothers ordered the carpenters to start doing the lumber work outside the booth. The puzzled information booth clerks wondered what was going on. At exactly 9 o'clock, Tony Fortunato approached the booth and ordered the clerks out. The clerks then began asking the questions, with the indignant Fortunatos shouting answers. Railroad guards appeared, trying to clear away the carpenters, who were blocking travelers from getting to the information booth.

Finally, one hour and one melee later, the Fortunatos were escorted into the administrative offices of the New York Central Railroad. They flaunted their written contract but were told that there was no such thing as the Grand Central Holding Corp.

Undaunted, the Fortunato brothers promptly led the officials to the offices of that firm—or at least where the offices had been. The officials of the railroad tried to explain to them that they had been the victims of a confidence scheme. The brothers were convinced that a rich American corporation was trying to cheat two foreigners out of $100,000 and then lease the booth to another fruit dealer. In the end, they were forcibly ejected from the terminal. The brothers took their complaint to leaders of New York's Italian community, who complained to the police. But while the police had extensive files on confidence game operators, they could not identify Grenfell or Blodgett. It had been a perfect crime, one that many in the Italian community continued to believe had been cooked up by a rich corporation to take advantage of naive Italians. For many years thereafter, Tony and Nick Fortunato would come into Grand Central Station and glare at the poor information clerks, hurling insults of shaking their fists at them, thus becoming, after a fashion, another strange sight for tourists arriving in Gotham.

Grand Street School criminal institution

Operations of Fagin-type schools for crime were common in 19th-century America, but few achieved the stature of the so-called Grand Street School in New York City in the 1870s.

Run by the celebrated Marm Mandelbaum, the leading fence and perhaps the greatest criminal organizer of the era, the establishment was virtually within sight of police headquarters. Marm's staff of expert pickpockets and sneak thieves taught small boys and girls, many under the age of 10, the secrets of their profession, and there were also advanced courses in safecracking and burglars, confidence rackets and blackmail techniques.

No charges were levied for the instructions, but virtually all the income from "class work" went to Marm and her cohorts. Upon completion of the courses, several of the more proficient students were put on straight salary, binding them to turn in everything they stole. Marm Mandelbaum abandoned this practice after she discovered that several of her top employees were instead selling a considerable portion of their loot to rival fences while still drawing their regular pay. This realization that there was no honor among thieves and Marm's conclusion that the crime school had become too blatant when the young son of a prominent police officer applied for training forced her to cease operations after a half-dozen years.

See also: FREDERICKA "MARM" MANDELBAUM.

Grannan, Riley (1868–1908) gambler and gunfighter

Although he was reputed to be fast on the draw, Riley Grannan is best remembered as a truly successful Western gambler, a brilliant student of horse racing and the inventor of modern form-betting. He once bet $275,000 on a horse and won.

Born in Paris, Ky. in 1868, Grannan arrived on the Western scene fairly late and soon grasped that with the closing of the frontier, the old style of the cheating gambler was outdated. He came up with the idea of establishing a gambling palace that could offer customers satisfaction for all their desires and, an idea still relatively unique for the West, honest gambling. For the locale of this great dream, Grannan picked out a plot of land at Rawhide, Nev. in 1907 and plunked down $40,000 for its purchase. There were those who considered it a foolish idea to try to build a great gambling center in the desert, and they appeared to be right. When Grannan died suddenly in April 1908, he was flat broke, his dream having drained away virtually all his funds.

Four decades later, a leading hoodlum named Bugsy Siegel would come up with the same dream and lose millions of the crime syndicate's money building the Flamingo. Eventually, the gambling paradise of Las Vegas was to prove that Siegel, and Riley Grannan before him, were right.

Grant, Joe (?–1880?) Billy the Kid victim

Joe Grant was a mean Texas gunman who "leaned on" Billy the Kid in a saloon at Fort Sumner, N.M. in January 1880 and was shot dead after falling for a clever ruse by the Kid. At least, that's the way the story is told in many of the more colorful biographies of Billy the Kid.

Over the years Joe Grant was built up from an unknown to a vicious gunman who drifted up from Texas for the specific purpose of ridding New Mexico of the Kid. But when he challenged Billy in that saloon, he did not exactly behave like a seasoned gunman. According to the legend, Billy smoothtalked him into showing him his gun, from which Grant had already fired a few shots. The Kid admired the .45 and—unknown to Grant—spun the barrel around to an empty chamber. When the shooting started, Joe Grant was embarrassed to hear his gun click on the empty chamber, but his embarrassment was short lived as the Kid gunned him down. Writer after writer has embellished the account, but more recently, experts, such as James D. Horan and Paul Sann, have argued that the so-called duel might well have been an "invention." And it may be that not only was the duel apocryphal, but so was Joe Grant himself, living—and dying—only in the legend of Billy the Kid.

Grant, Ulysses S. (1822–1885) traffic offender

Both before and after he entered the White House, Ulysses S. Grant was a notorious speedster with horse and rig. On at least two occasions, Grant, while in command of the Union armies, was fined $5 in precinct court. Such an offense was not so readily handled during Grant's first presidential term. President Grant was apprehended in the nation's capital for racing his horse and buggy at breakneck speed on M Street between 11th and 12th. The arresting constable, a man named William H. West, was dragged some 50 feet after seizing the horse's bridle. When Constable West recognized Grant, he started to apologize, but the president said, "Officer, do your duty." The horse and rig were impounded for a time but finally returned to Grant when no charges were pressed. A constitutional dilemma developed, much as it would a century later in the Watergate scandal, about whether it was possible to indict a president without first impeaching him.

Gravano, Sammy "the Bull" (1945–) highest-ranking Mafia informer

Without doubt, he was the most important Mafia bigwig to turn informer in the entire history of the battle against organized crime in America. Federal prosecutors were never able to bring down John Gotti, the boss of the powerful Gambino crime family, until his underboss, Salvatore Gravano, better known as "Sammy the Bull" "flipped" and testified against Gotti, dubbed by the media as the "Teflon Don" for his ability to beat rap after rap.

This time the Feds could be said to have Gotti with "the meat in his mouth," doomed by 100 hours of taped conversations he conducted. Later criticism was raised that the prosecutors needlessly let Gravano "walk." Experts found that prosecutors were "tape-shy," since

Mafia turncoat Sammy "the Bull" Gravano achieved best-seller status with his account of his life in the Mafia. (Author's collection)

cases had previously been lost even though there were plenty of tapes for the government to use. In those cases Gotti's lawyers tore into the tapes, saying they were misleading and just plain "garbage." Jurors seemed to agree.

Faced with that reality the government decided Gravano was vital to their case. The Bull—so named for his compact muscular body and thick bovine neck—had witnessed the events Gotti talked about so damningly and was able to provide personal corroboration that prosecutors were never able to come up with before. That hardly meant that Gravano put a "human face" on the case. More accurately what made the Bull so fascinating to the authorities, the media and the public was his very unwholesomeness. Without a qualm or real note of regret, Gravano confessed to 19 murders, and a reading of his testimony made a number of observers conclude that in some cases Gravano pushed the killings on Gotti rather than the reverse.

Gravano enumerated his 19 murders stretching from 1970 to some two decades later. Still the prosecution had to have him on the stand, immunity for him a small price to pay for tying Gotti to the curbside murder of Paul Castellano, the head of the Gambinos whom Gotti had to eliminate to achieve power.

Gotti went to prison for life with no parole, and he was to be only one of dozens of mobsters to end up in prison, as were corrupt union officials, having been convicted of racketeering. So too fell a crooked cop who supplied information to Gotti and a corrupt juror who aided the Gotti cause in a previous prosecution.

Since it was true that Gravano very easily would have been convicted without testimony from Gotti on the basis of the taped conversations and gotten at least 50 years, some have argued that obviously Gotti could have been convicted without Gravano's testimony. Gravano made it clear he felt Gotti's "big mouth" on the tapes was what had doomed him. The fact was that Gravano probably knew he was in a top-dog position because the prosecutors knew this was their last chance to get Gotti on all the charges under the RICO law. If they lost the case, Gotti could never be charged again on any of that evidence.

That meant, some legal experts say, Gravano actually was in a position to dictate the terms of his own treatment. In 1985 he drew a five-year sentence, but since he had been held for five years, mostly for his own protection, he went free.

Gravano at first went into the witness protection program. He was supposed to crawl into the most remote cave and stay there, fingers firmly crossed and hoping the mob wouldn't find him. That was not the Bull's way. He left the program and increasingly appeared in the open. In 1999 he was living in Phoenix, Ariz., having popped up on television to promote his 1997 biography, *Underboss*. He also returned to the construction business, which is where he operated during his crime days, and even talked to a local newspaper as long as it did not reveal his new name.

Apparently, Gravano concluded the Gambinos were not about to go after him. True, family members all hated him, but secretly many agreed that Gotti was the one who had caused their woes, starting by his insistence that all his capos and other underlings appear regularly at the gang's Manhattan headquarters, the Ravenite. This allowed the FBI years of surveillance that eventually identified them.

As for Gotti himself, it became a fair bet he would not order the Bull's murder, if he still maintained the power to do so. Gotti had come down with cancer, which might in time allow him his freedom. The killing of the Bull would certainly "queer" that hope.

About the only ones really after Gravano were the kin of several of the Bull's hits. They launched a legal campaign to deprive him of any financial rewards from his book and they filed a $25 million suit against him. Despite his dark past, Gravano was making no deals and not giving up any of his money, rumored to include funds he got for his many "legitimate" businesses.

Apparently he felt secure in what the *New York Times* called his "all-American sun-belt future."

Even more amazing was another act of daring. Some newsmen have been trying to confirm that Sammy the Bull turned up in 1998 or 1999 walking around the New York's Howard Beach section, the heart of Gotti country. True or not, Sammy the Bull seemed to have a way about him.

See also: PAUL CASTELLANO, JOHN GOTTI.

Graves, Thomas T. (1843–1893) murderer

The murder of a rich elderly lady named Josephine Barnaby by Dr. Thomas Graves in 1891 ranked as New England's second most celebrated mystery during the 1890s, surpassed only by the case of Lizzie Borden. What especially offended the Victorian mores of the day was that a physician had done in his patient for profit. It was something "doctors don't do," a contemporary account noted.

The estranged wife of a Providence, R.I. businessman, Mrs. Barnaby inherited a paltry $2,500 upon her husband's death. Dr. Graves, who had treated the woman for a number of years, masterminded Mrs. Barnaby's campaign to reverse the will and eventually succeeded. The grateful widow gave her doctor power of attorney over her finances, whereupon the good doctor proceeded to loot her assets.

To make the task easier, Dr. Graves prescribed long trips for his patient's health. The old woman eventually grew suspicious, and when she insisted upon returning home and taking charge of her own affairs, the doctor warned her that he might have her declared incompetent and put in a home for the aged. Initially, Mrs. Barnaby was too petrified to protest any further, but then she let the doctor know she was returning from California and planned to take care of her estate personally.

On her trip back home, Mrs. Barnaby stopped off in Denver, Colo. to visit with a friend, a Mrs. Worrell. When she arrived there, she was greeted with a package from the East. It contained a bottle of whiskey on which was pasted a note reading: "Wish you a Happy New Year's. Please accept this fine old whiskey from your friend in the woods."

The two women used the whiskey in mixed drinks, found it rather "vile" but downed it all. Both of them died six days later. When the gift of whiskey was discovered, one of Mrs. Barnaby's daughters financed an autopsy on her body that turned up evidence of poison. Suspicion soon centered on Dr. Graves, who was much reviled in the press despite his denials of the crime. But suspicion was one thing and proof another, and although Dr. Graves was arrested, he was soon released on $30,000 bail. The lack of proof of any connection between the doctor and the poisoned whiskey made it appear that he would eventually be cleared, and numerous patients continued to visit him, declaring their belief in his innocence.

However, at Dr. Graves' trial the prosecution brought forth a newly discovered witness, a young man named Joseph Breslyn who told of Dr. Graves approaching him in November 1890 in the Boston train station and asking him to write a note, claiming he himself could not write. This was the note pasted on the poisoned whiskey bottle. Convicted, Graves was awaiting a retrial after a successful appeal when he committed suicide in April 1893 with poison smuggled into his jail cell.

graves of criminals

The headstone and marble shaft stands on Plot 48 in Chicago's Mount Olivet Cemetery. An inscription reads:

> *QUI RIPOSA*
> *Alphonse Capone*
> *Nato: Jan. 17, 1899*
> *Morto: Jan. 25, 1947*

The tourists still visit the grave, but there is no body. Even in death, Al Capone continues to be involved in deceit. When the Capone family realized, after Al's death, that the public would keep coming to the grave site to gawk, they secretly had the caskets of all the family's members moved across town to Mount Carmel Cemetery where the real graves are clustered around a granite slab, each headstone bearing the words "My Jesus Mercy."

A similar deception was practiced two decades earlier by the wife of Chicago gangster Dion O'Banion, who was murdered by Capone gunners. Originally, he was buried in November 1924 under a headstone bearing his name, in unconsecrated ground at Mount Carmel, as directed by Cardinal George Mundelein. A spokesman for the archdiocese explained: "One who refuses the ministrations of the Church in life need not expect them in death. O'Banion was a notorious criminal. The Church did not recognize him in his days of lawlessness and when he died unrepented in his iniquities, he had no claims to the last rites for the dead." In 1925 Anna O'Banion had the remains of her husband disinterred and reburied in consecrated ground under a granite shaft inscribed, "My Sweetheart." The cardinal was outraged when he heard of it and ordered the monument removed. He relented, however, about having O'Banion's body moved again and allowed it to remain, marked only by a simple headstone.

Most Mafia big shots, with few exceptions, prefer the same type of anonimity in death that they seek in life. The body of Thomas Lucchese reposes in Calvary Cemetery in Queens, New York City under a headstone with his name oddly misspelled Luckese, a version never used by the family. The theory is that it was his or the family's way of misdirecting the curious.

Another Queens cemetery, St. John's, has become known as the Mafia's Boot Hill. Charles "Lucky" Luciano (1897–1962) personally picked out his future resting place at St. John's in 1935. His Grecian mausoleum near the entrance (Section 3, Range C) provided the final resting ground for a number of his family who died before him. Twenty-five years after selecting the site, Luciano was fortunate to be able to be interred there. Since at the time of his death he was in exile in his native Italy, permission had to be obtained so that his body could be returned to the United States for burial.

Vito Genovese (1897–1969) also lies buried in St. John's. Once an ally of Luciano, he became his mortal enemy in later years. Now they are closer than ever. Genovese reposes very near Luciano (Section 11, Range E, Plot 9) in a simple tomb.

Also near the Luciano mausoleum is the Romanesque tomb of Joseph Profaci (1897–1962), former head of one of New York's five crime families. Profaci's resting place, another mausoleum, is the largest of all the dons, located on a circular road fronting the Cloister building that contains the body of Carlo Gambino, the model for Mario Puzo's *Godfather,* in a private family vault on the fifth floor. Among others buried at St. John's in more recent years are Joseph Colombo (1914–78) and Carmine Galante (1910–79).

Walkie-talkie-equipped keepers guard the privacy of all the underworld big shots at St. John's. Picture takers are given the bum's rush by guards, especially at the Luciano and Genovese grave sites, with the explanation that the families of the deceased do not appreciate such activities. One crime writer, Philip Nobile, advised readers recently that if they wished to "shoot" the Profaci grave, "do it from a moving car, a tactic perfected by the Mafia itself."

By comparison, it is relatively easy to snap pictures at other cemeteries, such as St. Michael's, also in Queens, where Frank Costello (1891–1973) lies. St. Michael's is nonsectarian, which is perhaps most fitting for Costello, the most "non-Italian" of the syndicate. Like that of Luciano, Costello's tomb is positioned just to the left of the main entrance, almost like a greeting to visitors.

Ironically, both Albert Anastasia, born Anastasio, (1902–57) and Crazy Joe Gallo (1929–72) lie buried in Brooklyn's Greenwood Cemetery, the former's death being the result of the latter's plotting. Guards at the cemetery will direct visitors to Gallo's grave. But then, Crazy Joe was always one of the more exhibitionist characters in the underworld.

Graves of criminals are probably raided more often than those of other people. When Billy the Kid was laid to rest in 1881, after being shot dead by Sheriff Pat Garrett, he was dressed in a borrowed white shirt by Deluvina Maxwell, the Indian servant girl who loved him, and buried under a wooden cross bearing the legend *"Duerme bien. Querido"* ("Sleep well, beloved"). But before long, the cross was carried off by ardent souvenir hunters. Today, Billy is buried in a common grave in Old Fort Sumner with two of his fellow outlaws, Tom O'Folliard and Charlie Bowdre. A stone marker with the inscription "Pals" identifies the trio and their dates. The grave is surrounded by a high-wire fence, the only enclosure to successfully contain the Kid.

Gray, Henry Judd   See RUTH SNYDER.

great diamond hoax

In 1872 two seedy prospectors named John Slack and Philip Arnold pulled off a monumental fraud, fooling some of the best business brains of this country and the diamond experts of Tiffany's.

Slack and Arnold visited the Bank of California in San Francisco and asked to have a leather pouch deposited in the vault. After first refusing to say what it contained, they finally shrugged and spilled out the pouch's glittering contents, a hoard of uncut diamonds. By the time they left the bank, the head teller was already in the office of the bank's president, William C. Ralston. A former miner himself, and probably selected by Slack and Arnold for that very reason, Ralston soon went looking for the two prospectors. His offer: to form a mining syndicate for harvesting the diamonds. Slack and Arnold conceded they could use some help, but they were not about to reveal the source of the diamonds until they had cash in hand. The diamonds were sent over to a jeweler's office in San Francisco to determine their genuineness and the answer came back that they were indeed the real thing. Still, caution prompted Ralston and his associates to double-check with Tiffany's in New York. Tiffany's proved even more enthusiastic, suggesting the diamonds sent them meant that those in hand were worth at least $1.5 million.

Now convinced there was a pot of diamonds at the end of the rainbow, Ralston & Co.'s next step was to find a way to separate the diamond find from the grizzled prospectors. Slack and Arnold were first brought into the mining syndicate and then offered $300,000 apiece for their shares—provided they would reveal the source of the diamonds. The two prospectors rubbed their whiskers and said that was a good enough offer since they weren't the greedy kind. The fact that the mining company had in its possession an estimated $1.5 million in gems made it a very good deal for Ralston and the others, some might even say a swindle. That, of course, is the secret behind many a great swindle—the cheated must believe they are cheating the cheaters.

Before the money was turned over to the pair, they would have to prove the diamond field existed. This they agreed to provided the man sent with them to check its authenticity, mining expert John Janin, went and returned blindfolded. Slack and Arnold stated they would not reveal the field's location until they were paid. They traveled a day and a half by train and then two days by pack mule with Janin blindfolded all the way. What the mining expert found at the end of the trip made him ecstatic. There were diamonds all over the place, just below the ground, between rocks, in ant hills! When the three returned to San Francisco, Janin refused to make his report until he was permitted to buy into the mining corporation. That ignited the whole thing. A diamond craze hit the West. Ralston's company paid off the prospectors, who headed east, and then prepared to mine the diamond field before other fortune hunters found it. The company sent out phony search groups to mislead other prospectors. At least 25 expeditions were launched to find diamonds. However, before the Ralston combine could really get its operation off the ground (the company first wanted to set up its own, and the country's first, diamond-cutting industry in San Francisco), the bubble burst. A prominent geologist, Clarence King and two others set out to find the field. When they did, King quickly determined it had been "salted." Some of the diamonds found by King showed lapidary marks.

The news was electrifying. The *San Francisco Evening Bulletin* headlined the story:

THE DIAMOND CHIMERA
It Dissolved Like the Baseless
Fabric of a Dream
The Most Dazzling Fraud of the Age

Investigation in Europe revealed that Slack and Arnold had come to Amsterdam with $25,000 they'd won gambling and bought up a huge amount of flawed uncut diamonds. This was what they salted the desert with. Very few reputations came through the scandal unmarred. Charles Lewis Tiffany had to admit that his experts, who were the best in America, hadn't ever worked with uncut diamonds and thus simply were not aware how much of a raw stone was lost when fashioned into a jewel. Many of California's tycoons dropped huge amounts of money and Ralston's bank collapsed. Ralston committed suicide.

Slack and Arnold fared better. Private detectives found Arnold living quite happily in his original home in Elizabethtown, Ky. on his $300,000 take. The courts there did not look kindly on efforts to have him extradited to California. He and Slack were admired, even lionized, by much of the country. After all, even if they had taken some supposedly sharp tycoons for $600,000, hadn't those greedy men swindled them out of a "billion dollar" mine? Finally, in return for giving back $150,000 of his haul, Arnold had all charges against him dropped. Nothing more was heard of Slack for many years. Just before leaving California, he had told his friends that he intended to drink up his $300,000 or die in the effort. Then years later, he turned up as a well-to-do coffin maker in White Oaks, N.M.

Great Michigan "free land" swindle

There have been any number of swindles involving the sale of vacation or retirement plots, but never has there been anything to rival the fantastic ripoff worked early in the 20th century by two colorful rogues, Col. Jim Porter, a former Mississippi steamboat gambler, and his young assistant, who over the years would become famous as Yellow Kid Weil.

Col. Porter had a cousin who was a county recorder up in Michigan and the owner of several thousand acres of undesirable or submarginal land. Porter and his assistant bought a large chunk of this land at $1 an acre and then set up a Chicago sales office, showing the usual artist's concept of a clubhouse, marina and other features that would be built. However, they said nothing was ready for sale yet. Meanwhile, Porter, posing as an eccentric millionaire, and Weil started ingratiating themselves with hundreds of people by giving away free lots. No one was immune to the offer. Porter on certain evenings would give away 30 to 40 lots to prostitutes, madams, waiters and bartenders. Weil even gave some to Chicago police detectives. But they admonished each recipient not to mention the gift because then everyone else would want one. Naturally, they would also inform the happy recipients that they should immediately write and have the transaction recorded at the county seat. The fee for this, it developed, was $30; it had been just $2 before the swindle, but Porter's cousin had raised the fee to $30 with the understanding that $15 of it would go to Porter and Weil, netting the pair $16,000, and the rest he would keep for himself. The operation was entirely legal since all they had done was give away some valueless land, and not taken a penny from any recipient.

Green, Eddie   See JUG MARKERS.

Green, Edward (1833–1866) bank robber

In a sense, Edward Green, often mistakenly called America's first bank robber, represents a criminal trend that has come full circle. When Green, who was postmaster of Malden, Mass., robbed that town's bank on December 15, 1863, he was an amateur, it was his first crime and he did it on impulse. Today, that is the description of the average bank robber, the professionals having long since deserted the field.

Green, a cripple, visited the bank and discovered that the president's son, 17-year-old Frank Converse, was alone there. Green went home, returned to the bank with his pistol and shot Converse in the head, killing him. He then scooped up $5,000 in cash and ambled out. Behaving like the amateur he was, Green, who was deep in debt, suddenly paid all his bills; a heavy drinker, he drank even more and spent money lavishly. When the police brought him in for questioning, Green quickly confessed the robbery and murder and was duly hanged on February 27, 1866. Shortly after Green's bank robbery, the James and Younger boys, the Missouri badmen, went into the bank-robbing business and raised the crime to an art form in America.

See also: BANK ROBBERIES.

"Green, Ballad of Baldy"   frontier song

Not too much is known about the life of Baldy Green, but his accomplishments were, in a manner of speaking, impressive. As a stagecoach whip, Baldy drove the trails of the Nevada gold camps for Wells Fargo in the 1860s. This was not a safe occupation, considering the number of highwaymen that plagued Wells Fargo. Many drivers got shot but never Baldy Green. It was said that Baldy was just about the most polite victim a stagecoach robber could wish for, and he became celebrated for his ability to throw his hands up and the strongbox to the ground in one motion.

According to one story, Wells Fargo finally fired Baldy while they still had some strongboxes left. While Baldy's fate is lost to history, his fame as a Wells Fargo driver was and is still celebrated in the rollicking "Ballad of Baldy Green."

Green Chair Curse   Chicago underworld superstition

One of the most colorful legends in crime is that of the Green Chair Curse, also sometimes referred to by the chroniclers of Chicago crime as the Undertaker's Friend. The curse was named after a green leather chair in the office of William "Shoes" Schoemaker, who became Chicago's chief of detectives in 1924. Several of Chicago's top gangsters were hauled into Schoemaker's office for grilling and ordered to sit in the green chair. Several of them died violent deaths shortly thereafter. This could hardly be considered a startling coincidence in view of the death rate in Chicago's gang wars during Prohibition.

The newspapers, however, quickly seized on a great story and belief in the curse of the green chair began to grow. In time, Schoemaker started keeping a record of the criminals who sat in the chair and later died violently. When the "inevitable" event occurred, Shoes put an X by the gangster's name. There were the bloody brothers Genna (Angelo, Tony and Mike), Porky Lavenuto, Mop Head Russo, Samoots Amatuna, Antonio "the Scourge" Lombardo, John Scalise, Albert Anselmi, Schemer Drucci, Zippy Zion, Pickle Puss DePro, Antonio "the Cavalier" Spano. Undoubtedly aprocryphal tales had it that other gangsters, including Al Capone, absolutely refused to sit down in the chair.

When Shoes retired in 1934, there were 35 names in his notebook and 34 had Xs after them. Only one criminal, Red Holden, was still alive and he was doing time in Alcatraz for train robbery. "My prediction still stands," Shoes informed reporters. "He'll die a violent death. Maybe it'll happen in prison. Maybe we'll have to wait until he gets out. But, mark my words, it'll happen."

Holden, however, outlived Shoes, who died four years later. The chair passed to Capt. John Warren, Shoes' aide, and he continued to seat an occasional hoodlum in it. By the time Warren died in September 1953, the green chair death rate was said to stand at 56 out of 57. Only Red Holden was still alive. He had been released from Alcatraz in 1948 and thereafter was involved in several shoot-outs, which he survived. Then he was convicted of murder and sent to prison for 25 years. On December 18, 1953, he died in the infirmary of Illinois' Statesville Penitentiary. The newspapers reported he was "smiling" because he had "beaten the chair"—the green one rather than the electric one.

Holden's passing set off a newspaper search for the illustrious green chair that had so cursed the underworld, but alas, it was no more. The chair was traced to the Chicago Avenue police station, where it had been confined to the cellar after Capt. Warren's death. When it was found to be infested with cockroaches, it was chopped up and consigned to the furnace before

Holden died in his hospital bed. Otherwise, some claimed, Holden would never have escaped its curse.

Green Corn Rebellion   antiwar movement

Antiwar sentiment during World War I was much more pronounced than it was during the Vietnam conflict, but it produced only one major and premeditated violent incident: the Green Corn Rebellion of eastern Oklahoma.

The organization behind the rebellion was the Working Class Union (WCU), a syndicalist movement associated with the Industrial Workers of the World, which was formed before the beginning of the war. In August 1917 several hundred angry WCU farmers assembled to march on Washington, take over the government and end the war. While they awaited the arrival of thousands of other antiwar, antidraft protestors to swell their ranks, the farmers subsisted on unripe green corn. They managed to cut some telegraph wires and tried unsuccessfully to blow up railroad bridges. Before the movement was fully mobilized, they were attacked and scattered by patriotic posses. A total of 450 farmers were arrested. Many were released, but the leaders drew prison sentences of three to 10 years and many lesser supporters were given 60 days to two years.

There were several shootings and hangings during the war period, but in all cases save the Green Corn Rebellion, the violence was initiated by supporters of the war.

green goods swindle   confidence game

The green goods game is an old swindle by which a victim is sold what he thinks is an extraordinarily well-executed set of counterfeit money, only to find out later he has bought a bundle of worthless paper.

The racket made its first appearance in 1869. The mark would be shown a batch of genuine bills, told they were perfect counterfeits and given the chance to buy them at an extremely reasonable rate. Invariably, the victim would jump at the opportunity, but just before the sale was completed, the money package would be switched for one containing cut-up green paper.

By the 1880s several green goods gangs flourished in this country. They set about picking their victims in a scientific manner. First, a list of people who regularly bought lottery tickets was compiled and scouts were sent out to determine whether they were likely to go for a dishonest scheme and whether they had the funds to make fleecing them worthwhile. In this fashion quite a number of small-town bankers and businessmen were targeted and then caught in the swindlers' net. Rather

brazenly, the approach would even be made by mail. One circular issued in 1882 read:

Dear Sir:

I will confide to you through this circular a secret by which you can make a speedy fortune. I have on hand a large amount of counterfeit notes of the following denominations: $1, $2, $5, $10 and $20. I guarantee every note to be perfect, as it is examined carefully by me as soon as finished, and if not strictly perfect is immediately destroyed. Of course it would be perfectly foolish to send out poor work, and it would not only get my customers into trouble, but would break up my business and ruin me. So for personal safety, I am compelled to issue nothing that will not compare with the genuine. I furnish you with my goods at the following low price, which will be found as reasonable as the nature of my business will allow:

For $ 1,200 in my goods (assorted) I charge 100
For $ 2,500 in my goods (assorted) I charge 200
For $ 5,000 in my goods (assorted) I charge 350
For $10,000 in my goods (assorted) I charge 600

Faced with the glowing prospect of making a considerable sum of money, very few carefully screened recipients of such letters notified the authorities. In a few rare cases the sellers of the "counterfeit" money were seized when they appeared to close the deal, but they were released when an examination showed their money was genuine. In one case a fast-talking swindler convinced a New England police chief that he represented a bank executive who was planning to offer an important position to a local banker but wanted to test his honesty first.

Among the swindlers who worked the green goods game over the years were Reed Waddell, Tom O'Brien, George Post, Pete Conlish, Yellow Kid Weil and Fred Buckminster. For a time the New Orleans Mafia pulled green goods swindles, and even Mafia godfather Carlo Gambino supposedly worked it several times. Although most victims never reveal that they have been swindled, police bunco squads get a few such reports each year.

See also: REED WADDELL.

Green Parrot murder

The murder at the Green Parrot Restaurant and Bar on Third Avenue near 100th Street on July 12, 1942 was a run-of-the-mill crime, the slaying of the proprietor during an apparent holdup; yet it is remembered today by New York police as a case with a most unusual solution. Although there had been 20 patrons in the bar at the time of the shooting, none would admit seeing anything, insisting they had been at the far end of the bar or in booths lining the wall.

It was not unusual in this tough section of East Harlem to find such a group of uncommunicative witnesses. A few acknowledged that they had seen a man with a gun, heard a shot and ducked. When they lifted their heads, the patrons said, the man with the gun was gone, and owner Max Geller was lying on the floor behind the bar in a pool of blood. Had the man simply walked in, drawn a gun and shot the bar owner? Or had it been an attempted robbery? None of the witnesses was certain. Only one of them had yelled "Robber, robber, robber!" And that was the establishment's green parrot, kept on a perch behind the bar.

The Green Parrot Bar was actually a community landmark because of the bird. It was a reason to bring guests and tourists to the place, for this was no ordinary talking pet with a few limited phrases but a crotchety old creature with the vocabulary of a longshoreman. An unsuspecting visitor might be told to offer the parrot a cracker. If he did so and expected a grateful reaction, he was sadly disillusioned. Such acts of friendship only provoked outrage from the bird, who would cut loose with a torrent of sulfurous language. But the creature was clearly the keen sort. Evidently, Geller had cried out "robber" during the attack on him, and the parrot had picked up the cry.

Knowing that a robbery had been attempted and finding a solution to the case were two separate matters, however. For almost two years the case remained unsolved, forgotten by almost everyone except Detective John J. Morrisey, who occasionally would return to the neighborhood in an attempt to dredge a forgotten fact from the memories of the witnesses. Finally, he learned that in addition to cursing the bird had been taught to greet several patrons by name. It was a long, tedious process but after a number of weeks the bird would pick up a patron's name and repeat it, appealing to the vanity of the customer.

The detective returned to the Green Parrot and tried to teach the bird his name and some other expressions. If the bird was smart, it was also stubborn and took weeks to pick up what the police officer taught it. Suddenly, Morrisey realized it was impossible for the parrot to have picked up the word *robber* after just hearing it once. No, the bird hadn't been saying "robber" but something else.

A short time later, Morrisey arrested Robert Butler, a former resident of the area, in Baltimore, Md., where he was working as a lathe operator. He had vanished from New York right after the Geller murder. As the case turned out, the bird had not been shrieking "robber" but had actually been repeating a name he had learned earlier: "Robert, Robert, Robert!" Butler was

the only bar patron greeted by that name, and it was he whom the parrot had identified as the murderer. Indeed, he had not tried to commit a robbery but had shot Geller in a drunken rage because the bar owner had refused to serve him, claiming he was intoxicated when he entered.

On February 10, 1944 the only killer ever convicted because of a parrot was sentenced to seven to 15 years in Sing Sing.

Green River Killer   the one that got away

Quite possibly the most prolific unidentified serial killer is the "Green River Killer," so called because the 49 victims attributed to him or her were dumped in or near Washington State's Green River. The victims started appearing on January 21, 1982, when 16-year-old Leann Wilcox of Tacoma was found strangled 8 miles from Seattle. Then in the fall of 1984, the parade of corpses abruptly stopped. There have been no further attributable Green River killings since then, but a law enforcement Green River Task Force remained in place to find the killer. That goal was not achieved, but over the next several years the force solved seven unrelated murders and three rapes. In what some observers thought a bizarre development, serial killer Ted Bundy was used as an adviser to the task force. Bundy was himself facing conviction and the death penalty. In point of fact Bundy contributed little to the investigation and clearly was motivated by a desire to postpone his own death sentence.

Why did the Green River Killer stop? Some have speculated that he or she died or was in prison or a mental institution, his or her Green River crimes not suspected by authorities. Another theory held by some experts was that the killer had simply left the area. These experts noted that in 1985, a series of murders started in San Diego, Cal. that seemed related to the Green River cases. The number of murders attributed to the unknown San Diego serial killer ranged from 10 to perhaps 18 by a recent count. This would raise the combined toll to anywhere from 59 to 67.

Green Tree dance house

The dime-a-dance halls of this century trace back to the much more bawdy dance houses of the 19th century. All such dance houses featured three attractions: liquor, women and, least important, dancing. Most dance houses would have at least 20 to 30 girls who not only were unsalaried but indeed had to pay rent for rooms or cubicles on the upper floors of the building. They made their living from the customers they could lure to their room to engage in paid sex or to be robbed. When business was especially good, harlots would be imported from a nearby brothel. The general rule was that the nearer the dance house was to the waterfront, the rougher and meaner it was. The Green Tree on Gallatin Street in New Orleans was a good example of one of the more depraved dancehall establishments.

The Green Tree opened its doors in 1850. An old woman ran the place with a firm hand. The first floor of the establishment was divided into two rooms. The first room, much bigger than the second, sported a long bar, which could accommodate as many as 250 patrons elbow to elbow. A smaller room in back was for dancing and featured a piano and a fiddle, occasionally supplemented by a few brass instruments. At times, the bouncers would have to enforce a minimum of decorum on the dance floor, where some of the girls would try to stimulate business by suddenly whipping off their dresses and dancing in the nude. The clients would sometimes follow suit, and the bouncers would have to clear the floor of couples doing everything else but dancing.

The bouncers, as many as six at a time, were always armed at least with clubs and brass knuckles. Besides maintaining order in the back room, they were needed to handle trouble at the bar. They were not too concerned with ordinary fights or an occasional knifing, provided the culprit showed the decency to clean up afterward by dumping his victim or victims outside the premises. The bouncers' main concern was to prevent physical damage to the house, and they would move in quickly and viciously the second any furnishings were splintered.

The history of violence at the Green Tree can be traced through the fate of its various owners. The first owner, the old woman, disappeared from the scene in the mid-1850s. Her place was filled by Harry Rice, who lasted until 1864, when he was almost stoned to death by a group of Union soldiers objecting to the high water content of the liquor served. It took a detachment of U.S. cavalrymen to save him, and Rice, maimed for life, closed shop. The resort was reopened the following year by Mary Rich, better known as One-Legged Duffy because of her wooden leg. She failed to last a year, being murdered on the premises by her lover, Charley Duffy, who not only knifed her to death but also smashed her skull in with her own wooden leg. Paddy Welsh, a veteran saloon keeper, took over but got in trouble with one of the worst criminal gangs of the district, the Live Oak Boys, who wrecked the dive, admonishing Welsh not to open up again. Welsh paid no heed to their warning, however, and a few days later, his body was found floating in the Mississippi.

William Lee, a former drum major in the U.S. Army, remained in New Orleans after the Civil War and eventually took charge of the Green Tree. He was stabbed to death by a gangster in an argument over a woman.

The last owner of the Green Tree was Tom Pickett, who saw the place torn apart by Live Oak bullies in 1876. After brooding about the fact that it would take a fortune to try to refurbish the establishment, Pickett went out hunting with a revolver. He found several Live Oak men in a saloon and shot two of them dead. He was sent to the state penitentiary for life but escaped in 1885 when it caught fire. Pickett was later identified in New York, but the authorities apparently made no effort to return him to justice. As for the Green Tree, it became regarded as a jinx. When the premises next opened, it was a bakery.

See also: LIVE OAK BOYS.

Greenlease, Robert C., Jr. (1947–1953) kidnap-murder victim

The first major kidnapping of the post–World War II period was the abduction of six-year-old Bobby Greenlease, Jr., the son of a wealthy Kansas City, Mo. automobile dealer, on September 28, 1953. Using the ruse that the child's mother had suffered a heart attack and was calling for her son, one of the kidnappers, 41-year-old Bonnie Brown Heady, posed as the boy's aunt to get him out of the French Institute of Notre Dame de Scion, one of the city's most exclusive schools for small children.

She and her accomplice, Carl Austin Hall, the 34-year-old ne'er-do-well son of a respected lawyer and an alcoholic who had turned to crime, then drove the Greenlease boy across the state line to Kansas, where Hall attempted to strangle him in a field. The feisty youngster fought back fiercely, several times breaking from Hall's grasp and striking back. Finally, Hall drew a revolver from his pocket and shot the child twice.

The kidnappers put the corpse back in their car and later buried it in the garden of Mrs. Heady's home in St. Joseph, Mo. Then, by letter and telephone, they demanded and received $600,000 in ransom from their victim's frantic parents. It took several fouled-up efforts to get the money to the kidnappers, but the child was not returned. On October 6, 1953 the two were arrested by police in St. Louis after they had gone on a drunken spree and attracted the suspicions of a cab driver.

Justice came swiftly. They were found guilty the following month, and on December 18, 1953 they died together in the gas chamber. As they were strapped into their chairs, Bonnie Heady's main concern was that her lover not be bound too tightly. "You got plenty of room, honey?" she asked. Hall replied, "Yes, Mama." The gas was turned on and they died.

An unanswered question was what happened to that part of the ransom money that Hall had placed in two metal suitcases. After the pair's arrest the suitcases were brought to the Eleventh Precinct Station in St. Louis.

When the money was counted, it totaled only $295,140. Since the couple had spent just a few thousand dollars, the FBI determined, the missing amount was $301,960. It was an open secret that the FBI suspected a member or members of the St. Louis police force, but no charges were ever lodged.

Guadalupe Canyon massacre

Actually, there was not one but two Guadalupe Canyon massacres, the second of which came close to being commemorated as a national holiday in Mexican border towns because so many *gringos* had been killed. The first massacre was the work of the notorious Clanton gang. In July 1881 Old Man Clanton, the leader of the outlaws, learned that a Mexican mule train was freighting bullion through the Chiricahua Range. Clanton scouted the area and decided the best place for his cutthroats to ambush the mule train was in Guadalupe Canyon. With about 20 men, among them Curly Bill Brocius, Johnny Ringo and several of Clanton's own brood, Old Man Clanton led an attack on the train when the 19 Mexican muleteers were in an exposed position. They killed several of the Mexicans and—on Clanton's orders—lined up the survivors and executed them. The gang escaped with $75,000 in loot and left a large section of the Chiricahua country mourning their dead.

Less than two weeks later, Old Man Clanton and five of his men attempted to drive a herd of stolen Mexican cattle through the same canyon, totally unmindful that the Mexicans might have learned something from their ambush. A band of relatives and friends of the massacre victims ambushed the small Clanton contingent, killing all but one of them, including Old Man Clanton.

While there was considerable rejoicing in Mexican adobes after the massacre of the *gringos*, the joy was short lived. Later that same month Curly Bill Brocius, who had taken over the leadership of the gang, ambushed a Mexican trail herd in the San Luis Pass and killed six *vaqueros*. Eight others surrendered and were tortured to death by Curly Bill and his men.

See also: NEWMAN "OLD MAN" CLANTON.

Guiteau, Charles Julius (1844–1882) assassin of James A. Garfield

It is generally agreed that no assassin today could kill a president of the United States with the ease that Charles J. Guiteau, a disgruntled office seeker, shot President James A. Garfield in a Washington railroad station on July 2, 1881. First of all, it is doubtful an assassin could get as close as he got. Moreover, Guiteau fired and missed on his first shot: now, he would almost certainly be dropped before he had a chance to squeeze the trigger a second time.

Only after Guiteau's second shot did the president's guards pin his arms behind him and hustle him off to jail. It may have been the quietest assassination on record. But the president did not die immediately, lingering the whole hot summer with a bullet lodged so deep behind his pancreas that an operation to remove it was impossible. He finally died, after much suffering, on September 19, 1881.

"How could anybody be so cold-hearted as to want to kill my baby?" Garfield's mother asked.

Guiteau was eager to answer the question. He was busy in his jail cell writing his memoirs. He had had an erratic background as a sort of self-styled lawyer. Abandoning his wife, a 16-year-old waif he found in the streets, he had moved to Washington, D.C., where he did volunteer work for the Republican Party and picked up syphilis. When Garfield won the nomination, Guiteau mailed the candidate a disjointed speech he had written for Garfield to use and passed printed copies of it at meetings. Garfield never utilized the unsolicited speech, but Guiteau became convinced that his words provided Garfield with his margin of victory and thereby petitioned the newly elected president for the post of ambassador to France. He did not get it and resolved to gain vengeance by shooting Garfield. He bought a .44-caliber pistol and practiced shooting at trees along the Potomac. When he considered himself a credible marksman, he started dogging Garfield. When he was unsure of the president's schedule on a certain day, he simply asked the White House doorman, who told him. He once got near to Garfield in church but decided not to shoot because he feared others would be hit. On another occasion he passed up a golden opportunity to shoot the president because Mrs. Garfield was present, and Guiteau considered her "a dear soul."

Shortly before he finally shot Garfield Guiteau visited the District of Columbia jail to see what his future accommodations would be like and concluded it was "an excellent jail."

Brought to trial two months after the president's death, Guiteau subjected the courtroom to venomous outbursts during the 10½-week trial. He leaped up and launched into long diatribes against the witnesses and called them "dirty liars." The prosecutor was alternately "a low-livered whelp" and an "old hog." At other times, he was most civil; after the Christmas and New Year's recesses, Guiteau assured the judge that he "had a very happy holiday."

When in his cell, Guiteau made a point of strutting back and forth behind the bars so that visitors and crowds outside could gawk at him. In his own defense, he told the jurors that God had told him to kill. "Let your verdict be, it was the Deity's act, not mine," he demanded. When he was found guilty, he shook his finger at the jury box and snarled, "You are all low, consummate jackasses!"

In the days before his scheduled execution, Guiteau was relaxed and unrepentant during his waking hours, but his jailers insisted he moaned all night and slept in terror with his blankets over his head. At dawn on June 30, 1882, the date of his execution, Guiteau insisted on shining his shoes. He ate a hearty meal and memorized a poem he had written to recite on the scaffold. Guiteau went silently to the gallows, but after mounting the scaffold, he wept for a moment and, as the hangman came forward, recited his verse. "I am going to the Lordy," it started.

Then Guiteau was gone.

Charles J. Guiteau shoots President Garfield in a Washington railroad station.

gunfighting, western

It happened just the way good Western gunfights were supposed to happen. One day in late 1876 Turkey Creek Jack Johnson got into an argument with a couple of card-playing miners in Deadwood and invited them outside to settle matters. The trio headed out to the cemetery followed by a large crowd. Each of Johnson's opponents strapped on an extra gunbelt as Johnson started toward them from one end of the cemetery. The pair started from the other end and at 50 yards began firing at Johnson. Before they had gone 10 yards, each of Johnson's foes had finished one six-shooter and shifted to the other. Johnson had not yet fired a shot. Finally, at 30 yards Johnson fired his first shot and killed one of the men. Johnson stopped walking and let his remaining opponent move closer to him. The man approached, firing three more shots. Then Johnson shot him dead. When they rolled the man over, his finger was still on the trigger of his cocked gun. Johnson had fired just two shots.

That was how gunfights were supposed to be fought in the Wild West, and once in a rare while, they were. Turkey Creek Johnson's feat is notable for its rarity. Wyatt Earp once expounded that fighting a duel was a matter of "going into action with the greatest speed of which a man's muscles are capable, but mentally unflustered by an urge to hurry or the need for complicated nervous and muscular actions which trick shooting involves." Earp's detractors, on the other hand, insist the controversial lawman seldom if ever lived up to those words, engaging instead in what amounted to cold-blooded murder without giving his opponent a chance. Few Western "gunfights" really fit the bill; most consisted of sneaking up behind a man and shooting him or drawing down on him at a bar without giving him the opportunity to go for his gun. Even when both sides were able to shoot it out fairly, what usually resulted was a wild shooting spree in which neither protagonist was hurt, although this was not always the case with onlookers. Such duels ended when the fighters simply ran out of ammunition. This was even true in cases where the opponents faced each other at almost point-blank range. In 1882 Cockeyed Frank Loving and Jack Allen fought a storied duel in Trinidad, Colo. in which they fired a total of 16 shots without drawing blood. The next day, however, Allen got Loving—coming up behind him and shooting him down in cold blood, some said.

Few supposedly great gunfighters deserved their reputations. Bat Masterson killed only one man and that in self-defense after being shot by a drunken, brawling cavalryman. Jesse James was a notoriously bad shot. He once fired at a bank cashier at point-blank range and missed. On another occasion, attempting to kill a train robbery victim, he fired six shots at the man from a close distance but failed to hit him once. Billy the Kid certainly did not qualify as a great gunfighter, and there is no evidence that he ever gave any of his victims, variously estimated from four to 21, any kind of chance to draw. The Kid also was not much of a two-gun man, as he is often portrayed. Not many were—since two guns with belt and cartridges weighed at least 8 pounds.

Even gunfights fought on "fair" terms generally amounted to little more than murder, since it was usually evident beforehand which man was the better and quicker shot. A case in point occurred when a cowboy named Red Ivan dispatched a cardslick named Pedro Arondondo in Canon City, Colo. in 1889. Ivan accused the gambler of stacking the deck, which meant an automatic duel. Arondondo asked for a delay long enough to take care of a few matters. He bought himself a black suit and ordered a headstone with the inscription "Pedro Arondondo, born 1857—died 1889, from a bullet wound between the eyes fired by Red Ivan." Which is exactly what happened.

See also: GWIN-MCCORKLE DUEL, COCKEYED FRANK LOVING.

Gunness, Belle (1859–?) murderess

It would be difficult to estimate whether Belle Gunness or Jane Tappan holds the record as America's greatest murderess. The latter did not keep score, and the former just plain never told. The best estimate on Belle Gunness was given by Roy L'Amphere, a Canadian farmhand who became her on-and-off lover. He said she killed at least 49 persons—42 would-be husbands, two legal husbands, a young girl left in her care, three of her own children and an unknown saloon wench she'd hired as a servant and whose body she used as a stand-in corpse for herself.

Belle turned up in La Porte, Ind. at the age of 42 as the Widow Sorenson from Chicago. She was not the friendly sort and kept neighbors off her property with a high-wire fence. All the local folks seemed to know about her was that she slaughtered hogs for a living. Actually, she also carried on another very profitable slaughtering business, that of killing off would-be suitors. She would place advertisements in matrimonial magazines announcing she was seeking a husband with two fine attributes. He had to be "kind and willing to help pay off a mortgage." The first man to answer an ad was an amiable Norwegian named Peter Gunness. Belle married him, insured him and then he died. One of Belle's children told a schoolmate that her mother had killed her father. "She hit him with a cleaver." But Belle explained her unfortunate husband had met his

end when a meat grinder toppled off a shelf. Naturally, the widow Gunness was believed, children being given to overactive imaginations.

After that, Belle never bothered going to the trouble of marrying her mail-order suitors. She'd have them bring their money with them, and if they didn't have enough, she'd send them back home for more. Then she murdered them and buried them within a day or two on her farm. Once, according to L'Amphere, Belle got $20,000 from a victim, but in most other cases it was around the $1,000 mark. In all, it was estimated she collected well over $100,000 from 1901 until 1908, when her murder spree ended. It probably ceased because a relative or two of the murdered men began writing in an effort to locate their missing relatives. Belle must have concluded it was only a matter of time before the law would close in on her.

On April 28, 1908 the Gunness farmhouse burned to the ground. Inside were found the bodies of Belle's three children, aged 11, nine and five, and Belle herself. Well, it could have been Belle except the woman was shorter and weighed about 150 pounds while Belle was a good 250, at least. And to top it off, the head was missing. The head, of course, would have contained teeth that could have been traced. Belle was known to wear a false plate anchored to a tooth, and this was found in the ashes. The obvious conclusion was that Belle had even ripped out her anchor tooth and plate to deceive the law. No one was fooled, but that didn't do much good. Belle Gunness had disappeared. It was soon proven that mass murder had taken place on the Gunness farm. All or parts of the bodies of at least 14 different men were dug up before the law stopped looking. It would have been virtually impossible to unearth completely 40 acres of farmland. And there was already more than enough evidence to convict Belle, if she were ever found. She was not. Over the years various bulky ladies from coast to coast would be identified as Belle Gunness and then cleared with the law's apologies.

L'Amphere was sent to prison in 1909 for his part in the activities of the Lady Bluebeard of La Porte. He died there two years later after revealing all he knew about Belle's murderous activities. He said Belle was supposed to get in touch with him after she had settled elsewhere but she never did. About the only legacy Belle Gunness left was a bit of bad poetry written about her. The last stanza went:

There's red upon the Hoosier moon
For Belle was strong and full of doom;
And think of all them Norska men
Who'll never see St. Paul again.

Guzik, Jake "Greasy Thumb" (1887–1956) Capone mob financial manager

A pimp in his early teens, Moscow-born Jake "Greasy Thumb" Guzik rose to become one of the most powerful men in the Chicago syndicate both during Al Capone's reign and for a quarter of a century afterward. During all that time, it is believed that Guzik never carried a gun. He was the trusted treasurer and financial wizard of the mob and, in the years after Capone's fall, was considered the real brains of the organization, along with Paul "the Waiter" Ricca. The intense loyalty Jake showed his fellow criminals was repaid many times over. He was the only man that Capone ever killed for out of pure friendship.

It happened in 1924, just a few years after Guzik had joined the mob and was promoted to a high position because (so the story goes) without previously knowing Capone he had saved the mob leader from an ambush after accidently overhearing two hit men from a rival gang talking about the plot. One evening in May, Guzik got into an argument with a freelance hijacker named Joe Howard, who slapped and kicked him around. Incapable of fighting back, Guzik waddled off to Capone and told him what had happened. Capone hunted down Howard and found him in Heinie Jacobs' saloon on South Wabash Avenue, boasting about how he had "made the little Jew whine."

When Howard saw Capone, he extended his hand and said, "Hello, Al." Capone seized his shoulders and, shaking him, demanded to know why he had assaulted his friend. "Go back to your girls, you dago pimp," Howard replied. Without another word Capone put six bullets in Howard's head.

After that killing—which required a considerable amount of fixing—Capone had in Guzik a faithful dog who remained loyal to him and who, it is said, did much to support him financially when Capone was in his deteriorating stage during his final years.

One of Jake Guzik's most important duties for the mob was acting as a bagman in payoffs to police and politicos, hence the origin of the nickname Greasy Thumb. Actually, the name was first applied to Jake's older brother, procurer Harry Guzik, of whom it was said that his "fingers are always greasy from the money he counts out for protection." Later, the title was transferred to Jake, whose thumb was much more greasy since he handled much more money. One of his chores was to sit nightly at a table in St. Hubert's Old English Grill and Chop House, where district police captains and the sergeants who collected graft for some of them could pick up their payoffs. Other visitors to Guzik included bagmen for various Chicago mayors and their aides.

Like Capone, Guzik eventually was nailed on tax charges but handled his few years behind bars with aplomb and returned ready to take up his money chores. He was one of the hits, if not a very communicative one, of the Kefauver hearings with his refusal to answer because any such response might tend to "discriminate against me."

Guzik's position in the mob was never questioned, and all of Capone's successors—Nitti, Ricca, Giancana, Accardo, Battaglia—allowed Jake complete freedom to make the financial arrangements for the mob. When he died on February 21, 1956, he was at his table in the restaurant partaking a simple meal of lamb chops and a glass of Mosel while making his usual payoffs. He collapsed of a heart attack. During his services there were more Italians in the temple than ever in its history.

Jake was buried in an ornate bronze coffin that cost $5,000. "For that money," one of the hoods said, "we could have buried him in a Cadillac."

Gwin-McCorkle duel

Gun duels in the Old West seldom fit the picture portrayed by Hollywood. An excellent example was the gunfight between William M. Gwin, a judge, and Joseph McCorkle in California in 1855. The duel took place on a marsh north of the Presidio, some miles from the Gwin home on Jackson Street in San Francisco. Gwin arranged to have relays of horses ready for a messenger to carry the news of the gunfight to his wife. In due course, the messenger came riding down Jackson Street and rushed into the Gwin house reportedly shouting, "The first fire has been exchanged and no one is hurt!"

"Thank God!" Mrs. Gwin cried and dropped to her knees in prayer with the rest of her family.

Sometime later, the messenger dashed into the house again and yelled, "The second fire has been exchanged and no one is hurt!"

"Praised be the Lord!" Mrs. Gwin replied.

On the third occasion, the messenger knocked on the door, tendered his card and was brought into the parlor. When Mrs. Gwin greeted him, he said, "The third fire has been exchanged and no one is hurt."

"That's good," Mrs. Gwin said.

The next time, the messenger on arriving was asked to stay for dinner. He did, ate heartily and joined in the customary dinner table conversation. Then he announced in passing: "Oh, by the way, the fourth fire has been exchanged and no one is hurt. What do you think of that, Mrs. Gwin?"

"I think," the lady said, "that there has been some mighty poor shooting!"

The poor shooting continued and both emerged unscathed, a fact that, if nothing else, later allowed Mr. Gwin to become the first U.S. senator from California.

See also: GUNFIGHTING.

Gyp the Blood (1889–1914) gangster and killer

One of the most vicious gangsters in New York during the early 1900s, Gyp the Blood (real name Harry Horrowitz) worked on commission for Big Jack Zelig as a slugger, bomber and killer. He filled in slow periods as a mugger and, at times, as a bouncer in East Side dance halls, gaining the reputation as the best bouncer since Monk Eastman, which was high praise indeed. Having enormous strength, he boasted he could break a man's back by bending him across his knee, and he lived up to the claim a number of times. Once, he won a $2 bet by seizing an unfortunate stranger and cracking his spine in three places. Gyp the Blood truly loved violence; Gyp's explanation for his eagerness to take on bombing assignments was, "I likes to hear de noise."

When the violence business got a bit slow, Gyp the Blood formed his own gang, the Lenox Avenuers, who engaged in muggings, burglaries and stickups around 125th Street. Gyp the Blood and three of his underlings, Whitey Lewis, Dago Frank and Lefty Louie, murdered gambler Herman Rosenthal on July 16, 1912 because he had begun revealing to District Attorney Charles S. Whitman the tie-ins between gamblers and the police. All four were apprehended despite a police slowdown on the investigation. Gyp the Blood, in an effort to save himself, said they had been hired to do the killing by Big Jack Zelig at the behest of Lt. Charles E. Becker. Zelig then talked about Becker, and although Big Jack was assassinated before he could testify in court, Becker was convicted and executed. Gyp the Blood and his three henchmen went to the electric chair on April 13, 1914.

See also: CHARLES E. BECKER, LENOX AVENUE GANG, BIG JACK ZELIG.

Gypsy Curse swindle enduring con game

The Gypsy Curse is a concept that goes back many centuries in Europe and endures to the present in this country. Witch doctors have gouged the gullible since colonial times, placing on or removing curses from believing victims.

The greatest practitioners of the art in the 20th century were two audacious swindlers, Mrs. William McBride and Edgar Zug, who produced terror in hundreds of people and then bilked them of fortunes. Dressed in weird ceremonial costumes, the pair told wealthy victims they, their property and money were under evil spells. Then they explained that Zug, as the sole living white witch doctor in the United States, could be the instrument of their salvation. "The only way to relieve this deadly spell," Zug would intone, "is to buy your way out of it. These evil spirits respect cash."

In 1902 Zug and Mrs. McBride put the curse on an elderly rich couple, Mrs. Susan Stambaugh and her palsy-ridden husband. "I see your profiles on the side of a distant mountain . . . and through the brains of these profiles, evil spirits have thrust long needles. This was done many years ago and the needles are now rusty. When these needles break, a day not long off, you both will die."

Upon hearing this prediction Mrs. Stambaugh fainted and her husband had a spasmodic fit. When they came to, Mrs. McBride had some good news; Edgar Zug could save them from their awful fate. There was a way Zug could convince the spirits to withdraw the fatal needles. Zug nodded but warned, "It will take money, a lot of money." Within seven days the scheming pair had stripped the Stambaughs of all their savings and the deeds to their many properties. Then Zug had some bad news for them. The spirits were not satisfied. "You are going to die," he intoned with an air of resignation, "unless you can come up with at least another five thousand." But there was then some good news; the Stambaughs would end up getting more back than they paid in through a hidden treasure that the spirits would reveal to them.

The now desperate but hopeful couple hysterically hunted for more money, trying to secure loans from friends. Finally, one of them revealed the reason for the cash and the Gypsy Curse swindlers were arrested and convicted of fraud. As they were being led from the courtroom, Zug cried, "That's what I get for being kind!"

Police report that variations of the Gypsy Curse swindle are still worked today on the elderly rich in almost every ethnic community in big cities.

gypsy swindles See HANDKERCHIEF SWITCH.

Hahn, Anna (1906–1938) mass poisoner

The first woman electrocuted in the state of Ohio, Anna Hahn specialized in being a companion to well-off elderly men who had no relatives, providing them with tender loving care and a little arsenic. After each one died, she either produced a will naming her the beneficiary or simply looted her victim's bank accounts before moving on to brighten up the last days of another old gentleman. Exactly how many men she killed is not known. Anna was not cooperative on the subject, and the authorities stopped exhuming bodies after they found five loaded with arsenic.

Anna Hahn arrived in Cincinnati from her native Fussen, Germany in 1927, married a young telegraph operator named Philip Hahn and opened a bakery in the "Over the Rhine" German district. Then Anna's husband became afflicted with a strange illness and finally was taken to a hospital, where he recovered, by his mother over Anna's protests. In retrospect, it seemed likely that her husband was suffering from something he ate, but in any event, Anna Hahn took the opportunity to move in with a septuagenarian burgher named Ernest Koch, who seemed remarkably vigorous despite his age. Under Anna's ministrations that condition did not continue for long. On May 6, 1932 a much weakened Koch died. When his will was probated, Anna was bequeathed his house.

Anna's next victim was Albert Palmer, an aged and ailing railroad retiree who lasted almost no time at all. Anna avoided the embarrassing coincidence of twice being named heir to an old man's estate by simply borrowing Palmer's money before he died. She insisted on giving him an IOU for the money, but after he expired, she simply tore up the note and no one was the wiser. Anna then sold the Hahn house and moved to another part of the city.

Next on her list was a man named Jacob Wagner, who left an estate of $17,000 to his "niece" Anna. She earned another $15,000 taking care of one George Gsellman for a few months until his demise. One who escaped her deadly attention was a man named George Heiss. As he revealed after Anna's arrest, Heiss became suspicious when flies sipping the beer she brought him kept flipping over and dying. He demanded that Anna share his stein, and when she refused, he ordered her from his house.

Not quite as careful was Anna's last victim, George Obendoerfer. Anna lured him to Colorado with a story about a ranch she had there. Obendoerfer never made it to the ranch however, expiring in a Denver hotel. In the meantime Anna had gained possession of his bankbook and looted it of $5,000. But when it came time to pay for Obendoerfer's burial, she refused, claiming she had just met him on a train and had pretended to be his wife at his suggestion. Police became suspicious when they discovered the bank transfer, and an autopsy was performed, revealing lethal amounts of arsenic in the dead man's viscera. Upon her return to Cincinnati, Anna was arrested. The bodies of four other of Anna's old gentlemen were exhumed and post mortems confirmed the presence of arsenic in each case.

After a sensation-packed trial a jury of 11 women and one man convicted Anna with no recommendation of mercy. She exhibited iron nerve until shortly before her execution on June 20, 1938. But when strapped into the electric chair, Anna broke and screamed hysterically. She regained her composure with the help of a prison chaplain. As she removed her hand from his, Anna said, "You might be killed, too, Father."

Hairtrigger Block   Chicago "shoot-out" area

During the Civil War, Chicago gambling thrived as it probably did in no other city, North or South. In the gamblers' vernacular, the city was a "sucker's paradise," teeming with army officers and, more important, paymasters, soldiers from the front with many months pay, speculators rich with war contracts and so on, all ready and eager to lose their money at cards. The center of the gambling industry, which was illegal but well protected through heavy payments to the police, was on Randolph and Clark Streets, which contained palatial "skinning houses" for trimming the suckers. Naturally, with fortunes won and lost so easily, shootings and killings were common and probably far more frequent than could be found in any town of the Wild West. In fact, Randolph Street between Clark and State was commonly referred to as Hairtrigger Block because of the many shootings that took place there.

Some of the shootings were between professional gamblers themselves over matters such as possession of a "mark" or out of just plain nastiness. The most famous feud on Hairtrigger Block was between two big gamblers, George Trussell, the dandy of Gambler's Row, and Cap Hyman, described as "an insufferable egotist, an excitable, emotional jack-in-the-box." They could barely tolerate each other when sober, but when drunk they would immediately start shooting at each other; each probably shot at and was shot at by the other at least 50 times. Both, especially when intoxicated, were incredibly bad marksmen, and the usual damage was to windows, bar mirrors and street signs. So long as the shooting was confined to Hairtrigger Block, the police did not intervene; unfortunately, the two gamblers often staggered off to other areas in search of each other and continued their shooting sprees, leading the *Chicago Tribune* to declare that "the practice is becoming altogether too prevalent in this city."

In 1862 Hyman once staggered into the lobby of the Tremont House hunting for Trussell, fired several shots and allowed no one to leave or enter the hotel for an hour. Hyman was frequently arrested and fined for his forays, and after paying the penalty, he would meticulously deduct the amount from his usual police payoffs. Whenever a Trussell-Hyman duel started, the inhabitants and habitués of Hairtrigger Block immediately wagered on which one would be killed. As it turned out, neither of the two ever prevailed over the other.

Trussell was shot to death by his mistress in 1866; Hyman went insane and died in 1876.

See also: GEORGE TRUSSELL.

Halberstam, Dr. Michael   See BERNARD CHARLES WELCH, JR.

Hall, Lee (1849–1911)   Texas Ranger

One of the most famous Texas Rangers, Lee Hall started out as a schoolteacher in Texas after relocating there in 1869 from his native North Carolina. Two years later, he made the rather unlikely switch to the post of city marshal of Sherman. He subsequently served as a deputy sheriff and in 1876 joined the Texas Rangers. Assigned to clamp down on the brutal Taylor-Sutton feud, Hall gained wide acclaim for fearlessness, once entering unarmed into a room full of the feuding cowboys and marching out seven men wanted for murder. In 1877 Hall was promoted to captain, and within two years he and his men had made some 400 arrests and successfully quelled the murderous feud.

Hall ran up an enviable record of capturing lawbreakers; he was involved in tracking down and shooting the noted outlaw Sam Bass. In 1880 Hall resigned from the Rangers to become a successful rancher. For two years he harbored an ill young man named Will Porter on his ranch, where Porter gathered much of the material for the stories he would write under the name O. Henry.

In 1885 Hall was made an Indian agent, but he was removed in 1887 on trumped-up graft charges. It took him two years to clear his name. Later, Hall held various law enforcement positions and in 1899 served as an army officer in the Philippines. After contracting malaria there, he was forced to resign from the army. Hall died in 1911.

Hall-Mills Murders   unsolved double killing

It was once said that no American murder case had more words written about it than did the unsolved Hall-Mills case of 1922. On September 16 the bodies of a man and woman were found in a lovers lane in New Brunswick, N.J., with cards and personal letters strewn around them. The contents of the letters and the identity of the couple caused a sensation. The man was Rev. Edward Wheeler Hall, 41, rector of St. John's Episcopal Church, and the woman was Mrs. Eleanor Mills, 34, a member of his flock, a choir singer and the wife of the church sexton. The letters had been written by Mrs. Mills to the pastor; they would become some of the juiciest newspaper reading of the 1920s. Hall had been shot with a bullet in the head, and Mrs. Mills had suffered three such wounds and her throat had been cut for good measure. Someone had arranged the bodies in delicate intimacy in keeping with the tone of the letters.

Nothing much came of the case despite its explosive nature. The local police insisted they were stumped. Then in 1926 the *New York Daily Mirror* uncovered a secret witness whose testimony resulted in the indictment of Mrs. Frances Stevens Hall, seven years the pastor's senior and a woman of position and wealth, for the two murders. Also indicted were Mrs. Hall's two devoted brothers, William and Henry Stevens, and her cousin, Henry de la Bruyere Carpender, a member of the New York Stock Exchange. According to the *Mirror* the four had bribed witnesses and the police and had soft-soaped the local prosecutor to avoid arrest in 1922.

When the trial of Mrs. Hall and her brothers began, 300 reporters from around the nation and the world were on hand. Sixty wires were required to handle the incredible flow of words going out to a waiting public. Five million words were transmitted the first 11 days and a total of 9 million during the 18 days of the trial. Even the august *New York Times* had four stenographers on hand so that its readers would not lose a precious syllable of testimony.

In the trial it was alleged that Mrs. Hall had been trying to catch her husband in a compromising position with the choir singer. The star prosecution witness was 56-year-old Mrs. Jane Gibson, called the Pig Woman because she raised Poland China pigs. She was dying of cancer and testified from a hospital bed with a nurse and doctor in attendance. Mrs. Gibson said that as she was passing the murder spot, De Russey's Lane, she recognized Mrs. Hall and her brother Henry in the bright moonlight among a group of four figures huddled around a crab-apple tree, under which the bodies were later found. She heard snatches of conversation, she testified, such as "explain those letters," and someone being hit continuously. "I could hear somebody's wind going out, and somebody said, 'Ugh.'"

Then Mrs. Gibson said a flashlight went on and she saw two men wrestling. The light went out and she heard a shot. Had she heard a woman's voice? "Yes. One said, 'Oh, Henry,' easy, very easy; and the other began to scream, scream, scream so loud, 'Oh my, oh my, oh my.' so terrible loud." The Pig Woman testified she had heard three shots and then mounted her mule Jenny and rode away as quickly as she could.

Clearly, the main thrust of the prosecution's case depended on the credibility of the Pig Woman. All through her testimony her aged mother sat in a front row muttering, "She's a liar, she's a liar, she's a liar." Mrs. Hall's defense team, called the Million Dollar

Defense (actually their fee came to $400,000), found small discrepancies between the Pig Woman's testimony before a grand jury in 1922 and her current testimony. But they impugned her supposedly superior memory by getting her to testify that she couldn't remember when she had married, if she had been divorced, if she had remarried and if she knew the names of a number of men.

As the Pig Woman was removed from the courtroom, she shook a finger at Frances Hall and cried, "I've told the truth, so help me God, and you know it, you know it."

Henry Stevens presented evidence that he was bluefishing in Barnegat Bay the weekend of the murder and produced witnesses to back him up. Mrs. Hall took the stand and testified in an icy calm that earned her the journalistic sobriquet the Iron Widow. When asked if Mr. Hall was "a loving, affectionate husband," she answered, "Always." She denied all involvement in the murders.

After only five hours of deliberations, the jury acquitted Mrs. Hall. Her brothers were cleared as well and the indictment against Carpender was thrown out. Mrs. Hall and her brothers sued the *Daily Mirror* for $3 million and accepted an out-of-court settlement.

Hamer, Frank (1884–1955) Texas Ranger and killer of Bonnie and Clyde

The most legendary Texas Ranger of the 20th century, one who would have fit the mold even a century earlier, was Frank Hamer. He is best remembered, if in a distorted fashion, as the killer of Bonnie Parker and Clyde Barrow. His career started when portions of the West were still wild, with cattle rustlers, horse thieves, bank robbers on horseback, six-shooters and "walkdowns" in dusty cowtown streets. It lasted through the gangster era of the late 1920s and early 1930s, with speeding black sedans and chattering tommy guns. Hamer spanned both eras and remained a top-notch officer through the 1940s, when the development of sophisticated methods of crime detection began making oldstyle criminal operations all but obsolete. Before his long and distinguished career ended, he was involved in more than 50 gunfights, was wounded 20 times and was ambushed four times. On two occasions he was shot up so badly that his assailants left him for dead. It was the criminals who ended up dead—100 of them, according to some biographers. Others place the estimate lower, anywhere from 40 to 55. Even Hamer probably didn't know the exact number.

In 1906 Frank Hamer became a Texas Ranger after some stints as a cowboy. Although only 22, he soon demonstrated he could get the job done on lone assignments, the way the Rangers generally operated. In 1907 he was sent to clean up Doran, Tex. It was typical of the towns that had sprung up during the turn-of-the-century oil boom—rough, dirty, jerry-built, boisterous, with more than its share of toughs, con men, fancy women, cardsharps and other ruthless characters out for a dishonest buck. Unlike the other towns, most of the vice in Doran was controlled by one man, a clever, vicious operator named Haddon Slade. Criminals who wanted to "work" in Doran either worked directly for Slade or kicked in a healthy percentage of their take for what Slade called "franchise rights." He was so sure of himself that he even had his men murder the local sheriff.

Hamer was sent in to solve that killing and at 23 he probably looked like easy pickings, although Slade no doubt knew better than to murder a Ranger unless he could come up with a good story. Apparently, he tried his best. There was evidence he planned to shoot Hamer from ambush, use the Ranger's gun to kill two of his own men and then plant the gun he used to murder Hamer on one of them. This would leave everything tidy for the law. But the plot backfired when Hamer spotted Slade and dropped him with three bullets in the chest. With Slade gone, Doran was an easy place to tame. Over the years Hamer gained a reputation for catching bank robbers, once tracking three robbers to a job and killing two of them as they tried to shoot their way out. Although wounded in the leg, Hamer marched the surviving bandit to the local jail before taking what he called a "medical lay-down."

Hamer's most bizarre case involved one of the state's scandals: the killing of innocent men by local Texas law officers to collect bounties for dead bank robbers. The bounties were the ill-conceived idea of the Texas Bankers Association to stop a rising tide of bank thefts. The bankers group posted the following notice in every bank in the state:

REWARD
$5,000 for Dead Bank Robbers
Not One Cent For Live Ones

In no time at all, bank robbers started turning up dead as a result of this throwback to the bounty system of the Old West. Frank Hamer was appalled at the practice. He started a lone investigation that shocked the state with the discovery that local lawmen, hungry for reward money, had actually formed murder combines and sought out drifters and other homeless men to kill. Law enforcement officials expressed disbelief over his findings, and the Texas Bankers Association refused to withdraw the reward system. Finally, Hamer took his charges to the newspapers. The resulting stories broke the scandal wide open and led to the filing of charges against some of the murder ring leaders. Hamer arrested them and they subsequently confessed.

In 1934 Hamer resigned from the Texas Rangers because it was being corrupted by the cronyism of controversial Gov. "Ma" Ferguson, who had just taken office. He went to work as a plant security specialist at a salary of $500 a month, a considerable sum at the time, but he soon left to join the Texas Highway Patrol at $150 a month. Unlike the Rangers, the Highway Patrol was not under the governor's tight control. He was offered a very special assignment—capture the notorious outlaws Bonnie and Clyde.

The highly popular movie *Bonnie and Clyde* portrayed Hamer as a not-too-bright "flatfoot" who viciously gunned down the handsome, daring Clyde Barrow and the beautiful Bonnie Parker. Nothing could have been further from the truth. Hamer took the assignment because Clyde Barrow had killed a number of his fellow law officers. Methodically, he learned all he could about the two desperadoes, from first-hand sources, from people who knew them and from newspaper stories of their bloody deeds. In his own words: "On February 10th, I took the trail and followed it for exactly 102 days. Like Clyde Barrow, I used a Ford V-8, and like Clyde, I lived in the car most of the time."

Hamer decided that Barrow "played a circle from Dallas to Joplin, Missouri, to Louisiana and back to Dallas." Occasionally, he would leave his beat, but he would always come back to it, as most criminals do. "It was necessary for me to make a close study of Barrow's habits. I have never seen him and I never saw him until May 23rd."

On May 23 Hamer's persistence finally paid off. An informer told him the couple, driving a gray Ford sedan, would travel a certain road. With some other officers, he set up a secret roadblock, and when the car appeared, Hamer sprang the trap.

"At the command of 'stick 'em up,' both turned," Hamer recalled. "But instead of obeying the order . . . they clutched the weapons which they held in their hands or in their laps. When the firing started, Barrow's foot released the clutch, and the car, in low gear, moved forward on the decline and turned into the ditch on the left."

Before the pair ever got a chance to lift their weapons, the officers had sent a hail of rifle bullets and shotgun blasts into the car. Clyde Barrow and Bonnie Parker were wiped out.

About a year later, Ma Ferguson's control on the Texas Rangers having been loosened by the voters, Hamer returned to the Rangers, serving until his retirement in 1949. He died July 10, 1955 at home in his bed in Austin.

See also: BANK ROBBERIES—BOUNTIES, BONNIE AND CLYDE.

Hamilton, Ray (1912–1935) robber and murderer

Remembered best as a part-time accomplice of Bonnie and Clyde, Hamilton had a career in crime that was in many respects more spectacular than that of Clyde Barrow, with whom he started off as a juvenile criminal in the sneak thief Square Root Gang in Houston, Tex. From that time on, Hamilton would be linked with Bonnie and Clyde in several short but bloody stints.

In 1932 Hamilton served time with Barrow at the Eastham Prison Farm in Texas. Two years later, Bonnie and Clyde broke Hamilton, Henry Methvin and Joe Palmer out of the prison. However, as a trio, Bonnie, Clyde and Hamilton could not continue for long. A major reason was sexual jealousy. When the three traveled together, it was Hamilton who slept with Bonnie Parker. This was not, as portrayed in the movie *Bonnie and Clyde,* because Clyde Barrow was impotent, but rather because he was homosexual, a preference he developed at Eastham. At times, Hamilton also slept with Barrow. Such an arrangement couldn't last, and Hamilton would keep dropping in and out of the ménage.

Hamilton's crime record, which began in earnest in January 1932—when he was 19—and lasted a short three years, was awesome. Alone or with Barrow or other accomplices, Hamilton held up at least two dozen places, including seven banks, two oil refineries, a packing plant, a post office and even the National Guard Armory at Fort Worth, where he stole boxes of shotguns, automatic rifles and machine guns. Although apprehended a number of times, he escaped two road traps "no human could escape," as one reporter described them, including one manned by a posse of 20, all of whom he disarmed and whose leader he took with him as a hostage. Even when Hamilton was caught, holding him was another matter. In all, he escaped four times, and thus, while he had committed several murders, it took five trials to get him convicted and sentenced to the chair for just one of them. In 1934 Hamilton broke out of the death house in the state penitentiary at Huntsville, Tex. After a 10-month manhunt he was recaptured and, on May 10, 1935, executed.

See also: BONNIE AND CLYDE.

hams smuggling technique

"Hams" were first used during Prohibition by rumrunners bringing their contraband to shore. If they found themselves pursued by the Coast Guard, the smugglers would jettison gunny sacks, or hams, containing several bottles of liquor wrapped in straw. Attached to each ham was a bag of salt and a red marker. Weighted by the salt, the ham would sink to the bottom. When the salt melted sometime later, the red marker would float to the surface. By then the danger above would have passed, and the smugglers could return to retrieve the treasured hams. The ham remains a favorite method of narcotics smugglers.

Hand, Dora (?–1878) murder victim

Dora Hand (also known as Fannie Keenan) was called the First Lady of Dodge City when it was truly the Gomorrah of the Plains. Her early life was shrouded in mystery, although the West had no trouble coming up with an impressive set of "facts." She was allegedly from a most genteel family in Boston, had been educated in Europe and had enjoyed a brilliant operatic career before coming to Dodge City, where she had been brought by Mayor James H. "Dog" Kelley to oversee his whorehouse operations.

Chronicler Stuart Lake described her in these words:

Saint or sinner, Dora Hand was the most graciously beautiful woman to reach the camp in the heyday of its iniquity. . . . By night, she was the Queen of the Fairybelles, as old Dodge termed its dance-hall women, entertaining drunken cowhands after all the fashions that her calling demanded. By day, she was the Lady Bountiful of the prairie settlement, a demurely clad, generous woman to whom no appeal would go unheeded.

Once, Dora Hand had been a singer in Grand Opera. In Dodge, she sang of nights in the bars and honkey-tonks. On Sundays, clad in simple black, she crossed the Dead Line to the little church on the North Side to lead the hymns and anthems in a voice at which those who heard her forever marvelled. A quick change of attire after the Sunday evening service, and she was back at her trade in the dance hall. . . .

At least 12 men supposedly died fighting one another to win Dora's heart in Dodge and in her previous ports of call, Abilene and Hays. Her main man in Dodge was the mayor himself, who exhibited a rather violent jealousy when other suitors tried to show their affections. This led to a smoldering feud with young James Kennedy, son of Mifflin Kennedy of Texas' King Ranch. Finally, one night when Kennedy became particularly attentive to Dora in the Alhambra, Dog's showcase establishment, Kelley tossed him out. Kennedy left town, vowing revenge. In October 1878 Kennedy attempted to make good on his threat, sneaking up on Dog's frame house and pumping a couple of shots in the direction of the mayor's bedroom. Unfortunately for Kennedy, Dog Kelley wasn't even there at the time. But Dora was asleep in the bed and was killed instantly. Kennedy rode out of town without knowing the damage done by his bullets.

Sheriff Bat Masterson quickly organized a posse that included Wyatt Earp, Neal Brown, Bill Tilghman and Charlie Bassett. The posse ran Kennedy to earth; Masterson put a rifle slug through his right arm, shattering it, and Earp shot the fugitive's horse from under him. Kennedy cursed his captors, swore to get even and then asked if he had killed Kelley. When told that Dora Hand had been his victim, he turned morose and said he wished the posse had killed him.

Dora was given a lavish funeral, some say the best Dodge ever had. The procession was certainly an unusual one, consisting of dance hall girls, gunslingers, saloon keepers, gamblers, cowboys and even some of the more respectable ladies of the town. Epitomizing the ways of the frontier, a minister admonished, "He that is without sin among you, let him first cast a stone at her."

The overwhelming sentimentality, however, did not carry over to the cause of justice. While Kennedy's remorse had its limits, his wealthy father's purse had none. The best lawyers were hired and much was made of Kennedy's shattered arm, now 4 inches shorter. The defendant went free for "lack of evidence," and a father took his errant son home.

See also: WILLIAM B. "BAT" MASTERSON.

handkerchief switch   gypsy bunco operation

A famous confidence game dating back as far as gypsy fortune-tellers, palmists and card readers, the handkerchief switch has been used to bilk thousands of gullible Americans out of millions of dollars annually.

At first, the victim is told his fortune for a small fee, during which the fortune-teller gauges his or her gullibility and means. The victim is then told that the fortune-teller's power of prayer will solve his or her problems. The prayer must be accompanied by the burning of a candle, and the size and price of the candle determine how long these potent prayers will continue. Once a likely prospect has been found, the fortune-teller informs the victim that evil spirits are within him or her, and must be routed. The victim may be asked to bring a raw egg on the next visit, at which time the fortune-teller, by sleight of hand, breaks the egg, displaying a black mass inside. This, the victim is informed, constitutes the evil spirits that transfer their potent bad luck on everything the victim comes in contact with.

By further prayers, the fortune-teller discovers the reasons these evil spirits remain in the victim's body. It is because of the money the victim has. If he or she gets rid of the money, the evil spirits will depart. The victim is then instructed to bring a large sum of money, preferably in big bills. The fortune-teller places the money in a very large handkerchief, which is then folded up and sewn together at the ends. In the process, another stuffed handkerchief is substituted while the victim is not looking, and the substituted handkerchief is buried in a cemetery, flushed down a toilet or thrown in a river or the ocean. Sometimes the victim himself is permitted to throw the handkerchief in the ocean or to flush it down the toilet. Occasionally when the money is to be flushed down a toilet, the use of the handkerchief is discarded, and the victim is permitted to watch the roll of money flush away. In such cases, the toilet's plumbing has been altered so that the money is trapped in the pipes, to be extracted later.

Hanks, O. C. "Camilla" (1863–1902)   train robber

As a member of the Wild Bunch, Camilla, or as he sometimes was called, Deaf Charley Hanks, was considered to be the best and most fearless train robber of the gang. As Kid Curry once said, he could rob a train "as slick as a whistle." Butch Cassidy would think nothing of having Hanks cover all the passengers in a train car alone, feeling certain no one could get the drop on him. One story tells how a passenger did get the drop on him, leveling and cocking a derringer at Hanks as he was going up the aisle collecting loot. When the passenger ordered Hanks in a low menacing hiss to drop his piece, the outlaw turned and fired first. The tale may be a bit overdramatized, since Hanks was deaf in his right ear and later said he'd heard neither the command nor the gun being cocked.

In 1892 Hanks was captured after robbing a Northern Pacific train at Big Timber, Mont. and drew a 10-year term at Deer Lodge Penitentiary. Released on April 30, 1901, Hanks headed for Hole in the Wall country, located Butch Cassidy at Brown's Hole and went back in the train-robbing business. Hanks took part in every job the Wild Bunch pulled over the next year and accumulated a big pile of cash. He headed for Texas to do some wild living. He got into a saloon brawl, and when the law wondered where his money had come from, Hanks went for his gun. A lawman named Pink Taylor was faster, and on October 22, 1902 the slickest of the train robbers was shot dead.

See also: WILD BUNCH.

Hansen, Robert (1940–) Alaskan serial killer

It could be said that Robert Hansen came out of Iowa to open up Alaska for serial killing. This was facilitated by the immense size of the state and the fact that Hansen had his own private Piper Super Cub bush plane. By his own admission he killed 17 women and consulted his aviation chart to pick out likely burial spots in forsaken areas of snow and ice.

Hansen came to Alaska at the age of 20 with a brand new wife and, following his father's profession, obtained work as a baker. He prospered at his trade and soon had his own business. His marriage, however, ended in six months, but he remarried six years later. His new wife had no idea of the degree to which her husband was mad. By the early 1970s he was making his mark as an outdoorsman and pilot-hunter who stalked Dahl sheep, wolves and bears with a rifle and bow and arrow.

Hansen began to send his wife and children to visit relations in Iowa and also on a European vacation. By 1973 Hansen was killing women in earnest. Over the next decade, he committed 17 murders and more than 30 rapes. His usual targets were prostitutes, exotic dancers and those he lured through singles ads. Some he took into his Anchorage home, pulled a rifle on them and marched into his trophy room. His usual practice in such cases was to have sex with his captives and then kill them, consult his charts and fly off with the body to be dumped where it was hardly likely to be found. Others he forced into the plane at gunpoint and then threatened with death if they did not do as he said. Many did, and he returned them to town with a warning that if they said anything about what happened he would have them prosecuted as prostitutes through connections he had with the police.

The key to the women's survival was to obey his every whim, and if they did not displease him they might be spared. Unfortunately Hansen's displeasure was easily aroused. The slightest resistance or a request for payment was, as far as Hansen was concerned, a capital offense. If a woman was particularly offensive to him, he would turn her loose in the wilderness and stalk her with rifle or bow and arrow. There were no survivors in that sporting game.

No suspicions fell on Hansen, and indeed it appeared the authorities had no idea a serial killer was in their midst for six to seven years. Discovery of a couple of bodies, one in a gravel pit near Seward and another in a shallow grave along the Knik River where hunters made the grim find, caused authorities to begin to suspect the worst.

Hansen was not unmasked until 1983 when a 17-year-old captive broke free as he was taking her to his plane hangar. She cried for help with a handcuff still dangling from one wrist. Hansen quickly confessed his killing spree and on a flying tour of the wilderness pointed out the spots where he had buried his victims. Eleven bodies were recovered in this manner. Some of the women were never identified, and Hansen had no idea what their names were. It was assumed that several were among the women listed as missing in police files.

Hansen was prosecuted for four murders, which resulted in his receiving a life with 461 additional years sentence.

Hardin, John Wesley (1853–1895) gunfighter and murderer

John Wesley Hardin was one of the dedicated gunfighters of the West who delighted in showing a gun full of notches. In his case the boast was deserved. By his own count Wes Hardin killed 44 men. Some historians credit him with 40, and even the most skeptical will grant him 34 or 35.

Hardin started killing in his native Texas in 1868 at the age of 15. He shot a black who had taken his new citizenship rights too seriously, a not unpopular crime of that era. Then he gunned down three Yankee soldiers who came after him for the shooting. Hardin went on the run and received the ready assistance of most folks who knew him. By 1871, at about 18 years of age, he was a trail cowboy driving cattle from Texas to Kansas, and his murder toll stood at about a dozen, give or take a corpse or two. Many of his victims had died in face-to-face confrontations, but Wes was certainly not fussy about putting a slug in a man's back. Around Abilene he knocked off another eight or so and for a time escaped the wrath of Marshal Wild Bill Hickok, who clearly wanted no trouble with this fast-drawing young hellion.

When Hardin killed a man in his hotel, however, Hickok came after him. Hardin later claimed the man had tried to knife him because he had made some big gambling winnings the night before. The other version was that Hardin had shot him because his snoring in the next room had disturbed the gunfighter's sleep. Fleeing out a second-story window in his long johns, Hardin avoided being arrested by Hickok. On the trail he trapped three members of a posse sent out by Hickok, and in a rare gallant gesture, Hardin refrained from killing them. Instead, he made them strip off their pants and sent them back toward Abilene in that condition. Through the years Hardin supported himself mostly by gambling and only occasionally by punching cattle. A man who was especially fast on the draw had a way of facing down an opponent in a disputed hand. If a man got into a lone game of poker with a young feller who he later learned was the notorious Wes Hardin and was then informed that a straight beat a flush, why that was an unarguable proposition as long as Hardin had his gun. And Hardin always did, and did something about it if anyone tried to take it away from him. In his memoirs he wrote of an incident in Willis, Tex.: "Some fellows tried to arrest me for carrying a pistol. They got the contents of it instead."

In 1874 Wes Hardin celebrated his 21st birthday by shooting Deputy Sheriff Charley Webb of Brown County between the eyes. By now his murder toll stood somewhere between 35 or 36 and 44. Hardin himself was no authority on the matter, preferring to ignore some of his back-shooting escapades. With a $4,000 price on his head, the gunfighter decided to head for points east. He moved through Louisiana to Alabama and into Florida. He gambled and drank but avoided killing anyone, so as not to mark his trail. Despite his care, Hardin was captured by Texas Rangers aboard a train at Pensacola Junction on August 23, 1877.

Back in Texas, Hardin got only 25 years instead of the death sentence, a fact that produced a bitter protest from a condemned gunman, William P. Longley. He had only killed half as many men as Hardin—at most— and he was due to be hanged. Where was the justice in that, Longley demanded in a death cell letter to the governor. The governor didn't bother to respond, and Longley was hanged, while Hardin went to prison.

Hardin studied law behind bars, and when he was released in 1894 with a full pardon, he set up a law office. However, he did most of his lawyering in saloons and at the gaming tables. In El Paso he gained the enmity of a nasty old lawman, John Selman, who was a sterling advocate of the principle that one shot in the back was worth more than two up front. On August 19, 1895 Hardin was standing at the bar, being his loud and boisterous self, when Constable Selman walked in and put a bullet in the back of his head. Selman was acquitted, claiming self-defense. He said it had been a fair fight since Hardin had seen him in the mirror. They might not have bought that one even in Texas had not Wes Hardin been the notorious character he was.

See also: JACK HELM, JOHN SELMAN, SUTTON-TAYLOR FEUD.

Further reading: *The Life of John Wesley Hardin* by John Wesley Hardin.

Hare, Joseph Thompson (?–1818) highwayman

At the beginning of the 19th century the most celebrated highwayman in America was Joseph Thompson Hare, who led a gang of cutthroats along the Natchez Trace and the Wilderness Road for years. Not only was Hare uncommonly successful, pulling some most lucrative robberies, he was also an elegant dresser and a dandy who excited the public's imagination.

Born in Chester, Pa., Hare grew up in the slums of New York City and Baltimore and then went to sea. When his windjammer docked in New Orleans, Hare, never having seen a city at the same time so vile and so enticing, jumped ship. He soon became an accepted and successful member of the New Orleans underworld and in time ventured out on the Natchez Trace, where he became notorious for his "stand and deliver" escapades. He was a legend on the Trace, a phantom the

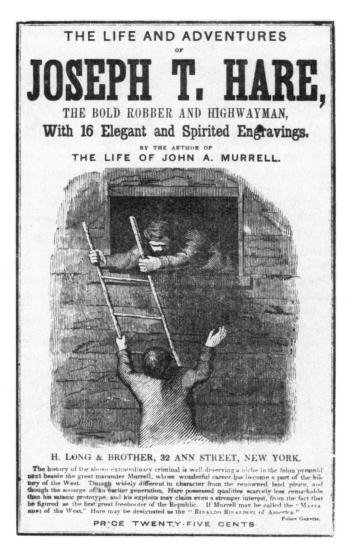

Joseph Thompson Hare's career inspired many literary efforts, which usually included his advice to others to avoid the ways of the highwayman "as it is a desperate life, full of danger, and sooner or later it ends on the gallows."

law could not catch since, despite his fame, there was no firm description of him. He frequently returned to New Orleans without hindrance to sample its fleshpots until the time he once more needed loot to sustain his life as a rogue and blade.

When he was finally captured in 1813, Hare expected to be hanged but got off with only a five-year prison term. When he was released, he returned immediately to his highwayman's career. Robbing the Baltimore night coach near Havre de Grace, Md., he netted $16,000, a tremendous haul for the period. Two days later, he was apprehended in a fashionable tailor shop in Baltimore while purchasing a coat, which he described in his memoirs as "in the style of an officer's, at the price of $75, very dashy." Hare was hanged in Baltimore on September 10, 1818, leaving his diary in his cell. It ended with a somber warning for readers not to take to the highway "as it is a desperate life, full of danger, and sooner or later it ends on the gallows."

Hargraves, Dick (1824–1882) gambler and killer

Probably the epitome of the Mississippi gambler, Dick Hargraves cut a dapper and deadly figure on the river in the 1840s and 1850s.

A fashion plate who ordered boots from Paris and clothing from his native England, Hargraves came to New Orleans at the age of 16 and went to work as a bartender. He turned to professional gambling after winning $30,000 in a legendary poker game. Thereafter, he was a fixture on the river, where he became famous as an honest but pitiless gambler. Since at least 90 percent of all Mississippi gamblers were dishonest operators, Hargraves prided himself on being "square" and always felt that characteristic made it totally unnecessary for him to feel any sympathy for those he won money from. He supposedly shot at least eight or 10 men who sought vengeance after losing their money and often all their possessions to him. At the peak of his prosperity, Hargraves was worth an estimated $2 million.

As the best-known gambler in New Orleans, it was inevitable that women would be attracted to Hargraves. One of his numerous affairs resulted in scandal and death rivaling a Greek tragedy. Hargraves became involved with a banker's wife and was challenged to a duel by the enraged husband. He killed the banker with dispatch, and when the dead man's brother warned he would shoot the gambler on sight, Hargraves met him at a Natchez-under-the-Hill gambling den and killed him in a desperate battle. When Hargraves returned to New Orleans, the banker's widow stabbed him and then committed suicide. He recovered from his wounds and married a girl whose life he had saved in a fire.

Tired of river gambling, he joined a filibustering campaign to Cuba and during the Civil War served as an officer in the Union Army. After the war Hargraves, a wealthy but ill man, moved to Denver, where he died of tuberculosis in 1882.

See also: RIVERBOAT GAMBLERS.

Harpe brothers 18th-century highwaymen

For more than 50 years during the latter part of the 18th century, the Natchez Trace, which was little more than a narrow path from Natchez to Nashville, was probably the most crime-infested area in America.

Among the bandits who roamed the Trace and the Wilderness Road were two brothers, Micajah and Wiley Harpe, better known as Big and Little Harpe. There is no accurate record of how many men, women and children the Harpes butchered in the 1790s, but it was well up in the scores. In 1799 a large posse of frontiersmen cornered the Harpes in the Ohio wilds. Little Harpe escaped, but Big Harpe was shot from his horse and, while still alive, had his head cut off by a man whose wife and children he had slaughtered; Big Harpe was 31 at the time. After his escape Little Harpe, two years his brother's junior, joined up with the bandit gang of Samuel Mason, a strange character who had turned to outlawry in middle age after being a soldier and justice of the peace in Kentucky. Mason would boastfully carve on a tree at the scene of one of his many murders, "Done by Mason of the Woods."

Late in 1803 Little Harpe, now going under the name of Setton, and Sam Mays, another member of the Mason gang, axed their chieftain's head off. They packed it in clay and went to Natchez to claim a reward. Unfortunately, while waiting for their money, they were accused of stealing horses, and Setton was identified as Little Harpe. Little Harpe and Mays were hanged at Greenville, Miss. on February 8, 1804. Their heads were cut off, and Harpe's head was stuck on a pole and displayed on the Trace to the north of the town. May's head was placed on view to the south of town, a warning to other outlaws that the murderous days of the Natchez Trace were coming to a close.

See also: SAM MASON.

Harper, Richard (?–c. 1839) early Chicago thief

The record is unclear concerning Chicago's first thief, or, more correctly, the first to get caught. His name was listed as Richard Harper, and he was lodged in the city's first jail, constructed in 1833 of "logs firmly bolted together."

Various historical accounts differ on Harper's background and crimes. One describes him as a young loafer from Maryland, but another relates he was a young man of considerable education and breeding who was brought down by a devotion to whiskey. All sources agree he enjoyed stealing better than working. In 1833 Harper was put up for sale under the Illinois vagrancy law, making him the first white man in the area to be auctioned. That act caused considerable controversy, but despite strong feelings on the subject, no one in the large crowd would raise the 25¢ bid made by George White, the Negro town crier, and Harper was led away by his new owner at the end of a chain. One historian reported that he escaped that very night and was never seen again. However, Chicago's first directory, published in 1839, contained the listing "Harper, Richard, called 'Old Vagrant.'"

Harris, Jean (1923–) "he done her wrong"

Certain cases rise little above the level of the tawdry in their facts but take on special import because of the role they play in influencing social attitudes affecting the American scene. Many crime aficionados would eschew Jean Harris' murder of famous "Scarsdale Diet" doctor Herman Tarnower as a minor event in the annals of homicide. She shot him, made no real effort to escape, was easily apprehended and insisted it was an accident resulting from a lover's quarrel. However, the Harris-Tarnower case had an important impact on the nation's views, occurring as it did on the tide of rising female expectations and demands for social equality with men. For decades, verdicts delivered in "heat of the moment" legal cases were seldom harsh. Jean Harris represented fair turnaround, or, as one female put it in a reversal of a popular refrain, "He done her wrong."

On March 10, 1980, Dr. Tarnower, the 69-year-old cardiologist and author of the best-selling book *The Complete Scarsdale Medical Diet,* which brought him millions, was shot and killed in the bedroom of his luxurious home in Purchase, N. Y. The police were summoned by the Tarnower maid and picked up 56-year-old Jean S. Harris before she drove away.

Harris, a cultured woman and headmistress of the exclusive Madeira School for Girls in McLean, Va., had had a love affair with Tarnower for 14 years. Known to her students as "Integrity Harris," she had spent many weekends and vacations with the doctor and had helped him in the writing of his book. Over the years, Tarnower had spoken often of marriage to Harris but had called off an impending wedding on one occasion. During the years, Harris had shut her eyes to the more than 30 relationships Tarnower had maintained with

Jean Harris' murder of the famous "Scarsdale Diet" doctor, Herman Tarnower, energized many women in their demands for social equality in court.

other women, and she had tolerated other women's nightclothes, underwear, cosmetics, and the like, which littered the Tarnower bedroom.

But it was Mrs. Lynne Tryforos, 18 years younger than Harris, whom the headmistress came to regard as her main threat. The two women carried on a fierce struggle for the doctor's affections, cutting up each other's clothes, and Harris accusing Tryforos of making obscene phone calls. Harris contemplated plastic surgery as a means to regain the doctor's affections.

Just a few days before Tarnower's death, Harris mailed him a letter from Virginia, calling Tryforos a "dishonest adultress . . . a slut and a psychotic whore."

Hoping to spend the weekend with Tarnower, Harris drove up from Virginia and arrived in advance of her letter. She and the doctor got into a violent argument in the bedroom after Harris came across a nightgown and hair curlers belonging to some other woman. In the ensuing struggle, Harris pulled a .32-caliber handgun from her purse, and the doctor began pushing her and was heard to cry out, "Get out of here. You're crazy."

Four shots were fired, and Tarnower keeled over, bleeding profusely. He died about an hour later in the hospital. Meanwhile, Harris gave a rambling statement to the police who apprehended her. "He wanted to live," she said. "I wanted to die." She claimed she had carried the revolver and a number of amphetamines to give her courage, saying she had planned to persuade Tarnower to shoot her and that her shooting of him (with three hits) had been accidental.

Harris' three-month-long trial started in November 1980 and was a field day for the tabloid press, as much testimony centered on Tarnower's lifestyle and love affairs. A great deal was made of the intimate clothing so many women had left behind. At one point, even Harris' own underwear was introduced as evidence, much to her discomfort.

Although many women sympathized with Harris and felt she had been demeaned by Tarnower, the jury of eight women and four men found that she had deliberately set out to kill the lover who had spurned her. On March 20, 1981, she was sentenced to a mandatory term of 15 years to life imprisonment. An attempt to gain clemency, which was supported by many women, failed, and she was confined at Bedford Hills Correctional Facility, not eligible for parole until 1996. Harris became active in prison reform and, in 1988, wrote a book entitled *They Always Call Us Ladies* about her prison experience.

Harris began experiencing heart problems and in January 1993, Harris, then 69, had her sentence commuted by Gov. Mario Cuomo, after serving not quite 12 years of her minimum 15-year term.

Harris, William and Emily kidnappers of Patricia Hearst

The bizarre hunt for kidnapped heiress Patricia Hearst ended on September 18, 1975, when Hearst and 32-year-old Wendy Yoshimura were captured by the FBI in an apartment in the Mission District of San Francisco. About an hour earlier, William and Emily Harris, 30 and 26, respectively, were picked up on a street corner by FBI agents. The Harrises were considered to be the last of the Symbionese Liberation Army, a radical terrorist group that had taken Hearst from her Berkeley, Calif. apartment in February 1974. Some three months after her abduction, Hearst renounced her parents and said she was joining her SLA captors.

It appeared the Harrises had been with Hearst during virtually the entire period of her kidnapping and witnessed her startling behavioral conversion from prisoner to willing partner. In the San Francisco apartment agents found a portion of William Harris' autobiography describing the Hearst abduction and her later transformation to a willing member of the SLA, a development that startled the Harrises. The manuscript quoted Hearst as labeling her parents racists.

In August 1978 the Harrises pleaded guilty to "simple kidnapping" rather than to the more serious charge of "kidnapping for ransom and with great bodily harm." Before they were sentenced in October, William Harris accused Patricia Hearst and her family of "lies, distortions and exaggerations" about her life with the SLA. He said: "She was not brainwashed, beaten, tortured or raped. She was not coerced into rejecting her family and remaining with the people of the SLA." This had been Hearst's defense at her own trial on charges of taking part in a bank robbery with other SLA members.

With credit for time served and good behavior, the Harrises were released in 1983 and went their separate ways.

See also: PATRICIA HEARST.

Harrison, Carter (1825–1893) corrupt Chicago mayor

In a city where crooked politicians were the rule, Chicago mayor Harrison Carter, who served five separate terms in the 19th century, was perhaps the most audacious of the lot. While newspapers were constantly exposing Harrison's involvement in the ownership of many vice properties and connected him with known criminals and corrupters, Chicago voters kept right on electing him to office.

Born in Kentucky in 1825 and a graduate of Yale, Harrison came to Chicago in 1850 and quickly made a fortune in real estate, becoming a financial and political power. Elected mayor, he soon realized he could rent out a number of his properties for three or four times their former rental values by giving them over to saloon, gambling and prostitution enterprises. In 1877 the *Chicago Times* pointed out that an entire block occupied by buildings housing every sort of vice activity was owned by "Our Carter." Despite this intelligence, the voters of Chicago promptly reelected Harrison on his next try for the mayorality.

Harrison's close connections with the underworld started in the 1880s, when he formed a working relationship with Mike McDonald, the crime king of Chicago. McDonald handled the "fix," charging most criminals a percentage of their take in exchange for a guarantee of immunity from official persecution. Gamblers, vice operators, swindlers, pickpockets and other crooks were allowed to keep from 40 to 65 percent of their take, with the rest going to McDonald, who in turn paid off the police, judges, aldermen and other city officials and supplied bribe money to fix juries. Describing this arrangement, the famed muckraker

William T. Steed wrote: "Many people had a finger in the pie before the residue reached Mr. Harrison. But however many there were who fingered the profit en route, there was enough left to make it well worth the Mayor's while."

As part of the agreement between Harrison and McDonald, the latter retained an important say in the police department, replacing an honest police chief, Simon O'Donnell, with the more compliant William J. McGarigle. In 1882 McGarigle was shifted to the wardenship of the Cook County Hospital, where he then hired McDonald's contracting firm to paint a public building for $128,500. A number of bribes were given to aldermen to approve the deal and the paint job was done—with a mixture of chalk and water. When the scandal broke, McGarigle left town without packing a bag, and a number of aldermen were sent to jail. McDonald and Harrison were unscathed, however.

Harrison was elected to his fifth term in office by promising Chicagoans an open town for the Columbian Exposition of 1893. And he certainly kept his promise, simultaneously insuring that the public was fleeced as expeditiously as possible by the underworld with, above all, no scandal to taint the good name of the fair and the city. Typical of these arrangements was the one made with the pickpockets via McDonald. Under an agreement reached by the politicians and the pickpockets, whose negotiations were handled by Eddie Jackson, the dean of the dips, no fair visitor was to be robbed at the entrance gates, since if they were, they would have no money to spend inside. The terms of the agreement required that a pickpocket seized at the gate return the loot to the victim if he could be found; if not, the money went to the police. Regardless of what finally happened to the loot, the pickpocket would be required to pay the arresting officer $10 for his release. This was a harsh measure, but as a sop to the pickpockets, they were promised that any thief arrested in the downtown area between 8 A.M. and 4 P.M. would be released when brought to the Central Station House.

With such arrangements the fair was a bonanza for the underworld as well as the business interests of Chicago. On American Cities Day, October 28, 1893, three days before the fair closed, Harrison delivered a speech at the fairgrounds and then returned home ahead of his family and servants. When he went to answer his door bell, Harrison was shot dead by a disgruntled office seeker named Prendergast. The public display of grief was overwhelming, and Harrison was given a funeral that rivaled anything since the grand passage of Abraham Lincoln's body. Over the next two decades the late mayor's son, Carter Harrison II, held sway in Chicago, much of the time as mayor, while McDonald and his successors in the underworld noticed little change in their relationship with City Hall.

See also: BILER AVENUE, MICHAEL CASSIUS "MIKE" MCDONALD.

Harrison, Lester (1923–) serial killer with unusual bid for freedom

Lester Harrison had a long history of killing and a habit based on his obvious insanity, of never being convicted for his most gruesome murders. While confined in a state hospital in 1951, Harrison killed another inmate but was deemed incompetent to stand trial. Two decades later Harrison was found competent for trial on robbery counts and was given a term of 18 months. He served less than that when he was subjected to psychiatric evaluations.

When he was released, he was not even suspected of beating a woman to death in Chicago's Park in 1970. And immediately after his being put back on the streets, a number of women were murdered, subjected to nightmarish sexual abuse in the process. In one case, Harrison gnawed his victim's body. In August 1973 Harrison stabbed to death a 28-year-old woman in a park restroom. The victim's husband observed Harrison running from the women's bathroom, gave chase and apprehended him without knowing his wife had been killed.

Harrison then confessed to at least four murders, although authorities were sure he had committed many more in the area. He was found competent to stand trial, but the defense succeeded in delaying trial for five years and Harrison was subjected to several psychiatric examinations.

A jury acquitted Harrison by virtue of insanity, but authorities then resorted to a special and seldom invoked measure by which Harrison could be found in a hearing to be "sexually dangerous" and subject to confinement as long as he remained a menace.

It was hard to dispute an affirmative verdict, which resulted, and Harrison was put away. That proved to be but the prelude to a bizarre occurrence eight years later. By that time Harrison's health had deteriorated to the extent that at age 62 he was now a quadriplegic. Lawyers taking Harrison's case insisted he should be released since he was barely able to move at all and thus unlikely to do harm to others. The state attorney's office fought the claim, a representative stating that if Harrison "were able to get his hands on any woman that woman would be in danger of being killed. If he could use one arm, he would use it to try to beat somebody to death."

Testimony from guards at Belleville State Hospital where Harrison was being held indicated that Harrison could raise his arms. More important testimony was given that he became what was euphemistically referred to as "visibly aroused" when nurses he liked entered the room.

The case failed to become a matter of some special legal interpretation when the petition for the patient's release was withdrawn.

Harsh, George S. (1907–1980) murderer and war hero

Once sentenced to death for a senseless "thrill killing," George S. Harsh went on to become a much storied World War II hero and an author and spokesman against capital punishment.

In 1929 Harsh and Richard G. Gallory confessed to the shooting of a drugstore clerk during an Atlanta holdup that the newspapers called a thrill killing. The two were also charged in six other robberies and the killing of another clerk. Both defendants came from wealthy and socially prominent families. Harsh's family put up an elaborate and expensive defense, including testimony from 12 psychiatrists that he suffered from "psychological irresponsibility and hereditary taints." Harsh was nonetheless found guilty and sentenced to die in the electric chair, but this was later commuted to life imprisonment on a Georgia work gang. In 1940 he was granted a parole after helping to save a fellow inmate's life by performing an appendectomy on him.

Harsh joined the Royal Canadian Air Force. Shot down by the Germans, he was captured and sent to a Nazi prison camp. He played a key role in the tunnel breakout of 126 Allied soldiers from the camp, 50 of whom were later apprehended and executed. The movie entitled *The Great Escape* was based on this incident. Harsh was eventually freed from captivity, and after the war he turned to writing about his life and his moral redemption, relating his experiences in a book entitled *A Lonesome Road*. He also crusaded against capital punishment, writing in 1972: "Capital punishment is a law zeroed in on the poor, the underprivileged, the friendless, the uneducated and the ignorant. I was convicted of a senseless crime and sentenced to die in the electric chair. This sentence would have been carried out had I not come from a white, wealthy and influential family. This Mosaic law of death is drawn from the worst of all human motives, revenge."

Harsh died on January 25, 1980 in Toronto, Canada.

Hart, Brooke (1911–1933) kidnapping and murder victim

The kidnap-murder of a 22-year-old hotel and department store heir in California in 1933 probably triggered more official approval of vigilantism than any other crime in this century.

Brooke Hart was seized by two 24-year-old youths of comfortable middle-class backgrounds, John Maurice Holmes and Thomas H. Thurmond, the latter having no criminal record at all. The pair abducted Hart as he left the family's department store in San Jose on November 9 and, using the victim's car, drove to the San Mateo–Hayward Bridge. Hart was knocked unconscious and his body, weighted down with cement blocks, heaved into the bay. Hart regained consciousness on hitting the water and, screaming, tried to stay afloat whereupon Thurmond shot him several times until his body disappeared. An hour later, the kidnappers were on the telephone to the victim's father, Alex Hart, demanding a ransom of $40,000 for the safe return of his son. Several more calls were necessary to arrange a pickup spot for the money, and on November 15 police traced a call to a San Jose garage and arrested Thurmond while he was still on the phone with the elder Hart. Thurmond confessed and named Holmes as his accomplice, each man accusing the other of devising the plot and committing the murder.

On November 24, young Hart's body washed ashore and the San Jose community, especially the college students who knew Hart as a recent graduate, were enraged. By that evening, a crowd of 15,000 had gathered outside the jail where the two quarreling killers were being held in separate cells. The college students took up a cry of "We want a touchdown," a chant that chilled not only the prisoners but Sheriff William Emig as well. He called Gov. James "Sunny Jim" Rolfe requesting troops, but his plea was rejected. Gov. Rolfe insisted there was no need. For the next several hours local and state police held off the crowd, which was growing bigger and more ugly by the minute. They held them back with high-powered hoses and tear gas but the mob continued to surge toward the jail. Alex Hart appeared on the scene and begged the would-be vigilantes to leave, but he was ignored. Not long before midnight, the mob moved in, battered down the jail door and poured past the handful of police guards. Holmes was attacked in his cell, stripped of his clothes and beaten so badly an eyeball dangled from its socket. When the mob located Thurmond's cell, they found it empty. Then while everyone grew silent, they could hear labored breathing and spotted him hiding in the pipes over the cell's toilet. Thurmond was beaten badly, dragged outside to a

Thomas Thurmond's body dangled from a tree after he was dragged from his cell by angry Californians and hanged. Gov. Sunny Jim Rolfe called the lynching "the best lesson ever given the country."

park and hanged from a tree. A pleading Holmes was hanged next, while the crowd chanted, "Get that ball!"

Authorities never charged anyone in the lynchings, although many identifications could have been made. Newspapers in California and the rest of the nation condemned the lynchings, but it was clear the popular and official California reaction approved of the acts. Gov. Rolfe described the lynchings as "the best lesson ever given the country. I would pardon those fellows if they were charged. I would like to parole all kidnappers in San Quentin and Folsom to the fine patriotic citizens of San Jose."

Hart, Gene Leroy (1944–1979) wrong man

A full-blooded Cherokee Indian and an escaped convict, Gene Leroy Hart became an Oklahoma folk hero in his successful battle against charges that he killed three Girl Scouts in 1977. Serving sentences totaling

140 years for rape, kidnapping and burglary, Hart escaped from the Mayes County, Okla. jail in 1973. He was still at large on June 13, 1977 when three Girl Scouts—Lori Lee Farmer, Michele Guse and Doris Denise Milner, aged 8, 9 and 10—were sexually assaulted and beaten to death at a camp near Pryor. Within two weeks of the crime, law enforcement officials announced that Hart was their principal suspect. Many local people believed in Hart's innocence, and they helped him to continue to hide out from the law. Finally, after a 10-month manhunt that attracted a small army of police officers and civilian volunteers, Hart was caught.

Brought to trial for the murders, Hart had to defend himself against a case that was both highly technical and circumstantial. During his trial, Oklahoma's longest, his family and friends held support meetings for him and raised money for his defense by selling chili suppers. After a former jailer testified that some of the state's evidence against the popular Indian had been in the officials' possession up to three years before the crime was committed and other Girl Scouts identified photographs of a convicted Kansas rapist as looking like the murderer, Hart was acquitted in March 1979. While he went back to prison, his supporters held a champagne celebration. On June 4, 1979 the 35-year-old Cherokee died of a heart attack after jogging in the prison yard. An estimated 1,000 mourners attended the funeral of the man whose case was said to have done much to further the cause of Indian rights. However, even as Hart was being buried, officials insisted they had new evidence that proved his guilt.

Hart, Pearl (1878–?) last stagecoach robber
Pearl Hart was a failure at stagecoach robbing, but she did have the distinction of taking part in the last stage robbery in the United States.

Pearl, who described herself as "slightly married," had left her husband in her native Canada and headed for the Wild West at the age of 20, having devoured all the tales about Jesse James and Butch Cassidy. She was determined to become the greatest woman outlaw in history. Slinging hash in an Arizona mining camp, she met up with Joe Boot, a cash-short miner, and convinced him there was more money in robbing stage coaches than in mining. Apparently, Pearl didn't even know that Wells Fargo had by that date stopped shipping money in stage strongboxes. On May 30, 1899 Pearl and Boot held up the Benson-Globe stage. As Joe Boot collected the loot from the three passengers—a traveling salesman, $390, an Eastern dude, $36 and a Chinese man, $5—Pearl, her long brunette locks stuffed under a hat, trained a six-gun on the driver and the victims. As the pair took off, Pearl, elated at their magnificent take of $431, broke into song, her spirits undampened by a sudden rain squall. Then the last of the stagecoach robbers got lost. After traveling three days and nights in the rain, they finally lay down to sleep, and that was how the law found them. Taken to Florence by Sheriff William Truman, they were greeted by a large crowd. A reporter asked Pearl, "Would you do it again?" Giving him a "savage look," she snarled "Damn right, podner."

Joe Boot was sentenced to 35 years. Being a woman, Pearl got only five years. She was the only female inmate at the Yuma Territorial Prison and became quite an attraction. Sunday visitors often asked her to pose for pictures in the jail yard and she always obliged. Released after doing almost two and a half years, Pearl toured theaters billed as the Arizona Bandit, with her record somewhat embellished. Pearl's footlight glory lasted about a year, and then nothing was heard of her until 1905, when she was arrested in Deming, New Mexico Territory for conspiring to rob a train. Released for lack of evidence, she dropped out of sight. In 1924 Pearl, now a white-haired little woman in her late forties, turned up at the Pima County Courthouse and asked to be allowed to look around for old time's sake. Treated as a celebrity, Pearl Hart got the grand tour and then vanished again, this time for good.

Hartley Mob 19th-century New York gang
Probably the most colorful of New York's 19th-century gangs was the Hartley Mob, which dominated an area around Broadway and Houston Street. Numbering in its membership some of the city's most cunning thieves and vicious killers, the Hartley Mob thrived in the 1870s. Even the contemporary Whyos, probably the worst gang of the century and often described as the forerunners of Murder, Inc., made it a practice of not tangling with the Hartley Mob.

The gang's criminal technique was daring and original. While an obliging traffic officer would hold up the flow of other vehicles, the very well-armed gangsters, dressed in solemn black, would transport their stolen goods hidden behind the drapes of a hearse and on the floors of accompanying funeral carriages. The Hartleys discovered the combat uses of the hearse in a noted battle with a vicious Five Points Gang, which had been encroaching on their territory. The Five Pointers stationed themselves on Mulberry Street to take the onslaught of the Hartleys but respectfully parted ranks to allow a hearse and some funeral carriages to pass. They were then overwhelmed from behind by two dozen Hartley Mob battlers who swarmed out of the vehicles.

The Hartley Mob was too mean and deadly a gang to last. Unlike other gangs, the mob saw no need to seek political protection, and within a few years most of the members were imprisoned.

Harvey, Donald (1952–) medical serial killer
While any attempt to catalog the full extent of nurse's aide Donald Harvey's brutality results in a mind-boggling numbers game, there is little doubt that he was easily the most lethal medical serial killer of the 20th century.

At 18 Harvey became an orderly at a hospital in London, Ky. in May 1970. He stayed on the job 10 months and later confessed to killing about 12 patients. He would reveal he had smothered two with pillows and hooked another 10 to virtually empty oxygen tanks because he wanted to "ease their suffering." He left the job after being arrested for burglary and got away with only a small fine from a judge who recommended he get psychiatric treatment. Instead, Harvey joined the air force but was discharged ahead of time for unstated reasons. He was committed a couple of times to a Veteran's Administration medical center suffering from mental disorders, which may have included a suicide attempt. He got a number of electroshock treatments but was released with no obvious improvement.

Despite this, he served as a nurse's aide in two hospitals at the same time in Lexington. After holding clerical jobs at another hospital, he then moved on to the Cincinnati V.A. Medical Center, holding nursing positions, including that of an autopsy assistant. In that job he sometimes smuggled out tissue samples to take home to "study."

He did not ignore his "mercy murders" and disposed of some 15 patients by his former methods as well as by poison. Now that he was playing God, Harvey took to putting people who weren't hospitalized out of their misery, apparently deciding that anyone who annoyed him was clearly in misery. Angered by a neighbor, he gave her hepatitis serum to drink. By the heroic efforts of doctors the woman was saved.

In July 1985 Harvey was forced to resign his job after he was found leaving work with hypodermic needles and other medical gear as well as a cocaine spoon. In February 1986 he turned up as a part-time nurse's aide in another Cincinnati hospital and was soon promoted to full time. During a period of just over a year, 23 patients fell victim to his murderous rampage. Some had their life support system disconnected or were injected with mixtures of cyanide, arsenic and a petroleum-based cleanser.

In addition, he poisoned his live-in lover, Carl Hoeweler, after a dispute and then nursed him back to health. Harvey also poisoned Carl's parents; Hoeweler's mother died.

But 23 murders in a hospital were too many to get away with. Patient John Powell was given an autopsy and found to have lethal doses of cyanide in his body. Charged with murder in the case, Harvey pleaded not guilty by reason of insanity. Over the next few months Harvey confessed to a total of 33 murders. Harvey kept adding victims to his list until it climbed to 52. Subjected to a number of psychiatric examinations, Harvey nonetheless was found to be sane and competent although a compulsive killer.

In August 1987 Harvey pleaded guilty to 25 counts of aggravated murder and sundry other charges. He was given four consecutive life sentences with no eligibility for parole for 80 years. Kentucky tacked on nine counts of murder in November. That got him eight more life terms plus 20 years. In February the following year he got three more homicide convictions as well as convictions on other charges. It was said that Harvey was impressed that he had surpassed John Wayne Gacy in total murders committed.

Harvey, Captain Julian (1916–1961) mass murderer

At first regarded as the fortunate sole survivor of a cruising yacht that had sunk, a 45-year-old adventurer, Capt. Julian Harvey, was later unmasked as the perpetrator of one of this country's worst mass murders at sea.

On November 13, 1961 Harvey was rescued from a dinghy, which also contained the drowned body of a little girl. Harvey explained he was the skipper of the ketch *Bluebelle*, which had caught fire and sunk the day before some 50 miles from Nassau. He said that because of the flames he had been unable to save any of his passengers, Mr. and Mrs. Arthur Dupperrault, their 14-year-old son Brian, their 11-year-old daughter Terry Jo, their seven-year-old daughter Renee or his own 34-year-old wife Mary, although he was able to fish Renee's dead body from the water.

There seemed little reason to doubt the captain's story, despite the fact that he had taken out a $20,000 double-indemnity life insurance policy on his wife shortly before the *Bluebelle* sailed from Fort Lauderdale, Fla. on November 8 with the Dupperrault family as passengers. Then, three and a half days after Harvey was rescued, 11-year-old Terry Jo Dupperrault was found floating on a cork raft. The story she told was far different from Harvey's tale. She revealed that Harvey had slaughtered her parents and brother and his own wife. She saw the bodies of her mother and brother covered with blood "all over." Harvey had left her on the deck of the sinking ketch after opening the sea cocks, but she managed to escape on a raft before the craft went down.

Harvey was attending a Coast Guard hearing into the sinking when word came that the girl had been rescued. He walked from the room, shaking his head. He went back to a Miami motel and killed himself by slashing his veins with a razor blade. Subsequent inquiry revealed Mary Harvey had been the second wife of Julian Harvey to die in a violent accident. In 1949, while he was an air force lieutenant colonel, Harvey crashed the car he was driving through a bridge railing into a Florida bayou. He told investigators he was thrown free but his wife, Joan, and her mother, Mrs. Myrtle Boylen, were trapped and drowned.

As he had requested in a suicide note, Harvey was buried at sea by friends. A blue ribbon emblazoned with gold letters read, "Bon voyage, Julian."

Hastings, Mary (1863–?) madam

A young prostitute from Brussels, Belgium with previous experience in Paris, Toronto, British Columbia, San Francisco, Portland and Denver, Mary Hastings arrived in Chicago at the age of 25 and immediately set about earning her reputation as the worst madam in the city's history. She boasted that her first bordello at 144 Custom House Place contained only harlots who were thrown out of "decent houses." To satisfy some customers' desires, however, she hired procurers to kidnap girls as young as 13 from other cities. Frequently, she would go on such forays herself, returning with girls between 13 and 17, whom she had lured to Chicago with the promise of jobs. Once the girls were safely confined in one of her houses, they would be subjected to a process of brutalization and rape to introduce them to "the life." In one typical case, three young girls were locked in a room overnight with six men. Those girls Madam Hastings had no need for in her own houses she would sell to other establishments for sums varying from $50 to $300, depending on their age and beauty.

Madam Hastings bought police protection by paying cops on the beat $2.50 a week plus free drinks, meals and girls whenever they desired. Naturally, the payoffs to ward politicians and the higher brass at the Harrison Street police station were much higher. When she once complained that the charges were excessive, a police captain stormed back, "Why, damn you, what are you made for but to be plundered?"

While virtually all the police accepted bribes for overlooking mere prostitution, many refused to be bought when the offense involved was the forceful procuring of young girls. In 1895 hard evidence against her was finally supplied by four girls from Cleveland who had escaped a Hastings house by climbing down a rope made of sheets and reached a police station. A raiding party crashed into the house and freed five other girls. After bail was posted by her "solid man," Tom Gaynor, Madam Hastings was indicted. She promptly fled to Canada, and the bail was forfeited. When she returned, however, strings were pulled, and the funds were returned to Gaynor. Then Madam Hastings decamped again for Canada, this time signing over all her property to Gaynor so that it could not be seized by the courts. By mid-1897 she was able to return once more because the witnesses against her had scattered. However, when she tried to reclaim her brothels, Gaynor threw her out on the street, to the cheers of the inmates. Finally, he let her have $200, and Mary Hastings left the city for good.

Hatcher, Charles (1929–1984) serial child killer

When serial child killer Charles Hatcher was brought to justice in the early 1980s and started making wholesale confessions, there was at least one fortunate consequence. Melvin Reynolds, serving a life sentence for the sex murder of four-year-old Eric Christgen, was freed when Hatcher was discovered to have been the actual murderer.

From 1969 onward Hatcher confessed to some 16 child murders, the first being that of 12-year-old William Freeman, who vanished in Antioch, Cal., in August of 1969. Ironically the day after the Freeman murder, Hatcher was charged in a child molestation case in San Francisco. In the aftermath of the Freeman disappearance Hatcher was later convicted in California and several Midwest states several times in cases involving sexual assaults and kidnappings of children. What the law was unaware of was that there were intervening murders of children.

Early in 1982 Hatcher was committed to a state mental institution for the abduction of a young boy. After psychiatrists studied Hatcher for two months they sent him free. Then on July 29 the nude, violated body of 11-year-old Michelle Steele turned up on a bank by the Missouri River outside St. Louis. Hatcher was taken into custody the following day when he attempted to check in at the St. Joseph State Hospital. It was in this period that Hatcher began confessing to his cross-country child murders, which proved eminently verifiable. Using a rough map drawn by Hatcher, searchers found the body of James Churchill on the grounds of an army arsenal near Davenport, Iowa.

Hatcher was at first tried only for the Christgen killing for which Reynolds had previously been convicted. He was given a life sentence with no parole for a minimum of 50 years. In 1984, tried and convicted for the Steele killing in Missouri, Hatcher asked for the death penalty, but the jury declined, recommending life. Four days after that sentence was imposed, Hatcher was found hanged in his prison cell. Prison authorities in Jefferson City were satisfied that the child killer had committed suicide and that it was not a case of murder.

But why had Hatcher killed himself? Remorse? A desire to avoid a life sentence that he regarded as worse than execution? Or was there recognition on his part that he faced years of torment from fellow inmates in an institution where child killers can be subjected to extreme violence at any moment?

hate crimes A part of American culture

Hate crimes have always been part of the fabric of America, sometimes fueled by Old World hatreds.

Among the early Irish-American criminal elements, attacks, robberies and murders of Englishmen hardly seemed a crime at all. And newcomers had no qualms at all of nurturing new hatreds. It was easy enough to hate the red man, the black man, the Spanish-speaking elements, some of whom were the first to settle in this new world.

The history of hate in America constantly exploded in eras of unspeakable violence, such as the anti-Chinese riots, the Civil War Draft Riots, which were soon translated in New York beyond protests against the draft into an anti-black pogrom. In the South, but certainly in the North and West as well, lynching of blacks became a monotonous norm. In 1923 it was said that 59 blacks were lynched in southern and neighboring states. Actually the figure was much higher, when riotous bloodletting was included. Certainly the figures for 1921, for example, numbered in the hundreds, with the inclusion of the terrible Tulsa riots, details of which have only been explored in the 1990s. White invasions of black areas produced mass killings; of past estimates of about 125 dying and 1,000 more wounded in the riot in Tulsa, Okla., virtually all the victims were black. The 125 figure is no longer taken seriously. The Tulsa Race Riot Commission set up in 1997, with its work hardly completed, drew a picture far more devastating. What has been learned was that hundreds of African Americans were shot, tied to cars and dragged to death or burned alive. There were recent reports of corpses stacked at street corners like cordwood, and dead bodies loaded on wagons, in dump trucks and along railroad sidings. A report indicated that some 123 blacks were clubbed to death in a tunnel and buried there. Many bodies were dumped into the Arkansas River and washed away.

An even more graphic example occurred in 1923 in Rosewood, Fla., a community that sported a number of blacks living in relatively middle-class circumstances. A riot in Rosewood was triggered by a white woman's lie about being attacked by blacks (the same thing that had happened in Tulsa), but the real cause of the explosion was the festering jealousy of whites fearing some blacks' becoming their social equals. Armed with the lie, a white "army" moved into Rosewood, determined to wipe out the entire settlement. The death toll was less than in Tulsa, simply because the population was less, but the end result was even better from the rioters' view. It was said that 40 to 150 men, women and children died in the attack, and that virtually all who survived fled forever. The community of Rosewood in effect disappeared overnight.

It may indicate a measure of changing attitudes when in 1999 three whites were convicted of first-degree murder for the dragging death of an African

American man in Texas and faced the death penalty, with much support from whites. In fact, such dragging deaths were a killing method of choice in previous years especially in southern states and probably occurred dozens of times in Tulsa alone.

Nevertheless hate crimes remain a "sport" in the United States. Feelings of jealousy, greed, desperation and stoked hatred can be the hallmarks of such crimes. Officially when bias is directed against another person's religion, race, disability, sexual orientation or ethnicity, the offense is classified under the 1990 Hate Crime Statistics Act, with the FBI charged with determining such facts.

The agency's 1997 statistical report, the most recent available, demonstrates some revealing—to some very startling—facts. Hate crimes of course remain a mostly white offense, in every category studied. In the matter of single-bias incidents, fully 80 percent are anti-Jewish out of a total of 1,483. By contrast anti-Catholic acts amount to only 2 percent, about the same figure for anti-Islamic attacks. Among the incidents where the suspected offender's race was known, whites committed 240 anti-Jewish attacks as opposed to only 30 perpetrated by blacks, a figure probably surprising to the victims themselves.

On the matter of ethnicity or national origin, whites were known to have committed 544 offenses, mostly against Hispanics, in comparison to 73 such offenses by blacks.

When sexual orientation is considered, 701 offenses are attributed to whites and 154 to blacks.

On race, as always, the chief victims remained African Americans. The offenders were mainly white (2,336 among suspected offenders), while blacks were involved in 718 offenses against whites. Whites also were known to have committed 214 racial attacks on whites and 200 against Asians and Pacific Islanders, compared to 41 in total committed by blacks.

In the late 1990s coverage of hate crimes in the media became a staple in the news, far different from years earlier when such offenses drew less—and sometimes scant—attention. Typical of the more notorious cases was the random shooting of Sasezley Richardson, a 19-year-old black, by two whites, aged 18 and 19, in Elkhart County, Ind. The authorities said the alleged killers had confessed the murder. A local newspaper reported that one of the whites told friends that he hoped the killing would earn him membership in the Aryan Brotherhood, a white supremacist prison gang so that he would be able to wear the gang's spiderweb tattoo. Elkhart County police estimated that the Aryan Brotherhood had just under 100 members in the area.

Looking for group approval is sometimes a hallmark of the hate criminal. Benjamin N. Smith, a former student at first the University of Illinois and then the

University of Indiana, was known to espouse the views of the White Nationalist Party and the Church of the Creator, an anti-black, anti-Christian, anti-Jewish organization based in East Peoria, Ill. He was to become a hate murderer.

He was known to have been very close to Matthew F. Hale, the leader of the Church of the Creator, which did not worship any God, was opposed to other organized religions and had faith only in the white race. After Smith turned killer, Hale insisted his group did not advocate killing non-whites and Jews, proposing rather to "crowd them off the planet in self-defense," and at the same time "straightening out the thinking of white people." Hale described the church as supporting the views of Hitler in many respects, but differing on a few. The church's Golden Rule was: "That which is good for the White Race is the highest virtue. That which is bad for the White Race is the ultimate sin."

Smith, who went under the name of August rather than Benjamin because it sounded "too Jewish," moved on from violent talk to murderous violence on July 2, 1999, when a state administrative board turned down Hale's appeal after being denied a law license because of his racial views.

That same night Smith went on a shooting rampage. Around 8:30 P.M. he started shooting at Orthodox Jews in Northern Chicago sometimes on foot and sometimes from his car. Six were wounded, but not seriously.

The first fatality occurred in Skokie, just north of Chicago. Ricky Birdsong, a 43-year-old black, the former coach of the Northwestern Wildcats, and previously at five other schools, was walking with his son and daughter near their home. Smith opened up with one of his two handguns, missing the children but hitting Birdsong in the back.

The shooting spree continued as Smith continued firing one handgun and then another at Jews, blacks and Asians. Some were hit but not seriously until the following morning, July 4, when Smith fired four shots into a group of people leaving the Korean United Methodist Church in Bloomington. Won-Joon Yoon, a 26-year-old University of Indiana student, was shot twice in the back and killed. Witnesses said the killer had sped off in a blue Taurus, running several traffic lights. Police were aware of Smith's anti-Semitic and anti-black activities and issued a warrant for him.

After 10 P.M. that evening police received a report of a stolen van. The police picked up the trail for the vehicle and after an hourlong chase, ran Smith down in Salem, Ill. Smith then shot himself and crashed the van. He was rushed to the hospital but died, the hate finally draining out of Benjamin "August" Smith.

See also: HATE CRIMES—HOMOSEXUAL ATTACKS.

hate crimes—homosexual attacks

Like all hate crimes, those against homosexuals are basically carried out by whites. In an FBI breakdown of such crimes for 1997, the latest available figures with the race of the perpetrator known, there were 714 sexual bias incidents by whites and 160 by blacks. Only a handful of cases represent attacks the FBI referred to as "Anti-Heterosexual" or "Anti-Bisexual," and they were statistically too little to be considered, although virtually all of these were also carried out by whites as well.

Among the more prominent cases of violence against homosexuals in the last two years of the 20th century was that of Matthew Shepard, a 21-year-old student at the University of Wyoming, who was lured from a bar near campus to an isolated area by three young men who robbed and blugeoned him, subjected him to awesome abuse and then left him trussed up to die a slow agonizing death there. In two other cases in 1999 gay haters slashed Billy Jack Gaither's throat, smashed his head open with an ax handle, planted him on top of some kerosene-soaked tires and set him ablaze. And another victim was decapitated and his head carried a mile away from the body and deposited on a busy footbridge known as a gay cruising area.

Some experts find there has been a marked increase in the number of extremely vicious attacks and killings of homosexuals. Veteran police, used to such brutal crimes, still suspect many cases start out as robbery attempts that escalate to vile practices as though the perpetrators can later claim their actions were caused by a frenzy or panic rather than premeditated brutality.

Gay bashings can frequently occur in localities with a large homosexual community, but it is also true that homophobes do operate in surroundings that are more "heterosexual friendly," such as university areas and very frequently in the armed services. Critics have insisted such codes as "don't ask, don't tell" have proven a disaster and have actually created a climate that incites more violence against those the policy allegedly attempts to aid.

In 1999 the murder of a gay soldier, Pfc. Barry Winchell, created a firestorm of protest that the "don't ask, don't tell" policy was a failure without strong enforcement from higher brass. In the case, an 18-year-old private, Calvin Glover, crept up on a sleeping Winchell in a barracks in Fort Campbell, Ky. and beat him to death with a baseball bat, egged on by a buddy.

The investigation and court-martial record showed that Glover and many other GIs habitually harassed Winchell for his sexual preference, which he never apparently stated. Such activities were unaccompanied by any superiors' reprimands of notice. Testimony indicated all such regulations were ignored—as was a complaint about a master sergeant who referred to Private Winchell as "that faggot"—and that harassment complaints were positively discouraged. In fact, the trial indicated that army authorities did not begin to hold sessions down the ranks on gay policy until after Winchell was killed, other than a brief parody of activity. An army private told CBS news program *60 Minutes* that a superior said with obvious disgust, "This is a meeting about fags. Don't bother them; they won't bother you." The same private told of his drill sergeant keeping homophobic cadence in a 5-mile run: "Faggot, faggot down the street/ Shoot him, shoot 'til he retreats.

While Pvt. Glover drew a life sentence for the crime and investigation continued concerning an accomplice or accomplices, the Winchell case indicated how deeply ingrained homophobic attitudes would probably remain in the military under "don't tell, don't ask."

See also: MATTHEW SHEPARD.

Hatfields and McCoys   mountaineer feud

America's classic mountain feud between the Hatfields in West Virginia and the McCoys in Kentucky was in many respects an extension of the Civil War. The Hatfields, under the leadership of young Anderson "Devil Anse" Hatfield, had sided with the South, while the family of Randolph McCoy took up the Union cause. Both families rode with border guerrilla bands and built up a hatred that would long outlive the war.

After the war, although relations were strained, there was no important confrontation until 1873, when Randolph McCoy accused Floyd Hatfield of stealing a hog. The case finally came for adjudication before Parson Anse, a Baptist minister who dispensed justice in the backcountry. Mountaineers streamed to the trial, all armed with long knives, or "toothpicks," and long-barreled rifles. Supporting the Hatfields were the Mahons, Vances, Ferrels, Statons and Chafins. On the McCoy side were the Sowards, Stuarts, Gateses, Colemans, Normans and Rutherfords. Six supporters of each side were placed on a jury, and it appeared matters would be deadlocked. However, one of the jurors, Selkirk McCoy, who was married to a Hatfield, voted in favor of the Hatfields, breaking the tie. He pointed out that both men had presented sound arguments, but in the final analysis possession was what counted and there did not seem to be enough grounds to take the hog away from Floyd Hatfield.

The decision ended the legal battle but ill feelings festered. It was only a matter of time before violence erupted. The first to die was Bill Staton, a Hatfield supporter who had vowed to kill McCoys. How many died after that was never accurately counted; both clans were close-mouthed on such matters, but the bloodbath esca-

lated. When Ellison Hatfield, a brother of Devil Anse, was shot by McCoys in an election day dispute in 1882, the Hatfields took three McCoy brothers hostage and warned them they would die if Ellison died. Two days later, Ellison died and the three McCoy brothers were tied to papaw bushes along a stream and shot to death.

Word about the various murders seeped out to the cities of Kentucky, and the governor of the state finally posted rewards for the capture of any Hatfields. Since the majority of the Hatfields and their supporters lived in West Virginia, and the McCoys and their followers mostly resided in Kentucky, the matter soon flared into a dispute between the two states. In 1888 the Hatfields, who resented the fact that the McCoys kept trying to bring in the law, decided a major drive was necessary to eliminate their foe. A large Hatfield contingent attacked the home of Randolph McCoy. Wearing masks, they yelled out, "Come out, you McCoys, and surrender as prisoners of war!" When the call went unanswered (Randolph McCoy was not present), they shot in the windows and set fire to the house. Randolph's young daughter ran out and was slain. Then his son Calvin emerged and went down in a fusillade. Old Mrs. McCoy tried to run to her daughter and was clubbed over the head and left for dead. This would be the last great reprisal in the feud.

Newspapers all over the country reported the atrocity. Kentucky law officers made several raids into West Virginia, and at least two Hatfield clansmen were killed and nine others captured. West Virginia appealed to the Supreme Court to have the captives returned. The High Court handed down a quick decision stating the law provided no method of compelling one state to return parties wrongfully abducted from another state. Of the nine, two were executed and the others sent to state prison.

By 1890 the feud was about over. A year later, Cap Hatfield wrote a letter to a local newspaper stating the Hatfields were declaring a general amnesty and that "the war spirit in me has abated." Shortly thereafter, Devil Anse came out of hiding, finally sure no Kentucky lawmen would be waiting to apprehend him.

By the time Devil Anse died in 1921 at about 100 years of age, the two clans had intermarried frequently. In the younger generations the feud was nothing more than ancient history, like the Civil War itself.

Haun's Mill Massacre   anti-Mormon killings

For about three decades from the time of the establishment of the Church of Jesus Christ of Latter-day Saints by Joseph Smith in 1830, the history of Mormonism was one of persecution and murder, first in New York State, then in Ohio and later in Missouri. It was common for Mormons to be beaten, robbed, tarred and feathered, whipped and killed. On October 30, 1838 a group of 200 Missourians under the leadership of Nehemiah Comstock attacked an encampment of Mormons at Haun's Mill. The death toll was about 20, with many more seriously wounded. Men, women and children were among the victims. One victim was a small boy who had sought refuge with other children in a blacksmith shop. When he was found, the child begged for his life. But a gun was placed to his temple and his brains blown out; the killer bragged of his deed long after. The attackers threw the corpses down a well and then plundered the camp. Not only were there no prosecutions following these killings, but Gov. Lillburn W. Boggs shortly thereafter announced, "The Mormons must be treated as enemies, and must be exterminated or driven from the state for the public peace." The Haun's Mill Massacre, as well as the murder of Joseph Smith, set the precedent for the 1857 slaughter of more than 120 wagon train emigrants by a Mormon attacking party in the Mountain Meadows Valley, Utah Territory.

See also: MOUNTAIN MEADOWS MASSACRE, JOSEPH SMITH.

Hauptmann, Bruno Richard   See LINDBERGH KIDNAPPING.

Havana Convention   underworld conference

Probably the most important underworld conference in the post–World War II period was the Havana meeting in December 1946, convened to heal the rifts that were appearing in the national crime syndicate. With Lucky Luciano in exile in Italy, serious rivalries developed as Vito Genovese attempted to extend his power over the New York crime families. Luciano had left Frank Costello in charge of his crime family, just as he had been during the period when he was serving time in American prisons. Genovese, who had recently been returned to the United States from his self-imposed exile in Italy to face a murder charge (which he had beaten), was attempting to fill the Luciano vacuum.

The Luciano–Meyer Lansky combination had called the meeting to bring about order and to reassert the former's position of control. Luciano clearly felt he could bide his time in Havana for a couple of years while he waited for the proper political strings to be pulled so that he could come back to the United States.

Among those present at the conclave were Costello, Tommy Lucchese, Joe Profaci, Genovese, Joe Bananas Bonanno, Willie Moretti, Augie Pisano, Joe Adonis, Giuseppe Magliocco and Mike Miranda, all from New York–New Jersey; Steve Magaddino, from Buffalo; Carlos Marcello, from New Orleans; Santo Trafficante,

from Florida; and Tony Accardo and Charlie and Rocco Fischetti, from Chicago. Also present, although in nonvoting roles (this was essentially an Italian Mafia conference), were Meyer Lansky and the syndicate's partner in New Orleans, Dandy Phil Kastel, both Jews. Another attendee was a popular young singer, an Italian American from New Jersey named Frank Sinatra, whom Luciano would describe as "a good kid and we was all proud of him."

Sinatra was not there to take part in the deliberations. He had come with his friends the Fischetti brothers to be the guest of honor at a gala party. As such, he provided good cover for the many Italian mobsters in attendance, giving them an alibi, if necessary, for being in Havana.

The conference proved less than a total success for Luciano in many respects. Genovese actually had the nerve to suggest privately to Luciano that he "retire" from the syndicate. Luciano handled this effrontery by easily facing down Genovese, but he soon learned his word was no longer law.

Luciano effectively blocked Genovese from taking more power and stifled Genovese-inspired complaints about Albert Anastasia, the Lord High Executioner of the mob, who was accused of becoming kill crazy. Anastasia apparently was advocating the assassination of Bureau of Narcotics director Harry Anslinger. Luciano evidently curbed Anastasia but did not "defang" him, realizing he would be a valuable weapon in any future war with Genovese.

However, Luciano lost on another important issue: narcotics. Like Lansky, Costello, Magaddino and a few others, Luciano wanted to take the syndicate out of the narcotics business, but the profits were so enormous that many important crime chiefs would not or, perhaps because of opposition from their own underlings, could not give up the trade. Luciano was forced to leave the decision up to the individual crime families.

Another serious matter of business for the convention was the passing of the death sentence on Bugsy Siegel. A longtime underworld partner of Luciano and, in particular, of Lansky, Siegel had squandered huge sums of money building a great financial lemon, a Las Vegas gambling casino–hotel called the Flamingo. Besides being a bad businessman, Siegel was suspected of also being a crook, skimming off money the mob had put up to construct the hotel. It was Lansky's motion that sealed Siegel's doom: "There's only one thing to do with a thief who steals from his friends. Benny's got to be hit."

In due course, Siegel was hit.

Luciano had taken up residence in Cuba with two passports (the extra was in case one was taken from him) made out in his real name, Salvatore Lucania, but his presence in Cuba could not be kept secret for long and he was soon found out. It was Luciano's belief that Genovese had tipped off the U.S. government. Finally, the Cuban government, despite its gambling operation arrangements with the mob, was forced to make Luciano return to Italy. The crime leader's dream of returning to the United States was permanently shattered, and slowly over the years his influence over criminal matters in America waned.

Hawthorne Inn Capone's Cicero headquarters

Located at 4833 22nd Street, the Hawthorne Inn was the Capone headquarters in Cicero, Ill. A two-story structure of brown brick with white tiles set in the upper face, it was completely redone on Capone's orders. Bulletproof steel shutters were affixed to every window, armed guards were posted at every entrance and the entire second floor was refurbished for Capone's private use. Eventually, the Hawthorne Inn was a regular stop for sightseeing buses, whose conductors referred to it as the Capone Castle.

On September 20, 1926 it almost became Capone's tomb. Eleven automobiles packed with gangsters loyal to Hymie Weiss, the successor to Capone's late rival and assassination victim Dion O'Banion, drove slowly past the inn and fired more than 1,000 bullets at the building, as shoppers and lunch-tour promenaders screamed and ducked for cover. Capone, eating in the restaurant on the ground floor, was raising a cup of coffee to his lips when the Thompson submachine guns began blasting. He was saved by a quick-thinking bodyguard, Frankie Rio, who knocked him to the floor. After the attack bullet holes were found in 35 automobiles parked at the curb. Inside the inn, doors and woodwork were splintered, plate glass and mirrors shattered, plaster torn from the walls and office, and lobby furniture ripped apart.

Mrs. Clyde Freeman, sitting with her infant son in a car that took 30 bullets, was hit by a shot that plowed a furrow across her forehead and injured her eyes. Capone paid doctors $5,000 to save the woman's sight.

Capone refused to name any suspects in the shooting, but he told reporters: "Watch the morgue. They'll show up there." Twenty days later Hymie Weiss turned up at the morgue.

Haymarket affair terrorist bombing

One of the most tragic instances of labor turmoil in this country was the Haymarket affair in Chicago on May 4, 1886. Fifteen thousand workers jammed Haymarket Square in a rally to demand shorter work hours, con-

demn police brutality and protest the killing of a worker four days earlier in a strike-breaking battle at the McCormick-Harvester plant. Suddenly, as Samuel Fielden, a 40-year-old teamster who had immigrated to the United States from England, was speaking, 180 police officers appeared and one of the officers in charge said, "In the name of the people of the State of Illinois, I command this meeting immediately and peaceably to disperse."

Fielden responded, "We are peaceable."

As he and other speakers began to descend from the truck wagon being used as a podium, a dynamite bomb flew through the air and exploded in front of the police. Several fell. The police re-formed and started firing. Those workers who had guns fired back. In all, seven policemen and two civilians died, and 130 others were wounded.

The public uproar against anarchists and Reds was instant and widespread. The color red was cut out of street signs, and the press all around the country attacked anarchists, socialists and aliens, especially Germans since most of the speakers were German.

Nine men, most of them speakers at the rally, were indicted for murder; they were Albert Parsons, Samuel Fielden, Michael Schwab, August Spies, Adolph Fischer, Oscar Neebe, George Engel, Louis Lingg, who was charged with making the bomb, and Rudolph Schnaubelt, who was reported to have thrown it. Parsons and Schnaubelt disappeared before the trial opened; the latter was believed to have gone back to his native Germany.

When the trial began on June 21, 1886, Parsons, who had been in hiding in Wisconsin, walked into the courtroom and sat down with the other defendants. A veteran of the Confederate Army from Alabama, he had long alienated his socially prominent family by embracing radical causes. He later explained his reappearance by saying, "They will kill me, but I could not bear to be at liberty, knowing that my comrades were here and were to suffer for something of which they were as innocent as I."

With the aid of the prosecution, Judge Joseph Eaton Gary refused to bar from the jury one individual who had a relative among the dead policeman and another who had been a close friend of one of the officers. The strategy was to force the defense to use up its challenges on such potential jurors and then it would be forced to take whomever was offered. The jurors selected were all either businessmen or white-collar workers; none was an industrial worker.

The prosecution's case was exceptionally weak. It presented no evidence concerning who had thrown the bomb, nor did it connect the unknown bomb thrower to any of the speakers at the rally. Amazingly, Judge

Gary ruled that it was not necessary for the prosecution to identify the bomb-thrower or even to prove that the murderer had been influenced by the anarchist beliefs of the defendants.

All the defendants were found guilty. Neebe was sentenced to 15 years imprisonment and the remaining eight, including the disappeared Schnaubelt, were sentenced to death. The verdict was hailed throughout Chicago and the nation, although not in foreign countries and U.S. labor circles. But with delays in the execution, public opinion started to shift and pressures for a commutation began building. Finally, Fielden and Schwab's sentences were reduced to life imprisonment, but the other five were still scheduled to hang.

The day before the executions Louis Lingg placed a small bomb in his mouth and blew off half his face, dying six and a half hours later. The next day the remaining four, Parsons, Engel, Fischer and Spies, died on the scaffold. They shouted anarchist slogans, and Parsons said: "Will I be allowed to speak, O men of America? Let me speak, Sheriff Matson! Let the voice of the people be heard!" The executioner at that moment sprang the trap.

In 1892 John P. Altgeld, a wealthy property owner, was elected governor of Illinois. He ordered a complete study made of the Haymarket affair and trial and then condemned Judge Gary for unfairness. He pardoned the three defendants still alive, Fielden, Schwab and Neebe, declaring them and their executed comrades innocent. Altgeld was severely criticized for his act by most newspapers, many of which pointed to his own German birth. Earning the sobriquet of John "Pardon" Altgeld, his political career was wrecked.

Perhaps the real vindication of the wrongfully hanged men came in the next century, when labor finally achieved the prime objective of the Haymarket rally—the eight-hour day.

See also: JOHN P. ALTGELD.

Haynes, Richard "Racehorse" (1923–) defense attorney

Without a doubt, the most colorful defense lawyer practicing today is a square-jawed Texan named Richard "Racehorse" Haynes. Nothing quite like him has been seen in a courtroom since the days of such legendary figures as Bill Fallon, Clarence Darrow or Moman Pruiett. If anything, he may be more successful than all of them. Noted for his lurid defenses in murder trials, which are generally marked by some very rich defendants on one side and some very damning evidence on the other, Racehorse, who was given the nickname by his high school football coach for his moves on the field, is now regarded by many as America's premier criminal

defender. In any event, he may well be the highest paid. Based in Houston, Haynes does not reveal his fees, but at least two of his cases supposedly commanded million-dollar sums. Randolph Hearst for a time considered employing Haynes to defend his daughter Patty but settled on F. Lee Bailey, in part, it is believed, because Bailey's charges were much lower.

Haynes insists he is "worth every dollar" he charges. With a smile he says, "What's money when you're faced with spending 25 years to life in the Crossbar Hotel?"

Few deny that Haynes is now "the best lawyer money can buy," but a prosecutor who has dueled with him in the courtroom is less than enthused, commenting: "He's good, he's very good. But on account of him, there are a couple dozen people walking free in Texas who wouldn't blink before blowing somebody's head off. He's a menace to society."

Haynes' response is the one always used by defense attorneys: "I sleep fine at night. It isn't my job to be judge and jury, but to do the best I can on behalf of the citizen accused."

Texas citizens successfully defended by him have included the late Dr. John Hill, the defendant in the Houston case made famous by the best-selling book *Blood and Money,* and oilman T. Cullen Davis, the richest man in America ever tried for murder. Davis was charged with staging a shooting spree in his $6 million family mansion during which his 12-year-old stepdaughter and his wife's lover were killed, his estranged wife was severely wounded and a family friend was crippled. Despite the fact that three eyewitnesses named Davis as the killer, Haynes won an acquittal for him, with the jury deliberating a mere four hours. Later, Haynes' client beat additional charges, considered ironclad by the prosecution, and left court a free man.

While Haynes is regarded as a master of the theatrical defense, the fact is he solidly grounds his cases in scientific analysis and often can pick apart prosecution testimony on ballistics, pathology, stains, hair and other supposedly damning evidence. Haynes was involved in the first case allegedly solved by the use of nuclear techniques. In that case scientists had analyzed the hairs of a dead woman by nuclear activation and linked the victim's strangle murder to an aircraft mechanic. The scientists were awarded medals for their accomplishment, but at the subsequent trial Haynes proceeded to debunk their findings and got the judge to bar the evidence as failing to meet the court's standards for scientific proof. As a result, the jury ended up voting nine to three for acquittal.

Another Haynes' feat still commands awe in Texas legal circles. He defended a man accused of battering a woman to death with a replica of a sword and spiked-ball and chain. Although his client had confessed and signed a statement and blood on his clothes matched the type of the victim, Haynes produced a hung jury at the first trial and won an acquittal at the second.

The key to most of Haynes' defenses revolves around jury selection. "I can usually raise real doubt in the minds of at least a couple of jurors if I've picked the jury right." Haynes uses social scientists and psychologists to profile the ideal juror in any given case. In the first Cullen Davis trial, he spent $30,000 for a jury study and utilized the services of a Ph.D. in psychology when making the actual jury selections.

In 1971 Haynes won freedom for two Houston police officers accused of violating the civil rights of a black man by kicking him to death in the station house. They had arrested the man for "stealing" a car that turned out to be his own. The lawyer got the trial moved out of Houston to New Braunfels, Tex., a conservative German-American community. "I knew we had that case won when we seated the last bigot on the jury," he told a reporter at the end of the trial.

Haynes takes no more than 15 percent of the cases brought to him, often basing his selection on the degree of challenge they offer. The high fees he commands allow him to take other cases at no charge. He once won freedom for a motorcycle gang accused of punishing an errant female member by nailing her to a tree. A typical Haynes case is far from the Perry Mason variety, in which a dramatic last-minute act of deduction frees the defendant. "My clients admit they pulled the trigger, plunged the knife, swung the club," he says. "I have to show why, because sometimes the pulling, plugging or swinging was justified. When all else fails, I just ask the jury for mercy. They usually oblige me."

A Haynes defense seldom relies on a single factor to sway a jury. He tends to develop several possible scenarios for a jury to pick from, and in his summation he follows the argument he feels has the best chance of

Charles Moyers, Big Bill Haywood and George Pettibone (left to right) were acquitted of conspiracy in the bomb assassination of former Idaho governor Frank Steunenberg.

working. Haynes once outlined his defense strategy for an American Bar Association seminar in New York. "Say you sue me because you say my dog bit you. Well, now this is my defense: my dog doesn't bite. And second, in the alternative, my dog was tied up that night. And third, I don't believe you really got bit. And fourth, I don't have a dog."

Haywood, William D. "Big Bill" (1869–1928) radical and labor leader

Big Bill Haywood, a leader of the radical labor movement during the most turbulent era in the history of American unions, was tried for murder in a case considered to be the most important judicial confrontation between capital and labor in this country.

Haywood, a miner, cowboy and homesteader in his youth, joined the Western Federation of Miners in 1896 and quickly rose to position among the nation's union leaders. In 1905 former governor Frank Steunenberg was assassinated by a bomb. The confessed assassin, Harry Orchard, insisted he was carrying out Haywood's orders, as he said he had done in many previous acts of terrorism and murder. In a 1906–07 trial Haywood was charged with two others, Charles H. Moyers and George A. Pettibone, of conspiring in the bomb assassination. The 78-day courtroom drama had numerous stars: besides Haywood and Orchard, there were Clarence Darrow, the defense attorney, and future Senator William E. Borah, prosecutor. The state's case was that Steunenberg had been murdered in retaliation for his antilabor actions during a strike in the Coeur d'Alene mines. Considered a classic today, Darrow's defense shredded the prosecution's case of any supporting evidence other than Orchard's confession, which had been written with the assistance of the Pinkertons. In his summary, Darrow conducted a eulogy on the righteousness of labor as opposed to the evils of capitalism. The defendants were acquitted.

From 1905 to 1917 Haywood remained the most charismatic labor leader in America and had a devoted following. He was arrested in the 1917 Palmer Raids and convicted of sedition, a vague charge most legal scholars agree would never be upheld today. He was sentenced to Leavenworth Penitentiary but on appeal was released on $30,000 bail. Haywood jumped bail and fled to Soviet Russia in 1921. He spent his last few years lonely and sick in Moscow, where on May 18, 1928, after a party at the home of foreign correspondent Eugene Lyons, he died.

See also: CLARENCE DARROW, JAMES MCPARLAND, HARRY ORCHARD, PALMER RAIDS, PINKERTON'S NATIONAL DETECTIVE AGENCY, FRANK STEUNENBERG.

Hearst, Patricia (1955–) kidnap victim

Few crimes in recent history were as sensational and involved as many bizarre twists as the kidnapping of Patricia Hearst, who was taken from her Berkeley, Calif. apartment on February 5, 1974 by members of the Symbionese Liberation Army (SLA), a radical terrorist organization.

At first, the kidnappers offered to return the 19-year-old heiress if her father, newspaper publisher Randolph Hearst, would start a food program for the poor in the San Francisco Bay area. Later, however, a tape-recorded message from Patty said she had "chosen to stay and fight" with the SLA for the "freedom of the oppressed people." She adopted the SLA name of "Tania" and was subsequently linked to the armed robbery of a San Francisco bank on April 15. Hearst refused to believe his daughter was acting of her own free will, but photographs of the bank robbery and reports by eyewitnesses indicated she "absolutely was a participant." In later tapes sent by the SLA, Patty ridiculed the idea that she had been brainwashed.

Meanwhile, law enforcement authorities pressed their hunt for the handful of SLA members and cornered six of them in a Los Angeles hideout on May 17. All six including Donald DeFreeze, alias "Field Marshal Cinque," the alleged leader of the group died in an ensuing gun battle and fire. Actually, subsequent evidence indicated the real leaders were a dynamic female trio Patricia Soltysik, Nancy Ling Perry and Camilla Hall, all of whom perished with guns in their hands during the desperate shoot-out. Fears that Patty was among the dead proved unfounded, and although she was still missing, she was indicted on a charge of bank robbery.

Finally, 19 months after her original kidnapping, Patty Hearst was captured in a hideout in San Francisco. With her was 32-year-old Wendy Yoshimura, who had joined her after she had gone into hiding. The hunt ended with Patty telling FBI agents, "Don't shoot. I'll go with you." Just an hour earlier agents had arrested William and Emily Harris, the last remaining members of the SLA group that originally seized Patty.

At Patty's trial, defense attorney F. Lee Bailey stressed the brutality of the kidnapping by the SLA and claimed she had endured hardships and constant terrorization during her captivity. He argued the bank robbery had been staged by the SLA just to make Patty believe she could not return to society. The lawyer also said that DeFreeze had familiarity with brainwashing techniques and "knew just enough about this process to start it moving" on "a particularly vulnerable, frightened 19-year-old girl."

In her own testimony Patty said her early treatment by her abductors had included a number of death threats. She insisted she had been forced to have sexual intercourse with DeFreeze and another SLA member, William Wolfe. The prosecution presented psychiatric testimony to refute any contention that Patty had been anything but a "voluntary member of the SLA." Dr. Joel Fort cast doubt on her tale of sexual abuse while with the SLA, noting that she had been "sexually active at age 15," and Dr. Harry Kozol described her at the time of her kidnapping as a "rebel in search of a cause."

Patty Hearst was found guilty of the bank robbery charge and sentenced to seven years imprisonment. She served a total of 28 months, including time in prison before and after her trial. William and Emily Harris were given 10 years to life for the kidnapping.

When Patty Hearst was released, she married and settled into what was described as a very establishment lifestyle.

See also: DOROTHY ALLISON, F. LEE BAILEY, WILLIAM AND EMILY HARRIS.

Heath, John   See BISBEE MASSACRE.

Hecht, Ben (1894–1964) crime reporter

Many of the fascinating facts that typified novelist and playwright Ben Hecht's writing were drawn from his earlier experiences as a Chicago crime reporter. He started out as what was called a "picture chaser" for the *Chicago Journal,* assigned to acquire, by any means possible, photographs of ax murderers and the like and their victims, sometimes pilfering them from the family mantelpiece. Before long he advanced to reporter, which in the Chicago journalism of the day did not require an undue concern for accuracy.

Hecht became expert at writing stories that began, e.g., "If Fred Ludwig is hanged for the murder of his wife, Irma, it will be because of the little gold band he slipped on her finger on his wedding day, inscribed with the tender words, 'Irma—Love Forever—Fred.'"

If Hecht and his favorite crony, Charles MacArthur of the rival *Examiner* and later the *Daily News,* sometimes purpled their facts, they also solved many a case that had the police stumped. It was basically Hecht who cracked Chicago's famed Case of the Ragged Stranger, in which a pregnant woman named Mrs. Ruth Wanderer was shot by a ragged stranger as she and her husband were returning from a movie the night of June 21, 1920. At the time, her husband, Carl, according to his statement, was carrying the Colt .45 service automatic that he had kept upon discharge from the army after World War I, and he blazed back at the attacker. A total of 14 shots were fired, and when the smoke cleared, Mrs. Wanderer was dead and so was the ragged stranger. Only Carl Wanderer was unscathed.

Wanderer was celebrated in the press and by a public fearful about the rise in violent crime. But Hecht and MacArthur both were skeptical. MacArthur traced the gun found on the ragged stranger back to a relative of Carl Wanderer's. That man, a cousin, had given it to Wanderer. Hecht in the meantime befriended Wanderer and learned much of his private life, including that he was a homosexual who was appalled at the thought of being father to a woman's baby. When Hecht found letters Wanderer had written to a male lover, the husband confessed he had tricked an unidentified stranger, whom he had met in a skid row bar, into waiting in the vestibule for him. When he and his wife arrived, Wanderer pulled two guns and opened up on both his wife and the stranger.

Ironically, the two reporters spent much time with Wanderer in the death house at the Cook County Jail, playing cards with him (and winning his money), and prevailed upon him to read attacks on their city editors as his last words on the gallows. The reporters forgot that a condemned man is bound hand and foot when hanged. At his execution Wanderer could only glance unavailing at the speeches strapped to his side. Shrugging at the reporters, he did the next best thing he could think of, bursting forth in a rollicking version of "Dear Old Pal O' Mine."

After the trap was sprung, MacArthur turned to Hecht and said, "You know, Ben, that son of a bitch should have been a song plugger."

Even after Hecht went on to bigger and better things as an author, playwright and screenwriter, his Chicago crime-writing days came back to haunt him. In Hollywood during the early 1930s Hecht wrote the screenplay for *Scarface,* starring Paul Muni, for Howard Hughes' studio. One night there was a knock at his hotel room in Los Angeles, and two sinister-looking gentlemen confronted him with a copy of the screenplay.

"You the guy who wrote this?" one said, brandishing the script.

Hecht couldn't deny it.

"Is this stuff about Al Capone?"

"God, no!" Hecht assured them. "I don't even know Al." He rattled off the names of Chicago underworld characters he had known—Big Jim Colosimo, Dion O'Banion, Hymie Weiss.

His visitors seemed satisfied, one saying: "O.K. then. We'll tell Al this stuff you wrote is about them other guys." As they started to leave, however, the other one had a thought. "If this stuff isn't about Al Capone, why are you calling it *Scarface?* Everybody'll think it's him."

"That's the reason. Al is one of the most famous and fascinating men of our time. If you call the movie *Scarface,* everybody will want to see it, figuring it's about Al. That's part of the racket we call showmanship."

"I'll tell Al. Who's this fella Howard Hughes?"

"He got nothing to do with it. He's the sucker with the money."

"O.K. The hell with him." And Capone's men left placated.

Hedgepeth, Marion (?–1910) outlaw

Marion Hedgepeth did not have the look, or the name, of a Western outlaw, but, as Robert Pinkerton noted, "He was one of the really bad men of the West." Immaculately dressed (his "Wanted" posters observed that his shoes were usually well polished) in a well-cut suit and topcoat with his hair slicked down under a bowler hat, Hedgepeth often looked like easy pickings to other gunfighters. But he was exceedingly fast on the draw, once killing a foe who already had his gun out before Hedgepeth even started to draw.

Not much is known about Hedgepeth's early life except that he ran away from his Missouri home in his mid-teens and became a cowboy in Wyoming and a holdup man in Colorado during the 1880s. He killed men in both states. By 1890 he was the leader of a small band of train robbers known as the Hedgepeth Four. The other members of the group, all daring and cunning killers, were Albert D. Sly, Lucius Wilson and James Francis, better known as "Illinois Jimmy." They pulled their first train job in Nebraska, netting only $1,000, but a week later, they knocked off a train in Wisconsin and got away with $5,000. Eventually, the gang made its biggest score in a train robbery at Glendale, Mo., making off with $50,000. Hedgepeth became something of a new folk hero in the area, which was Jesse James' old stamping grounds.

The gang scattered after that hit, but the Pinkertons eventually ran Hedgepeth to earth in San Francisco in 1893 and brought him back to Missouri for trial. The dapper outlaw became the toast of St. Louis, and dour-faced lawmen were forced to fill his cell with flowers sent by feminine well-wishers. His popularity with women did not prevent him from being found guilty and drawing a 25-year prison term.

While awaiting transfer to the penitentiary, Hedgepeth shared a cell with a man called H. H. Holmes, whose real name was Herman Webster Mudgett. Holmes was being held on a swindling charge, but what was not known then was that he was also the worst killer of women in America's history. In his "murder castle" in Chicago he may well have killed 200 women, collecting on the insurance policies and obtaining the dowries of many of them. Holmes offered Hedgepeth $500 if he could put him in touch with a "shrewd lawyer." Hedgepeth did and Holmes was eventually sprung from jail, but not before he had made some incriminating statements to Hedgepeth. The outlaw might have kept Holmes' secrets had he gotten the $500 promised him, but Holmes, no spendthrift, never paid him the money. Hedgepeth wrote a letter to the St. Louis police chief in which he exposed an insurance plot in Philadelphia that Holmes was involved in. The authorities checked on it and discovered Holmes had killed a man named Herman Pitezel there. They took Holmes into custody and then discovered his wholesale murders in Chicago.

Meanwhile, Hedgepeth was sent to the pentitentiary. For 12 years committees, most composed of women, mounted efforts to win his freedom, pointing out he was a "friend of society" because his actions had resulted in the capture of the terrible woman killer Holmes. Finally, Hedgepeth was pardoned in 1906.

A happy Hedgepeth said he was going to live an honest life thereafter and went to Nebraska, where he immediately started blowing safes. He was caught in 1907 and got 10 years but was released after doing less than two. In late 1908 he formed a new gang, but they were a pale imitation of the old Hedgepeth Four. After a few minor jobs the outlaw pulled out and went on his own. By this time he was suffering from the ravages of tuberculosis, however, and no longer resembled the old bandit dandy. On January 1, 1910 he walked into a bar in Chicago and threatened the bartender with a six-gun while he proceeded to clean out the cash register. A passing policeman saw him through the window and rushed in with pistol drawn.

The officer shouted, "Surrender!"

Hedgepeth coughed and replied, "Never!"

Both fired at the same time. Hedgepeth, weakened by his illness, missed, probably for the first time in his life. The policeman's shot caught Hedgepeth in the chest and spun him around. Hedgepeth fell to his knees, raised his gun by instinct and, holding it with both hands, fired again. A bullet went through the officer's coat. Hedgepeth died still firing his weapon.

See also: H. H. HOLMES.

Heinrich, Edward Oscar (1881–1953) criminologist

Known by the press as the "Edison of crime detection," Edward O. Heinrich trailblazed in the use of scientific methods in criminal detection. A criminologist in private practice and a lecturer on the subject at the University of California at Berkeley, he was utilized by police departments all over the country. Over a 45-year career, he was credited with solving 2,000 major and minor mysteries. He did so by being a master of all trades; he was a geologist, a physicist, a handwriting expert, an authority on inks and papers, and a biochemist. He was fond of saying that no criminal ever departs the scene of his crime without leaving several clues and that it was up to a scientific investigator to find and interpret them correctly. He proved a number of alleged suicides to be murders and a number of suspected murders to be suicides or accidents. His work in the investigation of the 1916 Black Tom explosion, which he was able to lay at the door of a German sabotage ring, brought him considerable fame, as did his presentation of scientific evidence in the bestial sex murder involved in the Fatty Arbuckle case.

Probably his most famous case, because it demonstrated his deductive powers so well, was the attempted robbery of a 1923 Southern Pacific Railroad mail train and the resultant quadruple murders. On October 11 the train with its coaches filled with passengers was moving slowly through a tunnel in the Siskiyou Mountains of southern Oregon when two men armed with shotguns climbed over the tender and ordered the engineer and fireman to halt as soon as the engine, tender and next car, the mail car, cleared the tunnel. They followed instructions and watched helplessly as a third man appeared outside the tunnel with a bulky package, which he carried to the side of the mail car. Running back to a detonator, the man set off an enormous explosion. The mail car and its contents were consumed in flames, which obviously ruined the robbery attempt. It also incinerated the lone mail clerk inside the car. Before the trio left, they cold-bloodedly shot down the engineer, fireman and a brakeman who had come forward through the tunnel to investigate the explosion.

The attempted train robbery, reminiscent of the Wild West days, became front-page news as railroad police, postal detectives, sheriff's deputies and other lawmen converged on the scene. Posses set out to track the bandits but came up empty. All that was found was a detonator with batteries, a revolver, a pair of well-worn and greasy blue denim overalls and some shoe covers made of gunnysack soaked in creosote, apparently to keep pursuing dogs off the criminals' scent.

As days and weeks passed with no discernible leads, the authorities asked Heinrich to help. He was sent the overalls for examination with information that a garage mechanic who worked not far from the tunnel had been taken into custody because his work clothes appeared to have the same greasy stains. Heinrich started out with a magnifying glass and microcopic examination of the garment and its "contents," such as scrapings of the grease stains and lint and other tiny items from the pockets.

The first thing he discovered was that the garage mechanic should be released. "The stains are not auto grease," he said, referring to the overalls from the scene of the crime. "They're pitch from fir trees." Then he went on to stun detectives with a full description of the man they sought: he was a left-handed lumberjack who'd worked the logging camps of the Pacific Northwest. He was thin, had light brown hair, rolled his own cigarettes and was fussy about his appearance. He was 5 feet 10 and was in his early twenties.

All of Heinrich's conclusions were backed up with solid evidence that he had "properly interpreted." He had quickly identified the grease as being fir stains, and in the pockets of the overalls he had found bits of Douglas fir needles, common to the forests of the Pacific Northwest. The pockets on the left side of the overalls were more heavily worn than those on the right. In addition, the garment was regularly buttoned from the left side. Therefore, the wearer obviously was left-handed. From the hem of a pocket, Heinrich extracted several carefully cut fingernail trimmings. Such manicuring was somewhat incongruous for a lumberjack unless he was fastidious about his appearance. The scientist found a single strand of light brown hair clinging to one button. More than merely determining the suspect's hair coloring, however, Heinrich used his own techniques to make a close estimate of the man's age. Heinrich also found one other clue, which other investigators had totally overlooked. Using a delicate forceps, he was able to dig out from the hem of the narrow pencil pocket a tiny wad of paper, apparently rammed down inadvertently with a pencil. The paper appeared to have gone through a number of washings with the overalls and was blurred beyond all legibility, but by treating it with iodine vapor, Heinrich was able to identify it as a registered-mail receipt and establish its number.

The receipt was traced to one Roy d'Autremont of Eugene, Ore. In Eugene authorities found Roy's father, who, it turned out, was worried about his twin sons, Roy and Ray, and another son, Hugh, who had all disappeared on October 11, the date of the train holdup. Inquiries about Roy showed he was left-handed, rolled his own tobacco (confirming Heinrich's findings of tobacco samples) and was known to be fussy about his appearance. Authorities later said Heinrich had virtually furnished them with a photograph of the suspect.

Following Heinrich's cracking of the mystery, one of the most intensive manhunts in American history was launched. Circulars were printed in 100 languages and sent to police departments throughout the world. Records of the men's medical histories, dental charts and eye prescriptions were supplied to doctors, dentists and oculists. Finally, three years and six months after the crime, Hugh d'Autremont was captured in Manila, the Philippines. In April the twins were found working in a steel mill in Steubenville, Ohio under the name of Goodwin. All three were convicted and given life imprisonment.

Edward Heinrich returned to his laboratory, where he continued to supply his expertise to police forces faced with baffling crimes until his death in 1953.

Heirens, William (1929–) murderer

Beginning at the age of nine, William Heirens committed hundreds of thefts, most often slipping into women's bedrooms and stealing their underthings, which he would later fondle in his room. He dressed in women's clothing and stared at pictures of Nazi leaders for hours. At the age of 13 he was arrested on a charge of carrying a loaded pistol. In his home police found an impressive arsenal of weapons. Heirens was sent to private corrections home. Since he was an above-average student, he was enrolled in Chicago University at the age of 16. But he continued to commit burglaries.

In March 1945 he disturbed a sleeping woman, Mrs. Josephine Ross, slit her throat and stabbed her several times. Three months later, another victim saw him, but he merely knocked her out. In October he killed Frances Brown, shooting her twice and stabbing her. Her body was draped over the tub in the bathroom; the top part of her pajamas was around her neck and a long bread-knife was stuck in her neck just below the left ear.

Young Heirens knew he was being overwhelmed by madness. On the wall of Miss Brown's living room, he scrawled in bright red lipstick: "For heavens sake catch me before I kill more I cannot control myself."

Unfortunately, the police did not catch William Heirens until after he committed his most shocking crime, kidnapping six-year-old Suzanne Degnan from her home and slaughtering her in January 1946. He dismembered the body and scattered the parts in Chicago sewers.

While his killings were gory almost beyond description, he had always cleaned the blood off his victim's body. Both Miss Brown and Mrs. Ross had been washed clean. The parts of the child, which were found inside bags, had also been immaculately washed.

Heirens was caught the following June 26 by a caretaker and a tenant in an apartment complex he was trying to enter. For a time he denied the killings, insisting they had been done by one George Murman, who psychiatrists discovered was his alter ego. Even when Heirens made a full confession, he seemed less remorseful about the murders than the fact that his school grades were only average. "I should have been a 'B' level student," he said, "but my grades slipped due to my messing around and cutting up."

Judged insane, Heirens was sentenced to three consecutive life terms with a provision that he never be paroled.

Heitler, Mike "de Pike" (?–1931) brothel keeper and murder victim

A wizened, ageless brothel keeper who looked something like a Surinam toad, Mike "de Pike" Heitler could be described as Chicago's "grand old man" of merchandised vice, with a career that spanned about half a century.

Heitler got his nickname de Pike, from the fact that he ran the cheapest fancy house in Illinois and hence was a piker. But Mike actually prided himself on being the first to introduce modern assembly line methods in the world's oldest profession. He operated a 50¢ house at Peoria and West Madison. The customers stood in line at the foot of the stairs and handed Mike half a dollar, which he rang up on a cash register. When a girl came downstairs with a satisfied customer, Mike gave her a brass check that she could redeem for two bits, and then the man at the head of the line took her back upstairs.

Helping de Pike keep the traffic moving was another quaint character, Charlie "Monkey Face" Genker. Monkey Face would scurry up the doors of Heitler's houses and poke his homely face through the transom to urge the prostitute and her customer to hurry up. The sudden appearance of that monkey face proved disconcerting to many customers, and the more knowledgeable regulars would go through their paces quickly in hope of beating Genker to the punch.

Heitler operated with certain peacefulness for many years, aside from an occasional arrest and conviction for white slavery, but he lost much of his personal clout when Al Capone tightened his hold on the entire prostitution racket in Chicago and the surrounding area. Heitler's choice was either to come in as a paid employee or simply be declared "out." Through the 1920s his position continued to deteriorate as Capone turned more to Harry Guzik to look after prostitution operations. Smarting over this lack of respect, which he considered his due, Heitler took to informing on other Capone activities.

He told Judge John H. Lyle about the mob's part-time headquarters in a resort called the Four Deuces. As recounted in *The Dry and Lawless Years*, Heitler told the judge:

> They snatch guys they want information from and take them to the cellar. They're tortured until they talk. Then they're rubbed out. The bodies are hauled through a tunnel into a trap door opening in the back

of the building. Capone and his boys put the bodies in cars and then they're dumped out on a country road, or maybe in a clay hole or rock quarry.

Heitler made the mistake of passing on information to others who evidently were not as hostile toward Capone as he assumed. He wrote an anonymous letter to the state attorney's office revealing many secrets about the Capone brothel empire. Not long afterward, the letter turned up on Capone's desk. Heitler was summoned to appear before the mob leader at his office in the Lexington Hotel. Capone insisted only Heitler could have imparted the specific information and told him, "You're through."

Still, Heitler continued to write letters. In one, which he gave to his daughter, he named eight Capone figures as being responsible for the murder of *Chicago Tribune* reporter Jake Lingle. Unfortunately for Heitler, he apparently gave another copy of the letter to the wrong people and on April 30, 1931 his charred remains were found in the smoldering wreckage of a suburban house.

Hellier, Thomas (?–1678) murderer

Long before Nat Turner's 1831 slave uprising, a bonded white man struck fear into the hearts of Virginians by killing his masters. Because of his act, he later became, in a manner of speaking, a local tourist attraction.

A lifelong troublemaker and thief, Hellier was finally sold into bondage in early 1678. He passed from one owner to the other, eventually becoming the property of a gentleman farmer named Cutbeard Williamson, who had a plantation appropriately dubbed Hard Labour. The place was true to its name, Hellier discovered, and in a fit of vengeance he entered his master's mansion late one night and axed to death Williamson and his wife and the couple's maid.

Hellier fled but was soon captured by other farmers. He was hanged on August 5, 1678 at Westover, Va., and his body was chained to a giant tree that overlooked the James River, to be viewed not only by all travelers on the waterway but, most important, by other bonded servants being barged upriver. The body remained a gruesome sight for a number of years until it deteriorated completely.

Hell's Kitchen New York crime area

Hell's Kitchen, known for a time as New York City's most crime-ridden area, was originally a notorious pre–Civil War dive, but after that conflict the name was applied to a large area to the north and south of 34th Street west of Eighth Avenue. The dominant gang of the area was the original Hell's Kitchen Gang, bossed by one of the true ruffians of the late 1860s and 1870s, Dutch Heinrichs. According to one contemporary account, Heinrichs and his toughs exacted tribute from every merchant and factory owner in the district. The gang thought nothing of breaking into private houses in broad daylight and beating and robbing pedestrians at will. About 1870 Heinrichs absorbed the Tenth Avenue Gang led by Ike Marsh, the mastermind of New York City's first train robbery, and quickly grasped the wisdom of raiding the railroads. Thereafter, much of the gang's activities focused on looting the Hudson River Railroad yards and depot on 30th Street.

The railroad hired its own detectives to try to curb the gang's activities. When that action proved insufficient, it began to pay bounties to police officers for each arrest of a Hell's Kitchen gangster. Under this steady harassment, Heinrichs was finally sent to prison for five years. Even though the power of the original Hell's Kitchen Gang eventually waned, the area remained a stronghold of other gangs well into the 20th century. Only the advent of Prohibition caused these gangs to lose their distinctive neighborhood character, as they spread their activities over more of the city.

See also: TENTH AVENUE GANG.

Helm, Boone (1824–1864) killer and vigilante victim

The tales told about Boone Helm describe him as one of the grisliest and most depraved killers ever to set foot on the Western scene. Among his multitude of crimes, he once killed a companion as they crossed the mountains in deep snow and then ate his flesh. When drunk he could be coaxed to talk about it and he would freely admit the act. "You don't think I was damned fool enough to starve to death, do you?" he would snarl. While the vigilantes of the 1860s would later receive considerable criticism for being "excessive" in their hanging, there was never a harsh word said about their elimination of Helm.

A vacant-faced Missourian who somehow inspired fear just by the way he could look at a person, Helm committed his first murder at the age of 27, stabbing a man to death in a drunken dispute. Deserting his wife and young daughter, Helm fled to Indian Territory in the vicinity of what is now Oklahoma, where he was captured and returned to Missouri. His trial was postponed three times because of the difficulty of finding material witnesses. Helm claimed he had acted in self-defense and wondered out loud how the witnesses against him would feel when he was acquitted. The three main witnesses apparently gave some thought to this prospect and finally decided that they hadn't seen a thing.

Deserting his family a second time, Helm next turned up in Oregon, where, despite an unsavory record of violence, he was hired by Elijah Burton to guide a small party through the mountains to Salt Lake City. The trek was disastrous, as Helm was anything but a competent guide. Along the way, members of the group dropped out to await warmer weather, but Burton himself pressed on with Helm, not realizing he would be killed and eaten by his scout. When Helm arrived in Salt Lake City, he looked rather well fed. He did not remain there long enough for firm suspicion to be established against him, however. After killing a gambler in a particularly brutal fashion, he was driven out of town.

Nothing was heard from Helm until he turned up on San Francisco, where he slaughtered a customer in a brothel parlor who had insisted he should be served before Helm. The eager lover was hacked to death with a variety of hatchet and bowie knife blows, causing the establishment's madam to complain that her parlor looked like a butcher shop. Helm committed his next murder in Idaho and then drifted into Canada, where the law became suspicious of him after he had gone trapping with a man named Angus McPherson and returned alone with a rich load of furs. However, since nobody could be found, the authorities were forced to release him. Helm was then escorted to the Montana border.

In Montana he joined up with Henry Plummer's murderous gang of road agent killers known as the Innocents. Helm became one of Sheriff Plummer's deadliest gunmen and was probably responsible for a dozen slayings. When the vigilantes finally rode against the Innocents, one of their main targets was, of course, Helm. Captured on the morning of January 14, 1864, he was hanged along with four others that same afternoon. Helm had never shown any pity for his victims and showed none for himself. "I have looked at death in all forms and I am not afraid to die," he said. He scorned those of his companions who pleaded for mercy. As George Lane swung from the gallows, he commented, "There's one gone to hell." When Jack Gallagher strangled to death, he called out: "Kick away, old fellow. My turn next. I'll be in hell with you in a minute!"

Helm, Jack (c. 1838–1873) lawman and murderer

A captain of the Texas state police and sheriff of DeWitt County, Jack Helm has been called "the most cold-blooded murderer ever to wear a badge." The contention is debatable, but there is no question that killings happened fast when he was around.

The facts about Helm's early life are hazy, but he fought on the side of the Confederacy and, during that conflict, killed a black man on the spot for whistling a Yankee tune. In the early 1870s Helm was a captain in the Texas state police and commanded a force, official and unofficial, of 200 men, whom he involved on the side of the Suttons in the bloody Sutton-Taylor feud that engulfed DeWitt County. In 1873 Helm's men arrested two Taylor supporters, brothers Bill and Henry Kelley, on a minor charge of disturbing the peace, but the two captives never reached town. Their bodies, riddled with bullets, were found in a clearing near their ranch. Helm's deputies said they had been shot trying to escape, while Helm said he hadn't seen a thing. Because of the furor the newspapers raised, Gov. E. J. Davis dismissed Helm from the state police force, but he remained sheriff of DeWitt County.

Helm might have continued as the biggest gun in the Sutton-Taylor feud but for the appearance in 1873 of John Wesley Hardin. Wes Hardin was distantly related to the Taylor clan but close enough to join in the killing. He shot down Helm's deputy and almost got Helm on a couple of occasions. The sheriff apparently saw the handwriting on the wall and tried to negotiate a truce. One armistice meeting ended in a free-for-all that left two Sutton men dead. In another one, held in a saloon, Hardin drew his guns and backed out on Helm simply because he didn't trust him. The final confrontation occurred in a blacksmith's shop. There are many versions of what happened: according to one, it was to be an unarmed truce meeting. In any event, the three participants, Helm, Hardin and Jim Taylor were all armed to the teeth. Helm apparently pulled a knife and stabbed Taylor, and then Hardin produced a hidden shotgun and cut Helm to the floor with a double blast. Taylor then produced a six-gun and finished off the dying sheriff with three shots to the head.

Thus, as Hardin stated later in his memoirs, died a man "whose name was a horror to all law-abiding citizens." The authorship of this statement was rather ironic, but the sentiment was not entirely inaccurate.

See also: JOHN WESLEY HARDIN, SUTTON-TAYLOR FEUD.

Helter Skelter   Manson murder code

Originally the title of a rock song by the Beatles, "Helter Skelter" took on a grim meaning within the notorious Charles Manson "family." In August 1969 the words were found printed in blood outside the home of two of the Manson family's murder victims, Leno and Rosemary LaBianca. The words meant, according to Manson, that blacks were destined to rise up and wipe out the entire white race, with only Manson and his family permitted to survive.

See also: CHARLES MANSON.

Hendrick's Lake   pirate treasure trove

Of all the tales about buried or lost pirate treasure, perhaps the most dependable is one that claims $2 million in silver lies somewhere at the bottom of Hendrick's Lake in Texas. It was the loot of Jean Lafitte, the French pirate who ravaged the Gulf of Mexico in the early 1800s. In his last apparent act of piracy before settling down to the staid business of smuggling and slave trading, Lafitte seized the silver aboard the Spanish brig *Santa Rosa*. He then had it transported to what is now Galveston and there loaded onto wagons to be sent to St. Louis for disposal. Lafitte entrusted this task to Gaspar Trammell, an aide who generally handled fencing operations.

The silver convoy made it as far as Hendrick's Lake, a small body of water fed by the Sabine River, when 200 Mexican troops searching for the loot cut the pirates off. Trammell knew he and his men faced certain death but resolved at least to prevent the enemy from getting the silver. Under cover of night he had the heavily ladened wagons shoved into the lake, where they sank quickly in some 50 feet of water with a 15-foot mud bottom. In the ensuing battle Trammell and all but two of his men apparently were killed. These two, a man named Robert Dawson and another who remains unidentified, escaped being slaughtered by the cavalrymen by slipping into the cold water of the lake and breathing through reeds. The troops made a half-hearted effort to retrieve the silver and then pulled out.

Robert Dawson reached St. Louis and related what had happened to the loot, and the other man returned to Lafitte with the same intelligence. Lafitte reportedly made an effort to salvage the treasure but gave it up as a hopeless task. The Mexican government also tried until they became involved in other troubles with Americans who had settled in Texas. Thereafter, nothing was done about the lost silver for perhaps half a century, when treasure hunters again took up the hunt. In 1927 a fisherman snagged his line on something in the lake and pulled a silver ingot to the surface. In all, he salvaged four bars of the Spanish silver. Each year thereafter, fortune seekers have continued to search, but the only thing found since then was an iron rim believed to have been one of Trammell's wagon wheels.

Lafitte's loot is still in the lake, now more valuable than ever since the value of silver has increased to the point that the treasure would be worth, depending on the fluctuation of price, somewhere between $20 million and $50 million.

See also: JEAN LAFITTE.

Hendrickson, John, Jr. (1833–1853)   poisoner

A lame-brained youth, John Hendrickson, Jr. is nonetheless given credit as the first American murderer to make use of what was at the time a little-known vegetable poison, aconitine, to get rid of his young wife in 1853.

John Hendrickson had married his 19-year-old fiancée Maria and taken her to live with the other seven members of his family in Bethlehem, N.Y. In almost no time, Maria was ordering not only John but the rest of the family about. Members of the Hendrickson family told John he would have to get rid of her. Whether they meant murder can be disputed, but that is what young John did. The family thereafter tried to cover up the poisoning but authorities ordered an examination of the body and found evidence of the substance. Because it was doubted that a dimwit like John could have carried out such a plot on his own, all the Hendricksons came under suspicion and talk pervaded the community of a family of poisoners. In the end, however, only John was prosecuted, and on March 6, 1853 he was hanged.

Henley, Elmer Wayne, Jr.   See DEAN CORLL.

Henry Street Gang   Chicago gang

The most prosperous and vicious of the criminal gangs in Chicago during the last two decades of the 19th century was the Henry Street Gang, bossed by Chris Merry, who was finally hanged in the 1890s for kicking his invalid wife to death. The *Chicago Tribune* labeled Merry "one of the worst criminals that ever lived in Chicago."

Merry was ostensibly a peddler but his wagon was little more than a ready container for stolen goods. The Henry Street Gang would simply ride along Maxwell and Halstead Streets in broad daylight taking anything they wanted from stores and outside stands. Eventually, the gang moved on to bigger things and developed the "kick in." With a half-dozen thieves in his wagon, Merry would drive to a store selected for a robbery. One man would stay in the wagon holding the reins while two others stood on the sidewalk brandishing revolvers, threatening passersby and looking out for police. Meanwhile, Merry and the other gangsters would kick in the door of the store and cart off the loot, holding the store employees at bay with their guns until ready to take off at breakneck speed in the wagon.

Merry was a huge bull of a man with enormously long arms and huge hands and feet. He was usually sullen and morose but was given to terrible fits of anger. At such times, as the *Tribune* described him, he was "a demon unleashed, and acted more like a mad animal than like a human being." When Merry engaged in physical combat, he used his teeth, fists, feet and any weapon that was handy. He permanently maimed or disfigured many men who had dared to challenge him. The police generally left Merry alone, although they frequently suspected him of specific crimes. When it became necessary to bring Merry in, a squad of at least six or eight men was sent on the difficult mission.

With Merry's trial and ultimate execution, the Henry Street Gang broke up and, oddly, the kick-in technique more or less disappeared for better than a quarter of a century. It was reintroduced with the automobile by John Dillinger and other gangsters.

Herrin Massacre   labor dispute

The Herrin Massacre gave Williamson County, Ill. its nickname Bloody Williamson. On June 22, 1922, 47 nonunion scabs brought in to operate a strip mine during a coal strike were besieged by several hundred union men and surrendered under a promise of safe conduct. Instead, they were herded to an area outside Herrin and told to run for their lives under a fusillade of fire. Twenty-one of the scabs were killed and many others wounded: many women and children allegedly took part in the slaughter. A large number of arrests were made and several accused strikers were tried on charges of murder and other crimes. After a five-month trial all were acquitted. It was apparent that because of public opinion in the county no guilty verdicts would ever be returned, and the charges against all the other indicted individuals were dropped.

Herring, Robert (1870–1930)   outlaw

To this day in the Wichita Mountains of Oklahoma, treasure seekers still hunt for the "traitor's gold." The traitor was Bob Herring, a Texas outlaw with an incorrigible habit of betraying his accomplices. While still a teenager, Herring and two other youngsters once robbed a herd of Mexican horses and drove them to New Mexico for quick sale. Along the way, he kept cutting horses from the pack and trying them out, saying he wanted to keep the fastest one for himself. His reason became clear when the trio sold the herd. Herring simply grabbed the money, hopped on his fast horse and galloped off into the sunset.

In 1894 Herring hooked up with Joe Baker, an active outlaw on the Texas trail, and two of his sidekicks, known only as Six Toes and Buck. The quartet pulled a number of minor jobs and a major one that netted them $35,000 in gold. Herring put the gold in his saddlebags and rode off once more. Joe Baker was enraged and swore he would catch up with the dishonest crook, a chase that became known in Texas as the "Herring hunt."

Baker ranged as far north as Montana in his search for Herring but couldn't resist such distractions as horse stealing and was shot dead during one such misdeed. Six Toes also met an untimely end when he tried to break out of a jail where he was being held for a minor offense. All of which calmed Herring's nerves enough for him to return to Texas. He settled down in Dallas, sure that the otherwise anonymous Buck was no longer tracking him. Buck wasn't, but a few years later, in 1899, Buck and Herring bumped into each other in Dallas. During a rather heated argument, Herring offered to take Buck to the hidden loot in Oklahoma. Apparently, Buck did not relish the thought of many nights sleeping on the trail with Herring and decided he'd just as soon have his revenge. In the shooting melee that followed, Buck was killed. It is entirely possible that Herring could have successfully pleaded self-defense but for the fact that he also had killed two innocent bystanders in the battle. Herring was sentenced to 35 years, talking for years afterwards about getting out and retrieving his buried loot. However, he never had the chance, dying in prison in 1930, his 30th year behind bars. The secret of the "traitor's gold" died with him.

Hickman, Edward (1904–1928)   kidnapper and murderer

In the years before the Lindbergh baby was kidnapped, the abduction of 12-year-old Marion Parker was considered the most heinous. Little Marion was kidnapped near her Los Angeles suburb home on December 15, 1927 by Edward Hickman, a 23-year-old college student who later claimed he did it to cover his tuition costs. Hickman then sent Perry Parker, the girl's businessman father, a ransom note demanding $7,500. The note was signed, "The Fox." Several other notes followed, with "DEATH" elaborately scrawled across the top of them. There was also a letter written by little Marion that read:

Dear Daddy and Mother:
I wish I could come home. I think I'll die if I have to be like this much longer. Won't somebody tell me why all this had to happen to me? Daddy please do what the man tells you or he'll kill me if you don't.

Your loving daughter,

Marion Parker

P.S. Please Daddy, I want to come home tonight.

The first effort by Perry Parker to pay the ransom failed because of the kidnapper's caution, and there followed another letter from the child.

Dear Daddy and Mother:

Daddy please don't bring anyone with you today. I am sorry for what happened last night. We drove right by the house and I cryed all the time last night. If you don't meet us this morning, you'll never see me again.

Love to All,

Marion Parker

Accompanying this note was one from the kidnapper that advised, "If you want aid against me, ask God, not man."

By the time Parker received the notes it was too late to receive aid from any quarter. Hickman had strangled Marion immediately after she wrote the letter and then, inexplicably, cut off her limbs and almost severed her head. The following morning Parker drove to an appointed rendezvous on the outskirts of Los Angeles to exchange the money for his daughter. Hickman drove his car up next to Parker's and, holding a blanket-wrapped figure, said he would take the money and then leave the girl farther along the road. Parker threw the money into the kidnapper's car and after a moment's delay proceeded up the road until he saw the blanket-wrapped bundle. He jumped from his auto and anxiously unwrapped the blanket to find the grisly remains of his daughter.

Hickman was not able to enjoy the fruits of his gruesome crime for long. He drove to Seattle, Wash. where local police, armed with a description of the kidnapper given by Parker and flashed across the country, noticed his free-spending activities and arrested him. Hickman did not deny the crime and was put on a train for the trip back to Los Angeles. Thousands of curious onlookers gathered at each station stop to catch a glimpse of the vicious murderer. Hickman waved to them. Some simply gawked, but others waved back.

Along the way, Hickman made two superficial attempts to take his own life in the train's washroom, which authorities later insisted were merely efforts to lay the groundwork for a plea of insanity. That was how Hickman pleaded, but he failed to convince a jury. He was hanged at San Quentin on October 19, 1928.

Hickok, James Butler "Wild Bill" (1837–1876)
gunfighter and lawman

In some respects James Butler "Wild Bill" Hickok was a genuine Western hero despite the fact that he was a master of the art of back-shooting as he demonstrated in his great gun battle with the "McCanles Gang" in 1861. However, most of his so-called great accomplishments, except for those during his tour as an army scout, were probably false. Sifting out the truth from Hickok's tall tales could occupy a lifetime. As a scout in 1868, he saved 34 men in an Indian siege in the Colorado Territory by riding through the attackers' ranks to get help. But he did not, as he boasted to the Eastern press, knock off 50 Confederate soldiers with 50 bullets fired from a new-fangled rifle.

Born in Troy Grove, Ill. in 1837, Hickok was originally called "Duck Bill" because of a long nose and protruding lip. Once he had demonstrated his great ability with a gun, however, the other young blades thought it wiser to call him Wild Bill.

The Hickok legend began in 1861, when, as was described later in a ridiculous profile in *Harpers Monthly,* he wiped out the so-called McCanles Gang of nine "desperadoes, horse-thieves, murderers and regular cutthroats" in "the greatest one-man gunfight in history." In fact, there was no McCanles gang. Dave McCanles was a rancher who was owed money by a freighting company for which Hickok was working.

Wild Bill Hickok's reputation as a fearless lawman was built on the numerous ridiculous stories told of him by dime novel writers who overlooked his many less laudable traits.

With his 12-year-old son in tow, McCanles, probably unarmed, came to the branch office at Rock Creek Station, Neb. for his money. Two of his ranch hands, most certainly unarmed, waited outside. An argument ensued inside the building between the manager and McCanles; Hickok, hiding behind a calico curtain, shot the rancher dead. The two ranch hands outside the building were then killed by other members of the depot crew; one possibly was shot by the depot manager's wife. McCanles' 12-year-old son survived only by running away. Hickok was charged with murder, but the boy was not permitted to testify and the charge got lost in the shuffle.

A few years later, Hickok demonstrated he did have great shooting ability by gunning down Dave Tutt in a face-to-face duel at a distance of 75 yards. As his fame in that exploit spread, the Hickok legend grew and was expanded on with every retelling. Tutt, like McCanles, became a savage outlaw, when in fact he and Hickok had been friends since youth and their quarrel was over a girl.

In 1869 Hickok was elected sheriff of Ellis County and promptly killed two men in Hays City, the county seat. One of these killings was a remarkable performance. He had his back turned on a troublemaker named Sam Strawan when the latter started to draw. Hickok whirled, drew and shot first, killing Strawan. That November, in spite of these accomplishments, Hickok was voted out of office, apparently for taking more graft from brothels and gaming saloons than the average sheriff.

Hickok left town but returned in July 1880 and promptly got into a drunken brawl with five cavalry troopers. He shot two, one fatally; the others backed off. Hickok fled town again.

In April 1871 he was hired as city marshal of Abilene, Kan. with orders from the city fathers to clean up the town. Wild Bill did some shooting, but basically, he found it more gratifying to take protection money from gamblers and pimps rather than to interfere with their business. He spent his afternoons at the card table and almost every night in the town's red-light district.

In October 1871 Wild Bill got into a gunfight with a gambler named Phil Coe and mortally wounded him. As Coe fell, Hickok's deputy, Mike Williams, came rushing through the crowd, guns drawn, to help Hickok. Hearing Williams' footsteps, the marshal whirled and fired off two quick shots before he saw who it was. Williams died instantly of two bullets in the head. That was all the citizens of Abilene could take, and within a few weeks Wild Bill was fired and forced to leave town. Although his record in Abilene actually was a sorry one, it is still sighted today as one of the greatest reigns by a lawman in the history of the West.

The remaining five years of Hickok's life were pretty much downhill. He joined Buffalo Bill Cody's Wild West Show for a time but found the work both tiresome and degrading. He quit and tried his hand at prospecting and gambling, not having too much success in either. He was arrested several times in the Wyoming Territory, said a newspaper report, "as a vagrant, having no visible means of support."

In June 1876 Hickok turned up in Deadwood, Dakota Territory with Calamity Jane, an amazon whore. Hickok, who had accumulated a spot of cash, ensconced himself at Mann's Saloon Number 10 along the main street. On August 2, 1876 Wild Bill was playing poker and mulling over what to do with his hand—two pairs, aces and eights—when a saddlebum named Jack McCall slipped up behind him and shot him through the brain. Thereafter, the hand of aces and eights became known as a "dead man's hand." McCall claimed he was avenging his brother, whom he said Hickok had killed. Asked why he hadn't met Hickok face to face, McCall shrugged. "I didn't want to commit suicide," he said.

See also: PHIL COE, DEAD MAN'S HAND, JACK MCCALL, MCCANLES GANG, SHAME OF ABILENE, SAMUEL STRAWAN.

Hickok, Richard E. See CLUTTER FAMILY MURDERS.

Hicks, Albert E. (?–1860) gangster and murderer

One of New York's most legendary thugs in the 1850s was Albert Hicks, a freelance gangster who eschewed working with any of the great gangs of the period because he felt he could fare better as a lone wolf criminal. The record bears out his judgment; he lived a carefree existence and never appeared to worry about money. The police suspected Hicksie, as he was called, of a number of robberies and possibly a dozen murders but, as he often said, "suspecting it and proving it are two different things." His reputation was such that when he was working a certain street along the waterfront, gangs of footpads knew they would be wise to move elsewhere.

Remarkably, Hicksie's downfall came about simply because he was not recognized by a Cherry Street shanghaier in whose establishment he had wandered dead drunk. The crimp operator put laudanum in his rum, and when Hicksie awakened the next morning, he was aboard the sloop *E. A. Johnson*, headed for Deep Creek, Va. on an oyster run. After ascertaining that the captain, named Burr, had a money bag along to pay for his cargo, the unwilling sailor resolved to murder the skipper and the other crewmen, two brothers named Smith and Oliver Watts. He did so in particularly bloody fashion, decapitating two of them and dazing the other and then chopping off that victim's fingers and hands as he clutched the rail in a futile attempt to avoid being thrown overboard.

After looting the sloop and letting it drift off, Hicksie returned to Manhattan with quite a substantial booty. Soon, he fled the city for Providence, R.I. with his wife and child. But he left a trail. Having flashed large sums of money, he came under suspicion when the bloodstained *Johnson* was discovered and put under tow five days after the murders. Hicksie was located in Providence and found in possession of the personal belongings of the captain and one of the Watts brothers.

He was tried for piracy and murder on the high seas and sentenced to be hanged on July 13, 1860. About a week before his scheduled execution, he made a full confession to the warden of the Tombs. Hicks was certainly one of the most celebrated villains of the day and his confession made him all the more infamous. There was a steady stream of visitors to the Tombs to see the noted blackguard shackled to the floor of his cell. For a small fee paid to the jailers, a visitor was permitted to speak a few words with the murderer.

Among those calling on Hicksie was Phineas T. Barnum, the great showman, whose American Museum enjoyed enormous popularity. Barnum told the flattered villain that he wished to obtain a plaster cast of his head and bust for display in the museum. After hag-

gling the entire day, Hicksie agreed to pose for $25 and two boxes of 5¢ cigars. After the cast was made, the magnanimous Barnum returned with a new suit of clothes, which he traded to Hicks for his old suit, with which he wished to adorn a display dummy. Later, Hicks complained to the warden that Barnum had cheated him, that the new suit was shoddy and inferior to his old one.

Hicks was to be hanged on Bedloe's Island. He was ushered from the Tombs to the mainland dock by a fife and drum corps and a procession of carriages full of dignitaries. Thousands lined the procession route and cheered Hicksie, who graciously waved back to them. His only protest was that his suit did not fit, for which he cursed Barnum, but the warden informed him there was no time for alterations.

It was estimated that at least 10,000 persons witnessed the execution on Bedloe's Island. The scaffold was positioned only 30 feet from the water and hundreds of boats, from small craft to large excursion vessels, formed a solid line offshore. Hicksie's body was left suspended for half an hour and then cut down and transported back to Manhattan. His corpse was buried in Calvary Cemetery, but within a matter of days it was stolen by ghouls, who sold it to medical students more than willing to pay a premium for the chance to study the brain of such a notorious and bloodthirsty criminal.

Hicks, Jeffrey Joe (1959–) sex murderer and prison snitch

Much is made that imprisoned sex murderers, especially those whose victims are children, are among the most hated by other inmates. Compounding that hatred, however, is a genuine fear that such a vulnerable prisoner could be forced by his keepers to turn snitch. In Hicks' case it was not illogical that he should be suspected of snitching on an elaborate escape plan worked out by his cellmate. According to the plan Hicks and the cellmate were to be rescued from Leavenworth Penitentiary by a helicopter pilot who would swoop down in the prison yard and pick up the two of them. Negotiations were said to be going on for hiring a pilot when suddenly prison officials swept down on the pair.

As punishment for having conceived the plot—which obviously never got off the ground—the cellmate was sent to the federal penitentiary in Marion, Ill., where he would be locked up in an individual cell 23 hours a day and denied virtually all privileges. Hicks was moved to an isolation cell in Leavenworth for a time. The thought of many inmates was that Hicks had snitched.

Still no retribution was taken on Hicks since it was not absolutely certain that he had snitched—or had a

"Hicksie" was a freelance killer whom even the organized waterfront gangs steered clear of.

reason to snitch. Hicks had been an inmate in a Michigan state prison when suddenly he was transferred to Leavenworth. In general there were only two reasons for that to have happened: he was a problem prisoner Michigan couldn't control or he was in personal danger.

The truth surfaced when a prisoner came across an issue of *Inside Detective* that reported on the case of a sexual sadist who had snatched a 13-year-old boy off his bicycle in Green Oak Township, Mich., in October 1986 and driven away in his jeep. The boy's naked body was found in the woods a few days later. He had been molested and strangled. The magazine referred to other kidnappings and molestation to which he had subjected other young boys.

Hicks was sentenced to life plus 65 to 100 years and was serving his time in state prison. It was obvious to Leavenworth convicts that Hicks had to be transferred to Leavenworth for his own protection, and according to accepted criminal protocol, such a prisoner is accepted only when it is made clear to him that in return for "sanctuary," he must turn informer. Naturally in such cases prison authorities deny any such deal has taken place.

In Hicks' case the harassment became so intense that it was only a matter of time before he would be murdered. He disappeared from Leavenworth, undoubtedly transferred to a much lower-security federal prison in another state where he could hope no one would learn of his past so that he might live to serve his sentence without constant fear.

Higgins, John Calhoun Pinckney "Pink"
(1848–1914) rancher and gunfighter

A fiery Texas rancher of the "I am the law" school, John Calhoun Pinckney "Pink" Higgins was probably as mean and sadistic as Print Olive, perhaps the West's most notorious big-spread owner. Higgins had the good sense to confine his excesses to Texas, which tolerated a lot from the high and mighty. Olive, also a Texan, made the mistake of shifting his operations, including his practice of "man burning," to Nebraska, a state that eventually sided with the homesteaders.

In the art of killing, Higgins was cut from the Olive mold. Typical was his treatment of a cowboy he caught butchering one of his cows just after he had shot it. Higgins gunned him down with a Winchester at 90 yards, disemboweled the dead animal and stuffed the would-be rustler's corpse inside. He then rode to town and informed authorities of a miracle he had just witnessed: a cow giving birth to a man.

From the time he was a young man, Pink exhibited a penchant for direct action. He was twice wounded by Indians and was an officer in the Ku Klux Klan. When he started his own ranch, he was brutal in his treatment of rustlers or those he considered rustlers. Pink also was the key figure in the bloody Horrell-Higgins feud that shook Lampasas County in the 1870s. On the surface, the feud started after the owners of a huge neighboring spread, the Horrells, killed three lawmen, including one of Pink's kin. But the real reason was the disappearance of cattle. When the fighting broke out, Pink took up his Winchester without hesitation. He gunned down Zeke Terrell, a rider for the Horrells, and then gave him the cow-birth treatment. Next, he shot Ike Lantier, another Horrell cowboy, for having the temerity to use the same water hole for watering his stock. Higgins' most callous act in the feud was the murder of Merritt Horrell as he sat in a saloon. Horrell was unarmed when Higgins marched in through the back door and pumped four slugs into him without giving his foe a fighting chance.

Lampasas became a regular battleground for the feudists, with Higgins and his men ambushing the Horrells as they rode in. A major shoot-out occurred in the town on June 14, 1877, when Higgins and three of his men took on seven of the Horrells. The gunfight lasted for several hours. It finally ended when the townsfolk convinced both sides to stop shooting and ride out their separate ways, but not before Higgins' brother-in-law died in the fighting. The following month Higgins led all his riders in an attack on the Horrell ranch. The siege ended after 48 hours, as the Higgins men started running low on ammunition.

The Texas Rangers arrived in the region in July and prevailed upon Higgins and the Horrells to sign a treaty, bringing peace to the county. Despite his excesses, Higgins did not suffer any major loss of popularity, since the Horrells were not exactly models of virtue. Two of the brothers, Mart and Tom Horrell were lynched the year after the truce for some other indiscretions they were suspected of having committed.

Higgins' last known killing, one of his fairest, occurred in 1903, when Pink met up with Bill Standifer, a longtime opponent of his. Both expert riflemen, they exchanged shots at a distance of 60 yards. Standifer hit Higgins' horse, but Pink put a Winchester bullet through his foe's heart. Higgins died of a heart attack in 1914.

See also: HORRELL-HIGGINS FEUD.

highbinder societies   Chinese gangs

Highbinder societies were strong-arm groups that engaged in blackmail, kidnapping and murder on assignment. These gangs never achieved the power or influence of the Chinese tongs, although their hatchet men were often hired by the tongs. Little Pete, the infamous Chinese tong warrior, started his career as a member of the Gin Sin Seer highbinders, but because of his cunning and ability, he soon moved up to the Sum Yop tong.

See also: LITTLE PETE, TONG WARS.

hijack   word origin

During Prohibition, when the commandeering of trucks loaded with illegal booze became a common occurrence, the usual greeting given by an armed gunman sticking up was a terse "High, Jack"—meaning raise your hands high, Jack; hence *hijack*.

hijacking

In its various forms, hijacking goes back to early colonial times, but it hit a peak during Prohibition, when the stealing of liquor shipments by one gang from another reached bloody and epidemic proportions. Today, hijacking is a highly professional art committed by gangs that limit their criminal activities to this one lucrative field. The theft of entire shipments of television sets, refrigerators, furs, clothing, cigarettes, drugs, oil and liquor is handled with smooth efficiency based on precise advance planning. By surveillance or bribery, a hijack gang will learn a truck's schedule and type of cargo and plan exactly when and how to steal that cargo. One Chicago gang had special "scouts" to tip them off about valuable shipments, and its "work cars" were equipped with high-powered engines, police radios and switches to extinguish rear lights when desired. A special "crash car" was utilized to cut off the arrival of police during the operations.

Usually, hijackers are thought to work on lonely stretches of road in the middle of the night, but some of the lushest operating areas for these thieves are crowded business centers in broad daylight, a typical example being New York's garment district. Two members of a hijacking mob will climb up to the cab of a truck, perhaps when it is halted at a red light or still parked at the curb on a side street, and force the driver and his helper to get out at gunpoint. They will be ordered to walk quietly to a car right behind the truck. Inside the car, the driver and helper are bound and blindfolded. They are then driven off to some quiet spot to cool their heels for three or four hours while one of the hijackers drives the truck away, empties its load into another truck—or a warehouse—and finally disposes of it. Once the job is over, the driver and helper are released.

A particularly daring breed of hijacker is the so-called switch man. This operator drives through the garment district in his own truck looking for another truck that the driver has had to park and leave for some reason. The switch man generally likes to see the driver go into a luncheonette where he will be sure to stay for several minutes. While the driver is gone, the switch man and a helper or two will clean the truck out in a matter of minutes and load the contents in their own truck. The switch man, of course, does not operate like the sophisticated crook of the more traditional hijacking gangs, but he does get the job done.

Another approach has been perfected in recent years by a New York area crook who takes jobs with parcel delivery companies under assumed names. His first day on the job, he is given a truck full of merchandise and sent out on his assigned rounds. It is the last the delivery service sees of the driver or the merchandise. All that is ever recovered is an abandoned delivery truck.

Overall figures on hijacking indicate it is a relatively "low incidence, high profit" crime. Losses, according to insurance officials, probably exceed $100 million a year, but estimates are inexact because of the difficulty of determining whether an actual hijacking or a case of employee theft has occurred. When an area experiences a sudden increase in hijackings, insurance firms and associations may send in undercover agents who use trucks as bait. A single arrest can cause hijacking in an area to cease for a considerable time, as apparently the news spreads rapidly. Similarly, insurance groups sometimes pass the word among truckers that an area is under surveillance, and as a result complaints of hijackings usually decrease. In such cases it is suspected that the drivers themselves are doing the looting and decide to "cool it" for a while.

Probably the greatest hijacking gang in history was Detroit's Purple Gang, which during Prohibition sent convoys of liquor from Canada across the border into the United States and hijacked the trucks of rival shippers to augment their supply. Police believe that remnants of the old Purples are still responsible for much of the hijackings in Michigan and neighboring states.

Hill, Joan Robinson (1930–1969) alleged murder victim

One of the most notorious, headline-provoking murder cases in modern American history was the alleged "murder by omission" of beautiful and wealthy Joan Robinson Hill by her husband, a leading plastic surgeon in Houston, Tex. After he walked out free as a result of a mistrial, he was assassinated by a paid gunman, which kept the case boiling for years.

Joan Robinson was the daughter of oil multimillionaire Ash Robinson, a man who epitomized Texas-style money and power. Robinson was highly influential in state politics and had the ability to get what he wanted. But few things meant as much to him as Joan. She had been through a couple of marriages when she met Dr. John Hill in 1957. The two were married in a mammoth, Texas-sized wedding paid for by Ash Robinson. Hill's career kept him away from his wife a good deal, but Joan, an accomplished horsewoman, didn't seem to mind and old Ash was perfectly happy because he still had his daughter around so much of the time.

By 1968, however, the marriage was breaking up. Joan became aware that Hill was seeing other women. They argued often. In March 1969 Joan grew ill, and after considerable delay her husband put her in a small hospital, which didn't have the facilities to handle what developed into a very serious condition. During the course of her treatment, she had a sudden heart failure and died. The following morning a most peculiar event occurred. When doctors arrived to perform an autopsy, they found the body had been sent to a funeral home "by accident." Upon reaching the funeral home, they discovered the body had already been drained of fluids and was partly embalmed, making a really thorough autopsy most difficult. Back at the hospital a brain said to be Joan Hill's showed signs of meningitis, but there was some reason to suspect it was not Joan's brain since the brain stem in the body failed to produce the same symptoms.

From the time of Joan's funeral, old Ash Robinson pressured the district attorney to get a murder charge brought against Hill. In addition, Robinson had a parade of his important friends approach the DA with the same demand. Then, three months after the death of his first wife, John Hill married a woman with whom he had been linked while his marriage to Joan was disintegrating. That galvanized Robinson to further action. He hired detectives to follow Hill and lined up medical testimony, even bringing in the New York City medical examiner to reexamine the body. Two grand juries were convened but both refused to indict Hill. A third grand jury, however, received some additional material. By that time, Hill's second wife, Ann, had divorced him and testified Hill had confessed to her that he had killed Joan. Moreover, she claimed Hill had tried to kill her on more than one occasion. Hill was indicted for murder by neglect, technically "murder by omission," in that he willfully denied his wife adequate medical attention.

Hill's murder trial ended in a mistrial when his second wife blurted out that Hill had told her he had killed Joan. Such a statement could not be permitted in court, since under the law she could only testify about the period before she married Hill.

Before a new trial could be held, Dr. Hill married a third time. Just after returning from his honeymoon in September 1972, he was shot and killed by an assassin wearing a Halloween mask. The murderer was identi-fied as a young Houston hood, Bobby Vandiver, who had brought along a prostitute to keep him company while he waited to ambush Hill in the latter's home. Vandiver confessed he had gotten $5,000 for the job, and his story implicated a number of people, among them Ash Robinson. The killer said that Ash had let it be known he would pay for the execution of his ex-son-in-law and that his intermediary in the hit contract was a Houston woman named Lilla Paulus, a former prostitute and madam. The Paulus woman was indicted, but before her trial began, Bobby Vandiver was killed while attempting to escape jail. Despite this development, Paulus was convicted on the testimony of the young prostitute who had accompanied Vandiver. The prostitute, however, could produce no admissible evidence linking anyone else to the crime. Lilla Paulus was sentenced to life imprisonment but refused to implicate anyone else in the murder.

Following the verdict, Ash Robinson continued to deny to the press any involvement in Hill's murder. He successfully fended off a civil suit against him by the Hill family, and it appeared that with Joan Robinson dead, John Hill dead and Ash Robinson growing old, the Hill-Robinson murders were destined to remain one of the most bizarre mysteries of modern times. In 1981 a four-hour miniseries dramatization of the case was shown on television; it had already been the subject of a best-selling book, *Blood and Money* by Thomas Thompson. Joan Robinson was played by Farrah Fawcett, and the actress, or her publicity agent, took special pains to let it be known that Ash Robinson, the surviving principal in the case and then 84 years old, had voiced his "casting approval" of Farrah as the "ideal choice" to play his deceased daughter. Rumor also had it that Robinson had suggested he portray himself in the film.

Hill, Joe (1879–1915) labor organizer and alleged murderer

A handsome Swedish immigrant, Joel Hagglund became the troubadour of the Industrial Workers of the World, a radical labor union founded in 1905. Soon the songs of "Joe Hill" were known throughout America. He composed many of the Wobblies' favorite songs and is perhaps most famous for the refrain of "pie in the sky" in "The Preacher and the Slave."

In 1915 two Salt Lake City policemen were shot in a grocery store holdup. Hill was charged with the crime, convicted and sentenced to die. The verdict was most controversial and the IWW and the rest of the American left considered it a frame-up. Just before he was executed by a Utah firing squad, Hill wired Big Bill Haywood, the head of the IWW: "Don't waste any time in mourning. Organize."

Hill, Virginia (1918–1966) syndicate girlfriend and bagwoman

Mistakenly dubbed the Queen of the Mob by newspapers in the early 1950s during the Kefauver Committee hearings into organized crime, Virginia Hill was no more than a trusted bedmate to many of the syndicate's top gangsters and a bagwoman for the mob, delivering funds to secret Swiss bank accounts or elsewhere as instructed. From the time she arrived in Chicago to be a cooch dancer in the 1934 World's Fair Hill took a series of husbands and lovers. First came Joe Epstein, the bookmaking king and tax expert for the Capone mob, followed by the brothers Fischetti, Tony Accardo, Murray Humphreys, Frank Nitti, Joe Adonis, Frank Costello, and lastly her true love, Benjamin "Bugsy" Siegel.

Hill was truly in love with Siegel, yet was conveniently away in Europe when the Bug was shot to death in her living room by an underworld assassin in 1947. After his death she still spoke lovingly of Siegel (he had named the Flamingo Hotel in Las Vegas in honor of her nickname) without being critical of the syndicate, which had ordered his execution because his Las Vegas deals had cost them a fortune.

Virginia Hill, the so-called Queen of the Mob, added a touch of glamour and, at one point, violence to the Kefauver hearings.

She provided the Kefauver hearings with one of its high points as she parried questions about why so many gangsters gave her money. (It was strictly because of her personal charms, she said.) She also added some off-the-stand excitement by tossing a right cross to the jaw of reporter Marjorie Farnsworth of the *New York Journal American* and screaming at other reporters: "You goddamn bastards. I hope an atom bomb falls on all of you."

After that dramatic peak in her life, Virginia took a new husband and wandered the pleasure spots of Europe. According to some, she oversaw the Swiss bank accounts of several mobsters. It is generally believed that Hill supplied much of the funds that allowed Lucky Luciano to live out his exile in Italy in comfort.

But Hill missed the action of the old mob days and hated growing old. She attempted suicide a number of times, and finally, in March 1966 she swallowed a large number of sleeping pills and lay down in the snow outside Salzburg, Austria to watch the clouds as death closed in on her.

See also: BAGMAN, FLAMINGO HOTEL, KEFAUVER INVESTIGATION, BENJAMIN "BUGSY" SIEGEL.

"Hillside Strangler" duo   Bianchi and Buono

In addition to being more adept than other serial killers, the so-called Hillside Strangler eluded apprehension for some time due to the fact that the law enforcement authorities were not suspecting two perpetrators of the crimes. The Strangler's modus operandi was readily recognizable: it started out in imitation of that of Caryl Chessman, California's notorious "Red Light Bandit" of the 1940s. Chessman would approach parked couples in lonely spots, flashing a red light resembling that on a police car. He robbed the drivers and sometimes took off with their female companions and forced them to perform sexual acts with him.

Chessman never killed his victims, but the Hillside Strangler murdered at least 10 women, starting in 1977. What prevented the police from catching him sooner was, again, the fact that the Hillside Strangler was not one man but two—cousins Kenneth Bianchi, born in 1952, and Angelo Buono, Jr., born in 1935. At times, the cousins killed together. They first planned their murder rampage after a long drinking bout in which they speculated how it would feel to kill someone. (This statement may be giving them the benefit of the doubt. It is still not clear whether one or both had previously committed murders on their own.) Both decided that Chessman's method of pretending to be a law officer was the perfect way to grab women.

Their technique was to stop women motorists or streetwalkers, flash badges, demand identification, and force them into their car, supposedly an undercover police vehicle. The women were invariably raped, sodomized, then strangled to death. Most of the bodies were left in spots where they were certain to be found. The bodies were generally washed clean—apparently at Buono's suggestion—so as to leave no clues for the police to follow.

After a while, Bianchi decided a change of scene was called for, and he moved to the state of Washington, where, in Bellingham, he found work as a security guard. Eventually, he was linked to the murder of two young women who had been lured by him to investigate a nonexistent house-sitting job. A search of Bianchi's home turned up evidence tying him to the killings, and cooperation with California authorities linked him to at least five Hillside Strangler slayings. Fearful of a possible death penalty in Washington State, Bianchi offered to identify his cousin as the "real" Hillside Strangler. Based on Bianchi's evidence, Buono was convicted in 1983 of nine murders. Despite Buono's care in always fixing up the death scene after one of the pair's murders—he always cleaned his home after Bianchi left so that no fingerprints of any victims were found—a meticulous scientific search turned up a single eyelash from one of the murder victims. Also, some strands of fiber from a chair in Buono's home were discovered on one body.

One witness in the Buono trial was 27-year-old Catherine Lorre, who identified the two cousins as the men who had stopped her on a Hollywood street in the late 1970s and demanded identification. She had produced her driver's license, next to which was a picture of herself as a little girl sitting on the lap of her proud father, actor Peter Lorre. Bianchi testified that he decided not to ensnare her, for fear that murdering the daughter of a celebrity might put too much heat on the homicidal partners.

Buono was sentenced to nine terms of life imprisonment without parole, while Bianchi was returned to Washington to a life sentence with no possibility of parole before 2005.

Like several other serial murderers, the Hillside Strangler—or at least Bianchi—maintained a romantic liaison, with a woman drawn to him because of his crimes as Carol Bundy was to Douglas Clark. While Bianchi was in California prior to Buono's trial, a 23-year-old poet and aspiring playwright named Veronica Lynn Compton sought Bianchi's opinion of her new play about a female serial killer. Correspondence and conversations followed, which reveal how close Veronica's tastes came to serial killing. Bianchi then concocted a plan to spring him from his own guilty verdict in the Bellingham murders by having Veronica strangle a woman and leave specimens of Bianchi's semen at the scene to convince authorities that the real killer was still at large.

Compton visited Bianchi in prison and got from him a book in which he had hidden part of a rubber glove containing his semen. Compton went to Bellingham and attempted a murder but botched the job. She was convicted and was sent to prison with no hope of parole before 1994. For a time, she continued to correspond with Bianchi, but finally her ardor for him cooled, and she shifted to corresponding with Douglas Clark, then in San Quentin waiting execution as the Sunset Slayer. A typical ghoulish passage in one letter to Clark read: "Our humor is unusual. I wonder why others don't see the necrophilic aspects of existence as we do."

In 1988 Compton escaped from prison and disappeared.

See also: DOUGLAS CLARK, SERIAL KILLERS.

Hinckley, John W., Jr. (1955–) accused assailant of Ronald Reagan

On March 30, 1981 Ronald Reagan became the eighth sitting president of the United States to be subjected to an assassination attempt and the fourth—after Andrew Jackson, Harry Truman and Gerald Ford—to survive. Reagan was shot by a 25-year-old drifter, John W. Hinckley of Evergreen, Colo., as he left the Washington Hilton Hotel, where he had addressed a labor audience. The assailant was seized immediately after having fired four to six shots from a .22-caliber revolver, a type known popularly as a Saturday Night Special. The president was hit by a bullet that entered under the left armpit, pierced the chest, bounced off the seventh rib and plowed into the left lower lobe of the lung. Reagan froze for a moment at the door of his limousine and then was brusquely pushed inside the car by a Secret Service agent. Remarkably, the president did not realize he had been shot but thought he had simply been injured when shoved into the car. Only upon arrival at the hospital was it determined that he had been shot.

Also wounded were three others: the president's press secretary, James S. Brady; a Secret Service agent, Timothy J. McCarthy; and a District of Columbia police officer, Thomas K. Delahanty. All three survived, although Brady remained hospitalized for many months after the assassination attempt.

Hinckley turned out to be the son of an oil executive who had grown up in affluence in Dallas and moved with his family to Colorado in 1974. He had attended Texas Tech University on and off through 1980 but never graduated. At times he had traveled across the country, and in 1978 he had enrolled himself in the National Socialist

Party of America, generally known as the Nazi Party of America. A spokesman for that organization said the group had not renewed Hinckley's membership the following year because of his "violent nature."

Hinckley had evidently flown from Denver to Los Angeles on March 25 and then boarded a Greyhound bus for Washington the following day, arriving March 29, the day before the attack. Following Hinckley's arrest for the attack on President Reagan, it was discovered that he had been in Nashville, Tenn. on October 9, 1980, when then-President Jimmy Carter was there. Hinckley was arrested at the airport in Nashville when X-ray equipment disclosed he had three handguns and some ammunition in his carry-on bag. The weapons were confiscated, and he paid a fine of $62.50. Despite his arrest, federal authorities did not place Hinckley under security surveillance thereafter. Four days after his release, Hinckley turned up in Dallas, where he purchased two .22-caliber handguns in a pawnshop. One of these weapons was alleged to have been used in the attack on Reagan.

A bizarre sidelight to the case was the discovery that Hinckley had been infatuated with movie star Jodie Foster, then a student at Yale University. He had written her several letters, and an unmailed letter dated March 30, 1981, 12:45 P.M.—one and three-quarter hours before the attack—was found in his Washington hotel room. It read:

Dear Jody,
> *There is a definite possibility that I will be killed in my attempt to get Reagan. It is for this very reason that I am writing to you now.*

Hinckley went on to say he loved her and that

> *although we talked on the phone a couple of times, I never had the nerve to simply approach you and introduce myself . . . Jody, I would abandon this idea of getting Reagan in a second if I could only win your heart and live out the rest of my life with you, whether it be in total obscurity or whatever. I will admit to you that the reason I'm going ahead with this attempt now is because I just cannot wait any longer to impress you. I've got to do something now to make you understand in no uncertain terms that I am doing all this for your sake. By sacrificing my freedom and possibly my life, I hope to change your mind about me.*

It appeared that Hinckley had been influenced in his alleged actions by the film *Taxi Driver,* in which Foster had played a child prostitute. At one point in the film, the protagonist, a taxi driver, is planning to assassinate a presidential candidate.

In August 1981 Hinckley was indicted by a federal grand jury in Washington, D.C. on charges of attempting to kill President Reagan as well as the other three men. The FBI reportedly concluded that Hinckley had acted alone. In a verdict that shocked the nation, he was acquitted by a jury on grounds of insanity. He was then committed to a mental institution.

Hite, Wood (1848–1881) James gang outlaw

A cousin of Jesse and Frank James, Wood Hite was shot and killed in 1881 in what has been characterized by some as a "dress rehearsal" for Jesse James' murder some four months later.

Born in Logan County, Ky. in 1848, Hite rode with the James gang from 1870 until 1881. By that year the gang was in disarray. Many of its key members had been killed or imprisoned while others had apparently contacted law enforcement officials about betraying Jesse James in return for leniency. In 1881 Hite had the misfortune to choose the home of a relative of Bob Ford, James' eventual assassin, as a hideout. Also seeking refuge there was Dick Little, another gang member who like the Fords, was seeking to turn traitor. According to certain accounts Hite somehow got wind of the plot or came to suspect that the Fords and Little were planning to turn him in. He accused them of it and died in a blazing gun battle in the kitchen. Other accounts, such as that of contemporary James biographer Frank Triplett, insist the killing was more dastardly: "Creeping one night lightly to his room, Dick and Bob Ford put a pistol to his head, and he was soon weltering in his gore."

Jesse James partisans have since maintained that had Hite managed to get his information to Jesse, the latter would have trusted the Ford brothers even less than he already did and thus might have saved his own life.

See also: JAMES BROTHERS, DICK LITTLE.

Hobbs, James (1819–1879) scalp hunter

Together with James Kirker, James Hobbs was a partner in America's most lethal scalp-hunting team.

As a boy Hobbs was taken prisoner by Indians and instead of being killed was adopted by them. Thereafter, he seems to have had a love-hate relationship with the Indians, living with them, marrying them, deserting them, scalping them for bounties and aiding them against other white men. Hobbs had the same sort of attitude toward whites. He might help them against Indians, or if they happened to be dark-skinned and dark-haired, he was just as likely to scalp them since their hair would be indistinguishable from that of an Indian and would bring the same bounty.

Hobbs left his original tribe, the Comanche, in 1839 and became a trapper and hunter of both buffalo and scalps. He formed an alliance with another scalp hunter, James Kirker, and together they took scalps by the hundreds. In one Indian village, aided by Shawnee friendly to Hobbs, they lifted 300 scalps. Eventually they accumulated an extremely valuable load, which they took to Mexico to turn in for a bounty. Kirker stole the down payment they received for the scalps and deserted Hobbs, but in time Hobbs received the balance of the money due from the Mexican authorities, which made him a wealthy man. He also gained added fame when he started killing Navajo, much to the Mexicans' delight. Later though, Hobbs joined the American cause in the war against Mexico and came out of the conflict a captain. He then headed for the gold fields of California, getting as far as Yuma Indian country. He settled with the tribe for a while, and in 1850 he even helped them to dispose of a vicious scalp hunter named John Glanton. Hobbs lived out his life in this contradictory fashion, sometimes scalping Indians and sometimes joining their cause, until his death in Grass Valley, Calif. in 1879.

See also: JOHN GLANTON, JAMES KIRKER, SCALP HUNTING.

Hoch, Johann (1855–1906) mass murderer

In 1905 Chicago police inspector labeled a Chicago packinghouse employee named Johann Hoch "the greatest mass murderer in the history of the United States." No accurate list of victims could ever be compiled, so the claim cannot be verified statistically, but Hoch's record was certainly formidable in many respects. From about 1890 until 1905 it was estimated that he married bigamously as many as 55 women. The lucky ones he robbed of all their possessions and deserted; the unlucky ones he not only robbed but poisoned as well. While the more sensationalist newspapers placed his murder toll at about 25, diligent police work determined the number to be about 15. He was convicted of only one homicide, however, that of his next-to-last known bride, 46-year-old Marie Walcker, the owner of a small candy shop. His other 14 unfortunate spouses all died rather quickly after exchanging vows with him. All their bodies were found to contain traces of arsenic, but virtually all embalming fluid at the time contained some arsenic, and Hoch always saw to it that each of his dearly departed was very heavily embalmed.

Hoch located his victims by simply advertising in German-language newspapers. The ad that attracted Mrs. Walcker read:

WIDOWER, quiet and home-loving, with comfortable income and well-furnished house wishes acquaintance of congenial widow without children. Object, matrimony. Write Box B-103.

Mrs. Walcker did write and within days became Mrs. Hoch. She managed to live only a month following the wedding, taken mysteriously ill shortly after she'd transferred all her life savings to her husband. In keeping with Hoch's record of the most marriages in the shortest period of time, he promptly married his widow's sister four days later. He did not kill her, but instead took her money and ran. Unaware of his intentions, Hoch's new wife reported him missing. In the ensuing police hunt, Hoch's picture appeared in newspapers around the country, and woman after woman came forward to say he, under the name of Hoch or various other aliases, was her husband as well. Other persons came forward to identify Hoch as the short-term husband of a departed member of their family. Hoch was finally located in New York City as he was popping his favorite question to the landlady of a boardinghouse.

By this time, authorities were convinced they had a monstrous mass murderer on their hands. The newspapers named him Stockyard Bluebeard, a reference to his sometime work in Chicago packinghouses. Arsenic traces were found in a number of Hoch's dead wives, and he was returned to Chicago to be tried for Marie Walcker's death. It was a prudent choice, the one case in which Hoch could not use his pat defense that the traces of arsenic in the dead body came from the embalming fluid. By this time science had made advances in the undertaking field, and the newest embalming agents contained no arsenic. The undertaker who'd embalmed Marie Walcker had switched to one of the new fluids just two weeks before. That fact and the testimony of several of Hoch's wives about how he had absconded with their money—one told of him stealing off in the night, even taking the gold bridgework she had left in a water glass beside her bed—sealed the verdict against the defendant. He was hanged on February 23, 1906 before 100 witnesses at the Cook County Jail.

Forty-nine years later, some very old human bones were found in the wall of a cottage where Hoch had lived. The police had searched the premises at the time hoping to find evidence of additional killings by Hoch but had discovered nothing.

Hodges, Thomas See TOM BELL.

423

Hoffa, James R. (1913–1975?) labor leader and alleged murder victim

Theoretically, the disappearance in 1975 of former Teamster labor boss James R. Hoffa is still under investigation by federal and local law enforcement agencies in Michigan. Actually, the handful of FBI agents still assigned to the Hoffa case do little more than check out an occasional lead. In fact, the FBI considers the case—one of murder—solved.

Hoffa had for decades been a controversial union leader, one with established links to organized crime. Yet despite his underworld connections and a long list of nefarious dealings, he remained immune to prosecution until he became the target of Robert F. Kennedy, first as chief counsel to the Senate Select Committee on Improper Activities in the Labor or Management Field, more popularly known as the McClellan Committee, and later as attorney general.

Subjected to a persistent "Get Hoffa" campaign by Kennedy, the labor leader was finally brought to trial in 1962 for demanding and receiving illegal payments from a firm employing Teamsters. The result was a hung jury, but Hoffa was later convicted of attempting to bribe one of the jurors and sentenced to eight years. In 1964 he was also convicted of misappropriating $1.7 million in Teamster pension funds. Finally entering prison in 1967, Hoffa served a total of 58 months.

In 1975 Hoffa was in the midst of a struggle to retake control of the union from his former protégé, Frank Fitzsimmons. His sentence had been commuted in 1971 by President Richard Nixon with the provision that he stay out of union politics for 10 years. He was challenging that legal stipulation and, perhaps more critically, the will of various organized crime fiefdoms within the Teamsters whose leaders did not want a strongman like Hoffa back in power, fearing he would upset or take over their operations.

On July 30, 1975 the 62-year-old Hoffa left his suburban Detroit home and drove to a restaurant, Manchus Red Fox, allegedly to meet a member of the Detroit underworld, a Detroit labor leader and a power in New Jersey Teamster affairs. Hoffa arrived for the meeting at 2 P.M.; at 2:30 P.M. he called his wife to tell her the others had not yet shown up. That was the last ever heard from him. He was seen getting into a car with several other men in the restaurant parking lot about 2:45. According to the most popular police theory, he was garroted and then his body was run through a mob controlled fat-rendering plant that was later destroyed by fire.

The government's list of suspects, gathered through information received from underworld characters and convicts seeking to reduce their own sentences, has long included reputed Pennsylvania crime kingpin Russell Bufalino, Anthony "Tony Pro" Provenzano and two of his underlings, Gabriel Briguglio and Thomas Andretta. Another suspect, Gabriel's brother, Salvatore Briguglio, was reported to be talking to the FBI when he was shot to death in front of a New York City restaurant in March 1978. According to the FBI scenario, Tony Pro set up the so-called peace meeting with Hoffa and instead ordered him murdered. Provenzano denied even being in Detroit on the date of the Hoffa disappearance and produced an alibi that placed him in Hoboken N.J., visiting various union locals.

One of the more curious aspects of the case is the question of why, if he had ordered Hoffa's execution, would Tony Pro link himself to the murder by setting up a meeting with the victim, a fact that Hoffa had made known to a number of individuals. Even more confusing is why Hoffa's killers would pick him up some 45 minutes late, an unlikely display of tardiness for mob hit men. However, the FBI's theory, backed up by such facts as the finding of traces of Hoffa's blood and hair in the back seat of the abduction car, appears more convincing than any other plausible explanation. One Teamster foe of Hoffa under suspicion told investigators, with a perfectly straight face, he had it on good authority that the missing union leader "ran off to Brazil with a black go-go dancer."

Since the former union leader's disappearance, those suspects mentioned most often have either started serving sentences or been convicted of other crimes, some on evidence uncovered during the Hoffa investigation. But convictions in the Hoffa case clearly will depend on the authorities' ability to get some lower-level hoodlum in organized crime to talk or the possibility that one of the conspirators will say the wrong thing to the wrong person. Otherwise, the authorities have no court case. "We all know who did it," one unidentified Teamster vice president has been quoted as saying. "It was Tony with those guys of his from New Jersey. It's common knowledge. But the cops need a corroborating witness, and it doesn't look like they're about to get one, does it?"

Hoffman, Harold Giles (1896–1954) governor and embezzler

One of the most flamboyant politicians in recent American history, Harold G. Hoffman lived a double life, that of an elected public official and an embezzler, whose total depredations remain undetermined. At the high point of his career, in 1936, he was boomed by New Jersey Republicans for president of the United States. At the low point in his life, in 1954, investigators closed in on him and he became an almost certain candidate for prison.

Hoffman was an army captain in World War I, a small-town banker, mayor of South Amboy, assemblyman, congressman, state commissioner of motor vehicles and, lastly, governor of New Jersey. At the age of 33, he began looting money. By the time he left the governorship in 1937, he had stolen at least $300,000, a considerable sum in Depression dollars. He spent the last 18 years of his life juggling monies in order to cover his embezzlements.

As near as could be determined, Hoffman started stealing from his South Amboy bank, dipping into dormant accounts to keep up his free-spending ways. Whenever an inactive account became active, Hoffman was able to shift money from another quiet account to cover his looting. Some of Hoffman's stolen funds went to promote his political career. Eventually, he reached Congress. Happily, Washington was not too far away from South Amboy, so he could keep a lid on things at the bank. When Hoffman suddenly left Congress to take the post of state commissioner of motor vehicles, which to many seemed a political step-down, some observers theorized that the move was part of Hoffman's plan to eventually run for governor, but the real reason was that he needed access to public funds. Sooner or later, an examiner might discover the shortages at the bank, so it was extremely advantageous for Hoffman to be able to juggle the funds of the motor vehicle department. When money had to be at the bank, it was there; when it had to be in the state coffers, it was there. In the process, more and more stuck to Hoffman's fingers.

When Hoffman won the governorship at the age of 39, he enjoyed wide popularity in his state and grew to be a national political power. However, he became a center of controversy in the sensational Lindbergh kidnapping case. His interference and attempts to reopen the investigation after Bruno Richard Hauptmann was convicted brought him widespread criticism. When he granted Hauptmann a few months' reprieve, he provoked a storm of criticism. He would never again be elected to any public office. Upon completing his term, Hoffman was named director of the unemployment compensation commission, an agency with a budget of $600 million, and he was able to continue his money-juggling operations.

While still governor, Hoffman had become president of the Circus Saints and Sinners, a group devoted to the twin duties of providing help to old circus folk and providing themselves with a good time. Hoffman became known as a boisterous buffoon, but inside he must have been a frightened, lonely man trying to keep his crimes hidden.

In 1954 newly elected Gov. Robert B. Meyner suspended Hoffman pending investigation of alleged financial irregularities in his department. Exorbitant rentals were apparently being paid for some department offices, and the state's attorney general subsequently found that favored groups stood to make nearly $2 million from a modest investment of $86,854. Other irregularities appeared in the purchase of supplies.

Hoffman put up a joyous front. The day following his suspension he appeared before the Circus Saints and Sinners. Harry Hershfield, the famous wit, cracked, "I knew you'd get into trouble in Jersey, fooling with a Meyner." Hoffman answered, "I can't even laugh." And he broke into raucous laughter.

The next two months, however, were lonely ones for Hoffman as he waited for the ax to fall. One morning in June he got up in the two-room Manhattan hotel suite provided by the Saints and keeled over with a fatal heart attack.

Later, more and more facts came out. The state became concerned when they discovered Hoffman had deposited $300,000 of public money in his own bank in a non-interest-bearing account. Officials then learned that not only was the interest missing but so was the principal.

Hoffman had written a confession to one of his daughters to be opened only upon his death. It said, ". . . until rather recently I have always lived in hope that I would somehow be able to make good, to get everything straight."

See also: LINDBERGH KIDNAPPING, ELLIS PARKER.

Holdberg Technicality   legal technicality

Much has been made of criminal cases being thrown out on technicalities, sometimes with sound legal justification but sometimes for what seem the most absurd of reasons. Probably the leading example of the latter was a criminal case in Illinois in 1919 in which a man named Goldberg was indicted on 50 criminal counts and convicted on all of them. However, the conviction was reversed on appeal and the case remanded because on one of the 50 court documents, the defendant's name was spelled Holdberg instead of Goldberg, a simple typographical error. To this day a discussion of the Holdberg Technicality is part of the regular course work at a number of law schools.

hole, the   prison punishment cell

Known by various names in different penal institutions, the hole is reserved for "incorrigible inmates." Few persons have ever understood the horrors the hole represented until the courts in recent years started taking up the question of whether such cells were unconstitutional.

They have steadily rejected the claims of prison administrators that such cells are a necessary part of institutional discipline.

The strip cell at California's Soledad Prison was one that the courts have closed down. Each such cell measured 8 feet 4 inches by 6 feet, with side and rear walls and floor of solid concrete. One prisoner, cited in a court case, spent his first eight days totally naked, sleeping on the floor with only a stiff canvas mat that "could not be folded to cover the inmate." The only other furnishing was a toilet which was flushed by a guard outside the cell, once in the morning and once at night. The cell was without light or heat and was never cleaned, so that the floors and walls were "covered with the bodily wastes of previous inhabitants."

A federal court found solitary confinement cells at New York's Dannemora Prison little different, although the cells did have sinks ("encrusted with slime, dirt, and human excremental residue"). The court also found that the prisoners were kept entirely nude for days while the windows just across from the cell were left wide open during the night—even in subfreezing temperatures.

A University of Connecticut professor of law, Leonard Orland, has a program in which his students are sent to prison for a weekend as part of their class work. He himself once spent 24 hours in the hole in a Connecticut institution. His cell was a windowless 4 by 8 foot steel box, with a single lightbulb and a small peephole controlled from outside. He was not alone in the cell—there were three cockroaches in the sink. In his book *Prisons: Houses of Darkness*, Orland described his experience as being confined in a "very small stalled elevator." And he added:

Its effect on me was devastating: I was terrified; I hallucinated; I was cold (I was nude and the temperature was in the low 60's). When the time came for my disciplinary hearing, I was prepared to say or do anything not to return to the hole. And yet I could not have experienced a tenth of the desperation of those men for whom the situation is a genuine one.

Hole in the Wall   Western outlaw stronghold

Probably the best known of all the Western badman hideouts, Hole in the Wall was located in Wyoming some 50 miles south of Buffalo and about a day's ride from Casper. East of the Hole lay the lush grazing lands of the Powder River country.

At first strictly a refuge for outlaws, particularly horse thieves and renegade Indians, Hole in the Wall soon became a haven for unemployed cowboys, especially after the drought of 1883. For a while, it appeared that Hole in the Wall was getting bigger and badder, but in reality, it was being civilized. Some of the cowboys did pilfer a cow or two, but they were homesteading the land and slowly pushing the badmen out. Still, people spoke of something called the Hole in the Wall Gang, a band that never existed. There were many gangs that periodically headquartered at Hole in the Wall, but the concept of a specific "gang" was an oversimplification. Certainly, there was little loyalty among the resident thieves, as full-time and part-time bandits shifted allegiance from one outfit to another whenever a new leader looked like he was about to produce something worthwhile. In time, Butch Cassidy lost his taste for Hole in the Wall and hid out thereafter in Brown's Hole or Robber's Roost. When the Hole in the Wall Gang is mentioned, what is meant is the Wild Bunch, of which Cassidy was the acknowledged leader. Other Hole-in-the-Wallers included the Black Jack Ketchum gang and the Laughing Sam Carey gang.

Laughing Sam might well be considered the founder of the outlaw community at Hole in the Wall, turning up there some time before 1880. Carey, a mean-streaked bank robber and train robber who killed a number of men, fled to the Hole whenever a posse was closing in on him. Somehow he never had trouble recruiting renegades and cowboys to follow him on forays, even though he was not really a very successful bandit. Once when he and his gang attempted to hold up the Spearfish Bank in South Dakota, Laughing Sam was the only one to get away alive, and he was badly shot up. He struggled back to Hole in the Wall, where a cowboy took three slugs out of him. Ten days later, he was off again with a full complement of men to hold up a train. As Butch Cassidy is supposed to have said to the Sundance Kid, "Kid, there's a lot of dummies at Hole in the Wall."

See also: BROWN'S HOLE, ROBBER'S ROOST, WILD BUNCH.

Hole-In-The-Wall Saloon   19th-century New York dive

One of the toughest saloons in New York City between the 1850s and the 1870s was the legendary Hole-In-The-Wall, located at Dover and Water Streets in the heart of the crime-ridden Fourth Ward. A stranger happening into the Hole-In-The-Wall, operated by One-Armed Charley Monell, could be mugged while standing at the bar. If he survived, he was tossed out into the street; if he was wise, he dusted himself off and left without further protest. When such an assault proved fatal, the mugger was expected to bring a cart to the side door after dark and carry the corpse away.

The dive was famous for its two women bouncers, Gallus Mag and Kate Flannery. Gallus Mag would have been enough on her own. A 6-foot Englishwoman of indeterminate age, she earned her nickname because she wore galluses, or suspenders, to hold her skirt up. She always carried a pistol in her belt and a bludgeon strapped to her wrist. While she was expert with either weapon, Gallus Mag's routine method for maintaining order in the dive was to beat a troublesome customer to the floor, grab his ear with her teeth and drag him to the door. If the man still resisted, Gallus Mag would bite his ear off. She kept these trophies in a jar of alcohol behind the bar.

It was at the Hole-In-The-Wall that one of the underworld's most infamous duels was fought in 1855 by Slobbery Jim and Patsy the Barber, two vicious members of the violent Daybreak Boys. The pair had mugged a portly immigrant by the seawall at the Battery, knocking him unconscious and relieving him of all his wealth, 12¢. Then Slobbery Jim lifted the unconscious victim over the wall and deposited him in the harbor, where he drowned. The two killers adjourned to the Hole-In-The-Wall to divide their loot, such as it was. Since he had done the heavy labor of lifting the victim over the wall, Jim insisted he should get 8¢. Certainly, he would not settle for less than 7¢. Patsy the Barber was furious, pointing out that he had done the original clubbing of the victim and was thus entitled to an equal share.

The dispute turned violent when Slobbery Jim bit down and chewed on Patsy the Barber's nose. Patsy promptly drew a knife and stuck it in Jim's ribs. The blow had no effect on Jim, however, and the pair wrestled on the floor. The fight went on, incredibly, for some 30 minutes without interference from Monell or Gallus Mag or anyone else, since this, after all, was no drunken brawl but a professional dispute. The battle finally ended in Slobbery Jim's favor when he got hold of the knife and slashed his opponent's throat. As the blood gushed from the wound, Jim proceeded to kick the Barber to death. It was the last seen of Slobbery Jim, who fled the city and was not heard of again until the Civil War, when some New York soldiers insisted they'd seen him in the uniform of a Confederate Army captain.

The Hole-In-The-Wall was too deadly a place even for the Fourth Ward and it was finally shut down by the police in 1871 after the occurrence of seven murders in two months; no one knew how many other unreported slayings had happened there.

See also: GALLUS MAG.

Holliday, John Henry "Doc" (1852–1887) gunfighter and dentist

Suffering from tuberculosis, John Henry "Doc" Holliday, an Atlanta, Ga. dentist, came west in 1873 seeking to extend his life span after being given no more than a year or two to live. He practiced dentistry now and then when he could be coaxed out of a saloon but spent most of his time gambling, usually as a house gambler, and gunning men down. Of the so-called Dodge City Gang, Doc Holliday was one of the few genuine killers, unlike Wyatt Earp, who exaggerated his kill record, and Bat Masterson, who only killed once. Doc killed often and cruelly. During the infamous gunfight at the O.K. Corral, in which he stood with the Earps, Holliday pulled a shotgun out from under his long coat and blasted Tom McLowery, who stood by his horse unarmed except for a rifle in his saddle scabbard.

Friends of the Earps never approved of their association with Holliday, whom they considered a pathological killer, but the Earps appreciated a man who was always there when they needed him. Holliday first met Wyatt Earp during the latter's days as a lawman in Dodge City, and Earp credited Doc with saving his life once when he was surrounded by a bunch of gunslinging Texas cowboys. From then on, the friendship was never to be broken. In 1879 Holliday left Dodge at about the same time as Earp departed. He ran a saloon for a time in Las Vegas, New Mexico Territory by the rule of the gun. When a love-struck former army scout named Mike Gordon tried to lure one of the saloon's prostitutes away to a better life, Holliday shot him dead.

When Wyatt Earp located in Tombstone, Doc Holliday drifted in and took a job as a gambler-bouncer at the Oriental Saloon, a lavish gambling joint in which Earp had an interest. Holliday rode out of town a lot—coincidentally while he was out riding, stagecoaches seemed to get robbed quite frequently. In March 1881 the Kinnear and Co. stage was held up near Conception. Holliday was suspected of having pulled the job, and the Earps were suspected of having planned it. The charge may have been false and spread by the Earp-hating Clanton gang, but it was indicative of Holliday's low esteem among the public.

In Griffin, Tex., Holliday got into an argument over cards with a man named Edward Bailey and killed him with a bowie knife. Doc was arrested by the town marshal. The town of Griffin having no jail available, he was locked up in a hotel room. By early evening the locals were getting liquored up and talking about a lynching. Big Nose Kate Elder, a prostitute and long-time girlfriend of Holliday, heard the rumblings and distracted the forming mob by setting fire to a shack.

While the crowd was busy with the fire, Kate helped her lover escape.

Kate's devotion to Holliday rose and fell depending on how much he beat her. At the time of the Kinnear stagecoach robbery, Doc had been particularly unkind to her, so she signed a statement that he had pulled the job and committed the murders involved. After the Earps got her away from their enemy, Sheriff John Behan, and put her in a cell in Tombstone to sober up, she retracted her statement and said her fancy man was innocent. Later, Holliday reputedly married her, a fortuitous arrangement since a wife could not testify against her husband.

After the O.K. Corral battle, Virgil Earp was injured and Morgan Earp killed by Clanton men. Holliday rode with Wyatt Earp to gun down the suspected assassins. In the Hollywood version of what followed, one Clanton supporter is depicted sneaking up on Earp in the train yard at Tucson to shoot him in the back. In truth, Earp, Holliday and three other horsemen ran the Clanton supporter down in the Southern Pacific yards and pumped 30 bullets into him. Two days later, Holliday helped corner another Clanton follower, Florentino Cruz, and executed him with 10 or 12 shots.

Over the next few years Holliday drifted around the West gambling and gunfighting, but it was apparent he was losing his big battle in life. He entered a sanatorium at Glenwood Springs, Colo. in the spring of 1887 and lasted another six months. Just before he died, on November 8, 1887, he downed a large glass of whiskey, looked at his bootless feet and said, "I'll be damned!" He had fully expected—and perhaps hoped—to die with his boots on. He was 35.

See also: DODGE CITY PEACE COMMISSION, WYATT EARP, O.K. CORRAL, ORIENTAL SALOON AND GAMBLING HOUSE.

Holmes, Alexander William (1812–?) sailor accused of murder

Alexander Holmes was a robust, handsome Finnish seaman who became involved in one of the greatest legal decisions in American history.

Holmes' ship, *William Brown,* hit an iceberg in April 1841 on its voyage from Liverpool to Philadelphia. In the rush for the two lifeboats, far fewer than could accommodate all those on board, the captain and eight seamen took refuge in one, a jolly boat, while First Mate Francis Rhodes, Holmes and seven other sailors crammed 32 passengers and themselves into the other, a longboat designed to carry 20 persons. The survivors then watched the *William Brown* go under, as they listened to the pitiful cries from the four men, eight women and 19 children stranded on board.

The two boats drifted together for a while until Capt. George L. Harris cut the jolly loose, saying he was going to try to make Newfoundland. He ignored pleas from Rhodes to take a few more from the longboat aboard the jolly. Instead he told Rhodes he was in charge and to do whatever he had to do but "only as a last resort."

At dusk it started to rain and the seas began to rise. Finally, giant waves battered the longboat. All aboard bailed water, which rose steadily to within 4 or 5 inches of the gunwales. It was soon evident that another giant wave would capsize the boat. Rhodes, who seemed about to collapse, said to Holmes, "We must go to work." Holmes looked away. Another wave slapped at the boat. "Men, fall to work or we will all perish," Rhodes screamed hysterically. This time Holmes motioned to another seaman and together they seized a passenger, Owen Riley, and heaved him overboard. Then a second man went. A third asked to be allowed to pray first and then let himself be thrown over the side. Several women clawed their way to the far end of the boat to get further away from Holmes. Even though the craft had been lightened by some 500 pounds, it still sat perilously low in the water. A man named Frank Askins was heaved overboard, and immediately, his two screaming sisters followed him. Later, there would be a dispute about whether Holmes had ordered them cast overboard or whether they had hysterically jumped after their brother. In the next 10 minutes, eight more men were jettisoned.

By morning the longboat was riding easier, now weighing a full ton less. Then crewmen found two more male passengers hiding under women's skirts. Holmes ordered them forward to bail. After a while, the sea grew rough again and the danger of sinking returned. Without a word, Holmes and three sailors seized the two men and cast them over the side. "How cruel, how cruel!" a voice moaned. It was Rhodes. He was no longer capable of clear thought after nine hours of killing. It was obvious that Seaman Holmes was in charge of the craft. Some sailors wanted to throw some of the women over, but Rhodes stopped them, saying, "No, we will go before the women."

A little after 9 o'clock, the sun appeared in brightening skies, and Holmes said to the passengers, who still eyed him warily: "Be of good cheer. There will be no more killing. We will all live or perish together." An hour later, they were picked up by a passing schooner bound for Le Havre. After reaching Le Havre, the survivors were put on another vessel and sent to New York. When they got there, they discovered that Capt. Harris and the jolly boat had made it safely and the news of their survival and the ordeal had preceded them. Public debate was raging over whether or not the frightful events aboard the longboat had been justified.

Newspapers throughout the country demanded murder trials be held. The *New York Courier* wrote, "Every soul aboard that boat had the same right to such protection as she afforded as the mate and the seamen and until a fair and equal chance was given by lot for a decision as to who should be sacrificed, no man could throw his fellow man overboard without committing murder." And the *Philadelphia Public Ledger* declared, "No human being is authorized to kill another in self-preservation unless against an attempt of that other to kill."

U.S. attorney William Meredith brought murder indictments against Rhodes and Holmes in Philadelphia. Capt. Harris was allowed to leave and immediately shipped out. Rhodes disappeared and was believed to have left with Capt. Harris. Only Holmes surrendered to face trial. The prosecution, aided by the testimony of three women, hammered away at the point that no seaman had died and no lots had been drawn. However, most of the survivors testified in Holmes' behalf. The defense was headed by David Paul Brown, the Clarence Darrow of his day, who was hired to represent Holmes by the Female Seamen's Friend Society. Brown hit hard at the prosecution charges:

Whoever heard of casting lots at midnight in a sinking boat, in the midst of darkness, of rain, of terror, and of confusion. This case, in order to embrace all its horrible relations, ought to be decided in a longboat, hundreds of leagues from shore, loaded to the very gunwales with 41 half-naked victims, with provision only sufficient to prolong the agonies of famine and of thirst, with all the elements combined against her, leaking from below, filling also from above, surrounded by ice, unmanageable from her condition and subject to destruction from the least change of wind and the waves—most variable and most terrible of all elements. Decided at such a tribunal, nature would at once pronounce a verdict not only of acquittal but of commendation.

Following an eight-day trial, the case went to the jury. After 16 hours the jury advised the court it couldn't agree and was sent back for more deliberations. Ten hours later, the jury returned a verdict of guilty, with a recommendation of mercy. By this time, public opinion had shifted entirely in Holmes' favor. Before he was sentenced, even the *Philadelphia Public Ledger*—the very newspaper that had once said, "An act of greater atrocity could scarcely be conceived of"—now warned that an effort would "be made to have him pardoned by the President if anything more than a nominal sentence be passed upon him."

Holmes got six months and was fined $20, and even this light sentence brought many protests. He served his time and then disappeared back to sea. His six-month punishment established the precedent that a sailor "is bound to set a greater value on the life of others than on his own."

Holmes, H. H. (1858–1896) mass murderer

His real name was Herman Webster Mudgett, but he became infamous as H. H. Holmes—probably the greatest mass killer in American history. At various times, he admitted killing anywhere from 20 to 27 persons, being a master of inconsistency, and undoubtedly he murdered many more. Some wild-eyed biographers credit him with killing 200 women in his "murder castle" in Chicago during the 1890s, while a more reasonable count would fall somewhere between 40 and 100.

If there was any question about his arithmetic, there was none about his dedication. Holmes killed with a bizarre fervor to make the last possible cent out of his victims, mostly marriage-starved women whom he murdered for their money. He kept a keen eye out for newspaper ads requesting skeletons, and when he found such an ad, he would scrape his latest victim's bones clean and sell the skeleton to an interested medical student or institution.

As a medical school student, Herman Mudgett had always shown the greatest interest in bodies, more so in those of women than those of men. However, he lost interest in his studies of female anatomy and in time, despite a marriage before he was 20 and a second bigamous one before he was 30, became adept at such additional careers as horse thieving, forging and swindling. He finally went into murder in a big way. With the proceeds from his various crimes, he built a massive "hotel" in 1892 at Sixty-third and Wallace, in anticipation of the Columbian Exposition the following year.

The first floor consisted of stores and the second and third floors of about 100 rooms. Holmes used several as his office and his living quarters. The remaining rooms were for guests, many of whom were never seen alive again. A newspaper subsequently described one of the rooms as an "asphyxiation chamber" with "no light—with gas connections." The room had no windows; the door was equipped with stout bolts; and the walls were padded with asbestos. All Holmes had to do was get a victim in the room and turn on the gas. Most of the rooms featured these gas connections and certain ones had false-bottom floors, which covered small airless chambers. Some of the rooms were lined with iron plates and some had blowtorchlike appliances. Various rooms had chutes that carried human cargo to the basement. Here, Holmes maintained a crematory, complete with vats of corrosive acid and quicklime pits. The pits later yielded up bone and skull fragments of many women he had held prisoner and killed. All the "prison" rooms had an alarm that buzzed in Holmes' quarters if a victim attempted to break out. The evidence indicated that he kept many of the women prisoners for months before he decided to dispose of them.

Holmes obtained most of his victims through ads offering good jobs in a big city or through offers of marriage. If the offer was for a job, he would describe several in detail, and a young woman on her first visit would select the one she wanted. Holmes then sent her home to pack her things and withdraw all her money from the bank since she would need the money to get set up. He would require that the woman not reveal his name to anyone and he would not tell her where the job was until she returned with her money, claiming he had business competitors who were trying to steal his clients. When the woman returned and Holmes was satisfied she had revealed nothing about him, he would take her prisoner. If he was not satisfied, he would say the job had been canceled and send her away. Those whom he offered to marry got the same sort of line. If they came back with less than all their worldly goods, Holmes would use various types of torture apparatuses to make them reveal the whereabouts of their remaining valuables. He then would imprison the women while he went to get their property.

Amazingly, Holmes was able to keep his wholesale murder operation secret for four years. His trouble started when he got involved in an insurance swindle with a shady character named Benjamin F. Pitzel. To pull it off, they both traveled around the country, and in the process Holmes was arrested in St. Louis. He revealed part of the insurance scam to a cell mate, a notorious bank robber named Marion Hedgepeth. Holmes offered Hedgepeth money to put him in touch with a good lawyer. Hedgepeth obliged and Holmes got out, promptly forgetting to pay Hedgepeth. He went to Philadelphia and met up with Pitzel. The two had a falling out, and Holmes killed his partner in crime. About this time, Hedgepeth decided his former cell mate had stiffed him and told the authorities what he knew. Holmes was captured and the Pitzel murder discovered. When Chicago police searched his "hotel," the results were awesome.

Before he was hanged in Philadelphia on May 7, 1896, for the Pitzel murder, since that city refused to surrender him to Chicago for his more gruesome deeds, Holmes made a number of confessions concerning the women he had killed. He accepted an offer of $5,000 from a Chicago newspaper for his story and then perversely concocted a death list that included several women who were still alive and omitted others who had been identified among his victims.

See also: MARION HEDGEPETH.

Honeymoon Gang 19th-century New York gang

One of the most brutal New York gangs in the mid-1800s was the Honeymoon Gang, whose members were considered so beyond the pale that they were denied protection by the politicians who took care of most other organized gangsters because of their value as electoral enforcers.

By 1853 the Honeymooners had so terrorized the East Side's 18th Ward that it became literally unsafe to walk there. Every evening the gang would place their men at each corner of Madison Avenue and 29th Street and attack every well-dressed citizen who came along. At midnight the Honeymooners' "basher patrol" would adjourn to a drinking establishment to spend a portion of the night's ill-gotten gains.

The Honeymooners were not molested by police until George W. Walling was appointed captain of the district in late 1853. Organizing the city's first Strong Arm Squad, he picked out his six burliest men, put them in plain clothes and sent them into the Honeymooners' turf armed with locust clubs. The beefy officers simply walked right up to the gangsters and battered them senseless before they could bring their own bludgeons and brass knuckles into play. A few nights of this treatment convinced the Honeymooners to evacuate their ambush posts. But this did not satisfy Walling, who then provided every policeman on his roster with the identifications of all the Honeymooners. Whenever one was sighted, he was attacked and beaten mercilessly. Within two weeks the Honeymoon Gang vanished, its members scattering to other wards where police tactics were not so rough.

See also: STRONG ARM SQUAD.

hoodlum

Hoodlum is as American as apple pie. The word refers to a member of any gang of thugs. The explanations for its origin are varied and many, but there is no doubt that the term was first applied to the San Francisco underworld in the late 1860s. One theory holds that the term was initially used to describe several vicious brothers whose name was Hoodler and that the name was corrupted into "hoodlum" with the passage of time. Another explanation is that it arose from the street thugs' practice of turning up the collar and lapels of their jackets to act, as much as possible, as a hood while they stalked and molested their victims.

The *Los Angeles Express* of August 25, 1877, seemed to offer the most plausible theory:

A gang of bad boys from fourteen to nineteen years of age were associated for the purpose of stealing. These boys had a rendezvous, and when danger threatened them their words of warning were 'Huddle 'em! Huddle 'em!' An article headed 'Huddle 'Em' describing the gang and their plans of operation, was published in the San Francisco Times. The name applied to them was soon contracted to hoodlum.

Hoodoo War   See MASON COUNTY WAR.

Hook Gang   19th-century New York waterfront gang

The Hook Gang was composed of thugs who worked the East River area around the Corlears' Hook section of New York from the late 1860s to the late 1870s.

Known as the daffiest of all river pirates, the Hookers were captained by Terry Le Strange, James Coffee, Tommy Shay and Suds Merrick. Neither the gang nor its individual members thought any job was too big for them. Coffee and Shay once rowed up to the boat of an eight-man rowing club and, with guns leveled, ordered them to head for the Brooklyn shore. When they got within 50 yards of shore, they forced the rowers to jump and swim for it and headed back to Manhattan with their prize boat. Long before the rowers got back to sound the alarm, the pair had transported the outsized craft to the Hudson docks and sold it to the skipper of a canal boat.

Another gang member, the redoubtable Slipsey Ward, finally overstepped himself when he mounted the

The Hook Gang, 19th-century river pirates, fought pitched battles with police for more than a decade before finally being driven from the East River.

deck of a schooner at Pike Street and attempted single-handedly to overpower the crew of six. He had downed three before he was stopped; he ended up with a long sentence at Auburn Prison for this crime. On more than one occasion, the Hookers would pull a number of wagons up to a likely boat in dock and, after simply cordoning off the street, loot it at their leisure. Once, an officer a few blocks away saw their barricades and, thinking there was some authorized work going on, helpfully diverted traffic onto a side street.

In a manner of speaking, the Hookers had no one to blame but themselves for their eventual demise. It all started when one of their number, Nigger Wallace, tried to rob three men in a rowboat. They turned out to be three detectives taking the sun on their day off, and Wallace ended up dunked and towed off to jail. This started the police thinking that if they had some decoy craft on the river, they could catch the pirates in their act. Thus, in 1876 the Steamboat Squad was organized. By the end of the decade, the police had cleared the Corlears' Hook area. Many of the Hookers were imprisoned, others scattered and the rest shifted their activities to safer, onshore thefts and burglaries.

See also: SUDS MERRICK, STEAMBOAT SQUAD.

Hoover, Herbert Clark (1874–1964)   Al Capone's nemesis

"That bastard," Al Capone was to repeat many times after his conviction on income tax charges. "That bastard got me." He was referring to President Herbert Hoover; underworld opinion held that Capone had been railroaded because of the personal vindictiveness of a bitter president of the United States. According to mob legend, Hoover had come to hate Capone for either of two reasons or both. One was that shortly after his victory over Al Smith in the 1928 election, Hoover had visited the J. C. Penney estate on Belle Isle in Florida, not far from the Capone retreat on Palm Island. As the story went, there was so much shouting, females screaming and shooting during the night from the Capone compound that Hoover could not fall asleep, and he vowed to crush the mobster once he took office. According to the second story, Hoover watched in chagrin as a crowd of newsmen in a Miami hotel lobby deserted the president-elect for what they regarded as a more important interviewee, Capone.

In fact, both stories are apocryphal, but it is true that Hoover had determined to bring down Capone, whom he regarded as a blot on the national honor. The method used was suggested to Hoover by Col. Frank Knox, publisher of the *Chicago Daily News,* who came to him in despair over the unwillingness or inability of local and state authorities to jail Capone. He suggested to Hoover that the best way to catch the mobster was to charge him with two federal offenses: bootlegging and income tax evasion.

Thereafter, Hoover hounded the Treasury Department to eliminate Capone. Andrew Mellon, who was secretary of the treasury at the time, later recalled the activities of Hoover's so-called Medicine Cabinet, a small group of high officials the president invited to the White House each morning to toss around a medicine ball. "Every morning when the exercising started, Mr. Hoover would bring up the subject," Mellon said. "He'd ask me, 'Have you got that fellow Al Capone yet?' And at the end of the session, he'd tell me, 'Remember now, I want that Capone in jail.'"

In another era, or in another economic climate, Herbert Hoover might well have won the reelection just for successfully putting Capone behind bars. But not in the early 1930s. The public clearly agreed with a minor Capone follower quoted by the press as saying, "President Hoover should be worrying more about putting people to work than sending a simple bootlegger to prison."

Hoover, J. Edgar (1895–1972) FBI director

For better or worse, the history of the Federal Bureau of Investigation can be told in the life of its longtime director, J. Edgar Hoover. Hoover more than typified the agency, he was in a very real sense *the* FBI. The agency's successes were attributable to him, just as its excesses and abuses often resulted from his personal failings. Despite scandals that were revealed after Hoover's death, such as the agency's deliberate attempts to destroy individuals not accused of crimes by leaking damaging information—sometimes true, often false—about them, the FBI is recognized as one of the most brilliant and efficient investigative forces in any country.

It was not always that way, especially when Hoover joined the U.S. Department of Justice in 1917 as a young attorney. The agency, then known as the Bureau of Investigation, was a disorganized body of about 200 poorly supervised agents, some political hacks, others outright crooks. The agency was virtually worthless in any battle against crime and proved totally incapable of preventing sabotage during World War I. The great sabotage and espionage ring organized by German ambassador Johann von Bernstorff had almost a free hand to operate in this country. Defense plants were wrecked and wheat fields in the West set afire. The great "Black Tom" explosion in New York Harbor destroyed the nation's biggest arsenal, producing a tremendous roar heard more than 100 miles away.

Hoover rose rapidly in the ranks and became special assistant to Attorney General A. Mitchell Palmer.

Despite his later denials, Hoover played a vital role in the Palmer Raids inspired by the postwar Red Scare. He planned and executed mass raids against aliens, built up a card file on 450,000 radicals and organized his first informer network, a technique Hoover developed to the level of a science, far better than any other American law official.

By 1924 the Bureau of Investigation was mired in scandal, much like the late Harding administration. Hoover was named to head the agency and cleanse it. To his credit, he did so with ruthless efficiency, forcing out scores of incompetents and cheats and establishing professional standards for agents, such as the requirement that new recruits have training as either lawyers or accountants. During the 1930s Hoover toughened the FBI into a highly mobile crime-busting organization. He laid heavy emphasis on scientific detection methods and established the FBI Laboratory. The FBI National Academy was formed to train local police officers in the newest law enforcement techniques.

In 1933 Hoover launched a highly publicized war on the so-called public enemies—Dillinger, the Barkers, Alvin Karpis, Pretty Boy Floyd, Baby Face Nelson, Machine Gun Kelly and others of their ilk, all 20th-century versions of the desperadoes of the Old West. They were relatively easy targets, certainly compared to the Mafia and the emerging national crime syndicate formed by the great ex-bootlegging gangs of the Prohibition era. Since he was a Republican holdover in a Democratic administration, Hoover needed some sort of spectacular display. Speaking of the campaign years later, a high ex-FBI official, William C. Sullivan, said, "The whole of the FBI's main thrust was not investigation but public relations and propaganda to glorify its director."

Hoover needed all the public relations he could get in the 1930s. When John Dillinger was killed, a conservative Virginia newspaper editor assailed the FBI's work on the case. "Any brave man," he editorialized, "would have walked down the aisle and arrested Dillinger . . . why were there so many cowards afraid of this one man? The answer is that the federal agents are mostly cowards."

Later it was revealed that the Secret Service was secretly investigating the conduct of FBI agents in the Dillinger case and the case of another gang member, Eddie Green, who had been described as shot while attempting an armed escape from FBI custody. Green was found to be unarmed, however. Clearly, the Secret Service was trying to show that the G-men were trigger-happy amateurs at best. In 1936 Hoover himself came under rigorous attack in Congress. Sen. Kenneth D. McKellar of Tennessee grilled him at an appropriations hearing about his background and experience, bringing out the fact that Hoover had never personally handled an investigation or made an arrest.

Hoover reacted to this attack on his courage and competence the following month by personally arresting public enemy Alvin "Creepy" Karpis in New Orleans. Karpis was later to insist that Hoover had hidden out of sight until after other agents had seized him in a car and called to Hoover that it was safe to approach. On the other hand, Don Whitehead in *The FBI Story* credited Hoover as having "reached into the car and grabbed Karpis before he could reach for a rifle on the back seat." There is some question about this accomplishment, since the car had no back seat. The arrest proved to be a bit of a fiasco when none of the dozens of agents present could carry out Hoover's orders to "put the handcuffs on him." None of them had thought to bring along handcuffs.

In 1939 Hoover's FBI was handed the responsibility of guarding the nation against sabotage and subversion. It was these wartime duties, carried out with efficiency, that did the most to upgrade Hoover's image to one of unquestioned authority and wisdom. By 1943 Sen. McKellar was calling him a "grand man."

In the post-1945 cold war years, Hoover rediscovered the Red Menace that had launched his career. The FBI's war on the Communist Party reached the stage of the ridiculous when agency informers in the organization probably outnumbered bona fide members. As the party dropped in size and influence, Hoover assured conservatives this merely indicated that the members were going underground and that more concentrated efforts—and larger budgets—were needed to combat the remaining threat. Hoover long ago had discovered that while conservatives might bewail the crime menace, their hold on the purse strings did not loosen much to combat such danger. However, given a good Red Scare, the money simply gushed forth.

In all, Hoover served under eight presidents, none of whom dared take the political consequences of attempting to oust him. Few attorneys general, technically his superiors, countered his views, especially in the 1940s and 1950s. The first to give Hoover genuine orders was Robert Kennedy in 1961, when he insisted the FBI concentrate on battling organized crime, truly an affront to its director, who for years had denied the existence of organized crime and the Mafia. Critics of Hoover said he took this tack because fighting the syndicate was not an easy matter, certainly more difficult than battling the great threat to the Republic posed by car thieves, probably 90 percent of whom were joyriding teenagers.

In the early 1960s it was clear that President John Kennedy wished to replace Hoover, who had reached retirement age, but having been elected by a thin majority, he felt incapable of withstanding the political repercussions. Undoubtedly, though, Kennedy planned to oust him if reelected to a second term. After Kennedy's assassination Lyndon Johnson is said to have exploited his power to force Hoover to step down by demanding the director perform illegal political investigations for him. According to ex-FBI official Sullivan, "There was absolutely nothing Johnson wouldn't ask of the FBI, and Hoover hotfooted it to Johnson's demands."

By the time he reached his late sixties, Hoover had turned crotchety and vindictive, launching secret operations against real and perceived personal enemies, including a particularly vicious campaign to discredit Martin Luther King based on sexual misbehavior. A lifelong bachelor, Hoover was never tainted by any innuendos of sexual improprieties.

Perhaps the best example of the tenor within the FBI in this period occurred during a top-level FBI meeting in 1968 presided over by Clyde Tolson, the number two man in the agency and Hoover's alter ego. When Robert Kennedy's name came up, Tolson declared, "I hope someone shoots and kills the son of a bitch." Shortly thereafter, someone did.

By 1970 President Richard Nixon had resolved to get rid of Hoover. The president invited him to the Oval Office to inform him that his tenure was at an end. Sullivan, who obviously was Nixon's man within the FBI, wrote in his book *The Bureau—My Thirty Years in Hoover's FBI* that Hoover "started talking non-stop. It was his usual line of conversation, starring Dillinger, Ma Barker and a cast of thousands, and he kept talking until the President ended the interview.

"Assistant Attorney General Robert Mardian called me later and said: 'Christ almighty, Nixon lost his guts. He had Hoover there in his office, he knew what he was supposed to tell him, but he got cold feet. He couldn't go through with it.'"

Later, when Hoover forced Sullivan out of the FBI, Nixon, Mardian, John Mitchell, John Ehrlichman and Bob Haldeman determined that Hoover would go after Nixon's reelection. Hoover died, however, in May 1972, six months before the election. Had he lived, he undoubtedly would have survived this new threat to his reign, as his would-be purgers became immersed in the Watergate scandal, from which none would survive politically. They would have needed Hoover more than he would have needed them.

After Hoover's death and especially after the disclosure of his latter-day excesses, such as the notorious COINTELPRO program aimed at punishing Hoover targets who were neither convicted nor even suspected of illegal activities, some of his critics demanded

Hoover's name be taken off the new FBI headquarters building. It was a senseless exercise. To separate Hoover from the FBI in such fashion would be a silly attempt to rewrite history. The FBI itself, not the building, was Hoover's monument. The agency in 1972 was and, indeed, still is—"warts and all"—the embodiment of J. Edgar Hoover.

See also: BRIEFCASE AGENTS, COSA NOSTRA, ALVIN "CREEPY" KARPIS, GASTON BULLOCK MEANS, PALMER RAIDS, MELVIN PURVIS, CLYDE A. TOLSON.

Hope, Jimmy (1840–?) police fixer and bank burglar

One of the most important underworld figures of the 19th century, Jimmy Hope was a crooked ex-cop in New York who handled "the fix" for the Shang Draper–George Leonidas Leslie mob of bank burglars.

Maintaining a fifth column of crooked officers within the New York Police Department, Hope could get the law to do anything he wanted, an ability he demonstrated stunningly in the great $2,747,000 looting of the Manhattan Savings Institution in 1878. In preparation for that job, he paid off many of the officers in the Detective Bureau just as he had in the past. Ordered to ensure the bank watchman would not interfere, Hope determined that the man could not be bribed. He solved the dilemma by having him hired away to a better-paying job on the recommendation of several police officers. When Manhattan Savings officials asked the police department to suggest a replacement, Hope saw to it that a 60-year-old Irishman named Patty Shevlin got the job. Shevlin was perfect. Whenever safecracker George Leonidas Leslie wanted to study the layout of the bank or the safe, Shevlin was told to take a nap in the basement and stay there until morning.

Hope also arranged that on the day of the burglary, Sunday morning, October 27, the policeman on the beat, John Nugent, would remain at a suitable distance away from the bank, yet close enough to guard the retreat of the burglars and, if necessary, to delay or mislead pursuit. As it was, the mob had so much loot packed in their small satchels that Nugent had to be summoned to carry one of them.

It took almost a year for the police to make arrests in this case. Two of the gang, Abe Coakley and Banjo Pete Emerson, were acquitted, but Bill Kelly and, ironically, Jimmy Hope were convicted. Patrolman Nugent was said to have won his freedom by bribing a juror, but within a few months he was convicted and sent to prison for highway robbery. Kelly and Hope got long prison terms. When the ex-fixer was set free near the turn of the century, he quickly disappeared.

See also: GEORGE LEONIDAS LESLIE.

Horn, Tom (1860–1903) hired killer

In recent years there have been efforts by some writers and even by Hollywood—in a 1980 movie—to "rehabilitate" Tom Horn, probably the most callous hired gun and bushwacker the Old West ever saw. Much is made of Horn's early years and his heroism as an army scout under the celebrated Al Sieber and as a lawman and cowboy. Some of the more unquestioning also applaud his four years as a Pinkerton, although during that period he can only be described as a roving gun for the agency, with a toll of victims reputedly amounting to 17. Horn quit the Pinkertons, announcing he "had no more stomach for it" Agency apologists said that indicated he found the job too boring; others thought it meant Horn felt he was underpaid for the work. Immediately thereafter, he offered his lethal services to Wyoming cattlemen. There was no one Tom Horn wouldn't kill for $500. "Killing men is my specialty," he once remarked. "I look at it as a business proposition and I think I have a corner on the market."

Born in Missouri in 1860, he left home at about age 13, after an altercation with his father, and headed west. A tough, headstrong youth, he is believed to have had a row with Billy the Kid and slapped his face. No one was ever to accuse Horn of lacking guts. At 15 he was a stagecoach driver and from 1875 to 1886 he worked off and on for Al Sieber, chief army scout at the San Carlos Indian Reservation. It was Horn who arranged the final surrender of Geronimo to Gen. Nelson Miles in 1886. After that, he became a deputy sheriff in the Arizona Territory.

By the time he went to work for the Pinkertons, he had quite a reputation, one that only worsened while he served in the agency. He ached with the desire for big money, but his only real talent was his skill with guns. The law paid peanuts, the Pinks somewhat more. The real money lay in working directly for the big cattlemen, settling old scores for them and eliminating small ranchers and rustlers (in Cheyenne's cattle baron circles the two terms were used interchangeably). Members of the Wyoming Cattlemen's Association bid high for Horn's services and Horn gloried in their attentions. He smoked their cigars, drank their liquor, backslapped with them and murdered for them.

Horn was a tidy butcher and regarded his assassinations as works of art. Testimony at his later trial would reveal how even in a driving rain, he waited for hours chewing on cuds of raw bacon, to get the one sure shot at a victim. After the kill he always left behind his trademark, a small rock under the victim's head, so that there could be no argument over who had carried out the assignment.

Horn once even offered his deadly services to Gov. W. A. Richards of Wyoming. The governor, who owned a large ranch in the Big Horn country, was fearful of having the gunman seen at his office in the state capital, so he used the premises of the state Board of Livestock Commissioners. Another big stockman, William Irvine, who took part in the meeting, later recollected:

The Governor was quite nervous, so was I, Horn perfectly cool; told the Governor he would either drive every rustler out of the Big Horn County, or take no pay other than $350 advanced to buy two horses and a pack outfit; that when he had finished the job to the Governor's satisfaction he should receive $5,000 because, he said in conclusion, "Whenever everything else fails, I have a system which never does." He placed no limit on the number of men to be gotten rid of.

Irvine said the governor clearly got cold feet when Horn matter-of-factly made his murder proposition. The killer saw this immediately and tactfully ended the discussion by saying: "I presume that is about all you wanted to know, Sir. I shall be glad to hear from you at any time I can be of service."

Horn's murder dealing became so well known that rustlers and other desperadoes often cleared out of an area when he appeared on the scene. But the small rancher, his entire life tied up in his meager holdings, could not. And if a big cattleman said a small rancher was rustling his cattle, that was good enough for Horn.

Because of his powerful connections, Horn was considered immune from the law. But in 1901 he murdered a 14-year-old boy, Willie Nickell, from ambush. Hired to shoot the boy's sheepman father, Horn mistook the youth for the father in the early dawn light. The case remained unsolved until Joe Lefors, a deputy U.S. marshal who led the famous posse that chased Butch Cassidy and the Sundance Kid, took over the investigation. He wormed his way into Horn's confidence, and when the latter was drinking heavily, he got him to boast of his killings, including the Nickell affair, while hidden witnesses and a stenographer listened.

Horn was thrown in jail. When he sobered up, he insisted he had merely been telling tall tales and accused the stenographer of adding statements he had not made. Horn had brilliant legal talent defending him at his trial, with some $5,000 donated to his defense fund by an unknown "admirer." However, the case against him was overwhelming and he was sentenced to hang.

While he awaited execution, people wondered if Horn would start naming all his powerful employers, and it appears that employers wondered too. In August 1903 someone smuggled a pistol to him, and he escaped with another prisoner. He was quickly recaptured, how-ever, and spent much of the rest of his time hurriedly penning his memoirs, leaving out, of course, all references to his murderous "range detecting." With the streets of Cheyenne patrolled by militiamen, Tom Horn was hanged on November 20, 1903, his lips still sealed.

A Wyoming cattleman was to recall, "He died without 'squealing,' to the great relief of many very respectable citizens of the West."

In recent years some effort has been made to discredit the Lefors testimony. Dean Krakel, Horn's chief biographer and author of *The Saga of Tom Horn*, insists the Horn confession was a frame-up and would be inadmissible in modern courts and that Horn was innocent of the Nickell shooting.

See also: RANGE DETECTIVES.

Horrell-Higgins feud

One of Texas' bloodiest feuds, the Horrell-Higgins conflict broke out in central Texas in 1873 over charges of cattle rustling around the frontier town of Lampasas, northwest of Austin. Suspicion centered on the men of the Horrell spread. When the sheriff attempted to arrest one of the Horrell men, he was promptly killed. A squad of state officers were dispatched to Lampasas to take care of the Horrells, once again with fatal consequences for the law officers. A group of Horrells were found in the Gem Saloon and ordered to give up their guns and surrender. Shooting broke out immediately. When the gunsmoke cleared, four officers lay dead or dying. Only Mart Horrell, who was wounded, was arrested. However, when he was placed in the jail at Georgetown, his friends and brothers broke in and freed him. The Horrells then moved their herds into New Mexico to avoid further problems with the Texas authorities.

Finding themselves ensnarled in similar rustling disputes in New Mexico, the Horrells returned to Texas, where two of them were tried and acquitted in the killing of the four law officers. Meanwhile, new suspicions about the Horrells rustling cattle were voiced, especially by the Higgins clan, which had lost a considerable amount of stock. Pink Higgins led his family in a war against the Horrells. Higgins, a fiery gunfighter, threatened to wipe out every Horrell. In January 1877 Pink killed Merritt Horrell at the Gem.

With all sorts of legal charges against both clans, someone broke into the courthouse one night in July 1877 and removed the records of all pending criminal cases. The families then prepared to settle the matter between themselves. Later that same month the two factions fought a bitter gun battle for several hours in the streets of Lampasas. At least one innocent bystander was among those killed.

Finally, in July the Texas Rangers moved into the area in force. A detachment under Sgt. N. O. Reynolds entered the Horrell ranch house before dawn and captured the family and its supporters without a fight. Other Rangers simultaneously captured the Higgins clan. Realizing that a few prison sentences would hardly end the shooting, the Rangers had long discussions with each group. Eventually, members of both families signed a formal peace treaty. Such agreements had been tried in other feuds without success, but in this case all the participants faithfully observed the treaty and the Horrell-Higgins feud ended.

See also: JOHN CALHOUN PINCKNEY "PINK" HIGGINS.

horse poisoners

Common during the early decades of this century in New York, horse poisoning was one of the most detested of all crimes, viewed with horror by the public, the police and even much of the underworld. The horse was the lifeline of many businesses, such as the produce, ice cream, beer and seltzer trades. Businessmen faced with stiff competition would often hire gangsters to destroy the competition's trade. The simplest way to do this was to poison a rival's horses, thus destroying his distribution system. It was a common sight on the Lower East Side to see a produce seller with two dead horses desperately trying to sell his stock at half price to clamoring housewives before it was all ruined.

By 1913 three gangs of horse poisoners under the leaderships of Yoske Nigger, whose real name was Joseph Toplinsky, Charley the Cripple, whose real name was Charles Vitoffsky, and Johnny Levinsky dominated the field. They would steal or poison horses to order. Unlike their clients, these three did not engage in cutthroat competition among themselves. Instead they divided the field into separate monopolies, with Yoske Nigger handling the produce markets, truckmen and livery stables; Charley the Cripple the seltzer and soda water dealers and manufacturers; and Levinsky the ice cream trade. Whenever an order came in from some area not covered by this jurisdictional agreement, the three handled the matter jointly.

A defecting member of one of the gangs finally revealed to the police the trio's scale of fees:

hooting, fatal	$500
Shooting, not fatal	$100
Poisoning a team	$50
Poisoning one horse	$35
Stealing a horse and rig	$25

The first two items, of course, referred to human victims and were much higher than the rates a client could find elsewhere. Since many gangsters at the time hired out to do a murder for as little as $10 to $20, it was not surprising that most of the trio's business was limited to horses. Yet the horse poisoners were hated by other gangsters who had no qualms about shooting humans but found the poisoning of dumb beasts despicable.

Eventually, the three poisoners felt the full wrath of the law when a chicken dealer named Barnett Baff was shot to death in 1914. According to the police theory, Baff's competitors had paid the staggering sum of $4,200 for his violent demise. This money, was supposedly given to Levinsky, Yoske Nigger and Charley the Cripple, who divided it up after paying a mere $50 to the actual hit man. Under close surveillance and harassment by the police, the trio abandoned their poisoning practices and retired to reputable business lives in the wilds of Brooklyn, remaining honest, it was said, until the bootlegging era beckoned them back to criminality.

horse stealing

As an old quip has it, "One day the first man tamed the first horse; the next day another man stole it." Certainly, horse stealing was one of the most prevalent crimes in colonial America, and horse thieves flourished during the Revolution, selling animals to both sides and often the same beasts at that. However, horse stealing in America is most often associated with the West, where it was considered a crime without equal. Stealing horses was regarded as murder, and indeed, it often amounted to as much since a man without his horse in open spaces was at the mercy of the elements or of Indian raiders as well as vulnerable to death by starvation or thirst.

T. A. McNeal in *When Kansas Was Young* summed up the utter necessity of a horse:

A horse was about the only means of conveyance, and in the cattle business it was essential. It was necessary, too, to let the horses run on the range unguarded. The cattlemen reasoned that unless the men who lusted for the possession of good horses were restrained by fear of prompt and violent death, no man would be sure that when he turned his horses out at night he would be able to gather any of them in the morning.

In 1878 a Houston, Tex. newspaper bemoaned the fact that 100,000 horses had been stolen in the state during the preceding three years.

It further estimated that 750 men are regularly engaged in this business and that not more than one in ten is ever captured and brought to justice. By common prac-

tice in the rural districts, every man caught is either shot on the spot or hanged to the nearest tree. No instance is yet recorded where the law paid the slightest attention to lynchers of this kind. It is conceded that the man who steals a horse forfeits his life to the owner. It is a game of life and death. Men will pursue these thieves for 500 miles, go any length, spend any amount of money to capture them, and fight them to the death when overtaken. That they will be totally exterminated admits of no doubt. The poor scoundrels cannot last long when the feeling of all civilization is so much aroused against them as it now is in Texas.

When vigilantes in Fort Griffin hanged a horse thief from a pecan tree and put a pick and shovel there for anyone with a mind to bury him, a correspondent for the *Dallas Herald* recorded the event and added: "So far, so good. As long as the committee strings up the right parties, it has the well wishes of every lover of tranquility."

Lynching of horse thieves became common throughout the entire West, but it was not a very effective deterrent. The horse thieves thrived. One, Dutch Henry, known as the King of the Horse Thieves, had some 300 men working during one period for him. Because horses could easily be recognized on sight by former owners, thieves would often drive them hundreds, even a thousand miles, to sell them. The famed Horse-Thief Trail ran from Salt Lake City in the north to the Mexican border in the south without ever once following the frequently used commercial trails. Horse thieves worked both ends of their run: a gang stealing horses in Texas would drive them to Kansas and in Kansas collar a herd and drive it back to Texas.

Perhaps the futility of using the death penalty as a deterrent is illustrated by the history of this crime. Even the threat of hangings on the spot did not deter horse thieves from stealing thousands of horses each year. Their ranks were slowly thinned only after the development of efficient range detective methods and, more important, after the invention of the horseless carriage.

See also: DUTCH HENRY, HORSE-THIEF TRAIL, HENRY TUFTS.

Horse-Thief Trail

In the post–Civil War West it was possible for outlaws to drive stolen horses all the way from Salt Lake City, Utah through Arizona, New Mexico and Texas to Mexico without once running into the law or an honest rider. The route they followed was the famous but unmarked Horse-Thief Trail, and any man who knew the entire route had his fortune made, the only source of danger being other horse thieves.

Hot Corn Girls   See EDWARD COLEMAN.

Hot Springs, Arkansas   See WHITE FRONT CIGAR STORE.

Hotsy Totsy Club   New York speakeasy

Among all the notorious New York speakeasies that thrived during Prohibition, none had a worse reputation than the Hotsy Totsy Club, a second-floor joint on Broadway between 54th and 55th Streets. Although Hymie Cohen fronted as the proprietor, a big chunk of the place was owned by gangster Legs Diamond. Diamond utilized the club to hold court and directed several rackets from there. He also used it as an execution site. Many crime figures whom Diamond wished to prevail upon would be invited there for some revelry and a business discussion. If they failed to go along with Diamond's view of things, they were murdered in a back room and later carried out "drunk."

The Hotsy Totsy's bloodiest claim to fame came in 1929, when Diamond and sidekick Charles Entratta gunned down a hoodlum named Red Cassidy. Also killed in the wild shoot-out at the bar was an innocent bystander, Simon Walker, who nonetheless happened to be wearing two loaded revolvers in his belt. Unlike the pair's other murders in the club, a great number of witnesses were present during the shooting causing Diamond and Entratta to flee.

From hiding, Diamond directed a reign of killings to clear his name. That meant the bartender had to be rubbed out, along with three customers who had seen what had happened. The cashier, a waiter, the hat check girl and another club, hanger-on disappeared, although their fate was not entirely a mystery to police or the newspapers. But suspicions meant little. Diamond and Entratta surrendered and were charged with the killings at the club. But they were soon freed because the authorities had no witnesses to present evidence against them.

See also: JACK "LEGS" DIAMOND.

Hounds   19th-century San Francisco anti-foreigner gang

Officially bearing the high-sounding title of the San Francisco Society of Regulators, the Hounds, as they were more commonly called, were a collection of young thugs organized to contain the peril to Anglo-Americans presented by Spanish Americans in San Francisco in 1849.

Under the pretense of a fiery patriotism, flamed by the influence of the Know Nothings, the Hounds set about driving the foreigners out of the gold fields, a goal that had a good deal of public support. They beat, stabbed and shot helpless Mexicans and Chileans whenever they had the chance and extorted money and gold from those few who had managed to accumulate any wealth. Officials made no effort to stop these outrages until the Hounds got the idea that the good people of San Francisco should pay them for their protection of the community. Then no man's property or life—be he Spanish or Anglo-American—was safe. The Hounds roamed the streets in bands, robbing stores and pedestrians in broad daylight. Merchants trying to stop them were stabbed. The gang victimized saloons, gorging themselves on the best of food and drink and telling the proprietor to collect from the city as they walked out. If there were objections, the building was set on fire. The Hounds increased their atrocities against the "greasers" and blacks. They cut off the ears of a black man who had accidentally brushed a Hound in passing. A Mexican who talked back to a Hound had his tongue ripped out by the roots.

In the summer of 1849 the Hounds, in full battle array—almost all were veterans of the Mexican War—made their most violent onslaught against the Mexican tents and shanties. The authors of a contemporary account wrote:

These they violently tore down, plundering them of money and valuables, which they carried away, and totally destroying on the spot such articles as they did not think it worth while to seize. Without provocation, and in cold blood, they barbarously beat with sticks and stones, and cuffed and kicked the offending foreigners. Not content with that, they repeatedly and wantonly fired among the injured people, and amid the shrieks of terrified women and the groans of wounded men, recklessly continued their terrible course in different quarters, wherever in fact malice or thirst for plunder led them. . . . There were no individuals brave or foolhardy enough to resist the progress of such a savage mob, whose exact force was unknown, but who were believed to be both numerous and desperate.

This outrage at last galvanized the whole town. Money was collected for the relief of the destitute Spanish-Americans and 230 volunteers were deputized to round up the Hounds. Many of the gang immediately fled the city, but 20-odd Hounds, including one of their leaders, Sam Roberts, were taken. Several witnesses, including a number of injured Spanish-Americans who later died, testified against the prisoners. Roberts and a man named Saunders were sentenced to 10 years at hard labor, while others drew shorter punishments. But within a few days political supporters of the gang won their release and none of the sentences were ever car-

Using a patriotic pretense, the Hounds first attacked Hispanics in San Francisco and then turned their violence on whites as well.

ried out. However, the Hounds were too frightened ever to reorganize and within a short time virtually all of them left the area.

House of All Nations   celebrated brothel

While the Everleigh Club was undoubtedly Chicago's, America's and perhaps the world's most famous brothel, another much more reasonably priced contemporary at the turn of the century was almost as well known in the Windy City. It was the celebrated House of All Nations, a bordello on Armour Avenue that was considered a must-stop for on-the-town sports.

The House of All Nations was famed for two qualities: its employees allegedly came from all parts of the globe (or at least could affect the proper accents) and they came in different price ranges. There was both a $2 and a $5 entrance, and in typical whoredom flimflammery, the ladies of the house all worked both entrances, dispensing the same services for either price tag. One commonly held belief in Chicago was that Asian prostitutes working in the house plied their profession during the winter months clad in long underwear because they were unable to take the chilly Chicago climate. The practice gave the Oriental harlots an added "exotic" quality that made them even more popular, but it should be noted that for a small additional fee they would strip down to the skin and brave the elements.

The House of All Nations was shuttered prior to the start of World War I, a victim of the great vice cleanup of the notorious Levee section on Chicago's South Side.

Houston, Temple L. (1860–1905) criminal lawyer

The son of Texas patriot Sam Houston, Temple Houston became one of the West's most colorful lawyers. Tall, with hair down to his shoulders, he cut a flamboyant figure in long Prince Albert coats, white sombreros and ties fashioned out of rattlesnake skin.

As a courtroom orator, Houston had few equals. Defending a prostitute named Millie Stacy for plying her trade in 1899, he mesmerized the jury with oratory. Proclaiming that, "where the star of purity once glittered on her girlish brow, burning shame has set its seal forever," he begged the all-male jury to let Millie "go in peace." They did.

Some of his tactics were most unusual. Representing a man who had shot first when facing a skilled gunfighter, Houston, in an effort to demonstrate the speed the victim possessed, whipped out a pair of Colt .45s and blazed away at the judge and jury. When peace was restored, the lawyer got around to mentioning that the guns had been loaded with blanks. It was an effective demonstration, but the jury still convicted his client. Undismayed, Houston argued for a new trial on the grounds that when the jurors had scattered after he started shooting they had mingled with the courtroom crowd and therefore could no longer be considered sequestered. The lawyer won his appeal and the eventual freedom of his client.

Houston was himself an expert gunman and easily outpointed Bat Masterson in a shooting contest. Besides being called on many times to lead posses after criminals, he fought several duels and never sustained a wound. Once, he got into a saloon shoot-out with another lawyer at the conclusion of a trial and killed his opponent. He then defended himself successfully in court, pleading self-defense.

Temple Houston died of a stroke in Woodward, Okla. A newspaper called him "a mingling of nettles and flowers" and observed that the Southwest "probably will never see his counterpart."

Howard, Joseph See CIVIL WAR GOLD HOAX.

Howe and Hummel shyster lawyers

Howe and Hummel were easily the grandest shysters ever to seek out a loophole, suborn a witness or free a guilty man. Practicing in New York from 1869 to 1906, they made a mockery of the law. Rotund, walrus-mustached William F. Howe was a great courtroom pleader who could bring sobs to any jury. Young Abe Hummel was a little man who was marvelously adept at ferreting out loopholes in the law, to the extent that once he almost succeeded in making murder legal.

At the age of 32, Howe came to America from England, where his career as a medical practitioner had terminated in a prison term for performing an illegal operation on a woman patient. He studied law and within three years he opened up shop on New York's Centre (later called Center) Street. Howe was an instant success because of his resonant voice and a face that could turn on and off any emotion he wished to display for a jury. Years later, David Belasco, the theatrical producer, watched Howe's tearful performance winning an acquittal for a woman who had shot her lover full of holes. "That man," he said, "would make a Broadway star."

In the late 1860s Howe hired young Abe Hummel as his law clerk and in almost no time promoted him to partner. Anyone so adept at finding holes in the law was too good to lose. One case that illustrated Hummel's ability involved a professional arsonist named Owen Reilly. Hummel suggested they save the prosecution the trouble of a trial by pleading Reilly guilty to attempted arson. Only after the plea was accepted did anyone notice that there was no penalty for the crime of attempted arson. However, the statutes did say that the sentence for any crime attempted but not actually committed was to be one-half of the maximum allowable for the actual commission of the crime. Since the penalty for arson at the time was life imprisonment, obviously the defendant's sentence had to be half a life. Howe made nonsense of that standard.

"Scripture tells us that we knoweth not the day nor the hour of our departure," he told the judge. "Can this court sentence the prisoner at the bar to half of his natural life? Will it, then, sentence him to half a minute or to half the days of Methuselah?" The judge gave up and set Reilly free; the state legislature rushed to revise the arson statutes shortly thereafter.

On another occasion the pair almost managed to make murder legal in New York State. It happened in November 1888, when a client named Handsome Harry Carlton was convicted of having killed a cop. Since the jury failed to recommend mercy, the death penalty was mandatory. Little Abe studied the statutes very carefully and pointed out to Howe that in the month of November there was no death penalty for murder on the books, the state having abolished hanging the previous June, with the provision that it be replaced by the electric chair. The new death-dealing apparatus was to start functioning on the following

January 1, and as Hummel noted, the law specifically said that electrocution should apply to all convictions punishable by death on and after January 1.

When Carlton came up for sentencing, early in December, Howe objected as the judge prepared to pronounce the death penalty. In fact, he objected to any sentence being passed on Carlton. If the jury had recommended mercy, Carlton could be sentenced to life imprisonment, the lawyer noted. "However, my client has been convicted of first-degree murder with no recommendation of mercy and there is no law on the books covering such a crime.

He then read the precise language in the new law and concluded that all the judge could do was turn his client free. Nonplussed, the judge delayed sentencing while the case moved to the state supreme court. Quite naturally, Howe and Hummel's contention made headlines across the country. In New York the public reaction was one of utter shock. According to the lawyers' contention, anyone committing murder between June and the new year could not be executed. Other murderers confined in death cells clamored to be released on the ground that they were being wrongfully held and could not be executed.

The district attorney's office vowed to fight the matter, and Inspector Thomas Byrnes of the New York Police Department's Detective Bureau pledged to the public that his men would continue to clap murderers behind bars, law or no law.

In the end, Howe and Hummel lost out on their interpretation; the high court ruled that no slip in syntax could be used as an excuse to legalize murder. Harry Carlton swung from the gallows two days after Christmas, a nick-of-time execution. However, if Carlton had lost out, Howe and Hummel did not; their crafty efforts brought many felons and murderers to their office door.

Buoyed by the publicity, the two shysters coauthored a book entitled *In Danger, or Life in New York: A True History of the Great City's Wiles and Temptations.* They explained in the preface that it was published in the interest of justice and to protect the innocent from the guilty, but what they actually turned out was a primer on every type of crime—blackmail, house burglary, card sharping, safecracking, shoplifting, jewel thievery and, of course, murder.

It became an immediate best-seller, with bookstore owners noticing a lot of traffic in their shops by persons who did not appear to be frequent book buyers. The book became required reading for every professional or would-be lawbreaker, from streetwalkers to killers. More and more when Howe and Hummel asked a new client, "Who sent you?" the stock reply was, "I read about you in the book."

No one ever computed exactly what percentage of murderers Howe and Hummel got off scot-free, but a prosecutor once estimated it was at least 70 percent, and "90 percent of them were guilty."

Whenever they had a client who was obviously as guilty as could be, the pair went into their bandage routine, having the defendant appear swathed in yards of white bandage, as though to suggest so frail a mind that his brains might fall out at any moment. One contemporary account tells of a Howe and Hummel client who simulated a village idiot's tic by "twitching the right corner of the mouth and simultaneously blinking the left eye." As soon as he was cleared, the defendant's face "resumed its normal composure, except for the large grin that covered it as he lightly removed the cloths from about his forehead." Another client, whose supposedly blithering insanity was accompanied by muteness and an ability to communicate only by sign language, seized Howe's hand gratefully when the verdict was announced in his favor and boomed, "Silence is golden."

The pair did not always resort to such trickery. When it was more convenient, they simply bribed witnesses and appropriate officials to get records changed, yet somehow they never ran into deep trouble until after Howe died in 1906. The following year Hummel was caught paying $1,000 to facilitate a divorce action. He was sentenced to two years in prison. Released at the age of 60, Hummel retired to Europe and died in London in January 1926, a regular to the end in the visitors' section during trials at the Old Bailey.

See also: HANDSOME HARRY CARLTON, *IN DANGER,* FREDERICKA "MARM" MANDELBAUM.

Hoyt, George (?–1877) Wyatt Earp victim

George Hoyt, a Texas cowboy and alleged outlaw, was killed by Wyatt Earp in Dodge City, which in itself was a distinction. Despite the reputation he gained there as a gun-toting lawman, Earp killed only one man in Dodge City, and his chief deputy, Bat Masterson, killed none. The fact that Earp and Masterson were nicknamed the Fighting Pimps perhaps indicates what they meant by "cleaning up" the town. Not that Earp's brand of justice didn't include plenty of violence, especially against cowboys, for whom he always showed considerable contempt. Earp proudly recalled, "As practically every prisoner heaved into the calaboose was thoroughly buffaloed (crowned with a revolver barrel) in the process, we made quite a dent in cowboy conceit."

One cattleman subjected to this treatment was Tobe Driskill. Following his experience Driskill supposedly put, in true Texas style, a $1,000 reward on Earp's head. There was some indication that a couple of drunken cowboys tried to collect that reward, but they missed Earp and he missed them. Finally, George Hoyt gave it a try. Hoyt was allegedly a wanted outlaw in Texas, and as a further inducement to kill Earp, Driskill is said to have promised to use his influence in order to get the charges against Hoyt dropped. On July 26, 1877 Hoyt rode into the town's plaza and fired six shots at Earp, who was standing in front of the Comique Theater, where Eddie Foy was at the moment singing "Kalamazoo in Michigan." Three of the bullets whizzed by Earp and plowed through the door of the theater and into the audience section, hitting nobody but causing Foy to drop flat on his face. Hoyt's mount bucked furiously, making him a poor target, but Earp still spilled the cowboy in the dirt with his third shot. Hoyt lingered a month before dying and never told Earp who had hired him to do the job.

Hughes, John R. (1855–1946) Texas Ranger

Illinois-born John Hughes was one of the most productive of all Texas Rangers. He compiled an outstanding record of captures, even crossing the Rio Grande, with or without permission, to bring back an outlaw. In 1877 Hughes gave up running his Texas horse ranch after he had been forced to go after a gang of six rustlers who had taken his stock. He killed four of them and captured the other two, but he also realized that as the sole operator of his ranch, he would continue to suffer losses from his herd. Hughes eventually decided that if he had to chase rustlers, he might as well get paid for it, and he joined the Rangers.

By 1883 Hughes had risen to captain, a high rank in the law organization, and single-handedly had brought in the notorious outlaw Juan Perales. Over the years he was also responsible for wiping out such gangs as the Ybarras, Friars and Massays. Hughes ended his career in 1915 at the age of 60 and died in 1946.

humming bird, the   prison torture

It is perhaps futile to attempt to single out the most hideous and brutal torture ever practiced on the inmates of prisons in the United States, but "the hummingbird" was certainly among the worst. This innocuous-sounding name was applied to a technique that involved placing a prisoner, chained hand and foot, in a steel bathtub filled with water. He was then rubbed down with a sponge attached to an electric battery. According to one description of the torture's agonizing effects, "Two or three minutes and the victim is ready for the grave or the mad house."

Bloody riots at the Oregon State Prison at Salem during World War I were in large measure aimed at eliminating this cruel instrument of torture. Needless to say, the leaders of riots were subjected to the humming bird, although its use in Oregon prisons was discontinued shortly thereafter.

Hunt, Sam "Golf Bag" (?–1956) Capone mob enforcer

Together with Machine Gun McGurn, Sam "Golf Bag" Hunt was perhaps the toughest of the Capone mob enforcers, or "blazers," as they were more commonly called. Placed on the Chicago Crime Commission's list of the city's public enemies, Hunt was often described as the killer of no less than 20 men. He got his nickname as a result of one of his more colorful assassinations, the victim of which remains a mystery.

One day in 1927 a Chicagoan was taking an early morning stroll along Lake Michigan's beautiful South Shore when the boom of shotgun blasts disturbed the tranquil air. He hurried in the direction of the shots and found a corpse, so recently rendered dead that blood was still oozing forth. The morning stroller rushed to a telephone and informed the police. The officers who responded came across Hunt and McGurn less than a half mile away. When asked about the golf bag he was carrying, Hunt gave a reasonable explanation: "Jack and I were going out to play a little golf."

This answer, however, did not prevent the policemen from peering into the bag and finding among the golf clubs a semiautomatic shotgun. The weapon was still warm, a fact that convinced the police they had a hot clue. But it didn't turn out that way. The good citizen led them to the spot where he had found the body, but it was no longer there. Either the dead man had walked away or he had been carted away, and all that remained was a splatter of blood on the dewy grass.

In any event, there was nothing to link Hunt to a crime, and the only thing he was tagged with was a permanent nickname. The athletically inclined assassin outlived his mentor Capone and most of the other blazers, dying in 1956 in his late fifties.

hurrahing the town   cowboy custom

In the quiet lives of Western town dwellers, one of the most disruptive events was when the cowboys came into town, "yippeeing" their ponies along the plank walks and into the saloons. These "ruffians" on horseback would later ride out of town firing their six-shooters in the air. Undeniably there was gunplay, drunken brawling and wanton vandalism, the same that existed back east in the infamous dives of New York,

Cincinnati and Chicago, where huge street gangs literally would take apart a saloon or a whole row of saloons when the notion struck them. Indeed, Western cowboys, even when "hurrahing the town," were restrained by comparison.

Historian Ramon F. Adams describes the practice from the cowhand's perspective:

> Let's follow a newly paid-off puncher with $100—three or four months' pay—burning a hole in his pocket. First he visits a barber, has a tangle of beard removed and his hair cut. Then he drops into a dry goods store and buys himself a new outfit. Now he is ready to celebrate. The saloon men, the gamblers, the pimps, are all waiting to filch his hard-earned pay. The bartender sets out a bottle of cheap frontier whiskey, "two bits a throw." A little heady after a few drinks, the puncher heads for the poker table, where a flashy gambler is waiting with his marked cards. Our puncher watches the dealer's pile of chips grow and his own melt away. Convinced he is being robbed, he can't prove it. Finally, pockets empty, he pulls away from the table, mounts his pony, races up and down the street and blazes a few indignant shots at the stars. Then, with a yell, he spurs the pony and gallops out of town, heading for the security of his cow camp. And yet, because of this type of conduct, he became known to the Easterner as a bloodthirsty demon, reckless and rowdy, weighted down with guns and itching to use them.

Writers of the day insisted the cowboys were semisavages and lionized the likes of Hickok, Earp, Masterson and Holliday—the men who regarded the gamblers, whoremasters and saloonkeepers as clients and the cowboys as foes. Wyatt Earp especially held the cowboy in contempt. For some time he operated a con game with Mysterious Dave Mather in Mobeetie, Tex. selling phony gold bricks to gullible trail hands.

See also: WYATT EARP, GOLD BRICK SWINDLE.

hypnotism and crime

Can a person under hypnosis be made to commit murder or another crime? For years the possible use of hypnotism in murders and other crimes has been a subject of debate in scientific circles, with the weight of opinion apparently slowly shifting to the side of those who think it possible. Even legal authorities have admitted the need to deal with the problem. In the 1950s a New York prosecutor, Assistant District Attorney Sheldon S. Levy, raised the possibility of law-abiding citizens being hypnotized against their will and made, by various means, to commit acts they would not do if they had their usual control over themselves. Writing in the *Journal of Criminal Law*, he quoted findings of some psychologists that "a hypnotist who really wished a murder could almost certainly get it."

Of course, it has never been proven that a hypnotist can actually get another person to commit a murder for him, since such a test, obviously, cannot be carried out. Yet numerous stage hypnotists have demonstrated the ability to get people to commit other crimes against their conscience. In a well-publicized demonstration at New York City's Carnegie Hall, one hypnotist called several people to the stage and induced them to rob members of the audience when they returned to their seats. He did so by hypnotizing them and giving them cards that read: "You must raise money for a charity that will save hundreds of children from starvation. The people from whom you are taking things are wicked and do not deserve their ill-gotten gains. You cannot possibly be caught."

The hypnotized persons returned to their seats without the audience being informed about what they had been instructed to do. When they were told to return to the stage, they had with them a number of wallets and a woman's handbag, all stolen without the victims' knowledge.

The note, according to student of hypnotism, had broken down all mental resistance by the subjects. While no one can be forced to perform an act that he knows is wrong, they say, he can be induced to commit an illegal act if he is convinced it is right. The note had the added value of assuring the subjects they would not be caught, thus overcoming any fear factor. Similarly, in tests at various universities hypnotized subjects threw sulfuric acid into a person's face, which unknown to them, was protected by an invisible sheet of glass. Some subjects threw the acid with an obvious pleasurable display of violence, while others shuddered and only threw it after considerable hesitation.

Disbelievers say such experiments prove nothing because the subject, although in a trance, is still aware that the experiments are being conducted in a laboratory or entertainment atmosphere and thus knows he will not be permitted to do anything wrong. Since a hypnotized person "knows" he won't be called upon to commit murder, he will pick up a gun and fire it, reasoning the weapon will be loaded with blanks. Assistant District Attorney Levy countered this view by pointing out that all a hypnotist bent on homicide would have to do was convince a person that he was merely undergoing a psychological test and that the gun contained blanks and then substitute real bullets.

Occasionally newspaper stories report a person's claim that he or she was hypnotized into committing a crime, but there is no recent record of any such story being accepted. Indeed, the California Supreme Court once said that "the law of the United States does not recognize hypnotism."

One classic murder case that seems to come closest to proving the murder by hypnosis theory occurred in Minnesota in 1894. Harry Hayward was a young blade about Minneapolis who was known as a lady's man as well as a hard-drinking, heavy-gambling, all-around sport. He was also a student of hypnotism, having taken a course on the subject. Some students of crime are convinced that he used this power to win the favors and money of Katherine Ging and to get her to assign her insurance—$10,000 worth—over to him.

Hayward was also practicing his power of hypnosis on a local handyman named Claus Blixt, whom he convinced to carry out relatively minor crimes, such as burning down a small factory on which Kitty Ging held a mortgage. Kitty collected the insurance money, and Hayward collected from her. Soon, the lady was down to no assets but her life insurance. For days Hayward talked to the handyman, always making him look into his eyes as he spoke. Hayward later confessed, "I would repeat over a few times how easy it was to kill someone, and pretty soon he would be saying right after me, 'Sure, that's easy; nothing to that.'"

Whether the handyman was actually under hypnosis at the time he murdered Katherine Ging or whether his will to resist the idea had simply been broken by suggestions made during earlier trances was never made clear. But either way, Blixt committed the murder while Hayward was miles away establishing an alibi. Hayward was later hanged for the killing, but the handyman, a relatively pathetic character, was allowed to plead guilty and drew a lesser sentence.

Another supposed hypnotic murderer, convicted in 1894, was Dr. Henry Meyer, who left a string of corpses from New York to Chicago. Before setting himself up as a doctor in the Midwest, Meyer had studied hypnotism in Leipzig, Germany under Professor Herbert Flint, one of the celebrated mesmerists of the era.

Meyer murdered several persons to collect on their insurance polices. He killed his first wife and then the husband of another woman so that he could marry her. When he saw a chance to kill his second wife for $75,000, he conceived a murder plan involving hypnosis. Meyer chose as the tool of his plot a plumber named Peter Bretz, an ideal hypnotic subject who soon fell under his spell. He convinced the plumber that he was in love with Mrs. Meyer, who apparently was ready herself for an affair of the heart, and should run away with her. Bretz was to take the second Mrs. Meyer to Arizona, offer to show her the Grand Canyon and, when nobody was around, shove her over the canyon lip. The plumber and the intended victim had actually reached the Grand Canyon when he broke out of the spell. The couple then returned to Chicago and revealed the plot to authorities. But since the authorities at that time could not possibly get a grand jury to swallow such a tale, Meyer went free to commit another murder before being brought to justice. Students of hypnotic crime insist the Meyer case deserves closer study. Basically, despite the claims of some believers in the feasibility of hypnotic murder, the justice system continues to ignore the question.

See also: KATHERINE "KITTY" GING.

hypnotism and detection

Experts agree that hypnotism, if properly used, can play an important role in fighting crime, far greater than the potential danger that it may be when employed in the commission of crimes. In the 1976 kidnapping of 26 children in a school bus in Chowchilla, Calif. hypnosis helped the bus driver remember part of the license plate number of a van used in the kidnapping so that the police were able to trace the vehicle to the criminals. New York police made an arrest in the murder of a young female cellist at the Metropolitan Opera House after a ballerina who had seen a man with the musician was enabled by hypnosis to give a description for a police sketch. Part of what convinced police that Albert DeSalvo was the Boston Strangler was his description under hypnosis of gory details concerning the sex murders and the tortured thoughts that made him commit his terrible crimes.

Similarly, hypnotic examination of a young man, Allen Curtis Lewis, who had admitted to pushing a young woman, Renee Katz, onto the New York City subway tracks in 1979, as well as of a Connecticut teenager, Peter Reilly, who had confessed murdering his mother, helped clear them, revealing, among other things, how their confessions had been produced by subtle coercion.

There are, however, a number of obstacles to widespread police use of hypnosis. One is that attempts have been made to interrogate suspects under hypnosis against their will. The second objection is that hypnotized persons do not necessarily give reliable information. In the $2.7 million Brinks robbery during the 1950s, police traced a license plate number furnished under hypnosis only to find it belonged to a college president who had an iron-clad alibi not only for himself but for his car as well. In another case a man charged with the murder of a child supplied "hypnotized" evidence that indicated his wife, rather than he, was the guilty party. However, discrepancies turned up indicating that the suspect had used the opportunity to try to shift the guilt away from himself.

A classic example of the perils of accepting as legal evidence a confession obtained by hypnosis is the case of Camilo W. Leyra, Jr., who was convicted and sentenced to death for the 1950 hammer slaying of his 74-year-old father and 80-year-old mother. He was released from the death house in 1956 after an appeals court overturned his conviction for a third time because the only evidence against him was his original confession obtained through hypnosis. Stated the New York Court of Appeals:

The prosecution has produced not a single trustworthy bit of affirmative, independent evidence connecting the defendant with the crime. Under the circumstances, a regard for the fundamental concept of justice and fairness, if not due process, imposes upon the court the duty to write finis to further prosecution against the

defendant. . . . It seems quite probable that the police and the District Attorney, relying too heavily on the confessions that they had obtained . . . failed to do the essential careful and intensive investigation that should be done before a defendant is charged with a crime, certainly one as serious as murder.

Despite the dangers of misuse, there is little doubt that the practice of hypnosis will continue to grow. The New York Police Department has firm rules against using the method on any person even slightly suspected of being guilty of the crime. At one time Los Angeles police had 11 officers trained in hypnosis and have used the method in 600 cases. In 90 percent of the cases the hypnotic probes were said to have provided information that led to an arrest.

Ice Cream Bar Robbery   minor crime, major sentence
Few minor crime convictions in the 1990s provoked more nationwide anger than what was facetiously dubbed in the media "The Great Ice Cream Bar Robbery." A black teenager, Dehundra Caldwell, a first offender, was convicted in 1992 for stealing ice cream bars from the cafeteria of a Thomaston, Ga., middle school.

White superior court judge Andrew Whalen sentenced the 17-year-old to three years in prison. Following outcries throughout the country that the judge had been racist and unfair, Caldwell was released after serving 10 days of his sentence. The board of pardons then put Caldwell on two years' probation.

ice pick kill   murder technique
Long a favorite rub-out method of Mafia hit men, the so-called ice pick kill is employed to make a murder victim's death appear to be the result of natural causes. Generally, the victim is forced into a men's room or some isolated place, and while two or three of the hit men hold him still, the killer wielding the ice pick jams the weapon through his eardrum into the brain. The pick produces only a tiny hole in the ear and only a small amount of bleeding, which is carefully wiped clean, but massive bleeding occurs in the brain, causing death. Examination of the victim by a doctor generally results in a finding that the person has died of a cerebral hemorrhage. Only expert medical examiners are capable of uncovering murder. When a gangland murder victim is found with numerous ice pick wounds, police generally theorize the victim struggled so much

that the normally meticulous execution proved impossible and the victim was simply ice-picked to death.

Ida the Goose War   New York underworld feud
If Homeric Greece had its Helen of Troy, the New York underworld had its Ida the Goose. Despite her rather unromantic name, the only one that has come down through posterity, Ida the Goose was a noted beauty, a maiden whose favors were traditionally reserved for the leaders of the notorious Gopher Gang of Hell's Kitchen. Ida was the last woman, so far as is known, to have caused a full-scale gang war over an affair of the heart.

In the early 1900s the Gophers were one of the most prominent gangs of the city, especially following the fractionalization of the powerful and bloody Eastman gang as a result of the imprisonment of their leader, Monk Eastman. One group of Eastmans, perhaps 400 to 500 strong, rallied to the banner of Chick Tricker, who maintained his headquarters at his own Cafe Maryland on West 28th Street. The Tricker gangsters engaged in all sorts of criminality from robbery to homicide. Their main battles generally were fought against other former members of the Eastman gang who had joined up with Big Jack Zelig or Jack Sirocco. Tricker hardly wanted an additional war with the Gophers, but he proved powerless against the momentum of events that bore down on him.

It started when a tough Tricker gangster, Irish Tom Riley, who, despite his name, was probably a Spanish Jew, won the heart of Ida the Goose and lured her from the bosom of the Gophers to the Cafe Maryland. The enraged Gophers sent a delegation to retrieve their lost princess, but both she and her new lover refused to agree to her return to Hell's Kitchen. Tricker merely shrugged. He would not order the surrender of Ida, since that would represent a loss of face. Over the next several weeks the Gophers and the Trickers had numerous hand-to-hand confrontations, including a few nonfatal stabbings, but after a while finally it appeared the Gophers had lost interest in launching a total war to regain Ida the Goose.

Thus, it was a surprise when on a snowy night in October 1909 four Gophers brazenly strolled into the Maryland and ordered beer at the bar. About a half-dozen Trickers, their noted leader absent, sat at tables eyeing the intrusion with both shock and disbelief. Had Tricker himself been present, he probably would have ordered an immediate attack on the hated intruders. As it was, only Ida the Goose spoke up with indignation. "Say! Youse guys got a nerve!"

The Gophers silently drained their mugs and then one said, "Well, let's get at it!"

They whirled around, each man holding two revolvers, and opened fire. Five of the surprised Trickers went down, several mortally wounded. Only Ida's lover was unscathed, and he scrambled across the floor and dove under his lady's voluminous skirts. The Gophers made no move to shoot him, instead watching Ida the Goose to see what she would do.

The lady surveyed the scene a moment, shrugged and contemptuously raised her skirts. "Say, youse!" she said. "Come out and take it!"

Trembling on his hands and knees, her lover crawled out to the middle of the floor. Four revolvers barked, and he fell dead with four slugs in him. One of the Gophers strode forward and put another bullet in his brain. The four assassins then turned and walked out to the street, followed at a respectful distance by Ida the Goose. She fully understood the honor bestowed on her by having been the cause of such a great battle, and it was said that she nevermore strayed from her place of adornment in Hell's Kitchen.

See also: KISS OF DEATH GIRLS.

immigration, illegal   See POLLOS.

In Danger   primer for criminals

Probably no book ever published in America was more blatantly an instruction guide to criminality than *In Danger, or Life in New York: A True History of a Great City's Wiles and Temptations*, which appeared in 1888. The book was signed, "Howe and Hummel, the Celebrated Criminal Lawyers." Howe and Hummel

indeed were celebrated attorneys and probably the most corrupt New York has ever seen. As they declared in a moral-toned preface, the two wrote the book after being moved by a clergyman's sermon in which he had declared, "It had been well for many an honest lad and unsuspecting country girl that they had never turned their steps cityward nor turned them from the simplicity of their country home toward the snares and pitfalls of crime and vice that await the unwary in New York." That was the last piece of high-minded drivel to appear in the book, the rest of which was given over to a detailed guide on what to steal and how.

By way of invitation, Howe and Hummell wrote of "elegant storehouses, crowded with the choicest and most costly goods, great banks whose vaults and safes contain more bullion than could be transported by the largest ships, colossal establishments teeming with diamonds, jewelry, and precious stones gathered from all the known and uncivilized portions of the globe—all this countless wealth, in some cases so insecurely guarded."

Having thus whetted the appetites of novice and would-be criminals, they hastened to add that "all the latest developments in science and skill are being successfully pressed into the service of the modern criminal." The ever-helpful authors went into detailed technical descriptions of various devices used by jewel thieves and shoplifters, such as "the traveling bag with false, quick-opening sides . . . the shoplifter's muff . . . the lady thieves' corsets." There were instructions for making one's own burglar tools and descriptions of the methods used in various skin games and the mathematical formulas used for rigging cards. And did crime pay? Howe and Hummel never said so in so many words, but, e.g., of shoplifting they stated, "In no particular can the female shiplifter be distinguished from other members of her sex except perhaps that in most cases she is rather more richly and attractively dressed."

The great shysters also touted certain legal services available at "what we may be pardoned for designating the best-known criminal law offices in America."

In Danger was severely criticized by the police and denounced from the pulpits, but each fresh denunciation merely produced more sales of the book.

See also: HOWE AND HUMMEL.

Indian police

One of the few techniques of self-government introduced by the white man to the Indian that had a modicum of success was the Indian police force and court system. The system proved popular with the Indians themselves because it took them away from the white man's justice, which for the red man simply did not exist.

The first to experiment with the concept of Indian police were Gen. George Crook and Indian agent John P. Clum, both of whom persisted despite being called the "Indian lovers." Even the anti-Indian Interior Department saw that the Indian police had value because they relieved the government of the need and expense of supplying troops to preserve peace on the reservations. Indians charged with committing crimes against other Indians were brought to Indian courts for trial and given justice that average Indians would accept as valid.

Clum made the most effective use of Indian police, and with their aid he brought in Geronimo in April 1877, scoring a great coup. Shortly thereafter, he informed the government he was prepared to supervise all the Apache in Arizona without the help of army troops provided he be allowed to raise two companies of Indian police. The government, however, would not accept the proposal because it was assuming a more restrictive policy, including forced migration of the Indians. During those later migrations the loyal Indian police were treated as roughly and unfairly as any other Indians. By then Indian police were hated by most other Indians. From a certain perspective, they played the same sort of role performed by the police of the Warsaw ghetto during World War II. Certainly, the murder of Sitting Bull in 1890 by a number of Indian police was done at the instigation of white men wishing to avoid any direct involvement.

See also: JOHN P. CLUM.

infanticide

Next to spouse slaying, the most common type of murders within families is infanticide. It is estimated that parents kill about 600 or 700 children a year, or about 3 percent of the total murder toll. However, if killings not reported as murders could be counted, the infanticide rate would probably be much higher.

Very few cases of infanticide are committed by fathers, but experts agree this is simply because they have far less contact with babies than mothers have. Mothers who murder their offspring usually suffer from emotional disturbances and build up to the deed over a long period of time. Generally, less severe forms of child abuse provide warning signals of the impending tragedy. Some mothers become fearful of the possibility of what they might do to their children and have themselves committed. A California mother recently signed herself into Napa Hospital after trying to kill her two tiny sons. She received some therapy and was sent home. Later she killed both boys and then failed in a suicide attempt.

Judith Catchpole may or may not have been the first woman tried for infanticide in America, but she did establish a first of a kind. While surviving details of the case are somewhat sketchy, it is known that in September 1656 the first all-female jury in the colonies was empaneled in the General Provincial Court at Patuxent, Md. to hear evidence concerning the charge that she had murdered her child. Catchpole claimed she had never even been pregnant, and after hearing her evidence, the jury acquitted her.

In a bizarre case in Maryland in 1976, a 19-year-old mother killed her baby boy as she was dressing him to go to church service, while a young woman friend watched in horror. The mother started screaming she could see the devil trying to enter her baby and she tried to stop him by slapping the child and scratching at his navel—while he screamed in agony—and, finally, wringing the baby's neck. When the mother appeared in court five months later, all the parties—prosecution defense and psychiatrists—agreed she had been insane at the time of the act, and an insanity plea of not guilty was accepted. However, when the judge asked for testimony on her current condition, psychiatrists would not certify her as insane, and she was freed. Yet, the horror of society toward the crime of infanticide was exhibited in the legal treatment accorded to the woman friend who had watched the killing. Because she had not attempted to stop the mother's insane acts, for whatever reason, she was sentenced to a seven-year prison term.

When fathers do commit infanticide, the victim is almost always a boy, rarely either a daughter or a baby. The underlying motive may be an attempt to gain supremacy in the household, but occasionally, the motive has been monetary. On Halloween night 1974, in Pasadena, Tex. Ronald O'Bryan poisoned his eight-year-old son, Tim, with cyanide to collect the boy's $65,000 life insurance policy. O'Bryan was sentenced to the electric chair.

Because of the close-knit relationships involved and the horror of the crime, experts agree that a large number of infanticide cases are hushed up by families that, having one loss, see nothing to be gained from having another. Thus, it is generally believed that the rate of infanticide is greatly understated. Society also simply ignores other forms of infanticide. In a classic study of the subject, *Infanticide: Past and Present*, Maria W. Piers refers to babies who are "forgotten," or left behind, by their young mothers immediately after delivery. This happens especially in impoverished sections. Piers states: "Many of them probably assume that their babies will survive, but the assumption is incorrect. Because of insufficient hospital staff and the inefficiency of adoption procedures, human babies die in misery from sheer neglect, while authorities avert their eyes."

informer   See SQUEALER.

Ingalls, Oklahoma Territory, Battle of

One of the great gunfights of the West, the Battle of Ingalls on September 1, 1893 added significantly to the folklore of a dying era. The battle resulted from a disastrous effort by the law to capture the Bill Doolin gang, a hell-for-leather outfit that probably enjoyed greater down-home esteem than was ever achieved by the James gang or Butch Cassidy's Wild Bunch.

One of the gang's many headquarters was the clapboard town of Ingalls, some 10 miles east of Stillwater. In Ingalls they felt safe because the locals were friendly and sympathizers would hurry in with reports whenever a posse approached.

On the night of August 31, the U.S. marshal's office in Guthrie got a tip that the Doolin gang was carousing in Ingalls, and the following day a posse of marshals slipped into town in a covered wagon to wipe out the gang in one swoop. The lawmen might have succeeded in their mission had not one of the gang, Bitter Creek Newcomb, spotted them as he came out of Murray's Saloon. There is some indication that Newcomb had been tipped off. What followed was the celebrated Battle of Ingalls, which proved to be a resounding triumph for the outlaws. Three deputy marshals were killed, while all of the gang survived and only one of them, Arkansas Tom, who was asleep in his hotel room at the time, was captured as the rest were escaping. Bill Dalton's horse went down. Bill Doolin rode back for him, and the two of them shared the same mount in a daring dash to freedom. The most amazing escape of all, however, was Bitter Creek Newcomb's, who for a time was literally enveloped in mushrooming dust caused by the posse's bullets. He was wounded but survived to get away, an accomplishment so incredible that a very special savior was invented for him. The legend developed that Newcomb had lived through the battle because a daring young lass who loved him came charging to his rescue with an extra gunbelt of ammunition, that she shielded him with her own body and that she even provided protective fire for him. The best evidence is that there was no girl involved in any way in the fighting, but the myth grew nonetheless.

The Battle of Ingalls became the Doolin gang's greatest feat, the lore of it persisting even after the outfit had disbanded and each member had been blasted into extinction. They sang praises of the great fight, and song and story recorded the heroic love of Newcomb

and the "Rose of Cimarron," who supposedly had saved his life.

See also: BILL DOOLIN, GEORGE "BITTER CREEK" NEWCOMB, ROSE OF CIMARRON.

Innocents   western outlaws

A particularly inappropriate name, the Innocents were members of the most efficient gang of the frontier West, bossed by a magnetic personality, Henry Plummer, doubling as the Montana sheriff whose duty it was to contain the sudden rampage of criminality. The full story of the Innocents can never be told since it is impossible to pinpoint each of the hundreds of crimes they committed; the murders attributed to the band have been fixed by most historians at 102.

In 1862 Plummer, a lawman in California until he got into trouble because of a couple of messy murders and other, lesser infractions, drifted into what is now southwest Montana, where gold had been discovered. He assembled a large group of outlaws, including a number he had used in previous criminal endeavors in Idaho. Most were in their teens or early twenties. Plummer himself, a handsome rogue who had a way with women, was only 25 or so. Some historians have insisted that the Plummer gang was composed of murderous juvenile delinquents. But this overlooks the fact that it was traditional in the West for men to hit the outlaw trail at an extremely young age.

The Innocents operated with a certain childlike fervor and enthusiasm, terrorizing stagecoaches and miners hauling ore in and out of Bannack. Since at one time the Innocents totaled over 100 men, they needed secret ways of identifying themselves to one another and thus wore red bandanas with special sailor knots. They used a secret handclasp and the password *innocent* when meeting, under the assumption that saying such a word could hardly imply any kind of guilt.

The only recourse for the victims of the Innocents was the local sheriff, Henry Plummer, who, while sympathetic, seemed incapable of stemming the criminal tide. The Innocents, however, were too vast an organization not to spring leaks, and in time, suspicion spread to Plummer himself. A Montana vigilante movement sprang up, and in a six-week period in late 1863 and early 1864, they hung no less than 26 outlaws, including Plummer, who met his doom on a scaffold he had built himself as part of his legal duties. The rest of the gang scattered, although some others were to receive the same rough-hewn justice throughout the rest of the year.

Over the years Henry Plummer and his Innocents became the inspiration of a near-endless string of stories, books and movies depicting the nefarious activities of a crooked sheriff unmasked in the dramatic denouement.

See also: BANNACK, MONTANA; THOMAS J. DIMSDALE; BOONE HELM; HAZE LYONS; HENRY PLUMMER; CYRUS SKINNER; VIGILANTES OF MONTANA; ERASTUS "RED" YAGER.

insanity defense

Most jurisdictions have statutes that protect insane or incompetent persons from criminal prosecution, but the legal responsibility of such persons varies considerably from place to place. Courts recognize that a person afflicted with insanity or a mental disorder may not be responsible for his actions and therefore not liable to prosecution. However, the legal tests for insanity have long been the subject of much confusion. Some states apply the "wild beast test," which requires that to be judged insane, the defendant must be so devoid of reason that he no more knows what he is doing than would an infant, a brute or a wild beast. Others call for a "delusion test," whereby an accused criminal must be shown to have been suffering from delusions before he can be cleared of responsibility. A little over half the states abide by M'Naghten Rules, which hold an accused not responsible if he "was laboring under such a defect of reason, from disease of the mind, as not to know the nature and the quality of the act he was doing, or if he did know it, that he did not know he was doing what was wrong."

Some states adhere to the "right and wrong test," which centers on a defendant's ability to tell right from wrong. Another standard used is the "irresistible impulse test," which requires that in order to be considered sane there needs to exist, in addition to the capacity for intellectual judgment, the possibility of doing what is considered right and to refrain from doing what is thought to be wrong.

A striking case was that of William Milligan who was charged in 1977 with raping four Ohio State University coeds. Milligan was found to have 10 distinct personalities, only one of which was criminal. The four coeds had the misfortune of meeting the wrong one of the 10. He was found not guilty by reason of insanity and shipped off to a mental institution. Similarly, Howard Unruh, the New Jersey mass murderer who killed 13 neighbors and strangers in the streets of Camden in 1949 never faced trial for his crimes. Instead, he was sent to the Trenton State Hospital where some three decades later he was described as quiet and withdrawn, a man in his late fifties who mostly read or sat around.

The law's treatment of insane persons charged with crimes has been the subject of much criticism because such persons are frequently released from confinement.

If it were merely a simple choice of finding a murderer, for instance, either guilty and sending him to prison or finding him insane and sending him to a mental institution, such criticism would be muted. However, the decision is not always so clear-cut. A not unusual case, which occurred in California in 1976, involved a mother who had killed her baby in a religious frenzy. She pleaded guilty on the ground of insanity, a contention of considerable merit considering her many previous acts of crazed violence. It appeared logical that she would simply be sent to a mental institution when the judge accepted her plea. However, while a number of mental experts agreed the woman had been of unsound mind when she killed her infant, the preponderance of opinion on her "current condition" was that she was not certifiably insane. Under the circumstances, the judge was forced to release her and, legally, could not even require her to undergo psychiatric treatment.

Because of numerous publicized cases of this type, jurors have developed a form of "sophistication," rightly or wrongly, leading to their refusal in many cases to bring in a verdict of insanity for fear the defendant might at some later date be inflicted upon society again. As a result, several observers agree, obviously insane persons are being convicted and placed in prison, a terrible ordeal both for the person and the institution.

A typical example of this sort was mass murderer Herbert William Mullin, who, between October 1972 and February 1973, killed at least 13 persons. Mullin called his victims "sacrifices" and killed them because he was convinced their deaths were necessary to ward off a predicted cataclysmic earthquake in California. Mullin's record showed five previous hospital releases after he had voluntarily committed himself each time. The jurors were described as fearful of what would happen if they judged him insane and he was later discharged from the hospital for the sixth time. Consequently, they were said to have ignored all the evidence concerning his mental condition when they brought in a guilty verdict, requiring him to be sent to prison.

Perhaps because of this trend, the courts in recent years have become more concerned with protecting the rights of allegedly insane persons charged with crimes. Juan Corona was convicted in 1972 for the murders of 25 itinerant farm workers, whose mutilated bodies had been found in shallow graves in the peach orchards around Yuba City, Calif. However, in 1978 the courts ordered a new trial for Corona on the ground that his attorney had failed to provide him with proper representation. Corona had a history of hallucinations and mental illness, but his lawyer had refused a psychiatric examination for him and presented no witnesses on the subject of his mental state. The appeal judges made it clear they did not doubt the evidence against Corona, but ruled he was entitled to mental competency hearings. At the time of the ruling, a number of California legal authorities predicted Corona would never be returned to prison. He was sent to a mental institution but then retried, convicted and sent back to prison to serve 25 life sentences. Because of the state of the law on insanity questions, a number of new causes célébres will no doubt emerge in the coming years.

Insull, Samuel (1860–1938) stock manipulator

Among the most grandiose swindlers of the 20th century, Samuel Insull built up a multibillion-dollar Midwest utility empire, one of the great financial marvels of the 1920s, by merging troubled small electric companies into an apparently smooth-running combine. He was hailed by the nation's press as the financial genius of the age, and lucky was the banker from whom Mr. Insull deigned to borrow money.

Clearly outdoing even Horatio Alger, Insull began his career as a 14-year-old dropout in his native London and rose to the pinnacle of high finance. He first worked as an office boy for $1.25 a week and later became a clerk for Thomas A. Edison's London agent. He was so impressive that he was recommended to Edison as a youth worth bringing to America, and the great inventor made him his secretary in 1881; Insull was 21 at the time.

Soon, Insull was handling the organization of several Edison companies, and by 1902 he was president of Chicago Edison. In 1907 he merged all the electric companies there into Commonwealth Edison. He then struck out on his own, joining small, often poorly run utilities into one operation. By the 1920s he was among the nation's richest men, worth $100 million, and people felt they were making the smartest investment in America when they purchased his stock.

The secret of Insull's success was to have one of his electric companies sell properties to another of his companies at a handsome profit over the original cost. The second company would not be hurt because it would later sell other properties to yet another Insull company. Thus, even in 1931, at the depths of the Depression, Insull's Middle West Utilities group reported the second most profitable year in its history. Of course, by this time Insull had to do more than sell properties to himself. He started cutting depreciation allowances in his various utilities or eliminating them entirely.

Then Insull had to spend huge sums—which he took in from gullible investors—to fight off takeover bids from other Wall Street operators eager to latch onto a strong financial organization. The problem was that if a takeover occurred the buyers would soon discover

that Insull had done it all with mirrors. The swindler spent $60 million in the battle and won, but his financial empire was now so weak the bubble had to burst. The collapse came in June 1932, with investor losses estimated at $750 million.

Broke at the age of 72, Insull fled to Paris, where he lived on a yearly pension of $21,000 from a few companies of his that hadn't gone under. Facing extradition back to the United States on embezzlement and mail fraud charges, the old man left France and went to Greece. The Greek government let him stay a year but then bowed to U.S. pressure and ordered him out. For a time Insull drifted about the Mediterranean in a leased tramp steamer, but he finally had to put in at Instanbul for supplies. The Turks arrested him and shipped him back home for trial.

Because Insull's financial capers were so involved and often fell into areas where the law was not really clear, the government failed to prove its charges and he was able to go back to Paris. He dropped dead on a street there at the age of 78. At the time, he had assets of $1,000 cash and debts of $14 million.

insurance frauds—faked deaths

Cases of "dead men" turning up alive are common in insurance company fraud files, although the industry has never seen the virtue of publishing any statistics on the subject. There is, of course, even less information on those who have gotten away with such fraud. One of the most publicized disappearance frauds of all was perpetrated in the 1930s by John H. Smith, who had once run for governor of Iowa. Smith made it look as if he had been burned to death in an auto accident, substituting an embalmed body in his fire-gutted car. Mrs. Smith later confessed her husband had faked his own death to fleece an insurance firm out of $60,000 stating, "Under our plan, I was to collect the insurance or accept it when the insurance company paid it to me, and then meet John when he got in communication with me, which might be from one to two years."

Smith might have gotten away with his plot had he not developed a roving eye. He committed bigamy during his disappearance by marrying an 18-year-old Kansas farm girl. That was something Mrs. Smith hadn't agreed to, and since her wounded pride meant more to her than $60,000, she screamed for the law as soon as she learned what her husband had done.

Probably the longest successful insurance disappearance was pulled off by socially prominent Thomas C. Buntin of Nashville, Tenn. who vanished in 1931. Shortly thereafter, Buntin's 22-year-old secretary also disappeared. Buntin had $50,000 in insurance, and after waiting the customary seven years, the insurance company paid off the claim. However, the firm, New York Life, did not close the case. It kept up a search for Buntin, and in 1953—some 22 years after he vanished—the company found him living in Orange, Tex. with his ex-secretary under the name Thomas D. Palmer. For 22 years the couple had posed as Mr. and Mrs. Palmer and had even raised a family.

A trust fund had been established with the money from Buntin's insurance policy, and there was still $31,000 left when he turned up alive. The insurance company immediately launched legal action to get the money. As for Buntin, he obviously had not benefitted personally from the fraud. What was the reason? Very often a husband wishing to leave his wife and knowing he cannot expect a divorce will use a disappearing act to get out from under. Along with acquiring his freedom, the man can feel he has discharged all his duties as a husband and father by defrauding an insurance company into providing for his family. In the end, Buntin and his former secretary suffered no penalties from the law. In fact, after they were exposed, their neighbors sent them flowers.

Of course, producing a dead body will make a faked death even more convincing, but this often entails murder. In the 1930s Philadelphia's notorious Bolber-Petrillo murder ring specialized in killing off husbands so their wives could claim the insurance. Occasionally, they worked with a loving couple who wanted to enjoy the fruits of the husband's life insurance policy while he was still alive. In such cases the ring would kill an itinerant stranger and use him as a stand-in corpse for the husband.

Another famous insurance fraud murderer was Charles Henry Schwartz, a sort of mad scientist. When Schwartz ran his business into the ground in the 1920s, he looked for someone to use as a substitute corpse so that he could collect $200,000 in insurance. He settled on a traveling evangelist, Warren Gilbert Barbe, and murdered him in his Berkeley, Calif. laboratory. Since Barbe didn't look much like him, Schwartz worked hard on his substitute. Because Schwartz had a scar on his own chest, he burned away a section of Barbe's chest. He pulled out two teeth from the murdered man's upper jaw to match his own missing teeth. To take care of the difference in eye color between the two, Schwartz punctured his victim's eyeballs, and then for added protection, he blew up the laboratory. Despite all this, the corpse was soon identified as someone other than Schwartz and the latter was exposed. To avoid imprisonment he committed suicide.

Beyond doubt the prize victim of all insurance swindles was a beautiful but gullible model named Marie Defenbach. She was persuaded by a Dr. August M. Unger to join him and two accomplices in a fraud in which she was to take out $70,000 worth of life insurance and then fake her own death. The men were to be her beneficiaries and were to give her half the money. Dr. Unger assured Marie he would personally handle her "demise." He would give her a special medicine of his own that would induce a deathlike sleep. Later, the doctor convinced her, she would be revived in the back room of an undertaking establishment and spirited away, with an unclaimed body left in her place for cremation. If Marie had had any sense, she would have realized that it would save the man a lot of bother and money if they just fed her some old-fashioned poison. But Marie was already mentally counting her loot.

On the evening of August 25, 1900, Marie blithely informed her Chicago landlady she was feeling ill, and she sent a messenger to get her some medicine. Fifteen minutes after taking it, she died in terrible agony. In due course, the true nature of Marie's death was uncovered by a suspicious uncle, whose investigation finally led to the arrest and conviction of the culprits.

In a curious sidelight to insurance frauds, the man responsible for the fact that few insurance company investigators carry weapons while on the job was a New Jersey man named J. R. Barlow, who had a wife and a $200,000 life insurance policy. One day he swam out from a beach and never swam back. His wife reported him as missing and applied for the insurance. The insurance company was suspicious, however, and after an intensive investigation traced Barlow to Mexico. When he was confronted by an insurance agent, Barlow turned violent, and in the ensuing struggle the investigator was forced to shoot him. Ironically, the insurance company was then compelled to pay off on his death. Soon after, the company issued a rule forbidding investigators to carry weapons.

See also: WARREN GILBERT BARBE, BOLBER-PETRILLO MURDER RING, MARIE DEFENBACH.

Internet crime   keyboards beat guns

A 28-year-old Los Gatos, Calif. woman suddenly discovered she was much "richer" than she thought. She possessed a new $22,000 Jeep, five credit cards, an apartment and a $3,000 loan listed in her name. The trouble was she never asked for any of it. It turned out the woman had been a victim of "identity theft" via the Internet.

Another woman was impersonating her. All the second woman needed was to get hold of the woman's employee-benefits form and it was shopping time. The victim spent months and months straightening out the mess. There were scores of angry phone calls, court appearances and lots of legal expenses. And she constantly had to demonstrate she was the real her, rather than her impersonator!

Internet identity theft is getting to be a very common crime, committed by very sophisticated swindlers. One expert calls it "the next growth industry in crime." All a crook has to do is have a keyboard—no guns necessary. All he or she needs is your full name or Social Security number to access Internet databases that spew out your address, phone number, name of employer or driver's license. Then they use your good name to get great credit, and leave you to explain later if you can.

Everyone notes how amazingly the Internet is growing. Well so is Internet fraud. The Internet Fraud Watch, operated by the National Consumers League, reports that complaints from 1997 to early 1999 shot up by an astonishing 600 percent. The number one complaint involves auctions. In 1997 auctions made up 26 percent of the total frauds reported, and the following year increased to 68 percent. The top auction companies work with authorities to try to cut auction scams, but the fact is as a Internet Fraud Watch spokesperson notes, "More people are online, and more people are being scammed. Consumers need to remember that con artists are everywhere—even in cyberspace."

While most frauds on the Internet are in auctions, many consumers do well in auctions, but with the traffic soaring the need for consumer protection and increased education is a must.

The top 10 scams on the Internet in order are auctions, general merchandise sales, computer equipment and software, Internet services, work-at-home, business opportunities and franchises, multilevel marketing and pyramids, credit card offers, advance fee loans and employment offers.

Anyone can be a target for Internet frauds, even those who don't have a computer. Hacker programs have turned up on the Web allowing people to generate credit card numbers using the same algorithms as the ones used by banks. Crooks open accounts with created numbers and then order products on-line—without even having the plastic.

In some cases consumers using auto-buying services have paid money on the assumption the service will search auctions looking for the car they want. Result: no car and no money back.

interrogation methods See CONFESSIONS.

Irving, Clifford (1930–) Howard Hughes book forger

In 1971 writer Clifford Irving pulled off what was undoubtedly the most celebrated literary hoax of the 20th century when he swindled the McGraw-Hill Book Co. out of $765,000 for a fake autobiography of billionaire recluse Howard R. Hughes. Irving also conned *Life* magazine, which planned to print excerpts of the book with 20 pages of handwritten letters by Hughes. After examining the letters, a number of handwriting experts had declared all of them to be genuine.

Together with a friend who was a children's book author, Richard Suskind, Irving wrote an engrossing 1,200 page book, which veteran newsmen who had long covered the enigmatic Hughes found to be most "authentic." The scheme was so daring and so outrageous it was widely accepted even after Hughes said in a telephone call from his hideaway in the Bahamas that he had never met with Irving and that the work was "totally fantastic fiction." Irving's hoax was finally wrecked when a Swiss bank broke its vow of secrecy to reveal that a $650,000 check from the book publisher to Hughes had been cashed in one Swiss bank by "H. R. Hughes" and deposited in another under the name "Helga R. Hughes"—actually Irving's wife.

Clifford Irving's phony biography of Howard Hughes earned him a dubious distinction from *Time* magazine.

On March 13, 1972 Irving pleaded guilty to federal conspiracy charges. He was forced to return what was left of the publisher's money and was sentenced to two and a half years in prison. He served 17 months.

In 1977 Irving was asked by the editors of the *Book of Lists* to compile a list of the 10 best forgers of all time. He listed Clifford Irving as number nine.

Israel, Harold (1901–?) wrong man

One of America's most famous "wrong man" murder cases wrecked the elective political career of a prosecutor named Homer S. Cummings in the 1920s. The case was the murder of a popular minister in Bridgeport, Conn.

In 1924 an unidentified person shot Father Hubert Dahme, pastor of St. Joseph's Episcopal Church, in the back of the head, throwing the city into an uproar. Both the city government and a local newspaper offered rewards, and the public demanded the police come up with a solution to the crime. This they appeared to do by arresting an itinerant young man, 23-year-old Harold Israel. After many hours of questioning, Israel made a confession. He later tried to retract it, but there was no denying that when apprehended, he had been carrying a gun of the same caliber as the murder weapon. In addition, police had the testimony of a ballistic expert that Israel's gun had been the murder weapon.

Since Father Dahme was one of Bridgeport's most popular citizens, the pressure on prosecutor Cummings was enormous. There was press speculation that a conviction in the case would earn the state's attorney a sure nomination for governor. Cummings was a former chairman of the Democratic National Committee, keynote speaker at the 1920 national convention in San Francisco and, indeed, Connecticut's favorite son for the presidential nomination. Under the circumstances, it would have been quite logical for Cummings to have accepted the sure conviction handed him. Amazingly, he did not.

Even though the public defender announced that Israel would plead guilty by reason of insanity, Cummings had strong misgivings about the case. The prosecution regarded some of the witnesses who had sworn Israel was the priest's killer as less than reliable. When he checked the area where the murder had occurred and where the witnesses said they had been standing, he determined it would have been too dark for them to recognize anyone. Cummings also had his doubts about the ballistics expert, who struck him as overly anxious to help the police solve the crime. He asked six other experts in the field to make their own findings without telling any of them that others were doing the same

work. All six agreed that Israel's gun had not fired the fatal bullet.

When Israel's case came to trial, Cummings made an opening presentation outlining the findings that had weakened the prosecution's case. He then calmly proceeded to load the so-called murder gun. He aimed it downward at a 45° angle—the position the murder gun had been in—and pulled the trigger. Nothing happened. The gun, Cummings explained, had a defective firing pin and would not fire when held in that particular position.

On Cummings' motion, Israel was released. The prosecutor personally escorted the happy youth to the train station and saw him off to his home in Pennsylvania. It's possible that Cummings felt his presence was necessary to keep the police from rearresting Israel.

Years later, the Israel case was made into a movie called *Boomerang*. While Cummings won considerable praise in many circles for his work in the case, he did not get quite as much as he deserved in his native state. When Israel was cleared, Cummings' chance for the governorship fizzled. In 1933, however, he was named by President Franklin D. Roosevelt to be attorney general. As for Israel himself, he faded into obscurity, to which Cummings felt he was entitled. Still, Cummings wondered if his clearing of the young man had paid off and in the late 1930s he ordered the FBI to make a secret check on him. The agency reported that Israel was a respectable miner in Pennsylvania, a married man, the father of two children and a pillar of the Methodist Church.

Italian Dave gang 19th-century New York pickpocket gang

From the 1840s to the 1860s the most notorious Fagin in America was the New York criminal mastermind named Italian Dave. He always had some 40 or so boys aged nine to 15 whom he instructed in the art of pickpocketing and sneak thievery. He provided the boys with room and board in an old tenement on Paradise Square and conducted daily classes in various techniques of theft. They were shown how to pinch articles from store windows and counters, how to beg and, with the aid of fully dressed dummies of men and women in various positions, how to pick pockets and snatch purses and muffs. Whenever a boy fumbled his assignment, Italian Dave would ceremoniously dress himself in a policeman's uniform and work him over with a nightstick. Other thieves and gangs would rent out squads of boys for specific criminal assignments such as lookouts, with all money paid directly to Italian Dave.

Dave took advanced students out into the streets himself and would point out victims to be robbed, observing his pupils' modus operandi with a most critical eye. When a student failed to use a club on a mugging victim with sufficient stunning effect, Italian Dave would step forward and demonstrate how to do it properly. His most apt pupils deserted him within a couple of years because he was so miserly, giving them only pennies out of what they stole. However, long after Italian Dave passed from the scene, his pupils continued to benefit from his harsh lessons; among his students were master pickpockets Blind Mahoney and Jimmy Dunnigan and the redoubtable gang leader Jack Mahaney, who later became known as the American version of Jack Sheppard, the famous British escape artist, because of his ability to escape from custody.

See also: JACK MAHANEY.

Ivers, Alice   See POKER ALICE.

Izzy and Moe   revenue agents

Prohibition brought many things to the American scene: speakeasies, rot-gut liquor, gangsters, hijacking and "the ride." But Prohibition had its comic side as well, as demonstrated by the merry antics of those dry clowns Izzy and Moe. They were the greatest and wackiest Prohibition agents of all time and they fit right into the Roaring Twenties. The newspapers gave front-page coverage to their capers, one joyously announcing, "IZZY IS BIZZY AND SO IS MOE." Hundreds of hilarious newspaper stories were written about the pair, and a great many of them were no doubt true.

In 1920 Isadore Einstein was a short, smiling cherub of 225 pounds who worked as a clerk for the New York Post Office. Previously, he had been a dry goods salesman. One day Izzy showed up at the Federal Prohibition Bureau headquarters and announced his availability. That got a laugh. "Izzy," one official said, "you don't even look like a Prohibition agent." On reflection, it was decided that Izzy might thus be handy to have around, and he got the job. A product of the polyglot Lower East Side, he could speak fluent Yiddish, Hungarian, Polish, German and Italian.

Bureau officials figured the worst that could happen was that a few tough assignments would send Izzy in hasty retreat back to the post office. They decided to send him out to hit a 52nd Street speakeasy. A dozen agents had previously tried and failed to bust the place. A few had gotten past the front door, but they were served nothing stronger than beer because they couldn't produce a regular customer as a sponsor.

Izzy talked his way into the speakeasy, waddled up to the bar, plunked down his newly acquired badge and

Bizzy Izzy and Moe, as the newspapers dubbed them, were the clown princes of Prohibition enforcement, using many disguises to make their busts.

said to the bartender, 'How about a good stiff drink for a thirsty revenue agent?"

The bartender nearly doubled up with laughter. "Get a load of this funny fat man!" he called to his customers. Then, fingering Izzy's badge, he asked, "Where did you buy this?"

"Give me a drink and I'll take you to the place sometime," Izzy replied.

The bartender obliged. So did Izzy. He took the man down to the Revenue Office.

Izzy's superiors were stunned . . . and immediately assigned him to another tough case. Izzy made that pinch as well.

After a few weeks on the job, Izzy started to miss his old coffeehouse buddy, Moe Smith. He asked if they had a job for Moe as well. The only trouble was, Izzy noted, that Moe didn't look like an agent either; he was fat like Izzy. Moe got the job, and the pair worked as a team, a sort of Laurel and Hardy of the Revenuers—except both were Hardy. They were so effective that some speakeasies posted pictures of the two, but that proved futile. The pair disguised themselves with false whiskers and noses. On occasion they wore blackface. Once, they donned football uniforms to bust a joint serving the thirsty athletes playing in Van Cortlandt Park in the Bronx. To crack a Coney Island speakeasy in midwinter, Izzy went swimming with a polar bear cub and was then carried quivering into the establishment by a solicitous Moe. "Quick," Moe cried, "some liquor before he freezes to death." A tenderhearted bartender complied and was arrested.

Another time, the pair marched into a speakeasy arguing loudly about the name of a particular revenue sleuth. Was it Einstein or Epstein? The bartender agreed it was Einstein. Nonsense, said Izzy, and bet the bartender double the price for two drinks. The bartender won the bet and got pinched.

Because they needed to produce liquor served them as proof of a crime, Izzy and Moe designed special funnels to be strapped inside their vests. One time, they started out at 5 A.M. and made 24 arrests by 9 A.M., just working up an appetite for breakfast. The pair's all-time record was 65 raids in one day. Their standard line when making a pinch was "Dere's sad news here." Over a five-year period their combined score was 5 million bottles of liquor confiscated, 4,392 persons arrested and convictions achieved in 95 percent of their cases, which was 20 percent of all the successful illegal liquor prosecutions in the New York district. Everybody loved Izzy-and-Moe stories. Stanley Walker once said, "Izzy and Moe almost made prohibition popular."

Once Izzy met his namesake—Albert Einstein. He asked him what he did for a living. "I discover stars in the sky," the scientist replied. "I'm a discoverer too," Izzy said, "only I discover in the basements."

Izzy and Moe became so famous that other bureaus began asking for the pair's help in busting some problem spots in their cities. In Pittsburgh they made a pinch within 11 minutes of leaving the train depot. In Atlanta it took 17 minutes, and Chicago and St. Louis, 21. They set their record in New Orleans: 35 seconds.

Unfortunately, Izzy and Moe were called on the carpet often because of their penchant for publicity. They were warned that the service had to be dignified in its procedures. Finally, in November 1925 the boys turned in their badges. Izzy explained, "I fired myself," because they were to be transferred away from their beloved New York to the wilds of Chicago. Bureau officials insisted they had been dismissed "for the good of the service."

Both men went into the insurance business and soon numbered among their clients many of the people they had arrested for liquor violations. Izzy even published an autobiography, *Prohibition Agent Number 1,* which didn't sell very well. It seemed the public had had enough of Prohibition.

See also: PROHIBITION.

Jackson, Andrew   victim of assassination attempt

On January 3, 1835 the first attempt on the life of a United States president took place when Andrew Jackson was attacked in the rotunda of the Capitol while attending the funeral of a South Carolina congressman, Warren Ransom Davis. A house painter named Richard Lawrence stepped up to President Jackson and, at a distance of 6 feet, fired two pistols at him. Both misfired and Jackson's would-be slayer was seized. Lawrence, who believed he was the rightful heir to the English throne, was committed to an insane asylum.

Jackson, Eddie (1873–1932) pickpocket

Among authorities on the subject, there are those who say that Eddie Jackson was the most proficient pickpocket America has ever produced. Jackson lifted his first poke when he was 14 and is said to have been the greatest "kiss-the-sucker" operator of all times. Kissing the sucker is walking right up to the victim, bumping him in front and lifting his wallet from his inside coat pocket in one quick motion. It is not a technique that many pickpockets, or "dips," like to employ since there are far easier and safer methods. Of course, Jackson used other techniques as well. Generally operating with three or four accomplices, he would use his nimble fingers to lift a victim's money while the others jostled him and diverted his attention. He usually worked Chicago's Loop district, often making as much as $1,500 a week, an incredible sum for the 1890s and early 1900s.

Jackson kept a famous lawyer and politician, Black Horton, on retainer, and when he and his mob were working, they would report to Horton every hour. Whenever they failed to report, Horton immediately hurried to the police station with bail money and a writ of habeas corpus. Over a career that spanned 40 years, Jackson was arrested some 2,000 times. Pickpockets are subject to frequent arrests, especially on loitering charges but he generally avoided prosecution by giving back a portion of his loot. He was only convicted twice, sentenced once to 10 days and another time to a year. In later years the "Jackson touch" abandoned him, and he died a pauper in 1932.

Jackson, Frank (1856–?) Texas outlaw

In the folklore of Texas outlaws, Frank Jackson is remembered for his refusal to betray his legendary outlaw chief, Sam Bass, and perhaps more important, as a man whose loyalty was probably rewarded with the secret of Bass' hidden treasure troves.

Born in Llano County, Texas, in 1856 and orphaned when he was seven, Jackson grew up with relatives, training as a tinsmith. The occupation held little attraction for the youth, and by 1876 he was working as a cowhand at the Murphy Ranch in Denton County. From time to time, the Murphys harbored the notorious outlaw Sam Bass. Making the outlaw's acquaintance, Jackson quickly enlisted in the gang, thereafter taking part in all the gang's Texas train robberies.

Bass accumulated a considerable amount of his loot in the form of $20 gold pieces and buried it in several places in the hills and hollows northwest of Dallas. Frank Jackson's last ride with Sam Bass occurred in July 1878, when he, Bass and Seaborn Barnes

THE ATTEMPTED ASSASSINATION,

OF THE PRESIDENT OF UNITED STATES, JAN. 30.1835.

As the Funeral Procession of the Hon. Warren R. Davis, was about moving from the Capitol of the United States, Richard Lawrence, a supposed maniac, rushed from the crowd, and snapped two heavily loaded pistols immediately at the body of President Jackson, both of which Providentially missed fire! Lawrence was instantly arrested by persons present, examined by Judge Cranch, and committed for trial.

Andrew Jackson remained convinced that the attempt on his life by an insane house painter was inspired by his political foes.

attempted to hold up a small bank in Round Rock. They were betrayed by another gang member, Jim Murphy of the ranching family. Barnes was killed and Bass badly wounded in the ensuing gun battle. With Jackson's help Bass was able to ride out of town. The next day trackers found Bass dying in a woodland. For 24 hours lawmen questioned the outlaw, trying to get him to reveal his accomplices on various robberies and the hiding places of his loot before he died. Bass kept his silence to the end, and Frank Jackson was never seen again. The circumstances fueled speculation in Texas cow country that Bass must have encouraged the steadfast Jackson to leave him to die and told him where the

gang's accumulated loot had been buried. Jackson was presumed to have retired from the outlaw trail a wealthy man.

See also: SAM BASS, JIM MURPHY.

Jackson, Humpty (?–1914) New York gang leader and murderer

One of New York's most feared gang leaders at the turn of the century, Humpty Jackson was an odd combination of cold-blooded murderer and bibliophile. A man with a superior education, although a hazy past,

457

he bossed some 50 gangsters, many of whom later became notorious in their own right. Among them were Spanish Louie, Nigger Ruhl, the Grabber and the Lobster Kid.

Humpty was never without a book on his person. His favorite writers were Voltaire, Darwin, Huxley and Spencer, and he often read various tomes in Greek and Latin. His scholarly pursuits, however, did not carry over into his professional life, which was thoroughly dedicated to crime. He always carried three revolvers on his person—one in his pocket, another slung under his hunchback, which is why he was called Humpty, and the third in a special holder in his derby hat.

Jackson's headquarters was an old graveyard between First and Second Avenues bound by 12th and 13th Streets. Sitting on a tombstone, he would dispense criminal assignments to his thugs. If a customer wanted someone blackjacked or otherwise assaulted, he or she simply approached Humpty, and for $100, in the case of blackjacking, he would see the job was done. Naturally, Jackson never soiled his own hands on such chores but merely handed them out to one of his men. Similarly, he would plan burglaries or warehouse lootings but seldom lead the forays himself. Nevertheless, Jackson was a man with a volatile temper who committed many acts of violence, which earned him more than 20 arrests and convictions. In 1909 he was sentenced to 20 years for ordering the execution of a man he'd never met. He died behind bars in 1914.

See also: SPANISH LOUIE.

Jackson, Mary Jane "Bricktop" (1836–?) female ruffian and murderess

Nicknamed Bricktop because of her flaming red hair, Mary Jane Jackson was reputedly the most vicious street criminal, male or female, New Orleans has ever produced. Any number of the Live Oak gangsters, the city's toughest gang, backed off from confrontations with her. In about a decade of battling, Bricktop Jackson never lost a fight, killed four men and sent at least two dozen more to the hospital, from which many emerged permanently maimed. When she took up living with a notorious criminal named John Miller, the pair became known as New Orleans' toughest couple.

Born on Girod Street in 1836, Bricktop, a husky, well-endowed girl, became a prostitute at age 13. The next year she attained a measure of security when a saloon keeper took her as his mistress. When he tired of her after three years and threw her out, she charged into his saloon and gave him a fearsome beating, sending him to the hospital minus an ear and most of his nose. Bricktop then entered a Dauphine Street whorehouse, where, while she gained a following with the customers, she terrified the other girls. She was turned out of the Dauphine Street establishment and subsequently, several other brothels. Bricktop was headed for the dance halls of New Orleans' toughest thoroughfare, Gallatin Street, and got a job with the redoubtable Archie Murphy in his notorious Dance-House. Nothing was considered too rough for Murphy's place, but Bricktop Jackson proved the exception to the rule. She had to be forcibly evicted from there as well as many other tough dance houses, whose owners had foolishly thought they could control her. Bricktop finally became a freelance prostitute and street mugger. In 1856 she killed her first man and in 1857 her second; one had called her a "whore" and gotten clubbed to death for the insult, and the other, Long Charley, had been cut down with Bricktop's made-to-order knife following an argument over which way he would fall if stabbed (the nearly 7-foot-tall Charley was reported to have fallen forward when Bricktop tested her hypothesis).

One of Bricktop's more famous murders occurred on November 7, 1859, when she visited a beer garden with two other vicious vixens, America Williams and Ellen Collins. A man at the next table, Laurent Fleury, objected to Bricktop's language and told her to shut up. Bricktop cursed even more and threatened to cut Fleury's heart out. Fleury, who had not recognized the scourge of Gallatin Street, slapped her. In a second the three women were all over him, and the luckless Fleury disappeared in a mass of flailing hands, swirling skirts and flashing knives. Joe Seidensahl, the owner of the beer garden, tried to come to his rescue but was driven back, severely cut up. A Seidensahl employee shot at the women from a second-floor window, but they drove him off with a barrage of bricks. By the time the police arrived, they found Fleury dead and his pants pocket cut out. The pocket, with money still inside, was found tucked under Bricktop's skirt. She was locked up in Parish Prison but eventually freed when an autopsy failed to show the victim's cause of death. Bricktop's lawyer contended he had died of heart disease.

It was in Parish Prison that Bricktop Jackson met a man who was, for the time, the love of her life, a jailer and ex-criminal named John Miller. The pair became a colorful item, even by Gallatin Street standards. Miller had lost an arm in a previous escapade and now walked about with a chain and iron ball attached to his stump, which made an awesome weapon. The couple supported themselves by close teamwork based on their respective skills. Bricktop would start up a romance with a stranger in a French Quarter dive and repair to the back streets with him. The man would end up with a very sore skull, no recollection of what happened and empty pockets.

The romance between Bricktop and Miller was marred by a dispute over who was the master of their nest. One day in 1861 Miller came home and decided to bullwhip Bricktop into subservience. She snatched the whip away from him, however, and gave him a bloody beating. He lashed out with his iron ball but she seized the chain in midair and began dragging him around the room. Miller pulled out a knife and slashed at Bricktop, who bit the knife free, grabbed it and then stabbed her lover five times. It was a fatal end to their relationship and one that caused Bricktop to be sent to prison for 10 years. She was released after only nine months when Gen. George F. Shepley, the military governor of the state, practically emptied the penitentiary with blanket pardons. Upon her release, Bricktop Jackson disappeared from New Orleans, a loss that went totally unlamented by honest and dishonest citizens alike.

See also: JOHN MILLER.

Jackson-Dickinson duel

In the famous, or infamous, duel between Andrew Jackson and Charles Dickinson in 1806, there was no quarter given. Although Dickinson was considered to be the best shot in Tennessee, Jackson had challenged him after he had made disparaging remarks about Jackson's wife, Rachel. The duel was fought at a range of 24 feet. Dickinson got off the first shot, which crashed into Jackson's chest, missing his heart by only an inch. Blood gushed through his clothes, but Jackson managed to keep his feet, though unsteadily. He took dead aim at Dickinson, who broke and ran from the line of fire. The seconds ordered Dickinson back to his previous position, as the dueling code required, and he stood awaiting Jackson's shot with his arms crossed to protect his heart. Jackson aimed a bit lower at his target and fired, hitting Dickinson in the groin. Death came slowly and excruciatingly to Dickinson. Jackson carried the lead ball he had received until the end of his days, it being too close to the heart to be removed.

jailhouse shopping network   convict's credit card con

Credit card fraud is a billion-dollar business, but there are some frauds, in a manner of speaking, more fraudulent than others. That is perhaps the only way to describe the scam that became known as the "nationwide jailhouse shopping network" in the early 1990s. It was conceived in Miami's Dade County jail, where there was a legal requirement that inmates be provided with access to telephones. The scam was thought up by Danny Ferris, a shrewd con man convicted of murder who, for more than four years, made local calls and 1-800 calls free of charge.

What Ferris did was simply order all sorts of merchandise over the telephone and steal an estimated $2 million in that fashion. It turned out that Ferris' accomplices on the outside provided him with hundreds of credit card numbers (retrieved from hotel dumpsters and the like), and the convict in turn used the numbers to order from catalogs by telephone. He arranged to have the goods delivered overnight to his accomplices who then sold the goods and split the profits with Ferris. Ferris ordered incredible numbers of video camcorders, Rolex watches, champagne, gourmet gift baskets and gold and silver coins and raked in a fortune.

Later he admitted to interviewers, "I split right half with everybody. I mean, I never took more than half. I got robbed a lot, but, again, you kind of take it on the chin. You know what I mean? It was like you said, 'Heck, it was all free.'"

When at last Ferris was exposed, jail officials found they could not legally deprive him of his phone rights. They did, however, raid his cell and confiscate hundreds of credit card numbers.

That failed to knock Ferris out of business, as he managed to salvage a single number and used it to order a newspaper ad and a telephone answering service. He ran the ad in USA Today offering, "Cosmetics package, $89.95 value for only $19.95. All major credit cards accepted. Please call Regina Donovan Cosmetics." Danny supplied a 1-800 number but never sold any cosmetics. But he got what he really was after—a brand new batch of credit card numbers.

Eventually Danny Ferris was sentenced to five years for credit card fraud. Since that was in addition to the life sentence he was already serving, that hardly upset him. However, he was transferred to a tougher Florida state prison, where more stringent controls were placed on telephone calls. Meanwhile, back at Dade County jail it was discovered that other inmates were pulling Danny's surefire scam, one con even operated in the departed Danny's personal cell. Finally after the CBS television program 60 Minutes featured the case, Dade County jail officials removed the in-cell telephones, requiring prisoners to make their calls in open corridors and the like, figuring that would put a serious crimp in their operations.

Without the old master's tutelage, the restrictions appeared to work.

James brothers

The James brothers, especially Jesse, who was born in 1847, were probably the best-known outlaws in America, leading a gang of robbers from 1866 to 1882, when Jesse was assassinated for the reward on his head. Since then his niche in American folklore has remained secure, perhaps typified by a ballad that surfaced instantly after his death. It started:

Jesse James was a lad who killed many a man.
He robbed the Glendale train.
He stole from the rich and he gave to the poor.
He'd a hand and a heart and a brain.

Jesse James was the American version of Robin Hood, as the loving tales told about him reveal. He was the holdup man who stole money from the wicked banker about to foreclose and gave it to the poor widow to pay off her mortgage (and then—perhaps to embellish the fantasy—he restole the money from the banker). He fought for the oppressed, saved the frail from the bully and so on. But the truth is that he and his brother Frank, four years his elder, never once gave a penny to the poor. What they stole they kept. They were ruthless, desperate men who killed anyone who got in their way.

Yet they were popular. Reflecting the political alignment of a border state in the aftermath of the Civil War,

Cole
Younger

Bob
Younger
(rear)

Jesse
James

Frank
James

The alliance between the James brothers and the Youngers eventually foundered over Jesse's readiness to sacrifice any member of the gang as the price for escape.

Jesse became a hero to the defeated Rebels and those who had sympathized with the South and was invariably described as having been driven to his crimes because of persecution of Northerners, particularly businessmen. Ex-Unionists and abolitionists called the Jameses and their frequent allies, the Youngers, murderers and thieves and said they were deserving of hanging.

The James boys were born in Clay County, Mo., the sons of a preacher, the Rev. Robert James, who died when Jesse was three. During the Civil War, Frank joined Quantrill's Raiders and continued to ride with him even after it became apparent he was nothing more than a plunderer and butcher. In 1864, at the age of 17, Jesse hooked up with Confederate guerrillas under Bloody Bill Anderson and took part in the Centralia massacre that year, in which he is reputed to have brutally murdered a Union officer.

Jesse came out of the war badly wounded and was nursed back to health by a cousin, Zerelda Mimms, whom he would eventually marry. Even though the conflict was over, neither the James boys nor Cole Younger and his brothers saw any reason to stop their looting. They formed a gang and robbed $17,000 from a bank in Liberty, Mo. on February 13, 1866, killing a bystander in the process. It is known that they committed a number of additional bank robberies, but later practically every bank job in Missouri from 1866 to 1869 was attributed to them. There is no doubt that the James-Younger gang robbed the bank at Gallatin in 1869, since all of them were well identified. After that, they ranged as far afield as Alabama and Iowa. Jesse often provided a touch of verve to the capers. Once, they hit a bank while a political rally was taking place, and Jesse, on the way out, stopped in front of the crowd and earnestly informed them he thought there might be something wrong back at the bank. Perhaps their most audacious outing occurred at a fair in Kansas City where Jesse and his men rode right up into a crowd of 10,000 people and robbed the box office of $10,000. Many persons thought it was all part of the show until a little girl was shot.

What made the James boys popular in much of Missouri was their harassment of railroad officials, perhaps the most hated group in the state because of their seizure of private lands under condemnation orders, for which they paid a mere pittance. The gang's first known train robbery was in 1873, when they derailed the Chicago and Rock Island express near Adair, Iowa. As happened during many of their jobs, someone died during the holdup, in this case the engineer when the train derailed.

The James-Younger move into train robberies put them in the big time and the Pinkertons on their trail. In January 1875, the Pinkertons were convinced the

James brothers were holed up in their mother's home and laid siege to it. In an effort to flush them out, the detectives threw in a bomb—the agency later insisted it was only a flare—and when the smoke cleared, Frank and Jesse's nine-year-old brother, Archie, was dead and their mother, Mrs. Zerelda Samuels, had had most of her right arm blown off. The incident stoked great resentment toward the Pinkertons and brought forth a rash of sympathy for the James boys, not only in Missouri but throughout the country. Lost in the shuffle of support for the outlaws was an recollection of their own long list of victims. The bungling Pinkertons had done as much as anybody to make them respectable.

In 1876 disaster struck the gang when they attempted to rob the First National Bank of Northfield, Minn. Of the eight gang members, including the James brothers and three Younger brothers, only Jesse and Frank escaped when things went wrong and the citizenry came out shooting. The rest were either killed or captured there or in the ensuing chase.

For the next three years the James boys were relatively inactive, living off accumulated loot, but in 1879 Jesse reconstituted the gang. Although he didn't feel comfortable with some of the new men, including Bob and Charles Ford, he made do. After two more murders by the gang in 1881, the state of Missouri posted $5,000 rewards on each of the James brothers. The Fords then made a deal with Gov. Thomas Crittenden to assassinate Jesse James for a $10,000 reward.

On April 3, 1882 Jesse summoned the Fords to his home in St. Joseph, where he was living under the name of Howard, to plan their next job. When Jesse climbed up on a chair to straighten a picture, Bob Ford shot him dead.

The James legend didn't die with Jesse. He was lionized by much of the press. The *Kansas City Journal* headlined his death with a mournful farewell: "GOODBYE JESSE."

He was buried in a corner of his mother's yard and later an inscription was put on the marker:

Jesse W. James,
Died April 3, 1882.
Aged 34 years, six months, 28 days.
Murdered by a coward whose name is not worthy
to appear here.

Of course, few killers ever get their names inscribed on the headstones of their victims. But no matter, a legend was being constructed, one that continues to the present day.

In October 1882 Frank James, tired of running, walked into Gov. Crittenden's office and surrendered his guns. He too was now part of the legend, and he was treated like one. Mobs cheered him as he stood on train platforms during a trip back to Clay County to stand trial for a couple of murders. The authorities were wasting their time; there was no way Frank James was going to be convicted. He was then shipped to Alabama to stand trial for a robbery charge but was found not guilty. Missouri tried again on another robbery count. Again he went free.

Thereafter Frank James lived in retirement from crime, working at a number of jobs, such as a horse race starter, shoe salesman and farmer. He died in 1915, a much respected citizen.

See also: THOMAS T. CRITTENDEN; CHARLES FORD; ROBERT NEWTON FORD; WOOD HITE; JESSE JAMES—IMPOSTORS; NORTHFIELD, MINNESOTA BANK RAID; ALLAN PINKERTON; YOUNGER BROTHERS.

James, Jesse—impostors

Almost from the time Jesse James was laid in his grave, impostors came forth claiming to be the real Jesse James, insisting he hadn't been shot at all. Most were proven liars and disappeared. Oddly, the last one seemed to be the most convincing. In 1948 a man named J. Frank Dalton, citing his age at 101, claimed to be the real Jesse James. At the time he was bedridden in Lawton, Okla.

Rudy Turilli, a noted authority on Jesse James, asserted that Bob Ford hadn't killed Jesse but rather another member of the gang, Charlie Bigelow. According to this theory, Bigelow looked like Jesse, having often passed himself off as the famous outlaw. He was due for extinction anyway because he was suspected of being an informer. Among those involved in the hoax, said Turilli, were James' mother and wife, the Ford brothers, and even Gov. Thomas Crittenden, who, he alleged, was a longtime friend of the James family.

In 1966 Turilli published a booklet, in cooperation with the Jesse James Museum of Stanton, Mo. entitled *I Knew Jesse James*, relating how he had found Dalton in Oklahoma through a tip. Turilli rounded up two of Jesse's old cronies: 108-year-old James R. Davis, a former U.S. marshal, and 111-year-old John Trammell, a black who had cooked for the James gang. Both men identified Dalton as Jesse James. Dalton was interviewed by dozens of reporters; writer Robert Ruark spent three days with Dalton and the other old-timers and was absolutely convinced that Dalton was no hoaxer.

One of those not convinced was Homer Croy, among the more reliable Jesse James' biographers. He visited Dalton before the old man had a chance to school himself on all the details of Jesse's life that unbelievers might ask about. When Croy asked him who or what was Red Fox, Dalton identified the name as that of a scout for Quantrill, a part Indian. Actually, Red Fox was Jesse's race horse.

The real stumbling block, however, was the fact that the tip of Dalton's left-hand middle finger was intact. Supposedly, Jesse accidentally had blown part of that finger off while cleaning his pistol during the period in the Civil War when he rode with Bloody Bill Anderson, though some experts are unsure whether the fingertip was really shot off or not. Turilli challenged anyone to produce a photo of Jesse showing a missing fingertip. Probably because of the dearth of photographs of Jesse James, the challenge went unanswered. However, at the coroner's inquest into Jesse James' death, several witnesses testified they recognized the dead man as James, including Sheriff James H. Timberlake of Clay County, who knew well what Jesse looked like. Timberlake, who had last seen the outlaw in 1870, said he recognized Jesse's face. And

Much of the speculation that Jesse James was not killed by Bob Ford stemmed from the fact that the only known photograph taken after his death failed to show that the tip of his left-hand middle finger was missing.

he stated, "He had the second joint of his third finger shot off, by which I also recognize him." Other witnesses besides Timberlake mentioned the missing part of the finger.

J. Frank Dalton died on August 16, 1951, just short of Jesse James' 104th birthday.

See also: AL JENNINGS.

Jennings, Al (1864–1961) alleged outlaw

One of the classic frauds in American crime writing is the effort to paint Al Jennings as the "last of the Western outlaws." He was not, despite a famous lurid article on his career in the *Saturday Evening Post* and a Hollywood movie about him and the so-called Al Jennings gang, whose rampage one authority described as "the shortest and funniest on record."

Jennings grew up one of the four sons of a frontier judge in the Oklahoma Territory. In later years he said he began his life of crime at the age of 16, but we have only his word for it. No court or law enforcement records list any charges against him or against his brothers, who, he stated were his partners in crime. The fact that all four were admitted to the bar tends to cast suspicion on Jennings' later claims. Two of his brothers did end up in a murderous affair, but as victims rather than perpetrators. Ed and John Jennings got into a saloon dispute with flamboyant lawman-gunman Temple Houston in 1894. Ed was shot dead while John was badly wounded and died a short time later.

People who didn't know Al Jennings—and thus were unaware that he was a notoriously poor shot—expected him to go after Houston. He never did. Instead, he and brother Frank hit the outlaw trail together with three stumblebums. The road agents "ran riot" for 109 days, during which they abandoned two efforts to hold up trains before finally robbing a Rock Island train on October 1, 1897. This achievement, on which Jennings subsequently built his reputation, netted the five outlaws $60 apiece. Four of the gang, including Al and Frank Jennings, were arrested single-handedly by lawman Bud Ledbetter without firing a shot. When he cornered the two brothers, he told them to drop their guns and tie themselves up. They did.

For their trivial crime the Jennings brothers got life sentences, this was a period when long sentences were meted out and later reduced (the pardon business was thriving and lucrative). Al did five years and Frank seven. After that, both returned to the straight life, Al even running unsuccessfully for governor of Oklahoma. He also hit the lecture circuit, far from Oklahoma, where folks knew better about his wild and wooly past. The *Post* article eased his way into Hollywood, where filmmakers and afterward, the filmgoers simply ate up the tales of his fanciful life of crime. Highly intelligent, Jennings proved a huge success as both an author and a film producer.

In 1948 Jennings was able to carry his outlaw hoax a little further. In that year 101-year-old J. Frank Dalton turned up, announcing he was the real Jesse James. He was brought together with 85-year-old Jennings, who said: "Boys, there isn't a bit of doubt on earth. It's him. It's Jesse James." Of course, Jennings had never even met Jesse James. It was the reverse side of the pot calling the kettle black. When he died in 1961, the obituary writers paid due tribute to Al Jennings, "last of the Western outlaws."

See also: JESSE JAMES—IMPOSTORS.

Jewett, Helen (1813–1836) murder victim

The murder of Helen Jewett in 1836 remains one of New York's most infamous unsolved cases, particularly since it was all too evident that the public didn't want the case solved. Helen Jewett at the time was the city's most desirable and most sought-after prostitute, always the "star woman" in whatever scarlet establishment she deigned to grace, and she was, according to one contemporary biographer, "kind to excess to all who required her assistance." However, she did have a troubling side to her nature, being quick to defend her rights whatever the consequences.

When a drunken British naval officer ripped up all her dresses and drowned her pet canary, she hauled him into court and collected damages. And when a wealthy rake got annoyed with her and knocked her down in a theater, she promptly had him arrested for assault and battery, charges ladies of her profession seldom brought, regarding such affronts as one of the perils of the profession.

Raised in a New England foster home under the tutelage of a kindly judge, she had grown up in an atmosphere of music, literature and the social graces that undoubtedly put her a cultural cut above most of her customers. Helen handpicked many of her lovers. If a man proved attractive to her, she would attempt to seduce him by missive. Taking a liking to an actor she had seen in *Othello,* she wrote:

> *Othello is in my opinion a great lout and a great fool, and has not one half so much to cry about as Iago. . . . I should like to see you in Damon or in Romeo. I should like above all things to be your Juliet, or to rehearse the character with you in private, at any rate. I have some notions on the philosophy of her character and likewise on that of Romeo, which would perhaps amuse you.*

In 1834 Helen enticed a young rake named Richard P. Robinson into her regular army of admirers. Like many other blades of the day, he conducted much of his nightlife under an alias, that of Frank Rivers, but as his affair with Helen bloomed, he readily revealed to her his true identity. Robinson also developed a jealous streak, the thought of her having an interest, other than financial, in any other man obsessed him. Of course, Robinson never gave a thought to marrying Helen, and when he decided to wed a respectable young lady of considerable means, a second note of friction entered his relationship with the haughty harlot.

For whatever reason, at 3 o'clock on Sunday morning April 10, 1836, Robinson entered Mrs. Rosina Townsend's famed brothel, where Helen Jewett was in residence. He was wearing his usual flashy visored cap and billowing Spanish cloak so that Madam Townsend and another prostitute readily recognized him. What they didn't know was that Robinson carried a hatchet under the cloak. Helen Jewett was found brutally murdered several hours later, her skull savagely hacked in.

Helen Jewett's death exposed New York's false morality. At first, the newspapers treated the murder as a sensational affair, but it soon became evident that nobody wanted Robinson arrested, including the police and several important protectors of Madam Townsend. Robinson apparently felt so safe that he did not bother to flee the city. Finally, after what can only be described as a lethargic investigation, he was arrested.

A public cry of sympathy went up, with one newspaper regretting that so young a person as Robinson should be sacrificed for "ridding the city of so great a disgrace to her sex." A Methodist minister pleaded from the pulpit for mercy for him, and young rakes adopted a new heroic dress, striding up Broadway in "Frank Rivers" caps and "Robinson" cloaks and chanting, "No man should hang for the murder of a whore."

No man did. Robinson's trial was a five-day farce, with most newspapers printing nothing but laudatory comments about the accused and somber warnings to prostitutes to stay away from the City Hall area because of threats of violence. By his attitude, it was clear Mayor Philip Hone considered the accused innocent; he later wrote in his diary, "He certainly looks as little like a murderer as any person I ever saw."

During the trial prosecution witnesses who had furnished damaging evidence against Richardson, both regarding the murder and his general dissolute life, became shaky in their testimony. A grocer named Robert Furlong gave the defendant a dubious alibi, but his subsequent suicide somewhat spoiled the effect. Just to make sure nothing went wrong, a few of Robinson's more ardent supporters bribed at least one juror. The effort proved unnecessary, as a not-guilty verdict was quickly brought in. That evening Robinson was honored at a great celebration.

Obviously, good had triumphed over evil, although James Gordon Bennett's *Herald,* which alone held Robinson guilty wrote:

The evidence in this trial and the remarkable disclosure of the manners and morals of New York form one of those events that must make philosophy pause, religion stand aghast, morals weep in the dust, and female virtue droop her head in sorrow.
A number of young men, clerks in fashionable stores, are dragged up to the witness stand, but where are the married men, where the rich merchants, where the devoted church members who were caught in their shirts and drawers on that awful night? The publication and perusal of the evidence in this trial will kindle up fires that nothing can quench.

Nonetheless, the good burghers of New York had an unsolved mystery on their hands and obviously preferred it that way. After Richard Robinson was freed and left the city, rumor had it that he became a desperado along the Mississippi.

Jewish Mafia

There has been a long-standing argument over whether or not the Mafia, Italian style, exists. Of course, the real argument lies in the definition of the term *Mafia* and how close a relationship can be assumed to exist among various "crime families." Certainly, in a looser context, there is an Italian Mafia, and years ago there was a Jewish Mafia. Like the Italian Mafia, there were Jewish gangs that cooperated with one another, and this did not change just because a Monk Eastman or a Jack Zelig, to name two brutes, or an Arnold Rothstein, to name a brain, were removed from the scene. Meyer Lansky was able to put the pieces back together again and lead a new Jewish Mafia in cooperation with the Italian Mafia. Lansky first did some missionary work around the country, bringing in the Moe Dalitz forces from Cleveland and the Purple Gang from Detroit, among others. Then he organized a convention of East Coast forces at the Franconia Hotel in New York City on November 11, 1931. Those attending included Bugsy Siegel, Joseph "Doc" Stacher, Louis "Lepke" Buchalter, Hyman "Curly" Holtz, Jacob "Gurah" Shapiro, Philip "Little Farvel" Kovalick, Louis "Shadows" Kravitz, Harry Tietlebaum and Harry "Big Greenie" Greenberg.

The conference closely followed a revolutionary change in the operation of the Italian Mafia. Just two months earlier, Lucky Luciano had effectively seized control of the Italian underworld by the assassination of Salvatore Maranzano, the so-called boss of bosses. Luciano's plan, which was at least 50 percent Lansky's idea was to establish a new "combination," or national crime syndicate. Lansky's job was to bring in the Jewish mobsters, and the final scene in that act was the Franconia conference, which established the firm rule that "the yids and dagos would no longer fight each other."

The new "interfaith" combination was to be paramount. If there were any doubters, they were converted when one of the Franconia participants, Big Greenie, was eliminated by Bugsy Siegel, filling a contract that came down from the national board of the syndicate. When Siegel was later erased for defying the same board, his erstwhile tutor and partner Lansky would simply say with a shrug, "I had no choice."

Joe the Boss   See GIUSEPPE "JOE THE BOSS" MASSERIA.

Johnny Behind the Deuce (1862–1882) gambler and killer

One of the West's most colorful and deadly gamblers, Johnny Behind the Deuce won a fortune at cards, killed several men, was saved from a lynch mob by Wyatt Earp and went to his own reward in a blazing gunfight—all before he reached his 21st birthday.

Nothing is known of his early life, but Johnny turned up in Tucson, Arizona Territory in early 1878 at the age of 16, giving his surname, at various times, as O'Rourke and his Christian name as either Michael or John. He worked as a hotel porter and seemed to spend all his free moments learning to manipulate a gun and a deck of cards. By 1880 he was famous throughout the territory as Johnny Behind the Deuce, a hard man to beat at any game of cards. In time, a suspicion developed that as he sat in the saloon gambling, Johnny would watch for a man passing out from drink and then leave the table for a short period. When the drunk sobered up the next day, he would find his belongings had been burglarized. Hardly anyone accused Johnny Behind the Deuce of such crimes, since he had already demonstrated a deadly knack for dealing with critics.

In January 1881 in Charleston a miner named Henry Schneider dared to call Johnny a thief when he found his poke had disappeared from his shack. He died with a bullet between the eyes after, Johnny Behind the Deuce alleged, drawing a knife. Marshal George McKelvey hustled the gambler off to Tombstone before the miners could start thinking of a lynching. Upon his arrival in Tombstone a crowd quickly gathered but a shotgun-armed Wyatt Earp held them off long enough for the prisoner to be moved to Tucson, where he was able to break out of jail. Since Johnny Behind the Deuce often dealt in the Oriental Saloon, of which Earp owned a piece, it is very likely that the latter felt he owed the young gambler something.

What happened next is guesswork, but a popular theory that summer was that the fugitive gambler came across the notorious Johnny Ringo, Wyatt Earp's mortal enemy, sleeping off a powerful drunk under a gnarled oak in Turkey Creek Canyon. Johnny Behind the Deuce supposedly figured he owed Earp one, so he shot the outlaw through the head. Whether true or not, the story was generally believed by Ringo's gunfighter friends. One of these, Pony Deal, got into a card game with Johnny Behind the Deuce in Sulphur Springs Valley. After a few hands Deal called Johnny a four-flusher, cheater and murderer. Angered, the gambler went for his gun, but Deal outdrew him and shot him dead.

See also: JOHNNY RINGO.

Johnson, George (?–1882) lynch victim

Since George Johnson was lynched for a murder that didn't happen, his case pricked the conscience of Tombstone, Ariz. Not that Johnson didn't deserve hanging, as old-timers would relate years later, but it didn't seem quite just.

In October 1882 Johnson held up, or at least attempted to hold up, the Tombstone-Bisbee stage, firing a shot to bring it to a halt. Inside the coach one of the two passengers, Mrs. M. E. Kellogg, felt her husband slump down beside her when the shot was fired. He was dead. The woman screamed, and that frightened the would-be bandit's horse, which then bolted, unseating its rider. Johnson lost his weapon on hitting the ground and then did the only thing he could do under the circumstances: he ran off on foot.

The stage driver jumped down and seeing that Mr. Kellog was dead, unhitched two horses. He put the new widow on one horse and sent her back to Tombstone to request aid while he took off after the bandit on the other. Mrs. Kellogg got back to Tombstone in hysterical shape but was able to tell the sheriff what had happened. He and a doctor headed for the scene of the crime. Meanwhile, the stage driver ran Johnson to earth and brought him back to town. Unfortunately for Johnson, they came back by a different road and missed the sheriff.

By the time the sheriff, the doctor and the corpse returned, they found Tombstone justice had been done. Johnson had been strung up by a lyncher mob. The sheriff was angry and the doctor upset, and for good reason. The dead man had not been shot at all. He had

suffered a heart attack and died when the stagecoach was stopped. George Johnson had not killed anyone; he hadn't even robbed anyone. Under the circumstances a necktie party did seem somewhat extreme. Business in the saloons and brothels reportedly was a bit subdued that night. Conscience finally got the better of folks and a collection was taken up. The sum of $800 was presented to Johnson's widow to ease her loss. In addition, the words "Hanged By Mistake" were put on his tombstone.

Johnson, John (?–1824) murderer

John Johnson's crime in 1824 was in many respects a most pedestrian murder; at the same time it was probably the most publicized homicide in New York City's history.

When Johnson's roommate, James Murray, collected his pay, Johnson decided to appropriate it. Splitting Murray's skull with an ax he packed the dead man in a blanket and lugged his grim load toward the harbor to dispose of it. On the way he was challenged by a suspicious police officer. Johnson dropped his gory bundle and ran, managing to elude capture.

Stuck with a corpse they could not identify, officials ordered the dead man put on display at City Hall Park in the hope that someone would recognize it. For days an estimated 50,000 persons made the trek to view the body, many of them using the occasion as an excuse for a picnic in the area. Finally, a neighbor identified Murray, and the police quickly arrested Johnson. His execution was held at Second Avenue and 13th Street on April 2, 1824. Due the previous publicity the murder had attracted, the execution drew a crowd of 50,000.

Johnson, Mushmouth (?–1907) gambler

Perhaps the most successful black gambler in America, John V. "Mushmouth" Johnson dominated black gambling enterprises in Chicago from the mid-1880s until his death in 1907. Johnson, a flamboyant man with the obligatory cigar in mouth, controlled the city's policy racket, as well as scores of faro, poker and crap games in the black sections. His influence also extended over the Chinese quarter, where he charged all gambling enterprises a fee for protection. Mushmouth had considerable clout with the law as a result of his ability to deliver large blocks of black votes in elections.

Generally believed to have been a native of St. Louis, Mushmouth Johnson first appeared on the Chicago scene as a waiter at the Palmer House in the 1870s. In the early 1880s Andy Scott hired him as a floor man in his gambling emporium on South Clark Street and soon became so impressed with Mushmouth's abilities that he gave him a small interest in the operation. Mushmouth decided that what Chicago needed was a good nickel gambling house. A few years later, he opened his own place at 311 South Clark and did a thriving business with tables that catered to all races, offering bets as low as 5¢ in any of the games. Mushmouth sold off his interest in the place in 1890 and opened a saloon and gambling hall at 464 State Street, which operated without interruption for the next 17 years despite reform waves that shut down other gambling resorts at various times.

Together with two other big-time gamblers, Bill Lewis and Tom McGinnis, Mushmouth opened the Frontenac Club on 22nd Street. The club catered strictly to whites, and to be admitted, one was required to display a certain amount of cash. The fact that the Frontenac excluded blacks did not hurt Mushmouth's standing with his fellows; on the contrary, his success in the white world was a matter of black pride.

A total nongambler himself, Mushmouth is generally believed to have accumulated a quarter of a million dollars, a sizable sum for any man in that day and a colossal sum for a black man. Yet, shortly before his death in 1907, Johnson told a friend he had only $15,000, all the proceeds of his saloon business, and that he had lost money on his gambling ventures through the years. He said that he had spent $100,000 on fines and that police protection had always drained him, claiming, "I have had to pay out four dollars for every one I took in at the game." Johnson also implied he had been forced to pay more than his white counterparts because of the color of his skin.

When the claim gained currency following Mushmouth's death, an unnamed police official was outraged, denouncing Mushmouth Johnson as a "whiner" and a "damnable liar." It was unclear whether the official objected to Johnson's statement that he had paid for protection or, simply, that he had been discriminated against in the rates charged.

Johnson County War   range conflict

In 1892, under the guise of driving out "rustlers," the great cattle barons of Johnson County, Wyo. waged a war of extermination against small ranchers and homesteaders. There is no question that the big stockmen, mostly absentee owners residing in Cheyenne and members of the Wyoming Stock Growers' Association, had been losing cattle and that some had been taken by the "long rope," which was the traditional way most ranchers got started, picking up mavericks on the open range, and, indeed, the way most of the big stockmen themselves had gotten started. However, there were other reasons for the losses, including poor management and overstocking of the ranges, prairie fires, grass-destroying grasshoppers and bad weather. Tradi-

tionally too, many foremen on absentee-owner ranches built up small herds of their own and blamed the shortages on outside rustlers.

The stockmen followed the usual procedure of sending in "range detectives" to kill a few rustlers but found the results in Johnson County unsatisfactory. Whenever a small rancher or homesteader was arrested on rustling charges, a friendly jury of homesteaders invariably released him. The stockmen soon discovered, however, they could control not only the state administration, which they already owned, but the press as well. Their newfound power came about after a posse of cattlemen lynched a prostitute named Cattle Kate because she apparently had accepted beef from cowboys in payment for services rendered, and the beef the stockmen alleged, was stolen. To avoid any legal repercussions as a result of the lynching, they claimed Cattle Kate was a "bandit queen" who had masterminded a vast rustling operation. The press eagerly accepted the story and printed ridiculous accounts about the depredations of Cattle Kate. Encouraged by the public relations coup, the cattle barons decided to launch a full-scale war of extermination by going into the county in force with an army of gunmen to wipe out their arch enemies, one or two at a time.

For a period of a few months, members of the Wyoming Stock Growers' Association were invited to forward the names of deserving victims to the secretary of the organization. The executive committee then selected who would go on the death list (it was later estimated that a total of 70 victims were chosen), and sent 46 "regulators" under command of Col. Frank Wolcott and Frank H. Canton, a wanted murderer, into the county on a brutal murder mission.

Their first victims were two small ranchers, Nick Ray and Nate Champion who were killed in cold blood. Sickened by the murders, a doctor and one of the reporters accompanying the invaders left the expedition. But the shootings delayed the murder army and word spread of their presence. They soon found themselves besieged by a possee of 200 county residents.

The stockmen's army was forced to seek refuge in a ranch 13 miles south of Buffalo. They faced certain extinction until the U.S. Cavalry rode to their rescue. The killers then laid down their arms, surrendered to the army and were escorted back to Cheyenne. The local sheriff, Red Angus, unsuccessfully requested that the invaders be turned over to his custody. Had they been, there undoubtedly would have been 40-odd lynchings that evening.

The Johnson County "war" ended in a total disaster for the stockmen, who spent the next few years attempting to conceal their culpability. When a muckraker of the period, Asa Mercer published *The Banditti of the Plains* the following year, the cattle barons used their power to have the book suppressed; its plates were destroyed and Mercer was even jailed for a time for sending "obscene matter" through the mails. Copies of the book were torn up and burned and even the Library of Congress copy vanished.

While the stockmen had failed to exterminate the homesteaders of Johnson County, none were ever prosecuted for their offenses.

See also: JAMES AVERILL, *THE BANDITTI OF THE PLAINS*, FRANK M. CANTON, CATTLE KATE, NATHAN D. CHAMPION, RED SASH GANG.

Johnston, James A. (1876–1958) warden of Alcatraz

In 1934 James A. Johnston, a veteran penologist, was appointed by the U.S. Department of Justice to be the first warden of a new maximum-security, minimum-privilege federal prison on Alcatraz Island in San Francisco Bay. Johnston had previously served as warden of both Folsom and San Quentin prisons, California's toughest, but he had a reputation as a reformer. As such, his appointment caused something of a surprise. Old prison hands wanted someone tougher in the job, and many of Johnston's supporters were perplexed that he had accepted the post, which by the nature of the prison, had to be a repressive one.

From the beginning, Alcatraz was Johnston's creation; he personally designed the cell blocks and composed the most restrictive regulations ever used in a federal prison in the United States. In the popular press, Johnston was referred to as being "tough but kindly." The convicts thought differently, however, calling him Saltwater Johnston because they considered him as bitter as saltwater.

The rules that Johnston laid down were so severe that they are credited with having driven any number of convicts "stir crazy." For the first four years a rigid "rule of silence" prohibited the convicts from speaking a word in the cell blocks, in the mess hall or at work. A single word uttered without permission meant instant punishment, often in solitary confinement for periods up to several months. It was an abrupt change for a warden who in a dozen years had reformed San Quentin in more ways than had been accomplished in the previous 50. There, he had introduced individual treatment of convicts, established honor camps, abolished corporal punishment and did away with the ugly striped prison uniform. At Alcatraz the hole became a standard punishment. In the cramped space a convict slept on concrete and received only water and four slices of bread a day. Solitary was a little better, since the prisoner got a bunk and one regular meal a day.

During the so-called Alcatraz Prison Rebellion of 1946, really just an escape attempt by six convicts, Johnston proposed an all-out attack on the cell blocks by armed guards and grenade-tossing marines. When his superior in Washington, Bureau of Prisons head James Bennett, said he was worried about "what public reaction will be if a large number of innocent inmates were unnecessarily killed," Johnston responded rather stiffly, "Mr. Director, there are no *innocent* inmates in here."

The investigation following the 1946 rebellion revealed that one prisoner had been held in total isolation for more than seven years. Johnston bristled when asked how much longer the man would remain there and said, "As long as necessary for discipline." The warden insisted that the FBI agents preparing a murder case against three members of the six-man escape team interview them in the dungeon, relenting only when the officers explained that any statements they got from the prisoners under those conditions might not be admitted in court.

There is little doubt that Johnston was personally brave. Even in periods of unrest—and Alcatraz was almost constantly beset by strikes, sit-ins and riots—Johnston always entered the dining hall alone and unarmed; of course, machine-gun toting guards patrolled the catwalk outside. He would taste the soup and then take his position by the door, exposing his back to the convicts marching out. During a strike in September 1937, a young convict known to be mentally deficient attacked the 61-year-old warden, battering his face in, knocking out several teeth and stomping on his chest before guards could tear him away. It was a week before Johnston could get out of bed. His assailant went to the hole for a long stay. As a lifer, he faced death for attacking a prison officer, but the warden never brought charges.

Johnston retired as warden in 1948, a man who had believed in rehabilitation but who had during 14 years molded a prison incapable of rehabilitating anyone. Summing up his tenure, he said: "Atlanta and Leavenworth had sent me their worst. I had done my best with them." Johnston died at the age of 82, having outlived many a younger con who had sworn to celebrate on the day the warden died.

See also: ALCATRAZ PRISON, ALCATRAZ PRISON REBELLION, ATLANTA BOYS CONVOY, RUFUS "WHITEY" FRANKLIN, RULE OF SILENCE, ROBERT STROUD.

Johnstown flood looting

The flood that struck Johnstown, Pa., in 1889 was easily the worst disaster to occur in the United States during the late 19th century. When a 100-foot-high earthen dam broke, the resulting cataclysm killed at least 2,000 people—an average of about one out of

"DEATH TO THE FIENDS!" A contemporary sketch revealed the swift justice meted out to looters and mutilators of the dead at Johnstown in the aftermath of the great flood there.

every 10 persons living in the way of the flood—and bodies were still being found as late as 1906. However, much as the public was upset by the tragedy and the almost certain criminal negligence in the construction and supervision of the dam, it became more outraged by the looting, especially of the bodies of dead victims, that took place in the aftermath of the disaster.

As soon as the waters started to settle, hordes of looters descended on the scene to pillage business establishments and to strip the dead of cash, watches, wedding rings and the like. Dozens of looters were arrested, but they were the lucky ones. Outraged citizens killed others on the spot.

A Miss Wayne from Altoona, Pa. reported she was swept off a ferryboat by the rampaging waters and ended up on a beach, where she awakened to find herself stripped naked by looters. She feigned death and watched bands of thieves "slice off with wicked knives" the fingers of women to get their rings.

So outraged was the citizenry over this story that many persons lost interest in rescue work and set out in vigilante style to hunt for looters. One looter captured with a ring-bearing severed finger in his pocket was summarily drowned. Others were shot. Even the police, overburdened with rescue work, were caught up in the frenzy of catching looters. A publication of the period reported:

> A trap was laid for a crook undertaker, who was robbing the bodies in the Fourth Ward morgue. A female was brought in, and before it was dressed for burial a diamond ring was placed upon one of her fingers, and the pseudo undertaker was assigned to take charge of the body. He was detected in the act of stealing the jewelry, and was promptly arrested by the chief of police.

Jon, Gee (?–1924) first gas chamber victim

In 1924 Gee Jon became the first man to die in the gas chamber in Carson City, Nev. Reformers in that state were sure they had come up with a humane execution method when they pushed through a bill to have condemned men killed by poison gas that would be piped into their cells. The idea was that the execution would take place while the prisoner was asleep so that no prior notice would have to be given. Jon, the first man facing such a fate, would thus be spared the macabre preparations for the execution as well as having to await a preestablished time of death. However, these well-laid plans had to be scrapped because prison officials couldn't figure out how to carry out such an execution without having the gas spread and kill off a considerable number of the prison population. An airtight chamber was then constructed, and Jon had to endure all the frightful preparations the reformers had hoped to spare him. He was led into the chamber with a stethoscope attached to his chest and strapped into a chair under which cyanide pellets tied in a gauze sack hung on a hook. The chamber was cleared and a lever was pulled allowing the cyanide "eggs" to drop into a pan filled with a mixture of water and sulfuric acid. Within a matter of seconds, deadly fumes rose and, in a short time, the condemned man's heartbeat stopped. An effusive Carson City reporter informed his readers that Nevada had moved "one step further from the savage state."

See also: EXECUTION, METHODS OF.

Jones, Frank (1856–1893) Texas Ranger

One of the most colorful and storied Texas Rangers, Frank Jones had become a Ranger in his native Texas at the age of 17 and a hero in the organization at 18. Sent after a gang of Mexican horse thieves, Jones saw the two Rangers accompanying him cut down in an ambush. Carrying on alone, he killed two of the enemy and took one prisoner. Later, as a sergeant, he led a seven-man force after a group of rustlers. In a bitter gunfight three Rangers were killed, and Jones and three others were captured. Then, in an act of heroism befitting the storybook reputation of the Texas Rangers, Jones managed to seize the rifle of one of the rustlers and shoot his five captors dead. In 1880, as a captain, Jones was sent out with a murder warrant to arrest the notorious Scott Cooley, the instigator of the Mason County War of 1875. In a rare failure, Jones did not find Cooley (no one ever did and there is some reason to believe Cooley was dead at the time), but he did turn up three other desperadoes, one of whom he gunned down, the others he captured. After a while, Jones killed a rustler in a stand-up gun duel in a saloon, and in another barroom shoot-out he wounded and captured a notorious gunman named Tex Murietta. The list of Jones' daring accomplishments lengthened until June 29, 1893, when he went after a father-son outlaw team named Olguin. In a withering gun battle Jones, long regarded as "unkillable," was riddled with bullets. Ironically, the gunfight took place on an island in the Rio Grande that was actually on the Mexican side of the border, where the Olguins were immune to Texas justice.

See also: SCOTT COOLEY, MASON COUNTY WAR.

Jones, William "Canada Bill" (?–1877) gambler

Probably the greatest three-card monte cheater this country has ever produced and a fine all-round gambler, Canada Bill Jones cut a mangy figure along the Mississippi in the middle of the 19th century. In his autobiography *Forty Years a Gambler on the Mississippi*, George Devol, another legendary gambler, described Canada Bill as

a character one might travel the length and breadth of the land and never find his match, or run across his equal. Imagine a medium-sized, chicken-headed, tow-haired sort of a man with mild blue eyes, and a mouth nearly from ear to ear, who walked with a shuffling, half-apologetic sort of a gait, and who, when his countenance was in repose, resembled an idiot. His clothes were always several sizes too large, and his face was as smooth as a woman's and never had a particle of hair on it.

Canada was a slick one. He had a squeaking, boyish voice, and awkward gawky manners, and a way of asking fool questions and putting on a good natured sort of a grin, that led everybody to believe that he was the rankest kind of sucker—the greenest sort of country jake. Woe to the man who picked him up, though. Canada was, under all his hypocritical appearance, a regular card shark, and could turn monte with the best of them. He was my partner for a number of years, and many are the suckers we roped in, and many the huge roll of bills we corralled.

Normally, three-card monte favored the dealer two-to-one, but Canada Bill seldom gave a sucker such a decent break. He was probably the century's greatest manipulator of cards and could show a victim two aces and a queen and then, virtually in the act of throwing the cards, palm the queen and introduce a third ace so that the sucker could never find the queen. About 1850 Canada Bill formed a partnership with Devol and two other talented gamblers, Tom Brown and Hally Chappell. The larcenous quartet operated on the Mississippi and Ohio and other navigable streams for close to a decade. When the partnership dissolved, each man's share of the profits was more than $200,000.

As quickly as both he and Devol made their money, however, they squandered it, both being suckers for faro. Canada Bill, who truly loved gambling for its own sake, was the originator of what was to become a classic gamblers' comment. He and a partner were killing time between boats in a small Mississippi River town when Bill found a faro game and started to lose consistently. His partner, tugging at his sleeve, said, "Bill, don't you know the game's crooked!"

"I know it," Bill replied, "but it's the only game in town!"

When river traffic dwindled and then virtually disappeared by the start of the Civil War, Canada Bill shifted his operations to the rails. The railroads, however, did not always exhibit the same tolerance for gamblers that the riverboats had, and three-card monte players were ejected when spotted. In 1867 Canada Bill wrote to one of the Southern lines offering $25,000 a year in exchange for the right to operate without being molested. He promised to give the railroad an additional percentage of the profits and said he would limit his victims to very rich men and preachers. Alas, his offer was refused.

Alternately flush and broke Canada Bill continued his itinerant gambling style until 1874, when he settled in Chicago and, with Jimmy Porter and Charlie Starr, established some very lucrative and dishonest gambling dens. Within six months he was able to pull out with $150,000, but in a short time, he lost his entire poke at faro. Canada Bill worked Cleveland a bit, winning and then losing, and in 1877 he wound up in Reading, Pa., an area noted as a refuge for gamblers. While down on funds he was committed to Charity Hospital and died there in 1877. He was buried by the mayor of the city, who was later reimbursed by Chicago gamblers for the cost. As two old gambling buddies watched Canada Bill's coffin being lowered into the grave, one offered to bet $1,000 to $500 that the notorious cheat was not in the box.

"Not with me," the other gambler said. "I've known Bill to squeeze out of tighter holes than that."

See also: GEORGE DEVOL.

Juanita (1828–1851) first woman hanged in California

The hanging of a Mexican woman named Juanita, who comes down through history by that name alone, in the town of Downieville, Calif. in 1851 brought denunciations of American border justice from as far away as England.

Downieville was at the time a mining camp full of violent miners and harlots of all ages and hues, but Juanita was unquestionably the prize beauty. One account testifies: "Her dusky hair, long and glossy, was pulled low over delicate olive features and knotted loosely at the nape of her graceful neck. It gave her a Madonna-like expression. No doubt, many a rough miner stood in awe of her beauty and bared his head in reverence mingled with a certain human admiration." But she also had some faults, being described as, among other things, "a live volcano, an enraged lioness, a fighting wildcat."

In mid-1851 Juanita found true love with a young Mexican miner and set up housekeeping. She was henceforth not available as in the past. On the Fourth of July a celebrating miner named Jack Cannon came knocking on Juanita's door, brandishing a bag of gold dust. Juanita screamed at him in Spanish to let her alone. Cannon ignored her protestations and forced his way into the cabin, actually smashing the cabin door from its hinges. A knife flashed in the Mexican girl's hand, and Cannon fell bleeding to death on the floor.

Cannon was known in the camp as a rowdy, but he was a popular one, and an angry crowd soon gathered and began talk of lynching. Juanita was dragged to Craycroft's saloon for what was supposed to be a trial, but in the meantime some of her clothing had been dipped in Cannon's blood so that her crime would be more evident. A "prosecutor" was appointed to present the case, and a young unidentified lawyer who had journeyed over the mountains from Nevada to hear the Fourth of July speeches in Downieville was permitted to defend Juanita. While the "trial" proceeded, a number of miners argued over whose rope should be used for the girl's execution. When the young attorney started making a strong case of self-defense, he was knocked off the barrel he was standing on and flung out to the street. The jury then was ready to bring in a verdict, which, of course, turned out to be guilty.

Then a Dr. C. D. Aikin, who had come to the camp only weeks before, interrupted the proceedings to declare he was treating Juanita for pregnancy. An angry murmur arose in the crowd, which numbered in the hundreds. Three other local medical men were charged with examining the girl and came back to announce the claim was a hoax. Dr. Aiken quickly was held in contempt for his humane effort to save the girl and was given 24 hours to get out of town or be hanged himself.

Juanita was dragged back to her cabin and given an hour to prepare for her fate, while a crowd gathered outside the cabin and started shouting curses at her and stoning the flimsy structure. A priest was not allowed to go to her. After the hour was up, Juanita was marched to Durgan Bridge, from which a noose hung out over the wide Yuba. Extending from the bridge was a 6-foot plank, on which the condemned woman was to stand. As she took her position, Juanita was silent, unlike during her courtroom appearance when she voluably had attacked the kangaroo proceedings in Spanish. Now she merely observed the crowd and smiled in contempt. When she spotted a friendly face, she called out, "Adiós, amigo, adiós." Then the plank was kicked out from under her.

When news of the execution reached the outside world, the press from one end of the country to the other condemned the bloodthirsty affair. Even the *Times of London* printed severe and caustic criticism of the manner in which border justice had been dispensed. Juanita was described as the first and only woman ever hanged in California, which was not true. Many Mexican and Indian women had been hanged, but hers was the first to follow a "trial."

Judd, Winnie Ruth (1909–1993) murderess

Winnie Judd was called the Tiger Woman by a devoted press, which kept her supplied with clippings for 40 years after her conviction in the trunk murders of two young women in Phoenix, Ariz.

Winnie had been friendly with 27-year-old Agnes LeRoi, a nurse who worked at the same medical clinic as herself, and Hedvig Samuelson, with whom Agnes shared an apartment, and often stayed with them. On October 16, 1931, screams were heard coming from the apartment. The next day Winnie showed up for work but Agnes did not. On October 18 Winnie went by train to Los Angeles with a large trunk and a small one. Upon her arrival she asked a baggage room employee to help her load them in her car. The employee noticed a dark red fluid dripping from a corner of one of them and demanded to know what was inside, suspecting the trunks might contain contraband deer meat. Winnie said the keys were in the car and went to get them. She drove off, but the baggage clerk managed to write down her license number.

When authorities opened the trunks, they found the body of Agnes LeRoi in the large one and most of the dismembered body of Hedvig in the smaller one. She had been cut up to make her fit. An alarm went out for Winnie, who finally surrendered five days later after an appeal from her Los Angeles husband, from whom she had been separated for some time.

The public was enthralled by the trunk murderess, but it was difficult to tell whether people were more taken by the grisliness of the crime or letters that Winnie had written but never sent to her husband, which revealed strange heterosexual, bisexual and homosexual activities that were common at the LeRoi-Samuelson apartment.

Winnie insisted she had killed in self-defense after Hedvig pulled out a gun and shot her in the hand following a bitter argument. She said she had struggled for the gun, managed to wrest it from Hedvig and in the ensuing melee shot both women. At her trial the prosecution made the point that no one had noticed the gun wound in Winnie's hand until two days after the killings.

Winnie was found guilty and sentenced to hang. Pressure around the country built up for Winnie to be spared the death penalty in light of her claims of self-defense and her lawyer's insistence that she was mentally ill. Thirty state legislators and 34 priests and ministers signed a petition, and thousands of letters poured in on her behalf, including from Mrs. Eleanor Roosevelt.

The governor granted her a stay and a sanity hearing 72 hours before her scheduled execution. At the hearing the Tiger Woman put on a show that delighted the newspapers. She clapped, laughed and yelled at the jury. She got up once and told her husband she was "going out the window." Winnie's mother testified that she herself was feeble-minded and that her daughter had "been more or less insane all her life." Her father produced a family tree that traced insanity back 125 years to Scotland. Winnie emphasized the point by ripping at her hair and trying to pull off her clothes. She finally had to be removed from the hearing room and ultimately was judged insane and sentenced to life imprisonment in the state mental institution.

When she arrived at the institution Winnie no longer acted crazy. She was quiet, helpful and plotting. She fashioned a dummy of herself, put it in her bed and escaped. She was found some days later, and it was discovered that strangers had helped her on a number of occasions.

Winnie was brought back and tightly confined. It did no good. Over the years she escaped seven times, each time sparking headlines. One of her escapes lasted six years. It got so that in newsrooms on dull news days an editor would say, "Well, maybe Winnie Ruth Judd will escape again." One of the more sensational crime publications warned its readers. "When you read this story, the country's cleverest maniac may be at large again, perhaps walking down your street, or sitting next to you!"

In 1969, after one of her long-term escapes, attorney Melvin Belli fought Winnie's extradition from California to Arizona, but Gov. Ronald Reagan ordered her returned. Doctors then ruled Winnie was perfectly sane and she was sent to prison. In 1971 Winnie won a parole. She was then in her 60s and no one seemed to be upset about the Tiger Woman being on the loose, possibly because she had had so much free time before.

Winnie Ruth Judd (center), the trunk murderess, being returned to prison after one of her many escapes.

judicial corruption

The roster of corrupt judges in the American judicial system is, sadly, a long one. It is least serious in the federal judiciary. As Donald Dale Jackson states in *Judges* (1974), "Manton, Kerner, Ritter, perhaps three dozen others in the history of the republic is not bad." But Jackson goes on to add: "Corruption in state courts is oceanic in comparison to federal courts. Salaries are lower, prestige is lower, and inevitably the quality declines. Most important, the state courts are too often havens for failed politicians and mediocre lawyers. Character, given these limitations, is a sometime thing."

Unscrupulous judges have for generations taken advantage of the opportunity to milk estates through their authority to appoint special guardians and appraisers. This practice can profit a judge's political allies, personal friends, members of his family and others. Some have believed in garnering the rewards more directly. Clem McClelland, a probate judge in Harris County, Tex. even went so far as to set up a dummy corporation, the Tierra Grande Corp. in which his appointees could buy stock and thereby contribute to his personal fortune. The judge was finally convicted of stealing $2,500 from an estate in his court and in 1965 was sentenced to 10 years imprisonment.

About the same time as the McClelland affair broke, the judicial system of Oklahoma was rocked by a scandal involving four justices of the state's nine-man Supreme Court. In his confession one of the jurists, Nelson S. Corn, said he and three other members of the court had shared $150,000 for reversing a tax decision against an investment company. Corn and Justice Earl Welch avoided impeachment by resigning. Another judge died before the plot was revealed and the fourth, Justice Napoleon Bonaparte Johnson, a part-Cherokee honored as Indian of the Year in 1964, was impeached by the state senate. Perhaps the most sordid testimony of the investigation occurred when Corn was asked if there had been any year during his 24 on the bench when he had failed to take a bribe. He answered, "Well, I don't know."

Perhaps the most prolific fixer ever to preside over a court was the late New York Circuit judge Martin T. Manton. Manton's method of trying a lawsuit was to decide in favor of the highest bidder. He told one prospective victim, "While I'm sitting on the bench, I have my right and my left hand." This particular victim, who happened to be as underhanded as Manton himself had the judge's fix offer wire-recorded. After Manton heard the recording, he rushed back to court and handed down the required verdict for not so much as a thin dime. Manton was not caught on that particular caper, but he was on some 17 others. He served a prison term, was disbarred and died in disgrace.

The last federal judge impeached and removed from office by the U.S. Congress was Halsted L. Ritter in 1936. Among other charges brought against him were continuing to practice law while serving on the federal bench and giving his former law partner an excessive $75,000 fee as receiver of a Palm Beach hotel and taking in exchange a kickback of $4,500. He also accepted a number of other kickbacks and appointed his sister-in-law manager of a bankrupt hotel where he then received free room and board and other services. Ritter had failed to report any of these items on his income tax returns.

Removed from office, Ritter ignored the removal order of the Senate and refused to leave his office until forcefully ejected by a U.S. marshal.

See also: MARTIN T. MANTON, HALSTED RITTER.

Judson, Edward Z. C. (1823–1886) writer and rioter

While Edward Judson is best remembered as Ned Buntline, the author of those hokey, bloodcurdling dime novels that brought fame to Buffalo Bill Cody and Wild Bill Hickok, he also had a long record in the annals of crime. Among other things, he killed a cuckolded husband in a messy love triangle, was shot at while on the witness stand by his victim's brother, narrowly escaped a lynching and was imprisoned for his part in inciting New York's notorious Astor Place Riots of 1849.

Born in Stamford, N.Y. in 1823, he went to sea at the age of 10 as a cabin boy after quarreling with his father, a minor writer named Levi C. Judson. He returned to land at the age of 20 and, almost overnight, became a writer. By late 1843 he was publishing a gutter journal in Nashville, Tenn. called *Ned Buntline's Own.*

In Nashville, Judson had an affair with a married woman whose husband, Robert Porterfield, came after him with a gun. While he was testifying at a hearing into the killing in magistrate's court, the dead man's brother fired three shots at him, all of which gave him skin burns but did no other damage. Judson was released, but the local citizenry felt that justice had not been done and pursued him to his hotel. He was forced to jump from a third-floor window to escape his pursuers, a leap that gave him a permanent limp. Judson was then put in jail for his own protection until the lynch mood subsided. Later on, he wrote that lynchers took him from his cell and actually strung him up, leaving him for dead, and that some friends cut him down before he expired. This, however, might well be taken with the same skepticism due when reading his writings on the heroics of Cody and Hickok. Lynchers seldom left a body before it was stone-cold dead, and sporting bets were usually made over when the victim would twitch his last twitch.

A few years later, Judson moved to New York City, where he became a writer and henchman for the notorious political leader and rogue Capt. Isaiah Rynders. In 1849 Judson was sent to prison for his part in the Astor Place Riots, in which 23 persons had been killed mainly because of the anti-British hysteria whipped up by Rynders and Judson. When Judson came out of Blackwell's Island after serving his one-year term, he published a book called *The Convict's Return or Innocence Vindicated.* After that, the rest of Judson's life was free of rascality and criminality—except for the hyperbole of his dime-novel writings.

See also: ASTOR PLACE RIOTS.

jug markers

When the desperadoes of the 1920s and 1930s turned to bank robbing as a major occupation, a need developed for the services of a "jug marker," a caser who would know which bank to rob and when. The great bank robber Baron Lamm, who first organized bank gangs into specialized, militarylike units, was his own jug marker, considering it the most important role in the operation. A good jug marker not only learned the particulars of a bank's security system but also ascertained who had responsibility to open which safe and when, as well as what day of the week the most money would be on hand.

John Dillinger's favorite jug marker was Eddie Green, although he sometimes utilized the brash Harry Pierpont who once cased a bank by interviewing the president in the guise of a newsman. Green was perhaps the most thorough at his trade. He kept an "active list" of banks and checked back on them to see if anything had changed since his last go-round. Even while in jail he was able to sell his information to bank-robbing gangs and to receive a share in the profits. When he joined the Dillinger gang, Dillinger asked him to name a good bank. Green cited one in Sioux Falls, S.D. and started rattling off details. The gang then went out and robbed it.

On some jobs Green went so far as to find a reason for visiting bank officials in their homes just to study them more carefully, to be able to judge how they would act under stress. Green found the First National Bank of Mason City, Iowa for the Dillinger mob and discovered the bank's vault contained more than $240,000. Through no fault of Green's the gang botched the operation and got only $52,000. Green was shot dead by FBI agents in St. Paul, Minn. in April 1934. His death put a considerable crimp in Dillinger's short-lived operations thereafter.

With Dillinger's demise, Baby Face Nelson emerged as the great bank-robbing public enemy. Nelson's idea of jug marking was to charge through a bank's front door blazing away. Obviously, an era in bank robbing was ending. Following Green's death probably the greatest jug marker, and some say the only really good one, to appear on the scene was Slick Willie Sutton. In the late 1960s and through the 1970s, the impulsive amateurs took over and, as Sutton noted, "jug marking plain went to hell."

Jukes alleged criminal clan

For many years the Juke clan of New York State was regarded as the most depraved family in America, having produced, from the mid-1700s to the 1870s, seven generations of rapists, thieves, prostitutes, disease carriers and murderers. Begun in the 1870s, a criminal-genealogical study—*The Jukes, A Study in Crime, Pauperism, Disease and Heredity* by Richard L. Dugdale—established, to the author's satisfaction, that criminal traits could be inherited just as much as hair coloring.

Dugdale started his study with a mid-18th century Dutch tavern keeper he called Max, who was well known as a gambler and drinker and was the father of two sons. The sons in turn married two illegitimate sisters, whom Dugdale described as harlots. He dubbed one of these sisters, "Margaret, mother of criminals" and indicted her as "the progenitor of the distinctly criminal line of the family."

Dugdale traced 540 "blood relatives" and 169 others related by marriage or cohabitation. Of these, 140 were criminals and offenders of various stripes, almost 300 were wards of the state and the remainder generally a debased, foul and diseased lot. Dugdale enraged his readers by estimating that the price of imprisonment, public assistance and the like had cost the taxpayers something like $1.3 million.

During the early 20th century, critics began to question Dugdale's research methods and findings. The famous prison reformer Thomas Mott Osborne marveled at Dugdale's supposed ability to trace family bloodlines among the illegitimately born. Not a scientific researcher but merely a functionary of the Prison Association of New York, Dugdale seemed to rely very heavily on reciting the criminal backgrounds of various unnamed wretches who, he was satisfied, were related to the original Margaret. Osborne soon became convinced that Dugdale had simply operated under the assumption that every criminal he happened upon must have been a Juke and every Juke was probably a criminal. The shoddiness of Dugdale's research was shown by some of the "criminals" he unearthed: "a reputed sheep-stealer"; a man "supposed to have attempted rape"; an "unpunished and cautious thief"; "a petty thief but never convicted"; and a particularly offensive lad about whom it was "impossible to get any reliable information, but it is evident that at nineteen he was a leader in crime."

Many sociologists attacked the Juke thesis, but it received a new lease on life when in 1916 Arthur H. Estabrook took up the Dugdale mantle, claiming that since the 1870s the Jukes had continued to spawn more criminals and unworthiness. Estabrook admitted there was a lot of "good" Jukes around but insisted that since in recent years the Jukes had taken to marrying outside the breed, the theory of hereditary criminality and immorality was not weakened. Today, Dugdale and Estabrook alike enjoy little support because of their failure to give any weight to the influence of cultural and environmental factors on the development of criminal behavior.

Julian Street Cripple Creek, Colorado vice center

Cripple Creek, the last of the Colorado gold towns, was as wicked as any of its predecessors and perhaps even a bit more open about it. Train travelers passing through the town were treated to a full view of Myers Avenue and its "line," replete with such signs as "MEN TAKEN IN AND DONE FOR." A leading turn-of-the-century journalist, Julian Street, exposed the shame of Myers Avenue to a national audience in a searing article in *Colliers* magazine, calling the thoroughfare a disgrace to the entire country. The outraged city fathers of Cripple Creek fought back by bestowing a special honor on the journalist: they renamed Myers Avenue "Julian Street."

Jump, John (?–1943) murder victim

When one December morning in 1943 the dismembered body of John Jump was found on the train tracks near Fort Valley, Ga., the authorities' first theory was that the man had obviously been drunk and fallen in front of the train. However, the police soon discarded this theory and began looking for a murderer.

Inspection of the Jump home showed that the kitchen walls had recently been washed halfway to the ceiling and chemical tests revealed blood stains on the walls. Finally, Jump's young widow admitted killing him, claiming self-defense. After splitting the victim's head open with an ax, she cut the body in three parts and in two trips in the dark, carried the pieces to a desolate section of train tracks.

Given a long prison term for second-degree murder, she might well have gotten away with the crime but for one glaring miscalculation. There were three sets of tracks on the right-of-way where the body was found, but she had chosen to place its parts on the one set of tracks over which no train had run for eight months.

juvenile delinquency

In one sense, juvenile delinquency was not a problem in early colonial times. Until the Revolution settlers in this land lived under England common law, which held that juvenile offenders from the age of seven were accountable for their acts and could face the same penalties imposed on adults for various offenses. While a judge had discretion to determine the culpability of children between seven and 14 years of age, there were numerous executions of children as young as one eight-year-old hanged for burning a barn with "malice, revenge, craft and cunning." One well-known case was that of 12-year-old Hannah Ocuish, hanged for the murder of a six-year-old child. A contemporary account, which in tone approved of the execution, did comment that "she said very little and appeared greatly afraid, and seemed to want somebody to help her." Protests that she was too young to die drew very little public support.

Still, the punishment of juveniles was much more lenient in the colonies than in England. Corporal punishment and incarceration were gradually replacing the hangman's rope, especially in the post–Revolutionary

An early 19th-century woodcut depicts Boston authorities in pursuit of suspected youthful thieves who flooded the town. Not even the sight of a hanging figure (in background) could deter the juvenile criminals, many of whom were homeless.

War period. The Society for the Prevention of Pauperism was established in New York in 1817 to improve the lot of "those unfortunate children from 10 to 18 years of age, who from neglect of parents, from idleness and misfortune have . . . contravened some penal statute without reflecting on the consequences, and for hasty violations, been doomed to the penitentiary by the condemnation of the law." Funded by private donations, the House of Refuge was established in 1825 in New York to admit children convicted of crimes and those so destitute or neglected that they were in imminent danger of becoming delinquent. This marked the first time that children and adults were jailed separately.

By today's standards, the House of Refuge was a harsh institution, but it merely reflected the general practices of the day, when children were often put in irons, whipped, placed in solitary confinement, forced to survive on a reduced food supply and subjected to the silent treatment. The institution had the right to act as a parent for neglected or criminal children, and parents who objected were generally unable to win the release of their offspring. Houses of refuge were set up in Boston and Philadelphia, and both instituted reforms in treating juveniles. Boston prohibited corporal punishment; Philadelphia housed each child in a cell of his own. By 1834 the New York house took the revolutionary step of accepting black children. In 1856 the first girls' reformatory, the Massachusetts State Industrial School for Girls, opened.

In the 1860s, an ill-fated experiment was attempted with "ship schools," whereby young offenders were sent to sea on special vessels. Disciplinary problems, heavy operating expenses and protests from adult seamen fearful of losing jobs dealt the ship schools a quick death. In the 1870s and 1880s the so-called child-saving movement started under the leadership of a number of women's clubs. As a result of such efforts, separate courts for juveniles were established in 1899 in the states of Illinois and Rhode Island and the city of Denver, Colo.

The first federal effort to combat juvenile delinquency came with the establishment of the Children's Bureau in 1912. Under federal encouragement many states and large cities opened special reformatories for juveniles. These institutions did not solve the juvenile delinquency problem or clarify how juveniles could be rehabilitated through confinement. To this day, brutality, homosexuality and rioting remain ever present problems. Following the new approaches to aiding troubled juveniles expounded by John Dewey, Karen Horney, Carl Rogers, Erich Fromm and others, a new era of get-tough approaches to juvenile delinquency began in the 1970s.

The new public attitude was bolstered by such horrors as New York City's "laugh killing" in July 1978, the senseless slaying of a 16-year-old seminary student by a 13-year-old boy, a tragedy some experts say will have as great an impact on America's attitude toward juvenile crime as any offense has ever had. The killing took place in front of Teachers College at Columbia University when the 13-year-old and a 15-year-old companion came up to the seminary student, Hugh McEvoy, and a friend, Peter Mahar, 15, who were sitting on a railing. According to later testimony, the 13-year-old boy asked McEnvoy, "What are you laughing at?"

Mahar replied, "We're not laughing at anything."

With that, the 13-year-old pulled out a .22-caliber pistol, placed it to McEvoy's head and pulled the trigger. McEvoy was fatally wounded.

Under the existing law, the 13-year-old, who had a record of 10 arrests, nine within the previous 18 months, could only be tried in family court and receive a maximum sentence of 18 months in a "secure facility," with the option that his sentence could be renewed. After the first 18 months the 13-year-old would automatically be able to receive home passes and furloughs. The uproar over the laugh killing brought speedy passage of what some reporters called "Carey's law," named after New York governor Hugh L. Carey, which allowed juveniles to be tried for murder like adults and be sentenced to life in prison. It was predicted that the laugh-killing law would spread throughout the country.

The chief deficiency in any serious study of juvenile delinquency (as pointed out in the entry on Age and Crime) the absence of reliable statistics concerning juvenile crime in the 19th century, or even the first three decades of the 20th until the first appearance of the FBI *Uniform Crime Reports*. Even use of the *Uniform Crime Reports* is not that helpful and can cause misleading conclusions about a "juvenile crime wave" based on increase in juvenile arrests. Certain types of crime, both violent and nonviolent, are typically juvenile offenses and explode upward when a crop of baby boom youths hits the crime-prone ages.

See also: AGE AND CRIME, SHIP SCHOOLS, WALSH SCHOOL FEUD.